FOURTEENTH EDITION

MW01006400

Criminal Justice Today

AN INTRODUCTORY TEXT
FOR THE TWENTY-FIRST CENTURY

ANNOTATED INSTRUCTOR'S EDITION

Frank Schmalleger, Ph.D.

Distinguished Professor Emeritus, The University of North Carolina at Pembroke

PEARSON

Boston   Columbus   Indianapolis   New York   San Francisco   Amsterdam
Cape Town   Dubai   London   Madrid   Milan   Munich   Paris   Montreal   Toronto
Delhi   Mexico City   São Paulo   Sydney   Hong Kong   Seoul   Singapore   Taipei   Tokyo

NOTICE:
This work is protected by U.S. copyright laws and is provided solely for the use of college instructors in reviewing course materials for classroom use. Dissemination or sale of this work, or any part (including on the World Wide Web), will destroy the integrity of the work and is not permitted. The work and materials from it should never be made available to students except by instructors using the accompanying text in their classes. All recipients of this work are expected to abide by these restrictions and to honor the intended pedagogical purposes and the needs of other instructors who rely on these materials.

Editorial Director: Andrew Gilfillan
Senior Acquisitions Editor: Gary Bauer
Editorial Assistant: Lynda Cramer
Director of Marketing: David Gesell
Marketing Manager: Thomas Hayward
Product Marketing Manager: Kaylee Carlson
Marketing Assistant: Les Roberts
Program Manager Team Lead: Laura Weaver
Program Manager: Tara Horton
Project Manager Team Lead: Bryan Pirrmann
Project Manager: Susan Hannahs
Operations Specialist: Deidra Smith
Creative Director: Andrea Nix
Art Director: Diane Six

Manager, Product Strategy: Sara Eilert
Product Strategy Manager: Anne Rynearson
Team Lead, Media Development & Production: Rachel Collett
Media Project Manager: Maura Barclay
Cover Designer: Melissa Welch, Studio Montage
Cover Image: Samxmeg/Getty Images, Antbphotos/Fotolia, Oleg Golovnev/Fotolia, Senk/Fotolia, Patrik Dietrich/Shutterstock, and Manfredxy/Shutterstock
Full-Service Project Management: Abinaya Rajendran, Integra Software Services, Pvt Ltd
Composition: Integra Software Services, Pvt Ltd
Text Printer/Binder: RR Donnelley
Cover Printer: Lehigh-Phoenix Color/Hagerstown
Text Font: Bembo MT Pro 10/13

Credits and acknowledgments for content borrowed from other sources and reproduced, with permission, in this textbook appear on the appropriate page within the text.

Acknowledgements of third party content appear on page with the borrowed material, which constitutes an extension of this copyright page.

Unless otherwise indicated herein, any third-party trademarks that may appear in this work are the property of their respective owners and any references to third-party trademarks, logos or other trade dress are for demonstrative or descriptive purposes only. Such references are not intended to imply any sponsorship, endorsement, authorization, or promotion of Pearson's products by the owners of such marks, or any relationship between the owner and Pearson Education, Inc. or its affiliates, authors, licensees or distributors.

Many of the designations by manufacturers and sellers to distinguish their products are claimed as trademarks. Where those designations appear in this book, and the publisher was aware of a trademark claim, the designations have been printed in initial caps or all caps.

Library of Congress Cataloging-in-Publication Data
Schmalleger, Frank, author.
    Criminal justice today: an introductory text for the twenty-first century/Frank Schmalleger, Ph.D.,
Distinguished Professor Emeritus, The University of North Carolina at Pembroke.—Fourteenth edition.
    pages cm
    ISBN 978-0-13-414561-7 (alk. paper)—ISBN 0-13-414561-5 (alk. paper) 1. Criminal justice,
Administration of—United States. 2. Criminal procedure—United States. I. Title.
HV9950.S35 2017
364.973--dc23
                                                                    2015036928

10 9 8 7 6 5 4 3 2 1
V011

ISBN 13: 978-0-13-414561-7
ISBN 10:   0-13-414561-5

This book is dedicated to my beautiful wife,
Ellen "Willow" Szirandi Schmalleger, my true companion,
whose wonderful, happy, and free spirit
is a gift to all who know her.

Brief Contents

Contents

PART ONE ▪ Crime in America   2

Chapter 1 | What Is Criminal Justice?   2

Chapter 2 | The Crime Picture   30

Chapter 3 | The Search for Causes   72

PART TWO ▪ Policing   137

Chapter 5 | Policing: History and Structure   138

Chapter 6 | Policing: Purpose and Organization   163

Chapter 7 | Policing: Legal Aspects   195

PART THREE ■ Adjudication 277

Chapter 9 | The Courts: Structure and Participants 278

Chapter 11 | Sentencing   344

PART FOUR   ■   Corrections   389

Chapter 12 | Probation, Parole, and Intermediate Sanctions   390

PART FIVE ■ Special Issues   503

Chapter 15 | Juvenile Justice   504

New to This Edition

Chapter 1: What Is Criminal Justice?

- The chapter opening story now describes the 2015 justice system crisis that arose following refusals by grand jurors in Missouri and New York to indict police officers in the death of two black suspects in separate incidents.
- "Milestones in crime history" now recognize the present-day impact of computer and high-technology crimes
- The late-2014 assassination of two New York City police officers as they sat in their marked patrol car on a Brooklyn Street is now discussed.
- The 2014 trial of Oscar Pistorius, the South African Paralympic athlete known as the "Blade Runner", who was convicted of the shooting death of his model girlfriend, Reeva Steenkamp is now discussed.
- Mention is made of Justin Bieber's Miami Beach, Florida arrest in 2014, where he was charged with speeding in a yellow Lamborghini, for driving with an expired license, and for driving under the influence of alcohol, marijuana, and prescription drugs.
- A new key term, "procedural fairness," has been added to the chapter.
- The 2015 "work stoppage" by NYPD officers is described.

Chapter 2: The Crime Picture

- The chapter opening story now illustrates the growing significance of cybercrimes with a tale about how a county sheriff's office was made to pay a fee via ransomeware to regain access to their important files. The discussion of cybercrimes has been enhanced, recognizing them as contributing to a higher rate of crime than is commonly acknowledged.
- Updated crime statistics are found throughout the chapter.
- A new and detailed box on marijuana legalization and decriminalization is included, along with a map of marijuana legalization initiatives.
- A new definition of "rape" is provided, reflecting a change by the FBI in it's Uniform Crime Reporting terminology.
- A new example of the crime of larceny is provided.
- The CJ Issues box dealing with race and the justice system has been modified and updated to include recent incidents in Ferguson, Missouri, and elsewhere.
- New photos are used to illustrate racial tensions affecting the justice system.

- A new "Freedom v. Safety" box now describes the FBI's concern with encryption technology, and asks if citizens can have too much privacy.
- The discussion of cybercrime has been enhanced.
- The URL for the federal government's Elder Justice website is now provided.
- The information on hate crimes has been updated.
- A new study on gun control laws and their effectiveness at preventing gun crime is discussed.
- The potential for new 3-D printers to be used in the fabrication of handguns is now discussed, and a photo of such a weapon is provided.

Chapter 3: The Search for Causes

- A new chapter opening photo indicates the importance of new technologies to law enforcement agencies.
- The arrest of rap music mogul, "Surge" Knight on murder charges now opens the chapter.
- New line art depicts the number of persons convicted of homicide, by gender and region of the world.
- Statistics and crime data throughout the chapter have been updated.

Chapter 4: Criminal Law

- A new chapter opening photo has been added.
- The CJ News box detailing the rule of law has been updated, including the photos it contains.
- A discussion of former New Orleans mayor, Ray Nagin, has been added. Nagin was convicted of 20 counts of bribery, conspiracy, and money laundering—crimes that he committed while serving as mayor.
- The offenses of treason and espionage have been better separated in the text, and a new story describing the crime of espionage has been added.
- A story and photo of Saiqa Akhter, the Texas woman who was found not guilty by reason of insanity in 2014 after admitting to the murder of her two young children by strangulation, has been added.

Chapter 5: Policing: History and Structure

- Added photo and brief discussion of the Center for Evidence-Based Crime Policy (CEBCP) at Virginia's George Mason University.

- Replaced photo of the International Law Enforcement Academy in Budapest, Hungary. The new photo shows the author visiting the academy.
- Added a new CJ News box discussing the Federal Bureau of Investigation's Next Generation Identification (NGI) System. The System was developed to expand the Bureau's biometric identification capabilities, ultimately replacing the FBI's Integrated Automated Fingerprint Identification System (IAFIS).
- Three new key terms and their definitions have been added to this chapter: hot-spot policing, predictive policing, and smart policing.
- A new CJ Careers box focusing on private security has been added to the chapter.

Chapter 6: Policing: Purpose and Organization

- The discussion of police officer discretion has been removed from this chapter and has been moved to a later chapter.
- The discussion of police officer professionalism and ethics has been removed from this chapter and has been moved to a later chapter.
- A graphic detailing policing purposes has been added.
- The 2014 death of 18-year-old Michael Brown, who was shot and killed by a Ferguson, Missouri, police officer is now the chapter opening story. The shooting sparked days of racially-charged protests and revealed a deep distrust of the police by minorities.
- The discussion of the police use of recording devices, especially body cameras, has been enhanced.
- Issues box has been added focusing on the use of social media in policing.

Chapter 7: Policing: Legal Aspects

- The chapter opening story has been updated.
- The chapter now includes discussion of the 2014 U.S. Supreme Court case of *Prado Navarette* v. *California,* in which the court held that an anonymous and uncorroborated tip can provide a sufficient basis for a police officer's reasonable suspicion to make an investigative stop.
- The 2014 U.S. Supreme Court case of *Feernandez* v. California is now discussed. In that case, the court ruled that where multiple occupants are involved, the search of a dwelling is permissible without a warrant if one person living there consents after officers have removed another resident who objects.

- A new CJ News box has been added that discusses the 2014 case of *Riley* v. *California,* in which the U.S. Supreme Court ruled that under most circumstances police officers are required to obtain a warrant before accessing and searching the data stored on a suspect's cell phone.
- Additional information on the legal issues surrounding the use of GPS tracking by the police is now included in the chapter.

Chapter 8: Policing: Issues and Challenges

- The material on police discretion has been moved here from Chapter 6.
- A discussion of the dangers of police work has been moved here from Chapter 6.
- The discussion of police professionalism has been moved to this chapter.
- A new key term, police subculture, has been added to the chapter and a definition is provided.
- The corruption and integrity section now includes a story about Puerto Rican police officers who ran a criminal organization out of their department's offices.
- Recent initiatives by the COPS office are now discussed.
- Some new photographs have been added, while others have been updated.
- The need for first responders to protect themselves against diseases such as Ebola is now discussed.
- The diagram depicting stress and fatigue among police officers has been enhanced.
- The Freedom or Safety? box on religion and public safety has been updated.
- The graphic depicting the police use of force continuum has been updated, along with the discussion of such force.
- The discussion of racial profiling has been expanded.
- Discussion has been added of one of the earliest lawsuits (Thurman v. City of Torrington) brought against a city police department for ignoring domestic abuse restraining orders.

Chapter 9: The Courts: Structure and Participants

- A new chapter opening story highlights the importance of courts as a central component of the American system of justice.
- A new graphic depicts that structure of state courts in two contrasting jurisdictions.

- Two new key terms have been added to the chapter: courts of general jurisdiction, and courts of limited jurisdiction.
- The CJ News box on America's judiciary has been updated and expanded.
- The information on judges' pay has been updated.
- The information on public defenders has been updated, and a revised graphic now shows state government indigent defense expenditures.
- A new CJ News box on DNA sampling has been added to the chapter.
- An update is provided on the use of camera in the chambers of the U.S. Supreme Court.

Chapter 10: Pretrial Activities and the Criminal Trial

- A new CJ Careers box has been added to the chapter, featuring a bail bond agent.
- The discussion of the grand jury system, used in some states, has been updated and expanded.
- The case of Oscar Pistorius, the South African Paralympic athlete, who was convicted in 2014 of the shooting death of his girlfriend is featured, and a photo of Pistorius is included.
- The CJ News box on the use of social media by jurors has been modified and expanded.

Chapter 11: Sentencing

- The discussion of how "get-tough on crime" legislation has led to heightened prison populations has been clarified.
- Two new key terms have been added to the chapter: recidivism and recidivism rate.
- Recent changes in California's three-strikes law are highlighted and discussed.
- Discussion of the proposed federal Smarter Sentencing Act has been updated.
- A new top-level heading, "Sentencing and Today's Prison Crisis," has been added to the chapter. That discussion includes a new figure comparing historical rates of imprisonment with crime rates.
- A new CJ Careers box has been added featuring a medicolegal death investigator.
- A new piece of line art depicting the four traditional sentencing options available to criminal court judges has been added.
- Statistics and data have been updated throughout the chapter.

- Convicted child-killer Kevin Ray Underwood is now discussed and a photo of him has been added.
- Discussion of the 2014 U.S. Supreme Court case of Hall v. Florida has been added. In that case, the Court ruled that states cannot rely solely on an IQ score to bar an inmate from claiming mental disability n the face of execution.

Chapter 12: Probation, Parole, and Intermediate Sanctions

- All data in the chapter have been completely updated.
- A new Paying for It box describing cost-efficient parole has been added.
- The discussion of the use of GPS technology in parole supervision has been expanded.
- A new key term (desistance) and its definition have been added to the chapter.

Chapter 13: Prisons and Jails

- A 2014 federal court ruling ordering California parole officials to implement a plan to free all nonviolent second-strike offenders (except sex offenders) on parole after serving half of their sentences, is described.
- All data, statistics, and graphics detailing the prison population in various states, and in federal government facilities, have been updated.
- The discussion of the evidence-based movement in corrections has been enlarged.
- The chapter's discussion of the purpose of imprisonment has been clarified.
- A number of the photographs have been replaced in order to keep abreast of changes now afoot in corrections.
- A discussion of California's Proposition 47 has been added. The ballot measure changed many felonies to misdemeanors and is anticipated to lead to a decrease in correctional populations in the state.
- A new graphic showing the impact of realignment on prison populations in the state of California has been added.
- A new figure, explaining federal Bureau of Prisons institutional security levels and terminology has been added.
- The CJ Issues box containing arguments for and against the privatization of prisons has been substantially updated.

Chapter 14: Prison Life

- Data on both male and female prisoners have been updated.

- A new CJ Issues box describing the (United Nations) Bangkok Rules on the Treatment of Female Prisoners is now included.
- A description of the federal Bureau of Prisons Mothers and Infants Together program has been added.
- A photograph depicting the role of women in correctional administration has been added.
- A table describing the ten most influential security threat groups (gangs) in American prisons has been added.
- The 2015 U.S. Supreme Court case of Holt v. Hobbs, regarding a prisoner's rights to "religious exercise" has been added.
- Information on mentally ill prisoners has been expanded.
- A discussion of the 2015 attack by Islamic terrorists on the offices of French newspaper Charlie Hebdo, is now included in the context of prisoner radicalization.

Chapter 15: Juvenile Justice

- The chapter now begins with a discussion of the U.S. Supreme Court's recognition of recent advances in understanding of adolescent brain development—to include the Court's decisions of Graham v. Florida (2010) and Miller v. Alabama (2012).
- The U.S. Supreme Court case of J.D.B. v. North Carolina (2011) has been added to the graphic depicting the legal environment of juvenile justice.
- All statistics have been updated, to include those regarding juveniles held in public and private facilities.

Chapter 16: Drugs and Crime

- The chapter opening story about Joaquin "El Chapo" Guzman has been updated to account for his arrest by Mexican authorities and a request by the U.S. to extradite him from that country.
- The discussion of marijuana legalization and decriminalization has been expanded in the wake of the substance's new legal status in a number of states.
- Lunesta (eszopiclone) and Ambien (zolpidem) have been added to the table of major controlled substances under the federal Controlled Substances Act.
- All of the data and statistics on drug use and abuse have been updated throughout.
- A photograph of Denver's 2015 Cannabis Cup celebration is now included in the chapter.
- The information and graphic on federal drug control spending has been updated.

- Asset forfeiture is now discussed in the context of the purchase by the St. Louis Police Department of a new headquarters building using forfeited funds.
- A new timeline depicting the development of federal drug control legislation has been added.

Chapter 17: Terrorism, Multinational Criminal Justice and Global Issues

- The title of this chapter has changed to better reflect its contents.
- A new story opens the chapter and focuses on "lone wolf" would-be terrorist Christopher Lee Cornell who was arrested by the FBI in 2015.
- The case of Raif Badawi, the Saudi Arabian blogger sentenced to 1,000 lashes, is now discussed. A photo of Badawi has also been added.
- Data throughout the chapter have been updated.
- The 13th United Nations crime congress, held in Qatar in 2015, is now discussed.
- The discussion of the International Criminal Court (ICC) has been updated.
- Cyberterrorism is now better distinguished from other forms of terrorism.
- The list of foreign terrorist organizations has been updated, as has the map showing the location of such organizations.

Chapter 18: High-Technology Crimes

- The chapter opening story has changed to describe the cyberattack on Sony Pictures by North Korean agents.
- The case of Russian national Aleksandr Andreevich Panin, who plead guilty in U.S. federal court to conspiracy to commit wire and bank fraud is now discussed.
- All data (on cybercrimes) throughout the chapter have been updated.
- The 2015 Social Media Internet Law Enforcement (SMILE) national conference is now discussed.
- The discussion of the use of automatic plate recognition (APR) technology by law enforcement agencies has been expanded.
- The CJ News box describing the activities of Kim Dotcom (AKA Megaupload) has been updated.
- A new key term, sentinel event, has been added, along with its description. A detailed description of sentinel events in criminal justice is now included.

Preface

Many students are attracted to the study of criminal justice because it provides a focus for the tension that exists within our society between individual rights and freedoms, on the one hand, and the need for public safety, security, and order, on the other. Recently, 21st century technology in the form of social media, smartphones, and personal online videos, has combined with perceived injustices in the day-to-day operations of the criminal justice system, culminating in an explosion of demands for justice for citizens of all races and socioeconomic status—especially those whose encounters with agents of law enforcement turn violent. A "Black Lives Matter" movement that began with the shooting of an unarmed black teenager in Ferguson, Missouri, in 2014, has developed into a widespread social movement that demands justice for all.

The tension between individual rights and public order is the theme around which all editions of this textbook have been built. That same theme is even more compelling today because of the important question we have all been asking in recent years: How much personal freedom are we willing to sacrifice to achieve a solid sense of individual and group security?

Although there are no easy answers to this question, this textbook guides criminal justice students in the struggle to find a satisfying balance between freedom and security. True to its origins, the 14th edition focuses on the crime picture in America and on the three traditional elements of the criminal justice system: police, courts, and corrections. This edition has been enhanced with additional "Freedom or Safety" boxes, which time and again question the viability of our freedoms in a world that has grown ever more dangerous. This edition also asks students to evaluate the strengths and weaknesses of the American justice system as it struggles to adapt to an increasingly multicultural society and to a society in which the rights of a few can threaten the safety of many—especially in the modern context of a War Against Terrorism.

It is my hope that this TEXT will ground students in the important issues that continue to evolve from the tension between the struggle for justice and the need for safety. For it is on that bedrock that the American system of criminal justice stands, and it is on that foundation that the future of the justice system—and of this country—will be built.

FRANK SCHMALLEGER, PH.D.
Distinguished Professor Emeritus,
The University of North Carolina at Pembroke

Key Features Include

Freedom OR safety? YOU decide boxes in each chapter highlight the book's ever-evolving theme of individual rights versus public order, a hallmark feature of this text since the first edition. In each chapter of the text, Freedom or Safety boxes build on this theme by illustrating some of the personal rights issues that challenge policymakers today. Each box includes critical-thinking questions that ask readers to ponder whether and how the criminal justice system balances individual rights and public safety.

CJ Careers boxes outline the characteristics of a variety of criminal justice careers in a Q&A format, to introduce today's pragmatic students to an assortment of potential career options and assist them in making appropriate career choices.

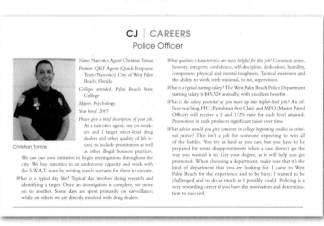

CJ News boxes in each chapter present case stories from the media to bring a true-to-life dimension to the study of criminal justice and allow insight into the everyday workings of the justice system.

CJ | NEWS

Evidence of "Warrior Gene" May Help Explain Violence

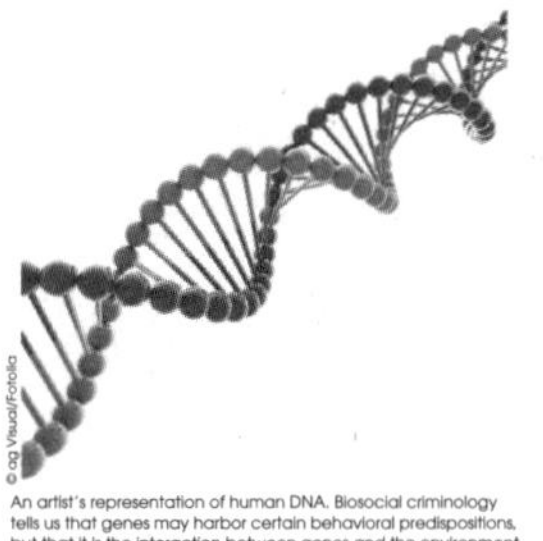
© ag Visual/Fotolia

An artist's representation of human DNA. Biosocial criminology tells us that genes may harbor certain behavioral predispositions, but that it is the interaction between genes and the environment that produces behavior. What forms might such interaction take?

As scientists study the DNA of the mass shooter at the elementary school in Newtown, Connecticut, some experts are hoping that it might lead to discovery of a gene that identifies violent criminals and helps prevent future killings. But be careful what you wish for. If a genetic link to violence were firmly identified, could it be used to falsely stigmatize people who haven't committed any crime at all? Or could such a link help convicted criminals get reduced sentences?

The argument that "my DNA made me do it" has, in fact, already been successfully used in the courts for a particular gene linked to violence. Monoamine oxidase A, known as MAOA, produces an enzyme that breaks down serotonin and other neurotransmitters in the brain that are identified with aggression. Studies have shown that a variant of the gene, known as MAOA-L, can lead to violent behavior when coupled with serious mistreatment in childhood. The link has only been identified in men, leaving women seemingly immune from the effects of this genetic anomaly.

The media nicknamed MAOA-L the "warrior gene" after it was identified as highly prevalent in a constantly warring Maori tribe. Another study found that boys with an MAOA variation were more likely to join gangs and become some of the most violent members. Researchers now know that MAOA-L may alter the very structure of the brain. Using structural magnetic resonance imaging (MRI) scanning, a 2006 study found that men with the gene variant were much more likely to have abnormalities in an area of the brain associated with behavior than were other men. Functional MRI scanning then showed that these men had difficulty inhibiting strong emotional impulses. Lawyers for violent defendants have latched on to the growing science. In the 2009 murder trial of Bradley Waldroup, who was convicted of chopping up his wife with a machete (she survived) and shooting her female friend to death, lawyers were able to demonstrate that Waldroup had the MAOA gene variant. Although the jury convicted him of murder and of attempted murder, its members concluded that his actions weren't premeditated due to the influence that his genes had on him—sparing him the death penalty. Also in 2009, an Italian appeals court cut the sentence of a convicted murderer by one year on the grounds that he, too, had the MAOA-L gene.

Judges are warming up to genetic defenses. In a 2012 study in *Science*, when trial judges were given the MAOA variant as evidence in mock trials, they tended to reduce sentences by one year in comparison to cases with no such evidence. Critics, however, argue that these defendants should be behind bars longer. Because their trait is baked into their DNA, such people say, they are likely to commit violence again. "Trying to absolve people of responsibility by attributing their behavior to their genes or environment is not new," wrote Ronald Bailey, author of the book *Liberation Biology*. He urged courts to take a tough stance against defendants with a genetic predilection to violence: "Knowing that you will be held responsible for criminal acts helps inhibit antisocial impulses that we all feel from time to time." Also, scientists want their findings to be taken with a grain of salt in the courts, arguing that science and the law have different aims. "Science is focused on understanding universal phenomena; we do this by averaging data across groups of individuals," wrote Joshua Buckholtz for the NOVA series on PBS. "Law, on the other hand, only cares about specific individual people—the individual on trial." Buckholtz observed that "Genetic differences rarely affect human behavior with the kind of selectivity or specificity desired and required by the law."

Resources: Mark Lallanilla, "Genetics May Provide Clues to Newtown Shooting," *Live Science*, December 28, 2012, http://www.livescience.com/25853-newtown-shooter-dna.html; Joshua W. Buckholtz, "Neuroprediction and Crime," *NOVA*, October 18, 2012, http://www.pbs.org/wgbh/nova/body/neuroprediction-crime.html; and Patricia Cohen, "Genetic Basis for Crime: A New Look," *New York Times*, June 19, 2011, http://www.nytimes.com/2011/06/20/arts/genetics-and-crime-at-institute-of-justice-conference.html?pagewanted=all&_r=0.

NEW! Paying for It boxes in the first four parts of the text explore how the criminal justice system is affected by today's financial realities. Financial necessity in the form of budget shortfalls and limits on available resources is leading police, courts, and corrections to become more cost-efficient.

paying for it

Cost-Efficient Policing

In January 2011, Newark, New Jersey, ranked 23rd on the list of the most dangerous cities in America, laid off almost half of its police force as budget constraints forced the city to reduce the services it offered to its citizens. The layoffs came after city revenues dipped by one-third amid declining income from taxes on hotel stays and local payrolls, and parking fees collected by the city fell sharply. Adding to the city's woes was an additional decline of 40% in aid from the state of New Jersey.

In the four-month period immediately following the layoffs, crime in Newark surged. The murder rate climbed 73% above what it was in the same period for the previous year; auto thefts were up 40%; and carjackings increased fourfold. The number of shooting victims taken to area hospitals doubled. Although some claim that not all of those crime increases can be directly attributed to declines in police staffing, others are not so sure. As police personnel were cut, so were crime-prevention programs that had served the city well. One of them was Operation Impact, which targeted high-crime areas and resulted in a 35% decrease in crime in those neighborhoods. The program was eliminated as uniformed personnel were moved to street patrol.

The city of Newark, which has since rehired some of its officers, is not alone in facing financial pressures. A year after the layoffs were announced in Newark, Camden city officials, also in New Jersey, announced that they were considering eliminating the entire Camden Police Department, and were working to create a countywide police force to be named the Camden County Police Department. Theoretically, the department, which would include other cities and towns in the area, would bring about cost savings from a combination of resources and personnel that were previously performing redundant tasks. Current plans, however, which are still developing as this book goes to press, do not ask for the department to combine operations with the Camden County Sheriff's Office, which serves unincorporated areas of the county.

Although today's combined departments represent one approach to cost savings, others include the following: prioritizing activities, reducing services, and modifying service delivery; reorganizing and rightsizing agencies; partnering with other agencies and organizations; using proactive policing methods instead of reactive ones; adopting preventative and problem-solving service models; increasing efficiency; outsourcing services; recycling confiscated criminal resources; and implementing force multipliers.

Force multipliers, the last of the options listed here, refers to using technologies that permit a few personnel to do the work of many. Cameras placed in crime-prone areas, for example, and monitored by police employees can sometimes reduce the need for active police patrols, thereby saving huge expenditures on personnel, vehicles, communications, and administrative expenses. Cross-training, in which personnel are trained to perform a number of roles—such as police officer, EMT, and firefighter—can also save money by eliminating duplicate positions.

Finally, another initiative, **smart policing**, makes use of techniques shown to work at both reducing and solving crimes. **Hot-spot policing**, in which agencies focus their resources on known areas of criminal activity, is one such technique; whereas **predictive policing**, which provides the ability to anticipate or predict crime through the use of statistical techniques, helps guide enforcement operations, and is an increasingly important concept in policing today (see the "CJ News box" in Chapter 6 for more information on hot-spot policing).

Two programs that support effective policing are the Smart Policing Initiative (SPI), and the National Law Enforcement and Corrections Technology Center (NLECTC). The NLECTC works to identify emerging technologies, as well as to assess their efficiency; the SPI, a collaborative consortium composed of the Bureau of Justice Assistance, the nonprofit CNA Corporation, and over 30 local law enforcement agencies, works to build evidence-based law enforcement strategies that are effective, efficient, and economical. The SPI is also discussed in a "Paying for It" box in Chapter 6. Visit SPI on the Web at http://www.smartpolicinginitiative.com. The NLECTC can be accessed at http://www.justnet.org.

References: William Alden, "Newark Police Layoffs Threaten Crime-Fighting as Budget Cuts Spark Fears," *Huffington Post*, February 25, 2011, http://www.huffingtonpost.com/2011/02/25/newark-police-layoffs-budget-cuts_n_827993.html (accessed May 28, 2012); Claudia Vargas, "Camden City Council Urges Officials to Advance Plan for County Police Force," *The Philadelphia Inquirer*, December 28, 2011, http://articles.philly.com/2011-12-28/news/30565451_1_county-force-police-force-police-officers (accessed May 21, 2012); Joe Cordero, *Reducing the Costs of Quality Policing: Making Community Safety Cost Effective and Sustainable* (The Cordero Group), http://www.njlmef.org/policy-papers/FoLG_v_3_1.pdf (accessed May 29, 2012); Charlie Beck, "Predictive Policing: What Can We Learn from Wal-Mart and Amazon about Fighting Crime in a Recession?" *The Police Chief*, April 2012, http://www.policechiefmagazine.org/magazine/index.cfm?fuseaction=display_arch&article_id=1942&issue_id=112009 (accessed May 25, 2012); and JustNet, "About NLECTC," https://www.justnet.org/About_NLECTC.html (accessed May 29, 2012); James R. Coldren, Jr., Alissa Huntoon, and Michael Medaris, "Introducing Smart Policing: Foundations, Principles, and Practice," *Police Quarterly*, Vol. 16, No. 3 (2013), pp. 275–286.

Issues boxes throughout the text showcase selected issues in the field of criminal justice, including topics related to multiculturalism, diversity, and technology.

CJ | ISSUES

Gender Issues in Criminal Justice

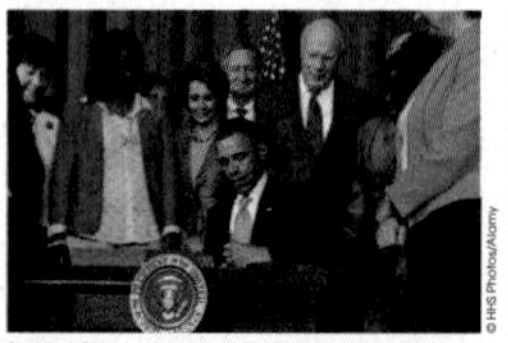
© HHS Photos/Alamy

President Obama signing the Violence against Women Act (VAWA) reauthorization legislation in 2013. Intimate partner violence is a problem of special concern to the criminal justice system, and violence against women is an area that is receiving legislative attention, as evidenced by the federal VAWA. How might laws designed to protect women be improved?

The Violent Crime Control and Law Enforcement Act of 1994 included significant provisions intended to enhance gender equality throughout the criminal justice system. Title IV of the Violent Crime Control and Law Enforcement Act, known as the Violence against Women Act (VAWA) of 1994, contains the Safe Streets for Women Act. This act increased federal penalties for repeat sex offenders and requires mandatory restitution for sex crimes, including costs related to medical services (including physical, psychiatric, and psychological care); physical and occupational therapy or rehabilitation; necessary transportation, temporary housing, and child-care expenses; lost income; attorneys' fees, including any costs incurred in obtaining a civil protection order; and any other losses suffered by the victim as a result of the offense. The act requires that compliance with a restitution order be made a condition of probation or supervised release (if such a sentence is imposed by the court) and provides that violation of the order will result in the offender's imprisonment. The law also extends "rape shield law" protections to civil cases and to all criminal cases in order to bar irrelevant inquiries into a victim's sexual history.

Chapter 2 of the VAWA provided funds for grants to combat violent crimes against women. The purpose of funding was to assist states and local governments to "develop and strengthen effective law enforcement and prosecution strategies to combat violent crimes against women, and to develop and strengthen victim services in cases involving violent crimes against women." The law also provided funds for the "training of law enforcement officers and prosecutors to more effectively identify and respond to violent crimes against women, including the crimes of sexual assault and domestic violence"; for "developing, installing, or expanding data collection and communication systems, including computerized systems, linking police, prosecutors, and courts or for the purpose of identifying and tracking arrests, protection orders, violations of protection orders, prosecutions, and convictions for violent crimes against women, including the crimes of sexual assault and domestic violence"; and for developing and strengthening "victim services programs, including sexual assault and domestic violence programs."

The act also created the crime of crossing state lines in violation of a protection order and the crime of crossing state lines to commit assault on a domestic partner. It established federal penalties for the latter offense of up to life in prison in cases where death results.

Chapter 3 of the act provided funds to increase the "safety for women in public transit and public parks." It authorized up to $10 million in grants through the Department of Transportation to enhance lighting, camera surveillance, and security telephones in public transportation systems used by women.

Chapter 5 of VAWA funded the creation of hotlines, educational seminars, informational materials, and training programs for professionals who provide assistance to victims of sexual assault. Another portion of the law, titled the Safe Homes for Women Act, increased grants for battered women's shelters, encouraged arrest in cases of domestic violence, and provided for the creation of a national domestic violence hotline to provide counseling, information, and assistance to victims of domestic violence. The act also mandates that any protection order issued by a state court must be recognized by the other states and by the federal government and must be enforced "as if it were the order of the enforcing state."

The VAWA was reauthorized by Congress in 2000, 2005, and again in 2013.[1] The 2005 VAWA reauthorization included a new statute known as the International Marriage Broker Regulation Act (IMBRA), which provides potential life-saving protections to prospective foreign brides who may immigrate to the United States. Finally, the 2013 reauthorization made $659 million available each year for five years for programs that strengthen the justice system's response to crimes against women and some men, including protections for gays, lesbians, bisexual, and transgender Americans.

[1] VAWA 2013 was signed into law by President Obama on March 7, 2013. It is officially known as the Violence against Women Reauthorization Act of 2013.

Instructor Supplements

The 14th edition of *Criminal Justice Today* is supported by a complete package of instructor and student resources:

Instructor's Manual with Test Bank. Includes content outlines for classroom discussion, teaching suggestions, and answers to selected end-of-chapter questions from the text. This also contains a Word document version of the test bank.

TestGen. This computerized test generation system gives you maximum flexibility in creating and administering tests on paper, electronically, or online. It provides state-of-the-art features for viewing and editing test bank questions, dragging a selected question into a test you are creating, and printing sleek, formatted tests in a variety of layouts. Select test items from test banks included with TestGen for quick test creation, or write your own questions from scratch. TestGen's random generator provides the option to display different text or calculated number values each time questions are used.

PowerPoint Presentations. Our presentations offer clear, straightforward outlines and notes to use for class lectures or study materials. Photos, illustrations, charts, and tables from the book are included in the presentations when applicable.

Annotated Instructors Edition (AIE). The AIE of Criminology Today 8e contains notes in the top margins identifying key topics with suggestions for stimulating and guiding class discussion.

To access supplementary materials online, instructors need to request an instructor access code. Go to www.pearsonhighered.com/irc, where you can register for an instructor access code. Within 48 hours after registering, you will receive a confirming email, including an instructor access code. Once you have received your code, go to the site and log on for full instructions on downloading the materials you wish to use.

Alternate Versions

eBooks. This text is also available in multiple eBook formats. These are an exciting new choice for students looking to save money. As an alternative to purchasing the printed textbook, students can purchase an electronic version of the same content. With an eTextbook, students can search the text, make notes online, print out reading assignments that incorporate lecture notes, and bookmark important passages for later review. For more information, visit your favorite online eBook reseller or visit www.mypearsonstore.com.

REVEL™ is Pearson's newest way of delivering our respected content. Fully digital and highly engaging, REVEL replaces the textbook and gives students everything they need for the course. Seamlessly blending text narrative, media, and assessment, REVEL enables students to read, practice, and study in one continuous experience—for less than the cost of a traditional textbook. Learn more at pearsonhighered.com/revel.

CourseConnect Online Course to Accompany *Criminal Justice Today,* 14e

Criminal Justice Today is supported by online course solutions that include interactive learning modules, a variety of assessment tools, videos, simulations, and current event features. Go to **www.pearsonhighered.com** or contact your local representative for the latest information.

Acknowledgments

My thanks to all who assisted in so many different ways in the development of this textbook. Thanks to Lynda Cramer, Tara Horton, Susan Hannahs, and Maura Barclay, and all the past and present Pearson staff with whom I have worked. They are true professionals and have made the task of manuscript development enjoyable.

A very special thank-you goes to Leah Jewel, Andrew Gilfillan and David Gesell, for their stewardship and support; and to my editor, Gary Bauer; field marketing manager, Thomas Hayward; and product marketing manager, Kaylee Carlson.

I'd also like to thank my supplements author, Ellen Cohn, for her support and help in preparing the Instructor's Manual, PowerPoints, and TestBank. I am grateful, as well, to the manuscript reviewers involved in this and previous editions for holding me to the fire when I might have opted for a less rigorous coverage of some topics—especially Darl Champion of Methodist College, Jim Smith at West Valley College, Cassandra L. Renzi of Keiser University, and Bryan J. Vila formerly of the National Institute of Justice for their insightful suggestions as this book got under way.

I thank the reviewers of the manuscript for this 14th edition. They include:

Mkay Bonner, University of Louisiana at Monroe
Salih Hakan Can, Penn State University - Schuylkill
    Campus
Nadine Connell, The University of Texas at Dallas
Erin Grant, Washburn University
Pearl Jacobs, Sacred Heart University
Daniel Moeser, East Tennessee State University
Michael Paquette, Middlesex County College
Mary Pyle, Tyler Junior College
Stephen Wofsey, Northern Virgina Community College

I also thank the following reviewers of previous editions,
    including:

Howard Abadinsky, St. Johns University
Stephanie Abramoske-James, Collin County
    Community College
Reed Adams, Elizabeth City State University
Jonathan Appel, Tiffin University
Earl Ballou, Palo Alto College
Earl Ballou, Jr., Palo Alto College
Kevin Barrett, Palomar College
Larry Bassi, State University of New York
    (SUNY)–Brockport
Kevin Beaver, Florida State University
Richard Becker, North Harris College

Todd Beitzel, University of Findlay
Gad Bensinger, Loyola University–Chicago
Robert Bing, University of Texas - Arlington
Michael Bisciglia, Southeastern Louisiana University
Gary Boyer, Dabney S. Lancaster CC
Gary Boyer, Sr., Dabney S. Lancaster Community College
Mindy Bradley, University of Arkansas
Alton Braddock, University of Louisiana–Monroe
Pauline Brennan, University of Nebraska
Chip Burns, Texas Christian University
Ronald Burns, Texas Christian University
Theodore P. Byrne, California State University–
    Dominguez Hills
W. Garret Capune, California State University–Fullerton
Mike Carlie, Southwest Missouri State University
Geary Chlebus, James Sprunt Community College
Steven Christiansen, Joliet Junior College
Dr. Joseph Ciccone, WWCC
Joseph Ciccone, WWCC & CCI/Everest College
Jon E. Clark, Temple University
Lora C. Clark, Pitt Community College
Warren Clark, California State University–Bakersfield
Lisa Clayton, Community College of Southern Nevada
Lisa Clayton, College of Southern Nevada
Ellen G. Cohn, Florida International University
Gary Colboth, California State University–Long Beach
Kimberly Collica, Monroe College
Tomasina Cook, Erie Community College
William Corbet, New Mexico State University
Catherine Cowling, Campbell University
Susan C. Craig, University of Central Florida
Fredrick Crawford, Missouri Baptist University
Jannette O. Domingo, John Jay College of Criminal Justice
Vicky Doworth, Montgomery College
Daniel P. Doyle, University of Montana
Martha Earwood, University of Alabama–Birmingham
Steven Egger, University of Houston–Clearlake
Ron Fagan, Pepperdine University
Robert Franzese, University of Oklahoma
Alan S. Frazier, Glendale Community College
Harold A. Frossard, Moraine Valley Community College
Barry J. Garigen, Genesee Community College
S. Marlon Gayadeen, Buffalo State College
Michael Gray, Wor-Wic Community College
Alex Greenberg, Niagara County Community College
Tim Griffin, St. Xavier University
Julia Hall, Drexel University

Ed Heischmidt, Rend Lake College

Gary Herwald, Central Texas College and University of Phoenix

Dennis Hoffman, University of Nebraska at Omaha

Michael Hooper, California Department of Justice

William D. Hyatt, Western Carolina University

Nicholas H. Irons, County College of Morris

Galan M. Janeksela, University of Tennessee at Chattanooga

Jeffrie Jinian, Florida Gulf Coast University

Steve Johnson, Eastern Arizona College

Terry L. Johnson, Owens Community College

David M. Jones, University of Wisconsin–Oshkosh

Victor Kappeler, Eastern Kentucky State University

P. Ray Kedia, Grambling State University

David Keys, New Mexico State University

Lloyd Klein, Louisiana State University–Shreveport

Sylvia Kuennen, Briar Cliff College

Karel Kurst-Swanger, Oswego State University of New York

Hamid R. Kusha, Texas A&M International University

Tony LaRose, University of Tampa

David Legere, New England College

David S. Long, St. Francis College

Barry Langford, Columbia College

Joan Luxenburg, University of Central Oklahoma

Michael Lyman, Columbia College

Francis Marrocco, Triton College

Adam Martin, South Florida Community College

Dena Martin, Ivy Tech Community College of Indiana

Richard H. Martin, Elgin Community College

Theresa McGuire, DeVry University

David C. May, Eastern Kentucky University

G. Larry Mays, New Mexico State University

Thomas P. McAninch, Scott Community College

William McGovern, Sussex County Community College

Susan S. McGuire, San Jacinto College North

Robert J. Meadows, California Lutheran University

Jim Mezhir, Niagara County Community College

Rick Michelson, Grossmont College

Jeffrey D. Monroe, Xavier University

Harvey Morley, California State University–Long Beach

Jacqueline Mullany, Indiana University Northwest

Charles Myles, California State University–Los Angeles

Bonnie Neher, Harrisburg Area Community College

David Neubauer, University of New Orleans–Lakefront

Melanie Norwood, Southeastern Louisiana University

Ken O'Keefe, Prairie State College

David F. Owens, Onondaga Community College

Michael J. Palmiotto, Wichita State University

Lance Parr, Grossmont College

William H. Parsonage, Penn State University

Allison Payne, Villanova University

Ken Peak, University of Nevada–Reno

Joseph M. Pellicciotti, Indiana University Northwest

Roger L. Pennel, Central Missouri State University

Joseph L. Peterson, University of Illinois at Chicago

Morgan Peterson, Palomar College

Caryl Poteete, Illinois Central College

Gary Prawel, Keuka College

Philip J. Reichel, University of Northern Colorado

Albert Roberts, Rutgers University

Christopher Rosbough, Florida State University

Carl E. Russell, Scottsdale Community College

Paul Sarantakos, Parkland College

Wayne J. Scamuffa, ITT Technical Institute

Benson Schaffer, IVAMS Arbitration and Mediation Services

Stephen J. Schoenthaler, California State University–Stanislaus

Jeff Schrink, Indiana State University

Tim Schuetzle, University of Mary

Scott Senjo, Weber State University

Bart Scroggins, Columbia College

Judith M. Sgarzi, Mount Ida College

Louis F. Shepard, West Georgia Technical College

John Siler, Georgia Perimeter College

Ira Silverman, University of South Florida

Loretta J. Stalans, Loyola University–Chicago

Domenick Stampone, Raritan Valley Community College

Z. G. Standing Bear, University of Colorado

Mark A. Stetler, Montgomery College

B. Grant Stitt, University of Nevada–Reno

Norma Sullivan, College of DuPage; Troy University

Robert W. Taylor, University of North Texas

Lawrence F. Travis III, University of Cincinnati

Ron Vogel, California State University–Long Beach

David Whelan, Western Carolina University

Dianne A. Williams, North Carolina A&T State University

Kristin Williams, Ball State University

Lois Wims, Salve Regina University

Francis Williams, Plymouth State University

L. Thomas Winfree, Jr., New Mexico State University
John M. Wyant, Illinois Central College
Jeffrey Zack, Fayetteville Technical Community College

My thanks to everyone! I would also like to extend a special thanks to the following individuals for their invaluable comments and suggestions along the way: Gordon Armstrong, Jack Brady, Avon Burns, Kathy Cameron-Hahn, Alex Obi Ekwuaju, Gene Evans, Joe Graziano, Donald J. Melisi, Greg Osowski, Phil Purpura, Victor Quiros, John Robich, Barry Schreiber, Dave Seip, Ted Skotnicki, Stewart Stanfield, Bill Tafoya, Tom Thackery, Joe Trevalino, Howard Tritt, Bill Tyrrell, Tim Veiders, and Bob Winslow.

Thanks are also due to everyone who assisted in artistic arrangements, including Sergeant Michael Flores of the New York City Police Department's Photo Unit, Michael L. Hammond of the Everett (Washington) Police Department, Mikael Karlsson of Arresting Images, Assistant Chief James M. Lewis of the Bakersfield (California) Police Department, Tonya Matz of the University of Illinois at Chicago, and Monique Smith of the National Institute of Justice—all of whom were especially helpful in providing a wealth of photo resources. I am especially indebted to University of Illinois Professor Joseph L. Peterson for his assistance with sections on scientific evidence and to George W. Knox of the National Gang Crime Research Center for providing valuable information on gangs and gang activity.

I'd also like to acknowledge Chief J. Harper Wilson and Nancy Carnes of the FBI's Uniform Crime Reporting Program; Mark Reading of the Drug Enforcement Administration's Office of Intelligence; Kristina Rose at the National Institute of Justice; Marilyn Marbrook and Michael Rand at the Office of Justice Programs; Wilma M. Grant of the U.S. Supreme Court's Project Hermes; Ken Kerle at the American Jail Association; Lisa Bastian, survey statistician with the National Crime Victimization Survey Program; Steve Shackelton with the U.S. Parks Service; Ronald T. Allen, Steve Chaney, Bernie Homme, and Kenneth L. Whitman, all with the California Peace Officer Standards and Training Commission; Dianne Martin at the Drug Enforcement Administration; and George J. Davino of the New York City Police Department for their help in making this book both timely and accurate.

Last, but by no means least, Taylor Davis, H. R. Delaney, Jannette O. Domingo, Al Garcia, Rodney Hennigsen, Norman G. Kittel, Robert O. Lampert, and Joseph M. Pellicciotti should know that their writings, contributions, and valuable suggestions at the earliest stages of manuscript development continue to be very much appreciated. Thank you, everyone!

FRANK SCHMALLEGER, PH.D.

About the Author

Frank Schmalleger, Ph.D., is Distinguished Professor Emeritus at the University of North Carolina at Pembroke. He holds degrees from the University of Notre Dame and The Ohio State University, having earned both a master's (1970) and a doctorate in sociology (1974) from The Ohio State University with a special emphasis in criminology. From 1976 to 1994, he taught criminology and criminal justice courses at the University of North Carolina at Pembroke. For the last 16 of those years, he chaired the university's Department of Sociology, Social Work, and Criminal Justice. The university named him Distinguished Professor in 1991.

Schmalleger has taught in the online graduate program of the New School for Social Research, helping build the world's first electronic classrooms in support of distance learning on the Internet. As an adjunct professor with Webster University in St. Louis, Missouri, Schmalleger helped develop the university's graduate program in security administration and loss prevention. He taught courses in that curriculum for more than a decade. An avid Web user and website builder, Schmalleger is also the creator of a number of award-winning websites, including some that support this textbook.

Frank Schmalleger is the author of numerous articles and more than 40 books, including the widely used *Criminal Justice: A Brief Introduction* (Pearson, 2016), *Criminology Today* (Pearson, 2017), and *Criminal Law Today* (Pearson, 2014).

Schmalleger is also founding editor of the journal *Criminal Justice Studies.* He has served as editor for the Pearson series *Criminal Justice in the Twenty-First Century* and as imprint adviser for Greenwood Publishing Group's criminal justice reference series.

Schmalleger's philosophy of both teaching and writing can be summed up in these words: "In order to communicate knowledge we must first catch, then hold, a person's interest—be it student, colleague, or policymaker. Our writing, our speaking, and our teaching must be relevant to the problems facing people today, and they must in some way help solve those problems." Visit the author's website at **http://www.schmalleger.com**.

Justice is truth in action!
—*Benjamin Disraeli (1804–1881)*

Injustice anywhere is a threat to justice everywhere.
—*Martin Luther King, Jr. (1929–1968)*

THE CRIMINAL

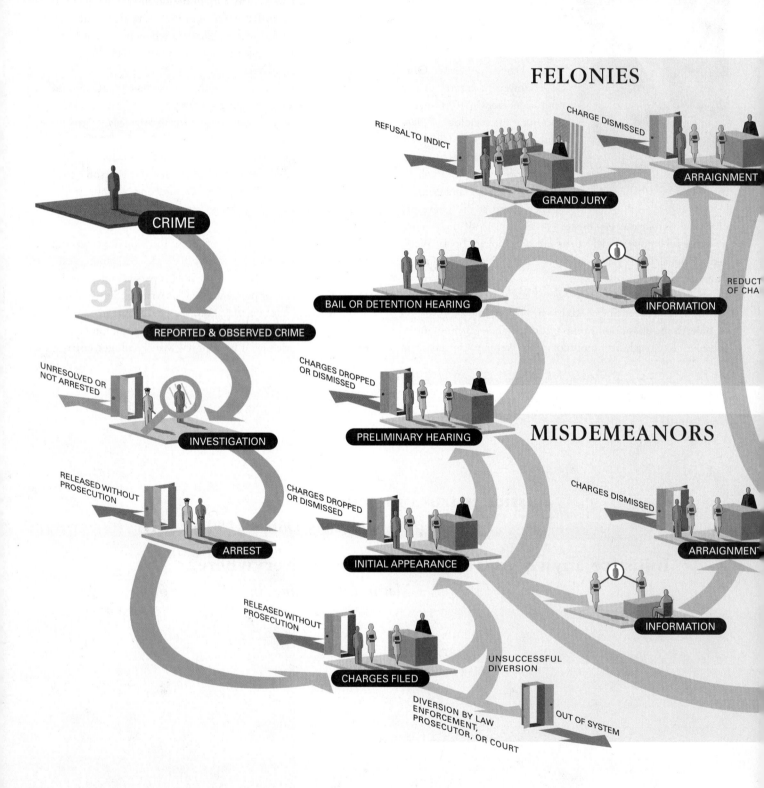

FELONIES

REFUSAL TO INDICT

CHARGE DISMISSED

ARRAIGNMENT

GRAND JURY

CRIME

BAIL OR DETENTION HEARING

REDUCT
OF CHA

911

INFORMATION

REPORTED & OBSERVED CRIME

CHARGES DROPPED
OR DISMISSED

UNRESOLVED OR
NOT ARRESTED

PRELIMINARY HEARING

MISDEMEANORS

INVESTIGATION

RELEASED WITHOUT
PROSECUTION

CHARGES DROPPED
OR DISMISSED

CHARGES DISMISSED

ARRAIGNMEN

ARREST

INITIAL APPEARANCE

RELEASED WITHOUT
PROSECUTION

INFORMATION

CHARGES FILED

UNSUCCESSFUL
DIVERSION

DIVERSION BY LAW
ENFORCEMENT,
PROSECUTOR, OR COURT

OUT OF SYSTEM

USTICE SYSTEM

SENTENCING & SANCTIONS   **PROBATION**   **PRISON**   **PAROLE**

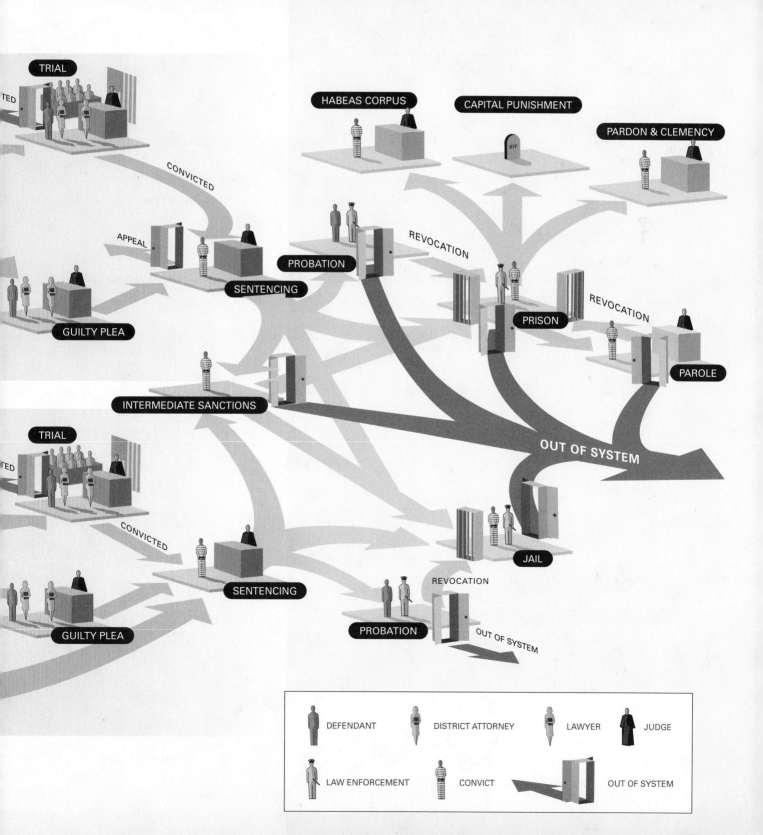

TRIAL

TED

CONVICTED

HABEAS CORPUS

CAPITAL PUNISHMENT

PARDON & CLEMENCY

RIP

APPEAL

PROBATION

REVOCATION

SENTENCING

REVOCATION

GUILTY PLEA

PRISON

REVOCATION

PAROLE

INTERMEDIATE SANCTIONS

OUT OF SYSTEM

TRIAL

TED

CONVICTED

SENTENCING

JAIL

REVOCATION

GUILTY PLEA

PROBATION

OUT OF SYSTEM

DEFENDANT   DISTRICT ATTORNEY   LAWYER   JUDGE

LAW ENFORCEMENT   CONVICT   OUT OF SYSTEM

PART 1

CRIME IN AMERICA

INDIVIDUAL RIGHTS VERSUS PUBLIC ORDER

The accused has these common law, constitutional, statutory, and humanitarian rights:

- Justice for the individual
- Personal liberty
- Dignity as a human being
- The right to due process

Those individual rights must be effectively balanced against these community concerns:

- Social justice
- Equality before the law
- The protection of society
- Freedom from fear

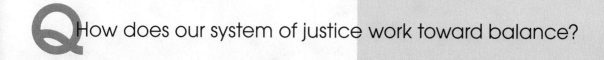 How does our system of justice work toward balance?

The Will of the People Is the Best Law

The great American statesman and orator Daniel Webster (1782–1852) once wrote, "Justice is the great interest of man on earth. It is the ligament which holds civilized beings and civilized nations together." Although Webster lived in a relatively simple time with few problems and many shared rules, justice has never been easily won. Unlike Webster's era, society today is highly complex. It is populated by groups with a wide diversity of interests, and it faces threats and challenges unimaginable in Webster's day. It is within this challenging context that the daily practice of American criminal justice occurs.

The criminal justice system has three central components: police, courts, and corrections. The history, the activities, and the legal environment surrounding the police are discussed in Part 2 of this book. Part 3 describes the courts, and Part 4 deals with prisons, probation, and parole. Part 5 provides a guide to the future of the justice system and describes the impact of the threat of terrorism on enforcement agencies. We begin here in Part 1, however, with an overview of that grand ideal that we call *justice*, and we consider how the justice ideal relates to the everyday practice of criminal justice in the United States today. To that end, in the four chapters that make up this section, we will examine how and why laws are made. We will look at the wide array of interests that

impinge upon the justice system, and we will examine closely the dichotomy that distinguishes citizens who are primarily concerned with individual rights from those who emphasize the need for individual responsibility and social accountability—a dichotomy that has existed since the start of our country, but has become especially significant in the wake of the September 11, 2001, terrorist attacks. In the pages that follow, we will see how justice can mean personal freedom and protection from the power of government to some people and greater safety and security to others. In this section, we will also lay the groundwork for the rest of the text by painting a picture of crime in America today, suggesting possible causes for it, and showing how policies for dealing with crime have evolved.

As you read about the complex tapestry that is the practice of criminal justice in America today, you will learn of a system in flux, perhaps less sure of its purpose than at any time in its history. You may also catch the sense, however, that very soon a new and reborn institution of justice may emerge from the ferment that now exists. Whatever the final outcome, it can only be hoped that *justice*, as proffered by the American system of criminal justice, will be sufficient to hold our civilization together—and to allow it to prosper in the twenty-first century and beyond.

Tony Avelar-Pool/Getty Images

1 WHAT IS CRIMINAL JUSTICE?

LEARNING OBJECTIVES

After reading this chapter, you should be able to

- Summarize the history of crime in America and corresponding changes in the American criminal justice system.
- Describe the public-order (crime-control) and individual-rights (due process) perspectives of criminal justice, concluding with how the criminal justice system balances the two perspectives.
- Explain the relationship of criminal justice to general concepts of equity and fairness.
- Describe the American criminal justice system in terms of its three major components and their respective functions.
- Describe the process of American criminal justice, including the stages of criminal case processing.
- Define *due process of law*, including where the American legal system guarantees due process.
- Describe the role of evidence-based practice in contemporary criminal justice.
- Explain how multiculturalism and diversity present challenges to and opportunities for the American system of criminal justice.

People expect both safety and justice and do not want to sacrifice one for the other.

CHRISTOPHER STONE, President, Open Society Foundations[1]

■ **crime** Conduct in violation of the criminal laws of a state, the federal government, or a local jurisdiction for which there is no legally acceptable justification or excuse.[i]

■ **Follow the author's tweets about the latest crime and justice news @schmalleger.**

Introduction

Ask anyone who has come into contact with it, and you will hear that the American criminal justice system wields a lot of power. Agencies of the justice system have the authority to arrest, to convict, and to imprison. In the most serious cases, the system even has control over who lives and who dies. For those who commit **crimes**, the "full weight and power" of the system comes crashing down on them, beginning with arrest. Yet, for all of it's power, the American system of justice is a consensual system that relies upon both public acceptance and public cooperation for it to function effectively. Were citizens to lose faith in the justice process and question its legitimacy, then the day-to-day work of law enforcement officers, court personnel, and corrections officers would become insurmountably difficult—and their jobs would be impossible to perform.

In late 2014 and early 2015, the criminal justice system in this country was teetering on the edge of just such a crisis. It was a crisis that arose quickly and spontaneously, fed in large part by social media, following refusals by grand jurors in Missouri and New York to indict police officers in the death of two black suspects in separate incidents. The first involved Michael Brown, an 18-year-old unarmed African American man who died in hail of bullets fired by a Ferguson, Missouri, police officer after an initial confrontation between the two turned violent.[2] The second involved Eric Garner, another unarmed black man who died after an NYPD officer placed him in a choke hold while they struggled—apparently preventing him from being able to breathe.[3] Garner, a father of six, had been arrested numerous times before the fatal encounter for illegally selling cigarettes on city streets—a minor offense.

Protests followed both grand jury decisions, with demonstrators in Ferguson rioting, looting, and burning down stores over a period of days. New York City protestors emblazoned the slogan "No justice, No Peace" on placards they carried, and Missouri protestors chanted "Hands up, don't shoot!" in the belief that Brown was surrendering to police when he was shot (the grand jury, however, concluded otherwise).

Confrontations between police and demonstrators remained largely peaceful but led to an especially surprising result. Police officers in Ferguson made no arrests during the first few nights of looting and rioting, even though arsonists and thieves were in plain sight; and NYPD officers stopped making "quality of life arrests"—or arrests for minor crimes. By December 2014, arrests in New York City for minor crimes such as traffic violations, and public drinking and urination, had plummeted 94% from the year before.[4] Arrests for other crimes nose-dived by 66% from only a week earlier. Police in New York City were reported to

Kateleen Foy/Getty Images

New York City police officers mourn the loss of two of their own. In late December 2014, NYPD officers Rafael Ramos and Wenjian Liu were assassinated while they sat in their marked patrol car on a Brooklyn Street. The shooter, 28-year-old Ismaaiyl Brinsley, may have wanted to avenge the deaths of two unarmed black men at the hands of police months earlier. The killings led to debates over the fairness of the American criminal justice system. How would *you* assess that system's fairness?

■ **theme**   Why do you think the increased emphasis on individual rights beginning in the 1960s was associated with an increase in reported crime?

■ **procedural fairness**   The process by which procedures that feel fair to those involved are made.

■ **individual rights**   The rights guaranteed to all members of American society by the U.S. Constitution (especially those found in the first ten amendments to the Constitution, known as the *Bill of Rights*). These rights are particularly important to criminal defendants facing formal processing by the criminal justice system.

■ **social disorganization**   A condition said to exist when a group is faced with social change, uneven development of culture, maladaptiveness, disharmony, conflict, and lack of consensus.

be making arrests "only when they have to."[5] In Seattle, police chief Kathleen O'Toole, made the rounds of her department's stations telling officers that it was OK to arrest people. "If you get agitators who threaten the police or the public, you have to arrest them," she said.[6] It was as though police officers in Ferguson, New York City, and elsewhere—perhaps wary of stoking more public unrest—had become afraid to enforce the law.

Matters became even uglier when assaults on police officers rose significantly following the protests. On December 20, 2014, two uniformed NYPD police officers were shot dead as they sat in their marked police cruiser on a Brooklyn street corner.[7] The assassination-style attack was carried out by 28-year-old Ismaaiyl Brinsley, who soon shot and killed himself on a nearby subway platform. Prior to the killings, Brinsley had posted anti-police threats on his Instagram page, referencing the "unjust" killings of Garner and Brown. "I'm putting wings on pigs today," he wrote, "They take 1 of ours . . . Let's take 2 of Theirs." Soon, police officers around the country were doubling up on patrol and bracing for further attacks.

American society is built upon a delicate balance between the demand for personal freedoms and the need for public safety.

Then, on New Year's Eve, as 2015 was about to begin, activists stormed St. Louis police headquarters and pushed their way inside, saying that they had an eviction notice and were reclaiming the building for "the people." Protestors were pepper sprayed, and five ended up being arrested.[8]

About the same time someone spray-painted an image on a wall of a Detroit, Michigan, youth center that was close to the city's police department, depicting a small figure with wings and a halo pointing a gun at a police officer whose hands were raised in the air.[9]

Although the antipolice movement was embraced by only a relatively small portion of the American population, it signified distrust not only of the police, but also reflected a fundamental sense of injustice about how suspects—especially African Americans—were being treated by the entire justice system. Some saw the protests as releasing pent-up frustration that resulted from a decades-long war on drugs, during which a hugely disproportionate number of young blacks were arrested, and a get-tough-on-crime era that resulted in dramatically overcrowded prisons throughout the country. Whatever the cause, it soon became clear that public acceptance of the justice system's authority is based significantly on the perception of fair and equitable treatment by all of its component agencies.[10] One of the lessons learned from the events of 2014–2015 was that fairness

has a wider meaning than ensuring just outcomes and upholding due process (issues that we will later discuss).

As we shall see throughout this text, **procedural fairness**, which is the process by which decisions that *feel* fair are made, is a vital component of our American justice system.

A Brief History of Crime in America

What we call *criminal activity* has undoubtedly been with us since the dawn of history, and crime control has long been a primary concern of politicians and government leaders worldwide. Still, the American experience with crime during the last half century has been especially influential in shaping the criminal justice system of today (Figure 1-1). In this country, crime waves have come and gone, including an 1850–1880 crime epidemic, which was apparently related to social upheaval caused by large-scale immigration and the Civil War.[11] A spurt of widespread organized criminal activity was associated with the Prohibition years of the early twentieth century. Following World War II, however, American crime rates remained relatively stable until the 1960s

The 1960s and 1970s saw a burgeoning concern for the rights of ethnic and racial minorities, women, people with physical and mental challenges, and many other groups. The civil rights movement of the period emphasized equality of opportunity and respect for individuals, regardless of race, color, creed, gender, or personal attributes. As new laws were passed and suits filed, court involvement in the movement grew. Soon a plethora of hard-won individual rights and prerogatives, based on the U.S. Constitution, the Bill of Rights, and new federal and state legislation, were recognized and guaranteed. By the 1980s, the civil rights movement had profoundly affected all areas of social life—from education and employment to the activities of the criminal justice system.

This emphasis on **individual rights** was accompanied by a dramatic increase in reported criminal activity. Although some researchers doubted the accuracy of official accounts, reports by the Federal Bureau of Investigation (FBI) of "traditional" crimes like murder, rape, and assault increased considerably during the 1970s and into the 1980s. Many theories were advanced to explain this leap in observed criminality. Some analysts of American culture, for example, suggested that the combination of newfound freedoms and long-pent-up hostilities of the socially and economically deprived worked to produce **social disorganization**, which in turn increased criminality.

The American experience with crime during the last half century has been especially influential in shaping the criminal justice system of today.

By the mid-1980s, the dramatic increase in the sale and use of illicit drugs threatened the foundation of American society. Cocaine, and later laboratory-processed "crack," spread to every corner of America. Large cities became havens for drug gangs, and many inner-city areas were all but abandoned to highly armed and well-financed drug racketeers. Cities experienced dramatic declines in property values, and residents wrestled with an eroding quality of life.

By the close of the 1980s, neighborhoods and towns were fighting for their communal lives. Huge rents had been torn in the national social fabric, and the American way of life, long taken for granted, was under the gun. Traditional values appeared in danger of going up in smoke along with the "crack" being consumed openly in some parks and resorts. Looking for a way to stem the tide of increased criminality, many took up the call for "law and order." In response, President Ronald Reagan created a cabinet-level "drug czar" position to coordinate the "war on drugs." Careful thought was given at the highest levels to using the military to patrol the sea-lanes and air corridors through which many of the illegal drugs entered the country.

1850–1880 A crime epidemic spurred by social upheaval brought on by large-scale immigration and the Civil War.

1920–1933 Prohibition spurs the growth of organized crime.

Following World War II, American crime rates remained relatively stable until the 1960s.

1960–1970 The civil rights movement of the period emphasized equality of opportunity and respect for individuals regardless of race, color, creed, gender, or personal attributes. This period also saw a dramatic increase in reported criminal activity.

1970s Reports of crimes such as murder, rape, and assault increased considerably.

1980s By the mid-1980s, the dramatic increase in sale and use of illicit drugs led to increased crime. Large cities became havens for drug gangs and cities experienced dramatic declines in property values and quality of life. President Reagan declared a "war on drugs."

1992 The videotaped beating of Rodney King, an African American, by Los Angeles–area police officers was seen as an example of the abuse of police power.

By the late **1990s,** the public perception was that crime rates were growing and that many offenders went unpunished. This led to a growing emphasis on responsibility and punishment and the development of a "get tough on crime" era.

2001 A series of terrorist attacks on New York City, Washington, D.C., and elsewhere changed the focus of law enforcement to a proactive and more global approach.

2001 USA PATRIOT Act dramatically increases the investigatory authority of federal, state, and local police agencies.

The incidence of personal crime declined throughout the 1990s.

2009 Bernard Madoff pleads guilty to the largest Ponzi scheme in history. The crimes of Madoff, and widespread suspicions about the activities of Wall Street financiers, led to a number of white-collar crime investigations. White-collar crime came into focus as a serious threat to the American way of life.

2011 FBI most-wanted terrorist Osama Bin Laden was killed by U.S. special operations forces in Pakistan, leading to fears of a renewed terrorist onslaught on American targets throughout the world.

2012–2015 Epidemic of mass shootings and random violence sweeps public venues across the U.S.

2015–present Cybercrimes become commonplace and threaten both national security and corporate and personal financial integrity.

Photo sources (from top): Courtesy of the Library of Congress; Darryl Jacobson / Everett Collection / Superstock; Darryl Jacobson / Superstock; Steven Hirsch/ Newscom; NetPics / Alamy

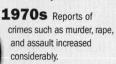

FIGURE 1-1 | Milestones in Crime History

Source: Pearson Education, Inc.

© ACE STOCK LIMITED/Alamy

A street-corner drug deal. By the mid-1980s, the American criminal justice system had become embroiled in a war against illicit drugs, filling the nation's prisons and jails with drug dealers, traffickers, and users. Has the war been won?

President George H. W. Bush, who followed Reagan into office, quickly embraced and expanded the government's antidrug efforts.

A decade later, a few spectacular crimes that received widespread coverage in the news media fostered a sense among the American public that crime in the United States was out of hand and that strict new measures were needed to combat it. One such crime was the 1995 bombing of the Alfred P. Murrah Federal Building in Oklahoma City by antigovernment extremists. Another was the 1999 Columbine High School massacre in Colorado that left 12 students and one teacher dead.[12]

The public's perception that crime rates were growing, coupled with a belief that offenders frequently went unpunished or received only a judicial slap on the wrist, led to a burgeoning emphasis on responsibility and punishment. By the late 1990s, a newfound emphasis on individual accountability began to blossom among an American public fed up with crime and fearful of its own victimization. Growing calls for enhanced responsibility quickly began to replace the previous emphasis on individual rights. As a juggernaut of conservative opinion made itself felt on the political scene, Senator Phil Gramm of Texas observed that the public wants to "grab violent criminals by the throat, put them in prison [and] stop building prisons like Holiday Inns."[13]

> By the late 1990s, a newfound emphasis on individual accountability began to blossom among an American public fed up with crime and fearful of its own victimization.

Then, in an event that changed the course of our society, public tragedy became forever joined with private victimization in our collective consciousness after a series of highly destructive and well-coordinated terrorist attacks on New York City and Washington, D.C., on September 11, 2001. Those attacks resulted in the collapse and total destruction of the twin 110-story towers of the World Trade Center and a devastating explosion at the Pentagon. Thousands of people perished, and many were injured. Although law enforcement and security agencies were unable to prevent the September 11 attacks, many have since moved from a reactive to a proactive posture in the fight against terrorism—a change that is discussed in more detail in Chapter 6, "Policing: Purpose and Organization."

The September 11 attacks also made clear that adequate law enforcement involves a global effort at controlling crime and reducing the risk of injury and loss to law-abiding people both at home and abroad. The attacks showed that criminal incidents that take place on the other side of the globe can affect those of us living in the United States, and they illustrated how the acquisition of skills needed to understand diverse cultures can help in the fight against crime and terrorism.

As Chapter 17, "Terrorism, Multinational Criminal Justice and Global Issues," points out, terrorism is a criminal act, and preventing terrorism and investigating terrorist incidents after they occur are highly important roles for local, state, and federal law enforcement agencies.

A different kind of offending, corporate, and white-collar crime took center stage in 2002 and 2003 as Congress stiffened penalties for unscrupulous business executives who knowingly falsify their company's financial reports.[14] The changes came amidst declining stock market values, shaken investor confidence, and threats to the viability of employee pension plans in the wake of a corporate crime wave involving criminal activities that had been planned and undertaken by executives at a number of leading corporations. In an effort to restore order to American financial markets, President George W. Bush signed the Sarbanes-Oxley Act on July 30, 2002.[15] The law, which has been called "the single most important piece of legislation affecting corporate governance, financial disclosure, and the practice of public accounting since the US securities laws of the early 1930s,"[16] is intended to deter corporate fraud and to hold business executives accountable for their actions.

Today, white-collar crime continues to be a focus of federal prosecutors. In 2012, for example, Texas billionaire R. Allen Stanford, 61, was convicted by a federal jury in a $7 billion Ponzi scheme that he ran for almost 20 years.[17] Prosecutors convinced the jury that Stanford illegally funneled money from investors in his financial services firm to his personal accounts, allowing him to pay for an extravagant lifestyle including private jets, yachts, and a number of mansions for himself and his family. Following conviction, Stanford received a sentence of 110 years in prison.

Freedom Tower under construction at the World Trade Center site in New York City. The tower opened in 2014. It stands 1,776 feet tall and will be surrounded by several other buildings, and a memorial to the nearly 3,000 people who were killed in the terrorist attacks that demolished the Twin Towers in 2001. How did those attacks change the American justice system?

If we were to examine all forms of criminal activity, and if we were to become fully aware of all of today's hidden offenses, we would probably find that crimes today have undergone a significant shift away from historical forms of offending to more innovative schemes involving computers and other digital devices.

Illinois, are seeing record homicide rates.[20] Similarly, as Chapter 2 explains in greater detail, many other types of crimes today are Internet-based or involve other forms of high-technology. Criminal perpetrators who illegally gain access to digital information (and money) through social media or Internet-based transactions are responsible for a significant level of criminal activity in the virtual world. Such crimes can have very significant impacts on people's lives. Moreover, crimes committed through the medium of cyberspace frequently remain undiscovered, or are found out only with the passage of time. Computer-related crimes are discussed in Chapter 18, "High-Technology Crimes." For a detailed look at crimes, both historical and contemporary, visit **http://www.trutv.com/library/crime**.

The Theme of This Book

This book examines the American system of criminal justice and the agencies and processes that constitute it. It builds on a theme that is especially valuable for studying criminal justice today: *individual rights versus public order*. This theme draws on historical developments that have shaped our legal system and our understandings of crime and justice. It is one of the primary determinants of the nature of contemporary criminal justice—including criminal law, police practice, sentencing, and corrections.

A strong emphasis on individual rights rose to the forefront of American social thought during the 1960s and 1970s, a period known as the *civil rights era*. The civil rights era led to the recognition of fundamental personal rights that had previously been denied illegally to many people on the basis of race, ethnicity, gender, sexual preference, or disability. The civil rights movement soon expanded to include the rights of many other groups, including criminal suspects, parolees and probationers, trial participants, prison and jail inmates, and victims. As the emphasis on civil rights grew, new laws and court decisions broadened the rights available to many.

The treatment of criminal suspects was afforded special attention by those who argued that the purpose of any civilized society should be to secure rights and freedoms for each of its citizens—including those suspected and convicted of crimes. Rights advocates feared unnecessarily restrictive government action and viewed it as an assault on basic human dignity and individual liberty. They believed that at times it was necessary to sacrifice some degree of public safety and predictability to

Similarly, in a 2009 story that most readers will remember, investment fund manager Bernard Madoff pleaded guilty to operating a Ponzi scheme that defrauded investors out of as much as $50 billion.[18] Madoff pleaded guilty to 11 felony counts, including securities fraud, mail fraud, wire fraud, money laundering, and perjury. Madoff was sentenced to serve 150 years in federal prison—three times as long as federal probation officers had recommended.[19] White-collar crime is discussed in more detail in Chapter 2, "The Crime Picture."

The current era is characterized by low and declining rates of "traditional" crimes such as rape, robbery, and burglary (see Chapter 2 for more details), but the specter of random mass shootings, a high number of inner-city murders, and novel forms of criminal activity complicates today's crime picture. In 2012, for example, the year of the mass shootings in Aurora, Colorado, and Newtown, Connecticut, both Camden, New Jersey, and Detroit, Michigan, reported more murders than at any time in their history, and other cities, including Chicago,

Lucas Jackson/Reuters/Landov Media

Ponzi schemer Bernard Madoff is escorted by police and photographed by the media as he departs U.S. federal court after a hearing in New York, January 5, 2009. Madoff, whose financial crimes may have cost investors as much as $50 billion, was sentenced to 150 years in prison in 2009. What happened to the money he stole?

Public perspectives in the late twentieth century largely shifted away from seeing the criminal as an unfortunate victim of poor social and personal circumstances who is inherently protected by fundamental human and constitutional rights to seeing him or her as a dangerous social predator who usurps the rights and privileges of law-abiding citizens. Reflecting the "get tough on crime" attitudes of recent times, many Americans demanded to know how offenders can better be held accountable for violations of the criminal law. In late 2010, for example, California state senators unanimously passed Chelsea's Law, a bill intended to increase prison sentences and extend parole terms for offenders who commit sex crimes against minors. The bill, named after 17-year-old Chelsea King, who was raped and murdered by a convicted sex offender earlier in 2010, was signed into law by the state's governor soon after it passed the legislature.[21] Even in an era of difficult budgetary challenges, a number of states are continuing to extend prison sentences for sex offenders, restrict where released sex offenders can live, and improve public notification of the whereabouts of sex offenders.[22]

> By the start of the Twenty-First Century public opinion had shifted away from seeing the criminal as an unfortunate victim of poor social and personal circumstances who is inherently protected by fundamental human and constitutional rights, to seeing him or her as a dangerous social predator who usurps the rights and privileges of law-abiding citizens.

Although financial constraints and social concerns like those identified in the story that opens this chapter have tempered the zeal of legislators to expand criminal punishments, the tension between individual rights and social responsibility still forms the basis for much policymaking activity in the criminal justice arena. Those who fight for individual rights continue to carry the banner of civil and criminal rights for the accused and the convicted, while public-order activists loudly proclaim the rights of the victimized and call for an increased emphasis on social responsibility and criminal punishment for convicted criminals. In keeping with these realizations, the theme of this book can be stated as follows:

> There is widespread recognition in contemporary society of the need to balance (1) the freedoms and privileges of our nation's citizens and the respect accorded the rights of individuals faced with criminal prosecution against (2) the valid interests that society has in preventing future crimes, in public safety, and in reducing the harm caused by criminal activity. While the personal freedoms guaranteed to law-abiding citizens as well as to criminal suspects by the Constitution, as interpreted by the U.S.

guarantee basic freedoms. Hence criminal rights activists demanded a justice system that limits police powers and that holds justice agencies accountable to the highest procedural standards.

During the 1960s and 1970s, the dominant philosophy in American criminal justice focused on guaranteeing the rights of criminal defendants while seeking to understand the root causes of crime and violence. The past 30 years, however, have witnessed increased interest in an ordered society, in public safety, and in the rights of crime victims. This change in attitudes was likely brought about by national frustration with the perceived inability of our society and its justice system to prevent crimes and to consistently hold offenders to heartfelt standards of right and wrong. Increased conservatism in the public-policy arena was given new life by the September 11, 2001, terrorist attacks and by widely publicized instances of sexual offenses targeting children. It continues to be sustained by the many stories of violent victimization, like random mass shootings, that seem to be the current mainstay of the American media.

■ **theme** Do you identify more with what the book calls the individual-rights perspective or the public-order perspective? What experiences have you had that might explain your affinity for that perspective?

■ **theme** What are the relative merits of the individual-rights perspective, and what are the merits of the public-order point of view? How can the goals of both perspectives be balanced in contemporary society?

■ **theme** Do you see a trend in our society in favor of individual-rights or public-order interests? What recent examples support your opinion?

■ **activity** Poll students to determine their identification with either the individual-rights perspective or the public-order perspective. After polling is complete, assign students to presentation groups by asking those who most closely identify with the public-order perspective to defend individual rights, and vice versa. Such role reversal can be interesting in its own right, but it may also serve to broaden students' appreciation for the values of others.

■ **individual-rights advocate** One who seeks to protect personal freedoms within the process of criminal justice.

■ **social order** The condition of a society characterized by social integration, consensus, smooth functioning, and lack of interpersonal and institutional conflict. Also, a lack of social disorganization.

■ **public-order advocate** One who believes that under certain circumstances involving a criminal threat to public safety, the interests of society should take precedence over individual rights.

freedom OR safety? YOU decide

Clarence Thomas Says: "Freedom Means Responsibility"

In 2009, U.S. Supreme Court Justice Clarence Thomas spoke to a group of high school essay contest winners in a Washington, D.C., hotel ballroom. Thomas used the occasion, which was dedicated to our nation's Bill of Rights, to point out the importance of obligations as well as rights. "Today there is much focus on our rights," said Thomas. "Indeed, I think there is a proliferation of rights." But then he went on to say, "I am often surprised by the virtual nobility that seems to be accorded those with grievances. Shouldn't there at least be equal time for our Bill of Obligations and our Bill of Responsibilities?"

Today, the challenge for the criminal justice system, it seems, is to balance individual rights and personal freedoms with social control and respect for legitimate authority. Years ago, during the height of what was then a powerful movement to win back control of our nation's cities and to rein in skyrocketing crime rates, the New York Post sponsored a conference on crime and civil rights. The keynote speaker at that conference was New York City's mayor, Rudolph W. Giuliani. In his speech, Giuliani identified the tension between personal freedoms and individual responsibilities as the crux of the

crime problem then facing his city and the nation. We mistakenly look to government and elected officials, Giuliani said, to assume responsibility for solving the problem of crime when, instead, each individual citizen must become accountable for fixing what is wrong with our society. "We only see the oppressive side of authority . . . . What we don't see is that freedom is not a concept in which people can do anything they want, be anything they can be. Freedom is about authority. Freedom is about the willingness of every single human being to cede to lawful authority a great deal of discretion about what you do."

You Decide

How can we, as Justice Thomas suggests, achieve a balance of rights and obligations in American society? What did Giuliani mean when he said, "What we don't see is that freedom is not a concept in which people can do anything they want, be anything they can be"? Is it possible to balance individual rights and personal freedoms with social control and respect for legitimate authority?

References: Adam Liptak, "Reticent Justice Opens Up to a Group of Students," New York Times, April 13, 2009, http://www.nytimes.com/2009/04/14/us/14bar.html (accessed September 2, 2009); and Philip Taylor, "Civil Libertarians: Giuliani's Efforts Threaten First Amendment," Freedom Forum Online, http://www.freedomforum.org (accessed September 5, 2011).

Supreme Court, must be closely guarded, the urgent social needs of communities to control unacceptable behavior and to protect law-abiding citizens from harm must be recognized. Still to be adequately addressed are the needs and interests of victims and the fear of crime and personal victimization that is often prevalent in the minds of many law-abiding citizens. It is important to recognize, however, that the drama between individual rights and public safety advocates now plays out in a tenuous economic environment characterized by financial constraints and a concern with effective public policy.

Figure 1-2 represents our theme and shows that most people today who intelligently consider the criminal justice system assume one of two viewpoints. We will refer to those who seek

> We seek to look at ways in which the individual-rights and public-order perspectives can be balanced to serve both sets of needs.

to protect personal freedoms and civil rights within society, and especially within the criminal justice process, as **individual-rights advocates**. Those who suggest that under certain circumstances involving criminal threats to public safety, the interests of society, especially crime control and **social order**, should take precedence over individual rights will be called **public-order advocates**. Recently, retired U.S. Supreme Court Justice Sandra Day O'Connor summed up the differences between these two perspectives by asking, "At what point does the cost to civil

■ **justice** The principle of fairness; the ideal of moral equity.

■ **social justice** An ideal that embraces all aspects of civilized life and that is linked to fundamental notions of fairness and to cultural beliefs about right and wrong.

■ **civil justice** The civil law, the law of civil procedure, and the array of procedures and activities having to do with private rights and remedies sought by civil action. Civil justice cannot be separated from social justice because the justice enacted in our nation's civil courts reflects basic American understandings of right and wrong.

■ **criminal justice** In the strictest sense, the criminal (penal) law, the law of criminal procedure, and the array of procedures and activities having to do with the enforcement of this body of law. Criminal justice cannot be separated from social justice because the justice enacted in our nation's criminal courts reflects basic American understandings of right and wrong.

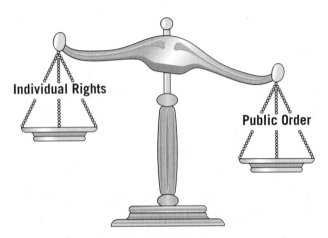

FIGURE 1-2 | **The Theme of This Book**

Balancing the concern for individual rights with the need for public order through the administration of criminal justice is the theme of this book.

Source: Pearson Education, Inc.

liberties from legislation designed to prevent terrorism [and crime] outweigh the added security that that legislation provides?"[23] In this book, we seek to look at ways in which the individual-rights and public-order perspectives can be balanced to serve both sets of needs. Hence you will find our theme discussed throughout this text, and within "Freedom or Safety?" boxes.

Criminal Justice and Basic Fairness

On the eve of the national election in November 2008, as final votes were being counted, President-elect Barack H. Obama gave an inspiring victory speech addressed to the nation and the world. In it, he said, "A new dawn of American leadership is at hand. To those who would tear this world down—we will defeat you. To those who seek peace and security—we support you. And to all those who have wondered if America's beacon still burns as bright—tonight we proved once more that the true strength of our nation comes not from the might of our arms or the scale of our wealth, but from the enduring power of our ideals: democracy, liberty, opportunity, and unyielding hope." The president concluded that night's remarks with an enduring

phrase, telling listeners that "the arc of the moral universe is long, but it bends toward justice."[24] The phrase, a favorite of the president's, had been adapted from remarks that Martin Luther King, Jr., made before the Southern Christian Leadership Conference in 1967.[25]

There is no denying that the word *justice* is powerful, and—at the time—the president's choice of words spoke to all Americans. The reality, however, is that *justice* is an elusive term. Although most listeners came away inspired that night, few who heard the president's speech knew exactly what *justice* might mean and what form it might eventually take. Even to those living within the same society, *justice* means different things. And just as *justice* can be an ambiguous term for politicians, it is not always clear how justice can be achieved in the criminal justice system. For example, is "justice for all" a reasonable expectation of today's—or tomorrow's—system of criminal justice? The answer is unclear because individual interests and social needs often diverge. From the perspective of a society or an entire nation, justice can look very different than it does from the perspective of an individual or a small group of people. Because of this dilemma, we now turn our attention to the nature of justice.

British philosopher and statesman Benjamin Disraeli (1804–1881) defined **justice** as "truth in action." A popular dictionary defines it as "the principle of moral rightness, or conformity to truth."[26] **Social justice** is a concept that embraces all aspects of civilized life. It is linked to notions of fairness and to cultural beliefs about right and wrong. Questions of social justice can arise about relationships between individuals, between parties (such as corporations and agencies of government), between the rich and the poor, between the sexes, between ethnic groups and minorities—between social connections of all sorts. In the abstract, the concept of social justice embodies the highest personal and cultural ideals.

Civil justice, one component of social justice, concerns itself with fairness in relationships between citizens, government agencies, and businesses in private matters, such as those involving contractual obligations, business dealings, hiring, and equality of treatment. **Criminal justice**, on the other hand, refers to the aspects of social justice that concern violations of the criminal law. As mentioned earlier, community interests in the criminal justice sphere demand the apprehension and punishment of

■ **administration of justice** The performance of any of the following activities: detection, apprehension, detention, pretrial release, post-trial release, prosecution, adjudication, correctional supervision, or rehabilitation of accused persons or criminal offenders.[ii]

Demonstrators gathering on the steps of New York City's Federal Hall to protest provisions of the USA PATRIOT Act. Federal Hall served as the venue for President George Washington's inauguration in 1789 and was the meeting place of the First Congress, which wrote our nation's Bill of Rights. The PATRIOT Act was passed by Congress with little debate just 45 days after the terrorist attacks of September 11, 2001. Rights advocates claim that the act, which has since been modified, unfairly restricts individual liberties. What do you think?

law violators. At the same time, criminal justice ideals extend to the protection of the innocent, the fair treatment of offenders, and fair play by the agencies of law enforcement, including courts and correctional institutions.

Criminal justice, ideally speaking, is "truth in action" within the process that we call the **administration of justice**. It is therefore vital to remember that justice, in the truest and most satisfying sense of the word, is the ultimate goal of criminal justice—and of the day-to-day practices and challenges that characterize the American criminal justice system. Reality, unfortunately, typically falls short of the ideal and is severely complicated by the fact that justice seems to wear different guises when viewed from diverse vantage points. To some people, the criminal justice system and criminal justice agencies often seem biased in favor of the powerful. The laws they enforce seem to emanate more from well-financed, organized, and vocal interest groups than they do from any idealized sense of social justice. As a consequence, disenfranchised groups, those who do not feel as though they share in the political and economic power of society, are often wary of the agencies of justice, seeing them more as enemies than as benefactors.

On the other hand, justice practitioners, including police officers, prosecutors, judges, and corrections officials, frequently complain that their efforts to uphold the law garner unfair public criticism. The realities of law enforcement and of "doing justice," they say, are often overlooked by critics of the system who have little experience in dealing with offenders and victims. We must recognize, practitioners often tell us, that those accused of violating the criminal law face an elaborate process built around numerous legislative, administrative, and organizational concerns. Viewed realistically, although the criminal justice process can be fine-tuned to take into consideration the interests of ever-larger numbers of people, it rarely pleases everyone. The outcome of the criminal justice process in any particular case is a social product, and like any product that is the result of group effort, it must inevitably be a patchwork quilt of human emotions, reasoning, and concerns.

Whichever side we choose in the ongoing debate over the nature and quality of criminal justice in America, it is vital that we recognize the plethora of pragmatic issues involved in the administration of justice while also keeping a clear focus on the justice ideal.[27] Was justice done, for example, in the 2013 first-degree murder trial of Jodi Arias on charges that she killed her

CJ | NEWS

Surveillance Technology Has Been Blanketing the Nation Since 9-11

Charles Rex Arbogast/AP Wide World Photos

A Chicago Police Department surveillance camera system and microphone unit positioned high above the street. This surveillance system includes a camera, high-bandwidth wireless communication, a strobe light, and a gunshot-recognition system, all in a bulletproof enclosure. The city is installing the surveillance system to spot crimes or terrorist activity. Do such units infringe on the personal freedoms of Chicago residents?

In the book *1984*, written more than 60 years ago, George Orwell envisioned a totalitarian regime that created an extensive surveillance network to monitor people's every move. Today, in the wake of the terrorist attacks of September 11, 2001, America has built a surveillance network that rivals that of *1984*, but without a totalitarian regime involved.

A decade after 9-11, there were an estimated 30 million surveillance cameras in the United States, says IMS Research. U.S. law enforcement is also implementing facial recognition technology, license plate readers, and gunfire alert systems. These developments prompted Jay Stanley of the American Civil Liberties Union to warn that the nation is heading toward "a total surveillance society in which your every move, your every transaction, is duly registered and recorded by some computer."

Most Americans, however, are not alarmed and actually welcome the trend. A 2007 ABC News/Washington Post poll showed that 71% of respondents favored increased video surveillance. In addition, courts have indicated that surveillance cameras, placed in plain view in public spaces, do not violate the Fourth Amendment, which bars governments from conducting unreasonable searches or seizures.

Technology has come a long way since surveillance cameras took small, grainy photos of two 9-11 hijackers boarding their plane at Boston's Logan Airport. Today's cameras collect and store images with many more pixels of information, making it possible to enlarge the photographs and capture previously undetected details.

In 2003, the city of Chicago began building what has become one of the most extensive surveillance systems in the United States, with 2,000 cameras operated by the police department and central monitoring over additional cameras operated by the transit system, school system, and private entities.

A 2011 study by the Urban Institute examining the use of surveillance cameras in three Chicago neighborhoods found they reduced crime in two of the neighborhoods. In the Humboldt Park neighborhood, for example, drug-related offenses and robberies fell by nearly 33% and violent crime declined by 20%.

Chicago has spent more than $60 million on its video surveillance network. Although that cost was supplemented by federal Homeland Security grants, such systems have high maintenance costs and compete for scarce tax dollars with other law enforcement activities, such as patrolling. The Urban Institute, however, found that Chicago saved $4.30 for every dollar spent on cameras in Humboldt Park.

Chicago uses wireless cameras mounted on poles with a "pan-tilt-zoom" technology that allows operators to follow subjects and focus in on them. Officers can do this manually, but as images proliferate, law enforcement has been increasingly turning to video analytic software that can sort through thousands of pictures to look for a specific image. This involves use of sophisticated software that recognizes faces or specific shapes and colors. The same technology is also used for scanners that read license plates and automatically check the number through a direct feed with state car license databases.

Police departments across the country are also implementing new sound-wave technology to monitor gunshots. This type of system, the best known of which is Shotspotter™, requires installing sensors throughout the city that can triangulate sound waves and identify the location of the gunshot within five yards. The Boston Police Department spent about $1.5 million to install gunshot detection systems and spends $150,000 to $175,000 in annual maintenance fees.

The effectiveness of gunfire alert systems has not been independently studied. According to the manufacturer, about one-third of reports are false alarms involving backfiring cars, construction, and other urban noises. But one definite advantage is that gunshot reports arrive in one to two minutes faster than 911 calls, bringing officers to the scene more quickly. And sometimes the systems pick up gunshots that were never called in.

Resources: "Surveillance Society: New High-Tech Cameras Are Watching You," *Popular Mechanics*, October 2, 2009, http://www.popularmechanics.com/technology/military/4236865; "Surveillance Cameras Cost-Effective Tools for Cutting Crime, 3-Year Study Concludes," *Urban Institute*, September 19, 2011, http://www.urban.org/publications/901450.html; and "Surveillance Technology Helps Boston Police Find Location of Gunfire," *WBUR*, December 23, 2011, http://www.wbur.org/2011/12/23/shotspotter.

boyfriend, Travis Alexander (the case is discussed in more detail in Chapter 10, "Pretrial Activities and the Criminal Trial"). What about in the 2005 criminal trial of pop-music superstar Michael Jackson on charges of child molestation? After Jackson's death, was the 2011 trial of his personal physician, Conrad Murray, just? Has justice been served in the case of Casey Anthony, whom authorities say killed her young daughter? Similarly, we might ask,

was justice done in the 2014 trial of Oscar Pistorius, the South African Paralympic athlete known as the "Blade Runner", who was convicted of the shooting death of his model girlfriend, Reeva Steenkamp?[28] Although answers to such questions may reveal a great deal about the American criminal justice system, they also have much to say about the perspectives of those who provide them.

■ **criminal justice system**   The aggregate of all operating and administrative or technical support agencies that perform criminal justice functions. The basic divisions of the operational aspects of criminal justice are law enforcement, courts, and corrections.

■ **lecture note**   Explain that the consensus model of criminal justice envisions the components of the criminal justice system as functioning together to achieve the goal of justice.

■ **consensus model**   A criminal justice perspective that assumes that the system's components work together harmoniously to achieve the social product we call *justice*.

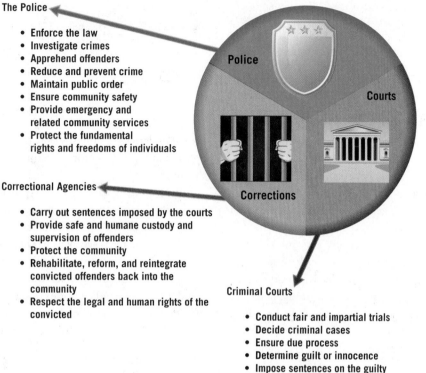

The Police

- Enforce the law
- Investigate crimes
- Apprehend offenders
- Reduce and prevent crime
- Maintain public order
- Ensure community safety
- Provide emergency and related community services
- Protect the fundamental rights and freedoms of individuals

Correctional Agencies

- Carry out sentences imposed by the courts
- Provide safe and humane custody and supervision of offenders
- Protect the community
- Rehabilitate, reform, and reintegrate convicted offenders back into the community
- Respect the legal and human rights of the convicted

Criminal Courts

- Conduct fair and impartial trials
- Decide criminal cases
- Ensure due process
- Determine guilt or innocence
- Impose sentences on the guilty
- Uphold the law
- Require fairness throughout the justice process
- Protect the rights and freedoms of anyone facing processing by the justice system
- Provide a check on the exercise of power by other justice system agencies*

*Fairness, professionalism, integrity, and impartiality are expected of all criminal justice personnel at every stage of criminal case processing, and it is a special duty of the courts to ensure that these expectations are met.

FIGURE 1-3 | The Core Components of the American Criminal Justice System and Their Functions

Source: Pearson Education, Inc.

American Criminal Justice: System and Functions

The Consensus Model

So far, we have described a **criminal justice system**[29] consisting of the component agencies of police, courts, and corrections. Each of these components can, in turn, be described in terms of its functions and purpose (Figure 1-3).

The systems perspective on criminal justice is characterized primarily by its assumption that the various parts of the justice system work together by design to achieve the wider purpose we have been calling *justice*. Hence the systems perspective on criminal justice generally encompasses a point of view called the **consensus model**. The consensus model assumes that each of the component parts of the criminal justice system strives toward a common goal and that the movement of cases and people through the system is smooth due to cooperation between the various components of the system.

The systems model of criminal justice is more an analytic tool than a reality, however. An analytic model, whether in the hard sciences or in the social sciences, is simply a convention chosen for its explanatory power. By explaining the actions of criminal justice officials—such as arrest, prosecution, and sentencing—as though they were systematically related, we are able to envision a fairly smooth and predictable process (which is described in more detail later in this chapter).

■ **lecture note**   Explain that the conflict model of criminal justice envisions the components of the criminal justice system as serving their own interests and competing with one another over scarce resources, public recognition, and various other forms of accomplishment.

■ **conflict model**   A criminal justice perspective that assumes that the system's components function primarily to serve their own interests. According to this theoretical framework, justice is more a product of conflicts among agencies within the system than it is the result of cooperation among component agencies.

■ **lecture note**   Compare and contrast the consensus and conflict models of criminal justice and discuss the importance of both models in the study of the criminal justice system

■ **theme**   Why does the author say that the various agencies of justice are linked closely enough to be termed a *system* while at the same time agreeing with Skolnick's idea of a criminal justice *nonsystem*?

■ **theme**   Which model, in your opinion, your mind, best describes the American system of criminal justice: the consensus model or the conflict model? Why?

■ **activity**   Ask representatives from community criminal justice agencies to visit your class, either in person or virtually through computer conferencing. Create a master schedule for speakers, linking it to the topics covered in the class syllabus and in the textbook.

■ **lecture note**   Explain the criminal justice system in terms of its main components: the police, the courts, and corrections.

The systems model has been criticized for implying a greater level of organization and cooperation among the various agencies of justice than actually exists. The word *system* calls to mind a near-perfect form of social organization. The modern mind associates the idea of a system with machine-like precision in which the problems of wasted effort, redundancy, and conflicting actions are quickly corrected. In practice, the justice system has nowhere near this level of perfection, and the systems model is admittedly an oversimplification. Conflicts among and within agencies are rife, individual actors within the system often do not share immediate goals, and the system may move in different directions depending on political currents, informal arrangements, and personal discretion.

The Conflict Model

The **conflict model** provides another approach to the study of American criminal justice. The conflict model says that the interests of criminal justice agencies tend to make actors within the system self-serving. According to this model, the goals of individual agencies often conflict, and pressures for success, promotion, pay increases, and general accountability fragment the efforts of the system as a whole, leading to a criminal justice *non*system.[30]

A classic study of clearance rates by criminologist Jerome H. Skolnick provides support for the idea of a criminal justice nonsystem.[31] Clearance rates are a measure of crimes solved by the police. The more crimes the police can show they have solved, the better they look to the public they serve. Skolnick discovered an instance in which a burglar was caught red-handed during the commission of a burglary. After his arrest, the police suggested that he confess to many unsolved burglaries that they knew he had not committed. In effect they said, "Help us out, and we will try to help you out!" The burglar did confess—to more than 400 other burglaries. Following the confession, the police were satisfied because they could say they had "solved" many burglaries, and the suspect was pleased as well because the police and the prosecutor agreed to speak on his behalf before the judge.

Both models have something to tell us. Agencies of justice with a diversity of functions (police, courts, and corrections) and at all levels (federal, state, and local) are linked closely enough for the term *system* to be meaningfully applied to them. On the other hand, the very size of the criminal justice undertaking makes effective cooperation between component agencies difficult. The police, for example, have an interest in seeing offenders put behind bars. Prison officials, on the other hand, are often working with extremely overcrowded facilities. They may favor early-release programs for certain categories of offenders, such as those judged to be nonviolent. Who wins out in the long run might just be a matter of internal politics and quasi-official wrangling. Everyone should be concerned, however, when the goal of justice is affected, and sometimes even sacrificed, because of conflicts within the system.

> Everyone should be concerned when the goal of justice is affected, and sometimes even sacrificed, because of conflicts within the system.

American Criminal Justice: The Process

Whether part of a system or a nonsystem, the agencies of criminal justice must process the cases that come before them. An analysis of criminal justice case processing provides both a useful guide to this book and a "road map" to the criminal justice system itself. The figure in the front matter of this book illustrates the processing of a criminal case through the federal justice system in some detail, beginning with the investigation of reported crimes; while Figure 1-4 provides a summary of the process. The process in most state systems is similar.

■ **sustainable justice** Criminal laws and criminal justice institutions, policies, and practices that achieve justice in the present without compromising the ability of future generations to have the benefits of a just society.[iii]

paying for it

Cost-Efficient Criminal Justice

Crimesolutions.gov website

The federal Office of Justice Programs' website, CrimeSolutions.gov. The site facilitates research into the effectiveness of criminal justice–related programs. How can the site be of help to policymakers?

The Great Recession of the past few years has forced state and local governments to make some hard choices about budgets. As government revenues declined due to a drop in taxable income, consumer spending, lower property values, and fewer licensing fees, officials in many locales have been forced to reduce expenditures and to curb services. Criminal justice agencies have not been immune to the impact of budget cuts, and many are looking for ways to offer quality services at a lower cost. Noteworthy is the fact that today's emphasis on the efficient use of resources has combined with calls for greater accountability and transparency in government spending.

To discuss today's concern with cost efficiency throughout the justice system, a number of boxes like this one appear throughout the text and describe what police departments, courts, and corrections agencies are doing as they move toward increasingly responsible stewardship of taxpayer dollars. Noteworthy is the fact that today's emphasis on the efficient use of resources has combined with calls for greater accountability and transparency in government spending.

In an effort to help justice agencies utilize resources wisely, the U.S. Department of Justice announced a new website in 2012. Located at **http://crimesolutions.gov**, the site is designed to provide policymakers, justice system administrators, and taxpayers with the ability to assess the effectiveness of state and local anticrime programs. The site, run by the Washington, D.C.-based National Institute of Justice (NIJ), has been described by federal officials as a "single, credible, online resource to inform practitioners and policymakers about what works in criminal justice, juvenile justice, and crime victim services."

Once criminal justice programs have been selected for review, experts working with the NIJ analyze available research documenting the program's effectiveness and cost efficiency. Programs are then scored on CrimeSolutions.gov according to established criteria and identified as either: (1) effective, (2) promising, or (3) no effect. Where evidence on a program is insufficient or inconsistent, it receives no ranking. As of this writing, 33% of programs reviewed have been scored as "effective," whereas another 57% were identified as "promising."

Finally, the concept of **sustainable justice** was advanced by Melissa Hickman Barlow, in her 2012 presidential address to the Academy of Criminal Justice Sciences. Sustainable justice, said Barlow, can be defined as "criminal laws and criminal justice institutions, policies, and practices that achieve justice in the present without compromising the ability of future generations to have the benefits of a just society." Sustainable justice, in other words, refers to criminal justice practices and institutions that are affordable now, and into the future. Visit the topics page of CrimeSolutions.gov at **http://www.crimesolutions.gov/topics.aspx** to learn more about the categories of programs being evaluated.

References: CrimeSolutions.gov; Melissa Hickman Barlow, "Sustainable Justice: 2012 Presidential Address to the Academy of Criminal Justice Sciences," *Justice Quarterly*, Vol. 30, No. 1 (2013), pp. 1–17.

■ **lecture note**   Discuss the background of the *Miranda v. Arizona* decision and the type of impact it has had on criminal justice.

■ **warrant**   In criminal proceedings, a writ issued by a judicial officer directing a law enforcement officer to perform a specified act and affording the officer protection from damages if he or she performs it.

■ **booking**   A law enforcement or correctional administrative process officially recording an entry into detention after arrest and identifying the person, the place, the time, the reason for the arrest, and the arresting authority.

Investigation and Arrest

The modern justice process begins with investigation. After a crime has been discovered, evidence is gathered at the scene when possible, and a follow-up investigation attempts to reconstruct the sequence of activities. Although a few offenders are arrested at the scene of the crime, most are apprehended later. In such cases, an arrest **warrant** issued by a judge provides the legal basis for an apprehension by police.

An arrest, in which a person is taken into custody, limits the arrestee's freedom. Arrest is a serious step in the process of justice and involves a discretionary decision made by the police seeking to bring criminal sanctions to bear. Most arrests are made peacefully, but if a suspect tries to resist, a police officer may need to use force. Only about half of all people arrested are eventually convicted, and of those, only about a quarter are sentenced to a year or more in prison.

> The *Miranda* decision requires only that police advise a person of his or her rights prior to questioning. An arrest without questioning does not require a warning.

During arrest and before questioning, defendants are usually advised of their constitutional rights, as enumerated in the famous U.S. Supreme Court decision of *Miranda* v. *Arizona*.[32] Defendants are told:

(1) "You have the right to remain silent." (2) "Anything you say can and will be used against you in court." (3) "You have the right to talk to a lawyer for advice before we ask you any questions, and to have him with you during questioning." (4) "If you cannot afford a lawyer, one will be appointed for you before any questioning if you wish." (5) "If you decide to answer questions now without a lawyer present, you will still have the right to stop answering at any time. You also have the right to stop answering at any time and may talk with a lawyer before deciding to speak again." (6) "Do you wish to talk or not?" and (7) "Do you want a lawyer?"[33]

Although popular television programs about the criminal justice system almost always show an offender being given a rights advisement at the time of arrest, the *Miranda* decision requires only that police advise a person of his or her rights prior to questioning. An arrest without questioning does not require a warning. When an officer interrupts a crime in progress, public-safety considerations may make it reasonable for the officer to ask a few questions prior to a rights advisement. Many officers, however, feel they are on sound legal ground only by advising suspects of their rights immediately after arrest. Investigation and arrest are discussed in detail in Chapter 7, "Policing: Legal Aspects."

Booking

Following arrest, suspects are booked. During **booking**, which is an administrative procedure, pictures are taken, fingerprint records are made, and personal information such as address, date of birth, weight, and height is gathered. Details of the charges are recorded, and an administrative record of the arrest is created. At this time suspects are often advised of their rights again and are asked to sign a form on which each right is written. The written form generally contains a statement acknowledging the advisement of rights and attesting to the fact that the suspect understands them.

Investigation ▶ After a crime has been discovered, evidence is gathered and follow-up investigations attempt to reconstruct the sequence of activities leading up to and including the criminal event. Efforts to identify suspects are initiated.

Warrant ▶ An arrest warrant issued by a judge provides the legal basis for an apprehension of suspects by police.

Arrest ▶ In an arrest, a person is taken into custody, limiting the arrestee's freedom. Arrest is a serious step in the process of justice. During arrest and before questioning, defendants are usually advised of their constitutional rights, or Miranda rights.

Booking ▶ Following arrest, suspects are booked. Booking is an administrative procedure where pictures, fingerprints, and personal information are obtained. A record of the events leading up to and including the arrest is created. In some jurisdictions, DNA evidence may be collected from arrestees.

FIGURE 1-4 | The American Criminal Justice Process
Source: Pearson Education, Inc.

■ **lecture note**   Explain probable cause by showing that as actors in the criminal justice system develop a case against a suspect, the information available to them and their belief about the defendant's culpability generally build according to the following steps: (1) reasonable suspicion, (2) probable cause, (3) a preponderance of the evidence, (4) clear and convincing proof, and, finally, (5) proof beyond a reasonable doubt.

■ **lecture note**   Discuss the concerns and criticisms of the grand jury system and ask students to discuss whether the grand jury system should be abolished.

■ **bail**   The money or property pledged to the court or actually deposited with the court to effect the release of a person from legal custody.

■ **preliminary hearing**   A proceeding before a judicial officer in which three matters must be decided: (1) whether a crime was committed, (2) whether the crime occurred within the territorial jurisdiction of the court, and (3) whether there are reasonable grounds to believe that the defendant committed the crime.

■ **probable cause**   A set of facts and circumstances that would induce a reasonably intelligent and prudent person to believe that a specified person has committed a specified crime. Also, reasonable grounds to make or believe an accusation. Probable cause refers to the necessary level of belief that would allow for police seizures (arrests) of individuals and full searches of dwellings, vehicles, and possessions.

Pretrial Activities

First Appearance

Within hours of arrest, suspects must be brought before a magistrate (a judicial officer) for an initial appearance. The judge will tell them of the charges against them, will again advise them of their rights, and may sometimes provide the opportunity for **bail**.

Most defendants are released on recognizance into their own care or the care of another or are given the chance to post a bond during their first appearance. A bond may take the form of a cash deposit or a property bond in which a house or other property serves as collateral against flight. Those who flee may be ordered to forfeit the posted cash or property. Suspects who are not afforded the opportunity for bail because their crimes are very serious or who do not have the needed financial resources are taken to jail to await the next stage in the justice process.

If a defendant doesn't have a lawyer, one will be appointed at the first appearance. To retain a court-appointed lawyer, the defendant may have to demonstrate financial hardship. The names of assigned lawyers are usually drawn off the roster of practicing defense attorneys in the county. Some jurisdictions use public defenders to represent indigent defendants.

All aspects of the first appearance, including bail bonds and possible pretrial release, are discussed in detail in Chapter 10, "Pretrial Activities and the Criminal Trial."

Preliminary Hearing

The primary purpose of a **preliminary hearing**, also sometimes called a *preliminary examination*, is to establish whether sufficient evidence exists against a person to continue the justice process. At the preliminary hearing, the hearing judge will seek to determine whether there is **probable cause** to believe that (1) a crime has been committed and (2) the defendant committed it. The decision is a judicial one, but the process provides the prosecutor with an opportunity to test the strength of the evidence at his or her disposal.

The preliminary hearing also allows defense counsel the chance to assess the strength of the prosecution's case. As the prosecution presents evidence, the defense is said to "discover" what it is. Hence the preliminary hearing serves a discovery function for the defense. If the defense attorney thinks the evidence is strong, he or she may suggest that a plea bargain be arranged. All defendants, including those who are indigent, have a right to be represented by counsel at the preliminary hearing.

First Appearance ▶

Within hours of arrest suspects must be brought before a magistrate (a judicial officer) for an initial appearance. The judge will tell them of the charges against them, advise them of their rights, and may provide the opportunity for bail.

Preliminary Hearing ▶

The purpose of a preliminary hearing is to establish whether sufficient evidence exists against a person to continue the justice process. At the preliminary hearing, the hearing judge will seek to determine whether there is probable cause. The process provides the prosecutor with an opportunity to test the strength of the evidence.

Information or Indictment ▶

In some states the prosecutor may seek to continue the case against a defendant by filing an information with the court. Other states require an indictment be returned by a grand jury. The grand jury hears evidence presented by the prosecutor and decides whether the case should go to trial.

Arraignment ▶

At arraignment the accused stands before a judge and hears the information or indictment against him. Defendants are again notified of their rights and asked to enter a plea. Pleas include not guilty, guilty, and no contest. No contest may result in a conviction but cannot be used in trial as an admission of guilt.

■ **information**   A formal, written accusation submitted to a court by a prosecutor, alleging that a specified person has committed a specified offense.

■ **indictment**   A formal, written accusation submitted to the court by a grand jury, alleging that a specified person has committed a specified offense, usually a felony.

■ **grand jury**   A group of jurors who have been selected according to law and have been sworn to hear the evidence and to determine whether there is sufficient evidence to bring the accused person to trial, to investigate criminal activity generally, or to investigate the conduct of a public agency or official.

■ **arraignment**   Strictly, the hearing before a court having jurisdiction in a criminal case in which the identity of the defendant is established, the defendant is informed of the charge and of his or her rights, and the defendant is required to enter a plea. Also, in some usages, any appearance in criminal court before trial.

Information or Indictment

In some states, the prosecutor may seek to continue the case against a defendant by filing an **information** with the court. An information, which is a formal written accusation, is filed on the basis of the outcome of the preliminary hearing.

Other states require that an **indictment** be returned by a **grand jury** before prosecution can proceed. The grand jury hears evidence from the prosecutor and decides whether the case should go to trial. In effect, the grand jury is the formal indicting authority. It determines whether probable cause exists to charge the defendant formally with the crime. Grand juries can return an indictment on less than a unanimous vote.

The grand jury system has been criticized because it is one-sided. The defense has no opportunity to present evidence; the grand jury is led only by the prosecutor, often through an appeal to emotions or in ways that would not be permitted in a trial. At the same time, the grand jury is less bound by specific rules than a trial jury. For example, a grand jury member once told the author that a rape case had been dismissed because the man had taken the woman to dinner first. Personal ignorance and subcultural biases are far more likely to play a role in grand jury hearings than in criminal trials. In defense of the grand jury system, however, defendants who are clearly innocent will likely not be indicted. A grand jury's refusal to indict can save the system considerable time and money by preventing cases lacking in evidence from further processing by the criminal justice system.

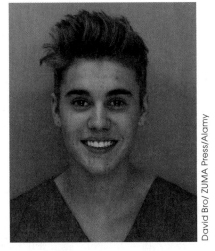

Canadian singer Justin Bieber's mugshot. Bieber, 19, was arrested in Miami Beach, Florida, on January 23, 2014, and charged with speeding in a yellow Lamborghini, driving with an expired license, and driving under the influence of alcohol, marijuana, and prescription drugs. The justice process starts when a crime has been committed and a perpetrator arrested. What are the three main components of the justice system?

Arraignment

The **arraignment** is "the first appearance of the defendant before the court that has the authority to conduct a trial."[34] At arraignment, the accused individuals stand before a judge and hear the information, or indictment, against them as it is read. Defendants are again notified of their rights and are asked to enter a plea.

Adjudication ▶	Sentencing ▶	Corrections ▶	Reentry
A criminal trial may be held, or the defendant may decide to enter a guilty plea. A criminal trial involves an adversarial process that pits the prosecution against the defense. In most trials, a jury hears the evidence and decides issues of guilt or innocence, while the judge ensures the fairness of the proceedings.	After the person has been convicted, it is up to the judge to determine the punishment. Prior to sentencing, a sentencing hearing is sometimes held in which attorneys for both sides can present information to influence the judge's decision.	The corrections period begins following sentencing. Corrections involves a variety of sentences that can be imposed on a defendant.	Not everyone who has been convicted of a crime goes to prison. Probation imposes requirements or restrictions upon offenders. Offenders are required to check in with a probation officer on a regular basis. Similarly, after a defendant has served a portion of his prison term he may be freed on parole. Like probation, parole may come with obligations and requires the offender to check in with a parole officer.

FIGURE 1-4 (continued)

■ **lecture note**   The text mentions the large percentage of cases that are plea bargained. Briefly discuss the implications of plea bargaining on the defendant, including giving up the right to trial and the presumption of innocence.

■ **trial**   In criminal proceedings, the examination in court of the issues of fact and relevant law in a case for the purpose of convicting or acquitting the defendant.

■ **theme**   What factors do you think a judge might consider when deciding between consecutive or concurrent sentences?

Acceptable pleas generally include (1) not guilty, (2) guilty, and (3) no contest (*nolo contendere*), which may result in conviction but can't be used later as an admission of guilt in civil proceedings. Civil proceedings, or private lawsuits, while not covered in detail in this book, provide an additional avenue of relief for victims or their survivors. Convicted offenders increasingly face suits brought against them by victims seeking to collect monetary damages.

The Federal Rules of Criminal Procedure specify that "arraignment shall be conducted in open court and shall consist of reading the indictment or information to the defendant or stating to him the substance of the charge and calling on him to plead thereto. He shall be given a copy of the indictment or information before he is called upon to plead."[35]

Guilty pleas are not always accepted by the judge. If the judge believes a guilty plea is made under duress or is due to a lack of knowledge on the part of the defendant, the plea will be rejected and a plea of "not guilty" will be substituted for it. Sometimes defendants "stand mute"—that is, they refuse to speak or to enter a plea of any kind. In that case, the judge will enter a plea of "not guilty" on their behalf.

The arraignment process is discussed in detail in Chapter 10, "Pretrial Activities and the Criminal Trial."

Adjudication

Under the Sixth Amendment to the U.S. Constitution, every criminal defendant has a right to a **trial** by jury. The U.S. Supreme Court, however, has held that petty offenses are not covered by the Sixth Amendment guarantee and that the seriousness of a case is determined by the way in which "society regards the offense." For the most part, "offenses for which the maximum period of incarceration is six months or less are presumptively petty."[36] In *Blanton* v. *City of North Las Vegas* (1989), the Court held that "a defendant can overcome this presumption and become entitled to a jury trial, only by showing that . . . additional penalties [such as fines and community service] viewed together with the maximum prison term, are so severe that the legislature clearly determined that the offense is a serious one."[37] The *Blanton* decision was further reinforced in the case of *U.S.* v. *Nachtigal* (1993).[38]

In most jurisdictions, many criminal cases never come to trial. Most are "pleaded out"; that is, they are dispensed of as the result of a bargained plea, or they are dismissed for one of a variety of reasons. Studies have found that as many as 82% of all sentences are imposed in criminal cases because of guilty pleas rather than trials.[39]

In cases that do come to trial, the procedures governing the submission of evidence are tightly controlled by procedural law and precedent. *Procedural law* specifies the type of evidence that may be submitted, the credentials of those allowed to represent the state or the defendant, and what a jury is allowed to hear.

Precedent refers to understandings built up through common usage and also to decisions rendered by courts in previous cases. Precedent in the courtroom, for example, requires that lawyers request permission from the judge before approaching a witness. It also can mean that excessively gruesome items of evidence may not be used or must be altered in some way so that their factual value is not lost in the strong emotional reactions they may create.

Some states allow trials for less serious offenses to occur before a judge if defendants waive their right to a trial by jury. This is called a *bench trial*. Other states require a jury trial for all serious criminal offenses.

Trials are expensive and time-consuming. They pit defense attorneys against prosecutors. Regulated conflict is the rule, and jurors are required to decide the facts and apply the law as the judge explains it to them. In some cases, however, a jury may be unable to decide. Such a jury is said to be *deadlocked*, and the judge declares a mistrial. The defendant may be tried again when a new jury is impaneled.

> Everyone facing criminal prosecution in the United States is guaranteed a constitutional right to due process, meaning that defendants must be afforded a fair opportunity to participate in every stage of criminal proceedings.

The criminal trial and its participants are described fully in Chapter 9, "The Courts: Structure and Participants," and Chapter 10, "Pretrial Activities and the Criminal Trial."

Sentencing

Once a person has been convicted, it becomes the responsibility of the judge to impose some form of punishment. The sentence may take the form of supervised probation in the community, a fine, a prison term, or some combination of these. Defendants will often be ordered to pay the costs of the court or of their own defense if they are able.

Prior to sentencing, a sentencing hearing may be held in which lawyers on both sides present information concerning the defendant. The judge may also ask a probation or parole officer to compile a presentence report, which contains information on the defendant's family and business situation, emotional state,

■ **consecutive sentence**   One of two or more sentences imposed at the same time, after conviction for more than one offense, and served in sequence with the other sentence. Also, a new sentence for a new conviction, imposed upon a person already under sentence for a previous offense, which is added to the previous sentence, thus increasing the maximum time the offender may be confined or under supervision.

■ **concurrent sentence**   One of two or more sentences imposed at the same time, after conviction for more than one of-fense, and served at the same time. Also, a new sentence for a new conviction, imposed upon a person already under sentence for a previous offense, served at the same time as the previous sentence.

■ **due process**   A right guaranteed by the Fourth, Fifth, Sixth, and Fourteenth Amendments of the U.S. Constitution and generally understood, in legal contexts, to mean the due course of legal proceedings according to the rules and forms established for the protection of individual rights. In criminal proceedings, due process of law is generally understood to include the follow-ing basic elements: a law creating and defining the offense, an impartial tribunal having jurisdictional authority over the case, accusation in proper form, notice and opportunity to defend, trial according to established procedure, and discharge from all restraints or obligations unless convicted.

social background, and criminal history. This report helps the judge make an appropriate sentencing decision.

Judges traditionally have had considerable discretion in sen-tencing, although new state and federal laws now place limits on judicial discretion in some cases, requiring that a sentence "presumed" by law be imposed. Judges still retain enormous discretion, however, in specifying whether sentences on mul-tiple charges are to run consecutively or concurrently. Offenders found guilty of more than one charge may be ordered to serve one sentence after another is completed, called a **consecutive sentence**, or may be told that their sentences will run at the same time, which is called a **concurrent sentence**.

Many convictions are appealed. The appeals process can be complex and can involve both state and federal judiciaries. An appeal is based on the defendant's claim that rules of procedure were not followed properly at some earlier stage in the justice process or that the defendant was denied the rights guaranteed by the U.S. Constitution.

Chapter 11, "Sentencing," outlines modern sentencing prac-tices and describes the many modern alternatives to imprisonment.

Corrections

Once an offender has been sentenced, the corrections stage be-gins. Some offenders are sentenced to prison, where they "do time" for their crimes. Once in the correctional system, they are classified according to local procedures and are assigned to con-finement facilities and treatment programs. Newer prisons today bear little resemblance to the massive bastions of the past, which isolated offenders from society behind huge stone walls. Many modern prisons, however, still suffer from a "lock psychosis" (a preoccupation with security) among top- and mid-level adminis-trators as well as a lack of significant rehabilitation programs.

Chapter 13, "Prisons and Jails," discusses the philosophy be-hind prisons and sketches their historical development. Chapter 14, "Prison Life," portrays life on the inside and delineates the social structures that develop in response to the pains of imprisonment.

Reentry

Not everyone who is convicted of a crime and sentenced ends up in prison. Some offenders are ordered to prison only to have

their sentences suspended and a probationary term imposed. They may also be ordered to perform community-service ac-tivities as a condition of their probation. During the term of probation, these offenders are required to submit to supervision by a probation officer and to meet other conditions set by the court. Failure to do so results in revocation of probation and imposition of the original prison sentence.

Offenders who have served a portion of their prison sen-tences may be freed on parole. They are supervised by a parole officer and assisted in their readjustment to society. As in the case of probation, failure to meet the conditions of parole may result in revocation of parole and a return to prison.

Chapter 11, "Sentencing," and Chapter 12, "Probation, Parole, and Intermediate Sanctions," deal with the practice of probation and parole and with the issues surrounding reentry. Learn more about the criminal justice process at **http://www .justicestudies.com/pubs/perspectives.pdf**. For a critical look at the justice system, visit **http://www.360degrees.org**.

Due Process and Individual Rights

The U.S. Constitution requires that criminal justice case process-ing be conducted with fairness and equity; this requirement is referred to as **due process**. Simply put, *due process* means proce-dural fairness.[40] It recognizes the individual rights of criminal de-fendants facing prosecution by a state or the federal government. Under the due process standard, rights violations may become the basis for the dismissal of evidence or of criminal charges, espe-cially at the appellate level. Table 1-1 outlines the basic rights to which defendants in criminal proceedings are generally entitled.

Due process underlies the first ten amendments to the Constitution, which are collectively known as the *Bill of Rights*. Due process is specifically guaranteed by the Fourth, Fifth, Sixth, and Fourteenth Amendments and is succinctly stated in the Fifth, which reads, "No person shall be . . . deprived of life, lib-erty, or property, without due process of law."[41] The Fourteenth Amendment makes due process binding on the states—that is, it requires individual states to respect the due process rights of U.S. citizens who come under their jurisdiction.

■ **theme**   What is due process? Why is due process such a central notion in American criminal justice? What would our justice system be like without due process? Would you want to live in a society that did not guarantee due process rights?

■ **lecture note**   Discuss the concept of separation of powers and the implications of allowing Supreme Court decisions to carry as much weight as legislative actions.

TABLE 1-1 | Individual Rights Guaranteed by the Bill of Rights[a]

A right to be assumed innocent until proven guilty
A right against unreasonable searches of person and place of residence
A right against arrest without probable cause
A right against unreasonable seizure of personal property
A right against self-incrimination
A right to fair questioning by the police
A right to protection from physical harm throughout the justice process
A right to an attorney
A right to trial by jury
A right to know the charges
A right to cross-examine prosecution witnesses
A right to speak and present witnesses
A right not to be tried twice for the same crime
A right against cruel or unusual punishment
A right to due process
A right to a speedy trial
A right to assistance of counsel in criminal proceedings
A right against excessive bail
A right against excessive fines
A right to be treated the same as others, regardless of race, sex, religious preference, and other personal attributes

[a]As interpreted by the U.S. Supreme Court.

The courts, and specifically the U.S. Supreme Court, have interpreted and clarified the guarantees of the Bill of Rights. The due process standard was set in the 1960s by the Warren Court (1953–1969), following a number of far-reaching Supreme Court decisions that affected criminal procedure. Led by Chief Justice Earl Warren, the Warren Court is remembered for its concern with protecting the innocent against the massive power of the state in criminal proceedings.[42] As a result of its tireless efforts to institutionalize the Bill of Rights, the daily practice of modern American criminal justice is now set squarely upon the due process standard.

The Role of the Courts in Defining Rights

Although the Constitution deals with many issues, what we have been calling *rights* are open to interpretation. Many modern rights, although written into the Constitution, would not exist in practice were it not for the fact that the U.S. Supreme Court

decided, at some point in history, to recognize them in cases brought before it. In the well-known case of *Gideon* v. *Wainwright* (1963),[43] for example, the Supreme Court embraced the Sixth Amendment guarantee of a right to a lawyer for all criminal defendants and mandated that states provide lawyers for defendants who are unable to pay for them. Before *Gideon* (which is discussed in detail in Chapter 9, "The Courts: Structure and Participants"), court-appointed attorneys for defendants unable to afford their own counsel were practically unknown, except in capital cases and in some federal courts. After the *Gideon* decision, court-appointed counsel became commonplace, and measures were instituted in jurisdictions across the nation to select attorneys fairly for indigent defendants. It is important to note, however, that although the Sixth Amendment specifically says,

> The U.S. Supreme Court is very powerful, and its decisions often have far-reaching consequences.

among other things, that "in all criminal prosecutions, the accused shall enjoy the right . . . to have the Assistance of Counsel for his defense,"[44] it does not say, in so many words, that the state is *required* to provide counsel. It is the U.S. Supreme Court, interpreting the Constitution, that has said that.

The U.S. Supreme Court is very powerful, and its decisions often have far-reaching consequences. The decisions rendered by the justices in cases like *Gideon* become, in effect, the law of the land. For all practical purposes, such decisions often carry as much weight as legislative action. For this reason, we speak of "judge-made law" (rather than legislated law) in describing judicial precedents that affect the process of justice.

Rights that have been recognized by court decisions are subject to continual refinement, and although the process of change is usually very slow, new interpretations may broaden or narrow the scope of applicability accorded to constitutional guarantees.

The Ultimate Goal: Crime Control through Due Process

Two primary goals were identified in our discussion of this book's theme: (1) the need to enforce the law and to maintain public order and (2) the need to protect individuals from injustice, especially at the hands of the criminal justice system. The first of these principles values the efficient arrest and conviction of criminal offenders. It is often referred to as the **crime-control model** of justice. The crime-control model was first brought to the attention of the academic community in Stanford

■ **crime-control model**   A criminal justice perspective that emphasizes the efficient arrest and conviction of criminal offenders.

■ **due process model**   A criminal justice perspective that emphasizes individual rights at all stages of justice system processing.

■ **social control**   The use of sanctions and rewards within a group to influence and shape the behavior of individual members of that group. Social control is a primary concern of social groups and communities, and it is their interest in the exercise of social control that leads to the creation of both criminal and civil statutes.

■ **evidence-based practice**   Crime-fighting strategies that have been scientifically tested and are based on social science research.

University law professor Herbert Packer's cogent analysis of the state of criminal justice in the late 1960s.[45] For that reason, it is sometimes referred to as *Packer's crime-control model.*

The second principle is called the **due process model** because of its emphasis on individual rights. Due process is intended to ensure that innocent people are not convicted of crimes; it is a fundamental part of American criminal justice. It requires a careful and informed consideration of the facts of each individual case. Under the due process model, police are required to recognize the rights of suspects during arrest, questioning, and handling. Similarly, prosecutors and judges must recognize constitutional and other guarantees during trial and the presentation of evidence.

The dual goals of crime control and due process are often assumed to be opposing goals. Indeed, some critics of American criminal justice argue that the practice of justice is too often concerned with crime control at the expense of due process. Other analysts of the American scene maintain that our type of justice coddles offenders and does too little to protect the innocent. Although it is impossible to avoid ideological conflicts like these, it is also realistic to think of the American system of justice as representative of *crime control through due process*—that is, as a system of **social control** that is fair to those whom it processes. This model of *law enforcement infused with the recognition of individual rights* provides a workable conceptual framework for understanding the American system of criminal justice.

Evidence-Based Practice in Criminal Justice

In 2011, John H. Laub, then-director of the National Institute of Justice (NIJ), called for the creation of a "culture of science and research within the institute." What that means, said Laub, "is embracing empirical data, embracing transparency and also embracing a critical perspective." Science, Laub continued, challenges conventional wisdom and has the ability to evaluate programs and strategies to show what works in the area of criminal justice. The NIJ, said Laub, should be thought of "as a science agency." You can view Laub's comments online at **http://nij .ncjrs.gov/multimedia/video-laub1.htm**.

Only a year earlier, in June 2010, Assistant Attorney General Laurie O. Robinson announced a new initiative at the Office of Justice Programs (OJP), an arm of the U.S. Department of Justice that funds implementation of state-of-the-art practices in criminal justice agencies across the country.[46] The initiative, which Robinson said was intended to help "criminal and juvenile justice professionals expand their base of scientific knowledge and transform research into practice," is known as the Evidence Integration Initiative (E2I). E2I is an ongoing, OJP-wide effort to integrate science and research throughout the agency and the work it sponsors. "Most importantly," Robinson said, "we are working to move evidence into practice by funding evidence-based programs."

As the word is used here, *evidence* does not refer to evidence of a crime but means, instead, findings that are supported by studies. Hence, **evidence-based practice** refers to crime-fighting strategies that have been scientifically tested and are based on social science research. Scientific research has become a major element in the increasing professionalization of criminal justice, both as a career field and as a field of study. As Robinson recognized, there is a strong call today within criminal justice policymaking circles for the application of evidence-based practices throughout the justice field.

As noted in the "Paying for It" feature, in 2012, in support of the evidence-based movement in criminal justice, the U.S. Department of Justice announced a new website, **http:// crimesolutions.gov**, featuring an innovative online program evaluation tool created by the federal Office of Justice Programs (OJP). The website, which is meant to help citizens and policymakers assess the effectiveness of state and local crime-fighting programs, has been described as a "single, credible, online resource to inform practitioners and policymakers about what works in criminal justice, juvenile justice, and crime victim services."[47]

> Evidence-based practices can be expected to play an expanded role in policymaking and in the administration of criminal justice in the years to come.

CJ | CAREERS
Careers in Criminal Justice

Throughout this book, you will find a number of "CJ Career" boxes showcasing individuals currently working in the justice field. Those boxes highlight job opportunities within various kinds of criminal justice agencies, and provide brief interviews with people employed in the field. A list of some of the many kinds of criminal justice career opportunities available today is provided in this table.

Arson/fire investigator
Bailiff
Bounty hunter
Computer forensic technician
Correctional officer
Correctional treatment specialist
Court clerk
Court reporter
Crime laboratory analyst
Crime prevention specialist
Crime scene investigator
Crime scene technician
Criminal investigator
Criminalist
Criminologist
Criminology researcher/research associate
Deputy sheriff
Electronic crime scene investigator
Federal Bureau of Investigation (FBI) forensic accountant
Federal Bureau of Investigation (FBI) special agent
Federal Protective Service (FPS) officer
Fish and game warden
Forensic nurse
Forensic psychologist
Forensic science technician
Fraud investigator
Gaming surveillance officer
Highway patrol officer
Information security manager
Judge
Juvenile probation officer
K-9 officer
Lawyer/attorney
Legal clerk
Loss prevention specialist (retail)
Magistrate
Motorcycle officer
National Security Agency (NSA) police officer
Native American tribal police officer
Nuclear security officer
Paralegal
Park ranger
Parole officer
Penologist
Police detective

Police dispatcher
Police officer
Police sniper
Private detective
Private investigator
Private security manager
Probation officer
Railroad police officer
Sheriff
Social worker
State trooper
Substance abuse counselor
Surveillance officer
SWAT team member
Transit Authority police officer
University/College Campus Police Officer
U.S. Air Force Office of Special Investigations (OSI) special agent
U.S. Air Marshal
U.S. Army criminal investigator (CID)
U.S. Army military police officer
U.S. Bureau of Alcohol, Tobacco, Firearms and Explosives (ATF) special agent
U.S. Bureau of Indian Affairs (BIA) correctional officer
U.S. Bureau of Indian Affairs (BIA) drug enforcement special agent
U.S. Bureau of Indian Affairs (BIA) investigator
U.S. Bureau of Indian Affairs (BIA) police officer
U.S. Bureau of Reclamation Security, Safety, and Law Enforcement officer
U.S. Coast Guard (USCG) compliance officer
U.S. Coast Guard (USCG) sea marshal
U.S. Customs and Border Protection (CBP) special agent
U.S. Department of Agriculture (USDA) compliance officer
U.S. Department of Agriculture (USDA) criminal investigator
U.S. Department of Agriculture (USDA) investigative attorney
U.S. Department of State Civilian Response Corps team member
U.S. Department of State diplomatic security officer
U.S. Department of Veterans Affairs (VA) police officer
U.S. Drug Enforcement Administration (DEA) special agent
U.S. Fish and Wildlife Service, Division of Refuge Law Enforcement officer
U.S. Immigration and Customs Enforcement (ICE) special agent
U.S. Internal Revenue Service (IRS) special agent
U.S. Marine Corps criminal investigator
U.S. Marine Corps military police officer
U.S. marshal
U.S. Navy criminal investigator (NCIS)
U.S. Navy law enforcement officer
U.S. Navy security officer
U.S. Park Police
U.S. Secret Service special agent
U.S. Secret Service uniformed division officer
U.S. Transportation Security Administration (TSA) screener

■ **criminology**   The scientific study of the causes and prevention of crime and the rehabilitation and punishment of offenders.

As Chapter 5, "Policing: History and Structure," of this text points out, evidence-based practices can be expected to play an expanded role in policymaking and in the administration of criminal justice in the years to come. For additional insight into some of the issues facing criminal justice policymakers today, read the U.S. Department of Justice's "Smart on Crime" report at **http://www.justice.gov/sites/default/files/ag/legacy/2013/08/12/smart-on-crime.pdf**. See the last chapter of this text for a discussion of "sentinel events"—a term used by the National Institute of Justice to refer to problematic justice system outcomes whose study could benefit from an evidence-based approach.

The Start of Academic Criminal Justice

The study of criminal justice as an academic discipline began in this country in the late 1920s, when August Vollmer (1876–1955), then police chief of Berkeley, California, persuaded the University of California to offer courses on the subject.[48] Vollmer was joined by his former student Orlando W. Wilson (1900–1972) and by William H. Parker (who later served as chief of the LAPD from 1950 to 1966) in calling for increased professionalism in police work through better training.[49] Largely as a result of Vollmer's influence, early criminal justice education was practice-oriented; it was a kind of extension of on-the-job training for working practitioners. Hence, in the early days of the discipline, criminal justice students were primarily focused on the application of general management principles to the administration of police agencies. Criminal justice came to be seen as a practical field of study concerned largely with issues of organizational effectiveness.

By the 1960s, however, police training came to be augmented by criminal justice education[50] as students of criminal justice began to apply the techniques of social scientific research—many of them borrowed from sister disciplines like **criminology**, sociology, psychology, and political science—to the study of all aspects of the justice system. Scientific research into the operation of the criminal justice system was encouraged by the 1967 President's Commission on Law Enforcement and Administration of Justice, which influenced passage of the Safe Streets and Crime Control Act of 1968. The Safe Streets Act led to the creation of the National Institute of Law Enforcement and Criminal Justice, which later became the National Institute of Justice (NIJ). As a central part of its mission, the NIJ continues to support research in the criminal justice field through substantial funding for scientific explorations into all aspects of the discipline, and it funnels much of the $3 billion spent annually

by the U.S. Department of Justice to local communities to help fight crime.

Now, almost 100 years after its beginnings as a field of study, criminal justice is being revitalized by an evidence-based approach to its subject matter (described earlier). Former Assistant Attorney General Robinson put it this way: "Justice professionals have been collecting, analyzing, and using evidence for centuries—in laboratories and courtrooms. As financial realities demand more innovative approaches, social science research is forming the basis for new programs in areas ranging from reentry to victim services. Evidence has found a new home: in the field."[51]

Multiculturalism and Diversity in Criminal Justice

In 2011, polygamist Warren Jeffs, a former leader of the Fundamentalist Church of Jesus Christ of Latter-day Saints (FLDS), an offshoot of the mainstream Mormon church, was sentenced to life in prison for sexually assaulting two underage female followers whom he took as wives. During his trial, prosecutors played an audio recording of what they said was Jeffs raping a 12-year-old girl. Jeffs, who had been on the FBI's Ten Most Wanted list, won't be eligible for parole for at least 45 years.[52]

The FLDS brought plural marriage to Utah in the early nineteenth century, but the state legislature banned the practice more than 100 years ago. Today, the church officially excommunicates polygamists, although members of the FLDS practice polygamy as a central tenet of their religion. Some estimate the number of polygamists living in Utah and Arizona today at over 30,000.[53] The existence of such alternative family lifestyles is just one indicator that the United States is a multicultural and diverse society.

Multiculturalism describes a society that is home to a multitude of different cultures, each with its own set of norms, values, and routine behaviors. Although American society today is truly a multicultural society, composed of a wide variety of racial and ethnic heritages, diverse religions, incongruous values, disparate traditions, and distinct languages, multiculturalism in America is not new. For thousands of years before Europeans arrived in the Western Hemisphere, tribal nations of Native Americans each spoke their own language, were bound to customs that differed significantly from one another, and practiced a wide range of religions. European immigration, which began in earnest in the seventeenth century, led to greater diversity still. Successive waves of immigrants, along with the slave trade

■ **multiculturalism** The existence within one society of diverse groups that maintain unique cultural identities while frequently accepting and participating in the larger society's legal and political systems.[iv] *Multiculturalism* is often used in conjunction with the term *diversity* to identify many distinctions of social significance.

of the early and mid-nineteenth century,[54] brought a diversity of values, beliefs, and patterns of behavior to American shores that frequently conflicted with those of prevailing cultures. Differences in languages and traditions fed the American melting pot of the late nineteenth and early twentieth centuries and made effective communication between groups difficult.

The face of multiculturalism in America today is quite different than it was in the past, due largely to relatively high birthrates among some minority populations and the huge but relatively recent immigration of Spanish-speaking people from Mexico, Cuba, Central America, and South America. Part of that influx consists of substantial numbers of undocumented immigrants who have entered the country illegally and who, because of experiences in their home countries, may have a special fear of police authority and a general distrust for the law. Such fears make members of this group hesitant to report being victimized, and their undocumented status makes them easy prey for illegal scams involving extortion, blackmail, and documentation crimes. Learn more about immigration and crime via **http://www.justicestudies.com/pubs/immcrime.pdf**.

Diversity characterizes both immigrant and U.S.-born individuals. Census Bureau statistics show that people identifying themselves as white account for 71% of the U.S. population—a percentage that has been dropping steadily for at least the past 40 years. People of Hispanic origin constitute approximately 12% of the population and are the fastest-growing group in the country. Individuals identifying themselves as African American make up another 12% of the population, and people of Asian and Pacific Island origin make up almost 4% of the total. Native Americans, including American Indians, Eskimos, and Aleuts, account for slightly less than 1% of all Americans.[55] Statistics like these, however, are only estimates, and their interpretation is complicated by the fact that surveyed individuals may be of mixed race. Nonetheless, it is clear that American society today is ethnically and racially quite diverse.

Race and *ethnicity* are only buzzwords that people use when they talk about multiculturalism. After all, neither race nor ethnicity determines a person's values, attitudes, or behavior. Just as there is no uniquely identifiable "white culture" in American society, it is a mistake to think that all African Americans share

A group of immigrants who have just completed taking the pledge of allegiance during a naturalization ceremony in Washington, D.C. American society is multicultural, composed of a wide variety of racial and ethnic heritages, diverse religions, incongruous values, disparate traditions, and distinct languages. What impact does the multicultural nature of our society have on the justice system?

Jim Lo Scalzo/Newscom

the same values or that everyone of Hispanic descent honors the same traditions or even speaks Spanish.

Multiculturalism, as the term is used today, is but one form of *diversity*. Taken together, these two concepts—multiculturalism and diversity—encompass many distinctions of social significance. The broad brush of contemporary multiculturalism and social diversity draws attention to variety along racial, ethnic, subcultural, generational, faith, economic, and gender lines. Lifestyle diversity is also important. The fact that influential elements of the wider society are less accepting of some lifestyles than others doesn't mean that such lifestyles aren't recognized from the viewpoint of multiculturalism. It simply means that at least for now, some lifestyles are accorded less official acceptability than others. As a result, certain lifestyle choices, even within a multicultural society that generally respects and encourages diversity, may still be criminalized, as in the case of polygamy.

Multiculturalism and diversity will be discussed in various chapters throughout this textbook. For now, it is sufficient to recognize that the diverse values, perspectives, and behaviors characteristic of various groups within society have a significant impact on the justice system. Whether it is the confusion that arises from a police officer's commands to a non-English-speaking suspect, the need for interpreters in the courtroom, a deep-seated distrust of the police in some minority communities, a lack of willingness

> The demands and expectations placed on justice agencies in multicultural societies involve the dilemma of how to protect the rights of individuals to self-expression while ensuring social control and the safety and security of the public.

among some immigrants to report crime, the underrepresentation of women in criminal justice agencies, or some people's irrational suspicions of Arab Americans following the September 11 terrorist attacks, diversity and multiculturalism present special challenges to the everyday practice of criminal justice in America. Finally, as we shall see, the demands and expectations placed on justice agencies in multicultural societies involve a dilemma that is closely associated with the theme of this text: how to protect the rights of individuals to self-expression while ensuring social control and the safety and security of the public.

For an overview of crime rates, corrections statistics, and additional resources about crime and justice in the United States, see the 181-page *Crime and Justice Atlas* created by the U.S. Department of Justice at **http://www.jrsa.org/programs/Crime_Atlas_2000.pdf**. An updated version of the atlas is available at **http://www.jrsa.org/programs/Crime_Atlas_2001-update.pdf**.

SUMMARY

- The American experience with crime during the last half century has been especially influential in shaping the criminal justice system of today. Although crime waves have come and gone, some events during the past century stand out as especially significant, including a spurt of widespread organized criminal activity associated with the Prohibition years of the early twentieth century, the substantial increase in "traditional" crimes during the 1960s and 1970s, the threat to the American way of life represented by illicit drugs around the same time, and the terrorist attacks of September 11, 2001.

- The theme of this book is one of individual rights versus public order. As this chapter points out, the personal freedoms guaranteed to law-abiding citizens as well as to criminal suspects by the Constitution must be closely guarded. At the same time, the urgent social needs of communities for controlling unacceptable behavior and protecting law-abiding citizens from harm must be recognized. This theme is represented by two opposing groups: individual-rights advocates and public-order advocates. The fundamental challenge facing the practice of American criminal justice is in achieving efficient and cost-effective enforcement of the laws while simultaneously recognizing and supporting the legal rights of suspects and the legitimate personal differences and prerogatives of individuals.

- Even though justice may be an elusive concept, it is important to recognize that criminal justice is tied closely to other notions of justice, including personal and cultural beliefs about equity and fairness. As a goal to be achieved, criminal justice refers to those aspects of social justice that concern violations of the criminal law. Although community interests in the administration of criminal justice demand the apprehension and punishment of law violators, criminal justice ideals extend to the protection of the innocent, the fair treatment of offenders, and fair play by justice administration agencies.

- In this chapter, we described the process of American criminal justice as a system with three major components—police, courts, and corrections—all of which can be described as working together toward a common goal. We warned, however, that a systems viewpoint is useful primarily for the simplification that it provides. A more realistic approach to understanding criminal justice may be the nonsystem approach. As a nonsystem, the criminal justice process is depicted as a fragmented activity in which individuals and agencies within the process have interests and goals that at times coincide but often conflict.

- The stages of criminal case processing include investigation and arrest, booking, a first appearance in court, the defendant's preliminary hearing, the return of an indictment by the grand jury or the filing of an information by the prosecutor, arraignment of the defendant before the court, adjudication or trial, sentencing, and corrections. As a field of study, corrections include jails, probation, imprisonment, and parole.

- The principle of due process, which underlies the first ten amendments to the U.S. Constitution, is central to American criminal justice. Due process (also called *due process of law*) means procedural fairness and requires that criminal case processing be conducted with fairness and equity. The ultimate goal of the criminal justice system in America is achieving crime control through due process.

- The study of criminal justice as an academic discipline began in this country in the late 1920s and is well-established today. Scientific research has become a major element in the increasing professionalization of criminal justice, and there is an increasingly strong call for the application of evidence-based practices in the justice field. Evidence-based practices are crime-fighting strategies that have been scientifically tested and that are based on social science research.

- American society today is a multicultural society, composed of a wide variety of racial and ethnic heritages, diverse religions, incongruous values, disparate traditions, and distinct languages. Multiculturalism complicates the practice of American criminal justice because there is rarely universal agreement in our society about what is right or wrong or about what constitutes "justice." As such, multiculturalism represents both challenges and opportunities for today's justice practitioners.

KEY TERMS

administration of justice, 11
arraignment, 18
bail, 17
booking, 16
civil justice, 10
concurrent sentence, 20
conflict model, 14
consecutive sentence, 20
consensus model, 13
crime, 3
crime-control model, 22
criminal justice, 10
criminal justice system, 13
criminology, 24
due process, 20
due process model, 22
evidence-based practice, 22
grand jury, 18

indictment, 18
individual rights, 4
individual-rights advocate, 9
information, 18
justice, 10
multiculturalism, 25
preliminary hearing, 17
probable cause, 17
public-order advocate, 9
procedural fairness, 4
social control, 22
social disorganization, 4
social justice, 10
social order, 9
sustainable justice, 15
trial, 19
warrant, 16

QUESTIONS FOR REVIEW

1. Describe the American experience with crime during the last half century. What noteworthy criminal incidents or activities can you identify during that time, and what social and economic conditions might have produced them?

2. What is the theme of this book? According to that theme, what are the differences between the individual-rights perspective and the public-order perspective?

3. This chapter also says that the drama of individual rights versus public order plays out in an economic environment constrained by today's financial considerations. How can evidence-based strategies help to meet the goals of both individual-rights and public-order advocates?

4. What is justice? What aspects of justice does this chapter discuss? How does criminal justice relate to other, wider notions of equity and fairness?

5. What are the main components of the criminal justice system? How do they interrelate? How might they conflict?

6. List the stages of case processing that characterize the American system of criminal justice, and describe each stage.

7. What is meant by *due process of law*? Where in the American legal system are guarantees of due process found?

8. What is the role of research in criminal justice? What is evidence-based practice? How can research influence crime-control policy?

9. What is multiculturalism? What is social diversity? What impact do multiculturalism and diversity have on the practice of criminal justice in contemporary American society?

QUESTIONS FOR REFLECTION

1. Reiterate the theme of this textbook. How might this book's theme facilitate the study of criminal justice?

2. Why is public order necessary? Do we have enough public order or too little? How can we tell? What might a large, complex society like ours be like without laws and without a system of criminal justice? Would you want to live in such a society? Why or why not?

3. What must we, as individuals, sacrifice to facilitate public order? Do we ever give up too much in the interest of public order? If so, when?

4. This chapter describes two models of the criminal justice system. What are they and how do they differ? Which model do you think is more useful? Which is more accurate? Why?

NOTES

i. All boldfaced terms are explained whenever possible using definitions provided by the Bureau of Justice Statistics under a mandate of the Justice System Improvement Act of 1979. That mandate found its most complete expression in the *Dictionary of Criminal Justice Data Terminology* (Washington, DC: Bureau of Justice Statistics, 1982), the second edition of which provides the wording for many definitions in this text.

ii. Adapted from U.S. Code, Title 28, Section 20.3 (2[d]). Title 28 of the U.S. Code defines the term administration of criminal justice.

iii. Melissa Hickman Barlow, "Sustainable Justice: 2012 Presidential Address to the Academy of Criminal Justice Sciences," *Justice Quarterly*, Vol. 30, No. 1 (2013), pp. 1–17.

iv. Adapted from Robert M. Shusta et al., *Multicultural Law Enforcement*, 2nd ed. (Upper Saddle River, NJ: Prentice Hall, 2002), p. 443.

1. As quoted in "Communities: Mobilizing Against Crime," *National Institute of Justice Journal*, August 1996.

2. Emily Brown, "Timeline: Michael Brown Shooting in Ferguson, Mo.," *USA Today*, December 2, 2014, http://www.usatoday.com/story/news/nation/2014/08/14/michael-brown-ferguson-missouri-timeline/14051827 (accessed January 30, 2015).

3. J. David Goodman and Al Baker, "Wave of Protests After Grand Jury Doesn't Indict Officer in Eric Garner Chokehold Case," *New York Times*, December 3, 2014, http://www.nytimes.com/2014/12/04/nyregion/grand-jury-said-to-bring-no-charges-in-staten-island-chokehold-death-of-eric-garner.html (accessed February 3, 2015).

4. Simon McCormack, "Cops Reportedly Say They're Not Making Arrests After Cop Killings," *Huffington Post*, December 27, 2014, http://www.huffingtonpost.com/2014/12/30/arrests-drop-nyc_n_6397452.html (accessed February 3, 2015).

5. Matt Taibbi, "The NYPD's 'Work Stoppage' Is Surreal," *Rolling Stone*, December 31, 2014, http://www.rollingstone.com/politics/news/the-nypds-work-stoppage-is-surreal-20141231?page=2 (accessed March 4, 2015).

6. John R. Emshwiller, "Seattle Police Chafe Under New Marching Orders," *Wall Street Journal*, December 30, 2014, http://www.wsj.com/articles/seattle-police-chafe-under-new-marching-orders-1419981603 (accessed March 2, 2015).

7. Benjamin Mueller and Al Baker, 2 N.Y.P.D. Officers Killed in Brooklyn Ambush; Suspect Commits Suicide, *New York Times*, December 20, 2015, http://www.nytimes.com/2014/12/21/nyregion/two-police-officers-shot-in-their-patrol-car-in-brooklyn.html?_r=0 (accessed February 28, 2015).

8. Andy Campbell, "Protesters Storm St. Louis Police Headquarters," *Huffington Post*, December 31, 2014, http://www.huffingtonpost.com/2014/12/31/protesters-st-louis-police_n_6402150.html (accessed February 28, 2015).

9. Louise Boyle, "Disturbing Graffiti of an Angel Shooting a Police Officer in Detroit Sparks Fears of More Anti-cop Violence," *Daily Mail*, http://www.dailymail.co.uk/news/article-2893469/Disturbing-graffiti-Detroit-sparks-fears-anti-cop-violence.html (accessed February 28, 2015).

10. Emily Gold Lagratta and Phil Bowen, *To Be Fair: Procedural Fairness in Courts* (New York; Criminal Justice Alliance, October 2014).

11. For a thorough discussion of immigration as it relates to crime, see Ramiro Martinez, Jr., and Matthew T. Lee, "On Immigration and Crime," in National Institute of Justice, *Criminal Justice 2000, Vol. 1: The Nature of Crime—Continuity and Change* (Washington, DC: U.S. Dept. of Justice, Office of Justice Programs, 2000).

12. "Inside Columbine," *Rocky Mountain News*, http://www.rockymountainnews.com/drmn/columbine (accessed July 4, 2007).

13. "Cries of Relief," *Time*, April 26, 1993, p. 18; and "King II: What Made the Difference?" *Newsweek*, April 26, 1993, p. 26.

14. Laurence McQuillan, "Bush to Urge Jail for Execs Who Lie," *USA Today*, July 9, 2002, http://www.usatoday.com/news/washdc/2002/07/09/bush-business.htm (accessed July 9, 2006).

15. Sarbanes-Oxley Act of 2002 (officially known as the Public Company Accounting Reform and Investor Protection Act), Public Law 107–204, 116 Stat. 745 (July 30, 2002).

16. PricewaterhouseCoopers, "The Sarbanes-Oxley Act," http://www.pwcglobal.com/Extweb/NewCoAtWork.nsf/docid/D0D7F79003C6D64485256CF30074D66C (accessed July 8, 2007).

17. "Texas Tycoon R. Allen Stanford Convicted of $7 Billion Ponzi Fraud," CBS News Crimesider, http://www.cbsnews.com/8301-504083_162-57391629-504083/texas-tycoon-r-allen-stanford-convicted-of-$7-billion-ponzi-fraud. March 6, 2012 (accessed March 9, 2012).

18. Richard Esposito, Eloise Harper, and Maddy Sauer, "Bernie Madoff Pleads Guilty to Ponzi Scheme, Goes Straight to Jail, Says He's 'Deeply Sorry,'" ABCNews.com, March 12, 2009, http://abcnews.go.com/Blotter/WallStreet/Story?id=7066715&page=1 (accessed July 4, 2009).

19. Robert Lenzner, "Bernie Madoff's $50 Billion Ponzi Scheme," Forbes.com, December 12, 2008, http://www.forbes.com/2008/12/12/madoff-ponzi-hedge-pf-ii-in_rl_1212croesus_inl.html (accessed September 28, 2009).

20. Jeremy Gorner, "In Chicago, Killings and Questions on the Rise," *Chicago Tribune*, December 30, 2012, http://www.chicagotribune.com/news/local/ct-met-chicago-violence-2012-20121230,0,186137.story (accessed January 3, 2013); Darran Simon, "Cracking Camden's Killings," *Philadelphia Inquirer*, December 30, 2012, http://articles.philly.com/2012-12-30/news/36065156_1_homicide-unit-reluctant-witnesses-killings (accessed January 3, 2013); and George Hunter and Mike Wilkinson, "Detroit Homicides Climb 10%," *The Detroit News*, December 31, 2012 (accessed January 4, 2013).

21. Elliot Spagat, "Chelea's Law Signed by Schwarzenegger, Will Give Some Sex Offenders Life in Prison," *Huffington Post*, September 9, 2010, http://www.huffingtonpost.com/2010/09/09/chelseas-law-signed-by-sc_n_711115.html (accessed April 4, 2012).

22. Wendy Koch, "States Get Tougher with Sex Offenders," *USA Today*, May 24, 2006, p. 1A.

23. See "Justice Questions Should Terrorists Be Treated Differently Than Criminals," Free Library, http://www.thefreelibrary.com/Justice+questions+should+terrorists+be+treated+differently+than. . .-a079412926 (accessed September 12, 2009).

24. Barack Obama, Speech in Chicago, November 4, 2008.

25. Martin Luther King, Jr., in an address to the Tenth Anniversary Convention of the Southern Christian Leadership Conference in Atlanta, Georgia, on August 16, 1967. It was abolitionist and Unitarian minister Theodore Parker who first used a similar phrase in the mid-1800s, saying "I do not pretend to understand the moral universe; the arc is a long one . . .. And from what I see I am sure it bends toward justice."

26. The American Heritage Dictionary on CD-ROM (Boston: Houghton Mifflin, 1991).

27. For a good overview of the issues involved, see Judge Harold J. Rothwax, *Guilty: The Collapse of Criminal Justice* (New York: Random House, 1996).

28. For one perspective on the detention of Muslims following September 11, 2001, see the plaintiff's motion to stay proceedings on defendant's summary judgment motion pending discovery, in *Center for National Security Studies* v. *U.S. Department of Justice*, U.S. District Court for the District of Columbia (Civil Action No. 01-2500; January 2002), http://www.aclu.org/court/cnssjan22.pdf (accessed September 24, 2007).

29. The systems model of criminal justice is often attributed to the frequent use of the term *system* by the 1967 Presidential Commission in its report *The Challenge of Crime in a Free*

Society (Washington, DC: U.S. Government Printing Office, 1967).

30. One of the first published works to use the nonsystem approach to criminal justice was the American Bar Association's *New Perspective on Urban Crime* (Washington, DC: ABA Special Committee on Crime Prevention and Control, 1972).

31. Jerome H. Skolnick, *Justice without Trial* (New York: John Wiley, 1966), p. 179.

32. *Miranda v. Arizona*, 384 U.S. 436, 16 L.Ed.2d 694, 86 S.Ct. 1602 (1966).

33. North Carolina Justice Academy, *Miranda Warning Card* (Salemburg: North Carolina Justice Academy, n.d.).

34. John M. Scheb and John M. Scheb II, *American Criminal Law* (St. Paul, MN: West, 1996), p. 32.

35. Federal Rules of Criminal Procedure, 10.

36. *Blanton v. City of North Las Vegas*, 489 U.S. 538, 103 L.Ed.2d 550, 109 S.Ct. 1289 (1989).

37. Ibid.

38. *U.S. v. Nachtigal*, 122 L.Ed.2d 374, 113 S.Ct. 1072, 1073 (1993), per curiam.

39. Barbara Borland and Ronald Sones, *Prosecution of Felony Arrests* (Washington, DC: Bureau of Justice Statistics, 1991).

40. "The Defendants' Rights at a Criminal Trial," http://www.mycounsel.com/content/arrests/court/rights.html (accessed February 10, 2007).

41. U.S. Constitution, Amendment V.

42. For a complete and now-classic analysis of the impact of decisions made by the Warren Court, see Fred P. Graham, *The Due Process Revolution: The Warren Court's Impact on Criminal Law* (New York: Hayden Press, 1970).

43. U.S. Consitution, Amendment VI.

44. *Gideon v. Wainwright*, 372 U.S. 353 (1963).

45. Herbert Packer, *The Limits of the Criminal Sanction* (Stanford, CA: Stanford University Press, 1968).

46. "Understanding and Using Evidence-Based Practices," Justice Resource Update, http://www.ojp.gov/justiceresourceupdate/june2010 (accessed June 3, 2010).

47. "Criminal Justice: What Works? What Doesn't?" *The Crime Report*, June 21, 2011, http://www.thecrimereport.org/archive/criminal-justice-reform-what-works-what-doesnt-what-dont-we-know (accessed August 13, 2011).

48. For an excellent history of policing in the United States, see Edward A. Farris, "Five Decades of American Policing, 1932–1982," *Police Chief* (November 1982), pp. 30–36.

49. Gene Edward Carte, "August Vollmer and the Origins of Police Professionalism," *Journal of Police Science and Administration*, Vol. 1, No. 1 (1973), pp. 274–281.

50. Chris Eskridge distinguishes between police training, which is "job specific" and is intended to teach trainees how to do something (like fire a weapon), and justice education, whose purpose is to "develop a general spirit of inquiry." See C. W. Eskridge, "Criminal Justice Education and Its Potential Impact on the Sociopolitical-Economic Climate of Central European Nations," *Journal of Criminal Justice Education*, Vol. 14, No. 1 (spring 2003), pp. 105–118; and James O. Finckenauer, "The Quest for Quality in Criminal Justice Education," *Justice Quarterly*, Vol. 22, No. 4 (December 2005), pp. 413–426.

51. "Understanding and Using Evidence-Based Practices."

52. "Polygamist Jeffs Gets Life for Underage Sex Assault," *USA Today*, August 10, 2011, p. 5A.

53. "Polygamist Wins Parole from Utah State Prison," Associated Press, August 27, 2007.

54. On March 22, 1794, the U.S. Congress barred American citizens from transporting slaves from the United States to another nation or between foreign nations. On January 1, 1808, the importation of slaves into the United States became illegal, and Congress charged the U.S. Revenue Cutter Service (now known as the U.S. Coast Guard) with enforcing the law on the high seas. Although some slave ships were seized, the importation of Africans for sale as slaves apparently continued in some southern states until the early 1860s. See U.S. Coast Guard, "U.S. Coast Guard in Illegal Immigration (1794–1971)," http://www.uscg.mil/hq/g-o/g-opl/mle/amiohist.htm (accessed October 13, 2007).

55. U.S. Census Bureau website, http://www.census.gov (accessed March 22, 2010). Population statistics are estimates because race is a difficult concept to define and because Census Bureau interviewers allow individuals to choose more than one race when completing census forms.

© David R. Frazier Photolibrary, Inc./Alamy

2

THE CRIME PICTURE

LEARNING OBJECTIVES

After reading this chapter, you should be able to

- Describe the FBI's UCR/NIBRS Program, including its purpose, history, and what it tells us about crime in the United States today.
- Describe the National Crime Victimization Survey (NCVS) program, including its purpose, history, and what it tells us about crime in the United States today.
- Compare and contrast the UCR and NCVS data collection and reporting programs.
- Describe how the special categories of crime discussed in this chapter are significant today.

No one way of describing crime describes it well enough.
PRESIDENT'S COMMISSION ON LAW ENFORCEMENT AND ADMINISTRATION OF JUSTICE

■ **theme**   Why are crime statistics valuable to policy makers and to the criminal justice system?

■ **lecture note**   Explain the historical circumstances that led to the development of the NCVS and the UCR, and discuss how new and innovative types of crime (such as some high-technology offenses) might not be fully counted under those programs.

Introduction

In 2014, officials with the Dickson (Tennessee) County Sheriff's Office reported that the department had been extorted into paying a fee to unknown cybercriminals after ransomware had locked detectives and deputies out of more than 72,000 files stored on the agency's computers. Ransomware (discussed in more detail in Chapter 18) is malicious software that takes over personal computers and forces their users to pay a fee in order to regain control. After consulting with the FBI and military security experts, the department was forced to pay $500 in Bitcoins to recover the data. Jeff McCliss, the agency's Information Technology director told *Police Magazine*, "It's a very bad feeling to be the victim instead of the investigator."[1] A video describing the event was posted on the Web at **http://www.policemag .com/videos/channel/technology/2014/11/video -tennessee-sheriff-s-office-pays-ransom-for-case-files.aspx.**

As this story shows, a wide range of new forms of crime are victimizing all areas of contemporary society—and they are not always easy to solve, or even to discover!

> A wide range of new forms of crime are victimizing all areas of contemporary society—and they are not always easy to solve, or even to discover!

This chapter has a dual purpose. First, it provides a statistical overview of crime in contemporary America by examining information on reported and discovered crimes. Second, it identifies special categories of crime that are of particular interest today, including crime against women, crime against the elderly, hate crime, corporate and white-collar crime, organized crime, gun crime, drug crime, cybercrime, and terrorism.

Although we will look at many crime statistics in this chapter, it is important to remember that statistical aggregates of reported crime, whatever their source, do not reveal the lost lives, human suffering, lessened productivity, and reduced quality of life that crime causes. Unlike the fictional characters on TV crime shows, real-life crime victims as well as real-life offenders lead intricate lives—they have families, hold jobs, and dream dreams. As we examine the crime statistics, we must not lose sight of the people behind the numbers.

Crime Data and Social Policy

Crime statistics provide an overview of criminal activity. If used properly, a statistical picture of crime can serve as a powerful tool for creating social policy. Decision makers at all levels, including

Public safety personnel in Sacramento, California, work on laptops. This chapter opens with a story about a sheriff's office that was victimized by ransomware. What other new forms of crime can you think of that were not known a generation ago?

CBS/Cliff Lipson/Landov

legislators, other elected officials, and administrators throughout the criminal justice system, rely on crime data to analyze and evaluate existing programs, to fashion and design new crime-control initiatives, to develop funding requests, and to plan new laws and crime-control legislation. Many "get tough" policies, such as the three-strikes movement that swept the country during the 1990s, were based in large part on the measured ineffectiveness of existing programs to reduce the incidence of repeat offending.

However, some people question just how objective—and therefore how useful—crime statistics are. Social events, including crime, are complex and difficult to quantify. Even the decision of which crimes should be included and which excluded in statistical reports is itself a judgment reflecting the interests and biases of policymakers. As mentioned in Chapter 1, the number of Internet-based offenses and crimes making use of other forms of high technology are constantly increasing, and statistical reporting programs that were designed years ago may not fully count such crimes. As famed criminologist Herbert Packer once observed, "We can have as much or as little crime as we please; depending on what we choose to count as criminal."[2]

> How much crime we have depends on what we count as criminal.

Finally, we should note that public opinion about crime is not always realistic. As well-known criminologist Norval Morris points out, the news media do more to influence public perceptions of crime than any official data do.[3] During the four-year period (in the mid-1990s) covered by Morris's study, for example, the frequency of crime stories reported in the national

■ **lecture note**   Explain the different types of information on crime that may be obtained from the UCR Program, the NCVS, and offender self-reports and that the choice of data source may depend on the type of information required.

■ **Uniform Crime Reporting (UCR) Program**   A statistical reporting program run by the FBI's Criminal Justice Information Services (CJIS) division. The UCR Program publishes *Crime in the United States*, which provides an annual summation of the incidence and rate of reported crimes throughout the United States.

■ **National Crime Victimization Survey (NCVS)**   An annual survey of selected American households conducted by the Bureau of Justice Statistics to determine the extent of criminal victimization—especially unreported victimization—in the United States.

■ **lecture note**   Explain how data from the UCR and NIBRS, which includes crimes reported to the police, can lead to a far different picture of crime in America than information obtained from a random survey of self-reporters such as the NCVS.

■ **lecture note**   Explain the criminal justice funnel and how many cases fall out as they move through the criminal justice system.

■ **Bureau of Justice Statistics (BJS)**   A U.S. Department of Justice agency responsible for the collection of criminal justice data, including the annual National Crime Victimization Survey.

■ **self-reports**   Crime measures based on surveys that ask respondents to reveal any illegal activity in which they have been involved.

media increased fourfold. During the same time period, crime was at the top of the list in subject matter covered in news stories at both the local and national levels. The irony, says Morris, is that "the grossly increasing preoccupation with crime stories came at a time of steadily declining crime and violence." However, as Morris adds, "aided and abetted by this flood of misinformation, the politicians, federal and state and local, fostered the view that the public demands … 'get tough' policies."

The Collection of Crime Data

Nationally, crime statistics come from two major sources: (1) the Federal Bureau of Investigation's (FBI's) **Uniform Crime Reporting (UCR) Program** (also known today as the UCR/NIBRS Program), which produces an annual overview of major crime titled *Crime in the United States*; and (2) the **National Crime Victimization Survey (NCVS)** of the **Bureau of Justice Statistics (BJS)**. The most widely quoted numbers purporting to describe crime in America today probably come from the UCR/NIBRS Program, although the statistics it produces are based largely on *reports* to the police by victims of crime.

> Social events, including crime, are complex and difficult to quantify. Even the decision of which crimes should be included and which excluded in statistical reports is itself a judgment reflecting the interests and biases of policymakers.

A third source of crime data is offender **self-reports** based on surveys that ask respondents to reveal any illegal activity in which they have been involved. Offender self-reports are not discussed in detail in this chapter because surveys utilizing them are not national in scope and are not undertaken regularly. Moreover, offenders are often reluctant to accurately report ongoing or recent criminal involvement, making information derived from these surveys somewhat unreliable and less than current. However, the available information from offender self-reports reveals that serious criminal activity is considerably more widespread than most "official" surveys show (Figure 2-1).

Other data sources also contribute to our knowledge of crime patterns throughout the nation. One important source is the *Sourcebook of Criminal Justice Statistics*—an annual compilation of national information on crime and on the criminal justice system. *Sourcebook* data are produced by the BJS, and made available on the Web through the auspices of the State University of New York at Albany. The National Institute of Justice (NIJ), which is the primary research arm of the U.S. Department of Justice, the Office of Juvenile Justice and Delinquency Prevention (OJJDP), the Federal Justice Statistics Resource Center, and the National Victim's Resource Center provide still more information on crime patterns. The *Sourcebook* is available online at **http://www.albany.edu/sourcebook**.

The UCR/NIBRS Program

Development of the UCR Program

In 1930, Congress authorized the U.S. attorney general to survey crime in America, and the FBI was designated to implement the program. In short order, the bureau built on earlier efforts by the International Association of Chiefs of Police (IACP) to create a national system of uniform crime statistics. As a practical measure, the IACP had recommended the use of readily available information, and so it was that citizens' crime reports to the police became the basis of the FBI's plan.[4]

During its first year of operation, the FBI's UCR Program received reports from 400 cities in 43 states. Twenty million people were covered by that first comprehensive survey. Today, approximately 18,000 law enforcement agencies provide crime information for the program, with data coming from city, county, and state departments. To ensure uniformity in reporting, the FBI has developed standardized definitions of offenses and terminologies used in the program. Numerous publications,

■ **Crime Index**   A now defunct but once inclusive measure of the UCR Program's violent and property crime categories, or what are called *Part I offenses*. The Crime Index, long featured in the FBI's publication *Crime in the United States*, was discontinued in 2004. The index had been intended as a tool for geographic (state-to-state) and historical (year-to-year) comparisons via the use of crime rates (the number of crimes per unit of population). However, criticism that the index was misleading arose after rese archers found that the largest of the index's crime categories, larceny-theft, carried undue weight and led to an underappreciation of changes in the rates of more violent and serious crimes.

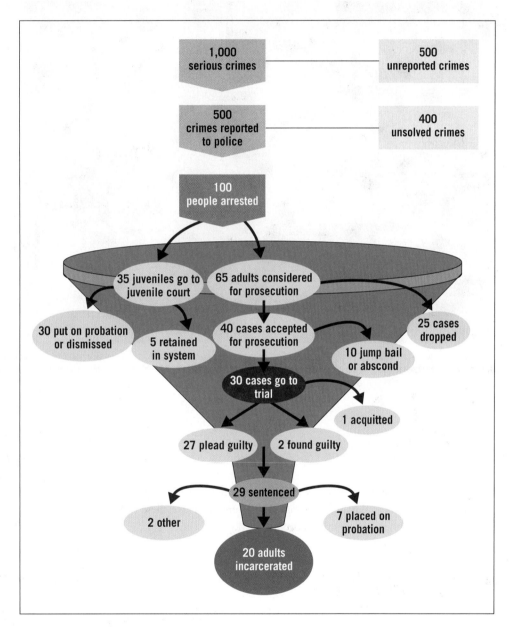

FIGURE 2-1 | The Criminal Justice Funnel

Source: Pearson Education, Inc.

including the *Uniform Crime Reporting Handbook* and the *Manual of Law Enforcement Records,* are supplied to participating agencies, and training for effective reporting is available through FBI-sponsored seminars and instructional literature.

Following the IACP recommendations, the original UCR Program was designed to permit comparisons over time through construction of a **Crime Index**. As originally constituted, the index summed the occurrences of seven major offenses—murder, forcible rape, robbery, aggravated assault, burglary, larceny-theft, and motor vehicle theft—and expressed the result as a crime rate based on population. In 1979, by congressional mandate, an eighth offense—arson—was added to the index. The Crime Index, first published in *Crime in the United States* in 1960, was the title used for a simple aggregation of the

■ **lecture note**   Explain why the FBI believed it was necessary to develop NIBRS. Review the differences between the UCR system and NIBRS, using Table 2-1 as a reference.

■ **Follow the author's tweets about the latest crime and justice news @schmalleger.**

■ **National Incident-Based Reporting System (NIBRS)**   An incident-based reporting system that collects detailed data on every single crime occurrence. NIBRS data are replacing the kinds of summary data that have traditionally been provided by the FBI's Uniform Crime Reporting Program.

Los Angeles emergency personnel working at the scene of an apparent gang-related shooting at Sunset Boulevard and Pacific Coast Highway. Some experts fear that violent crime may be starting to rise in big cities after two decades of decline. What would be the consequences for American cities if crime were to increase?

seven main offense classifications (called Part I offenses). The Modified Crime Index refers to the original Crime Index offenses plus arson.

Over the years, however, concern grew that the Crime Index did not provide a clear picture of criminality because it was skewed by the offense with the highest number of reports—typically larceny-theft. The sheer volume of larceny-theft offenses overshadowed more serious but less frequently committed offenses, skewing perceptions of crime rates for jurisdictions with high numbers of larceny-thefts, but low numbers of serious crimes such as murder and rape. In 2004, the FBI's Criminal Justice Information Services (CJIS) Advisory Policy Board officially discontinued the use of the Crime Index in the UCR/NIBRS Program and in its publications and directed the FBI to instead publish simple violent crime totals and property crime totals until a more viable index could be developed.[5]

Although work to develop such an index is still ongoing, UCR/NIBRS Program crime categories continue to provide useful comparisons of specific reported crimes over time and between jurisdictions. It is important to recognize, as you read through the next few pages, that today's UCR/NIBRS Program categories tend to parallel statutory definitions of

criminal behavior, but they are not legal classifications—only conveniences created for statistical-reporting purposes. Because many of the offense definitions used in this textbook are derived from official UCR/NIBRS Program terminology, you should remember that these definitions may differ from statutory definitions of crimes.

The National Incident-Based Reporting System (NIBRS)

Beginning in 1988, the FBI's UCR Program initiated development of a new national crime-collection effort called the **National Incident-Based Reporting System (NIBRS)**. NIBRS represents a significant redesign of the original Uniform Crime Reporting Program. Whereas the original UCR system was "summary based," the enhanced National Incident-Based Reporting System is incident driven (Table 2-1). Under NIBRS, city, county, state, and federal law enforcement agencies throughout the country furnish detailed data on crime and arrest activities at the incident level either to the individual state incident-based reporting programs or directly to the federal NIBRS Program.

TABLE 2-1 | Differences between the Traditional UCR and Enhanced UCR/NIBRS Reporting

TRADITIONAL UCR	ENHANCED UCR/NIBRS
Consists of monthly aggregate crime counts	Consists of individual incident records for the 8 major crimes and 38 other offenses, with details on offense, victim, offender, and property involved
Records one offense per incident, as determined by the hierarchy rule, which suppresses counts of lesser offenses in multiple-offense incidents	Records each offense occurring in an incident
Does not distinguish between attempted and completed crimes	Distinguishes between attempted and completed crimes
Collects assault information in five categories	Restructures definition of assault
Collects weapon information for murder, robbery, and aggravated assault	Collects weapon information for all violent offenses
Provides counts on arrests for the 8 major crimes and 21 other offenses	Provides details on arrests for the 8 major crimes and 49 other offenses
Distinguishes between personal (violent) and property crimes	General categories of crime consist of crimes against persons, property, and society
Sees robbery as a personal crime	Classifies robbery as a property crime

Source: Adapted from *Effects of NIBRS on Crime Statistics*, BJS Special Report (Washington, DC: Bureau of Justice Statistics, 2000), p. 1, and FBI, *National Incident-Based Reporting System: Crimes against Persons, Property, and Society* (https://www.fbi.gov/about-us/cjis/ucr/nibrs/2013/resources/crimes-against-persons-property-and-society), accessed July 30, 2015.

NIBRS is not a separate report; rather, it is the new methodology underlying the contemporary UCR system—hence our use of the term *UCR/NIBRS* in describing today's Uniform Crime Reporting Program. Whereas the old UCR system depended on statistical tabulations of crime data, which were often little more than frequency counts, the new UCR/NIBRS system gathers many details about each criminal incident. Included is information on place of occurrence, weapon used, type and value of property damaged or stolen, the personal characteristics of the offender and the victim, the nature of any relationship between the two, and the disposition of the complaint.

Under UCR/NIBRS, the traditional distinctions between Part I and Part II offenses are being replaced with 23 general offenses: arson, assault, bribery, burglary, counterfeiting, embezzlement, extortion, forcible sex offenses, fraud, gambling, homicide, kidnapping, larceny, motor vehicle theft, narcotics offenses, nonforcible sex offenses, pornography, prostitution, receiving stolen property, robbery, vandalism, and weapons violations. Other offenses on which UCR/NIBRS data are being gathered include bad checks, vagrancy, disorderly conduct, driving under the influence, drunkenness, nonviolent family offenses, liquor-law violations, "peeping Tom" activity, trespass, and a general category of all "other" criminal law violations. UCR/NIBRS also collects data on an expanded array of attributes involved in the commission of offenses, including whether the offender is suspected of using alcohol, drugs, or narcotics, or a computer, in the commission of the offense.

The FBI began accepting crime data in the NIBRS format in January 1989. Although the bureau intended to have NIBRS fully in place by 1999, delays have been routine, and the NIBRS format has not yet been fully adopted. Because it is a flexible system, changes continue to be made in the data gathered under UCR/NIBRS. In 2003, for example, three new data elements were added to the survey to collect information on law enforcement officers killed and assaulted. Another new data element has since been added to indicate the involvement of gang members in reported offenses.

The goals of the innovations introduced under NIBRS are to enhance the quantity, quality, and timeliness of crime-data collection by law enforcement agencies and to improve the methodology used for compiling, analyzing, auditing, and publishing the collected data. A major advantage of UCR/NIBRS, beyond the sheer increase in the volume of data collected, is the ability that NIBRS provides to break down and combine crime offense data into specific information.[6] The latest crime statistics from the FBI can be viewed at **http://www.fbi.gov/stats-services/crimestats**.

Other changes in crime reporting were brought about by the 1990 Crime Awareness and Campus Security Act, which requires colleges to publish annual security reports.[7] Most campuses share crime data with the FBI, increasing the reported national incidence of a variety of offenses. The U.S. Department of Education reported that 24 murders and 5,054 forcible sex offenses occurred on U.S. college campuses in 2013—the most recent year for which data are available. Also reported were 1,568 robberies, 2,303 aggravated assaults, 16,010 burglaries, and 3,261 motor vehicle thefts.[8] Although these numbers may seem high, it is important to realize that, except for the crimes of rape and sexual assault, college students experience violence at average annual rates that are lower than those for nonstudents in the same age group.[9] Rates of rape and sexual assault do not differ statistically between students and nonstudents. For the latest campus crime information, see **http://clerycenter.org.**

Historical Trends

Most UCR/NIBRS information is reported as a rate of crime. Rates are computed as the number of crimes *per* some unit of population. National reports generally make use of large units of population, such as 100,000 people. Hence the rate of rape reported by the UCR/NIBRS Program for 2014 was 36.6 rapes per every 100,000 inhabitants of the United States.[10] Rates allow for a meaningful comparison over areas and across time. The rate of reported rape for 1960, for example, was only about 10 per 100,000 inhabitants. We expect the number of crimes to increase

A fourth shift in crime trends may be on the horizon and could lead to sustained increases in crime.

as population grows, but rate increases are cause for concern because they indicate that reports of crime are increasing faster than the population is growing. Rates, however, require interpretation. Although there is a tendency to judge an individual's risk of victimization based on rates, such judgments tend to be inaccurate because they are based purely on averages and do not take into consideration individual life circumstances, such as place of residence, wealth, and educational level. Although rates may tell us about aggregate conditions and trends, we must be very careful when applying them to individual cases.

Since the FBI's UCR Program began, there have been three major shifts in crime rates—and we now seem to be witnessing the beginning of a fourth (Figure 2-2). The first occurred during the early 1940s, when crime decreased sharply due to the large number of young men who entered

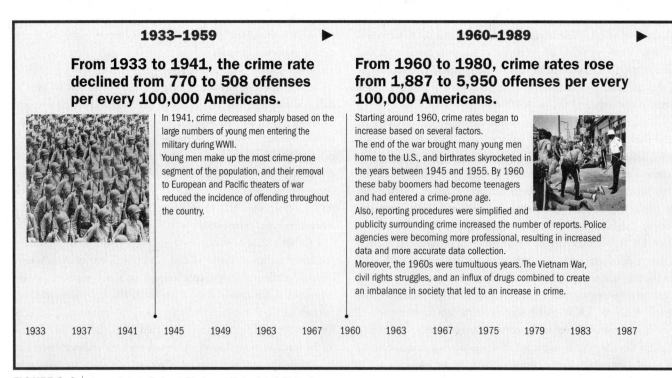

1933–1959 ▶

From 1933 to 1941, the crime rate declined from 770 to 508 offenses per every 100,000 Americans.

In 1941, crime decreased sharply based on the large numbers of young men entering the military during WWII.
Young men make up the most crime-prone segment of the population, and their removal to European and Pacific theaters of war reduced the incidence of offending throughout the country.

1960–1989 ▶

From 1960 to 1980, crime rates rose from 1,887 to 5,950 offenses per every 100,000 Americans.

Starting around 1960, crime rates began to increase based on several factors.
The end of the war brought many young men home to the U.S., and birthrates skyrocketed in the years between 1945 and 1955. By 1960 these baby boomers had become teenagers and had entered a crime-prone age.
Also, reporting procedures were simplified and publicity surrounding crime increased the number of reports. Police agencies were becoming more professional, resulting in increased data and more accurate data collection.
Moreover, the 1960s were tumultuous years. The Vietnam War, civil rights struggles, and an influx of drugs combined to create an imbalance in society that led to an increase in crime.

| 1933 | 1937 | 1941 | 1945 | 1949 | 1963 | 1967 | 1960 | 1963 | 1967 | 1975 | 1979 | 1983 | 1987 |

FIGURE 2-2 | American Crime Rates: Historical Trends
Source: Pearson Education, Inc.

■ **theme**   There have been three major shifts in crime rates since the UCR Program began. What factors have affected crime? What factors may affect crime in the near future?

military service during World War II. Young males make up the most "crime-prone" segment of the population, and their deployment overseas did much to lower crime rates at home. From 1933 to 1941, the Crime Index declined from 770 to 508 offenses per every 100,000 members of the American population.[11]

The second noteworthy shift in offense statistics was a dramatic increase in most forms of crime between 1960 and the early 1990s. Several factors contributed to the increase in reported crime during this period. One was also linked to World War II. With the end of the war and the return of millions of young men to civilian life, birthrates skyrocketed between 1945 and 1955, creating a postwar baby boom. By 1960, the first baby boomers were teenagers—and had entered a crime-prone age. This disproportionate number of young people produced a dramatic increase in most major crimes.

Other factors contributed to the increase in reported crime during the same period. Modified reporting requirements made it less stressful for victims to file police reports, and the publicity associated with the rise in crime sensitized victims to the importance of reporting. Crimes that might have gone undetected in the past began to figure more prominently in official statistics. Similarly, the growing professionalization of some police departments resulted in greater and more accurate data collection, making some of the most progressive departments appear to be associated with the largest crime increases.[12]

The 1960s were tumultuous years. The Vietnam War, a vibrant civil rights struggle, the heady growth of secularism, a dramatic increase in the divorce rate, diverse forms of "liberation," and the influx of psychedelic and other drugs all combined to fragment existing institutions. Social norms were blurred, and group control over individual behavior declined substantially. The "normless" quality of American society in the 1960s contributed greatly to the rise in crime.

From 1960 to 1980, crime rates rose from 1,887 to 5,950 offenses per every 100,000 U.S. residents. In the early 1980s, when postwar boomers began to age out of the crime-prone years and American society emerged from the cultural drift that had characterized the previous 20 years, crime rates leveled out briefly. Soon, however, an increase in drug-related criminal activity led crime rates—especially violent crime rates—to soar once again. Crime rates peaked during the early 1990s.

A third major shift came with a significant decline in the rates of most major crimes being reported between 1991 and 2014. During these years, the rate of reported crime dropped

1990–2014 ▶

From 1991 to 2014, crime rates dropped from 5,897 to 2,962 offenses per every 100,000 Americans.

Strict laws, an expanded justice system, and increased police funding for personnel and for crime-fighting technologies are cited as reasons for the drop in crime. Other changes beyond the control of the police may have played a role as well and include economic expansion and an aging population. During the 1990s, unemployment decreased by 36% and likely contributed to the decline in crime rates.

2015–present

Some cities have recently experienced increases in violent crime, but online criminal activity is difficult to measure using existing reporting practices.

A fourth shift in rates of traditional crime may be about to begin, but online forms of crime may soon outnumber traditional offenses. Economic uncertainty, a growing number of ex-convicts back on the streets as well as an increase in teen populations and gang activity may soon lead to sustained increases in traditional offenses.

| 1990 | 1994 | 1997 | 2001 | 2005 | 2009 | 2010 | 2011 | 2012 | 2016 |

FIGURE 2-2 | (continued)

from 5,897 to 2,962 offenses per every 100,000 residents—sending it down to levels not seen since 1975. The U.S. Department of Justice suggests various reasons for the decline, including[13]

- A coordinated, collaborative, and well-funded national effort to combat crime, beginning with the Safe Streets Act of 1968 and continuing through the USA PATRIOT Act of 2001
- Stronger, better-prepared criminal justice agencies, resulting from increased spending by federal and state governments on crime-control programs
- The growth in popularity of innovative police programs, such as community policing (see Chapter 6, "Policing: Purpose and Organization")
- A strong victims' movement and enactment of the 1984 federal Victims of Crime Act (see Chapter 11, "Sentencing") and the 1994 Violence against Women Act (discussed later in this chapter), which established the Office for Victims of Crime in the U.S. Department of Justice
- Sentencing reform, including various "get tough on crime" initiatives (see Chapter 11)
- A substantial growth in the use of incarceration (see Chapter 13, "Prisons and Jails") due to changes in sentencing law practice (see Chapter 11)
- The "war on drugs," begun in the 1970s,[14] which resulted in stiff penalties for drug dealers and repeat drug offenders
- Advances in forensic science and enforcement technology, including the increased use of real-time communications, the growth of the Internet, and the advent of DNA evidence (see Chapter 11)

More important than new strict laws, an expanded justice system, police funding, or changes in crime-fighting technologies, however, may have been influential economic and demographic factors that were largely beyond the control of policymakers but that combined to produce substantial decreases in rates of crime—including economic expansion and a significant shift in demographics caused by an aging of the population. During the 1990s, unemployment decreased by 36% in the United States, while the number of people ages 20 to 34 declined by 18%. Hence it may have been the ready availability of jobs combined with demographic shifts in the population—not the official efforts of policymakers—that produced a noteworthy decrease in crime during the 1990s.

Confounding matters even more, the digital age has brought with it a plethora of new criminal opportunities—many of which were inconceivable only a decade or two ago. Shifts in crime patterns away from more "traditional" crimes (like those measured by the UCR and NCVS), and toward innovative forms of law violation using high technology, may mask the true face of crime in America—leading to a mistaken sense that the total number of criminal offenses in our society is lower than it actually is. Bank robbery, for example, is a "traditional" crime and is scored

by the FBI as one form of "robbery" in the crime statistics that it reports; but while bank robberies have fallen in number over the years, illicit computer attempts to access and misappropriate funds held by banks have risen significantly. A couple of years ago, for example, an international ring of computer criminals stole $45 million from thousands of ATM machines around the globe in a matter of hours. In New York City alone, members of the ring struck 2,904 ATM machines over a ten-hour period, illegally withdrawing more than $2.4 million leading the *New York Times* to comment that "the criminals never wore ski masks, threatened a teller or set foot in a vault."[15] Still, some computer crimes are not reportable under historical crime categories.[16]

It is important to recognize that today's law enforcement administrators often feel judged by their success in lowering crime rates. Consequently, police departments may put pressure on officers to artificially reduce crime rates through techniques such as downgrading crimes to lesser offenses when completing official paperwork. In fact, a recent study of nearly 2,000 retired New York Police Department (NYPD) officers found that the manipulation of crime reports has become a part of police culture in the NYPD.[17] Indications are that the underreporting of crime statistics by the police may be a nationwide phenomenon. Another investigation, for example, this one into the crime reporting practices of Milwaukee police officers, found hundreds of violent assaults that were misreported as minor offenses, and that were not counted in the city's violent crime rate. Following the report, Milwaukee Police Chief Edward Flynn ordered 70 members of the department to complete a refresher training course offered by the FBI on crime reporting.[18]

A fourth shift in crime trends may be on the horizon. Some think that recent economic uncertainty, an increased jobless rate among unskilled workers, the growing number of ex-convicts who are back on the streets, the recent growth in the teenage population in this country, the increasing influence of gangs, copycat crimes, and the lingering social disorganization brought on by natural disasters like Hurricane Katrina in 2005 and Super Storm Sandy in 2012 may lead to sustained increases in crime.[19] "We're probably done seeing declines in crime rates for some time to come," says Jack Riley, director of the Public Safety and Justice Program at RAND Corporation in Santa Monica, California. "The question," says Riley, "is how strong and how fast will those rates [rise], and what tools do we have at our disposal to get ahead of the curve."[20]

The specter of frequent but random mass shootings, and a high number of inner-city murders, is also changing the face of crime in America. One recent study, for example, showed that while rates of traditional crimes have been falling, some cities are experiencing dramatically higher rates of murder. In 2012, the year of the mass shootings in Aurora, Colorado, and Newtown, Connecticut, both Camden, New Jersey, and Detroit, Michigan, reported more murders than at any time in their history, and other cities, including Chicago, Illinois, were seeing record homicide rates.[21]

Finally, it is important to realize that while official U.S. crime rates may be close to multiyear lows, a number of other countries

■ **lecture note** Introduce the crime clock and stress that it does not mean crime occurs regularly or "like clockwork."

■ **violent crime** A UCR/NIBRS summary offense category that traditionally includes murder, rape, robbery, and aggravated assault.

■ **property crime** A UCR/NIBRS summary offense category that traditionally includes burglary, larceny-theft, motor vehicle theft, and arson.

■ **lecture note** Discuss clearance rates by referring to Table 2-2. Ask why some crimes have much higher clearance rates than others. Explain that personal crimes are cleared far more frequently than most property crimes because victims of violence are often able to identify their attackers.

■ **clearance rate** A measure of investigative effectiveness that compares the number of crimes reported or discovered to the number of crimes solved through arrest or other means (such as the death of the suspect).

Morgue workers place a coffin holding an unidentified body into a grave on the outskirts of the Mexican border city of Ciudad Juarez. Mexico's drug war has claimed more than 70,000 lives in the past eight years. Should cross-national killings be a concern of American law enforcement officials?

are experiencing high levels of criminal activity. Mexico, for example, where an ongoing war between the government and drug cartels has led to the deaths of more than 70,000 people and the disappearance of 27,000 more in the past eight years, is caught up in a rapid rate of violent crime escalation.[22] Violent crime, much of it associated with tribal and political conflicts, now extends across borders in Africa, the Middle East, and parts of Europe, leading one writer to comment that "crime has become a global anxiety, alongside climate change, banking crises, and outbreaks of disease."[23] Keep up with headlines in the Mexican drug war via the *Los Angeles Times* at **http://projects.latimes.com/mexico-drug-war/#/its-a-war.**

UCR/NIBRS in Transition

Reports of U.S. crime data available through the UCR/NIBRS Program are now going through a transitional phase, as the FBI integrates more NIBRS-based data into its official summaries. The transition to NIBRS reporting is complicated by the fact that not only does NIBRS gather more kinds of data than the older summary UCR Program did, but the definitions used for certain kinds of criminal activity under NIBRS differ from what they were under the traditional UCR Program. The standard reference publication that the FBI designates for use by police departments in

scoring and reporting crimes that occur within their jurisdiction is the *Uniform Crime Reporting Handbook*, and it is the most recent edition of that *Handbook* that guides and informs the discussion of crime statistics in the pages that follow. You can access the entire 164-page *Uniform Crime Reporting Handbook* at **http://www.justicestudies.com/pubs/ucrhandbook.pdf.** A thorough review of that document shows that much of the traditional UCR summary data reporting terminology and structure remains in place.

Figure 2-3 shows the FBI crime clock, which has long been calculated annually as a shorthand way of diagramming crime frequency in the United States. It should not be taken to imply regularity in the commission of crime.[24] Also, although the crime clock is a useful diagrammatic tool, it is not a rate-based measure of criminal activity and does not allow easy comparisons over time. Seven major crimes are included in the figure: murder, rape, robbery, aggravated assault, burglary, larceny-theft, and motor vehicle theft.

The crime clock distinguishes between two categories of offenses: violent crimes and property crimes. **Violent crimes** (also called *personal crimes*) include murder, rape, robbery, and aggravated assault. It is worth noting that in California and in some other states, almost all violent crimes are referred to as "strikable," as two- and three-strikes laws in those states can result in long prison terms for anyone who commits two or more such crimes. **Property crimes** are motor vehicle theft, burglary, arson (which is not shown in the crime clock) and larceny-theft. Other than the use of this simple dichotomy, UCR/NIBRS data do not provide a clear measure of the severity of the crimes they cover.

Like most UCR/NIBRS statistics, crime clock data are based on crimes reported to (or discovered by) the police. For a few offenses, the numbers reported are probably close to the numbers that actually occur. Murder, for example, is a crime that is difficult to conceal because of its seriousness. Even where the crime is not immediately discovered, the victim is often quickly missed by family members, friends, and associates, and someone files a "missing persons" report with the police. Auto theft is another crime that is reported in numbers similar to its actual rate of occurrence, probably because insurance companies require that the victim file a police report before they will pay the claim.

A commonly used term in today's UCR/NIBRS reports is **clearance rate**, which refers to the proportion of reported

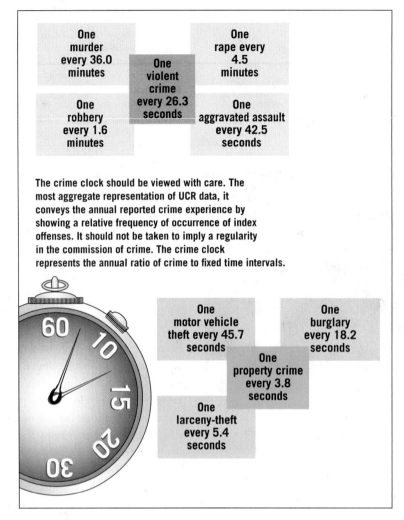

One murder every 36.0 minutes

One violent crime every 26.3 seconds

One rape every 4.5 minutes

One robbery every 1.6 minutes

One aggravated assault every 42.5 seconds

The crime clock should be viewed with care. The most aggregate representation of UCR data, it conveys the annual reported crime experience by showing a relative frequency of occurrence of index offenses. It should not be taken to imply a regularity in the commission of crime. The crime clock represents the annual ratio of crime to fixed time intervals.

One motor vehicle theft every 45.7 seconds

One burglary every 18.2 seconds

One property crime every 3.8 seconds

One larceny-theft every 5.4 seconds

FIGURE 2-3 | The FBI Crime Clock, Which Shows the Frequency of the Commission of Major Crimes in 2014

Source: Adapted from Federal Bureau of Investigation, *Crime in the United States, 2014* (Washington, DC: U.S. Department of Justice, 2015).

crimes that have been "solved." Clearances are judged primarily on the basis of arrests and do not involve judicial disposition. Once an arrest has been made, a crime is regarded as having been "cleared" for reporting purposes. Exceptional clearances (sometimes called *clearances by exceptional means*) can result when law enforcement authorities believe they know who committed a crime but cannot make an arrest. The perpetrator may, for example, have fled the country or died. Table 2-2 summarizes UCR/NIBRS Program statistics for 2014.

Part I Offenses

Murder

Murder is the unlawful killing of one human being by another.[25] UCR/NIBRS statistics on murder describe the yearly incidence of all willful and unlawful homicides within the United States. Included in the count are all cases of nonnegligent manslaughter that have been reported to or discovered by the police. Not included in the count are suicides, justifiable homicides (that

TABLE 2-2 | Major Crimes Known to the Police, 2014 (UCR/NIBRS Part I Offenses)

OFFENSE	NUMBER	RATE PER 100,000	CLEARANCE RATE
Personal/Violent Crimes			
Murder	14,249	4.5	64.5%
Rape	116,645	36.6	39.3
Robbery	325,802	102.2	29.6
Aggravated assault	741,291	232.5	56.3
Property Crimes			
Burglary	1,729,806	542.5	13.6
Larceny-theft	5,858,496	1,837.3	23.0
Motor vehicle theft	689,527	216.2	12.8
Arson[a]	42,934	14.2	21.7
U.S. Total	**9,518,750**	**2,986.0**	

[a]Arson can be classified as either a property crime or a violent crime, depending on whether personal injury or loss of life results from its commission. It is generally classified as a property crime, however. Arson statistics are incomplete for 2014.

Source: Adapted from Federal Bureau of Investigation, *Crime in the United States, 2014* (Washington, DC: U.S. Dept. of Justice, 2015).

■ **lecture note**   Review the eight major UCR Part I offenses crimes and their definitions.

■ **lecture note**   Research your state's crime-reporting program, and develop a PowerPoint presentation or other teaching materials showing the incidence of reported Part I offenses in your state during the past year.

■ **lecture note**   Remind the class that official definitions (including UCR/NIBRS terminology) for each of the Part I offenses are provided in the glossary.

■ **murder**   The unlawful killing of a human being. *Murder* is a generic term that in common usage may include first- and second-degree murder, manslaughter, involuntary manslaughter, and other similar offenses.

■ **lecture note**   Discuss the differences between first- and second-degree murder. Explain that although all murders are felonies, the category of felony murder, in some jurisdictions, refers to the (often unintentional) death of a person during the commission of another crime, such as the bank patron who dies of a heart attack during a bank robbery.

■ **Part I offenses**   A UCR/NIBRS offense group used to report murder, rape, robbery, aggravated assault, burglary, larceny-theft, motor vehicle theft, and arson, as defined under the FBI's UCR/NIBRS Program.

freedom OR safety? YOU decide

A Dress Code for Bank Customers?

© David Kilpatrick/Alamy

Many banks and some retail establishments require customers to remove hats, hoodies, and sunglasses before entering their place of business. Do you see such requests as limitations on personal rights and freedoms, or as reasonable and necessary precautions?

Hoodies, or hooded sweatshirts, made the national news in 2012 following the fatal shooting of Trayvon Martin in Florida. Martin, a black 17-year-old, was wearing a hoodie when he was apparently confronted by George Zimmerman, a Hispanic community-watch volunteer working in a gated community. Following the shooting, hooded sweatshirts became a symbol of racial profiling, and inspired protests, including one by U.S. Representative Bobby Rush (D-Ill.), who wore sunglasses and a hoodie on the House floor.

Even before the Martin shooting, however, dark glasses, hooded sweatshirts, and hats had been banned by some banks—which called them the "uniform of choice" for bank robbers. In an effort to thwart an increase in robberies, many banks post requests for customers to remove hats, hoods, and sunglasses before entering financial establishments. In 2009, for example, Houston-area banks began putting up signs requiring that customers remove even their cowboy hats—a request that some saw as going too far. Since Sterling Bank, with 60 branches across Texas, asked customers to follow such rules, none of its branches has been robbed. Graham Painter, a Sterling Bank spokesman, said, "We don't want our regular customers thinking that we're telling them how they ought to dress. But it seems reasonable and not too much to ask to give us an advantage over the robber."

Not all banks, however, are following the trend. "I think what you have to weigh is convenience to customers versus the added benefits in terms of identifying suspects with a measure like this," said Melodie Jackson, spokeswoman for Citizens Bank of Massachusetts. "We're taking a very close look at things."

Nonetheless, dress code signs are now commonplace at banks throughout the country, and it is likely that this request will soon become the de facto standard at all financial venues.

You Decide

Are bank "dress codes" asking too much of customers? How would you feel about doing business with a bank that posts requests like those described here? Would you discriminate against certain members of the public if they dressed in ways that you considered suspicious? If so, what type of clothing would arouse your suspicions?

References: Cindy Horswell, "Some Banks Strike Hats, Sunglasses from Dress Code," *Houston Chronicle*, April 23, 2009; Michael S. Rosenwald and Emily Ramshaw, "Banks Post Dress Code to Deter Robbers," *Boston Globe*, July 13, 2002; and "Missouri Banks Attempt Unmasking Robbers," *Police Magazine* online, October 25, 2002, http://www.policemag.com/t_newspick.cfm?rank571952 (accessed August 8, 2014).

is, those committed in self-defense), deaths caused by negligence or accident, and murder attempts. In 2014, some 14,249 murders came to the attention of police departments across the United States. First-degree murder is a criminal homicide that is planned. Second-degree murder is an intentional and unlawful killing but one that is generally unplanned and that happens "in the heat of the moment."

Murder is the smallest numerical category in the **Part I offenses**. The 2014 murder rate was 4.5 homicides for every 100,000 residents of the United States. Generally, murder

■ **activity**   Ask students to research FBI crime statistics for their home states (and/or counties and cities) for the past few years. Have students compare crime rates for each geographic area and discuss possible reasons for the variations in rates.

■ **lecture note**   Explain the differences between spree killings, mass murder, and serial murder.

■ **lecture note**   Explain why murder consistently has the highest clearance rate of any index crime.

rates peak in the warmest months; in 2014, the greatest number of murders occurred in August. Geographically, murder is most common in the southern states. However, because those states are also the most populous, a meaningful comparison across regions of the country is difficult.

Age is no barrier to murder. Statistics for 2014 reveal that 177 infants (children under the age of one) were victims of homicide, as were 271 people age 75 and over.[26] Young adults between 20 and 24 were the most likely to be murdered. Murder perpetrators were also most common in this age group.

Firearms are the weapon used most often to commit murder. In 2014, guns were used in 67.9% of all killings. Handguns outnumbered shotguns almost 15 to 1 in the murder statistics, with rifles used almost as often as shotguns. Knives were used in approximately 13.1% of all murders. Other weapons included explosives, poison, narcotics overdose, blunt objects like clubs, hands, feet, and fists.

Only 10.5% of all murders in 2014 were perpetrated by offenders classified as "strangers." In 45.5% of all killings, the relationship between the parties had not yet been determined. The largest category of killers was officially listed as "acquaintances," which probably includes a large number of former friends. Arguments cause most murders, but murders also occur during the commission of other crimes, such as robbery, rape, and burglary. Homicides that follow from other crimes are more likely to be impulsive rather than planned.

> Because murder is such a serious crime, it consumes substantial police resources. Consequently, over the years, the offense has shown the highest clearance rate of any index crime.

Murders may occur in sprees, which "involve killings at two or more locations with almost no time break between murders."[27] One spree killer, John Allen Muhammad, 41, part of the "sniper team" that terrorized the Washington, D.C., area in 2002, was arrested along with 17-year-old Jamaican immigrant Lee Boyd Malvo in the random shootings of 13 people in Maryland, Virginia, and Washington over a three-week period. Ten of the victims died.[28] In 2003, Muhammad and Malvo were convicted of capital murder; Muhammad was sentenced to die. Malvo was given a sentence of life without the possibility of parole in 2006 after he struck a deal with prosecutors in an effort to avoid the death penalty.[29]

In contrast to spree killing, mass murder entails "the killing of four or more victims at one location, within one event."[30] Recent mass murderers have included Newtown, Connecticut, shooter Adam Lanza (who killed 20 first graders and six adults

at Sandy Hook Elementary School); Aurora, Colorado, movie theater shooter James Eagan Holmes (who killed 12 people and injured 58 others); Seung-Hui Cho (who killed 33 people and wounded 20 on the campus of Virginia Polytechnic Institute and State University in Blacksburg, Virginia, in 2007); Timothy McVeigh (the antigovernment Oklahoma City bomber); and Mohammed Atta and the terrorists whom he led in the September 11, 2001, attacks against American targets.

Yet another kind of murder, serial murder, happens over time and officially "involves the killing of several victims in three or more separate events."[31] In cases of serial murder, days, months, or even years may elapse between killings.[32] Some of the more infamous serial killers of recent years are confessed 43-year-old Gary, Indiana, sex-killer, Darren Vann (unconvicted as of this writing), Wichita BTK[33] murderer Dennis Rader; Jeffrey Dahmer, who received 936 years in prison for the murders of 15 young men (and who was himself later murdered in prison); Ted Bundy, who killed many college-aged women; Henry Lee Lucas, now in a Texas prison, who confessed to 600 murders but later recanted (yet was convicted of 11 murders and linked to at least 140 others);[34] Ottis Toole, Lucas's partner in crime; cult leader Charles Manson, still serving time for ordering followers to kill seven Californians, including famed actress Sharon Tate; Andrei Chikatilo, the Russian "Hannibal Lecter," who killed 52 people, mostly schoolchildren;[35] David Berkowitz, also known as the "Son of Sam," who killed six people on lovers' lanes around New York City; Theodore Kaczynski, the Unabomber, who perpetrated a series of bomb attacks on "establishment" figures; Seattle's Green River Strangler, Gary Leon Ridgway, a 54-year-old painter who in 2003 confessed to killing 48 women in the 1980s; and the infamous "railroad killer" Angel Maturino Resendiz. Although Resendiz was convicted of only one murder—that of Dr. Claudia Benton, which occurred in 1998—he is suspected of many more.[36]

Federal homicide laws changed in 2004, when President George Bush signed the Unborn Victims of Violence Act.[37] The act, which passed the Senate by only one vote, made it a separate federal crime to "kill or attempt to kill" a fetus "at any stage of development" during an assault on a pregnant woman. The fetal homicide statute, better known as Laci and Conner's Law, after homicide victims Laci Peterson and her unborn son (whom she had planned to name Conner), specifically prohibits the prosecution of "any person for conduct relating to an abortion for which the consent of the pregnant woman, or a person authorized by law to act on her behalf, has been obtained."

Because murder is such a serious crime, it consumes substantial police resources. Consequently, over the years, the offense has

■ **lecture note**   Discuss why the UCR revised its definition of rape in 2012 and explain the differences between the previous definition and the new definition.

■ **lecture note**   Use Table 2-2 to illustrate the rate of rape in the United States. Explain that age is no barrier to the crime of rape. Explain that very young girls and the oldest of women have reported being raped.

■ **rape**   Unlawful sexual intercourse achieved through force and without consent. More specifically, penetration, no matter how slight, of the vagina or anus with any body part or object, or oral penetration by a sex organ of another person, without the consent of the victim. *Statutory rape* differs from other types of rape in that it generally involves nonforcible sexual intercourse with a minor. Broadly speaking, the term rape has been applied to a wide variety of sexual attacks and may include same-sex rape and the rape of a male by a female. Some jurisdictions refer to same-sex rape as sexual battery.

■ **lecture note**   Explain that criminologists believe that many rapes go unreported and discuss some of the reasons why victims do not report this crime.

■ **theme**   Why do you think that certain crimes, such as rape, assault, and robbery, seem to show seasonal variations?

■ **theme**   Is rape a crime of power or one of sexual gratification?

■ **sexual battery**   Intentional and wrongful physical contact with a person, without his or her consent, that entails a sexual component or purpose.

■ **date rape**   Unlawful forced sexual intercourse with a person, without his or her consent, that occurs within the context of a dating relationship. Date rape, or acquaintance rape, is a subcategory of rape that is of special concern today.

Self-confessed serial killer Gary L. Ridgway. Known as the Green River Strangler, Ridgway is said to be the nation's worst captured serial killer. In 2003, Ridgway admitted to killing 48 women over a 20-year period in the Pacific Northwest. He is now serving life in prison without possibility of parole. What's the difference between serial killers and mass murderers?

Elaine Thompson/AP Wide World Photos

shown the highest clearance rate of any index crime. More than 64.5% of all homicides were cleared in 2014. Figure 2-4 shows expanded homicide data from the FBI.

Rape

The terms **rape** and *forcible rape* are often applied to a wide variety of sexual attacks, including same-sex rape and the rape of a male by a female. Under the FBI's UCR program, the term forcible rape historically meant "the carnal knowledge of a person forcibly and against their will."[38] Today, rape is defined by the UCR program as "penetration, no matter how slight, of the vagina or anus with any body part or object, or oral penetration by a sex organ of another person, without the consent of the victim."[39] The FBI began using that terminology in 2012, after it abandoned an earlier definition of the phrase that allowed only for the rape of a female. Previously, violent sexual crimes committed against men were termed **sexual battery**, sexual assault, or something similar under the FBI's reporting program. It is worth noting that, in a number of jurisdictions, rape is called *sexual assault* or *aggravated sexual assault* (especially when the victim is under a certain age or if the victim suffers serious physical injuries). Statutory rape, where no force is involved but the victim is younger than the age of consent, is not included in rape statistics, but attempts to commit rape by force or the threat of force are.

Rape is the least reported of all violent crimes. Estimates are that only one out of every four rapes is reported to the police. An even lower figure was reported by a 1992 government-sponsored study, which found that only 16% of rapes were reported.[40] The victim's fear of embarrassment was the most commonly cited reason for nonreports. In the past, many states routinely permitted a person's past sexual history to be revealed in detail in the courtroom if a trial ensued. But the past few decades have seen many changes designed to facilitate accurate reporting of rape and other sex offenses. Trained female detectives often interview female victims, physicians have become better educated in handling the psychological needs of victims, and sexual histories are no longer regarded as relevant in most trials.

The UCR/NIBRS statistics show 116,645 reported rapes for 2014, an increase over the number of offenses reported for the previous year. Comparisons of such numbers over time, however, can be tricky due to changes in UCR terminology. The offense of rape follows homicide in its seasonal variation. The greatest numbers of rapes in 2014 were reported in the hot summer months, and the lowest numbers were recorded in January, February, November, and December.

Rape is frequently committed by a person known to the victim, as in the case of **date rape**. Victims may be held captive and subjected to repeated assaults.[41] In the crime of heterosexual

■ **lecture note**   Discuss date rape. Ask whether the phenomenon is of recent origin or has existed for generations. Why has it received so much media attention recently?

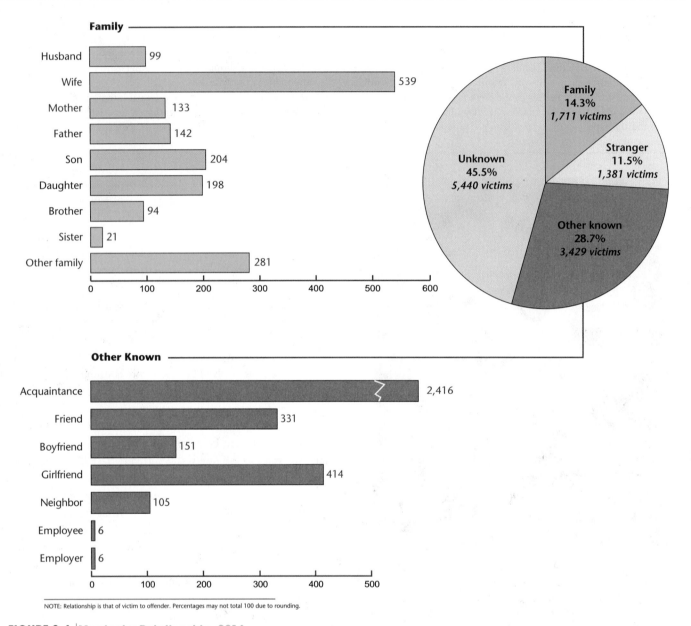

FIGURE 2-4 | Murder by Relationship, 2014

Source: Pearson Education, Inc.

rape, any female—regardless of age, appearance, or occupation—is a potential victim. Through personal violation, humiliation, and physical battering, rapists seek a sense of personal aggrandizement and dominance. Victims of rape often experience a lessened sense of personal worth; feelings of despair, helplessness, and vulnerability; a misplaced sense of guilt; and a lack of control over their personal lives.

Contemporary wisdom holds that rape is often a planned violent crime that serves the offender's need for power rather than sexual gratification.[42] The "power thesis" has its origins in the writings of Susan Brownmiller, who argued in 1975 that the primary motivation leading to heterosexual rape is the rapist's desire to "keep women in their place" and to preserve gender inequality through violence.[43] Although many writers on the subject of heterosexual rape have generally accepted the power thesis, at least one study has caused some to rethink it. In a survey of imprisoned serial rapists, for example, Dennis Stevens found that "lust" was reported most often (41%) as "the primary motive for predatory rape."[44]

■ **lecture note**   Point out that most people tend to confuse the terms *robbery* and *burglary*, using them interchangeably. Explain the differences between the two terms, and show why they are not the same.
■ **theme**   Why is the hierarchy rule a concern for the UCR? Why has it been eliminated in NIBRS?

■ **robbery (UCR/NIBRS)**   The unlawful taking or attempted taking of property that is in the immediate possession of another by force or violence and/or by putting the victim in fear. Armed robbery differs from unarmed, or strong-arm, robbery in that it involves a weapon. Contrary to popular conceptions, highway robbery does not necessarily occur on a street—and rarely in a vehicle. The term *highway robbery* applies to any form of robbery that occurs outdoors in a public place.

Peter Dokus/Getty Images, Inc.

A crime in progress? Date rape is unlawful sexual intercourse that occurs within the context of a dating relationship. "Date rape drugs" like Rohypnol are sometimes secretly placed in drinks, rendering victims unable to resist. How can people guard against being victimized?

Statistically speaking, most rapes are committed by acquaintances of the victims and often betray a trust or friendship. Date rape, which falls into this category, appears to be far more common than previously believed. Recently, the growing number of rapes perpetrated with the use of the "date rape drug" Rohypnol have alarmed law enforcement personnel. Rohypnol, which is discussed in Chapter 16, "Drugs and Crime," is an illegal pharmaceutical substance that is virtually tasteless. Available on the black market, it dissolves easily in drinks and can leave anyone who consumes it unconscious for hours, making them vulnerable to sexual assault.

Rape within marriage, which has not always been recognized as a crime, is a growing area of concern in American criminal justice, and many laws have been enacted during the past few decades to deter it. Similarly, even though some state laws on rape continue to encompass only the rape or attempted rape of a female by a male, they also criminalize the sexual abuse of a male by a female. When it occurs, this offense is typically charged as statutory rape, or falls under some other state statute.

Robbery

Robbery is a personal crime involving a face-to-face confrontation between a victim and a perpetrator. It is often confused with burglary, which is primarily a property crime. (We'll examine burglary later.) Weapons may be used in robbery, or strong-arm robbery may occur through intimidation. Purse snatching and pocket picking are not classified as robbery by the UCR/NIBRS Program but are included under the category of larceny-theft.

In 2014, as Figure 2-5 shows, individuals were the most common target of robbers (shown under the category of "street/highway" robbery). Banks, gas stations, convenience stores, and other businesses were the second most common target, with residential robberies accounting for only 16.8% of the total. In 2014, 325,802 robberies were reported to the police. Of that number, 41% were highway robberies, meaning that the crime occurred outdoors, most commonly as the victim was walking in a public place. Strong-arm robberies, in which the victim was intimidated but no weapon was used, accounted for 43% of the total robberies reported. Guns were used in 40.3% of all robberies, and knives were used in 7.9%. Armed robbers are dangerous; guns are actually discharged in 20% of all robberies.[45]

When a robbery occurs, the UCR Program would score the event as one robbery, even when numerous victims were robbed during the event. With the move toward incident-driven reporting, however, the revised UCR/NIBRS Program now

■ **lecture note**   Define *highway robbery* as any robbery that occurs outdoors in a public place. Explain that highway robbery does not necessarily occur on the road or in a vehicle.

■ **lecture note**   Explain the difference between simple and aggravated assault. Explain that some states use the term "assault" to refer to an attempt and "battery" to refer to a completed assault.

■ **assault (UCR/NIBRS)**   An unlawful attack by one person upon another. Historically, *assault* meant only the attempt to inflict injury on another person; a completed act constituted the separate offense of battery. Under modern statistical usage, however, attempted and completed acts are grouped together under the generic term *assault*.

■ **aggravated assault**   The unlawful, intentional inflicting, or attempted or threatened inflicting, of serious injury upon the person of another. Although *aggravated assault* and *simple assault* are standard terms for reporting purposes, most state penal codes use labels like *first-degree* and *second-degree* to make such distinctions.

■ **burglary (UCR/NIBRS)**   The unlawful entry of a structure to commit a felony or a theft (excludes tents, trailers, and other mobile units used for recreational purposes). Under the UCR/NIBRS Program, the crime of burglary can be reported if (1) an unlawful entry of an unlocked structure has occurred, (2) a breaking and entering (of a secured structure) has taken place, or (3) a burglary has been attempted.

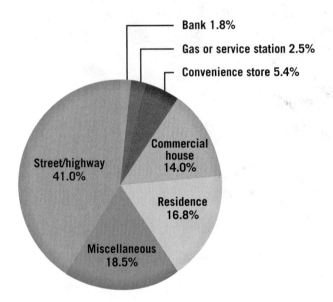

FIGURE 2-5 | Robbery Locations, 2014
Source: Pearson Education, Inc.

makes data available on the number of individuals robbed in each incident. UCR statistics on crime follow what's known as the *hierarchy rule*, and show only the most serious offense that occurred during a particular episode. Hence robberies are often hidden in UCR data when they occur in conjunction with more serious crimes. For example, 3% of robbery victims are also raped, and a large number of homicide victims are robbed.[46]

Robbery is primarily an urban offense, and most arrestees are young male minorities. The robbery rate in large cities in 2014 was 261.3 per every 100,000 inhabitants, whereas it was much lower in rural areas. Of those arrested for robbery in 2014, 86% were male, 59% were under the age of 25, and 58% were minorities.[47]

Aggravated Assault

In April 2006, Arthur J. McClure, 22, of Fort Myers, Florida, was arrested when he allegedly took the head off an Easter Bunny costume that he was wearing and punched Erin Johansson of Cape Coral, Florida, after the young mother apparently became upset that a mall photo set was closing 10 minutes early.[48] The incident was witnessed by dozens of people, including many children who had gathered to have their pictures taken with the rabbit. McClure, who denied he struck Johansson, was fired after the incident.

Assaults are of two types: simple (misdemeanor) and aggravated (felonious). For statistical-reporting purposes, simple assaults typically involve pushing and shoving. Although simple assault may also at times include fistfights, the correct legal term to describe such incidents is *battery*. **Aggravated assaults** are distinguished from simple assaults in that either a weapon is used or the assault victim requires medical assistance. When a deadly weapon is employed, an aggravated assault may be charged as attempted murder even if no injury results.[49] In some cases, the UCR/NIBRS Program scores these attempted assaults as aggravated assault because of the potential for serious consequences.

In 2014, 741,291 cases of aggravated assault were reported to law enforcement agencies in the United States. Assault reports were most frequent in summer months and least frequent in February, November, December, and January. Most aggravated assaults were committed with blunt objects or objects near at hand, and hands, feet, and fists were also commonly used (27%). Less frequently used were knives (18%) and firearms (22%). Because those who commit assaults are often known to their victims, aggravated assaults are relatively easy to solve. About 56% of all aggravated assaults reported to the police in 2014 were cleared by arrest.

Burglary

Although it may involve personal and even violent confrontation, **burglary** is primarily a property crime. Burglars are interested in financial gain and usually fence (that is, illegally sell) stolen items, recovering a fraction of their cash value. About 1.7 million burglaries were reported to the police in 2014. Dollar losses to burglary victims totaled $3.9 billion, with an average loss per offense of $2,251.

The UCR/NIBRS Program employs three classifications of burglary: (1) forcible entry, (2) unlawful entry where no force is used, and (3) attempted forcible entry. In most jurisdictions, force need not be employed for a crime to be classified as burglary. Unlocked doors and open windows are invitations to burglars, and the legal essence of burglary consists not so much of a forcible entry as it does of the intent to trespass and steal. In 2014,

■ **lecture note** Discuss the three categories of burglary: forcible entry, unlawful entry where no force is used, and attempted forcible entry.

■ **theme** Why do you think the clearance rate for burglary tends to be low?

CJ | NEWS
"Flash Robs"—The Next Social Media Phenomenon

The immediate aftermath of a flash robbery showing young people streaming out of a store that they just attacked. How have social media changed the nature of criminal activity in this country?

"Flash mobs," where text messaging or Twitter brings together large groups of people for spontaneous events, have irked police because they lack permits and may be disruptive. Now, however, police are facing a more serious problem: "flash robs," where social media directs people—often teenagers—to go to retail stores and rob them.

Unlike conventional robberies, flash robs have the feel of a mob looting a store. When social media bring people together, the individuals often don't even know each other and very little planning has taken place. Videos on YouTube show scores of jubilant teenagers filing into a convenience store and helping themselves to snacks and sodas, as employees helplessly look on. It all lasts a matter of minutes.

This is "mob behavior but it has some premeditation, which is a new thing," said Read Hayes, a University of Florida research scientist, in an interview with the *Wall Street Journal*.

According to a July 2011 poll by the National Retail Federation, 10% of storeowners reported they were victims of flash robs in the past 12 months, and half of them said they experienced two to five incidents in that period. Social media or texting was involved in at least 42% of cases where suspects were apprehended, and 83% of incidents involved juveniles.

Because flash robs involve as many as 50 people, store employees can do little to stop them and may even suffer injury. Participants have been known to punch an employee on the way out. In addition to the loss of merchandise, retailers are concerned about losing customers. "A frenzied group of teens snatching merchandise and running through store aisles creates panic and potential safety issues for customers and store employees," according to a 2011 white paper by the National Retail Federation.

One flash robbery at a convenience store can involve hundreds of dollars worth of goods, and the toll can be far greater at high-end retailers. About 20 flash robbers stole $20,000 worth of merchandise from a Washington, D.C., clothing store in April 2011.

Swarms of young people assembled through social media may also commit acts of violence or vandalism, without stealing. In Philadelphia, for example, teens knocked down passers-by and assaulted shoppers in an upscale department store. Such incidents prompted Mayor Michael A. Nutter to intensify police patrols and move a curfew for teens to 9 p.m. in 2011.

In many cases, flash robbers are recorded by surveillance cameras, making it easier to arrest and convict them. They may also be identified on social media or be apprehended leaving the scene. Police simply have to look for large groups of young people who have items from the store but no receipts (although the legal issues involved in stopping and searching people can pose problems for law enforcers).

Even though the total value of stolen goods can be high, the value of what each person stole is often quite low, making it difficult to charge the participants with a serious crime. Typically, the charges are third-degree theft and riot. Guns are not used and criminal conspiracy charges don't apply when participants don't even know each other.

After several flash robs occurred in Maryland in 2011, a bill introduced in the state legislature would make each participant in a flash rob responsible for the total value stolen, thus allowing for harsher sentences. In a different tack, the city of Cleveland considered making it a criminal offense to summon any kind of flash mob through social media, but the proposal was withdrawn.

Resources: "Flash Mobs Aren't Just for Fun Anymore," NPR, May 26, 2011, http://www.npr.org/2011/05/26/136578945/flash-mobs-arent-just-for-fun-anymore; "Flash Robs" Vex Retailers, *Wall Street Journal*, October 21, 2011, http://online.wsj.com/article/SB10001424052970203752604576643422390552158.html; and "Multiple Offender Crimes," *National Retail Federation White Paper*, August 2011, http://www.nrf.com/modules.php?name=News&op=viewlive&sp_id=1167.

58.3% of all burglaries were forcible entries, 35.2% were unlawful entries, and 6.5% were attempted forcible entries.[50] The most dangerous burglaries were those in which a household member was home (about 10% of all burglaries).[51] Residents who were home during a burglary suffered a greater than 30% chance of becoming the victim of a violent crime.[52] However, although burglary may evoke images of dark-clothed strangers breaking into houses in which families lie sleeping, burglaries more often are of unoccupied homes and take place during daylight hours.

The clearance rate for burglary, as for other property crimes that we'll look at later, is generally low. In 2014, the clearance rate for burglary was only 13.6%. Burglars usually do not know their victims, and in cases where they conceal their identity by committing their crime when the victim is not present.

■ **lecture note** Explain that larceny-theft is the most common of all offenses and that it is often not reported because the value of the property taken is very small.

■ **larceny-theft (UCR/NIBRS)** The unlawful taking or attempted taking, carrying, leading, or riding away of property, from the possession or constructive possession of another. Motor vehicles are excluded. Larceny is the most common of the eight major offenses, although probably only a small percentage of all larcenies are actually reported to the police because of the small dollar amounts involved.

Larceny-Theft

In 2014, a pair of women in the United Kingdom were caught on a surveillance camera stealing an entire front lawn of newly placed sod.[53] The theft occurred in Skelmersdale, England, and the homeowner posted the recording on YouTube.

Larceny is another name for theft and, as is true in this example, almost anything of value can be stolen. The UCR/NIBRS Program uses the term **larceny-theft** to describe theft offenses (Figure 2-6) of all kinds. Some states distinguish between simple larceny and grand larceny, categorizing the crime based on the dollar value of what is stolen. Larceny-theft, as defined by the UCR/NIBRS Program, includes the theft of valuables of any dollar amount. The reports specifically list the following offenses as types of larceny (listed here in order of declining frequency):

- Thefts from motor vehicles
- Shoplifting
- Thefts from buildings
- Thefts of motor vehicle parts and accessories
- Bicycle thefts
- Thefts from coin-operated machines
- Purse snatching
- Pocket picking

Because larceny has traditionally been considered a crime that requires physical possession of the item appropriated, some computer crimes, including thefts engineered through online access or thefts of software and information, have not been scored as larcenies unless computer equipment, electronic circuitry, or computer media were actually stolen.

Thefts of farm animals (known as *rustling*) and thefts of most types of farm machinery also fall into the larceny category. In fact, larceny is such a broad category that it serves as a kind of catchall in the UCR/NIBRS Program. In 1995, for example, Yale University officials filed larceny charges against 25-year-old-student Lon Grammer, claiming that he had fraudulently obtained university funds.[54] The university maintained that Grammer had stolen his education by forging college and high school transcripts and concocting letters of recommendation prior to admission. Grammer's alleged misdeeds, which Yale University officials said misled them into thinking that Grammer, a poor student before attending Yale, had an exceptional scholastic record, permitted him to receive $61,475 in grants and loans during the time he attended the school. Grammer was expelled.

Reported thefts vary widely, in terms of both the objects stolen and their value. Stolen items range from pocket change to a $100 million aircraft. For reporting purposes, crimes entailing embezzlement, con games, forgery, and worthless checks are specifically excluded from the count of larceny. Because larceny has traditionally been considered a crime that requires physical possession of the item appropriated, some computer crimes, including thefts engineered through online access or thefts of software and information, have not been scored as larcenies unless computer equipment, electronic circuitry, or computer media were actually stolen.

From a statistical stand-point, the most common form of larceny in recent years has been theft of motor vehicle parts, accessories, and contents. Tires, wheels, GPS devices, radar detectors, satellite radios, CD players, and cellular phones account for many of the items reported stolen.

Reports to the police in 2014 showed 5,858,496 larcenies nationwide, with the total value of property stolen placed at $5.5 billion. Larceny-theft is the most frequently reported major crime, according to the UCR/NIBRS Program. It may also be the program's most underreported crime category

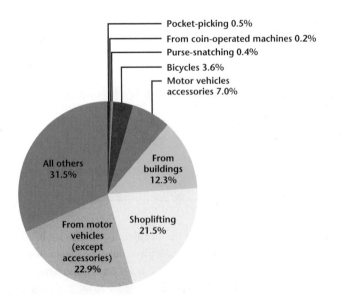

Pocket-picking 0.5%
From coin-operated machines 0.2%
Purse-snatching 0.4%
Bicycles 3.6%
Motor vehicles accessories 7.0%

All others 31.5%
From buildings 12.3%
From motor vehicles (except accessories) 22.9%
Shoplifting 21.5%

FIGURE 2-6 | Larceny-Theft Distribution, 2014

Note: Due to rounding, the percentages may not total 100.

Source: Pearson Education, Inc.

CJ | ISSUES
Race and the Criminal Justice System

Protestors in Ferguson, Missouri, following the shooting of 18-year-old Michael Brown in 2014. Brown was black and unarmed; the officer who shot him was white, leading to claims of racial injustice—especially after a grand jury called to investigate the incident declined to indict the officer. Is the American criminal justice system equitable? Explain your answer.

In 2015, Gallup Poll researchers reported that black Americans saw race relations and unemployment as the most important problems facing the United States. More significant, however, was the disparity between perceptions of blacks and whites about the state of race relations in this country. Only 4% of whites identified race relations as the number one issue, and the percentage-point gap between blacks' and whites' perception of race relations as the top U.S. problem is significantly wider than narrower gaps of no more than four points in most recent years.

Sensitivity to race relations in the United States escalated quickly among African Americans after a series of police shootings of unarmed young black men by white officers in 2014 and 2015. Many of the killings happened over seemingly minor offenses. When almost none of the officers involved in the shootings were charged with the use of excessive force, protestors took to the streets, riots broke out in a number of cities, police property was destroyed by angry mobs, and intense media coverage of disaffected black leaders

stoked a sense of injustice that had long festered in minority areas. The social upheaval that followed led some to compare it to the Civil Rights era of the 1960s.

In June 2015, members of Harvard University's Executive Session on Policing and Public Safety found that "concern about race seemed to become stalled in discussion rather than advancing to action." They recognized that American criminal justice personnel "confront issues of race daily in almost everything they do." That confrontation can be found in the geographic distribution of criminality and in the fear of crime found especially in the inner city, as well as "in assumptions about what criminals look like." The police, they said, "confront race in the suspicion and hostility of many young African American men they encounter on the street." And, they found, charges of racial profiling and unequal justice are often intertwined with hiring practices of justice agencies, including the promotion and assignment of personnel.

One of the most difficult problems to address is the fact that the highest rates of violent crime are in minority neighborhoods. This, said the Harvard writers, "creates the impression that race or ethnicity is implicated in criminality and that serious crime in America is particularly a 'black problem.'" Such reasoning, they argued, "gets the causality backward." Race is not a causal factor in criminality; instead, "the circumstances that create compacted disadvantage for minority groups also create criminality." Due to a long history of exclusion from important economic and social opportunities, residents of disadvantaged urban neighborhoods are primarily minorities and often black. Lost in all of this, said the report, is the fact that minorities are more likely than the majority of white people to be victims of crime—and hence most in need of help from the justice system. Those who say that "black-on-black" crime is the major problem that needs to be addressed may be statistically correct, but according to a second paper by Harvard researchers, "To the vast majority of urban black residents who are not involved in violence or criminal behavior, the term invokes visions of indiscriminate and aggressive police enforcement responses applied to a broad range of black people."

While it will not be easy to address today's concerns over race, one solution might see justice system agencies begin to focus more on procedural fairness than on objective statistics like the number of crimes solved. For a continuation of this discussion, see the CJ Issues box in Chapter 8 on "Rightful Policing."

References: Katherine J. Rosich, Race, Ethnicity, and the Criminal Justice System (Washington, DC: American Sociological Association, 2007), p. 4; Jeffrey M. Jones, "Drop Among Nonwhites Drives U.S. Police Honesty Ratings Down," Gallup, January 5, 2015 (http://www.gallup.com/poll/180230/drop-among-nonwhites-drives-police-honesty-ratings-down.aspx (accessed January 7, 2015); Katheryn K. Russell, "The Racial Hoax as Crime: The Law as Affirmation," Indiana Law Journal, Vol. 71 (1996), pp. 593–621; William Wilbanks, The Myth of a Racist Criminal Justice System (Monterey, CA: Brooks/Cole, 1987); Quoted in "For the Record," Washington Post wire service, March 3, 1994.

Larceny-theft is the most frequently reported major crime, according to the UCR/NIBRS Program. It may also be the program's most underreported crime category because small thefts rarely come to the attention of the police.

because small thefts rarely come to the attention of the police. The average value of items reported stolen in 2014 was about $941. Because larceny is the most frequently reported of the UCR's

major crimes, it is important to note that the FBI's official position is that "Computer Crime actually involves the historical common-law offenses of larceny, embezzlement, trespass, etc., which are being perpetrated through the use of a new tool, the computer." Therefore, according to the FBI, "if larcenies, embezzlements, and trespasses relating to computers were to be reported under a new classification called Computer Crime, the national UCR Program's traditional time series relating to such crimes would be distorted." To avoid such a result,

■ **identity theft**   A crime in which an impostor obtains key pieces of information, such as Social Security and driver's license numbers, to obtain credit, merchandise, and services in the name of the victim. The victim is often left with a ruined credit history and the time-consuming and complicated task of repairing the financial damage.[i]

High speed commuter trains. The FBI defines motor vehicles as self-propelled vehicles that run on the ground and not on rails. How might the theft of a train be classified under the UCR?

© Aygul Bulté/Fotolia

NIBRS provides the capability to indicate whether a computer was the object of the crime, and/or to indicate whether the offenders used computer equipment to perpetrate a crime. The FBI says that "this ensures the continuance of the traditional crime statistics and at the same time flags incidents that involve Computer Crime." Unfortunately, however, this strategy does not account for all forms of cybercrime, leaving UCR/NIBRS crime statistics vulnerable to the kinds of undercounting referred to elsewhere in this chapter.[55]

Identity Theft: A New Kind of Larceny   In September 2014, JPMorgan Chase, one of the largest financial institutions in the world, announced that cyberattackers operating from overseas had stolen account information on 76 million American households and seven million businesses that the company had stored in its computers.[56] Bank executives had to scramble to assure customers that no money had been stolen from their accounts, and that financial information remained secure. While Chase executives admitted that names, mailing addresses, phone numbers and email addresses of customers had been obtained by the hackers, they denied that passwords and Social Security numbers had been stolen. The revelations at Chase followed an announcement by the large retail chain Target, that credit card and other information of 110 million customers had been taken in a cyber-theft at its headquarters; and an admission by Home Depot that the credit card numbers of 56 million shoppers had been stolen.[57]

Identity theft, which involves obtaining credit, merchandise, or services by fraudulent personal representation, is a special kind of larceny. According to a recent federal survey, 17.6 million Americans were victims of identity theft in 2014, although most did not report the crime.[58] Information from the Bureau of Justice Statistics (BJS) shows that 7.0% of United States residents 16 or older had been a victim of one or more types of identity theft in 2014.[59] The BJS also says that identity theft is the fastest-growing type of crime in America.[60]

Identity theft became a federal crime in 1998 with the passage of the Identity Theft and Assumption Deterrence Act.[61] The law makes it a crime whenever anyone "knowingly transfers or uses, without lawful authority, a means of identification of another person with the intent to commit, or to aid or abet, any unlawful activity that constitutes a violation of federal law, or that constitutes a felony under any applicable state or local law."

■ **lecture note** Explain that motor vehicles are defined for UCR/NIBRS purposes as self-propelled vehicles that run on land and not on rails, and point out that the theft of other types of vehicles are classified as larceny-theft.
■ **theme** Why are people more likely to report motor vehicle theft than many other types of crimes?
■ **lecture note** Explain that carjacking is considered to be a robbery rather than a motor vehicle theft by the UCR/NIBRS program.

■ **motor vehicle theft (UCR/NIBRS)** The theft or attempted theft of a motor vehicle. A *motor vehicle* is defined as a self-propelled road vehicle that runs on land surface and not on rails. The stealing of trains, planes, boats, construction equipment, and most farm machinery is classified as larceny under the UCR/NIBRS Program, not as motor vehicle theft.

JPMorgan Chase headquarters in New York City. In 2014, the company revealed that cyber thieves had stolen the personal information of 70 million households and seven million businesses that had been stored on its computers. Why is identity theft so prevalent today? How can it be stopped?

Aaron Showalter/Sipa/Newscom

card numbers and expiration dates, along with their name and address.[63] Identity theft perpetrated through the use of high technology depends on the fact that a person's legal and economic identity in contemporary society is largely "virtual" and supported by technology. Read the National Strategy to Combat Identity Theft at **http://www.justicestudies .com/pubs/natlstrategy.pdf.**

Motor Vehicle Theft

For record-keeping purposes, the UCR/NIBRS Program defines *motor vehicles* as self-propelled vehicles that run on the ground and not on rails. Included in the definition are automobiles, motorcycles, motor scooters, trucks, buses, and snowmobiles. Excluded are trains, airplanes, bulldozers, most farm and construction machinery, ships, boats, and spacecraft; the theft of these would be scored as larceny-theft.[64] Vehicles that are temporarily taken by individuals who have lawful access to them are not thefts. Hence spouses who jointly own all property may drive the family car, even though one spouse may think of the vehicle as his or her exclusive personal property.

As we said earlier, because most insurance companies require police reports before they will reimburse car owners for their losses, most occurrences of **motor vehicle theft** are reported to law enforcement agencies. Some reports of motor vehicle thefts, however, may be false. People who have damaged their own vehicles in single-vehicle crashes or who have been unable to sell them may try to force insurance companies to "buy" them through reports of theft.

In 2014, 689,527 motor vehicles were reported stolen. The average value per stolen vehicle was $6,537 making motor vehicle theft a $4.1 billion crime. The clearance rate for motor vehicle theft was only 12.8% in 2014. Large city agencies reported the lowest rates of clearance, and rural counties had the highest rate. Many stolen vehicles are quickly disassembled and the parts resold, as auto parts are much more difficult to identify and trace than are intact vehicles. In some parts of the country, chop shops—which take stolen vehicles apart and sell their components—operate like big businesses, and one shop may strip a dozen or more cars per day.

Motor vehicle theft can turn violent, as in cases of carjacking—a crime in which offenders usually force the car's occupants onto the street before stealing the vehicle. The BJS estimates that around 34,000 carjackings occur annually and account for slightly more than 1% of all motor vehicle thefts.[65] Arrest reports for motor vehicle theft show that the typical offender is a

The 2004 Identity Theft Penalty Enhancement Act[62] added two years to federal prison sentences for criminals convicted of using stolen credit card numbers and other personal data to commit crimes. It also prescribed prison sentences for those who use identity theft to commit other crimes, including terrorism, and it increased penalties for defendants who exceed or abuse the authority of their positions in unlawfully obtaining or misusing means of personal identification.

According to the National White Collar Crime Center, identity thieves use several common techniques. Some engage in "dumpster diving," going through trash bags, cans, or dumpsters to get copies of checks, credit card and bank statements, credit card applications, or other records that typically bear identifying information. Others use a technique called "shoulder surfing," which involves looking over the victim's shoulder as he or she enters personal information into a computer or on a written form. Eavesdropping is another simple, yet effective, technique that identity thieves often use. Eavesdropping can occur when the victim is using an ATM machine, giving credit card or other personal information over the phone, or dialing the number for a telephone calling card. Criminals can also obtain personal identifying information from potential victims through the Internet. Some Internet users, for example, reply to "spam" (unsolicited e-mail) that promises them all sorts of attractive benefits while requesting identifying data, such as checking account or credit

■ **arson (UCR/NIBRS)**   Any willful or malicious burning or attempt to burn, with or without intent to defraud, a dwelling house, public building, motor vehicle or aircraft, personal property of another, and so on. Some instances of arson result from malicious mischief, some involve attempts to claim insurance money, and some are committed in an effort to disguise other crimes, such as murder, burglary, or larceny.

■ **Part II offenses**   A UCR/NIBRS offense group used to report arrests for less serious offenses. Agencies are limited to reporting only arrest information for Part II offenses, with the exception of simple assault.

young male. Nearly 42% of all arrestees in 2014 were under the age of 25, and 81% were male.

Arson

The UCR/NIBRS Program received crime reports from more than 15,000 law enforcement agencies reported 42,934 arsons in 2014.[66] Of these, only 14,646 submitted expanded **arson** data. Even fewer agencies provided complete data as to the type of arson (the nature of the property burned), the estimated monetary value of the property, the ownership, and so on. Arson data include only the fires that are determined through investigation to have been willfully or maliciously set. Fires of unknown or suspicious origin are excluded from arson statistics.[67]

The intentional and unlawful burning of structures (houses, storage buildings, manufacturing facilities, and so on) was the type of arson reported most often in 2014 (17,854 instances). The arson of vehicles was the second most common category, with 9,154 such burnings reported. The average dollar loss per instance of arson in 2014 was $16,055, and total nationwide property damage was placed at close to $1 billion.[68] As with most property crimes, the clearance rate for arson was low—only 21.8% nationally. The crime of arson exists in a kind of statistical limbo. In 1979, Congress ordered that it be added as an eighth Part I offense. Today, however, many law enforcement agencies still have not begun making regular reports to the FBI on arson offenses in their jurisdictions.

Some of these difficulties have been resolved through the Special Arson Program, authorized by Congress in 1982. In conjunction with the National Fire Data Center, the FBI now operates a Special Arson Reporting System, which focuses on fire departments across the nation. The reporting system is designed to provide data to supplement yearly UCR arson tabulations.[69]

Part II Offenses

The UCR Program also includes information on what the FBI calls **Part II offenses**. Part II offenses, which are generally less serious than those that make up the Part I offense category, include a number of social-order, or so-called victimless, crimes. The statistics on Part II offenses are for *recorded arrests*, not for crimes reported to the police. The logic inherent in this form of scoring is that most Part II offenses would never come to the attention of the police were it not for arrests. Part II offenses are shown in Table 2-3, with the number of estimated arrests made in each category for 2014. You can access the BJS data analysis tool at **http://www.bjs.gov/index .cfm?ty=datool&surl=/arrests/index.cfm** to view customized national and local arrest data by age, sex, and race for many different offenses.

A Part II arrest is counted each time a person is taken into custody. As a result, the statistics in Table 2-3 do not report the number of suspects arrested but rather the number of arrests made. Some suspects were arrested more than once.

TABLE 2-3 | **UCR/NIBRS Part II Offenses, 2014**

OFFENSE CATEGORY	NUMBER OF ARRESTS
Simple assault	1,093,258
Forgery and counterfeiting	56,783
Fraud	141,293
Embezzlement	16,227
Stolen property (e.g., receiving)	88,946
Vandalism	198,400
Weapons (e.g., carrying)	140,713
Prostitution and related offenses	47,598
Sex offenses (e.g., statutory rape)	55,456
Drug-law violations	1,561,231
Gambling	5,637
Offenses against the family (e.g., nonsupport)	102,336
Driving under the influence	1,117,852
Liquor-law violations	321,125
Public drunkenness	414,854
Disorderly conduct	436,014
Vagrancy	27,380
Curfew violation/loitering	53,654
Source: Pearson Education, Inc.	

freedom OR safety? YOU decide

Can Citizens Have Too Much Privacy?

In 2015, FBI director James B. Comey spoke at Fordham University about the "cyber threat" challenging the American justice system. Comey's main concern was about new encryption technologies that put many types of information (including text messages, e-mail, and other forms of Internet-based communication) beyond the reach of investigators—even when enforcement officials are armed with a warrant. What follows is excerpted from his talk.

Let me start by telling you what you know, which is that everything has changed in ways that are so fundamental that it's difficult to describe what it means when we say the world is changing because of cyber. ....

I always look for ways to describe just how fundamental the transformation we're standing in the middle of is.

....Cisco provided some stats that I saw recently that I just wanted to mention as I start. In 2003 there were 6.3 billion human beings on the earth and 500 million devices connected to the Internet. In 2010 there were 6.8 billion people on the earth and 12.5 billion devices connected to the Internet. One-point-eight-four per person.

Cisco projects that in 2020, now just four years away, there will be seven billion people on the earth and 50 billion devices connected to the Internet. Six-and-a-half devices on average per person....

There is no doubt that everything has changed because we've connected our entire lives to the Internet. That is why, because all of life is there, that all of the parts of life that the FBI is responsible for trying to protect—whether it is criminal, counterintelligence, counterterrorism, protecting children, fighting fraud—it all happens there because that's where life is.

.... I actually try to describe to people in very simple ways what we're talking about today because I don't see cyber as a thing, I see it as a way. As a vector. Because my children play on the Internet. Because that's where I bank. Because that's where my health care is. Because that's—I don't have a social life, but if I had one, that's where I'm sure it would be. That's where our nation's critical infrastructure is, that's where our government's secrets are and that's—because life is there, that's where bad people come who want to hurt children, who want to steal money, who want to take identities, who want to steal secrets, who want to damage dams and critical infrastructure in the United States. It's the way they come at us because that's where life is.

...Dillinger or Bonnie and Clyde could not do a thousand robberies in all 50 states in the same day from their pajamas from Belarus. That's the challenge we face today. The traditional notions of space and time and venue and border and my jurisdiction and your jurisdiction are blown away by a threat that moves not at 40 miles an hour or 50 downhill, but at 186,000 miles per second. The speed of light.

Traditional notions, frameworks, are destroyed by that kind of threat. That requires every part of the FBI, those who are spending their days protecting kids, fighting fraud, fighting spies, fighting terrorism, protecting intellectual property, all of those things; it requires those people to be digitally literate. It requires me to have the right kind of people, the right kind of equipment and deploy them in a way that deals with a vector change that is mind boggling compared to the Dillinger era.

...We need to equip our state and local partners to be able to be digitally literate and to conduct their investigations in responding to the same threats coming through the vector that is cyber. And so one of the things we're trying to do is work with the Secret Service to offer training to the 17,000 state and local law enforcement organizations in this country to equip their people to be digitally literate. A ton of work going on there. Lots more needs to be done.

Before I leave you though I want to mention something ... the problem of what we call Going Dark.

This is very, very important to us in law enforcement.... We are drifting to a place in this country without serious public discussion that I don't think a democracy should drift to without discussion.

....We're making it increasingly difficult for us with lawful authority, especially in our criminal work, to be able to intercept the communications of drug dealers, organized criminals, of bad people of all sorts with court approval.

But there's another dimension to it that made it blink even more brightly—directly in front of me... Increasingly what we're finding ourselves up against is data ... that is sitting in a place or in a device that, even with a search warrant, we can't get access to. And this is everywhere in law enforcement.

This ... is about us drifting to a place where there will be zones beyond the reach of the law in the United States. The Fourth Amendment is one of the most important parts of this entire democracy because the government may not search and seize the people's papers and effects without a warrant. But now we're drifting to a place that, even with a warrant, there will be papers and effects, even with court authority, that are beyond the reach of the law. Maybe we want to go there. Maybe that's where we want to end up as a democracy. Maybe people decide that privacy is that important. But I don't think we're talking about it enough. I don't think we're thinking about, "So what are the trade-offs involved there?"

My job, I don't believe, is to tell people what to do. I mean, in a democracy, the people should decide what to do. My job, I think, is simply to say there are significant public safety implications here and let's talk about it before we get to the place ... Where people look at us with tears in their eyes and say, "What do you mean you can't? What do you mean you can't? This little girl has disappeared. What do you mean you can't tell me who she was texting with before she disappeared? You've got the phone. You've got a court order." Before we get to "what do you mean you can't," I think we've got to talk about it as a people.

You decide

What does Director Comey mean when he asks, "So, what are the trade-offs involved there?" Can you identify any of those "trade-offs"? How comfortable are you with them?

Reference: James B. Comey, remarks made before the *International Conference on Cyber Security*, Fordham University, New York, January 7, 2015, http://www.fbi.gov/news/speeches/addressing-the-cyber-security-threat?utm_campaign=email-Immediate&utm_medium=email&utm_source=executive-speeches&utm_content=391299 (accessed March 7, 2015).

■ **lecture note** Discuss the origins of the NCVS, and explain that it was developed as a way to obtain a more complete picture of crime than the UCR could provide.
■ **lecture note** Define the "dark figure of crime" and explain how the NCVS can be used to help uncover information about it.
■ **lecture note** Ask the class why the NCVS does not collect data on homicide.

■ **lecture note** Discuss recent NCVS statistics and ask the class what these findings may indicate about the underlying nature and causes of crime in America.
■ **dark figure of crime** Crime that is not reported to the police and that remains unknown to officials.

The National Crime Victimization Survey

A second major source of statistical data about crime in the United States is the National Crime Victimization Survey (NCVS), which is based on victim self-reports rather than on police reports. The NCVS is designed to estimate the occurrence of all crimes, whether reported or not.[70] The NCVS was first conducted in 1972. It built on efforts in the late 1960s by both the National Opinion Research Center and the President's Commission on Law Enforcement and the Administration of Justice to uncover what some had been calling the **dark figure of crime**. This term refers to those crimes that are not reported to the police and that remain unknown to officials. Before the development of the NCVS, little was known about such unreported and undiscovered offenses.

Early data from the NCVS changed the way criminologists thought about crime in the United States. The use of victim self-reports led to the discovery that crimes of all types were more prevalent than UCR statistics indicated. Many cities were shown to have victimization rates that were more than twice the rate of reported offenses. Others, like Saint Louis, Missouri, and Newark, New Jersey, were found to have rates of victimization that very nearly approximated reported crime. New York, often thought of as a high-crime city, was discovered to have one of the lowest rates of self-reported victimization. The NCVS for 2014 data showed that 54% of all violent victimizations, and 63% of property crimes were not reported to the police.[71]

NCVS data are gathered by the BJS through a cooperative arrangement with the U.S. Census Bureau.[72] Twice each year, Census Bureau personnel interview household members in a nationally representative sample of approximately 90,000 households (about 160,000 people). Only individuals age 12 or older are interviewed. Households stay in the sample for three years, and new households rotate into the sample regularly.

The NCVS collects information on crimes suffered by individuals and households, whether or not those crimes were reported to law enforcement. It estimates the proportion of each crime type reported to law enforcement, and it summarizes the reasons that victims give for reporting or not reporting. BJS statistics are published in annual reports made available on the Internet titled *Criminal Victimization* and *Crime and the Nation's Households*.

Using definitions similar to those employed by the UCR/NIBRS Program, the NCVS includes data on the national incidence of rape, sexual assault, robbery, assault, burglary, personal and household larceny, and motor vehicle theft. Not included are murder, kidnapping, and victimless crimes (crimes that, by their nature, tend to involve willing participants). Commercial robbery and the burglary of businesses were dropped from NCVS reports in 1977. The NCVS employs a hierarchical counting system similar to that of the pre-NIBRS system: It counts only the most "serious" incident in any series of criminal events perpetrated against the same individual. Both completed and attempted offenses are counted, although only people 12 years of age and older are included in household surveys.

NCVS statistics for recent years reveal the following:

- Approximately 9% of American households are touched by crime every year.
- About 21 million victimizations occur each year.
- City residents are almost twice as likely as rural residents to be victims of crime.
- About half of all violent crimes, and slightly more than one-third of all property crimes, are reported to police.[73]
- Victims of crime are more often men than women.
- Younger people are more likely than the elderly to be victims of crime.
- Blacks are more likely than whites or members of other racial groups to be victims of violent crimes.
- Violent victimization rates are highest among people in lower-income families.

Since 1993, the rate of violent crime reported by the NCVS has declined from 79.8 to 20.1 victimizations per 1,000 persons age 12 or older.[74] Since 1993, the rate of property crime has declined from 351.8 to 118.1 victimizations per 1,000 households. The decline in theft accounted for the majority of the decrease in property crime. However, UCR statistics, which go back almost another 40 years, show that today's crime rate is still many times what it was in the early and middle years of the twentieth century.[75] Like the UCR, however, NCVS major data categories do not fully encompass the shifting nature of criminal activity in the United States. Nonetheless, some researchers trust NCVS data more than UCR/NIBRS data because they believe that victim self-reports provide a more accurate gauge of criminal incidents than do police reports in which victims had to initiate the reporting process. A comparison of UCR/NIBRS and NCVS data for 2014 can be found in Table 2-4.

You can also explore the NCVS Victimization Analysis Tool (NVAT) at **http://www.bjs.gov/index.cfm?ty=nvat**. The tool, which became available in 2012, analyzes data on victims, households, and incidents, and instantly generates tables

TABLE 2-4 | Comparison of UCR/NIBRS and NCVS Data, 2014

OFFENSE	UCR/NIBRS	NCVS[a]
Personal/Violent Crimes—victims 12 or older		
Homicide	14,249	—
Rape[b]	116,645	284,350
Robbery	325,802	664,210
Aggravated assault	741,291	1,092,090
Property Crimes—victims 12 or older		
Burglary[c]	1,729,806	2,993,480
Larceny	5,858,496	11,760,620
Motor vehicle theft	689,527	534,370
Arson[d]	42,934	—
Total of All Crimes Recorded	9,518,750	20,629,120[e]

[a]NCVS data on property crimes cover "households touched by crime," not absolute numbers of crime occurrences. More than one victimization may occur per household, but only the number of households in which victimizations occur enters the tabulations.

[b]NCVS statistics include both rape and sexual assault.

[c]NCVS statistics include only household burglary and attempts.

[d]Arson data are incomplete in the UCR/NIBRS and are not reported by the NCVS.

[e]Includes NCVS crimes not shown in the table, including 3.3 million simple assaults.

Source: Pearson Education, Inc.

with national estimates of the numbers, rates, and percentages of both violent and property victimization from 1993 to the most recent year for which NCVS data are available.

Comparisons of the UCR and NCVS

As mentioned earlier in this chapter, crime statistics from the UCR/NIBRS and the NCVS reveal crime patterns that are often the bases for social policies that intend to deter or reduce crime. These policies also build on explanations for criminal behavior found in more elaborate interpretations of the statistical information. Unfortunately, however, researchers too often forget that statistics, which are merely descriptive, can be weak in explanatory power. For example, NCVS data show that "household crime rates" are highest for households (1) headed by blacks, (2) headed by younger people, (3) with six or more members, (4) headed by renters, and (5) located in central cities.[76] Such findings, combined with statistics that show that most crime occurs among members of the same race, have led some researchers to conclude that values among certain black subcultural group members both propel them into crime and make them targets of criminal victimization. The truth may be, however, that

> Like most statistical data-gathering programs in the social sciences, the UCR/NIBRS and the NCVS programs are not without problems.

crime is more a function of inner-city location than of culture. From simple descriptive statistics, it is difficult to know which is the case.

Like most statistical data-gathering programs in the social sciences, the UCR/NIBRS and the NCVS programs are not without problems. Because UCR/NIBRS data are based primarily on citizens' crime reports to the police, there are several inherent difficulties. First, not all people report when they are victimized. Some victims are afraid to contact the police, whereas others may not believe that the police can do anything about the offense. Second, certain kinds of crimes are reported rarely, if at all. These include victimless crimes, also known as *social-order offenses*, such as drug use, prostitution, and gambling. Similarly, white-collar offenses, such as embezzlement—because they often go undiscovered, or because they are difficult to score in terms of traditional UCR categories—probably enter the official statistics only rarely. The FBI acknowledges such shortcomings by saying that "it is well documented that the major limitation of the traditional Summary Reporting System is its failure to keep up with the changing face of crime and criminal activity. The inability to grasp the extent of white-collar crime is a specific example of that larger limitation."[77] Third, high-technology and computer crime, like white-collar crime, don't always "fit" well with traditional reporting categories, leading to their possible underrepresentation in today's crime statistics.[78] Fourth, victims' reports may not be entirely accurate. A victim's memory may be faulty, victims may feel the need to impress or please the police, or they may be under pressure from others to misrepresent the facts. Finally, all reports are filtered through a number of bureaucratic levels, which increases the likelihood that inaccuracies will enter the data. As noted methodologist Frank Hagan points out, "The government is very keen on amassing statistics. They collect them, add to them, raise them to the nth power, take the cube root, and prepare wonderful diagrams. But what you must never forget is that every one of these figures comes in the first instance from the *chowty dar* [village watchman], who puts down what he damn pleases."[79]

In contrast to the UCR/NIBRS dependence on crimes reported by victims who seek out the police, the National Crime Victimization Survey relies on door-to-door surveys and personal interviews for its data. Survey results, however, may be skewed for several reasons. First, no matter how objective survey questions may appear to be, survey respondents inevitably provide their personal interpretations and descriptions of what may or may not have been a criminal event. Second, by its very nature, the survey includes information from those people who are most willing to talk to surveyors; more reclusive people are less likely to respond regardless of the level of victimization they may have suffered. Also, some victims are afraid to report crimes even to nonpolice interviewers, and others may invent victimizations for the interviewer's sake. As the first page of the NCVS report admits, "Details about the crimes come directly from the victims, and no attempt is made to validate the information against police records or any other source."[80]

Finally, because both the UCR/NIBRS and the NCVS are human artifacts, they contain only data that their creators think appropriate. UCR/NIBRS statistics for 2001, for example, do not include a tally of those who perished in the September 11, 2001, terrorist attacks because FBI officials concluded that the events were too "unusual" to count. Although the FBI's 2001 *Crime in the United States* acknowledges "the 2,830 homicides reported as a result of the events of September 11, 2001," it goes on to say that "these figures have been removed" from the reported data.[81] Crimes that result from an anomalous event, but are excluded from reported data, highlight the arbitrary nature of the data collection process itself.

Special Categories of Crime

A **crime typology** is a classification scheme used in the study and description of criminal behavior. There are many typologies, all of which have an underlying logic. The system of classification that derives from any particular typology may be based on legal criteria, offender motivation, victim behavior, the characteristics of individual offenders, or the like. Criminologists Terance D. Miethe and Richard C. McCorkle note that crime typologies "are designed primarily to simplify social reality by identifying homogeneous groups of crime behaviors that are different from other clusters of crime behaviors."[82] Hence one common but simple typology contains only two categories of crime: violent and property. In fact, many crime typologies contain overlapping or nonexclusive categories—just as violent crimes may involve property offenses, and property offenses may lead to violent crimes. Thus no one typology is likely to capture all of the nuances of criminal offending.

Social relevance is a central distinguishing feature of any meaningful typology, and it is with that in mind that the remaining sections of this chapter briefly highlight crimes of special importance today. They are crime against women, crime against the elderly, hate crime, corporate and white-collar crime, organized crime, gun crime, drug crime, cybercrime, and terrorism.

Crime against Women

The victimization of women is a special area of concern, and both the NCVS and the UCR/NIBRS contain data on gender as it relates to victimization. Statistics show that women are victimized less frequently than men in every major personal crime category other than rape.[83] The overall U.S. rate of violent victimization is about 12 per 1,000 males age 12 or older, and 11 per 1,000 females.[84]

> Many crime typologies contain overlapping or nonexclusive categories—just as violent crimes may involve property offenses, and property offenses may lead to violent crimes. Thus no one typology is likely to capture all of the nuances of criminal offending.

When women become victims of violent crime, however, they are more likely than men to be injured (29% vs. 22%, respectively).[85] Moreover, a larger proportion of women than men make modifications in the way they live because of the threat of crime.[86] Women, especially those living in cities, have become increasingly careful about where they travel and the time of day they leave their homes—particularly if they are unaccompanied—and in many settings are often wary of unfamiliar males.

Date rape, familial incest, spousal abuse, **stalking**, and the exploitation of women through social-order offenses like prostitution and pornography are major issues facing American society today. Testimony before Congress tagged domestic violence as the largest cause of injury to American women.[87] Former Surgeon General C. Everett Koop once identified

■ **theme** Why do the elderly tend to experience lower rates of victimization than other age groups?

■ **cyberstalking** The use of the Internet, e-mail, and other electronic communication technologies to stalk another person.[ii]

■ **theme** Why is elder victimization of special concern? How can the effect of crime be more serious for an elderly victim?

violence against women by their partners as the number one health problem facing women in America.[88] Findings from the National Violence against Women Survey[89] (NVAWS) and the National Intimate Partner and Sexual Violence Survey[90] reveal the following:

- Physical assault is widespread among American women. Fifty-two percent of surveyed women said that they had been physically assaulted as a child or as an adult.
- Approximately 1.9 million women are physically assaulted in the United States each year.
- Eighteen percent of women experienced a completed or attempted rape at some time in their lives.
- Of those reporting rape, 22% were under 12 years old, and 32% were between 12 and 17 years old when they were first raped.
- Native American and Alaska Native women were most likely to report rape and physical assault, and Asian/ Pacific Islander women were least likely to report such victimization. Hispanic women were less likely to report rape than non-Hispanic women.
- Women report significantly more partner violence than men. Twenty-five percent of surveyed women, and only 8% of surveyed men, said they had been raped or physically assaulted by a current or former spouse, cohabiting partner, or date.
- Violence against women is primarily partner violence. Seventy-six percent of the women who had been raped or physically assaulted since age 18 were assaulted by a current or former husband, cohabiting partner, or date, compared with 18% of the men.
- Women are significantly more likely than men to be injured during an assault. Thirty-two percent of the women and 16% of the men who had been raped since age 18 were injured during their most recent rape.
- Eight percent of surveyed women and 2% of surveyed men said they had been stalked at some time in their lives. According to survey estimates, approximately 1 million women and 371,000 men are stalked annually in the United States.
- Twenty-seven percent of women and 12% of men report significant short- or long-term impacts from sexual or physical violence or from stalking by an intimate partner.

Survey findings like these show that more must be done to alleviate the social conditions that result in the victimization of women. Suggestions already under consideration call for

expansion in the number of federal and state laws designed to control domestic violence, a broadening of the federal Family Violence Prevention and Services Act, federal help in setting up state advocacy offices for battered women, increased funding for battered women's shelters, and additional funds for prosecutors and courts to develop spousal abuse units. The federal Violent Crime Control and Law Enforcement Act of 1994 was designed to meet many of these needs through a subsection titled the Violence against Women Act (VAWA). That act signified a major shift in our national response to domestic violence, stalking (which is often part of the domestic violence continuum), and sexual assault crimes. For the first time in our nation's history, violent crimes against women were addressed in relation to the more general problem of gender inequality.[91] VAWA is discussed in greater detail in a "CJ Issues" box in this chapter.

Finally, the passage of antistalking legislation by all 50 states and the District of Columbia provides some measure of additional protection to women (as women comprise 80% of all stalking victims[92]). On the federal level, the seriousness of stalking was addressed when Congress passed the interstate stalking law in 1996.[93] The law[94] also addresses **cyberstalking**, or the use of the Internet by perpetrators seeking to exercise power and control over their victims by threatening them directly or by posting misleading and harassing information about them Cyberstalking can be especially insidious because it does not require that the perpetrator and the victim be in the same geographic area. Similarly, electronic communication technologies lower the barriers to harassment and threats; a cyberstalker does not need to confront the victim physically.[95]

Crime against the Elderly

Relative to other age groups, older victims rarely appear in the crime statistics. Criminal victimization seems to decline with age, suggesting that older people are only infrequently targeted by violent and property criminals. Moreover, older people are more likely than younger individuals to live in secure areas and to have the financial means to provide for their own personal security.

Victimization data pertaining to older people come mostly from the NCVS, which, for such purposes, looks at people age 65 and older. The elderly generally experience the lowest rate of victimization of any age group in both violent and property crime categories.[96] Some aspects of crime against older people

CJ | ISSUES
Gender Issues in Criminal Justice

President Obama signing the Violence against Women Act (VAWA) reauthorization legislation in 2013. Intimate partner violence is a problem of special concern to the criminal justice system, and violence against women is an area that is receiving legislative attention, as evidenced by the federal VAWA. How might laws designed to protect women be improved?

The Violent Crime Control and Law Enforcement Act of 1994 included significant provisions intended to enhance gender equality throughout the criminal justice system. Title IV of the Violent Crime Control and Law Enforcement Act, known as the Violence against Women Act (VAWA) of 1994, contains the Safe Streets for Women Act. This act increased federal penalties for repeat sex offenders and requires mandatory restitution for sex crimes, including costs related to medical services (including physical, psychiatric, and psychological care); physical and occupational therapy or rehabilitation; necessary transportation, temporary housing, and child-care expenses; lost income; attorneys' fees, including any costs incurred in obtaining a civil protection order; and any other losses suffered by the victim as a result of the offense. The act requires that compliance with a restitution order be made a condition of probation or supervised release (if such a sentence is imposed by the court) and provides that violation of the order will result in the offender's imprisonment. The law also extends "rape shield law" protections to civil cases and to all criminal cases in order to bar irrelevant inquiries into a victim's sexual history.

Chapter 2 of the VAWA provided funds for grants to combat violent crimes against women. The purpose of funding was to assist states and local governments to "develop and strengthen effective law enforcement and prosecution strategies to combat violent crimes against women, and to develop and strengthen victim services in cases involving violent crimes against women." The law also provided funds for the "training of law enforcement officers and prosecutors to more effectively identify and respond to violent crimes against women, including the crimes of sexual assault and domestic violence"; for "developing, installing, or expanding data collection and communication systems, including computerized systems, linking police, prosecutors, and courts or for the purpose of identifying and tracking arrests, protection orders, violations of protection orders, prosecutions, and convictions for violent crimes against women, including the crimes of sexual assault and domestic violence"; and for developing and strengthening "victim services programs, including sexual assault and domestic violence programs."

The act also created the crime of crossing state lines in violation of a protection order and the crime of crossing state lines to commit assault on a domestic partner. It established federal penalties for the latter offense of up to life in prison in cases where death results.

Chapter 3 of the act provided funds to increase the "safety for women in public transit and public parks." It authorized up to $10 million in grants through the Department of Transportation to enhance lighting, camera surveillance, and security telephones in public transportation systems used by women.

Chapter 5 of VAWA funded the creation of hotlines, educational seminars, informational materials, and training programs for professionals who provide assistance to victims of sexual assault. Another portion of the law, titled the Safe Homes for Women Act, increased grants for battered women's shelters, encouraged arrest in cases of domestic violence, and provided for the creation of a national domestic violence hotline to provide counseling, information, and assistance to victims of domestic violence. The act also mandates that any protection order issued by a state court must be recognized by the other states and by the federal government and must be enforced "as if it were the order of the enforcing state."

The VAWA was reauthorized by Congress in 2000, 2005, and again in 2013.[1] The 2005 VAWA reauthorization included a new statute known as the International Marriage Broker Regulation Act (IMBRA), which provides potential life-saving protections to prospective foreign brides who may immigrate to the United States. Finally, the 2013 reauthorization made $659 million available each year for five years for programs that strengthen the justice system's response to crimes against women and some men, including protections for gays, lesbians, bisexual, and transgender Americans.

[1] VAWA 2013 was signed into law by President Obama on March 7, 2013. It is officially known as the Violence against Women Reauthorization Act of 2013.

---

are worth noting. In general, elderly crime victims are more likely than younger victims to

- Be victims of property crime—nine out of ten crimes committed against the elderly are property crimes, compared to fewer than four in ten crimes against people between age 12 and 24.

- Face offenders who are armed with guns
- Be victimized by strangers
- Be victimized in or near their homes during daylight hours
- Report their victimization to the police, especially when they fall victim to violent crime
- Be physically injured

■ **lecture note** Define hate crimes, explain the various categories of bias that may motivate a hate crime, and explain that laws continue to expand to include more categories, such as disability, sexual orientation, gender, and gender identity. Discuss groups that are not yet protected under the law, such as the homeless.

■ **theme** Do you think that the number and intensity of hate crimes will increase or decrease throughout the 21st century and why?

■ **hate crime (UCR/NIBRS)**   A criminal offense motivated, in whole or in part, by the offender's bias against a race, gender, gender identity, religion, disability, sexual orientation, or ethnicity, and committed against persons, property, or society.

In addition, elderly people are less likely to attempt to protect themselves when they are victims of violent crime.

The elderly face special kinds of victimizations that only rarely affect younger adults, such as physical abuse at the hands of caregivers. Criminal physical abuse of the elderly falls into two categories: domestic and institutional. Domestic abuse often occurs at the hands of caregivers who are related to their victims; institutional abuse occurs in residential settings such as retirement centers, nursing homes, and hospitals. Both forms of elder abuse may also involve criminal sexual victimization.

The elderly are also more often targeted by con artists. Confidence schemes center on commercial and financial fraud (including telemarketing fraud), charitable donation fraud, funeral and cemetery fraud, real estate fraud, caretaker fraud, automobile and home repair fraud, living trust fraud, health-care fraud (e.g., promises of "miracle cures"), and health-provider fraud (overbilling and unjustified repeat billing by otherwise legitimate health-care providers). "False friends" may intentionally isolate elderly targets from others in the hopes of misappropriating money through short-term secret loans or outright theft. Similarly, a younger person may feign romantic involvement with an elderly victim or pretend to be devoted to the senior in order to solicit money or receive an inappropriate gift or inheritance.

Finally, crime against the elderly will likely undergo a significant increase as baby boomers enter their retirement years. Not only will the elderly comprise an increasingly larger segment of the population as boomers age, but it is anticipated that they will be wealthier than any preceding generation of retirees, making them attractive targets for scam artists and property criminals.[97] The National Center on Elder Abuse, which provides additional information for researchers and justice system participants, can be reached at **http://www.ncea.aoa .gov/ncearoot/Main_Site/index.aspx.** Likewise, the U.S. Department of Justice's new Elder Justice Website can be visited at **http://www.justice.gov/elderjustice**.

Hate Crime

A significant change in crime reporting practices resulted from the Hate Crime Statistics Act,[98] signed into law by President George H. W. Bush in 1990. The act mandates a statistical tally of **hate crimes**; data collection under the law began in 1991.

Congress defined *hate crime* as an offense "in which the defendant's conduct was motivated by hatred, bias, or prejudice, based on the actual or perceived race, color, religion, national origin, ethnicity, gender, or sexual orientation of another individual or group of individuals."[99] In 2013, police agencies reported a total of 5,922 hate-crime incidents, including eight murders, across the country. As Figure 2-7 shows, 17.4% of the incidents were motivated by religious bias, 48.5% were caused by racial hatred, and 11.1% were driven by prejudice against ethnicity or national origin. Another 20.8% of all hate crimes were based on sexual orientation, most committed against males believed by their victimizers to be homosexuals.[100] A relatively small number of hate crimes targeted people with physical or mental disabilities.

Following the terrorist attacks of September 11, 2001, authorities in some jurisdictions reported a dramatic shift in the nature of hate crime, with race-motivated crimes declining and crimes motivated by religion or ethnicity increasing sharply.[101] Islamic individuals, in particular, became the target of many such crimes.

Most hate crimes consist of intimidation, although vandalism, simple assault, and aggravated assault also account for a number of hate-crime offenses. A few robberies and rapes were also classified as hate crimes in 2013.

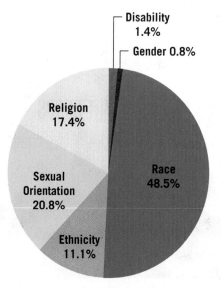

FIGURE 2-7 | Motivation of Hate-Crime Offenders, 2013

Note: Total may be more than 100% due to rounding.

Source: Pearson Education, Inc.

■ **theme**   How do hate crimes and the existence of survivalist organizations highlight the dichotomy between individual rights and the need for public order?

■ **lecture note**   Explain the difference between corporate and white collar crime.

■ **theme**   Do you think that there are differences in the characteristics of offenders committing traditional Part I crimes and those committing white-collar and corporate crime? Why?

Although hate crimes are popularly conceived of as crimes motivated by racial enmity, the Violent Crime Control and Law Enforcement Act of 1994 created a new category of "crimes of violence motivated by gender." Congress defined this crime as "a crime of violence committed because of gender or on the basis of gender, and due, at least in part, to an animus based on the victim's gender." The 1994 act did not establish separate penalties for gender-motivated crimes, anticipating that they would be prosecuted as felonies under existing laws. The 1994 act also mandated that crimes motivated by biases against people with disabilities be considered hate crimes.

In 2010, President Obama signed the Matthew Shepard and James Byrd, Jr. Hate Crimes Prevention Act into law. The act expanded the definition of federal hate crimes to include crimes based on sexual orientation, gender identity, or disability. The law also amended the Hate Crimes Statistics Act[102] to include crimes motivated by gender and gender identity, as well as hate crimes committed by and against juveniles.

Hate crimes are sometimes called *bias crimes*. One form of bias crime that bears special mention is homophobic homicide—the murder of homosexuals by those opposed to their lifestyles. The Southern Poverty Law Center, which tracks hate groups, recently identified 939 such groups operating in the United States.[103] The center, which is based in Montgomery, Alabama, says that the number of hate groups has jumped 66% since 2000, mostly because of the formation of new anti-immigrant and antigovernment "patriot" organizations. So-called patriot groups are "sovereign citizen" extremists who don't recognize government authority, including its power to tax and to enforce laws. According to the center, California has the most hate groups (77). Nationwide, the center has identified 170 neo-Nazi, 136 white nationalist, 136 racist skinhead, 36 anti-Muslim, 26 Christian identity, 149 black separatist, 42 neoconfederate, and 221 Ku Klux Klan groups. Another 122 general hate groups—or those that "espouse a variety of hateful doctrines"—were also identified. Learn more about hate crime and what can be done to address it at **http://www.justicestudies.com/pubs/hcv2014** and **http://www.justicestudies.com/pubs/hatecrimes.pdf**.

Corporate and White-Collar Crime

In 2012, Texas financier R. Allen Stanford was convicted by a federal trial jury of 13 out of 14 counts of financial fraud for his involvement in an illegal investment scheme that cost nearly 30,000 investors in 113 countries $7 billion.[104] Stanford's fraud occurred over more than 20 years, and included staged hoaxes designed to convince clients that their investments were safe. Following conviction, he was sentenced to 110 years in prison.

The most infamous financial crime of recent years involved investment fund manager Bernard ("Bernie") Madoff, who pled guilty in 2009 to operating a Ponzi scheme that defrauded investors out of as much as $50 billion.[105] Called "Wall Street's biggest fraud" by some, Madoff's shenanigans purportedly cost investors $50 billion in money that seemed to simply disappear.[106] Madoff, a former chairman of the NASDAQ stock market, pleaded guilty to 11 felony counts, including securities fraud, mail fraud, wire fraud, money laundering, and perjury. He was sentenced to 150 years in prison.[107]

The recent economic downturn, combined with the collapse of the housing market and a loss of jobs in many sectors of the economy, sparked a rapid growth in mortgage fraud scams. Mortgage fraud, which is a federal crime, can involve making false or misleading statements about one's identity, personal income, assets, or debts during the mortgage application process. It also includes efforts to knowingly overvalue land or property to defraud purchasers and lenders.

Essentially, there are three types of mortgage fraud. The first, "fraud for profit," involves a scheme by "ghost buyers" to collect cash, with no interest in owning the property against which money is being borrowed. The second is "fraud for housing,"

AP WideWorld Photos

Emanuel AME Church in Charleston, South Carolina. In 2015, the church was the scene of a mass shooting allegedly carried out by 21-year-old Dylann Roof. Roof is white, but the nine victims who died were black; and federal officials charged Roof with a hate crime in the killings. Why are hate crimes given special attention under the law?

■ **corporate crime** A violation of a criminal statute by a corporate entity or by its executives, employees, or agents acting on behalf of and for the benefit of the corporation, partnership, or other form of business entity.[iii]

■ **white-collar crime** Violations of the criminal law committed by a person of respectability and high social status in the course of his or her occupation. Also, nonviolent crime for financial gain utilizing deception and committed by anyone who has special technical or professional knowledge of business or government, irrespective of the person's occupation.

■ **organized crime** The unlawful activities of the members of a highly organized, disciplined association engaged in supplying illegal goods or services, including gambling, prostitution, loan-sharking, narcotics, and labor racketeering, and in other unlawful activities.[iv]

or application fraud, in which otherwise legitimate homebuyers fake documents in order to appear eligible for a loan that they would not otherwise get. According to one report, 61% of all reported mortgage frauds in 2008 involved misrepresentations made on applications for a mortgage. The third type of mortgage fraud involves overestimating a property's value or submitting a false appraisal.

The recent economic downtown, combined with the collapse of the housing market and a loss of jobs in many sectors of the economy, sparked a rapid growth in mortgage fraud scams.

A recent study by the Mortgage Asset Research Institute concluded that mortgage fraud was more prevalent at the time of the study than it had been at the height of the nation's building boom just a few years earlier.[108] Federal agencies, already inundated with mortgage fraud cases, are starting to look into a new breed of scams perpetrated by those who offer to refinance homes or save them from foreclosure. In one of the new scams, criminals offer to help people who are about to lose their homes, collect several thousand dollars up front, and then disappear.[109] In early 2009, the Federal Trade Commission announced a wave of law enforcement actions against operations using deceptive tactics to market mortgage modification and home foreclosure relief services, including firms that marketed their "services" by falsely implying an affiliation with the federal government.[110]

Under the American system of criminal justice, corporations can be treated as separate legal entities and can be convicted of violations of the criminal law under a legal principle known as the *identification doctrine*. In 2002, for example, a federal jury convicted global accounting firm Arthur Andersen of obstruction of justice after its employees shredded documents related to Enron's bankruptcy in an effort to impede an investigation by securities regulators. The conviction, which was overturned by a unanimous U.S. Supreme Court in 2005,[111] capped the firm's demise, and it ended U.S. operations in August 2002.[112]

Although corporations may be convicted of a crime, the human perpetrators of **corporate crime** are business executives known as *white-collar criminals*. **White-collar crime** was first defined in 1939 by Edwin H. Sutherland in his presidential address to the American Sociological Society.[113] Sutherland

proposed that "crime in the suites" (a reference to corporate offices) rivaled the importance of street crime in its potential impact on American society.

In July 2002, President George W. Bush created a Corporate Fraud Task Force within the federal government and proposed a new law providing criminal penalties for corporate fraud. A few months later, the president signed into law the Sarbanes-Oxley Act.[114] The new law created tough provisions designed to deter and punish corporate and accounting fraud and corruption and to protect the interests of workers and shareholders. Under the Sarbanes-Oxley Act, corporate officials (chief executive officers and chief financial officers) must personally vouch for the truth and accuracy of their companies' financial statements. The act also substantially increased federal penalties for obstructing justice and, specifically, for shredding or destroying documents that might aid in a criminal investigation of business practices. Learn more about corporate and white-collar crime at the National White Collar Crime Center (NW3C) via **http://www.nw3c .org**. Established in 1992, the NW3C provides a national support system for the prevention, investigation, and prosecution of multijurisdictional economic crimes.

Organized Crime

For many people, the term **organized crime** conjures up images of the Mafia (also called the *Cosa Nostra*) or the hit HBO TV series *The Sopranos* and *Boardwalk Empire*. Although organized criminal activity is decidedly a group phenomenon, the groups involved in such activity in the United States today display a great deal of variation. During the past few decades in the United States, the preeminence of traditional Sicilian American criminal organizations has fallen to such diverse criminal associations as the Black Mafia, the Cuban Mafia, the Haitian Mafia, the Colombian cartels, and Asian criminal groups like the Chinese Tongs and street gangs, Japanese yakuza, and Vietnamese gangs. Included here as well might be inner-city gangs, the best known of which are probably the Los Angeles Crips and Bloods and the Chicago Vice Lords; international drug rings; outlaw motorcycle gangs like the Hell's Angels and the Pagans; and other looser associations of small-time thugs, prison gangs, and drug dealers. Noteworthy among these groups—especially for their involvement in the lucrative drug trade—are the Latino organized bands, including the

■ **theme**   Why is transnational organized crime such a serious concern today?
■ **activity**   Conduct a debate on gun control. Divide students into groups and assign one group to research and argue in favor of gun control and the other group to research and argue in favor of the Constitutional right to bear arms.

■ **transnational organized crime**   Unlawful activity undertaken and supported by organized criminal groups operating across national boundaries.

David J. Phillip/AP Wide World Photos

Texas financier R. Allen Stanford, who was convicted by a federal trial jury in 2012 of 13 out of 14 counts of financial fraud for his involvement in an illegal investment scheme that cost nearly 30,000 investors in 113 countries $7 billion. Stanford received a sentence of 110 years in prison. How is white collar crime different from other crimes? How is it similar?

Dominican, Colombian, Mexican, and Cuban importers of cocaine, heroin, marijuana, and other controlled substances.

The unlawful activities of organized groups that operate across national boundaries are especially significant. Such activity is referred to as **transnational organized crime**. Transnational criminal associations worthy of special mention are the Hong Kong–based Triads, the South American cocaine cartels, the Italian Mafia, the Japanese yakuza, the Russian *Mafiya*, and the West African crime groups—each of which extends its reach well beyond its home country. In some parts of the world, close links between organized crime and terrorist groups involve money laundering, which provides cash to finance the activities of terrorist cells and to finance paramilitary efforts to overthrow established governments.

Former Central Intelligence Agency (CIA) Director R. James Woolsey points out that "while organized crime is not a new phenomenon today, some governments find their authority besieged at home and their foreign policy interests imperiled abroad. Drug trafficking, links between drug traffickers and terrorists, smuggling of illegal aliens, massive financial and bank fraud, arms smuggling, potential involvement in the theft and

sale of nuclear material, political intimidation, and corruption all constitute a poisonous brew—a mixture potentially as deadly as what we faced during the cold war."[115] The challenge for today's criminal justice student is to recognize that crime does not respect national boundaries. Crime is global, and what happens in one part of the world could affect us all.[116]

Gun Crime

Guns and gun crime seem to pervade American culture. The 2012 Newtown, Connecticut, school shootings took 28 lives, including the shooter and 20 first graders. A month earlier, on July 20, 2012, a gunman who apparently identified with the Joker, a character in Batman movies, attacked a crowded theater in Aurora, Colorado, during a midnight showing of the movie *The Dark Knight Rises*, killing 12 people and injuring 58 others. The shooter, James Egan Holmes, used a shotgun, a semiautomatic rife with a 100-round magazine, and a handgun. Eighteen months earlier, in January 2011, another random mass shooting claimed the lives of six people

Guns and gun crime seem to pervade American culture.

■ **theme** Do you agree with the legalization of recreational marijuana? How might this affect the criminal justice system?

A fully functional plastic handgun created using a 3-D printing process. The weapon is undetectable by standard metal detectors. What's your position on gun ownership and gun control?

and wounded 13 people, including U.S. Representative Gabrielle Giffords, who was shot through the head. These three events, happening in rapid succession, led to strident calls for gun control at both the state and national level.

Constitutional guarantees of the right to bear arms have combined with historical circumstances to make ours a well-armed society. Guns are used in many types of crimes. Each year, approximately 1 million serious crimes—including homicide, rape, robbery, and assault—involve the use of a handgun. In a typical year, approximately 9,800 murders are committed in the United States with firearms. A recent report by the BJS found that 18% of state prison inmates and 15% of federal inmates were armed at the time they committed the crime for which they were imprisoned.[117] Nine percent of those in state prisons said they fired a gun while committing the offense for which they were serving time.[118]

Both federal and state governments have responded to the public concern over the ready availability of handguns. In 1994, Congress passed the Brady Handgun Violence Prevention Act, which President Bill Clinton signed into law. The law was named for former Press Secretary James Brady, who was shot and severely wounded in an attempt on President Ronald Reagan's life on March 30, 1981. The law mandated a five-day waiting period before the purchase of a handgun, and it established a national instant criminal background check system that firearms dealers must use before selling a handgun. The five-day waiting period was discontinued in 1998 when the instant computerized background checking system became operational.

Although federal law limits retail purchases of handguns by felons, a BJS study found that most offenders obtain weapons from friends or family members or "on the street" rather than attempt to purchase them at retail establishments.[119] One recent study, for example, found no evidence that stringent gun-control laws have an impact on crime.[120] The study, which used data from all 50 states, found that gun-control laws do not have an impact on the crime rate or on the occurrence of any specific type of serious crime. Such laws are ineffective in reducing crime, the study authors said, because they do not substantially reduce the availability of firearms to criminal offenders.

In Congress, debate continues about whether to require gun manufacturers to create and retain "ballistic fingerprints" (the marks left on a bullet by the barrel of the gun from which it was fired) of each weapon they produce. Although a national ballistics fingerprinting requirement may still be years away, three states—California, Maryland, and New York—and the District of Columbia already require that a record be kept of the "fingerprint" characteristics of each new handgun sold.[121]

Microstamping uses laser engraving to encode a weapon's serial number on each cartridge that it fires, and California authorities believe that the technology will allow handguns to be traced to their manufacturer and then to the first purchaser, using only spent cartridges left at crime scenes.

For the latest information on gun violence and gun laws, visit the Brady Center to Prevent Gun Violence via **http://www .bradycenter.org**. The National Rifle Association site at **http://home.nra.org** provides support for responsible access to firearms.

Drug Crime

Unlike many crimes tracked by the FBI, drug-related crime has continued to rise even in years when other crimes have been decreasing. The seemingly relentless increase in drug violations has largely accounted for the continued growth in America's prison populations, even when official crime rates (which count the eight major crimes discussed earlier) have been declining. Chapter 16, "Drugs and Crime," discusses illicit drugs and drug-law violations in detail. As that chapter shows, the rate of drug-related crime commission has more than doubled in the United States since 1975.

Alone, drug-law violations are themselves criminal, but many studies have linked drug abuse to other serious crimes. An early survey by the RAND Corporation found that most of the "violent predators" among prisoners had extensive

CJ | ISSUES
Gun Control

The issue of gun control took center stage on January 30, 2013, when Senator Dianne Feinstein, astronaut Mark Kelly (husband of former Representative Gabrielle Giffords, who was seriously injured at a mass shooting in Arizona), National Rifle Association (NRA) vice president Wayne LaPierre, and others testified before the U.S. Senate Judiciary in a hearing on gun violence. During the hearing, LaPierre emphasized the constitutional right of people to bear arms, while Feinstein and others told committee members that the American people have a fundamental right to be safe. As with so many other issues in criminal justice, the debate that the committee heard that day centered on the tension between individual rights and public safety.

By the time the hearing had ended, the committee heard pleas to stiffen federal gun control legislation by outlawing the possession of assault weapons, to place limits on the capacity of ammunition magazines, and to increase the range of background checks to which potential gun owners would be subjected.

Only a few years earlier, however, the U.S. Supreme Court came down heavily in support of the individual's right to bear arms. The Second Amendment to the U.S. Constitution reads, "A well regulated Militia, being necessary to the security of a free State, the right of the people to keep and bear Arms, shall not be infringed." In the 2008 case of *District of Columbia* v. *Heller*, the U.S. Supreme Court struck down a District of Columbia gun control regulation and ruled that "the Second Amendment protects an individual's right to possess firearms and that the city's total ban on handguns, as well as its requirement that firearms in the home be kept nonfunctional even when necessary for self-defense, violated that right."[1] The Court's holding in *Heller* was sweeping and unambiguous. The decision clearly declared the Second Amendment protection of "an individual right to possess a firearm unconnected with service in a militia, and to use that arm for traditionally lawful purposes, such as self-defense within the home."

Following Heller, some questioned whether the Court's ruling might be limited to federal enclaves, like the District of Columbia, or whether it was applicable to other jurisdictions. In 2010, in the case of *McDonald* v. *City of Chicago*,[2] the U.S. Supreme Court answered that question when it struck down gun-banning ordinances in Chicago and the city of Oak Park, Illinois. The Justices found that "the right to keep and bear arms must be regarded as a substantive guarantee" inherent in the U.S. Constitution.

One of the most significant laws enacted prior to *Heller* was the Violent Crime Control and Law Enforcement Act of 1994,[3] which regulated the sale of firearms within the United States and originally banned the manufacture of 19 military-style assault weapons, including those with specific combat features, such as high-capacity ammunition clips capable of holding more than ten rounds. The ban on assault weapons ended in 2004, however, when it was not renewed by Congress. The 1994 law also prohibited the sale or transfer of a gun to a juvenile, as well as the possession of a gun by a juvenile, and it prohibits gun sales to, and possession by, people subject to family violence restraining orders.

The 1996 Domestic Violence Offender Gun Ban[4] prohibits individuals convicted of misdemeanor domestic violence offenses from

Former Arizona Representative Gabrielle Giffords, who was seriously injured in a Tucson, Arizona, mass shooting in 2011, testifies with her husband before a U.S. Senate Judiciary Committee in 2013. The committee was examining issues of gun violence. What's your position on gun ownership and gun control?

owning or using firearms. Following the 1999 Columbine High School shooting, a number of states moved to tighten controls over handguns and assault weapons. The California legislature, for example, restricted gun purchases to one per month and tightened a ten-year-old ban on assault weapons. Similarly, Illinois passed a law requiring that gun owners lock their weapons away from anyone under age 14.

In 2004, at the urging of major police organizations, the U.S. Senate scuttled plans for a gun-industry protection bill. However, the bill was revived in 2005 and passed both houses of Congress before being signed into law by President George W. Bush on October 31. Known as the Protection of Lawful Commerce in Firearms Act, the law grants gunmakers and most gun dealers immunity from lawsuits brought by victims of gun crimes and their survivors. The law removes negligence as viable grounds for a civil suit against a gun dealer who carelessly sells a gun to someone who is at risk for using it in a crime; the law states that the dealer can be sued only if he or she knew of the gun buyer's criminal intent before the purchase. Gunmakers were made similarly immune from suits alleging product liability for having manufactured potentially lethal items.

Recently, however, as signaled by the Senate hearings with which this box opened, the need for greater gun control measures has been highlighted by a series of random mass shootings that shocked the nation (and that are described earlier in this chapter). Consequently, that year President Obama signed 23 executive orders on gun safety and called upon Congress to address the problem of gun violence in America.[5] Read the executive orders signed by President Obama at http://justicestudies.com/pubs/wh_orders.pdf.

[1] *District of Columbia, et al.* v. *Dick Anthony Heller* (2008). Available at http://www.law.cornell.edu/supct/html/07-290.ZO.html (accessed August 4, 2009).

[2] *McDonald* v. *Chicago*, 561 U.S. 3025, 130 S.Ct. 3020 (2010).

[3] Public Law 103-322, 108 Stat. 1796 (codified as amended in scattered sections of 18, 21, 28, 42, etc., U.S.).

[4] Public Law 104-208, an amendment to U.S. Code, Title 18, Section 921(a). Also known as the Lautenberg Amendment.

[5] Rick Ungar, "Here Are the 23 Executive Orders on Gun Safety Signed Today by the President," *Forbes*, January 16, 2013, http://www.forbes.com/sites/rickungar/2013/01/16/here-are-the-23-executive-orders-on-gun-safety-signed-today-by-the-president/ (accessed January 16, 2015).

■ **lecture note** Explain that many computer crimes are traditional crimes committed using technology in some way.

■ **cybercrime** Any crime perpetrated through the use of computer technology. Also, any violation of a federal or state cybercrime statute.

histories of heroin abuse, often in combination with alcohol and other drugs.[122] Some cities reported that a large percentage of their homicides were drug related.[123] More recent studies also link drug abuse to other serious crimes. Community leaders perceive, and data analyses confirm, that the crack cocaine epidemic of a couple of decades ago had a profound impact on violent crime, with homicide rates closely tracking cocaine-use levels among adult male arrestees.[124] Prisoner survey data show that 19% of state inmates and 16% of federal prisoners report committing their current offense to obtain money for drugs.[125] One study found that 13.3% of convicted jail inmates said that they had committed their offense to get money for drugs.[126]

Enforcement of drug laws has another side, and that is the conviction and imprisonment of many nonviolent offenders whose only interest is in recreational use of "soft" drugs such as marijuana. Consequently, within the past few years some states (notably Washington, Oregon, and Colorado) have modified their laws to allow for personal nonpublic use of recreational marijuana. Alaska voters approved a ballot initiative in 2014 that decriminalizes possession of small amounts of marijuana, but does not permit sale of the drug. Whether other states will follow those that have already legalized recreational use of marijuana remains to be seen. Even so, it is apparent that public attitudes toward at least some drugs are changing. That change is likely to break part of the relationship between drug use and continued criminal involvement which in part may be due to exclusion from the workforce and the virtual nonemployability which so often results from a drug conviction of any kind.

> Cybercrime, sometimes called *computer crime* or *information-technology crime*, uses computers and computer technology as tools in crime commission.

Cybercrime

Cybercrime, sometimes called *computer crime* or *information-technology crime*, uses computers and computer technology as tools in crime commission. Computer criminals manipulate the information stored in computer systems in ways that violate the law. (Thefts of computer equipment, although sometimes spectacular, are not computer crimes but are instead classified as larcenies.) The incidence of cybercrime is shown graphically in Figure 2-9, which displays the number of complaints filed with the Internet Crime Complaint Center (IC3) from 2000 to 2014. Although the figure shows an almost twenty-fold increase in cybercrimes since 2000, traditional crime measures (like those used by the UCR and NCVS) were only "designed to count the kinds of direct contact predatory crimes typical of the 1940s and 1950s, where victims and offenders came together in time and space."[127].

Many crimes committed via the Internet, however, such as prostitution, drug sales, theft, and fraud, are not new forms of offending. Rather, they are traditional offenses that use technology in their commission or that build on the possibilities for criminal activity that new technologies make possible. In 2013, for example, an international operation led by U.S. Immigration and Customs Enforcement agents led to arrest of 245 suspected child pornographers who communicated through the Internet.[128] Of those arrested, 213 were from the United States, and 23 from other countries. The enforcement effort, known as Operation Sunflower, led to the identification of 123 victims of child exploitation and the removal of 44 children from the control of alleged abusers. Five of the rescued children were three years old, and nine were between the ages of four and six.

Chapter 18, "The Future of Criminal Justice," provides additional information about cybercrime, including computer malware, software piracy, and phishing, and the law enforcement technologies used to fight it.

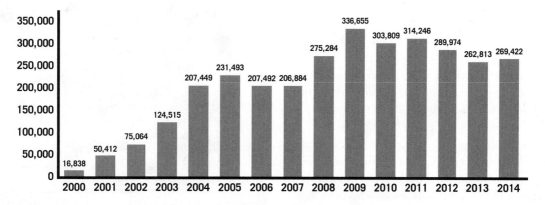

FIGURE 2-9 | Computer Crime Complaints, 2000–2014
Source: Based on data from Internet Crime Complaint Center.

CJ | NEWS
Most Americans Favor Legalizing Marijuana

Marijuana remains a Level I controlled substance under the 1970 Federal Comprehensive Drug Abuse Prevention and Control Act (CSA). That puts it into the same category as drugs such as heroin, LSD, peyote, mescaline, and other potent hallucinogenics. Now, however, public opinion polls reveal that most Americans are in favor of legalizing the drug, and a number of state and local governments have already okayed possession of small amounts of marijuana for nonpublic recreational use. One recent Gallup poll, for example (Figure 2-8), found 58% of Americans in favor of marijuana legalization, whereas only 39% of those polled wanted to keep the drug illegal. Young Americans (ages 18 to 29) were most in favor of legalization (67% in favor), whereas older Americans (aged 65 and older) were most opposed (53% against).

As of this writing, three states (Washington, Oregon, and Colorado) have legalized recreational marijuana, whereas Alaska voters approved a 2014 ballot initiative that decriminalized possession of small amounts of marijuana for personal use, although it does not provide for legal sales of the drug. A number of other states (including California, Florida, and Maine) are planning legislative action that might soon lead to legalization. Some cities, most notably Philadelphia, have told their police departments to avoid arrests for the possession of small amounts of marijuana. Even in states where recreational marijuana remains illegal, a strong medical marijuana movement has led to the drug's use on a prescription basis. Consequently, by early 2015, twenty-one states and the District of Columbia had laws legalizing marijuana in some form.

Advocates of legalization argue that by controlling and taxing drug sales states can enhance revenues, while eliminating the social stigma and overcrowded jails associated with arrests for possession of small amounts of the drug.

For its part, the U.S. Department of Justice, under an Obama administration mandate, issued a memorandum to federal prosecutors in 2013 asking them to refrain from marijuana prosecutions unless the drug was sold through criminal enterprises or cartels, or made available to children.

Even so, huge disparities exist between jurisdictions, and some law enforcement officials see marijuana as a gateway drug to more serious drug abuse. Chapter 16 contains more information on the marijuana legalization debate.

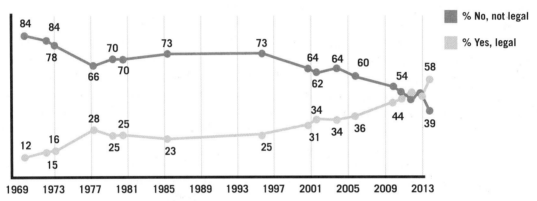

% No, not legal

% Yes, legal

FIGURE 2-8 | American's Views on Legalizing Marijuana

Do you think the use of marijuana should be made legal, or not?

Source: Pearson Education, Inc.

References: Art Swift, "For First Time, Americans Favor Legalizing Marijuana," *Gallup*, http://www.gallup.com/poll/165539/first-time-americans-favor-legalizing-marijuana.aspx, October 22, 2013; U.S. Dept. of Justice, Memorandum for all United States Attorneys, "Guidance Regarding Marijuana Enforcement," August 29, 2013; Marc Fisher, "Even as Marijuana Gains Ground, Some Tightly Enforce Laws," *Washington Post*, June 21, 2014, http://www.washingtonpost.com/politics/even-as-marijuana-gains-ground-some-tightly-enforce-laws/2014/06/21/2d0f8230-d21d-11e3-9e25-188ebe1fa93b_story.html.

Terrorism

Following the September 11, 2001, attacks on the World Trade Center and the Pentagon, terrorism and its prevention became primary concerns of American justice system officials. Long before September 11, however, terrorism was far from unknown. In 2001, for example, terrorist attacks totaled 864 worldwide—down from the 1,106 reported a year earlier.[129]

To assist in developing protection for the nation's critical infrastructure, the Homeland Security Act of 2002 created the Department of Homeland Security and made its director a cabinet member. Visit the Department of Homeland Security via **http://www.dhs.gov**. Terrorism and efforts to combat it are discussed in detail in Chapter 17, "Terrorism and Multinational Criminal Justice and Global Issues."

A commuter being helped away from the Edgware Road Underground Station following terrorist bombings in London's subway system in 2005. How might future acts of terrorism be prevented?

Jane Mingay/AP Wide World Photos

SUMMARY

- The FBI's UCR Program began in the 1930s when Congress authorized the U.S. attorney general to survey crime in America. Today's UCR/NIBRS Program provides annual data on the number of reported Part I offenses, or major crimes, as well as information about arrests that have been made for less serious Part II offenses. The Part I offenses are murder, rape, robbery, aggravated assault, burglary, larceny-theft, motor vehicle theft, and arson. The Part II offense category covers many more crimes, including drug offenses, driving under the influence, and simple assault. Modifications to the UCR Program, which has traditionally provided only summary crime data, are occurring with the implementation of the new National Incident-Based Reporting System (NIBRS). NIBRS, which represents a significant redesign of the original UCR Program, gathers many details about each criminal incident, such as place of occurrence, weapon used, type and value of property damaged or stolen, the personal characteristics of the offender and the victim, the nature of any relationship between the two, and the disposition of the complaint.

- The National Crime Victimization Survey (NCVS) is the second major source of statistical data about crime in the United States. The NCVS, which was first conducted in 1972, is based on victim self-reports rather than on police reports. The NCVS originally built on efforts by both the National Opinion Research Center and the 1967 President's Commission on Law Enforcement and the Administration of Justice to uncover what some had been calling the *dark figure of crime*—that is, those crimes that are not reported to the police and that are relatively hidden from justice system officials. An analysis of victim self-report data led to the realization that crimes of all types were more prevalent than UCR statistics had previously indicated.

- Significant differences exist between the UCR/NIBRS and the NCVS. For example, UCR/NIBRS data are primarily based on citizens' crime reports to the police, whereas NCVS data are gathered by field researchers who interview randomly selected households throughout the country. These and other differences lead to significant variation in the crime rates reported under both programs.

- It is important to recognize that UCR/NIBRS and NCVS data do not necessarily provide a complete picture of crime in America not only because they fail to capture what we have called the dark figure of crime, but also because the traditional reporting categories that they employ do not always encompass more innovative forms of crime such as those committed through the use of high technology or certain forms of white-collar crime.

- This chapter introduces a number of special categories of crime, including crime against women, crime against the elderly, hate crime, corporate and white-collar crime, organized crime, gun crime, drug crime, cybercrime, and terrorism. Each of these categories is of special concern in contemporary society and most are covered in greater detail in later chapters.

KEY TERMS

aggravated assault, 46
arson, 52
assault, 46
Bureau of Justice Statistics (BJS), 32
burglary, 46
clearance rate, 39
corporate crime, 61
Crime Index, 33
crime typology, 56
cybercrime, 65
cyberstalking, 57
dark figure of crime, 54
date rape, 43
hate crime, 59
identity theft, 50
larceny-theft, 48
motor vehicle theft, 51
murder, 41

National Crime Victimization Survey (NCVS), 32
National Incident-Based Reporting System (NIBRS), 34
organized crime, 61
Part I offenses, 41
Part II offenses, 52
property crime, 39
rape, 43
robbery, 45
self-reports, 32
sexual battery, 43
stalking, 56
transnational organized crime, 62
Uniform Crime Reporting (UCR) Program, 32
violent crime, 39
white-collar crime, 61

QUESTIONS FOR REVIEW

1. Describe the historical development of the FBI's Uniform Crime Reporting Program, and list the crimes on which it reports. How is the ongoing implementation of the National Incident-Based Reporting System (NIBRS) changing the UCR Program? How will data reported under the new UCR/NIBRS differ from the crime statistics reported under the traditional UCR Program?

2. Describe the history of the National Crime Victimization Survey (NCVS). What do data from the NCVS tell us about crime in the United States today?

3. What significant differences between the UCR/NIBRS and NCVS programs can be identified?

4. What are the special categories of crime discussed in this chapter? Why are they important?

QUESTIONS FOR REFLECTION

1. What can crime statistics tell us about the crime picture in America? How has that picture changed over time?

2. What are the potential sources of error in the nation's major crime reports? Can you think of some popular use of crime statistics today that might be especially misleading?

3. Why are many crime statistics expressed as rates? How does the use of crime rates instead of simple numerical tabulations improve the usefulness of crime data?

4. Do "traditional" UCR/NIBRS and NCVS categories accurately reflect the changing nature of crime in America? Why or why not?

5. This chapter recognizes the changing nature of crime. What might crime rates look like if all types of crime today could be captured by traditional crime reporting systems?

6. Do some property crimes have a violent aspect? Are there any personal crimes that could be nonviolent? If so, what might they be?

7. What is a clearance rate? What does it mean to say that a crime has been "cleared"? What are the different ways in which a crime can be cleared?

NOTES

i. Identity Theft Resource Center website, http://www.idtheftcenter.org (accessed November 24, 2014).

ii. Ibid.

iii. Andrew Backover, "Two Former WorldCom Execs Charged," *USA Today* online, August 1, 2002, http://www.usatoday.com/money/industries/telecom/2003-08-01-worldcom-execs-surrender_x.htm (accessed August 2, 2006).

iv. The Organized Crime Control Act of 1970.

1. "Video: Tennessee Sheriff's Office Pays Ransom for Case Files," *Police Magazine*, November 13, 2014, http://www.policemag.com/channel/technology/news/2014/11/13/video-tennessee-sheriff-s-office-pays-ransom-for-case-files.aspx?utm_campaign=OnTarget-Thursday-New-20141113&utm_source=Email&utm_medium=Enewsletter (accessed February 4, 2015).

2. Herbert Packer, *The Limits of Criminal Sanction* (Stanford: Stanford University Press, 1968), p. 364.

3. Norval Morris, "Crime, the Media, and Our Public Discourse," National Institute of Justice, Perspectives on Crime and Justice video series, recorded May 13, 1997.

4. Federal Bureau of Investigation, *Crime in the United States, 1987* (Washington, DC: U.S. Dept. of Justice, 1988), p. 1.

5. Federal Bureau of Investigation, "Uniform Crime Reports," http://www2.fbi.gov/ucr/ucr.htm (accessed May 4, 2015).

6. See the FBI's UCR/NIBRS website at http://www.fbi.gov/hq/cjisd/ucr.htm (accessed November 24, 2014).

7. The 1990 Crime Awareness and Campus Security Act (Public Law 101-542) required college campuses to commence publishing annual security reports beginning in September 1992.

8. U.S. Department of Education, The Campus Safety and Security Data Analysis Cutting Tool, http://ope.ed.gov/security/GroupDetails.aspx (accessed May 4, 2015).

9. Katrina Baum and Patsy Klaus, *Violent Victimization of College Students, 1995–2002* (Washington, DC: Bureau of Justice Statistics, 2005).

10. Federal Bureau of Investigation, *Crime in the United States, 2014* (Washington, DC: U.S. Dept. of Justice, 2015).

11. The President's Commission on Law Enforcement and Administration of Justice, *The Challenge of Crime in a Free Society* (Washington, DC: U.S. Government Printing Office, 1967). The commission relied on Uniform Crime Reports data.

The other crime statistics reported in this section come from Uniform Crime Reports for various years.

12. Frank Hagan, *Research Methods in Criminal Justice and Criminology* (New York: Macmillan, 1982).

13. U.S. Department of Justice, *Fiscal Years 2000–2005 Strategic Plan* (Washington, DC: U.S. Government Printing Office, 2000).

14. The "war on drugs," and the use of that term, can be traced back to the Nixon administration. See Dan Baum, *Smoke and Mirrors: The War on Drugs and the Politics of Failure*, reprint ed. (Boston: Little, Brown, 1997).

15. Marc Santora, "In Hours, Thieves Took $45 Million in A.T.M. Scheme," *The New York Times*, May 9, 2013.

16. Some such crimes are reportable as crimes of theft. See, Jack Nicas, "Crime That No Longer Pays," *Wall Street Journal*, February 4, 2013, professional.wsj.com/article/SB10001424127887323926104578274541161239474.html (accessed March 3, 2015).

17. Wendy Ruderman, "Crime Report Manipulation Is Common among New York Police, Study Finds," *New York Times*, June 28, 2012, http://www.nytimes.com/2012/06/29/nyregion/new-york-police-department-manipulates-crime-reports-study-finds.html (accessed July 10, 2014).

18. Ben Poston and John Diedrich, "Flynn Orders Training on FBI Crime Reporting Standards," *Milwaukee Journal Sentinel*, http://www.jsonline.com/watchdog/watchdogreports/flynn-orders-training-on-fbi-crime-reporting-standards-db628gg-162006545.html (accessed June 11, 2014).

19. John J. DiIulio, Jr., "The Question of Black Crime," *Public Interest* (fall 1994), pp. 3–12.

20. Quoted in Dan Eggen, "Major Crimes in U.S. Increase: 2001 Rise Follows Nine Years of Decline," *Washington Post*, June 23, 2002.

21. Jeremy Gorner, "In Chicago, Killings and Questions on the Rise," *Chicago Tribune*, December 30, 2012, http://www.chicagotribune.com/news/local/ct-met-chicago-violence-2012-20121230,0,186137.story (accessed January 3, 2014); Darran Simon, "Cracking Camden's Killings," *Philadelphia Inquirer*, December 30, 2012, http://articles.philly.com/2012-12-30/news/36065156_1_homicide-unit-reluctant-witnesses-killings (accessed January 3, 2014); and George Hunter and Mike Wilkinson, "Detroit Homicides Climb 10%," *The Detroit News*, December 31, 2012 (accessed January 4, 2013).

22. See Tim Johnson, "Mexico's War on Crime Now Ranks among Latin America's Bloodiest Conflicts," *McClatchy Newspapers*, February 21, 2013, www.mcclatchydc.com/2013/02/21/183820/mexicos-war-on-crime-now-ranks.html (accessed May 2, 2014); and Alan Taylor, "Mexico's Drug War: 50,000 Dead in Six Years," *The Atlantic*, May 17, 2012, http://www.theatlantic.com/infocus/2012/05/mexicos-drug-war-50-000-dead-in-6-years/100299/ (accessed May 2, 2014).

23. Paul Knepper, "Measuring the Threat of Global Crime: Insights from Research by the League of Nations into the Traffic in Women," *Criminology*, April 2012, doi: 10.1111/j.1745-9125.2012.00277.x.

24. That is, whereas crime clock data may imply that one murder occurs every half hour or so, most murders actually occur during the evening, and only a very few take place around sunrise.

25. Most offense definitions in this chapter are derived from those used by the UCR/NIBRS Program and are taken from the FBI's *Crime in the United States, 2014* or from the Bureau of Justice Statistics, *Criminal Justice Data Terminology*, 2nd ed. (Washington, DC: BJS, 1981).

26. These and other statistics in this chapter are derived primarily from the FBI's *Crime in the United States, 2014.*

27. Bureau of Justice Statistics, *Report to the Nation on Crime and Justice,* 2nd ed. (Washington, DC: U.S. Government Printing Office, 1988), p. 4.

28. "Feds Deny Thwarting Sniper Suspect's Confession," CNN.com, October 31, 2002, http://www.cnn.com/2002/US/10/30/snip ers.interrogation/index.html (accessed October 31, 2002).

29. "Sniper Malvo Given Second Life Sentence," *USA Today,* October 27, 2004.

30. BJS, *Report to the Nation on Crime and Justice,* p. 4.

31. Ibid.

32. For excellent coverage of serial killers, see Steven Egger, *The Killers among Us: An Examination of Serial Murder and Its Investigation* (Upper Saddle River, NJ: Prentice Hall, 1998); Steven A. Egger, *Serial Murder: An Elusive Phenomenon* (Westport, CT: Praeger, 1990); and Stephen J. Giannangelo, *The Psychopathology of Serial Murder: A Theory of Violence* (New York: Praeger, 1996).

33. "BTK" stands for "Bind, Torture, and Kill," an acronym that Rader applied to himself in letters he sent to the media during the 1970s.

34. Several years ago, Lucas recanted all of his confessions, saying that he had never killed anyone—except possibly his mother, a killing he said he didn't remember. See "Condemned Killer Admits Lying, Denies Slayings," *Washington Post,* October 1, 1995.

35. Chikatilo was executed in 1994.

36. See Mark Babineck, "Railroad Killer Gets Death Penalty," Associated Press, May 22, 2000, http://cnews.tribune.com/news/tribune/story/0,1235,tribune-nation-37649,00.html (accessed March 3, 2002).

37. Public Law 108-212.

38. Email communication with the Criminal Justice Information Services Division of the FBI, January 6, 2012.

39. FBI, "UCR Offense Definitions," http://ucrdatatool.gov/offenses.cfm (accessed May 5, 2014).

40. "Study: Rape Vastly Underreported," Associated Press, April 26, 1992.

41. Ronald Barri Flowers, *Women and Criminality: The Woman as Victim, Offender, and Practitioner* (Westport, CT: Greenwood Press, 1987), p. 36.

42. A. Nichols Groth, *Men Who Rape: The Psychology of the Offender* (New York: Plenum Press, 1979).

43. Susan Brownmiller, *Against Our Will: Men, Women, and Rape* (New York: Simon and Schuster, 1975).

44. Dennis J. Stevens, "Motives of Social Rapists," *Free Inquiry in Creative Sociology,* Vol. 23, No. 2 (November 1995), pp. 117–126.

45. BJS, *Report to the Nation on Crime and Justice,* p. 5.

46. Under NIBRS, one offense is recorded for each victim of a crime against person; one offense for each distinct operation of a crime against property (with the exception of motor vehicle theft, where one offense is counted for each stolen vehicle); and one offense for each crime against society.

47. FBI, *Crime in the United States, 2014.* For UCR reporting purposes, minorities are defined as African Americans, Native Americans, Asians, Pacific Islanders, and Alaska Natives.

48. "Easter Bunny Charged with Battery for Mall Attack," Associated Press, April 18, 2006.

49. This offense is sometimes called assault with a deadly weapon with intent to kill (AWDWWITK).

50. FBI, *Crime in the United States, 2014.*

51. BJS, *Report to the Nation on Crime and Justice,* p. 6.

52. Ibid.

53. Ed Mazza, "Grass Thieves Allegedly Caught on Video Stealing Freshly Laid Sod From Home," *The Huffington Post,* August 26, 2014, http://www.huffingtonpost.com/2014/08/26/grass-thieves-caught-on-video_n_5713215.html (accessed January 5, 2015).

54. "Yale Says Student Stole His Education," *USA Today,* April 12, 1995.

55. FBI, Criminal Justice Information Services Division, *National Incident-Based Reporting System, Volume 1: Data Collection Guidelines* (Washington, DC: USDOJ, 2000), pp. 19-20.

56. Jessica Silver-Greenberg, Matthew Goldstein, and Nicole Perlroth, "Cyberattacks Against JPMorgan Chase Affects 76 Million Households," *The New York Times,* October 2, 2014, http://dealbook.nytimes.com/2014/10/02/jpmorgan-discovers-further-cyber-security-issues (accessed January 5, 2015).

57. Ibid.

58. Erika Harrell, *Victims of Identity Theft, 2014* (Washington, DC: Bureau of Justice Statistics, 2015).

59. Ibid.

60. Katrina Baum, *Identity Theft, 2005* (Washington, DC: Bureau of Justice Statistics, 2007).

61. U.S. Code, Title 18, Section 1028.

62. Public Law 108–275.

63. Much of the information in this paragraph is adapted from National White Collar Crime Center, "Identity Theft," http://www.nw3c.org/research/site_files.cfm?fileid=935cdacc-b138-483a-8d05-83e6fd3d9004&mode=w (accessed November 24, 2014).

64. FBI, *Uniform Crime Reporting Handbook, 2004,* p. 28.

65. Patsy Klaus, *Carjacking, 1993–2002* (Washington, DC: Bureau of Justice Statistics, July 2004).

66. FBI, *Crime in the United States, 2014.*

67. As indicated in the UCR definition of arson. See Federal Bureau of Investigation, *Crime in the United States, 1998* (Washington, DC: U.S. Dept. of Justice, 1999).

68. FBI, *Crime in the United States, 2014.*

69. Ibid.

70. "Trends in Crime and Victimization," *Criminal Justice Research Reports,* Vol. 2, No. 6 (July/August 2001), p. 83.

71. Jennifer Truman and Lynn Langton, *Criminal Victimization, 2014* (Washington, DC: Bureau of Justice Statistics, September 2015).

72. For additional information, see Jennifer L. Truman and Lynn Langton, *Criminal Victimization, 2014* (Washington, DC: Bureau of Justice Statistics, 2015); and Patsy A. Klaus, *Crime and the Nation's Households, 2006* (Washington, DC: Bureau of Justice Statistics, 2007).

73. Truman and Langton, *Criminal Victimization, 2014.*

74. Ibid.

75. See, for example, President's Commission on Law Enforcement and Administration of Justice, *The Challenge of Crime in a Free Society,* pp. 22–23.

76. BJS, *Report to the Nation on Crime and Justice,* p. 27.

77. FBI, Criminal Justice Information Services Division, *The Measurement of White-Collar Crime Using Uniform Crime Reporting (UCR) Data* (Washington, DC: FBI, no date), http://www.fbi.gov/about-us/cjis/ucr/nibrs/nibrs_wcc.pdf (accessed November 24, 2014).

78. It is the national UCR Program's official position that "Computer crime actually involves the historical common-law offenses of larceny, embezzlement, trespass, etc., which are

being perpetrated through the use of a new tool, the computer." Therefore, according to the FBI, "if larcenies, embezzlements, and trespasses relating to computers were to be reported under a new classification called Computer Crime, the national UCR Program's traditional time series relating to such crimes would be distorted." To avoid such a result, NIBRS provides the capability to indicate whether a computer was the object of the crime and/ or to indicate whether the offenders used computer equipment to perpetrate a crime. The FBI says that "this ensures the continuance of the traditional crime statistics and at the same time flags incidents that involve Computer Crime." FBI, Criminal Justice Information Services Division, *National Incident-Based Reporting System, Volume 1: Data Collection Guidelines* (Washington, DC: USDOJ, 2000), pp. 19–20.

79. Hagan, *Research Methods in Criminal Justice and Criminology*, p. 89.

80. Bureau of Justice Statistics, *Criminal Victimization in the United States, 1985* (Washington, DC: U.S. Government Printing Office, 1987), p. 1.

81. FBI, *Crime in the United States, 2001*, preliminary data, http:// www.fbi.gov./ucr/01prelim.pdf (accessed August 27, 2002).

82. Terance D. Miethe and Richard C. McCorkle, *Crime Profiles: The Anatomy of Dangerous Persons, Places, and Situations* (Los Angeles: Roxbury, 1998), p. 19.

83. Following a recent change in UCR/NIBRS offense definitions, same-sex rape is now included in the official count for crimes of rape.

84. Truman and Langton, *Criminal Victimization, 2015*, p. 6.

85. Thomas Simon et al., *Injuries from Violent Crime, 1992–98* (Washington, DC: Bureau of Justice Statistics, 2001), p. 5.

86. See, for example, Elizabeth Stanko, "When Precaution Is Normal: A Feminist Critique of Crime Prevention," in Loraine Gelsthorpe and Allison Morris, eds., *Feminist Perspectives in Criminology* (Philadelphia: Open University Press, 1990).

87. For more information, see Eve S. Buzawa and Carl G. Buzawa, *Domestic Violence: The Criminal Justice Response* (Thousand Oaks, CA: Sage, 1996).

88. "Battered Women Tell Their Stories to the Senate," *Charlotte (NC) Observer*, July 10, 1991, p. 3A.

89. Patricia Tjaden and Nancy Thoennes, *Full Report of the Prevalence, Incidence, and Consequences of Violence against Women: Findings from the National Violence against Women Survey* (Washington, DC: National Institute of Justice, 2000).

90. Michele C. Black, et al., *The National Intimate Partner and Sexual Violence Survey: 2010 Summary Report* (Atlanta, GA: National Center for Injury Prevention and Control, 2011).

91. VAWA 2005 was signed into law by President George W. Bush on January 5, 2006. It is officially known as the Violence against Women and Department of Justice Reauthorization Act of 2005 (Public Law 109–162).

92. Violence against Women Office, *Stalking and Domestic Violence: Report to Congress* (Washington, DC: U.S. Dept. of Justice, 2001).

93. U.S. Code, Title 18, Section 2261A.

94. As modified through VAWA 2000.

95. Violence against Women Office, *Stalking and Domestic Violence*.

96. Many of the data in this section come from Bureau of Justice Statistics, *Crimes against Persons Age 65 or Older, 1993–2002* (Rockville, MD: BJS, 2005).

97. Lamar Jordan, "Law Enforcement and the Elderly: A Concern for the Twenty-First Century," *FBI Law Enforcement Bulletin*, May 2002, pp. 20–23.

98. Public Law 101–275.

99. H.R. 4797, 102d Cong. 2d Sess. (1992).

100. FBI, "Bias Breakdown," http://www.fbi.gov/news/stories/2014/ december/latest-hate-crime-statistics-report-released/latest-hate -crime-statistics-report-released (accessed January 10, 2015).

101. "Sept. 11 Attacks Cited in Nearly 25 Percent Increase in Florida Hate Crimes," Associated Press, August 30, 2002.

102. Title 18 U.S. Code, Section 245.

103. Southern Poverty Law Center, "Extremist Files," http://www .splcenter.org/node/3502/activegroups (accessed January 6, 2015).

104. Clifford Krauss, "Jury Convicts Stanford in $7 Billion Ponzi Fraud," *New York Times*, March 6, 2012, http://www.nytimes .com/2012/03/07/business/jury-convicts-stanford-in-7-billion -ponzi-fraud.html (accessed May 15, 2014).

105. Richard Esposito, Eloise Harper, and Maddy Sauer, "Bernie Madoff Pleads Guilty to Ponzi Scheme, Goes Straight to Jail, Says He's 'Deeply Sorry,'" ABC News, March 12, 2009, http:// abcnews.go.com/Blotter/WallStreet/Story?id=7066715&page=1 (accessed July 4, 2009).

106. Joanna Chung and Henny Sender, "Investors Fear $50bn Loss in Madoff's 'Big Lie,'" *Financial Times*, December 14, 2008.

107. Diana B. Henriques, "Madoff Is Sentenced to 150 Years for Ponzi Scheme," *New York Times*, June 29, 2009, http://www .nytimes.com/2009/06/30/business/30madoff.html (accessed September 28, 2010).

108. Dina ElBoghdady, "Mortgage Fraud Up as Credit Tightens," *Washington Post*, March 17, 2009, http://www.washingtonpost .com/wp-dyn/content/article/2009/03/16/AR2009031601612 .html (accessed May 13, 2009).

109. Jennifer Liberto, "More Muscle Sought in Fraud Fight," CNNMoney.com, May 8, 2009, http://money.cnn.com/2009/ 05/08/news/economy/mortgage_fraud/index.htm (accessed May 13, 2009).

110. Federal Trade Commission, "Federal and State Agencies Crack Down on Mortgage Modification and Foreclosure Rescue Scams," http://www.ftc.gov/opa/2009/04/hud.shtm (accessed November 24, 2014).

111. *Andersen v. U.S.*, 544 U.S. 696 (2005).

112. Public Broadcasting System, "Enron: After the Collapse," http:// www.pbs.org/newshour/bb/business/enron/player6.html (accessed August 27, 2005).

113. Edwin H. Sutherland, "White-Collar Criminality," *American Sociological Review* (February 1940), p. 12.

114. Public Law 107-204.

115. R. James Woolsey, as quoted on the Transnational Threats Initiative home page of the Center for Strategic and International Studies (CSIS), http://www.csis.org/tnt/index.htm (accessed August 22, 2007).

116. These ideas were originally expressed by Assistant U.S. Attorney General Laurie Robinson in an address given at the Twelfth International Congress on Criminology, Seoul, Korea, August 28, 1998.

117. Caroline Wolf Harlow, *Firearm Use by Offenders* (Washington, DC: Bureau of Justice Statistics, 2001).

118. Ibid, p. 1.

119. Ibid.

120. John C. Moorhouse and Brent Wanner, "Does Gun Control Reduce Crime or Does Crime Increase Gun Control?" *CATO Journal*, Vol. 103 (2006), pp. 103–124.

121. Sarah Brady, "Statement on the Sniper Shootings," October 8, 2002, http://www.bradycampaign.org/press/release .asp?Record 5429 (accessed October 16, 2005).

122. J. M. Chaiken and M. R. Chaiken, *Varieties of Criminal Behavior* (Santa Monica, CA: RAND Corporation, 1982).

123. D. McBride, "Trends in Drugs and Death," paper presented at the annual meeting of the American Society of Criminology, Denver, 1983.

124. National Criminal Justice Reference Service, "The Micro Domain: Behavior and Homicide," p. 140, http://www.ncjrs .org/pdffiles/167262-3.pdf (accessed February 23, 2007).

125. Bureau of Justice Statistics, *Substance Abuse and Treatment: State and Federal Prisoners* (Washington, DC: U.S. Dept. of Justice, January 1999).

126. Bureau of Justice Statistics, *Drug Use, Testing, and Treatment in Jails* (Washington, DC: U.S. Dept. of Justice, May 2000).

127. M. Tcherni, A. Davies, G. Lopes, and A. Lizotte, "The Dark Figure of Online Property Crime: Is Cyberspace Hiding a Crime Wave?" *Justice Quarterly*, DOI: 10.1080/07418825.2014.994658.

128. Details for this story come from Carol Cratty, "245 Arrested in U.S.-Led Child Sex Abuse Operation," CNN, January 4, 2013, http://www.cnn.com/2013/01/03/us/ice-child-abuse-arrests (accessed November 24, 2014).

129. Emergency Response and Research Institute, "Summary of Emergency Response and Research Institute Terrorism Statistics: 2000 and 2001," http://www.emergency.com/2002/ terroris00-01.pdf (accessed August 22, 2011).

TOP 10 MOST WANTED

Yaser Abdel Said

Capital Murder - Multiple

1-800-CALL-FBI

2006 PHOTO

© Ice Tea Media/Alamy

3

THE SEARCH FOR CAUSES

OUTLINE

- Introduction
- Criminological Theory
- Classical and Neoclassical Theory
- Early Biological Theories
- Biosocial Theories
- Psychological Theories
- Sociological Theories
- Social Process Theories
- Conflict Theories
- Emergent Perspectives

LEARNING OBJECTIVES

After reading this chapter, you should be able to

- Summarize the development of criminological theory, including the role of social research in that development.
- Describe the Classical School of criminology, including how it continues to influence criminological theorizing through neoclassical thought.
- Describe the basic features of biological theories of crime causation and their shortcomings.
- Explain biosocial criminology and show how biosocial understanding of criminal behavior focus on the interaction between biology and the social and physical environments.
- Describe the fundamental assumptions of psychological explanations for crime and their shortcomings.
- Describe the basic features of sociological theories of crime causation.
- Describe social process theories of criminology, including the kinds of crime-control policies that might be based on them.
- Describe conflict theories of criminality, including the kinds of crime-control policies that might be based on them.
- Summarize two emerging theories of criminology.

Society prepares the crime; the criminal commits it.

HENRY THOMAS BUCKLE

■ **Follow the author's tweets about the latest crime and justice news @schmalleger.**
■ **lecture note** Review the definitions of crime and deviant behavior, and the differences between them.

■ **deviance** A violation of social norms defining appropriate or proper behavior under a particular set of circumstances. Deviance often includes criminal acts.

Introduction

In 2015, Marion "Surge" Knight, the founder of Death Row Records, was arrested and charged with murder following an incident in which two men were allegedly run over by the rap musician's red pickup truck in Compton, California. One of the men died, while the other was seriously injured. Knight's attorney claimed that his client had accidentally run over the men as he was fleeing attackers. Knight has a long history of arrests and run-ins with the law, with charges ranging from gun law violations to assaults and robbery. Months before the incident, he had been shot six times at a Los Angeles nightclub.[1]

Violent crime is no stranger to the world of hard-core rap music. In 2013, aspiring Oakland (California) rapper Kenny Clutch (Kenneth Cherry, Jr.) died after the Maserati he was driving was peppered with bullets from a passing Range Rover and crashed into a Yellow cab at a Las Vegas intersection, causing a fiery explosion.[2] The shooting, which happened at 4:20 a.m. on Las Vegas Boulevard, apparently stemmed from a dispute at a nearby hotel. The incident happened just two blocks from the location of a 1996 shooting in which rapper Tupac Shakur was killed.

Similarly, in an event that is still discussed today, hip-hop artist Curtis "50 Cent" Jackson, a rising star in the world of hard-core rap music, was shot nine times in front of his grandmother's home in New York City in 2000.[3] One of the bullets hit him in the face. "50," as the singer is known to his fans, survived the shooting but spent months recovering. Murdered rap stars include Tupac Shakur, Notorious B.I.G., Big L., and the Lost Boyz's hip-hop hype man Raymond "Freaky Tah" Rogers.

Whether rap music merely reflects the social conditions under which its artists come of age or whether it is a direct cause of the violence that surrounds them is a question to which we will return shortly. One clue is provided by Pusha T (aka Push), who has performed with Ross, as he explains: "It's tough out here as an artist and being in rap it's like this is the only profession where you don't really leave your core. You don't really leave your upbringing. You don't really leave that behind; you stay in it lyrically and so on and so forth. So it's like you can't really get out of it, you can't really get away from it. I don't care how much money you have."[4]

No discussion of crime and of the criminal justice system would be complete without considering the *causes* of crime and **deviance**, and the idea that certain types of music lead to law violation provides one theory of crime causation. Criminologists search for answers to the fundamental questions about what causes crime: Why do people commit crime? What are the root causes of violence and aggression? Are people basically good, or are they motivated only by self-interest? More precisely, we might ask why a particular person commits a particular crime on a given occasion and under specific circumstances.

In this chapter, we will look at the causes of crime. Before we begin, however, some brief definitions are in order. *Crime*, as noted in Chapter 1, is a violation of the criminal law without acceptable legal justification,[5] whereas *deviant behavior* is a violation of social norms that specify appropriate or proper behavior under a particular set of circumstances. Deviant behavior is a broad category that often includes crime.

Many theories have been advanced to explain all sorts of rule-violating behavior. As is the case with the story that opened this chapter, some observers of the contemporary scene blame much of today's crime on commonplace episodes of violence in the

Deviant behavior is a broad category that often includes crime, but not all deviance is criminal.

© Randy Miramontez/Alamy

Rapper and Death Row Records founder, Surge Knight. In 2015, Knight was charged with murder after allegedly running over two men in a California parking lot. Some claim that rap and other forms of hip-hop music lead to crime. What do you think?

■ **activity**   Some prisons provide inmate speakers. These are usually "honor-grade" inmates who have progressed through a speaker's training program and who can be depended on to provide a good classroom experience. If a prison in your area has such a program, arrange to have an inmate speaker brought to the classroom. Have students outline selected theories of criminal behavior from this chapter and be ready to present them briefly to the speaker during a question-and-answer session. Students can then ask which theoretical approach the inmate speaker finds most applicable in terms of his or her own experience.

■ **theme**   How do we judge when a theory is useful? Can the same theory be useful in different ways for different people? Can we agree on an ultimate criterion of usefulness for a "good" theory?

■ **lecture note**   Explain the concept of a theory. Describe the similarities and differences between the physical and social sciences as they relate to theory building.

■ **lecture note**   Refer to Figure 3-1 and review the basic steps in building theories and creating social policies.

■ **theory**   A set of interrelated propositions that attempt to describe, explain, predict, and ultimately control some class of events. A theory is strengthened by its logical consistency and is "tested" by how well it describes and predicts reality.

American media—especially on television, in music, and on film. Experts who study the media estimate that the aver-age American child watches 8,000 murders and 100,000 acts of violence while growing up.[6] At an international conference, Suzanne Stutman, president of the Institute for Mental Health Initiatives, a nonprofit organization in Washington, D.C., reported that studies consistently show that the extent of exposure to television violence in childhood is a good predictor of future criminal behavior.[7] One particular study found that watching just one hour of television a day can make a person more violent toward others.[8] The study, which was conducted over a 25-year period at New York's Columbia University and published in 2002, used police records to confirm that 45% of young men who had watched three or more hours of television a day went on to commit at least one aggressive act against another person, compared to 9% of young men who had watched TV for less than one hour per day.

An African American critic of gangsta rap puts it this way: "The key element is aggression—in rappers' body language, tone, and witty rhymes—that often leaves listeners hyped, on edge, angry about … something. Perhaps the most important element in gangsta rap is its messages, which center largely around these ideas: that women are no more than 'bitches and ho's,' disposable playthings who exist merely for men's abusive delight; that it's cool to use any means necessary to get the material things you want; and most importantly, it's admirable to be cold-blooded and hard."[9] The Reverend Arthur L. Cribbs, Jr., an African American social commentator, agrees. Cribbs calls gangsta rap "nothing but modern-day violence and vulgarity wrapped and packaged in blackface."[10]

Most people agree that media violence harms society. According to one survey, "57% of the public thinks violence in the media is a major factor in real-life violence" of all kinds.[11] But it is less than clear whether violence in the media and aggressive themes in popular music are indeed a cause of crime, as many believe, or merely a reflection of the social conditions that exist in many American communities today. Findings from studies on the effect of television viewing, for example, may be inadvertently spotlighting existing criminal tendencies among lower-class undereducated teenagers with enough time on their hands for extensive TV viewing. Hence getting legislators to address the issue of violence in the media is sometimes difficult. Moreover, in 2011, the U.S. Supreme Court weighed in with an important decision in the case of *Brown* v. *Entertainment Merchants Association*, in which it ruled that a state law in California restricting the sale or rental of violent computer games to minors was a violation of the First Amendment's guarantee of free speech.[12] The majority of justices held that computer games, "like protected books, plays, and movies, communicate ideas through familiar literary devices and features distinctive to the medium."[13]

Criminological Theory

It is easy to understand why the entertainment industry and the media are often targeted as the cause of crime and criminal violence.

> There is no single cause of crime; it is rooted in a diversity of causes and takes a variety of forms, depending on the situation in which it occurs.

However, many other types of explanations for crime are also viable, such as individual psychological differences, including personality disorders; variations in patterns of early socialization that may predispose some people to crime and violence; and biosocial perspectives that say crime arises out of a causal brew formed by the interaction of biological predispositions and the social environment. Similarly, it is prudent to examine social institutions such as the family, schools, churches, and even the police for their role in reducing or enhancing the likelihood of criminality among people.

One thing is certain: There is no single cause of crime; it is rooted in a diversity of causes and takes a variety of forms, depending on the situation in which it occurs. Nonetheless, some theories of human behavior help us understand why certain people engage in acts that society defines as criminal or deviant, while others do not. A **theory** is a kind of model. Theories posit relationships, often of a causal sort, between events and things under study. A theory's explanatory power derives primarily from its inherent logical consistency, and theories are tested by how well they describe and predict reality. In other words, a good theory fits the facts, and it stands up to continued scrutiny. Figure 3-1 uses the association between poverty and crime as an example to diagram the important aspects of theory creation in the social sciences.

History is rife with theories purporting to explain rule-violating behavior. For example, an old Roman theory, based on ancient observations that more crime and deviance occur on nights with a full moon, proposed that the moon causes a kind of temporary insanity, or *lunacy*. According to this theory,

■ **lecture note** Establish some criteria for a "good" theory, such as predictability. Ask students to rank those criteria in terms of importance.

■ **hypothesis** An explanation that accounts for a set of facts and that can be tested by further investigation. Also, something that is taken to be true for the purpose of argument or investigation.[i]

■ **lecture note** Explain why some theories are better than others—that is, why some are better at explaining, predicting, and so on. Discuss the fact that some theories serve the political ends of interest groups that find their world-views reaffirmed by a theory's assertions.

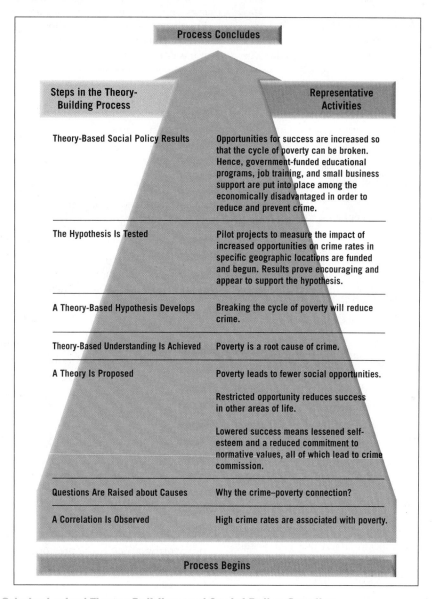

FIGURE 3-1 | Steps in Criminological Theory Building and Social Policy Creation

Source: Pearson Education, Inc.

deviant behavior isn't random; it waxes and wanes in cadence with the lunar cycle. Although modern statisticians have noted an association between phases of the moon and crime rates, the precise mechanism by which the moon influences behavior—if it does—has never been adequately explained.

As mentioned, a complete theory attempts to flesh out all of the causal links between phenomena that are associated or *correlated*. For example, some comprehensive theories of lunacy suggest that light from the full moon stimulates the reticular-activating system (RAS) in the limbic portion of the human brain, which makes people more excitable and hyperactive—and thus more likely to behave in deviant ways and to commit crime. Others have suggested, quite simply, that people commit more crimes when the moon is full because it is easier to see.

Theories, once created, must be tested to determine whether they are valid, and modern criminology has become increasingly scientific.[14] Theory testing usually involves the development of **hypotheses** based on what the theory under scrutiny would predict. A theory of lunacy, for example, might be tested in a variety of ways, including (1) observing rates of

■ **lecture note**　As you cover the various historical and contemporary perspectives on criminality, relate each school of thought to the criteria for a "good" theory.

■ **lecture note**　Suggest that each theoretical approach to crime causation can be characterized by the "locus" that it assigns to the root cause of crime. Explain that biological theories point to physiological causes, sociological theories highlight cultural circumstances, and so on.

■ **lecture note**　As you discuss the various theoretical approaches, show how particular treatment and rehabilitative strategies might derive from each school of thought on crime causation. For example, you could discuss imposing the death penalty or of life in prison without possibility of parole for offenders who are thought to be criminal by virtue of some biological defect.

■ **research**　The use of standardized, systematic procedures in the search for knowledge.

■ **lecture note**　Emphasize that the classical school emphasized free will and individual choice.

■ **interdisciplinary theory**　An approach that integrates a variety of theoretical viewpoints in an attempt to explain something, such as crime and violence.

■ **Classical School**　An eighteenth-century approach to crime causation and criminal responsibility that grew out of the Enlightenment and that emphasized the role of free will and reasonable punishment. Classical thinkers believed that punishment, if it is to be an effective deterrent, has to outweigh the potential pleasure derived from criminal behavior.

crime and deviance on nights when the light of the full moon is obscured by clouds (we would expect no rise in crime rates if the RAS or visibility explanations are correct) and (2) examining city crime rates on full-moon nights—especially in well-lit city areas where the light of the moon hardly increases visibility. If the predictions made by a theory are validated by careful observation, the theory gains greater acceptability.

Generally accepted research designs—coupled with careful data-gathering strategies and statistical techniques for data analysis—have yielded considerable confidence in certain explanations for crime, while at the same time disproving others. Theories of crime causation that have met rigorous scientific tests for acceptability give policymakers the intellectual basis they need to create informed crime-control strategies. The ultimate goal of **research** and theory building in criminology is to provide models that permit a better understanding of criminal behavior and that enhance the development of strategies, or policies, intended to address the problem of crime.

Although we will use the word *theory* in describing various explanations for crime throughout this chapter, it should be recognized that the word is only loosely applicable to some of the perspectives we will discuss. As noted, many social scientists insist that to be considered "theories," explanations must consist of sets of clearly stated, logically interrelated, and measurable propositions. The fact that few of the "theories" that follow rise above the level of organized conjecture, and that many others are not readily amenable to objective scrutiny through scientific testing, is one of the greatest failures of social science today.

Also, many contemporary theories of deviant and criminal behavior are far from complete, offering only limited ideas rather than comprehensive explanations for the behavior in question. Moreover, when we consider the wide range of behaviors regarded as criminal—from murder to drug use to terrorism to white-collar crime—it is difficult to imagine a theory that can explain them all.

For our purposes, explanations of criminal behavior fall into eight general categories:

- Classical and neoclassical
- Early biological
- Biosocial
- Psychological
- Sociological
- Social process
- Conflict
- Emergent

The differences among these approaches are summarized in Table 3-1. A ninth category could be **interdisciplinary theories**. Interdisciplinary approaches integrate a variety of theoretical viewpoints in an attempt to explain crime and violence. The Project on Human Development in Chicago Neighborhoods (PHDCN) is one example of an ongoing interdisciplinary study of the causes of crime. Described in more detail later in this chapter, the PHDCN project involves an examination of the roles of personality, school, and community as they contribute to juvenile delinquency and criminal behavior. See **http://www .justicestudies.com/pubs/phdcn.pdf** for more information on the project.

Classical and Neoclassical Theory

Theories of the **Classical School** of crime causation dominated criminological thought for much of the late eighteenth and early nineteenth centuries. These theories represented a noteworthy advance over previous thinking about crime because they moved beyond superstition and mysticism as explanations for deviance. As noted criminologist Stephen Schafer puts it, "In the eighteenth-century individualistic orientation of criminal law, the act was judged and the man made responsible."[15] A product of the Enlightenment then sweeping through Europe, the Classical School demanded recognition of rationality and the ability to exercise informed choice in human social life.

Most classical theories of crime causation, both old and new, make certain basic assumptions. Among them are these:

- Crime is caused by the individual exercise of free will. Human beings are fundamentally rational, and most human behavior is the result of free will coupled with rational choice.
- Pain and pleasure are the two central determinants of human behavior.

TABLE 3-1 | Types of Criminological Theory

TYPE & CONCEPTS	THEORISTS	CHARACTERISTICS
Classical and Neoclassical		
Free will theories	Beccaria	Crime is caused by the individual exercise of free will.
Hedonistic calculus Rational choice theory	Bentham Cohen & Felson	Prevention is possible through swift and certain punishment that offsets any gains to be had through criminal behavior.
Routine activities theory	Cohen & Felson	Lifestyles significantly affect both the amount and type of crime found in any society, and the risk of criminal victimization varies according to the circumstances and locations in which people place themselves and their property.
Early Biological		
Phrenology Atavism Criminal families Somatotypes Body types	Gall Lombroso Dugdale Goddard Sheldon	"Criminal genes" cause deviant behavior. Criminals are identifiable through physical characteristics or genetic makeup. Treatment is generally ineffective, but aggression may be usefully redirected.
Biosocial		
Gender ratio problem Genetics/chromosomes Hormones Nutrition Body chemistry Heredity/heritability Brain dysfunction	Wilson & Herrnstein Beaver Ellis Walsh Jacobs Raine	The interactions between human biology and the physical and social environments are key to understanding human behavior, including criminality.
Psychological		
Behavioral conditioning Psychoanalysis Psychopathology	Pavlov Freud Cleckley	Crime is the result of inappropriate behavioral conditioning or a diseased mind. Treatment necessitates extensive behavioral therapy.
Sociological		
Social disorganization Anomie	Park & Burgess Shaw & McKay Durkheim Merton	The structure of society and its relative degree of organization or disorganization are important actors contributing to the prevalence of criminal behavior.
Subcultures Focal concerns Subculture of violence	Cohen Miller Wolfgang & Ferracuti	Group dynamics, group organization, and subgroup relationships form the causal nexus out of which crime develops. Effective social policy may require basic changes in patterns of socialization and an increase in accepted opportunities for success.
Social Process		
Differential association Social learning Containment Social control Neutralization	Sutherland Burgess & Akers Reckless Hirschi Sykes & Matza	Crime results from the failure of self-direction, inadequate social roles, or association with defective others. Social policy places responsibility for change on the offender.
Labeling	Becker	The source of criminal behavior is unknown, but an understanding of crime requires recognition that the definition of crime is imposed on behavior by the wider society. Individuals defined as "criminal" may be excluded by society from "normal" opportunities. Therapy requires a total reorientation of the offender.
Social development Life course perspective	Terrie Moffitt Sampson & Laub	Human development occurs simultaneously on many levels, including psychological, biological, familial, interpersonal, cultural, societal, and ecological. The life course perspective notes that criminal behavior tends to follow an identifiable pattern throughout a person's life cycle.
Conflict		
Radical criminology	Turk Vold Chambliss	Conflict is fundamental to social life. Crime is a natural consequence of social, political, and economic inequities.
Peacemaking criminology	Pepinsky Quinney	Fundamental changes to the structure of society are needed to eliminate crime.
Emergent		
Feminist criminology	Adler Simon Daly & Chesney-Lind	Feminist criminology emphasizes the need for gender awareness in the criminological enterprise.
Postmodern criminology	Henry & Milovanovic	Deconstructionist approaches challenge existing theories in order to replace them with perspectives more relevant to the modern era.

Source: Pearson Education, Inc.

■ **theme**   How does neoclassical criminology differ from classical criminology? Why do you think the distinction is important?

■ **neoclassical criminology**   A contemporary version of classical criminology that emphasizes deterrence and retribution and that holds that human beings are essentially free to make choices in favor of crime and deviance or conformity to the law.

■ **rational choice theory**   A perspective on crime causation that holds that criminality is the result of conscious choice. Rational choice theory predicts that individuals will choose to commit crime when the benefits of doing so outweigh the costs of disobeying the law.

■ **routine activities theory (RAT)**   A neoclassical perspective that suggests that lifestyles contribute significantly to both the amount and the type of crime found in any society.

- Crime erodes the bond that exists between individuals and society and is therefore an immoral form of behavior.
- Punishment, a necessary evil, is sometimes required to deter law violators from repeating their crimes and to serve as an example to others who would also violate the law.
- Crime prevention is possible through swift and certain punishment that offsets any gains to be had through criminal behavior.

Cesare Beccaria: Crime and Punishment

In 1764, Cesare Beccaria (1738–1794) published his *Essays on Crimes and Punishment*. The book was an immediate success and stirred a hornet's nest of controversy over the treatment of criminal offenders. Beccaria proposed basic changes in the criminal laws of his day to make them more "humanitarian." He called for the abolition of physical punishment and an end to the death penalty. Beccaria is best remembered for his suggestion that punishment should be just sufficient to deter criminal behavior but should never be excessive. Because Beccaria's writings stimulated many other thinkers throughout the eighteenth and early nineteenth centuries, he is referred to today as the founder of the Classical School of criminology.

Jeremy Bentham: Hedonistic Calculus

Among those influenced by Beccaria was the Englishman Jeremy Bentham (1748–1832). Bentham devised a "hedonistic calculus," which essentially said that the exercise of free will would cause an individual to avoid committing a crime as long as the punishment for committing that crime outweighed the benefits to be derived from committing it. Bentham termed this philosophy of social control *utilitarianism*. Both Bentham and Beccaria agreed that punishment had to be "swift and certain"—as well as just—to be effective. Learn more about Jeremy Bentham at **http://www.ucl.ac.uk/Bentham-Project**.

The Neoclassical Perspective

A contemporary theory with roots in the Classical School, **neoclassical criminology** is a perspective that owes much to the early classical thinkers. Although classical criminology focuses primarily on pleasure and pain as motivators of human behavior, neoclassical criminology places greater emphasis on rationality and cognition. Central to such perspectives is **rational choice theory**, which holds that criminality is largely the result of conscious choices that people make. According to the theory, offenders choose to violate the law when they believe that the benefits of doing so outweigh the costs.

Rational choice theory is represented by a somewhat narrower perspective called **routine activities theory**, and referred to by the somewhat humorous acronym, **RAT**. Routine activities theory was first proposed by Lawrence Cohen and Marcus Felson in 1979.[16] Cohen and Felson argued that lifestyles significantly affect both the amount and type of crime found in any society, and they noted that "the risk of criminal victimization varies dramatically among the circumstances and locations in which people place themselves and their property."[17] Lifestyles that contribute to criminal opportunities are likely to result in crime because they increase the risk of potential victimization.[18] For example, a person who routinely uses an ATM late at night in an isolated location is far more likely to be preyed on by robbers than is someone who stays home after dark. Rational choice theorists concentrate on "the decision-making process of offenders confronted with specific contexts" and have shifted "the focus of the effort to prevent crime … from broad social programs to target hardening, environmental design or any impediment that would [dissuade] a motivated offender from offending."[19]

> Although classical criminology focuses primarily on pleasure and pain as determinants of human behavior, neoclassical criminology places greater emphasis on rationality and cognition.

Central to the routine activities approach is the claim that crime is likely to occur when a motivated offender and a suitable target come together in the absence of a *capable guardian*. Capable guardians are those who effectively discourage crime and prevent it from occurring. Members of neighborhood watch groups, for example, might be capable guardians. Capable guardians do not necessarily have to confront would-be offenders directly but might be people who have completed classes in crime prevention and who have taken steps to reduce their chances of victimization.

■ **lecture note**   Explain how biological theories (and other positivist theories) differ from classical criminology, particularly in their move away from the belief in free will.

■ **Biological School**   A perspective on criminological thought that holds that criminal behavior has a physiological basis.

■ **lecture note**   Remind students that not all theories are equally valid and that many are no longer accepted by criminologists.

■ **phrenology**   The study of the shape of the head to determine anatomical correlates of human behavior.

Social Policy and Classical Theories

Much of the practice of criminal justice in America today is built on concepts provided by Classical School theorists. Many

> Much of the practice of criminal justice in America today is built on concepts provided by Classical School theorists.

contemporary programs designed to prevent crime, for example, have their philosophical roots in the classical axioms of deterrence and punishment. Modern heirs of the Classical School see punishment as central to criminal justice policy, use evidence of high crime rates to argue that punishment is a necessary crime preventive, and believe punishment is a natural and deserved consequence of criminal activity. Such thinkers call for greater prison capacity and new prison construction. In Chapter 1, we used the term *public-order advocate*, which can be applied to modern-day proponents of classical theory who frequently seek stiffer criminal laws and greater penalties for criminal activity. The emphasis on punishment as an appropriate response to crime, however, whether founded on principles of deterrence or revenge, and the resulting packed courtrooms and overcrowded prisons, has left many contemporary criminal justice policy initiatives floundering.

Early Biological Theories

Biological theories of crime causation, which had fallen into disrepute during the past few decades, are beginning to experience something of a contemporary resurgence. It is important to distinguish, however, between early biological perspectives, which have been largely discounted by contemporary criminologists, and the rather sophisticated biosocial perspectives offered by some cutting-edge criminologists today. Biosocial theories will be discussed later in this chapter, but most early theories of the **Biological School** of crime causation built on inherited or bodily characteristics and features and made certain fundamental assumptions. Among them are these:

- Basic determinants of human behavior, including criminal tendencies, are constitutionally or genetically based.
- The basic determinants of human behavior, including criminality, may be passed on from generation to

generation. In other words, a penchant for crime may be inherited.
- At least some human behavior is the result of biological propensities inherited from more primitive developmental stages in the evolutionary process. Some human beings may be further along the evolutionary ladder than others, and their behavior may reflect it.

Franz Joseph Gall: Phrenology

The idea that the quality of a person can be judged by a study of the person's face is as old as antiquity. Even today, we often judge people on their looks, saying, "He has an honest face" or "She has tender eyes." Horror movies play on unspoken cultural themes to shape the way a "maniac" might look. Jack Nicholson's portrayal of a crazed killer in *The Shining* and Anthony Hopkins's role as a serial killer in *The Silence of the Lambs* turned that look into fortunes at the box office. More recently, TV series such as NBC's *Hannibal* have capitalized on scary looks and frightening scenes.

Franz Joseph Gall (1758–1828) was one of the first thinkers to theorize about the idea that bodily constitution might reflect personality. Gall was writing at a time when it was thought that organs throughout the body determined one's mental state and behavior. People were said to be "hard-hearted" or to have a "bad spleen" that filled them with bile. Gall focused on the head and the brain and called his approach *cranioscopy*. It can be summarized in four propositions:

- The brain is the organ of the mind.
- The brain consists of localized faculties or functions.
- The shape of the skull reveals the underlying development (or lack of development) of areas within the brain.
- The personality can be revealed by a study of the skull.

Gall never systematically tested his theory in a way that would meet contemporary scientific standards. Even so, his approach to predicting behavior, which came to be known as **phrenology**, quickly spread throughout Europe. Gall's student, Johann Gaspar Spurzheim (1776–1853), brought phrenology to America in a series of lectures and publications on the subject. By 1825, 29 phrenological journals were being produced in the United States and Britain.[20] Until the turn of the twentieth century, phrenology remained popular in some American circles, where it was used in diagnostic schemes to classify new prisoners.

■ **atavism**   A condition characterized by the existence of features thought to be common in earlier stages of human evolution.

■ **Positivist School**   An approach that stresses the application of scientific techniques to the study of crime and criminals.

Cesare Lombroso: Atavism

Gall's theory was "deterministic" in the sense that it left little room for choice. What a person did depended more on the shape of the skull than on the exercise of free will. Other biological theories would soon build on that premise. One of the best known is that created by the Italian psychologist Cesare Lombroso (1835–1909).

Lombroso began his criminal anthropology with a postmortem evaluation of famous criminals, including one by the name of Vilella. Before Vilella died, Lombroso had the opportunity to interview him on a number of occasions. After Vilella's death, Lombroso correlated earlier observations of personality traits with measurable physical abnormalities. As a result of this and other studies, Lombroso concluded that criminals were atavistic human beings—throwbacks to earlier stages of evolution who were not sufficiently mentally advanced for successful life in the modern world. **Atavism** was identifiable in suspicious individuals, Lombroso suggested, through measures designed to reveal "primitive" physical characteristics.

In the late nineteenth century, Charles Darwin's theory of evolution was rapidly being applied to a wide range of fields. It was not surprising, therefore, that Lombroso linked evolution and criminality. What separated Lombroso from his predecessors, however, was that he continually refined his theory through ongoing observation. Based on studies of known offenders, whom he compared to conformists, Lombroso identified a large number of atavistic traits, which he claimed characterized criminals. Among them were long arms, large lips, crooked noses, an abnormally large amount of body hair, prominent cheekbones, two eyes of different colors, and ears that lacked clearly defined lobes.

Atavism implies that certain people are born criminals. Throughout his life, Lombroso grappled with the task of determining what proportion of the total population of offenders were born criminals. His estimates ranged at different times between 70% and 90%. Career criminals and those who committed crimes of opportunity without atavistic features he termed *criminaloids*, and he recognized the potential causative roles of greed, passion, and circumstance in their behavior.

Today, Lombroso is known as the founder of the **Positivist School** of criminology because of the role observation played in the formulation of his theories. Stephen Schafer calls Lombroso "the father of modern criminology"[21] because most contemporary criminologists follow in the tradition that Lombroso began—scientific observation and a comparison of theory with fact.

Cesare Lombroso, who has been dubbed "the father of modern criminology," in a rare photograph from 1909. What concepts developed by Lombroso might still be applicable today?

The Evidence for and against Atavism

After Lombroso died, two English physicians, Charles Goring and Karl Pearson, conducted a test of atavism, studying more than 3,000 prisoners and comparing them along physiological criteria to an army detachment known as the Royal Engineers. No significant differences were found between the two groups, and Lombroso's ideas rapidly began to fall into disrepute.

A further study of atavism was published in 1939 by Earnest A. Hooton, a distinguished Harvard University anthropologist. Hooton spent 12 years constructing anthropometric profiles—profiles based on human body measurements—of 13,873 male convicts in ten different American states. He measured each inmate in 107 different ways and compared them to 3,203 volunteers from National Guard units, firehouses, beaches, and hospitals. Surprisingly, Hooton did find some basis for

■ **somatotyping**   The classification of human beings into types according to body build and other physical characteristics.

Lombroso's beliefs, and he concluded that the inmate population in his study demonstrated a decided physical "inferiority."

However, Hooton never recognized that the prisoners he studied were only a subgroup of the population of all offenders throughout the country. They were, in fact, the least successful offenders—the ones who had been caught and imprisoned. Hooton may have unknowingly measured other criminals—the ones who had avoided capture—among his "conformist" population. Hence the "inferiority" Hooton observed may have been an artificial product of a process of selection (arrest) by the justice system.

Criminal Families

The concept of biological inheritance has been applied to "criminal families" as well as to individuals. The idea of mental degeneration as an inherited contributor to crime was first explored by Richard Dugdale.[22] Dugdale used the family tree method to study a family he called the Jukes, publishing his findings in 1877. The Juke lineage had its beginning in America with "Max" (whose last name is unknown), a descendant of Dutch immigrants to New Amsterdam in the early eighteenth

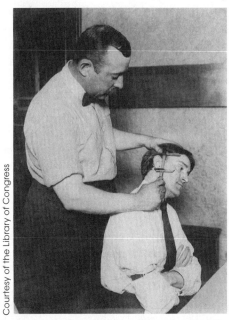

Courtesy of the Library of Congress

The Bertillion system of identification being applied to a subject in the years before the development of fingerprinting. The theory of atavism, based on the ideas of Charles Darwin, supported the use of physical anthropology in the identification of offenders. Why have sociological theories largely replaced simple biological approaches to explaining crime?

century. Two of Max's sons married into the notorious "Juke family of girls," six sisters, all of whom were illegitimate. Male Jukes were reputed to have been "vicious," while Ada, one of the sisters, had an especially bad reputation and eventually came to be known as "the mother of criminals."

Dugdale found that, during the next 75 years, Ada's heirs included 1,200 people, most of whom were "social degenerates." Only a handful of socially productive progeny could be identified. In 1915, Dugdale's study of the Jukes was continued by Arthur A. Estabrook, who extended the line to include 2,094 descendants and found just as few conformists.

A similar study was published by Henry Goddard in 1912.[23] Goddard examined the Kallikak family, which contained two clear lines of descent. One emanated from an affair that Revolutionary War soldier Martin Kallikak had with a "feebleminded" barmaid. She bore a son, and the line eventually produced 480 identifiable descendants. After the war, Kallikak returned home and married a "virtuous" Quaker woman in Philadelphia. This legitimate line produced 496 offspring by 1912, of whom only three were abnormal; not one was criminal. The illegitimate group, however, contained over half "feebleminded" or deviant progeny.

The underlying suppositions of these studies are that degenerate and feebleminded people are produced and propagated through bad genetic material and that crime is an outlet for degenerate urges. However, these studies fail to recognize any effect that socialization and life circumstances have on the development of criminal behavior.

William Sheldon: Somatotypes

"Constitutional" theories of crime causation refer to the *physical constitution*, or bodily characteristics, of offenders. The last of the famous constitutional theorists was William Sheldon (1893–1977), who developed the idea of **somatotyping**.

Sheldon studied 200 juvenile delinquents between the ages of 15 and 21 at the Hayden Goodwill Institute in Boston and decided that the young men possessed one of three somatotypes (or body types). The types of bodies described by Sheldon were (in his words):

- *Mesomorphs* with a relative predominance of muscle, bone, and connective tissue
- *Endomorphs* with a soft roundness throughout the various regions of the body; short tapering limbs; small bones; and soft, smooth, velvety skin
- *Ectomorphs* characterized by thinness, fragility, and delicacy of body

Sheldon developed a system of measurements by which an individual's physique could be expressed as a combination of numbers, and believed that predominantly mesomorphic individuals were most prone to aggression, violence, and delinquency.[24]

Social Policy and Early Biological Theories

Because traditional biological theories of crime causation attribute the cause of crime to fundamental physical characteristics that are not easily modified, they suggest the need for extreme social policies. During the 1920s and early 1930s, for example, biological theories of crime causation, especially those focusing on inherited mental degeneration, led to the eugenics movement, under which mentally handicapped people were sometimes sterilized to prevent them from bearing offspring. The eugenics movement was institutionalized by the 1927 U.S. Supreme Court case of *Buck* v. *Bell*, in which Justice Oliver Wendell Holmes, Jr., writing in support of a Virginia statute permitting sterilization, said, "It is better for all the world, if instead of waiting to execute degenerate offspring for crime, or to let them starve for their imbecility, society can prevent those persons who are manifestly unfit from continuing their kind."[25] Visit **http://www.crimetimes.org** to learn more about early biological theories of crime and violence.

Biosocial Theories

During the past few years, numerous researchers have taken a sophisticated approach to biological theorizing. Consequently, most contemporary biological theories of crime causation fall under the heading of **biosocial criminology**. The biosocial perspective sees the interaction between biology and the physical and social environments as key to understanding human behavior, including criminality. While recognizing the role of human DNA, heritability, environmental contaminants, nutrition, hormones, physical trauma (especially to the brain), and body chemistry in human cognition, feeling, and behavior, biosocial theorists emphasize that it is the *interaction* between biology and the cultural and social environments that produces behavior, and that both conformity and criminality are a consequence of such interaction. Some biosocial theories, including those offered by University of Pennsylvania criminologist Adrian Raine, stress the importance of the interaction between a cluster of biological markers—including brain dysfunction, glucose metabolism, poor nutrition, and physiological reactivity (such as skin resistance and heart rate)—with the social environment in producing deviance and criminality.[26] Raine argues that measurements of biological indicators and observations of the social environment can be used to accurately predict which people will turn to crime in later life.[27]

> The biosocial perspective sees the interaction between biology and the physical and social environments as key to understanding human behavior, including criminality.

The Gender Ratio Problem

One of the most telling issues in contemporary criminology is what biosocial criminologists Kevin Beaver and Anthony Walsh call the **gender ratio problem**. The gender ratio problem refers to the fact that in all societies, regardless of the historical period, men are always far more involved in criminal activity than are women. That is not to say that some forms of crime, like prostitution, do not disproportionately involve women (although there are likely far more male "Johns" than there are female prostitutes), or that women commit a few specific types of crimes more often than men (but such crimes, like teller theft, are usually associated with a significant gender imbalance, as in the case of bank tellers, who are predominately women).

Anthony Walsh explains the gender ratio problem this way: "In virtually every study ever conducted, males are much more likely than females to engage in violence, aggression, and serious crimes. As the seriousness of the offense/behavior increases, the gender gap also tends to increase, such that the most violent criminal acts are almost exclusively a male phenomenon."[28] Figure 3-2 shows, for example, gender differences in the rate of homicide convictions for various regions of the world for 2012.

As Walsh explains, the gender ratio problem is only a problem if biological explanations for criminality are ignored.

■ **chromosomes**   Bundles of genes.
■ **genes**   Distinct portions of a cell's DNA that carry coded instructions for making everything the body needs.
■ **supermale**   A male individual displaying the XYY chromosome structure.

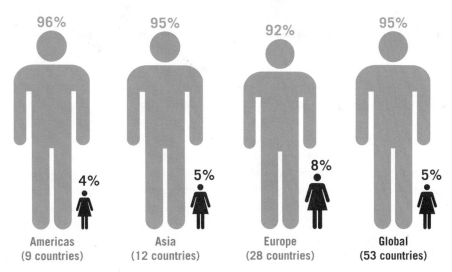

FIGURE 3-2 | Persons Convicted of Homicide, by Gender and Region, 2012.

Source: From: Percentage of persons convicted of homicide from: Global Study on Homicide (http://www.unodc.org/documents/gsh/pdfs/2014_GLOBAL_HOMICIDE_BOOK_web.pdf). Reprinted with the permission of the United Nations

Sociological theories, psychological perspectives, and approaches such as the Classical School tend to deny the important role that inherent physiological differences between the sexes can play in crime causation. Primary among such differences is the role that the male sex hormone testosterone plays in increasing the propensity toward violence and aggression among men. A few authors have suggested that testosterone is the agent primarily responsible for male criminality and that its relative lack in women leads them to commit fewer crimes. A growing body of evidence supports just such a hypothesis. Studies have shown, for example, that female fetuses exposed to elevated testosterone levels during gestation develop masculine characteristics, including a muscular build and a demonstrably greater tendency toward aggression later in life. Other studies show that testosterone strongly influences behavior, and that it creates what some have called "sexually dismorphic brains"—including physical and functional differences between the brains of men and women.

Chromosome Theory

In 2013, Connecticut Chief Medical Examiner H. Wayne Carver, ordered the testing of Newton, Connecticut, school shooter Adam Lanza's DNA in an effort to determine "if he possessed any genetic abnormalities that could have led to his violent behavior." The detailed mapping of human DNA and other recent advances in the field of recombinant DNA have rekindled interest in genetic correlates of deviant behavior. More sophisticated than their historical counterparts, the biosocial theories of today often draw on the latest medical advances or build on popular health concerns.

Chromosomes are bundles of genes, and **genes** are distinct portions of a cell's DNA that carry coded instructions for making everything the body needs.[29] The links between chromosome patterns and crime were first explored in the 1960s. A normal female has a chromosome structure often diagrammed as "XX" because of how the sex-determining gene pair looks in an electron microscope. A male has a Y chromosome in place of the second X, for a typical male XY pattern. Although it had been known for some time that a few people have abnormal patterns that include "extra" chromosomes (such as XXX females, XXY males with Klinefelter's syndrome, and XXYY "double males"), it wasn't until 1965 that the respected English journal *Nature* reported on the work of Patricia Jacobs, who identified **supermales**—men with an extra Y chromosome whose chromosome structure is diagrammed XYY. Jacobs found that supermales were more common in prisons than in the general population.[30]

Other early studies claimed that the XYY male was more aggressive than other males and that he possessed a number of specific physical and psychological traits, such as height (taller than 6 feet, 1 inch), thinness, acne, a tendency toward homosexuality, a somewhat low IQ, and "a marked tendency to commit a succession of apparently motiveless property crimes."[31] Later studies disputed many of these findings, and today's criminologists largely disregard the relationship between XYY patterns and criminal behavior.

Instead, contemporary biosocial researchers have turned their attention to the study of gene deficits, enzymes, and hormones. Some recent studies, for example, have found that an overabundance of the enzyme monoamine oxidase A (MAOA) in the brain may lead to overstimulation of the nervous system, and to a defect in the DRD2 A1 allele gene, which some have called the pleasure-seeking gene. This combination can result in uncontrollable urges and, ultimately, criminal behavior (see the "CJ News" box in this chapter).[32] Defects in the DRD2 A1 allele gene can drive a person to seek stimulation and to engage in dangerous or threatening behavior.[33] Similarly, in 2007, researchers at the University of Texas Southwestern Medical Center discovered that mice carrying certain mutations in what is called the clock gene exhibited manic behaviors, such as recklessness and hyperactivity, and also displayed a preference for addictive substances, such as cocaine.

Unfortunately, things are not as simple as they might seem when considering the link between genes and crime. New understandings about how genes operate seem to call into question previous notions that genes are strong determinants of human behavior. Researchers in the field of neurobiology, for example, have found 17 genes, known as CREB genes, that are switched on and off in response to environmental influences. The CREB genes lay down neural pathways in the brain and form the basis of memory; the act of learning turns the CREB genes on and is made possible by them.[34] Hence, the CREB genes respond to human experience rather than determine it. One writer explains it this way: "These genes are at the mercy of our behavior, not the other way around."[35]

Biochemical Factors and Imbalances

Research in the area of nutrition has produced some limited evidence that the old maxim "You are what you eat" may contain more than a grain of truth. Some biocriminologists have linked violent or disruptive behavior to eating habits, vitamin deficiencies, genetics, and other conditions that affect body tissues.

One of the first studies to focus on chemical imbalances in the body as a cause of crime was reported in the British medical journal *Lancet* in 1943.[36] Authors of the study linked murder to hypoglycemia (low blood sugar), which is caused by too much insulin in the blood or by near-starvation diets. Some researchers believe that hypoglycemia reduces the mind's capacity to reason effectively or to judge the long-term consequences of behavior.

Allergic reactions to common foods have been reported as the cause of violence and homicide in a number of studies.[37] Foods said to produce allergic reactions in sensitive individuals, leading to a swelling of the brain and brain stem, include milk, citrus fruit, chocolate, corn, wheat, and eggs. Involvement of the central nervous system in such allergies, it has been suggested, reduces the amount of learning that occurs during childhood and may contribute to delinquency as well as to adult criminal behavior. Some studies have implicated food additives, such as monosodium glutamate, dyes, and artificial flavorings, in producing criminal behavior.[38]

Other research has found that the amount of coffee and sugar consumed by inmates is considerably greater than in the outside population.[39] Theorists have suggested that high blood levels of caffeine and sugar produce antisocial behavior.[40] It is unclear whether inmates consume more coffee due to boredom or whether those with "excitable" personalities need the kind of stimulation coffee drinking produces. On the other hand, habitual coffee drinkers in nonprison populations have not been linked to crime, and other studies, such as that conducted by Mortimer Gross of the University of Illinois, show no link between the amount of sugar consumed and hyperactivity.[41] Similarly, studies "have not yielded evidence that a change in diet will result in [a] significant reduction in aggressive or antisocial behavior" among inmate populations.[42] Nonetheless, some prison programs have limited the intake of dietary stimulants through nutritional management and the substitution of artificial sweeteners for refined sugar.

Vitamins have also been examined for their impact on delinquency. Abram Hoffer found that disruptive children consumed far less than the optimum levels of vitamins B3 and B6 than did nonproblem youths.[43] He claimed that the addition of these vitamins to the diets of children who were deficient in them could control unruly behavior and improve school performance.

Recently, Ap Zaalberg, an official at the Dutch Ministry of Justice, implemented a program of nutritional supplementation in 14 prisons in the Netherlands. Under the program, inmates were provided with healthy diets, devoid of added sugar, and supplemented with vitamins and important micronutrients, including fish oils.[44] Zaalberg's study, which showed a reduction in rule-breaking among prisoners,[45] followed on the heels of a nutritional experiment conducted a few years earlier in British prisons by Oxford University professor C. Bernard Gesch.[46] Gesch added dietary supplements to prisoners' diets, and reported finding a significant decrease in violent incidents and other offenses among study participants.

Hormones have also come under scrutiny as potential behavioral determinants. The male sex hormone, testosterone, has been linked to aggressiveness in males. Some studies of blood-serum levels of testosterone have shown a direct relationship[47] between the amount of hormone present and the degree of violence used by sex offenders,[48] and steroid abuse among bodybuilders has been linked to destructive urges and psychosis.[49] One 1998 study found that high levels of testosterone, especially when combined with low socioeconomic status, produced antisocial personalities, resulting in deviance and criminality.[50] Recently, researchers at the University of Michigan

> Research in the area of nutrition has produced some limited evidence that the old maxim "You are what you eat" may contain more than a grain of truth.

■ **heritability** A statistical construct that estimates the amount of variation in the traits of a population that is attributable to genetic factors.

■ **Psychological School** A perspective on criminological thought that views offensive and deviant behavior as the product of dysfunctional personality. Psychological thinkers identify the conscious, and especially the subconscious, contents of the human psyche as major determinants of behavior.

at Ann Arbor found that the higher the blood levels of testosterone in young men, the more they enjoyed provoking anger in others.[51]

Some studies of brain chemistry have led researchers to conclude that low levels of certain neurotransmitters, especially serotonin, are directly related to a person's inability to control aggressive impulses.[52] The presence of adequate serotonin levels in the human brain buffers irritating experiences that might otherwise result in anger and aggression. Low serotonin levels may result from the ingestion of toxic pollutants, such as the metals lead and manganese, according to one study.[53] Reduced serotonin levels, say other researchers, are sometimes found in men with an extra Y chromosome.[54]

Researchers have also implicated a malfunctioning endocrine system as a cause of physical abuse, antisocial behavior, and psychopathology. One Swedish study that focused on variations in blood-serum levels of two thyroid hormones, triiodothyronine (T3) and thyroxine (FT4), found that elevated T3 levels were related to alcoholism and criminality.[55] Serum levels of FT4 were found to be negatively correlated to such behavior.

Heredity and Heritability

Studies have shown that the behavior of biological children of criminals who are adopted at birth tends to reflect the criminality of biological parents, independent of the environment in which the children were raised.[56] Also, identical twins exhibit a greater similarity in behavior than do nonidentical (or "fraternal") twins, and studies have shown that identical twins are more alike in patterns and degree of criminal involvement than are fraternal twins.[57]

One of the earliest modern-day biological perspectives on crime was proposed by James Q. Wilson and Richard Herrnstein in their book *Crime and Human Nature*, published in 1985.[58] Wilson and Herrnstein argue that inherited traits, such as maleness, aggressiveness, mesomorphic body type, and low intelligence, combine with environmental influences, including poor schools and strained family life, to produce crime. Although the authors reject a firm determinism, asserting that it is the interaction between genetics and environment that determines behavior, they do claim that children who will eventually grow up to be criminals can sometimes be identified early in their lives.

In 2011, making a genetic argument for at least some forms of callous-unemotional behavior, Nathalie Fontaine of Indiana University and colleagues reported that **heritability** (which is

a statistical construct that estimates the amount of variation in the traits of a population that is attributable to genetic factors) leads to persistently high levels of such behavior among twin boys. The data on which Fontaine reported were derived from the United Kingdom's ongoing Twin Early Development Study (TEDS), which uses information gathered from over 15,000 families to explore how people change through childhood and adolescence.

Social Policy and Biological Theories

Early criminologists concerned with crime and its causes had hoped to find biological techniques that could be applied to the prevention and control of crime. If a crime-causing gene or chemical imbalance could somehow be identified, such researchers hoped that a drug or gene alteration might turn off criminal behavior.

However, at least in the case of gene alterations, today's criminologists do not see such an easy solution. Lee Ellis and Anthony Walsh, two contemporary biosocial researchers, note that "in the case of behavior, nearly all of the effects of genes are quite indirect because they are mediated through complex chains of events occurring in the brain. This means that there are almost certainly no genes for something as complex as criminal behavior. Nevertheless," Ellis and Walsh concluded, "many genes may affect brain functioning in ways that either increase or reduce the chances of individuals learning various complex behavior patterns, including behavior patterns that happen to be so offensive to others that criminal sanctions have been instituted to minimize their recurrence."[59] In sum, it is important to recognize that genes are both the cause and the consequence of our actions—and that they do not so much *determine* human action as *enable* it.

Psychological Theories

Sociological theories are the most common approach to explaining crime today. Some, however, have pointed out that it is individuals who actually commit crimes. They argue that "ecological and societal factors must be included in any full explanation of crime," but that "individual factors always intervene between them and a criminal act."[60] For this reason, they say, "individual factors need to be at the center of any description of the causes of crime." Theories of the **Psychological School** of

■ **behavioral conditioning**   A psychological principle that holds that the frequency of any behavior can be increased or decreased through reward, punishment, and association with other stimuli.

■ **personality**   The relatively stable characteristic patterns of thoughts, feelings, and behaviors that make a person unique, and that influence that person's behavior.

■ **lecture note**   Discuss conditioning as a psychological theory. Relate the concepts of reward and punishment to the free will and hedonistic ideas of the Classical School. Discuss the implications of the conditioning approach for treatment strategies that might be based on it.

■ **psychoanalysis**   A theory of human behavior, based on the writings of Sigmund Freud, that sees personality as a complex composite of interacting mental entities.

crime causation make certain fundamental assumptions. Among them are these:

- The individual is the primary unit of analysis.
- Personality is the major motivational element within individuals, as it is the source of drives and motives.
- Crimes result from inappropriately conditioned behavior or from abnormal, dysfunctional, or inappropriate mental processes within the personality.
- Defective or abnormal mental processes may have a variety of causes, including a diseased mind and inappropriate learning or improper conditioning—often occurring in early childhood.

Behavioral Conditioning

Two threads were woven through early psychological theories. One emphasized **behavioral conditioning**, while the other focused on **personality**—including personality disturbances and diseases of the mind. Taken together, these two foci constituted the early field of psychological criminology.

Conditioning is a psychological principle that holds that the frequency of any behavior, including criminal or deviant behavior, can be increased or decreased through reward, punishment, and association with other stimuli. The concept of conditioned behavior was popularized through the work of the Russian physiologist Ivan Pavlov (1849–1936), whose research with dogs won him the Nobel Prize in physiology and medicine in 1904. Similarly, behavioral psychologists suggest that criminal behavior, which may be inherently rewarding under many circumstances, tends to be more common in those who are able to avoid punishment when involved in rule-breaking behavior.

Freudian Psychoanalysis

The name most widely associated with the field of psychology is that of Sigmund Freud (1856–1939). Freudian theory posits the existence of an id, an ego, and a superego within the personality.[61] The id is the source of drives, which are seen as primarily sexual. The ego is a rational mental entity, which outlines paths through which the desires of the id can be fulfilled. The ego is often called the *reality principle* because of the belief that it relates desires to practical behavioral alternatives. The superego is a guiding principle, often compared to conscience, that judges the quality of the alternatives presented by the ego according to the standards of right and wrong acquired by the personality of

which it is a part. Freud wrote very little about crime, but his followers, who developed the school of Freudian **psychoanalysis**, believe that crime can result from at least three conditions.

The first possible source of criminal behavior is a weak superego, which cannot responsibly control the drives that emanate from the id. Sex crimes, crimes of passion, murder, and other violent crimes are thought to follow inadequate superego development. People who lack fully developed superegos are often called *psychopaths* or *sociopaths* to indicate that they cannot see beyond their own interests. Canadian criminologist Gwynn Nettler observes that "civilization is paid for through development of a sense of guilt."[62]

Freud also created the concept of sublimation to explain the process by which one thing is symbolically substituted for another. He believed that sublimation was necessary when the direct pursuit of one's desires was not possible. Freud suggested, for example, that many children learned to sublimate negative feelings about their mothers. In the society in which Freud developed his theories, mothers closely controlled the lives of their children, and Freud saw the developing child as continually frustrated in seeking freedom to act on his or her own. The strain produced by this conflict could not be directly expressed by the child because the mother also controlled rewards and punishments. Hence dislike for one's mother (which Freud thought was especially strong in boys) might show itself symbolically later in life. Crimes against women could then be explained as being committed by men expressing a symbolic hatred.

A final Freudian explanation for criminality is based on the death instinct, or Thanatos, which Freud believed each of us carries. Thanatos is the often-unrecognized desire of animate matter to return to the inanimate. Potentially self-destructive activities, including smoking, speeding, skydiving, bad diets, "picking fights," and so on, can be explained by Thanatos. The self-destructive wish may also motivate offenders to commit crimes that are themselves dangerous or self-destructive—such as burglary, assault, murder, prostitution, and drug use—or it may result in unconscious efforts to be caught. Criminals who leave evidence behind may be responding to some basic need for apprehension and punishment.

Psychopathology and Crime

From a psychiatric point of view, crime might also occur because of a diseased mind or a disordered personality—conditions that may collectively be referred to as *psychopathy*.

■ **psychopathology**   The study of pathological mental conditions—that is, mental illness.

■ **psychopath**   A person with a personality disorder, especially one manifested in aggressively antisocial behavior, which is often said to be the result of a poorly developed superego.
■ **psychosis**   A form of mental illness in which sufferers are said to be out of touch with reality.
■ **schizophrenic**   A mentally ill individual who suffers from disjointed thinking and possibly from delusions and hallucinations.

Cleckley described the **psychopath** as a "moral idiot" whose central defining characteristic is the inability to empathize with others.

The study of psychopathic mental conditions is called **psychopathology**. The role of a disordered personality in crime causation was central to early psychiatric theorizing. In 1944, for example, the well-known psychiatrist David Abrahamsen wrote, "When we seek to explain the riddle of human conduct in general and of antisocial behavior in particular, the solution must be sought in the personality."[63] Later, some psychiatrists went so far as to claim that criminal behavior itself is only a symptom of a more fundamental psychiatric disorder.[64]

By the 1930s, psychiatrists had begun to develop the concept of a psychopathic personality. This personality type, which by its very definition is asocial, was fully developed by Hervey Cleckley in his 1941 book *The Mask of Sanity*.[65] Cleckley described the **psychopath**, also called a *sociopath*, as a "moral idiot" whose central defining characteristic is the inability to empathize with others. Hence it becomes possible for a psychopath to inflict pain and engage in cruelty without appreciation for the victim's suffering. Charles Manson, for example, whom some have called a psychopath, once told a television reporter, "I could take this book and beat you to death with it, and I wouldn't feel a thing. It'd be just like walking to the drugstore."[66] According to Cleckley, psychopathic indicators appear early in life, often in the teenage years. They include lying, fighting, stealing, and vandalism. Even earlier signs may be found, according to some authors, in bed-wetting, cruelty to animals, sleepwalking, and fire setting.[67]

Although the terms *psychopath* and *criminal* are not synonymous, individuals manifesting characteristics of a psychopathic personality are likely, sooner or later, to run afoul of the law.

Although the terms *psychopath* and *criminal* are not synonymous, individuals manifesting characteristics of a psychopathic personality are likely, sooner or later, to run afoul of the law. As one writer says, "The impulsivity and aggression, the selfishness in achieving one's own immediate needs, and the disregard for society's rules and laws bring these people to the attention of the criminal justice system."[68]

Although much studied, the causes of psychopathy are unclear. Somatogenic causes, or those that are based on physiological aspects of the human organism, include (1) a malfunctioning

Charles Manson, one of the most photographed criminal offenders of all time, is shown at a parole hearing decades after he and his "family" shocked the world with their gruesome crimes. What can we learn from offenders like Manson?

AP Wide World Photos

central nervous system characterized by a low state of arousal, which drives the sufferer to seek excitement, and (2) brain abnormalities, which may be present in most psychopaths from birth. Psychogenic causes, or those rooted in early interpersonal experiences, include the inability to form attachments to parents or other caregivers early in life, sudden separation from the mother during the first six months of life, and other forms of insecurity during the first few years of life. In short, a lack of love or the sensed inability to unconditionally depend on one central loving figure (typically the mother in most psychological literature) immediately following birth is often posited as a major psychogenic factor contributing to psychopathic development.

The Psychotic Offender

Another form of mental disorder is called **psychosis**. Psychotic people, according to psychiatric definitions, are out of touch with reality in some fundamental way. They may suffer from hallucinations, delusions, or other breaks with reality. For example, a psychotic may believe that he or she is a famous historical figure or may see spiders crawling on a bare wall. Psychoses may be either organic (i.e., caused by physical damage to, or abnormalities in, the brain) or functional (i.e., with no known physical cause). Psychotic people have also been classified as schizophrenic or paranoid schizophrenic. **Schizophrenics** are characterized by disordered or disjointed thinking, in which the types of logical associations they make are atypical of those of other people. Paranoid schizophrenics suffer from delusions and hallucinations.

■ **lecture note**   Define psychological profiling as the attempt to derive a composite picture of an offender's social and psychological characteristics from the crime he or she committed and the manner in which it was committed. Explain how Adolf Hitler became the first subject for psychological profiling when the Allied forces sought to find possible weaknesses in his psyche.

■ **traits**   Stable personality patterns that tend to endure throughout the life course and across social and cultural contexts.

■ **psychological profiling**   The attempt to categorize, understand, and predict the behavior of certain types of offenders based on behavioral clues they provide.

Psychoses may lead to crime in a number of ways. Following the Vietnam War, for example, a number of former American soldiers suffering from a kind of battlefield psychosis killed friends and family members, thinking they were enemy soldiers. These men, who had been traumatized by battlefield experiences in Southeast Asia, relived their past on American streets.

Trait Theory

In 1964, Hans J. Eysenck, a British psychologist, published *Crime and Personality*, a book in which he explained crime as the result of fundamental personality characteristics, or **traits**, which he believed are largely inherited.[69] Psychological traits are stable personality patterns that tend to endure throughout the life course and across social and cultural contexts. According to trait theory, as an individual grows older or moves from one place to another, his or her personality remains largely intact—defined by the traits that comprise it. Trait theory links personality (and associated traits) to behavior, and holds that it is an individual's personality, combined with his or her intelligence and natural abilities,[70] that determines his or her behavior in a given situation.[71]

> Trait theories of personality build on five basic traits known as the Big Five.

Generally speaking, trait theories of personality build on five basic traits: (1) openness to experience, (2) extraversion, (3) conscientiousness, (4) neuroticism, and (5) agreeableness. People are said to possess more or less of any one trait, and the combination of traits and the degree to which they are characteristic of an individual define that person's personality. Psychologists call these traits the Big Five, and they are referenced in most contemporary literature on personality. According to many psychologists, "the Big Five are strongly genetically influenced, and the genetic factor structure of the Big Five appears to be invariant across European, North American, and East Asian samples,"[72] which suggests that personality traits, to a greater or lesser degree, are universally shared by all peoples.

Eysenck, in contrast, believed that the degree to which just three universal supertraits are present in an individual accounts for his or her unique personality. He termed these supertraits: (1) introversion/extraversion, (2) neuroticism/emotional stability, and (3) psychoticism. Eysenck, like many other psychologists, accepted the fact that personality holds steady throughout much of life, but stressed that it is largely determined by genetics. In support of his idea of the genetic basis of personality, Eysenck pointed to twin studies, which showed that identical twins display strikingly similar behavioral tendencies, whereas fraternal twins demonstrate far less likelihood of similar behaviors. Eysenck also argued that psychological conditioning occurs more rapidly in some people than in others because of biological differences, and that antisocial individuals are difficult to condition (or to socialize) because of underlying genetic characteristics. He believed that up to two-thirds of all "behavioral variance" could be strongly attributed to genetics.[73]

Of Eysenck's three personality dimensions, one in particular—psychoticism—was thought to be closely correlated with criminality at all stages.[74] According to Eysenck, psychoticism is defined by such characteristics as lack of empathy, creativeness, tough-mindedness, and antisociability. Psychoticism, added Eysenck, is also frequently characterized by hallucinations and delusions, leading to the personality type described as psychotic. Extroverts, Eysenck's second personality group that was associated with criminality, are described as carefree, dominant, and venturesome, operating with high levels of energy. "The typical extrovert," Eysenck wrote, "is sociable, likes parties, has many friends, needs to have people to talk to, and does not like reading or studying by himself."[75] Neuroticism, the third of the personality characteristics Eysenck described, is said to be typical of people who are irrational, shy, moody, and emotional.

According to Eysenck, psychotics are the most likely to be criminal because they combine high degrees of emotionalism with similarly high levels of extroversion; individuals with such characteristics are especially difficult to socialize and to train and do not respond well to the external environment. Eysenck cited many studies in which children and others who harbored characteristics of psychoticism performed poorly on conditioning tests designed to measure how quickly they would respond appropriately to external stimuli. Because conscience is fundamentally a conditioned reflex, Eysenck said, an individual who does not take well to conditioning will not fully develop a conscience and will continue to exhibit the asocial behavioral traits of a very young child. In essence, criminality can be seen as a personality type characterized by self-centeredness, indifference to the suffering and needs of others, impulsiveness, and low self-control—which, taken together, lead to law-violating behavior.

Psychological Profiling

Psychological profiling is the attempt to derive a composite picture of an offender's social and psychological characteristics from the crime he or she committed and from the manner in which

■ **theme** How do sociological theories differ from other perspectives on crime—especially psychological theories?

■ **dangerousness** The likelihood that a given individual will later harm society or others. Dangerousness is often measured in terms of recidivism, or the likelihood that an individual will commit another crime within five years following arrest or release from confinement.

■ **Chicago School** A sociological approach that emphasizes demographics (the characteristics of population groups) and geographics (the mapped location of such groups relative to one another) and that sees the social disorganization that characterizes delinquency areas as a major cause of criminality and victimization.

■ **social disorganization** A condition said to exist when a group is faced with social change, uneven development of culture, maladaptiveness, disharmony, conflict, and lack of consensus.

which it was committed. Psychological profiling began during World War II as an effort by William Langer (1896–1977), a government psychiatrist hired by the Office of Strategic Services, to predict Adolf Hitler's actions.[76] Profiling in criminal investigations is based on the belief that criminality, because it is a form of behavior, can be viewed as symptomatic of the offender's personality. Psychological evaluations of crime scenes, including the analysis of evidence, are used to re-create the offender's frame of mind during the commission of the crime. A profile of the offender is then constructed to help in the investigation of suspects.

During the 1980s, the Federal Bureau of Investigation (FBI) led the movement toward psychological profiling[77] through its focus on violent sex offenses[78] and arson.[79] FBI profilers described "lust murderers" and serial arsonists. Often depicted as loners with an aversion to casual social contact, lust murderers were shown to rarely arouse suspicions in neighbors or employers. Other personality types became the focus of police efforts to arrest such offenders through a prediction of what they might do next.

New areas for psychological profiling include hostage negotiation[80] and international terrorism.[81] Right-wing terrorist groups in the United States have also been the subject of profiling efforts.

Social Policy and Psychological Theories

Crime-control policies based on psychological perspectives are primarily individualistic. They are oriented toward individualized treatment, characteristically exposing the individual offender to various forms of therapy intended to overcome the person's propensity for criminality.

Most crime-control strategies based on psychological theories emphasize assessing personal **dangerousness**, through psychological testing and other efforts to identify personality-based characteristics that predict interpersonal aggression. Although the ability to accurately predict future dangerousness is of great concern to today's policymakers, definitions of *dangerousness* are fraught with difficulty. As some authors have pointed out, "Dangerousness is not an objective quality like obesity or brown eyes; rather it is an ascribed quality like trustworthiness."[82] Hence, dangerousness is not necessarily a personality trait that is stable or easily identifiable. Even if it were, some studies of criminal careers show that involvement in crime decreases with

age.[83] As one author puts it, if "criminality declines more or less uniformly with age, then many offenders will be 'over the hill' by the time they are old enough to be plausible candidates for preventive incarceration."[84]

Before crime-control policies can be based on present understandings of dangerousness, research must answer several questions: Can past behavior predict future behavior? Do former instances of criminality foretell additional ones? Are there other identifiable characteristics that violent offenders might manifest that could serve as warning signs to criminal justice decision makers faced with the dilemma of whether to release convicted felons?

Sociological Theories

Sociological theories are largely an American contribution to the study of crime causation. In the 1920s and 1930s, the famous **Chicago School** of sociology explained criminality as a product of society's impact on the individual. The structure of prevailing social arrangements, the interaction between individuals and groups, and the social environment were all seen as major determinants of criminal behavior.

Sociological perspectives on crime causation are quite diverse. Most, however, build on certain fundamental assumptions. Among them are these:

- Social groups, social institutions, the arrangements of society, and social roles all provide the proper focus for criminological study.
- Group dynamics, group organization, and subgroup relationships form the causal nexus out of which crime develops.
- The structure of society and the relative degree of social organization or **social disorganization** are important factors contributing to the prevalence of criminal behavior.

All sociological perspectives on crime share the foregoing characteristics, but particular theories may give greater or lesser weight to the following aspects of social life:

- The clash of norms and values among variously socialized groups
- Socialization and the process of association between individuals
- The existence of subcultures and varying types of opportunities

■ lecture note   Explain the concept of anomie and why it is important to criminological theorists.

■ **anomie**   A socially pervasive condition of normlessness. Also, a disjunction between approved goals and means.

Social Ecology Theory

In the 1920s, during the early days of sociological theorizing, the University of Chicago brought together such thinkers as Robert Park, Ernest Burgess,[85] Clifford Shaw, and Henry McKay.[86] Park and Burgess recognized that Chicago, like most cities, could be mapped according to its social characteristics. Their map resembled a target with a bull's-eye in the center. Shaw and McKay adapted these concentric zones to the study of crime when they realized that the zones nearest the center of the city had the highest crime rates. In particular, zone 2 (once removed from the center) consistently showed the highest crime rate over time, regardless of the groups or nationalities inhabiting it. This "zone of transition"—so called because new immigrant groups moved into it as earlier ones became integrated into American culture and moved out—demonstrated that crime was dependent to a considerable extent on aspects of the social structure of the city itself. Structural elements identified by Shaw and McKay included poverty, illiteracy, lack of schooling, unemployment, and illegitimacy. In combination, these elements were seen to lead to social disorganization, which in turn produced crime.

Anomie Theory

Opportunities are not equally distributed throughout society, and some people turn to illegitimate means to achieve the goals they feel pressured to reach.

The French word **anomie** has been loosely translated as a condition of "normlessness." Anomie entered the literature as a socio-logical concept with the writings of Émile Durkheim (1858–1917) in the late nineteenth century.[87] Robert Merton (1910–2003) applied anomie to criminology in 1938 when he used the term to describe a disjunction between socially acceptable goals and means in American society.[88]

Merton believed that although the same goals and means are held out by society as desirable for everyone, they are not equally available to all. Socially approved goals in American society, for example, include wealth, status, and political power. The acceptable means to achieve these goals are education, wise investment, and hard work. Unfortunately, however, opportunities are not equally distributed throughout society, and some people turn to illegitimate means to achieve the goals they feel pressured to reach. Still others reject both acceptable goals and legitimate means of reaching them.

TABLE 3-2 | Merton's Anomie Theory and Implied Types of Criminality

CATEGORY	GOALS	MEANS	EXAMPLES
Conformist	+	+	Law-abiding behavior
Innovator	+	−	Property offenses, white-collar crimes
Retreatist	−	−	Drug use/addiction, vagrancy, some "victimless" crimes
Ritualist	−	+	A repetitive and mundane lifestyle
Rebel	±	±	Political crime (e.g., environmental activists who violate the law, violence-prone antiabortionists)

Source: Adapted from Robert K. Merton, "Social Structure and Anomie," *American Sociological Review*, Vol. 3, No. 5 (October 1938), pp. 672–682.

Merton represented his theory with a chart, shown in Table 3-2. *Conformists* accept both the goals and means that society holds out as legitimate, whereas *innovators* accept the goals but reject the means, instead using illegal means to gain money, power, and success. It is the innovators whom Merton identified as criminal. The inherent logic of the model led Merton to posit other social types. *Ritualists* are those who reject success goals but still perform their daily tasks in conformity with social expectations. They might hold regular jobs but lack the desire to advance in their careers or in other aspects of their lives. *Retreatists* reject both the goals and the means and usually drop out of society by becoming derelicts, drug users, hermits, or the like. *Rebels* constitute a special category. Their desire to replace the existing system of socially approved goals and means with some other system more to their liking makes them the revolutionaries of the theory.

Merton believed that categories are not intentionally selected by the individuals who occupy them but rather are imposed on people by structural aspects of society. Where people live, how wealthy their families are, and what ethnic background they come from are all significant determinants of the "box" into which people are placed.

Modern writers on anomie recognize that normlessness is not likely to be expressed as criminality unless people who experience it also feel that they are capable of doing something to change their lives. As Catherine Ross and John Mirowsky put it, "A person who has high levels of normlessness and powerlessness is less likely to get in trouble with the law than a person who has a high level of normlessness and a high level of instrumentalism."[89]

CJ | NEWS

Evidence of "Warrior Gene" May Help Explain Violence

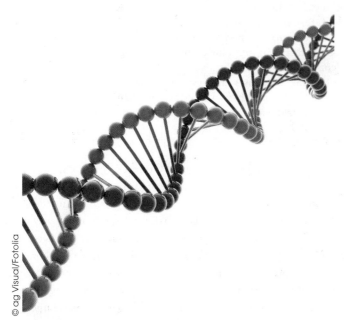

© ag Visual/Fotolia

An artist's representation of human DNA. Biosocial criminology tells us that genes may harbor certain behavioral predispositions, but that it is the interaction between genes and the environment that produces behavior. What forms might such interaction take?

As scientists study the DNA of the mass shooter at the elementary school in Newtown, Connecticut, some experts are hoping that it might lead to discovery of a gene that identifies violent criminals and helps prevent future killings. But be careful what you wish for. If a genetic link to violence were firmly identified, could it be used to falsely stigmatize people who haven't committed any crime at all? Or could such a link help convicted criminals get reduced sentences?

The argument that "my DNA made me do it" has, in fact, already been successfully used in the courts for a particular gene linked to violence. Monoamine oxidase A, known as MAOA, produces an enzyme that breaks down serotonin and other neurotransmitters in the brain that are identified with aggression. Studies have shown that a variant of the gene, known as MAOA-L, can lead to violent behavior when coupled with serious mistreatment in childhood. The link has only been identified in men, leaving women seemingly immune from the effects of this genetic anomaly.

The media nicknamed MAOA-L the "warrior gene" after it was identified as highly prevalent in a constantly warring Maori tribe. Another study found that boys with an MAOA variation were more likely to join gangs and become some of the most violent members. Researchers now know that MAOA-L may alter the very structure of the brain. Using structural magnetic resonance imaging (MRI) scanning, a 2006 study found that men with the gene variant were much more likely to have abnormalities in an area of the brain associated with behavior than were other men. Functional MRI scanning then showed that these men had difficulty inhibiting strong emotional impulses. Lawyers for violent defendants have latched on to the growing science. In the 2009 murder trial of Bradley Waldroup, who was convicted of chopping up his wife with a machete (she survived) and shooting her female friend to death, lawyers were able to demonstrate that Waldroup had the MAOA gene variant. Although the jury convicted him of murder and of attempted murder, its members concluded that his actions weren't premeditated due to the influence that his genes had on him—sparing him the death penalty. Also in 2009, an Italian appeals court cut the sentence of a convicted murderer by one year on the grounds that he, too, had the MAOA-L gene.

Judges are warming up to genetic defenses. In a 2012 study in *Science*, when trial judges were given the MAOA variant as evidence in mock trials, they tended to reduce sentences by one year in comparison to cases with no such evidence. Critics, however, argue that these defendants should be behind bars longer. Because their trait is baked into their DNA, such people say, they are likely to commit violence again. "Trying to absolve people of responsibility by attributing their behavior to their genes or environment is not new," wrote Ronald Bailey, author of the book *Liberation Biology*. He urged courts to take a tough stance against defendants with a genetic predilection to violence: "Knowing that you will be held responsible for criminal acts helps inhibit antisocial impulses that we all feel from time to time." Also, scientists want their findings to be taken with a grain of salt in the courts, arguing that science and the law have different aims. "Science is focused on understanding universal phenomena; we do this by averaging data across groups of individuals," wrote Joshua Buckholtz for the NOVA series on PBS. "Law, on the other hand, only cares about specific individual people—the individual on trial." Buckholtz observed that "Genetic differences rarely affect human behavior with the kind of selectivity or specificity desired and required by the law."

Resources: Mark Lallanilla, "Genetics May Provide Clues to Newtown Shooting," *Live Science*, December 28, 2012, http://www.livescience.com/25853-newtown-shooter-dna.html; Joshua W. Buckholtz, "Neuroprediction and Crime," *NOVA*, October 18, 2012, http://www.pbs.org/wgbh/nova/body/neuroprediction-crime.html; and Patricia Cohen, "Genetic Basis for Crime: A New Look," *New York Times*, June 19, 2011, http://www.nytimes.com/2011/06/20/arts/genetics-and-crime-at-institute-of-justice-conference.html?pagewanted=all&_r=0.

Merton's anomie theory drew attention to the lack of equal opportunity that existed in society at the time he was writing. Although considerable efforts have been made to eradicate it, much of that inequality continues today.

Subcultural Theory

Another sociological contribution to criminological theory is the idea of a subculture. A subculture is a group of people who participate in a shared system of values and norms that are at variance with those of the larger culture. Subcultural explanations of crime posit the existence of group values that support criminal behavior. Subcultures were first recognized in the enclaves formed by immigrants who came to America during the early part of the twentieth century. Statistics have shown that certain immigrant groups had low crime rates.[90] Among them were the Scandinavians, Chinese, Dutch, Germans, and Japanese. Other immigrant groups, including the Italians, Mexicans, Puerto

■ **theme** What is a subculture? Do you believe that there are criminal subcultures?

■ **reaction formation** The process whereby a person openly rejects that which he or she wants or aspires to but cannot obtain or achieve.

■ **subculture of violence** A cultural setting in which violence is a traditional and often accepted method of dispute resolution.

■ **social process theory** A perspective on criminological thought that highlights the process of interaction between individuals and society. Most social process theories highlight the role of social learning.

■ **defensible space theory** The belief that an area's physical features may be modified and structured so as to reduce crime rates in that area and to lower the fear of victimization that residents experience.

■ **broken windows theory** A perspective on crime causation that holds that the physical deterioration of an area leads to higher crime rates and an increased concern for personal safety among residents.

Ricans, and Africans, demonstrated a significantly greater propensity for involvement in crime.[91]

Albert Cohen (b. 1918) coined the term **reaction formation** to encompass the rejection of middle-class values by status-seeking lower-class youths who find they are not permitted access to approved opportunities for success.[92] In Cohen's eyes, reaction formation leads to the development of gangs and perpetuates the existence of subcultures. Walter Miller described the focal concerns of subcultural participants in terms of "trouble," "toughness," "excitement," "smartness," "fate," and "autonomy."[93] It is a focus on such concerns, Miller suggested, that leads members of criminal subcultures into violations of the law. Richard Cloward and Lloyd Ohlin proposed the existence of an illegitimate opportunity structure that permits delinquent youths to achieve in ways that are outside of legitimate avenues to success.[94]

During the 1950s, Marvin Wolfgang and Franco Ferracuti examined homicide rates in Philadelphia and found that murder was a way of life among certain groups.[95] They discovered a "wholesale" and a "retail" price for murder—which depended on who was killed and who did the killing. Killings that occurred within violent subgroups were more likely to be partially excused than those that happened elsewhere. The term **subculture of violence** has come to be associated with their work and has since been applied to other locations across the country.

Critiques of subcultural theory have been numerous. A major difficulty for these theories lies in the fact that studies involving self-reports of crime commission have shown that much violence and crime occur outside of "criminal" subcultures. Many middle- and upper-class lawbreakers are able to avoid the justice system and therefore do not enter the "official" crime statistics. Hence, criminal subcultures may be those in which crime is more visible rather than more prevalent.

Social Policy and Sociological Theories

Theoretical approaches that fault the social environment as the root cause of crime point to social action as a panacea. A contemporary example of intervention efforts based on sociological theories can be found in Targeted Outreach,[96] a program operated by the Boys and Girls Clubs of America. The program's philosophy is based on studies undertaken at the University of Colorado that showed that at-risk youths could be effectively diverted from the juvenile justice system through the provision of positive alternatives. The program recruits at-risk youngsters—many as young as seven years old—and diverts them into activities that are intended to promote a sense of belonging, competence, usefulness, and power. Social programs like Targeted Outreach are intended to change the cultural conditions and societal arrangements that are thought to lead people into crime.

Social Process Theories

Whereas psychological approaches to crime causation seek to uncover aspects of the personality hidden even from the mind in which they reside, and sociological theories look to institutional arrangements in the social world to explain crime, social process approaches focus on the interaction between individuals and society. Most **social process theories** highlight the role of social learning. They build on the premise that behavior—both "good" and "bad"—is learned, and they suggest that "bad" behavior can be unlearned. Social process theories are often the most attractive to contemporary policymakers because they demand that responsibility be placed on the offender for actively participating in rehabilitation efforts and because they are consistent with popular cultural and religious values centered on teaching right from wrong.

Differential Association Theory

In 1939, Edwin Sutherland (1883–1950) published the third edition of his *Principles of Criminology*. It contained, for the first time, a formalized statement of his theory of differential association, a perspective that Sutherland based on the "laws of imitation" described by Gabriel Tarde (1843–1904), a French sociologist.

The theory of differential association explains crime as a natural consequence of the interaction with criminal lifestyles.

CJ | ISSUES
The Physical Environment and Crime

Social ecology theory—an outgrowth of the Chicago School of sociological thought, which flourished during the 1920s and 1930s—posited a link between physical location and crime. A modern perspective, called crime prevention through environmental design (CPTED), bears a strong resemblance to such earlier ecological theories. CPTED, which was first formulated in the 1960s and 1970s, focuses on the settings in which crimes occur and on techniques for reducing vulnerability within those settings. Because defensible space concepts are being increasingly applied to the design of physical facilities, including housing, parking garages, public buildings, and even entire neighborhoods, it is highly likely that applications of CPTED will accelerate throughout the twenty-first century.

Second-generation **defensible space theory**, upon which contemporary CPTED is built, developed around 1980 and considered more carefully how the impact of physical features on fear and victimization depends on other social and cultural features in the setting. Second-generation defensible space theory employed the **broken windows theory**, which holds that physical deterioration and an increase in unrepaired buildings lead to increased concerns for personal safety among area residents. Heightened concerns, in turn, lead to further decreases in maintenance and repair and to increased delinquency, vandalism, and crime among local residents, which spawn even further deterioration both in a sense of safety and in the physical environment. Offenders from other neighborhoods are then increasingly attracted by the area's perceived vulnerability.

Research on CPTED has shown environmental design to be effective in lowering crime and crime-related public-order problems. Effective use of CPTED to alter features of the physical environment can affect potential offenders' perceptions about a possible crime site,

A run-down city street. To explain crime, criminologists sometimes use the "broken windows" approach, which says that neighborhood deterioration leads to rising crime rates. Similarly, poverty, unemployment, a relative lack of formal education, and low skill levels, which often characterize inner-city populations, seem to be linked to criminality. Why?

their evaluations of the opportunities associated with that site, and the availability and visibility of one or more natural guardians at or near the site. CPTED is based on the belief that offenders decide whether to commit a crime in a particular location after they evaluate the area's features, including (1) the ease of entry to the area, (2) the visibility of the target to others—that is, the chance of being seen, (3) the attractiveness or vulnerability of the target, (4) the likelihood that criminal behavior will be challenged or thwarted if discovered, and (5) the ease of egress—that is, the ability to quickly and easily leave the area once the crime has been committed.

According to the National Institute of Justice, CPTED suggests four approaches to making a location more resistant to crime and to crime-related public-order problems:

- *Housing design or block layout*—making it more difficult to commit crimes by (1) reducing the availability of crime targets, (2) removing barriers that prevent easy detection of potential offenders or of an offense in progress, and (3) increasing physical obstacles to committing a crime.

- *Land use and circulation patterns*—creating safer use of neighborhood space by reducing routine exposure of potential offenders to crime targets. This can be accomplished through careful attention to walkways, paths, streets, traffic patterns, and locations and hours of operation of public spaces and facilities. Street closings or revised traffic patterns that decrease vehicular volume may, under some conditions, encourage residents to better maintain the sidewalks and streets in front of their houses.

- *Territorial features*—encouraging the use of territorial markers or fostering conditions that will lead to more extensive marking to indicate that the block or site is occupied by vigilant residents. Sponsoring cleanup and beautification contests and creating controllable, semiprivate outdoor locations may encourage such activities. This strategy focuses on small-scale, private, and semipublic sites, usually within predominantly residential locales. It is most relevant at the street-block level and below. It enhances the chances that residents themselves will generate semifixed features that demonstrate their involvement in and watchfulness over a particular delimited location.

- *Physical maintenance*—controlling physical deterioration to reduce offenders' perceptions that areas are vulnerable to crime and that residents are so fearful they would do nothing to stop a crime. Physical improvements may reduce the signals of vulnerability and increase commitment to joint protective activities. Physical deterioration, in all probability, not only influences the cognition and behavior of potential offenders but also shapes how residents behave and what they think about other residents.

For additional information on CPTED via the Crime Mapping Research Center, see **http://www.justicestudies.com/pubs/cpted.pdf**.

References: Derek J. Paulsen and Matthew B. Robinson, *Spatial Aspects of Crime: Theory and Practice* (Boston: Allyn and Bacon, 2004); Oscar Newman, *Defensible Space* (New York: Macmillan, 1972); Oscar Newman, *Creating Defensible Space* (Washington, DC: HUD, 1996); James Q. Wilson and George Kelling, "Broken Windows," *Atlantic Monthly*, March 1982; Dan Fleissner and Fred Heinzelmann, *Crime Prevention through Environmental Design and Community Policing* (Washington, DC: NIJ, 1996); Ralph B. Taylor and Adele V. Harrell, *Physical Environment and Crime* (Washington, DC: NIJ, 1996); Mary S. Smith, *Crime Prevention through Environmental Design in Parking Facilities* (Washington, DC: NIJ, 1996); and Corey L. Gordon and William Brill, *The Expanding Role of Crime Prevention through Environmental Design in Premises Liability* (Washington, DC: NIJ, 1996).

■ **lecture note**   Give an example of how Sutherland's principles might play out in the life of a criminal and in the life of a conformist.

■ **theme**   Why is it important to study the reasons why some people do *not* commit crime?

■ **social learning theory**   A psychological perspective that says that people learn how to behave by modeling themselves after others whom they have the opportunity to observe.

Sutherland suggested that children raised in crime-prone environments were often isolated and unable to experience the values that would otherwise lead to conformity. Differential association provides the basis for much research in modern criminology.[97] Even popular stories of young drug pushers, for instance, often refer to the fact that inner-city youths imitate what they see. Some residents of poverty-ridden ghettos learn quickly that fast money can be made in the illicit drug trade, and they tend to follow the examples of material "success" that they see around them.

Differential association views crime as the product of socialization and sees it as being acquired by criminals according to the same principles that guide the learning of law-abiding behavior in conformists. Differential association removes criminality from the framework of the abnormal and places it squarely within a general perspective applicable to all behavior. In the 1947 edition of his text, Sutherland wrote, "Criminal behavior is a part of human behavior, has much in common with noncriminal behavior, and must be explained within the same general framework as any other human behavior."[98] A study of the tenets of differential association (listed in Table 3-3) shows that Sutherland believed that even the sources of behavioral motivation are much the same for conformists and criminals—that is,

TABLE 3-3 | Sutherland's Principles of Differential Association

1. Criminal behavior is learned.
2. Criminal behavior is learned in interaction with others in a process of communication.
3. The principal part of the learning of criminal behavior occurs within intimate personal groups.
4. When criminal behavior is learned, the learning includes (a) techniques of committing the crime, which are sometimes very complicated, sometimes very simple, and (b) the specific direction of motives, drives, rationalizations, and attitudes.
5. The specific direction of motives and drives is learned from definitions of the legal codes as favorable or unfavorable.
6. A person becomes delinquent because of an excess of definitions favorable to violations of law over definitions unfavorable to violations of law.
7. Differential associations may vary in frequency, duration, priority, and intensity.
8. The process of learning criminal behavior by association with criminal and anticriminal patterns involves all the mechanisms that are involved in any other learning.
9. Although criminal behavior is an expression of general needs and values, it is not explained by those general needs and values because noncriminal behavior is an expression of the same needs and values.

Source: Sutherland's Principles of Differential Association from *Principles of Criminology* by Edwin Sutherland. Copyright (c) 1992 Rowman and Littlefield Publishing. Reproduced by permission of Patricia Zline.

both groups strive for money and success but choose different paths to the same goal.

However, differential association theory fails to explain why people have the associations they do and why some associations affect certain individuals more than others. Why, for example, are most prison guards unaffected by their constant association with offenders, while a few take advantage of their position to smuggle contraband? The theory has also been criticized for being so general and imprecise as to allow for little testing.[99] Complete testing of the theory would require that all of the associations a person has ever had be recorded and analyzed from the standpoint of the individual—a clearly impossible task.

Other theorists continue to build on Sutherland's early work. Robert Burgess and Ronald Akers, for example, have constructed a differential association–reinforcement theory that seeks to integrate Sutherland's original propositions with the work of American psychologist B. F. Skinner's work on conditioning.[100] Burgess and Akers suggest that although values and behavior patterns are learned in association with others, the primary mechanism through which such learning occurs is operant conditioning. Reinforcement is the key, they say, to understanding any social learning as it takes place. The name **social learning theory** has been widely applied to the work of Burgess and Akers. It is somewhat of a misnomer, however, because the term can easily encompass a wide range of approaches and should not be limited to one specific combination of the ideas found in differential association and reinforcement theory.

Restraint Theories

As we have seen throughout this chapter, most criminological theories posit a cause of crime.[101] Some theories, however, focus less on causes than on constraints—those forces that keep people from committing a crime. These theories are called *restraint theories*. However, because they focus primarily on why people do not break the law, restraint theories provide only half of the causal picture. They are especially weak in identifying the social-structural sources of motivations to commit crimes.[102] Also, the ways in which bonds with different institutions interact with one another and with personal attributes, as well as the variety of bonds that operate throughout the life cycle, have yet to be clarified.[103]

Containment Theory

Containment theory, a type of restraint theory offered by Walter Reckless (1899–1988), assumes that all of us are subject to inducements to crime.[104] Some of us resist these "pushes" toward criminal behavior, whereas others do not. The difference, according to Reckless, can be found in forces that contain, or control, behavior.

■ **lecture note**   Explain labeling theory as a product of the tumultuous 1960s. Ask students what form of "treatment" labeling theorists might suggest for convicted offenders.

■ **containment**   The aspects of the social bond and of the personality that act to prevent individuals from committing crimes and engaging in deviance.

■ **labeling theory**   A social process perspective that sees continued crime as a consequence of the limited opportunities for acceptable behavior that follow from the negative responses of society to those defined as offenders.

Reckless described two types of **containment**: outer and inner. Outer containment depends on social roles and the norms and expectations that apply to them. People who occupy significant roles in society find themselves insulated from deviant tendencies. A corporate executive, for example, is less apt to hold up a liquor store than is a drifter. The difference, according to Reckless, is not due solely to income, but also to the pressure the executive feels to conform.

Inner containment involves a number of factors, such as conscience, a positive self-image, a tolerance for frustration, and aspirations that are in line with reality. Reckless believed that inner containment is more powerful than outer containment; inner containment functions even in secret. For example, an inner-directed person who comes across a lost purse feels compelled to locate its rightful owner and return it. If theft or greed crosses the mind of an inner-directed person, he will say to himself, "I'm not that kind of person. That would be wrong."

Reckless studied small close-knit societies—including the Hutterites, Mennonites, and Amish—in developing his theory. He realized that the "containment of behavior … is … maximized under conditions of isolation and homogeneity of culture, class, and population."[105] Hence its applicability to modern American society, with its considerable heterogeneity of values and perspectives, is questionable.

Social Control Theory

Travis Hirschi emphasized the bond between individuals and society as the primary operative mechanism in his *social control theory*.[106] Hirschi identified four components of that bond: (1) emotional attachments to significant others, (2) a commitment to appropriate lifestyles, (3) involvement or immersion in conventional values, and (4) a belief in the "correctness" of social obligations and the rules of the larger society. These components act as social controls on deviant and criminal behavior; as they weaken, social control suffers, and the likelihood of crime and deviance increases. Using self-reports of delinquency from high school students in California, Hirschi concluded that youngsters who were less attached to teachers and parents and who had few positive attitudes about their own accomplishments were more likely to engage in crime and deviance than were others.[107]

Neutralization Techniques

Complementing restraint theory is the *neutralization approach* of Gresham Sykes and David Matza.[108] The neutralization approach centers on rationalizations that allow offenders to shed feelings of guilt and responsibility for their behavior. Sykes and Matza believed that most people drift into and out of criminal behavior but will not commit a crime unless they have available to them techniques of neutralization. Their study primarily concerned juveniles for whom, they suggested, neutralization techniques provided only a temporary respite from guilt. That respite, however, lasted long enough to avoid the twinges of conscience while a crime was being committed. Neutralization techniques include the following:

- Denial of responsibility ("I'm a product of my background.")
- Denial of injury ("No one was really hurt.")
- Denial of the victim ("They deserved it.")
- Condemnation of the condemners ("The cops are corrupt.")
- Appeal to higher loyalties ("I did it for my friends.")

Like containment theory, restraint theories tend to depend on a general agreement as to values, or they assume that offenders are simply conformists who suffer temporary lapses. Neutralization techniques, by definition, are needed only when the delinquent has been socialized into middle-class values or where conscience is well developed. Even so, neutralization techniques do not in themselves explain crime. Such techniques are available to us all, if we make only a slight effort to conjure them up. The real question is why some people readily allow proffered neutralizations to affect their behavior, while others effortlessly discount them.

Labeling Theory

As we saw earlier in this chapter, the worth of any theory of behavior is proved by how well it reflects the reality of the social world. In practice, however, theoretical perspectives find acceptance in the academic environment via a number of considerations. **Labeling theory**, for example, became fashionable in the 1960s. Its popularity may have been due more to the cultural environment into which it was introduced rather than to any inherent quality of the theory itself.

Labeling theory was first introduced by Frank Tannenbaum (1893–1969) in 1938 under the rubric of *tagging*.[109] He wrote, "The young delinquent becomes bad because he is defined as bad and because he is not believed if he is good." He went on to say, "The process of making the criminal, therefore, is a process of tagging. … It becomes a way of stimulating … and evolving the very traits that are complained of. … The person becomes the thing he is described as being."[110] Tannenbaum focused on society's power to *define* an act or an individual as bad and drew attention to the

■ **lecture note**   Explain that social development theory is a fairly recent perspective and discuss how it differs from the other theories already discussed in this chapter.

■ **moral enterprise**   The process undertaken by an advocacy group to have its values legitimated and embodied in law.

■ **social development theory**   An integrated view of human development that points to the process of interaction among and between individuals and society as the root cause of criminal behavior.

■ **life course perspective**   An approach to explaining crime and deviance that investigates developments and turning points in the course of a person's life.

group need for a scapegoat in explaining crime. The search for causes inherent in individuals was not yet exhausted, however, and Tannenbaum's theory fell mostly on deaf ears.

By the 1960s, the social and academic environments in America had changed, and the issue of responsibility was seen more in terms of the group than the individual. In his book *Outsiders*, published in 1963, Howard Becker pointed out that criminality is not a quality inherent in an act or in a person. Crime, said Becker, results from a social definition, through law, of unacceptable behavior. That definition arises through **moral enterprise**, by which groups on both sides of an issue debate and eventually legislate their notion of what is moral and what is not. Becker wrote, "The central fact about deviance [is that] it is created by society. … Social groups create deviance by making the rules whose infraction constitutes deviance."[111]

The criminal label, however, produces consequences for labeled individuals that may necessitate continued criminality. In describing the criminal career, Becker wrote, "To be labeled a criminal one need only commit a single criminal offense. … Yet the word carries a number of connotations specifying auxiliary traits characteristic of anyone bearing the label."[112] The first time a person commits a crime, the behavior is called *primary deviance* and may be a merely transitory form of behavior.

However, in the popular mind, a "known" criminal is not to be trusted, should not be hired because of the potential for crimes on the job, and would not be a good candidate for the military, marriage, or any position requiring responsibility. Society's tendency toward such thinking, Becker suggested, closes legitimate opportunities, ensuring that the only new behavioral alternatives available to the labeled criminal are deviant ones. Succeeding episodes of criminal behavior are seen as a form of secondary deviance that eventually becomes stabilized in the behavioral repertoire and self-concept of the labeled person.[113]

Labeling theory can be critiqued along a number of dimensions. First, it is not really a "theory" in that labeling does not uncover the genesis of criminal behavior. It is more useful in describing how such behavior continues than in explaining how it originates. Second, labeling theory does not recognize the possibility that the labeled individual may make successful attempts at reform and may shed the negative label. Finally, the theory does not provide an effective way of dealing with offenders. Should people who commit crimes not be arrested and tried so as to avoid the consequences of negative labels? It would be exceedingly naïve to suggest that all repeat criminal behavior would cease, as labeling theory might predict, if people who commit crimes are not officially "handled" by the system.

Social Development and the Life Course

Some of the most recent perspectives on crime causation belong to a subcategory of social process thought called **social development theory**. According to the social development perspective, human development occurs simultaneously on many levels, including the psychological, biological, familial, interpersonal, cultural, societal, and ecological levels. Hence social development theories tend to be integrated theories—that is, theories that combine various points of view on the process of development. Theories that fall into this category, however, highlight the process of interaction between individuals and society as the root cause of criminal behavior. In particular, they emphasize that a critical period of transition occurs in a person's life as he or she moves from childhood to adulthood.

One social development approach is the dual taxonomy theory of offending offered by Terrie Moffitt in the 1990s.[114] Moffitt identifies two types of offenders: *adolescent limited offenders* and *life course persistent offenders*. The first type, adolescent limited offenders, are prone to antisocial behavior only during adolescence; the second type, life course persisters, continue to reoffend throughout life. Moffitt was interested in explaining the continuity and stability of antisocial behavior, and noted that life course persisters evidence significant antisocial attitudes and behavior early on in life. Moffitt's theory, while it is concerned with the development of antisocial behavior, combines biological factors (genetic influences, brain injury, and the like) with social ones (childhood abuse and neglect, bad parenting, and other factors) and proposes that initial biological predispositions can combine with a negative childhood environment to produce antisocial behavior that persists over time.

> Initial biological predispositions can combine with a negative childhood environment to produce antisocial behavior that persists over time.

Another social development perspective of special significance is the **life course perspective**. According to Robert Sampson and John Laub, who named the life course perspective in 1993, criminal behavior typically follows an identifiable pattern throughout a person's life cycle.[115] In the lives of those who eventually become criminal, crime-like or deviant behavior is relatively rare during early childhood, tends to begin as sporadic instances during early adolescence, becomes more common during the late-teen and early-adult years, and then gradually diminishes as the person gets older.

Sampson and Laub also use the idea of *transitions* in the life course, or turning points that identify significant events in a person's life and represent the opportunity for people to turn either away from or toward deviance and crime. An employer who gives an employee a second chance, for example, may provide a unique opportunity that helps determine the future course of that person's life. Similarly, the principle of *linked lives*, also common to life course theories, highlights the fact that no one lives in isolation. Events in the life course are constantly being influenced by family members, friends, acquaintances, employers, teachers, and so on. Not only might such influences determine the life course of any given individual, but they are active throughout the life course. Figure 3-3 diagrams some of the life course influences experienced by most adolescents. Also shown in the diagram are desired outcomes and positive and negative indicators of development.

In 1986, the federal Office of Juvenile Justice and Delinquency Prevention (OJJDP) began funding a study of life pathways as they lead to criminality. The Program of Research on the Causes and Correlates of Delinquency continues to

produce results.[116] Over a period of years, researchers examined how delinquency, violence, and drug use develop within and are related to various social contexts, including the family, peer groups, schools, and the surrounding community. To date, the study, for which data continue to be analyzed, has identified three distinct pathways to delinquency, which are shown in Figure 3-4. These pathways are not mutually exclusive and can sometimes converge:

- The *authority conflict pathway*, along which children begin to move during their early years (as early as three or four years old), involves stubborn behavior and resistance to parental authority. Defiance of authority begins around age 11, and authority avoidance (i.e., truancy, running away) begins about the same time.
- The *covert pathway*, which starts around age ten with minor covert acts such as shoplifting and lying, quickly progresses to acts of vandalism involving property damage. Moderate to severe delinquency frequently begins a year or two later.
- The *overt pathway* is marked by minor aggression, such as bullying, that develops around age 11 or 12. The overt

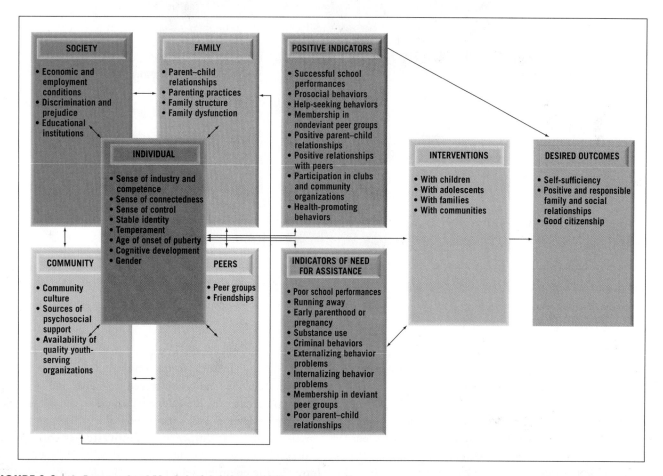

FIGURE 3-3 | A Conceptual Model of Adolescent Development
Source: Family and Youth Services Bureau, *Understanding Youth Development: Promoting Positive Pathways of Growth* (Washington, DC: U.S. Dept. of Health and Human Services, 2000).

■ **lecture note**   Explain the concept of an interdisciplinary theory of criminal behavior that combines elements of all the schools of thought described in this chapter. Suggest that such a perspective, at the very least, might combine biological, psychological, and sociological elements in one perspective.

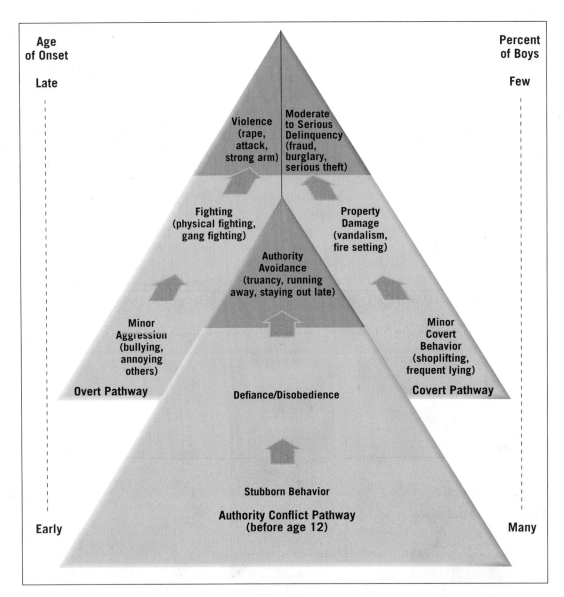

FIGURE 3-4 | Three Pathways to Disruptive Behavior and Delinquency

Source: Barbara Tatem Kelley et al., *Developmental Pathways in Boys' Disruptive and Delinquent Behavior* (Washington, DC: Office of Juvenile Justice and Delinquency Prevention, 1997).

pathway leads to fighting and physical violence during the teenage years and tends to eventuate in serious violent criminality that may include rape, robbery, and assault.

A similar study is under way at the Project on Human Development in Chicago Neighborhoods (PHDCN), mentioned earlier in this chapter. PHDCN researchers are "tracing how criminal behavior develops from birth to age 32."[117] Participating researchers come from a variety of scientific backgrounds and include psychiatrists, developmental psychologists, sociologists,

criminologists, physicians, educators, statisticians, and public health officials. The study focuses on the influence of communities, peers, families, and health-related, cognitive, and emotional factors to decipher the lines along which crime and delinquency are likely to develop. Learn more about the OJJDP's causes and correlates study at **http://www.justicestudies.com/pubs/ccdp.pdf**, and find out more about the PHDCN project at **http://ccf.tc.columbia.edu/neighborhood03.html**. A related effort, the Pathways to Desistance Study, can be reviewed at **http://justicestudies.com/pubs/pathways2015.pdf**.

■ **lecture notes**   Explain that the other theories in this chapter are mainly based on a consensus view, as contrasted with the conflict perspective.

■ **conflict perspective**   A theoretical approach that holds that crime is the natural consequence of economic and other social inequities. Conflict theorists highlight the stresses that arise among and within social groups as they compete with one another for resources and for survival. The social forces that result are viewed as major determinants of group and individual behavior, including crime.

■ **lecture note**   Describe radical criminology. Explain how radical criminologists see the causes of crime as rooted in social inequities. Ask students what form of "treatment" radical criminologists might suggest for convicted offenders.

radical criminology   A conflict perspective that sees crime as engendered by the unequal distribution of wealth, power, and other resources, which adherents believe is especially characteristic of capitalist societies.

Conflict Theories

Basic to the **conflict perspective** is the belief that conflict is a fundamental aspect of social life and can never be fully resolved. From the conflict point of view, formal agencies of social control at best merely coerce the unempowered or the disenfranchised to comply with the rules established by those in power. Laws become tools of the powerful, tools that are useful in keeping others from wresting control over important social institutions. Social order, rather than being the result of any consensus or process of dispute resolution, rests on the exercise of power through law. The conflict perspective can be described in terms of four key elements:[118]

- Society is composed of diverse social groups, and diversity is based on distinctions that people hold to be significant, such as gender, sexual orientation, and social class.
- Conflict among groups is unavoidable because of differing interests and differing values. Hence conflict is inherent in social life.
- The fundamental nature of group conflict centers on the exercise of political power. Political power is the key to the accumulation of wealth and to other forms of power.
- Laws are the tools of power and further the interests of those powerful enough to make them. Laws allow those in control to gain what they define (through the law) as legitimate access to scarce resources and to deny (through the law) such access to the politically disenfranchised.

Radical Criminology

Criminological theory took a new direction during the 1960s and 1970s, brought about in part by the turmoil that characterized American society during that period. **Radical criminology** placed the blame for criminality and deviant behavior squarely on officially sanctioned cultural and economic arrangements. The distribution of wealth and power in society was held to be the primary cause of criminal behavior, especially among those who were disenfranchised. Poverty and discrimination were seen to lead to frustration and pent-up hostilities that were expressed through murder, rape, theft, and other crimes.

Radical criminology had its roots in early conflict theories and in the thought of Dutch criminologist Willem Bonger (1876–1940). Some authors have distinguished between conflict theory and radical criminology by naming them "conservative

conflict theory" and "radical conflict theory," respectively.[119] The difference between the two theories, however, is mostly in the rhetoric of the times. Conservative conflict theories held that conflict was a natural part of any society and that struggles for power and control would always occur. "Losers" of conflicts were defined as "criminal," and constraints on their behavior would be legislated. Characteristic of this perspective are the approaches of Austin Turk[120] (b. 1934) and George Vold (1896–1967). An even earlier conflict perspective can be found in the culture conflict notions of Thorsten Sellin (1896–1994), who was concerned with the clash of immigrant values and traditions with those of established American culture.[121]

Radical criminology went a step further. It recognized that the struggle to control resources is central to society, and it encompassed the notion that the law is a tool of the powerful. The focus of radical criminology, however, was capitalism and the evils that capitalism was believed to entail. The ideas of Karl Marx (1818–1883) entered the field of criminology through the writings of William Chambliss[122] (b. 1933) and Richard Quinney[123] (b. 1934). According to Marx, the labor of the lower classes provides the basis for the accumulated wealth of the upper classes, and the lower classes are always exploited by the "owners" in society. The poor were trained to believe that capitalism was in their best interests and the working classes suffered under the consequences of a "false class consciousness"

Joel Steffenheim/Corbis

A homeless man walking by an expensive home. Radical criminologists claim that the inequitable distribution of wealth in society produces frustrations and pent-up hostilities that lead to criminality. In this view, the powerful use the criminal law as a tool to maintain their privileged place in the social world. Do you agree? Why or why not?

peacemaking criminology   A perspective that holds that crime-control agencies and the citizens they serve should work together to alleviate social problems and human suffering and thus reduce crime.

perpetrated by the powerful. Marx believed that only when the exploited workers realized their exploitation would they rebel and change society for the better.

American radical criminology built on the ideals of the 1960s and charged that the "establishment," controlled by the upper classes, perverted justice through the unequal application of judicial sanctions. As David Greenberg observes, "Many researchers attributed the overrepresentation of blacks and persons from impoverished family backgrounds in arrest and conviction statistics to the discriminatory practices of the enforcement agencies. It was not that the poor stole more, but rather that when they did, the police were more likely to arrest them."[124] Conflict theories of criminality face the difficulty of realistic implementation. Radical criminology, in particular, is flawed by its narrow emphasis on capitalist societies. It fails to recognize adequately the role of human nature in the creation of social classes and in the perpetuation of the struggle for control of resources. Radical criminology implies that a utopian social arrangement—perhaps communism—would eliminate most crime. Such a belief is contrary to historical experience: A close look at any contemporary communist society will reveal both social conflict and crime.

Peacemaking Criminology

Peacemaking criminology, which some theorists see as a mature expression of earlier conflict theories, holds that crime-control agencies and the citizens they serve should work together to alleviate social problems and human suffering and thus reduce crime.[125] Criminology as peacemaking has its roots in ancient Christian and Eastern philosophies, as well as in traditional conflict theory. Peacemaking criminology, which includes the notion of service and has also been called *compassionate criminology*, suggests that "compassion, wisdom, and love are essential for understanding the suffering of which we are all a part, and for practicing a criminology of nonviolence."[126] Peacemaking criminology also holds that official agents of social control need to work with both the victimized and the victimizers to achieve a new world order that is more just and fair to all who live in it. In a fundamental sense, peacemaking criminologists exhort their colleagues to transcend personal dichotomies to end the political and ideological divisiveness that separates people. "If we ourselves cannot know peace … how will our acts disarm hatred and violence?" they ask.[127]

> Criminology as peacemaking has its roots in ancient Christian and Eastern philosophies, as well as in traditional conflict theory.

Peacemaking criminology was popularized by the works of Harold Pepinsky[128] and Richard Quinney[129] beginning in 1986. Both Pepinsky and Quinney restate the problem of crime control from one of "how to stop crime" to one of "how to make peace" within society and among citizens and criminal justice agencies. Peacemaking criminology draws attention to many issues, among them the perpetuation of violence through the continuation of social policies based on dominant forms of criminological theory, the role of education in peacemaking, "common sense theories of crime," crime control as human rights enforcement, and conflict resolution within community settings.[130]

Social Policy and Conflict Theories

Because radical and conflict criminologists view social inequality as the cause of crime, many suggest that the only way to achieve real change in the rate of crime is through revolution. Revolution—because it holds the promise of greater equality for underrepresented groups and because it mandates a redistribution of wealth and power—is thought necessary for any lasting reduction in crime.

Some contemporary writers on radical criminology, however, have attempted to address the issue of what can be done under our current system, because they recognize that a sudden and total reversal of existing political arrangements within the United States is highly unlikely. Hence they have begun to focus on promoting "middle-range policy alternatives" to the present system, including "equal justice in the bail system, the abolition of mandatory sentences, prosecution of corporate crimes, increased employment opportunities, and promoting community alternatives to imprisonment."[131] Likewise, programs to reduce prison overcrowding, efforts to highlight injustices within the current system, the elimination of racism and other forms of inequality in the handling of both victims and offenders, growing equality in criminal justice system employment, and the like are all frequently mentioned as mid-range strategies for bringing about a justice system that is fairer and closer to the radical ideal.

Raymond Michalowski summarizes the policy directions envisioned by today's radical criminologists when he says, "We cannot be free from the crimes of the poor until there are no more poor; we cannot be free from domination of the powerful until we reduce the inequalities that make domination possible; and we cannot live in harmony with others until we begin to limit the competition for material advantage over others that alienates us from one another."[132]

■ **theme** How does female criminality differ from male offending?
■ **feminist criminology** A developing intellectual approach that emphasizes gender issues in criminology.

Emergent Perspectives

A number of new and developing criminological perspectives deserve special mention. They include feminist, biosocial, and postmodern criminology. Biosocial criminology has already been discussed earlier in this chapter. Now, however, we will briefly discuss feminist and postmodern criminology.

Feminist Criminology

As some writers in the developing field of **feminist criminology** have observed, "Women have been virtually invisible in criminological analysis until recently and much theorizing has proceeded as though criminality is restricted to men."[133] Another puts it this way: "[Traditional] criminological theory assumes a woman is like a man."[134] Feminist criminologists are now working to change long-cherished notions of crime and of criminal justice so that the role of women in both crime causation and crime control might be better appreciated.[135]

One of the first writers to attempt a definitive explanation of the criminality of women was Otto Pollak. Pollak's book, *The Criminality of Women*,[136] written in 1950, suggested that women commit the same number of offenses as men but that most of their criminality is hidden. Pollak claimed that women's roles at the time, primarily those of homemaker and mother, served to disguise their criminal undertakings. He also proposed that chivalrous treatment by a male-dominated justice system acted to bias every stage of criminal justice processing in favor of women. Hence, according to Pollak, although women are just as criminal as men, they are rarely arrested, tried, or imprisoned. In fact, although the criminality of women may approach or exceed that of men in selected offense categories, today it is safe to say that Pollak was incorrect in his assessment of the degree of female criminality; overall, women commit far fewer crimes than men.

Early works in the field of feminist criminology include Freda Adler's *Sisters in Crime*[137] and Rita Simon's *Women and Crime*.[138] Both books were published in 1975, and in them the authors claimed that the existing divergences in crime rates between men and women were due primarily to socialization rather than biology. Women, claimed these authors, were taught to believe in personal limitations, faced reduced socioeconomic opportunities, and, as a result, suffered from lowered aspirations. As gender equality increased, they said, it could be expected that male and female criminality would take on similar characteristics. More recent researchers, however, have not found this to be true; substantial differences between the criminality of men and women remain, even as gender equality grows.[139]

Contemporary feminist thinking in criminology is represented by the works of writers like Kathleen Daly and Meda Chesney-Lind.[140] Daly and Chesney-Lind emphasize the need for a "gender-aware" criminology and stress the usefulness of applying feminist thinking to criminological analysis. Gender, say these writers, is a central organizing principle of contemporary life. Feminist criminology suggests that theories of crime causation and prevention must include women and that more research on gender-related issues in the field is badly needed. Additionally, some authors say, "Criminologists should begin to appreciate that their discipline and its questions are a product of white, economically privileged men's experiences."[141] They suggest that rates of female criminality, which are lower than those of males, may show that criminal behavior is not as "normal" as once thought. Because modern-day criminological perspectives were mostly developed by white middle-class males, the propositions and theories they advance fail to take into consideration women's "ways of knowing."[142] Hence the fundamental challenge posed by feminist criminology is this: Do existing theories of crime causation apply as well to women as they do to men? Or, as Daly and Chesney-Lind put it, given the current situation in theory development, "do theories of men's crime apply to women?"[143]

Recent perspectives on female criminality stress that "a key to understanding and responding to women as offenders is understanding their status as crime victims."[144] Psychologist Cathy Spatz Widom, for example, examined the life cycle of female offenders, looking for links between childhood abuse and neglect and later criminality. Widom suggests that the successful socialization of girls can be "derailed" by early victimization through mechanisms such as "running away, deficits in cognitive ability and achievement, growing up without traditional social controls, engaging in relationships with deviant or delinquent individuals, and failing to learn the social and psychological skills necessary for successful adult development."[145]

Contemporary statistics tell us that although females make up 51% of the population of the United States, they are arrested for only 20.2% of all violent crimes and 39.2% of property crimes. The relatively limited involvement of women in the FBI's eight major crimes can be seen in Table 3-4. Data show that the number of female offenders is increasing faster than the number of male offenders, however. Between 1970 and 2000, an era of significant crime increases, the number of crimes committed by men grew by 46%, while crimes committed by women increased 144%. Violent crimes by men increased 82% during the period; by women, 260%. Property crimes perpetrated by men grew by 3%; by women, 85%.[146]

■ **theme**   Which of the emergent perspectives discussed in this chapter seems to hold the most promise? Why?

■ **theme**   Which theory of criminality described in this chapter do you think is most useful for understanding criminal behavior? Are some theories more applicable to certain forms of criminality than to others?

■ **activity**   Have students rate each major theoretical perspective in terms of its usefulness in understanding what motivates individual offenders who perpetrate particular crimes, such as the FBI's Part I offenses.

■ **activity**   Have students choose a crime that is currently in the news and apply to it the various theoretical perspectives described in this chapter. What kind of insight can each perspective provide into understanding the offender's motivation? Given the nature of the crime, which of the perspectives holds the most hope for rehabilitation? Which holds the least?

■ **theme**   Which of the theories described in this chapter are most likely to appeal to individual-rights advocates? Which are likely to appeal to public order advocates? What elements of each group's worldview are affirmed by the theories you selected? Does popular appeal make the theories in question any more or any less valid? Any more or any less useful?

■ **activity**   Have students arrange in-person or online interviews with various representatives of the criminal justice system. Ask students to do the following: Briefly explain to each practitioner interviewed the theories of criminal behavior described in this chapter. Ask the practitioners which of the theoretical approaches they think is most applicable to the kinds of offenders with whom they have dealt. Find out why these professionals think as they do, and report back to the class.

■ **postmodern criminology**   A branch of criminology that developed after World War II and that builds on the tenets of postmodern social thought.

■ **deconstructionist theory**   One of the emerging approaches that challenges existing criminological perspectives to debunk them and that works toward replacing them with concepts more applicable to the postmodern era.

TABLE 3-4 | Male and Female Involvement in Crime: Offense Patterns, 2014

UCR INDEX CRIME	PERCENTAGE OF ALL ARRESTS	
	MALES	FEMALES
Murder and nonnegligent manslaughter	88.5	11.5
Rape	97.2	2.8
Robbery	86.1	13.9
Aggravated assault	77.0	23.0
Burglary	82.2	17.8
Larceny-theft	56.9	43.2
Motor vehicle theft	79.7	20.3
Arson	80.5	19.5

Gender Differences

• Men are more likely than women to be arrested for serious crimes, such as murder, rape, robbery, and burglary.
• Arrest, jail, and prison data all suggest that more women than men who commit crimes are involved in property crimes, such as larceny, forgery, fraud, and embezzlement, and in drug offenses.

Source: Pearson Education, Inc.

Relative increases in the FBI's Part II offenses tell a similar story. Arrests of women for embezzlement, for example, increased by more than 228% between 1970 and 2000, versus only 8.5% for men—reflecting women's increased entry into positions of financial responsibility. Arrests of women for drug abuse grew by 289%, and liquor-law violations by women increased 285% (versus 96% for men).[147] In two officially reported categories—prostitution and runaways—women outnumber men in the volume of offenses committed.[148] Other crimes in which significant numbers of women (relative to men) are involved include larceny-theft (where 43.1% of reported crimes are committed by women), forgery and counterfeiting (37.4%), fraud (39.9%), and embezzlement (48.8%).[149] Nonetheless, as Table 3-4 shows, female offenders still account for only a small proportion of all

serious crimes. Statistics on female criminality are difficult to interpret because reports of increasing female criminality may reflect the greater equality of treatment accorded women in contemporary society more than they do actual increases in criminal activity. In the past, when women committed crimes, they were dealt with less formally than is likely to be the case today.

When women do commit serious crimes, they are more often followers than leaders. A study of women in correctional settings, for example, found that women are far more likely to assume "secondary follower roles during criminal events" than "dominant leadership roles."[150] Only 14% of women surveyed played primary roles, but those who did "felt that men had little influence in initiating or leading them into crime." African American women were found to be more likely to play "primary and equal crime roles" with men or with female accomplices than were white or Hispanic women. Statistics such as these dispel the myth that the female criminal in America has taken her place alongside the male offender—in terms of either leadership roles or the absolute number of crimes committed.

Postmodern Criminology

Before concluding this chapter, it is important to note that **postmodern criminology** is a term applied to a wide variety of novel perspectives that have developed in recent decades. It encompasses evolving paradigms with such intriguing names as *chaos theory*, *discourse analysis*, *topology theory*, *critical theory*, *realist criminology*, *constitutive theory*, and *anarchic criminology*.[151] Postmodern criminology builds on the belief that past criminological approaches have failed to realistically assess the true causes of crime and have therefore failed to offer workable solutions for crime control—or if they have, that such theories and solutions may have been appropriate at one time but no longer apply to the postmodern era. Because postmodern criminology challenges and debunks existing perspectives, it is referred to as *deconstructionist*, and such theories are sometimes called **deconstructionist theories**.

SUMMARY

- A theory is a proposed model of causal relationships between events and things under study. This chapter defines *theory* as a series of interrelated propositions that attempt to describe, explain, predict, and ultimately control some class of events. A good theory fits the facts and stands up to continued scrutiny. The goal of social research in criminology is to assist in the development of theoretical models that permit a better understanding of criminal behavior and that enhance the development of strategies intended to address the problem of crime.

- The Classical School of criminology, which was in vogue throughout the late eighteenth and early nineteenth centuries, held that crime is caused by the individual exercise of free will and that it can be deterred through the promise of swift and certain punishment. Classical criminology continues to be influential through today's neoclassical thought, represented by rational choice and routine activities theories.

- Traditional biological theories of crime posit a genetic or a physiological basis for deviant and criminal behavior. The notion of a "weak" gene that might predispose some people toward criminal activity has been expanded to include the impact of environmental contaminants, poor nutrition, and food additives on behavior. Studies of fraternal twins and chromosome structure have helped bring biological theories into the modern day. Such theories, however, have their shortcomings, including attributing the cause of crime to fundamental physical characteristics that are not easily modified.

- Biosocial criminology, a contemporary biological perspective, sees the interaction between biology and the physical, cultural, and social environments as key to understanding human behavior, including criminality. Biosocial criminology recognizes the role that human DNA, environmental contaminants, nutrition, hormones, physical trauma, and body chemistry play in behavior that violates the law. The detailed mapping of human DNA and other recent advances in the field of recombinant DNA have rekindled interest in genetic correlates of criminal behavior.

- Psychological explanations of crime are individualistic. Some psychoanalytic theories see offenders as psychotic, psychopathic, or sociopathic. Other psychological theories claim that criminal behavior is a type of conditioned response. The stimulus-response model sees criminal behavior as the consequence of a conditioning process that extends over the entire life span of an individual. Trait theory links personality (and associated traits) to behavior, and holds that it is an individual's personality, combined with his or her intelligence and natural abilities that produces criminality. Psychological traits are stable personality patterns that tend to endure throughout the life course and across social and cultural contexts. As with most other theories, psychological perspectives remain plagued by shortcomings. Among them are questions about whether past behavior can accurately predict future behavior and whether there are identifiable characteristics that violent offenders might manifest that could serve as warning signs of impending criminal activity.

- Sociological theories hold that the individual is a product of his or her social environment. They emphasize the role that social structure, inequality, and socialization play in criminality. Although they are today's perspective of choice, the danger of most sociological approaches is that they tend to deny the significance of any influences beyond those that are mediated through social interaction.

- Social process theories of criminology claim that crime results from the failure of self-direction, from inadequate social roles, or from associating with others who are already criminal. Social policies based on such theories place responsibility for change largely on the offender.

- Conflict perspectives attempt to explain crime by noting that conflict is fundamental to social life and by claiming that crime is a natural consequence of social, political, and economic inequity. Conflict criminologists believe that fundamental changes in the structure of society are needed if crime is to be eliminated or curtailed.

- Included among emergent approaches to explaining crime are feminist criminology and postmodern criminology. Feminist criminology challenges some long-held notions of crime and criminal justice that have been based solely on understandings of male criminality. Postmodern criminology, the last of the approaches discussed in this chapter, is often more an effort to debunk previous perspectives than it is a theoretical perspective in its own right.

KEY TERMS

anomie, 90
atavism, 80
behavioral conditioning, 86
Biological School, 79
biosocial criminology, 82
broken windows theory, 93
Chicago School, 89
chromosomes, 83
Classical School, 76
conflict perspective, 99
containment, 95
dangerousness, 89
deconstructionist theory, 102
defensible space theory, 93
deviance, 73
feminist criminology, 101
gender ratio problem, 82
genes, 83
heritability, 85
hypothesis, 75
interdisciplinary theory, 76
labeling theory, 95

life course perspective, 96
moral enterprise, 96
neoclassical criminology, 78
peacemaking criminology, 100
personality, 86
phrenology, 79
Positivist School, 80
postmodern criminology, 102
psychoanalysis, 86
psychological profiling, 88
Psychological School, 85
psychopath, 87
psychopathology, 87
psychosis, 87
radical criminology, 99
rational choice theory, 78
reaction formation, 92
research, 76
routine activities theory (RAT), 78
schizophrenic, 87
social development theory, 96

KEY CASES

QUESTIONS FOR REVIEW

1. What is a theory? Describe the steps in criminological theory building, and explain the role that social research plays in the development of theories about crime.

2. List the basic assumptions of classical theories of crime causation, and describe the neoclassical perspective.

3. Describe the basic features of biological theories of crime causation. What shortcomings of the biological perspective can you identify?

4. What is biosocial criminology? How do biosocial theories of criminality differ from other biological theories?

5. Describe the basic features of psychological explanations for crime. What are the shortcomings of this perspective?

6. Describe the basic features of sociological explanations for crime. What are the shortcomings of this perspective?

7. Describe social process theories of crime causation, including labeling theory and the life course perspective. What types of crime-control policies might be based on such theories?

8. Describe conflict theories of crime causation, including radical criminology and peacemaking criminology. What sorts of crime-control policies might be predicated on the basis of such theories?

9. What is meant by "emergent perspectives"? List and describe two emergent perspectives on crime causation.

QUESTIONS FOR REFLECTION

1. Chapter 1 referred briefly to evidence-based practices. What evidence-based practices might be developed as a result of the studies discussed in this chapter?

2. What is the relationship between punishment and classical and neoclassical thought? With what types of offenders might punishment be the most effective in reducing recidivism?

3. Do you think that biological theories successfully explain the causes of crime? Why or why not?

4. How do biosocial theories of crime differ from early biological theories? What is the central feature of biosocial theories?

5. Do you think that psychological theories of crime causation are sound? Why or why not?

6. Do you think that sociological theories of crime causation are sound? Why or why not?

NOTES

i. The American Heritage Dictionary and Electronic Thesaurus on CD-ROM (Boston: Houghton Mifflin, 1987).

1. Jayme Deerwester, "Surge Knight Arrested in Fatal Hit-and-Run," USA Today, January 30, 2015, http://www.usatoday.com/story/life/people/2015/01/29/the-wrap-suge-knight-fatal-car-crash/22561575/ (accessed May 20, 2015).

2. "Oakland Rapper 'Kenny Clutch' Killed in Las Vegas Strip Shooting," *Los Angeles Times*, February 22, 2013, http://latimes blogs.latimes.com/lanow/2013/02/oakland-rapper-kenny-clutch-killed-in-vegas-strip-shooting.html (accessed March 14, 2013).

3. "50 Cent Biography," *Sing365.com*, http://www.sing365.com/music/lyric.nsf/50-Cent-Biography/83CE63737F6CE6CB4825 6C79000EA96F (accessed June 1, 2013).

4. Rob Markman, "Rick Ross Is 'Layin' Back' after Shooting, Pusha T Says," *MTV.com*, January 29, 2013, http://www.mtv .com/news/articles/1700995/rick-ross-shooting-pusha-t -comments.jhtml (accessed January 29, 2013).

5. As we will see in Chapter 4, behavior that violates the criminal law may not be "crime" if accompanied by an acceptable legal justification or excuse. Justifications and excuses that are recognized by the law may serve as defenses to a criminal charge.

6. This and many of the statistics in these opening paragraphs come from Jonathan Wright, "Media Are Mixed Blessing, Criminologists Say," *Reuters*, May 2, 1995.

7. See "Comments of James T. Hamilton before the Federal Communications Commission, in the Matter of Industry Proposal for Rating Video Programming," May 23, 1997, citing Suzanne Stutman, Joanne Cantor, and Victoria Duran, *What Parents Want in a Television Rating System: Results of a National Survey* (Madison: University of Wisconsin, 1996); Wes Shipley and Gary Cavender, "Murder and Mayhem at the Movies," *Journal of Criminal Justice and Popular Culture*, Vol. 9, No. 1 (2001), pp. 1–14; and Suzanne Stutman, Joanne Cantor, and Victoria Duran, *What Parents Want in a Television Rating System: Results of a National Survey* (Washington, DC: National Parent Teacher Association, 2002), http://www.pta .org/ptacommunity/tvreport.asp (accessed August 21, 2007).

8. Jeffrey Johnson, "Television Viewing and Aggressive Behavior during Adolescence and Adulthood," *Science*, Vol. 295 (2002), pp. 2468–2471.

9. Nathan McCall, "My Rap against Rap," Washington Post wire service, November 14, 1993.

10. Arthur L. Cribbs, Jr., "Gangsta Rappers Sing White Racists' Tune," *USA Today*, December 27, 1993.

11. U.S. News/UCLA Survey on the Media and Violence, reported in "Hollywood: Right Face," *U.S. News and World Report*, May 15, 1995.

12. *Brown v. Entertainment Merchants Association*, U.S. Supreme Court, No. 08–1448 (decided June 27, 2011).

13. Ibid.

14. The word *scientific* is used here to refer to the application of generally accepted research strategies designed to reject explanations that rival the one under study.

15. Stephen Schafer, *Theories in Criminology* (New York: Random House, 1969), p. 109.

16. L. E. Cohen and Marcus Felson, "Social Change and Crime Rate Trends: A Routine Activity Approach," *American Sociological Review*, Vol. 44, No. 4 (August 1979), pp. 588–608. Also see Marcus Felson and L. E. Cohen, "Human Ecology and Crime: A Routine Activity Approach," *Human Ecology*, Vol. 8, No. 4 (1980), pp. 389–406; Marcus Felson, "Linking Criminal Choices, Routine

Activities, Informal Control, and Criminal Outcomes," in Derek B. Cornish and Ronald V. Clarke, eds., *The Reasoning Criminal: Rational Choice Perspectives on Offending* (New York: Springer-Verlag, 1986), pp. 119–128; and Ronald V. Clarke and Marcus Felson, eds., *Advances in Criminological Theory: Routine Activity and Rational Choice* (New Brunswick, NJ: Transaction, 1993).

17. Cohen and Felson, "Social Change and Crime Rate Trends," p. 595.

18. For a test of routine activities theory as an explanation for victimization in the workplace, see John D. Wooldredge, Francis T. Cullen, and Edward J. Latessa, "Victimization in the Workplace: A Test of Routine Activities Theory," *Justice Quarterly*, Vol. 9, No. 2 (June 1992), pp. 325–335.

19. Werner Einstadter and Stuart Henry, *Criminological Theory: An Analysis of Its Underlying Assumptions* (Fort Worth, TX: Harcourt Brace, 1995), p. 70.

20. For a modern reprint of a widely read nineteenth-century work on phrenology, see Orson Squire Fowler and Lorenzo Niles Fowler, *Phrenology: A Practical Guide to Your Head* (New York: Chelsea House, 1980).

21. Schafer, *Theories in Criminology*, p. 123.

22. Richard Louis Dugdale, *The Jukes: A Study in Crime, Pauperism, Disease, and Heredity*, 3rd ed. (New York: G. P. Putnam's Sons, 1985).

23. Henry Herbert Goddard, *The Kallikak Family: A Study in the Heredity of Feeblemindedness* (New York: Macmillan, 1912).

24. For more information, see Richard Herrnstein, "Crime File: Biology and Crime," a study guide (Washington, DC: National Institute of Justice, n.d.).

25. *Buck v. Bell*, 274 U.S. 200, 207 (1927).

26. Adrian Raine et al., "Prefrontal Glucose Deficits in Murderers Lacking Psychosocial Deprivation," *Neuropsychiatry, Neuropsychology, and Behavioral Neurology*, Vol. 11, No. 1 (1998), pp. 1–7.

27. Josh Fischman, "Criminal Minds," *Chronicle of Higher Education*, June 12, 2011, http://chronicle.com/article/Can-This-Man-Predict-Whether/127792 (accessed June 2, 2013).

28. Anthony Walsh.

29. Mary Kugler, "What Are Genes, DNA and Chromosomes?" About.com, http://rarediseases.about.com/od/geneticdisorders/a/genesbasics.htm (accessed December 6, 2012).

30. Patricia Jacobs et al., "Aggressive Behavior, Mental Subnormality, and the XYY Male," *Nature*, Vol. 208 (1965), pp. 1351–1352.

31. Schafer, *Theories in Criminology*, p. 193.

32. H. G. Brunner, M. Nelen, X. O. Breakefield, H. H. Ropers, and B. A. van Oost, "Abnormal Behavior Associated with a Point Mutation in the Structural Gene for Monoamine Oxidase A," *Science*, Vol. 262, No. 5133 (October 22, 1993), pp. 578–580.

33. A. E. Baum et al., "A Genome-Wide Association Study Implicates Diacylglycerol Kinase Eta (DGKH) and Several Other Genes in the Etiology of Bipolar Disorder," *Molecular Psychiatry*, advance online publication, http://doi:10.1038/sj.mp.4002012 (accessed May 8, 2007).

34. See "The Genome Changes Everything: A Talk with Matt Ridley," http://www.edge.org/3rd_culture/ridley03/ridley_print.html (accessed February 10, 2007).

35. Matt Ridley, "What Makes You Who You Are?" *Time*, June 2, 2003, pp. 55–63.

36. D. Hill and W. Sargent, "A Case of Matricide," *Lancet*, Vol. 244 (1943), pp. 526–527.

37. See, for example, A. R. Mawson and K. J. Jacobs, "Corn Consumption, Tryptophan, and Cross-National Homicide Rates," *Journal of Orthomolecular Psychiatry*, Vol. 7 (1978), pp. 227–230; and A. Hoffer, "The Relation of Crime to Nutrition," *Humanist in Canada*, Vol. 8 (1975), p. 8.

38. See, for example, C. Hawley and R. E. Buckley, "Food Dyes and Hyperkinetic Children," *Academy Therapy*, Vol. 10 (1974),

pp. 27–32; and Alexander Schauss, *Diet, Crime, and Delinquency* (Berkeley, CA: Parker House, 1980).

39. "Special Report: Measuring Your Life with Coffee Spoons," *Tufts University Diet and Nutrition Letter*, Vol. 2, No. 2 (April 1984), pp. 3–6.

40. See, for example, "Special Report: Does What You Eat Affect Your Mood and Actions?" *Tufts University Diet and Nutrition Letter*, Vol. 2, No. 12 (February 1985), pp. 4–6.

41. See *Tufts University Diet and Nutrition Letter*, Vol. 2, No. 11 (January 1985), p. 2; and "Special Report: Why Sugar Continues to Concern Nutritionists," *Tufts University Diet and Nutrition Letter*, Vol. 3, No. 3 (May 1985), pp. 3–6.

42. Diana H. Fishbein and Susan E. Pease, "Diet, Nutrition, and Aggression," in Marc Hillbrand and Nathaniel J. Pallone, eds., *The Psychobiology of Aggression: Engines, Measurement, Control* (New York: Haworth Press, 1994), pp. 114–117.

43. A. Hoffer, "Children with Learning and Behavioral Disorders," *Journal of Orthomolecular Psychiatry*, Vol. 5 (1976), p. 229.

44. See, Megan Visscher, "How Food Can Cut Crime," *Ode Magazine*, February 9, 2010, http://www.care2.com/greenliving/how-food-can-cut-crime.html?page=4 (accessed March 11, 2012).

45. Ap Zaalberg, Henk Nijman, Erik Bulten, Luwe Stroosma, and Cees van der Staak, "Effects of Nutritional Supplements on Aggression, Rule-Breaking, and Psychopathology among Young Adult Prisoners," *Aggressive Behavior*, Vol. 35 (2009), pp. 1–10.

46. C. B. Gesch, S. M. Hammond, S. E. Hampson, A. Eves, and M. J. Crowder, "Influence of Supplementary Vitamins, Minerals and Essential Fatty Acids on the Antisocial Behavior of Young Adult Prisoners: Randomized, Placebo-Controlled Trial," *British Journal of Psychiatry*, Vol. 181 (July 2002), pp. 22–28.

47. See, for example, R. T. Rada, D. R. Laws, and R. Kellner, "Plasma Testosterone Levels in the Rapist," *Psychomatic Medicine*, Vol. 38 (1976), pp. 257–268.

48. Later studies, however, have been less than clear. See, for example, J. M. Dabbs, Jr., "Testosterone Measurements in Social and Clinical Psychology," *Journal of Social and Clinical Psychology*, Vol. 11 (1992), pp. 302–321.

49. "The Insanity of Steroid Abuse," *Newsweek*, May 23, 1988, p. 75.

50. E. G. Stalenheim et al., "Testosterone as a Biological Marker in Psychopathy and Alcoholism," *Psychiatry Research*, Vol. 77, No. 2 (February 1998), pp. 79–88.

51. Michelle M. Wirth and Oliver C. Schultheiss, "Basal Testosterone Moderates Responses to Anger Faces in Humans," *Physiology and Behavior*, Vol. 90 (2007), pp. 496–505.

52. For a summary of such studies, see Serena-Lynn Brown, Alexander Botsis, and Herman M. Van Praag, "Serotonin and Aggression," in Hillbrand and Pallone, eds., *The Psychobiology of Aggression*, pp. 28–39.

53. Roger D. Masters, Brian Hone, and Anil Doshi, "Environmental Pollution, Neurotoxicity, and Criminal Violence," in J. Rose, ed., *Environmental Toxicology* (London and New York: Gordon and Breach, 1997).

54. B. Bioulac et al., "Serotonergic Functions in the XYY Syndrome," *Biological Psychiatry*, Vol. 15 (1980), pp. 917–923.

55. E. G. Stalenheim, L. von Knorring, and L. Wide, "Serum Levels of Thyroid Hormones as Biological Markers in a Swedish Forensic Psychiatric Population," *Biological Psychiatry*, Vol. 43, No. 10 (May 15, 1998), pp. 755–761.

56. R. B. Cattell, *The Inheritance of Personality and Ability: Research Methods and Findings* (New York: Academic Press, 1982).

57. Karl Christiansen, "A Preliminary Study of Criminality among Twins," in Sarnoff Mednick and Karl O. Christiansen, eds., *Biosocial Bases of Criminal Behavior* (New York: Gardner Press, 1977).

58. James Q. Wilson and Richard J. Herrnstein, *Crime and Human Nature* (New York: Simon and Schuster, 1985).

59. Lee Ellis and Anthony Walsh, "Gene-Based Evolutionary Theories in Criminology," *Criminology*, Vol. 35, No. 2 (1997), pp. 229–230.

60. Peter J. Richerson, "Crime and Criminality," http://www.des .ucdavis.edu/faculty/Richerson/BooksOnline/He16-95.pdf (accessed March 1, 2013).

61. Sigmund Freud, *A General Introduction to Psychoanalysis* (New York: Boni and Liveright, 1920).

62. Gwynn Nettler, *Killing One Another* (Cincinnati, OH: Anderson Publishing Co., 1983).

63. David Abrahamsen, *Crime and the Human Mind* (reprint, Montclair, NJ: Patterson Smith, 1969), p. 23.

64. See Adrian Raine, *The Psychopathology of Crime: Criminal Behavior as a Clinical Disorder* (Orlando, FL: Academic Press, 1993).

65. Hervey M. Cleckley, *The Mask of Sanity: An Attempt to Reinterpret the So-Called Psychopathic Personality* (St. Louis, MO: Mosby, 1941).

66. Charles Manson, Interview by Heidi Schulman, 1987.

67. Nettler, *Killing One Another*, p. 179.

68. Albert I. Rabin, "The Antisocial Personality—Psychopathy and Sociopathy," in Hans Toch, ed., *Psychology of Crime and Criminal Justice* (Prospect Heights, IL: Waveland Press, 1979), p. 330.

69. Hans J. Eysenck, *Crime and Personality* (Boston: Houghton Mifflin, 1964).

70. Intelligence may also be seen as an ability. See, for example, Colin G. DeYoung, "Intelligence and Personality," in R. J. Sternberg and S. B. Kaufman, eds., *The Cambridge Handbook of Intelligence* (New York: Cambridge University Press, 2011), pp. 711–737.

71. Some early personality theorists considered intelligence to be part of personality. See, for example, R. B. Cattell, *Personality* (New York: McGraw-Hill, 1950); and J. P. Guilford, *Personality* (New York: McGraw-Hill, 1959).

72. DeYoung, "Intelligence and Personality."

73. Eysenck, *Crime and Personality*, p. 92.

74. Hans J. Eysenck, "Personality and Criminality: A Dispositional Analysis," in William S. Laufer and Freda Adler, eds., *Advances in Criminology Theory*, Vol. 1 (New Brunswick, NJ: Transaction, 1989), p. 90.

75. Eysenck, *Crime and Personality*, pp. 35–36.

76. Richard L. Ault and James T. Reese, "A Psychological Assessment of Crime Profiling," *FBI Law Enforcement Bulletin* (March 1980), pp. 22–25.

77. John E. Douglas and Alan E. Burgess, "Criminal Profiling: A Viable Investigative Tool against Violent Crime," *FBI Law Enforcement Bulletin* (December 1986), pp. 9–13.

78. Robert R. Hazelwood and John E. Douglass, "The Lust Murderer," *FBI Law Enforcement Bulletin* (April 1980), pp. 18–22.

79. A. O. Rider, "The Firesetter—A Psychological Profile," *FBI Law Enforcement Bulletin* (June 1980), pp. 4–11.

80. M. Reiser, "Crime-Specific Psychological Consultation," *Police Chief* (March 1982), pp. 53–56.

81. Thomas Strentz, "A Terrorist Psychosocial Profile: Past and Present," *FBI Law Enforcement Bulletin* (April 1988), pp. 13–19.

82. Jill Peay, "Dangerousness—Ascription or Description," in M. P. Feldman, ed., *Violence*, Vol. 2 of *Developments in the Study of Criminal Behavior* (New York: John Wiley, 1982), p. 211, citing N. Walker, "Dangerous People," *International Journal of Law and Psychiatry*, Vol. 1 (1978), pp. 37–50.

83. See, for example, Michael Gottfredson and Travis Hirschi, *A General Theory of Crime* (Stanford, CA: Stanford University Press, 1990); and Travis Hirschi and Michael Gottfredson, "Age and the Explanation of Crime," *American Journal of Sociology*, Vol. 89 (1983), pp. 552–584.

84. David F. Greenberg, "Modeling Criminal Careers," *Criminology*, Vol. 29, No. 1 (1991), p. 39.

85. Robert E. Park and Ernest Burgess, *Introduction to the Science of Sociology*, 2nd ed. (Chicago: University of Chicago Press, 1924); and Robert E. Park, ed., *The City* (Chicago: University of Chicago Press, 1925).

86. Clifford R. Shaw and Henry D. McKay, "Social Factors in Juvenile Delinquency," in *Report on the Causes of Crime, National Commission on Law Observance and Enforcement*, report no. 13, Vol. 2 (Washington, DC: U.S. Government Printing Office, 1931); and Clifford R. Shaw, *Juvenile Delinquency in Urban Areas* (Chicago: University of Chicago Press, 1942).

87. Émile Durkheim, *Suicide* (reprint, New York: Free Press, 1951).

88. Robert K. Merton, "Social Structure and Anomie," *American Sociological Review*, Vol. 3 (1938), pp. 672–682.

89. Catherine E. Ross and John Mirowsky, "Normlessness, Powerlessness, and Trouble with the Law," *Criminology*, Vol. 25, No. 2 (May 1987), p. 257.

90. See Nettler, *Killing One Another*, p. 58.

91. This is not to say that all members of these groups engaged in criminal behavior, but rather that statistics indicated higher average crime rates for these groups than for certain others immediately after immigration to the United States.

92. Albert K. Cohen, *Delinquent Boys: The Culture of the Gang* (Glencoe, IL: Free Press, 1958).

93. Walter B. Miller, "Lower Class Culture as a Generating Milieu of Gang Delinquency," *Journal of Social Issues*, Vol. 14 (1958), pp. 5–19.

94. Richard Cloward and Lloyd Ohlin, *Delinquency and Opportunity: A Theory of Delinquent Gangs* (New York: Free Press, 1960).

95. Marvin Wolfgang, *Patterns in Criminal Homicide* (Philadelphia: University of Pennsylvania Press, 1958). See also Marvin Wolfgang and Franco Ferracuti, *The Subculture of Violence: Toward an Integrated Theory in Criminology* (London: Tavistock, 1967).

96. "Gang Prevention through Targeted Outreach—Boys and Girls Clubs of America," http://ojjdp.ncjrs.org/pubs/gun_violence/ sect08-k.html (accessed April 10, 2007).

97. See, for example, James D. Orcutt, "Differential Association and Marijuana Use: A Closer Look at Sutherland (with a Little Help from Becker)," *Criminology*, Vol. 25, No. 2 (1987), pp. 341–358.

98. Edwin Sutherland, *Principles of Criminology*, 4th ed. (Chicago: J. B. Lippincott, 1947), p. 4.

99. John E. Conklin, *Criminology*, 3rd ed. (New York: Macmillan, 1989), p. 278.

100. Robert L. Burgess and Ronald L. Akers, "A Differential Association-Reinforcement Theory of Criminal Behavior," *Social Problems*, Vol. 14 (fall 1996), pp. 128–147.

101. Some theories are multicausal and provide explanations for criminal behavior that include a diversity of "causes."

102. For a more elaborate criticism of this sort, see Conklin, *Criminology*, p. 260.

103. Ibid.

104. Walter C. Reckless, *The Crime Problem*, 4th ed. (New York: Appleton-Century-Crofts, 1961).

105. Ibid., p. 472.

106. Travis Hirschi, *Causes of Delinquency* (Berkeley: University of California Press, 1969).

107. Ibid., p. 472.

108. Gresham Sykes and David Matza, "Techniques of Neutralization: A Theory of Delinquency," *American Sociological Review*, Vol. 22 (1957), pp. 664–670.

109. Many of the concepts used by Howard Becker in explicating his theory of labeling were, in fact, used previously not only by Frank Tannenbaum but also by Edwin M. Lemert. Lemert wrote of "societal reaction" and "primary and secondary deviance" and even used the word *labeling* in his book *Social Pathology* (New York: McGraw-Hill, 1951).

110. Frank Tannenbaum, *Crime and the Community* (Boston: Ginn, 1938), pp. 19–20.

111. Howard Becker, *Outsiders: Studies in the Sociology of Deviance* (New York: Free Press, 1963), pp. 8–9.

112. Ibid.

113. Ibid., p. 33.

114. Terrie E. Moffitt, "Adolescence-Limited and Life-Course Persistent Antisocial Behavior: A Developmental Taxonomy," *Psychological Review*, Vol. 100 (1993), pp. 674–701.

115. Robert J. Sampson and John H. Laub, *Crime in the Making: Pathways and Turning Points through the Life Course* (Cambridge, MA: Harvard University Press, 1993).

116. Katharine Browning et al., "Causes and Correlates of Delinquency Program," *OJJDP Fact Sheet* (Washington, DC: U.S. Dept. of Justice, April 1999).

117. MacArthur Foundation, "The Project on Human Development in Chicago Neighborhoods," http://www.macfound.org/research/hcd/hcd_5.htm (accessed January 5, 2007).

118. Adapted from Raymond Michalowski, "Perspectives and Paradigm: Structuring Criminological Thought," in Robert F. Meier, ed., *Theory in Criminology* (Beverly Hills, CA: Sage, 1977).

119. See George B. Vold, *Theoretical Criminology* (New York: Oxford University Press, 1986).

120. Austin T. Turk, *Criminality and the Legal Order* (Chicago: Rand McNally, 1969).

121. Thorsten Sellin, *Culture Conflict and Crime* (New York: Social Science Research Council, 1938).

122. William J. Chambliss and Robert B. Seidman, *Law, Order, and Power* (Reading, MA: Addison-Wesley, 1971).

123. Richard Quinney, *The Social Reality of Crime* (Boston: Little, Brown, 1970).

124. David F. Greenberg, *Crime and Capitalism* (Palo Alto, CA: Mayfield, 1981), p. 3.

125. For examples of how this might be accomplished, see F. H. Knopp, "Community Solutions to Sexual Violence: Feminist/Abolitionist Perspectives," in Harold E. Pepinsky and Richard Quinney, eds., *Criminology as Peacemaking* (Bloomington: Indiana University Press, 1991), pp. 181–193; and S. Caringella-MacDonald and D. Humphries, "Sexual Assault, Women, and the Community: Organizing to Prevent Sexual Violence," in Pepinsky and Quinney, eds., *Criminology as Peacemaking*, pp. 98–113.

126. Richard Quinney, "Life of Crime: Criminology and Public Policy as Peacemaking," *Journal of Crime and Justice*, Vol. 16, No. 2 (1993), pp. 3–9.

127. Ram Dass and P. Gorman, *How Can I Help? Stories and Reflections on Service* (New York: Alfred A. Knopf, 1985), p. 165, as cited in Richard Quinney and John Wildeman, *The Problem of Crime: A Peace and Social Justice Perspective*, 3rd ed. (Mayfield, CA: Mountain View Press, 1991), p. 116, originally published as *The Problem of Crime: A Critical Introduction to Criminology* (New York: Bantam, 1977).

128. See, for example, Harold E. Pepinsky, "This Can't Be Peace: A Pessimist Looks at Punishment," in W. B. Groves and G. Newman, eds., *Punishment and Privilege* (Albany, NY: Harrow and Heston, 1986); Harold E. Pepinsky, "Violence as Unresponsiveness: Toward a New Conception of Crime," *Justice Quarterly*, Vol. 5 (1988), pp. 539–563; and Pepinsky and Quinney, eds., *Criminology as Peacemaking*.

129. See, for example, Richard Quinney, "Crime, Suffering, Service: Toward a Criminology of Peacemaking," *Quest*, Vol. 1 (1988), pp. 66–75; Richard Quinney, "The Theory and Practice of Peacemaking in the Development of Radical Criminology," *Critical Criminologist*, Vol. 1, No. 5 (1989), p. 5; and Quinney and Wildeman, *The Problem of Crime*.

130. All of these themes are addressed, for example, in Pepinsky and Quinney, eds., *Criminology as Peacemaking*.

131. Michael J. Lynch and W. Byron Groves, *A Primer in Radical Criminology*, 2nd ed. (Albany, NY: Harrow and Heston, 1989), p. 128.

132. Raymond J. Michalowski, *Order, Law, and Crime: An Introduction to Criminology* (New York: Random House, 1985), p. 410.

133. Don C. Gibbons, Talking about Crime and Criminals: Problems and Issues in Theory Development in Criminology (Upper Saddle River, NJ: Prentice Hall, 1994), p. 165, citing Loraine Gelsthorpe and Alison Morris, eds., *Feminist Perspectives in Criminology* (Bristol, England: Open University Press, 1990).

134. Sally S. Simpson, "Feminist Theory, Crime, and Justice," *Criminology*, Vol. 27, No. 4 (1989), p. 605.

135. For an excellent overview of feminist theory in criminology and for a comprehensive review of research regarding female offenders, see Joanne Belknap, *The Invisible Woman: Gender Crime and Justice* (Belmont, CA: Wadsworth, 1996).

136. Otto Pollak, *The Criminality of Women* (Philadelphia: University of Pennsylvania Press, 1950).

137. Freda Adler, *Sisters in Crime: The Rise of the New Female Criminal* (New York: McGraw-Hill, 1975).

138. Rita J. Simon, *Women and Crime* (Lexington, MA: Lexington Books, 1975).

139. See, for example, Darrell J. Steffensmeir, "Sex Differences in Patterns of Adult Crime, 1965–1977: A Review and Assessment," *Social Forces*, Vol. 58 (1980), pp. 1098–1099.

140. See, for example, Kathleen Daly and Meda Chesney-Lind, "Feminism and Criminology," *Justice Quarterly*, Vol. 5, No. 5 (December 1988), pp. 497–535.

141. Ibid., p. 506.

142. Ibid.

143. Ibid., p. 514.

144. Cathy Spatz Widom, "Childhood Victimization and the Derailment of Girls and Women to the Criminal Justice System," in Beth E. Richie et al., eds., *Research on Women and Girls in the Justice System* (Washington, DC: National Institute of Justice, 2000), p. iii.

145. Ibid., pp. 27–36.

146. Federal Bureau of Investigation, *Crime in the United States, 1970* (Washington, DC: U.S. Dept. of Justice, 1971); and Federal Bureau of Investigation, *Crime in the United States, 2000* (Washington, DC: U.S. Dept. of Justice, 2001).

147. Ibid.

148. Federal Bureau of Investigation, *Crime in the United States, 2000*.

149. Federal Bureau of Investigation, *Crime in the United States, 2013* (Washington, DC: U.S. Dept. of Justice, 2014).

150. Leanne Fiftal Alarid et al., "Women's Roles in Serious Offenses: A Study of Adult Felons," *Justice Quarterly*, Vol. 13, No. 3 (September 1996), pp. 432–454.

151. For an excellent and detailed discussion of many of these approaches, see Milovanovic, *Postmodern Criminology*.

Alamy

4
CRIMINAL LAW

LEARNING OBJECTIVES

After reading this chapter, you should be able to

- Summarize the purpose, primary sources, and development of law.
- Define the *rule of law*, including its importance in Western democratic societies.
- Summarize the various categories of law, including the purpose of each.
- Describe six general categories of crimes and their characteristics.
- Describe the eight general features of crime.
- Explain what is meant by the elements of a specific criminal offense.
- Compare and contrast the four general categories of accepted criminal defense.

Law is the art of the good and the fair.

ULPIAN, ROMAN JUDGE (CIRCA A.D. 200)

Every law is an infraction of liberty.

JEREMY BENTHAM (1748-1832)

■ **theme**   This chapter describes the various purposes of the law. As you read, consider the following: With which of these purposes would individual rights advocates most likely agree? What about public-order advocates? Why?

■ **lecture note**   When discussing the purposes of law, question students regarding their preconceptions about what the law is supposed to be and what it is supposed to do.

■ **law**   A rule of conduct, generally found enacted in the form of a statute, that proscribes or mandates certain forms of behavior.

■ **lecture note**   Describe the purposes of the law. Ask whether laws that enforce moral beliefs serve any significant purpose today and whether they are even enforceable given society's increasing diversity.

■ **lecture note**   Point out the difference between laws intended to prevent harm and laws designed to promote social good. Ask students to identify instances of both in the criminal code of their home state.

■ **statutory law**   Written or codified law; the "law on the books," as enacted by a government body or agency having the power to make laws.

Introduction

In October, 2012, seven prominent Italian seismologists were convicted of manslaughter and sentenced to six years in prison for failing to warn residents of the historic town of L'Aquila of a coming earthquake.[1] The scientists, who denied responsibility by claiming that earthquake prediction is not an exact science, were also ordered to pay court costs and to reimburse the city for $10.2 million in damages. The trial and verdict came more than three years after a 6.3-magnitude earthquake destroyed L'Aquila's city center, in the Abruzzo region—a bucolic area east of Rome. The earthquake left 309 people dead, and thousands more homeless or injured. In rendering the verdict, the court agreed with prosecution arguments that "it is possible to predict risk and to adopt measures that mitigate that risk." The scientists' failure to do so resulted in the manslaughter convictions against them.[2]

A society needs laws to uphold fairness and to prevent the victimization of innocents.

Laws govern many aspects of our lives, and we are expected to know what the **law** *says* as it applies to our daily lives and to *follow* it. As this chapter will show, laws provide for predictability because people can study the law and know exactly what is required of them. In the case of the convicted scientists, however, no one had ever been found guilty of a crime for failing to make an accurate seismic prediction, and their murder convictions jolted the international scientific community into fearing an onslaught of criminal trials for failed or inaccurate scientific assessments.

The Nature and Purpose of Law

Imagine a society without laws. Without civil law, people would not know what to expect from one another, nor would they be able to plan for the future with any degree of certainty. Without criminal law, people wouldn't feel safe because the more powerful could take what they wanted from the less powerful. Without constitutional law, people could not exercise the basic rights that are available to them as citizens of a free nation. A society needs laws to uphold fairness and to prevent the victimization of innocents.

Practically speaking, laws regulate relationships between people and also between parties, such as government agencies and individuals. They channel and simultaneously constrain human behavior, and they empower individuals while contributing to public order. Laws also serve other purposes. They ensure that the philosophical, moral, and economic perspectives of their creators are protected and made credible. They maintain values and uphold established patterns of social privilege. They sustain existing power relationships, and, finally, they support a system for the punishment and rehabilitation of offenders. (See Table 4-1.) Modifications of the law, when gradually introduced, promote orderly change in the rest of society.

Our laws are found in statutory provisions and constitutional enactments,[3] as well as in hundreds of years of rulings by courts at all levels. According to the authoritative *Black's Law Dictionary*, the word *law* "generally contemplates both statutory and case law."[4] **Statutory law** is "the law on the books."

REUTERS/Alessandro Bianchi

L'Aquila, Italy, damaged by an earthquake in October, 2012. Seven prominent Italian seismologists were convicted of manslaughter and sentenced to six years in prison for failing to warn residents of the historic town of the coming quake. Were their conviction and sentence just?

TABLE 4-1 | What Do Laws Do?

- Laws maintain order in society.
- Laws regulate human interaction.
- Laws enforce moral beliefs.
- Laws define the economic environment.
- Laws enhance predictability.
- Laws support the powerful.
- Laws promote orderly social change.
- Laws sustain individual rights.
- Laws redress wrongs.
- Laws identify wrongdoers.
- Laws mandate punishment and retribution.

Source: Pearson Education, Inc.

■ **lecture note**   Explain what law is by referring to both statutory law and case law.

■ **lecture note**   Explain how statutory law is the result of powerful interest groups that have succeeded in having their values formally endorsed.

■ **theme**   Why is common law necessary?

■ **theme**   Why is the rule of law so important?

■ **penal code**   The written, organized, and compiled form of the criminal laws of a jurisdiction.

■ **case law**   The body of judicial precedent, historically built on legal reasoning and past interpretations of statutory laws, that serves as a guide to decision making, especially in the courts.

■ **lecture note**   Distinguish among criminal, civil, and administrative law, and explain why we draw distinctions among these various categories of law.

■ **common law**   Law originating from usage and custom rather than from written statutes. The term refers to an unwritten body of judicial opinion, originally developed by English courts, that is based on nonstatutory customs, traditions, and precedents that help guide judicial decision making.

■ **rule of law**   The maxim that an orderly society must be governed by established principles and known codes that are applied uniformly and fairly to all of its members.

■ **jurisprudence**   The philosophy of law. Also, the science and study of the law.

It results from legislative action and is often thought of as "the law of the land." Written laws exist in both criminal and civil areas and are called *codes*. Once laws have been written down in an organized fashion, they are said to be *codified*. Federal statutes are compiled in the U.S. Code (U.S.C.), which is available online in its entirety at **http://uscode.house.gov**. State codes and municipal ordinances are also readily available in written, or statutory, form. The written form of the criminal law is called the **penal code**. **Case law**, which we will discuss in detail a bit later, is the law that results from judicial decisions.

But the laws of our country are not unambiguous. If all of "the law" could be found in written legal codes, it would be plain to nearly everyone, and we would need far fewer lawyers than are practicing today. But some laws—the precedents established by courts—do not exist "on the books," and even those that do are open to interpretation. This is where common law comes into play. **Common law** is the traditional body of unwritten historical precedents created from everyday social customs, rules, and practices, many of which were supported by judicial decisions during early times. Common law principles are still used to interpret many legal issues in quite a few states. Hence it is not uncommon to hear of jurisdictions within the United States referred to as "common law jurisdictions" or "common law states."

The Rule of Law

The social, economic, and political stability of any society depends largely on the development and institutionalization of a predictable system of laws. Western democratic societies adhere to the **rule of law**, which is sometimes also referred to as the *supremacy of law*. The rule of law centers on the belief that an orderly society must be governed by established principles and known codes that are applied uniformly and fairly to all of its members. Under this tenet, no one is above the law, and those who make or enforce the law must also abide by it. The principle was well illustrated when, in 2011, former House Majority Leader Tom DeLay was sentenced to three years in prison for taking part in a money-laundering scheme stemming from the 2002 elections.

> The rule of law has been called the greatest political achievement of our culture.

Delay was convicted of illegally funneling almost $200,000 in corporate donations through the Republican National Committee in an effort to elect Republicans to the Texas Legislature.[5]

The rule of law has been called the greatest political achievement of our culture. Without it, few other human achievements—especially those that require the coordinated efforts of a large number of people—would be possible. President John F. Kennedy eloquently explained the rule of law, saying, "Americans are free to disagree with the law, but not to disobey it; for [in] a government of laws and not of men, no man, however prominent and powerful, no mob, however unruly or boisterous, is entitled to defy a court of law."[6]

The rule of law has also been called "the foundation of liberties in the Western world,"[7] for it means that due process (which was discussed in Chapter 1) has to be followed in any criminal prosecution, and it is due process that serves as a check on arbitrary state power.

The American Bar Association notes that the rule of law includes these elements:[8]

- Freedom from private lawlessness provided by the legal system of a politically organized society
- A relatively high degree of objectivity in the formulation of legal norms and a like degree of evenhandedness in their application
- Legal ideas and juristic devices for the attainment of individual and group objectives within the bounds of ordered liberty
- Substantive and procedural limitations on governmental power in the interest of the individual for the enforcement of which there are appropriate legal institutions and machinery

Jurisprudence is the philosophy of law or the science and study of the law, including the rule of law. To learn more about the rule of law, including its historical development, visit **http://www.lexisnexis.com/about-us/rule-of-law**.

Types of Law

Criminal and civil law are the best-known types of modern law. However, scholars and philosophers have drawn numerous distinctions between categories of law that rest on the source, intent, and application of the law (Figure 4-1).

CJ | NEWS
Politicians Who Violate the "Rule of Law" Get Tough Prison Sentences

Former Detroit mayor Kwame Kilpatrick (left), former New Orleans mayor Ray Nagin (second from left), former Virginia governor Bob McDonnell (right), and former U.S. Representative William Jefferson (second from right). As their cases demonstrate, the rule of law means that no one is above the law—not even those who make it. Kilpatrick, charged with ten felony counts, pleaded guilty to reduced charges and served 99 days in jail before being released in February 2009; he reentered prison in 2010 for violating probation, and was again found guilty in 2013 of using his office as mayor to execute a wide-ranging racketeering conspiracy. Nagin was convicted in 2014 and sentenced to 10 years in federal prison for participation in a half-million dollar bribery and conspiracy scheme that ran through most of his time in office. Jefferson served nine terms in the U.S. House of Representatives prior to being sentenced in 2009 to 13 years in prison for using his office to solicit bribes. McDonnell was convicted, along with his wife, in 2014 of public corruption charges. How would you explain the rule of law to someone who is unfamiliar with it?

The United States has always embraced the principle that no one, not even a powerful politician, can violate the law with impunity. As President Theodore Roosevelt said, "No man is above the law and no man is below it."

Today, enforcement of "the rule of law" appears to be stricter than ever, producing some eye-popping prison terms for convicted politicians. Illinois Democratic governor Rod Blagojevich was sentenced to 14 years in prison in 2011, more than twice the 6½-year term given to his predecessor, former Republican governor George Ryan.

Blagojevich made headlines for his most notable crime: trying to sell President Obama's former senate seat—and he was unrepentant until almost the end. But was he twice as guilty as Ryan, who sold truck drivers' licenses to unqualified people, leading to highway deaths? And was Ryan twice as guilty as former Democratic governor Otto Kerner of Illinois, who got three years in prison in 1973 for accepting bribes from a racetrack owner?

Sentencing is a matter for individual judges to decide, but the overall trend for convicted politicians is increased prison time. In 2009, former Rep. William J. Jefferson (D-La.), who famously stored bribe money in his freezer, was given 13 years in prison. It was the longest sentence ever given to a former congressman, easily topping the eight years and four months in prison given in 2006 to former Rep. Randy Cunningham (R-Calif.), who accepted bribes for tens of millions of dollars in defense contracts.

Pleas for mercy now seem to fall on deaf ears. In the 1970s, Kerner was released early due to terminal cancer, but in 2011 a judge refused a request from former Governor Ryan to leave to visit his wife who was dying of cancer. The only way Ryan got to see her at all was through the mercy of his prison warden.

Some judges compare the destruction of citizens' trust in the political system to violent crimes. According to former U.S. Attorney Patrick Collins, who prosecuted Ryan, "judges are now looking at these corruption cases like guns and drug cases." As U.S. District Judge James Zagel put it in sentencing Blagojevich, "When it is the governor who goes bad, the fabric of Illinois is torn and disfigured and not easily or quickly repaired."

Some errant politicians still get relatively short sentences but are hammered if convicted again. In 2008, former Democratic mayor Kwame Kilpatrick of Detroit was sentenced to four months in prison for covering up an affair with his chief of staff and assaulting a police officer. But when he violated parole, the judge lambasted him for his "lack of contriteness and lack of humility," and he received 18 months to 5 years in prison in 2010. In 2012, Kilpatrick was convicted by a federal jury of using his position as mayor and as a Michigan State House Representative to execute a wide-ranging racketeering conspiracy.

Finally, in 2014, former New Orleans mayor Ray Nagin was convicted of 20 counts of bribery, conspiracy, and money laundering—crimes that he committed while serving as mayor.

Resources: "Former Detroit Mayor Kwame Kilpatrick, His Father Bernard Kilpatrick, and City Contractor Bobby Ferguson Convicted on Racketeering, Extortion, Bribery, Fraud, and Tax Charges," FBI press release, March 11, 2013, http://www.fbi.gov/detroit/press-releases/2013/former-detroit-mayor-kwame-kilpatrick-his-father-bernard-kilpatrick-and-city-contractor-bobby-ferguson-convicted-on-racketeering-extortion-bribery-fraud-and-tax-charges; "'Sorry' Blagojevich Gets 14-Year Prison Sentence," Chicago Sun-Times, December 7, 2011, http://www.suntimes.com/news/metro/blagojevich/9300810-452/sorry-blagojevich-gets-14-year-prison-sentence.html; "Ex-New Orleans Mayor Ray Nagin Reports to Federal Prison to Begin 10-year Sentence," Associated Press, September 8, 2014, http://www.foxnews.com/politics/2014/09/08/ex-new-orleans-mayor-ray-nagin-reports-to-federal-prison-to-begin-10-year; and "Former Rep. William Jefferson Sentenced to 13 Years in Prison," Christian Science Monitor, November 13, 2009, http://www.csmonitor.com/USA/Politics/2009/1113/former-rep-william-jefferson-sentenced-to-13-years-in-prison.

■ **lecture note**   Explain the difference between substantive and procedural law.

■ **criminal law**   The body of rules and regulations that define and specify the nature of and punishments for offenses of a public nature or for wrongs committed against the state or society. Also called *penal law.*

■ **substantive criminal law**   The part of the law that defines crimes and specifies punishments.

■ **procedural law**   The part of the law that specifies the methods to be used in enforcing substantive law.

CRIMINAL LAW

Criminal law is defined as the body of rules and regulations that define and specify the nature of and punishments for offenses of a public nature or for wrongs committed against the state or society. Fundamental to the concept of criminal law is the assumption that criminal acts injure not just individuals but society as a whole. Criminal law is also called *penal law.*

These crimes not only offend their victims but also disrupt the peaceful order of society. It is for this reason that the state begins the official process of bringing the offender to justice. The state will be the plaintiff in the criminal proceeding. Those found guilty of violating a criminal law are punished.

EXAMPLES: Murder, rape, robbery, and assault are examples of criminal offenses against which there are laws.

ADMINISTRATIVE LAW

Administrative law is the body of regulations that governments create to control the activities of industries, businesses, and individuals. For the most part, a breach of administrative law is not a crime.

Administrative agencies will sometimes arrange settlements that fall short of court action but that are considered binding on individuals or groups that have not followed the rules of administrative law.

EXAMPLES: Tax laws, health codes, restrictions on pollution and waste disposal, vehicle regulation laws, and building codes are examples of administrative laws.

STATUTORY LAW

Refers to the law on the books; written, codified laws.

EXAMPLE: The acts of legislatures.

Substantive criminal law is a form of statutory law that describes what constitutes particular crimes and specifies the appropriate punishment for the offense.

Procedural law is a type of statutory law. It is a body of rules that determines the proceedings by which legal rights are enforced. These laws regulate the gathering of evidence and the processing of offenders by the criminal justice system.

CIVIL LAW

Civil law governs relationships between and among people, businesses and other organizations, and agencies of government. In contrast to the criminal law, whose violation is against the state or the nation, civil law governs relationships between parties.

Typically civil suits seek compensation (usually in the form of property or money). A violation of the civil law is not a crime. It may be a contract violation or a tort. A tort is a wrongful act, damage, or injury not involving a breach of contract. Because a tort is a personal wrong and not a crime, it is left to the aggrieved individual to bring the case to court. Civil law is more concerned with assessing liability than it is with intent. Civil suits can also be brought against a crime where the intent is clear. His or her victim may decide to seek monetary compensation.

EXAMPLES: Includes things such as rules for contracts, divorces, child support and custody, the creation of wills, property transfers, libel, and many other contractual and social obligations.

CASE LAW

Case law comes from judicial decisions and is also referred to as the law of precedent. It represents the accumulated wisdom of trial and appellate courts. Once a court decision is rendered, it is written down. At the appellate level, the reasoning behind the decision is recorded as well.

The Supreme Court is the highest-level appellate court. *Stare decisis* refers to the principle of recognizing previous decisions as precedents for guiding future deliberations.

A vertical rule requires that decisions made by a higher court be taken into consideration by lower courts.

The horizontal dimension refers to cases handled by the same court that should be decided in a similar way.

EXAMPLES: Under the law of precedent, the reasonings of previous courts should be taken into consideration by other courts in settling similar future cases.

COMMON LAW

Common law is that body of law originating from usage and custom rather than from written statutes.

EXAMPLE: English common law is the basis for much American criminal law, although most states have codified common law principles in their written statutes.

FIGURE 4-1 | Types of Law

Source: Pearson Education, Inc.

Criminal Law

Criminal law, also called *penal law*, refers to the body of rules and regulations that define and specify the nature of and punishments for offenses of a public nature or for wrongs committed against the state or society. Public order is compromised whenever a criminal act occurs, and those found guilty of violating the criminal law are punished. Punishment for crime is philosophically justified by the fact that the offender *intended* the harm and is responsible for it. Criminal law, which is built on constitutional principles and operates within an established set of procedures applicable to the criminal justice system, is composed of both statutory (written law) and case law.

Statutory Law

Written law, or statutory law, is of two types: substantive and procedural. **Substantive criminal law** describes what constitutes particular crimes, such as murder, rape, robbery, and assault, and specifies the appropriate punishment for each particular offense. **Procedural law** is a body of rules that determines the proceedings

■ **theme**   How do civil and criminal law overlap?

■ **lecture note**   Discuss "frivolous" litigation and the consequences of such lawsuits for the American system of civil law.

■ **civil law**   The branch of modern law that governs relationships between parties.

■ **tort**   A wrongful act, damage, or injury not involving a breach of contract. Also, a private or civil wrong or injury.

■ **precedent**   A legal principle that ensures that previous judicial decisions are authoritatively considered and incorporated into future cases.

■ **lecture note**   Demonstrate the significance of case law, or the law of precedent, by discussing Senate hearings over Supreme Court nominees (such as Judges Robert Bork and Clarence Thomas) in which senators realized that the philosophical leanings of judicial nominees could affect the social order.

■ **lecture note**   Explain how felonies, misdemeanors, and infractions differ. Suggest that the distinction between these categories is an artificial one, with the main difference being the level of seriousness of the criminal act and the severity of the punishment specified by the criminal law.

■ ***stare decisis***   A legal principle requiring that, in subsequent cases on similar issues of law and fact, courts be bound by their own earlier decisions and by those of higher courts having jurisdiction over them. The term literally means "standing by decided matters."

by which legal rights are enforced. The law of criminal procedure, for example, regulates the gathering of evidence and the processing of offenders by the criminal justice system. General rules of evidence, search and seizure, procedures to be followed in an arrest, trial procedures, and other specified processes by which the justice system operates are all contained in procedural law. Each state has its own set of criminal procedure laws, as does the federal government. Laws of criminal procedure balance a suspect's rights against the state's interests in the speedy and efficient processing of criminal defendants. View the Federal Rules of Criminal Procedure at **http://www.law.cornell.edu/rules/frcrmp** and the Federal Rules of Evidence at **http://www.uscourts.gov/uscourts/rules/rules-evidence.pdf.**

Civil Law

Civil law, much of which takes the form of statutory law, stands in contrast to criminal law. Civil law governs relationships between and among people, businesses and other organizations, and agencies of government. It contains rules for contracts, divorces, child support and custody, the creation of wills, property transfers, negligence, libel, unfair practices in hiring, the manufacture and sale of consumer goods with hidden hazards for the user, and many other contractual and social obligations. When the civil law is violated, a civil suit may follow. Typically, civil suits seek compensation (usually in the form of property or monetary damages), not punishment. A violation of the civil law is not a crime. It may be a contract violation or a **tort**—which is a wrongful act, damage, or injury not involving a breach of contract. Because a tort is a personal wrong and not a crime, it is left to the aggrieved individual to set the machinery of the court in motion—that is, to bring a suit. The parties to a civil suit are referred to as the *plaintiff*, who seeks relief, and the *defendant*, against whom relief is sought. Civil suits are also sometimes brought by crime victims against those whose criminal intent is clear. Once the perpetrator of a crime has been convicted, the victim may decide to seek monetary compensation from him or her through our system of civil laws.

Administrative Law

Still another kind of law, *administrative law,* is the body of regulations that governments create to control the activities of industries,

businesses, and individuals. Tax laws, health codes, restrictions on pollution and waste disposal, vehicle registration laws, and building codes are examples of administrative laws. Other administrative laws cover practices in the areas of customs (imports and exports), immigration, agriculture, product safety, and most areas of manufacturing. For the most part, a breach of administrative law is not a crime. However, criminal law and administrative regulations may overlap. For instance, organized criminal activity is prevalent in the area of toxic waste disposal—an area covered by many administrative regulations—which has led to criminal prosecutions in several states.

Case Law

Legal experts also talk about case law, or the law of **precedent**. Case law comes from judicial decisions and represents the accumulated wisdom of trial and appellate courts (those that hear appeals) in criminal, civil, and administrative law cases over the years. Once a court decision is rendered, it is written down. At the appellate level, the reasoning behind the decision is recorded as well. Under the law of precedent, this reasoning is then taken into consideration by other courts in settling similar future cases. The principle of recognizing previous decisions as precedents to guide future deliberations, called ***stare decisis***, forms the basis for our modern law of precedent. *Stare decisis* makes for predictability in the law. The court with the greatest influence, of course, is the U.S. Supreme Court, and the precedents it establishes are used as guidelines in the process of legal reasoning by which lower courts reach conclusions.

Learn more about the evolution of American criminal law at **http://schmalleger.com/pubs/evolution.pdf.** Some online criminal law journals may be accessed at **http://www.law.berkeley.edu/228.htm** and **http://wings.buffalo.edu/law/bclc/bclr.htm.**

General Categories of Crime

Violations of the *criminal* law can be of many different types and can vary in severity. Six general categories of criminal law violations can be identified: (1) felonies, (2) misdemeanors, (3) offenses, (4) treason, (5) espionage, and (6) inchoate offenses (Figure 4-2).

■ **felony**   A criminal offense punishable by death or by incarceration in a prison facility for at least one year.

■ **misdemeanor**   An offense punishable by incarceration, usually in a local confinement facility, for a period whose upper limit is prescribed by statute in a given jurisdiction, typically one year or less.

■ **offense**   A violation of the criminal law. Also, in some jurisdictions, a minor crime, such as jaywalking, that is sometimes described as *ticketable*.

■ **infraction**   A minor violation of state statute or local ordinance punishable by a fine or other penalty or by a specified, usually limited, term of incarceration.

■ **treason**   A U.S. citizen's actions to help a foreign government overthrow, make war against, or seriously injure the United States.[i] Also, the attempt to overthrow the government of the society of which one is a member.

FELONY
A criminal offense punishable by death or by incarceration in a prison facility for at least one year.

OFFENSE
A violation of the criminal law. Also, in some jurisdictions, a minor crime, such as jaywalking, that is sometimes described as *ticketable*. Such minor offenses are also known as *infractions*.

TREASON
A U.S. citizen's actions to help a foreign government overthrow, make war against, or seriously injure the United States. Also, the attempt to overthrow the government of the society of which one is a member.

INCHOATE OFFENSE
An offense not yet completed. Also, an offense that consists of an action or conduct that is a step toward the intended commission of another offense.

MISDEMEANOR
An offense punishable by incarceration, usually in a local confinement facility, for a period whose upper limit is prescribed by statute in a given jurisdiction, typically one year or less.

ESPIONAGE
The "gathering, transmitting, or losing" of information related to the national defense in such a manner that the information becomes available to enemies of the United States and may be used to their advantage.

FIGURE 4-2 | General Categories of Crime
Source: Pearson Education, Inc.

Felonies

Felonies are serious crimes; they include murder, rape, aggravated assault, robbery, burglary, and arson. Today, many felons receive prison sentences, although the range of potential penalties includes everything from probation and a fine to capital punishment in many jurisdictions. Under common law, felons could be sentenced to death, could have their property confiscated, or both. Following common law tradition, people who are convicted of felonies today usually lose certain privileges. Some states, for example, make a felony conviction and incarceration grounds for uncontested divorce. Others prohibit offenders from voting, running for public office, or owning a firearm and exclude them from some professions, such as medicine, law, and police work.

Misdemeanors

Misdemeanors are relatively minor crimes, consisting of offenses such as petty theft, which is stealing items of little worth; simple assault, in which the victim suffers no serious injury and in which none was intended; breaking and entering; possessing burglary tools; being disorderly in public; disturbing the peace; filing a false crime report; and writing bad checks, although the amount for which the check is written may determine the classification of this offense. In general, misdemeanors are any crime punishable by a year or less in prison. In fact, most misdemeanants receive suspended sentences involving a fine and supervised probation.

Offenses

A third category of crime is the **offense**. Although, strictly speaking, all violations of the criminal law can be called *criminal offenses*, the term *offense* is sometimes used to refer specifically to minor violations of the law that are less serious than misdemeanors. When the term is used in that sense, it refers to such things as jaywalking, spitting on the sidewalk, littering, and committing certain traffic violations, including the failure to wear a seat belt. Another word used to describe such minor law violations is **infraction**. People committing infractions are typically ticketed and released, usually on a promise to appear later in court. Court appearances may often be waived through payment of a small fine that can be mailed to the court.

Treason

Felonies, misdemeanors, offenses, and the people who commit them constitute the daily work of the justice system. However, special categories of crime do exist and should be recognized. They include treason and espionage, two crimes that are often regarded as the most serious of felonies. **Treason** can be defined

freedom OR safety? YOU decide

Should Violent Speech Be Free Speech?

In 2005, a state jury in Alexandria, Virginia, convicted 42-year-old Muslim scholar Ali al-Timimi of a number of offenses, including the crime of incitement, conspiring to carry firearms and explosives, and soliciting others to make war against the United States. The U.S.-born Islamic spiritual adviser had spoken frequently at the Center for Islamic Information and Education—also known as the Dar al Arqam Islamic Center—in Falls Church, Virginia. Prosecutors told jurors that al-Timimi had verbally encouraged his followers to train with terrorist organizations and to engage in violent Jihad, or holy war, against America and its allies. al-Timimi, who lived much of his life in the Washington, D.C., area, earned a doctorate in computational biology from George Mason University and is the author of at least 12 articles published in scientific journals, most dealing with how to use computers to analyze genes found in various kinds of cancer. As a teenager, al-Timimi had spent two years in Saudi Arabia with his family, where he became interested in Islam.

Following conviction, al-Timimi was sentenced to life in prison without the possibility of parole, plus 70 years—a sentence meant to guarantee that he would never leave prison. He is currently appealing, and there is some chance that his case will be sent back for retrial based on claims that the National Security Agency illegally gathered information about his activities.

The al-Timimi case raises a number of interesting issues—among them the issue of when violent speech crosses the line from free expression into criminal advocacy.

The First Amendment to the U.S. Constitution guarantees the right to free speech. It is a fundamental guarantee of our democratic way of life. So, for example, the speech of those who advocate a new form of government in the United States is protected, even though their ideas may appear anti-American and ill-considered.

In the 1957 case of *Roth* v. *United States,* the U.S. Supreme Court held that "the protection given speech and press was fashioned to assure unfettered interchange of ideas for the bringing about of political and social changes desired by the people."

It is important to remember, however, that constitutional rights are not without limit—that is, they have varying applicability under differing conditions. Some forms of speech are too dangerous to be allowed, even under our liberal rules.

Freedom of speech does not mean, for example, that you have a protected right to stand up in a crowded theater and yell "Fire!" That's because the panic that would follow such an exclamation would likely cause injuries and would put members of the public at risk of harm.

Hence, the courts have held that although freedom of speech is guaranteed by the Constitution, there are limits to it. (Shouting "Fire!" in a public park would likely not be considered an actionable offense.)

Similarly, saying, "The president deserves to die," horrific as it may sound, may be merely a matter of personal opinion. Anyone who says, "I'm going to kill the president," however, can wind up in jail because threatening the life of the president is a crime—as is the act of communicating threats of imminent violence in most jurisdictions.

al-Timimi's mistake may have been the timing of his remarks, which were made to a public gathering in Virginia five days after the September 11, 2001, attacks. In his speech, al-Timimi called for a "holy war" and "violent Jihad" against the West. He was later quoted by converts with whom he met as referring to American forces in Afghanistan as "legitimate targets."

Critics of al-Timimi's conviction point to a seeming double standard under which people can be arrested for unpopular speech, but not for popular speech—regardless of the degree of violence it implies. They note, for example, that conservative columnist Ann Coulter has suggested in writing that "we should invade (Muslim) countries, kill their leaders and convert them to Christianity," but she was never arrested for what she said.

In 2010, in an effort to distinguish what would otherwise be protected free speech from speech that constitutes criminal support of terrorist organization, the U.S. Supreme Court decided the case of *Holder* v. *Humanitarian Law Project.* In that case, Chief Justice John G. Roberts, Jr., wrote that for speech to constitute criminal support of terrorist organizations, "it has to take the form of training, expert advice or assistance conveyed in coordination with or under the direction of a foreign terrorist organization."

You Decide

Should al-Timimi's advocacy of violence be unlawful? Why or why not? Do you think that al-Timimi's rhetoric rises to the level of criminal support of terrorist organizations according to the standard set in Holder v. Humanitarian Law Project? Might we have more to fear from the suppression of speech (even speech like al-Timimi's) than from its free expression? If so, how?

References: "Virginia Man Convicted of Urging War on U.S.," *USA Today,* April 27, 2005; Jonathan Turley, "When Is Violent Speech Still Free Speech?" *USA Today,* May 3, 2005; Eric Lichtblau, "Administration Continues Eavesdropping Defense," *The New York Times,* January 24, 2006; and *Holder* v. *Humanitarian Law Project,* 561 U.S. 1 (2010).

■ **theme**   How can an incomplete act be a crime?

■ **lecture note**   Discuss the three features or elements of crime and explain that unless all are present, there can be no crime.

■ **espionage**   The "gathering, transmitting, or losing"ii of information related to the national defense in such a manner that the information becomes available to enemies of the United States and may be used to their advantage.

■ **inchoate offense**   An offense not yet completed. Also, an offense that consists of an action or conduct that is a step toward the intended commission of another offense.

■ ***actus reus***   An act in violation of the law. Also, a guilty act.

as "a U.S. citizen's actions to help a foreign government overthrow, make war against, or seriously injure the United States."9

Espionage

Espionage, an offense akin to treason but that can be committed by noncitizens, is the "gathering, transmitting, or losing" of information related to the national defense in such a manner that the information becomes available to enemies of the United States and may be used to their advantage.10 In 2014, for example, 40-year-old Robert Patrick Hoffman, II, of Virginia Beach, Virginia, was sentenced to 30 years in prison for attempting to commit espionage against the United States.11 While serving in the U.S. Navy, Hoffman held a cryptologic technician position, which gave him access to various forms of sensitive information. After Hoffman initiated efforts to sell information to representatives of the Russian Federation, FBI agents posed as Russian operatives and contacted him. The undercover agents arranged with Hoffman to fill a drop site with encrypted thumb drives containing answers to questions posed to him by people he believed to be Russian agents. In his answers, Hoffman supplied classified national defense information.

Inchoate Offenses

Another special category of crime is called *inchoate*. The word *inchoate* means "incomplete or partial," and **inchoate offenses** are those that have not been fully carried out. Conspiracies are

Steve Earley/AP Images

Former navy submariner, Robert Patrick Hoffman, II. In 2014, Hoffman was sentenced to 30 years in prison for attempting to sell classified information to the Russians. What's the difference between espionage and treason?

an example. When a person conspires to commit a crime, any action undertaken in furtherance of the conspiracy is generally regarded as a sufficient basis for arrest and prosecution. For instance, a woman who intends to kill her husband may make a phone call or conduct an Internet search to find a hit man to carry out her plan. The call or search are themselves evidence of her intent and can result in her imprisonment for conspiracy to commit murder.

Conventional legal wisdom holds that the essence of crime consists of three conjoined elements: (1) the criminal act, which in legal parlance is termed the *actus reus*; (2) a culpable mental state, or *mens rea*; and (3) a concurrence of the two.

Another type of inchoate offense is the attempt to commit a crime, which occurs when an offender is unable to complete the intended crime. For example, homeowners may arrive just as a burglar is beginning to enter their residence, causing the burglar to drop his tools and run. In most jurisdictions, this frustrated burglar can be arrested and charged with attempted burglary.

General Features of Crime

From the perspective of Western jurisprudence, all crimes can be said to share certain features (Figure 4–3), and the notion of crime itself can be said to rest on such general principles. Taken together, these features, which are described in this section, make up the legal essence of the concept of crime. Conventional legal wisdom holds that the essence of crime consists of three conjoined elements: (1) the criminal act, which in legal parlance is termed the *actus reus*; (2) a culpable mental state, or *mens rea*; and (3) a concurrence of the two. Hence, as we shall see in the following paragraphs, the essence of criminal conduct consists of a concurrence of a criminal act with a culpable mental state.

The Criminal Act (*Actus Reus*)

A necessary first feature of any crime is some act in violation of the law. Such an act is termed the ***actus reus*** of a crime. The term means "guilty act." Generally, a person must commit some voluntary act before he or she is subject to criminal sanctions. To *be something* is not a crime; to *do something* may be. For example, someone who is caught using drugs can be arrested, whereas

By definition, a crime requires *actus reus*, *mens rea*, and the concurrence of the two:

Actus Reus

A necessary feature of any crime is some act in violation of the law. This violation is called the *actus reus* (guilty act). Generally, a person must commit the act voluntarily for it to be considered a crime.

Mens Rea

A second component of crime is *mens rea*, or guilty mind. This refers to the person's state of mind when they commit the act. There are four types of *mens rea*.

Concurrence

Concurrence requires that the act and the mental state occur together in order for a crime to have taken place.

Purposeful (intentional) is an act that is undertaken to achieve some goal.

Knowing behavior is undertaken with awareness. A person who acts purposefully always acts knowingly, but a person may act in a knowing way, but without criminal intent.

Reckless behavior is activity that increases the risk of harm. In this activity, the person may not have intended harm but should know that his behavior could endanger others.

Negligent behavior refers to a situation where the person should have known better and her act, or failure to act, endangers others.

Motive is not the same as *mens rea*. A motive refers to a person's reason for committing a crime. Motive is not an essential feature of a crime.

Special Categories of Crime

Strict liability (or absolute liability) is a special category of crime that requires no culpable mental state and presents a significant exception to the principle that all crimes require *actus reus* and *mens rea*. These offenses make it a crime to simply do something without the intention of violating the law. Routine traffic offenses are considered an example of strict liability.

Four different states of mind

KNOWING: She needed to be taught a lesson for roaming carelessly in the street. If it cost her her life, then so be it.

RECKLESS: Maybe if I hadn't been going 20 mph over the speed limit, I would have seen the stop sign.

PURPOSEFUL: I'm glad I killed her the first time so I didn't have to go back and finish the job.

NEGLIGENT: I should have been watching the road instead of talking on my cell phone and using my GPS.

FIGURE 4-3 | Features of a Crime

Source: Illustration from Frank A. Schmalleger, Daniel E. Hall, and John J. Dolatowski, *Criminal Law Today*, 4th ed. (Upper Saddle River, NJ: Pearson Education, 2010), p. 46. Reprinted by permission of Pearson Education, Inc., Upper Saddle River, NJ.

someone who simply admits that he or she is a drug user (perhaps on a TV talk show or in a tweet) cannot be arrested on that basis. Police who hear the drug user's admission might begin gathering evidence to prove some specific law violation in that person's past, or perhaps they might watch that individual for future behavior in violation of the law. A subsequent arrest would then be based on a specific action in violation of the law pertaining to controlled substances.

Vagrancy laws, popular in the early part of the twentieth century, have generally been invalidated by the courts because they did not specify what act violated the law. In fact, the less a person did, the more vagrant he or she was. An omission to act, however, may be criminal where the person in question is required by law to do something. Child-neglect laws, for example, focus on parents and child guardians who do not live up to their responsibility to care for their children.

Threatening to act can be a criminal offense. For example, threatening to kill someone can result in an arrest for the offense of communicating threats. Such threats against the president of the United States are taken seriously by the Secret Service, and individuals are arrested for boasting about planned violence directed at the president. Attempted criminal activity is also illegal. An attempt to murder or rape, for example, is a serious crime, even when the planned act is not accomplished.

■ **activity**   Have students locate current news articles on crime and discuss the type of *mens rea* that may have been present.
■ **theme**   Do you agree with the doctrine of transferred intent? Should criminal liability in this type of situation be reduced? Why or why not?
■ ***mens rea***   The state of mind that accompanies a criminal act. Also, a guilty mind.
■ **reckless behavior**   Activity that increases the risk of harm.

■ **lecture note**   Explain the difference between reckless behavior and criminal negligence.
■ **criminal negligence**   Behavior in which a person fails to reasonably perceive the substantial and unjustifiable risks of dangerous consequences.
■ **motive**   A person's reason for committing a crime.

Conspiracies, mentioned earlier in this chapter, are another criminal act. When a conspiracy unfolds, the ultimate act that it aims to bring about does not have to occur for the parties to the conspiracy to be arrested. When people plan to bomb a public building, for example, they can be legally stopped before the bombing. As soon as they take steps to "further" their plan, they have met the requirement for an act. Buying explosives, telephoning one another, and drawing plans of the building may all be actions in furtherance of the conspiracy. But not all conspiracy statutes require actions in furtherance of the "target crime" before an arrest can be made. Technically speaking, crimes of conspiracy can be seen as entirely distinct from the target crimes that the conspirators are contemplating. For example, in 1994 the U.S. Supreme Court upheld the drug-related conviction of Reshat Shabani when it ruled that, in the case of certain antidrug laws,[12] "it is presumed that Congress intended to adopt the common law definition of conspiracy, which does not make the doing of any act other than the act of conspiring a condition of liability."[13] Hence, according to the Court, "The criminal agreement itself," even in the absence of actions directed toward realizing the target crime, can be grounds for arrest and prosecution.

The importance of *mens rea* as a component of crime cannot be overemphasized.

A Guilty Mind (*Mens Rea*)

Mens rea is the second general component of crime. The term, which literally means "guilty mind," refers to the defendant's specific mental state at the time the behavior in question occurred. The importance of *mens rea* as a component of crime cannot be overemphasized. It can be seen in the fact that some courts have held that "[a]ll crime exists primarily in the mind."[14] The extent to which a person can be held criminally responsible for his or her actions generally depends on the nature of the mental state under which he or she was laboring at the time of the offense.

Four levels, or types, of *mens rea* can be distinguished: (1) purposeful (or intentional), (2) knowing, (3) reckless, and (4) negligent. Purposeful or intentional action is that which is undertaken to achieve some goal. Sometimes the harm that results from intentional action may be unintended; however, this does not reduce criminal liability. The doctrine of *transferred intent*, for example, which operates in all U.S. jurisdictions, holds a person guilty of murder if that individual took aim and shot at an intended victim but missed, killing another person instead.

The philosophical notion behind the concept of transferred intent is that the killer's intent to kill, which existed at the time of the crime, transferred from the intended victim to the person who was struck by the bullet and died.

Knowing behavior is action undertaken with awareness. A person who acts purposefully always acts knowingly, but a person may act in a knowingly criminal way but for a purpose other than criminal intent. For example, an airline captain who allows a flight attendant to transport cocaine aboard an airplane may do so to gain sexual favors from the attendant, but without the purpose of drug smuggling. Knowing behavior involves near certainty. In this scenario, if the airline captain allows the flight attendant to carry cocaine aboard the plane, it *will* be transported, and the pilot knows it. In another example, if an HIV-infected individual knowingly has unprotected sexual intercourse with another person, the partner *will* be exposed to the virus.

Reckless Behavior and Criminal Negligence

Reckless behavior is activity that increases the risk of harm. In contrast to knowing behavior, knowledge may be part of recklessness, but it exists more in the form of probability than certainty. As a practical example, reckless driving is a frequent charge in many jurisdictions; it is generally brought when a driver engages in risky activity that endangers others.

Nevertheless, *mens rea* is said to be present when a person should have known better, even if the person did not directly intend the consequences of his or her action. A person who acts negligently and thereby endangers others may be found guilty of **criminal negligence** when harm occurs, even though no negative consequences were intended. For example, a parent who leaves a 12-month-old child alone in the tub can be prosecuted for negligent homicide if the child drowns.[15] It should be emphasized, however, that negligence in and of itself is not a crime. Negligent conduct can be evidence of crime only when it falls below some acceptable standard of care. That standard is applied today in criminal courts through the fictional creation of a *reasonable person*. The question to be asked in a given case is whether a reasonable person, in the same situation, would have known better and acted differently from the defendant. The reasonable person criterion provides a yardstick for juries faced with thorny issues of guilt or innocence.

It is important to note that *mens rea*, even in the sense of intent, is not the same thing as motive. A **motive** refers to a person's reason for committing a crime. Although evidence of

■ **theme** Do you agree with the concept of strict liability crimes? Should an individual be punished for a crime if he or she had no intent to violate the law?
■ **strict liability** Liability without fault or intention. Strict liability offenses do not require *mens rea*.
■ **concurrence** The coexistence of (1) an act in violation of the law, and (2) a culpable mental state.

■ **lecture note** Discuss the five additional features of crime and explain why they are important to our understanding of crime.
■ **legal cause** A legally recognizable cause. A legal cause must be demonstrated in court in order to hold an individual criminally liable for causing harm.

motive may be admissible during a criminal trial to help prove a crime, motive itself is not an essential element of a crime. As a result, we cannot say that a bad or immoral motive makes an act a crime.

Mens rea is a tricky concept. Not only is it philosophically and legally complex, but a person's state of mind during the commission of an offense can rarely be known directly unless the person confesses. Hence, *mens rea* must generally be inferred from a person's actions and from all the circumstances surrounding those actions. Pure accident, however, which involves no recklessness or negligence, cannot serve as the basis for either criminal or civil liability. "Even a dog," the famous Supreme Court Justice Oliver Wendell Holmes once wrote, "distinguishes between being stumbled over and being kicked."[16]

Strict Liability

A special category of crimes, called **strict liability** offenses, requires no culpable mental state and presents a significant exception to the principle that all crimes require a concurrence of *actus reus* and *mens rea*. Strict liability offenses, also called *absolute liability offenses*, make it a crime simply to *do* something, even if the offender has no intention of violating the law. Strict liability is philosophically based on the presumption that causing harm is in itself blameworthy, regardless of the actor's intent.

Routine traffic offenses are generally considered strict liability offenses. Driving 65 miles per hour in a 55-mph zone is a violation of the law, even though the driver may be listening to music, thinking, or simply going with the flow of traffic, entirely unaware that his or her vehicle is exceeding the posted speed limit. Statutory rape is another example of strict liability.[17] This crime generally occurs between two consenting individuals; it requires only that the offender have sexual intercourse with a person under the age of legal consent. Statutes describing the crime routinely avoid any mention of a culpable mental state. In many jurisdictions, it matters little whether the "perpetrator" knew the exact age of the "victim" or whether the "victim" lied about his or her age or had given consent, as statutory rape laws are "an attempt to prevent the sexual exploitation of persons deemed legally incapable of giving consent."[18]

Concurrence

The concurrence of an unlawful act and a culpable mental state provides the third basic component of crime. **Concurrence** requires that the act and the mental state occur together in order for a crime to take place. If one precedes the other, the requirements of the criminal law have not been met. A person may intend to kill a rival, for example. He drives to the intended victim's house, with his gun, fantasizing about how he will commit the murder. Just as he nears the victim's home, the victim crosses the street on the way to the grocery store. If the two accidentally collide and the intended victim dies, there has been no concurrence of act and intent.

Other Features of Crime

Some scholars contend that the three features of crime that we have just outlined—*actus reus*, *mens rea*, and concurrence—are sufficient to constitute the essence of the legal concept of crime. Other scholars, however, see modern Western law as more complex. They argue that recognition of five additional principles is necessary to fully appreciate contemporary understandings of crime. These five principles are (1) causation, (2) resulting harm, (3) the principle of legality, (4) the principle of punishment, and (5) necessary attendant circumstances. We will now discuss each of these additional features in turn.

Causation

Causation refers to the fact that the concurrence of a guilty mind and a criminal act may cause harm. Whereas some statutes criminalize only conduct, others require that the offender *cause* a particular result before criminal liability can be incurred. Sometimes, however, a causal link is unclear. For example, let's consider a case of assault with a deadly weapon with intent to kill. A person shoots another, and the victim is seriously injured but is not immediately killed. The victim, who remains in the hospital, survives for more than a year. The victim's death occurs due to a blood clot that forms from lack of activity. In such a case, it is likely that defense attorneys will argue that the defendant did not cause the death; rather, the death occurred because of disease. If a jury agrees with the defense's claim, the shooter may go free or be found guilty of a lesser charge, such as assault.

To clarify the issue of causation, the American Law Institute suggests use of the term **legal cause** to emphasize the notion of a legally recognizable cause and to preclude any assumption that such a cause must be close in time and space to the result it produces. Legal causes can be distinguished from those causes that may have produced the result in question but do not provide the basis for a criminal prosecution because they are too complex, too indistinguishable from other causes, not knowable, or not provable in a court of law.

■ *ex post facto*   Latin for "after the fact." The Constitution prohibits the enactment of *ex post facto* laws, which make acts committed before the laws in question were passed punishable as crimes.

■ **attendant circumstances**   The facts surrounding an event.
■ **element (of a crime)**   In a specific crime, one of the essential features of that crime, as specified by law or statute.

Harm

A harm occurs in any crime, although not all harms are crimes. When a person is murdered or raped, harm can be clearly identified. Some crimes, however, can be said to be *victimless*. Perpetrators (and their attorneys) maintain that in committing such crimes they harm no one but themselves; rather, they say, the crime may actually be pleasurable for those involved. Prostitution, gambling, and drug use are commonly classified as "victimless." What these offenders fail to recognize, say legal theorists, is the social harm caused by their behavior. In areas afflicted with chronic prostitution, drug use, and illegal gambling, property values fall, family life disintegrates, and other, more traditional crimes increase as money is sought to support the "victimless" activities. Law-abiding citizens abandon the area.

In a criminal prosecution, however, it is rarely necessary to prove harm as a separate element of a crime because it is subsumed under the notion of a guilty act. In the crime of murder, for example, the "killing of a human being" brings about a harm but is, properly speaking, an act. When committed with the requisite *mens rea*, it becomes a crime. A similar type of reasoning applies to the criminalization of *attempts* that cause no harm. A scenario commonly raised to illustrate this dilemma is one in which attackers throw rocks at a blind person, but because of bad aim, the rocks hit no one, and the intended target remains unaware that anyone is trying to harm him. In such a case, should throwing rocks provide a basis for criminal liability? As one authority on the subject observes, "Criticism of the principle of harm has ... been based on the view that the harm actually caused may be a matter of sheer accident and that the rational thing to do is to base the punishment on the *mens rea*, and the action, disregarding any actual harm or lack of harm or its degree."[19] This observation also shows why we have said that the essence of crime consists only of three things: (1) *actus reus*, (2) *mens rea*, and (3) the concurrence of an illegal act and a culpable mental state.

Legality

The principle of legality highlights the fact that a behavior cannot be criminal if no law exists that defines it as such. For example, as long as you are of drinking age, it is all right to drink beer because there is no statute on the books prohibiting it. During Prohibition, of course, the situation was quite different. (In fact, some parts of the United States are still "dry," and the purchase or public consumption of alcohol can be a law violation regardless of age.) The principle of legality also includes the notion that *ex post facto* laws are not binding, which means that a law cannot be created tomorrow that will hold a person legally responsible for something he or she does today. Rather, laws are binding only from the date of their creation or from some future date at which they are specified as taking effect.[20]

Punishment

The principle of punishment holds that no crime can be said to occur where punishment has not been specified in the law. Larceny, for example, would not be a crime if the law simply said, "It is illegal to steal." Punishment for the crime must be specified so that if a person is found guilty of violating the law, sanctions can be lawfully imposed.

Necessary Attendant Circumstances

Finally, statutes defining some crimes specify that certain additional elements, called **attendant circumstances**, must be present for a conviction to be obtained. Generally speaking, attendant circumstances are the "facts surrounding an event"[21] and include such things as time and place. Attendant circumstances that are specified by law as necessary elements of an offense are sometimes called *necessary attendant circumstances*, indicating that the existence of such circumstances is necessary, along with the other elements included in the relevant statute, for a crime to have been committed. Florida law, for example, makes it a crime to "[k]nowingly commit any lewd or lascivious act in the presence of any child under the age of 16 years."[22] In this case, the behavior in question might not be a crime if committed in the presence of someone who is older than 16. Sometimes attendant circumstances increase the degree, or level of seriousness, of an offense.

Circumstances surrounding a crime can also be classified as aggravating or mitigating and may, by law, increase or lessen the penalty that can be imposed on a convicted offender. Aggravating and mitigating circumstances are not elements of an offense, however, because they are primarily relevant at the sentencing stage of a criminal prosecution. They are discussed in Chapter 11.

Elements of a Specific Criminal Offense

Now that we have identified the principles that constitute the *general* notion of crime, we can examine individual statutes to see what particular statutory **elements** constitute a *specific* crime. Written laws specify exactly what conditions are necessary for a person to be charged in a given instance of criminal activity,

■ **lecture note** Distinguish between homicide (the killing of a human being) and murder or "criminal homicide" (the unlawful killing of a human being). Discuss justifiable and excusable homicide, both of which are non-criminal homicides.

■ **lecture note** Distinguish between the *corpus delicti* and the physical body of a murder victim. Show that the two are not the same by demonstrating that it is possible to convict a person of murder even though the body of the victim is never recovered.

■ **lecture note** Explain the difference between the *corpus delicti* of a crime and the statutory elements necessary to convict a particular person of having committed a specific crime.

■ *corpus delicti* The facts that show that a crime has occurred. The term literally means "the body of the crime."

and they do so for every offense. Hence, elements of a crime are specific legal aspects of a criminal offense that the prosecution must prove to obtain a conviction. In almost every jurisdiction in the United States, for example, the crime of first-degree murder involves four quite distinct elements:

1. An unlawful killing
2. Of a human being
3. Intentionally
4. With planning (or "malice aforethought")

The elements of any specific crime are the statutory minimum without which that crime cannot be said to have occurred. Because statutes differ between jurisdictions, the specific elements of a particular crime may vary. To convict a defendant of a particular crime, prosecutors must prove to a judge or jury that all of the required statutory elements are present[23] and that the accused was responsible for producing them. If even one element of an offense cannot be established beyond a reasonable doubt, criminal liability will not have been demonstrated, and the defendant will be found not guilty.

The Example of Murder

Every statutory element of a crime serves a purpose. As mentioned, the crime of first-degree murder includes an *unlawful killing* as one of its required elements. Not all killings are unlawful. In war, for instance, human beings are killed. These killings are committed with planning and sometimes with "malice." They are certainly intentional. Yet killing in war is not unlawful as long as the belligerents wage war according to international conventions.

The second element of first-degree murder specifies that the killing must be *of a human being*. People kill all the time. They kill animals for meat, they hunt, and they practice euthanasia on aged and injured pets. Even if the killing of an animal is planned and involves malice (perhaps a vendetta against a neighborhood dog that overturns trash cans), it does not constitute first-degree murder. Such a killing, however, may violate statutes pertaining to cruelty to animals.

The third element of first-degree murder, *intentionality*, is the basis for the defense of accident. An unintentional or non-purposeful killing is not first-degree murder, although it may violate some other statute.

Finally, murder has not been committed unless *malice* is involved. There are different kinds of malice. Second-degree murder involves malice in the sense of hatred or spite. A more

extreme form of malice is necessary for a finding of first-degree murder. Sometimes the phrase used to describe this requirement is *malice aforethought*. This extreme kind of malice can be demonstrated by showing that planning was involved in the commission of the murder. Often, first-degree murder is described as "lying in wait," a practice that shows that thought and planning went into the illegal killing.

A charge of second-degree murder in most jurisdictions would necessitate proving that a voluntary (or intentional) killing of a human being had taken place—although without the degree of malice necessary for it to be classified as first-degree murder. A crime of passion is an example of second-degree murder. In a crime of passion, the malice felt by the perpetrator is hatred or spite, which is considered less severe than malice aforethought. Manslaughter, or third-degree murder, another type of homicide, can be defined simply as the unlawful killing of a human being. Not only is malice lacking in third-degree murder cases, but so is intention; in fact, the killer may not have intended that *any* harm come to the victim.

Manslaughter charges are often brought when a defendant acted in a negligent or reckless manner. The 2001 sentencing of 21-year-old Nathan Hall to 90 days in jail on charges of criminally negligent homicide following a fatal collision with another ski racer on Vail Mountain near Eagle, Colorado, provides such an example.[24] Hall had been tried on a more serious charge of reckless manslaughter, which carries a sentence of up to 16 years under Colorado law, but the jury convicted him of the lesser charge.

Manslaughter statutes, however, frequently necessitate some degree of negligence on the part of the killer. When a wanton disregard for human life is present—legally defined as "gross negligence"—some jurisdictions permit the offender to be charged with a more serious count of murder.

The *Corpus Delicti* of a Crime

The term **corpus delicti** literally means "the body of the crime." One way to understand the concept of *corpus delicti* is to realize that a person cannot be tried for a crime unless it can first be shown that the offense has, in fact, occurred. In other words, to establish the *corpus delicti* of a crime, the state has to demonstrate that a criminal law has been violated and that someone violated it (Figure 4-4). This term is often confused with the statutory elements of a crime, and sometimes it is mistakenly thought to refer to the body of a murder victim or some other physical result of criminal activity. It actually means something quite different.

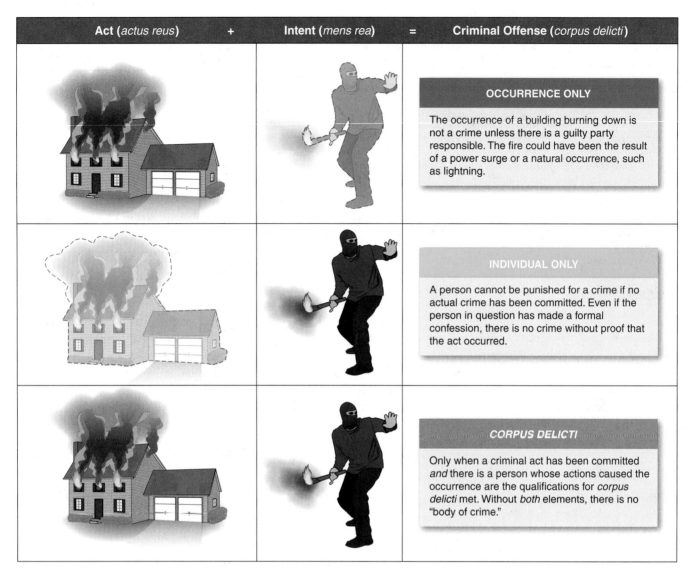

| Act (*actus reus*) | + | Intent (*mens rea*) | = | Criminal Offense (*corpus delicti*) |

OCCURRENCE ONLY

The occurrence of a building burning down is not a crime unless there is a guilty party responsible. The fire could have been the result of a power surge or a natural occurrence, such as lightning.

INDIVIDUAL ONLY

A person cannot be punished for a crime if no actual crime has been committed. Even if the person in question has made a formal confession, there is no crime without proof that the act occurred.

CORPUS DELICTI

Only when a criminal act has been committed *and* there is a person whose actions caused the occurrence are the qualifications for *corpus delicti* met. Without *both* elements, there is no "body of crime."

FIGURE 4-4 | Body of Crime

Source: Frank A. Schmalleger, Daniel E. Hall, and John J. Dolatowski, *Criminal Law Today*, 4th ed. (Upper Saddle River, NJ: Pearson Education, 2010), p. 61. Reprinted by permission of Pearson Education, Inc., Upper Saddle River, NJ.

There are two aspects to the *corpus delicti* of an offense: (1) that a certain result has been produced, and (2) that a person is criminally responsible for its production. For example, the crime of larceny requires proof that the property of another has been stolen—that is, unlawfully taken by someone whose intent it was to permanently deprive the owner of its possession.[25] Hence, evidence offered to prove the *corpus delicti* in a trial for larceny is insufficient if it fails to prove that any property was stolen or if property found in a defendant's possession cannot be identified as having been stolen. Similarly, "[i]n an arson case, the *corpus delicti* consists of (1) a burned building or other property, and (2) some criminal agency which caused the burning.... In other words, the *corpus delicti* includes not only the fact of burning, but it must also appear that the burning was by the willful act of some person, and not as a result of a natural or accidental cause."[26]

We should note that the identity of the perpetrator is not an element of the *corpus delicti* of an offense. Hence, the fact that a crime has occurred can be established without having any idea who committed it or even why it was committed. This principle was clearly enunciated in a Montana case when that state's supreme court held that "the identity of the perpetrator is not an element of the *corpus delicti*." In *State* v. *Kindle* (1924),[27] the court said, "We stated that '[i]n a prosecution for murder, proof of the *corpus delicti* does not necessarily carry with it the identity of the slain nor of the slayer.' ... The essential elements of the *corpus delicti* are ... establishing the death and the fact that the death was caused by a criminal agency, nothing more." *Black's Law Dictionary* puts it another way: "The *corpus delicti* [of a crime] is the fact of its having been actually committed."[28]

■ **lecture note**   Explain the four categories of defenses recognized by the legal system. Point out that the category of "alibi" is actually a single defense, rather than an overarching category containing multiple types of defenses.

■ **defense (to a criminal charge)**   Evidence and arguments offered by a defendant and his or her attorney to show why the defendant should not be held liable for a criminal charge.

■ **alibi**   A statement or contention by an individual charged with a crime that he or she was so distant when the crime was committed, or so engaged in other provable activities, that his or her participation in the commission of that crime was impossible.

■ **justification**   A legal defense in which the defendant admits to committing the act in question but claims it was necessary in order to avoid some greater evil.

■ **theme**   How can you defend yourself in court by admitting that you committed the criminal act of which you are accused?

■ **excuse**   A legal defense in which the defendant claims that some personal condition or circumstance at the time of the act was such that he or she should not be held accountable under the criminal law.

■ **procedural defense**   A defense that claims that the defendant was in some significant way discriminated against in the justice process or that some important aspect of official procedure was not properly followed in the investigation or prosecution of the crime charged.

Types of Defenses to a Criminal Charge

When a person is charged with a crime, he or she typically offers some defense (Figure 4-5). A **defense** consists of evidence and arguments offered by the defendant to show why he or she should not be held liable for a criminal charge. Our legal system generally recognizes four broad categories of defenses: (1) **alibi**, (2) **justifications**, (3) **excuses**, and (4) **procedural defenses**. An alibi, if shown to be valid, means that the defendant could not have committed the crime in question because he or she was somewhere else (and generally with someone else) at the time of the crime. When a defendant offers a justification as a defense, he or she admits committing the act in question but claims that it was necessary to avoid some greater evil. A defendant who offers an excuse as a defense, on the other hand, claims that some personal condition or circumstance at the time of the act was such that he or she should not be held accountable under the criminal law. Procedural defenses make the claim that the defendant was in some significant way discriminated against in the justice process or that some important aspect of official procedure was not properly followed in the investigation or prosecution of the crime charged.

Alibi

A reference book for criminal trial lawyers says, "Alibi is different from all of the other defenses … because … it is based upon the premise that the defendant is truly innocent."[29] The defense of alibi denies that the defendant committed the act in question. All of the other defenses we are about to discuss grant that the defendant committed the act, but they deny that he or she should be held criminally responsible. Whereas justifications and excuses may produce findings of "not guilty," the defense of alibi claims outright innocence.

Alibi is best supported by witnesses and documentation. A person charged with a crime can use the defense of alibi to show that he or she was not present at the scene when the crime was alleged to have occurred. Hotel receipts, eyewitness identification, and participation in social events have all been used to prove alibis.

ALIBI: The defendant could not have committed the offense because he or she was somewhere else at the time of the crime.

EXCUSE: Some personal condition or circumstance at the time of the act was such that the actor should not be held accountable under the criminal law.
EXAMPLES: Duress, age, mistake, involuntary intoxication, unconsciousness, provocation, insanity, diminished capacity, and mental incompetence are examples of excuse defenses.

JUSTIFICATION: The defendant admits committing the act in question but claims that it was necessary to avoid some greater evil.
EXAMPLES: Self-defense, necessity, defense of others, consent, defense of home and property, and resisting unlawful arrest are examples of justification defenses.

PROCEDURAL DEFENSE: The defendant was in some significant way discriminated against in the justice process, or some important aspect of official procedure was not properly followed in the investigation or prosecution of the crime charged.
EXAMPLES: Entrapment, denial of a speedy trial, double jeopardy, prosecutorial misconduct, *collateral estoppel*, police fraud, and selective prosecution are examples of procedural defenses.

FIGURE 4-5 | Types of Defenses to a Criminal Charge
Source: Pearson Education, Inc.

■ **self-defense**   The protection of oneself or of one's property from unlawful injury or from the immediate risk of unlawful injury. Also, the justification that the person who committed an act that would otherwise constitute an offense reasonably believed that the act was necessary to protect self or property from immediate danger.

■ **reasonable force**   A degree of force that is appropriate in a given situation and is not excessive. Also, the minimum degree of force necessary to protect oneself, one's property, a third party, or the property of another in the face of a substantial threat.

Justifications

As defenses, justifications claim a kind of moral high ground. Justifications may be offered by people who find themselves forced to choose between "two evils." Generally speaking, conduct that a person believes is necessary to avoid harm to him- or herself or to another is justifiable if the harm he or she is trying to avoid is greater than the harm the law defining the offense seeks to avoid. For example, a firefighter might set a controlled fire to create a firebreak to head off a conflagration threatening a community. Although intentionally setting a fire might constitute arson, destroying property to save a town by creating a firebreak may be justifiable behavior in the eyes of the community and in the eyes of the law. Included under the broad category of justifications are: (1) self-defense, (2) defense of others, (3) defense of home and property, (4) necessity, (5) consent, and (6) resisting unlawful arrest.

Self-Defense

In May 2009, when Oklahoma City pharmacist Jerome Ersland was confronted by two holdup men, he pulled a gun and shot one of them in the head.[30] The second man ran away. Then, in a scene recorded by the drugstore's security camera, Ersland went behind the counter, got another gun, and pumped five more bullets into the wounded robber as he lay on the floor, killing him. Following the incident, Ersland, whose store had been robbed before and is located in a crime-ridden part of the city, was charged with first-degree murder in a case that stirred a furious debate over vigilante justice and self-defense. Many people praised him for defending himself and for his actions in protecting two female employees at the store. Not everyone thought that Ersland was a hero, however. In 2011, more than two years after the shooting, the 59-year-old Ersland was found guilty of first-degree murder by an Oklahoma City jury, and was sentenced to life in prison without the possibility of parole.[31]

Self-defense is probably the best known of the justifications. This defense strategy makes the claim that it was necessary to inflict harm on another to ensure one's own safety in the face of near-certain injury or death. A person who harms an attacker can generally use this defense. However, the courts have generally held that where a "path of retreat" exists for a person being attacked, it should be taken. In other words, the safest use of self-defense, legally speaking, is only when cornered, with no path of escape. Some states, such as Florida, have enacted "stand-your-ground" laws, which remove the retreat requirement, and allow for the use of force without the need for a victim to evade his or her attacker or to give ground. By 2013, close to 30 states had passed stand-your-ground laws,[32] although the statutes came under close scrutiny after the acquittal on murder charges of Florida neighborhood watchman George Zimmerman, who shot and killed 17-year-old Trayvon Martin during a physical confrontation. Ironically, Zimmerman's defense did not invoke any stand-your-ground claims, but relied instead on a traditional self-defense strategy.

> "Stand your ground" laws remove the retreat requirement, and allow for the use of force without the need for a victim to evade his or her attacker or to give ground.

The amount of defensive force used must be proportional to the amount of force or the perceived degree of threat that one is seeking to defend against. Hence, **reasonable force** is the degree of force that is appropriate in a given situation and that is not excessive. Reasonable force can also be thought of as the minimum degree of force necessary to protect oneself, one's

George Zimmerman is shown wearing restraints as he is escorted by a sheriff's deputy to his chair in the Seminole County courthouse in Orlando, Florida. Zimmerman was acquitted in 2013 on charges of second-degree murder and manslaughter in the Florida shooting death of 17-year-old Trayvon Martin. If you were on the jury, would you have found Zimmerman guilty?

Gary Green/UPI/Newscom

■ **alter ego rule** In some jurisdictions, a rule of law that holds that a person can defend a third party only under circumstances and only to the degree that the third party could legally act on his or her own behalf.

property, a third party, or the property of another in the face of a substantial threat. Deadly force, the highest degree of force, is considered reasonable only when used to counter an immediate threat of death or great bodily harm. Deadly force cannot be used against nondeadly force.

Force, as the term is used within the context of self-defense, means physical force and does not extend to emotional, psychological, economic, psychic, or other forms of coercion. A person who turns the tables on a robber and assaults him during a robbery attempt, for example, may be able to claim self-defense, but a businessperson who physically assaults a financial rival to prevent a hostile takeover of her company will have no such recourse.

Self-defense has sometimes been claimed in killings of abusive spouses. A jury is likely to accept as justified a killing that occurs while the physical abuse is in progress, especially where a history of such abuse can be shown. On the other hand, wives who suffer repeated abuse but coldly plan the killing of their husbands have not fared well in court.

Defense of Others

The use of force to defend oneself has generally been extended to permit the use of reasonable force to defend others who are or who appear to be in imminent danger. The defense of others, sometimes called *defense of a third person*, is circumscribed in some jurisdictions by the **alter ego rule**. The alter ego rule holds that a person can defend a third party only under circumstances and only to the degree that the third party could act. In other words, a person who aids another whom he or she sees being attacked may become criminally liable if that person initiated the attack or if the assault is a lawful one—for example, the use of physical force by a law enforcement officer conducting a lawful arrest of a person who is resisting. A few jurisdictions, however, do not recognize the alter ego rule and allow a person to act in defense of another if the actor reasonably believes that his or her intervention is immediately necessary to protect the third person.

Defense of others cannot be claimed by an individual who joins an illegal fight merely to assist a friend or family member. Likewise, one who intentionally aids an offender in an assault, even though the tables have turned and the offender is losing the battle, cannot claim defense of others. Under the law, defense of a third person always requires that the defender be free from fault and that he or she act to aid an innocent person who is in the process of being victimized. The same restrictions that apply to self-defense also apply to the defense of a third party. Hence a defender may act only in the face of an immediate threat to another person, cannot use deadly force against nondeadly force, and must act only to the extent and use only the degree of force needed to repel the attack.

Defense of Home and Property

In most jurisdictions, the owner of property can justifiably use reasonable, *nondeadly* force to prevent others from unlawfully taking or damaging it. As a general rule, the preservation of human life outweighs the protection of property, and the use of deadly force to protect property is not justified unless the perpetrator of the illegal act may intend to commit, or is in the act of committing, a violent act against another human being. A person who shoots and kills an unarmed trespasser, for example, could not claim "defense of property" to avoid criminal liability.[33] However, a person who shoots and kills an armed robber while being robbed can make such a claim.

The use of mechanical devices to protect property is a special area of law. Because deadly force is usually not permitted in defense of property, the setting of booby traps, such as spring-loaded shotguns, electrified gates, and explosive devices, is generally not permitted to protect property that is unattended and unoccupied. If an individual is injured as a result of a mechanical device intended to cause death or injury in the protection of property, criminal charges may be brought against the person who set the device.

On the other hand, acts that would otherwise be criminal may carry no criminal liability if undertaken to protect one's home. For purposes of the law, one's "home" is one's dwelling, whether owned, rented, or merely borrowed. Hotel rooms, rooms aboard vessels, and rented rooms in houses belonging to others are all considered, for purposes of the law, one's home. The retreat rule referred to earlier, which requires a person under attack to retreat when possible before resorting to deadly force, is subject to what some call the *castle exception*. The castle exception can be traced to the writings of the sixteenth-century English jurist Sir Edward Coke, who said, "A man's house is his castle—for where shall a man be safe if it be not in his house?"[34] The castle exception generally recognizes that a person has a fundamental right to be in his or her home and that the home is a final and inviolable place of retreat (i.e., the home offers a place of retreat from which a person can be expected to retreat no further). Hence, it is not necessary for one to retreat from one's home in the face of an immediate threat, even where such retreat is possible, before resorting to deadly force in protection of the home. Court decisions have extended the castle exception to include one's place of business, such as a store or an office.

Necessity

Necessity, or the claim that some illegal action was needed to prevent an even greater harm, is a useful defense in cases that do not involve serious bodily harm. A famous but unsuccessful

■ theme   Why is duress generally not a valid defense for crimes involving serious harm to another person? Do you agree with this? Why or why not?

use of this defense occurred in *The Crown* v. *Dudly & Stephens* in the late nineteenth century.[35] This British case involved a shipwreck in which three sailors and a cabin boy were set adrift in a lifeboat. After a number of days at sea without food, two of the sailors decided to kill and eat the cabin boy. At their trial, they argued that it was necessary to do so, or none of them would have survived. The court, however, reasoned that the cabin boy was not a direct threat to the survival of the men and rejected this defense. Convicted of murder, they were sentenced to death, although they were spared the gallows by royal intervention. Although cannibalism is usually against the law, courts have sometimes recognized the necessity of consuming human flesh where survival was at issue. Those cases, however, involved only "victims" who had already died of natural causes.

Consent

The defense of consent claims that whatever harm was done occurred only after the injured person gave his or her permission for the behavior in question.

In the "Condom Rapist Case," for example, Joel Valdez was found guilty of rape in 1993 after a jury in Austin, Texas, rejected his claim that the act became consensual once he complied with his victim's request to use a condom. Valdez, who was drunk and armed with a knife at the time of the offense, claimed that his victim's request was a consent to sex. After that, he said, "we were making love."[36]

> The castle exception generally recognizes that a person has a fundamental right to be in his or her home and that the home is a final and inviolable place of retreat.

Resisting Unlawful Arrest

All jurisdictions make resisting arrest a crime. Resistance, however, may be justifiable, especially if the arresting officer uses excessive force. Some states have statutory provisions detailing the limits imposed on such resistance and the conditions under which it can be used. Such laws generally say that a person may use a reasonable amount of force, other than deadly force, to resist arrest or an unlawful search by a law enforcement officer if the officer uses or attempts to use greater force than necessary to make the arrest or search. The rationale underlying such laws is that officers are no longer engaged in the performance of their duties under the law once they exceed the legal authority afforded to them under the law. Under California law, for example, an officer is not lawfully performing his or her duties when he or she "detains an individual without reasonable suspicion or arrests an individual without probable cause."[37] Resisting unlawful arrest as a defense is inapplicable in cases where the defendant is the first to resort to force. Deadly force to resist arrest is never justified unless the law enforcement officer resorts to deadly force when it is not called for.

Excuses

In contrast to a justification, an excuse does not claim that the conduct in question is justified by the situation or that it is moral. An excuse claims, rather, that the actor who engaged in the unlawful behavior was, at the time, not legally responsible for his or her actions and should not be held accountable under the law. For example, a person who assaults a police officer, thinking that the officer is really a disguised space alien who has come to abduct him, may be found "not guilty" of the charge of assault and battery by reason of insanity. Actions for which excuses are offered do not morally outweigh the wrong committed, but criminal liability may still be negated on the basis of some personal disability of the actor or because of some special circumstances that characterize the situation. Excuses recognized by the law include (1) duress, (2) age, (3) mistake, (4) involuntary intoxication, (5) unconsciousness, (6) provocation, (7) insanity, (8) diminished capacity, and (9) mental incompetence.

Duress

The defense of duress depends on an understanding of the situation. *Duress* has been defined as "any unlawful threat or coercion used by a person to induce another to act (or to refrain from acting) in a manner he or she otherwise would not (or would)."[38] A person may act under duress if, for example, he or she steals an employer's payroll to meet a ransom demand for kidnappers holding the person's children. Should the person later be arrested for larceny or embezzlement, the person can claim that he or she felt compelled to commit the crime to help ensure the safety of the children. Duress is generally not a useful defense when the crime committed involves serious physical harm, as the harm committed may outweigh the coercive influence in the minds of jurors and judges. Duress is sometimes also called *coercion*.

Age

Age offers another kind of excuse to a criminal charge, and the defense of "infancy"—as it is sometimes known in legal jargon—has its roots in the ancient belief that children cannot reason logically until around the age of seven. Early doctrine in the Christian church sanctioned that belief by declaring that rationality develops around that age. As a consequence, only older children could be held responsible for their crimes.

The defense of infancy today has been expanded to include young people well beyond the age of seven. Many states set the 16th birthday as the age at which a person becomes an adult for purposes of criminal prosecution. Others use the age of 17, and still others 18. When a person younger than the age required for adult prosecution commits a "crime," it is termed a *juvenile offense* (see Chapter 15). He or she is not guilty of a criminal violation of the law by virtue of youth.

In most jurisdictions, children below the age of 7 cannot be charged even with juvenile offenses, no matter how serious their actions may appear to others.

Mistake

Two types of mistakes can serve as a defense. One is mistake of law, and the other is mistake of fact. Rarely is mistake of law held to be an acceptable defense. Most people realize that it is their responsibility to know the law as it applies to them. "Ignorance of the law is no excuse" is an old dictum still heard today. On occasion, however, cases do arise in which such a defense is accepted by authorities. For example, an elderly woman raised marijuana plants because they could be used to make a tea that relieved her arthritis pain. When her garden was discovered, she was not arrested but was advised as to how the law applied to her.[39]

Mistake of fact is a much more useful form of the mistake defense. In 2000, for example, the statutory rape conviction of 39-year-old Charles Ballinger of Bradley County, Tennessee, was reversed by Tennessee's Court of Criminal Appeals at Knoxville on a mistake-of-fact claim.[40] Ballinger admitted that he had had sex with his 15-year-old neighbor, who was under the age of legal consent at the time of the act in 1998. In his defense, however, Ballinger claimed that he had had good reason to mistake the girl's age.

Involuntary Intoxication

The claim of involuntary intoxication may form the basis for another excuse defense. Either drugs or alcohol may produce intoxication. Voluntary intoxication itself is rarely a defense to a criminal charge because it is a self-induced condition. It is widely recognized in our legal tradition that an altered mental condition that is the product of voluntary activity cannot be used to exonerate guilty actions that follow from it. Some state statutes formalize this general principle of law and specifically state that voluntary intoxication cannot be offered as a defense against a charge of criminal behavior.[41]

Involuntary intoxication, however, is another matter. A person might be tricked into consuming an intoxicating substance. Secretly "spiked" punch, popular aphrodisiacs, or drug-laced desserts might be ingested unknowingly. Because the effects and taste of alcohol are so widely known in our society, the defense of involuntary intoxication due to alcohol consumption can be difficult to demonstrate.

Unconsciousness

A very rarely used excuse is that of unconsciousness. An individual cannot be held responsible for anything he or she does while unconscious. Because unconscious people rarely do anything at all, this defense is almost never seen in the courts. However, people afflicted with sleepwalking, epileptic seizure, or neurological dysfunction may unintentionally cause injuries to others. Under such circumstances, a defense of unconsciousness might be argued with success.

Provocation

Provocation recognizes that a person can be emotionally enraged by another who intends to elicit just such a reaction. Should the person then strike out at the tormentor, some courts have held, he or she may not be guilty of criminality or may be guilty of a lesser degree of criminality than might otherwise be the case. The defense of provocation is commonly used in cases arising from barroom brawls in which a person's parentage was called into question, although most states don't look favorably on verbal provocation alone. This defense has also been used in some spectacular cases where wives have killed their husbands, or children their fathers, citing years of verbal and physical abuse. In these latter instances, perhaps because the degree of physical harm inflicted—the death of the husband or father—appears to be out of proportion to the abuse suffered by the wife or child, the courts have not readily accepted the defense of provocation. As a rule, the defense of provocation is generally more acceptable in minor offenses than in serious violations of the law.

Insanity

From the point of view of the criminal law, *insanity* has a legal definition and not a medical one. This legal definition often has very little to do with psychological or psychiatric understandings of mental illness; rather, it is a concept developed to enable the judicial system to assign guilt or innocence to particular defendants. As a consequence, medical conceptions of mental illness do not always fit well into the legal categories of mental illness created by courts and legislatures. The differences between psychiatric and legal conceptualizations of insanity often lead to disagreements among expert witnesses who, in criminal court, may provide conflicting testimony as to the sanity of a defendant.

The **insanity defense** is given a lot of play in the entertainment industry; movies and television shows regularly employ it because it makes for good drama. In practice, however, the defense of insanity is rarely raised. According to an eight-state study funded by the National Institute of Mental Health, the insanity defense was used in less than 1% of the cases that came before county-level courts.[42] The study showed that only 26% of all insanity pleas were argued successfully and that 90% of those who employed the defense had been previously diagnosed with a mental illness. As the American Bar Association says, "The best evidence suggests that the mental nonresponsibility defense is raised in less than one percent of all felony cases in the United States and is successful in about a fourth of these."[43] Even so, there are several rules that guide the legal definition of insanity.

The M'Naghten Rule   The insanity defense, as we know it today, was nonexistent prior to the nineteenth century. Until then, insane people who committed crimes were punished in the same way as other law violators. It was Daniel M'Naghten (sometimes spelled McNaughten or M'Naughten), a woodworker from Glasgow, Scotland, who, in 1844, became the first person to be found not guilty of a crime by reason of insanity. M'Naghten had tried to assassinate Sir Robert Peel, the British prime minister. He mistook Edward Drummond, Peel's secretary, for Peel himself and killed Drummond instead. At his trial, defense attorneys argued that M'Naghten suffered from vague delusions centered on the idea that the Tories, a British political party, were persecuting him. Medical testimony at the trial supported the defense's assertion that he didn't know what he was doing at the time of the shooting. The jury accepted M'Naghten's claim, and the insanity defense was born. Later, the House of Lords defined the criteria necessary for a finding of insanity. The **M'Naghten rule**, as it is called, holds that *a person is not guilty of a crime if, at the time of the crime, the person either didn't know what he or she was doing or didn't know that what he or she was doing was wrong.* The inability to distinguish right from wrong must be the result of some mental defect or disability.

Today, the M'Naghten rule is still followed in many U.S. jurisdictions (Figure 4-6). In those states, the burden of proving insanity falls on the defendant. Just as defendants are assumed to be innocent, they are also assumed to be sane at the outset of any criminal trial. Learn more about the M'Naghten rule at **http://tinyurl.com/6yfbybh**.

Irresistible Impulse   The M'Naghten rule worked well for a time. Eventually, however, some cases arose in which defendants clearly knew what they were doing, and they knew it was wrong.

Saiqa Akhter, the Texas woman who was found not guilty by reason of insanity in 2014 after admitting to the murder of her two young children by strangulation. Akhter, who had been charged with two counts of capital murder, claimed the children were autistic and told first responders, "I want normal kids." What is the M'Naughten rule? What will likely happen to Akhter?

Courtney Perry/Dallas Morning News/MCT/Newscom

Even so, they argued in their defense that they couldn't stop doing what they knew was wrong. Such people are said to suffer from an *irresistible impulse*, and in a number of states today, they may be found not guilty by reason of that particular brand of insanity. Some states that do not use the irresistible-impulse test in determining insanity may still allow the successful demonstration of such an impulse to be considered in sentencing decisions.

In a spectacular 1994 Virginia trial, Lorena Bobbitt successfully employed the irresistible-impulse defense against charges of malicious wounding stemming from an incident in which she cut off her husband's penis with a kitchen knife as he slept. In the case, which made headlines around the world, Bobbitt's defense attorney told the jury, "What we have is Lorena Bobbitt's life juxtaposed against John Wayne Bobbitt's penis. The evidence will show that in her mind it was his penis from which she could not escape, that caused her the most pain, the most fear, the most humiliation."[44] The impulse to sever the organ, said the lawyer, became irresistible.

The irresistible-impulse test has been criticized on a number of grounds. Primary among them is the belief that all of us suffer from compulsions. Most of us, however, learn to control them. If we give in to a compulsion, the critique goes, then why not just say it was unavoidable so as to escape any legal consequences?

FIGURE 4-6 | Standards for Insanity Determinations by Jurisdiction

Source: Adapted from David B. Rottman and Shauna M. Strickland, *State Court Organization, 2004* (Washington, DC: Bureau of Justice Statistics, 2006), with updates by the author; pp. 199–202.

The Durham Rule Another rule for gauging insanity is called the *Durham rule*. Originally created in 1871 by a New Hampshire court, it was later adopted by Judge David Bazelon in 1954 as he decided the case of *Durham* v. *U.S.* for the court of appeals in the District of Columbia.[45] The Durham rule states that *a person is not criminally responsible for his or her behavior if the person's illegal actions were the result of some mental disease or defect.*

> The Durham rule is especially vague, and provides fertile ground for conflicting claims.

Courts that follow the Durham rule typically hear from an array of psychiatric specialists as to the mental state of the defendant. Their testimony is inevitably clouded by the need to address the question of cause. A successful defense under the Durham rule necessitates that jurors be able to see the criminal activity in question as the *product* of the defendant's mental deficiencies. And yet many people who suffer from mental diseases or defects never commit crimes. In fact, low IQ, mental retardation, and lack of general mental capacity are not allowable excuses for criminal behavior. Because the Durham rule is especially vague, it provides fertile ground for conflicting claims.

The Substantial-Capacity Test Nineteen states follow another guideline—the substantial-capacity test—as found in the Model Penal Code (MPC) of the American Law Institute (ALI).[46] Also called the *ALI rule* or the *MPC rule*, it suggests that insanity should be defined as the lack of a substantial capacity to control one's behavior. This test requires a judgment to the effect that the defendant either had or lacked "the mental capacity needed to understand the wrongfulness of his act or to conform his behavior to the requirements of the law."[47] The substantial-capacity test is a blending of the M'Naghten rule and the irresistible-impulse standard. "Substantial capacity" does not require total mental incompetence, nor does the rule require the behavior in question to live up to the criterion of total irresistibility. However, the problem of establishing just what constitutes "substantial mental capacity" has plagued this rule from its conception.

The Brawner Rule Judge Bazelon, apparently dissatisfied with the application of the Durham rule, created a new criterion for gauging insanity in the 1972 case of *U.S.* v. *Brawner*.[48] The Brawner rule, as it has come to be called, places responsibility for deciding insanity squarely with the jury. Bazelon suggested that the jury should be concerned with whether the defendant could justly be held responsible for the criminal act in the face of any claims of insanity. Under this proposal, juries are left with few rules to guide them other than their own sense of fairness.

The Insanity Defense and Social Reaction The insanity defense originated as a way to recognize the social reality of mental disease. However, the history of this defense has been rife with difficulty and contradiction. First, psychiatric testimony is expensive, and "expert" witnesses are often at odds with one another. Another difficulty with this defense is society's acceptance of it. When "not guilty due to insanity" findings have been made, the public has not always been satisfied that justice

■ **guilty but mentally ill (GBMI)**   A verdict, equivalent to a finding of "guilty," that establishes that the defendant, although mentally ill, was in sufficient possession of his or her faculties to be morally blameworthy for his or her acts.

has been served. Dissatisfaction with the jumble of rules defining legal insanity peaked in 1982, when John Hinckley was acquitted of trying to assassinate then President Ronald Reagan. At his trial, Hinckley's lawyers claimed that a series of delusions brought about by a history of schizophrenia left him unable to control his behavior. Government prosecutors were unable to counter defense contentions of insanity. The resulting acquittal shocked the nation and resulted in calls for a review of the insanity defense.

One response has been to ban the insanity defense from use at trial. A ruling by the U.S. Supreme Court in support of a Montana law allows states to prohibit defendants from claiming that they were insane at the time they committed their crimes. In 1994, without comment, the High Court let stand a Montana Supreme Court ruling that held that eliminating the insanity defense does not violate the U.S. Constitution. Currently, only three states—Montana, Idaho, and Utah—bar use of the insanity defense.[49]

Guilty but Mentally Ill

Another response to public frustration with the insanity and responsibility issue is the **guilty but mentally ill (GBMI)** verdict, now possible in at least 11 states. (In a few states, the finding is "guilty but insane.") A GBMI verdict means that a person can be held responsible for a specific criminal act even though a degree of mental incompetence may be present in his or her personality. In most GBMI jurisdictions, a jury must return a finding of "guilty but mentally ill" if (1) every element necessary for a conviction has been proved beyond a reasonable doubt, (2) the defendant is found to have been *mentally ill* at the time the crime was committed, and (3) the defendant was *not* found to have been *legally insane* at the time the crime was committed. The difference between mental illness and legal insanity is a crucial one, as a defendant can be mentally ill by standards of the medical profession but sane for purposes of the law.

Upon return of a GBMI verdict, a judge may impose any sentence possible under the law for the crime in question. Mandated psychiatric treatment, however, is often part of the commitment order. Once cured, the offender is usually placed in the general prison population to serve any remaining sentence.

In 1997, Pennsylvania multimillionaire John E. du Pont was found guilty but mentally ill in the shooting death of former Olympic gold medalist David Schultz during a delusional episode. Although defense attorneys were able to show that du Pont sometimes saw Nazis in his trees, heard the walls talking, and had cut off pieces of his skin to remove bugs from outer space, he was held criminally liable for Schultz's death and was sentenced to 13 to 30 years in confinement.

As some authors have observed, the GBMI finding has three purposes: "first, to protect society; second, to hold some offenders who were mentally ill accountable for their criminal acts; [and] third, to make treatment available to convicted offenders suffering from some form of mental illness."[50] The U.S. Supreme Court case of *Ford* v. *Wainwright* recognized an issue of a different sort.[51] The 1986 decision specified that prisoners who become insane while incarcerated cannot be executed. Hence, although insanity may not always be a successful defense to criminal prosecution, it can later become a block to the ultimate punishment.

Temporary Insanity

Temporary insanity is another possible defense against a criminal charge. Widely used in the 1940s and 1950s, temporary insanity means that the offender claims to have been insane only at the time of the commission of the offense. If a jury agrees, the defendant goes free. The defendant is not guilty of the criminal action by virtue of having been insane at the time, yet he or she cannot be ordered to undergo psychiatric counseling or treatment because the insanity is no longer present. This type of plea has become less popular as legislatures have regulated the circumstances under which it can be made.

The Insanity Defense under Federal Law

Yet another response to the public's concern with the insanity defense and responsibility issues is the federal Insanity Defense Reform Act (IDRA). In 1984, Congress passed this act, which created major revisions in the federal insanity defense. Insanity under the law is now defined as a condition in which the defendant can be shown to have been suffering under a "severe mental disease or defect" and, as a result, "was unable to appreciate the nature and quality or the wrongfulness of his acts."[52] This definition of insanity comes close to that set forth in the old M'Naghten rule.

The act also places the burden of proving the insanity defense squarely on the defendant—a provision that has been challenged a number of times since the act was passed. The Supreme Court supported a similar requirement prior to the act's passage. In 1983, in the case of *Jones* v. *U.S.*,[53] the Court ruled that defendants can be required to prove their insanity when it becomes an issue in their defense. Shortly after the act became law, the Court held, in *Ake* v. *Oklahoma* (1985),[54] that the government must ensure access to a competent psychiatrist whenever a defendant indicates that insanity will be an issue at trial.

Consequences of an Insanity Ruling

The insanity defense today is not an "easy way out" of criminal prosecution, as some people assume. Once a verdict of "not guilty by reason of insanity" is returned, the judge may order the defendant to undergo psychiatric treatment until cured. Because psychiatrists are reluctant to declare any potential criminal "cured," such

■ **diminished capacity** A defense based on claims of a mental condition that may be insufficient to exonerate the defendant of guilt but that may be relevant to specific mental elements of certain crimes or degrees of crime.

■ **lecture note** Explain the difference between insanity and mental incompetence. Point out that an individual may have been legally sane at the time of the crime but still be found mentally incompetent to stand trial.

■ **incompetent to stand trial** In criminal proceedings, a finding by a court that, as a result of mental illness, defect, or disability, a defendant is incapable of understanding the nature of the charges and proceedings against him or her, of consulting with an attorney, and of aiding in his or her own defense.

a sentence may result in more time spent in a psychiatric institution than would have been spent in a prison. In *Foucha v. Louisiana* (1992),[55] however, the U.S. Supreme Court held that a defendant found not guilty by reason of insanity in a criminal trial could not thereafter be institutionalized indefinitely without a showing that he or she was either dangerous or mentally ill.

Diminished Capacity

Diminished capacity, or *diminished responsibility*, is a defense available in some jurisdictions. In 2003, the U.S. Sentencing Commission issued a policy statement saying that *diminished capacity* may mean that "the defendant, although convicted, *has a significantly impaired ability* to (A) understand the wrongfulness of the behavior comprising the offense or to exercise the power of reason; or (B) control behavior that the defendant knows is wrongful."[56] Still, "the terms 'diminished responsibility' and 'diminished capacity' do not have a clearly accepted meaning in [many] courts."[57] Some defendants who offer diminished-capacity defenses do so in recognition of the fact that such claims may be based on a mental condition that would not qualify as mental disease or mental defect nor be sufficient to support the defense of insanity but that might still lower criminal culpability. According to Peter Arenella, professor of law at UCLA, "the defense [of diminished capacity] was first recognized by Scottish common law courts to reduce the punishment of the 'partially insane' from murder to culpable homicide, a non-capital offense."[58]

The diminished-capacity defense is similar to the defense of insanity in that it depends on a showing that the defendant's mental state was impaired at the time of the crime. As a defense, diminished capacity is most useful when it can be shown that because of some defect of reason or mental shortcoming, the defendant's capacity to form the *mens rea* required by a specific crime was impaired. Unlike an insanity defense, however, which can result in a finding of "not guilty," a diminished-capacity defense is built on the recognition that "[m]ental condition, though insufficient to exonerate, may be relevant to specific mental elements of certain crimes or degrees of crime."[59] For example, a defendant might present evidence of mental abnormality in an effort to reduce first-degree murder to second-degree murder, or second-degree murder to manslaughter, when a killing

> The diminished-capacity defense is similar to the defense of insanity in that it depends on a showing that the defendant's mental state was impaired at the time of the crime.

occurs under extreme emotional disturbance. Similarly, in some jurisdictions, very low intelligence will, if proved, serve to reduce first-degree murder to manslaughter.[60]

As is the case with the insanity defense, some jurisdictions have entirely eliminated the diminished-capacity defense. The California Penal Code, for example, abolished the defense of diminished capacity,[61] stating that "[a]s a matter of public policy there shall be no defense of diminished capacity, diminished responsibility, or irresistible impulse in a criminal action or juvenile adjudication hearing."[62]

Mental Incompetence

In January 2007, King County (Washington) Superior Court Judge Helen Halpert dismissed murder charges against 39-year-old Marie Robinson, finding her mentally **incompetent to stand trial** in the deaths of her two baby sons.[63] The sons, 6-week-old Raiden and 16-month-old Justice, were found dead in Robinson's apartment by police who were called to check on the family. The boys were later determined to have died from starvation and dehydration, and Robinson was discovered passed out in a bedroom amid hundreds of empty beer cans. Her blood alcohol level at the time of discovery was five times Washington's legal limit for intoxication.

Although she was charged with two counts of second-degree murder, Halpert declared that "Ms. Robinson is clearly incompetent to stand trial. Every psychiatrist or psychologist who has examined her during the past two years has reached this conclusion." Interviews with Robinson showed that she believed her children were still alive and had been kidnapped by a secret police organization that wanted to prevent her from doing some kind of imagined scientific research.

Halpert found Robinson to be dangerously mentally ill and ordered her committed to a state mental hospital. Months later, however, doctors at Washington's Western State Hospital determined that she was not sick enough to be held for additional treatment and prosecutors refiled murder charges against her.[64] In late 2007, Robinson pleaded guilty to two reduced counts of manslaughter and one count of reckless endangerment and was sentenced to 34 years in prison.[65]

In Washington, as in most states, a person deemed competent to stand trial must be capable of understanding the nature of the proceedings and must be able to assist in his or her own legal defense. Hence, whereas insanity refers to an assessment of the offender's mental condition at the time the crime was committed, mental incompetence refers to his or her condition immediately before prosecution.

■ **lecture note**   Explain that procedural defenses do not address the question of whether or not the defendant committee the crime had an excuse or justification. Instead, they focus on some failure by the criminal justice system to follow proper procedure. In other words, the defendant is released from criminal liability not because he or she has been shown to be innocent but because the system made a mistake.

■ **entrapment**   An improper or illegal inducement to crime by agents of law enforcement. Also, a defense that may be raised when such inducements have occurred.

■ **lecture note**   Discuss the use of the entrapment defense by various well-known individuals (e.g., automotive executive John DeLorean; Washington D.C. Mayor Marion Barry; and various members of Congress accused of taking bribes).

■ **theme**   What one consideration makes for the crucial distinction between guilt and innocence when the entrapment defense is used?

■ **double jeopardy**   A common law and constitutional prohibition against a second trial for the same offense.

Mental illness that falls short of incompetence to stand trial can bar a defendant from self-representation. In 2008, in the case of *Indiana* v. *Edwards*, the U.S. Supreme Court held that even defendants found competent to stand trial can be prohibited from representing themselves before the court if they are too mentally disturbed to conduct trial proceedings by themselves.[66]

Procedural Defenses

Procedural defenses make the claim that the defendant was in some manner discriminated against in the justice process or that some important aspect of official procedure was not properly followed. As a result, those offering this defense say, the defendant should be released from any criminal liability. The procedural defenses we will discuss here are (1) entrapment, (2) double jeopardy, (3) *collateral estoppel*, (4) selective prosecution, (5) denial of a speedy trial, (6) prosecutorial misconduct, and (7) police fraud.

Entrapment

Entrapment is an improper or illegal inducement to crime by enforcement agents. Entrapment defenses argue that enforcement agents effectively created a crime where there would otherwise have been none. For entrapment to occur, the idea for the criminal activity must originate with official agents of the criminal justice system. Entrapment can also result when overzealous undercover police officers convince a defendant that the contemplated law-violating behavior is not a crime. To avoid claims of entrapment, officers must not engage in activity that would cause a person to commit a crime that he or she would not otherwise commit. Merely providing an opportunity for a willing offender to commit a crime, however, is not entrapment.

Double Jeopardy

The Fifth Amendment to the U.S. Constitution makes it clear that no person may be tried twice for the same offense. People who have been acquitted or found innocent may not again be "put in jeopardy of life or limb" for the same crime. The same is true of those who have been convicted: They cannot be tried again for the same offense. Cases that are dismissed for a lack of evidence also come under the double jeopardy rule and cannot result in a new trial. The U.S. Supreme Court has ruled that "the Double Jeopardy Clause protects against three distinct abuses: a second prosecution for the same offense after acquittal; a second prosecution for the same offense after conviction; and multiple punishments for the same offense."[67]

Double jeopardy does not apply in cases of trial error. Hence a defendant whose conviction was set aside because of some error in proceedings at a lower court level (e.g., inappropriate instructions to the jury by the trial court judge) can be retried on the same charges. Similarly, when a defendant's motion for a mistrial is successful, or when members of the jury cannot agree on a verdict (resulting in a hung jury), a second trial may be held. Defendants, however, may be tried in both federal and state courts without necessarily violating the principle of double jeopardy.

Generally, because civil law and criminal law differ as to purpose, it is possible to try someone in civil court to collect damages for a possible violation of civil law, even if he or she was found "not guilty" in criminal court, without violating the principle of double jeopardy. For example, the 2005 civil trial of actor Robert Blake, following his acquittal at a criminal trial for murdering his wife, resulted in Blake's being ordered to pay $30 million to his wife's children.[68] In cases where civil penalties are "so punitive in form and effect as to render them criminal,"[69] however, a person sanctioned by a court in a civil case may not be tried in criminal court.

Collateral Estoppel

Collateral estoppel is similar to double jeopardy, but it applies to facts that have been determined by a "valid and final judgment."[70] Such facts cannot become the object of new litigation. For example, if a defendant has been acquitted of a murder charge by

A handcuffed man in police custody walks away from the female police officer who arrested him while posing as a prostitute in Pomona, California. How might entrapment be a defense in a case like this? How can police avoid claims of entrapment.

David McNew/Getty Images

■ **lecture note**   Review the various defenses to a criminal charge that are discussed in this chapter. Remind students that a defense to a criminal charge does not necessarily mean that the defendant denies committing the act in question.

virtue of an alibi, it would not be permissible to try that person again for the murder of a second person killed along with the first.

Selective Prosecution

The procedural defense of selective prosecution is based on the Fourteenth Amendment's guarantee of "equal protection of the laws."? This defense may be available where two or more individuals are suspected of criminal involvement, but not all are actively prosecuted. Selective prosecution based fairly on the strength of available evidence is not the object of this defense. But when prosecution proceeds unfairly on the basis of some arbitrary and discriminatory attribute, such as race, sex, friendship, age, or religious preference, this defense may offer protection. In 1996, however, in a case that reaffirmed reasonable limits on claims of selective prosecution, the U.S. Supreme Court ruled that for a defendant to successfully "claim that he was singled out for prosecution on the basis of his race, he must make a … showing that the Government declined to prosecute similarly situated suspects of other races."[71]

Denial of a Speedy Trial

The Sixth Amendment to the Constitution guarantees a right to a speedy trial. The purpose of the guarantee is to prevent unconvicted and potentially innocent people from languishing in jail. The federal government[72] and most states have laws (generally referred to as *speedy trial acts*) that define the time limit necessary for a trial to be "speedy." They generally set a reasonable period, such as 90 or 120 days following arrest. Excluded from the total number of days are delays that result from requests by the defense to prepare the defendant's case. If the limit set by law is exceeded, the defendant must be set free, and no trial can occur.

> The Sixth Amendment to the Constitution guarantees a right to a speedy trial.

Speedy trial claims became an issue in New Orleans after it was ravaged by Hurricane Katrina in August 2005 because hundreds of inmates in parish jails who had been arrested before the hurricane hit never came to trial. Nine months after the storm battered the city, Chief District Judge Calvin Johnson told reporters that his staff was continuing to find people who shouldn't have been in jail and who were doing "Katrina time."[73] "We're still finding people—they bubble up weekly," Johnson said. Most pre-Katrina arrestees discovered by Johnson's staff had been taken into custody for misdemeanors before the storm hit, and the judge said that he released them when they were found. "We can't have people in jail indeterminately," he said. Speedy trial laws are discussed in more detail in Chapter 10.

Prosecutorial Misconduct

Another procedural defense is prosecutorial misconduct. Generally speaking, legal scholars use the term *prosecutorial misconduct* to describe actions undertaken by prosecutors that give the government an unfair advantage or that prejudice the rights of a defendant or a witness. Prosecutors are expected to uphold the highest ethical standards in the performance of their roles. When they knowingly permit false testimony, when they hide information that would clearly help the defense, or when they make unduly biased statements to the jury in closing arguments, the defense of prosecutorial misconduct may be available to the defendant.

Police Fraud

The defense of police fraud is available to defendants victimized by the police through planted evidence, the fabrication of "facts" uncovered during police investigations, and false arrests. In 2011, for example, Stephen Anderson, a former New York Police Department (NYPD) narcotics detective, testified in court that the practice of "flaking," or the planting of drugs on innocent people, was common practice in the NYPD's narcotics division. Flaking, said Anderson, was a quick and easy way to boost arrest numbers and to impress supervisors.[74]

Similarly, during the 1995 double-murder trial of O. J. Simpson, defense attorneys suggested that evidence against Simpson had been concocted and planted by police officers with a personal dislike of the defendant.

Not all claims of police fraud are supportable, however, and some defendants will claim fraud as a defense even when they know that they are guilty. As one observer put it, however, the defense of police fraud builds on extreme paranoia about the government and police agencies. This type of defense, said Francis Fukuyama, carries "to extremes a distrust of government and the belief that public authorities are in a vast conspiracy to violate the rights of individuals."[75] As a defense strategy, the claim of police fraud, when it is not warranted, can subject otherwise well-meaning public servants to intense public scrutiny, effectively shifting attention away from criminal defendants and onto the police officers—sometimes with disastrous personal results. Anthony Pellicano, a private investigator hired by Fuhrman's lawyers, put it this way: "[Fuhrman's] life right now is in the toilet. He has no job, no future. People think he's a racist. He can't do anything to help himself. He's been ordered not to talk. His family and friends, he's told them not to get involved…. Mark Fuhrman's life is ruined. For what? Because he found a key piece of evidence."[76] The 43-year-old Fuhrman retired from police work before the Simpson trial concluded and has since written two books.

SUMMARY

- Laws are rules of conduct, usually found enacted in the form of statutes, that regulate relationships between people and also between parties. One of the primary functions of the law is to maintain public order. Laws also serve to regulate human interaction, enforce moral beliefs, define the economic environment of a society, enhance predictability, promote orderly social change, sustain individual rights, identify wrongdoers and redress wrongs, and mandate punishment and retribution. Because laws are made by those in power and are influenced by those with access to power brokers, they tend to reflect and support the interest of society's most powerful members.

- The rule of law, which is sometimes referred to as the *supremacy of law*, encompasses the principle that an orderly society must be governed by established principles and known codes that are applied uniformly and fairly to all of its members. It means that no one is above the law, and it mandates that those who make or enforce the law must also abide by it. The rule of law is regarded as a vital underpinning in Western democracies, for without it disorder and chaos might prevail.

- This chapter identified various types of law, including criminal law, civil law, administrative law, case law, and procedural law. We were concerned primarily with criminal law, which is the form of the law that defines, and specifies punishments for, offenses of a public nature or for wrongs committed against the state or against society.

- Violations of the criminal law can be of many different types and can vary in severity. Five categories of violations were discussed in this chapter: (1) felonies, (2) misdemeanors, (3) offenses, (4) treason and espionage, and (5) inchoate offenses.

- From the perspective of Western jurisprudence, all crimes can be said to share certain features. Taken together, these features make up the legal essence of the concept of crime. The essence of crime consists of three conjoined elements: (1) the criminal act, which in legal parlance is termed the *actus reus*; (2) a culpable mental state, or *mens rea*; and (3) a concurrence of the two. Hence the essence of criminal conduct consists of a concurrence of a criminal act with a culpable mental state. Five additional principles, added to these three, allow us to fully appreciate contemporary understandings of crime. These five principles are (1) causation, (2) a resulting harm, (3) the principle of legality, (4) the principle of punishment, and (5) necessary attendant circumstances.

- Written laws specify exactly what conditions are required for a person to be charged in a given instance of criminal activity. Hence the elements of a crime are specific legal aspects of the criminal offense that the prosecution must prove to obtain a conviction. Guilt can be demonstrated, and criminal

offenders convicted, only if all of the statutory elements of the particular crime can be proved in court.

- Our legal system recognizes four broad categories of defenses to a criminal charge: (1) alibi, (2) justifications, (3) excuses, and (4) procedural defenses. An alibi, if shown to be valid, means that the defendant could not have committed the crime in question because he or she was not present at the time of the crime. When a defendant offers a justification as a defense, he or she admits committing the act in question but claims that it was necessary to avoid some greater evil. A defendant who offers an excuse as a defense claims that some personal condition or circumstance at the time of the act was such that he or she should not be held accountable under the criminal law. Procedural defenses make the claim that the defendant was in some significant way discriminated against in the justice process or that some important aspect of official procedure was not properly followed in the investigation or prosecution of the crime charged.

KEY TERMS

actus reus, 116	infraction, 114
alibi, 123	insanity defense, 127
alter ego rule, 125	jurisprudence, 110
attendant circumstances, 120	justification, 123
case law, 110	law, 109
civil law, 113	legal cause, 119
common law, 110	*mens rea*, 118
concurrence, 119	misdemeanor, 114
corpus delicti, 121	M'Naghten rule, 128
criminal law, 112	motive, 118
criminal negligence, 118	offense, 114
defense (to a criminal charge), 123	penal code, 110
	precedent, 113
diminished capacity, 131	procedural defense, 123
double jeopardy, 132	procedural law, 112
element (of a crime), 120	reasonable force, 124
entrapment, 132	reckless behavior, 118
espionage, 116	rule of law, 110
excuse, 123	self-defense, 124
ex post facto, 120	*stare decisis*, 113
felony, 114	statutory law, 109
guilty but mentally ill (GBMI), 130	strict liability, 119
	substantive criminal law, 112
inchoate offense, 116	tort, 113
incompetent to stand trial, 131	treason, 114

KEY CASES

Ake v. Oklahoma, 130	*Foucha v. Louisiana*, 131
The Crown v. Dudly & Stephens, 126	*Holder v. Humanitarian Law Project*, 115
Durham v. U.S., 129	*U.S. v. Brawner*, 129
Ford v. Wainwright, 130	

QUESTIONS FOR REVIEW

1. What is the purpose of law? What would a society without laws be like?

2. What is the rule of law? What is its importance in Western democracies? What does it mean to say that "nobody is above the law"?

3. What types of law does this chapter discuss? What purpose does each serve?

4. What are the six general categories of criminal law violations? Describe each, and rank the categories in terms of seriousness.

5. List and describe the eight general features of crime. What are the "three conjoined elements" that comprise the legal essence of the concept of crime?

6. What is meant by the *corpus delicti* of a crime? How does the *corpus delicti* of a crime differ from the statutory elements that must be proved to convict a particular defendant of committing that crime?

7. What four broad categories of criminal defenses does our legal system recognize? Under what circumstances might each be employed?

QUESTIONS FOR REFLECTION

1. What is common law? What impact does common law have on contemporary American criminal justice?

2. How does the legal concept of insanity differ from psychiatric explanations of mental illness?

3. Does the insanity defense serve a useful function today? If you could create your own rule for determining insanity in criminal trials, what would it be? How would it differ from existing rules?

NOTES

i. Daniel Oran, *Oran's Dictionary of the Law* (St. Paul, MN: West, 1983), p. 306.

ii. Henry Campbell Black, Joseph R. Nolan, and Jacqueline M. Nolan-Haley, *Black's Law Dictionary*, 6th ed. (St. Paul, MN: West, 1990), p. 24.

1. Elisabetta Povoledo and Henry Fountain, "Italy Orders Jail Terms for 7 Who Didn't Warn of Deadly Earthquake," *New York Times*, October 22, 2012, http://www.nytimes.com/2012/10/23/world/europe/italy-convicts-7-for-failure-to-warn-of-quake.html?_r=0 (accessed May 2, 2013).

2. Ibid.

3. Henry Campbell Black, Joseph R. Nolan, and Jacqueline M. Nolan-Haley, *Black's Law Dictionary*, 6th ed. (St. Paul, MN: West, 1990), p. 884.

4. Ibid.

5. Catalina Camia, "DeLay Gets 3-Year Sentence for Corruption," *USA Today*, January 11, 2011, p. 2A.

6. John F. Kennedy, *Profiles in Courage* (New York: Harper and Row, 1956).

7. Fareed Zakaria, "The Enemy Within," *New York Times*, December 17, 2006.

8. American Bar Association Section of International and Comparative Law, *The Rule of Law in the United States* (Chicago: American Bar Association, 1958).

9. Daniel Oran, *Oran's Dictionary of the Law* (St. Paul, MN: West, 1983), p. 306.

10. Black, Nolan, and Nolan-Haley, *Black's Law Dictionary*, p. 24.

11. FBI, "Former Sailor Sentenced to 30 Years in Prison for Attempted Espionage," February 10, 2014, http://www.fbi.gov/norfolk/press-releases/2014/former-sailor-sentenced-to-30-years-in-prison-for-attempted-espionage (accessed February 3, 2015).

12. Specifically, U.S. Code, Title 21, Section 846.

13. *U.S. v. Shabani*, 510 U.S. 1108 (1994).

14. *Gordon v. State*, 52 Ala. 3008, 23 Am. Rep. 575 (1875).

15. But not for a more serious degree of homicide, as leaving a young child alone in a tub of water, even if intentional, does not necessarily mean that the person who so acts intends the child to drown.

16. O. W. Holmes, *The Common Law*, Vol. 3 (Boston: Little, Brown, 1881).

17. There is disagreement among some jurists as to whether the crime of statutory rape is a strict liability offense. Some jurisdictions treat it as such and will not accept a reasonable mistake about the victim's age. Others, however, do accept such a mistake as a defense.

18. *State v. Stiffler*, 763 P.2d 308 (Idaho App. 1988).

19. John S. Baker, Jr., et al., *Hall's Criminal Law*, 5th ed. (Charlottesville, VA: Michie, 1993), p. 138.

20. The same is not true for procedures within the criminal justice system, which can be modified even after a person has been sentenced, and hence become retroactive. See, for example, the U.S. Supreme Court case of *California Department of Corrections v. Morales*, 514 U.S. 499 (1995), in which the Court allowed changes in the length of time between parole hearings, even though those changes applied to offenders who had already been sentenced.

21. Black, Nolan, and Nolan-Haley, *Black's Law Dictionary*, p. 127.

22. The statute also says, "A mother's breastfeeding of her baby does not under any circumstance violate this section."

23. Common law crimes, of course, are not based on statutory elements.

24. "*People v. Hall*—Final Analysis," SkiSafety.com, http://www.skisafety.com/amicuscases-hall2.html (accessed August 28, 2013).

25. See *Maughs v. Commonwealth*, 181 Va. 117, 120, 23 S.E.2d 784, 786 (1943).

26. *State v. Stephenson*, Opinion No. 24403 (South Carolina, 1996). See also *State v. Blocker*, 205 S.C. 303, 31 S.E.2d 908 (1944).

27. *State v. Kindle*, 71 Mont. 58, 64, 227 (1924).

28. Black, Nolan, and Nolan-Haley, *Black's Law Dictionary*, p. 343.

29. Patrick L. McCloskey and Ronald L. Schoenberg, *Criminal Law Deskbook* (New York: Matthew Bender, 1988), Section 20.03[13].

30. Details for this story come from Tim Talley, "Folk Hero or Killer: Druggist Who Killed Robber," *Associated Press*, May 30, 2009, http://abcnews.go.com/US/wireStory?id=7713776 (accessed May 31, 2009).

31. "Pharmacist Gets Life for Killing Robber," *USA Today*, July 12, 2001, p. 3A.

32. Greg Allen, "Florida Governor Stands Firm on 'Stand Your Ground' Law," *NPR*, July 19, 2013, http://www.npr

.org/2013/07/19/203594004/florida-governor-stands-firm-on
-stand-your-ground-law (accessed July 19, 2013).

33. The exception, of course, is that of a trespasser who trespasses in order to commit a more serious crime.

34. Sir Edward Coke, *3 Institute*, 162.

35. *The Crown* v. *Dudly & Stephens*, 14 Q.B.D. 273, 286, 15 Cox C. C. 624, 636 (1884).

36. "Jury Convicts Condom Rapist," *USA Today*, May 14, 1993.

37. *Nuño* v. *County of San Bernardino* (C.D.Cal.1999) 58 F.Supp.2d 1127, 1134.

38. Black, Nolan, and Nolan-Haley, *Black's Law Dictionary*, p. 504.

39. Story originally appeared in the *Santa Cruz Sentinel* at http://forums.santacruzsentinel.com/cgi-bin/forums/ultimatebb.cgi?ubb=get_topic;f=7;t=000301. Link no longer available.

40. *State of Tennessee* v. *Charles Arnold Ballinger*, No. E2000-01339-CCA-R3-CD (Tenn.Crim.App. 01/09/2000).

41. See, for example, *Montana* v. *Egelhoff*, 116 S.Ct. 2013, 135 L.Ed.2d 361 (1996).

42. L. A. Callahan et al., "The Volume and Characteristics of Insanity Defense Pleas: An Eight-State Study," *Bulletin of the American Academy of Psychiatry and the Law*, Vol. 19, No. 4 (1991), pp. 331–338.

43. American Bar Association Standing Committee on Association Standards for Criminal Justice, *Proposed Criminal Justice Mental Health Standards* (Chicago: American Bar Association, 1984).

44. "Mrs. Bobbitt's Defense: 'Life Worth More Than Penis,'" *Reuters*, January 10, 1994.

45. *Durham* v. *U.S.*, 214 F.2d 867, 875 (D.C. Cir. 1954).

46. American Law Institute, *Model Penal Code: Official Draft and Explanatory Notes* (Philadelphia: American Law Institute, 1985).

47. Ibid.

48. *U.S.* v. *Brawner*, 471 F.2d 969, 973 (D.C. Cir. 1972).

49. See Joan Biskupic, "Insanity Defense: Not a Right; In Montana Case, Justices Give States Option to Prohibit Claim," *Washington Post* wire service, March 29, 1994.

50. Ibid.

51. *Ford* v. *Wainwright*, 477 U.S. 399, 106 S.Ct. 2595, 91 L.Ed.2d 335 (1986).

52. U.S. Code, Title 18, Section 401.

53. *Jones* v. *U.S.*, U.S. Sup. Ct., 33 CrL. 3233 (1983).

54. *Ake* v. *Oklahoma*, 470 U.S. 68, 105 S.Ct. 1087, 84 L.Ed.2d 53 (1985).

55. *Foucha* v. *Louisiana*, 504 U.S. 71 (1992).

56. U.S. Sentencing Commission, "Supplement to the 2002 Federal Sentencing Guidelines: Section 5K2.13. Diminished Capacity (Policy Statement)," April 30, 2003, http://www.ussc.gov/2002suppb/5K2_13.htm (accessed May 8, 2010). Italics added.

57. *U.S.* v. *Pohlot*, 827 F.2d 889 (1987).

58. Peter Arenella, "The Diminished Capacity and Diminished Responsibility Defenses: Two Children of a Doomed Marriage," *Columbia Law Review*, Vol. 77 (1977), p. 830.

59. *U.S.* v. *Brawner*, 471 F.2d 969 (1972).

60. Black, Nolan, and Nolan-Haley, *Black's Law Dictionary*, p. 458.

61. California Penal Code, Section 25(a).

62. Ibid., Section 28(b).

63. Tracy Johnson, "Charges Dropped against Mom Whose Kids Starved to Death," *Seattle Post-Intelligencer*, January 31, 2007, http://seattlepi.nwsource.com/local/301852_mom31ww.html (accessed June 15, 2010).

64. Natalie Singer, "Competence Issue Creates Dilemma in '04 Murder Case," *Seattle Times*, March 16, 2007.

65. Nancy Bartley, "Child Abuser Given 34 Years," *Seattle Times*, November 17, 2007, http://seattletimes.nwsource.com/html/localnews/2004019371_robinson17m.html (accessed August 8, 2009).

66. *Indiana* v. *Edwards*, U.S. Supreme Court, No. 07–208 (decided June 19, 2008).

67. *U.S.* v. *Halper*, 490 U.S. 435 (1989).

68. "Robert Blake Found Liable for Wife's Death," *Associated Press*, November 18, 2005.

69. See, for example, *Hudson* v. *U.S.*, 18 S.Ct. 488 (1997); and *U.S.* v. *Ursery*, 518 U.S. 267 (1996).

70. McCloskey and Schoenberg, *Criminal Law Deskbook*, Section 20.02[4].

71. *U.S.* v. *Armstrong*, 116 S.Ct. 1480, 134 L.Ed.2d 687 (1996).

72. Speedy Trial Act, U.S. Code, Title 18, Section 3161. Significant cases involving the U.S. Speedy Trial Act are those of *U.S.* v. *Carter*, 476 U.S. 1138, 106 S.Ct. 2241, 90 L.Ed.2d 688 (1986); and *Henderson* v. *U.S.*, 476 U.S. 321, 106 S.Ct. 1871, 90 L.Ed.2d 299 (1986).

73. Peter Whoriskey, "New Orleans Justice System Besieged," *Boston Globe*, April 17, 2006, http://www.boston.com/news/nation/articles/2006/04/17/new_orleans_justice_system_besieged/ (accessed May 10, 2007).

74. Stephen Anderson, "Ex-NYPD Cop: We Planted Evidence, Framed Innocent People to Reach Quotas," *Huffington Post*, October 13, 2011, http://www.huffingtonpost.com/2011/10/13/ex-nypd-cop-we-planted-ev_n_1009754.html?view=print&comm_ref=false (accessed March 23, 2012).

75. Francis Fukuyama, "Extreme Paranoia about Government Abounds," *USA Today*, August 24, 1995.

76. Lorraine Adams, "Simpson Trial Focus Shifts to Detective with Troubling Past," *Washington Post* wire service, August 22, 1995.

PART

2

POLICING

RIGHTS OF THE ACCUSED UNDER INVESTIGATION

The accused has these common law, constitutional, statutory, and humanitarian rights:

- A right against unreasonable searches
- A right against unreasonable arrest
- A right against unreasonable seizures of property
- A right to fair questioning by authorities
- A right to protection from personal harm

These individual rights must be effectively balanced against these community concerns:

- The efficient apprehension of offenders
- The prevention of crimes

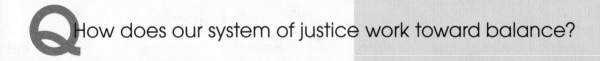 **Q** How does our system of justice work toward balance?

To Protect and to Serve

Famed police administrator and former New York City Police Commissioner Patrick V. Murphy once said, "It is a privilege to be a police officer in a democratic society." Although Murphy's words still ring true, many of today's law enforcement officers might hear in them only the echo of a long-dead ideal, unrealistic for today's times.

America's police officers form the front line in the unending battle against crime, drugs, and terrorism—a battle that seems to get more sinister and more demanding with each passing day. It is the police who are called when a crime is in progress or when one has been committed. They are the first responders to a terrorist event that strikes the homeland. The police are expected to objectively and impartially investigate law violations, gather evidence, solve crimes, and make arrests resulting in the successful prosecution of suspects—all the while adhering to the strict due process standards set forth in the U.S. Constitution and enforced by the courts. They are also expected to aid the injured, give succor to victims, and protect the

innocent. The chapters in this section of *Criminal Justice Today* provide an overview of the historical development of policing; describe law enforcement agencies at the federal, state, and local levels; explore issues related to police administration; and discuss the due process and legal environments surrounding police activity.

As you will see, although the police are ultimately charged with protecting the public, they often believe that members of the public do not accord them the respect they deserve, and they feel that the distance between the police and the public is not easily bridged. Within the last few decades, however, an image of policing has emerged that may do much to heal that divide. This model, known as *community policing*, goes well beyond traditional conceptions of the police as mere law enforcers and encompasses the idea that police agencies should take counsel from the communities they serve. Under this model, the police are expected to prevent crime, as well as solve it, and to help members of the community deal with other pressing social issues.

© ZUMA Press, Inc./Alamy

5 POLICING: HISTORY AND STRUCTURE

LEARNING OBJECTIVES

After reading this chapter, you should be able to

- Summarize the historical development of policing in America.
- Describe the three major levels of public law enforcement in the United States today.
- Briefly describe three federal law enforcement agencies, including their responsibilities.
- Identify the two major models of state law enforcement organization.
- Describe the various kinds of local law enforcement agencies and their roles in enforcing the law.
- Describe private protective services in the United States and their possible future roles.

Fidelity, bravery, and integrity.

MOTTO OF THE FEDERAL BUREAU OF INVESTIGATION

■ **theme** How do the needs of contemporary society help structure the activities of today's law enforcement agencies?

■ **lecture note** Review the development of the modern police, beginning with law enforcement practices in early England, continuing with the growth of American police forces, and culminating with a description of contemporary American law enforcement agencies.

■ ***comes stabuli*** A nonuniformed mounted law enforcement officer of medieval England. Early police forces were small and relatively unorganized but made effective use of local resources in the formation of posses, the pursuit of offenders, and the like.

■ **night watch** An early form of police patrol in English cities and towns.

■ **Statute of Winchester** A law, written in 1285, that created a watch and ward system in English cities and towns and that codified early police practices.

Introduction

Many of the techniques used by today's police differ quite a bit from those employed in days gone by. Listen to how a police officer, writing in the mid-1800s, describes the way pickpockets were caught in London 250 years ago: "I walked forth the day after my arrival, rigged out as the very model of a gentleman farmer, and with eyes, mouth, and pockets wide open, and a stout gold-headed cane in my hand, strolled leisurely through the fashionable thoroughfares, the pump-rooms, and the assembly-rooms, like a fat goose waiting to be plucked. I wore a pair of yellow gloves well wadded, to save me from falling, through a moment's inadvertency, into my own snare, which consisted of about fifty fish-hooks, large black hackles, firmly sewn barb downward, into each of the pockets of my brand new leather breeches. The most blundering 'prig' alive might have easily got his hand to the bottom of my pockets, but to get it out again, without tearing every particle of flesh from the bones, was a sheer impossibility. … I took care never to see any of my old customers until the convulsive tug at one or other of the pockets announced the capture of a thief. I then coolly linked my arm in that of the prisoner, and told him in a confidential whisper who I was."[1]

> The rise of the police as an organized force in the Western world coincided with the evolution of strong centralized governments.

Historical Development of the Police

Police tactics and strategy have changed substantially since historical times, and many different kinds of police agencies—some of them highly specialized—function within the modern criminal justice system. This chapter describes the development of organized policing in Western culture and discusses the function of contemporary American police forces at the federal, state and local levels. Agency examples are given at each level. The promise held by private protective services, the recent rapid growth of private security organizations, and the quasi-private system of justice are also discussed.

English Roots

The rise of the police as an organized force in the Western world coincided with the evolution of strong centralized governments. Although police forces have developed throughout the world, often in isolation from one another, the historical growth of the English police is of special significance to students of criminal justice in America, for it was on the British model that much of early American policing was based.

Law enforcement in early Britain, except for military intervention in the pursuit of bandits and habitual thieves, was not well organized until around the year 1200.[2] When a person committed an offense and could be identified, he or she was usually pursued by an organized posse. All able-bodied men who could hear a victim's cry for help were obligated to join the posse in a common effort to apprehend the offender. The posse was led by the shire reeve (the leader of the county) or by a mounted officer (the ***comes stabuli***). Our modern words *sheriff* and *constable* are derived from these early terms. The *comites stabuli* (the plural form of the term) were not uniformed, nor were they numerous enough to perform all the tasks we associate today with law enforcement. This early system, employing a small number of mounted officers, depended for its effectiveness on the ability to organize and direct the efforts of citizens toward criminal apprehension.

The offender, cognizant of a near-certain end at the hands of the posse, often sought protection from trusted friends and family. As a consequence, feuds developed among organized groups of citizens, some seeking revenge and some siding with the offender. Suspects who lacked the shelter of a sympathetic group might flee into a church and invoke the time-honored custom of sanctuary. Sanctuary was rarely an ideal escape, however, as pursuers could surround the church and wait out the offender, preventing food and water from being carried inside. The offender, once caught, became the victim. Guilt was usually assumed, and trials were rare. Public executions, often involving torture, typified this early justice and served to provide a sense of communal solidarity as well as group retribution.

The development of law enforcement in English cities and towns grew out of an early reliance on bailiffs, or watchmen. Bailiffs were assigned the task of maintaining a **night watch**, primarily to detect fires and spot thieves. Although too few in number to handle most emergencies, bailiffs were able to rouse the sleeping population, which could then deal with whatever crisis was at hand. Larger cities expanded the idea of bailiffs by creating both a night watch and a day ward.

British police practices became codified in the **Statute of Winchester**, written in 1285. The statute (1) specified the creation of the watch and the ward in cities and towns; (2) mandated the draft of eligible males to serve those forces; (3) institutionalized the use of the *hue and cry*, making citizens who disregarded a call for help subject to criminal penalties; and

■ **Follow the author's tweets about the latest crime and justice news @schmalleger.**
■ **Bow Street Runners**   An early English police unit formed under the leadership of Henry Fielding, magistrate of the Bow Street region of London.

■ **lecture note**   Discuss how the changing needs of society have contributed to a variety of law enforcement models at different times throughout history. For example, use the "Wild West" model of law enforcement personified by Wyatt Earp and others to show how a "six-gun" culture gave rise to a peculiarly American enforcement style.

© Howard Sayer/Alamy

British bobbies. Today's uniformed English police officers have a recognizable appearance rooted in the time of Sir Robert Peel. In what way were early American law enforcement efforts influenced by the British experience?

(4) required that citizens maintain weapons in their home for answering the call to arms.

Some authors have attributed the growth of modern police forces to the gin riots that plagued London and other European cities in the eighteenth and nineteenth centuries. The invention of gin around 1720 provided, for the first time, a potent and inexpensive alcoholic drink readily available to the massed populations gathered in the early industrial ghettos of eighteenth-century cities. Seeking to drown their troubles, huge numbers of people, far beyond the ability of the bailiffs to control, began binges of drinking and rioting. During the next hundred years, these gin riots created an immense social problem for British authorities. By this time, the bailiff system had broken down and was staffed by groups of woefully inadequate substitutes, hired by original draftees to perform duties in their stead. Incompetent and unable to depend on the citizenry for help in enforcing the laws, bailiffs became targets of mob violence and were often attacked and beaten for sport.

> The development of law enforcement in English cities and towns grew out of an early reliance on bailiffs, or watchmen.

The Bow Street Runners

The early eighteenth century saw the emergence in London of a large criminal organization led by Jonathan Wild. Wild ran a type of fencing operation built around a group of loosely organized robbers, thieves, and burglars who would turn their plunder over to him. Wild would then negotiate with the legitimate owners for a ransom of their possessions.

The police response to Wild was limited by disinterest and corruption. However, change began when Henry Fielding, a well-known writer, became the magistrate of the Bow Street region of London. Fielding attracted a force of dedicated officers, dubbed the **Bow Street Runners**, who soon stood out as the best and most disciplined enforcement agents that London had to offer. Fielding's personal inspiration and his ability to communicate what he saw as the social needs of the period may have accounted for his success.

In February 1725, Wild was arrested and arraigned on the following charges: "(1) that for many years past he had been a confederate with great numbers of highwaymen, pickpockets, housebreakers, shop-lifters, and other thieves, (2) that he had formed a kind of corporation of thieves, of which he was the head or director …, (3) that he had divided the town and country into so many districts, and appointed distinct gangs for each, who regularly accounted with him for their robberies …, (4) that the persons employed by him were for the most part felon convicts …, (5) that he had, under his care and direction, several warehouses for receiving and concealing stolen goods, and also a ship for carrying off jewels, watches, and other valuable goods, to Holland, where he had a superannuated thief for his benefactor, and (6) that he kept in his pay several artists to make alterations, and transform watches, seals, snuff-boxes,

■ **new police**   A police force formed in 1829 under the command of Sir Robert Peel. It became the model for modern-day police forces throughout the Western world.

■ **bobbies**   The popular British name given to members of Sir Robert (Bob) Peel's Metropolitan Police Service.

rings, and other valuable things, that they might not be known."[3] Convicted of these and other crimes, Wild attempted suicide by drinking a large amount of laudanum, an opium compound. The drug merely rendered him senseless, and he was hanged the following morning, having only partially recovered from its effects.

In 1754, Henry Fielding died. His brother John took over his work and occupied the position of Bow Street magistrate for another 25 years. The Bow Street Runners remain famous to this day for quality police work.

The New Police

In 1829, Sir Robert Peel, who later became prime minister of England, formed what many have hailed as the world's first modern police force. The passage of the Metropolitan Police Act that year allocated the resources for Peel's force of 1,000 handpicked men. The London Metropolitan Police Service (MPS), also known as the **new police** or more simply the *Met*, soon became a model for police forces around the world.

Members of the Metropolitan Police were quickly dubbed **bobbies**, after their founder. London's bobbies were organized around two principles: the belief that it was possible to discourage crime, and the practice of preventive patrol. Peel's police patrolled the streets by walking beats. Their predecessors, the watchmen, had occupied fixed posts throughout the city, awaiting a public outcry. The new police were uniformed, resembling a military organization, and adopted a military administrative style.

London's first two police commissioners were Colonel Charles Rowan, a career military officer, and Richard Mayne, a lawyer. Rowan believed that mutual respect between the police and the citizenry would be crucial to the success of the new force. As a consequence, early bobbies were chosen for their ability to reflect and inspire the highest personal ideals among young men in early-nineteenth-century Britain.

The new police were not immediately well received. Some elements of the population saw them as an occupying army, and open battles between the police and the citizenry ensued. The tide of sentiment turned, however, when an officer was viciously killed in the Cold Bath Fields riot of 1833. A jury, considering a murder charge against the killer, returned a verdict of "not guilty," inspiring a groundswell of public support for the much-maligned force.

The Early American Experience

Early American law enforcement efforts were based to some degree on the British experience. Towns and cities in colonial America depended on modified versions of the night watch and the day ward, but the unique experience of the American colonies

Sang Tan/AP Wide World Photos

An English policewoman directing subway riders in London following four terrorist explosions on the underground rail system and a bus in 2005. How has policing changed since the time of Sir Robert Peel?

quickly differentiated the needs of colonists from those of the masses remaining in Europe. Huge expanses of uncharted territory, vast wealth, a widely dispersed population engaged mostly in agriculture, and a sometimes ferocious frontier all combined to mold American law enforcement in a distinctive way. Recent writers on the history of the American police have observed that policing in America was originally "decentralized," "geographically dispersed," "idiosyncratic," and "highly personalized."[4]

The Frontier

One of the major factors determining the development of American law enforcement was the frontier, which remained vast and wild until late in the nineteenth century. The backwoods areas provided a natural haven for outlaws and bandits. Henry Berry Lowery, a famous outlaw of the Carolinas, the James Gang, and many lesser-known desperadoes felt at home in the unclaimed swamps and forests.

Only the boldest of settlers tried to police the frontier. Among them was Charles Lynch, a Virginia farmer of the late eighteenth century. Lynch and his associates tracked and punished offenders, often according to the dictates of the still well-known lynch law, or vigilante justice, which they originated. Citizen posses and vigilante groups were often the only law available to settlers on the western frontier. Judge Roy Bean ("the Law West of the Pecos"), "Wild Bill" Hickok, Bat Masterson, Wyatt Earp, and Pat Garrett were other popular figures of the nineteenth century who took it

■ **vigilantism**   The act of taking the law into one's own hands.

upon themselves, sometimes in a semiofficial capacity, to enforce the law on the books as well as the standards of common decency.

Although today **vigilantism** has a negative connotation, most of the original vigilantes of the American West were honest men and women trying to forge an organized and predictable lifestyle out of the challenging situations that they encountered. Often faced with unscrupulous, money-hungry desperadoes, they did what they could to bring the standards of civilization, as they understood them, to bear in their communities.

Policing America's Early Cities

Small-scale organized law enforcement came into being quite early in America's larger cities. In 1658, paid watchmen were hired by the city of New York to replace drafted citizens.[5] By 1693, the first uniformed officer was employed by the city, and in 1731, the first neighborhood station, or precinct, was constructed. Boston, Cincinnati, and New Orleans were among the American communities to follow the New York model and hire a force of watchmen in the early nineteenth century.

In 1829, American leaders watched closely as Sir Robert Peel created London's new police. One year later, Stephen Girard, a wealthy manufacturer, donated a considerable amount of money to the city of Philadelphia to create a capable police force. The city hired 120 men to staff a night watch and 24 to perform similar duties during the day.

In 1844, New York's separate day and night forces were combined into the New York City Police Department. Boston followed suit in 1855. Further advances in American policing were precluded by the Civil War. Southern cities captured in the war came under martial law and were subject to policing by the military.

The coming of the twentieth century, coinciding as it did with numerous technological advances and significant social changes, brought a flood of reform. The International Association of Chiefs of Police (IACP) was formed in 1902; it immediately moved to create a nationwide clearinghouse for criminal identification. In 1915, the Fraternal Order of Police (FOP) initiated operations. It was patterned after labor unions but prohibited strikes; it accepted personnel of all ranks, from patrol officer to chief. In 1910, Alice Stebbins Wells became the first policewoman in the world, serving with the Los Angeles Police Department.[6] Prior to Wells's appointment, women had served as jail matrons, and widows had sometimes been carried on police department payrolls if their officer-husbands had died in the line of duty, but they had not been fully "sworn" with carrying out the duties of a police officer. Wells became an outspoken advocate for the hiring of more policewomen, and police departments across the country

> In 1910, Alice Stebbins Wells became the first policewoman in the world, serving with the Los Angeles Police Department.

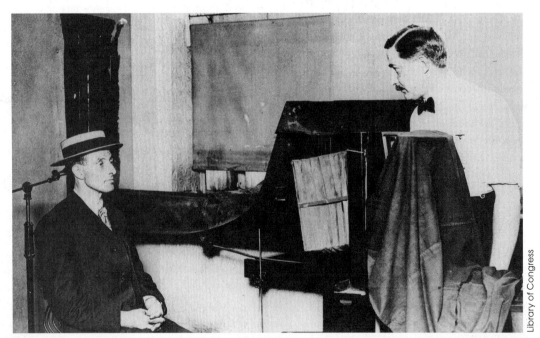

Library of Congress

A New York City police officer "mugging" a prisoner in the early days of police photography. How have advances in technology shaped policing?

■ **Wickersham Commission** The National Commission on Law Observance and Enforcement. In 1931, the commission issued a report stating that Prohibition was unenforceable and carried a great potential for police corruption.

■ **Law Enforcement Assistance Administration (LEAA)** A now-defunct federal agency established under Title I of the Omnibus Crime Control and Safe Streets Act of 1968 to funnel federal funding to state and local law enforcement agencies.

■ **lecture note** Review the origins and impact of the Eighteenth Amendment to the U.S. Constitution (on Prohibition), and trace its effects on crime and law enforcement.

began to hire female officers, especially to provide police services to children and to women and to "protect male officers from delicate and troublesome situations"[7]—such as the need to physically restrain female offenders.

In 1915, the U.S. Census reported that 25 cities employed policewomen. In that year, coinciding with the creation of the FOP, the International Association of Policewomen (now the International Association of Women Police) was formed in the city of Baltimore. In 1918, Ellen O'Grady became the first woman to hold a high administrative post in a major police organization when she was promoted to the rank of deputy police commissioner for the city of New York. As Dorothy Moses Schulz, a contemporary commentator on women's entry into policing, has observed, "The Policewomen's movement was not an isolated phenomenon, but was part of women's movement into other newly created or newly professionalized fields."[8]

During the early twentieth century, telephones, automobiles, and radios all had their impact on the American police. Teddy Roosevelt, the 26th president of the United States, began his career by serving as a police commissioner in New York City from 1895 to 1897. While there, he promoted the use of a call-box system of telephones, which allowed citizens to report crimes rapidly and made it possible for officers to call quickly for assistance. As president, Roosevelt helped organize the Bureau of Investigation, which later became the Federal Bureau of Investigation (FBI). Federal law enforcement already existed in the form of U.S. marshals, created by an act of Congress in 1789, and in the form of postal inspectors, authorized by the U.S. Postal Act of 1829. The FBI became a national investigative service designed to quickly identify and apprehend offenders charged with a growing list of federal offenses. Automobiles created an era of affordable, rapid transportation and gave police forces far-reaching powers and high mobility. Telephones and radios provided the ability to maintain regular communication with central authorities. State police agencies arose to counter the threat of the mobile offender, with Massachusetts and Pennsylvania leading the way to statewide forces.

Prohibition and Police Corruption

A dark period for American law enforcement agencies began in 1920 with the passage of a constitutional prohibition against all forms of alcoholic beverages. Until Prohibition was repealed in 1933, most parts of the country were rife with criminal activity, much of it supporting the trade in bootlegged liquor. Bootleggers earned huge sums of money, and some of them became quite wealthy. Massive wealth in the hands of law violators greatly increased the potential for corruption among police officials, some of whom were "paid off" to support bootlegging operations.

In 1931, the **Wickersham Commission**, officially called the National Commission on Law Observance and Enforcement and led by former U.S. Attorney General George W. Wickersham, recognized that Prohibition was unenforceable and reported that it carried a great potential for police corruption.[9] The commission, which released a number of reports, also established guidelines for enforcement agencies that directed many aspects of American law enforcement until the 1970s. The most influential of the Wickersham Commission reports was titled *Report on the Enforcement of the Prohibition Laws of the United States.* That report, the release of which became one of the most important events in the history of American policing, can be read in its entirety at **http://www .druglibrary.org/schaffer/library/studies/wick**.

The Last Half of the Twentieth Century

The rapid cultural change that took place throughout America in the 1960s and 1970s forever altered the legal and social environment in which the police must work. During that period, in conjunction with a burgeoning civil rights movement, the U.S. Supreme Court frequently enumerated constitutionally based personal rights for those facing arrest, investigation, and criminal prosecution. Although a "chipping away" at those rights, which some say is continuing today, may have begun in the 1980s, the earlier emphasis placed on the rights of defendants undergoing criminal investigation and prosecution will have a substantial impact on law enforcement activities for many years to come.

The 1960s and 1970s were also a period of intense examination of police operations, from day-to-day enforcement decisions to administrative organization and police–community relations. In 1967, the President's Commission on Law Enforcement and Administration of Justice issued its report, *The Challenge of Crime in a Free Society,* which found that the police were often isolated from the communities they served.[10] In 1969, the **Law Enforcement Assistance Administration (LEAA)** was formed to assist police forces across the nation in acquiring the latest in technology and in adopting new enforcement methods.

■ **lecture note**   Explain the rise of scientific police-management studies, beginning with the Kansas City Preventive Patrol Experiment of 1974. Ask how evidence-based policing represents a continuation of this earlier tradition.

■ **lecture note**   Consider briefly discussing other research into policing practices and how research findings have impacted policing. One example is the Minneapolis Domestic Violence Experiment (and the replications), which contributed to changes in legislation permitting warrantless arrest for domestic violence as well as to a move in policing towards mandatory arrest.

■ **scientific police management**   The application of social science techniques to the study of police administration for the purpose of increasing effectiveness, reducing the frequency of citizen complaints, and enhancing the efficient use of available resources.

Prohibition agents pouring liquor down a drain in 1921. How did the constitutional prohibition against alcoholic beverages during the 1920s and early 1930s affect American policing?

In 1973, the National Advisory Commission on Criminal Justice Standards and Goals issued a comprehensive report detailing strategies for combating and preventing crime and for improving the quality of law enforcement efforts at all levels.[11] Included in the report was a call for greater participation in police work by women and ethnic minorities and the recommendation that a college degree be made a basic prerequisite for police employment by the 1980s. The creation of a third major commission, the National Commission on Crime Prevention and Control, was authorized by the federal Violent Crime Control and Law Enforcement Act of 1994, but the commission never saw the light of day.[12]

Evidence-Based Policing

In 1968, with the passage of the Omnibus Crime Control and Safe Streets Act, the U.S. Congress created the Law Enforcement Assistance Administration. The LEAA was charged with combating crime through the expenditure of huge amounts of money in support of crime-prevention and crime-reduction programs. Some have compared the philosophy establishing the LEAA to that which supported the American space program's goal of landing people on the moon: Put enough money into any problem, and it will be solved! Unfortunately, the crime problem was more difficult to address than the challenge of a moon landing; even after the expenditure of nearly $8 billion,

the LEAA had not come close to its goal. In 1982, the LEAA expired when Congress refused it further funding.

The legacy of the LEAA is an important one for police managers, however. The research-rich years of 1969 to 1982, supported largely through LEAA funding, have left a plethora of scientific findings relevant to police administration and, more important, have established a tradition of program evaluation within police management circles. This tradition, which is known as **scientific police management**, is a natural outgrowth of LEAA's insistence that every funded program contain a plan for its evaluation. *Scientific police management* refers to the application of social science techniques to the study of police administration for the purpose of increasing effectiveness, reducing the frequency of citizen complaints, and enhancing the efficient use of available resources. The heyday of scientific police management occurred in the 1970s, when federal monies were far more readily available to support such studies than they are today.

The LEAA was not alone in funding police research during the 1970s. On July 1, 1970, the Ford Foundation announced the establishment of a Police Development Fund totaling $30 million, to be spent during the following five years to support major crime-fighting strategies of police departments. This funding led to the establishment of the Police Foundation, which continues today with the mission of "fostering improvement and innovation in American policing."[13] Police Foundation–sponsored studies during the past 30 years have added to the growing body of scientific knowledge about policing.

Today, federal support for criminal justice research and evaluation continues under the National Institute of Justice (NIJ) and the Bureau of Justice Statistics (BJS), both part of the Office of Justice Programs (OJP). The OJP, created by Congress in 1984, provides federal leadership in developing the nation's capacity to prevent and control crime. The National Criminal Justice Reference Service (NCJRS), a part of the NIJ, assists researchers nationwide in locating information applicable to their research projects. "Custom searches" of the NCJRS computer database can be done online and yield abundant information in most criminal justice subject areas. The NIJ also publishes a series of informative periodic reports, such as the *NIJ Journal* and *NIJ Research in Review*, which serve to keep criminal justice practitioners and researchers informed about recent findings. View the NIJ recent online publication list at **http://nij.ncjrs .org/App/publications/pubs_db.aspx**.

■ **lecture note** Explain the importance of systematic reviews, such as those conducted by the Campbell Collaboration.

■ **activity** Divide the class into groups. Ask each group to develop a plan to research and evaluate some aspect of local law enforcement operations with a focus on cost-effectiveness. Have students decide on how their proposed evaluation would be structured, what they would measure, who would conduct it, and what kinds of difficulties they can anticipate.

■ **lecture note** Explain the need to continue evaluating policing techniques to better fulfill law enforcement goals and to use resources wisely.

■ **Kansas City experiment** The first large-scale scientific study of law enforcement practices. Sponsored by the Police Foundation, it focused on the practice of preventive patrol.

The Kansas City Experiment

By far the most famous application of social research principles to police management was the Kansas City preventive patrol experiment.[14] The results of the year-long **Kansas City experiment** were published in 1974. The study, sponsored by the Police Foundation, divided the southern part of Kansas City into 15 areas. Five of these "beats" were patrolled in the usual fashion. In another group of five beats, patrol activities were doubled. The final third of the beats received a novel treatment indeed: No patrols were assigned to them, and no uniformed officers entered that part of the city unless they were called. The program was kept secret, and citizens were unaware of the difference between the patrolled and unpatrolled parts of the city.

The results of the Kansas City experiment were surprising. Records of "preventable crimes," those toward which the activities of patrol were oriented—such as burglary, robbery, auto theft, larceny, and vandalism—showed no significant differences in rate of occurrence among the three experimental beats. Similarly, citizens didn't seem to notice the change in patrol patterns in the two areas where patrol frequency was changed. Surveys conducted at the conclusion of the experiment showed no difference in citizens' fear of crime before and after the study. The 1974 study can be summed up in the words of the author of the final report: "The whole idea of riding around in cars to create a feeling of omnipresence just hasn't worked. … Good people with good intentions tried something that logically should have worked, but didn't."[15] This study has been credited with beginning the now-established tradition of scientific studies of policing.

A second Kansas City study focused on "response time."[16] It found that even consistently fast police response to citizen reports of crime had little effect on citizen satisfaction with the police or on the arrest of suspects. The study uncovered the fact that most reports made to the police came only after a considerable amount of time had passed. Hence, the police were initially handicapped by the timing of the report, and even the fastest police response was not especially effective.

Effects The Kansas City studies greatly affected managerial assumptions about the role of preventive patrol and traditional strategies for responding to citizen calls for assistance. As Joseph

Kansas City, Missouri, police crime scene technicians unload equipment as officers and agents prepare to search the woods in an effort to find 11-month-old Lisa Irwin in 2011. The girl was not found. Scientific police management was first supported by studies of preventive patrol undertaken in Kansas City in 1974. How does today's evidence-based policing build on that tradition?

Shane Keyser/The Kansas City Star/Newscom

■ **directed patrol**   A police-management strategy designed to increase the productivity of patrol officers through the scientific analysis and evaluation of patrol techniques.

■ **evidence-based policing (EBP)**   The use of the best available research on the outcomes of police work to implement guidelines and evaluate agencies, units, and officers.[i]

Lewis, then director of evaluation at the Police Foundation, said, "I think that now almost everyone would agree that almost anything you do is better than random patrol."[17]

Although the Kansas City studies called into question some basic assumptions about patrol, patrol remains the backbone of police work. New patrol strategies for the effective utilization of human resources have led to various kinds of **directed patrol** activities. One form of directed patrol varies the number of officers involved in patrolling according to the time of day or the frequency of reported crimes within an area, so as to put the most officers on the street where and when crime is most prevalent. Wilmington, Delaware, was one of the first cities to make use of split-force patrol, in which only a part of the patrol force performs routine patrol.[18] The remaining officers respond to calls for service, take reports, and conduct investigations.

As a result of the Kansas City study on response time, some cities have prioritized calls for service,[19] ordering a quick police response only when crimes are in progress or when serious crimes have occurred. Less significant offenses, such as minor larcenies and certain citizen complaints, are handled using the mail or by having citizens come to the police station to make a report.

Early policing studies, such as the Kansas City patrol experiment, were designed to identify and probe some of the basic assumptions that guided police work. The initial response to many such studies was "Why should we study that? Everybody knows the answer already!" As in the case of the Kansas City experiment, however, it soon became obvious that conventional wisdom was not always correct.

Evidence-Based Policing Today

At the close of the twentieth century, noted police researcher Lawrence W. Sherman addressed an audience of criminal justice policymakers, scholars, and practitioners at the Police Foundation in Washington, D.C., and called for a new approach to American policing that would use research to guide and evaluate practice. "Police practices should be based on scientific evidence about what works best," Sherman told his audience. Sherman's lecture, titled "Evidence-Based Policing: Policing Based on Science, Not Anecdote,"[20] popularized the term **evidence-based policing (EBP)**. EBP, says Sherman, "is the use of best available research on the outcomes of police work to implement guidelines and evaluate agencies, units, and officers."[21] In other words, evidence-based policing uses research into everyday police procedures to evaluate current practices and to guide officers and police executives in future decision making. In any discussion of evidence-based

policing, it is important to remember that the word *evidence* refers to scientific evidence, not criminal evidence.

"The basic premise of evidence-based practice," says Sherman, "is that we are all entitled to our own opinions, but not to our own facts."[22] Our own facts, or our beliefs about the way things should be done, says Sherman, often turn out to be wrong. During the civil rights movement of the 1960s and 1970s, for example, police executives in many areas took a heavy-handed approach in their attempts to control demonstrators. Images of tear-gas-filled streets, high-pressure fire hoses aimed at marchers, and police dogs biting fleeing demonstrators symbolize that era for many people. This heavy-handed approach had unintended consequences and served to inflame protesters. Situations that might have otherwise been contained with simple crowd-control tactics and the use of physical barriers became largely uncontrollable. Sherman reminds us that "the mythic power of subjective and unstructured wisdom holds back every field and keeps it from systematically discovering and implementing what works best in repeated tasks."

Some suggest that EBP offers a long-term approach for creating cost-effectiveness in policing that, in the current economic environment, "is the only alternative to current ways of operating."[23] "In an age of austerity and budget cuts," argue British writers Neil Wain and Alex Murray, it is necessary for police departments to invest wisely in programs and initiatives that have a proven track record at reducing or preventing crime.

Today's EBP model has been called the single "most powerful force for change" in policing today.[24] Leading the movement toward EBP are organizations like the FBI's Futures Working Group, the Campbell Crime and Justice Group, and the Center for Evidence-Based Crime Policy at George Mason University. FBI Supervisory Special Agent Carl J. Jensen III, a member of the Futures Working Group, notes that in the future "successful law enforcement executives will have to be consumers and appliers of research." They won't need to be researchers themselves, Jensen notes, "but they must use research in their everyday work."[25] The Campbell Crime and Justice Group, which emphasizes the use of experimental studies in crime and justice policymaking, can be accessed via the Campbell Collaboration web site.

A program of the Center for Evidence-Based Crime Policy (CEBCP) at George Mason University, the Evidence-Based Policing Hall of Fame, recognizes innovative law enforcement practitioners who have been central to the implementation of a high-quality research program in their respective agencies. Membership in the Hall of Fame highlights excellence in using and conducting policing research. An informative CEBCP YouTube channel is available at https://www.youtube.com/user/clsMason.

> Today's EBP model has been called the single "most powerful force for change" in policing today.

■ **theme**   The structure of modern-day American policing is very complex, with agencies functioning at the federal, state, and local levels. What kinds of problems arise as a consequence of this complex structure? How might these problems be reduced or eliminated?

■ **lecture note**   Describe the multidimensional structure of American law enforcement in terms of federal, state, local, and private agencies.

■ **theme**   Why does the United States have so many local police departments? Might we be better served by one national police agency, in lieu of the many local departments?

Alexis Glenn, George Mason University Creative Service.

The entrance to the Center for Evidence-Based Crime Policy (CEBCP) at Virginia's George Mason University. CEBCP seeks to make scientific research a key component in decisions about crime and justice policies. What is evidence-based policing?

The Institute of Criminology at Cambridge University has identified the following questions in the area of policing as goals to be answered by evidence-based studies:[26]

- How can policing produce greater public safety without eroding civil liberties?
- How can more value for the money be returned from investments in policing to cut the costs of crime?
- Can crime be better forecast for preventive policing by time and place?
- Can unsuccessful police methods be distinguished from cost-effective ones?
- Can better policing reduce the high costs of a growing prison population?
- Can evaluation tools used in evidence-based medicine be adopted by police?
- What are the possibilities for a police service based on cost-effectiveness?
- What are the prospects for developing the knowledge base for such evidence?

Finally, in 2010, innovative British police professionals and academics founded the British Society of Policing (BSEBP) to promote and facilitate the increased use of the best available research evidence to solve policing problems and the production of new research by police practitioners and researchers, and to communicate research evidence to police practitioners and the public.

Visit the Center for Evidence-Based Crime Policy at **http://cebcp.org**, and explore the Evidence-Based Policing Hall of Fame at **http://cebcp.org/hall-of-fame**. Read about the new paradigm in police science at Harvard's Kennedy School of Government at **http://tinyurl.com/5rs26l5**. Also, an evidence-based policing matrix is available at **http://gemini.gmu.edu/cebcp/Matrix.html**. The matrix, provided by the Center for Evidence-Based Crime Policy, is a research-to-practice translation tool that visually organizes strong EBP studies.

American Policing Today: From the Federal to the Local Level

The organization of American law enforcement has been called the most complex in the world. Three major legislative and judicial jurisdictions exist in the United States—federal, state, and local—and each has created a variety of police agencies to enforce its laws. Unfortunately, there has been little uniformity

■ **federal law enforcement agency**   A U.S. government agency or office whose primary functional responsibility is to enforce federal criminal laws.

■ **lecture note**   Discuss the difference between *police* and *law enforcement* agencies. Explain why the United States, unlike some countries, does not have a national police department.
■ **Outline**   how the FBI's function and primary activities have changed since the bureau's early days—and how terrorist attacks on the United States have had a special impact on the FBI's activities.

among jurisdictions as to the naming, function, or authority of enforcement agencies. The matter is complicated still more by the rapid growth of private security firms, which operate on a for-profit basis and provide services that have traditionally been regarded as law enforcement activities.

Federal Agencies

Dozens of **federal law enforcement agencies** are distributed among 14 U.S. government departments and 28 nondepartmental entities (Table 5-1). In addition to the enforcement agencies listed in the table, many other federal government offices are involved in enforcement through inspection, regulation, and control activities. The Government Accounting Office (GAO) reports that nonmilitary federal agencies employ a total of 137,929 law enforcement officers, which it defines as individuals authorized to perform any of four specific functions: (1)

conduct criminal investigations, (2) execute search warrants, (3) make arrests, or (4) carry firearms.[27]

Visit the home pages of many federal law enforcement agencies via **http://www.justicestudies.com/federal.html**.

The Federal Bureau of Investigation

The Federal Bureau of Investigation may be the most famous law enforcement agency in the country and in the world. The FBI has traditionally been held in high regard by many Americans, who think of it as an example of what a law enforcement organization should be and who believe that FBI agents are exemplary police officers.

> The Federal Bureau of Investigation may be the most famous law enforcement agency in the country and in the world.

TABLE 5-1 | American Policing: Federal Law Enforcement Agencies

Department of Agriculture U.S. Forest Service	**Department of Justice** Bureau of Alcohol, Tobacco, Firearms and Explosives Bureau of Prisons Drug Enforcement Administration Federal Bureau of Investigation U.S. Marshals Service
Department of Commerce Bureau of Export Enforcement National Marine Fisheries Administration	
Department of Defense Air Force Office of Special Investigations Army Criminal Investigation Division Defense Criminal Investigative Service Naval Investigative Service	**Department of Labor** Office of Labor Racketeering **Department of State** Diplomatic Security Service Department of Transportation Federal Air Marshals Program
Department of Energy National Nuclear Safety Administration Office of Mission Operations Office of Secure Transportation	**Department of the Treasury** Internal Revenue Service, Criminal Investigation Division Treasury Inspector General for Tax Enforcement
Department of Health and Human Services Food and Drug Administration, Office of Criminal Investigations	**Department of Veterans Affairs** Office of Security and Law Enforcement
Department of Homeland Security Federal Law Enforcement Training Center Federal Protective Service Transportation Security Administration U.S. Coast Guard U.S. Customs and Border Protection—includes U.S. Border Patrol U.S. Immigration and Customs Enforcement U.S. Secret Service	**U.S. Postal Service** Postal Inspection Service **Other Offices with Enforcement Personnel** AMTRAK Police Bureau of Engraving and Printing Police Environmental Protection Agency, Criminal Investigations Division Federal Reserve Board Tennessee Valley Authority U.S. Capitol Police
Department of the Interior Bureau of Indian Affairs Bureau of Land Management Fish and Wildlife Service National Park Service U.S. Park Police	U.S. Mint U.S. Supreme Court Police Washington, DC, Metropolitan Police Department

Note: Cunningham et al, The Hallcrest Report II: Private Security Trends, 1970-2000.

Source: Cunningham et al, The Hallcrest Report II: Private Security Trends, 1970-2000.

William Webster, former director of the FBI, reflected this sentiment when he said, "Over the years the American people have come to expect the most professional law enforcement from the FBI. Although we use the most modern forms of management and technology in the fight against crime, our strength is in our people—in the character of the men and women of the FBI. For that reason we seek only those who have demonstrated that they can perform as professional people who can, and will, carry on our tradition of fidelity, bravery, and integrity."[28]

The history of the FBI spans about 100 years. It began as the Bureau of Investigation in 1908, when it was designed to serve as the investigative arm of the U.S. Department of Justice. The creation of the bureau was motivated, at least in part, by the inability of other agencies to stem the rising tide of American political and business corruption.[29] Learn about the history of the FBI at **http://www.fbi.gov/about-us/history/brief-history**.

The official purpose of today's FBI is succinctly stated in the agency's mission statement: "The Mission of the FBI is to protect and defend the United States against terrorist and foreign intelligence threats, to uphold and enforce the criminal laws of the United States, and to provide leadership and criminal justice services to federal, state, municipal, and international agencies and partners."[30]

> Women account for more than 2,600 of the FBI's agents (nearly 20%), and 11 of the FBI's field offices have female special agents in charge.

FBI headquarters are located in the J. Edgar Hoover Building on Pennsylvania Avenue in Washington, D.C. Special agents and support personnel who work at the agency's headquarters organize and coordinate FBI activities throughout the country and around the world. Headquarters staffers determine investigative priorities, oversee major cases, and manage the organization's resources, technology, and personnel.

The daily work of the FBI is done by approximately 13,500 special agents and 20,100 civilian employees assigned to 56 field offices and 400 satellite offices (known as *resident agencies*). A special agent in charge oversees each field office, except for the three largest field offices in Washington, D.C., Los Angeles, and New York City, each of which is headed by an assistant director. Women account for more than 2,600 of the FBI's agents (nearly 20%), and 11 of the FBI's field offices have female special agents in charge.[31]

The FBI also operates "legal attaché offices" (called *Legats*) in a number of major cities around the world, including London and Paris. Such offices permit the international coordination of enforcement activities and facilitate the flow of law enforcement–related information between the FBI and police agencies in host countries. In 1995, a few years after the end of the cold war, the FBI opened a legal attaché office in Moscow. The Moscow office assists Russian police agencies in the growing battle against organized crime in that country and helps American officials track suspected Russian criminals operating in

Courtesy of the Justice Research Association

The author visiting the International Law Enforcement Academy in Budapest, Hungary. The ILEA is run by the FBI and the Hungarian government and serves as a global training ground for police executives and criminal justice leaders from across Eastern Europe and much of Asia. Why is it important to build bridges in international policing?

the United States. Also in 1995, an Eastern European version of the FBI Academy, known as the International Law Enforcement Academy (ILEA), opened in Budapest, Hungary. Its purpose is to train police administrators from all of Eastern Europe in the latest crime-fighting techniques.[32] Ten years later, in 2005, the FBI's then-director Robert S. Mueller III, spoke at the Budapest ILEA, telling gathered government ministers and diplomats that in times past, "Good fences make good neighbors." But today, he said, "seen from the perspective of the 21st-century global law enforcement community, dividing walls mean less security, not more. ... Today, good bridges make good neighbors."[33]

The FBI also operates the Combined DNA Index System (CODIS), a computerized forensic database of DNA "profiles" of offenders convicted of serious crimes (such as rape, other sexual assaults, murder, and certain crimes against children), as well as DNA profiles from unknown offenders.[34] CODIS, now a part of the National DNA Index System (NDIS), was formally authorized by the federal DNA Identification Act of 1994.[35] It is being enhanced daily through the work of federal, state, and local law enforcement agencies that take DNA samples from biological evidence gathered at crime scenes and from offenders themselves. The computerized CODIS system can rapidly identify a perpetrator when it finds a match between an evidence sample and a stored profile. By 1998, every state had enacted legislation establishing a CODIS database and requiring that DNA from offenders convicted of certain serious crimes be entered into the system. By mid-2014, the CODIS database contained more than 11 million DNA profiles.[36] Learn more about CODIS at **http://www.dna.gov/dna-databases/codis**.

The FBI Laboratory Division, located in Quantico, Virginia, operates one of the largest and most comprehensive crime laboratories in the world. It provides services related to the scientific solution and prosecution of crimes throughout the country. It is also the only full-service federal forensic laboratory in the United States. Laboratory activities include crime scene searches, special surveillance photography, latent-fingerprint examination, forensic examination of evidence (including DNA testing), court testimony by laboratory personnel, and other scientific and technical services. The FBI offers laboratory services, free of charge, to all law enforcement agencies in the United States. Visit the FBI on the Web at **http://www.fbi.gov**.

The FBI also runs a National Academy Program, which is part of its Training Division. The program offered its first class in 1935 and had 23 students. It was then known as the FBI National Police Training School. In 1940, the school moved from Washington, D.C., to the U.S. Marine Amphibious Base at Quantico, Virginia. In 1972, the facility expanded to 334 acres, and the FBI Academy, as we know it today, officially opened.[37] According to the most recent statistics available, the academy program has produced 43,229 graduates since it began operations. This includes international graduates from 176 foreign countries as well as graduates from U.S. territories and possessions. More than 200 sessions have been offered since inception of the training program. The FBI offers support personnel a variety of training opportunities throughout their careers, including classroom training, distance learning via satellite, and courses offered through the "Virtual Academy" on the FBI's intranet.

The FBI and Counterterrorism

Soon after the attacks of September 11, 2001, the FBI reshaped its priorities to focus on preventing future terrorist attacks. This effort is managed by the Counterterrorism Division at FBI headquarters and is emphasized at every field office, resident agency, and Legat. Headquarters administers a national threat

CJ | NEWS
The FBI's Next Generation Identification System

In late-2014, the Criminal Justice Information Services (CJIS) division of the Federal Bureau of Investigation (FBI) announced the achievement of full operational capability of the Bureau's Next Generation Identification (NGI) System. The NGI System was developed to expand the Bureau's biometric identification capabilities, ultimately replacing the FBI's Integrated Automated Fingerprint Identification System (IAFIS) in addition to adding new services and capabilities.

As part of NGI's full operational capability, the NGI team introduced two new services: Rap Back and the Interstate Photo System (IPS). Rap Back is a functionality that gives authorized entities the ability to receive ongoing status notifications of any criminal history reported on individuals holding positions of trust, such as school teachers. Rap Back should allow law enforcement agencies, probation and parole offices, and other criminal justice entities to improve their effectiveness by being automatically advised of subsequent or ongoing criminal activity of persons under investigation or supervision. The IPS facial recognition service provides the nation's law enforcement community with an investigative tool that provides an image-searching capability using photographs associated with criminal identities. IPS is a significant step forward for the criminal justice community in utilizing biometrics as an investigative tool.

The latest phase of NGI is only one portion of the FBI's NGI System. Since phase one was deployed in February 2011, the NGI system has introduced enhanced automated fingerprint and latent search capabilities, mobile fingerprint identification, and electronic image storage, all while adding enhanced processing speed and automation for electronic exchange of fingerprints to more than 18,000 law enforcement agencies and other authorized criminal justice partners.

Source: Adapted from FBI, Criminal Justice Information Services Division, *FBI Announces Full Operational Capability of the Next Generation Identification System*, http://www.fbi.gov/news/pressrel/press-releases/fbi-announces-full-operational-capability-of-the-next-generation-identification-system, September 15, 2014.

■ **lecture note**   Explain the advantages and the disadvantages of centralized and decentralized state police organizations.

warning system that allows the FBI to instantly distribute important terrorism-related bulletins to law enforcement agencies and public-safety departments throughout the country. "Flying Squads" provide specialized counterterrorism knowledge and experience, language capabilities, and analytic support as needed to FBI field offices and Legats.

> An essential weapon in the FBI's battle against terrorism is the Joint Terrorism Task Force (JTTF).

To combat terrorism, the FBI's Counterterrorism Division collects, analyzes, and shares information and critical intelligence with various federal agencies and departments—including the Central Intelligence Agency (CIA), the National Security Agency (NSA), and the Department of Homeland Security (DHS)—and with law enforcement agencies throughout the country. An essential weapon in the FBI's battle against terrorism is the Joint Terrorism Task Force (JTTF). A National JTTF, located at the FBI's Washington headquarters, includes representatives from the Department of Defense, the Department of Energy, the Federal Emergency Management Agency, the Central Intelligence Agency, the Customs Service, the Secret Service, and U.S. Immigration and Customs Enforcement. In addition, through 66 local JTTFs, representatives from federal agencies, state and local law enforcement personnel, and first responders coordinate efforts to track down terrorists and to prevent acts of terrorism in the United States.

State-Level Agencies

Most state police agencies were created in the late nineteenth or early twentieth century to meet specific needs. The Texas Rangers, created in 1835 before Texas attained statehood, functioned as a military organization responsible for patrolling the republic's borders.

> Most state police agencies were created in the late nineteenth or early twentieth century to meet specific needs.

The apprehension of Mexican cattle rustlers was one of its main concerns.[38] Massachusetts, targeting vice control, was the second state to create a law enforcement agency. Today, a wide diversity of state policing agencies exists. Table 5-2 lists typical state-sponsored law enforcement agencies.

TABLE 5-2 | American Policing: State Law Enforcement Agencies

Alcohol law enforcement agencies	Port authorities	State police
Fish and wildlife agencies	State bureaus of investigation	State university police
Highway patrols	State park services	Weigh station operations

Source: Pearson Education, Inc.

The Los Angeles Police Department's new $437 million headquarters building that opened in 2009. The 500,000-square-foot building is home to 2,300 LAPD officers and civilian employees. How do the roles of federal, state, and municipal law enforcement agencies differ?

State law enforcement agencies are usually organized after one of two models. In the first, a centralized model, the tasks of major criminal investigations are combined with the patrol of state highways. Centralized state police agencies generally do the following:

- Assist local law enforcement departments in criminal investigations when asked to do so.
- Operate centralized identification bureaus.
- Maintain a centralized criminal records repository.
- Patrol the state's highways.
- Provide select training for municipal and county officers.

The Pennsylvania Constabulary, known today as the Pennsylvania State Police, was the first modern force to combine these duties and has been called the "first modern state police agency."[39] Michigan, New Jersey, New York, Vermont, and Delaware are a few of the states that patterned their state-level enforcement activities after the Pennsylvania model.

The second state model, the decentralized model of police organization, characterizes operations in the southern United States but is found as well in the Midwest and in some western states. The model draws a clear distinction between traffic enforcement on state highways and other state-level law enforcement functions by creating at least two separate agencies. North Carolina, South Carolina, and Georgia are a few of the many states that employ both a highway patrol and a state bureau of investigation. The names of the respective agencies may vary, however, even though their functions are largely the same. In North Carolina, for example, the two major state-level law enforcement agencies are the North Carolina Highway Patrol and the State Bureau of Investigation. Georgia fields a highway patrol and the Georgia Bureau of Investigation, and South

■ **lecture note**   Discuss the pros and cons of appointing vs. electing police chiefs and/or sheriffs.

■ **activity**   Invite a representative from a local police agency to address students on departmental structure and operations. Ask students to question the speaker about how his or her agency has responded to the threat of terrorism. Computer conferencing may be considered as an alternative to a classroom visit.

Carolina operates a highway patrol and the South Carolina Law Enforcement Division.

States that use the decentralized model usually have a number of other adjunct state-level law enforcement agencies. North Carolina, for example, has created a State Wildlife Commission with enforcement powers, a Board of Alcohol Beverage Control with additional agents, and a separate Enforcement and Theft Bureau for enforcing certain motor vehicle and theft laws. Like

government agencies everywhere, state police agencies have seen their budgets impacted by the recent recession.

Local Agencies

Local law enforcement agencies, including city and county agencies, represent a third level of police activity in the United States. The term *local police* encompasses a wide variety of

CJ | NEWS
LAPD Adds Officers and Crime Falls—But Is There a Connection?

AURELIA VENTURA/LA OPINION/Newscom

New officers graduate from the LAPD academy. Why does the IACP say that the optimum ratio of police officers to citizens in a city depends on local conditions? What conditions would those be?

Ever since he successfully ran for office in 2005, Los Angeles mayor Antonio Villaraigosa has been intent on adding more sworn officers to the Los Angeles Police Department (LAPD) and reaching a record level of 10,000.

Battling huge budget shortfalls, he succeeded in adding a few hundred new officers through 2012, putting the LAPD just shy of the 10,000 mark. Facing the end of his tenure due to term limits, the mayor finally reached his goal on January 1, 2013, through a maneuver that didn't put any new officers on the streets. The LAPD simply annexed the city's General Services Department, which oversees parks, libraries, and other municipal buildings, and its 60 officers were sworn into the LAPD.

"I know some people think that 10,000 cops is a magical illusion, a meaningless number, that more officers don't necessarily lead to a reduction in crime," the mayor said. "Those critics talk a lot, but they're just plain wrong."

City officials noted that from 2011–2012, gang crime, one of the city's greatest scourges, fell by 10.5%. By 2012, Los Angeles had the

lowest overall crime rate of any major city. Using extra officers early in Villaraigosa's tenure, the LAPD could put more of them on the streets and open new stations, and response times fell from eight to nine minutes to six to seven minutes for calls for assistance.

But were extra officers the key factor in reducing crime? Skeptics point to other factors, such as a nationwide decline in crime rates and reshuffling existing officers into a new LAPD office targeting gang violence. Also, the city's budget shortages led to cutbacks in overtime, reducing the possible positive impact of having more officers on the payroll.

And if more officers reduce crime, then why do Chicago and New York, which have much higher ratios of officers to residents, have higher crime rates than LA? In 2005, the LAPD's ratio of officers to residents was about half the rate of the NYPD, even though Los Angeles has a much larger geographic area that should make it harder to patrol. Chicago, with markedly fewer people and a smaller area to patrol, actually has more officers than LA.

The varying circumstances among big-city police departments show there is no single ratio of officers to population that can be applied to all cities. The optimum ratio depends on local conditions, according to the International Association of Chiefs of Police (IACP). "Defining patrol staffing allocation and deployment requirements is a complex endeavor which requires consideration of an extensive series of factors and a sizable body of reliable, current data," the group says.

Therefore, a low crime rate might allow a city to have fewer officers. But without a universal standard for officer-to-population ratios, there will always be debate on what the right level for a city should be. For example, Charlie Beck, the current LAPD chief, insisted in a 2010 interview that LA should have 12,000 officers. With a lower number, "You're not able to spend any time working on solutions," he said. "You're just constantly chasing the symptoms."

But by January 2013, Beck was concerned about just maintaining the 10,000-officer level. If voters do not approve a sales tax increase in an upcoming ballot initiative, Beck warned that the number of officers might have to be cut.

Resources: David Zahniser, "LAPD Force Exceeds 10,000 for the First Time, Officials Say," *Los Angeles Times*, January 8, 2013, http://articles.latimes.com/2013/jan/08/local/la-me-lapd-size-20130108; Philip Rosenbaum, "LAPD Chief: The Thin Blue Line Keeps Getting Thinner," CNN, February 16, 2010, http://articles.cnn.com/2010-02-16/justice/california.lapd.beck_1_beck-transparency-cnn?_s=PM:CRIME; and Jerry Berrios, "LAPD Sees Force Grow to Record High," *Los Angeles Daily News*, March 2, 2009, http://www.dailynews.com/ci_11822848.

■ **sworn officer**   A law enforcement officer who is trained and empowered to perform full police duties, such as making arrests, conducting investigations, and carrying firearms.[ii]

■ **municipal police department**   A city- or town-based law enforcement agency.

■ **sheriff**   The elected chief officer of a county law enforcement agency. The sheriff is usually responsible for law enforcement in unincorporated areas and for the operation of the county jail.

Texas governor Rick Perry speaking to a group of Texas Rangers in Austin, Texas, in 2009. The Texas Rangers have long been held in high regard among state police agencies. How many levels of policing are there in the United States?

agencies. Municipal departments, rural sheriff's departments, and specialized groups like campus police and transit police can all be grouped under the "local" rubric. Large municipal departments are highly visible because of their vast size, huge budgets, and innovative programs. The nation's largest law enforcement agency, the New York City Police Department (NYPD), for example, has about 45,000 full-time employees, including about 34,500 full-time **sworn officers**.[40] Learn more about the NYPD via "Inside the Department" podcasts available at   **http://www.nyc.gov/html/nypd/html/pr/podcasts .shtml**.

Far greater in number, however, are small-town and county sheriff's departments. There are approximately 12,000 **municipal police departments** and 3,012 sheriff's departments in the United States.[41] Local police and sheriff's offices employ more than 1 million people, of which approximately 636,000 are sworn law enforcement officers.[42] Racial or ethnic minorities accounted for 27% of local police officers in 2013—up from about 15% in 1987.

Every incorporated municipality in the country has the authority to create its own police force. Some very small communities hire only one officer, who fills the roles of chief, investigator, and night watch—as well as everything in between.

About half of all local agencies employ fewer than ten full-time officers, and about 3,220 employ fewer than five full-time officers. These smaller agencies include 2,125 (or 12%) with just one full-time officer and 1,100 (or 6%) with only part-time officers.[43] A few communities contract with private security firms for police services, and still others have no active police force at all, depending instead on local sheriff's departments to deal with law violators.

City police chiefs are typically appointed by the mayor or selected by the city council. Their departments' jurisdictions are limited by convention to the geographic boundaries of their communities. **Sheriffs**, on the other hand, are elected public officials whose agencies are responsible for law enforcement throughout the counties in which they function. Sheriff's deputies mostly patrol the "unincorporated" areas of the county, or those that lie between municipalities. They do, however, have jurisdiction throughout the county, and in some areas they routinely work alongside municipal police to enforce laws within towns and cities.

Sheriff's departments are generally responsible for serving court papers, including civil summonses, and for maintaining security within state courtrooms. Sheriffs also run county jails and are responsible for more detainees awaiting trial than any other type of law enforcement department in the country.

For example, the Los Angeles County Jail System, operated by the Custody Operations Division of the LA County Sheriff's Department (LASD), is the largest in the world.[44] With eight separate facilities, the custody division of the LASD has an average daily population of 18,423 inmates—considerably more than the number of inmates held in many state prison systems. More than 2,200 uniformed officers and 1,265 civilian employees work in the custody division of the LASD, and that division alone operates with a yearly budget in excess of $200 million.[45] Overall, the LASD has more than 10,000 sworn and 8,000 civilian personnel, plus more than 830 reserve deputies and over 4,000 civilian volunteers.[46]

Sheriff's departments remain strong across most of the country, although in parts of New England, deputies mostly function as court agents with limited law enforcement duties. One report found that most sheriff's departments are small, with more than half of them employing fewer than 25 sworn officers.[47] Only 18 departments employ more than 1,000 officers. Even so, southern and western sheriffs are still considered the "chief law enforcement officers" in their counties. A list of conventional police agencies found at the local level is shown in Table 5-3.

Private Protective Services

Private protective services constitute a fourth level of enforcement activity in the United States today. Whereas public police are employed by the government and enforce public laws, private security personnel work for corporate employers and secure private interests.

Private security has been defined as "those self-employed individuals and privately funded business entities and organizations providing security-related services to specific clientele for a fee, for the individual or entity that retains or employs them, or for themselves, in order to protect their persons, private property, or interests from various hazards."[48] The growth in the size of private security in recent years has been phenomenal. In 2004, for example, official estimates put the total amount spent to secure the Olympic Games in Athens at $1.5 billion—or $283 per paid ticket.[49] Given Greece's geopolitical situation and its proximity to the Balkans and the Middle East, officials in Athens wanted to be sure they could prevent terrorist attacks. Eight years later, in 2012, England spent around $13.8 billion to host the Thirtieth Olympiad, of which $870 million was spent on security (more than twice what had been originally budgeted).[50] The London games involved 23,700 security personnel securing more than 100 venues—supplemented by British troops and police, adding another $65 million in expenses.[51]

ASIS International, with more than 33,000 members, is the preeminent international organization for private security professionals.[52] ASIS International members include corporate security managers and directors, as well as architects, attorneys, and federal, state, and local law enforcement personnel. Founded in 1955, ASIS International, formerly known as the American Society for Industrial Security, is dedicated to increasing the effectiveness and productivity of security professionals by developing educational and certification programs and training materials that address the needs of the security profession. ASIS also actively promotes the value of security management to business, the media, governmental entities, and the public. The organization publishes the industry magazine *Security Management*.

With 204 chapters worldwide, ASIS administers three certification programs: (1) the Certified Protection Professional (CPP) program, which provides for board certification in security management; (2) the Physical Security Professional (PSP) program, which provides a technical certification opportunity for specialists in physical plant security; and (3) the Professional Certified Investigator (PCI) program. Holders of PCI certification have satisfactorily demonstrated significant education and/or experience in the fields of case management, evidence collection, and case presentation. The ASIS also promotes the importance of ethical standards in the private security sector. The ASIS International Code of Ethics can be found in the "Ethics and Professionalism" box in this chapter. Visit ASIS online via **http://www.asisonline.org**.

A report released by the National Institute of Justice in 2001, titled *The New Structure of Policing*, found that "policing

TABLE 5-3 | American Policing: Local Law Enforcement Agencies

Campus police	Housing authority agencies	Sheriff's departments
City/county agencies	Marine patrol agencies	Transit police
Constables	Municipal police departments	Tribal police
Coroners or medical examiners		

Source: Pearson Education, Inc.

■ **smart policing**   A law enforcement initiative that makes use of techniques shown to work at both reducing and solving crimes.

■ **hot-spot policing**   A contemporary policing strategy in which law enforcement agencies focus their resources on known areas of criminal activity.

■ **lecture note**   Ask students whether they believe the rapid growth of private protective services can be expected to continue. Have students predict the problems as well as the benefits that continued expansion of private security services could entail for public law enforcement agencies.

■ **predictive policing**   A contemporary policing strategy that uses statistical techniques to analyze data in order to anticipate or predict the likelihood of crime occurrence in locations of interest.

paying for it

Cost-Efficient Policing

In January 2011, Newark, New Jersey, ranked 23rd on the list of the most dangerous cities in America, laid off almost half of its police force as budget constraints forced the city to reduce the services it offered to its citizens. The layoffs came after city revenues dipped by one-third amid declining income from taxes on hotel stays and local payrolls, and parking fees collected by the city fell sharply. Adding to the city's woes was an additional decline of 40% in aid from the state of New Jersey.

In the four-month period immediately following the layoffs, crime in Newark surged. The murder rate climbed 73% above what it was in the same period for the previous year; auto thefts were up 40%; and carjackings increased fourfold. The number of shooting victims taken to area hospitals doubled. Although some claim that not all of those crime increases can be directly attributed to declines in police staffing, others are not so sure. As police personnel were cut, so were crime-prevention programs that had served the city well. One of them was Operation Impact, which targeted high-crime areas and resulted in a 35% decrease in crime in those neighborhoods. The program was eliminated as uniformed personnel were moved to street patrol.

The city of Newark, which has since rehired some of its officers, is not alone in facing financial pressures. A year after the layoffs were announced in Newark, Camden city officials, also in New Jersey, announced that they were considering eliminating the entire Camden Police Department, and were working to create a countywide police force to be named the Camden County Police Department. Theoretically, the department, which would include other cities and towns in the area, would bring about cost savings from a combination of resources and personnel that were previously performing redundant tasks. Current plans, however, which are still developing as this book goes to press, do not ask for the department to combine operations with the Camden County Sheriff's Office, which serves unincorporated areas of the county.

Although today's combined departments represent one approach to cost savings, others include the following: prioritizing activities, reducing services, and modifying service delivery; reorganizing and rightsizing agencies; partnering with other agencies and organizations; using proactive policing methods instead of reactive ones; adopting preventative and problem-solving service models; increasing efficiency; outsourcing services; recycling confiscated criminal resources; and implementing force multipliers.

Force multipliers, the last of the options listed here, refers to using technologies that permit a few personnel to do the work of many. Cameras placed in crime-prone areas, for example, and monitored by police employees can sometimes reduce the need for active police patrols, thereby saving huge expenditures on personnel, vehicles, communications, and administrative expenses. Cross-training, in which personnel are trained to perform a number of roles—such as police officer, EMT, and firefighter—can also save money by eliminating duplicate positions.

Finally, another initiative, **smart policing**, makes use of techniques shown to work at both reducing and solving crimes. **Hot-spot policing**, in which agencies focus their resources on known areas of criminal activity, is one such technique; whereas **predictive policing**, which provides the ability to anticipate or predict crime through the use of statistical techniques, helps guide enforcement operations, and is an increasingly important concept in policing today (see the "CJ News box" in Chapter 6 for more information on hot-spot policing).

Two programs that support effective policing are the Smart Policing Initiative (SPI), and the National Law Enforcement and Corrections Technology Center (NLECTC). The NLECTC works to identify emerging technologies, as well as to assess their efficiency; the SPI, a collaborative consortium composed of the Bureau of Justice Assistance, the nonprofit CNA Corporation, and over 30 local law enforcement agencies, works to build evidence-based law enforcement strategies that are effective, efficient, and economical. The SPI is also discussed in a "Paying for It" box in Chapter 6. Visit SPI on the Web at http://www.smartpolicinginitiative.com. The NLECTC can be accessed at http://www.justnet.org.

References: William Alden, "Newark Police Layoffs Threaten Crime-Fighting as Budget Cuts Spark Fears," *Huffington Post*, February 25, 2011, http://www.huffingtonpost.com/2011/02/25/newark-police-layoffs-budget-cuts_n_827993.html (accessed May 28, 2012); Claudia Vargas, "Camden City Council Urges Officials to Advance Plan for County Police Force," *The Philadelphia Inquirer*, December 28, 2011, http://articles.philly.com/2011-12-28/news/30565451_1_county-force-police-force-police-officers (accessed May 21, 2012); Joe Cordero, *Reducing the Costs of Quality Policing: Making Community Safety Cost Effective and Sustainable* (The Cordero Group), http://www.njlmef.org/policy-papers/FoLG_v_3_1.pdf (accessed May 29, 2012); Charlie Beck, "Predictive Policing: What Can We Learn from Wal-Mart and Amazon about Fighting Crime in a Recession?" *The Police Chief*, April 2012, http://www.policechiefmagazine.org/magazine/index.cfm?fuseaction=display_arch&article_id=1942&issue_id=112009 (accessed May 25, 2012); and JustNet, "About NLECTC," https://www.justnet.org/About_NLECTC.html (accessed May 29, 2012); James R. Coldren, Jr., Alissa Huntoon, and Michael Medaris, "Introducing Smart Policing: Foundations, Principles, and Practice," *Police Quarterly*, Vol. 16, No. 3 (2013), pp. 275–286.

Source: Pearson Education, Inc.

is being transformed and restructured in the modern world" in ways that were unanticipated only a few decades ago.[53] Much of the change is due to the development of private protective services as an important adjunct to public law enforcement activities in the United States and throughout much of the rest of the world. The NIJ report says that "the key to understanding the transformation is that policing, meaning the activity of making societies safe, is no longer carried out exclusively by governments" and that the distinction between private and public police has begun to blur. According to the NIJ, "gradually, almost imperceptibly, policing has been 'multilateralized,'" meaning that "a host of nongovernmental agencies have undertaken to provide security services." As a result, the NIJ report says, "policing has entered a new era, an era characterized by a transformation in the governance of security." The report concludes the following:

- In most countries, certainly in the democratic world, private police outnumber public police.
- In these same countries, people spend more time in their daily lives in places where visible crime prevention and control are provided by nongovernmental groups rather than by governmental police agencies.
- The reconstruction of policing is occurring worldwide despite differences in wealth and economic systems.

According to the National Center for Policy Analysis, private security personnel outnumber public law enforcement officers in the United States by nearly three to one.[54] The widely cited *Hallcrest Report II*,[55] another important document describing the private security industry, says that employment in the field of private security is anticipated to continue to expand by around 4% per year, whereas public police agencies are expected to grow by only 2.8% per year for the foreseeable future. Still faster growth is predicted in private security industry revenues, which are expected to increase about 7% per year, a growth rate almost three times greater than that projected for the gross national product. Table 5-4 lists the ten largest private security agencies in business today and some of the services they offer.

Major reasons for the quick growth of the American proprietary security sector include "(1) an increase in crimes in the workplace, (2) an increase in fear (real or perceived) of crime and terrorism, (3) the fiscal crises of the states, which have limited public protection, and (4) an increased public and business awareness and use of ... more cost-effective private security products and services."[56]

Private agencies provide tailored policing funded by the guarded organization rather than through the expenditure of public monies. Experts estimate that the money spent on private security in this country exceeds the combined budgets of all law enforcement agencies—local, state, and federal.[57] Contributing to this vast expenditure is the federal government, which is itself a major employer of private security personnel, contracting for services that range from guards to highly specialized electronic snooping and computerized countermeasures at military installations and embassies throughout the world.

There are indications that private security activities are rapidly growing beyond traditional guard services to encompass dedicated efforts at security-related intelligence gathering.

There are indications that private security activities are rapidly growing beyond traditional guard services to encompass dedicated efforts at security related intelligence gathering. In August 2004, for example, the Department of Homeland Security warned that terrorists might be actively targeting Citigroup, Prudential, the New York Stock Exchange, and other large financial institutions on the East Coast of the United States. At the same time, however, Austin-based Stratfor, Inc., a low-profile private intelligence agency run by former CIA officers, was quietly assuring its clients that such an attack was very unlikely, saying that "Al Qaeda has never attacked into an alert."[58]

According to The Freedonia Group, a Cleveland-based industry research firm, U.S. demand for private contracted security services was around $66 billion in 2012.[59] The total includes spending on physical security, Internet safeguards, staff screening and training, and terrorist and related intelligence analysis. Not

TABLE 5-4 | American Policing: Private Security Agencies

THE LARGEST PRIVATE SECURITY AGENCIES IN THE UNITED STATES		
Advance Security, Inc.	Garda World Security Corp.	Security Bureau, Inc.
Allied Security, Inc.	G4S	Securitas, U.S.A.
American Protective Services	Globe Security	Wells Fargo Guard Services
Burns International Security Services	Guardsmark, Inc.	
	Pinkerton's, Inc.	
PRIVATE SECURITY SERVICES		
Airport security	Computer/information security	Nuclear facility security
ATM services	Executive protection	Railroad detectives
Bank guards	Hospital security	School security
Company guards	Loss-prevention specialists	Store/mall security

Sources: Pearson Education, Inc.

A security guard at a political gathering. Why has the privatization of policing become a major issue facing governments and public justice agencies everywhere?

included are federal and state government expenditures on aviation security, homeland security, or border security.

Integrating Public and Private Security

As the private security field grows, its relationship to public law enforcement continues to evolve. Some argue that "today, a distinction between public and private policing is increasingly meaningless."[60] As a result, the focus has largely shifted from an analysis of competition between the sectors to the recognition that each form of policing can help the other.

In 2012, Philip Cook, a professor of economics at Duke University, suggested that private security forces might have been largely responsible for the recent decade-long decline in reported crime. Although changes in crime rates are often attributed to effective policing, Cook reported that security contractors and anti-theft technology, such as LoJack devices and video surveillance systems, limit criminal opportunity. "Private action," said Cook, is a way "of controlling opportunity to potential criminals."[61] He predicted that crime rates will continue to fall with improving security technology and wider involvement by the private sector in crime prevention.

> As the private security field grows, its relationship to public law enforcement continues to evolve.

A private security officer conferring with a sworn public law enforcement officer at the Mall of America. How can cooperation between private security agencies and public law enforcement offices help solve and prevent crimes?

One government-sponsored report recommends that the resources of proprietary and contract security should be brought to bear in cooperative, community-based crime-prevention and security-awareness programs. Doing so, says the report, would maximize the cooperative crime-fighting potential of existing private and public security resources.[62]

One especially important policy area involves building private security–public policing partnerships to prevent terrorism and to respond to threats of terrorism. A national policy summit

CJ | CAREERS

Suzette Baker

Name. Suzette Baker

Position. Assistant Supervisor, G4S Security Solutions, Charlotte, NC

Colleges attended. Kaplan University

Majors. Criminal Justice/Juvenile Justice

Year hired. 2013

Please give a brief description of your job. As an assistant supervisor for a large private security company I assist with the professional operation, administration, profitability, and quality assurance of uniformed services for a single shift at a client's site. In addition, I assist with staffing, scheduling, and training of security officers assigned to my shift, ensure that contract-required training elements for security officers are met, ensure quality of service by inspecting the uniforms and security license/first aid/CPR cards of security officers on my shift, review and maintain incident reports, assist in preparation of post orders, and make recommendations for positive and negative personnel actions for officers on my shift. Customer service is a very important aspect of the security industry so I also respond to client requests.

What appealed to you most about the position when you applied for it? The security industry has greatly evolved from the days of the night watchman who drank coffee and watched TV or read the newspaper to pass the time. The industry has applied new technology to expand the services we offer to include CCTV cameras, computer programs, Secure Trax devices, and in-depth training in areas such as terrorism, fire and life safety, and access control to our sites. Because many security companies are going global, there are many fields of security that are now open to security officers both domestically and internationally. Some of these include special police forces, assisting with disaster relief, airports, and homeland security.

How would you describe the interview process? The interview process is a multi-step process that begins once an online application is reviewed and the applicant is scheduled for an interview with a site manager at the local office. During the interview the applicant will be asked why he or she wants to work in the security field and what strengths and/or skills they have to offer. The site manager will review the application and any questions he or she may have with the applicant, and if all criteria are met an offer of employment will be made. Once the offer of employment is accepted, the applicant is referred to office personnel to be scheduled for classes to obtain a PPSB (Private Protective Services Bureau) license. On completion of this class, the applicant will a take CPR/First Aid class and any other class(es) required by the company. Classes (orientation) can last anywhere from three to seven days and vary between security companies. Upon successful completion of all classes, the applicant will be considered an employee and assigned to the site of the manager who interviewed them.

What is a typical day like? A typical day varies depending on which shift is worked. Security officers on all shifts patrol designated areas inside and outside of buildings, ensuring that only authorized personnel gain access to certain areas of a site. The designated areas to be patrolled depend on the post the officer is working. For example, one officer may be assigned to parking decks and parking lots while another will check in vendors and contractors. Yet another officer will control access to the buildings and others will be responsible for interior and exterior patrols. Another officer will be responsible for checking in visitors and alerting key company personnel of their arrival. It is worth noting that some smaller sites only have one security officer per shift who is responsible for all of these job functions. Every security officer is responsible for reporting any fire or life safety issues to their supervisor.

What qualities/characteristics are most helpful for this job? Security officers encounter people from all walks of life, so it is vital that the officer remain unbiased and have the ability to keep personal opinions private. The ability to walk, stand, or sit for long periods of time; be flexible in working different posts, listen and respond to visitors and the customer's employees; accurately follow written and oral directions; patience; honesty; and attention to detail are important characteristics of security officers.

What is a typical starting salary? Starting salary varies between companies and locations. The salary for a security officer ranges from $17k–$34k. This is supplemented by medical and retirement benefits.

What is the salary potential as you move up into higher-level jobs? The salary potential varies depending on the company and location. Experience does not significantly affect salaries for this career. Moving into management positions does provide a small increase in salary ranging from $31k–$37 annually.

What career advice would you give someone in college beginning studies in criminal justice? If you are thinking about a career in the security industry, a bachelor's degree in criminal justice or other helping field is more valuable than an associate's degree. Adding a human resources component to your degree will allow for easier transition into administrative positions within a security company.

Source: Reprinted with permission of Suzette Baker. Photo courtesy of Suzette Baker.

---

report, jointly authored by the International Association of Chiefs of Police and the 30,000-member ASIS International, says that despite similar interests in protecting people and property in the United States, public police and private security agencies have rarely collaborated.[63] The report notes, however, that as much as 85% of the nation's critical infrastructure is protected by private security. It goes on to say that "the need for complex coordination, extra staffing, and special resources" in the light of possible terror attacks, "coupled with the significant demands of crime prevention and response, absolutely requires boosting the level of partnership between public policing and private security."[64] The full national policy summit report is available at **http://www.justicestudies.com/pubs/pubprivpart.pdf**.

ethics and professionalism

ASIS International Code of Ethics

Preamble

Aware that the quality of professional security activity ultimately depends upon the willingness of practitioners to observe special standards of conduct and to manifest good faith in professional relationships, the American Society for Industrial Security adopts the following Code of Ethics and mandates its conscientious observance as a binding condition of membership in or affiliation with the Society:

Code of Ethics

1. A member shall perform professional duties in accordance with the law and the highest moral principles.
2. A member shall observe the precepts of truthfulness, honesty, and integrity.
3. A member shall be faithful and diligent in discharging professional responsibilities.
4. A member shall be competent in discharging professional responsibilities.
5. A member shall safeguard confidential information and exercise due care to prevent its improper disclosure.
6. A member shall not maliciously injure the professional reputation or practice of colleagues, clients, or employers.

Article I

A member shall perform professional duties in accordance with the law and the highest moral principles.

Ethical Considerations

1. A member shall abide by the law of the land in which the services are rendered and perform all duties in an honorable manner.
2. A member shall not knowingly become associated in responsibility for work with colleagues who do not conform to the law and these ethical standards.
3. A member shall be just and respect the rights of others in performing professional responsibilities.

Article II

A member shall observe the precepts of truthfulness, honesty, and integrity.

Ethical Considerations

1. A member shall disclose all relevant information to those having the right to know.
2. A right to know is a legally enforceable claim or demand by a person for disclosure of information by a member.

Such a right does not depend upon prior knowledge by the person of the existence of the information to be disclosed.
3. A member shall not knowingly release misleading information nor encourage or otherwise participate in the release of such information.

Article III

A member shall be faithful and diligent in discharging professional responsibilities.

Ethical Considerations

1. A member is faithful when fair and steadfast in adherence to promises and commitments.
2. A member is diligent when employing best efforts in an assignment.
3. A member shall not act in matters involving conflicts of interest without appropriate disclosure and approval.
4. A member shall represent services or products fairly and truthfully.

Article IV

A member shall be competent in discharging professional responsibilities.

Ethical Considerations

1. A member is competent who possesses and applies the skills and knowledge required for the task.
2. A member shall not accept a task beyond the member's competence nor shall competence be claimed when not possessed.

Article V

A member shall safeguard confidential information and exercise due care to prevent its improper disclosure.

Ethical Considerations

1. Confidential information is nonpublic information, the disclosure of which is restricted.
2. Due care requires that the professional must not knowingly reveal confidential information, or use a confidence to the disadvantage of the principal or to the advantage of the member or a third person, unless the principal consents after full disclosure of all the facts. This confidentiality

(continues)

continues after the business relationship between the member and his principal has terminated.

3. A member who receives information and has not agreed to be bound by confidentiality is not bound from disclosing it. A member is not bound by confidential disclosures made of acts or omissions which constitute a violation of the law.

4. Confidential disclosures made by a principal to a member are not recognized by law as privileged in a legal proceeding. The member may be required to testify in a legal proceeding to the information received in confidence from his principal over the objection of his principal's counsel.

5. A member shall not disclose confidential information for personal gain without appropriate authorization.

Article VI

A member shall not maliciously injure the professional reputation or practice of colleagues, clients, or employers.

Ethical Considerations

1. A member shall not comment falsely and with malice concerning a colleague's competence, performance, or professional capabilities.

2. A member who knows, or has reasonable grounds to believe, that another member has failed to conform to the Society's Code of Ethics shall present such information to the Ethical Standards Committee in accordance with Article VIII of the Society's bylaws.

Thinking about Ethics

The ASIS code of ethics says, "A member shall observe the precepts of truthfulness, honesty, and integrity." Why are these qualities important in a security professional?

Why is it important for security personnel to "safeguard confidential information and exercise due care to prevent its improper disclosure"? What might happen if they didn't?

Source: ASIS International. Reprinted with permission.

SUMMARY

- American police departments owe a historical legacy to Sir Robert Peel and the London Metropolitan Police Service (MPS). Although law enforcement efforts in the United States were based to some degree on the British experience, the unique character of the American frontier led to the growth of a decentralized form of policing throughout the United States.

- Police agencies in the United States function to enforce the statutes created by lawmaking bodies, and differing types and levels of legislative authority are reflected in the diversity of police forces in our country today. Consequently, American policing presents a complex picture that is structured along federal, state, and local lines.

- Dozens of federal law enforcement agencies are distributed among 14 U.S. government departments and 28 non-departmental entities, and each federal agency empowered by Congress to enforce specific statutes has its own enforcement arm. The FBI may be the most famous law enforcement agency in the country and in the world. The mission of the FBI is to protect and defend the United States against terrorist and foreign intelligence threats, to uphold and enforce the criminal laws of the United States, and to provide leadership and criminal justice services to federal, state, municipal, and international agencies and partners.

- State law enforcement agencies have numerous functions, including assisting local law enforcement departments in criminal investigations when asked to do so, operating centralized identification bureaus, maintaining a centralized criminal records repository, patrolling the state's highways, and providing select training for municipal and county officers. State law enforcement agencies are usually organized after one of two models. In the first, a centralized model, the tasks of major criminal investigations are combined with the patrol of state highways. The second state model, the decentralized model, draws a clear distinction between traffic enforcement on state highways and other state-level law enforcement functions by creating at least two separate agencies.

- Local police agencies represent a third level of law enforcement activity in the United States. They encompass a wide variety of agencies, including municipal police departments, rural sheriff's departments, and specialized groups like campus police and transit police.

- Private protective services constitute another level of law enforcement. Whereas public police are employed by the government and enforce public laws, private security personnel work for corporate or private employers and secure private interests. Private security personnel outnumber public law enforcement officers in the United States by nearly three to one, and private agencies provide tailored protective services funded by the guarded organization rather than by taxpayers.

KEY TERMS

bobbies, 141
Bow Street Runners, 140
comes stabuli, 139
directed patrol, 146
evidence-based policing
  (EBP), 146
federal law enforcement
  agency, 148
hot-spot policing, 155
Kansas City experiment, 145
Law Enforcement Assistance
  Administration (LEAA), 143
municipal police
  department, 153

new police, 141
night watch, 139
predictive policing, 155
private protective service, 154
scientific police
  management, 144
sheriff, 153
smart policing 155
Statute of Winchester, 139
sworn officer, 153
vigilantism, 142
Wickersham Commission, 143

QUESTIONS FOR REVIEW

1. Describe the historical development of policing in America. What impact did the Prohibition era have on the development of American policing?
2. What are the three levels of public law enforcement described in this chapter?
3. Identify a number of significant federal law enforcement agencies, and describe the responsibilities of each.
4. Explain the role that state law enforcement agencies play in enforcing the law, and describe the two major models of state law enforcement organization.
5. What different kinds of local law enforcement agencies exist in the United States today? What role does each agency have in enforcing the law?
6. Describe the nature and extent of private protective services in the United States today. What role do you think they will play in the future?

QUESTIONS FOR REFLECTION

1. Why are there so many different types of law enforcement agencies in the United States? What problems, if any, do you think are created by having such a diversity of agencies?
2. What is evidence-based policing? What assumptions about police work have scientific studies of law enforcement called into question? What other assumptions made about police work today might be similarly questioned or studied?
3. Contrast the current deployment of private security personnel with the number of public law enforcement personnel.
4. How can the quality of private security services be ensured?
5. What is the relationship between private security and public policing in America today? How might the nature of that relationship be expected to change over time? Why?

NOTES

i. Lawrence W. Sherman, *Evidence-Based Policing* (Washington, DC: Police Foundation, 1998), p. 3.
ii. Adapted from Darl H. Champion and Michael K. Hooper, *Introduction to American Policing* (New York: McGraw-Hill, 2003), p. 166.

1. "A Reminiscence of a Bow-Street Officer," *Harper's New Monthly Magazine*, Vol. 5, No. 28 (September 1852), p. 484.
2. For a good discussion of the development of the modern police, see Sue Titus Reid, *Criminal Justice: Procedures and Issues* (St. Paul, MN: West, 1987), pp. 110–115; and Henry M. Wrobleski and Karen M. Hess, *Introduction to Law Enforcement and Criminal Justice*, 4th ed. (St. Paul, MN: West, 1993), pp. 3–51.
3. Camdem Pelham, *Chronicles of Crime*, Vol. 1 (London: T. Miles, 1887), p. 59.
4. Gary Sykes, "Street Justice: A Moral Defense of Order Maintenance Policing," *Justice Quarterly*, Vol. 3, No. 4 (December 1986), p. 504.
5. Law Enforcement Assistance Administration, *Two Hundred Years of American Criminal Justice: An LEAA Bicentennial Study* (Washington, DC: U.S. Government Printing Office, 1976), p. 15.
6. For an excellent discussion of the history of policewomen in the United States, see Dorothy Moses Schulz, *From Social Worker to Crimefighter: Women in United States Municipal Policing* (Westport, CT: Praeger, 1995); and Dorothy Moses Schulz, "Invisible No More: A Social History of Women in U.S. Policing," in Barbara R. Price and Natalie J. Sokoloff, eds., *The Criminal Justice System and Women: Offender, Victim, Worker*, 2nd ed. (New York: McGraw-Hill, 1995), pp. 372–382.
7. Schulz, *From Social Worker to Crimefighter*, p. 25.
8. Ibid., p. 27.
9. National Commission on Law Observance and Enforcement, *Wickersham Commission Reports*, 14 vols. (Washington, DC: U.S. Government Printing Office, 1931).
10. President's Commission on Law Enforcement and Administration of Justice, *The Challenge of Crime in a Free Society* (Washington, DC: U.S. Government Printing Office, 1967).
11. National Advisory Commission on Criminal Justice Standards and Goals, *A National Strategy to Reduce Crime* (Washington, DC: U.S. Government Printing Office, 1973).
12. Enacted as U.S. Code, Title 42, Chapter 136, Subchapter XII.
13. Thomas J. Deakin, "The Police Foundation: A Special Report," *FBI Law Enforcement Bulletin* (November 1986), p. 2.
14. George L. Kelling et al., *The Kansas City Patrol Experiment* (Washington, DC: Police Foundation, 1974).
15. Kevin Krajick, "Does Patrol Prevent Crime?" *Police Magazine* (September 1978), quoting Dr. George Kelling.
16. William Bieck and David Kessler, *Response Time Analysis* (Kansas City, MO: Board of Police Commissioners, 1977). See also J. Thomas McEwen et al., *Evaluation of the Differential Police Response Field Test: Executive Summary* (Alexandria, VA: Research Management Associates, 1984); and Lawrence Sherman, "Policing Communities: What Works?" in Michael Tonry and Norval Morris, eds., *Crime and Justice: An Annual Review of Research*, Vol. 8 (Chicago: University of Chicago Press, 1986).
17. Krajick, "Does Patrol Prevent Crime?"
18. Ibid.
19. Ibid.

20. "Evidence-Based Policing," Police Foundation press release, March 17, 1998, http://www.policefoundation.org/docs/evidence.html (accessed January 5, 2009).

21. Lawrence W. Sherman, *Evidence-Based Policing* (Washington, DC: Police Foundation, 1998), p. 3.

22. Much of the information in this section comes from Sherman, *Evidence-Based Policing.*

23. Neil Wain and Alex Murray, "Gathering Evidence," Police-Professional.com, March 24, 2001, http://gemini.gmu.edu/cebcp/BritishSocietyEBPolicing.pdf (accessed May 18, 2011).

24. Carl J. Jensen III, "Consuming and Applying Research: Evidence-Based Policing," *Police Chief*, Vol. 73, No. 2 (February 2006), http://policechiefmagazine.org/magazine/index.cfm?fuseaction=display_arch&article_id=815&issue_id=22006 (accessed May 17, 2009).

25. Ibid.

26. University of Cambridge, "Evidence-Based Policing: Possibilities and Prospects," revised and final program announcement, June 30, 2008.

27. Government Accounting Office, *Federal Law Enforcement: Survey of Federal Civilian Law Enforcement Functions and Authorities* (Washington, DC: U.S. GAO, December 2006), p. 17.

28. U.S. Department of Justice, *A Proud History … a Bright Future: Careers with the FBI*, pamphlet (October 1986), p. 1.

29. Much of the information in this section comes from U.S. Department of Justice, *The FBI: The First Seventy-Five Years* (Washington, DC: U.S. Government Printing Office, 1986).

30. Some of the information in this section is adapted from Federal Bureau of Investigation, "Today's FBI: Facts and Figures, 2010–11," http://www.fbi.gov/stats-services/publications/facts-and-figures-2010-2011 (accessed May 18, 2011).

31. "Rising to the Occasion," FBI News Blog, October 22, 2012, http://www.fbi.gov/news/news_blog/in-new-interviews-women-agents-reflect-on-40-years (accessed February 15, 2013).

32. Telephone conversation with FBI officials, April 21, 1995.

33. Federal Bureau of Investigation, "The Budapest International Law Enforcement Academy Turns Ten," May 13, 2005, http://www.fbi.gov/news/stories/2005/may/ilea051305 (accessed July 10, 2013).

34. Information in this section comes from Christopher H. Asplen, "National Commission Explores Its Future," *NIJ Journal* (January 1999), pp. 17–24.

35. The DNA Identification Act is Section 210301 of the Violent Crime Control and Law Enforcement Act of 1994.

36. Federal Bureau of Investigation, "CODIS-NDIS Statistics," http://www.fbi.gov/about-us/lab/biometric-analysis/codis/ndis-statistics (accessed January 10, 2015).

37. Much of the information in this paragraph comes from the FBI Academy website at http://www.fbi.gov/hq/td/academy/academy.htm (accessed January 23, 2009).

38. Henry M. Wrobleski and Karen M. Hess, *Introduction to Law Enforcement and Criminal Justice*, 4th ed. (St. Paul, MN: West, 1993), p. 34.

39. Ibid., p. 35.

40. New York City Police Department website, http://www.nyc.gov/html/nypd/html/faq/faq_police.shtml (accessed June 21, 2011).

41. Brian A. Reaves, *Local Police Departments, 2013: Personnel, Policies, and Practices* (Washington, DC, 2015).

42. Andrea M. Burch, *Sheriffs' Offices, 2007: Statistical Tables* (Washington, DC Bureau of Justice Statistics, 2012), p. 6.

43. Reaves, *Local Police Departments.*

44. Note, however, that New York City jails may have daily populations that, on a given day, exceed those of Los Angeles County.

45. The Police Assessment Resource Center, *The Los Angeles County Sheriff's Department—19th Semiannual Report* (Los Angeles: PARC, February 2005); and telephone communication with Deputy Ethan Marquez, Los Angeles County Sheriff's Department, Custodial Division, January 24, 2002.

46. Los Angeles County Sheriff's Department, "Employees," http://tinyurl.com/clq4eom (accessed February 15, 2013).

47. Burch, *Sheriffs' Offices, 2007: Statistical Tables*, p. 2.

48. *Private Security: Report of the Task Force on Private Security* (Washington, DC: U.S. Government Printing Office, 1976), p. 4.

49. "Securing the Olympic Games: $142,857 Security Cost per Athlete in Greece," *Wall Street Journal*, August 22, 2004, http://www.mindfully.org/Reform/2004/Olympic-Games-Security22aug04.htm (accessed May 17, 2007).

50. Christopher Elser, "London Olympics Doubles Spending on Security to $870 Million for Next Year," *Bloomberg*, December 5, 2011, http://www.bloomberg.com/news/2011-12-05/london-olympics-doubles-spending-on-security-to-870-million-for-next-year.html (accessed February 15, 2013).

51. John-Paul Ford Rojas, "£9 Billion Olympics 'Good Value,' Says Spending Watchdog," *The London Telegraph*, December 5, 2012 (accessed February 15, 2013).

52. The information and some of the wording in this paragraph come from the ASIS International website at http://www.asisonline.org (accessed August 5, 2009).

53. David H. Bayley and Clifford D. Shearing, *The New Structure of Policing: Description, Conceptualization, and Research Agenda* (Washington, DC: National Institute of Justice, 2001).

54. National Center for Policy Analysis, *Using the Private Sector to Deter Crime* (Washington, DC: NCPA, 2001).

55. William C. Cunningham, John J. Strauchs, and Clifford W. Van Meter, *The Hallcrest Report II: Private Security Trends, 1970–2000* (McLean, VA: Hallcrest Systems, 1990).

56. Ibid., p. 236.

57. See http://www.spyandsecuritystore.com.conex.html (accessed June 25, 2009).

58. Peter Lewis, "Companies Turn to Private Spies," *Fortune*, August 9, 2004, p. 24.

59. "U.S. Demand for Private Security Services to Approach $66 B in 2012," *Security Newswire*, July 29, 2008 (accessed February 15, 2013).

60. Bayley and Shearing, *The New Structure of Policing*, p. 15.

61. John Sodaro, "Move over, Police?" *The Crime Report*, http://www.thecrimereport.org/news/inside-criminal-justice/2012-02-move-over-police, February 10, 2012 (accessed February 15, 2013).

62. W. C. Cunningham, *Crime and Protection in America: A Study of Private Security and Law Enforcement Resources and Relationships* (Washington, DC: National Institute of Justice, 1985), pp. 59–72.

63. International Association of Chiefs of Police, *National Policy Summit: Building Private Security/Public Policing Partnerships to Prevent and Respond to Terrorism and Public Disorder: Vital Issues and Policy Recommendations, 2004* (Washington, DC: U.S. Dept. of Justice, 2004).

64. Ibid., p. 1.

UpperCut Images/Getty Images

6

POLICING: PURPOSE AND ORGANIZATION

LEARNING OBJECTIVES

After reading this chapter, you should be able to

- Explain the police mission in democratic societies.
- Discuss the five core operational strategies of today's police departments.
- Summarize the typical organizational structure of a police department.
- Compare and contrast the three most common policing styles.
- Compare the role of American police today in the post-9/11 environment with their pre-9/11 role.
- Describe three ethnic and gender diversity issues in policing, including ways to resolve them.

The police in the United States are not separate from the people. They draw their authority from the will and consent of the people, and they recruit their officers from them.

POLICE - REPORT OF THE NATIONAL ADVISORY COMMISSION ON CRIMINAL JUSTICE STANDARDS AND GOALS

■ **theme**   What is the police mission in a democratic society? How is it subservient to the rule of law discussed in Chapter 4?

■ **lecture note**   Discuss each of the five basic elements of the police mission. Explain how they may complement or conflict with each other at various times.

■ **activity**   Divide students into five groups and assign each group one of the five elements of the police mission. Have each group explain why its element should take precedence over the others in policing. If you like, you could set this up as a mock campaign, with each group campaigning for its element to be elected "most important" in the police mission.

■ **theme**   What are the possible implications of the inability of the police to enforce all of the laws. *Should* the police strive to enforce all laws at all times? Who should be responsible for determining which laws should be prioritized for enforcement?

Introduction

In 2014, 18-year-old Michael Brown was shot and killed by 28-year-old Ferguson, Missouri, police officer Darren Wilson, sparking days of racially charged protests. Brown, who was shot multiple times, had been unarmed at the time he died. Witnesses at the scene provided conflicting stories, with some saying that the 6-foot 4-inch, 292-lb. Brown had been raising his arms in surrender, while others said that he lunged at the officer. Tensions increased as police released video of a store robbery in which Brown was said to have participated immediately before the shooting, and detailed serious facial injuries that Wilson suffered during the encounter. A grand jury refused to indict Wilson in the shooting.

The death of Michael Brown revealed a deep distrust of the police by minorities—something that national opinion polls continue to document. Combined Gallup Poll data from 2011 to 2014, for example, show that 59% of whites have a "great deal" or "quite a lot" of confidence in the police, compared with only 37% of blacks.[1] The police department in Ferguson, a suburb of St. Louis, was more than 90% white at the time of Brown's shooting, while the town's population was nearly 70% African American.

A post-Brown analysis by *The New York Times* of nearly 400 police departments nationwide found that, in general, the "share of white officers was greater than the share of white residents by more than 50 percentage points."[2] Critics point out, however, that "it's very, very, very difficult" to hire qualified minorities for police

Police in Ferguson, Missouri, arrest a looter during a night of rioting following the shooting death of an unarmed black teenager by a white police officer in 2014. What aspects of the police mission can you identify?

FIGURE 6-1 | The Basic Purposes of Policing in Democratic Societies

Source: Pearson Education, Inc.

work; and that "there is little hard evidence that diversity correlates with better performance . . ."[3] Consequently, while the police mission may seem relatively straightforward, it is complicated by the many calls for individual and civil rights that surround police work.

The Police Mission

The basic purposes of policing in democratic societies are to (1) enforce and support the laws of the society of which the police are a part, (2) investigate crimes and apprehend offenders, (3) prevent crime, (4) help ensure domestic peace and tranquility, and (5) provide the community with needed enforcement-related services (Figure 6-1). Simply put, as Sir Robert Peel, founder of the British system of policing, explained in 1822, "The basic mission for which the police exist is to reduce crime and disorder."[4]

> Most police officers spend the majority of their time answering nonemergency public-service calls.

In the paragraphs that follow, we turn our attention to these five basic elements of the police mission.

Enforcing the Law

The police operate under an official public mandate that requires them to enforce the law. Collectively speaking, police agencies are the primary enforcers of federal, state, and local criminal laws. Not surprisingly, police officers see themselves as crime fighters, a view shared by the public and promoted by the popular media.

■ **Follow the author's tweets about the latest crime and justice news @schmalleger.**

■ **crime prevention** The anticipation, recognition, and appraisal of a crime risk and the initiation of action to eliminate or reduce it.

Although it is the job of the police to enforce the law, it is not their *only* job. Practically speaking, most officers spend the majority of their time answering nonemergency public-service calls,[5] controlling traffic, or writing tickets. Most are not involved in intensive, ongoing crime-fighting activities. Research shows that only about 10 to 20% of all calls to the police involve situations that actually require a law enforcement response—that is, situations that might lead to arrest and eventual prosecution.[6]

Even when the police are busy enforcing laws, they can't enforce them all. Police resources—including labor, vehicles, and investigative assets—are limited, causing officers to focus more on certain types of law violations than on others. Old laws prohibiting minor offenses like spitting on the sidewalk hold little social significance today and are typically relegated to the dustbin of statutory history. Even though they are still "on the books," few officers, if any, even think about enforcing such laws. Police tend to tailor their enforcement efforts to meet the contemporary concerns of the populace they serve.[7] For example, if a community is upset about a "massage parlor" operating in its neighborhood, the local police department may bring enforcement efforts to bear that lead to the relocation of the business. However, although community interests significantly influence the enforcement practices of police agencies, individual officers take their cue on enforcement priorities from their departments, their peers, and their supervisors.

The police are expected to not only enforce the law but also support it. The personal actions of law enforcement personnel should inspire others to respect and obey the law. Off-duty officers who speed down the highway or smoke marijuana at a party, for example, do a disservice to the police profession and engender disrespect for all agents of enforcement and for the law itself. Hence, in an important sense, we can say that respect for the law begins with the personal and public behavior of law enforcement officers.

Apprehending Offenders

Some offenders are apprehended during the commission of a crime or immediately afterward. Fleeing Oklahoma City bomber Timothy McVeigh, for example, was stopped by an Oklahoma Highway Patrol officer on routine patrol only 90 minutes after the destruction of the Alfred P. Murrah federal building[8] for driving a car with no license plate. When the officer questioned McVeigh about a bulge in his jacket, McVeigh admitted that it was a gun. The officer then took McVeigh into custody for carrying a concealed weapon. Typically, McVeigh would then have made an immediate appearance before a judge and would have been released on bail. As fate would have it, however, the judge assigned to see McVeigh was involved in a protracted

divorce case. The longer jail stay proved to be McVeigh's undoing. As the investigation into the bombing progressed, profiler Clinton R. Van Zandt of the Federal Bureau of Investigation's Behavioral Science Unit concluded that the bomber was likely a native-born white male in his 20s who had been in the military and was probably a member of a fringe militia group—all of which were true of McVeigh.[9] Working together, the Federal Bureau of Investigation (FBI) and the Oklahoma State Police realized that McVeigh was a likely suspect and questioned him. While McVeigh's capture was the result of a bit of good luck, many offenders are caught only as the result of extensive police work involving a painstaking investigation. (Investigation is described in more detail later in this chapter.)

Preventing Crime

Crime prevention is a proactive approach to the problem of crime; it is "the anticipation, recognition and appraisal of a crime risk and initiation of action to remove or reduce it."[10] In preventing crime, police agencies act before a crime happens, thus preventing victimization from occurring. Although the term *crime prevention* is relatively new, the idea is not. The techniques of securing valuables, limiting access to sensitive areas, and monitoring the activities of suspicious people were used long before Western police forces were established in the 1800s.

Modern crime-prevention efforts aim not only to reduce crime and criminal opportunities and to lower the potential rewards of criminal activity, but also to lessen the public's fear of crime.[11] Crime-prevention efforts led by law enforcement make use of both techniques and programs. Techniques include access control, including barriers to entryways and

A warning sign telling looters to stay away from a flood-damaged home in Biloxi, Mississippi, following Hurricane Katrina in 2005. Effective law enforcement helps maintain social order and fills a critical need in the face of the widespread social disorganization that sometimes follows natural disasters or large-scale terrorist attacks. What other roles do the police fulfill?

Win McNamee/Getty Imagesw

■ **lecture note** Review the "broken windows" material from Chapter 3 and explain how this relates to this element of the police mission.

■ **CompStat** A crime-analysis and police management process, built on crime mapping, that was developed by the New York City Police Department in the mid-1990s.

■ **quality-of-life offense** A minor violation of the law (sometimes called a *petty crime*) that demoralizes community residents and businesspeople. Quality-of-life offenses involve acts that create physical disorder (e.g., excessive noise or vandalism) or that reflect social decay (e.g., panhandling and prostitution).

exits; video and other types of surveillance; the use of theft-deterrence devices like locks, alarms, and tethers; lighting; and visibility landscaping. In contrast to techniques, crime-prevention programs are organized efforts that focus resources on reducing a specific form of criminal threat. The Philadelphia Police Department's Operation Identification, for example, is designed to discourage theft and to help recover stolen property.[12] The program educates citizens on the importance of identifying, marking, and listing their valuables to deter theft (because marked items are more difficult to sell) and to aid in their recovery. Through Operation Identification, the police department provides engraving pens, suggests ways of photographing valuables, and provides window decals and car bumper stickers that identify citizens as participants in the program. Other crime-prevention programs typically target school-based crime, gang activity, drug abuse, violence, domestic abuse, identity theft, vehicle theft, and neighborhood crimes such as burglary.

Today's crime-prevention programs depend on community involvement and education and effective interaction between enforcement agencies and the communities they serve. For example, neighborhood watch programs build on active observation by homeowners and businesspeople on the lookout for anything unusual. Crime Stoppers International and Crime Stoppers USA are examples of privately sponsored programs that accept tips about criminal activity that they pass on to the appropriate law enforcement organization. Crime Stoppers International can be accessed via **http://www.c-s-i.org**, and the National Crime Prevention Council can be found at **http://www.ncpc.org.**

Predicting Crime

Law enforcement's ability to prevent crimes relies in part on the ability of police planners to predict when and where crimes will occur. Effective prediction means that valuable police resources can be correctly assigned to the areas with the greatest need. One technique for predicting criminal activity is **CompStat**.[13] While CompStat may sound like a software program, it is actually a process of crime analysis and police management developed by the New York City Police Department in the mid-1990s[14] to help police managers better assess their performance and foresee the potential for crime. The CompStat process involves first collecting and analyzing the information received from 9-1-1 calls and officer reports.[15] Then, this detailed and timely information is mapped using special software developed for the purpose. The resulting map sequences, generated over time, reveal the time

and place of crime patterns and identify "hot spots" of ongoing criminal activity. The maps also show the number of patrol officers active in an area, ongoing investigations, arrests made, and so on, thus helping commanders see which anticrime strategies are working.

CrimeStat, a Windows-based spatial statistics-analysis software program for analyzing crime-incident locations, is a second technique for predicting criminal activity. It produces results similar to CompStat's.[16] Developed by Ned Levine and Associates with grants from the National Institute of Justice (NIJ), CrimeStat provides statistical tools for crime mapping and analysis—including identification of crime hot spots, spatial distribution of incidents, and distance analysis—which help crime analysts target offenses that might be related to one another. A link to chicagocrime.org, which overlays crime statistics on maps of the city, is available at **http://chicago.everyblock.com/crime**.

Preserving the Peace

Enforcing the law, apprehending offenders, and preventing crime are all daunting tasks for police departments because there are many laws and numerous offenders. Still, crimes are clearly defined by statute and are therefore limited in number. Peacekeeping, however, is a virtually limitless police activity involving not only activities that violate the law (and hence the community's peace) but many others as well. Law enforcement officers who supervise parades, public demonstrations, and picketing strikers, for example, attempt to ensure that the behavior of everyone involved remains "civil" so that it does not disrupt community life.

Robert Langworthy, who has written extensively about the police, says that keeping the peace is often left up to individual officers.[17] Basically, he says, departments depend on patrol officers "to define the peace and decide how to support it," and an officer is doing a good job when his or her "beat is quiet, meaning there are no complaints about loiterers or traffic flow, and commerce is supported."

Many police departments focus on quality-of-life offenses as a crime-reduction and peacekeeping strategy. **Quality-of-life offenses** are minor law violations, sometimes called *petty crimes*, that demoralize residents and businesspeople by creating disorder. Examples of petty crimes include excessive noise, graffiti, abandoned cars, and vandalism. Other quality-of-life offenses reflect social decay and include panhandling and aggressive begging, public urination, prostitution, roaming youth gangs, public consumption of alcohol, and street-level substance abuse.[18] Homelessness, although not necessarily a violation of

Chief Deputy Paula Townsend of the Watauga County (North Carolina) Sheriff's Department carrying 11-month-old Breanna Chambers to safety in 2005 after the capture of the child's parents. The parents, who were already wanted on charges related to methamphetamine manufacture, were charged with additional counts of child abduction, felonious restraint, and assault with a gun after they abducted Breanna and her two-year-old brother, James Paul Chambers, from a foster home. Today's police officers are expected to enforce the law while meeting the needs of the community. Do those goals conflict? If so, how?

the law unless it involves some form of trespass,[19] is also typically addressed under quality-of-life programs. Through police interviews, many of the homeless are relocated to shelters or hospitals or are arrested for some other offense. Some researchers claim that reducing the number of quality-of-life offenses in a community can restore a sense of order, reduce the fear of crime, and lessen the number of serious crimes that occur. However, quality-of-life programs have been criticized by those who say that the police should not be taking a law enforcement approach to social and economic problems.[20]

A similar approach to keeping the peace can be found in the broken windows model of policing.[21] This thesis (which is also discussed in the "CJ Issues" box in Chapter 3) is based on the notion that physical decay in a community, such as litter and abandoned buildings, can breed disorder and lead to crime by signaling that laws are not being enforced.[22] Such decay, the theory postulates, pushes

> Many police departments focus on quality-of-life offenses as a crime-reduction and peacekeeping strategy.

law-abiding citizens to withdraw from the streets, which then sends a signal that lawbreakers can operate freely.[23] The broken windows theory suggests that by encouraging the repair of run-down buildings and controlling disorderly behavior in public spaces, police agencies can create an environment in which serious crime cannot easily flourish.[24]

Although desirable, public order has its own costs. Noted police author Charles R. Swanson says, "The degree to which any society achieves some amount of public order through police action depends in part upon the price that society is willing to pay to obtain it."[25] Swanson goes on to describe the price to be paid in terms of (1) police resources paid for by tax dollars and (2) "a reduction in the number, kinds, and extent of liberties" that are available to members of the public.

> Although desirable, public order has its own costs.

Providing Services

As writers for the National Institute of Justice observe, "any citizen from any city, suburb, or town across the United States can mobilize police resources by simply picking up the phone and placing a direct call to the police."[26] "Calling the cops" has been described as the cornerstone of policing in a democratic society. About 70% of the millions of daily calls to 9-1-1 systems across the country are directed to the police, although callers can also request emergency medical and fire services.

Calls received by 9-1-1 operators are prioritized and then relayed to patrol officers, specialized field units, or other emergency personnel. An online service, **http://crimereports.com,** provides a map overlaid with crime-related incidents and calls to 9-1-1 dispatchers. You can use it to view incidents in your neighborhood. Some cities have also adopted nonemergency "Citizen Service System" call numbers in addition to 9-1-1. More than a dozen metropolitan areas, including Baltimore, Dallas, Detroit, Las Vegas, New York, and San Jose, now staff 3-1-1 nonemergency systems around the clock. Plans are afoot in some places to adopt the 3-1-1 system statewide. Learn more about a career in policing at **http://discoverpolicing.org.**

Operational Strategies

The police mission offers insight into general law enforcement goals, which help shape the various operational strategies that departments employ.[27] There are five core operational strategies—preventive patrol, routine incident response, emergency response, criminal investigation, and problem solving—and one ancillary operational strategy—support services.[28] The first four core strategies constitute the conventional way in which police have worked, at least since the 1930s; problem solving is relatively new. Each strategy has unique features, and each represents a particular way to approach situations that the police encounter.

■ **lecture note**   Review the research into the effectiveness of preventive patrol discussed in Chapter 5 and ask students why the police continue to engage in patrol despite the research results.

■ **response time**   A measure of the time that it takes for police officers to respond to calls for service.

■ **lecture note**   Discuss the research into the relationship between police response time and the likelihood of arresting a suspect (discussed in Chapter 5) and ask students why so much importance is placed on response time given the research findings.

Preventive Patrol

Preventive patrol, the dominant operational policing strategy,[29] has been the backbone of police work since the time of Sir Robert Peel. Routine patrol activities, which place uniformed police officers on the street in the midst of the public, consume most of the resources of local and state-level police agencies.

The purpose of patrol is fourfold: to deter crimes, to interrupt crimes in progress, to position officers for quick response to emergency situations, and to increase the public's feelings of safety and security. Patrol is the operational mode uniformed officers are expected to work in when not otherwise involved in answering calls for service. Most departments use a computer-aided dispatch (CAD) system to prioritize incoming service calls into different categories and to record dispatches issued, time spent on each call, the identities of responding personnel, and so on.

> The majority of police patrol activity is *interactive* because officers on patrol commonly interact with the public.

The majority of patrol activity is *interactive* because officers on patrol commonly interact with the public. Some forms of patrol, however, involve more interaction than others. The many types of patrol include foot, automobile, motorcycle, mounted, bicycle, boat, K-9, and aerial. Although some scientific studies of policing have questioned the effectiveness of preventive patrol in reducing crime (discussed in Chapter 5), most citizens expect police to patrol.

An NYPD station in Times Square. The provision of services is an important part of police work. What kinds of services do police departments provide?

Routine Incident Response

Police officers on patrol frequently respond to routine incidents, such as minor traffic accidents. Routine incident responses comprise the second most common activity of patrol officers.[30] Officers responding to routine incidents must collect information and typically file a written report. As noted by the National Institute of Justice, "the specific police objective will . . . vary depending on the nature of the situation, but generally, the objective is to restore order, document information or otherwise provide some immediate service to the parties involved."[31]

One important measure of police success that is strongly linked to citizen satisfaction is **response time**—the time it takes for police officers to respond to calls for service. It is measured from the time a call for service is received by a dispatcher until an officer arrives on the scene. During the first four months of the 2007 fiscal year, for example, police response times in New York City to crimes in progress averaged 7 minutes and 6 seconds—24 seconds better than the same period in the previous year. The average time required for an NYPD officer to arrive on the scene when responding to an incident rated by dispatchers as "critical" was 4.3 minutes. Response times to both critical incidents and crimes in progress in New York City in 2007 were the quickest times recorded in the city in more than a decade.[32]

Emergency Response

In May 2003, Pomona, California, police officers on routine patrol responded to a dispatcher's instructions to assist in an emergency at a local coin-operated laundry.[33] On arrival, they found a two-year-old girl trapped inside an industrial-size washing machine. The officers used their batons to smash the locked glass-paned door. The girl, unconscious and nearly drowned when pulled from the machine, was taken to a local hospital where she was expected to recover. Her mother, 35-year-old Erma Osborne, was arrested at the scene and charged with child endangerment when the onsite video surveillance cameras showed her placing her daughter in the machine and shutting the door.

Although police respond to emergencies far less frequently than to routine incidents,[34] emergency response is a vital aspect of what police agencies do. Emergency responses, often referred to as *critical incidents*, are used for crimes in progress, traffic accidents with serious injuries, natural disasters, incidents of terrorism, officer requests for assistance, and other

Courtesy of the Justice Research Association

■ **lecture note**   Point out to students that, unlike their television counterparts, crime scene investigators generally focus on gathering evidence at a
crime scene and analyzing that evidence in the lab (rather than on conducting follow-up investigations and arresting suspects) Explain that many crime
scene investigators are not police officers but civilians with scientific backgrounds and special training.

■ **criminal investigation**   "The process of discovering,
collecting, preparing, identifying, and presenting evidence to
determine *what happened and who is responsible*"[1] when a crime has
occurred.

■ **crime scene**   The physical area in which a crime is
thought to have occurred and in which evidence of the crime is
thought to reside.

■ **preliminary investigation**   All of the activities undertaken by a police officer who responds to the scene of a crime,
including determining whether a crime has occurred, securing
the crime scene, and preserving evidence.

■ **crime scene investigator**   An expert trained in the use
of forensics techniques, such as gathering DNA evidence, collecting fingerprints, photographing the scene, sketching, and
interviewing witnesses.

situations in which human life may be in jeopardy. Emergency
responses take priority over all other police work, and until
an emergency situation is secured and some order restored,
the officers involved will not turn to other tasks. An important part of police training involves emergency response techniques, including first aid, hostage rescue, and the physical
capture of suspects.

Criminal Investigation

Another operational strategy, criminal investigation, dominates
media depictions of police work. Although central to the mission of the police, investigations actually constitute a relatively
small proportion of police work. A **criminal investigation** is
"the process of discovering, collecting, preparing, identifying,
and presenting evidence to determine *what happened and who is
responsible*"[35] when a crime occurs.

Criminal investigators are often referred to as *detectives*,
and it is up to them to solve most crimes and to produce
the evidence needed for the successful prosecution of suspects. But any police officer can be involved in the initial
stages of the investigative process, especially those responding to critical incidents. First-on-the-scene officers, or first
responders, can play a critical role in providing emergency
assistance to the injured and in capturing suspects. First responders, however, also have an important responsibility to
secure the crime scene, a duty that can later provide the basis
for a successful criminal investigation. A **crime scene** is the
physical area in which a crime is thought to have occurred
and in which evidence of the crime is thought to reside
(Figure 6-2). Securing the crime scene is particularly crucial,
for when a crime takes place, especially a violent one, confusion often results. People at the scene and curious onlookers
may unwittingly (or sometimes intentionally) destroy physical evidence, obliterating important clues like tire tracks, fingerprints, or footprints.

The preliminary investigation is an important part of the investigatory process. An effective preliminary investigation is the foundation on which the entire criminal investigation process is built.[36]

The Florida Highway Patrol's policy manual provides a broad definition of a **preliminary investigation**, saying that it refers to all
of the activities undertaken by a police officer who responds to the
scene of a crime.[37] Those activities include the following:

1. Responding to immediate needs and rendering aid to
   the injured
2. Noting such facts as the position of victims or injured
   subjects, recording spontaneous statements, noting unusual actions or activities, and notifying headquarters
   with an assessment of the scene
3. Determining that a crime has been committed
4. Initiating enforcement action, such as arresting or
   pursuing the offender or dispatching apprehension
   information
5. Securing the crime scene and protecting evidence, including limiting access, identifying and isolating witnesses, and protecting all evidence, especially short-lived
   evidence (such as impressions in sand or mud)
6. Determining the need for investigative specialists and ar-
   ranging for their notification
7. Compiling a thorough and accurate report of activities

A preliminary investigation begins when the call to respond has been received. Even before they arrive at the crime
scene, officers may observe important events related to the offense, such as fleeing vehicles or the presence of suspicious
people nearby. After they arrive, first responders begin collecting information through observation and possibly through
conversations with others who are already at the scene.
Typically, it is at this point that officers determine whether
there are sufficient grounds to believe that a crime has actually occurred. Even in suspected homicides, for example, it is
important to rule out accidental death, suicide, and death by
natural causes before the investigation can proceed beyond the
preliminary stage.

Next, specially trained crime scene investigators arrive, and
the detailed examination of a crime scene begins. **Crime scene
investigators** are expert in the use of specific forensics techniques, such as gathering DNA evidence, collecting fingerprints,

■ **solvability factor**   Information about a crime that forms the basis for determining the perpetrator's identity.

Note: This diagram pertains to crime scene analysis, although a wider investigation will include identifying the victim, interviews with significant others in her life, and an examination of her background, recent activities, and lifestyle. The area surrounding the swimming pool, to include the house and the electronic devices it contains, will also be searched for possible evidence, as will the victim's vehicle if she has one. The crime scene will be photographed and videos recordings will be made.

Computer forensic experts will examine the laptop found at the scene for possible digital evidence—including texts or e-mail communications, especially those involving recent conversations. Ownership of the laptop will be established, and any GPS information will be collected showing where the computer might have been recently used. A record of Internet connections will be logged, and social media applications and other communications software will be evaluated for possible recent use.

A medical examination by a pathologist or medical examiner will be ordered to determine the cause of death and to identify any injuries to (or marks on) the body. The pathologist will analyze the person's blood for the presence of prescription drugs, illegal substances, and alcohol. Evidence of any possible sexual activity will be recorded. Should the death be ruled a homicide, the evidence gathered in the other steps shown in this box will become relevant.

Persons living nearby or who were in the area at the time of the incident will be contacted and asked if they heard or saw anything of relevance to the investigation.

Pool water and pool equipment will be examined to see if they might have contributed to death (i.e., electrical shock, hair caught in drain, etc.).

The victim's clothing will be examined for possible trace evidence. Pocket contents, rents, and tears will be noted. Fingernails will be examined for any forensic DNA evidence resulting from a possible physical struggle.

The body of a young woman was found floating in a home swimming pool by neighbors who called 911; they also reported hearing screams and calls for help. First responders determined that the woman was dead, and crime scene investigators were called to examine and collect evidence to determine whether the death was an accident, a suicide, or a homicide. Although foul play was suspected, the investigators noted the absence of blood in the pool, and they considered that the woman could have been killed elsewhere and her body later dumped into the swimming pool.

The wine bottle and wine glass will be examined for fingerprints and for DNA traces—whether that of the victim or any possible perpetrators. Remnants of any toxic or other substances that might have been added to the wine will be identified.

The handgun found at the scene will be examined by ballistics experts to determine whether it has been fired recently, and the area will be searched for spent shell casings. Fingerprints might also be found on the weapon, and ownership of the pistol will be established.

FIGURE 6-2 | The Crime Scene Investigation Process
Source: Pearson Education, Inc.

photographing the scene, making sketches to show the position of items at the scene, and interviewing witnesses.

Crime scene investigators are commonly promoted to their posts internally after at least a few years of patrol work. However, large local police departments and those at the state and federal levels may employ civilian crime scene investigators. Follow-up investigations, based on evidence collected at the scene, are conducted by police detectives. Important to any investigation are solvability factors. A **solvability factor** is information about a crime that can provide a basis for determining the perpetrator's

■ **lecture note** Explain problem solving in policing and present an example of a problem that was solved using SARA (or CAPRA). Information on a wide variety of police problem-solving efforts may be found at the website for the Center for Problem-Oriented Policing (www.popcenter.org).

■ **theme** Why are many support services personnel civilians rather than sworn police officers?

■ **lecture note** Discuss contemporary police management by focusing on the chain of command and on the distinction between line operations and staff operations.

■ **police management** The administrative activities of controlling, directing, and coordinating police personnel, resources, and activities in the service of preventing crime, apprehending criminals, recovering stolen property, and performing regulatory and helping services.[ii]

■ **line operations** In police organizations, the field activities or supervisory activities directly related to day-to-day police work.

■ **staff operations** In police organizations, activities (such as administration and training) that provide support for line operations.

identity. If few solvability factors exist, a continuing investigation is unlikely to lead to an arrest.

Problem Solving

Another operational strategy of police work is problem solving. Also called *problem-oriented policing*, problem solving seeks to reduce chronic offending in a community. NIJ authors note that "historically, [this operational strategy] is the least well-developed by the police profession. While the police have

Problem-oriented policing seeks to reduce chronic offending in a community.

always used the mental processes of problem solving, problem solving as a formal operational strategy of police work has gained some structure and systematic attention only in the past 20 years."[38]

The methodology of police problem solving is known by acronyms such as SARA (scanning, analysis, response, and assessment) or CAPRA (clients, acquired/analyzed, partnerships, respond, assess). CAPRA was developed by the Royal Canadian Mounted Police, who built on the earlier SARA process. This is the CAPRA process:[39]

- The police begin by communicating with the *clients* most affected by community problems.
- Information is *acquired* and *analyzed* to determine the problem's causes.
- Solutions are developed through community *partnerships*.
- The police *respond* with a workable plan.
- After plan implementation, the police periodically *assess* the situation to ensure progress.

Support Services

Support services constitute the final operational strategy found in police organizations. They include such activities as dispatch, training, human resources management, property and evidence control, and record keeping. Support services keep police agencies running and help deliver the equipment, money, and resources necessary to support law enforcement officers in the field.

Managing Police Departments

Police management entails administrative activities that control, direct, and coordinate police personnel, resources, and activities in an effort to prevent crime, apprehend criminals, recover stolen property, and perform a variety of regulatory and helping services.[40] Police managers include sworn law enforcement personnel with administrative authority, from the rank of sergeant to captain, chief, or sheriff, and civilians like police commissioners, attorneys general, state secretaries of crime control, and public-safety directors.

Police Organization and Structure

Almost all American law enforcement organizations are formally structured among divisions and along lines of authority. Roles within police agencies generally fall into one of two categories: line and staff. **Line operations** are field or supervisory activities directly related to daily police work. **Staff operations** include support roles, such as administration. In organizations that have line operations only, authority flows from the top down in a clear, unbroken line;[41] no supporting elements (media relations, training, fiscal management divisions, and so on) exist. All line operations are directly involved in providing field services. Because almost all police agencies need support, only the smallest departments have just line operations.

Most police organizations include both line and staff operations. In such organizations, line managers are largely unencumbered with staff operations like budgeting, training, the scientific analysis of evidence, legal advice, shift assignments, and personnel management. Support personnel handle these activities, freeing line personnel to focus on the day-to-day requirements of providing field services.

In a line and staff agency, divisions are likely to exist within both line operations and staff operations. For example, field services, a line operation, may be broken down into enforcement and investigation. Administrative services, a staff operation, may be divided into human resources management, training and

paying for it

Policing in an Economic Downturn

© Tom Grill/Corbis

First responders. In some cities, public-safety officers are cross-trained as police officers, firefighters, and in emergency medical services. What advantages accrue to communities who cross-train their first responders?

In 2013, the Police Executive Research Forum (PERF) released a report entitled *Policing and the Economic Downturn*. The subtitle of the publication was "Striving for Efficiency Is the New Normal." The 50-page document was based on a series of four surveys that PERF bogan sending to police administrators across the nation in 2008 asking about their department's economic situation. In the words of the report, "The first three surveys produced findings that could be summarized as 'grim', meaning that almost all agencies reported facing budget cutbacks and were making plans to reduce services or layoff officers."

PERF found that during the depths of the economic crisis around 2008, 32% of agencies had eliminated recruitment of new officers, while 72% reported a reduction in the amount of money being spent on training. Similarly, 67% of agencies had eliminated pay raises, and 58% of departments were implementing plans to decease services. Thirty-one percent of agencies that responded to the survey also said that response time to citizens' request for services had increased, or would likely increase due to budget cuts. Although not all agencies reported laying off officers, 45% reported hiring freezes. Finally, slightly more than half of all agencies responding to the early PERF surveys reported eliminating plans to acquire new technology.

Police departments have also been restructured in the face of budget cutbacks. Almost half of all departments reported discontinuing or significantly reducing specialty units such as bike patrols, and 22% said that they had consolidated some services with other departments. Many law enforcement agencies also said that they had shifted more officers into the field by staffing some internal positions, such as dispatch, crime analysis, and desk work, with civilian employees and volunteers. Finally, 34% of agencies said that patrol levels, meaning the number of officers assigned to an area at any given time, or the number of hours that an area was patrolled, had been lowered.

Since those initial surveys, however, trends in police funding have improved, with some departments reporting stable or increased monetary inflows. Today, only half as many agencies have cut back on recruiting efforts than those responding to earlier surveys, and agencies today are making fewer cuts to training. Almost half are instituting pay increases for their officers.

Many departments now report paying their officers overtime, rather than expanding the number of full-time officers on their payrolls. Funding overtime hours can be less expensive in the long run than hiring more full-time officers whose employment benefits, including health insurance and retirement expenses, can add substantially to an agency's costs.

One good thing that appears to have resulted from police budget cuts over the past six or more years has been increased efficiency in many areas of law enforcement. Some have used the term "smart policing" to describe the shift in attitude that came about as a result of the economic squeeze that law enforcement administrators have been facing.

According to the Smart Policing Initiative (SPI), the goal of smart policing is to "develop tactics and strategies that are effective, efficient and economical—as measured by reduced crime and high case closure rates." (SPI is discussed and defined in a "Paying for It" box in Chapter 5.)

SPI, which is a collaborative effort between the Bureau of Justice Assistance, the nonprofit CNA Corporation, and dozens of police departments, says that "effective policing requires a tightly focused, collaborative approach that is measurable; based on sound, detailed analysis; and includes policies and procedures that promote and support accountability."

One form of smart policing is being used in Sunnyvale, California, a city of around 140,000. There, police officers and firefighters are cross-trained so that, in a pinch, they can fill in for one another. In 2012, for example, the city was able to call upon firefighters who were finishing their shifts to switch into police uniforms and help canvas an area of the city looking for a man who had killed three people in a workplace shooting. Studies show that, because of cross-training, Sunnyvale is able to spend less on public safety than do surrounding communities—$519 per capita, versus $950 in Palo Alto and $683 in Mountain View (California).

Another form of smart policing was initiated two years ago in the Los Angeles Police Department (LAPD), where computer models alert officers to crimes that are likely to happen, and tell dispatchers to send officers to likely crime scenes. The program, called "predictive policing" by the LAPD, identifies potential "hot spots" of crime (sometimes as small as a 500-square-foot "zone") and makes predictions about the likelihood of future crime occurrences in those locations. Officers who are on patrol are then directed to "go in the box." Both hot-spot and predictive policing are discussed an defined in Chapter 5.

Unless municipalities can implement effective smart policing strategies, however, saving money on policing might not be such a good idea. In 2012, researchers at the University of California at Berkeley who studied crime in medium to large U.S. cities between 1960 and 2010 found that "each dollar spent on police is associated with approximately $1.60 in reduced victimization costs, suggesting that U.S. cities employ too few police."

Learn more about smart policing from the SPI website at http://www.smartpolicinginitiative.com.

Resources: Police Executive Research Forum, *Policing and the Economic Downturn: Striving for Efficiency Is the New Normal* (Washington, DC: PERF, February 2013); Aaron Chalfin and Justin McCrary, "The Effect of Police on Crime: New Evidence from U.S. Cities, 1960–2010," unpublished manuscript (University of California at Berkeley, November 8, 2012); Greg Risling, "Sci-Fi Policing: Predicting Crime before It Occurs," Associated Press, July 2, 2012, http://news.yahoo.com/sci-fi-policing-predicting-crime-occurs-150157831.html (accessed July 1, 2013); Lee Romney, "Cross-Training of Public Safety Workers Attracting More Interest," *The Los Angeles Times*, January 1, 2013, http://articles.latimes.com/2013/jan/01/local/la-me-sunnyvale-20130101 (accessed August 1, 2013); Paul Heaton, *Hidden in Plain Sight: What Cost-of-Crime Research Can Tell Us about Investing in Police* (RAND Center on Quality Policing, 2010), http://www.rand.org/content/dam/rand/pubs/occasional_papers/2010/RAND_OP279.pdf (accessed May 5, 2013); and Smart Policing Initiative, "Background," http://www.smartpolicinginitiative.com/background (accessed May 2, 2013).

■ **chain of command** The unbroken line of authority that extends through all levels of an organization, from the highest to the lowest.

■ **span of control** The number of police personnel or the number of units supervised by a particular commander.

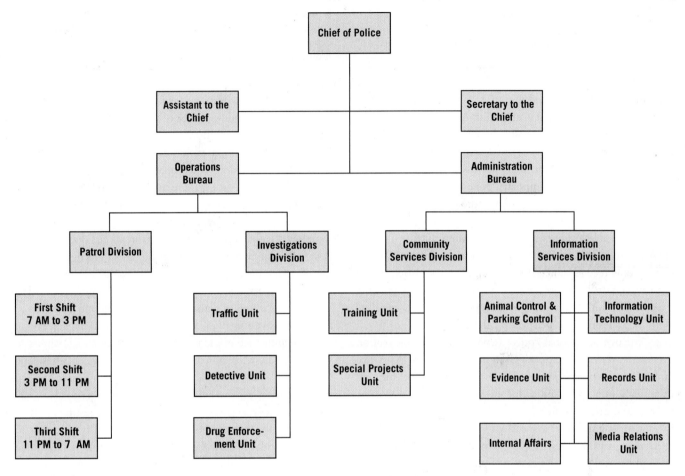

FIGURE 6-3 | Typical Organizational Chart of a Local Police Department

education, materials supply, finance management, and facilities management. The line and staff structure easily accommodates functional areas of responsibility within line and staff divisions. A typical organizational chart of a local police department is shown in Figure 6-3.[42]

Chain of Command

The organizational chart of any police agency shows a hierarchical **chain of command**, or the order of authority within the department. The chain of command clarifies who reports to whom. Usually, the chief of police or sheriff is at the top of the command chain—although his or her boss may be a police commissioner, city council, or mayor—followed by the subordinate leaders of each division.

Because law enforcement agencies employ a quasi-military chain-of-command structure, the titles assigned to personnel (captain, lieutenant, sergeant) are similar to those used by the military. It is important for individual personnel to know who is in charge; hence unity of command is an important principle

that must be firmly established within the department. When unity of command exists, every individual has only one supervisor to answer to and, under normal circumstances, to take orders from. **Span of control** refers to the number of police personnel or the number of units supervised by a particular commander. For example, one sergeant may be in charge of five or six officers; they represent the sergeant's span of control.

Policing Styles

The history of American policing can be divided into four epochs,[43] each distinguishable by the relative dominance of a particular approach to police operations (Figure 6-4). The first period, the political era, was characterized by close ties between police and public officials. It began in the 1840s and ended around 1930. Throughout the period, American police agencies tended to serve the interests of powerful politicians and their cronies, providing public-order-maintenance services almost as an afterthought. The second period, the reform era,

■ **lecture note**   Describe the watchman style of policing as one in which officers are concerned primarily with order maintenance in the communities they police. Ask students what the watchman style would mean within the context of their home communities.

■ **lecture note**   Describe the legalistic style of policing as one in which officers adhere to the letter of the law in making enforcement decisions. Ask students what the legalistic style would mean within the context of their home communities.

■ **watchman style**   A style of policing marked by a concern for order maintenance. Watchman policing is characteristic of lower-class communities where police intervene informally into the lives of residents to keep the peace.

■ **legalistic style**   A style of policing marked by a strict concern with enforcing the precise letter of the law. Legalistic departments may take a hands-off approach to disruptive or problematic behavior that does not violate the criminal law.

began in the 1930s and lasted until the 1970s. It was characterized by pride in professional crime fighting. Police departments during this period focused most of their resources on solving "traditional" crimes, such as murder, rape, and burglary, and on capturing offenders. The third period, which continues to characterize much of contemporary policing in America today, is the community policing era—an approach to policing that stresses the service role of police officers and envisions a partnership between police agencies and their communities.

A fourth period, which we call the *new era*, has made its appearance only recently and is still evolving. Some scholars say that the primary feature of this new law enforcement era is policing to secure the homeland, and they have dubbed it the *homeland security era*.[44] From their perspective, the homeland security era has grown out of national concerns with terrorism prevention born of the terrorist attacks of September 11, 2001. As police scholar Gene Stephens explains it, "The twenty-first century has put policing into a whole new milieu—one in which the causes of crime and disorder often lie outside the immediate community, demanding new and innovative approaches."[45] A decline in street crime, says Stephens, has been replaced by concern with new and more insidious types of offending, including terrorism and Internet-assisted crimes. These new kinds of crimes, says Stephens, although they threaten the integrity of local communities, often involve offenders thousands of miles away.

Others, however, see the new era as underpinned by an emphasis on intelligence-led policing (ILP), and they refer to it as the *ILP era*. (ILP is discussed in detail later in this chapter.) Michael Downing, commanding officer of the LAPD's Counter-Terrorism and Special Operations Bureau (CTSOB), for example, says that ILP represents the next evolutionary stage in how law enforcement officers should approach their work. "The necessity to successfully shift into a fifth era, the intelligence-led policing era," says Downing, "with seamless precision has never been more important considering the great threat we face as a nation."[46] The good news, some say, "is that ILP is not only an important strategic tool to thwart Al-Qaeda and other groups but also a practical one geared toward crime control and quality of life issues."[47] Hence the new era, whatever we choose to call it, is still emerging, but it clearly involves efforts to deal with threats to the homeland and to inform those efforts with situational awareness and shared intelligence.

The influence of each of the first three historical phases survives today in what noted social commentator and Presidential Medal of Freedom recipient James Q. Wilson[48] calls "policing styles."[49] A style of policing describes how a particular agency sees its purpose and chooses the methods it uses to fulfill that purpose. Wilson's three policing styles—which he does not link to any particular historical era—are (1) the watchman style (characteristic of the political era), (2) the legalistic style (professional crime fighting of the reform era), and (3) the service style (which is becoming more common today). These three styles characterize nearly all municipal law enforcement agencies now operating in the United States, although some departments are a mixture of two or more styles.

POLITICAL ERA

- Close ties between the police and political officials
- Police were organized in paramilitary style, focused on serving the politically powerful
- Politicians appointed/hired the police

1840s–1930

- Came about because of a need for social order and security in a dynamic and rapidly changing society

REFORM ERA

- Police gained pride in their profession
- Law enforcement focused on "traditional" crime-fighting and the capture of criminals
- Crackdown on organized crime

1930–1970s

- Progressive policing policy led by August Vollmer and O.W. Wilson
- Came about because citizens called for reform and the removal of politics from policing

FIGURE 6-4 | Historical Eras in American Policing
Source: Pearson Education, Inc.

■ **lecture note**   Describe the service style of policing as one in which officers strive to meet the needs of the citizens they serve. Ask students what the service style would mean within the context of their home communities.

■ **theme**   What happens when police administrators try to combine an order-maintenance (watchman style) orientation with a service mandate? What are the difficulties? How might differences be resolved?

■ **theme**   What are the differences between the original concept of police–community relations and the more contemporary notion of community policing? Which of these ideas do you think would appeal more to individual-rights advocates? To public-order advocates? Why?

■ **lecture note**   Describe community policing as an effort to involve the community in solving the problems faced by the police, and vice versa. Explain community policing as an ideational approach to policing that envisions the police and members of the community as sharing responsibility for the solution of problems within the community.

■ **service style**   A style of policing marked by a concern with helping rather than strict enforcement. Service-oriented police agencies are more likely to use community resources, such as drug-treatment programs, to supplement traditional law enforcement activities than are other types of agencies.

The Watchman Style of Policing

Police departments marked by the **watchman style** are chiefly concerned with achieving what Wilson calls "order maintenance" through control of illegal and disruptive behavior. Compared to the legalistic style, the watchman style uses discretion liberally. Watchman-style departments keep order through informal police "intervention," which may include persuasion, threats, or even "roughing up" disruptive people. Some authors condemn this style of policing, suggesting that it is typically found in lower- or lower-middle-class communities, especially where interpersonal relations include a fair amount of violence or physical abuse.

The watchman style was typified by the Los Angeles police officers who took part in the infamous beating of Rodney King in 1992. After the ensuing riots, the Christopher Commission, the independent commission on the LAPD, found that the Los Angeles police "placed greater emphasis on crime control over crime prevention, a policy that distanced cops from the people they serve."[50]

The Legalistic Style of Policing

Departments operating under the **legalistic style** enforce the letter of the law. For example, an officer who tickets a person going 71 miles per hour in a 70-mph speed zone is likely a member of a department that adheres to the legalistic style of policing. Conversely, legalistic departments routinely avoid community disputes arising from violations of social norms that do not break the law. Police expert Gary Sykes calls this enforcement style "laissez-faire policing" in recognition of its hands-off approach to behaviors that are simply bothersome or inconsiderate of community principles.[51]

The Service Style of Policing

In service-oriented departments, which strive to meet the needs of the community and serve its members, the police see themselves more as helpers than as soldiers in a war on crime. This type of department works with social services and other agencies to provide counseling for minor offenders and to assist community groups in preventing crimes and solving problems. Prosecutors may support the **service style** by agreeing not to prosecute law violators who seek psychiatric help or who voluntarily participate in programs like Alcoholics Anonymous, family counseling, or drug treatment. The service style is supported in part by citizens who seek to avoid the embarrassment that might result from a public airing of personal problems, thereby reducing the number of criminal complaints filed, especially in minor disputes. Although the service style of policing may seem more

COMMUNITY ERA ▶	THE NEW ERA
• Police departments work to identify and serve the needs of their communities • Envisions a partnership between the police and the community	• Policing to secure the homeland; emphasis on terrorism prevention and intelligence-led policing • Recent emphasis on procedural fairness
1970s–Today • Police focus on quality-of-life offenses • Broken windows model of policing • Came about because of a realization that effective community partnerships can help prevent and solve crimes	**2001–Today** • Creation of counterterrorism divisions and offices within police departments and the development of actionable intelligence • Came about because of the terrorist attacks of September 11, 2001, combined with recent claims of "overpolicing" and unnecessary use of force

■ **police–community relations (PCR)**   An area of police activity that recognizes the need for the community and the police to work together effectively. PCR is based on the notion that the police derive their legitimacy from the communities they serve. Many police agencies began to explore PCR in the 1960s and 1970s.

■ **team policing**   The reorganization of conventional patrol strategies into "an integrated and versatile police team assigned to a fixed district."[iii]

■ **strategic policing**   A type of policing that retains the traditional police goal of professional crime fighting but enlarges the enforcement target to include nontraditional kinds of criminals, such as serial offenders, gangs and criminal associations, drug-distribution networks, and sophisticated white-collar and computer criminals. Strategic policing generally makes use of innovative enforcement techniques, including intelligence operations, undercover stings, electronic surveillance, and sophisticated forensic methods.

appropriate to wealthy communities or small towns, it can also exist in cities with police departments that actively seek citizen involvement in identifying issues that the police can help address.

Police–Community Relations

The 1960s were fraught with riots, unrest, and student activism as the war in Vietnam, civil rights concerns, and other social issues produced large demonstrations and marches. The police, generally inexperienced in crowd control, were all too often embroiled in tumultuous encounters—even pitched battles—with citizen groups that viewed the police as agents of "the establishment." To manage these new challenges, the legalistic style of policing, so common in America until then, began to yield to the newer service-oriented policing.

As social disorganization increased, police departments across the nation, seeking to understand and better cope with the problems they faced, created **police–community relations (PCR)** programs. PCR programs represented a movement away from an exclusive emphasis on the apprehension of law violators toward an effort to increase the level of positive police–citizen interaction. At the height of the PCR movement, city police departments across the country opened storefront centers where citizens could air complaints and interact easily with police representatives. As police scholar Egon Bittner recognized in 1976, PCR programs need to reach to "the grassroots of discontent," where citizen dissatisfaction with the police exists,[52] if they are to be truly effective.

In many contemporary PCR programs, public-relations officers are appointed to provide an array of services, such as neighborhood watch programs, drug-awareness workshops, Project ID—using police equipment and expertise to mark valuables for identification in the event of theft—and victims' assistance programs. Modern PCR programs, however, often fail to achieve their goal of increased community satisfaction with police services because they focus on servicing groups already well satisfied with the police. PCR initiatives that do reach disaffected community groups are difficult to manage and may even alienate participating officers from the communities they are assigned to serve. Thus, as Bittner noted, "while the first approach fails because it leaves out those groups to which the program is primarily directed, the second fails because it leaves out the police department."

Team Policing

During the 1960s and 1970s, some communities experimented with **team policing**, which rapidly became an extension of the PCR movement. With team policing, a team of police officers was assigned semipermanently to particular neighborhoods, where it was expected that the officers would become familiar with the inhabitants and with their problems and concerns. Patrol officers were given considerable authority in processing complaints, from receipt through resolution. Crimes were investigated and solved at the local level, with specialists called in only if the resources needed to continue an investigation were not available locally. Some authors called team policing a "technique to deliver total police services to a neighborhood."[53] Others, however, dismissed it as "little more than an attempt to return to the style of policing that was prevalent in the United States over a century ago."[54]

Community Policing

Over the past quarter century, the role of the police in police–community relations has changed considerably. Originally, the PCR model was based on the fact that many police administrators saw police officers as enforcers of the law who were isolated from, and often in opposition to, the communities they policed. As a result, PCR programs were often a shallowly disguised effort to overcome public suspicion and community hostility.

Today, increasing numbers of law enforcement administrators embrace the role of service provider. Modern departments frequently help citizens solve a vast array of personal problems, many of which involve no law-breaking activity. For example, officers regularly aid sick or distraught people, organize community crime-prevention efforts, investigate domestic disputes, regulate traffic, and educate children and teens about drug abuse. Service calls far exceed calls directly related to law violations, and officers make more referrals to agencies like Alcoholics Anonymous, domestic violence centers, and drug-rehabilitation programs than they make arrests.

In contemporary America, some say, police departments function a lot like corporations. According to Harvard University's Executive Session on Policing, three generic kinds of "corporate strategies" guide American policing: (1) strategic policing, (2) problem-solving policing, and (3) community policing.[55]

Strategic policing, something of a holdover from the reform era, "emphasizes an increased capacity to deal with

freedom OR safety? YOU decide

Watch Out: You're on Camera!

In December 2014, in the wake of the shooting of an unarmed black teenager in Ferguson, Missouri, by a white police officer, President Obama asked Congress for $263 million to provide up to 50,000 body cameras for police across the country.

Most law enforcement officials agree that body cameras are the next step in recording technology—supplementing the thousands of patrol car-mounted video cameras currently in use. Recently, for example, all patrol officers in Atlantic City, NJ, were outfitted with body cameras in an effort to make police actions transparent.

Patrol cars equipped with video cameras have been on the nation's highways since the late 1980s, and the footage they've produced has been a staple of real-life police TV shows for years. In 2014, in what many see as a next step, Denver Police Chief Robert White called for equipping all of the city's 800 officers with body cameras, saying that "only bad cops fear wearing body cams." After cameras were introduced in the department in 2012, public complaints against Denver officers fell 88% compared to previous years, and officers' use of force fell by 60%. Also, in 2014, the NYPD announced the start of an "Omnipresence" initiative under which cameras and officers were deployed to high-crime areas throughout the city.

Many people believe that equipping both cars and personnel with continuous recording devices will lead to a reduction in police abuses, while serving to capture evidence of illegal behavior by suspects. Video footage can also be used for identification purposes and might be coupled with software that provides facial and license tag recognition, allowing officers to quickly identify stolen cars and wanted individuals.

Some, however, fear that the combination of video images and recognition software will lead to the creation of a suspect database that will inevitably include many otherwise innocent people and that might be improperly shared with other agencies or the popular media. At the same time, police officials worry that too many cameras may make citizens wary of interacting with officers. Chuck Wexler, executive director of the Police Executive Research Forum, warns that "Body-worn cameras can increase accountability, but police agencies

A Rialto Police Department (California) officer wears a body camera while he confers with another officer. Why do most departments favor the use of such equipment?

also must find a way to preserve the informal and unique relationships between police officers and community members."

Since 2000, the Justice Department's Office of Community Oriented Policing Services has provided $15 million to state law enforcement agencies to equip 3,563 cruisers with cameras. One study by the International Association of Chiefs of Police surveyed 47 state law enforcement agencies that received federal grants to buy in-car cameras and concluded that such cameras substantially improved public trust in the police and protected officers against unfounded lawsuits.

Finally, in 2015, NIJ announced the creation of a body-worn camera page on its website. The page, which is available at **http://www.nij.gov/topics/law-enforcement/technology/Pages/body-worn-cameras.aspx**, also provides a primer on body-worn cameras for law enforcement.

You Decide

Do you think that equipping all of the nation's patrol officers with body cameras is a good idea? What negative impact, if any, might such an initiative have on personal freedoms in our society? How might it affect policing?

References: "Atlantic City Becomes Latest N.J. City to Outfit Officers with Body Cameras," Associated Press, August 24, 2014; International Association of Chiefs of Police, *The Impact of Video Evidence on Modern Policing* (Alexandria, VA: IACP, 2005); Kendall Breitman, "White House Backs Body Cameras for Cops," *Politico*, September 16, 2014; Kevin Johnson, "Police Body Cameras Offer Benefits, Require Training," *USA Today*, September 12, 2014; Mark Landler, "Obama Offers New Standards on Police Gear," *The New York Times*, December 1, 2014, www.nytimes.com/2014/12/02/us/politics/obama-to-toughen-standards-on-police-use-of-military-gear.html (accessed January 30, 2015). and Andres Jaquregul, "Denver Police Chief: Only Bad Cops Fear Wearing Body Cams," *The Huffington Post*, August 28, 2014.

---

crimes that are not well controlled by traditional methods."[56] Strategic policing retains the traditional police goal of professional crime fighting but enlarges the enforcement target to include nontraditional kinds of criminals, such as serial offenders, gangs and criminal associations, drug-distribution networks, and sophisticated white-collar and computer criminals. To meet its goals, strategic policing generally makes use of innovative enforcement techniques, including intelligence operations, undercover stings, electronic surveillance, and sophisticated forensic methods.

■ **problem-solving policing**　A type of policing that assumes that crimes can be controlled by uncovering and effectively addressing the underlying social problems that cause crime. Problem-solving policing makes use of community resources, such as counseling centers, welfare programs, and job-training facilities. It also attempts to involve citizens in crime prevention through education, negotiation, and conflict management.

■ **community policing**　"A collaborative effort between the police and the community that identifies problems of crime and disorder and involves all elements of the community in the search for solutions to these problems."[iv]

Alamy

Charleston police officers comfort mourners gathered outside the Fieldings Funeral home in Charleston, South Carolina, in 2015. Scenes like this help foster the community policing ideal through which law enforcement officers and members of the public become partners in controlling crime and keeping communities safe. How does such a partnership help the police? The community?

The other two strategies give greater recognition to Wilson's service style. **Problem-solving policing** (sometimes called *problem-oriented policing*) takes the view that many crimes are caused by existing social conditions in the communities. To control crime, problem-oriented police managers attempt to uncover and effectively address these underlying social problems. Problem-solving policing makes thorough use of community resources, such as counseling centers, welfare programs, and job-training facilities. It also attempts to involve citizens in crime prevention through education, negotiation, and conflict management. For example, police may ask residents of poorly maintained housing areas to clean up litter, install better lighting, and provide security devices for their houses and apartments in the belief that clean, well-lighted, secure areas are a deterrent to criminal activity.

The third and newest strategy, **community policing** (sometimes called *community-oriented policing*), goes a step beyond the other two. It has been described as "a philosophy based on forging a partnership between the police and the community, so that they can work together on solving problems of crime, [and] fear of crime and disorder, thereby enhancing the overall quality of life in their neighborhoods."[57] This approach addresses the causes of crime to reduce the fear of crime and social disorder through problem-solving strategies and police–community partnerships.

The community policing concept evolved from the early works of police researchers George Kelling and Robert Trojanowicz. Their studies of foot-patrol programs in Newark, New Jersey,[58] and Flint, Michigan,[59] showed that "police could develop more positive attitudes toward community members and could promote positive attitudes toward police if they spent time on foot in their neighborhoods."[60] Trojanowicz's *Community Policing*, published in 1990,[61] may be the definitive work on this topic.

Community policing seeks to actively involve citizens in the task of crime control by creating an effective working partnership between citizens and the police.[62] Under the community policing ideal, the public and the police share responsibility for establishing and maintaining peaceful neighborhoods.[63] As a result, community members participate more fully than ever before in defining the police role. Police expert Jerome Skolnick says that community policing is "grounded on the notion that, together, police and public are more effective and more humane coproducers of safety and public order than are the police alone."[64] According to Skolnick, community policing involves at least one of four elements: (1) community-based crime prevention, (2) the reorientation of patrol activities to emphasize the importance of nonemergency services, (3) increased police accountability to the public, and (4) a decentralization of command, including a greater use of civilians at all levels of police decision making.[65] As one writer explains, "Community policing seeks to integrate what was traditionally seen as the different law enforcement, order maintenance and social service roles of the police. Central to the integration of these roles is a working partnership with the community in determining what neighborhood problems are to be addressed, and how."[66] Table 6-1 highlights the differences between traditional and community policing.

Community policing is a two-way street. It requires not only police awareness of community needs but also both involvement and crime-fighting action on the part of citizens themselves. As Detective Tracie Harrison of the Denver Police Department explains, "When the neighborhood takes stock in their community and they're serious [that] they don't want crime, then you start to see crime go down. . . . They're basically fed up and know the police can't do it alone."[67]

Police departments throughout the country continue to join the community policing bandwagon. A 2001 report by the Bureau of Justice Statistics (BJS) showed that state and local law enforcement agencies across the United States had nearly

■ **activity** Ask the class to describe the city or county police department that serves the community in which the university is located. Do they believe that the department is best characterized by the watchman, legalistic, or service style of policing? Explore the basis for this decision. In a distance learning class, students may describe the department in their individual home communities.

■ **theme** How might community policing alter the police subculture and the types of personalities that characterize it—especially in traditional departments?

TABLE 6-1 | Traditional versus Community Policing

QUESTION	TRADITIONAL POLICING	COMMUNITY POLICING
Who are the police?	The police are a government agency principally responsible for law enforcement.	The police are the public, and the public are the police. Police officers are paid to give full-time attention to the duties of every citizen.
What is the relationship of the police force to other public-service departments?	Priorities often conflict.	The police are one department among many responsible for improving the quality of life.
What is the role of the police?	To solve crimes.	To solve problems.
How is police efficiency measured?	By detection and arrest rates	By the absence of crime and disorder.
What are the highest priorities?	Crimes that are high value (e.g., bank robberies) and those involving violence.	Whatever problems disturb the community most.
What do police deal with?	Incidents.	Citizens' problems and concerns.
What determines the effectiveness of police?	Response times.	Public cooperation.
What view do police take of service calls?	They deal with them only if there is no "real" police work to do.	They view them as a vital function and a great opportunity.
What is police professionalism?	Providing a swift, effective response to serious crime.	Keeping close to the community.
What kind of intelligence is most important?	Crime intelligence (study of particular crimes or series of crimes).	Criminal intelligence (information about the activities of individuals or groups).
What is the essential nature of police accountability?	Highly centralized; governed by rules, regulations, and policy directives; accountable to the law.	Local accountability to community needs.
What is the role of headquarters?	To provide the necessary rules and policy directives.	To preach organizational values.
What is the role of the press liaison department?	To keep the "heat" off operational officers so they can get on with the job.	To coordinate an essential channel of communication with the community.
How do the police regard prosecutions?	As an important goal.	As one tool among many.

Source: Malcolm K. Sparrow, *Implementing Community Policing* (Washington, DC: National Institute of Justice, 1988), pp. 8–9.

113,000 full-time sworn personnel regularly engaged in community policing activities.[68] The BJS noted that only about 21,000 officers would have been so categorized in 1997. At the time of the report, 64% of local police departments serving 86% of all residents had full-time officers engaged in some form of community policing activity, compared to 34% of departments serving 62% of all residents in 1997.

The Chicago Police Department launched its comprehensive community policing program, called Chicago's Alternative Policing Strategy (CAPS), in 1993. The development of a strategic plan for "reinventing the Chicago Police Department," from which CAPS evolved, included significant contributions by Mayor Richard M. Daley, who noted that community policing "means doing more than responding to calls for service and solving crimes. It means transforming the Department to support a new, proactive approach to preventing crimes before they

occur. It means forging new partnerships among residents, business owners, community leaders, the police, and City services to solve long-range community problems."[69] Today, CAPS functions on a department-wide basis throughout the city. A review of Chicago's experience with community policing is available at **http://www.justicestudies.com/pubs/cpic.pdf**.

Although community policing efforts began in metropolitan areas, the community engagement and problem-solving spirit of these programs has spread to rural regions. Sheriff's departments operating community policing programs sometimes refer to them as "neighborhood-oriented policing" in recognition of the decentralized nature of rural communities. A Bureau of Justice Assistance (BJA) report on neighborhood-oriented policing notes that "the stereotypical view is that police officers in rural areas naturally work more closely with the public than do officers in metropolitan areas."[70] This view, warns the BJA,

■ **theme**   How might community policing help combat police corruption as well as crime?

may not be entirely accurate, and rural departments would do well "to recognize that considerable diversity exists among rural communities and rural law enforcement agencies."

Hence, as in metropolitan areas, effective community policing requires the involvement of all members of the community in identifying and solving problems.

Title I of the Violent Crime Control and Law Enforcement Act of 1994, known as the Public Safety Partnership and Community Policing Act of 1994, highlighted community policing's role in combating crime and funded (among other things) "increas[ing] the number of law enforcement officers involved in activities that are focused on interaction with members of the community on proactive crime control and prevention by redeploying officers to such activities." The avowed purposes of the Community Policing Act were to (1) substantially increase the number of law enforcement officers interacting directly with the public (through a program known as Cops on the Beat); (2) provide additional and more effective training to law enforcement officers to enhance their problem-solving, service, and other skills needed in interacting with community members; (3) encourage development and implementation of innovative programs to permit community members to assist local law enforcement agencies in the prevention of crime; and (4) encourage development of new technologies to assist local law enforcement agencies in reorienting their emphasis from reacting to crime to preventing crime.

In response to the 1994 law, the U.S. Department of Justice created the Office of Community Oriented Policing Services (COPS). The COPS Office administered the funds necessary to add 100,000 community policing officers to our nation's streets—the number originally targeted by law. In 1999, the Department of Justice and COPS reached an important milestone by funding the 100,000th officer ahead of schedule and under budget. Although the Community Policing Act originally provided COPS funding only through 2000, Congress has continued to fund COPS[71] In 2002, the COPS Office adopted the theme, "Homeland Security through Community Policing," which emphasizes the local police officer's crucial role in gathering information on terrorist suspects—a topic that is discussed later in this chapter. For fiscal year 2012, the federal budget included $200 million in COPS Office funding. The majority of the money was used to make grants to local police departments to hire full-time sworn officers, or to rehire officers who had been laid off. The 2012 expenditures extended hiring preferences to military veterans returning from the Gulf.[72] The federal COPS Office can be found at **http://www.cops.usdoj.gov**.

Critique of Community Policing

As some authors have noted, "Community policing has become the dominant theme of contemporary police reform in America,"[73] yet problems have plagued the movement since its inception.[74] For one thing, the range, complexity, and evolving nature of community policing programs make their effectiveness difficult to measure.[75] Moreover, "citizen satisfaction" with police performance can be difficult to conceptualize and quantify. Most early studies examined citizens' attitudes developed through face-to-face interaction with individual police officers. They generally found a far higher level of dissatisfaction with the police among African Americans than among most other groups. Recent findings continue to show that the attitudes of African Americans toward the police remain poor. The wider reach of these studies, however, led evaluators to discover that this dissatisfaction may be rooted in overall quality of life and type of neighborhood.[76] Because, on average, African Americans continue to experience a lower quality of life than most other U.S. citizens, and because they often live in neighborhoods characterized by economic problems, drug trafficking, and street crime, recent studies conclude that it is these conditions of life, rather than race, that are most predictive of citizen dissatisfaction with the police.

> Recent findings continue to show that the attitudes of African Americans toward the police remain poor.

Those who study community policing have often been stymied by ambiguity surrounding the concept of community.[77] Sociologists, who sometimes define a community as "any area in which members of a common culture share common interests,"[78] tend to deny that a community needs to be limited geographically. Police departments, on the other hand, tend to define communities "within jurisdictional, district or precinct lines, or within the confines of public or private housing developments."[79] Robert Trojanowicz and Mark Moore caution police planners that "the impact of mass transit, mass communications and mass media have widened the rift between a sense of community based on geography and one [based] on interest."[80]

Researchers who follow the police definition of *community* recognize that there may be little consensus within and between members of a local community about community problems and appropriate solutions. Robert Bohm and colleagues at the University of Central Florida have found, for example, that although there may be some "consensus about social problems and their solutions . . . the consensus

> Many citizens are not ready to accept a greater involvement of the police in their personal lives.

■ **lecture note**   Explore the idea of police agencies as businesses to which general management principles can apply.

■ **activity**   Invite a local police chief to speak to the class. Have students prepare and ask questions that will allow the class to later discuss the style of policing that is most characteristic of this department. Ask the chief how policing styles have changed, if at all, over the course of his or her career.

Chuck Eckert/Alamy

Chicago bike patrol officers talking with one another. The community policing concept requires that officers become an integral part of the communities they serve. How can community policing help to both prevent and solve crimes?

may not be community-wide." It may, in fact, exist only among "a relatively small group of 'active' stakeholders who differ significantly about the seriousness of most of the problems and the utility of some solutions."[81]

Finally, there is continuing evidence that not all police officers or managers are willing to accept nontraditional images of police work. One reason is that the goals of community policing often conflict with standard police performance criteria (such as arrests), leading to a perception among officers that community policing is inefficient at best and, at worst, a waste of time.[82] Similarly, many officers are loathe to take on new responsibilities as service providers whose role is more defined by community needs and less by strict interpretation of the law.

Some authors have warned that police subculture is so committed to a traditional view of police work, which is focused almost exclusively on crime fighting, that efforts to promote community policing can demoralize an entire department, rendering it ineffective at its basic tasks.[83] As the Christopher Commission found following the Rodney King riots, "Too many . . . patrol officers view citizens with resentment and hostility; too many treat the public with rudeness and disrespect."[84] Some analysts warn that only when the formal values espoused by today's innovative police administrators begin to match those of rank-and-file officers can any police agency begin to perform well in terms of the goals espoused by community policing reformers.[85]

Some public officials, too, are unwilling to accept community policing. Fifteen years ago, for example, New York City Mayor Rudolph W. Giuliani criticized the police department's Community Police Officer Program, saying that it "has resulted in officers doing too much social work and making too few arrests."[86] Similarly, many citizens are not ready to accept a greater involvement of the police in their personal lives. Although the turbulent, protest-prone years of the 1960s and early 1970s are long gone, some groups remain suspicious of the police. No matter how inclusive community policing programs become, it is doubtful that the gap between the police and the public will ever be entirely bridged. The police role of restraining behavior that violates the law will always produce friction between police departments and some segments of the community.

Terrorism's Impact on Policing

The terrorist attacks of September 11, 2001, have had a significant impact on policing in the United States. Although the core mission of American police departments has not changed, law enforcement agencies at all levels now devote an increased amount of time and resources to preparing for possible terrorist attacks and gathering the intelligence necessary to thwart them.

CJ | ISSUES
The Use of Social Media in Policing

Following the murder of two uniformed NYPD officers in their patrol car in 2014, it became clear that law enforcement agencies could make better use of social media. The gunman, Ismaaiyl Brinsley, had posted antipolice threats on Instagram before the execution-style murder took place, and his posts included an image of the handgun used in the attacks. Experts said that data analytics and data mining software, had they been in use, might have prevented the tragedy (or at least alerted officers to the threat).

That's not to say that law enforcement agencies are strangers to social media. In fact, many departments use it, but most are playing a game of "catch up," in which they are still learning how to use social networking sites to their advantage. Catching up is important, say experts, because social networking has become one of the primary forms of communication in our society.

In the fall of 2014, the International Association of Chiefs of Police (IACP) conducted its fifth annual survey on the use of social media by law enforcement agencies. A total of 600 agencies in 46 states responded to the survey. Included among the agencies were municipal police departments, sheriff's departments, state law enforcement agencies, school police units, and university law enforcement agencies.

The IACP survey found that 95% of surveyed agencies used social media for a variety of purposes, with the most common use being for criminal investigations (82% of agencies responding). Facebook (at 95%),

Twitter (66%), and YouTube (38%) were the most widely used social media (Figure 6-5). About 80% of police departments surveyed said that the use of social media has helped solve crimes in their jurisdiction, and 78% noted that the use of social media has improved police–community relations in their jurisdictions. The survey showed that most police agencies began using social media around 2012–2013, although departments without social media capabilities continue to join the networking bandwagon.

Many police departments responding to the survey reported using social media for purposes such as information dissemination, community outreach, public relations, and emergency/disaster notifications, but more than half reported using online tools for investigative purposes (Figure 6-6). Of those, 79% said that the use of social media helped solve crimes in their jurisdictions.

Social media sites contain huge amounts of information. Sorting through all of that information and analyzing it to produce actionable intelligence is a difficult job, but it is made easier by tools like LEEDIR (the Large Emergency Event Digital Information Repository), which pairs software apps with cloud storage to help investigators use their devices to identify items and persons of interest. Similarly, the nationwide online Law Enforcement Notification System (LENS) allows officers who log in to the system to query huge crime databases. LENS, developed by the federal judiciary, pulls data from the federal Probation and

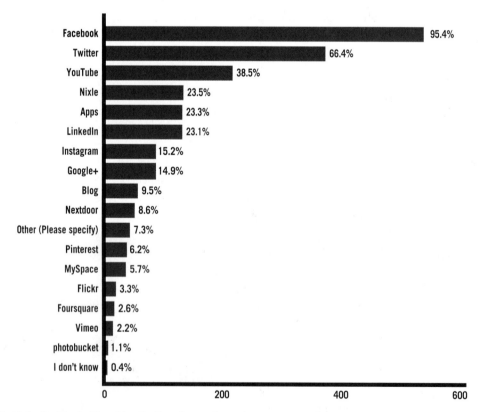

FIGURE 6-5 | Social Media Tools Used by Police Departments

Source: International Association of Chiefs of Police, Center for Social Media, *2014 Social Media Survey Results*, January, 2015, http://www.iacpsocialmedia.org/Resources/Publications/2014SurveyResults/AgenciesUsingSocialMedia.aspx (accessed March 7, 2015).

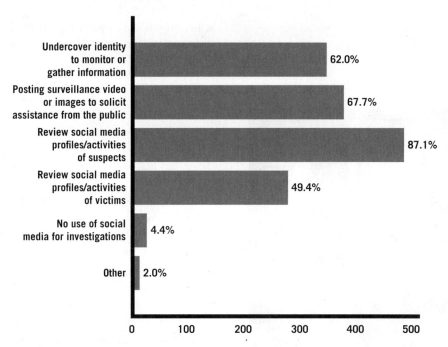

FIGURE 6-6 | The Use of Social Media in Police Investigations

Source: International Association of Chiefs of Police, Center for Social Media, *2014 Social Media Survey Results*, January, 2015, http://www.iacpsocialmedia.org/Resources/Publications/2014SurveyResults/AgenciesUsingSocialMedia.aspx (accessed March 7, 2015).

References: Edwin Chan and Alex Dobuzinskis, "U.S. Police Struggle to Uncover Threats on Social Media," *Reuters*, December 26, 2014, http://www.reuters.com/article/2014/12/26/us-usa-police-socialmedia-idUSKBN0K40MD20141226 (accessed March 7, 2015); Ashby Jones and Joe Palazzolo, "Police Seek Clues in Social Media," *The Wall Street Journal*, December 22, 2014, http://www.wsj.com/articles/police-seek-clues-in-social-media-1419301133 (accessed March 7, 2015); U.S. Courts, "With LENS, Offender Data Quickly Reaches Officers on the Beat," *The Third Branch News*, January 16, 2014; and Tami Abdollah, "Police Use New Tool to Source Crowds for Evidence," *Associated Press*, May 2, 2014, (accessed June 1, 2015).

Pretrial Services Automated Case Tracking System (PACTS) allowing investigators to access a wealth of information about convicted offenders. It also facilitates FBI Flash Notices—or push notifications from federal law enforcement agencies.

It should be noted, in keeping with the theme of this text, that some people fear that the use of social media and data analytics by the police, including the capture and analysis of data and messages intended for others, may violate personal privacy and threaten public freedoms. If so, we will need to ask ourselves whether the cost to privacy is worth the safety and security that such measures can secure.

Chapter 18 provides additional information on the use of social media by justice system personnel. An excellent online resource for learning more about the use of social media in policing can be found at **http://policesocialmedia.com**.

In today's post-9/11 world, local police departments play an especially important role in responding to the challenges of terrorism. They must help prevent attacks and respond when attacks occur, offering critical evacuation, emergency medical, and security functions to help stabilize communities following an incident. A survey of 250 police chiefs by the Police Executive Research Forum (PERF) found that the chiefs strongly believe that their departments can make valuable contributions to terrorism prevention by using community policing networks to exchange information with citizens and to gather intelligence.[87] Read the results of the PERF survey online at **http://tinyurl.com/69urerd**.

The Council on Foreign Relations, headquartered in New York City and Washington, D.C., agrees with PERF that American police departments can no longer assume that federal counterterrorism efforts alone will be sufficient to protect the communities they serve. Consequently, says the council, many police departments have responded to the terrorist threat by strengthening liaisons with federal, state, and local agencies (including fire departments and other police departments); by refining their training and emergency response plans; by creating antiterrorism divisions; and in a number of other ways.[88]

The extent of local departments' engagement in preventive activities depends substantially on budgetary considerations and is strongly influenced by the assessed likelihood of attack. The New York City Police Department (NYPD), for example, which has firsthand experience in responding to terrorist attacks (23 of its officers were killed when the World Trade Center towers collapsed), has created a special bureau headed by a deputy police commissioner responsible for counterterrorism training, prevention, and investigation.[89] One thousand officers have been reassigned to antiterrorism duties, and the department is training its entire 35,000-member force in how to respond to biological, radiological, and chemical attacks.[90] The NYPD has assigned detectives to work abroad with law enforcement agencies in Canada, Israel, Southeast Asia, and the Middle East to track terrorists who might target New York City,[91] and it now employs officers with a command of the Pashto, Farsi, and

■ **theme** How has policing changed since 9/11? What other changes do you see on the horizon?

■ **lecture note** Explain the concept of intelligence-led policing and why it is considered so important today.

■ **intelligence-led policing (ILP)** The collection and analysis of information to produce an intelligence end product designed to inform police decision-making at both the tactical and strategic levels.[v]

A Washington, D.C., Metro Transit police officer searching a train after subway bombings in London prompted increased security in 2005. How has the threat of terrorism altered the police role in America?

Urdu languages of the Middle East to monitor foreign television, radio, and Internet communications. The department has also invested heavily in new hazardous materials protective suits, gas masks, and portable radiation detectors.

In November 2004, in an effort to provide the law enforcement community and policymakers with guidance on critical issues related to antiterrorism planning and critical incident response, the International Association of Chiefs of Police (IACP) announced its Taking Command Initiative. The IACP described the initiative as "an aggressive project to assess the current state of homeland security efforts in the United States and to develop and implement the actions necessary to protect our communities from the specter of both crime and terrorism."[92] Initial deliberations under the initiative led the IACP to conclude that "the current homeland security strategy is handicapped by a fundamental flaw: It was developed without sufficiently seeking or incorporating the advice, expertise, or consent of public safety organizations at the state, tribal or local level."[93] Building on that premise, the IACP identified a number of key principles that it says must form the basis of any effective national homeland security strategy.[94]

Finally, in 2005, the IACP and its partners in the Post-9/11 Policing Project published *Assessing and Managing the Terrorism Threat*. The Post-9/11 Policing Project is a collaborative effort of the IACP, the National Sheriffs' Association (NSA), the National Organization of

Black Law Enforcement Executives (NOBLE), the Major Cities Chiefs Association (MCCA), and the Police Foundation.[95] Download the publication *Assessing and Managing the Terrorism Threat* at **http://www.justicestudies.com/pubs/amterrth .pdf**.

As the IACP recognizes, workable antiterrorism programs at the local level require effective sharing of critical information between agencies. FBI-sponsored Joint Terrorism Task Forces (JTTFs) facilitate this by bringing together federal and local law enforcement personnel to focus on specific threats. The FBI currently has established or authorized JTTFs in each of its 56 field offices. In addition to the JTTFs, the FBI has created Regional Terrorism Task Forces (RTTFs) to share information with local enforcement agencies. Through the RTTFs, FBI special agents assigned to terrorism prevention and investigation meet twice a year with their federal, state, and local counterparts for common training, discussion of investigations, and intelligence sharing. The FBI says that "the design of this non-traditional terrorism task force provides the necessary mechanism and structure to direct counterterrorism resources toward localized terrorism problems within the United States."[96] Six RTTFs are currently in operation: the Inland Northwest, South Central, Southeastern, Northeast Border, Deep South, and Southwest.

Another FBI counterterrorism component, Field Intelligence Groups (FIGs), was developed following recommendations of the 9/11 Commission. The commission said that the FBI should build a reciprocal relationship with state and local agencies, maximizing the sharing of information. FIGs, which now exist in all 56 FBI field offices, work closely with JTTFs to provide valuable services to law enforcement personnel at the state and local levels. According to the FBI, FIGs "generate intelligence products and disseminate them to the intelligence and law enforcement communities to help guide investigative, program, and policy decisions."[97]

Given the changes that have taken place in American law enforcement since the terrorist attacks of September 11, 2001, some say that traditional distinctions between crime, terrorism, and war are fading and that, at least in some instances, military action and civil law enforcement are becoming integrated. The critical question for law enforcement administrators in the near future may be one of discerning the role that law enforcement is to play in the emerging global context.

Intelligence-Led Policing and Antiterrorism

In 2005, the U.S. Department of Justice embraced the concept of **intelligence-led policing (ILP)** as an important technique to be employed by American law enforcement agencies in the

Workable antiterrorism programs at the local level require effective sharing of critical information between agencies.

■ **criminal intelligence** Information compiled, analyzed, or disseminated in an effort to anticipate, prevent, or monitor criminal activity.[vi]

battle against terrorism and organized and transnational crime.[98] Intelligence is information that has been analyzed and integrated into a useful perspective. The information used in the development of effective intelligence is typically gathered from many sources, such as surveillance, covert operations, financial records, electronic eavesdropping, interviews, newspapers, the Internet, and interrogations. Law enforcement intelligence, or **criminal intelligence**, is the result of a "process that evaluates information collected from diverse sources, integrates the relevant information into a cohesive package, and produces a conclusion or estimate about a criminal phenomenon by using the scientific approach to problem solving."[99] Although criminal investigation is typically part of the intelligence-gathering process, the intelligence function of a police department is more exploratory and more broadly focused than a single criminal investigation.[100]

> Intelligence is information that has been analyzed and integrated into a useful perspective.

ILP (also known as *intelligence-driven policing*) is the use of criminal intelligence to guide policing. A 2012 Bureau of Justice Assistance study noted that "ILP relies on analytically understanding multijurisdictional crime threats, developing a pathway toward solving the crime problems, and relying on proactive information sharing, both within the agency and externally with other law enforcement agencies, to maximize the number of law enforcement personnel who may identify indicators of threats and intervene."[101]

A detailed description of ILP and its applicability to American law enforcement agencies is provided in the FBI publication *The Law Enforcement Intelligence function* by David Carter of Michigan State University's School of Criminal Justice. The document is available at **http://tinyurl.com/6avb8fd**.

According to Carter, criminal intelligence "is a synergistic product intended to provide meaningful and trustworthy direction to law enforcement decision makers about complex criminality, criminal enterprises, criminal extremists, and terrorists." Carter goes on to point out that law enforcement intelligence consists of two types: tactical and strategic. Tactical intelligence "includes gaining or developing information related to threats of terrorism or crime and using this information to apprehend offenders, harden targets, and use strategies that will eliminate or mitigate the threat." Strategic intelligence, in contrast, provides information to decision makers about the changing nature of threats for the purpose of "developing response strategies and reallocating resources" to accomplish effective prevention.

Not every law enforcement agency has the staff or resources needed to create a dedicated intelligence unit. Even without an intelligence unit, however, a law enforcement organization should have the ability to effectively utilize the information and intelligence products that are developed and disseminated by organizations at all levels of government. In other words, even though a police agency may not have the resources necessary to analyze all the information it acquires, it should still be able to mount an effective response to credible threat information that it receives. Learn more about the law enforcement intelligence function and intelligence-led policing at **http://www.justicestudies.com/pubs/intelled.pdf**.

Information Sharing and Antiterrorism

The need to effectively share criminal intelligence across jurisdictions and between law enforcement agencies nationwide became apparent with the tragic events of September 11, 2001. Consequently, governments at all levels are today working toward the creation of a fully integrated criminal justice information system. According to a recent task force report, a fully integrated criminal justice information system is "a network of public safety, justice and homeland security computer systems, which provides to each agency the information it needs, at the time it is needed, in the form that it is needed, regardless of the source and regardless of the physical location at which it is stored."[102] The information that is provided should be complete, accurate, and formatted in whatever way is most useful for the agency's tasks. In a fully integrated criminal justice information system, information would be made available at the practitioner's workstation, whether that workstation is a patrol car, desk, laptop, or judge's bench. Within such a system, each agency shares information not only with other agencies in its own jurisdiction but with multiple justice agencies on the federal, state, and local levels. In such an idealized justice information system, accurate information is also available to nonjustice agencies with statutory authority and a legal obligation to check criminal histories before licensing, employment, weapons purchase, and so on.

> The need to effectively share criminal intelligence across jurisdictions and between law enforcement agencies nationwide became apparent with the tragic events of September 11, 2001.

One widely used information sharing system is Law Enforcement Online (LEO). LEO, an intranet intended exclusively for use by the law enforcement community, is a national interactive computer communications system and information service. This user-friendly system can be accessed by any

■ **NLETS**   The International Justice and Public Safety Information Sharing Network.

approved employee of a duly constituted local, state, or federal law enforcement agency or by an approved member of an authorized law enforcement special-interest group. LEO provides a state-of-the-art communication mechanism to link all levels of law enforcement throughout the United States. Members use LEO to support investigative operations, send notifications and alerts, and remotely access a wide variety of law enforcement and intelligence systems and resources. LEO also allows federal agencies, including the FBI, to immediately disseminate sensitive but unclassified information across agency boundaries.[103] The system includes password-accessed e-mail, Internet chat, an electronic library, an online calendar, special-interest topical focus areas, and self-paced distance learning modules.[104]

Another important information-sharing resource is **NLETS**, the International Justice and Public Safety Information Sharing Network. NLETS members include all 50 states, most federal agencies and territories, and the Royal Canadian Mounted Police. NLETS, which has been in operation for nearly 40 years, was formerly called the National Law Enforcement Telecommunications System. It has recently been enhanced to facilitate a variety of encrypted digital communications, and it now links 30,000 agencies and over half a million access devices in the United States and Canada. The system facilitates nearly 41 million transmissions each month. Information available through NLETS includes state criminal histories, homeland alert messages, immigration databases, driver records and vehicle registrations, aircraft registrations, Amber Alerts, weather advisories, and hazardous materials notifications and regulations. You can reach NLETS on the Web via **http://www.nlets.org.**

Fusion Centers

In 2014, the National Fusion Center Association (NFCA) held its annual training event in Alexandria, Virginia.[105] The annual event supports the goal of establishing an integrated national network of state and major urban area fusion centers. Fusion centers, a new concept in policing, "fuse" intelligence from participating agencies to create a more comprehensive threat picture, locally and nationally. They don't just collect information. They integrate new data into existing information, evaluate it to determine its worth, analyze it for links and trends, and disseminate their findings to the agency in the best position to do something about it.

Seventy-eight fusion centers currently operate in 49 states (there are another 20 regional centers) and have received $380 million in federal funding over the last five years. These centers are largely an outgrowth of one of the 9/11 Commission's criticisms that law enforcement agencies don't talk to each other as they should.

Guidelines for the development and operation of fusion centers have been created by a collaborative effort involving the U.S. Department of Justice (DOJ) and the U.S. Department of Homeland Security. According to those guidelines, a *fusion center* can be defined as a "collaborative effort of two or more agencies that provide resources, expertise, and information to the center with the goal of maximizing their ability to detect, prevent, investigate, and respond to criminal and terrorist activity."[106] Fusion centers vary greatly in size and in the equipment and personnel available to them. Some are small, consisting of little more than limited conference facilities and only a few participants. Others are large high-technology offices that make use of the latest information and computer technologies and that house representatives from many different organizations. Some fusion centers are physically located within the offices of other agencies. The Kentucky Fusion Center, for example, is housed within the state's Department of Transportation building in the state's capitol. Others operate out of stand-alone facilities and are physically separated from parent agencies.

Similarly, although information sharing is their central purpose, the activities of fusion centers are not uniform. Some centers perform investigations, some make arrests, and some exist only to share information. Certain fusion centers, such as the National Counterterrorism Center and the National Gang Intelligence Center, focus on clearly defined issues. Most of today's fusion centers do more than target terrorists, however; they work to collect information on a wide variety of offenders, gangs, immigrant smuggling operations, and other threats. Recognizing that actionable intelligence can come from seemingly unrelated areas, Michael Mines, the FBI's deputy assistant director of intelligence, says that the nation's network of fusion centers is intended to "maximize the ability to detect, prevent, investigate, and respond to criminal and terrorist activity."[107]

Fusion centers are still developing, and a number of problems remain. Obtaining security clearances for employees of local law enforcement agencies, for example, has sometimes been difficult or time consuming. Even representatives of federal agencies such as the Department of Homeland Security and the FBI sometimes refuse to accept each other's clearances. Nonetheless, a recent hearing before the House Intelligence Subcommittee shows that federal lawmakers are hopeful about the success of fusion centers and are willing to find the federal dollars needed to continue to support them. As Jane Harman (D-Calif.), chairwoman of the House Intelligence Subcommittee, said recently, "Everyone recognizes that fusion centers hold tremendous promise."[108] Read the *2014–2017 National Strategy for the National Network of Fusion Centers* at **http://tinyurl.com/p9smlju.**

The National Criminal Intelligence Sharing Plan

Although information-sharing efforts continue to evolve, most experts agree that a fully integrated nationwide criminal justice information system does not yet exist.[109] Efforts to create one, however, began in 2003 with the National Criminal Intelligence Sharing Plan (NCISP). The NCISP was developed under the auspices of the U.S. Department of Justice's Global Justice Information Sharing Initiative and was authored by its Global Intelligence Working Group.[110] Federal, local, state, and tribal law enforcement representatives all had a voice in the development of the plan. The NCISP provides specific steps that law enforcement agencies can take to participate in the sharing of critical law enforcement and terrorism prevention information.

Plan authors note that not every agency has the staff or resources needed to create a formal intelligence unit. However, the plan says that even without a dedicated intelligence unit, every law enforcement organization needs the ability to effectively consume the intelligence available from a wide range of organizations at all levels of government.[111] The NCISP is available in its entirety at **http://www.justicestudies.com/pubs/ncisp.pdf.**

CJ | NEWS

Fusion Centers: Unifying Intelligence to Protect Americans

Inside the Miami-Dade Police Department's Fusion Center, which serves much of South Florida. The center's combined technologies enhance the power of instant collaboration and information sharing among analysts and investigators from various law enforcement agencies. Why did fusion centers develop?

In Arizona, an international terrorism case was referred to local law enforcement after it was determined that the subjects of the case were involved in local criminal activity. In New Mexico, several individuals linked to FBI investigations—including an MS-13 gang member—were identified. In Tennessee, the FBI developed—with its partners—a formal process for collecting, sharing, and analyzing suspicious activity reports, looking for trends and patterns.

These cooperative efforts—and many more like them—have been made possible through the work of intelligence fusion centers around the country. These centers, usually set up by states or major urban areas and run by state or local authorities, are often supported by federal law enforcement, including the FBI. Fusion centers present a unified front against terrorism and other national security and criminal threats that put Americans at risk.

FBI Chief Intelligence Officer Don Van Duyn says that "while we still have work to do to make the information process more seamless,"

the FBI is committed to "expanding our interconnectedness" to help combat threats from terrorist and criminal networks. Van Duyn also said that during the past year the agency has rolled out—to all 56 field offices—standardized intelligence operations structures, roles, and procedures to enhance collaboration with its partners.

Although a few were already in existence before the terrorist attacks of September 11, 2001, fusion centers increased rapidly after the attacks when local and federal officials recognized the need to quickly coordinate information-sharing related to terrorism. Their number has been growing ever since. Today, there are some 70 centers around the country—50 state and 20 regional. Some have expanded their focus to include public-safety matters and major criminal threats.

Fusion center personnel "fuse" intelligence from participating agencies to create a more comprehensive threat picture, locally and nationally. They don't just collect information—they integrate new data into existing information, evaluate it to determine its worth, analyze it for links and trends, and disseminate their findings to the appropriate agency in the best position to do something about it.

The FBI currently has 114 employees working in 38 fusion centers—about 36% are agents, 61% are intelligence analysts, and the rest are language specialists, financial analysts, and the like. Fourteen of these centers also house an FBI *field intelligence group* or *joint terrorism task force*.

Elaine Cummins, the FBI's chief information-sharing officer, notes that "participating in a national network of fusion centers definitely helps us share timely, relevant, and actionable intelligence with our partners—an increasingly important component to our unique national-security and law enforcement mission."

The FBI says that "with fusion centers, everybody wins. State and local law enforcement agencies get access to certain federal databases and the benefit of big-picture terrorism and crime perspectives from their federal partners, along with grant funding, technical assistance, and training. Federal agencies like the FBI gain intelligence from the local level that may fuel terrorism or national security investigations elsewhere in the country or even overseas. And the public gets to sleep a little easier at night, knowing that their local, state, and federal officials are all working together to keep them safe."

Source: Adapted from Federal Bureau of Investigation, "Fusion Centers: Unifying Intelligence to Protect Americans," March 12, 2009, http://www.fbi.gov/page2/march09/fusion_031209.html (accessed May 6, 2013).

CJ | CAREERS
Police Officer

Christian Tomas

Name. Narcotics Agent Christian Tomas

Position. QRT Agent (Quick Response Team/Narcotics) City of West Palm Beach, Florida

Colleges attended. Palm Beach State College

Majors. Psychology

Year hired. 2007

Please give a brief description of your job. As a narcotics agent, my co-workers and I target street-level drug dealers and other quality of life issues, to include prostitution as well as other illegal business practices. We use our own initiative to begin investigations throughout the city. We buy narcotics in an undercover capacity and work with the S.W.A.T. team by writing search warrants for them to execute.

What is a typical day like? Typical day involves doing research and identifying a target. Once an investigation is complete, we move on to another. Some days are spent primarily on surveillance; while on others we are directly involved with drug dealers.

What qualities/characteristics are most helpful for this job? Common sense, honesty, integrity, confidence, self-discipline, dedication, humility, composure, physical and mental toughness, Tactical awareness and the ability to work with minimal, to no, supervision.

What is a typical starting salary? The West Palm Beach Police Department starting salary is $45,324 annually, with excellent benefits.

What is the salary potential as you move up into higher-level jobs? An officer reaching PFC (Patrolman first Class) and MPO (Master Patrol Officer) will receive a 2 and 1/2% raise for each level attained. Promotion in rank produces significant raises over time.

What advice would you give someone in college beginning studies in criminal justice? This isn't a job for someone expecting to win all of the battles. You try as hard as you can, but you have to be prepared for some disappointments when a case doesn't go the way you wanted it to. Get your degree, as it will help you get promoted. When choosing a department, make sure that it's the kind of department that you are looking for. I came to West Palm Beach for the experience and to be busy; I wanted to be challenged and to do as much as I possibly could. Policing is a very rewarding career if you have the motivation and determination to succeed.

Ethnic and Gender Diversity in Policing

In 2003, Annetta W. Nunn took the reins of the Birmingham (Alabama) Police Department. For many, Nunn, a 44-year-old African American mother and Baptist choir singer, symbolized the changes that had taken place in American policing during the past few decades. The new chief sat in a chair once occupied by Eugene "Bull" Connor, an arch segregationist and a national symbol of the South's fight against integration who jailed thousands of civil rights demonstrators during the 1960s. A 23-year veteran of the department, Nunn headed a force of 838 men and women. She left the department in 2008 to become an advocate for a domestic violence education program in municipal court.

More than 30 years before Nunn assumed the job of chief, a 1968 survey of police supervisors by the National Advisory Commission on Civil Disorders[112] (aka the Kerner Commission) found a marked disparity between the number of black and white officers in leadership positions. One of every 26 black police officers had been promoted to the rank of sergeant, whereas the ratio among whites was 1 in 12. Only 1 of every 114 black officers had become a lieutenant, whereas among whites the ratio was 1 in 26. At the level of captain, the disparity was even greater: One out of every 235 black officers had achieved the rank of captain, whereas 1 of every 53 whites had climbed to that rank.

Today, many departments, through dedicated recruitment efforts, have dramatically increased their complement of officers from underrepresented groups. The Metropolitan Detroit Police Department, for example, now has a force that is more than 30% black. Nationwide, racial and ethnic minorities comprised 25.3% of full-time sworn police personnel in 2007, up from 17.0% in 1990.[113] From 1990 to 2003, the number of African American local police officers

David R. Frazier Photolibrary/Photo Researchers, Inc.

African American and Hispanic police officers in Los Angeles. Ethnic minorities, although still underrepresented in the criminal justice field, have many opportunities for employment throughout the system. Can the same be said for women?

■ **theme** How important do you think it is to ensure ethnic and gender diversity in policing? Explain.

■ **theme** In your opinion, are police departments today doing enough to attract qualified ethnic minorities and women? Explain. How might hiring police officers from diverse groups help achieve the aims of community policing?

increased by 14,800, or 37% and the number of Hispanic officers increased by 22,300 or 98%. Moreover, a recent study of 123 African American police executives in the United States found that they were generally well accepted by their peers, well integrated into their leadership roles, and socially well adjusted.[114]

Although ethnic minorities are now employed in policing in numbers that approach their representation in the American population, women are still significantly underrepresented. The 2001 Status of Women in Policing Survey, conducted by the National Center for Women and Policing (NCWP), found that women fill only 12.7% of all sworn law enforcement positions nationwide.[115] On the other hand, the NCWP notes that women account for 46.5% of employed people over the age of 16 nationwide, meaning that they are "strikingly under-represented within the field of sworn law enforcement."[116]

It is unclear just how many women actually *want* to work in policing. Nonetheless, many departments aggressively recruit and retain women because they understand the benefits of having more women as sworn officers. Because female officers tend to use less physical force than male officers, for example, they are less likely to be accused of using excessive force. Female officers are also better at defusing and de-escalating potentially violent confrontations, often possess better communications skills than their male counterparts, and are better able to facilitate the cooperation and trust required to implement a community policing model. Moreover, the NCWP says that "female officers often respond more effectively to incidents of violence against women—crimes that represent one of the largest categories of calls to police departments. Increasing the representation of women on the force is also likely to address another costly problem for police administrators—the pervasive problem of sex discrimination and sexual harassment—by changing the climate of modern law enforcement agencies."[117] Finally, "because women frequently have different life experiences than men, they approach policing with a different perspective, and the very presence of women in the field will often bring about changes in policies and procedures that benefit both male and female officers."[118]

Women as Effective Police Officers

A recent report on female police officers in Massachusetts found that female officers (1) are "extremely devoted to their work," (2) "see themselves as women first, and then police officers," and (3) "are more satisfied when working in nonuniformed capacities."[119] The researcher identified two groups of female officers: (1) those who felt themselves to be well integrated into their departments and were confident in their jobs and (2) those who experienced strain and on-the-job isolation. The officers'

children were cited as a significant influence on their perceptions of self and their jobs. The demands of child rearing in contemporary society were found to be a major factor contributing to the resignation of female officers. The study also found that the longer female officers stayed on the job, the greater the stress and frustration they tended to experience, primarily because of the uncooperative attitudes of male officers. Some of the female officers identified networking as a potential solution to the stresses encountered by female officers, but also said that when women get together to solve problems, they are seen as "crybabies" rather than professionals. One of the participants in the study said that women who help each other are less likely to leave police work than those who don't. Peer support, she noted, is vital.[120] For more information on working in policing, visit **http://discoverpolicing.org.**

Some studies found that female officers are often underutilized and that many departments hesitate to assign women to patrol and other potentially dangerous field activities.[121] Consequently, some policewomen experience frustration and a lack of job satisfaction. An analysis of the genderization of the criminal justice workplace by Susan Ehrlich Martin and Nancy Jurik, for example, points out that gender inequality is part of a historical pattern of entrenched forms of gender interaction

ROGER L. WOLLENBERG/Newscom

Cathy Lanier, police chief of Washington, D.C. How do communities benefit from police agencies that are socially and culturally diverse?

relating to the division of labor, power, and culture.[122] Martin and Jurik contend that women working in the justice system are viewed in terms of such historically developed filters, causing them to be judged and treated according to normative standards developed for men. As a result, formal and informal social controls continue to disenfranchise women who wish to work in the system and make it difficult to recognize the specific contributions that they make as women.

SUMMARY

- The fundamental police mission in democratic societies includes five components: (1) enforcing the law (especially the criminal law), (2) investigating crimes and apprehending offenders, (3) preventing crime, (4) helping ensure domestic peace and tranquility, and (5) providing the community with needed enforcement-related services.
- This chapter presents five core law enforcement strategies: (1) preventive patrol, (2) routine incident response, (3) emergency response, (4) criminal investigation, and (5) problem solving. Support, an ancillary operational strategy, is also discussed.
- Police management involves the administrative activities of controlling, directing, and coordinating police personnel, resources, and activities in the service of preventing crime, apprehending criminals, recovering stolen property, and performing regulatory and helping services. Virtually all American law enforcement organizations are formally structured among divisions and along lines of authority. Roles within police agencies usually fall into one of two categories: line and staff. Line operations are field or supervisory activities directly related to daily police work. Staff operations include support roles, such as administration.
- Three policing styles are identified in this chapter: (1) the watchman style, (2) the legalistic style, and (3) the service style. The style of policing that characterizes a community tends to flow from the lifestyles of those who live there. Whereas the watchman style of policing, with its emphasis on order maintenance, was widespread during the mid-twentieth century, the service style, which is embodied in the community policing model, is commonplace today. Community policing is built on the principle that police departments and the communities they serve should work together as partners in the fight against crime.
- Policing in America was forever changed by the events of September 11, 2001. Local law enforcement agencies, many of which previously saw community protection and peacekeeping as their primary roles, are being called on to protect against potential terrorist threats with international roots. The contemporary emphasis on terrorism prevention, along with the need for a rapid response to threats of terrorism, has led to what some see as a new era of policing to secure the homeland. Homeland security policing builds on the established framework of community policing for the purpose of gathering intelligence to prevent terrorism.
- This chapter points out that ethnic minorities are now employed in policing in numbers that approach their representation in the general population. Women, however, are still significantly underrepresented. Questions can be raised about the degree of minority participation in the command structure of law enforcement agencies, about the desire of significant numbers of women to work in policing, and about the respect accorded to women and members of other underrepresented groups who work in law enforcement by their fellow officers.

KEY TERMS

chain of command, 173
community policing, 178
CompStat, 166
crime prevention, 165
crime scene, 169
crime scene investigator, 169
criminal intelligence, 185
criminal investigation, 169
intelligence-led policing (ILP), 184
legalistic style, 175
line operations, 171
NLETS, 186

police–community relations (PCR), 176
police management, 171
preliminary investigation, 169
problem-solving policing, 178
quality-of-life offense, 166
response time, 168
service style, 175
solvability factor, 170
span of control, 173
staff operations, 171
strategic policing, 176
team policing, 176
watchman style, 174

QUESTIONS FOR REVIEW

1. What are the basic purposes of policing in democratic societies? How are they consistent with one another? In what ways might they be inconsistent?
2. What are the five core operational strategies that police departments use today? What is the ancillary operational strategy?
3. Define the term *police management*, and describe the different types of organizational structures typical of American police departments.
4. What are the three styles of policing described in this chapter? How do they differ? Which one characterizes the community in which you live?

5. What new responsibilities have American police agencies assumed since the September 11, 2001, terrorist attacks? What new challenges are they facing?

6. What issues related to gender and ethnicity are important in American policing today? What problems still exist? How can those problems be addressed?

QUESTIONS FOR REFLECTION

1. Are there any aspects of the police mission that this chapter fails to recognize and that should be added to the basic purposes of policing identified here? If so, what are they?

2. How are police organizations managed? Might participatory or democratic management styles or the organizational styles of innovative high-technology firms be effective in policing? Why or why not?

3. What is community policing? How does it differ from what some might call traditional policing?

4. Does community policing offer an opportunity to improve policing services in the United States? Why or why not? Does it offer opportunities in the fight against terrorism? Why or why not?

NOTES

i. Wayne W. Bennett and Karen M. Hess, *Criminal Investigation*, 6th ed. (Belmont, CA: Wadsworth, 2001), p. 3.

ii. This definition draws on the classic work by O. W. Wilson, *Police Administration* (New York: McGraw-Hill, 1950), pp. 2–3.

iii. Sam S. Souryal, *Police Administration and Management* (St. Paul, MN: West, 1977), p. 261.

iv. Community Policing Consortium, *What Is Community Policing?* (Washington, DC: Community Policing Consortium, 1995).

v. Angus Smith, ed., *Intelligence-Led Policing* (Richmond, VA: International Association of Law Enforcement Intelligence Analysts, 1997), p. 1.

vi. Office of Justice Programs, *The National Criminal Intelligence Sharing Plan* (Washington, DC: U.S. Dept. of Justice, 2005), p. 27.

1. Frank Newport, "Gallup Review: Black and White Attitudes Toward Police," *Gallup*, August 20, 2014, http://www.gallup.com/poll/175088/gallup-review-black-white-attitudes-toward-police.aspx.

2. Jeremy Ashkenas and Haeyoun Park, "The Race Gap in America's Police Departments," *The New York Times*, September 4, 2014.

3. Shaila Dewan, "Mostly White Forces in Mostly Black Towns: Police Struggle for Racial Diversity," *The New York Times*, September 9, 2014, http://nyti.ms/1tIy4kU.

4. Andrew P. Sutor, *Police Operations: Tactical Approaches to Crimes in Progress* (St. Paul, MN: West, 1976), p. 68, citing Peel.

5. C. D. Hale, *Police Patrol: Operations and Management* (Upper Saddle River, NJ: Prentice Hall, 1994).

6. Victor Kappeler et al., *The Mythology of Crime and Criminal Justice* (Prospect Heights, IL: Waveland Press, 1996).

7. Darl H. Champion and Michael K. Hooper, *Introduction to American Policing* (New York: McGraw-Hill, 2003), p. 133.

8. Details for this story come from Ted Ottley, "Bad Day Dawning," Court TV's Crime Library, http://www.crimelibrary.com/serial_killers/notorious/mcveigh/dawning_1.html (accessed June 22, 2009).

9. Ibid.

10. This definition has been attributed to the National Crime Prevention Institute; see http://www.lvmpd.com/community/crmtip25.htm (accessed July 22, 2007).

11. See Steven P. Lab, *Crime Prevention at a Crossroads* (Cincinnati, OH: Anderson, 1997).

12. See the Philadelphia Police Department's Operation Identification website at http://www.ppdonline.org/ppd4_home_opid.htm (accessed July 25, 2008).

13. The term *CompStat* is sometimes thought to stand for computer statistics, comparative statistics, or computer comparative statistics, although it is not derived from any of those terms.

14. Learn more about CompStat from Vincent E. Henry, *The COMPSTAT Paradigm: Management Accountability in Policing, Business, and the Public Sector* (Flushing, NY: Looseleaf Law Publications, 2002).

15. Much of the information in this section comes from the Philadelphia Police Department, "The COMPSTAT Process," http://www.ppdonline.org/ppd_compstat.htm (accessed May 28, 2009).

16. See Ned Levine, *CrimeStat IV: A Spatial Statistics Program for the Analysis of Crime Incident Locations, Version 4.0* (Washington, DC: National Institute of Justice, 2013).

17. Robert H. Langworthy and Lawrence P. Travis III, *Policing in America: A Balance of Forces*, 2nd ed. (Upper Saddle River, NJ: Prentice Hall, 1999), p. 194.

18. Adapted from Bronx County (New York) District Attorney's Office, "Quality of Life Offenses," December 24, 2002, http://www.bronxda.net/fighting_crime/quality_of_life_offenses.html (accessed June 20, 2006).

19. Other violations may be involved, as well. On December 29, 2000, for example, Judge John S. Martin, Jr., of the federal district court in Manhattan, ruled that homeless people in New York City could be arrested for sleeping in cardboard boxes in public. Judge Martin held that a city Sanitation Department regulation barring people from abandoning cars or boxes on city streets could be applied to the homeless who were sleeping in boxes.

20. Norman Siegel, executive director of the New York Civil Liberties Union, as reported in "Quality of Life Offenses Targeted," *Western Queens Gazette*, November 22, 2000, http://www.qgazette.com/News/2000/1122/Editorial_pages/e01.html (accessed June 12, 2007).

21. The broken windows thesis was first suggested by George L. Kelling and James Q. Wilson in "Broken Windows: The Police and Neighborhood Safety," *Atlantic Monthly*, March 1982. The article is available online at http://www.theatlantic.com/politics/crime/windows.htm (accessed June 22, 2005).

22. For a critique of the broken windows thesis, see Bernard E. Harcourt, *Illusion of Order: The False Promise of Broken Windows Policing* (Cambridge, MA: Harvard University Press, 2001).

23. Peter Schuler, "Law Professor Harcourt Challenges Popular Policing Method, Gun Violence Interventions," *Chicago Chronicle*, Vol. 22, No. 12 (March 20, 2003).

24. George L. Kelling, Catherine M. Coles, and James Q. Wilson, *Fixing Broken Windows: Restoring Order and Reducing Crime in Our Communities* (reprint, New York: Touchstone, 1998).

25. Charles R. Swanson, Leonard Territo, and Robert W. Taylor, *Police Administration: Structures, Processes, and Behavior*, 4th ed. (Upper Saddle River, NJ: Prentice Hall, 1998), p. 1.

26. Lorraine Mazerolle et al., *Managing Citizen Calls to the Police: An Assessment of Nonemergency Call Systems* (Washington, DC: National Institute of Justice, 2001), pp. 1–11.

27. Michael S. Scott, *Problem-Oriented Policing: Reflections on the First 20 Years* (Washington, DC: U.S. Dept. of Justice, Office of Community Oriented Policing Services, 2000), p. 85, http://www.cops.usdoj.gov/Default.asp?Item5311 (accessed May 25, 2007).

28. Ibid., from which some of the wording and much of the material in this section is adapted.

29. Ibid., p. 86.

30. Ibid., from which much of this material is adapted.

31. Ibid., p. 86.

32. New York City Mayor's Office, *Fiscal 2007 Mayor's Management Report* (New York City: Office of the Mayor, 2007).

33. Details for this story come from Kurt Streeter, "Girl, 2, Rescued from Washer," *Los Angeles Times*, May 26, 2003, http://www.latimes.com/news/local/la-me-laundry26may26,1,7334286.story (accessed May 27, 2003).

34. See Scott, *Problem-Oriented Policing*, from which much of this material is adapted.

35. Wayne W. Bennett and Karen M. Hess, *Criminal Investigation*, 6th ed. (Belmont, CA: Wadsworth, 2001), p. 3 (italics in original).

36. Chief Gordon F. Urlacher and Lieutenant Robert J. Duffy, Rochester (New York) Police Department, "The Preliminary Investigation Process," http://www.surviveall.net/preliminary_investigation_proces.htm (accessed May 27, 2009).

37. Florida Highway Patrol, "Policy Number 22.01," *Policy Manual*, February 1, 1996, http://www.fhp.state.fl.us/html/Manuals/fh22-01.pdf (accessed June 1, 2009).

38. Scott, *Problem-Oriented Policing*, p. 88.

39. Adapted from Michigan State Police, *Annual Report 2000*, p. 12.

40. This definition draws on the classic work by O. W. Wilson, *Police Administration* (New York: McGraw-Hill, 1950), pp. 2–3.

41. Charles R. Swanson, Leonard Territo, and Robert W. Taylor, *Police Administration: Structures, Processes, and Behavior* (Upper Saddle River, NJ: Prentice Hall, 1998), p. 167.

42. For an organizational chart of a big-city police department, see one of the LAPD at http://assets.lapdonline.org/assets/pdf/Org_Chart_8-3-15-NEW-DP-9.pdf.

43. For more information on the first three categories, see Francis X. Hartmann, "Debating the Evolution of American Policing," *Perspectives on Policing*, No. 5 (Washington, DC: National Institute of Justice, 1988).

44. Willard M. Oliver, "The Homeland Security Juggernaut: The End of the Community Policing Era," *Crime and Justice International*, Vol. 20, No. 79 (2004), pp. 4–10. See also Willard M. Oliver, "The Era of Homeland Security: September 11, 2001 to . . .," *Crime and Justice International*, Vol. 21, No. 85 (2005), pp. 9–17.

45. Gene Stephens, "Policing the Future: Law Enforcement's New Challenges," *The Futurist* (March/April 2005), pp. 51–57.

46. Cited in Bernie G. Thompson, *A Law Enforcement Assistance and Partnership Strategy* (Washington, DC: U.S. Congress, 2008), p. 5. Congressman Thompson is a ranking member of the Democratic staff of the Committee on Homeland Security.

47. Ibid., p. 5.

48. To learn more about Wilson, see "Presidential Medal of Freedom Recipient James Q. Wilson," http://www.medaloffreedom.com/JamesQWilson.htm (accessed January 5, 2006).

49. James Q. Wilson, *Varieties of Police Behavior: The Management of Law and Order in Eight Communities* (Cambridge, MA: Harvard University Press, 1968).

50. Independent Commission on the Los Angeles Police Department, *Report of the Independent Commission on the Los Angeles Police Department* (Los Angeles: The Commission, 1991).

51. Gary W. Sykes, "Street Justice: A Moral Defense of Order Maintenance Policing," *Justice Quarterly*, Vol. 3, No. 4 (December 1986), p. 505.

52. Egon Bittner, "Community Relations," in Alvin W. Cohn and Emilio C. Viano, eds., *Police Community Relations: Images, Roles, Realities* (Philadelphia: J. B. Lippincott, 1976), pp. 77–82.

53. Paul B. Weston, *Police Organization and Management* (Pacific Palisades, CA: Goodyear, 1976), p. 159.

54. Hale, *Police Patrol*.

55. Mark H. Moore and Robert C. Trojanowicz, "Corporate Strategies for Policing," *Perspectives on Policing*, No. 6 (Washington, DC: National Institute of Justice, 1988).

56. Ibid., p. 6.

57. Community Policing Consortium, *Community Policing Is Alive and Well* (Washington, DC: Community Policing Consortium, 1995), p. 1.

58. George L. Kelling, *The Newark Foot Patrol Experiment* (Washington, DC: Police Foundation, 1981).

59. Robert C. Trojanowicz, "An Evaluation of a Neighborhood Foot Patrol Program," *Journal of Police Science and Administration*, Vol. 11 (1983).

60. Bureau of Justice Assistance, *Understanding Community Policing: A Framework for Action* (Washington, DC: Bureau of Justice Statistics, 1994), p. 10.

61. Robert C. Trojanowicz and Bonnie Bucqueroux, *Community Policing* (Cincinnati, OH: Anderson, 1990).

62. Moore and Trojanowicz, "Corporate Strategies for Policing," p. 8.

63. S. M. Hartnett and W. G. Skogan, "Community Policing: Chicago's Experience," *National Institute of Justice Journal* (April 1999), pp. 2–11.

64. Jerome H. Skolnick and David H. Bayley, *Community Policing: Issues and Practices around the World* (Washington, DC: National Institute of Justice, 1988).

65. Ibid.

66. William L. Goodbody, "What Do We Expect New-Age Cops to Do?" *Law Enforcement News*, April 30, 1995, pp. 14, 18.

67. Sam Vincent Meddis and Desda Moss, "Many 'Fed-Up' Communities Cornering Crime," *USA Today*, May 22, 1995.

68. Matthew J. Hickman and Brian A. Reaves, *Community Policing in Local Police Departments, 1997 and 1999*, Bureau of Justice Statistics Special Report (Washington, DC: U.S. Dept. of Justice, 2001).

69. Richard M. Daley and Matt L. Rodriguez, *Together We Can: A Strategic Plan for Reinventing the Chicago Police Department* (Chicago: Chicago Police Department, 1993), http://www.ci.chi.il.us/CommunityPolicing/Statistics/Reports/TWC.pdf (accessed March 5, 2002).

70. Bureau of Justice Assistance, *Neighborhood-Oriented Policing in Rural Communities: A Program Planning Guide* (Washington, DC: Bureau of Justice Statistics, 1994), p. 4.

71. See the COPS Office website at http://www.cops.usdoj.gov (accessed September 6, 2012).

72. U.S. Department of Justice press release, "White House, Justice Department Announce Law Enforcement Grants for Hiring of Veterans," June 25, 2012.

73. Jihong Zhao, Nicholas P. Lovrich, and Quint Thurman, "The Status of Community Policing in American Cities: Facilitators and Impediments Revisited," *Policing*, Vol. 22, No. 1 (1999), p. 74.

74. For a good critique and overview of community policing, see Geoffrey P. Alpert et al., *Community Policing: Contemporary Readings* (Prospect Heights, IL: Waveland Press, 1998).

75. Jack R. Greene, "Community Policing in America: Changing the Nature, Structure, and Function of the Police," in U.S. Department of Justice, *Criminal Justice 2000*, Vol. 3 (Washington, DC: U.S. Dept. of Justice, 2000).

76. Michael D. Reisig and Roger B. Parks, "Experience, Quality of Life, and Neighborhood Context: A Hierarchical Analysis of Satisfaction with Police," *Justice Quarterly*, Vol. 17, No. 3 (2000), p. 607.

77. Mark E. Correla, "The Conceptual Ambiguity of Community in Community Policing: Filtering the Muddy Waters," *Policing*, Vol. 23, No. 2 (2000), pp. 218–233.

78. Adapted from Donald R. Fessler, *Facilitating Community Change: A Basic Guide* (San Diego, CA: San Diego State University, 1976), p. 7.

79. Daniel W. Flynn, *Defining the "Community" in Community Policing* (Washington, DC: Police Executive Research Forum, 1998).

80. Robert C. Trojanowicz and Mark H. Moore, *The Meaning of Community in Community Policing* (East Lansing: Michigan State University's National Neighborhood Foot Patrol Center, 1988).

81. Robert M. Bohm, K. Michael Reynolds, and Stephen T. Holms, "Perceptions of Neighborhood Problems and Their Solutions: Implications for Community Policing," *Policing*, Vol. 23, No. 4 (2000), p. 439.

82. Ibid., p. 442.

83. Malcolm K. Sparrow, "Implementing Community Policing," *Perspectives in Policing*, No. 9 (Washington, DC: National Institute of Justice, 1988).

84. "L.A. Police Chief: Treat People Like Customers," *USA Today*, March 29, 1993.

85. Robert Wasserman and Mark H. Moore, "Values in Policing," *Perspectives in Policing*, No. 8 (Washington, DC: National Institute of Justice, 1988), p. 7.

86. "New York City Mayor Sparks Debate on Community Policing," *Criminal Justice Newsletter*, Vol. 25, No. 2 (January 18, 1994), p. 1.

87. Police Executive Research Forum, *Local Law Enforcement's Role in Preventing and Responding to Terrorism* (Washington, DC: PERF, October 2, 2001), http://www.policeforum.org/terrorismfinal.doc (accessed June 1, 2009).

88. Council on Foreign Relations, "Terrorism Questions and Answers: Police Departments," http://www.terrorismanswers.com/security/police.html (accessed April 19, 2005).

89. Ibid.

90. Michael Weissenstein, "NYPD Shifts Focus to Terrorism, Long Considered the Turf of Federal Agents," Associated Press, March 21, 2003, http://www.nj.com/newsflash/national/index.ssf?/cgi-free/getstory_ssf.cgi?a0801_BC_NYPD-Counterterror&&news&newsflash-national (accessed May 25, 2009).

91. Ibid.

92. International Association of Chiefs of Police, *From Hometown Security to Homeland Security: IACP's Principles for a Locally Designed and Nationally Coordinated Homeland Security Strategy* (Alexandria, VA: IACP, 2005).

93. Ibid.

94. Joseph G. Estey, *President's Message: Taking Command Initiative—An Update* (Washington, DC: International Association of Chiefs of Police, 2005), http://www.theiacp.org/documents/index.cfm?fuseaction5document&document_id5697 (accessed July 25, 2007).

95. Joel Leson, *Assessing and Managing the Terrorism Threat* (Washington, DC: Bureau of Justice Statistics, 2005).

96. Robert J. Jordan (FBI), Congressional Statement on Information Sharing before the U.S. Senate Committee on the Judiciary, Subcommittee on Administrative Oversight and the Courts, Washington, DC, April 17, 2002, http://www.fbi.gov/congress/congress02/jordan041702.htm (accessed April 19, 2003).

97. Suzel Spiller, "The FBI's Field Intelligence Groups and Police: Joining Forces," *FBI Law Enforcement Bulletin*, May 2006, pp. 2–6.

98. The concept of intelligence-led policing appears to have been first fully articulated in Angus Smith, ed., *Intelligence-Led Policing* (Richmond, VA: International Association of Law Enforcement Intelligence Analysts, 1997).

99. David L. Carter, *Law Enforcement Intelligence: A Guide for State, Local, and Tribal Law Enforcement Agencies* (Washington, DC: U.S. Dept. of Justice, 2004), p. 7.

100. Much of the information and some of the wording in this section is taken from Carter, *Law Enforcement Intelligence*.

101. *Reducing Crime through Intelligence-Led Policing* (Washington, DC: Bureau of Justice Assistance, 2012).

102. Governor's Commission on Criminal Justice Innovation, *Final Report* (Boston: The Commission, 2004), p. 57, from which much of the wording in the rest of this paragraph is taken.

103. Lesley G. Koestner, "LEO Roars into the Future," *FBI Law Enforcement Bulletin*, September 2006, p. 9.

104. Federal Bureau of Investigation, "Law Enforcement Online," http://www.fbi.gov/hq/cjisd/leo.htm (accessed September 1, 2006).

105. National Fusion Center Association, "Training," https://nfcausa.org/default.aspx/MenuItemID/166/MenuGroup/Public+Home.htm (accessed May 4, 2015).

106. Bureau of Justice Assistance, *Fusion Center Guidelines: Developing and Sharing Information in a New Era* (Washington, DC: U.S. Dept. of Justice, 2006), p. 2.

107. Michael C. Mines, "Statement before the House Committee on Homeland Security, Subcommittee on Intelligence, Information Sharing, and Terrorism Risk Assessment," September 27, 2007.

108. "State and Local Fusion Centers Face Challenges as They Grow," *Criminal Justice Newsletter*, September 18, 2007, p. 1.

109. Bernard H. Levin, "Sharing Information: Some Open Secrets and a Glimpse at the Future," *Police Futurist*, Vol. 14, No. 1 (winter 2006), pp. 8–9.

110. The plan was an outgrowth of the IACP Criminal Intelligence Sharing Summit, held in Alexandria, VA, in March 2002. The results of the summit are documented in International Association of Chiefs of Police, *Recommendations from the IACP Intelligence Summit, Criminal Intelligence Sharing*.

111. Office of Justice Programs, *The National Criminal Intelligence Sharing Plan* (Washington, DC: U.S. Dept. of Justice, 2003).

112. *Report of the National Advisory Commission on Civil Disorders* (New York: E. P. Dutton, 1968), p. 332.

113. Hickman and Reaves, *Community Policing*.

114. R. Alan Thompson, "Black Skin–Brass Shields: Assessing the Presumed Marginalization of Black Law Enforcement Executives," *American Journal of Criminal Justice*, Vol. 30, No. 2 (2006), pp. 163–175.

115. National Center for Women and Policing, *Equality Denied: The Status of Women in Policing, 2001* (Los Angeles: NCWP, 2002), p. 2.

116. Ibid.

117. National Center for Women and Policing, *Recruiting and Retaining Women: A Self-Assessment Guide for Law Enforcement* (Los Angeles: NCWP, 2001), p. 22.

118. Ibid.

119. C. Lee Bennett, "Interviews with Female Police Officers in Western Massachusetts," paper presented at the annual meeting of the Academy of Criminal Justice Sciences, Nashville, TN, March 1991.

120. Ibid., p. 9.

121. Carole G. Garrison, Nancy K. Grant, and Kenneth L. J. Mc-Cormick, "Utilization of Police Women," *Police Chief*, Vol. 32, No. 7 (September 1998).

122. Susan Ehrlich Martin and Nancy C. Jurik, *Doing Justice, Doing Gender: Women in Law and Criminal Justice Occupations* (Thousand Oaks, CA: Sage, 1996).

AP Photo/Adam Lau

7 POLICING: LEGAL ASPECTS

OUTLINE

LEARNING OBJECTIVES

After reading this chapter, you should be able to

- Explain how the Bill of Rights and democratically inspired legal restraints help protect our personal freedoms.
- Describe legal restraints on police action and instances of police abuse of power.
- Describe the circumstances under which police officers may conduct searches or seize property legally.
- Define arrest, and describe how popular depictions of the arrest process may not be consistent with legal understandings of the term.
- Describe the intelligence function, including the roles of police interrogation and the Miranda warning.

The touchstone of the Fourth Amendment is reasonableness. The Fourth Amendment does not proscribe all state-initiated searches and seizures. It merely proscribes those which are unreasonable.

FLORIDA V. JIMENO, 500 U.S. 248 (1991)

Introduction

In 2012, a $120 million civil suit alleging wrongful death was filed against the Los Angeles Police Department (LAPD) by the surviving parents of 19-year-old Abdul Arian, who was shot and killed by LAPD officers after he led them on a high-speed chase that ended when he swerved into the middle of the Hollywood Freeway in Woodland Hills, California. According to police reports supported by video taken from a helicopter at the scene, Arian fled his vehicle and repeatedly made threatening gestures toward pursuing officers, assuming the stance of a shooter and pointing what appeared to be a weapon at them.[1] Although he was later found to have been unarmed, he reportedly told 911 dispatchers, to whom he was speaking with during the chase, that he had a weapon and that he would "pull my gun out on them." Attorneys for the family explained that the amount of money asked for in the lawsuit was calculated using $1 million for each of the 120 bullets fired at Arian. Eventually the suit was dismissed in U.S. District Court, with the judge holding that "there were no issues that could be raised at trial."[2]

Law enforcement experts say that "contagious shooting"—gunfire that spreads "in the adrenaline-pumping, split-second heat of the moment"[3] among officers who believe that they, or their colleagues, are facing a deadly threat—likely explained the number of shots fired during the Arian shooting.[4] The incident was complicated by the fact that Arian had wanted to join the LAPD, but had been dismissed from its youth explorer program for disciplinary reasons.

Not all questionable cases of police use of force involve shootings. Two months after Hurricane Katrina devastated New Orleans, for example, members of the city's over-worked police department became embroiled in a public-relations nightmare when an Associated Press Television News (APTN) crew working in the French Quarter filmed two white officers beating an apparently dazed and unresisting 64-year-old African American retired elementary school teacher named Robert Davis. A third officer could be seen grabbing and shoving an APTN producer working with the news team. As the incident ended, Davis, whose family had property in the city, was arrested and charged with public intoxication, resisting arrest, battery on a police officer, and public intimidation. He later told reporters that he hadn't had an alcoholic drink in 25 years and that the trouble began when he asked a mounted officer for directions.[5] New Orleans Police Superintendent Warren Riley was quick to condemn the officers' behavior. "The actions that were observed on this video are certainly unacceptable [to] this department," Riley said as he announced the firings of officers Lance Schilling and Robert Evangelist and the suspension without pay of another officer, S. M. Smith.

> Not all questionable cases of police use of force involve shootings.

AP Photo/Reed Saxon

Mourners, many wearing T-shirts with images of Abdul Arian, a 19-year-old man shot and killed by members of the Los Angeles Police Department after a freeway chase, prepare to pray over his casket at his funeral at Valhalla Park in the North Hollywood district of Los Angeles. Attorneys filed a $120 million claim against the city on behalf of the family. The lawsuit was eventually dismissed. Might "contagious shooting" explain what happened on that fatal day?

■ **lecture note**   Explain how the potential for police abuse of power is anticipated by the Bill of Rights and how restraints on the police must be constantly balanced against the need for the police to be able to do their jobs.
■ **lecture note**   Explain that the due process environment surrounding police action extends to three important areas: search and seizure of evidence, arrest, and interrogation. Refer to Table 7-1 to highlight the rights of criminal defendants.

■ **lecture note**   Discuss the Rodney King case, which drew the spotlight of public attention to the abuse of police power—a spotlight that continues to shine more than two decades later. Ask students what, if anything, they know about the case and the media's portrayal of the event. Discuss the possibility that the Los Angeles officers were tried by the media, rather than by the courts, and that these officers, too, may have a story to tell.

Charges against Davis were dropped in April 2006, but he filed a federal lawsuit against the city claiming a denial of his civil rights resulting from the excessive use of police force. Lance Schilling was found dead on June 10, 2007, apparently from a self-inflicted gunshot wound. A month later, former officer Robert Evangelist was cleared of all criminal charges by Judge Frank Marullo, who said that the video evidence showed Davis struggling for several minutes with the police. "This event could have ended at any time if the man had put his hands behind his back," the judge wrote.[6] Finally, in late 2009, just as a civil trial was set to begin, a financial settlement was reached between the city and Davis. The terms of the settlement were not made public.[7]

The Abuse of Police Power

National publicity surrounding the Davis beating was considerably less intense than that which centered on the 2015 shooting of 50-year-old Walter Scott.[8] Scott, who was black and unarmed, was shot in the back eight times by Michael Slager, a 33-year-old Charleston, S.C., police officer as he ran away following a traffic stop. Much of the incident was captured on cell phone video by a bystander. The video evidence appeared to show Slager dropping his Taser by Scott's lifeless body after the shooting. Scott told his supervisors that Slager had attempted to gain control over the Taser before running away.

No one is above the law—not even the police.

Also in 2015, six Baltimore, Maryland, police officers were indicted in the death of 25-year-old Freddie Gray.[9] Gray, who was also black and unarmed, died a week after he was arrested and transported in a police van, apparently without proper safety restraints. Gray had reportedly asked for medical assistance a number of times while he was in the van, but prosecutors claimed that his pleas were ignored.

One year earlier, a 400-pound asthmatic Staten Island man who was selling untaxed cigarettes on a sidewalk died after NYPD officers slammed his head against the sidewalk and put him in a chokehold—a dangerous restraint tactic that was against department policy.[10] Like Scott, the man who died, Eric Garner, 43, was black and unarmed—and the incident was also recorded on cell phone video by others at the scene.

Organized public reaction to the police killing of unarmed black men culminated in the development of the "Black Lives Matter" movement—a social justice initiative that had its roots in the shooting death of unarmed 18-year-old Michael Brown by a white Ferguson, Missouri, police officer.[11] The incident, which is described in more detail in Chapter 6, occurred after Brown allegedly stole cigars from a nearby convenience store and later got into a scuffle with the officer. Although details of the shooting were in dispute, a grand jury later refused to indict the officer.

Prior to the incidents described here, the most widely discussed abuse of police power was the 1991 videotaped beating of motorist Rodney King by LAPD officers. King, an unemployed 25-year-old black man, was stopped by LAPD officers for an alleged violation of motor vehicle laws.[12] Police said King had been speeding and had refused to stop for a pursuing patrol car. Eventually King did stop, but then officers of the LAPD appeared to attack him, shocking him twice with stun guns and striking him with nightsticks and fists. Kicked in the stomach, face, and back, King was left with 11 skull fractures, missing teeth, a crushed cheekbone, and a broken ankle. A witness told reporters that she heard King begging officers to stop the beating but that they "were all laughing, like they just had a party."

In 1992, a California jury found four police defendants not guilty in the King beating—a verdict that resulted in days of rioting across Los Angeles. A year later, however, in the spring of 1993, two of the officers, Sergeant Stacey Koon and Officer Laurence Powell, were found guilty in federal court of denying King his constitutional right "not to be deprived of liberty without due process of law, including the right to be . . . free from the intentional use of unreasonable force."[13] Later that year, both were sentenced to two and a half years in prison. In 1994, King settled a civil suit against the city of Los Angeles for a reported $3.8 million. King's 1991 beating served for many years as a rallying point for individual-rights activists who wanted to ensure that citizens remain protected from the abuse of police power.

This chapter shows how no one is above the law—not even the police. It describes the legal environment surrounding police activities, from search and seizure through arrest and the interrogation of suspects. As we shall see throughout, democratically inspired legal restraints on the police help ensure individual freedoms in our society and prevent the development of a police state in America. Like anything else, however, the rules by which the police are expected to operate are in constant flux, and their continuing development forms the meat of this chapter. For a police perspective on these issues, visit **http://www.policedefense.org**.

■ **Follow the author's tweets about the latest crime and justice news @schmalleger.**
■ **Bill of Rights**   The popular name given to the first ten amendments to the U.S. Constitution, which are considered especially important in the processing of criminal defendants.

■ **lecture note**   Describe the growing conservatism of the U.S. Supreme Court. Begin with the liberal Warren Court era of the 1960s and move through the Burger, Rehnquist, and Roberts eras. Alluding to confirmation battles in the U.S. Congress over Robert Bork, David Souter, and Clarence Thomas, describe how such battles are a reflection of the ideological stances of members of Congress and of the nominees themselves.

TABLE 7-1 | **Constitutional Amendments of Special Significance to the American System of Justice**

THIS RIGHT IS GUARANTEED	BY THIS AMENDMENT
The right against unreasonable searches and seizures	Fourth
The right against arrest without probable cause	Fourth
The right against self-incrimination	Fifth
The right against "double jeopardy"	Fifth
The right to due process of law	Fifth, Sixth, Fourteenth
The right to a speedy trial	Sixth
The right to a jury trial	Sixth
The right to know the charges	Sixth
The right to cross-examine witnesses	Sixth
The right to a lawyer	Sixth
The right to compel witnesses on one's behalf	Sixth
The right to reasonable bail	Eighth
The right against excessive fines	Eighth
The right against cruel and unusual punishments	Eighth
The applicability of constitutional rights to all citizens, regardless of state law or procedure	Fourteenth
Note: The Fourteenth Amendment is not a part of the Bill of Rights.	
Source: Pearson Education, Inc.	

A Changing Legal Climate

The Constitution of the United States is designed—especially in its **Bill of Rights**—to protect citizens against abuses of police power (Table 7-1). However, the legal environment surrounding the police in modern America is much more complex than it was 50 years ago. Up until that time, the Bill of Rights was largely given only lip service in criminal justice proceedings around the country. In practice, law enforcement, especially on the state and local levels, revolved around tried-and-true methods of search, arrest, and interrogation that sometimes left little room for recognition of individual rights. Police operations during that period were often far more informal than they are today, and investigating officers frequently assumed that they could come and go as they pleased, even to the extent of invading someone's home without a search warrant. Interrogations could quickly turn violent, and the infamous "rubber hose," which was reputed to leave few marks on the body, was sometimes used during the questioning of suspects. Similarly, "doing things by the book" sometimes meant using thick telephone books to beat suspects, since the books spread out the force of blows and left few visible bruises.

Although these abuses were not day-to-day practices in all police agencies and characterized just a small proportion of all officers, such conduct pointed to the need for greater control over police activities so that even the *potential* for abuse could be curtailed.

In the 1960s, the U.S. Supreme Court, under the direction of Chief Justice Earl Warren (1891–1974), accelerated the process of guaranteeing individual rights in the face of criminal prosecution. Warren Court rulings bound the police to strict procedural requirements in the areas of investigation, arrest, and interrogation. Later rulings scrutinized trial court procedure and enforced humanitarian standards in sentencing and punishment. The Warren Court also seized on the Fourteenth Amendment and made it the basis for judicial mandates requiring that both state and federal criminal justice agencies adhere to the Court's interpretation of the Constitution. The apex of the individual-rights emphasis in Supreme Court decisions was reached in the 1966 case of *Miranda* v. *Arizona*,[14] which established the famous requirement of a police "rights advisement" of suspects. In wielding its brand of idealism, the Warren Court (which held sway from 1953 until 1969) accepted that a few guilty people would go free in order to protect the rights of the majority of Americans.

In the decades since the Warren Court, a new conservative Court philosophy has resulted in Supreme Court decisions that have brought about what some call a "reversal" of Warren-era advances in the area of individual rights. By creating exceptions to some of the Warren Court's rules and restraints and by allowing for the emergency questioning of suspects before they are read their rights, a changed Supreme Court has recognized the realities attending day-to-day police work and the need to ensure public safety.

Individual Rights

The Constitution of the United States provides for a system of checks and balances among the legislative, judicial, and executive (presidential) branches of government. By this we mean that one branch of government is always held accountable to the other branches. The system is designed to ensure that no one individual or agency can become powerful enough to usurp the rights and freedoms guaranteed under the Constitution. Accountability rules out the possibility of a police state in which the power of law enforcement is absolute and is related more to political considerations and personal vendettas than to objective considerations of guilt or innocence.

Under our system of government, courts are the arena for dispute resolution, not just between individuals but between citizens and the agencies of government. People who feel they have not received the respect and dignity from the justice system

■ **lecture note**   Describe checks on police action by the courts. Tell how police agencies in foreign countries are often not constrained by the rule of law, and explain why citizens of such countries often live in fear of unbridled police action.

■ **theme**   When police officers violate the "rules of fair play" that apply to criminal investigations, is it unusual for guilty people to go free? Can you think of another way of enticing officers to obey the law, without necessarily letting the guilty go free? Explain your idea.

■ **landmark case**   A precedent-setting court decision that produces substantial changes in both the understanding of the requirements of due process and the practical day-to-day operations of the justice system.

■ **lecture note**   Review the concept of "due process" as discussed in Chapter 1.

■ **lecture note**   Explain that the U.S. Constitution (through the Bill of Rights) requires law enforcement personnel to seek a warrant before making an arrest or executing a search. Note that warrants are generally issued by magistrates who check to see that the police have probable cause to believe that the person to be arrested is likely to be the person who committed the crime or that the place to be searched is the place where sought-after evidence is likely to be found.

■ **illegally seized evidence**   Evidence seized without regard to the principles of due process as described by the Bill of Rights. Most illegally seized evidence is the result of police searches conducted without a proper warrant or of improperly conducted interrogations.

that are due to them under the law can appeal to the courts for redress. Such appeals are usually based on procedural issues and are independent of more narrow considerations of guilt or innocence in a particular case.

In this chapter, we focus on cases that are important for having clarified constitutional guarantees concerning individual liberties within the criminal justice arena. They involve issues that most of us have come to call *rights*. Rights are concerned with procedure, that is, with how police and other actors in the criminal justice system handle each part of the process of dealing with suspects. Rights violations have often become the basis for the dismissal of charges, the acquittal of defendants, or the release of convicted offenders after an appeal to a higher court.

Due Process Requirements

As you may recall from Chapter 1, the Fourth, Fifth, Sixth, and Fourteenth Amendments to the U.S. Constitution require due process, which mandates that justice system officials respect the rights of accused individuals throughout the criminal justice process. Most due process requirements of relevance to the police pertain to three major areas: (1) evidence and investigation (often called *search and seizure*), (2) arrest, and (3) intelligence gathering. Each of these areas has been addressed by a plethora of landmark U.S. Supreme Court decisions. **Landmark cases** produce substantial changes both in the understanding of the requirements of due process and in the practical day-to-day operations of the justice system. Landmark cases significantly clarify the "rules of the game"—the procedural guidelines by which the police and the rest of the justice system must abide.

The three areas we will discuss have been well defined by decades of court precedent. Keep in mind, however, that judicial interpretations of the constitutional requirement of due process are always evolving. As new decisions are rendered and as the composition of the Court itself changes, major changes and additional refinements may occur.

Search and Seizure

The Fourth Amendment to the U.S. Constitution declares that people must be secure in their homes and in their persons

Hill Street Studios/Glowimages

A female officer patting down a suspect. The legal environment surrounding the police helps ensure proper official conduct. In a stop like this, inappropriate behavior on the part of the officer can later become the basis for civil or criminal action against the officer and the police department. What might constitute inappropriate behavior?

against unreasonable searches and seizures. This amendment reads, "The right of the people to be secure in their persons, houses, papers, and effects, against unreasonable searches and seizures, shall not be violated, and no Warrants shall issue, but upon probable cause, supported by Oath or affirmation, and particularly describing the place to be searched, and the persons or things to be seized." The Fourth Amendment, a part of the Bill of Rights, was adopted by Congress and became effective on December 15, 1791.

The language of the Fourth Amendment is familiar to all of us. "Warrants," "probable cause," and other phrases from the amendment are frequently cited in editorials, TV news shows, and daily conversation about **illegally seized evidence**. It is the interpretation of these phrases over time by the U.S. Supreme Court, however, that has given them the impact they have on the justice system today.

■ **lecture note**   Review the 1914 case of *Weeks* v. *U.S.* and describe the ruling of the U.S. Supreme Court that led to the development of the exclusionary rule, which excludes illegally seized evidence from use at trial. Explain that illegally seized evidence often involves evidence that was obtained without a search warrant.

■ **theme**   What is the exclusionary rule? What is the fruit of the poisoned tree doctrine? What would American criminal justice be like without these rules?

■ **exclusionary rule**   The understanding, based on U.S. Supreme Court precedent, that incriminating information must be seized according to constitutional specifications of due process or it will not be allowed as evidence in a criminal trial.

■ **lecture note**   Discuss the fruit of the poisonous tree doctrine. Use the example of an illegally seized list of names that details the structure of an elaborate illegal drug operation. Tell the class that although enforcement agents may set up complex investigative strategies based on the information in the list and may make hundreds of arrests over a period of months or years, the arrests themselves will be illegal (and the defendants will be set free) if it can be shown that the investigation was based solely on information from the illegally seized list.

■ **writ of *certiorari***   A writ issued from an appellate court for the purpose of obtaining from a lower court the record of its proceedings in a particular case. In some states, this writ is the mechanism for discretionary review. A request for review is made by petitioning for a writ of *certiorari*, and the granting of review is indicated by the issuance of the writ.

■ **fruit of the poisonous tree doctrine**   A legal principle that excludes from introduction at trial any evidence later developed as a result of an illegal search or seizure.

The Exclusionary Rule

The first landmark case concerning search and seizure was *Weeks* v. *U.S.* (1914).[15] Freemont Weeks was suspected of using the U.S. mail to sell lottery tickets, a federal crime. Weeks was arrested, and federal agents went to his home to conduct a search. Since at the time investigators did not routinely use warrants, the agents had no search warrant. Still, they confiscated many incriminating items of evidence, as well as some of the suspect's personal possessions, including clothes, papers, books, and even candy.

Prior to trial, Weeks's attorney asked that the personal items be returned, claiming that they had been illegally seized under Fourth Amendment guarantees. A judge agreed and ordered the materials returned. On the basis of the evidence that was retained, however, Weeks was convicted in federal court and was sentenced to prison. He appealed his conviction through other courts, and his case eventually reached the U.S. Supreme Court, where his lawyer reasoned that if some of his client's belongings had been illegally seized, then all were taken improperly. The Court agreed and overturned Weeks's earlier conviction.

The *Weeks* case forms the basis of what is now called the **exclusionary rule**, which holds that evidence illegally seized by the police cannot be used in a trial. The rule acts as a control over police behavior and specifically focuses on the failure of officers to obtain warrants authorizing them either to conduct searches or to make arrests, especially where arrest may lead to the acquisition of incriminating statements or to the seizure of physical evidence.

The decision of the Supreme Court in the *Weeks* case was binding, at the time, only on federal officers because it was federal agents who were involved in the illegal seizure. Learn more about *Weeks* v. *U.S.* at **http://tinyurl.com/59rsve**. See Figure 7-1 for more about the exclusionary rule and its development since *Weeks*.

Problems with Precedent

The *Weeks* case demonstrates the Supreme Court's power to enforce the "rules of the game," as well as the much more significant role that it plays in rule creation. Until the *Weeks* case was decided, federal law enforcement officers had little reason to think they were violating due process because they were not required to obtain a warrant before conducting searches. The rule that resulted from *Weeks* was new, and it would forever alter the enforcement activities of federal officers.

The *Weeks* case reveals that the present appeals system, focusing as it does on the "rules of the game," presents a ready-made channel for the guilty to go free. There is little doubt that Freemont Weeks had violated federal law. A jury had convicted him. Yet he escaped punishment because of the illegal behavior of the police—behavior that, until the Court ruled, had been widely regarded as legitimate. Even if the police knowingly violate the principles of due process, which they sometimes do, our sense of justice is compromised when the guilty go free. Famed Supreme Court Justice Benjamin Cardozo (1870–1938) once complained, "The criminal is to go free because the constable has blundered." One solution to the problem would be to allow the Supreme Court to address theoretical questions involving issues of due process. Concerned supervisors and officials could ask how the Court would rule "if …" As things now work, however, the Court can address only real cases and does so on a **writ of *certiorari***, in which the Court orders the record of a lower court case to be prepared for review.

The Fruit of the Poisonous Tree Doctrine

The Court continued to build on the rules concerning evidence with its decision in *Silverthorne Lumber Co.* v. *U.S.* (1920).[16]

The case against the Silverthornes, owners of a lumberyard, was built on evidence that was illegally seized. Although the tainted evidence was itself not used in court, its "fruits" (later evidence that derived from the illegal seizure) were and the Silverthornes were convicted. The Supreme Court overturned the decision, holding that any evidence that derives from a seizure that was in itself illegal cannot be used at trial.

The *Silverthorne* case articulated a new principle of due process that today we call the **fruit of the poisonous tree doctrine**. This doctrine is potentially far-reaching. Complex cases developed

THE FOURTH AMENDMENT TO THE U.S. CONSTITUTION

The right of the people to be secure in their persons, houses, papers, and effects, against unreasonable searches and seizures, shall not be violated, and no Warrants shall issue, but upon probable cause, supported by Oath or affirmation, and particularly describing the place to be searched, and the persons or things to be seized.

Based upon the Fourth Amendment, **the Exclusionary Rule** holds that evidence of an offense that is collected or obtained by law enforcement officers in violation of a defendant's constitutional rights is inadmissible for use in a criminal prosecution in a court of law.

SIGNIFICANT CASES

Weeks v. *U.S.* (1914)

Established the exclusionary rule at the federal level, holding that evidence that is illegally obtained cannot be used in a criminal trial; and that federal officer must have a valid warrant before conducting searches or seizing evidence. Prior to *Weeks*, common practice generally allowed all relevant evidence, no matter how it was obtained, to be used in court.

Silverthorne Lumber Co. v. *U.S.* (1920)

Set forth the **Fruit of the Poisonous Tree Doctrine,** which says that just as illegally seized evidence cannot be used in a trial, neither can evidence that derives from an illegal search or seizure. Under this doctrine, complex cases developed after years of police investigative effort may be ruined if defense attorneys are able to demonstrate that the prosecution's case was originally based on a search or seizure that, at the time it occurred, violated due process.

Mapp v. *Ohio* (1961)

Applied the exclusionary rule to criminal prosecutions at the state level. The Court held that the due process clause of the Fourteenth Amendment to the U.S. Constitution makes Fourth Amendment provisions applicable to state proceedings.

SUBSTANTIAL SOCIAL COSTS

U.S. v. *Leon* (1984) and *Hudson* v. *Michigan* (2006)

Recognized that the exclusionary rule generates "substantial social costs," which may include letting the guilty go free and setting the dangerous at large.

EXCEPTIONS TO THE EXCLUSIONARY RULE

THE GOOD-FAITH EXCEPTION

U.S. v. *Leon* (1984)

Allowed evidence that officers had seized in "reasonable good faith" to be used in court, even though the search was later ruled illegal.

Illinois v. *Krull* (1987)

The *good-faith exception* applied to a warrantless search supported by state law even though the state statute was later found to violate the Fourth Amendment.

Maryland v. *Garrison* (1987)

The use of evidence obtained by officers with a search warrant that was inaccurate in its specifics was allowed.

THE PLAIN-VIEW DOCTRINE

Harris v. *U.S.* (1968)

Police officers have the opportunity to begin investigations or to confiscate evidence, without a warrant, based on what they find in plain view and open to public inspection.

CLERICAL ERRORS EXCEPTION

Arizona v. *Evans* (1995)

A traffic stop that led to the seizure of marijuana was legal even though officers conducted the stop based on an arrest warrant that should have been deleted from the computer database to which they had access.

Herring v. *U.S.* (2009)

When police mistakes leading to an unlawful search are the result of isolated negligence rather than systemic error or reckless disregard of constitutional requirements, the exclusionary rule does not apply.

EMERGENCY SEARCHES OF PROPERTY/EMERGENCY ENTRY

Brigham City v. *Stuart* (2006)

Certain emergencies may justify a police officer's decision to search or enter premises without a warrant.

FIGURE 7-1 | The Exclusionary Rule

Source: Pearson Education, Inc.

after years of police investigative effort may be ruined if defense attorneys are able to demonstrate that the prosecution's case was originally based on a search or seizure that violated due process. In such cases, it is likely that all evidence will be declared "tainted" and will become useless.

The Warren Court (1953–1969)

Before the 1960s, the U.S. Supreme Court intruded only occasionally on the overall operation of the criminal justice system at the state and local levels. As one author observed, however, the 1960s were a time of idealism, and "without the distraction of a depression or world war, individual liberties were examined at all levels of society."[17] Hence, although the exclusionary rule became an overriding consideration in federal law enforcement from the time of its creation in 1914, it was not until 1961 that the Court, under Chief Justice Earl Warren, decided a case that changed the face of American law enforcement forever. Beginning with the now-famous *Mapp* v. *Ohio* (1961) case,[18] the Warren Court charted a course that would guarantee nationwide recognition of individual rights, as it understood them, by agencies at all levels

■ **lecture note**   Discuss the 1961 U.S. Supreme Court case of *Mapp* v. *Ohio* and explain that while the *Weeks* case applied the exclusionary rule to federal courts, *Mapp* extended it to the states as well.

■ **lecture note**   Consider explaining the "silver platter doctrine" which was also established by the *Weeks* case. This essentially was an exception to the exclusionary rule that covered situations in which local or state-level law enforcement officers obtained evidence illegally and then "handed it over on a silver platter" to federal law enforcement officers for use in federal courts. As long as the federal authorities were not involved in obtaining the evidence, it was admissible in court. The silver platter doctrine was repealed by the U.S. Supreme Court in the 1960 case of *Elkins* v. *U.S.*, one year before the *Mapp* case.

freedom OR safety? YOU decide

Liberty Is a Double-Edged Sword

This chapter builds on the following theme: For police action to be "just," it must recognize the rights of individuals while holding them accountable to the social obligations defined by law. It is important to realize that many democratically inspired legal restraints on the police stem from the Bill of Rights, which comprises the first ten amendments to the U.S. Constitution. Such restraints help ensure individual freedoms in our society and prevent the development of a police state in America.

In police work and elsewhere, the principles of individual liberty and social justice are cornerstones on which the American way of life rests. Ideally, the work of police agencies, as well as the American system of criminal justice, is to ensure justice while guarding liberty. The liberty–justice issue is the dual thread that holds the tapestry of the justice system together—from the simplest daily activities of police officers on the beat to the often complex and lengthy renderings of the U.S. Supreme Court.

For the criminal justice system as a whole, the question becomes, How can individual liberties be maintained in the face of the need for official action, including arrest, interrogation, incarceration, and the like? The answer is far from simple, but it begins with the recognition that liberty is a double-edged sword, entailing obligations as well as rights.

You Decide

What does it mean to say that "for police action to be 'just,' it must recognize the rights of individuals while holding them accountable to the social obligations defined by law"? How can police agencies accomplish this? What can individual officers do to help their agencies in this regard?

---

of the criminal justice system. Learn more about the case of *Mapp* v. *Ohio* at **http://tinyurl.com/66yotaz**.

Searches Incident to Arrest

Another important Warren-era case, *Chimel* v. *California* (1969),[19] involved both arrest and search activities by local law enforcement officers. Ted Chimel was convicted of the burglary of a coin shop based on evidence gathered at his home, where he was arrested. Officers, armed with an arrest warrant but not a search warrant, took Chimel into custody when they arrived at his residence and proceeded with a search of his entire three-bedroom house, including the attic, a small workshop, and the garage. Although officers realized that the search might be challenged in court, they justified it by claiming that it was conducted not so much to uncover evidence but as part of the arrest process. Searches that are conducted incident to arrest, they argued, are necessary for the officers' protection and should not require a search warrant. Coins taken from the burglarized coin shop were found in various places in Chimel's residence, including the garage, and were presented as evidence against him at trial.

> The Warren Court charted a course that would guarantee nationwide recognition of individual rights.

Chimel's appeal eventually reached the U.S. Supreme Court, which ruled that the search of Chimel's residence, although incident to arrest, became invalid when it went beyond the person arrested and the area subject to that person's "immediate control." The thrust of the Court's decision was that searches during arrest can be made to protect arresting officers but that without a search warrant, their scope must be strongly circumscribed. The legal implications of *Chimel* v. *California* are summarized in Table 7-2.

Since the early days of the exclusionary rule, other court decisions have highlighted the fact that "the Fourth Amendment protects people, not places."[20] In other words, people can reasonably expect privacy in their *homes*—even if those homes are not houses. "Homes" of all sorts—including apartments, duplex dwellings, motel rooms, and even the cardboard boxes or makeshift tents of the homeless—are protected places under the Fourth Amendment. In *Minnesota* v. *Olson* (1990),[21] for example, the U.S. Supreme Court extended the protection against warrantless searches to overnight guests residing in the home of another. The capacity to claim the protection of the Fourth Amendment, said the Court, depends on whether the *person* who makes that claim has a legitimate expectation of privacy in the place searched.

■ **lecture note** Discuss the way in which *Chimel v. California* (1969) defined *what* officers may search, *when* they may search, and *why*. Ask students why such directives are necessary and how they help individual suspects but may hinder police activity. How else might search parameters be defined?

■ **theme** What are some valid reasons for conducting a search? When does a search become illegal?
■ **theme** How did the Warren Court and the Burger Court differ? Why do you think the decisions of the Court changed over time?

TABLE 7-2 | Implications of *Chimel v. California* (1969)

What Arresting Officers May Search
The defendant
The physical area within easy reach of the defendant

Valid Reasons for Conducting a Search
To protect the arresting officers
To prevent evidence from being destroyed
To keep the defendant from escaping

When a Search Becomes Illegal
When it goes beyond the defendant and the area within the
defendant's immediate control
When it is conducted for other than a valid reason

Source: Pearson Education, Inc.

In 1998, in the case of *Minnesota* v. *Carter*,[22] the Court held that for a defendant to be entitled to Fourth Amendment protection, "he must demonstrate that he personally has an expectation of privacy in the place searched, and that his expectation is reasonable." The Court noted that "the extent to which the Amendment protects people may depend upon where those people are. While an overnight guest may have a legitimate expectation of privacy in someone else's home . . . one who is merely present with the consent of the householder may not." Hence, an appliance repair person visiting a residence is unlikely to be accorded privacy protections while on the job.

In 2006, in the case of *Georgia* v. *Randolph*,[23] the Court ruled that police officers may not enter a home to conduct a warrantless search if one resident gives permission but the other refuses it. The *Randolph* ruling was a narrow one and centered on the stated refusal by a physically present co-occupant to permit warrantless entry in the absence of evidence of abuse or other circumstances that might otherwise justify an immediate police entry.[24]

Finally, in 2013, in the case of *Baily* v. *U.S.*, the Court limited the power of police to detain people who are away from their homes when police conduct a search of their residence, unless they have probable cause for an arrest. One expert commenting on *Bailey* noted that "if you allow this, then whenever you do a search, people associated with that home could be arrested, no matter where they are, and that just goes too far."[25]

The Burger Court (1969–1986) and the Rehnquist Court (1986–2005)

During the 1980s and 1990s, the United States experienced a swing toward conservatism, giving rise to a renewed concern with protecting the interests—financial and otherwise—of those who live within the law. The Reagan–Bush years, and the popularity of the two presidents who many thought embodied "old-fashioned" values, reflected the tenor of a nation seeking a return to "simpler," less volatile times.

Chris O'Meara/AP Wide World Photos

Police officers examining suspected controlled substances after a drug raid. The exclusionary rule means that illegally gathered evidence cannot be used later in court, requiring that police officers pay close attention to how they gather and handle evidence. How did the exclusionary rule come into being?

■ **lecture note**   Describe the notion of good faith and good-faith exceptions to the exclusionary rule. Ask students what they think the impact of good-faith exceptions may be on American criminal justice and whether they think the Court should ever have created the good-faith exception.

■ **good-faith exception**   An exception to the exclusionary rule. Law enforcement officers who conduct a search or who seize evidence on the basis of good faith (that is, when they believe they are operating according to the dictates of the law) and who later discover that a mistake was made (perhaps in the format of the application for a search warrant) may still provide evidence that can be used in court.

■ **probable cause**   A set of facts and circumstances that would induce a reasonably intelligent and prudent person to believe that a particular other person has committed a specific crime. Also, reasonable grounds to make or believe an accusation. Probable cause refers to the necessary level of belief that would allow for police seizures (arrests) of individuals and full searches of dwellings, vehicles, and possessions.

Throughout the late 1980s, the U.S. Supreme Court mirrored the nation's conservative tenor by distancing itself from some earlier decisions of the Warren Court. Whereas the Warren Court embodied the individual rights heyday in Court jurisprudence, Court decisions beginning in the 1970s were generally supportive of a "greater good" era—one in which the justices increasingly acknowledged the importance of social order and communal safety. Under Chief Justice Warren E. Burger, the new Court adhered to the principle that criminal defendants who claimed violations of their due process rights needed to bear most of the responsibility of showing that police went beyond the law in the performance of their duties. This tenet is still held by the Court today.

Good-Faith Exceptions to the Exclusionary Rule

The Burger Court, which held sway from 1969 until 1986, "chipped away" at the strict application of the exclusionary rule originally set forth in the *Weeks* and *Silverthorne* cases. In the 1984 case of *U.S.* v. *Leon*,[26] the Court recognized what has come to be called the **good-faith exception** to the exclusionary rule. In this case, the Court modified the exclusionary rule to allow evidence that officers had seized in "reasonable good faith" to be used in court, even though the search was later ruled illegal. The suspect, Alberto Leon, was placed under surveillance for drug trafficking following a tip from a confidential informant. Burbank (California) Police Department investigators applied for a search warrant based on information gleaned from the surveillance, believing that they were in compliance with the Fourth Amendment requirement that "no Warrants shall issue, but upon probable cause." **Probable cause** is a tricky but important concept. Its legal criteria are based on facts and circumstances that would cause a reasonable person to believe that a particular other person has committed a specific crime. Before a warrant can be issued, police officers must satisfactorily demonstrate probable cause in a written affidavit to a magistrate[27]—a low-level judge who ensures that the police establish the probable cause needed for warrants to be obtained. Upon a demonstration of probable cause, the magistrate will issue a warrant authorizing law enforcement officers to effect an arrest or conduct a search.

In *U.S.* v. *Leon*, a warrant was issued, and a search of Leon's three residences yielded a large amount of drugs and other evidence. Although Leon was convicted of drug trafficking, a later ruling in a federal district court resulted in the suppression of evidence against him on the basis that the original affidavit prepared by the police had not, in the opinion of the reviewing court, been sufficient to establish probable cause.

> Before a warrant can be issued, police officers must satisfactorily demonstrate probable cause.

The federal government petitioned the U.S. Supreme Court to consider whether evidence gathered by officers acting in good faith as to the validity of a warrant should be fairly excluded at trial. The good-faith exception was presaged in the first paragraph of the Court's written decision: "When law enforcement officers have acted in objective good faith or their transgressions have been minor, the magnitude of the benefit conferred on such guilty defendants offends basic concepts of the criminal justice system." Reflecting the renewed conservatism of the Burger Court, the justices found for the government and reinstated Leon's conviction.

In that same year, the Supreme Court case of *Massachusetts* v. *Sheppard* (1984)[28] further reinforced the concept of good faith. In the *Sheppard* case, officers executed a search warrant that failed to accurately describe the property to be seized. Although they were aware of the error, a magistrate had assured them that the warrant was valid. After the seizure was complete and a conviction had been obtained, the Massachusetts Supreme Judicial Court reversed the finding of the trial court. Upon appeal, the U.S. Supreme Court reiterated the good-faith exception and reinstated the original conviction.

The cases of *Leon* and *Sheppard* represented a clear reversal of the Warren Court's philosophy, and the trend continued with the 1987 case of *Illinois* v. *Krull*.[29] In *Krull*, the Court, now under the leadership of Chief Justice William Rehnquist, held that the *good-faith exception* applied to a warrantless search permitted by an Illinois law related to automobile junkyards and vehicular parts sellers even though the state statute was later found to violate the Fourth Amendment. A 1987 Supreme Court case similar to *Sheppard*, *Maryland* v. *Garrison*,[30] supported the use of evidence obtained with a search warrant that was inaccurate in

■ **plain view** A legal term describing the ready visibility of objects that might be seized as evidence during a search by police in the absence of a search warrant specifying the seizure of those objects. To lawfully seize evidence in plain view, officers must have a legal right to be in the viewing area and must have cause to believe that the evidence is somehow associated with criminal activity.

■ **lecture note** Describe the plain-view doctrine. Ask students if they think this doctrine might be difficult for police officers to keep in mind in their daily work.

its specifics. In *Garrison*, officers had procured a warrant to search an apartment, believing it was the only dwelling on the building's third floor. After searching the entire floor, they discovered that it housed more than one apartment. Even so, evidence acquired in the search was held to be admissible based on the reasonable mistake of the officers.

The 1990 case of *Illinois* v. *Rodriguez*[31] further diminished the scope of the exclusionary rule. In *Rodriguez*, a badly beaten woman named Gail Fischer complained to police that she had been assaulted in a Chicago apartment. Fischer led police to the apartment (which she indicated she shared with the defendant), produced a key, and opened the door to the dwelling. Inside, investigators found the defendant, Edward Rodriguez, asleep on a bed, with drug paraphernalia and cocaine spread around him. Rodriguez was arrested and charged with assault and possession of a controlled substance.

Upon appeal, Rodriguez demonstrated that Fischer had not lived with him for at least a month and argued that she could no longer be said to have legal control over the apartment. Hence, the defense claimed, Fischer had no authority to provide investigators with access to the dwelling. According to arguments made by the defense, the evidence, which had been obtained without a warrant, had not been properly seized. The Supreme Court disagreed, ruling that "even if Fischer did not possess common authority over the premises, there was no Fourth Amendment violation if the police *reasonably believed* at the time of their entry that Fischer possessed the authority to consent."

In 1995, in the case of *Arizona* v. *Evans*,[32] the U.S. Supreme Court created a "computer errors exception" to the exclusionary rule. In *Evans*, the Court held that a traffic stop that led to the seizure of marijuana was legal even though officers conducted the stop based on an arrest warrant that should have been deleted from their computer database. The arrest warrant reported to the officers by their computer had actually been quashed a few weeks earlier, but due to an oversight, a court employee had never removed it from the database.

In reaching its decision, the high court reasoned that police officers could not be held responsible for a clerical error made by a court worker and concluded that the arresting officers had acted in good faith. In addition, the majority opinion said that "the rule excluding evidence obtained without a warrant was intended to deter police misconduct, not mistakes by court employees." In 2009, in the case of *Herring* v. *U.S.*, the Court reinforced its ruling in *Evans*, holding that "when police mistakes leading to an unlawful search are the result of isolated negligence . . . rather than systemic error or reckless disregard of constitutional requirements, the exclusionary rule does not apply."[33]

A general listing of established exceptions to the exclusionary rule, along with other investigative powers created by court precedent, is provided in Table 7-3.

During Rehnquist's tenure as chief justice, the Court invoked a characteristically conservative approach to many important criminal justice issues—from limiting the exclusionary rule[34] and generally broadening police powers to sharply limiting the opportunities for state prisoners to bring appeals in federal courts.[35] Preventive detention, "no knock" police searches,[36] the death penalty,[37] and habitual offender statutes[38] (often known as *three-strikes laws*) all were decisively supported under Chief Justice Rehnquist.[39] The particular cases in which the Court addressed these issues are discussed elsewhere in this text.

Following Rehnquist's death in 2005, John G. Roberts, Jr., became the nation's seventeenth chief justice. Roberts had previously served as a judge on the U.S. Court of Appeals for the District of Columbia Circuit.

The Plain-View Doctrine

Police officers have the opportunity to begin investigations or to confiscate evidence, without a warrant, based on what they find in **plain view** and open to public inspection. The plain-view doctrine was succinctly stated in the U.S. Supreme Court case of *Harris* v. *U.S.* (1968),[40] in which a police officer inventorying an impounded vehicle discovered evidence of a robbery.[41] In the *Harris* case, the Court ruled that "objects falling in the plain view of an officer who has a right to be in the position to have that view are subject to seizure and may be introduced in evidence."[42]

The plain-view doctrine is applicable in common situations like crimes in progress, fires, accidents, and other emergencies. For example, police officers who enter a residence responding to a call for assistance and find drugs or other contraband in plain view are within their legitimate authority to confiscate the materials and to effect an arrest if the owner of the contraband can be identified. However, the plain-view doctrine applies only to sightings by the police under legal circumstances—that is, in places where the police have a legitimate right to be and, typically, only if the sighting was coincidental. Similarly, the incriminating nature of the evidence seized must have been "immediately apparent" to the officers making the seizure.[43] If officers conspired to avoid the necessity for a search warrant by helping create a plain-view situation through surveillance, duplicity, or other means, the doctrine likely would not apply.

TABLE 7-3 | Selected Investigatory Activities Supported by Court Precedent

THIS POLICE ACTION	IS SUPPORTED BY
An anonymous and uncorroborated tip can provide a sufficient basis for an officer's reasonable suspicion to make an investigative stop.	*Prado Navarette v. California* (2014)
Where multiple occupants are involved, the search of a dwelling is permissible without a warrant if one person living there consents after officers have removed another resident who objects.	*Fernandez v. California.* (2014)
Arrest based on isolated clerical error	*Herring v. U.S.* (2009) *Arizona v. Evans* (1995)
Authority to enter and/or search an "open field" without a warrant	*U.S. v. Dunn* (1987) *Oliver v. U.S.* (1984) *Hester v. U.S.* (1924)
Authority to search incident to arrest and/or to conduct a protective sweep in conjunction with an in-home arrest	*Maryland v. Buie* (1990) *U.S. v. Edwards* (1974) *Chimel v. California* (1969)
Gathering of incriminating evidence during interrogation in noncustodial circumstances	*Yarborough v. Alvarado* (2004) *Thompson v. Keohane* (1996) *Stansbury v. California* (1994) *U.S. v. Mendenhall* (1980) *Beckwith v. U.S.* (1976)
Gathering of incriminating evidence during *Miranda*-less custodial interrogation	*Montejo v. Louisiana* (2009) *U.S. v. Patane* (2004)
Inevitable discovery of evidence	*Nix v. Williams* (1984)
"No knock" searches or quick entry	*Brigham City v. Stuart* (2006) *Hudson v. Michigan* (2006) *U.S. v. Barnes* (2003) *Richards v. Wisconsin* (1997) *Wilson v. Arkansas* (1995)
Prompt action in the face of threat to public or personal safety or destruction of evidence	*U.S. v. Banks* (2003) *Borchardt v. U.S.* (1987) *New York v. Quarles* (1984) *Warden v. Hayden* (1967)
Seizure of evidence in good faith, even in the face of some exclusionary rule violations	*Illinois v. Krull* (1987) *U.S. v. Leon* (1984)
Seizure of evidence in plain view	*Horton v. California* (1990) *Coolidge v. New Hampshire* (1971) *Harris v. U.S.* (1968)
Stop and frisk/request personal identification	*Arizona v. Johnson* (2009) *Hiibel v. Sixth Judicial District Court of Nevada* (2004) *Terry v. Ohio* (1968)
Use of police informants in jail cells	*Arizona v. Fulminante* (1991) *Illinois v. Perkins* (1990) *Kuhlmann v. Wilson* (1986)
Warrantless naked-eye aerial observation of open areas and/or greenhouses	*Florida v. Riley* (1989) *California v. Ciraolo* (1986)
Warrantless search incident to a lawful arrest	*U.S. v. Rabinowitz* (1950)
Warrantless seizure of abandoned materials and refuse	*California v. Greenwood* (1988)
Warrantless vehicle search where probable cause exists to believe that the vehicle contains contraband and/or that the occupants have been lawfully arrested	*Thornton v. U.S.* (2004) *Ornelas v. U.S.* (1996) *California v. Acevedo* (1991) *California v. Carney* (1985) *U.S. v. Ross* (1982) *New York v. Belton* (1981) *Carroll v. U.S.* (1925)

Source: Pearson Education, Inc.

The plain-view doctrine was restricted by later federal court decisions. In the 1982 case of *U.S. v. Irizarry*,[44] the First Circuit Court of Appeals held that officers could not move objects to gain a view of evidence otherwise hidden from view. In the U.S. Supreme Court case of *Arizona v. Hicks* (1987),[45] the requirement that evidence be in plain view, without requiring officers (who did not have a warrant, but who had been invited into a residence) to move or dislodge objects, was reiterated.

Most evidence seized under the plain-view doctrine is discovered "inadvertently"—that is, by accident.[46] However, in

■ **activity** Ask the class to look at the Supreme Court decisions noted in Table 7-3 and group the decisions according to the Court that rendered them (the Warren Court, the Rehnquist Court, etc.). Have students assign a score to each decision, indicating whether it would likely appeal more to individual-rights advocates or public-order advocates. Decisions that would have the greatest appeal to individual-rights advocates could be scored a 0, those with the greatest appeal to public-order advocates could be ranked 10, with other rankings in between.

■ **lecture note** Discuss the wide variety of police investigative activities that have been approved by the courts over the years by referring to Table 7-3. Ask students which of the police powers identified by the table are exceptions to the exclusionary rule and which are not. Which do they find acceptable?

CJ | ISSUES
Plain-View Requirements

Following the opinion of the U.S. Supreme Court in the case of *Horton v. California* (1990), items seized under the plain-view doctrine may be admissible as evidence in a court of law if both of the following conditions are met:

1. The officer who seized the evidence was in the viewing area lawfully.
2. The officer had probable cause to believe that the evidence was somehow associated with criminal activity.

Tarpon Springs, Florida, sheriff's deputies talk to a person inside of a home. How might the plain-view doctrine apply to this situation? How would you explain the concept of plain view?

1990, the U.S. Supreme Court ruled in the case of *Horton* v. *California*[47] that "even though inadvertence *is* a characteristic of most legitimate 'plain view' seizures, it is not a necessary condition."[48] In the *Horton* case, a warrant was issued authorizing the search of Terry Brice Horton's home for stolen jewelry. The affidavit, completed by the officer who requested the warrant, alluded to an Uzi submachine gun and a stun gun—weapons purportedly used in the jewelry robbery. It did not request that those weapons be listed on the search warrant. Officers searched the defendant's home but did not find the stolen jewelry. They did, however, seize a number of weapons, among them an Uzi, two stun guns, and a .38-caliber revolver. Horton was convicted of robbery in a trial in which the seized weapons were introduced into evidence. He appealed his conviction, claiming that

officers had reason to believe that the weapons were in his home at the time of the search and were therefore not seized inadvertently. His appeal was rejected by the Court. As a result of the *Horton* case, inadvertence is no longer considered a condition necessary to ensure the legitimacy of a seizure that results when evidence other than that listed in a search warrant is discovered.

Plain-view searches present a special problem in the area of electronic evidence (which is discussed in more detail later in this chapter). If, let's say, a police officer obtains a warrant to seize and search a computer that he suspects was used to commit a particular crime, he then has easy access to other documents and information stored on that computer. An officer conducting a fraud investigation, for example, might obtain a warrant to seize a personal computer, but then will need to examine individual files on

■ **emergency search**   A search conducted by the police without a warrant, which is justified on the basis of some immediate and overriding need, such as public safety, the likely escape of a dangerous suspect, or the removal or destruction of evidence.

■ **theme**   Given the advent of good-faith exceptions to the exclusionary rule, the plain-view doctrine, and the U.S. Supreme Court's recognition of the need for emergency searches, can we realistically argue that the exclusionary rule is still effective in contemporary American criminal justice? Has the exclusionary rule been so watered down by recent decisions as to be little more than a paper tiger? Defend your position.

■ **theme**   In your opinion, should the U.S. Supreme Court have created exceptions to the exclusionary rule? Why or why not?

it in order to determine which ones (if any) are related to the investigation. If, however, he discovers pirated videos stored on the machine, he can then generally charge the owner of the computer with illegally copying the digital media because it is protected by copyright law. Consequently, some legal experts have called for limiting the range of potential types of prosecution available in such cases—and confining them to the offense specified in the original warrant.[49] That no such limitations are currently in place has prompted some commentators to propose "statutory solutions eliminating plain view for computer searches."[50]

Emergency Searches of Property and Emergency Entry

Certain emergencies may justify a police officer's decision to search or enter premises without a warrant. In 2006, for example, in the case of *Brigham City* v. *Stuart*,[51] the Court recognized the need for emergency warrantless entries under certain circumstances when it ruled that police officers "may enter a home without a warrant when they have an objectively reasonable basis for believing that an occupant is seriously injured or imminently threatened with such injury." The case involved police entry into a private home to break up a fight.

According to the Legal Counsel Division of the Federal Bureau of Investigation (FBI), there are three threats that "provide justification for emergency warrantless action":[52] clear dangers (1) to life, (2) of escape, and (3) of the removal or destruction of evidence. Any one of these situations may create an exception to the Fourth Amendment's requirement of a search warrant.

Emergency searches, or those conducted without a warrant when special needs arise, are legally termed *exigent circumstances searches*. When emergencies necessitate a quick search of premises, however, law enforcement officers are responsible for demonstrating that a dire situation existed that justified their actions. Failure to do so successfully in court will, of course, taint any seized evidence and make it unusable.

The U.S. Supreme Court first recognized the need for emergency searches in 1967 in the case of *Warden* v. *Hayden*.[53]

> Certain emergencies may justify a police officer's decision to search or enter premises without a warrant.

In that case, the Court approved the warrantless search of a residence following reports that an armed robber had fled into the building. In *Hayden*, the Supreme Court held that "the Fourth Amendment does not require police officers to delay in

the course of an investigation if to do so would gravely endanger their lives or the lives of others."[54]

A 1990 decision, rendered in the case of *Maryland* v. *Buie*,[55] extended the authority of police to search locations in a house where a potentially dangerous person could hide while an arrest warrant is being served. The *Buie* decision was meant primarily to protect investigators from potential danger and can apply even when officers lack a warrant, probable cause, or even reasonable suspicion.

In 1995, in the case of *Wilson* v. *Arkansas*,[56] the U.S. Supreme Court ruled that police officers generally must knock and announce their identity before entering a dwelling or other premises, even when armed with a search warrant. Under certain emergency circumstances, however, exceptions may be made, and officers may not need to knock or to identify themselves before entering.[57] In *Wilson*, the Court added that the Fourth Amendment requirement that searches be reasonable "should not be read to mandate a rigid rule of announcement that ignores countervailing law enforcement interests." Hence, officers need not announce themselves, the Court said, when suspects may be in the process of destroying evidence, officers are pursuing a recently escaped arrestee, or officers' lives may be endangered by such an announcement. Because the *Wilson* case involved an appeal from a drug dealer who was apprehended by police officers who entered her unlocked house while she was flushing marijuana down a toilet, some said that it establishes a "drug-law exception" to the knock-and-announce requirement.

In 1997, in *Richards* v. *Wisconsin*,[58] the Supreme Court clarified its position on "no knock" exceptions, saying that individual courts have the duty in each case to "determine whether the facts and circumstances of the particular entry justified dispensing with the requirement." The Court went on to say that "[a] 'no knock' entry is justified when the police have a reasonable suspicion that knocking and announcing their presence, under the particular circumstances, would be dangerous or futile, or that it would inhibit the effective investigation of the crime. This standard strikes the appropriate balance," said the Court, "between the legitimate law enforcement concerns at issue in the execution of search warrants and the individual privacy interests affected by no knock entries."

In 2001, in the case of *Illinois* v. *McArthur*,[59] the U.S. Supreme Court ruled that police officers with probable cause to believe that a home contains contraband or evidence of criminal activity may reasonably prevent a suspect found outside the home from reentering it while they apply for a search warrant; and in 2003, in a case involving drug possession, the Court held

■ **anticipatory warrant**   A search warrant issued on the basis of probable cause to believe that evidence of a crime, while not presently at the place described, will likely be there when the warrant is executed.

■ **arrest**   The act of taking an adult or juvenile into physical custody by authority of law for the purpose of charging the person with a criminal offense, a delinquent act, or a status offense, terminating with the recording of a specific offense. Technically, an arrest occurs whenever a law enforcement officer curtails a person's freedom to leave.

that a 15- to 20-second wait after officers knocked, announced themselves, and requested entry before breaking open a door was sufficient to satisfy the Fourth Amendment requirements.[60]

In the 2006 case of *Hudson* v. *Michigan*,[61] the Court surprised many when it ruled that evidence found by police officers who enter a home to execute a warrant without first following the knock-and-announce requirement can be used at trial despite that constitutional violation. In the words of the Court, "The interests protected by the knock-and-announce rule include human life and limb (because an unannounced entry may provoke violence from a surprised resident), property (because citizens presumably would open the door upon an announcement, whereas a forcible entry may destroy it), and privacy and dignity of the sort that can be offended by a sudden entrance." But, said the Court, "the rule has never protected one's interest in preventing the government from seeing or taking evidence described in a warrant." The justices reasoned that the social costs of strictly adhering to the knock-and-announce rule are considerable and may include "the grave adverse consequence that excluding relevant incriminating evidence always entails—the risk of releasing dangerous criminals." In a ruling that some said signaled a new era of lessened restraints on the police, the Court's majority opinion said that since the interests violated by ignoring the knock-and-announce rule "have nothing to do with the seizure of the evidence, the exclusionary rule is inapplicable."

In 2011, in the case of *Kentucky* v. *King*, the U.S. Supreme Court overruled a Kentucky Supreme Court decision and found that Lexington, Kentucky, police officers had legally entered a suspected drug dealer's apartment without a warrant when they smelled marijuana outside the residence.[62] After knocking loudly and announcing their presence, the officers heard noises coming from inside the apartment that they believed indicated the destruction of evidence. They then kicked in the door and saw evidence of drug use in plain view. Writing for the majority, Justice Samuel Alito said, "Occupants who choose not to stand on their constitutional rights but instead elect to attempt to destroy evidence have only themselves to blame for the warrantless exigent-circumstances search that may ensue." Learn more about another type of exception to the exclusionary rule via **http://www.justicestudies.com/pubs/emergency.pdf**.

Anticipatory Warrants

Anticipatory warrants are search warrants issued on the basis of probable cause to believe that evidence of a crime, although not presently at the place described, will likely be there when the warrant is executed. Such warrants anticipate the presence of contraband or other evidence of criminal culpability but do not claim that the evidence is present at the time that the warrant is requested or issued.

Anticipatory warrants are no different in principle from ordinary search warrants. They require an issuing magistrate to determine (1) that it is probable that (2) contraband, evidence of a crime, or a fugitive will be on the described premises (3) when the warrant is executed.

The constitutionality of anticipatory warrants was affirmed in 2006 in the U.S. Supreme Court case of *U.S.* v. *Grubbs*.[63] In *Grubbs*, an anticipatory search warrant had been issued for Grubbs's house based on a federal officer's affidavit stating that the warrant would not be executed until a parcel containing a videotape of child pornography—which Grubbs had ordered from an undercover postal inspector—was received at and physically taken into his residence. After the package was delivered, law enforcement officers executed the anticipatory search warrant, seized the videotape, and arrested Grubbs.

Arrest

Officers seize not only property but people as well—a process referred to as *arrest*. Although many people think of arrest in terms of what they see on popular TV crime shows—the suspect is chased, subdued, and "cuffed" after committing a loathsome act in view of the camera—most arrests are far more mundane.

In technical terms, an **arrest** occurs whenever a law enforcement officer restricts a person's freedom to leave. There may be no yelling "You're under arrest!" No *Miranda* warnings may be offered, and in fact, the suspect may not even consider himself or herself to be in custody. Some arrests evolve as a conversation between the officer and the suspect develops. Only when the suspect tries to leave and tests the limits of the police response may the suspect discover that he or she is really in custody. In the 1980 case of *U.S.* v. *Mendenhall*,[64] Justice Potter Stewart set forth the "free to leave" test for determining whether a person has been arrested. Stewart wrote, "A person has been 'seized' within the meaning of the Fourth Amendment only if in view of all the circumstances surrounding the incident, a reasonable person would have believed that he was not free to leave." The "free to leave" test "has been repeatedly adopted by the Court as the test for a seizure."[65] In 1994, in the case of *Stansbury* v. *California*,[66] the Court once again used such a test in determining the point at which an arrest had been made. In *Stansbury*, where the focus was on the interrogation of a suspected child molester and murderer, the Court ruled, "In determining whether an individual was in custody, a court must examine all of the circumstances surrounding the interrogation,

■ **lecture note**   Explain the concept of arrest as the restriction of an individual's freedom to leave, even if the suspect does not actually consider himself or herself to be under arrest. Remind the class that the police are not required to give *Miranda* warnings immediately upon arrest, although many officers do.

■ **theme**   What is the purpose of a search incident to an arrest?

■ **search incident to an arrest**   A warrantless search of an arrested individual conducted to ensure the safety of the arresting officer. Because individuals placed under arrest may be in possession of weapons, courts have recognized the need for arresting officers to protect themselves by conducting an immediate search of arrestees without obtaining a warrant.

but the ultimate inquiry is simply whether there [was] a formal arrest or restraint on freedom of movement of the degree associated with a formal arrest." More recently, in 2012, Justice Samuel A. Alito, Jr., in the case of *Howes* v. *Fields*, explained that "custody is a term of art that specifies circumstances that are thought generally to present a serious danger of coercion."[67]

Probable cause is the basic minimum necessary for an arrest under any circumstances.

Youth and inexperience do not automatically undermine a reasonable person's ability to assess when they are free to leave. Hence, in the 2004 case of *Yarborough* v. *Alvarado*,[68] the U.S. Supreme Court found that a 17-year-old boy's two-hour interrogation in a police station without a *Miranda* advisement was not custodial, even though the boy confessed to his involvement in a murder and was later arrested. The boy, said the Court, had not actually been in police custody, even though he was in a building used by the police for questioning, because actions taken by the interviewing officer indicated that the juvenile had been free to leave. Whether a person is actually free to leave, said the Court, can be determined only by examining the totality of the circumstances surrounding the interrogation.[69]

Arrests that follow the questioning of a suspect are probably the most common type of arrest. When the decision to arrest is reached, the officer has come to the conclusion that a crime has been committed and that the suspect is probably the one who committed it. The presence of these elements constitutes the probable cause needed for an arrest. Probable cause is the basic minimum necessary for an arrest under any circumstances.

Arrests may also occur when the officer comes upon a crime in progress. Although such situations sometimes require apprehension of the offender to ensure the safety of the public, most arrests made during crimes in progress are for misdemeanors rather than felonies. In fact, many states do not allow arrest for a misdemeanor unless it is committed in the presence of an officer, since visible crimes in progress clearly provide the probable cause necessary for an arrest. In 2001, in a case that made headlines nationwide,[70] the U.S. Supreme Court upheld a warrantless arrest made by a Lago Vista, Texas, police officer for a seat belt violation. In what many saw as an unfair exercise of discretion, Patrolman Bart Turek stopped, then arrested, Gail Atwater, a young local woman whom he observed driving a pickup truck in which she and her two small children (ages three and five) were unbelted. Facts in the case showed that Turek verbally berated the woman after stopping her vehicle and that he handcuffed her, placed her in his squad car, and drove her to the local police station, where she was made to remove her

shoes, jewelry, and eyeglasses and empty her pockets. Officers took her "mug shot" and placed her alone in a jail cell for about an hour, after which she was taken before a magistrate and released on $310 bond. Atwater was charged with a misdemeanor violation of Texas seat belt law. She later pleaded no contest and paid a $50 fine. Soon afterward, she and her husband filed a Section 1983 lawsuit against the officer, his department, and the police chief, alleging that the actions of the officer violated Atwater's Fourth Amendment right to be free from unreasonable seizures. The Court, however, concluded that "the Fourth Amendment does not forbid a warrantless arrest for a minor criminal offense, such as a misdemeanor seat belt violation punishable only by a fine."

Most jurisdictions allow arrest for a felony without a warrant when a crime is not in progress, as long as probable cause can be established.[71] In jurisdictions that do require a warrant, arrest warrants are issued by magistrates when police officers can demonstrate probable cause. Magistrates will usually require that the officers seeking an arrest warrant submit a written affidavit outlining their reason for the arrest. In the case of *Payton* v. *New York* (1980),[72] the U.S. Supreme Court ruled that unless the suspect gives consent or an emergency exists, an arrest warrant is necessary if an arrest requires entry into a suspect's private residence.[73] In *Payton*, the justices held that "[a]bsent exigent circumstances," the "firm line at the entrance to the house…may not reasonably be crossed without a warrant." The Court reiterated its *Payton* holding in the 2002 case of *Kirk* v. *Louisiana*.[74] In *Kirk*, which involved an anonymous complaint about drug sales said to be taking place in the apartment of Kennedy Kirk, the justices reaffirmed their belief that "[t]he Fourth Amendment to the United States Constitution has drawn a firm line at the entrance to the home, and thus, the police need both probable cause to either arrest or search, and exigent circumstances to justify a nonconsensual warrantless intrusion into private premises."

Searches Incident to Arrest

The U.S. Supreme Court has established that police officers, to protect themselves from attack, have the right to conduct a search of a person being arrested, regardless of gender, and to search the area under the arrestee's immediate control. This rule regarding **search incident to an arrest** was created in the *Rabinowitz* and *Chimel* cases mentioned earlier. It became firmly established in other cases involving personal searches, such as the 1973 case of *U.S.* v. *Robinson*.[75] In Robinson, the Court upheld an officer's right to conduct a search without a warrant for purposes of personal protection and to use the fruits of the search when it turns

■ **reasonable suspicion**   The level of suspicion that would justify an officer in making further inquiry or in conducting further investigation. Reasonable suspicion may permit stopping a person for questioning or for a simple pat-down search. Also, a belief, based on a consideration of the facts at hand and on reasonable inferences drawn from those facts, that would induce an ordinarily prudent and cautious person under the same circumstances to conclude that criminal activity is taking place or that criminal activity has recently occurred. Reasonable suspicion is a *general* and reasonable belief that a crime is in progress or has occurred, whereas probable cause is a reasonable belief that a *particular* person has committed a *specific* crime.

Plain-clothes police detectives searching drug suspects in Harlem, New York City. The courts have generally held that to protect themselves and the public, officers have the authority to search suspects being arrested. What are the limits of such searches?

up contraband. In the words of the Court, "A custodial arrest of a suspect based upon probable cause is a reasonable intrusion under the Fourth Amendment; that intrusion being lawful, a search incident to the arrest requires no additional jurisdiction."[76]

The Court's decision in *Robinson* reinforced an earlier ruling in *Terry* v. *Ohio* (1968),[77] involving a seasoned officer who conducted a pat-down search of two men whom he suspected were casing a store, about to commit a robbery. The arresting officer was a 39-year veteran of police work who testified that the men "did not look right." When he approached them, he suspected they were armed. Fearing for his life, he quickly spun the men around, put them up against a wall, patted down their clothing, and found a gun on one of the men. The man, Terry, was later convicted in Ohio courts of carrying a concealed weapon.

Terry's appeal was based on the argument that the suspicious officer had no probable cause to arrest him and therefore no cause to search him. The search, he argued, was illegal, and the evidence obtained should not have been used against him. The Supreme Court disagreed, saying, "In view of these facts, we cannot blind ourselves to the need for law enforcement officers to protect themselves and other prospective victims of violence in situations where they may lack probable cause for an arrest."

The *Terry* case set the standard for a brief stop and frisk based on reasonable suspicion. Attorneys refer to such brief encounters as *Terry-type stops*. **Reasonable suspicion** can be defined as a belief, based on a consideration of the facts at hand and on reasonable inferences drawn from those facts, that would induce an ordinarily prudent and cautious person under the same circumstances to conclude that criminal activity is taking place or that criminal activity has recently occurred. It is the level of suspicion needed to justify an officer in making further inquiry or in conducting further investigation. Reasonable suspicion, which is a *general* and reasonable belief that a crime is in progress or has occurred, should be differentiated from probable cause. Probable cause, as noted earlier, is a reasonable belief that a *particular* person has committed a *specific* crime. It is important to note that the *Terry* case, for all the authority it conferred on officers, also made it clear that officers must have reasonable grounds for any stop and frisk that they conduct. Read more about the case of *Terry* v. *Ohio* at **http://tinyurl.com/yf2jhc2**.

In 1989, in the case of *U.S.* v. *Sokolow*,[78] the Supreme Court clarified the basis on which law enforcement officers, lacking probable cause to believe that a crime has occurred, may stop and briefly detain a person for investigative purposes. In *Sokolow*, the Court ruled that the legitimacy of such a stop must be evaluated according to a "totality of circumstances" criterion—in which all aspects of the defendant's behavior, taken in concert, may provide the basis for a legitimate stop based on reasonable suspicion.

■ **lecture note**   Explain the rule regarding search incident to arrest. Ask the class to discuss what they believe the limits on the scope of such a search should be.

■ **lecture note**   Discuss the 1968 Supreme Court case of *Terry* v. *Ohio* and explain why this case is considered to be a landmark case.

In this case, the defendant, Andrew Sokolow, appeared suspicious to police because, while traveling under an alias from Honolulu, he had paid $2,100 in $20 bills (from a large roll of money) for two airplane tickets after spending a surprisingly small amount of time in Miami. In addition, the defendant was obviously nervous and checked no luggage. A warrantless airport investigation by Drug Enforcement Administration (DEA) agents uncovered more than 1,000 grams of cocaine in the defendant's belongings. In upholding Sokolow's conviction, the Court ruled that although no single behavior was proof of illegal activity, taken together his behaviors created circumstances under which suspicion of illegal activity was justified.

In 2002, the Court reinforced the *Sokolow* decision in *U.S.* v. *Arvizu* when it ruled that the "balance between the public interest and the individual's right to personal security"[79] "tilts in favor of a standard less than probable cause in brief investigatory stops of persons or vehicles . . . if the officer's action is supported by reasonable suspicion to believe that criminal activity may be afoot."[80] In the words of the Court, "This process allows officers to draw on their own experiences and specialized training to make inferences from and deductions about the cumulative information available."[81]

In 1993, in the case of *Minnesota* v. *Dickerson*,[82] the U.S. Supreme Court placed new limits on an officer's ability to seize evidence discovered during a pat-down search conducted for protective reasons when the search itself was based merely on suspicion and failed to immediately reveal the presence of a weapon. In this case, the high court ruled that "if an officer lawfully pats down a suspect's outer clothing and feels an object whose contour or mass makes its identity immediately apparent, there has been no invasion of the suspect's privacy beyond that already authorized by the officer's search for weapons." However, in *Dickerson*, the justices ruled, "the officer never thought that the lump was a weapon, but did not immediately recognize it as cocaine." The lump was determined to be cocaine only after the officer "squeezed, slid, and otherwise manipulated the pocket's contents." Hence, the Court held, the officer's actions in this case did not qualify under what might be called a "plain-feel" exception. In any case, said the Court, the search in *Dickerson* went far beyond what is permissible under *Terry*, where officer safety was the crucial issue. The Court summed up its ruling in *Dickerson* this way: "While *Terry* entitled [the officer] to place his hands on respondent's jacket and to feel the lump in the pocket, his continued exploration of the pocket after he concluded that it contained no weapon was unrelated to the sole justification for the search under *Terry*" and was therefore illegal.

Just as arrest must be based on probable cause, officers may not stop and question an unwilling citizen whom they have no reason to suspect of a crime. In the case of *Brown* v. *Texas* (1979),[83] two Texas law enforcement officers stopped the defendant and asked for identification. Ed Brown, they later testified, had not been acting suspiciously, nor did they think he might have a weapon. The stop was made simply because officers wanted to know who he was. Brown was arrested under a Texas statute that required a person to identify himself properly and accurately when asked to do so by peace officers. Eventually, his appeal reached the U.S. Supreme Court, which ruled that under the circumstances of the *Brown* case, a person "may not be punished for refusing to identify himself."

In the 2004 case of *Hiibel* v. *Sixth Judicial District Court of Nevada*,[84] however, the Court upheld Nevada's "stop-and-identify" law that requires a person to identify himself to police if they encounter him under circumstances that reasonably indicate that he "has committed, is committing or is about to commit a crime." The *Hiibel* case was an extension of the reasonable suspicion doctrine set forth earlier in *Terry*.

In *Smith* v. *Ohio* (1990),[85] the Court held that an individual has the right to protect his or her belongings from unwarranted police inspection. In *Smith*, the defendant was approached by two officers in plain clothes who observed that he was carrying a brown paper bag. The officers asked him to "come here a minute" and, when he kept walking, identified themselves as police officers. The defendant threw the bag onto the hood of his car and attempted to protect it from the officers' intrusion. Marijuana was found inside the bag, and the defendant was arrested. Because there was little reason to stop the suspect in this case and because control over the bag was not thought necessary for the officers' protection, the Court found that the Fourth Amendment protects both "the traveler who carries a toothbrush and a few articles of clothing in a paper bag" and "the sophisticated executive with the locked attaché case."[86]

The following year, however, in what some Court observers saw as a turnabout, the Court ruled in *California* v. *Hodari D.* (1991)[87] that suspects who flee from the police and throw away items as they retreat may later be arrested based on the incriminating nature of the abandoned items. The significance of *Hodari* for future police action was highlighted by California prosecutors who pointed out that cases like *Hodari* occur "almost every day in this nation's urban areas."[88]

In 2000, the Court decided the case of William Wardlow.[89] Wardlow had fled upon seeing a caravan of police vehicles converge on an area of Chicago known for narcotics trafficking. Officers caught him and, searching for weapons, conducted a pat-down search of his clothing. After discovering a handgun,

> Suspects who flee from the police and throw away items as they retreat may later be arrested based on the incriminating nature of the abandoned items.

■ **theme** What conditions must exist for the police to conduct an emergency search of an individual without a warrant? Do you agree with all four conditions? Explain your views.

the officers arrested Wardlow on weapons charges, but his lawyer argued that police had acted illegally in stopping him because they did not have reasonable suspicion that he had committed an offense. The Illinois Supreme Court agreed with Wardlow's attorney, holding that "sudden flight in a high crime area does not create a reasonable suspicion justifying a *Terry* stop because flight may simply be an exercise of the right to 'go on one's way.'"[90] The case eventually reached the U.S. Supreme Court, which overturned the Illinois court, finding, instead, that the officers' actions did not violate the Fourth Amendment. In the words of the Court,

> This case, involving a brief encounter between a citizen and a police officer on a public street, is governed by *Terry*, under which an officer who has a reasonable, articulable suspicion that criminal activity is afoot may conduct a brief, investigatory stop. While 'reasonable suspicion' is a less demanding standard than probable cause, there must be at least a minimal level of objective justification for the stop. An individual's presence in a 'high crime area,' standing alone, is not enough to support a reasonable, particularized suspicion of criminal activity, but a location's characteristics are relevant in determining whether the circumstances are sufficiently suspicious to warrant further investigation. . . . In this case, moreover, it was also Wardlow's unprovoked flight that aroused the officers' suspicions. Nervous, evasive behavior is another pertinent factor in determining reasonable suspicion . . . and headlong flight is the consummate act of evasion.[91]

Emergency Searches of Persons

Situations in which officers have to search people based on quick decisions do arise. An emergency search of a person may be warranted when, for example, he matches the description of an armed robber, he is found unconscious, or he has what appears to be blood on his clothes. Such searches can save lives by disarming fleeing felons or by uncovering a medical reason for an emergency situation. They may also prevent criminals from escaping or destroying evidence.

Emergency searches of persons, like those of premises, fall under the exigent circumstances exception to the warrant requirement of the Fourth Amendment. In the 1979 case of *Arkansas* v. *Sanders*,[92] the Supreme Court recognized the need for such searches "where the societal costs of obtaining a warrant, such as danger to law officers or the risk of loss or destruction of evidence, outweigh the reasons for prior recourse to a neutral magistrate."[93]

The 1987 case of *U.S.* v. *Borchardt*,[94] decided by the Fifth Circuit Court of Appeals, held that Ira Eugene Borchardt could

be prosecuted for heroin uncovered during medical treatment, even though the defendant had objected to the treatment.

The Legal Counsel Division of the FBI provides the following guidelines for conducting emergency warrantless searches of individuals, where the possible destruction of evidence is at issue.[95] (Keep in mind that there may be no probable cause to *arrest* the individual being searched.) All four conditions must apply:

1. At the time of the search there was probable cause to believe that evidence was concealed on the person searched.
2. At the time of the search there was probable cause to believe an emergency threat of destruction of evidence existed.
3. The officer had no prior opportunity to obtain a warrant authorizing the search.
4. The action was no greater than necessary to eliminate the threat of destruction of evidence.

Vehicle Searches

Vehicles present a special law enforcement problem. They are highly mobile, and when a driver or an occupant is arrested, the need to search the vehicle may be immediate.

The first significant Supreme Court case involving an automobile was *Carroll* v. *U.S.*[96] in 1925, in which a divided Court ruled that a warrantless search of an automobile or other vehicle is valid if it is based on a reasonable belief that contraband is present. In 1964, however, in the case of *Preston* v. *U.S.*,[97] the limits of warrantless vehicle searches were defined. Preston was arrested for vagrancy and taken to jail. His vehicle was impounded, towed to the police garage, and later searched. Two revolvers were uncovered in the glove compartment, and more incriminating evidence was found in the trunk. Preston, convicted on weapons possession and other charges, eventually appealed to the U.S. Supreme Court. The Court held that the warrantless search of Preston's vehicle had occurred while the automobile was in secure custody and had therefore been illegal. Time and circumstances would have permitted acquisition of a warrant to conduct the search, the Court reasoned. Similarly, in 2009, the Court, in the case of *Arizona* v. *Gant*, found that vehicle searches "incident to a recent occupant's arrest" cannot be authorized without a warrant if there is "no possibility the arrestee could gain access to the vehicle at the time of the search."[98]

When the search of a vehicle occurs after it has been impounded, however, that search may be legitimate if it is undertaken for routine and reasonable purposes. In the case of *South Dakota* v. *Opperman* (1976),[99] for example, the Court held that a warrantless search undertaken for purposes of inventorying and safekeeping the personal possessions of the car's owner was not illegal. The intent of the search, which turned up marijuana, had not been

CJ | NEWS
Supreme Court Says Police Need Warrants before Searching Cell Phones

In 2014, in the case of *Riley* v. *California*, the U.S. Supreme Court ruled that under most circumstances police officers are required to obtain a warrant before accessing and searching the data stored on a suspect's cell phone. In the words of the Court,

> Riley was stopped for a traffic violation, which eventually led to his arrest on weapons charges. An officer searching Riley incident to the arrest seized a cell phone from Riley's pants pocket. The officer accessed information on the phone and noticed the repeated use of a term associated with a street gang. At the police station two hours later, a detective specializing in gangs further examined the phone's digital contents. Based in part on photographs and videos that the detective found, the State charged Riley in connection with a shooting that had occurred a few weeks earlier and sought an enhanced sentence based on Riley's gang membership. Riley moved to suppress all evidence that the police had obtained from his cell phone. The trial court denied the motion, and Riley was convicted. The California Court of Appeal affirmed.

> Held: The police generally may not, without a warrant, search digital information on a cell phone seized from an individual who has been arrested.

Here's how the Court reasoned:

> Cell phones differ in both a quantitative and a qualitative sense from other objects that might be carried on an arrestee's person. Notably, modern cell phones have an immense storage capacity. Before cell phones, a search of a person was limited by physical realities and generally constituted only a narrow intrusion on privacy. But cell phones can store millions of pages of text, thousands of pictures, or hundreds of videos. This has several interrelated privacy consequences. First, a cell phone collects in one place many distinct types of information that reveal much more

in combination than any isolated record. Second, the phone's capacity allows even just one type of information to convey far more than previously possible. Third, data on the phone can date back for years. In addition, an element of pervasiveness characterizes cell phones but not physical records. A decade ago officers might have occasionally stumbled across a highly personal item such as a diary, but today many of the more than 90% of American adults who own cell phones keep on their person a digital record of nearly every aspect of their lives.

> (ii) The scope of the privacy interests at stake is further complicated by the fact that the data viewed on many modern cell phones may in fact be stored on a remote server. Thus, a search may extend well beyond papers and effects in the physical proximity of an arrestee, a concern that the United States recognizes but cannot definitively foreclose.

> It is true that this decision will have some impact on the ability of law enforcement to combat crime. But the Court's holding is not that the information on a cell phone is immune from search; it is that a warrant is generally required before a search. The warrant requirement is an important component of the Court's Fourth Amendment jurisprudence, and warrants may be obtained with increasing efficiency. In addition, although the search incident to arrest exception does not apply to cell phones, the continued availability of the exigent circumstances exception may give law enforcement a justification for a warrantless search in particular cases.

Chief Justice John Roberts who wrote the decision acknowledged that the ruling would make police work harder. But, "Privacy comes at a cost," he said. Law enforcement officials, however, expressed disappointment with the ruling. Technology "is making it easier and easier for criminals to do their trade," said one district attorney, while the court "is making it harder for law enforcement to do theirs."

References: *Riley* v. *California*, U.S. Supreme Court (decided June 25, 2014); and "Private Lives," The 10-Point, *Wall Street Journal*, June 26, 2014.

---

to discover contraband but to secure the owner's belongings from possible theft. Again, in *Colorado* v. *Bertine* (1987),[100] the Court supported the right of officers to open closed containers found in a vehicle while conducting a routine search for inventorying purposes. In the words of the Court, such searches are "now a well-defined exception in the warrant requirement." In 1990, however, in the precedent-setting case of *Florida* v. *Wells*,[101] the Supreme Court agreed with a lower court's suppression of marijuana evidence discovered in a locked suitcase in the trunk of a defendant's impounded vehicle. In *Wells*, the Court held that standardized criteria authorizing the search of a vehicle for inventorying purposes were necessary before such a discovery could be legitimate. Standardized criteria, said the Court, could take the form of departmental policies, written general orders, or established routines.

Generally speaking, where vehicles are concerned, an investigatory stop is permissible under the Fourth Amendment if

supported by reasonable suspicion,[102] and a warrantless search of a stopped car is valid if it is based on probable cause.[103] Reasonable suspicion can expand into probable cause when the facts in a given situation so warrant. In the 1996 case of *Ornelas* v. *U.S.*,[104] for example, two experienced Milwaukee police officers stopped a car with California license plates that had been spotted in a motel parking lot known for drug trafficking after the Narcotics and Dangerous Drugs Information System (NADDIS) identified the car's owner as a known or suspected drug trafficker. One of the officers noticed a loose panel above an armrest in the vehicle's backseat and then searched the car. A package of cocaine was found beneath the panel, and the driver and a passenger were arrested. Following conviction, the defendants appealed to the U.S. Supreme Court, claiming that no probable cause to search the car existed at the time of the stop. The majority opinion, however,

■ fleeting-targets exception An exception to the exclusionary rule that permits law enforcement officers to search a motor vehicle based on probable cause and without a warrant. The fleeting-targets exception is predicated on the fact that vehicles can quickly leave the jurisdiction of a law enforcement agency.

■ **lecture note** Discuss the U.S. Supreme Court's rationale for allowing warrantless vehicle searches in cases in which the vehicle might quickly leave the jurisdiction of the investigating officers. Note that because motor vehicles are highly mobile, officers may have the authority to search vehicles they have stopped without a warrant if they have reason to believe that the vehicles may harbor contraband or other evidence.

AP Photo/The Hattiesburg American, Matt Bush

A Mississippi state trooper searches a car. Warrantless vehicle searches, where the driver is suspected of a crime, have generally been justified by the fact that vehicles are highly mobile and can quickly leave police jurisdiction. Can passengers in the vehicle also be searched?

noted that in the view of the court that originally heard the case, "the model, age, and source-State origin of the car, and the fact that two men traveling together checked into a motel at 4 o'clock in the morning without reservations, formed a drug-courier profile and . . . this profile together with the [computer] reports gave rise to a reasonable suspicion of drug-trafficking activity. . . . [I]n the court's view, reasonable suspicion became probable cause when [the deputy] found the loose panel."[105] Probable cause permits a warrantless search of a vehicle because it can quickly be driven out of a jurisdiction. This exception to the exclusionary rule is called the **fleeting-targets exception**.[106]

Warrantless vehicle searches can extend to any area of the vehicle if officers have probable cause to conduct a purposeful search or if officers have been given permission to search the vehicle. In the 1991 case of *Florida* v. *Jimeno*,[107] arresting officers stopped a motorist who gave them permission to search his car. A bag on the floor of the car was found to contain cocaine, and the defendant was later convicted on a drug charge. On appeal to the U.S. Supreme Court, however, he argued that the permission given to search his car did not extend to bags and other items within the car. In a decision that may have implications beyond vehicle searches, the Court held that "[a] criminal suspect's Fourth Amendment right to be free from unreasonable searches is not violated when, after he gives police permission to search his car, they open a closed container found within the car that might reasonably hold the object of the search. The amendment is satisfied

when, under the circumstances, it is objectively reasonable for the police to believe that the scope of the suspect's consent permitted them to open the particular container."[108]

In *U.S.* v. *Ross* (1982),[109] the Court found that officers had not exceeded their authority in opening a bag in the defendant's trunk that was found to contain heroin. The search was held to be justifiable on the basis of information developed from a search of the passenger compartment. The Court said, "If probable cause justifies the search of a lawfully stopped vehicle, it justifies the search of every part of the vehicle and its contents that may conceal the object of the search."[110] Moreover, according to the 1996 U.S. Supreme Court decision in *Whren* v. *U.S.*,[111] officers may stop a vehicle being driven suspiciously and then search it once probable cause has developed, even if their primary assignment centers on duties other than traffic enforcement or "if a reasonable officer would not have stopped the motorist absent some additional law enforcement objective" (which in the *Whren* case was drug enforcement).

Motorists and their passengers may be ordered out of stopped vehicles in the interest of officer safety, and any evidence developed as a result of such a procedure may be used in court.[112] In 1997, for example, in the case of *Maryland* v. *Wilson*,[113] the U.S. Supreme Court overturned a decision by a Maryland court that held that crack cocaine found during a traffic stop was seized illegally when it fell from the lap of a passenger ordered out of a stopped vehicle by a Maryland state trooper. The Supreme Court cited concerns for officer safety and held that the activities of passengers are subject to police control. Similarly, in 2007, in the case of *People v. Brendlin*, the Court ruled that passengers in stopped vehicles are necessarily detained as a result of the stop, and that they should expect that, for safety reasons, officers will exercise "unquestioned police command" over them for the duration of the stop.

In 1998, however, the U.S. Supreme Court placed clear limits on warrantless vehicle searches. In the case of *Knowles v. Iowa*,[114] an Iowa police officer stopped Patrick Knowles for speeding, issued him a citation, but did not make a custodial arrest. The officer then conducted a full search of his car without Knowles's consent and without probable cause. Marijuana was found, and Knowles was arrested. At the time, Iowa state law gave officers authority to conduct full-blown automobile searches when issuing only a citation. The Supreme Court found, however, that while concern for officer safety during a routine traffic stop may justify the minimal intrusion of ordering a driver and passengers out of a car, it does not by itself justify what it called "the considerably greater intrusion attending a full field-type search." In other words, while a search incident to arrest may be justifiable in the eyes of the Court, a search incident to citation clearly is not.

In the 1999 case of *Wyoming v. Houghton*,[115] the Court ruled that police officers with probable cause to search a car may inspect any passengers' belongings found in the car that are capable of concealing the object of the search. *Thornton v. U.S.* (2004) established the authority of arresting officers to search a car without a warrant even if the driver had previously exited the vehicle.[116]

In 2005, in the case of *Illinois v. Caballes*,[117] the Court held that the use of a drug-sniffing dog during a routine and lawful traffic stop is permissible and may not even be a search within the meaning of the Fourth Amendment. In writing for the majority, Justice John Paul Stevens said that "the use of a well-trained narcotics-detection dog—one that does not expose noncontraband items that otherwise would remain hidden from public view—during a lawful traffic stop generally does not implicate legitimate privacy interests."

Finally, in 2011, the Court created a good-faith exception to the exclusionary rule applicable to a search that was authorized by precedent at the time of the search but which was a type of search that was subsequently ruled unconstitutional. In that case, *Davis v. U.S.*, Willie Gene Davis was a passenger in a car stopped for a traffic violation in 2007.[118] He subsequently gave officers a false name, and was arrested for giving false information to a police officer. The vehicle in which he was riding was searched, and officers discovered a handgun in Davis's jacket, which he had left on the seat. Davis was charged and convicted for possession of an illegal weapon. Later, however, the U.S. Court of Appeals for the Eleventh Circuit found that the search was illegal, based on a previous Supreme Court ruling in the 2009 case of *Arizona v. Gant*.[119] Nonetheless, the lower court upheld Davis's conviction because the *Gant* ruling came after Davis's arrest. The Supreme Court agreed, saying, "Searches conducted in objectively reasonable reliance on binding appellate precedent are not subject to the exclusionary rule."

Roadblocks and Motor Vehicle Checkpoints

The Fourth and Fourteenth Amendments to the U.S. Constitution guarantee liberty and personal security to all people residing within the United States. Courts have generally held that, in the absence of probable cause to believe that a crime has been committed, police officers have no legitimate authority to detain or arrest people who are going about their business in a peaceful manner. In a number of instances, however, the U.S. Supreme Court has decided that community interests may necessitate a temporary suspension of personal liberty, even when probable cause is lacking. One such case is *Michigan Dept. of State Police v. Sitz* (1990),[120] which involved the legality of highway sobriety checkpoints, including those at which nonsuspicious drivers are subjected to scrutiny. In *Sitz*, the Court ruled that such stops are reasonable insofar as they are essential to the welfare of the community as a whole.

In a second case, *U.S. v. Martinez-Fuerte* (1976),[121] the Court upheld brief suspicionless seizures at a fixed international checkpoint designed to intercept illegal aliens. The Court noted that "to require that such stops always be based on reasonable suspicion would be impractical because the flow of traffic tends to be too heavy to allow the particularized study of a given car necessary to identify it as a possible carrier of illegal aliens. Such a requirement also would largely eliminate any deterrent to the conduct of well-disguised smuggling operations, even though smugglers are known to use these highways regularly."[122]

In fact, in 2004, in the case of *Illinois v. Lidster*,[123] the Court held that information-seeking highway roadblocks are permissible. The stop in *Lidster*, said the Court, was permissible because its intent was merely to solicit motorists' help in solving a crime. "The law," said the Court, "ordinarily permits police to seek the public's voluntary cooperation in a criminal investigation."

Watercraft and Motor Homes

The 1983 case of *U.S. v. Villamonte-Marquez*[124] widened the *Carroll* decision (the first U.S. Supreme Court case involving a vehicle, which was discussed earlier) to include watercraft. In this case, the Court reasoned that a vehicle on the water can easily leave the jurisdiction of enforcement officials, just as a car or truck can.

In *California v. Carney* (1985),[125] the Court extended police authority to conduct warrantless searches of vehicles to include motor homes. Earlier arguments had been advanced that a motor home, because it is more like a permanent residence than a vehicle, should not be considered a vehicle for purposes of search and seizure. In a 6–3 decision, the Court rejected those arguments, reasoning that a vehicle's appointments and size do not alter its basic function of providing transportation.

■ **compelling interest**   A legal concept that provides a basis for suspicionless searches when public safety is at stake. (Urinalysis tests of train engineers are an example.) It is the concept on which the U.S. Supreme Court cases of *Skinner* v. *Railway Labor Executives' Association* (1989) and *National Treasury Employees Union* v. *Von Raab* (1989) turned. In those cases, the Court held that public safety may sometimes provide a sufficiently compelling interest to justify limiting an individual's right to privacy.

■ **suspicionless search**   A search conducted by law enforcement personnel without a warrant and without suspicion. Suspicionless searches are permissible only if based on an overriding concern for public safety.

CJ | CAREERS
Patrol Officer

Name. Timothy D. Radtke

Position. Patrol officer, San Diego, California

Colleges attended. Winona State University (BS), University of Nevada–Las Vegas (MA)

Major. Criminal justice

Year hired. 2008

Please give a brief description of your job. Within a specified area of the city, I respond to radio calls for police service and perform self-initiated activities such as traffic stops and citizen contacts.

What appealed to you most about the position when you applied for it? While pursuing my degrees I worked closely with two police departments. The officers there inspired me to commit my life to a cause greater than myself—protecting communities. I was eager to put the knowledge I obtained through my education to practical use, to work closely with the community and apply the community-oriented policing and problem-oriented policing strategies I learned during my academic studies.

How would you describe the interview process? The testing process was strenuous. There were eight different tests: written test, preinvestigation questionnaire, physical ability test, comprehensive background investigation, polygraph, appointing authority interview, psychological screening, and medical exam.

The most challenging was the appointing authority interview, which was conducted by a lieutenant and a sergeant. They asked questions about my background and what I had done to prepare to serve as a police officer. I was asked to respond to a series of scenarios that

police officers often encounter in the field. This process helped them determine whether I could quickly find a logical and appropriate response when presented with an unexpected or stressful situation.

What is a typical day like? Patrol officers begin with "lineup," in which they are briefed about recent crimes and events and assigned to the specific patrol beat they will work throughout their shift. Patrol officers must be prepared to handle the unexpected. One day they may respond to a domestic disturbance, the next help establish a driving under the influence (DUI) checkpoint to deter drunk drivers, and the next be asked to locate warrant suspects.

What qualities/characteristics are most helpful for this job? A successful officer must know how to speak with people. The people [the officer interacts] with daily often need immediate help or have difficulty controlling their emotions. An officer may be faced with an individual who is attempting suicide or an individual who is angry and showing signs of assaultive behavior, or [the officer may be] called upon to interview a child who has suffered abuse. The ability to speak tactfully and quickly build rapport with others is crucial.

What is a typical starting salary? Between $40,000 and $50,000.

What is the salary potential as you move up into higher-level jobs? An officer's salary will increase after graduating from the academy and when promoted within the department. Those with an BA or MA will also receive percentage increases in pay.

What career advice would you give someone in college beginning studies in criminal justice? Classroom instruction in college will help students understand the basics of police work and give them the skills to interpret and appropriately apply laws. It will also increase students' problem-solving and critical thinking skills, which are necessary for finding solutions to the complex problems officers encounter daily.

Houseboats were brought under the automobile exception to the Fourth Amendment warrant requirement in the 1988 Tenth Circuit Court case of *U.S.* v. *Hill*.[126] Learn about vehicle pursuits and the Fourth Amendment at **http://www.justices-tudies.com/pubs/veh_pursuits.pdf.**

Suspicionless Searches

In two 1989 decisions, the U.S. Supreme Court ruled for the first time that there may be instances when the need to ensure public safety provides a **compelling interest** that negates the rights of

any individual to privacy, permitting **suspicionless searches**—those that occur when a person is not suspected of a crime. In the case of *National Treasury Employees Union* v. *Von Raab* (1989),[127] the Court, by a 5–4 vote, upheld a program of the U.S. Customs Service that required mandatory drug testing for all workers seeking promotions or job transfers involving drug interdiction and the carrying of firearms. The Court's majority opinion read, "We think the government's need to conduct the suspicionless searches required by the Customs program outweighs the privacy interest of employees engaged directly in drug interdiction, and of those who otherwise are required to carry firearms."

The second case, *Skinner* v. *Railway Labor Executives' Association* (1989),[128] was decided on the same day. In *Skinner*, the justices voted 7 to 2 to permit the mandatory testing of railway crews for the presence of drugs or alcohol following serious train accidents. The *Skinner* case involved evidence of drugs in a 1987 train wreck outside of Baltimore, Maryland, in which 16 people were killed and hundreds were injured.

The 1991 Supreme Court case of *Florida* v. *Bostick*,[129] which permitted warrantless "sweeps" of intercity buses, moved the Court deeply into conservative territory. The *Bostick* case came to the attention of the Court as a result of the Broward County (Florida) Sheriff's Department's routine practice of boarding buses at scheduled stops and asking passengers for permission to search their bags. Terrance Bostick, a passenger on one of the buses, gave police permission to search his luggage, which was found to contain cocaine. Bostick was arrested and eventually pleaded guilty to charges of drug trafficking. The Florida Supreme Court, however, found merit in Bostick's appeal, which was based on a Fourth Amendment claim that the search of his luggage had been unreasonable. The Florida court held that "a reasonable passenger in [Bostick's] situation would not have felt free to leave the bus to avoid questioning by the police," and it overturned the conviction.

The state appealed to the U.S. Supreme Court, which held that the Florida Supreme Court had erred in interpreting Bostick's *feelings* that he was not free to leave the bus. In the words of the Court, "Bostick was a passenger on a bus that was scheduled to depart. He would not have felt free to leave the bus even if the police had not been present. Bostick's movements were 'confined' in a sense, but this was the natural result of his decision to take the bus." In other words, Bostick was constrained not so much by police action as by his own feelings that he might miss the bus were he to get off. Following this line of reasoning, the Court concluded that warrantless, suspicionless "sweeps" of buses, "trains, planes, and city streets" are permissible as long as officers (1) ask individual passengers for permission before searching their possessions, (2) do not coerce passengers to consent to a search, and (3) do not convey the message that citizen compliance with the search request is mandatory. Passenger compliance with police searches must be voluntary for the searches to be legal.

In contrast to the tone of Court decisions more than two decades earlier, the justices did not require officers to inform passengers that they were free to leave nor that they had the right to deny officers the opportunity to search (although Bostick himself was so advised by Florida officers). Any reasonable person, the Court ruled, should feel free to deny the police request. In the words of the Court, "The appropriate test is whether, taking into account all of the circumstances surrounding the encounter, a reasonable passenger would feel free to decline the officers' requests or otherwise terminate the encounter." The Court continued, "Rejected, however, is Bostick's argument that he must have been seized because no reasonable person would freely consent to a search of luggage containing drugs, since the 'reasonable person' test presumes an innocent person."

Critics of the decision saw it as creating new "gestapo-like" police powers in the face of which citizens on public transportation will feel compelled to comply with police requests for search authority. Dissenting Justices Harry Blackmun, John Paul Stevens, and Thurgood Marshall held that "the bus sweep at issue in this case violates the core values of the Fourth Amendment." The Court's majority, however, defended its ruling by writing, "[T]he Fourth Amendment proscribes unreasonable searches and seizures; it does not proscribe voluntary cooperation." In mid-2000, however, in the case of *Bond* v. *U.S.*,[130] the Court ruled that physical manipulation of a carry-on bag in the possession of a bus passenger without the owner's consent violates the Fourth Amendment's proscription against unreasonable searches.

In the case of *U.S.* v. *Drayton* (2002),[131] the U.S. Supreme Court reiterated its position that police officers are not required to advise bus passengers of their right to refuse to cooperate with officers conducting searches or of their right to refuse to be searched.

In 2004, the Court made it clear that suspicionless searches of vehicles at our nation's borders are permitted, even when the searches are extensive. In the case of *U.S.* v. *Flores-Montano*,[132] customs officials disassembled the gas tank of a car belonging to a man entering the country from Mexico and found that it contained 37 kilograms of marijuana. Although the officers admitted that their actions were not motivated by any particular belief that the search would reveal contraband, the Court held that Congress has always granted "plenary authority to conduct routine searches and seizures at the border without probable cause or a warrant." In the words of the Court, "the Government's authority to conduct suspicionless inspections at the border includes the authority to remove, disassemble and reassemble a vehicle's fuel tank." Learn more about public-safety exceptions to *Miranda* at **http://www .justicestudies.com/pubs/psafety.pdf**.

High-Technology Searches

The burgeoning use of high technology to investigate crime and to uncover violations of the criminal law is forcing courts throughout the nation to evaluate the applicability of constitutional guarantees in light of high-tech searches and seizures. In 1996, the California appellate court decision in *People* v. *Deutsch*[133] presaged the kinds of issues that are being encountered as American law enforcement expands its use of cutting-edge technology. In *Deutsch*, judges faced the question of whether a warrantless scan of a private dwelling with a thermal-imaging device constitutes an unreasonable search within the meaning of the Fourth Amendment. Such devices (also called *forward-looking infrared [FLIR] systems*) measure radiant energy in the radiant heat portion of the electromagnetic spectrum[134] and display their readings as thermographs. The "heat picture" that a thermal imager produces can be used, as it was in the case of Dorian Deutsch, to reveal unusually warm areas or rooms that might be associated with the cultivation of drug-bearing plants, such as marijuana. Two hundred cannabis plants, which were being grown hydroponically under high-wattage lights in two walled-off portions of Deutsch's home, were seized following an exterior thermal scan of her home by a police officer who drove by at 1:30 in the morning. Because no entry of the house was anticipated during the search, the officer had acted without a search warrant. The California court ruled that the scan was an illegal search because "society accepts a reasonable expectation of privacy" surrounding "nondisclosed activities within the home."[135]

In a similar case, *Kyllo* v. *U.S.* (2001),[136] the U.S. Supreme Court reached much the same conclusion. Based on the results of a warrantless search conducted by officers using a thermal-imaging device, investigators applied for a search warrant of Kyllo's home. The subsequent search uncovered more than 100 marijuana plants that were being grown under bright lights. In overturning Kyllo's conviction on drug-manufacturing charges, the Court held, "Where, as here, the Government uses a device that is not in general public use, to explore details of a private home that would previously have been unknowable without physical intrusion, the surveillance is a Fourth Amendment 'search,' and is presumptively unreasonable without a warrant."[137]

Learn more about the issues surrounding search and seizure at **http://caselaw.lp.findlaw.com/data/constitution/amendment04**.

The Intelligence Function

In law enforcement parlance, useful information is known as *intelligence*, and the need for intelligence leads police investigators to question both suspects and informants—and even more often, potentially knowledgeable citizens who may have been witnesses or victims. Data gathering is a crucial form of intelligence; without it, enforcement agencies would be virtually powerless to plan and effect arrests.

> The importance of gathering intelligence in police work cannot be overstressed.

The importance of gathering intelligence in police work cannot be overstressed. Studies have found that the one factor most likely to lead to arrest in serious crimes is the presence of a witness who can provide information to the police. Undercover operations, neighborhood watch programs, "crime stopper" groups, and organized detective work all contribute this vital information.

Informants

Information gathering is a complex process, and many ethical questions have been raised about the techniques police use to gather information. The use of paid informants, for example, is an area of concern to ethicists who believe that informants are often paid while getting away with minor crimes that investigators are willing to overlook. Another concern is the police practice (endorsed by some prosecutors) of agreeing not to charge one offender out of a group if he or she will "talk" and testify against the others.

As we have seen, probable cause is an important aspect of both police searches and legal arrests. The successful use of informants in supporting requests for a warrant depends on the demonstrable reliability of their information. The case of *Aguilar* v. *Texas* (1964)[138] clarified the use of informants and established a two-pronged test. The U.S. Supreme Court ruled that informant information can establish probable cause if both of the following criteria are met:

1. The source of the informant's information is made clear.
2. The police officer has a reasonable belief that the informant is reliable.

The two-pronged test of *Aguilar* v. *Texas* was intended to prevent the issuance of warrants on the basis of false or fabricated information. The case of *U.S.* v. *Harris* (1971)[139] provided an exception to the two-pronged *Aguilar* test. The *Harris* case recognized the fact that when an informant provides information that is damaging to him or her, it is probably true. In *Harris*, an informant told police that he had purchased non-tax-paid whiskey from another person. Because the information also implicated the informant in a crime, it was held to be accurate, even though it could not meet the second prong of the *Aguilar* test. "Admissions of crime," said the Court, "carry their own indicia of credibility—sufficient at least to support a finding of probable cause to search."[140]

In 1983, in the case of *Illinois* v. *Gates*,[141] the Court adopted a totality-of-circumstances approach and held that sufficient probable cause for issuing a warrant exists where an informant can be reasonably believed on the basis of everything that the police know. The *Gates* case involved an anonymous informant who provided incriminating information about another person through a letter to the police. Although the source of the information was not stated and the police were unable to say whether the informant was reliable, the overall sense of things, given what was already known to police, was that the information supplied was probably valid. In *Gates*, the Court held that probable cause exists when "there is a fair probability that contraband or evidence of a crime will be found in a particular place."

In the 1990 case of *Alabama* v. *White*,[142] the Supreme Court ruled that an anonymous tip, even in the absence of other corroborating information about a suspect, could form the basis for an investigatory stop if the informant accurately predicted the *future* behavior of the suspect. The Court reasoned that the ability to predict a suspect's behavior demonstrates a significant degree of familiarity with the suspect's affairs. In the words of the Court, "Because only a small number of people are generally privy to an individual's itinerary, it is reasonable for the police to believe that a person with access to such information is likely to also have access to reliable information about that individual's illegal activities."[143]

In 2000, in the case of *Florida* v. *J. L.*,[144] the Court held that an anonymous tip that a person is carrying a gun does not, without more evidence, justify a police officer's stop and frisk of that person. Ruling that such a search is invalid under the Fourth Amendment, the Court rejected the suggestion of a firearm exception to the general stop-and-frisk rule.[145] The identity of informants may be kept secret only if sources have been explicitly assured of confidentiality by investigating officers or if a reasonably implied assurance of confidentiality has been made. In *U.S. Dept. of Justice* v. *Landano* (1993),[146] the U.S. Supreme Court required that an informant's identity be revealed through a request made under the federal Freedom of Information Act. In that case, the FBI had not specifically assured the informant of confidentiality, and the Court ruled that "the government is not entitled to a presumption that all sources supplying information to the FBI in the course of a criminal investigation are confidential sources."

Police Interrogation

In 2003, Illinois became the first state in the nation to require the electronic recording of police interrogations and confessions in homicide cases.[147] State lawmakers hoped that the use of recordings would reduce the incidence of false confessions as well as the likelihood of convictions based on such confessions. Under the law, police interrogators must create videotape or audiotape recordings of any questioning of suspects. The law prohibits the courtroom introduction of statements and confessions that have not been taped. Proponents of the law say that it will prevent the police intimidation of murder suspects and will put an end to coerced confessions.

Some argue that the mandatory recording of police interrogations offers overwhelming benefits at minimal cost. "By creating an objective and reviewable record," says Richard A. Leo of the University of San Francisco Law School, "electronic recording promotes truth-finding in the criminal process, relegates 'swearing contests' to the past, and saves scarce resources at multiple levels of the criminal justice system."[148] According to Leo, requiring that all interrogations be recorded will benefit police and prosecutors by increasing the accuracy of confessions and convictions and "will also reduce the number of police-induced false confessions and the wrongful convictions they cause."

INTERROGATION

The U.S. Supreme Court has defined interrogation as any behaviors by the police "that the police should know are reasonably likely to elicit an incriminating response from the suspect." The Court also noted that "police words or actions normally attendant to arrest and custody do not constitute interrogation" unless they involve pointed or directed questions. The interrogation of suspects, like other areas of police activity, is subject to constitutional limits as interpreted by the courts, and a series of landmark decisions by the U.S. Supreme Court has focused on police interrogations.

Physical Abuse:
The first in a series of significant cases was **Brown v. Mississippi**. In 1936, the court determined that physical abuse cannot be used to obtain a confession or elicit information from a suspect.

Inherent Coercion:
In the case of **Ashcraft v. Tennessee** (1944), the U.S. Supreme Court found that interrogation involving inherent coercion was not acceptable. Inherent coercion refers to any form of non-physical coercion, hostility, or pressure to try to force a confession from a suspect.

Psychological Manipulation:
Interrogation should not involve sophisticated trickery or manipulation. In the case of **Arizona v. Fulminante** (1991), the U.S. Supreme Court determined that it was not legal to allow an FBI informant posing as a fellow inmate to trick the suspect into a confession. Interrogators do not have to be scrupulously honest in confronting suspects, but there must be limits to the lengths that can be pursued in questioning a suspect.

Right to Lawyer at Interrogation:
Escobedo v. Illinois (1964) and **Minnick v. Mississippi** (1990).

FIGURE 7-2 | Police Interrogation
Source: Pearson Education, Inc.

■ **lecture note**   Begin a discussion of police interrogation with the 1936 U.S. Supreme Court case of *Brown* v. *Mississippi*, which outlawed the use of physical force in interrogative settings. Discuss how some forms of coercion are inherent rather than obvious and how psychological manipulation can be a form of unfair interrogation.

■ **interrogation**   The information-gathering activity of police officers that involves the direct questioning of suspects.

■ **inherent coercion**   The tactics used by police interviewers that fall short of physical abuse but that nonetheless pressure suspects to divulge information.

■ **psychological manipulation**   Manipulative actions by police interviewers that are designed to pressure suspects to divulge information and that are based on subtle forms of intimidation and control.

The U.S. Supreme Court has defined **interrogation** as any behaviors by the police "that the police should know are reasonably likely to elicit an incriminating response from the suspect."[149] Hence, interrogation may involve activities that go well beyond mere verbal questioning, and the Court has held that interrogation may include "staged lineups, reverse lineups, positing guilt, minimizing the moral seriousness of crime, and casting blame on the victim or society" (Figure 7-2). The Court has also held that "police words or actions normally attendant to arrest and custody do not constitute interrogation" unless they involve pointed or directed questions. Hence, an arresting officer may instruct a suspect on what to do and may chitchat with him or her without engaging in interrogation within the meaning of the law. Once police officers make inquiries intended to elicit information about the crime in question, however, interrogation has begun. The interrogation of suspects, like other areas of police activity, is subject to constitutional limits as interpreted by the courts, and a series of landmark decisions by the U.S. Supreme Court has focused on police interrogation.

Physical Abuse

The first in a series of significant cases regarding police interrogation was *Brown* v. *Mississippi*,[150] decided in 1936. The *Brown* case began with the murder of a white store owner in Mississippi in 1934 during a robbery. A posse formed and went to the home of a local African American man rumored to have been one of the perpetrators. They dragged the suspect from his home, put a rope around his neck, and hoisted and lowered him from a tree a number of times, hoping to get a confession from the man, but failing. The posse was headed by a deputy sheriff who then arrested other suspects in the case and laid them over chairs in the local jail and whipped them with belts and buckles until they "confessed." These confessions were used in the trial that followed, and all three defendants were convicted of murder. Their convictions were upheld by the Mississippi Supreme Court. In 1936, however, the case was reviewed by the U.S. Supreme Court, which overturned all of the convictions, saying that it was difficult to imagine techniques of interrogation more "revolting" to the sense of justice than those used in this case.

Inherent Coercion

Interrogation need not involve physical abuse for it to be contrary to constitutional principles. In the case of *Ashcraft* v. *Tennessee* (1944),[151] the U.S. Supreme Court found that interrogation involving **inherent coercion** was not acceptable. Ashcraft had

been charged with the murder of his wife, Zelma. He was arrested on a Saturday night and interrogated by relays of skilled interrogators until Monday morning, when he purportedly made a statement implicating himself in the murder. During questioning, he had faced a blinding light but was not physically mistreated. Investigators later testified that when the suspect requested cigarettes, food, or water, they "kindly" provided them. The Court's ruling, which reversed Ashcraft's conviction, made it plain that the Fifth Amendment guarantee against self-incrimination excludes any form of official coercion or pressure during interrogation.

A similar case, *Chambers* v. *Florida*, was decided in 1940.[152] In that case, four black men were arrested without warrants as suspects in the robbery and murder of an aged white man. After several days of questioning in a hostile atmosphere, the men confessed to the murder. The confessions were used as the primary evidence against them at their trial, and all four were sentenced to die. On appeal, the U.S. Supreme Court held that "the very circumstances surrounding their confinement and their questioning without any formal charges having been brought, were such as to fill petitioners with terror and frightful misgivings."[153] Learn more about the case of *Chambers* v. *Florida* at **http://tinyurl.com/4uy3c2w**.

Psychological Manipulation

Not only must interrogation be free of coercion and hostility, but it also cannot involve sophisticated trickery designed to ferret out a confession. Interrogators do not necessarily have to be scrupulously honest in confronting suspects, and the expert opinions of medical and psychiatric practitioners may be sought in investigations. However, the use of professionals skilled in **psychological manipulation** to gain confessions was banned by the Court in the case of *Leyra* v. *Denno*[154] in 1954, during the heyday of psychiatric perspectives on criminal behavior.

In 1991, in the case of *Arizona* v. *Fulminante*,[155] the U.S. Supreme Court further curtailed the use of sophisticated techniques to gain a confession. Oreste Fulminante was an inmate in a federal prison when he was approached by a fellow inmate who was an FBI informant. The informant told Fulminante that other inmates were plotting to kill him because of a rumor that he had killed a child. The informant offered to protect Fulminante if he divulged the details of his crime. Fulminante then

> Not only must interrogation be free of coercion and hostility, but it also cannot involve sophisticated trickery designed to ferret out a confession.

■ **lecture note**   Discuss the implications of the 1991 case of *Arizona* v. *Fulminante*, in which the U.S. Supreme Court held that under limited circumstances, the admission of a coerced confession into a criminal trial might be nothing more than a "trial error"—one that does not require the automatic reversal of a lower court's conviction.

■ **lecture note**   Explain that as a result of the 1964 U.S. Supreme Court case of *Escobedo* v. *Illinois*, suspects have the right to have a lawyer present during police interrogations.

■ **lecture note**   Point out to students that interrogation can be a subtle and complex process, wherein respect for individual rights and police mandates must be carefully balanced to ensure fairness and ultimately just trials and outcomes.

described his role in the murder of his 11-year-old stepdaughter. He was charged with that murder, tried, and convicted.

On appeal to the U.S. Supreme Court, Fulminante's lawyers argued that their client's confession had been coerced because of the threat of violence communicated by the informant. The Court agreed that the confession had been coerced and ordered a new trial at which the confession could not be admitted into evidence. Simultaneously, however, the Court found that the admission of a coerced confession should be considered a harmless "trial error" that need not necessarily result in reversal of a conviction if other evidence still proves guilt. The decision was especially significant because it partially reversed the Court's earlier ruling, in *Chapman* v. *California* (1967),[156] where it was held that forced confessions were such a basic form of constitutional error that they automatically invalidated any conviction to which they related. Fulminante was convicted again at his second trial, where his confession was not entered into evidence, and he was sentenced to die. The Arizona Supreme Court, however, overturned his conviction, ruling that testimony describing statements the victim had made about fearing for her life prior to her murder, and which had been entered into evidence, were hearsay and had prejudiced the jury.[157]

Finally, the area of eyewitness identification bears discussion. In 2011, in the case of *State* v. *Henderson*,[158] the New Jersey Supreme Court held that the current legal standard for assessing eyewitness identifications must be revised because it did not offer adequate measures for reliability; did not sufficiently deter inappropriate police conduct; and overstated the jury's ability to evaluate identification evidence.

In 2012, in the case of *Perry* v. *New Hampshire*,[159] the U.S. Supreme Court recognized problems with eyewitness identification, especially when such identification is obtained by skilled law enforcement interrogators. Still, the court denied that the due process clause of the U.S. Constitution requires a preliminary judicial inquiry into the reliability of an eyewitness identification when the identification was not procured under unnecessarily suggestive circumstances arranged by law enforcement.

Learn more about detecting deception from the FBI at **http://www.justicestudies.com/pdf/truth_deception.pdf**.

The Right to a Lawyer at Interrogation

In 1964, in the case of *Escobedo* v. *Illinois*,[160] the right to have legal counsel present during police interrogation was formally recognized.

In 1981, the case of *Edwards* v. *Arizona*[161] established a "bright-line rule" (that is, specified a criterion that cannot be violated) for investigators to use in interpreting a suspect's right to counsel. In *Edwards*, the Supreme Court reiterated its *Miranda* concern that once a suspect who is in custody and is being questioned requests the assistance of counsel, all questioning must cease until an attorney is present. In 1990, the Court refined the rule in *Minnick* v. *Mississippi*,[162] when it held that after the suspect has had an opportunity to consult his or her lawyer, interrogation may not resume unless the lawyer is present.

The 1986 case of *Michigan* v. *Jackson*[163] provided further support for *Edwards*. In *Jackson*, the Court forbade police from initiating the interrogation of criminal defendants who have invoked their right to counsel at an arraignment or similar proceeding.

Similarly, according to *Arizona* v. *Roberson* (1988),[164] the police may not avoid the suspect's request for a lawyer by beginning a new line of questioning, even if it is about an unrelated offense.

In 1994, however, in the case of *Davis* v. *U.S.*,[165] the Court "put the burden on custodial suspects to make unequivocal invocations of the right to counsel." In the *Davis* case, a man being interrogated in the death of a sailor waived his *Miranda* rights but later said, "Maybe I should talk to a lawyer." Investigators asked the suspect clarifying questions, and he responded, "No, I don't want a lawyer." He appealed his conviction, claiming that interrogation should have ceased when he mentioned a lawyer. The Court, in affirming the conviction, stated that "it will often be good police practice for the interviewing officers to clarify whether or not [the suspect] actually wants an attorney."

In the 2009 case of *Montejo* v. *Louisiana*,[166] however, in something of an about-face, the U.S. Supreme Court held that "*Michigan* v. *Jackson* should be and now is overruled." The justices found that strict interpretations of *Jackson* could lead to practical problems. Montejo had been charged with first-degree murder, and appointment of counsel was ordered at his arraignment. He did not, however, ask to see his attorney. Later that same day, the police read Montejo his *Miranda* rights, and he agreed to accompany them on a trip to locate the murder weapon. During the trip, he wrote an incriminating letter of apology to the victim's widow. Upon returning, he met with his court-appointed attorney for the first time. At trial, his letter was admitted over defense objection, and he was convicted and sentenced to death. In the words of the Court, "Both *Edwards* and *Jackson* are meant to prevent police from badgering defendants into changing their minds about the right to counsel once they have invoked it, but a defendant who never asked for counsel has not yet made up his mind." In effect, although an attorney

■ **theme** Examine the impact of *Miranda* warnings on American criminal justice. How might the justice system have functioned differently before 1966 (the date of the *Miranda* decision) than it does now as a result of this decision?

■ **lecture note** Discuss the 1966 U.S. Supreme Court case of *Miranda* v. *Arizona* (1966). Explain that this case requires that a criminal defendant who is in custody be advised of his or her rights prior to questioning. Review each of the five warnings that law enforcement officers are required to give to defendants.

■ **theme** Why are each of the five *Miranda* warnings important? What abuses does each prevent, and what police actions does each hamper?

■ ***Miranda* warnings** The advisement of rights due criminal suspects by the police before questioning begins. *Miranda* warnings were first set forth by the U.S. Supreme Court in the 1966 case of *Miranda* v. *Arizona*.

■ **activity** Encourage students to listen to old time radio productions of police dramas such as *Dragnet* that were produced prior to the wave of court cases expanding individual rights and guaranteeing individual due process, and identify examples of how "times have changed." Many of these programs are available online free to stream.

■ **theme** Are there any "rights" that you would add to, or remove from, the *Miranda* rights listed in the "CJ Issues" box on the *Miranda* warnings? If so, which ones?

■ **activity** Ask the class to consider each of the rights statements that make up the *Miranda* decision. Have students debate the wisdom of having law enforcement officers provide each rights statement to criminal suspects.

■ **activity** Divide the class into groups and have them debate the question of whether *Miranda* should be overturned.

had been appointed to represent Montejo, he had never actually invoked his right to counsel.

Finally, in 2010, in the case of *Maryland* v. *Shatzer*,[167] the Court held that police could reopen the interrogation of a suspect who has invoked his right to counsel following a 14-day or longer break in questioning. Even though the defendant (Shatzer) had been in state prison during the break, the justices said, he had been free "from the coercive power of an interrogator" during that time.

Suspect Rights: The *Miranda* Decision

In the area of suspect rights, no case is as famous as *Miranda* v. *Arizona* (1966),[168] which established the well-known **Miranda warnings**. Many people regard *Miranda* as the centerpiece of the Warren Court due process rulings.

The case involved Ernesto Miranda, who was arrested in Phoenix, Arizona, and was accused of having kidnapped and raped a young woman. At police headquarters, he was identified by the victim. After being interrogated for two hours, Miranda signed a confession that formed the basis of his later conviction on the charges.

On appeal, the U.S. Supreme Court rendered what some regard as the most far-reaching opinion to have affected criminal justice in the last half century. The Court ruled that Miranda's conviction was unconstitutional because "[t]he entire aura and atmosphere of police interrogation without notification of rights and an offer of assistance of counsel tends to subjugate the individual to the will of his examiner."

The Court continued, saying that the suspect "must be warned prior to any questioning that he has the right to remain silent, that anything he says can be used against him in a court of law, that he has the right to the presence of an attorney, and that if he cannot afford an attorney one will be appointed for him prior to any questioning if he so desires. Opportunity to exercise these rights must be afforded to him throughout the interrogation. After such warnings have been given, and such opportunity afforded him, the individual may knowingly and intelligently waive these rights and agree to answer the questions or make

Ernesto Miranda, shown here after a jury convicted him for a second time. Miranda's conviction on rape and kidnapping charges after arresting officers failed to advise him of his rights led to the now-famous *Miranda* warnings. What do the *Miranda* warnings say?

a statement. But unless and until such warnings and waiver are demonstrated by the prosecution at the trial, no evidence obtained as a result of interrogation can be used against him."

To ensure that proper advice is given to suspects at the time of their arrest, the now-famous *Miranda* rights are read before any questioning begins. These rights, as found on a *Miranda* warning card commonly used by police agencies, appear in the "CJ Issues" box.

Once suspects have been advised of their *Miranda* rights, they are commonly asked to sign a paper that lists each right, in order to confirm that they were advised of their rights and that they understand each right. Questioning may then begin, but only if suspects waive their rights not to talk and to have a lawyer present during interrogation.

In 1992, *Miranda* rights were effectively extended to illegal immigrants living in the United States. In a settlement of a class-action lawsuit against the Immigration and Naturalization Service, U.S. District Court Judge William Byrne, Jr., approved the printing of millions of notices in several languages to be given to arrestees. The approximately 1.5 million illegal aliens arrested each year must be told they may (1) talk with a lawyer, (2) make a phone call, (3) request a list of available legal services, (4) seek a hearing before an immigration judge, (5) possibly obtain release on bond, and (6) contact a diplomatic officer representing their country.[169] This was "long overdue," said Roberto Martinez of the American Friends Service Committee's Mexico–U.S. border program. "Up to now, we've had total mistreatment of civil rights of undocumented people."

When the *Miranda* decision was originally handed down, some hailed it as ensuring the protection of individual rights guaranteed under the Constitution. To guarantee those rights, they suggested, no better agency is available than the police themselves, since the police are present at the initial stages of the criminal justice process. Critics of *Miranda*, however, argued that the decision put police agencies in the uncomfortable and contradictory position not only of enforcing the law but also of having to offer defendants advice on how they might circumvent conviction and punishment. Under *Miranda*, the police partially assume the role of legal adviser to the accused.

In 1999, however, in the case of *U.S.* v. *Dickerson*,[170] the Fourth Circuit U.S. Court of Appeals upheld an almost-forgotten law that Congress had passed in 1968 with the intention of overturning *Miranda*. That law, Section 3501 of Chapter 223, Part II of Title 18 of the U.S. Code, says that "a confession . . . shall be admissible in evidence if it is voluntarily given." On appeal in 2000, the U.S. Supreme Court upheld its original

Miranda ruling by a 7–2 vote and found that *Miranda* is a constitutional rule (that is, a fundamental right inherent in the U.S. Constitution) that cannot be dismissed by an act of Congress. "*Miranda* and its progeny," the majority wrote in *Dickerson* v. *U.S.* (2000), will continue to "govern the admissibility of statements made during custodial interrogation in both state and federal courts."[171]

On June 28, 2004, the U.S. Supreme Court handed down two important decisions—*U.S.* v. *Patane*[172] and *Missouri* v. *Seibert*[173]—in a continuing refinement of its original 1966 ruling in *Miranda* v. *Arizona*.[174]

As described in this chapter, *Miranda* created a presumption of coercion in all custodial interrogations. Generally speaking, only a demonstration that *Miranda* warnings have been provided to a suspect has been sufficient to counter that presumption and to allow legal proceedings based on the fruits of an interrogation to move forward. Consequently, some scholars were surprised by *Patane*, in which the Court found that "a mere failure to give *Miranda* warnings does not, by itself, violate a suspect's constitutional rights or even the *Miranda* rule."

The *Patane* case began with the arrest of a convicted felon after a federal agent told officers that the man owned a handgun illegally. At the time of arrest, the officers tried to advise the defendant of his rights, but he interrupted them, saying that he already knew his rights. The officers then asked him about the pistol, and he told them where it was. After the weapon was recovered, the defendant was charged with illegal possession of a firearm by a convicted felon.

At first glance, *Patane* appears to contradict the fruit of the poisoned tree doctrine that the Court established in the 1920 case of *Silverthorne Lumber Co.* v. *U.S.*[175] and that *Wong Sun* v. *U.S.* (1963)[176] made applicable to verbal evidence derived

CJ | ISSUES
The *Miranda* Warnings

Adult Rights Warning

Suspects 18 years old or older who are in custody must be advised of the following rights before any questioning begins:

1. You have the right to remain silent.
2. Anything you say can be used against you in a court of law.
3. You have the right to talk to a lawyer and to have a lawyer present while you are being questioned.
4. If you want a lawyer before or during questioning but cannot afford to hire a lawyer, one will be appointed to represent you at no cost before any questioning.
5. If you answer questions now without a lawyer here, you still have the right to stop answering questions at any time.

Waiver of Rights

After reading and explaining the rights of a person in custody, an officer must also ask for a waiver of those rights before any questioning. The following waiver questions must be answered affirmatively, either by express answer or by clear implication. Silence alone is not a waiver.

1. Do you understand each of these rights I have explained to you? (Answer must be YES.)
2. Having these rights in mind, do you now wish to answer questions? (Answer must be YES.)
3. Do you now wish to answer questions without a lawyer present? (Answer must be YES.)

   The following question must be asked of juveniles ages 14, 15, 16, and 17.
4. Do you now wish to answer questions without your parents, guardians, or custodians present? (Answer must be YES.)

A suspect being read his *Miranda* rights immediately after arrest. Officers often read *Miranda* rights from a card or electronic device to preclude the possibility of a mistake. What might the consequences of a mistake be?

immediately from an illegal search and seizure. An understanding of *Patane*, however, requires recognition of the fact that the *Miranda* rule is based on the self-incrimination clause of the Fifth Amendment to the U.S. Constitution. According to the Court in *Patane*, "that Clause's core protection is a prohibition on compelling a criminal defendant to testify against himself at trial." It cannot be violated, the Court said, "by the introduction of nontestimonial evidence obtained as a result of voluntary statements." In other words, according to the Court, only (1) coerced statements and (2) those voluntary statements made by a defendant that might directly incriminate him or her at a later trial are precluded by a failure to read a suspect his or her *Miranda* rights. Such voluntary statements would, of course, include such things as an outright confession.

Significantly, however, oral statements must be distinguished, the Court said, from the "physical fruits of the suspect's unwarned but voluntary statements." In other words, if an unwarned suspect is questioned by police officers and tells the officers where they can find an illegal weapon or a weapon that has been used in a crime, the weapon can be recovered and later introduced as evidence at the suspect's trial. If the same unwarned suspect, however, tells police that he committed a murder, then his confession will not be allowed into evidence at trial. The line drawn by the court is against the admissibility of *oral statements*

made by an unwarned defendant, not the *nontestimonial physical evidence* resulting from continued police investigation of such statements. Under *Patane*, the oral statements themselves cannot be admitted, but the physical evidence derived from them can be. "Thus," wrote the justices in *Patane*, "admission of nontestimonial physical fruits (the pistol here) does not run the risk of admitting into trial an accused's coerced incriminating statements against himself."

The *Seibert* case addressed a far different issue: that of the legality of a two-step police interrogation technique in which suspects were questioned and—if they made incriminating statements—were then advised of their *Miranda* rights and questioned again. The justices found that such a technique could not meet constitutional muster, writing, "When the [*Miranda*] warnings are inserted in the midst of coordinated and continuing interrogation, they are likely to mislead and deprive a defendant of knowledge essential to his ability to understand the nature of his rights and the consequences of abandoning them. . . . And it would be unrealistic to treat two spates of integrated and proximately conducted questioning as independent interrogations . . . simply because *Miranda* warnings formally punctuate them in the middle."

Waiver of *Miranda* Rights by Suspects

Suspects in police custody may legally waive their *Miranda* rights through a *voluntary* "knowing and intelligent" waiver. A *knowing waiver* can be made only if a suspect is advised of his or her rights and is in a condition to understand the advisement. A rights advisement made in English to a Spanish-speaking suspect, for example, cannot produce a knowing waiver. Likewise, an *intelligent waiver* of rights requires that the defendant be able to understand the consequences of not invoking the *Miranda* rights. In the case of *Moran v. Burbine* (1986),[177] the U.S. Supreme Court defined an intelligent and knowing waiver as one "made with a full awareness both of the nature of the right being abandoned and the consequences of the decision to abandon it." Similarly, in *Colorado v. Spring* (1987),[178] the Court held that an intelligent and knowing waiver can be made even though a suspect has not been informed of all the alleged offenses about which he or she is about to be questioned.

Inevitable-Discovery Exception to *Miranda*

The case of Robert Anthony Williams provides a good example of the change in the U.S. Supreme Court philosophy, alluded to earlier in this chapter, from an individual-rights perspective toward a public-order perspective. The case epitomizes what many consider a slow erosion of the

Michael Newman/PhotoEdit Inc.

advances in defendant rights, which reached their apex in *Miranda*. This case began in 1969, at the close of the Warren Court era. Williams was apprehended as a suspect in the murder of ten-year-old Pamela Powers around Christmas time and was advised of his rights. Later, as Williams rode in a car with detectives who were searching for the girl's body, one of the detectives made what has since become known as the "Christian burial speech." The detective told Williams that since Christmas was almost upon them, it would be "the Christian thing to do" to see to it that Pamela had a decent burial rather than having to lie in a field somewhere. Williams confessed and led detectives to the body. However, because Williams had not been reminded of his right to have a lawyer present during his conversation with the detective, the Supreme Court in *Brewer* v. *Williams* (1977)[179] overturned Williams's conviction, saying that the detective's remarks were "a deliberate eliciting of incriminating evidence from an accused in the absence of his lawyer."

In 1977, Williams was retried for the murder, but his remarks in leading detectives to the body were not entered into evidence. The discovery of the body was used, however, and Williams was convicted, prompting another appeal to the Supreme Court based on the argument that the body should not have been used as evidence because it was discovered due to the illegally gathered statements. This time, in the 1984 case of *Nix* v. *Williams*,[180] the Supreme Court affirmed Williams's second conviction, holding that the body would have been found anyway, since detectives were searching in the direction where it lay when Williams revealed its location. This ruling came during the heyday of the Burger Court and clearly demonstrates a tilt by the Court away from suspects' rights and an acknowledgment of the imperfect world of police procedure. The *Williams* case, as it was finally resolved, is said to have created the inevitable-discovery exception to the *Miranda* requirements. The inevitable-discovery exception means that evidence, even if it was otherwise gathered inappropriately, can be used in a court of law if it would have invariably turned up in the normal course of events.

Public-Safety Exception to *Miranda*

In 2013, U.S. officials announced that they would question 19-year-old Dzhokhar Tsarnaev, the surviving Boston Marathon bomber, before reading him his *Miranda* rights.[181] The Boston attack killed three people and wounded more than 170. Tsarnaev had been wounded and was captured after his brother had been killed in a police shootout. Law enforcement officials said that they would question the hospitalized Tsarnaev under the well-established *public-safety exception* to the *Miranda*

rule which is intended to allow authorities to conduct an initial public-safety interview in order to quickly determine whether any danger to the public still exists. The *Tsarnaev* case raised questions, however, because it wasn't clear that taking the time for a rights advisement endangered public safety.

The public-safety exception was created in 1984, when the U.S. Supreme Court decided the case of *New York* v. *Quarles*.[182] That case centered on a rape in which the victim told police her assailant had a gun and had fled into a nearby supermarket. Two police officers entered the store and apprehended the suspect. One officer immediately noticed that the man was wearing an empty shoulder holster and, fearing that a child might find the discarded weapon, quickly asked, "Where's the gun?" Quarles was convicted of rape but appealed his conviction, requesting that the weapon be suppressed as evidence because officers had not advised him of his *Miranda* rights before asking him about it. The Supreme Court disagreed, stating that considerations of public safety were overriding and negated the need for rights advisement prior to limited questioning that focused on the need to prevent further harm. Following such reasoning, interrogators decided not to *Mirandize* Tsarnaev before questioning him, in the belief that he might be able to provide information about bombs or other plots that could pose an immediate danger to the public.

The U.S. Supreme Court has also held that in cases when the police issue *Miranda* warnings, a later demonstration that a person may have been suffering from mental problems does not necessarily negate a confession. *Colorado* v. *Connelly* (1986)[183] involved a man who approached a Denver police officer and said he wanted to confess to the murder of a young girl. The officer immediately informed him of his *Miranda* rights, but the man waived them and continued to talk. When a detective arrived, the man was again advised of his rights and again waived them. After being taken to the local jail, the man began to hear "voices" and later claimed that it was these voices that had made him confess. At the trial, the defense moved to have the earlier confession negated on the basis that it was not voluntarily or freely given because of the defendant's mental condition. On appeal, the U.S. Supreme Court disagreed, saying that "no coercive government conduct occurred in this case." Hence "self-coercion," due to either a guilty conscience or faulty thought processes, does not bar prosecution based on information revealed willingly by a suspect.

The 1986 case of *Kuhlmann* v. *Wilson*[184] represents another refinement of *Miranda*. In this case, the Court upheld a police informant's lawful ability to gather information for use at a trial from a defendant while the two were placed together in a jail cell. The passive gathering of information was judged to be

■ **lecture note** Explain the concept of *Miranda triggers* and discuss under what circumstances officers do *not* have to provide *Miranda* warnings.

■ **theme** What are the *Miranda* triggers? Why is it necessary for both to be present before a rights advisement is required? How would the meaning of *Miranda* change if the Court required only the first trigger?

■ ***Miranda* triggers**   The dual principles of custody and interrogation, both of which are necessary before an advisement of rights is required.

The immediate aftermath of a terrorist explosion at the finish line of the 2013 Boston Marathon. Dzhokhar Tsarnaev, one of two brothers who planted the explosive devices among the crowd, survived a citywide manhunt, but authorities invoked the public-safety exception to the *Miranda* requirement in not advising him of his rights for a couple of days following his arrest. Why did they do that, and what information were they hoping to uncover by questioning Tsarnaev?

acceptable, provided that the informant did not make attempts to elicit information.

In the case of *Illinois* v. *Perkins* (1990),[185] the Court expanded its position to say that under appropriate circumstances, even the active questioning of a suspect by an undercover officer posing as a fellow inmate does not require *Miranda* warnings. In *Perkins*, the Court found that, lacking other forms of coercion, the fact that the suspect was not aware of the questioner's identity as a law enforcement officer ensured that his statements were freely given. In the words of the Court, "The essential ingredients of a 'police-dominated atmosphere' and compulsion are not present when an incarcerated person speaks freely to someone that he believes to be a fellow inmate." Learn more about the public safety exception directly from the FBI at **http://www .justicestudies.com/pubs/public_safety.pdf**.

Miranda and the Meaning of Interrogation

Modern interpretations of the applicability of *Miranda* warnings turn on an understanding of interrogation. The *Miranda* decision, as originally rendered, specifically recognized the need for police investigators to make inquiries at crime scenes to determine facts or to establish identities. As long as the individual questioned is not yet in custody and as long as probable cause is lacking in the investigator's mind, such questioning can proceed without *Miranda* warnings. In such cases, interrogation, within the meaning of *Miranda*, has not yet begun.

The case of *Rock* v. *Zimmerman* (1982)[186] provides a different sort of example—one in which a suspect willingly made statements to the police before interrogation began. The suspect had set fire to his own house and shot and killed a neighbor. When the fire department arrived, he began shooting again and killed the fire chief. Cornered later in a field, the defendant, gun in hand, spontaneously shouted at police, "How many people did I kill? How many people are dead?"[187] This spontaneous statement was held to be admissible evidence at the suspect's trial.

It is also important to recognize that in the *Miranda* decision, the Supreme Court required that officers provide warnings only in those situations involving *both* arrest and custodial interrogation—what some call the ***Miranda* triggers**. In other words, it is generally permissible for officers to take a suspect into custody and listen, without asking questions, while he or she talks. Similarly, they may ask questions without providing a *Miranda* warning, even within the confines of a police station house, as long as the person questioned is not a suspect and is not under arrest.[188] Warnings are required only when officers begin to actively and deliberately elicit responses from a suspect whom they know has been indicted or who is in custody.

Officers were found to have acted properly in the case of *South Dakota* v. *Neville* (1983)[189] when they informed a man suspected of driving while intoxicated (DWI), without reading him his rights, that he would stand to lose his driver's license if he did not submit to a Breathalyzer test. When the driver responded, "I'm too drunk. I won't pass the test," his answer became evidence of his condition and was permitted at trial.

A third-party conversation recorded by the police after a suspect has invoked the *Miranda* right to remain silent may be used as evidence, according to a 1987 ruling in *Arizona* v. *Mauro*.[190] In *Mauro*, a man who willingly conversed with his wife in the presence of a police tape recorder, even after invoking his right to keep silent, was held to have effectively abandoned that right.

When a waiver is not made, however, in-court references to a defendant's silence following the issuing of *Miranda* warnings are unconstitutional. In the 1976 case of *Doyle* v. *Ohio*,[191] the U.S. Supreme Court definitively ruled that "a suspect's [post-*Miranda*] silence will not be used against him." Even so, according to the Court in *Brecht* v. *Abrahamson* (1993),[192] prosecution efforts to use such silence against a defendant may not invalidate a finding of guilt by a jury unless the "error had substantial and injurious effect or influence in determining the jury's verdict."[193]

■ **theme** What is nontestimonial evidence? Why does the collection of this type of evidence create legal complications for law enforcement?

Of course, when a person is *not* a suspect and is *not* charged with a crime, *Miranda* warnings need not be given. Such logic led to what some have called a "fractured opinion"[194] in the 2003 case of *Chavez v. Martinez*.[195] The case involved Oliverio Martinez, who was blinded and paralyzed in a police shooting after he grabbed an officer's weapon during an altercation. An Oxnard, California, police officer named Chavez persisted in questioning Martinez while he was awaiting treatment despite his pleas to stop and the fact that he was obviously in great pain. The Court held that "police questioning in [the] absence of *Miranda* warnings, even questioning that is overbearing to [the] point of coercion, does not violate constitutional protections against self-incrimination, as long as no incriminating statements are introduced at trial."[196] Nonetheless, the Court found that Martinez could bring a civil suit against Chavez and the Oxnard Police Department for violation of his constitutional right to due process.

In the 2010 case of *Florida v. Powell*, the U.S. Supreme Court held that although *Miranda* warnings are generally required prior to police interrogation, the wording of those warnings is not set in stone. The Court ruled that "in determining whether police warnings were satisfactory, reviewing courts are not required to examine them as if construing a will or defining the terms of an easement. The inquiry is simply whether the warnings reasonably convey to a suspect his rights as required by *Miranda*."

Also in 2010, in the case of *Berghuis v. Thompkins*, the Court held that a Michigan suspect did not invoke his Fifth Amendment right to remain silent by simply not answering questions that interrogators put to him.[197] Instead, the justices ruled, a suspect must unambiguously assert his right to remain silent before the police are required to end their questioning. In this case, the defendant, Van Chester Thompkins, was properly advised of his rights prior to questioning, and, although he was largely silent during a three-hour interrogation, he never said that he wanted to remain silent, that he did not want to talk with the police, or that he wanted an attorney. Near the end of the interrogation, however, he answered "yes" when asked whether he prayed to God to forgive him for the shooting death of a murder victim.

Finally, in 2013, in the case of *Salinas v. Texas*, the Supreme Court found that an offender must *expressly* invoke his Miranda privileges, and that failure to do so can later result in use at trial of the offender's silence as evidence of his guilt.[198] According to the Court, "A defendant normally does not invoke the privilege (against self-incrimination) by remaining silent."

Gathering Special Kinds of Nontestimonial Evidence

The role of law enforcement is complicated by the fact that suspects are often privy to special evidence of a nontestimonial sort. Nontestimonial evidence is generally physical evidence, and most physical evidence is subject to normal procedures of search and seizure. A special category of nontestimonial evidence, however, includes very personal items that may be within or part of a person's body, such as ingested drugs, blood cells, foreign objects, medical implants, and human DNA. Also included in this category are fingerprints and other kinds of biological residue. The gathering of such special kinds of nontestimonial evidence is a complex area rich in precedent. The Fourth Amendment guarantee that people be secure in their homes and in their persons has generally been interpreted by the courts to mean that the improper seizure of physical evidence of any kind is illegal and will result in exclusion of that evidence at trial. When very personal kinds of nontestimonial evidence are considered, however, the issue becomes more complicated.

The Right to Privacy

Two 1985 cases, *Hayes v. Florida*[199] and *Winston v. Lee*,[200] provide examples of limits the courts have placed on the seizure of very personal forms of nontestimonial evidence. The *Hayes* case established the right of suspects to refuse to be fingerprinted when probable cause necessary to effect an arrest does not exist. *Winston* demonstrated the inviolability of the body against surgical and other substantially invasive techniques that might be ordered by authorities against a suspect's will.

In the *Winston* case, Rudolph Lee, Jr., was found a few blocks from the scene of a robbery with a gunshot wound in his chest. The robbery had involved an exchange of gunshots by the store owner and the robber, with the owner noting that the robber had apparently been hit by a bullet. At the hospital, the store owner identified Lee as the robber. The prosecution sought to have Lee submit to surgery to remove the bullet in his chest, arguing that the bullet would provide physical evidence linking him to the crime. Lee refused the surgery, and in *Winston v. Lee*, the U.S. Supreme Court ruled that Lee could not be ordered to undergo surgery because intrusion into his body of that magnitude was unacceptable under the right to privacy guaranteed by the Fourth Amendment. The *Winston* case was based on precedent established in *Schmerber v. California* (1966).[201] The *Schmerber* case turned on the extraction against the defendant's

■ **lecture note**   Explain that body packing involves the swallowing or insertion into body cavities of drug-filled containers for the purpose of drug smuggling.

■ **theme**   Read what the text has to say about the case of *U.S. v. Montoya de Hernandez* (1985). In your opinion, did investigating officers have sufficient reason to detain the suspect in this case? Explain.

■ **theme**   Consider the types of electronic information that the typical person generates in an average day. Which types of information might form the basis for the criminal prosecution of those involved in illegal activities?

■ **activity**   Have students keep a daily log of the kinds of electronic signals and the forms of electronic information they generate over a week. Ask them to decide how each item of information (and each type of media involved) might be useful to criminal investigators if the students were to be involved in criminal activity.

will of a blood sample to be measured for alcohol content. In *Schmerber*, the Court ruled that warrants must be obtained for bodily intrusions unless fast action is necessary to prevent the destruction of evidence by natural physiological processes.

Body-Cavity Searches

In early 2005, officers of the Suffolk County (New York) Police Department arrested 36-year-old Terrance Haynes and charged him with marijuana possession.[202] After placing him in the back of a patrol car, Haynes appeared to choke and had difficulty breathing. Soon his breathing stopped, prompting officers to use the Heimlich maneuver, which dislodged a plastic bag from Haynes's windpipe. The bag contained 11 packets of cocaine. Although Haynes survived the ordeal, he now faces up to 25 years in prison.

Although some suspects might literally "cough up" evidence, some are more successful at hiding it *in* their bodies. Body-cavity searches are among the most problematic types of searches for police today. "Strip" searches of convicts in prison, including the search of body cavities, have generally been held to be permissible.

The 1985 Supreme Court case of *U.S.* v. *Montoya de Hernandez*[203] focused on the issue of "alimentary canal smuggling," in which the offender typically swallows condoms filled with cocaine or heroin and waits for nature to take its course to recover the substance. In the *Montoya* case, a woman known to be a "balloon swallower" arrived in the United States on a flight from Colombia. She was detained by customs officials and given a pat-down search by a female agent. The agent reported that the woman's abdomen was firm and suggested that X-rays be taken. The suspect refused and was given the choice of submitting to further tests or taking the next flight back to Colombia. No flight was immediately available, however, and the suspect was placed in a room for 16 hours, where she refused all food and drink. Finally, a court order for an X-ray was obtained. The procedure revealed "balloons," and the woman was detained another four days, during which time she passed numerous cocaine-filled plastic condoms. The Court ruled that the woman's confinement was not unreasonable, based as it was on the supportable suspicion that she was "body-packing" cocaine. Any discomfort she experienced, the Court ruled, "resulted solely from the method that she chose to smuggle illicit drugs."[204]

Electronic Eavesdropping

Modern technology makes possible increasingly complex forms of communication. One of the first Supreme Court decisions involving electronic communications was the 1928 case of *Olmstead* v. *U.S.*[205] In *Olmstead*, bootleggers used their home telephones to discuss and transact business. Agents tapped the lines and based their investigation and ensuing arrests on conversations they overheard. The defendants were convicted and eventually appealed to the high court, arguing that the agents had in effect seized information illegally without a search warrant in violation of the defendants' Fourth Amendment right to be secure in their homes. The Court ruled, however, that telephone lines were not an extension of the defendants' homes and therefore were not protected by the constitutional guarantee of security. However, subsequent federal statutes have substantially modified the significance of *Olmstead*.

Recording devices carried on the body of an undercover agent or an informant were ruled to produce admissible evidence in *On Lee* v. *U.S.* (1952)[206] and *Lopez* v. *U.S.* (1963).[207] The 1967 case of *Berger* v. *New York*[208] permitted wiretaps and "bugs" in instances where state law provided for the use of such devices and where officers obtained a warrant based on probable cause.

The Court appeared to undertake a significant change of direction in the area of electronic eavesdropping when it decided the case of *Katz* v. *U.S.* in 1967.[209] Federal agents had monitored a number of Katz's telephone calls from a public phone using a device separate from the phone lines and attached to the glass of the phone booth. The Court, in this case, stated that a warrant is required to unveil what a person makes an effort to keep private, even in a public place. In the words of the Court, "The government's activities in electronically listening to and recording the petitioner's words violated the privacy upon which he justifiably relied while using the telephone booth and thus constituted a 'search and seizure' within the meaning of the Fourth Amendment."

In 1968, with the case of *Lee* v. *Florida*,[210] the Court applied the Federal Communications Act[211] to telephone conversations that might be the object of police investigation and held that evidence obtained without a warrant could not be used in state proceedings if it resulted from a wiretap. The only person who has the authority to permit eavesdropping, according to that act, is the sender of the message.

CJ | NEWS
Supreme Court Says Police Need Warrant for GPS Tracking

A Las Vegas police officer tracks a suspect vehicle using GPS tracking technology. What role did such devices play in the 2012 U.S. Supreme Court case of *U.S.* v. *Jones*? Following the justices' reasoning in that case, under what circumstances can the police use GPS devices to track suspects' vehicles?

In 2014, NYPD officers tracked a pharmacy robber using a GPS device that they had hidden in a bottle of prescription painkillers. The robber, Scott Kato, 45, had a long criminal record and was soon cornered when his car was stopped in traffic. He was shot dead after he pointed a handgun at officers who surrounded the vehicle. Because the GPS device was hidden in a decoy bottle, its innovative use as a crime fighting technology was legal. However, until recently, law enforcement officers did not need a warrant to attach a geographic positioning system (GPS) tracking device to a suspect's car and see where it went.

After all, some said, police don't need a warrant to get into their cars and follow suspects through the streets, and GPS systems are basically doing the same thing, only digitally.

In 2012, however, the Supreme Court decided that GPS devices are far more intrusive than tailing a car. In the case of *U.S.* v. *Jones* the justices voted 9–0 that the FBI needed a warrant when placing a GPS device on the vehicle of a suspected drug dealer.

"GPS monitoring generates a precise, comprehensive record of a person's public movement that reflects a wealth of detail about her familial, political, religious and sexual associations," wrote Justice Sonia Sotomayor.

The *Jones* case was the first time that the court dealt with GPSs, which have become a common police tool only in recent years. The court also signaled that it won't be the last time it deals with the booming field of high-tech surveillance, which also includes using signals emitted from cellphones to track someone down.

Although all the justices agreed that the FBI had violated the Fourth Amendment, which protects against unreasonable search and seizure, they were spilt on how the violation took place.

A five-member majority held that when the FBI agents attached the GPS device, they were in effect trespassing. This opinion, which will be the basis for all future court renderings, holds that a private vehicle cannot be touched, in the same way that a house cannot be entered, even when that car is out on public streets.

But Justice Samuel Alito, speaking for the four-member minority, contended that the real violation was not touching the car, but rather that it lay in violating the driver's expectation of privacy. This is part of a legal theory the court has been applying for 45 years, which holds that the Fourth Amendment "protects people, not places," he wrote.

Alito explained there would be future cases when the majority's concept of trespassing would no longer apply to high-tech tracking. For instance, when a car comes with a GPS device already in it, the police do not even have to touch the car to link into the device. He added that more than 322 million cell phones in the nation have chips in them allowing phone companies to track customers' locations. Again, without touching the cell phone, police can simply obtain tracking data from the phone companies involved.

Justice Sotomayor wrote that it could take a while for the courts to sort out all the implications of tracking technology. "In the course of carrying out mundane tasks," she wrote, Americans disclose which phone numbers they dial, which URLs they visit, and "the books, groceries and medications they purchase."

Following *U.S.* v. *Jones*, the FBI was forced to turn off about 3,000 GPS tracking devices. In some cases, the agency had to get court orders to briefly turn the devices back on so they could be located and retrieved.

The bureau, like other law enforcement agencies, can still use GPS trackers if it gets a search warrant, but Andrew Weissmann, the FBI's chief legal counsel, said this could be tricky. The FBI would first need to justify its suspicions to a judge, showing "probable cause," but often the ability to show probable cause depends on the information agents obtain from tracking techniques like GPS, he said.

Resources: "Justices Rein in Police on GPS Trackers," *Wall Street Journal*, January 24, 2012, http://online.wsj.com/article/SB10001424052970203806504577178811800873358.html; "Supreme Court: GPS Devices Equivalent of a Search, Police Must Get Warrant," Fox News, January 23, 2012, http://www.foxnews.com/politics/2012/01/23/supreme-court-gps-devices -equivalent-search-police-must-get-warrant-469182072/; and "FBI Still Struggling with Supreme Court's GPS Ruling," NPR, March 21, 2012, http://www.npr.org/2012/03/21/149011887/ fbi-still-struggling-with-supreme-courts-gps-ruling; Joseph Goldstein and Michael Schwirtz, "Robbery Suspect Tracked by GPS and Killed," *The New York Times*, May 16, 2014, http://nyti .ms/S1ryFu (accessed January 5, 2015).

The Federal Communications Act, originally passed in 1934, does not specifically mention the potential interest of law enforcement agencies in monitoring communications. Title III of the Omnibus Crime Control and Safe Streets Act of 1968, however, mostly prohibits wiretaps but does allow officers to listen to electronic communications when (1) an officer is one of the parties involved in the communication, (2) one of the parties is not the officer but willingly decides to share the communication with the officer, or (3) officers obtain a warrant based on

probable cause. In the 1971 case of *U.S.* v. *White*,[212] the Court held that law enforcement officers may intercept electronic information when one of the parties involved in the communication gives consent, even without a warrant.

In 1984, the Supreme Court decided the case of *U.S.* v. *Karo*,[213] in which DEA agents had arrested James Karo for cocaine importation. Officers placed a radio transmitter inside a 50-gallon drum of ether purchased by Karo for use in processing the cocaine. The device was placed inside the drum with the

■ **theme**   What is electronic evidence? How does it differ from other types of evidence, if at all? How should police investigators secure and handle electronic evidence to protect its integrity?

■ **lecture note**   Explain the concept of electronic evidence. Explain that electronic evidence is similar in many ways to other forms of evidence and that crime scenes involving electronic evidence should be secured as soon as possible to avoid contamination or destruction of the evidence.

■ **lecture note**   Describe how the Electronic Communications Privacy Act, passed by Congress in 1986, limits the wiretapping and eavesdropping activities of law enforcement officers.

■ **Electronic Communications Privacy Act (ECPA)**
A law passed by Congress in 1986 establishing the due process requirements that law enforcement officers must meet in order to legally intercept wire communications.

consent of the seller of the ether but without a search warrant. The shipment of ether was followed to the Karo house, and Karo was arrested and convicted of cocaine-trafficking charges. Karo appealed to the U.S. Supreme Court, claiming that the radio beeper had violated his reasonable expectation of privacy inside his premises and that, without a warrant, the evidence it produced was tainted. The Court agreed and overturned his conviction.

Minimization Requirement for Electronic Surveillance

The Supreme Court established a minimization requirement pertinent to electronic surveillance in the 1978 case of *U.S. v. Scott*.[214] Minimization means that officers must make every reasonable effort to monitor only those conversations, through the use of phone taps, body bugs, and the like, that are specifically related to the criminal activity under investigation. As soon as it becomes obvious that a conversation is innocent, then the monitoring personnel are required to cease their invasion of privacy. Problems arise if the conversation occurs in a foreign language, if it is "coded," or if it is ambiguous. It has been suggested that investigators involved in electronic surveillance maintain logbooks of their activities that specifically show monitored conversations, as well as efforts made at minimization.[215]

The Electronic Communications Privacy Act of 1986

Passed by Congress in 1986, the **Electronic Communications Privacy Act (ECPA)**[216] brought major changes in the requirements law enforcement officers must meet to intercept wire communications (those involving the human voice). The ECPA deals specifically with three areas of communication: (1) wiretaps and bugs; (2) pen registers, which record the numbers dialed from a telephone; and (3) tracing devices, which determine the number from which a call emanates. The act also addresses the procedures to be followed by officers in obtaining records relating to communications services, and it establishes requirements for gaining access to stored electronic communications and records of those communications. The ECPA basically requires that investigating officers must obtain wiretap-type court orders to eavesdrop on *ongoing communications*. The use of pen registers and recording devices, however, is specifically excluded by the law from court order requirements.[217]

A related measure, the Communications Assistance for Law Enforcement Act (CALEA) of 1994,[218] appropriated $500 million to modify the U.S. phone system to allow for continued wiretapping by law enforcement agencies. The law also specifies a standard-setting process for the redesign of existing equipment that would permit effective wiretapping in the face of coming technological advances. In the words of the FBI's Telecommunications Industry Liaison Unit, "This law requires telecommunications carriers, as defined in the Act, to ensure law enforcement's ability, pursuant to court order or other lawful authorization, to intercept communications notwithstanding advanced telecommunications technologies."[219] In 2010, 3,194 wiretap requests were approved by federal and state judges, and approximately 5 million conversations were intercepted by law enforcement agencies throughout the country.[220]

The Telecommunications Act of 1996

Title V of the Telecommunications Act of 1996[221] made it a federal offense for anyone engaged in interstate or international communications to knowingly use a telecommunications device "to create, solicit, or initiate the transmission of any comment, request, suggestion, proposal, image, or other communication which is obscene, lewd, lascivious, filthy, or indecent, with intent to annoy, abuse, threaten, or harass another person." The law also provided special penalties for anyone who "makes a telephone call . . . without disclosing his identity and with intent to annoy, abuse, threaten, or harass any person at the called number or who receives the communication" or who "makes or causes the telephone of another repeatedly or continuously to ring, with intent to harass any person at the called number; or makes repeated telephone calls" for the purpose of harassing a person at the called number.

A section of the law, known as the Communications Decency Act (CDA),[222] criminalized the transmission to minors of "patently offensive" obscene materials over the Internet or other computer telecommunications service. Portions of the CDA were invalidated by the U.S. Supreme Court in the case of *Reno* v. *ACLU* (1997).[223]

The USA Patriot Act of 2001

The USA PATRIOT Act of 2001, which is also discussed in a "CJ Issues" box in this chapter, made it easier for police investigators to intercept many forms of electronic communications. Under previous federal law, for example, investigators could not obtain a wiretap order to intercept *wire* communications for violations of the Computer Fraud and Abuse Act.[224] In several well-publicized cases, hackers had stolen teleconferencing

■ **sneak-and-peek search**   A search that occurs in the suspect's absence and without his or her prior knowledge.

Explain how the USA PATRIOT Act has affected the ability of police investigators to intercept various forms of electronic communication.

CJ | ISSUES

The USA PATRIOT Act of 2001 and the USA PATRIOT Improvement and Reauthorization Act of 2005

On October 26, 2001, President George W. Bush signed into law the USA PATRIOT Act, also known as the Uniting and Strengthening America by Providing Appropriate Tools Required to Intercept and Obstruct Terrorism Act. The law, which was drafted in response to the September 11, 2001, terrorist attacks on the World Trade Center and the Pentagon, substantially increased the investigatory authority of federal, state, and local police agencies.

The act permits longer jail terms for certain suspects arrested without a warrant, broadens authority for **"sneak-and-peek" searches** (searches conducted without prior notice and in the absence of the suspect), and enhances the power of prosecutors. The law also increases the ability of federal authorities to tap phones (including wireless devices), share intelligence information, track Internet usage, crack down on money laundering, and protect U.S. borders. Many of the crime-fighting powers created under the legislation are not limited to acts of terrorism but apply to many different kinds of criminal offenses.

The 2001 law led individual-rights advocates to question whether the government unfairly expanded police powers at the expense of civil liberties. Although many aspects of the USA PATRIOT Act have been criticized as potentially unconstitutional, Section 213, which authorizes delayed notice of the execution of a warrant, may be the most vulnerable to court challenge. The American Civil Liberties Union (ACLU) maintains that under this section, law enforcement agents could enter a house, apartment, or office with a search warrant while the occupant is away, search through his or her property, and take photographs without having to tell the suspect about the search until later.[1] The ACLU also believes that this provision is illegal because the Fourth Amendment to the Constitution protects against unreasonable searches and seizures and requires the government to obtain a warrant and to give notice to the person whose property will be searched before conducting the search. The notice requirement enables the suspect to assert his or her Fourth Amendment rights.

In 2005, the U.S. Congress reauthorized most provisions of the USA PATRIOT Act, and in May 2011, President Barack Obama signed legislation providing for an extension of several terrorist surveillance provisions included in the USA PATRIOT Act and in the Intelligence Reform and Terrorism Prevention Act of 2004.

Read the original USA PATRIOT Act of 2001 in its entirety at **http://www.justicestudies.com/pubs/patriot.pdf**. Title 18 of the U.S. Code is available at **http://uscode.house.gov/browse/prelim@title18&edition.**

---

[1] Much of the material in this paragraph is taken from American Civil Liberties Union, "How the Anti-Terrorism Bill Expands Law Enforcement 'Sneak and Peek' Warrants," http://www.aclu.org/congress/l102301b.html (accessed August 28, 2007).

References: "Congressional Committee Votes to Reauthorize PATRIOT Act Provisions," Examiner.com, May 20, 2011, http://www.examiner.com/public-safety-in-national/congressional-committee-votes-to-reauthorize-patriot-act-provisions#ixzz1N65VSX33 (accessed May 22, 2011); USA PATRIOT Improvement and Reauthorization Act of 2005 (Public Law 109-177); U.S. Department of Justice, *Field Guidance on Authorities (Redacted) Enacted in the 2001 Anti-Terrorism Legislation* (Washington, DC: U.S. Dept. of Justice, no date), http://www.epic.org/terrorism/DOJguidance.pdf (accessed August 28, 2010); and USA PATRIOT Act, 2001 (Public Law 107-56).

---

services from telephone companies and then used those services to plan and execute hacking attacks.

The act[225] added felony violations of the Computer Fraud and Abuse Act to Section 2516(1) of Title 18 of the U.S. Code—the portion of federal law that lists specific types of crimes for which investigators may obtain a wiretap order for wire communications.

The USA PATRIOT Act also modified that portion of the ECPA that governs law enforcement access to stored electronic communications, such as e-mail, to include stored wire communications, such as voice mail. Before the modification, law enforcement officers needed to obtain a wiretap order rather than a search warrant to obtain unopened voice communications. Because today's e-mail messages may contain digitized voice "attachments," investigators were sometimes required to obtain both a search warrant and a wiretap order to learn the contents of a specific message. Under the act, the same rules now apply to both stored wire communications and stored electronic communications. Wiretap orders, which are often much more difficult to obtain than search warrants, are now required only to intercept real-time telephone conversations.

Before passage of the USA PATRIOT Act, federal law allowed investigators to use an administrative subpoena (that is, a subpoena authorized by a federal or state statute or by a federal or state grand jury or trial court) to compel Internet service providers to provide a limited class of information, such as a customer's name, address, length of service, and means of payment. Also under previous law, investigators could not subpoena certain records, including credit card numbers or details about other forms of payment for Internet service. Such information can be very useful in determining a suspect's true identity because, in some cases, users give false names to Internet service providers.

■ **electronic evidence**   Information and data of investigative value that are stored in or transmitted by an electronic device.[i]

■ **latent evidence**   Evidence of relevance to a criminal investigation that is not readily seen by the unaided eye.

■ **digital criminal forensics**   The lawful seizure, acquisition, analysis, reporting, and safeguarding of data from digital devices that may contain information of evidentiary value to the trier of fact in criminal events.[ii]

Before passage of the USA PATRIOT Act, federal law allowed investigators to use an administrative subpoena (that is, a subpoena authorized by a federal or state statute or by a federal or state grand jury or trial court) to compel Internet service providers to provide a limited class of information, such as a customer's name, address, length of service, and means of payment. Also under previous law, investigators could not subpoena certain records, including credit card numbers or details about other forms of payment for Internet service. Such information, however, can be highly relevant in determining a suspect's true identity because, in many cases, users register with Internet service providers using false names.

Previous federal law[226] was also technology-specific, relating primarily to telephone communications. Local and long-distance telephone billing records, for example, could be subpoenaed, but not billing information for Internet communications or records of Internet session times and durations. Similarly, previous law allowed the government to use a subpoena to obtain the customer's "telephone number or other subscriber number or identity" but did not define what that phrase meant in the context of Internet communications.

The USA PATRIOT Act amended portions of this federal law[227] to update and expand the types of records that law enforcement authorities may obtain with a subpoena. "Records of session times and durations," as well as "any temporarily assigned network address" may now be gathered. Such changes should make the process of identifying computer criminals and tracing their Internet communications faster and easier.

Finally, the USA PATRIOT Act facilitates the use of roving, or multipoint, wiretaps. Roving wiretaps, issued with court approval, target a specific individual and not a particular telephone number or communications device. Hence, law enforcement agents armed with an order for a multipoint wiretap can follow the flow of communications engaged in by a person as he switches from one cellular phone to another or to a wired telephone.

In 2006, President George W. Bush signed the USA PATRIOT Improvement and Reauthorization Act of 2005[228] into law. Also referred to as PATRIOT II, the act made permanent 14 provisions of the original 2001 legislation that had been slated to expire and extended others for another four years (including the roving wiretap provision and a provision that allows authorities to seize business records). It also addressed some of the concerns of civil libertarians who had criticized the earlier law as too restrictive. Finally, the new law provided additional protections for mass transportation systems and seaports, closed some legal loopholes in laws aimed at preventing terrorist financing, and includes a subsection called the Combat Methamphetamine Epidemic Act (CMEA). The CMEA contains significant provisions intended to strengthen federal, state, and local efforts designed at curtailing the spread of methamphetamine use.

In May 2011, President Barack Obama signed into law legislation extending a number of provisions of the PATRIOT Act that would have otherwise expired. The president's signature gave new life to the roving wiretap and business records provisions of the act, as well as some others.[229]

Gathering Electronic Evidence

The Internet, computer networks, and automated data systems present many new opportunities for committing criminal activity.[230] Computers and other electronic devices are increasingly being used to commit, enable, or support crimes perpetrated against people, organizations, and property. Whether the crime involves attacks against computer systems or the information they contain or more traditional offenses like murder, money laundering, trafficking, or fraud, **electronic evidence** is increasingly important.

Electronic evidence is "information and data of investigative value that is stored in or transmitted by an electronic device."[231] Such evidence is often acquired when physical items like computers, removable disks, cameras, CDs, DVDs, magnetic tape, flash memory chips, cellular telephones, and other electronic devices are collected from a crime scene or are obtained from a suspect.

Electronic evidence has special characteristics: (1) It is latent; (2) it can transcend national and state borders quickly and easily; (3) it is fragile and can easily be altered, damaged, compromised, or destroyed by improper handling or improper examination; and (4) it may be time sensitive. Like DNA or fingerprints, electronic evidence is **latent evidence** because it is not readily visible to the human eye under normal conditions. Special equipment and software are required to "see" and evaluate electronic evidence. In the courtroom, expert testimony may be needed to explain the acquisition of electronic evidence and the examination process used to interpret it.

In 2002, in recognition of the special challenges posed by electronic evidence, the Computer Crime and Intellectual Property Section (CCIPS) of the Criminal Division of the U.S. Department of Justice released a how-to manual for law enforcement officers called *Searching and Seizing Computers and Obtaining Electronic Evidence in Criminal Investigations*.[232] The manual, which explains procedures for **digital criminal forensics**, can be accessed at **http://www.justicestudies .com/pubs/electronic.pdf**.

About the same time, the Technical Working Group for Electronic Crime Scene Investigation (TWGECSI) released a detailed guide for law enforcement officers to use in gathering electronic evidence. The manual, *Electronic Crime Scene Investigation: A Guide for First Responders*,[233] grew out of a partnership formed in 1998 between the National Cybercrime Training Partnership, the Office of Law Enforcement Standards, and the National Institute of Justice. The working group was asked to identify, define, and establish basic criteria to assist federal and state agencies in handling electronic investigations and related prosecutions.

TWGECSI guidelines say that law enforcement must take special precautions when documenting, collecting, and preserving electronic evidence to maintain its integrity. The guidelines also note that the first law enforcement officer on the scene should take steps to ensure the safety of everyone at the scene and to protect the integrity of all evidence, both traditional and electronic. The entire TWGECSI guide, which includes many practical instructions for investigators working with electronic evidence, is available at **http://www.justicestudies.com/pubs/ecsi.pdf**.

Once digital evidence has been gathered, it must be analyzed. Consequently, in 2004, the government-sponsored Technical Working Group for the Examination of Digital Evidence (TWGEDE) published *Forensic Examination of Digital Evidence: A Guide for Law Enforcement*. Among the guide's recommendations are that digital evidence should be acquired in a manner that protects and preserves the integrity of the original evidence and that examination should be conducted only on a *copy* of the original evidence. The entire guide, which is nearly 100 pages long, can be accessed at **http://www.justicestudies.com/pubs/forensicexam.pdf**. An even more detailed guide, titled *Investigations Involving the Internet and Computer Networks*, was published by the National Institute of Justice in 2007 and is available at **http://www.justicestudies.com/pubs/internetinvest.pdf**.

Recently, the National Institute of Justice established the Electronic Crime Technology Center of Excellence (ECTCoE) to assist in building the capacity for electronic crime prevention and investigation and digital evidence collection and examination of state and local law enforcement. The ECTCoE works to identify electronic crime and digital evidence tools, technologies, and training gaps. In 2013, it developed a manual that outlines policies and procedures for gathering and analyzing digital evidence, which is available in Microsoft Word format through the National Law Enforcement and Corrections Technology Center (NLECTC) website at **http://www.justnet.org**.

Warrantless searches bear special mention in any discussion of electronic evidence. In the 1999 case of *U.S. v. Carey*,[234] a federal appellate court held that the consent a defendant had given to police for his apartment to be searched did not extend to the search of his computer once it was taken to a police station. Similarly, in *U.S. v. Turner* (1999),[235] the First Circuit Court of Appeals held that the warrantless police search of a defendant's personal computer while in his apartment exceeded the scope of the defendant's consent. Learn more about gathering digital evidence from the FBI at **http://www.justicestudies.com/digital_evidence.pdf**.

SUMMARY

- Legal restraints on police action stem primarily from the U.S. Constitution's Bill of Rights—especially the Fourth, Fifth, and Sixth Amendments, which, along with the Fourteenth Amendment, require due process of law. Most due process requirements of relevance to police work concern three major areas: (1) evidence and investigation (often called *search and seizure*), (2) arrest, and (3) interrogation. Each of these areas has been addressed by a number of important U.S. Supreme Court decisions, and it is the discussion of those decisions and their significance for police work that makes up the bulk of this chapter's content.
- The Bill of Rights was designed to protect citizens against abuses of police power. It does so by guaranteeing due process of law for everyone suspected of having committed a crime and by ensuring the availability of constitutional rights to all citizens, regardless of state or local law or procedure. Within the context of criminal case processing, due process requirements mandate that all justice system officials, not only the police, respect the rights of accused individuals throughout the criminal justice process.
- The Fourth Amendment to the Constitution declares that people must be secure in their homes and in their persons against unreasonable searches and seizures. Consequently, law enforcement officers are generally required to demonstrate probable cause in order to obtain a search warrant if they are to legally conduct searches and seize the property of criminal suspects. The Supreme Court has established that police officers, in order to protect themselves from attack, have the right to search a person being arrested and to search the area under the arrestee's immediate control.
- An arrest takes place whenever a law enforcement officer restricts a person's freedom to leave. Arrests may occur when an officer comes upon a crime in progress, but most jurisdictions also allow warrantless arrests for felonies when a crime is not in progress, as long as probable cause can later be demonstrated.

Information that is useful for law enforcement purposes is called *intelligence*, and as this chapter has shown, intelligence gathering is vital to police work. The need for useful information often leads police investigators to question suspects, informants, and potentially knowledgeable citizens. When suspects who are in custody become subject to interrogation, they must be advised of their *Miranda* rights before questioning begins. The *Miranda* warnings, which were mandated by the Supreme Court in the 1966 case of *Miranda* v. *Arizona*, are listed in this chapter. They ensure that suspects know their rights—including the right to remain silent—in the face of police interrogation.

KEY TERMS

anticipatory warrant, 209
arrest, 209
Bill of Rights, 198
compelling interest, 217
digital criminal forensics, 233
Electronic Communications
   Privacy Act (ECPA), 231
electronic evidence, 233
emergency search, 208
exclusionary rule, 200
fleeting-targets exception, 215
fruit of the poisonous tree
   doctrine, 200
good-faith exception, 204
illegally seized evidence, 199
inherent coercion, 221

interrogation, 221
landmark case, 199
latent evidence, 233
Miranda triggers, 227
Miranda warnings, 223
plain view, 205
probable cause, 204
psychological
   manipulation, 221
reasonable suspicion, 211
search incident to an
   arrest, 210
sneak-and-peek search, 232
suspicionless search, 217
writ of *certiorari*, 200

KEY CASES

Alabama v. White, 219
Arizona v. Fulminante, 221
Brecht v. Abrahamson, 227
Brown v. Mississippi, 221
California v. Hodari D., 212
Carroll v. U.S., 213
Chimel v. California, 202
Dickerson v. U.S., 224
Escobedo v. Illinois, 222
Florida v. Bostick, 218
Horton v. California, 207
Illinois v. Perkins, 227
Kyllo v. U.S., 219
Mapp v. Ohio, 201

Minnick v. Mississippi, 222
Miranda v. Arizona, 223
Nix v. Williams, 226
Richards v. Wisconsin, 208
Silverthorne Lumber Co. v.
   U.S., 224
Smith v. Ohio, 212
Terry v. Ohio, 211
U.S. v. Drayton, 218
U.S. v. Patane, 224
U.S. v. Robinson, 210
Weeks v. U.S., 200
Wilson v. Arkansas, 208

QUESTIONS FOR REVIEW

1. Name some of the legal restraints on police action, and list some types of behavior that might be considered abuse of police authority.

2. How do the Bill of Rights and democratically inspired legal restraints on the police help ensure personal freedoms in our society?

3. Describe the legal standards for assessing searches and seizures conducted by law enforcement agents.

4. What is an arrest, and when does it occur? How do legal understandings of the term differ from popular depictions of the arrest process?

5. What is the role of interrogation in intelligence gathering? List each of the *Miranda* warnings. Which recent U.S. Supreme Court cases have affected *Miranda* warning requirements?

QUESTIONS FOR REFLECTION

1. What is the Bill of Rights, and how does it affect our understandings of due process?

2. On what constitutional amendments are due process guarantees based? Can we ensure due process in our legal system without substantially increasing the risk of criminal activity?

3. What is the exclusionary rule? What is the fruit of the poisonous tree doctrine? What is their importance in American criminal justice?

4. Under what circumstances may police officers search vehicles? What limits, if any, are there on such searches? What determines such limits?

5. What are suspicionless searches? How does the need to ensure public safety justify certain suspicionless searches?

6. What is electronic evidence? How should first-on-the-scene law enforcement personnel handle it?

NOTES

i. Adapted from Technical Working Group for Electronic Crime Scene Investigation, *Electronic Crime Scene Investigation*, p. 2.
ii. Adapted from Larry R. Leibrock, "Overview and Impact on 21st Century Legal Practice: Digital Forensics and Electronic Discovery," http://www.courtroom21.net/FDIC.pps (accessed July 5, 2005).

1. Video: "LAPD Pursuit Ends in Gunfire," April 12, 2012, http://www.policemag.com/Videos/Channel/Patrol/2012/04/LAPD-Pursuit-Ends-In-Gunfire.aspx (accessed May 20, 2014).
2. Rick Orlov, "Abdul Arian's Family Weighing Appeal After Wrongful Death Lawsuit Dismissed," *San Jose Mercury News*, May 1, 2013, http://www.mercurynews.com/california/ci_23151122/abdul-arians-family-weighing-appeal-after-wrongful-death (accessed May 5, 2015).
3. Marcus Baram, "How Common Is Contagious Shooting?" ABC News, November 17, 2006, http://abcnews.go.com/Politics/story?id=2681947&page=1 (accessed May 21, 2010).
4. Michael Wilson, "50 Shots Fired, and the Experts Offer a Theory," *New York Times*, November 27, 2006, http://www.nytimes.com/2006/11/27/nyregion/27fire.html (accessed August 28, 2012).

5. "Victim of Police Beating Says He Was Sober," Associated Press, October 10, 2005, http://www.msnbc.msn.com/id/9645260 (accessed July 10, 2008).

6. "Police Officer Acquitted of Beating Man in Hurricane Katrina's Aftermath," Associated Press, July 25, 2007, http://www.foxnews.com/story/0,2933,290662,00.html (accessed August 30, 2009).

7. Michael Kunzelman, "New Orleans to Settle Lawsuit over Taped Beating," Associated Press, August 7, 2009, http://www.wtopnews.com/?nid=104&sid=1735442 (accessed August 30, 2009).

8. Mark Berman, Wesley Lowery and Kimberly Kindy, "South Carolina Police Officer Charged with Murder after Shooting man During Traffic Stop," The Washington Post, April 7, 2015, https://www.washingtonpost.com/news/post-nation/wp/2015/04/07/south-carolina-police-officer-will-be-charged-with-murder-after-shooting.

9. Alan Blinder and Richard Perez-Pena, "6 Baltimore Police Officers Charged in Freddie Gray Death," New York Times, May 1, 2015, http://www.nytimes.com/2015/05/02/us/freddie-gray-autopsy-report-given-to-baltimore-prosecutors.html.

10. Ken Murray, et al, "Staten Island Man Dies after NYPD Cop Puts Him in a Chokehold," Daily News, July 18, 2014, http://www.nydailynews.com/new-york/staten-island-man-dies-puts-choke-hold-article-1.1871486.

11. Emily Brown, "Timeline: Michael Brown Shooting in Ferguson, Mo.," USA Today, August 10, 2015, http://www.usatoday.com/story/news/nation/2014/08/14/michael-brown-ferguson-missouri-timeline/14051827.

12. "Police Brutality!" Time, March 25, 1991, p. 18.

13. "Koon and Powell Supreme Court Decision," PBS Newshour, http://www.pbs.org/newshour/bb/law-jan-june96-koon (accessed November 14, 2015).

14. Miranda v. Arizona, 384 U.S. 436 (1966).

15. Weeks v. U.S., 232 U.S. 383 (1914).

16. Silverthorne Lumber Co. v. U.S., 251 U.S. 385 (1920).

17. Clemmens Bartollas, American Criminal Justice (New York: Macmillan, 1988), p. 186.

18. Mapp v. Ohio, 367 U.S. 643 (1961).

19. Chimel v. California, 395 U.S. 752 (1969).

20. Katz v. U.S., 389 U.S. 347, 88 S.Ct. 507 (1967).

21. Minnesota v. Olson, 110 S.Ct. 1684 (1990).

22. Minnesota v. Carter, 525 U.S. 83 (1998).

23. Georgia v. Randolph, 547 U.S. 103 (2006).

24. The ruling left open the possibility that any evidence relating to criminal activity undertaken by the consenting party might be admissible in court. In the words of the Court, refusal by a co-occupant "renders entry and search unreasonable and invalid as to him."

25. Nina Totenberg, "High Court Rules on Detaining Suspects, Sniffer Dogs," NPR, February 19, 2013, http://www.npr.org/2013/02/19/172431555/latest-supreme-court-decisions-give-police-one-victory-one-loss, citing Cornell law professor Sherry Colb (accessed May 3, 2013).

26. U.S. v. Leon, 468 U.S. 897, 104 S.Ct. 3405, 82 L.Ed.2d 677, 52 U.S.L.W. 5155 (1984).

27. Judicial titles vary among jurisdictions. Many lower-level state judicial officers are called magistrates. Federal magistrates, however, generally have a significantly higher level of judicial authority.

28. Massachusetts v. Sheppard, 104 S.Ct. 3424 (1984).

29. Illinois v. Krull, 107 S.Ct. 1160 (1987).

30. Maryland v. Garrison, 107 S.Ct. 1013 (1987).

31. Illinois v. Rodriguez, 110 S.Ct. 2793 (1990).

32. Arizona v. Evans, 514 U.S. 1 (1995).

33. Herring v. U.S., 555 U.S. 135 (2009).

34. See California v. Acevedo, 500 U.S. 565 (1991); Ornelas v. U.S., 517 U.S. 690 (1996); and others.

35. See Edwards v. Balisok, 520 U.S. 641 (1997); Booth v. Churner, 532 U.S. 731 (2001); and Porter v. Nussle, 534 U.S. 516 (2002).

36. See Wilson v. Arkansas, 115 S.Ct. 1914 (1995); and Richards v. Wisconsin, 117 S.Ct. 1416 (1997).

37. See McCleskey v. Kemp, 481 U.S. 279, 107 S.Ct. 1756, 95 L.Ed.2d 262 (1987); McCleskey v. Zant, 499 U.S. 467, 493–494 (1991); Coleman v. Thompson, 501 U.S. 722 (1991); Schlup v. Delo, 115 S.Ct. 851, 130 L.Ed.2d 808 (1995); Felker v. Turpin, Warden, 117 S.Ct. 30, 135 L.Ed.2d 1123 (1996); Boyde v. California, 494 U.S. 370 (1990); and others.

38. See Ewing v. California, 538 U.S. 11 (2003); and Lockyer v. Andrade, 538 U.S. 63 (2003).

39. Richard Lacayo and Viveca Novak, "How Rehnquist Changed America," Time, June 30, 2003, pp. 20–25.

40. Harris v. U.S., 390 U.S. 234 (1968).

41. The legality of plain-view seizures was also confirmed in earlier cases, including Ker v. California, 374 U.S. 23, 42–43 (1963); U.S. v. Lee, 274 U.S. 559 (1927); U.S. v. Lefkowitz, 285 U.S. 452, 465 (1932); and Hester v. U.S., 265 U.S. 57 (1924).

42. As cited in Kimberly A. Kingston, "Look But Don't Touch: The Plain View Doctrine," FBI Law Enforcement Bulletin, December 1987, p. 18.

43. Horton v. California, 496 U.S. 128 (1990).

44. U.S. v. Irizarry, 673 F.2d 554, 556–567 (1st Cir. 1982).

45. Arizona v. Hicks, 107 S.Ct. 1149 (1987).

46. Inadvertence, as a requirement of legitimate plain-view seizures, was first cited in the U.S. Supreme Court case of Coolidge v. New Hampshire, 403 U.S. 443, 91 S.Ct. 2022 (1971).

47. Horton v. California, 496 U.S. 128 (1990).

48. Ibid.

49. Orin S. Kerr, "Searches and Seizures in a Digital World," Harvard Law Review, Vol. 119 (2005), p. 521, http://www.harvardlawreview.org/media/pdf/kerr.pdf (accessed May 1, 2013).

50. Caleb Mason, "Plain View Searches: Gen. Petraeus' Waterloo," The Crime Report, January 8, 2013, http://www.thecrimereport.org/viewpoints/2013-01-plain-view-searches-gen-petraeus-waterloo (accessed May 2, 2013).

51. Brigham City v. Stuart, 547 U.S. 398 (2006).

52. John Gales Sauls, "Emergency Searches of Premises, Part 1," FBI Law Enforcement Bulletin, March 1987, p. 23.

53. Warden v. Hayden, 387 U.S. 294 (1967).

54. Sauls, "Emergency Searches of Premises," p. 25.

55. Maryland v. Buie, 110 S.Ct. 1093 (1990).

56. Wilson v. Arkansas, 514 U.S. 927 (1995).

57. For additional information, see Michael J. Bulzomi, "Knock and Announce: A Fourth Amendment Standard," FBI Law Enforcement Bulletin, May 1997, pp. 27-31.

58. Richards v. Wisconsin, 117 S.Ct. 1416 (1997), syllabus.

59. Illinois v. McArthur, 531 U.S. 326, 330 (2001).

60. U.S. v. Banks, 540 U.S. 31 (2003).

61. Hudson v. Michigan, 547 U.S. 586 (2006).

62. Kentucky v. King, 563 U.S. ___ (2011).

63. U.S. v. Grubbs, 547 U.S. 90 (2006).

64. U.S. v. Mendenhall, 446 U.S. 544 (1980).

65. A. Louis DiPietro, "Voluntary Encounters or Fourth Amendment Seizures," FBI Law Enforcement Bulletin, January 1992, pp. 28–32.

66. Stansbury v. California, 114 S.Ct. 1526, 1529, 128 L.Ed.2d 293 (1994).

67. Howes v. Fields, U.S. Supreme Court, No. 10-680 (decided February 21, 2012).

68. *Yarborough v. Alvarado*, 541 U.S. 652 (2004).
69. *Thompson v. Keohane*, 516 U.S. 99, 112 (1996).
70. *Atwater v. Lago Vista*, 532 U.S. 318 (2001).
71. In 1976, in the case of *Watson v. U.S.* (432 U.S. 411), the U.S. Supreme Court refused to impose a warrant requirement for felony arrests that occur in public places.
72. *Payton v. New York*, 445 U.S. 573, 590 (1980).
73. In 1981, in the case of *U.S. v. Steagald* (451 U.S. 204), the Court ruled that a search warrant is also necessary when the planned arrest involves entry into a third party's premises.
74. *Kirk v. Louisiana*, 122 S.Ct. 2458, 153 L.Ed.2d 599 (2002).
75. *Atwater v. Lago Vista*, 532 U.S. 318 (2001).
76. Ibid.
77. *Terry v. Ohio*, 392 U.S. 1 (1968).
78. *U.S. v. Sokolow*, 109 S.Ct. 1581 (1989).
79. The Court was quoting from *U.S. v. Brignoni-Ponce*, 422 U.S. 873, 878 (1975).
80. 76 *U.S. v. Arvizu*, 534 U.S. 266 (2002).
81. Ibid.
82. *Minnesota v. Dickerson*, 113 S.Ct. 2130, 124 L.Ed.2d 334 (1993).
83. *Brown v. Texas*, 443 U.S. 47 (1979).
84. *Hiibel v. Sixth Judicial District Court of Nevada*, 542 U.S. 177 (2004).
85. *Smith v. Ohio*, 110 S.Ct. 1288 (1990).
86. Ibid., at 1289.
87. *California v. Hodari D.*, 111 S.Ct. 1547 (1991).
88. *Criminal Justice Newsletter*, May 1, 1991, p. 2.
89. *Illinois v. Wardlow*, 528 U.S. 119 (2000).
90. Ibid., syllabus, http://supct.law.cornell.edu/supct/html/98-1036.ZS.html (accessed April 1, 2009).
91. Ibid.
92. *Arkansas v. Sanders*, 442 U.S. 753 (1979).
93. Ibid.
94. *U.S. v. Borchardt*, 809 F.2d 1115 (5th Cir. 1987).
95. *FBI Law Enforcement Bulletin*, January 1988, p. 28.
96. *Carroll v. U.S.*, 267 U.S. 132 (1925).
97. *Preston v. U.S.*, 376 U.S. 364 (1964).
98. *Arizona v. Gant*, 556 U.S. 332 (2009).
99. *South Dakota v. Opperman*, 428 U.S. 364 (1976).
100. *Colorado v. Bertine*, 479 U.S. 367, 107 S.Ct. 741 (1987).
101. *Florida v. Wells*, 110 S.Ct. 1632 (1990).
102. *Terry v. Ohio*, 392 U.S. 1 (1968).
103. *California v. Acevedo*, 500 U.S. 565 (1991).
104. *Ornelas v. U.S.*, 517 U.S. 690, 696 (1996).
105. Ibid.
106. The phrase is usually attributed to the 1991 U.S. Supreme Court case of *California v. Acevedo* (500 U.S. 565 [1991]). See Devallis Rutledge, "Taking an Inventory," *Police*, November 1995, pp. 8–9. See also *Pennsylvania v. Labron*, 518 U.S. 938 (1996), in which the Court held that if a vehicle is readily mobile and probable cause exists to believe it contains contraband, the Fourth Amendment permits police to search the vehicle, and contraband seized from such a search should not be suppressed.
107. *Florida v. Jimeno*, 111 S.Ct. 1801 (1991).
108. Ibid., syllabus, http://laws.findlaw.com/us/500/248.html (accessed March 2, 2009).
109. *U.S. v. Ross*, 456 U.S. 798 (1982).
110. Ibid.
111. *Whren v. U.S.*, 517 U.S. 806 (1996).
112. See *Pennsylvania v. Mimms*, 434 U.S. 106 (1977).
113. *Maryland v. Wilson*, 117 S.Ct. 882 (1997).
114. *Knowles v. Iowa*, 525 U.S. 113 (1998).
115. *Wyoming v. Houghton*, 526 U.S. 295 (1999).
116. *Thornton v. U.S.*, 41 U.S. 615 (2004).
117. *Illinois v. Caballes*, 543 U.S. 405 (2005).
118. *Davis v. U.S.*, U.S. Supreme Court, No. 09-11328 (decided June 16, 2011).
119. *Arizona v. Gant*, 556 U.S. 332 (2009).
120. *Michigan Dept. of State Police v. Sitz*, 110 S.Ct. 2481 (1990).
121. *U.S. v. Martinez-Fuerte*, 428 U.S. 543 (1976).
122. Ibid., syllabus.
123. *Illinois v. Lidster*, 540 U.S. 419 (2004).
124. *U.S. v. Villamonte-Marquez*, 462 U.S. 579 (1983).
125. *California v. Carney*, 471 U.S. 386, 105 S.Ct. 2066, 85 L.Ed.2d 406, 53 U.S.L.W. 4521 (1985).
126. *U.S. v. Hill*, 855 F.2d 664 (10th Cir. 1988).
127. *National Treasury Employees Union v. Von Raab*, 489 U.S. 656 (1989).
128. *Skinner v. Railway Labor Executives' Association*, 489 U.S. 602 (1989).
129. *Florida v. Bostick*, 111 S.Ct. 2382 (1991).
130. *Bond v. U.S.*, 529 U.S. 334 (2000), http://supct.law.cornell.edu/supct/html/98-9349.ZS.html (accessed January 10, 2009).
131. *U.S. v. Drayton*, 122 S.Ct. 2105 (2002).
132. *U.S. v. Flores-Montano*, 541 U.S. 149 (2004).
133. *People v. Deutsch*, 96 C.D.O.S. 2827 (1996).
134. The thermal imager differs from infrared devices (such as night-vision goggles) in that infrared devices amplify the infrared spectrum of light, whereas thermal imagers register solely the portion of the infrared spectrum that we call heat.
135. *People v. Deutsch*, 96 C.D.O.S. 2827 (1996).
136. *Kyllo v. U.S.*, 533 U.S. 27 (2001).
137. Ibid.
138. *Aguilar v. Texas*, 378 U.S. 108 (1964).
139. *U.S. v. Harris*, 403 U.S. 573 (1971).
140. Ibid. at 584.
141. *Illinois v. Gates*, 426 U.S. 213 (1983).
142. *Alabama v. White*, 110 S.Ct. 2412 (1990).
143. Ibid., at 2417.
144. *Florida v. J. L.*, 529 U.S. 266 (2000).
145. Some of the wording in this paragraph is adapted from the *LII Bulletin*, "End of Term Wrap-Up," June 29, 2000 (e-mail bulletin of the Legal Information Institute, Cornell University School of Law).
146. *U.S. Dept. of Justice v. Landano*, 113 S.Ct. 2014, 124 L.Ed.2d 84 (1993).
147. Richard Willing, "Illinois Law First to Order Taping Murder Confessions," *USA Today*, July 18, 2003.
148. Richard A. Leo and Kimberly D. Richman, "Mandate the Electronic Recording of Police Interrogations," *Crime and Public Policy*, Vol. 6 (June 2008), http://ssrn.com/abstract=1141335 (accessed September 1, 2009).
149. *South Dakota v. Neville*, 103 S.Ct. 916 (1983).
150. *Brown v. Mississippi*, 297 U.S. 278 (1936).
151. *Ashcraft v. Tennessee*, 322 U.S. 143 (1944).
152. *Chambers v. Florida*, 309 U.S. 227 (1940).
153. Ibid.
154. *Leyra v. Denno*, 347 U.S. 556 (1954).
155. *Arizona v. Fulminante*, 111 S.Ct. 1246 (1991).
156. *Chapman v. California*, 386 U.S. 18 (1967).
157. *State v. Fulminante*, No. CR-95-0160.
158. *State v. Henderson*, August 24, 2011.
159. *Perry v. New Hampshire*, U.S. Supreme Court, No. 10-8974 (decided January 11, 2012).
160. *Escobedo v. Illinois*, 378 U.S. 478 (1964).

161. *Edwards* v. *Arizona*, 451 U.S. 477, 101 S.Ct. 1880, 68 L.Ed.2d 378 (1981).
162. *Minnick* v. *Mississippi*, 498 U.S. 146 (1990).
163. *Michigan* v. *Jackson*, 475 U.S. 625 (1986).
164. *Arizona* v. *Roberson*, 486 U.S. 675, 108 S.Ct. 2093 (1988).
165. *Davis* v. *U.S.*, 114 S.Ct. 2350 (1994).
166. *Montejo* v. *Louisiana*, 556 U.S. 778 (2009).
167. *Maryland* v. *Shatzer*, U.S. Supreme Court, No. 08-680 (2010).
168. *Miranda* v. *Arizona*, 384 U.S. 436 (1966).
169. "Immigrants Get Civil Rights," *USA Today*, June 11, 1992.
170. *U.S.* v. *Dickerson*, 166 F.3d 667 (1999).
171. *Dickerson* v. *U.S.*, 530 U.S. 428 (2000).
172. *U.S.* v. *Patane*, 542 U.S. 630 (2004).
173. *Missouri* v. *Seibert*, 542 U.S. 600 (2004).
174. *Miranda* v. *Arizona*, 384 U.S. 436 (1966).
175. *Silverthorne Lumber Co.* v. *U.S.*, 251 U.S. 385 (1920).
176. *Wong Sun* v. *U.S.*, 371 U.S. 471 (1963).
177. *Moran* v. *Burbine*, 475 U.S. 412, 421 (1986).
178. *Colorado* v. *Spring*, 479 U.S. 564, 107 S.Ct. 851 (1987).
179. *Brewer* v. *Williams*, 430 U.S. 387 (1977).
180. *Nix* v. *Williams*, 104 S.Ct. 2501 (1984).
181. "ACLU Eyes Boston Bombing Suspect's Miranda Rights," Associate Press, April 20, 2013, http://abcnews.go.com/US/wireStory/aclu-eyes-boston-bombing-suspects-miranda-rights-19007093#.UXPjlat4bYg (accessed April 21, 2013).
182. *New York* v. *Quarles*, 104 S.Ct. 2626, 81 L.Ed.2d 550 (1984).
183. *Colorado* v. *Connelly*, 107 S.Ct. 515, 93 L.Ed.2d 473 (1986).
184. *Kuhlmann* v. *Wilson*, 477 U.S. 436 (1986).
185. *Illinois* v. *Perkins*, 495 U.S. 292 (1990).
186. *Rock* v. *Zimmerman*, 543 F. Supp. 179 (M.D. Pa. 1982).
187. Ibid.
188. See *Oregon* v. *Mathiason*, 429 U.S. 492, 97 S.Ct. 711 (1977).
189. *South Dakota* v. *Neville*, 103 S.Ct. 916 (1983).
190. *Arizona* v. *Mauro*, 107 S.Ct. 1931, 95 L.Ed.2d 458 (1987).
191. *Doyle* v. *Ohio*, 426 U.S. 610 (1976).
192. *Brecht* v. *Abrahamson*, 113 S.Ct. 1710, 123 L.Ed.2d 353 (1993).
193. Citing *Kotteakos* v. *U.S.*, 328 U.S. 750 (1946).
194. See Linda Greenhouse, "The Supreme Court: Supreme Court Roundup—Police Questioning Allowed to the Point of Coercion," *New York Times*, May 28, 2003.
195. *Chavez* v. *Martinez*, 538 U.S. 760 (2003).
196. Ibid.
197. *Berghuis* v. *Thompson*, 560 U.S. 370 (2010).
198. *Salinas* v. *Texas*, U.S. Supreme Court, No. 12-246 (decided June 17, 2013).
199. *Hayes* v. *Florida*, 470 U.S. 811, 105 S.Ct. 1643 (1985).
200. *Winston* v. *Lee*, 470 U.S. 753, 105 S.Ct. 1611 (1985).
201. *Schmerber* v. *California*, 384 U.S. 757 (1966).
202. "Man Coughs Up Cocaine while in Custody," *Police Magazine* online, March 4, 2005, http://www.policemag.com/t_newspick.cfm?rank574703 (accessed January 4, 2006).
203. *U.S.* v. *Montoya de Hernandez*, 473 U.S. 531, 105 S.Ct. 3304 (1985).
204. Ibid.
205. *Olmstead* v. *U.S.*, 277 U.S. 438 (1928).
206. *On Lee* v. *U.S.*, 343 U.S. 747 (1952).
207. *Lopez* v. *U.S.*, 373 U.S. 427 (1963).
208. *Berger* v. *New York*, 388 U.S. 41 (1967).
209. *Katz* v. *U.S.*, 389 U.S. 347 (1967).
210. *Lee* v. *Florida*, 392 U.S. 378 (1968).
211. Federal Communications Act of 1934, U.S. Code, Title 47, Section 151.
212. *U.S.* v. *White*, 401 U.S. 745 (1971).
213. *U.S.* v. *Karo*, 468 U.S. 705 (1984).
214. *U.S.* v. *Scott*, 436 U.S. 128 (1978).
215. For more information, see *FBI Law Enforcement Bulletin*, June 1987, p. 25.
216. Electronic Communications Privacy Act of 1986, Public Law 99-508.
217. For more information on the ECPA, see Robert A. Fiatal, "The Electronic Communications Privacy Act: Addressing Today's Technology," *FBI Law Enforcement Bulletin*, April 1988, pp. 24–30.
218. Communications Assistance for Law Enforcement Act of 1994, Public Law 103-414.
219. U.S. Department of Justice, Office of the Inspector General, *Implementation of the Communications Assistance for Law Enforcement Act by the Federal Bureau of Investigation* (Washington, DC: U.S. Dept. of Justice, 2004).
220. Administrative Office of the United States Courts, "2010 Wiretap Report," http://www.uscourts.gov/Statistics/WiretapReports/WiretapReport2010.aspx (accessed June 1, 2013).
221. Telecommunications Act of 1996, Public Law 104-104, 110 Statute 56.
222. Title 47, U.S.C.A., Section 223(a)(1)(B)(ii) (Supp. 1997).
223. *Reno* v. *ACLU*, 117 S.Ct. 2329 (1997).
224. U.S. Code, Title 18, Section 1030.
225. Ibid., Section 202.
226. U.S. Code, Title 18, Section 2703(c).
227. Ibid.
228. Public Law 109-177.
229. "Obama Signs Last-Minute Patriot Act Extension," Fox News, http://www.foxnews.com/politics/2011/05/27/senate-clearing-way-extend-patriot-act, May 27, 2011 (accessed September 1, 2011).
230. Technical Working Group for Electronic Crime Scene Investigation, *Electronic Crime Scene Investigation: A Guide for First Responders* (Washington, DC: National Institute of Justice, 2001), from which much of the information in this section is taken.
231. Ibid., p. 2.
232. Computer Crime and Intellectual Property Section, U.S. Department of Justice, *Searching and Seizing Computers and Obtaining Electronic Evidence in Criminal Investigations* (Washington, DC: U.S. Dept. of Justice, 2002), http://www.usdoj.gov/criminal/cybercrime/s&smanual2002.htm (accessed August 4, 2007).
233. Technical Working Group, *Electronic Crime Scene Investigation*, p. 2.
234. *U.S.* v. *Carey*, 172 F. 3d 1268 (10th Cir. 1999).
235. *U.S.* v. *Turner*, 169 F. 3d 84 (1st Cir. 1999).

8

POLICING: ISSUES AND CHALLENGES

OUTLINE

LEARNING OBJECTIVES

After reading this chapter, you should be able to

- Describe the police personality and police subculture.
- Describe different types of police corruption and possible methods for building police integrity.
- Summarize the importance of police professionalism and integrity as well as three methods for building them.
- Describe the dangers, conflicts, challenges, and sources of stress that police officers face in their work.
- Summarize the guidelines for using force and for determining when excessive force has been used.
- Explain how police discretion affects contemporary law enforcement.
- Describe racial profiling and biased policing, including why they have become significant issues in policing.
- Describe civil liability issues associated with policing, including common sources of civil suits against the police.

The police at all times should maintain a relationship with the public that gives reality to the historic tradition that the police are the public and that the public are the police.

PERSONAL QUOTE FROM 1829[1]

■ **theme**   What elements of the police subculture and personality might lead to problems for female officers, both personally and in their underutilization in a police department?

■ **theme**   What forces gave rise to the police subculture? Which elements of the subculture do you see as particularly desirable or undesirable?

■ **Follow the author's tweets about the latest crime and justice news @schmalleger.**

■ **police subculture**   A particular set of values, beliefs, and acceptable forms of behavior characteristic of American police. Socialization into the police subculture begins with recruit training and continues thereafter.

Introduction

On a cold evening in late November, 2012, a young New York City Police Department (NYPD) officer was caught on a tourist's cell phone camera giving clean socks and shoes to a homeless man sitting on a sidewalk in Times Square. The photo was posted to Facebook and soon went viral, causing an outpouring of well wishes for the officer, Larry DePrimo. What DePrimo did that night was not part of his job, but a personal act of kindness that demonstrated the human side of police work.

NYPD officer Larry DePrimo. DePrimo made headlines in 2012 when he was photographed by a tourist giving shoes and socks to a homeless man on a cold winter night, and the photo went viral on Facebook. Is DePrimo a typical police officer?

Peter Kramer/NBC/NBC NewsWire via Getty Images

Interviewed later by *People Magazine*, DePrimo said, "Honestly, I feel undeserving of so much thanks. I just love to help people. That's why I became a cop."[2]

Today's police officers and administrators face many complex issues, and not all of the stories involving police work end well. Some concerns, such as corruption, on-the-job dangers, and the use of deadly force, derive from the very nature of policing. Others, like racial profiling and exposure to civil liability, have arisen due to common practices, characteristic police values, public expectations, legislative action, and ongoing societal change. Certainly, one of the most significant challenges facing American law enforcement today is policing a multicultural society. All of these issues are discussed in the pages that follow. We begin, however, with the police recruit socialization process. It is vital to understand this process because the values and expectations learned through it not only contribute to the nature of many important police issues but also determine how the police view and respond to those issues.

Police Personality and Culture

New police officers learn what is considered appropriate police behavior by working with seasoned veterans. Through conversations with other officers in the locker room, in a squad car, or over a cup of coffee, a new recruit is introduced to the value-laden subculture of police work. **Police subculture** can be understood as a particular set of values, beliefs, and acceptable forms of behavior characteristic of the police.[3] This process of informal socialization plays a much bigger role than formal police academy training in determining how rookies come to see police work. Through it, new officers gain a shared view of the world that can best be described as "streetwise." Streetwise cops know what official department policy is, but they also know the most efficient way to get a job done. By the time rookie officers become streetwise, they know which of the various informal means of accomplishing the job are acceptable to other officers. The police subculture creates few real mavericks, but it also produces few officers who view their jobs exclusively in terms of public mandates and official dictums.

■ **lecture note** Describe the police subculture according to the values that this chapter says are characteristic of that subculture. Explain how the police subculture influences the development of the police personality through socialization, and review the characteristics of the police personality by referring to Table 8-1.

■ **police working personality**   All aspects of the traditional values and patterns of behavior evidenced by police officers who have been effectively socialized into the police subculture. Characteristics of the police personality often extend to the personal lives of law enforcement personnel.

In the 1960s, renowned criminologist Jerome Skolnick described what he called the **police working personality**.[4] Skolnick's description of the police personality was consistent with William Westley's classic study of the Gary (Indiana) Police Department, in which he found a police culture with its own "customs, laws, and morality,"[5] and with Arthur Niederhoffer's observation that cynicism was pervasive among officers in New York City.[6] More recent authors have claimed that the "big curtain of secrecy" surrounding much of police work shields knowledge of the nature of the police personality from outsiders.[7] Taken in concert, these writers offer a picture of the police working personality shown in Table 8-1.

Some characteristics of the police working personality are essential for survival and effectiveness. For example, because officers are often exposed to highly emotional and potentially threatening confrontations with belligerent people, they must develop *efficient*, *authoritarian* strategies for gaining control over others. Similarly, a suspicious nature makes for a good police officer, especially during interrogations and investigations.

However, other characteristics of the police working personality are not so advantageous. For example, many officers are cynical, and some can be hostile toward members of the public who do not share their conservative values. These traits result from regular interaction with suspects, most of whom, even when they are clearly guilty in the eyes of the police, deny any wrongdoing. Eventually, personal traits that result from typical police work become firmly ingrained, setting the cornerstone of the police working personality.

There are at least two sources of the police personality. On the one hand, it may be that components of the police personality already exist in some individuals and draw them toward police work.[8] Supporting this view are studies that indicate that police officers who come from conservative backgrounds view themselves as defenders of middle-class morality.[9] On the other hand, some aspects of the police personality can be attributed to the socialization into the police subculture that rookie officers experience when they are inducted into police ranks.

Researchers have reported similar elements in police subculture throughout the United States. They have concluded that, like all cultures, police subculture is a relatively stable collection of beliefs and values that is unlikely to change from within.

TABLE 8-1 | **The Police Personality**

Authoritarian	Honorable	Loyal
Conservative	Hostile	Prejudiced
Cynical	Individualistic	Secret
Dogmatic	Insecure	Suspicious
Efficient		

Source: Pearson Education, Inc.

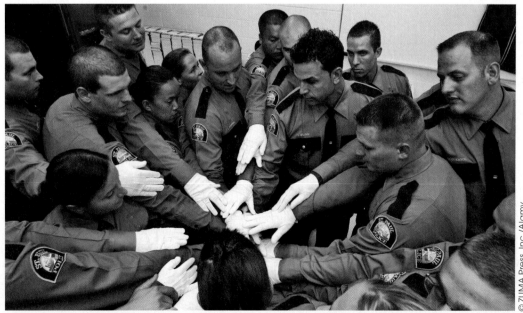

Police cadets in St. Paul, Minnesota, celebrate their graduation from the police academy. The police working personality has been characterized as authoritarian, suspicious, and conservative. How does the police working personality develop?

© ZUMA Press, Inc./Alamy

CJ | ISSUES
Rightful Policing

In 2015, in the wake of a heated national debate about racially biased police practices, the Program in Criminal Justice Policy and Management at Harvard University's Kennedy School released a report on what it called "rightful policing." The report's author, Tracey L. Meares, noted that success in police work has traditionally been measured in two ways: (1) the extent to which the police are successful at fighting crime; and (2) the degree to which police agencies and their officers adhere to the law.

Effectiveness at crime fighting has long been used to judge the success of police activities at all levels. Around the turn of the twenty-first century, for example, police administrators—along with politicians—took credit for declining crime rates, and "success stories" featuring city and local police departments were frequently heard.

The second criteria by which the police have often been judged, fidelity to the law, rests on the notion that law enforcement officers must respect legal strictures as much as anyone else. It means that authorities should be held accountable when they violate the rights guaranteed to suspects under the Constitution and by law—including statutes that authorize police action and the internal administrative rules and regulations that agencies develop to help ensure the lawful treatment of anyone who comes into contact with the police.

As the Harvard study notes, these two traditional criteria of police effectiveness can be objectively evaluated. Measures of declining crime rates, for example, would appear to indicate the success of police work. Likewise, the relative lack of civil lawsuits brought against departments, and success at making arrests that "stick" are common indicators of effective police work.

Nonetheless, recent widespread dissatisfaction with a number of grand jury decisions to exonerate police officers involved in the death of unarmed black suspects in a number of jurisdictions serve to show that a third way of assessing police effectiveness may be more important today than any other. Cases such as those in Ferguson, Missouri, Charleston, South Carolina, and Staten Island, New York, outraged many people who thought that the lives of the suspects could have been spared had the officers chosen to act differently. The fact that the officers who were involved in two of those incidents were not indicted meant that their actions had met strict legal requirements, but the lack of indictments brought about nationwide protests over what was seen as the unwarranted use of lethal force. Soon traditional and social media were inundated with debates over the quality of American policing, with discussions focused on claimed racial discrimination. The slogan "Black lives matter" quickly became a rallying cry for protestors.

On the heels of those events, the Harvard study examined how ordinary people assess their treatment by authorities. It concluded that "there is a third way, in addition to lawfulness and effectiveness, to evaluate policing—*rightful policing*." The concept of rightful policing does not depend on the lawfulness of police conduct; nor does it look to statistics demonstrating efficiency at crime fighting. "Rather," as the Harvard study says, "it depends primarily on . . . procedural justice or fairness of . . . conduct." In other words, rightful policing is about how to achieve fairness in policing and about how to engender trust in police. The Harvard study says:

Demonstrators protesting grand jury decisions in Missouri and New York that exonerated police officers in the deaths of two unarmed black men in 2014. What is "rightful policing?"

People typically care much more about how law enforcement agents treat them than about the outcome of the contact. Even when people receive a negative outcome in an encounter, such as a speeding ticket, they feel better about that incident than about an incident in which they do not receive a ticket but are treated poorly. In addition to being treated with dignity and respect, research demonstrates that people look for behavioral signals that allow them to assess whether a police officer's decision to stop or arrest them was made fairly—that is, accurately and without bias. These two factors—quality of treatment and indications of high-quality decision-making—matter much more to people than the outcome of the encounter.

The study also notes that people report higher levels of satisfaction with police encounters if they feel that they had the opportunity to explain their situation than if they did not; and people say that they want to believe that authorities are acting in a benevolent way—that is, in a way that is meant to protect and help them, rather than to harass and control them.

The study concludes that "all four of these factors—quality of treatment, decision-making fairness, voice, and expectation of benevolent treatment—constitute *procedural justice* in the minds of citizens who interact with the police; and that positive perceptions of procedural justice matter more to most people than do other criteria of assessing law enforcement success."

Study authors suggest that "a focus on the procedural justice of encounters can help policing agencies identify behavior, tactics, and strategies that many members of minority communities find problematic and that lead to disaffection, even though they may be lawful and, considered in isolation, appear effective."

References: Tracey L. Meares, *Rightful Policing*. New Perspectives in Policing Bulletin (Washington, DC: U.S. Department of Justice, National Institute of Justice, 2015); Tom R. Tyler and Jeffrey Fagan, "Legitimacy and Cooperation: Why Do People Help the Police Fight Crime in Their Communities?," *Ohio State Journal of Criminal Law*, Vol. 6 (2008), pp. 231 and 262; and Tom R. Tyler & Cheryl Wakslak, "Profiling and Police Legitimacy: Procedural Justice, Attributions of Motive, and Acceptance of Police Authority," *Criminology*, Vol. 42 (2004), pp. 253 and 255.

■ **theme**   What elements of the police subculture might be changed to fight police corruption? How could such changes be brought about?
■ **activity**   Ask students to list police activities that might be regarded as corrupt. Discuss the list, deciding on a "final" list of activities that most students agree are forms of corruption. Then have the class rank each of the items in the list from the least serious to the most serious.

■ **theme**   What is police corruption? What is the difference between police corruption and police deviance?
■ **police corruption**   The abuse of police authority for personal or organizational gain.[i]

Police subculture may, however, be changed through external pressures, such as new hiring practices, investigations into police corruption or misuse of authority, and commission reports that create pressures for police reform. Learn more about police subculture and police behavior at **http://clontz.mc-companies .com/additional_readings/subculture.htm**.

Corruption and Integrity

In 2014, sixteen current and former Puerto Rico police officers pled guilty to federal charges that they ran a criminal organization out of the police department.[10] Prosecutors for the U.S. Justice Department's Criminal Division said that the officers used their law enforcement positions to make money through robbery, extortion, manipulating court records, and selling illegal narcotics. At the time of the officers' arrest, Acting U.S. Assistant Attorney General David A. O'Neil said, "The criminal action today dismantles an entire network of officers who, we allege, used their badges and their guns not to uphold the law, but to break it." A second prosecutor noted that "Officers who use their badges as an excuse to commit egregious acts of violence and drug trafficking are an affront to the rule of law." According to court documents, the law enforcement officers who were charged took payoffs from drug dealers that they should have arrested. They also extorted money, planted evidence and stole from those individuals and from others. U.S. Attorney Rosa Emila Rodriquez-Velez summarized the gravity of the charges against the officers, saying, "They not only betrayed the citizens they were sworn to protect, they also betrayed the thousands of honest, hard-working law enforcement officers who risk their lives every day to keep us safe." Some of the officers were sentenced to 15 years in prison, while others received five-year sentences.

Police corruption has been a problem in American society since the early days of policing. It is probably an ancient and natural tendency of human beings to attempt to placate or win over those in positions of authority over them, while some people in authority will always be tempted to abuse. These tendencies become even more complicated in today's materialistic society by greed and by the personal and financial benefits to be derived from evading the law. The temptations toward illegality offered to police range from a free cup of coffee from a restaurant owner to huge monetary bribes arranged by drug dealers to guarantee

Diane Macdonald/Getty Images

The Police Monument in Old San Juan, Puerto Rico. The monument is flanked on either side by a long list of the names of fallen police officers. In 2014, sixteen Puerto Rico police officers were arrested and charged with corruption. How can police corruption, even if committed by only a few officers, detract from the police mission?

■ lecture note   Explain the events leading up to the Knapp Commission. Review the concepts of grass eaters and meat eaters and the differences between them.

■ **Knapp commission**   A committee that investigated police corruption in New York City in the early 1970s.

that the police will look the other way as an important shipment of contraband arrives. As noted criminologist Carl Klockars says, policing, by its very nature, "is an occupation that is rife with opportunities for misconduct. Policing is a highly discretionary, coercive activity that routinely takes place in private settings, out of the sight of supervisors, and in the presence of witnesses who are often regarded as unreliable."[11]

The effects of police corruption are far-reaching. As Michael Palmiotto of Wichita State University notes, "Not only does misconduct committed by an officer personally affect that officer, it also affects the community, the police department that employs the officer and every police department and police officer in America. Frequently, negative police actions caused by inappropriate police behavior reach every corner of the nation, and at times, the world."[12]

Exactly what constitutes corruption is not always clear. Ethicists say that police corruption ranges from minor offenses to serious violations of the law. In recognition of what some have called corruption's "slippery slope,"[13] most police departments now explicitly prohibit officers from accepting even minor gratuities. The slippery slope perspective holds that accepting even small thank-yous from members of the public can lead to a more ready acceptance of larger bribes. An officer who begins to accept, and then expect, gratuities may soon find that his or her practice of policing becomes influenced by such gifts and that larger ones soon follow. At that point, the officer may easily slide to the bottom of the moral slope, which was made slippery by previous small concessions.

Thomas Barker and David Carter, who have studied police corruption in depth, make the distinction between "occupational deviance," which is motivated by the desire for personal benefit, and "abuse of authority, which occurs most often to further the organizational goals of law enforcement, including arrest, ticketing, and the successful conviction of suspects."[14]

> Police corruption ranges from minor offenses to serious violations of the law.

FBI Special Agent Frank Perry, former chief of the bureau's ethics unit, distinguishes between police deviance and police corruption. Police deviance, according to Perry, consists of "unprofessional on- and off-duty misconduct, isolated instances of misuse of position, improper relationships with informants or criminals, sexual harassment, disparaging racial or sexual comments, embellished/falsified reporting, time and attendance abuse, insubordination, nepotism, cronyism, and noncriminal unauthorized disclosure of information."[15] Deviance, says Perry, is a precursor to individual and organizational corruption. It

may eventually lead to outright corruption unless police supervisors and internal affairs units are alert to the warning signs and actively intervene to prevent corruption from developing.

Figure 8-1 sorts examples of police corruption in terms of seriousness, though not everyone would agree with this ranking. In fact, a survey of 6,982 New York City police officers found that 65% did not classify excessive force, which we define later in this chapter, as a corrupt behavior.[16] Likewise, 71% of responding officers said that accepting a free meal is not a corrupt practice. Another 15% said that personal use of illegal drugs by law enforcement officers should not be considered corruption.

In the early 1970s, Frank Serpico made headlines when he testified before the **Knapp Commission** on police corruption in New York City.[17] Serpico, an undercover operative within the police department, revealed a complex web of corruption in which money and services routinely changed hands in "protection rackets" created by unethical officers. The authors of the Knapp Commission report distinguished between two types of corrupt officers, which they termed "grass eaters" and "meat eaters."[18] "Grass eating," the more common form of police corruption, was described as illegitimate activity that occurs from time to time in the normal course of police work. It involves mostly small bribes or relatively minor services offered by citizens seeking to avoid arrest and prosecution. "Meat eating" is a much more serious form of corruption, involving an officer's actively seeking illicit moneymaking opportunities. Meat eaters solicit bribes through threat or intimidation, whereas grass eaters commit the less serious offense of failing to refuse bribes that are offered.

In 1993, during 11 days of corruption hearings reminiscent of the Knapp Commission era, a parade of crooked New York police officers testified before a commission headed by former judge and Deputy Mayor Milton Mollen. Among the many revelations, officers spoke of dealing drugs, stealing confiscated drug funds, stifling investigations, and beating innocent people. Officer Michael Dowd, for example, told the commission that he had run a cocaine ring out of his station house in Brooklyn and had bought three homes on Long Island and a Corvette with the money he made. Most shocking of all, however, were allegations that high-level police officials attempted to cover up embarrassing incidents and that many officials may have condoned unprofessional and even criminal practices by the officers under their command. Honest officers, including internal affairs investigators, described how higher authorities had resisted their efforts to end corruption among their colleagues.

Repercussions from the Mollen Commission hearings continue to be felt. In 2004, for example, a New York State judge

■ **theme** The LAPD's infamous Rampart scandal in the late 1990s resulted in huge monetary settlements being given to drug dealers, gang members, and other criminals who claimed that they had been framed, shot, beaten, or otherwise mistreated by police. Do you agree with Los Angeles City Councilwoman Cindy Miscikowski who said, "Civil rights are civil rights, and they apply to everyone across the board"? Why or why not?

■ **lecture note** Discuss police corruption, and ask the class to identify pressures that officers are likely to face that might lead to corruption.

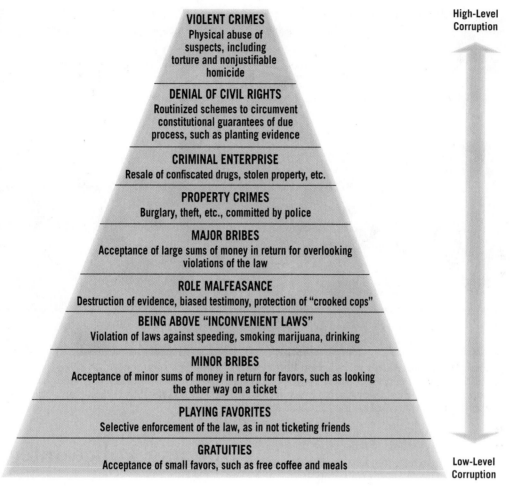

FIGURE 8-1 | Types and Examples of Police Corruption
Source: Pearson Education, Inc.

ruled that the city of New York had to pay special disability benefits to former police officer Jeffrey W. Baird, who served as an informant for the commission. Baird helped uncover corruption while working as an internal affairs officer but suffered from posttraumatic stress disorder after fellow officers threatened him, vandalized his work area, and sent obscene materials to his home.[19]

Money—The Root of Police Evil?

Years ago, Edwin Sutherland applied the concept of *differential association* (discussed in Chapter 3) to the study of deviant behavior.[20] Sutherland suggested that frequent, continued association of one person with another makes the associates similar. Of course, Sutherland was talking about criminals, not police officers.

Consider, however, the dilemma of average officers: Their job entails issuing traffic citations to citizens who try to talk their way out of a ticket, dealing with prostitutes who feel hassled by police, and arresting drug users who think it should be their right to do what they want as long as "it doesn't hurt anyone." Officers regularly encounter personal hostility and experience consistent and often quite vocal rejection of society's formalized norms. They receive relatively low pay, which indicates to them that their work is not really valued. By looking at the combination of these factors, it is easy to understand how officers often develop a jaded attitude toward the society they are sworn to protect.

Police officers' low pay may be a critical ingredient of the corruption mix.

Police officers' low pay may be a critical ingredient of the corruption mix. Salaries paid to police officers in this country have

■ **lecture note**   Discuss the importance of ethics training as a key element in the efforts to control police corruption.
■ **lecture note**   Explain that internal affairs divisions are charged with investigating wrongdoing by police officers, and discuss other methods departments can use to fight corruption.

■ **theme**   What are *Garrity rights*? Should police officers have these protections? How does their special (non-civilian) status affect their rights?

Tempe, Arizona, police officers Ratko Aleksis and Stephen Neff shown at an awards ceremony in 2014. The officers went to the aid of a shooting victim and saved his life using trauma skills they had acquired. The appropriate and timely recognition of outstanding and professional police activity can go a long way toward building police integrity and offsetting possible temptations for individual officers to engage in inappropriate behavior. What kinds of activities should be rewarded?

been notoriously low compared to those of other professions that require personal dedication, extensive training, high stress, and the risk of bodily harm. As police work becomes more professional, many police administrators hope that salaries will rise. However, no matter how much police pay increases, it will never be able to compete with the staggering amounts of money to be made through dealing in contraband. Working hand in hand with monetary pressures toward corruption are the moral dilemmas produced by unenforceable laws that provide the basis for criminal profit. During Prohibition, the Wickersham Commission warned of the potential for official corruption inherent in the legislative taboos on alcohol. The immense demand for drink called into question the wisdom of the law while simultaneously providing vast resources designed to circumvent it. Today's drug scene bears similarities to the Prohibition era. As long as there is a market for illegal drugs, the financial as well as societal pressures on the police to profit from the drug trade will remain substantial.

> As long as there is a market for illegal drugs, the financial as well as societal pressures on the police to profit from the drug trade will remain substantial.

Building Police Integrity

The difficulties of controlling corruption can be traced to several factors, including the reluctance of police officers to report corrupt activities by their fellow officers, the reluctance of police administrators to acknowledge the existence of corruption in their agencies, the benefits of corrupt transactions to the parties involved, and the lack of immediate victims willing to report corruption. However, high moral standards embedded in the principles of the police profession and effectively communicated to individual officers through formal training and peer-group socialization can raise the level of integrity in any department. Some law enforcement training programs are increasingly determined to reinforce the high ideals many recruits bring to police work and to encourage veteran officers to retain their commitment to the highest professional

> High moral standards embedded in the principles of the police profession and effectively communicated to individual officers through formal training and peer-group socialization can raise the level of integrity in any department.

■ **internal affairs**   The branch of a police organization tasked with investigating charges of wrongdoing involving members of the department.

standards. As one FBI publication explains it, "Ethics training must become an integral part of academy and in-service training for new and experienced officers alike."[21]

Ethics training, discussed later in this chapter, is part of a "reframing" strategy that emphasizes integrity to target police corruption. In 1997, for example, the National Institute of Justice (NIJ) released a report titled *Police Integrity: Public Service with Honor.* [22] The report, based on recommendations made by participants in a national symposium on police integrity, suggested (1) integrating ethics training into the programs offered by newly funded Regional Community Policing Institutes throughout the country, (2) broadening research activities in the area of ethics through NIJ-awarded grants for research on police integrity, and (3) conducting case studies of departments that have an excellent track record in the area of police integrity.

The NIJ report was followed in 2001 by a U.S. Department of Justice document titled *Principles for Promoting Police Integrity.*[23] The foreword to that document states, "For . . . policing to be successful, and crime reduction efforts to be effective, citizens must have trust in the police. All of us must work together to address the problems of excessive use of force and racial profiling, and—equally important—the perceptions of many minority residents that law enforcement treats them unfairly, if we are to build the confidence in law enforcement necessary for continued progress. Our goal must be professional law enforcement that gives all citizens of our country the feeling that they are being treated fairly, equally and with respect." The report covered such topics as the use of force; complaints and misconduct investigations; accountability and effective management; training; nondiscriminatory policing; and recruitment, hiring, and retention. Read the full report, which provides examples of promising police practices and policies that promote integrity, at **http://www.justice-studies .com/pubs/integrity.pdf**.

In 2000, the International Association of Chiefs of Police (IACP), in an effort to reinforce the importance of ethical standards in policing, adopted the Law Enforcement Oath of Honor. The IACP suggests that the Law Enforcement Oath of Honor should be seen by individual officers as a statement of commitment to ethical behavior. It is meant to reinforce the principles embodied in the IACP's Law Enforcement Code of Ethics, which is printed in the "Ethics and Professionalism" box later in this chapter.

In December 2005, the U.S. Department of Justice weighed in on the issue of police integrity with a Research for Practice report titled *Enhancing Police Integrity.*[24] The report said that "an

agency's culture of integrity, as defined by clearly understood and implemented policies and rules, may be more important in shaping the ethics of police officers than hiring the 'right' people."[25] The report's authors also noted that officers tend to evaluate the seriousness of various types of misconduct by observing and assessing their department's response in detecting and disciplining it. If unwritten policies conflict with written policies, the authors observed, then the resulting confusion undermines an agency's overall integrity-enhancing efforts. *Enhancing Police Integrity* is available online at **http://www.justicestudies.com/pubs/ epi.pdf**. An FBI-sponsored article on police corruption and ethics can be accessed at **http://www.justicestudies.com/pubs/ policecorrup.pdf**.

Most large-city law enforcement agencies have their own **internal affairs** divisions, which are empowered to investigate charges of wrongdoing made against officers. Where necessary, state police agencies may be called on to examine reported incidents. Federal agencies, including the FBI and the Drug Enforcement Administration, get involved when corruption violates federal statutes. The U.S. Department of Justice (DOJ), through various investigative offices, has the authority to examine possible violations of civil rights resulting from the misuse of police authority. The DOJ is often supported in these endeavors by the American Civil Liberties Union (ACLU), the National Association for the Advancement of Colored People (NAACP), and other watchdog groups.

> Internal affairs divisions are empowered to investigate charges of wrongdoing made against officers.

Officers suspected of law violations may invoke their *Garrity rights*—which are protections that officers have against self-incrimination in the face of questioning. Like the *Miranda* rights guaranteed to civilian criminal suspects who face questioning by police officers, Garrity rights protect officers themselves when being questioned by representatives of their department's internal affairs division or by their superior officers.

Drug Testing of Police Employees

On November 17, 2000, the U.S. Court of Appeals for the Fourth Circuit found that the chief of police in Westminster, Maryland, had acted properly in asking a doctor to test an officer's urine for the presence of heroin without the officer's knowledge.[26] Westminster Police Officer Eric Carroll had gone to the local hospital complaining of tightness in his chest and fatigue.

■ **theme**   Do you think police officers should be subject to random drug testing? Explain.

■ **lecture note**   Explain how the drug testing of police officers is important not just in keeping police departments drug free but also in fighting corruption.

■ **theme**   What are the hallmarks of a true profession? In your opinion, is police work a profession in America? Explain.

■ **lecture note**   Explain that a profession is characterized by a specialized body of knowledge and is capable of some kind of internal control over its members. Note that the Law Enforcement Code of Ethics and police training provide the rudimentary elements necessary for the professionalization of law enforcement. Ask students to read the Law Enforcement Code of Ethics in the "Ethics and Professionalism" box in this chapter, and have them comment on whether they think the code is realistic.

■ **police professionalism**   The increasing formalization of police work and the accompanying rise in public acceptance of the police.

The doctor who examined Carroll diagnosed him as suffering from high blood pressure. Carroll was placed on disability leave for three days. While Carroll was gone, the police chief received a call from someone who said that the officer was using heroin. The chief verified the caller's identity and then called the department doctor and asked him to test Carroll for drugs—but without informing the officer of the test. When Carroll returned to the physician for a follow-up visit, the doctor took a urine sample, saying that it was to test for the presence of blood. Although no blood was found in Carroll's urine, it did test positive for heroin. As a consequence, officer Carroll's employment with the department was terminated. He then sued in federal court, alleging conspiracy, defamation, and violations of his constitutional rights. The Fourth Circuit Court of Appeals, however, determined that the chief's actions were reasonable because, among other things, Carroll had signed a preemployment waiver that permitted the department to conduct drug tests at any time, with or without cause.[27]

The widespread potential for police corruption created by illicit drugs has led to focused efforts to combat drug use by officers. Drug-testing programs in local police departments are an example of such efforts. The IACP has developed a model drug-testing policy for police managers. The policy, designed to meet the needs of local departments, suggests the following:[28]

- Testing all applicants and recruits for drug or narcotics use
- Testing current employees when performance difficulties or documentation indicates a potential drug problem
- Testing current employees when they are involved in the use of excessive force or when they suffer or cause an on-duty injury
- Routine testing of all employees assigned to special "high-risk" areas, such as narcotics and vice

The courts have supported drug testing based on a reasonable suspicion that drug abuse has been or is occurring,[29] although random testing of officers was banned by the New York State Supreme Court in the case of *Philip Caruso, President of P.B.A.* v. *Benjamin Ward, Police Commissioner* (1986).[30] Citing overriding public interests, a 1989 decision by the U.S. Supreme Court upheld the testing of U.S. Customs personnel applying for transfer into drug-law enforcement positions or into positions requiring a firearm.[31] Many legal issues surrounding employee drug testing remain to be resolved in court, however.

Complicating this issue is the fact that drug and alcohol addictions are "handicaps" protected by the Federal Rehabilitation Act of 1973. As such, federal law enforcement employees, as well as those working for agencies with federal contracts, are entitled to counseling and treatment before action can be taken toward termination.

Employee drug testing in police departments, as in many other agencies, is a sensitive subject. Some claim that existing tests for drug use are inaccurate, yielding a significant number of "false positives." Repeated testing and high threshold levels for narcotic substances in the blood may eliminate many of these concerns. Less easy to address, however, is the belief that drug testing intrudes on the personal rights and professional dignity of individual employees.

Professionalism and Ethics

A profession is an organized undertaking characterized by a body of specialized knowledge acquired through extensive education[32] and by a well-considered set of internal standards and ethical guidelines that hold members of the profession accountable to one another and to society. Contemporary policing has many of the attributes of a profession.

Police professionalism requires that today's police officers have a great deal of specialized knowledge and that they adhere to the standards and ethics set out by the profession. Specialized knowledge in policing includes an understanding of criminal law, laws of procedure, constitutional guarantees, and relevant Supreme Court decisions; a working knowledge of weapons, hand-to-hand combat tactics, driving skills, vehicle maintenance, and radio communications; report-writing abilities; interviewing techniques; and media and human relations skills. Other specialized knowledge may include Breathalyzer operation, special weapons skills, polygraph operation, conflict resolution, and hostage negotiation. Supervisory personnel require an even wider range of skills, including administrative skills, management techniques, and strategies for optimum utilization of resources.

Police professionalism places important limits on the discretionary activities of individual enforcement personnel and helps

■ **theme**   What is accreditation? Why is it important for police agencies to be accredited if the only reward is that of peer recognition?

■ **police ethics**   The special responsibility to adhere to moral duty and obligation that is inherent in police work.

ethics and professionalism

The Law Enforcement Code of Ethics

As a Law Enforcement Officer, my fundamental duty is to serve mankind; to safeguard lives and property; to protect the innocent against deception, the weak against oppression or intimidation, and the peaceful against violence or disorder; and to respect the Constitutional rights of all men to liberty, equality, and justice.

I will keep my private life unsullied as an example to all; maintain courageous calm in the face of danger, scorn, or ridicule; develop self-restraint; and be constantly mindful of the welfare of others. Honest in thought and deed in both my personal and official life, I will be exemplary in obeying the laws of the land and the regulations of my department. Whatever I see or hear of a confidential nature or that is confided to me in my official capacity will be kept secret unless revelation is necessary in the performance of my duty.

I will never act officiously or permit personal feelings, prejudices, animosities, or friendships to influence my decisions. With no compromise for crime and with relentless prosecution of criminals, I will enforce the law courteously and appropriately without fear or favor, malice or ill will, never employing unnecessary force or violence and never accepting gratuities.

I recognize the badge of my office as a symbol of public faith, and I accept it as a public trust to be held so long as I am true to the ethics of the police service. I will constantly strive to achieve these objectives and ideals, dedicating myself before God to my chosen profession . . . law enforcement.

Thinking about Ethics

1. Why does the Law Enforcement Code of Ethics ask law enforcement officers "to respect the Constitutional rights of all men to liberty, equality, and justice"? Does such respect further the goals of law enforcement? Why or why not?

2. Why is it important for law enforcement officers to "keep (their) private life unsullied as an example to all"? What are the potential consequences of not doing so?

Source: International Association of Chiefs of Police. Reprinted with permission.

officers and the departments they work for gain the respect and regard of the public they police. Police work is guided by an ethical code developed in 1956 by the Peace Officers Research Association of California (PORAC) in conjunction with Dr. Douglas M. Kelley of Berkeley's School of Criminology.[33] The Law Enforcement Code of Ethics is reproduced in the "Ethics and Professionalism" box in this chapter. You can learn more about police professionalism from Harvard University's Executive Session on Policing and Public Safety at **http://www.hks.harvard.edu/programs/criminaljustice/research-publications/executive-sessions/policing**.

Ethics training has been integrated into most basic law enforcement training programs, and calls for expanded training in **police ethics** are being heard from many corners. A comprehensive resource for enhancing awareness of law enforcement ethics, called the Ethics Toolkit, is available from the IACP and the federal Office of Community Oriented Policing Services at **http://tinyurl.com/3ucxnla**.

Many professional associations support police work. One such organization, the Arlington, Virginia–based International Association of Chiefs of Police, has done much to raise professional standards in policing and continually strives for improvements in law enforcement nationwide. In like manner, the Fraternal Order of Police (FOP) is one of the best-known organizations of public-service workers in the United States. The FOP is the world's largest organization of sworn law enforcement officers, with more than 318,000 members in more than 2,100 lodges.

Accreditation is another avenue toward police professionalism. The Commission on Accreditation for Law Enforcement Agencies (CALEA) was formed in 1979. Police departments seeking accreditation through the commission must meet hundreds of standards in areas as diverse as day-to-day operations, administration, review of incidents involving the use of a weapon by officers, and evaluation and promotion of personnel. As of January 1, 2010, more than 800 (almost 4%) of the nation's 17,784 law enforcement agencies were accredited,[34] and a number of others were undergoing the accreditation process. Many accredited agencies are among the nation's largest; as a result, 25% of full-time law enforcement officers in the United States at the state and local levels are members of CALEA-accredited agencies.[35] Although accreditation makes possible the identification of high-quality police departments, it is often not valued by agency leaders because it offers few incentives. Accreditation does not guarantee

■ lecture note   Explain the importance of higher education to police officer training, especially in the era of community policing. Ask students how they think education might make a difference in their own approach to policing. Has it already changed their sense of the profession?

■ theme   Police standards and training vary greatly among jurisdictions. Do you think there should be a national standard that all police officers in the U.S. must meet? Explain.

■ activity   Have students research the education and training requirements in various departments in your state, or have each student (or group of students) research a different state. Discuss the wide variation in standards and the implications of this diversity. In a distance learning class, students may research requirements in their home states.

■ peace officer standards and training (POST) program The official program of a state or legislative jurisdiction that sets standards for the training of law enforcement officers. All states set such standards, although not all use the term *POST*.

ethics and professionalism

The FBI Oath

On their first day at the FBI Academy, new-agent trainees raise their right hands and take this oath as they are sworn in:

I (name) do solemnly swear (or affirm) that I will support and defend the Constitution of the United States against all enemies, foreign and domestic; that I will bear true faith and allegiance to the same; that I take this obligation freely, without any mental reservation or purpose of evasion; and that I will well and faithfully discharge the duties of the office on which I am about to enter. So help me God.

Similar ceremonies are conducted periodically in every state by every law enforcement agency for officers across the country, usually upon completion of their training. Although the wording of the oaths may vary, each officer promises to do one important thing—support and defend the Constitution of the United States.

Thinking about Ethics

1. How is the FBI oath similar to the Law Enforcement Code of Ethics presented earlier in this chapter? How does it differ?

2. What do the words "I will well and faithfully discharge the duties of the office" mean?

Source: "Our Oath of Office," The FBI Law Enforcement Bulletin, September, 2009.

a department any rewards beyond that of peer recognition. Visit CALEA online via **http://www.calea.org**.

Education and Training

Basic law enforcement training requirements were established in the 1950s by the state of New York and through a voluntary **peace officer standards and training (POST) program** in California. (Information on California's POST program can be accessed via **http://www.post.ca.gov**.) Today, every jurisdiction mandates POST-like requirements, although these requirements vary considerably. Modern police education generally involves training in subjects as varied as self-defense, human relations, firearms and weapons, communications, legal aspects of policing, patrol, criminal investigations, administration, report writing, ethics, computers and information systems, and cultural diversity. According to a 2009 Bureau of Justice Statistics report, the median number of hours of training required of new officers is 881 in state police agencies, 965 in county departments, 883 in municipal departments, and 719 in sheriff's departments.[36] Standards continue to be modified.

Accreditation is another avenue toward police professionalism.

Federal law enforcement agents receive schooling at the Federal Law Enforcement Training Center (FLETC) in Glynco, Georgia. The center provides training for about 60 federal law enforcement agencies, excluding the FBI and the Drug Enforcement Administration (DEA), which have their own training academies in Quantico, Virginia. FLETC also offers advanced training to state and local police organizations through the National Center for State and Local Law Enforcement Training, located on the FLETC campus. Specialized schools, like Northwestern University's Traffic Institute, are also credited with raising the level of police practice from purely operational concerns to a more professional level.

In 1987, in a move to further professionalize police training, the American Society for Law Enforcement Trainers was formed at the Ohio Peace Officer Training Academy. Now known as the American Society for Law Enforcement Training (ASLET), the Frederick, Maryland–based agency works to ensure quality in peace officer training and confers the title Certified Law Enforcement Trainer (CLET) on police-training professionals who meet its high standards. ASLET also works with the Police Training Network to provide an ongoing and comprehensive nationwide calendar of law enforcement training activities.

A recent innovation in law enforcement training is the Police Training Officer (PTO) program, the development of which was funded by the COPS Office starting in 1999.[37] The PTO program was designed by the Reno (Nevada) Police Department, in conjunction with the Police Executive Research Forum (PERF), as an alternative model for police field training. In fact, it represents the first new postacademy field-training program for law

■ **activity**   Have students research the various screening methods used by police departments and decide which methods are more common and which are rarely used. Have them rank them in order of importance. Encourage them to consider the difficulties or problems involved in some of the screening methods (e.g., cost, time).

■ **theme**   Do you agree with August Vollmer's comment regarding public expectations of the police? Why do you think he made this statement?

enforcement agencies in more than 30 years. The PTO program uses contemporary methods of adult education and a version of problem-based learning that is specifically adapted to the police environment. It incorporates community policing and problem-solving principles and, according to the COPS Office, fosters "the foundation for life-long learning that prepares new officers for the complexities of policing today and in the future."

As the concern for quality policing builds, increasing emphasis is also being placed on the formal education of police officers. As early as 1931, the National Commission on Law Observance and Enforcement (the Wickersham Commission) highlighted the importance of a well-educated police force by calling for "educationally sound" officers.[38] In 1967, the President's Commission on Law Enforcement and Administration of Justice voiced the belief that "the ultimate aim of all police departments should be that all personnel with general enforcement powers have baccalaureate degrees."[39] At the time, the average educational level of police officers in the United States was 12.4 years—slightly beyond a high school degree. In 1973, the National Advisory Commission on Criminal Justice Standards and Goals made the following rather specific recommendation: "Every police agency should, no later than 1982, require as a condition of initial employment the completion of at least four years of education . . . at an accredited college or university."[40]

However, recommendations do not always translate into practice. One report found that 1 in 3 state agencies have a college requirement for new officers, with 12% requiring a two-year degree, and 2% requiring a four-year degree. About 1 in 4 municipal and county police departments have a college requirement, with about 1 in 10 requiring a degree.[41] One in seven sheriff's offices have a college requirement, including 6% that require a minimum of a two-year degree for new hires.[42] A 2002 report on police departments in large cities found that the percentage requiring new officers to have at least some college rose from 19% in 1990 to 37% in 2000, and the percentage requiring either a two-year or four-year degree grew from 6 to 14% over the same period.[43] A Dallas Police Department policy requiring a minimum of 45 semester hours of successful college-level study for new recruits[44] was upheld in 1985 by the Fifth U.S. Circuit Court of Appeals in the case of *Davis* v. *Dallas*.[45]

An early survey of police departments by the PERF found that police agencies that hire educated officers accrue these benefits:[46] (1) better written reports, (2) enhanced communications with the public, (3) more effective job performance, (4) fewer citizen complaints, (5) greater initiative, (6) wiser use of discretion, (7) heightened sensitivity to racial and ethnic issues, and (8) fewer disciplinary problems. However, there are drawbacks to having more educated police forces. Educated officers are more likely than noneducated officers to leave police work, question orders, and request reassignment.

Today, most federal agencies require a four-year college degree for entry-level positions, and those degrees must be obtained from a college or university accredited by one of the regional or national institutional associations recognized by the U.S. Department of Education. Among agencies with such a requirement are the FBI; the Drug Enforcement Agency (DEA); the Bureau of Alcohol, Tobacco, Firearms and Explosives (ATF); the Secret Service; the Bureau of Customs and Border Protection, and the Bureau of Immigration and Customs Enforcement (ICE).[47] Learn more about the close relationship between professionalism and training at **http://justicestudies.com/pubs/letraining.pdf**.

Recruitment and Selection

All professions need informed, dedicated, and competent personnel. In its 1973 report on the police, the National Advisory Commission on Criminal Justice Standards and Goals bemoaned

Basketball great Shaquille O'Neal. In 2014, O'Neal, who has held adjunct law enforcement positions in the past, applied to be a reserve police officer in the town of Doral, Florida. What are the attractions of police work?

CBS/Cliff Lipson/Landov Media

■ **theme**   Identify some of the dangers of modern police work. What other, perhaps as yet unrealized, dangers can you anticipate for the future? How can police officers protect against each of the dangers you've identified?

■ **lecture note**   Explain the dangers of police work by referring to the risk of violence on the job, the danger of infectious diseases such as AIDS, terrorism, and the possibility of infection at accident sites and when dealing with injured people. Use Figure 8-2 to highlight the kinds of situations in which law enforcement officers are most likely to be killed.

the fact that "many college students are unaware of the varied, interesting, and challenging assignments and career opportunities that exist within the police service."[48] Today, police organizations consider education an important recruiting criterion, and they actively recruit new officers from two- and four-year colleges and universities, technical institutions, and professional organizations. The national commission report stressed the setting of high standards for police recruits and recommended a strong emphasis on minority recruitment, elimination of the requirement that new officers live in the area they were hired to serve, decentralized application and testing procedures, and various recruiting incentives.

A recent Bureau of Justice Statistics study found that local police departments use a variety of applicant-screening methods.[49] Nearly all use personal interviews, and a large majority use basic skills tests, physical agility measurements, medical exams, drug tests, psychological evaluations, and background investigations into the personal character of applicants. Among departments serving 25,000 or more residents, about eight in ten use physical agility tests and written aptitude tests, more than half check credit records, and about half use personality inventories and polygraph exams. After training, successful applicants are typically placed on probation for one year. The probationary period in police work has been called the "first true job-related test . . . in the selection procedure,"[50] providing the opportunity for supervisors to gauge the new officer's response to real-life situations.

Effective policing, however, may depend more on innate personal qualities than on educational attainment or credit history. One of the first people to attempt to describe the personal attributes necessary for a successful police officer, famed 1930s police administrator August Vollmer, said that the public expects police officers to have "the wisdom of Solomon, the courage of David, the strength of Samson, the patience of Job, the leadership of Moses, the kindness of the Good Samaritan, the strategic training of Alexander, the faith of Daniel, the diplomacy of Lincoln, the tolerance of the Carpenter of Nazareth, and finally, an intimate knowledge of every branch of the natural, biological, and social sciences."[51] More practically, Orlando (O. W.) Wilson, the well-known police administrator of the 1940s and 1950s, once enumerated some "desirable personal qualities of patrol officers": (1) initiative; (2) responsibility; (3) the ability to deal alone with emergencies; (4) the capacity to communicate effectively with people from diverse social, cultural, and ethnic backgrounds; (5) the ability to learn a variety of tasks quickly; (6) the attitude and ability necessary to adapt to technological changes;

(7) the desire to help people in need; (8) an understanding of others; (9) emotional maturity; and (10) sufficient physical strength and endurance.[52]

High-quality police recruits, an emphasis on training with an eye toward ethical aspects of police performance, and higher levels of education are beginning to raise police pay, which has traditionally been low. The acceptance of police work as a true profession should contribute to significantly higher rates of pay in coming years. Learn more about a career in policing at **http://discoverpolicing.org.**

The Dangers of Police Work

On October 15, 1991, the National Law Enforcement Officers' Memorial was unveiled in Washington, D.C. The memorial contained the names of 12,561 law enforcement officers killed in the line of duty, including U.S. Marshals Service Officer Robert Forsyth, who in 1794 was the nation's first law enforcement officer to be killed on the job. More than 6,000 names have been added since the opening day.[53] At the memorial, an interactive video system provides visitors with brief biographies and photographs of officers who have died. Tour the memorial by visiting **http://www.nleomf.com**.

As the memorial proves, police work is, by its very nature, dangerous. Although many officers never once fire their weapons

NYPD officer James Smith makes a rubbing of his wife Moira Smith's freshly engraved name at the National Law Enforcement Officers Memorial in Washington, D.C. Inscribed on the walls of the memorial are the names of the more than 18,000 police officers who gave their lives in the line of duty. In what other ways are fallen officers honored?

Roger L. Wollenberg UPI Photo Service/Newscom

■ **lecture note**   Point out that casual contact will not lead to AIDS, that there must be contact with fresh blood or other body fluids, and that breaks in the skin or mucous membranes provide the most likely route for infection to occur. Discuss the roles that accident scenes, rape crimes, cardiopulmonary resuscitation (CPR), bites, and cuts may play in AIDS transmission.

■ **lecture note**   Point out that although the police do face a risk of violent death in the line of duty, the actual rate of such death is extremely small.

■ **biological weapon**   A biological agent used to threaten human life (e.g., anthrax, smallpox, or any infectious disease).[ii]

in the line of duty, some die while performing their jobs. On-the-job police deaths occur from stress, training accidents, and auto crashes. However, it is violent death at the hands of criminal offenders that police officers and their families fear most.

Violence in the Line of Duty

Most officers who are shot are killed by lone suspects armed with a single weapon. In 2014, 133 American law enforcement officers were killed in the line of duty.[54] Figure 8-2 shows the number of officers killed in different types of incidents in 2014. In 2001, the attacks on the World Trade Center resulted in the greatest ever annual loss of life of on-duty law enforcement officers when 72 police officers perished.[55]

A study by the FBI found that, generally, slain officers were good natured and conservative in the use of physical force, "as compared to other law enforcement officers in similar situations. They were also perceived as being well-liked by the community and the department, friendly to everyone, laid back, and easy going."[56] Finally, the study, which was published before the September 11, 2001, terrorist attacks, also found that most officers who were killed failed to wear protective vests.

For statistics on police killings to have meaning beyond the personal tragedy they entail, it is necessary to place them within a larger framework. There are approximately 732,000 state and local (full- and part-time) sworn police employees in this country,[57] along with another 105,000 federal agents.[58] Such numbers demonstrate that the rate of violent death among law enforcement officers in the line of duty is small indeed.

Risk of Disease and Infected Evidence

Dangers other than violence also threaten law enforcement officers. The increase in serious diseases that can be transmitted by blood and other body fluids, the possible planned release of active **biological weapons** like anthrax or smallpox, and the fact that crime and accident scenes are inherently dangerous combine to make *caution* a necessary watchword among investigators and first responders. Routine criminal and accident investigations hold the potential for infection through minor cuts and abrasions resulting from contact with the broken glass and torn metal of a wrecked vehicle, the sharp edges of knives found at the scene of an assault or murder, and drug implements like razor blades and hypodermic needles secreted in vehicles, homes, and pockets. Such minor injuries, previously shrugged off by many police personnel, have become a focal point for warnings about the dangers of AIDS, Ebola, hepatitis B, tuberculosis, and other diseases spread through contact with bodily fluids.

Infection can also occur from the use of breath alcohol instruments on infected persons, the handling of evidence of all types, seemingly innocuous implements like staples, the emergency delivery of babies in squad cars, and the attack (especially bites) by infected individuals who are being questioned or who are in custody. Understandably, officers are concerned about how to handle the threat of AIDS and other diseases such as Ebola. However, as a publication of the NYPD reminds its officers, "Police officers have a professional responsibility to render assistance to those who are in need of our services. We cannot refuse to help. Persons with infectious diseases must be treated with the care and dignity we show all citizens."[59]

Of equal concern is the threat of biological agents. Although crime scenes and sites known to harbor (or that are suspected of harboring) dangerous active biological agents require a response by teams equipped with special protective equipment, all law enforcement officers should take reasonable precautions against exposure to

> All law enforcement officers should take reasonable precautions against exposure to the wide variety of infectious agents known to exist at even routine crime scenes.

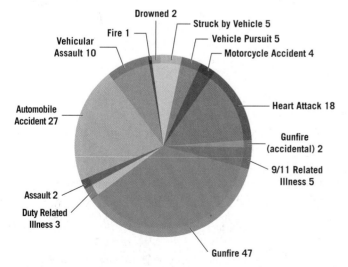

FIGURE 8-2 | U.S. Law Enforcement Officers Killed in the Line of Duty, 2014

Source: Pearson Education, Inc.

■ **lecture note** Discuss police stress as a major occupational hazard for law enforcement personnel, and identify some of the stressors that police officers face.
■ **theme** What are some of the main causes of stress among the police? How might the police department help to reduce some of these stressors?

■ **lecture note** Outline some of the techniques for stress reduction, such as exercise, meditation, breathing exercises, prayer, music, subliminal conditioning, and diet. Discuss techniques that are most likely to work with law enforcement personnel and those that are least likely to be effective.

the wide variety of infectious agents known to exist at even routine crime scenes. Emergency management agencies generally recommend a number of precautions, shown in Table 8-2, to defend against exposure to infectious substances.

To better combat the threat of infectious diseases among public-safety employees and health care professionals, the federal Bloodborne Pathogens Act of 1991[60] requires that police officers receive proper training in how to prevent contamination by bloodborne infectious agents. The act also requires that police officers undergo an annual refresher course on the topic.

Police departments will face an increasing number of legal challenges in the years to come in cases of infectious diseases and in cases involving the release of biological agents. Predictable areas of concern include (1) the need to educate officers and other police employees about AIDS, anthrax, Ebola, and other infectious diseases; (2) the responsibility of police departments to prevent the spread of infectious diseases in police lockups; and (3) the necessity of effective and nondiscriminatory enforcement activities

> Police departments will face an increasing number of legal challenges in the years to come in cases of infectious diseases like AIDS and in cases involving the release of biological agents.

and lifesaving measures by police officers in environments contaminated with active biological agents. With regard to nondiscriminatory activities, the National Institute of Justice has suggested that legal claims in support of an officer's refusal to render assistance to people with AIDS would probably not be effective in court.[61] The reason is twofold: The officer has a basic duty to render assistance to individuals in need of it, and the possibility of AIDS transmission by casual contact has been scientifically established as extremely remote. Viral infections that the CDC acknowledges can be spread by direct casual contact (i.e., touching saliva), such as Ebola, however, may fall into a different category.

A final issue of growing concern involves activities by police officers infected with the AIDS virus. Few statistics are currently available on the number of officers with AIDS, but public reaction to those officers may be a developing problem that police managers will soon need to address.

Stress and Fatigue among Police Officers

Traumatic events, like hurricanes, terrorist attacks, and violent confrontations, are instantly stressful. But long-term stress, whose debilitating effects accumulate over years, may be the

TABLE 8-2 | Biological Incident Law Enforcement Concerns

Suspicious material	Responding officers should not handle or come into close physical contact with suspicious material. If it is necessary to handle the material to evaluate it, officers should wear surgical gloves and masks and wash their hands thoroughly with soap and water after handling.
Human bites	The biter usually receives the victim's blood. Viral transmission through saliva is highly unlikely. If bitten by anyone, milk the wound to make it bleed, wash the area thoroughly, and seek medical attention.
Spitting	Viral transmission through saliva is possible in cases of Ebola, but highly unlikely with HIV.
Urine/feces	Unprotected contact with urine, feces, or vomit should be avoided.
Cuts/puncture wounds	Use caution in handling sharp objects and searching areas hidden from view. Needle-stick studies show risk of infection is very low.
CPR/first aid	To eliminate the risk associated with CPR, use masks/airways. Avoid blood-to-blood contact by keeping open wounds covered and wearing gloves when in contact with bleeding wounds.
Body removal	Observe crime scene rules; do not touch anything. Those who must come in contact with blood or other body fluids should wear gloves.
Casual contact	No cases of AIDS or AIDS virus infection have been attributed to casual contact.
Any contact with blood or body fluids	Wear gloves if contact with blood or body fluids is considered likely. If contact occurs, wash thoroughly with soap and water; clean up spills with one part water to nine parts household bleach.
Post-incident response	Notify health officials if you have had direct contact with blood or body fluids, such as but not limited to, feces, saliva, urine, vomit, and semen of a person who is sick with AIDS or Ebola. The Ebola virus can enter the body through broken skin or unprotected mucous membranes in the eyes, nose, or mouth.

References: Michigan Department of Community Health, "Anthrax (*Bacillus anthracis*) Information for Health Care Providers," http://www.michigan.gov/documents/Healthcare_provider_FAQ-anthrax_08-2004_104327_7.pdf (accessed June 11, 2014); Massachusetts Administrative Office of the Trial Court, "Personnel Policies and Procedures Manual, Section 24.000 (Statement of Policy and Procedures on AIDS)," http://www.state.ma.us/courts/admin/hr/section24.html (accessed June 5, 2013); Centers for Disease Control and Prevention, "Ebola Virus Disease," http://www.cdc.gov/vhf/ebola/prevention (accessed October 10, 2014); and "Collecting and Handling Evidence Infected with Human Disease-Causing Organisms," *FBI Law Enforcement Bulletin*, July 1987.

Source: Pearson Education, Inc.

most insidious and least visible of all threats facing law enforcement personnel today. Although some degree of stress can be a positive motivator, serious stress, over long periods of time, is generally regarded as destructive, even life threatening.

Stress is a natural component of police work (Figure 8-3).[62] The American Institute of Stress, based in Yonkers, New York, ranks policing among the top ten stress-producing jobs in the country.[63] The Bureau of Justice Statistics points out that "exposure to violence, suffering, and death is inherent to the profession of the law enforcement officer. There are other sources of stress as well. Officers who deal with offenders on a daily basis may perceive the public's opinion of police performance to be unfavorable; they often are required to work mandatory, rotating shifts; and they may not have enough time to spend with their families. Police officers also face unusual, often highly disturbing, situations, such as dealing with a child homicide victim or the survivors of vehicle crashes."[64]

Some stressors in police work are particularly destructive. One is frustration brought on by the inability to be effective, regardless of the amount of personal effort expended. Arrests may not lead to convictions. Evidence available to the officer may not be allowed in court. Imposed sentences may seem inadequate to the arresting officer. The feelings of powerlessness that come from seeing repeat offenders back on the streets and from witnessing numerous injustices to innocent victims may greatly stress police officers and cause them to question the purpose of their professional lives. These feelings of frustration and powerlessness may also lead to desperate attempts to find relief. As one researcher observes, "The suicide rate of police officers is more than twice that of the general population."[65]

Stress is not unique to the police profession, but because of the "macho" attitude that is traditionally associated with police work, police officers deny their stress more often than those in other occupations do. Some individuals are more susceptible to the negative effects of stress than others. The Type A personality, first identified almost 40 years ago, is most likely to perceive life in terms of pressure and performance. Type B people are more laid back and less likely to suffer from the negative effects of stress. Police ranks, drawn as they are from the general population, are filled with both stress-sensitive and stress-resistant personalities.

Stress Reduction

It is natural to want to reduce stress.[66] Humor helps, even if it's somewhat cynical. Health-care professionals, for example, are noted for their ability to joke while caring for patients who are seriously ill or even dying. At times, police officers use humor similarly to defuse their reactions to dark or threatening situations. Keeping an emotional distance from stressful events is another way of coping with them, although such distance is not always easy to maintain. Police officers who have had to deal with serious cases of child abuse often report that they experience emotional turmoil as a consequence.

Exercise, meditation, abdominal breathing, biofeedback, self-hypnosis, guided imaging, induced relaxation, subliminal conditioning, music, prayer, and diet have all been cited as useful techniques for stress reduction. Devices to measure stress levels are available in the form of handheld heart rate monitors, blood pressure devices, "biodots" (which change color according to the amount of blood flow in the extremities), and psychological inventories.

A new approach to managing stress among police officers holds that the amount of stress that officers experience is directly related to their reactions to potentially stressful situations.[67]

FIGURE 8-3 | **Stress and Fatigue among Police Officers**
Source: Pearson Education, Inc.

freedom OR safety? YOU decide

Religion and Public Safety

In 2014, 20-year-old Cassandra Belin was convicted by a French court and fined 150 Euros for wearing a full-face Islamic veil (or niqab) in public in violation of a 2011 French law. The French government initiated a ban on the wearing of veils, or Islamic burkas, following a number of terrorist incidents. French police can impose fines on women who wear veils in public, although recent reports reveal that few women have actually been ticketed.

The French ban was preceded by an incident in Florida in 2003, when state judge Janet Thorpe ruled that a Muslim woman could not wear a veil while being photographed for a state driver's license. The woman, Sultaana Freeman, claimed that her religious rights were violated when the state department of motor vehicles required that she reveal her face for the photograph. She offered to show her eyes, but not the rest of her face, to the camera.

Judge Thorpe said, however, that a "compelling interest in protecting the public from criminal activities and security threats" did not place an undue burden on Freeman's ability to practice her religion.

After the hearing, Freeman's husband, Abdul Maalik Freeman, told reporters, "This is a religious principle; this is a principle that's imbedded in us as believers. So, she's not going to do that." Howard Marks, the Freemans' attorney, supported by the American Civil Liberties Union (ACLU), filed an appeal claiming that the ruling was counter to guarantees of religious freedom inherent in the U.S. Constitution. Two years later, however, a Florida court of appeals denied further hearings in the case.

You Decide

Do the demands of public safety justify restrictions on religious practice? If so, would you go so far as the French practice of banning the wearing of veils in public? As an alternative, should photo IDs, such as driver's licenses, be replaced with other forms of identification (such as an individual's stored DNA profile) to accommodate the beliefs of individuals like the Freemans?

References: "French Court Upholds Controversial Burqa Ban," Al Arabiya News, http://english.alarabiya.net/en/News/world/2014/01/08/French-court-upholds-controversial-burqa-ban -.html (January 8, 2014); "Judge: No Veil in Driver's License Photo," Associated Press, June 6, 2003; Associated Press, "FL Appeals Court Upholds Ban of Veil in Driver's License Photo," September 7, 2005, http://www.newsday.com/news/nationworld/nation/orl-bk-freeman090705,0,2758466.story?coll=ny-leadnationalnews-headlines (accessed April 17, 2012); and Andrew Chung, "French Ban on Islamic Veil Turns Out to Be Toothless," Toronto Star, March 31, 2012, http://www.thestar.com/news/world/article/1154781--french-ban-on-islamic-veil-turns out-to-be-toothless (accessed May 20, 2013).

Robert Brenner/PhotoEdit Inc.

A New York City Police Department officer showing obvious signs of fatigue while working at a traffic barrier. Stress and fatigue are common problems in police work and can result from long work hours, grueling investigations, traumatic experiences, and even boredom. How can boredom be combated?

Officers who can filter out extraneous stimuli and who can distinguish between truly threatening situations and those that are benign are much less likely to report job-related stressors than those lacking these abilities. Because stress-filtering abilities are often closely linked to innate personality characteristics, some researchers suggest careful psychological screening of police applicants to better identify those who have a natural ability to cope with situations that others might perceive as stressful.[68]

Police officers' family members often report feelings of stress that are directly related to the officers' work. As a result, some departments have developed innovative programs to allay family stress. The Collier County (Florida) Spousal Academy, for example, is a family support program that offers training to spouses and other domestic partners of deputies and recruits who are enrolled in the department's training academy. The ten-hour program deals directly with issues that are likely to produce stress and informs participants of department and community resources that are available to help them. Peer-support programs for spouses and life partners and for the adolescent children of officers are also beginning to operate nationwide. One organization, Badge of Life, promotes mental health services for police officers. The organization has created an Emotional Self-care Training (ESC) initiative that asks officers to perform a periodic mental health check by visiting a licensed therapist at least once a year. Badge of Life can be reached on the Web at **http:// www.badgeoflife.com.**

Officer Fatigue

Like stress, fatigue can affect a police officer's performance. As criminologist Bryan Vila points out, "Tired, urban street cops are a national icon. Weary from overtime assignments, shift work, night

■ **theme**   What is excessive force? How does the situation affect the determination of an officer's actions as excessive or not?

■ **lecture note**   Discuss the police use of force continuum presented in Figure 8-5. Explain how the officer's perception of a situation affects his or her response to that situation.

■ **police use of force**   The use of physical restraint by a police officer when dealing with a member of the public.[iii]

■ **excessive force**   The application of an amount and/or frequency of force greater than that required to compel compliance from a willing or unwilling subject.[iv]

school, endless hours spent waiting to testify, and the emotional and physical demands of the job, not to mention trying to patch together a family and social life during irregular islands of off-duty time, they fend off fatigue with coffee and hard-bitten humor."[69] Vila found levels of police officer fatigue to be six times as high as those of shift workers in industrial and mining jobs.[70] As Vila notes, few departments set work-hour standards, and fatigue associated with the pattern and length of work hours may be expected to contribute to police accidents, injuries, and misconduct.

To address the problem, Vila recommends that police departments "review the policies, procedures, and practices that affect shift scheduling and rotation, overtime moonlighting, the number of consecutive work hours allowed, and the way in which the department deals with overly tired employees."[71] Vila also suggests controlling the working hours of police officers, "just as we control the working hours of many other occupational groups."[72] Learn more about police fatigue from the FBI at **http://justicestudies.com/pubs/police_fatigue.pdf**.

Police Use of Force

In 2013, U.S. District Court Judge Susie Morgan officially entered a consent decree into judgment mandating a plan to instill sweeping reforms in the New Orleans Police Department (NOPD).[73] Two years earlier, the Civil Rights Division (CRD) of the U.S. Department of Justice issued a stinging indictment of the NOPD[74] in a 158-page report detailing inadequacies within the department that had led to what the report's authors called "a pattern or practice of conduct that deprives individuals of rights, privileges, or immunities secured or protected by the Constitution or laws of the United States." The CRD investigation, which had been requested by the municipal administration of the City of New Orleans, was part of efforts by elected officials and concerned citizens to bring about the "complete transformation" of the NOPD. One of the most significant findings of the investigation was that the "NOPD, for at least the past several years, has been all too frequently indifferent to its officers' improper use of force." The report's authors explained it this way: "Police-civilian interactions only rarely require the use of force. In the small portion of interactions where it is necessary for officers to use force, the Constitution requires that officers use only the amount of force that is reasonable under the circumstances. We found that officers in NOPD routinely use unnecessary and unreasonable force in violation of the Constitution and NOPD policy." You can access the complete report at **http://justicestudies.com/pdf/nolpd.pdf**. The

2013 consent decree can be found at **http://justicestudies.com/pdf/noldconsentdecree.pdf**.

Police use of force can be defined as the use of physical restraint by a police officer when dealing with a member of the public.[75] Decisions to use force, including how much force to use, are within the discretion of individual police officers. However, as the Justice Department report on the NOPD noted, law enforcement officers are authorized to use only the amount of force that is reasonable and necessary given the circumstances facing them. Most officers are trained in the use of force and typically encounter numerous situations during their careers when the use of force is appropriate—for example, when making some arrests, restraining unruly combatants, or controlling a disruptive demonstration. Force may involve hitting; holding or restraining; pushing; choking; threatening with a flashlight, baton, or chemical or pepper spray; restraining with a police dog; or threatening with a gun. Some definitions of police use of force include handcuffing. It important to note that some police departments no longer use the phrase "use of force," preferring instead to talk about "response to resistance."

The National Institute of Justice estimates that more than 43.5 million people nationwide have face-to-face contact with the police over a typical 12-month period (nearly 18 million as a result of traffic stops) and that approximately 1.6%, or about 700,000, of these people become subject to the use of force or the threat of force.[76] When handcuffing is included in the definition of force, the number of people subjected to force increases to 1.2 million, or slightly more than 2.5% of those having contact with the police. Other studies show that police use weaponless tactics in approximately 80% of use-of-force incidents and that about 88% of all use-of-force incidents involve merely grabbing or holding the suspect.[77]

Studies show that police use force in fewer than 20% of adult custodial arrests. Even in instances where force is used, the police primarily use weaponless tactics. Female officers have been found to be less likely to use physical force and firearms, and more likely to use chemical weapons (mostly pepper spray), than their male counterparts.[78] Figure 8-4 shows the types of encounters in which the use of force is most likely to be employed.

A more complex issue is the use of excessive force. The IACP defines **excessive force** as "the application of an amount and/or frequency of force greater than that required to compel compliance from a willing or unwilling subject."[79] When excessive force is employed, the activities of the police often come under public scrutiny and receive attention from the media and from legislators. Police officers' use of excessive force can also result in lawsuits by members of the public who feel that they

■ **problem police officer**   A law enforcement officer who exhibits problem behavior, as indicated by high rates of citizen complaints and use-of-force incidents and by other evidence.[v]

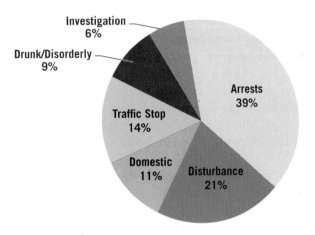

FIGURE 8-4 | Police Use of Force by Type of Encounter

Source: International Association of Chiefs of Police, *Police Use of Force in America, 2001* (Alexandria, VA: IACP, 2001), p. iii. Reprinted with permission.

have been treated unfairly. Whether the use of excessive force is aberrant behavior on the part of an individual officer or is a practice of an entire law enforcement agency, both the law and public opinion generally condemn it. Many police departments are now posting their use of force policy manuals online. See, for example, the UCLA Police Department's posting at **http://www.ucpd.ucla.edu/policy/300Use_of_force.pdf.**

Kenneth Adams, an associate dean at the University of Central Florida and an expert in the use of force by police, notes that there is an important difference between the terms *excessive force,* such as shoving or pushing when simply grabbing a suspect would be adequate, and *excessive use of force,* which refers to the phenomenon of force being used unacceptably, often on a department-wide basis. The term, says Adams, "deals with relative comparisons among police agencies, and there are no established criteria for judgment." *Use of excessive force* and the *excessive use of force* may be distinguished from the *illegal use of force,* which refers to situations in which the use of force by police violates a law or statute.[80]

In one study, Geoffrey Alpert and Roger Dunham found that the "force factor"—the level of force used by the police relative to the suspect's level of resistance—is a key element to consider in attempting to reduce injuries to both the police and suspects.[81] The force factor is calculated by measuring both the suspect's level of resistance and the officer's level of force on an equivalent scale and by then subtracting the level of resistance from the level of police force used. Results from the study indicate that, on average, the level of force that officers use is closely related to the type of training that their departments emphasize. Figure 8-5 shows a use of force continuum containing five levels of force starting with the

potential for force implied by the mere physical presence of a police officer, to deadly force. The figure conceptualizes of force not as a static concept but rather as a continuum of responses, ranging from the minor use of force such as verbal commands to deadly force, the maximum amount of force possible.[82]

Excessive force can also be symptomatic of **problem police officers**. Problem police officers are those who exhibit problem behavior, as indicated by high rates of citizen complaints, frequent involvement in use-of-force incidents, and other evidence.[83] The Christopher Commission, which studied the structure and operation of the Los Angeles Police Department (LAPD) in the wake of the Rodney King beating, found a number of "repeat offenders" on the LAPD force.[84] According to the commission, approximately 1,800 LAPD officers were alleged to have used excessive force or improper tactics between 1986 and 1990. Of these officers, more than 1,400 had only one or two allegations against them. Another 183 officers had four or more allegations, 44 had six or more, 16 had eight or more, and one had 16 such allegations. The commission also found that, generally speaking, the 44 officers with six complaints or more had received positive performance evaluations that failed to record "sustained" complaints or to discuss their significance. More recently, in 2014, New York City Police Commissioner William J. Bratton told police commanders that the agency's "gains against crime were being undercut by its most troublesome officers," and they had to be rooted out.[85]

Recent studies have found that problem police officers do not differ significantly in race or ethnicity from nonproblem officers, although they tend to be male and have disciplinary records

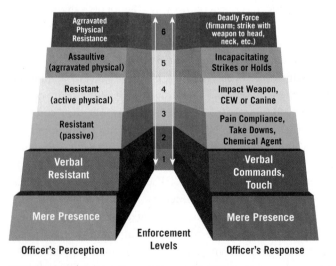

FIGURE 8-5 | Police Use of Force Continuum

Source: Charlie Mesloh, Mark Henych, Ross Wolf, "Less Lethal Weapon Effectiveness, Use of Force, and Suspect & Officer Injuries: A Five-Year Analysis," Report to the National Institute of Justice, 2008.
Note: "CEW" listed in Level 4 is an abbreviation for "Conducted Energy Weapon."

■ **theme**   How might a community policing approach alter police views of when deadly force is appropriate?

■ **deadly force**   Force likely to cause death or great bodily harm. Also, "the intentional use of a firearm or other instrument resulting in a high probability of death."[vi]

■ **lecture note**   Discuss the 1985 Supreme Court case of *Tennessee v. Garner* and explain how this case affected police use of deadly force.

■ **theme**   What elements of the police subculture and personality cause police officers and administrators to avoid acknowledging the psychological stress of using deadly force?

that are more serious than those of other officers. Some departments are developing early-warning systems to allow police managers to identify potentially problematic officers and to reduce problem behavior. Learn more about police use of force, as well as force used against the police, from **http://www.justicestudies.com/pubs/force.pdf** and **http://www.justicestudies.com/pubs/measureforce.pdf**. Two FBI articles on excessive force are available at **http://www.justicestudies.com/pubs/excessiveforce.pdf** and **http://www.justicestudies.com/pubs/excessiveforce02.pdf**.

Deadly Force

Generally speaking, **deadly force** is likely to cause death or significant bodily harm. The FBI defines *deadly force* as "the intentional use of a firearm or other instrument resulting in a high probability of death."[86]

The use of deadly force by law enforcement officers, especially when it is *not* considered justifiable, is one area of potential civil liability that has received considerable attention in recent years. Historically, the fleeing-felon rule applied to most U.S. jurisdictions. It held that officers could use deadly force to prevent the escape of a suspected felon, even when that person represented no immediate threat to the officer or to the public.

The 1985 U.S. Supreme Court case of *Tennessee* v. *Garner* [87] specified the conditions under which deadly force could be used in the apprehension of suspected felons. Edward Garner, a 15-year-old suspected burglar, was shot to death by Memphis police after he refused their order to halt and attempted to climb over a chain-link fence. In an action initiated by Garner's father, who claimed that his son's constitutional rights had been violated, the Court held that the use of deadly force by the police to prevent the escape of a fleeing felon could be justified only where the suspect could reasonably be thought to represent a significant threat of serious injury or death to the public or to the officer and where deadly force is necessary to effect the arrest. In reaching its decision, the Court declared that "[t]he use of deadly force to prevent the escape of *all* felony suspects, whatever the circumstances, is constitutionally unreasonable."

In the 1989 case of *Graham* v. *Connor*,[88] the Supreme Court established the standard of "objective reasonableness." The Court said that whether deadly force has been used appropriately should be judged from the perspective of a reasonable officer on the scene and not with the benefit of "20/20 hindsight." The justices wrote, "The calculus of reasonableness must embody allowance for the fact that police officers are often forced to make split-second judgments—in circumstances that are tense, uncertain, and rapidly evolving—about the amount of force that is necessary in a particular situation."

In 1995, following investigations into the actions of federal agents at the deadly siege of the Branch Davidian compound at Waco, Texas, and the tragic deaths associated with a 1992 FBI assault on antigovernment separatists in Ruby Ridge, Idaho (a case that is discussed later in the chapter), the federal government announced that it was adopting an "imminent danger" standard for the use of deadly force by federal agents. The imminent danger standard restricts the use of deadly force to those situations in which the lives of agents or others are in danger.

> The imminent danger standard restricts the use of deadly force to those situations in which the lives of agents or others are in danger.

When the new standard was announced, federal agencies were criticized for taking so long to adopt it. The federal deadly force policy, as adopted by the FBI, contains the following elements:[89]

- *Defense of life.* Agents may use deadly force only when necessary—that is, only when they have probable cause to believe that the subject poses an imminent danger of death or serious physical injury to the agent or to others.
- *Fleeing subject.* Deadly force may be used to prevent the escape of a fleeing subject if there is probable cause to believe that the subject has committed a felony involving the infliction or threatened infliction of serious physical injury or death and that the subject's escape would pose an imminent danger of death or serious physical injury to the agent or to others.
- *Verbal warnings.* If feasible, and if doing so would not increase the danger to the agent or to others, a verbal warning to submit to the authority of the agent should be given prior to the use of deadly force.
- *Warning shots.* Agents may not fire warning shots.
- *Vehicles.* Agents may not fire weapons solely to disable moving vehicles. Weapons may be fired at the driver or other occupant of a moving motor vehicle only when the agent has probable cause to believe that the subject poses an imminent danger of death or serious physical injury to the agent or to others and when the use of deadly force does not create a danger to the public that outweighs the likely benefits of its use.

Studies of killings by the police have often focused on claims of discrimination—that is, that minority suspects are more likely to be shot than whites. But research has not provided solid support for such claims. While individuals shot by police are more likely to be minorities, an early study by James Fyfe found that police officers will generally respond with deadly force when mortally threatened and that minorities are considerably more likely to use weapons in assaults on officers than are whites.[90] Complicating the picture further, Fyfe's study showed that minority officers are involved in the shootings of suspects more often than other officers, a finding that may be due to the assignment of minority officers to inner-city and ghetto areas. However, a later study by Fyfe, which analyzed police shootings in Memphis, Tennessee, found that black property offenders were twice as likely as whites to be shot by police.[91]

Although relatively few police officers ever fire their weapons at suspects during the course of their careers, those who do may become embroiled in social, legal, and personal complications. It is estimated that in an average year, 600 suspects are killed by public police in America, while another 1,200 are shot and wounded, and 1,800 are shot at and missed.[92] The personal side of police shootings is well summarized in the title of an article that appeared in *Police Magazine*. The article "I've Killed That Man Ten Thousand Times" demonstrates how police officers who have to use their weapons may be haunted by years of depression and despair.[93] Not long ago, according to author Anne Cohen, all departments did to help an officer who had shot someone was to "give him enough bullets to reload his gun." The stress and trauma that police officers suffer from having shot someone are only now being realized, and many departments have yet to develop mechanisms for adequately dealing with them.[94]

> The stress and trauma that police officers suffer from having shot someone are only now being realized, and many departments have yet to develop mechanisms for adequately dealing with them.

Police officers have particular difficulty dealing with instances of "suicide by cop," in which individuals bent on dying engage in behavior that causes responding officers to resort to deadly force. On March 10, 2005, for example, John T. Garczynski, Jr., a father of two preteen boys, died in a hail of 26 bullets fired by police officers who had surrounded his vehicle in a Boca Raton, Florida, condominium parking lot.[95] Garczynski, a Florida Power and Light Company employee, had been separated from his wife months earlier and appeared to have been despondent over financial problems and the breakup of his marriage. The night before his death, Garczynski met his wife at a bowling alley and handed her a packet containing a suicide note, a typed obituary, and a eulogy to be read at his funeral. After he left, Garczynski's wife called police, and officers used the help of a cell phone company to locate Garczynski. As deputies surrounded his 2003 Ford Explorer, he attempted to start the vehicle. One of the officers yelled "Freeze" and then "Let me see your hands." It was at that point, deputies said, that Garczynski pointed a gun at them and they fired.

Rebecca Stincelli, author of the book *Suicide by Cop: Victims from Both Sides of the Badge*,[96] says an incident like that involving Garczynski can be devastating for police officers. "In the past, people have used rope, a gun, gas, or jumped off a building. A police officer is just another method," said Stincelli. "They say it's nothing personal. [But] they are wrong. It's very personal" for the officers involved.[97] The FBI says that "suicide-by-cop incidents are painful and damaging experiences for the surviving families, the communities, and all law enforcement professionals."[98]

A study of fatal shootings by Los Angeles police officers found that an astonishingly large number—more than 10%—could be classified as "suicide by cop."[99] Recently, researchers have identified three main "suicide by cop" categories: direct confrontations, in which suicidal subjects instigate attacks on police officers for

UCLA students protesting the police use of Tasers. This less-lethal weapon, manufactured by Taser International, incapacitates potential attackers by delivering an electrical shock to the person's nervous system. The technology is intended to reduce injury rates to both suspects and officers. Why do some people oppose its use?

REED SAXON/AP Wide World Photos

■ **theme**   What are less-lethal weapons? What is their purpose? What might the risks be in using these weapons?

■ **less-lethal weapon**   A weapon that is designed to disable, capture, or immobilize—but not kill—a suspect. Occasional deaths do result from the use of such weapons, however.

■ **lecture note**   Explain the concept of discretion in policing and discuss the implications of allowing officers to have discretion in carrying out official duties, including the decision to arrest.

■ **theme**   Why is discretion an essential part of policing? What do you think might happen if police discretion was curtailed or eliminated altogether?

■ **police discretion**   The opportunity for police officers to exercise choice in their enforcement activities.

the purpose of dying; disturbed interventions, in which potentially suicidal subjects take advantage of police intervention in their suicide attempt in order to die; and criminal interventions, in which criminal suspects prefer death to capture and arrest.[100]

Less-Lethal Weapons

Less-lethal weapons offer what may be a problem-specific solution to potential incidents of "suicide by cop," as well as a generic solution to at least some charges of use of excessive force. Less-lethal weapons are designed to disable, capture, or immobilize a suspect rather than kill him or her. Efforts to provide law enforcement officers with less-lethal weapons like stun guns Tasers (aka conducted energy devices), rubber bullets, beanbag projectiles, and pepper spray began in 1987.[101] More exotic types of less-lethal weapons, however, are on the horizon. They include snare nets fired from shotguns, disabling sticky foam that can be sprayed from a distance, microwave beams that heat the tissue of people exposed to them until they desist in their illegal or threatening behavior or lose consciousness, and high-tech guns that fire bolts of electromagnetic energy at a target, causing painful sensory overload and violent muscle spasms. The National Institute of Justice says, "The goal is to give line officers effective and safe alternatives to lethal force."[102]

As their name implies, however, less-lethal weapons are not always safe. On October 21, 2004, for example, 21-year-old Emerson College student Victoria Snelgrove died hours after being hit in the eye with a plastic pepper-spray-filled projectile that police officers fired at a rowdy crowd celebrating the Red Sox victory over the New York Yankees in the final game of the American League Championship Series in 2004. Witnesses said that officers fired the projectile into the crowd after a reveler near Fenway Park threw a bottle at a mounted Boston police officer.[103] Learn more about less-lethal weapons from the FBI at **http://www.justicestudies.com/pubs/lesslethal.pdf.**

Discretion and the Individual Officer

Even as law enforcement agencies struggle to adapt to the threats posed by international terrorism, individual officers continue to retain considerable discretion in terms of their actions. **Police discretion** refers to the exercise of choice by law enforcement officers in the decision to investigate or apprehend, the disposition of suspects, the carrying out of official duties, and the application of sanctions. As one

author has observed, "Police authority can be, at once, highly specific and exceedingly vague."[104] Decisions to stop and question someone, arrest a suspect, and perform many other police tasks are made solely by individual officers and must often be made quickly and in the absence of any close supervision. Kenneth Culp Davis, who pioneered the study of police discretion, says, "The police make policy about what law to enforce, how much to enforce it, against whom, and on what occasions."[105] To those who have contact with the police, the discretionary authority exercised by individual officers is of greater significance than all of the department manuals and official policy statements combined.

Patrolling officers often decide against a strict enforcement of the law, preferring instead to handle situations informally. Minor law violations, crimes committed out of the officer's presence where the victim refuses to file a complaint, and certain violations of the criminal law where the officer suspects that sufficient evidence to obtain a conviction is lacking may all lead to the discretionary action short of arrest. The widest exercise of discretion is in routine situations involving relatively less serious violations of the law, but serious criminal behavior may occasionally result in discretionary decisions not to make an arrest. Underage drinking, possession of controlled substances, and assault are examples of crimes in which on-the-scene officers may choose to issue a warning or offer a referral instead of making an arrest. Figure 8-6 illustrates

> The widest exercise of police discretion is in routine situations involving relatively less serious violations of the law.

An officer writing a traffic ticket. Police officers wield a great amount of discretion, and an individual officer's decision to enforce a particular law or to effect an arrest is based not just on the law's applicability to a particular set of circumstances but also on the officer's subjective judgment about the nature of appropriate enforcement activity. What other factors influence discretion?

David Young-Wolff/PhotoEdit Inc.

CJ | NEWS

Is the Video Recording of Police Activity in a Public Place Legal?

New York City police officers arrest a demonstrator while a bevy of news photographers record the scene. Courts have held that the photographic recording of police activities that occur in public is permissible unless the recording interferes with or hinders those activities.

Simon Glik was walking in the Boston Common in 2007, when he saw police officers putting a suspected drug offender into a chokehold and heard someone yell, "You are hurting him, stop."

Glik pulled out his cell phone camera and began recording the scene, but the officers arrested him for filming them and confiscated the device. Taking him to jail, they charged him under a state law that bars secret recordings, even though the officers could plainly see the cell phone.

The charges against Glik were quickly dismissed in municipal court, but Boston Police continued over the next four years to seek qualified immunity for similar arrests. In August 2011, however, a federal appeals court once and for all denied any qualified immunity claims and confirmed that the video recording of an on-duty police officer is protected by the First Amendment, which also guarantees freedom of speech. An internal investigation by the Boston Police Department in January 2012 concluded that officers had shown poor judgment in arresting Glik, and the city agreed two months later to pay $170,000 to settle his civil rights lawsuit against the city.

Today, six years after the original incident, just about every cell phone in America has a camera built into it, and recordings like the one

Glik's made are occurring regularly. Yet arrests continue. In May 2011, for example, a police officer in Rochester, New York, arrested a woman standing in her own yard, taking pictures of him searching a man's car.

Before arresting her, the officer said, "I don't feel safe with you standing behind me." Clearly, some officers are not comfortable being filmed, even when doing nothing wrong. Perhaps they recall that when camera phones didn't exist some 20 years ago, a bystander's filming of the Los Angeles police beating of Rodney King literally caused a riot in South Central LA, resulting in $1 billion in property damage. Two of the officers caught on videotape in the King incident were sentenced to 30 months in prison.

In the *Glik* decision, the appeals court welcomed the filming the police by citizens. "Ensuring the public's right to gather information about their officials," the court declared, "not only aids in the uncovering of abuses but also may have a salutary effect on the functioning of government more generally." In any case, officers who make such arrests today often end up suffering public scorn and undergoing investigation by their department's internal affairs division. The Rochester woman who was mentioned earlier was acquitted and, after her video went viral on the Internet, Rochester police made an apology and initiated training programs about the right of people to record police activity that takes place in public.

Training programs may not be enough, however. Philadelphia police were trained on the use of cameras by members of the public, but in March 2012, they arrested a college student for taking photos of officers conducting a traffic stop in front of his house. He was charged with obstruction of justice, resisting arrest, and disorderly conduct.

Although the use of video cameras when recording police activity has generally been supported by the courts, the law on making recordings is not that easy to follow. For example, unlike photography and video, there is no general right to make audio recordings—especially those made without police knowledge. As Michael Allison found out in the tiny town of Bridgeport, Illinois, secret audio recordings are definitely out-of-bounds in many jurisdictions.

Told that there would be no court reporter provided for his legal hearing in late 2011, Allison taped it on a small digital recorder in his pocket, without telling the judge. When he was found out, Allison was arrested and charged with felony eavesdropping. Four more counts were added when other secret recordings were detected on his device, meaning he faced a possible 75-year prison sentence. The charges were thrown out, but the Illinois Attorney General later appealed the ruling to get them reinstated.

Resources: "Police Reverse Stance on Taping of Officers' Actions," *The Boston Globe*, January 10, 2012, http://www.bostonglobe.com/metro/2012/01/10/police-reverse-stance -taping-officers-actions/va6glfwq9L1mUElv6a33HK/story.html; "Chief Sheppard, the RPD, and Emily Good," *Rochester City Newspaper*, September 2, 2011, http://www.rochester citynewspaper.com/news/blog/2011/09/Chief-Sheppard-the-RPD-and-Emily-Good/; and "Eavesdropping Case in Tiny Illinois Town Makes Big Waves," *Chicago Tribune*, January 2, 2012, http://articles.chicagotribune.com/2012-01-02/news/ct-met-eavesdropping-law-sidebar-20120102_1_eavesdropping-case-tiny-illinois-town-big-waves.

a number of factors that studies of police discretion have found to influence the discretionary decisions of individual officers.

Racial Profiling and Biased Policing

In December, 2014, the U.S. Department of Justice released a 12-page document intended to provide guidance for federal law

enforcement officers regarding the use of personal characteristics in routine investigations. The document, which followed in the wake of two highly controversial deaths of black men at the hands of local police officers in Ferguson, Missouri, and New York City, stated that "Even-handed law enforcement is . . . central to the integrity, legitimacy, and efficacy of all Federal law enforcement activities."[106] It set forth two standards that were intended to "guide use by Federal law enforcement officers of race, ethnicity, gender, national origin, religion, sexual

■ **theme**   What is racial profiling? Why is it becoming such a problem in policing today? Why is behavioral profiling considered to be acceptable while racial profiling is not?

■ **activity**   Have students create a questionnaire designed to assess the degree of racial profiling by the police that respondents feel they have experienced, if any. Administer the questionnaire to people on campus, on the Web, or at a local shopping center.

■ **racial profiling (biased policing)**   Any police-initiated action that relies on the race, ethnicity, national origin, sexual orientation, gender, or religion, rather than (1) the behavior of an individual, or (2) information that leads the police to a particular individual who has been identified as being, or having been, engaged in criminal activity.

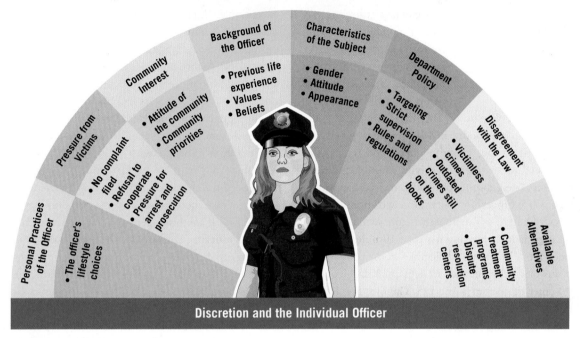

FIGURE 8-6 | Discretion and the Individual Officer
Source: Pearson Education, Inc.

orientation, or gender identity in law enforcement or intelligence activities." Those standards read:

1. In making routine or spontaneous law enforcement decisions, such as ordinary traffic stops, Federal law enforcement officers may not use race, ethnicity, gender, national origin, religion, sexual orientation, or gender identity to any degree, except that officers may rely on the listed characteristics in a specific suspect description. This prohibition applies even where the use of a listed characteristic might otherwise be lawful.

2. In conducting all activities other than routine or spontaneous law enforcement activities, Federal law enforcement officers may consider race, ethnicity, gender, national origin, religion, sexual orientation, or gender identity only to the extent that there is trustworthy information, relevant to the locality or time frame, that links persons possessing a particular listed characteristic to an identified criminal incident, scheme, or organization, a threat to national or homeland security, a violation of Federal immigration law, or an authorized intelligence activity. In order to rely on a listed characteristic, law enforcement officers must also reasonably believe that the law enforcement, security, or intelligence activity to be undertaken is merited under the totality of the

circumstances, such as any temporal exigency and the nature of any potential harm to be averted. This standard applies even where the use of a listed characteristic might otherwise be lawful.[107]

The document, which is available at **http://justicestudies .com/pubs/racialprofiling_feds.pdf**, includes a number of useful examples to guide law enforcement officers in their daily activities. While it applies only to federal agencies, the principles set forth in the document were meant to guide policing at all levels throughout the United States.

Racial profiling, also called biased policing, first received national attention in the late 1990s. Racial profiling can be defined as any police action initiated on the basis of the race, ethnicity, national origin, sexual orientation, gender, or religion of a suspect, rather than on the behavior of that individual or on information that leads the police to a particular individual who has been identified as being, or having been, engaged in criminal activity.[108]

It should be noted that racial profiling is significantly different from the practice of *behavioral profiling*, which makes use of a person's demeanor, actions, bearing, and manner to identify an offender before he can act.[109] As such, behavioral profiling can be both a useful predictive and proactive tool. Behavioral profiling has been successfully used, for example, by Israeli security forces to prevent acts of terrorism. In that country, potential offenders have been identified by their simple actions like wearing loose clothing (to conceal bombs or weapons), smoking on the Sabbath (something that Orthodox Jews would not do), or simply fidgeting and avoiding eye contact while standing in line.

Racial profiling is different because it uses an individual's personal characteristics as the sole or predominate factor in determining criminal intent or culpability.[110] The alleged use by police of racial profiling may take a number of forms. Minority accounts of disparate treatment at the hands of police officers include being stopped for being "in the wrong car" (e.g., a police stop of an African American youth driving an expensive late-model BMW); being stopped and questioned for being in the wrong neighborhood (i.e., police stops of members of minority groups driving through traditionally white residential neighborhoods); and perceived harassment at the hands of police officers for petty traffic violations like underinflated tires, failure to signal properly before switching lanes, vehicle equipment failures, driving less than 10 miles per hour above the speed limit, or having an illegible license plate.[111]

> Racial profiling uses a person's race as the sole or predominate factor in determining criminal intent or culpability.

Profiling was originally intended to help catch drug couriers attempting to enter the country. The U.S. Customs Service and the Drug Enforcement Administration developed a number of "personal indicators" that seemed, from the agency's day-to-day enforcement experiences, to be associated with increased likelihood of law violation. Among the indicators were these: speaking Spanish; entering the United States on flights originating in particular Central and South American countries; being an 18- to 32-year-old male; having purchased tickets with cash; and having a short planned stay (often of only a day or two) in the United States. Federal agents frequently used these criteria in deciding which airline passengers to search and which bags to inspect.

> *Profiling* was originally intended to help catch drug couriers attempting to enter the country.

Racial profiling has been derisively referred to as "driving while black" or "driving while brown," although it may also apply to situations other than those involving traffic violations. Racial profiling came to the attention of the public when police in New Jersey and Maryland were accused of unfair treatment of black motorists and admitted that race was a factor in traffic stops. Additional information about racial profiling studies focused on practices in New Jersey can be found in the expanded book.

In 2003, in response to widespread public outcry over racial profiling, the U.S. Department of Justice banned its practice in all federal law enforcement agencies, except in cases that involve the possible identification of terrorist suspects.[112] At the time, the DOJ said, "The guidance provides that in making routine law enforcement decisions—such as deciding which motorists to stop for traffic infractions—consideration of the driver's race or ethnicity is absolutely forbidden."[113] In contrast to the 2014 Department of Justice policy discussed at the start of this section, the 2003 ban was limited to race and ethnicity—and did not extend to religion, national origin, or sexual orientation.

Those who defend the use of racial profiling by the police argue that it is not a bigoted practice when based on facts (such as when a police department decides to increase patrols in a housing area occupied primarily by minorities because of exceptionally high crime rates there) or when significant criminal potential exists among even a few members of a group. An example of the latter is the widespread public suspicions that focused on Arabs and Arab Americans following the terrorist attacks of September 11, 2001. As soon as it was publicly announced that the hijackers had been of Middle Eastern origin, some flight crews demanded that Arab-looking passengers be removed from their airplanes before takeoff, and passengers refused to fly with people who looked like Arabs.[114]

None of this is to say, of course, that race, ethnicity, or other personal characteristics somehow inherently causes crime (or that it somehow causes poverty or increases the risk of victimization). If anything, personal characteristics may simply display a significant correlation with certain types of crime, as they do with certain kinds of victimization. Hence, although the *real* causes of criminality may be socialization into criminal subcultures, economically deprived neighborhoods, a lack of salable job skills, and intergenerational poverty, and not race per se, to some law enforcement officers race provides one more indicator of the likelihood of criminality. David Cole, a professor at Georgetown University's Law Center, for example, notes that in the minds of many police officials, "racial and ethnic disparities reflect not discrimination [or bigotry] but higher rates of offenses among minorities."[115] "Nationwide," says Cole, "blacks are 13 times more likely to be sent to state prisons for drug convictions than are whites, so it would seem rational for police to assume that all other things being equal, a black driver is more likely than a white driver to be carrying drugs." Similarly, a 2014 study showed that officer-initiated traffic stops were most likely to be influenced by criminal history, and not by the race of the driver—with black drivers being "1.8 times more likely to possess a criminal history relative to white citizens."[116] Statistics like this, of course, may further enhance police focus on minorities and may result in even more arrests, thereby reinforcing the beliefs on which racial profiling by some enforcement agents is based. Such observations led esteemed sociologist Amitai Etzioni following the turn of the century to declare that racial profiling, even though repugnant to most, is not necessarily racist.[117] Moreover, warned Etzioni, an end to racial profiling "would penalize those African American communities with high incidences of violent crime" because they would lose the levels of policing that they need to remain relatively secure.

Regardless of arguments offered in support of racial profiling as an enforcement tool, the practice has been widely condemned as being contrary to basic ethical principles, and national public

For each of the following situations, please say if you think the practice known as "racial profiling" is widespread or not?

Percentage saying "yes, widespread"

When motorists are stopped on roads and highways
- Non-Hispanic whites 50%
- Blacks 67%
- Hispanics 63%

When passengers are stopped at security checkpoints in airports
- Non-Hispanic whites 40%
- Blacks 48%
- Hispanics 54%

When shoppers in malls or stores are questioned about possible theft
- Non-Hispanic whites 45%
- Blacks 65%
- Hispanics 56%

FIGURE 8-7 | Racial Profiling and Biased Policing, Perceptions by Race

Source: From The Gallup Poll, http://www.gallup.com. Reprinted with permission of The Gallup Organization.

opinion polls conducted by the Gallup Organization show that more than 80% of respondents are morally opposed to the practice of racial profiling by the police,[118] although beliefs about the use of racial profiling vary widely by race (Figure 8-7). Figure 8-8 provides a map showing states that have officially banned the practice of racial profiling.[119] From a more pragmatic viewpoint, however, racial profiling is unacceptable because it weakens the public's confidence in the police, thereby decreasing police–citizen trust and cooperation.[120]

Racially Biased Policing

A decade ago, the Police Executive Research Forum (PERF) released a detailed report titled *Racially Biased Policing: A Principled Response*.[121] PERF researchers surveyed more than 1,000 police executives, analyzed material from more than 250 law enforcement agencies, and sought input from law enforcement agency personnel, community activists, and civil rights leaders about racial bias in policing. Researchers concluded that "the vast majority of law enforcement officers—of all ranks, nationwide—are dedicated men and women committed to serving all citizens with fairness and dignity."[122] Most police officers, said the report, share an intolerance for racially biased policing. The report's authors noted that some police behaviors may be misinterpreted as biased when, in fact, the officer is just doing his or her job. "The good officer continually scans the environment for anomalies to normalcy—for conditions, people and behavior that are unusual for that environment," they said. "In learning and practicing their craft, officers quickly develop a sense for what is normal and expected, and conversely, for what is not."[123] Hence for officers of any race to take special notice of unknown young white males who unexpectedly appear in a traditionally African American neighborhood, for example, might be nothing other than routine police procedure. Such an observation, however, is not in itself sufficient for an investigatory stop but might be used in conjunction with other trustworthy and relevant information already in the officer's possession—such as the officer's prior knowledge that young white men have been visiting a particular apartment complex in the neighborhood to purchase drugs—to justify such a stop.

The PERF report makes many specific recommendations to help police departments be free of bias. One recommendation, for example, says that "supervisors should monitor activity reports for evidence of improper practices and patterns. They should conduct spot-checks and regular sampling of in-car videotapes, radio transmissions, and in-car computer and central communications records to determine if both formal and informal communications are professional and free from racial bias and other disrespect."[124] Read the entire PERF report at **http://www.justicestudies.com/pubs/rbiasp.pdf**.

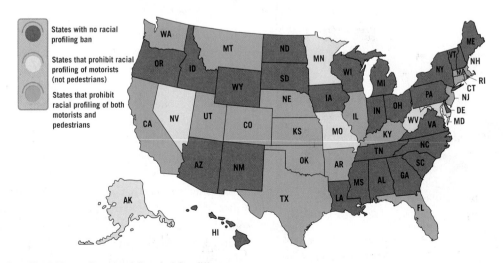

FIGURE 8-8 | States That Have Banned Racial Profiling

Source: Amnesty International USA, *Threat and Humiliation: Racial Profiling, Domestic Security, and Human Rights in the United States* (New York: Amnesty International USA Publications, 2004), p. 6. http://www.amnestyusa.org. © Amnesty International USA. Reprinted with permission.

freedom OR safety? YOU decide

Was the NYPD's Monitoring of Muslim Groups a Form of Religious Profiling?

In 2013, civil rights lawyers filed suit in federal court asking for the appointment of an independent commission to review the New York Police Department's monitoring of Muslim groups. Officials with the NYPD admitted to having conducted surveillance of Islamic mosques and Muslim groups in and around New York City over the past few years. At times, the surveillance involved planting undercover officers in Islamic groups and the monitoring of Muslim student groups at 16 colleges in the city and surrounding areas. The department was seeking to identify radical Islamists and Al-Qaida sympathizers who might represent a danger to the city's inhabitants.

Once news of the program became public, it drew quick criticism from many corners. Islamic leaders felt that it was a thinly disguised form of racial and religious profiling and that it was aimed unfairly at them and at members of their communities. New York City Comptroller John Liu also questioned the monitoring program, saying, "We should not as a matter of policy profile people based on religion or race—it goes against everything this city stands for." Robert Jackson, the sole Muslim on the New York City council, added, "When you step on one religious group, Muslims, then you're stepping on every religious group."

Even some law enforcement officials questioned the program. Michael Ward, director of the FBI's Newark office, told reporters that his agency had spent years building up trust in Muslim neighborhoods. "What we have now," he said, "is (Muslim communities) . . . that they're not sure they trust law enforcement in general, they're fearing being watched, they're starting to withdraw their activities." "The impact of that sinking tide of cooperation," said Ward, "means that we don't have our finger on the pulse of what's going on in the community, as well—we're less knowledgeable, we have blind spots, and there's more risk."

At the time, New York Police Commissioner Raymond Kelly made no apologies for the intelligence program and said that he and Mayor Michael Bloomberg are committed to doing whatever is needed to lawfully protect the city. "It is not as if would-be terrorists aren't trying," Kelly told city council members. "To the contrary, they've attempted to kill New Yorkers in 14 different plots." In mid-2014, however, after William Bratton took over as police commissioner, the monitoring program was discontinued and the unit's officers were assigned to other duties. One NYPD official, who chose to remain unnamed, told reporters, "it sends the message that the NYPD is going to back down on its counterterrorism effort in the name of political correctness."

You Decide

Was the NYPD's monitoring program really a form of religious and ethnic profiling? Should such profiling be permitted in order to safeguard the city? Why or why not?

References: Joseph Goldstein, "Lawyers Say Surveillance of Muslims Flouts Accord," New York Times, http://www.nytimes.com/2013/02/04/nyregion/police-department-flouts-surveillance-guidelines-lawyers-say.html (accessed February 4, 2013); Adam Peck, "FBI Officials: News of NYPD Muslim Surveillance Program Is 'Starting to Have a Negative Impact,'" Think Progress, March 8, 2012, http://thinkprogress.org/security/2012/03/08/440780/fbi-official-nypd-muslim-surveillance/?mobile=nc (accessed May 1, 2012); Michael Howard Saul, "Speaker Quinn Voices Support for NYPD Monitoring of Muslims," Wall Street Journal, February 27, 2012, http://blogs.wsj.com/metropolis/2012/02/27/speaker-quinn-voices-support-for-nypd-monitoring-of-muslims (accessed May 1, 2012); "NYPD Police Commissioner Ray Kelly Not Sorry about NJ Muslim Surveillance," Huffington Post, February 27, 2012, http://www.huffingtonpost.com/2012/02/27/nypd-police-commissioner-_n_1304710.html (accessed May 1, 2012); and "New York Police End Muslim Surveillance Program," USA Today, April 15, 2014, http://www.usatoday.com/story/news/nation/2014/04/15/nypd-muslim-surveillance/7758229 (accessed February 5, 2015).

Henny Ray Abrams/AP Wide World Photos

An elderly woman shows her displeasure with Transportation Security Administration (TSA) security requirements. Some people fear that the use of profiling techniques could unfairly discriminate against members of certain racial and ethnic groups. Others suggest that the careful use of profiling can provide an important advantage in an age of scarce resources. With which perspective do you agree?

Police Civil Liability

In 2013, officials with the city of Chicago, Illinois, agreed to pay $22.5 million to settle a lawsuit brought against the city's police department.[125] The award, paid to Chistina Eilman, members of her family, and her attorneys, was thought to be the largest amount of money ever offered to a single victim of police misconduct. The civil suit against the city stemmed from the arrest and relatively quick release of Eilman after she had spent less than 24 hours in police custody. Eilman, who was a 21-year-old small diminutive white woman at the time of her arrest, had been taken into custody at Chicago's Midway airport in May 2006 after airport officials alerted police officers to her erratic and aggressive behavior. She was taken to a police station where officers learned that she was suffering from bipolar disorder. Released the next day around sundown, she was offered no assistance as she stepped onto the streets of a gang-infested African American neighborhood. Soon after, she wandered away from the police

■ **theme**   What are the major sources of police civil liability? In what way might each of these sources affect individual police departments? Individual officers? Administrators (chiefs)? How can the potential for civil liability be reduced by all concerned?

■ **theme**   How might discretion lead to civil liability? What can departments do to train officers to use discretion wisely and to avoid major sources of civil liability through the proper exercise of discretion?

station, and was lured into a high-crime housing project, where a number of young men threatened to attack her sexually. In what appears to have been an effort to escape, Eilman flung herself out of a seven-story window and suffered serious injury—including a shattered pelvis, many broken bones, and serious brain injury. Although she survived, she lives today in a permanent childlike mental state. Faulting the police department, Chief Judge Frank Easterbrook of the Seventh U.S. Circuit Court of Appeals wrote that officers "might as well have released her into the lion's den at the Brookfield Zoo."

Civil liability suits brought against law enforcement personnel are of two types: state and federal. Suits brought in state courts have generally been the more common form of civil litigation involving police officers. In recent years, however, an increasing number of suits have been brought in federal courts on the claim that the civil rights of the plaintiff, as guaranteed by federal law, were denied.

Common Sources of Civil Suits

Police officers may become involved in a variety of situations that could result in civil suits against the officers, their superiors, and their departments. One of the earliest lawsuits (*Thurman v. City of Torrington*) was brought against the city of Torrington, Connecticut, police department by a woman who sued after she had been attacked, stabbed, and nearly killed by her husband. The woman claimed that police had ignored restraining orders that had been issued against her husband, telling him to stay away from his wife. The woman who brought the suit was awarded $2.3 million.

Major sources of police civil liability are listed in Table 8-3. Charles Swanson, an expert in police procedure, says that the most common sources of lawsuits against the police are "assault, battery, false imprisonment, and malicious prosecution."[126]

Of all complaints brought against the police, assault charges are the best known, being, as they are, subject to high media visibility. Less visible, but not uncommon, are civil suits charging the police with false arrest or false imprisonment. In the 1986 case of *Malley v. Briggs*,[127] the U.S. Supreme Court held that a police officer who effects an arrest or conducts a search on the basis of an improperly issued warrant may be liable for monetary damages when a reasonably well-trained officer, under the same circumstances, "would have known that his affidavit failed to establish probable cause and that he should not have applied for the warrant." Significantly, the Court ruled that an officer "cannot excuse his own default by pointing to the greater incompetence of the magistrate."[128] That is, the officer, rather than

TABLE 8-3 | **Major Sources of Police Civil Liability**

Failure to protect property in police custody	Negligence in the care of suspects in police custody
Failure to render proper emergency medical assistance	Failure to prevent a foreseeable crime
Lack of due regard for the safety of others	False imprisonment
Failure to aid private citizens	Unnecessary assault or battery
False arrest	Violations of constitutional rights
Inappropriate use of deadly force	Racial profiling
Malicious prosecution	Patterns of unfair and inequitable treatment

Source: Pearson Education, Inc.

the judge who issued the warrant, is ultimately responsible for establishing the basis for pursuing the arrest or search.

When an officer makes an arrest without just cause or simply impedes an individual's right to leave the scene without good reason, he or she may also be liable for the charge of false arrest. Officers who "throw their weight around" are especially subject to this type of suit, grounded as it is on the abuse of police authority. Because generally employers may be sued for the negligent or malicious actions of their employees, many police departments are being named as codefendants in lawsuits today.

Civil suits are also brought against officers whose actions are deemed negligent. High-speed vehicle pursuits are especially dangerous because of the potential for injury to innocent bystanders. In the case of *Biscoe v. Arlington County* (1984),[129] for example, Alvin Biscoe was awarded $5 million after he lost both legs as a consequence of a high-speed chase while he was waiting to cross the street. Biscoe, an innocent bystander, was struck by a police car that went out of control. The officer driving the car had violated department policies prohibiting high-speed chases, and the court found that he had not been properly trained.

> High-speed vehicle pursuits are especially dangerous because of the potential for injury to innocent bystanders.

The FBI states that "a traffic accident constitutes the most common terminating event in an urban pursuit."[130] Some cities are actively replacing high-speed vehicle pursuits with surveillance technologies employing unmanned aerial vehicles (UAVs). Although helicopters have long been used in this capacity, the advent of UAV technology promises to make the tracking of fleeing suspects much quicker and far safer for all involved.

Departments may protect themselves from lawsuits to a significant degree by providing proper and adequate training to

CJ | ISSUES
Investigating Crime in a Multicultural Setting

Two decades ago, the Washington, D.C.–based National Crime Prevention Council (NCPC) published an important guide for American law enforcement officers who work with multicultural groups. The principles it contains can be applied equally to most foreign-born individuals living in the United States and are especially important to patrol officers and criminal investigators.

The NCPC guide points out that it is important for well-intentioned newcomers to this country to learn that the law enforcement system in the United States is not a national police force but a series of local, state, and federal agencies that take seriously their obligation to "serve and protect" law-abiding residents. Newcomers need to know that police officers can teach them how to protect themselves and their families from crime. Many immigrants, especially political refugees, come from countries in which the criminal justice system is based on tyranny, repression, and fear.

The NCPC suggests that law enforcement officers and other members of the criminal justice system can help ease this transition by working not only to communicate with immigrants but also to understand them and the complexities of their native cultures. The mere absence of conflict in a neighborhood does not mean that residents of different cultures have found harmony and a cooperative working relationship, says the NCPC. True multicultural integration occurs when various cultures reach a comfortable day-to-day interaction marked by respect, interest, and caring.

Communities in which immigrants and law enforcement have established close positive ties benefit considerably, according to the NCPC. Immigrants gain greater access to police and other services,

such as youth programs, victims' assistance, parenting classes, medical assistance programs, business networking, and neighborhood groups. Crime decreases in communities where law enforcement officers help immigrants learn to protect themselves against crime.

For police officers working in communities in which "language is a serious barrier between cultures," the NCPC suggests the following pointers for communicating more effectively:

- Be patient when speaking with someone who does not clearly understand your language. Speak slowly and distinctly. Be willing to repeat words or phrases if necessary. Remember that shouting never helps a nonnative speaker understand better.
- Be careful with your choice of words, selecting those that are clear, straightforward, and simple to understand. Avoid colloquialisms and slang.
- Allow extra time for investigation when the people involved have not mastered English.
- Be sure that anyone who serves as an interpreter is fully qualified and has had experience. Interpreting under pressure is a difficult task; lack of training can lead to mistakes.
- Be candid about your ability to speak or understand a language. Trying to "fake it" just leads to confusion, misunderstanding, and misspent time.
- Never assume that someone is less intelligent just because he or she doesn't speak English well.

Visit the National Crime Prevention Council via http://www.ncpc.org.

Reference: Adapted from National Crime Prevention Council, *Building and Crossing Bridges: Refugees and Law Enforcement Working Together* (Washington, DC: NCPC, 1994).
Source: Pearson Education, Inc.

---

their personnel, and by creating regulations limiting the authority of employees. The Justice Department's investigation into the New Orleans Police Department, for example, which was mentioned earlier in this chapter, found that "the Department's failure to provide sufficient guidance, training, and support to its officers," along with "its failure to implement systems to ensure officers are wielding their authority effectively and safely," could be addressed by implementing policies and practices to "properly recruit, train, and supervise officers."[131] "This understanding," the report's authors pointed out, "serves as the foundation upon which to build sustainable reform that will reduce . . . and prevent crime more effectively, police all parts of the New Orleans' community fairly, respect the rights of all New Orleans' residents and visitors, and prepare and protect officers."

Law enforcement supervisors may be the object of lawsuits by virtue of the fact that they are responsible for the actions of their officers. If it can be shown that supervisors were negligent in hiring (as when someone with a history of alcoholism, mental problems, sexual deviance, or drug abuse is employed) or if supervisors failed in their responsibility to properly train officers before arming and deploying them, they may be found liable for damages.

In the 1989 case of the *City of Canton, Ohio v. Harris*,[132] the U.S. Supreme Court ruled that a "failure to train" can become

the basis for legal liability on the part of a municipality where the "failure to train amounts to deliberate indifference to the rights of persons with whom the police come in contact."[133] In that case, Geraldine Harris was arrested and taken to the Canton, Ohio, police station. While at the station, she slumped to the floor several times. Officers left her on the floor and did not call for medical assistance. Upon release, Harris's family took her to a local hospital, where she was found to be suffering from several emotional ailments. Harris was hospitalized for a week and received follow-up outpatient treatment for the next year.

> Law enforcement supervisors may be the object of lawsuits by virtue of the fact that they are responsible for the actions of their officers.

In the 1997 case of *Board of the County Commissioners of Bryan County, Oklahoma v. Brown*, however, the Supreme Court ruled that to establish liability, plaintiffs must show that "the municipal action in question was not simply negligent, but was taken with 'deliberate indifference' as to its known or obvious consequences."[134] Learn more about vehicle pursuits and the Fourth Amendment at **http://www.justicestudies.com/ubs/pursuits.pdf**. Law enforcement training is the topic of the FBI article at **http://justicestudies.com/pubs/letraining.pdf**.

A police car destroyed during a high-speed chase. Research shows that most of the suspects chased by police are not violent crimi-nals, and high-speed chases are especially dangerous because of their potential to injure innocent bystanders. When injuries do occur, a chase might provide a lawful basis for a civil suit against officers and their departments. How might a department protect itself from these kinds of suits?

freedom OR safety? YOU decide

Law Enforcement and Data Encryption

On October 16, 2014, FBI Director James B. Comey spoke at Washington, D.C.'s famed Brookings Institution. His talk focused on what Comey called "Going Dark," or advances in technology that can effectively put everyday communica-tions beyond the reach of legitimate law enforcement inves-tigative authority. What follows are excerpts from Comey's speech:

Technology has forever changed the world we live in. We're online, in one way or another, all day long. Our phones and computers have become reflections of our personalities, our interests, and our identities. They hold much that is impor-tant to us. And with that comes a desire to protect our privacy and our data. . . .

But the FBI has a sworn duty to keep every American safe from crime and terrorism, and technology has become the tool of choice for some very dangerous people.

Unfortunately, the law hasn't kept pace with technology, and this disconnect has created a significant public safety problem. We call it "Going Dark," and what it means is this: Those charged with protecting our people aren't always able to access the evidence we need to prosecute crime and prevent terrorism. We have the legal authority to intercept and access communications and information pursuant to court order, but we often lack the technical ability to do so.

FBI Director, James B. Comey

We face two overlapping challenges. The first concerns real-time court-ordered interception of what we call "data in motion," such as phone calls, e-mail and text messages, and chat sessions. The second challenge concerns court-ordered

■ **theme**   What do you think of the idea of police immunity from prosecution? How far should it extend? Should everyone be responsible for what they do, even public employees, without shelter of immunity? Explain.

■ **lecture note**   Explain the importance of department policy in reducing civil liability.

access to data stored on our devices, such as e-mail, text messages, photos, and videos—or what we call "data at rest." And both real-time communication and stored data are increasingly encrypted. . . .

In the past, conducting electronic surveillance was more straightforward. We identified a target phone being used by a bad guy, with a single carrier. We obtained a court order for a wiretap, and, under the supervision of a judge, we collected the evidence we needed for prosecution.

Today, there are countless providers, networks, and means of communicating. We have laptops, smart phones, and tablets. We take them to work and to school, from the soccer field to Starbucks, over many networks, using any number of apps. And so do those conspiring to harm us. They use the same devices, the same networks, and the same apps to make plans, to target victims, and to concoct cover-up stories. And that makes it tough for us to keep up . . .

Some believe that the FBI has these phenomenal capabilities to access any information at any time—that we can get what we want, when we want it, by flipping some sort of switch. It may be true in the movies or on TV. It is simply not the case in real life. . . .

I want people to understand that law enforcement needs to be able to access communications and information to bring people to justice. We do so pursuant to the rule of law, with clear guidance and strict oversight. But even with lawful authority, we may not be able to access the evidence and the information we need. . . .

And if the challenges of real-time interception threaten to leave us in the dark, encryption threatens to lead all of us to a very dark place.

Encryption is nothing new. But the challenge to law enforcement and national security officials is markedly worse, with recent default encryption settings and encrypted devices and networks—all designed to increase security and privacy. . .

Encryption . . . . will have very serious consequences for law enforcement and national security agencies at every level. Sophisticated criminals will come to count on these means of evading detection. It's the equivalent of a closet that can't be opened. A safe that can't be cracked. And my question is, at what cost?

. . . . With Going Dark, those of us in law enforcement and public safety have a major fear of missing out—missing out on predators who exploit the most vulnerable among us . . . missing out on violent criminals who target our communities . . . missing out on a terrorist cell using social media to recruit, plan, and execute an attack.

Criminals and terrorists would like nothing more than for us to miss out. And the more we as a society rely on these devices, the more important they are to law enforcement and public safety officials. We have seen case after case—from homicides and car crashes to drug trafficking, domestic abuse, and child exploitation—where critical evidence came from smartphones, hard drives, and online communication.

. . . . I hope you know, given my history, that I'm a huge believer in the rule of law. But I also believe that no one in this country is beyond the law. I like and believe very much that we need to follow the letter of the law to examine the contents of someone's closet or someone's smart phone. But the notion that the marketplace could create something that would prevent that closet from ever being opened, even with a properly obtained court order, makes no sense to me.

It might be time to ask: Where are we, as a society? Are we no longer a country governed by the rule of law, where no one is above or beyond that law? Are we so mistrustful of government—and of law enforcement—that we are willing to let bad guys walk away?

There will come a day—and it comes every day in this business—where it will matter a great deal to innocent people that we in law enforcement can't access certain types of data or information, even with legal authorization. . . . .

Some have suggested there is a conflict between liberty and security. I disagree. At our best, we in law enforcement, national security, and public safety are looking for security that enhances liberty . . . . .

You Decide

How would you answer FBI Director Comey when he asks, "Are we so mistrustful of government—and of law enforcement— that we are willing to let bad guys walk away?"

Source: Adapted from James B. Comey, "Going Dark: Are Technology, Privacy, and Public Safety on a Collision Course?," address given at the Brookings Institution, Washington, DC, October 16, 2014. Full text is available at: http://www.justicestudies.com/pubs/goingdark.pdf.

Federal Lawsuits

In April, 2012, five former officers of the New Orleans Police Department were sentenced to terms of imprisonment ranging from 6 to 65 years for violating the civil rights of unarmed residents on the city's Danziger Bridge during the breakdown of social order that followed Hurricane Katrina.[135] The officers, who claimed they thought that the residents were armed looters, shot six people, killing two of them.

Civil suits alleging police misconduct that are filed in federal courts are often called **1983 lawsuits** because they are based on Section 1983 of Title 42 of the U.S. Code—an act passed by

■ **1983 lawsuit**   A civil suit brought under Title 42, Section 1983, of the U.S. Code against anyone who denies others their constitutional right to life, liberty, or property without due process of law.

■ ***Bivens* action**   A civil suit, based on the case of *Bivens* v. *Six Unknown Federal Agents*, brought against federal government officials for denying the constitutional rights of others.

Congress in 1871 to ensure the civil rights of men and women of all races. That act requires due process of law before any person can be deprived of life, liberty, or property and specifically provides redress for the denial of these constitutional rights by officials acting under color of state law. It reads as follows:

> Every person who, under color of any statute, ordinance, regulation, custom, or usage, of any State or Territory, subjects, or causes to be subjected, any citizen of the United States or other person within the jurisdiction thereof to the deprivation of any rights, privileges, or immunities secured by the Constitution and laws, shall be liable to the party injured in an action at law, suit in equity, or other proper proceeding for redress.[136]

A 1983 suit may be brought, for example, against officers who shoot suspects under questionable circumstances, thereby denying them their right to life without due process. Similarly, an officer who makes an arrest based on accusations that he or she knows to be untrue may be subject to a 1983 lawsuit.

Another type of liability action, this one directed specifically at federal officials or enforcement agents, is called a **_Bivens_ action**. The case of *Bivens* v. *Six Unknown Federal Agents* (1971)[137] established a path for legal action against agents enforcing federal laws, which is similar to that found in a 1983 suit. *Bivens* actions may be addressed against individuals but not against the United States or its agencies.[138] Federal officers have generally been granted a court-created qualified immunity and have been protected from suits where they were found to have acted in the belief that their action was consistent with federal law.[139]

In the past, the doctrine of sovereign immunity barred legal actions against state and local governments. Sovereign immunity was a legal theory that held that a governing body could not be sued because it made the law and therefore could not be bound by it. Immunity is a much more complex issue today. Some states have officially abandoned any pretext of immunity through legislative action. New York State, for example, has declared that public agencies are equally as liable as private agencies for violations of constitutional rights. Other states, like California, have enacted statutory provisions that define and limit governmental liability.[140] A number of state immunity statutes have been struck down by court decisions. In general, states are moving in the direction of setting dollar limits on liability and adopting federal immunity principles to protect individual officers, including "good-faith" and "reasonable-belief" rules.

At the federal level, the concept of sovereign immunity is embodied in the Federal Tort Claims Act (FTCA),[141] which grants broad immunity to federal government agencies engaged in discretionary activities. When a federal employee is sued for a wrongful or negligent act, the Federal Employees Liability Reform and Tort

Major Juanita Walker-Kirkland of the Miami Police Department, left, listening to Manjit Singh, right, chair of Sikh Mediawatch and Task Force, during a Building Cultural Competency training program. The training program was sponsored by the U.S. Department of Justice in hopes of improving community relations between law enforcement officials and diverse cultural and religious groups. Why are such programs important?

Compensation Act of 1988, commonly known as the Westfall Act, empowers the attorney general to certify that the employee was acting within the scope of his or her office or employment at the time of the incident. Upon certification, the employee is dismissed from the action, and the United States is substituted as defendant. The case then falls under the governance of the FTCA. (See Chapter 14 for more information on the FTCA.)

The U.S. Supreme Court has supported a type of qualified immunity for individual officers (as opposed to the agencies for which they work). This immunity "shields law enforcement officers from constitutional lawsuits if reasonable officers believe their actions to be lawful in light of clearly established law and the information the officers possess." The Supreme Court has also described qualified immunity as a defense "which shields public officials from actions for damages unless their conduct was unreasonable in light of clearly established law."[142] According to the Court, "[T]he qualified immunity doctrine's central objective is to protect public officials from undue interference with their duties and from potentially disabling threats of liability."[143] In the context of a warrantless arrest, the Court said in *Hunter* v. *Bryant* (1991),[144] "even law enforcement officials who reasonably but mistakenly conclude that probable cause is present are entitled to immunity."[145]

The doctrine of qualified immunity, as it exists today, rests largely on the 2001 U.S. Supreme Court decision of *Saucier* v. *Katz*,[146] in which the Court established a two-pronged test for assessing constitutional violations by government agents.[147] First, the court hearing the case must decide whether the facts, taken in the light most favorable to the party asserting the injury, show that the defendant's conduct violated a constitutional right. Second, the court must then decide whether that right was clearly established. For a right to be clearly established, the Court ruled, "it would be clear to a reasonable [defendant] that his conduct was unlawful in the situation he confronted." In summary, qualified immunity protects law enforcement agents from being sued for damages unless they violate clearly established law which a reasonable official in the agent's position would have known. The *Saucier* decision has recently faced substantial legal challenges, leading the Court to rule in *Pearson et al. v. Callahan*[148] (2009) that "the rigid *Saucier* procedure" has serious shortcomings. The Court noted that "*stare decisis* does not prevent this Court from determining whether the *Saucier* procedure should be modified or abandoned."

Criminal charges can also be brought against officers who appear to overstep legal boundaries or who act in violation of set standards. In 2001, for example, in the case of *Idaho v. Horiuchi*,[149] the Ninth U.S. Circuit Court of Appeals ruled that federal law enforcement officers are not immune from state prosecution where their actions violate state law "either through malice or excessive zeal." The case involved FBI sharpshooter Lon Horiuchi, who was charged with negligent manslaughter by prosecutors in Boundary County, Idaho, following the 1992 incident at Ruby Ridge.

Today, most police departments at both state and federal levels carry liability insurance to protect themselves against the severe financial damage that can result from the loss of a large civil suit. Some officers also acquire private policies that provide coverage in the event they are named as individuals in a civil suit. Both types of insurance policies generally cover legal fees up to a certain amount, regardless of the outcome of the case. Police departments that face civil prosecution because of the actions of an officer may find that legal and financial liability extends to supervisors, city managers, and the community itself. Where insurance coverage does not exist or is inadequate, city coffers may be nearly drained to meet the damages awarded.[150]

One study of a large sample of police chiefs throughout Texas found that most believed that lawsuits or the threat of civil litigation against the police makes it harder for individual officers to do their jobs. Most of the chiefs espoused the idea that adequate training, better screening of applicants, close supervision of officers, and "treating people fairly" all reduced the likelihood of lawsuits.[151]

SUMMARY

- The police personality is created through informal pressures on officers by a powerful police subculture that communicates values that support law enforcement interests. This chapter described the police personality as, among other things, authoritarian, conservative, honorable, loyal, cynical, dogmatic, hostile, prejudiced, secret, and suspicious.

- Various types of police corruption were described in this chapter, including "grass eating" and "meat eating." The latter includes the most serious forms of corruption, such as an officer's actively seeking illegal moneymaking opportunities through the exercise of his or her law enforcement duties. Ethics training was mentioned as part of a "reframing" strategy that emphasizes integrity in an effort to target police corruption. Also discussed was a recent U.S. Department of Justice report that focused on enhancing policing integrity and that cited a police department's culture of integrity as more important in shaping the ethics of police officers than hiring the "right" people.

- Police professionalism requires that today's law enforcement officers adhere to ethical codes and standards established by the profession. Police professionalism places important limits on the discretionary activities of individual enforcement personnel and helps officers and the departments they work for gain the respect and regard of the public they police.

- The dangers of police work are many and varied. They consist of violent victimization, disease, exposure to biological or chemical toxins, stressful encounters with suspects and victims, and on-the-job fatigue. Stress-management programs, combined with department policies designed to reduce exposure to dangerous situations and agency practices that support officers' needs, can all help combat the dangers and difficulties that police officers face in their day-to-day work.

- Law enforcement officers are authorized to use the amount of force that is reasonable and necessary in a particular situation. Many officers have encounters where the use of force is appropriate. Nonetheless, studies show that the police use force in fewer than 20% of adult custodial arrests. Even in instances where force is used, police officers primarily use weaponless tactics. Excessive force is the application of an amount and/or frequency of force greater than that required to compel compliance from a willing or unwilling subject.

- Police discretion refers to the opportunity for police officers to exercise choice in their enforcement activities. Put another way, discretion refers to the exercise of choice by law enforcement officers in the decision to investigate or apprehend, the disposition of suspects, the carrying out of official duties, and the application of sanctions. The widest exercise of discretion can be found in routine situations involving relatively less serious violations of the law, but serious criminal behavior may also result in discretionary decisions not to make an arrest.

- Racial profiling, or racially biased policing, is any police action initiated on the basis of the race, ethnicity, or national origin of a suspect rather than on the behavior of that individual or on information that leads the police to a particular individual who has been identified as being, or having been, engaged in criminal activity. Racial profiling is a bigoted practice unworthy of the law enforcement professional. It has been widely condemned as contrary to basic ethical principles. Further, it weakens the public's confidence in the police, thereby decreasing police–citizen trust and cooperation. This chapter pointed out, however, that racial or ethnic indicators associated with particular suspects or suspect groups may have a place in legitimate law enforcement strategies if they accurately relate to suspects who are being sought for criminal law violations.

- Civil liability issues are very important in policing. They arise because officers and their agencies sometimes inappropriately use power to curtail the civil and due process rights of criminal suspects. Both police departments and individual police officers can be targeted by civil lawsuits. Federal suits based on claims that officers acted with disregard for an individual's right to due process are called *1983 lawsuits* because they are based on Section 1983 of Title 42 of the U.S. Code. Another type of civil suit that can be brought specifically against federal agents is a *Bivens* action. Although the doctrine of sovereign immunity barred legal action against state and local governments in the past, recent court cases and legislative activity have restricted the opportunity for law enforcement agencies and their officers to exercise claims of immunity.

KEY TERMS

1983 lawsuit, 270
biological weapon, 253
Bivens action, 271
civil liability, 267
deadly force, 259
excessive force, 257
internal affairs, 247
Knapp Commission, 244
less-lethal weapon, 261
peace officer standards
  and training (POST)
  program, 250

police corruption, 243
police discretion, 261
police ethics, 249
police professionalism, 248
police subculture, 240
police use of force, 257
police working personality, 241
problem police officer, 258
racial profiling, 263

KEY CASES

Biscoe v. *Arlington County*, 267
Bivens v. *Six Unknown Federal*
  Agents, 271
City of Canton, Ohio v. *Harris*, 268
Graham v. *Connor*, 259

Hunter v. *Bryant*, 271
Idaho v. *Horiuchi*, 272
Malley v. *Briggs*, 267
Tennessee v. *Garner*, 259

QUESTIONS FOR REVIEW

1. What is the police working personality? What are its central features? How does it develop? How does it relate to police subculture?

2. What are the different types of police corruption? What themes run through the findings of the Knapp Commission and the Wickersham Commission? What innovative steps might police departments take to reduce or eliminate corruption among their officers?

3. What is police professionalism? How can you tell when police action is professional? Why are professionalism and ethics important in policing today?

4. What are the dangers of police work? What can be done to reduce those dangers?

5. In what kinds of situations are police officers most likely to use force? When has too much force been used?

6. What is police discretion? How does the practice of discretion by today's officers reflect on their departments and on the policing profession as a whole?

7. What is racial profiling? What is racially biased policing? Why have they become significant issues in policing today?

8. What are some of the civil liability issues associated with policing? What are some of the common sources of civil suits against the police? How can civil liability be reduced?

QUESTIONS FOR REFLECTION

1. Do you think that this chapter has accurately described the police personality? Why or why not? Can you identify any additional characteristics of the police personality? Are there any listed here that you do not think are accurate?

2. What strategies can you think of for helping build police integrity? How might those strategies differ from one agency to another or from the local to the state or federal level?

3. What is it about racial profiling that most people find unacceptable? Are there any situations in which law enforcement's use of racial features or ethnic characteristics may be appropriate in targeting suspected criminals? If so, what would those situations be?

NOTES

i. Carl B. Klockars et al., "The Measurement of Police Integrity," *National Institute of Justice Research in Brief* (Washington, DC: National Institute of Justice, 2000), p. 1.

ii. Technical Working Group on Crime Scene Investigation, *Crime Scene Investigation: A Guide for Law Enforcement* (Washington, DC: National Institute of Justice, 2000), p. 12.

iii. National Institute of Justice, *Use of Force by Police: Overview of National and Local Data* (Washington, DC: National Institute of Justice, 1999).

iv. International Association of Chiefs of Police, *Police Use of Force in America, 2001* (Alexandria, VA: IACP, 2001), p. 1.

v. Samuel Walker, Geoffrey P. Albert, and Dennis J. Kenney, *Responding to the Problem Police Officer: A National Study of Early Warning Systems* (Washington, DC: National Institute of Justice, 2000).

vi. Sam W. Lathrop, "Reviewing Use of Force: A Systematic Approach," *FBI Law Enforcement Bulletin*, October 2000, p. 18.

vii. Adapted from Gerald Hill and Kathleen Hill, *The Real Life Dictionary of the Law*, http://www.law.com (accessed June 11, 2007).

1. Quoted in Jim Helihy, "Issues Affecting Irish Policing, 1922–1932," http://www.esatclear.ie/~garda/issues.html (accessed June 15, 2008).

2. "Caring and Courage: 2012 Heroes among Us Awards," *People*, December 17, 2012, p. 95.

3. For alternative definitions, see: Janine Rauch and Etienne Marasis, "Contextualizing the Waddington Report," http://www.wits.ac.za/csvr/papers/papwadd.html (accessed January 5, 2009).

4. Jerome H. Skolnick, *Justice without Trial: Law Enforcement in a Democratic Society* (New York: John Wiley, 1966).

5. William A. Westley, *Violence and the Police: A Sociological Study of Law, Custom, and Morality* (Cambridge, MA: MIT Press, 1970); and William A. Westley, "Violence and the Police," *American Journal of Sociology*, Vol. 49 (1953), pp. 34–41.

6. Arthur Niederhoffer, *Behind the Shield: The Police in Urban Society* (Garden City, NY: Anchor, 1967).

7. Thomas Barker and David L. Carter, *Police Deviance* (Cincinnati, OH: Anderson, 1986). See also Christopher P. Wilson, *Cop Knowledge: Police Power and Cultural Narrative in Twentieth-Century America* (Chicago: University of Chicago Press, 2000).

8. Richard Bennett and Theodore Greenstein, "The Police Personality: A Test of the Predispositional Model," *Journal of Police Science and Administration*, Vol. 3 (1975), pp. 439–445.

9. James Teevan and Bernard Dolnick, "The Values of the Police: A Reconsideration and Interpretation," *Journal of Police Science and Administration* (1973), pp. 366–369.

10. "Sixteen Former Puerto Rico Police Officers Plead Guilty to Running Criminal Organization from the Police Department," U.S. Dept. of Justice news release, August 25, 2014, http://www.justice.gov/opa/pr/2014/August/14-crm-891.html (accessed January 10, 2015).

11. Carl B. Klockars et al., "The Measurement of Police Integrity," *National Institute of Justice Research in Brief* (Washington, DC: NIJ, 2000), p. 1.

12. Michael J. Palmiotto, ed., *Police Misconduct: A Reader for the Twenty-First Century* (Upper Saddle River, NJ: Prentice Hall, 2001), preface.

13. Tim Prenzler and Peta Mackay, "Police Gratuities: What the Public Thinks," *Criminal Justice Ethics* (winter/spring 1995), pp. 15–25.

14. Thomas Barker and David L. Carter, *Police Deviance* (Cincinnati, OH: Anderson, 1986). For a detailed overview of the issues involved in police corruption, see Victor E. Kappeler, Richard D. Sluder, and Geoffrey P. Alpert, *Forces of Deviance: Understanding the Dark Side of Policing*, 2nd ed. (Prospect Heights, IL: Waveland Press, 1998); Dean J. Champion, *Police Misconduct in America: A Reference Handbook* (Santa Barbara, CA: Abo-Clio, 2002); and Kim Michelle Lersch, ed., *Policing and Misconduct* (Upper Saddle River, NJ: Prentice Hall, 2002).

15. L. Perry, "Repairing Broken Windows: Preventing Corruption within Our Ranks," *FBI Law Enforcement Bulletin*, February 2001, pp. 23–26.

16. "Nationline: NYC Cops—Excess Force Not Corruption," *USA Today*, June 16, 1995.

17. *Knapp Commission Report on Police Corruption* (New York: George Braziller, 1973).

18. Ibid.

19. Sabrina Tavernise, "Victory for Officer Who Aided Corruption Inquiry," *New York Times*, April 3, 2004.

20. Edwin H. Sutherland and Donald Cressey, *Principles of Criminology*, 8th ed. (Philadelphia: J. B. Lippincott, 1970).

21. Tim R. Jones, Compton Owens, and Melissa A. Smith, "Police Ethics Training: A Three-Tiered Approach," *FBI Law Enforcement Bulletin* (June 1995), pp. 22–26.

22. Stephen J. Gaffigan and Phyllis P. McDonald, *Police Integrity: Public Service with Honor* (Washington, DC: National Institute of Justice, 1997).

23. U.S. Department of Justice, *Principles for Promoting Police Integrity: Examples of Promising Police Practices* (Washington, DC: U.S. Dept. of Justice, 2001).

24. National Institute of Justice, *Enhancing Police Integrity* (Washington, DC: U.S. Dept. of Justice, 2005).

25. Ibid., p. ii.

26. *Carroll v. City of Westminster*, 4th Cir. No. 99-1556, November 17, 2000.

27. The material in this paragraph is adapted from Sharon Burrell, "Random Drug Testing of Police Officers Upheld," *Legal Views* (Office of the County Attorney, Montgomery County, Maryland), Vol. 6, No. 2 (February 2001), p. 4.

28. International Association of Chiefs of Police, *Employee Drug Testing* (St. Paul, MN: IACP, 1999).

29. *Maurice Turner v. Fraternal Order of Police*, 500 A.2d 1005 (D.C. 1985).

30. *Philip Caruso, President of P.B.A. v. Benjamin Ward, Police Commissioner*, New York State Supreme Court, Pat. 37, Index No. 12632-86, 1986.

31. *National Treasury Employees Union v. Von Raab*, 489 U.S. 656, 659 (1989).

32. Michael Siegfried, "Notes on the Professionalization of Private Security," *Justice Professional* (spring 1989).

33. See Edward A. Farris, "Five Decades of American Policing, 1932–1982: The Path to Professionalism," *Police Chief* (November 1982), p. 34.

34. Commission on Accreditation for Law Enforcement Agencies, *Annual Report 2009* (Gainesville, VA: CALEA, 2010), p. 3.

35. *CALEA Update*, No. 81 (February 2003), http://www.calea.org/newweb/newsletter/No81/81index.htm (accessed May 21, 2003).

36. Brian A. Reaves, *State and Local Law Enforcement Training Academies, 2006* (Washington, DC: Bureau of Justice Statistics, 2009), p. 6.

37. Information in this paragraph comes from "PTO Program," *COPS Office, U.S. Department of Justice*, http://www.cops.usdoj.gov/print.asp?Item_461 (accessed June 3, 2007).

38. National Commission on Law Observance and Enforcement, *Report on Police* (Washington, DC: U.S. Government Printing Office, 1931).

39. *Saucier v. Katz*, 533 U.S. 194 (2001).

40. *Brosseau v. Haugen*, 543 U.S. 194 (2004).

41. Brian A. Reaves and Matthew J. Hickman, *Law Enforcement Management and Administrative Statistics, 2000: Data for Individual State and Local Agencies with 100 or More Officers* (Washington, DC: Bureau of Justice Statistics, March 2004).

42. Ibid.

43. Brian A. Reaves and Matthew J. Hickman, *Police Departments in Large Cities, 1990–2000* (Washington, DC: Bureau of Justice Statistics, 2002), p. 1.

44. "Dallas PD College Rule Gets Final OK," *Law Enforcement News*, July 7, 1986, pp. 1, 13.

45. *Davis v. Dallas*, 777 F.2d 205 (5th Cir. 1985).

46. David L. Carter, Allen D. Sapp, and Darrel W. Stephens, *The State of Police Education: Policy Direction for the Twenty-First Century* (Washington, DC: Police Executive Research Forum, 1989), pp. xxii–xxiii.

47. The latter two were formerly part of the Immigration and Naturalization Service until its reorganization under the Homeland Security Act of 2002.

48. National Advisory Commission on Criminal Justice Standards and Goals, *Report on the Police*, p. 238.

49. Brian A. Reaves, *Local Police Departments, 2007* (Washington, DC: Bureau of Justice Statistics, 2010), p. 11.

50. Matthew J. Hickman and Brian A. Reaves, *Local Police Departments, 2003* (Washington, DC: Bureau of Justice Statistics, 2006), p. 270.

51. August Vollmer, *The Police and Modern Society* (Berkeley: University of California Press, 1936), p. 222.

52. O. W. Wilson and Roy Clinton McLaren, Police Administration, 4th ed. (New York: McGraw-Hill, 1977), p. 259.

53. National Law Enforcement Officers' Memorial Fund website, http://www.nleomf.com (accessed April 29, 2012).

54. From the Officer Down Memorial Page, http://www.odmp .org/search/year/2014?ref=sidebar (accessed October 29, 2015).

55. Ibid., http://www.odmp.org/year.php?year2001 (accessed January 16, 2011).

56. Anthony J. Pinizzotto and Edward F. Davis, "Cop Killers and Their Victims," *FBI Law Enforcement Bulletin*, December 1992, p. 10.

57. Brian A. Reaves, *Census of State and Local Law Enforcement Agencies, 2004* (Washington, DC: Bureau of Justice Statistics, 2007); and Matthew J. Hickman and Brian A. Reaves, *Local Police Departments, 2003* (Washington, DC: Bureau of Justice Statistics, 2006).

58. Brian A. Reaves, *Federal Law Enforcement Officers, 2004* (Washington, DC: Bureau of Justice Statistics, 2006).

59. *AIDS and Our Workplace*, New York City Police Department pamphlet, November 1987.

60. See Occupational Safety and Health Administration, OSHA Bloodborne Pathogens Act of 1991 (29 CFR 1910.1030).

61. *National Institute of Justice Reports*, No. 206 (November/December 1987).

62. See "On-the-Job Stress in Policing: Reducing It, Preventing It," *National Institute of Justice Journal* (January 2000), pp. 18–24.

63. "Stress on the Job," *Newsweek*, April 25, 1988, p. 43.

64. "On-the-Job Stress in Policing," p. 19.

65. Kevin Barrett, "Police Suicide: Is Anyone Listening?" *Journal of Safe Management of Disruptive and Assaultive Behavior* (spring 1997), pp. 6–9.

66. For an excellent review of coping strategies among police officers, see Robin N. Haarr and Merry Morash, "Gender, Race, and Strategies of Coping with Occupational Stress in Policing," *Justice Quarterly*, Vol. 16, No. 2 (June 1999), pp. 303–336.

67. Mark H. Anshel, "A Conceptual Model and Implications for Coping with Stressful Events in Police Work," *Criminal Justice and Behavior*, Vol. 27, No. 3 (2000), p. 375.

68. Ibid.

69. Bryan Vila, "Tired Cops: Probable Connections between Fatigue and the Performance, Health, and Safety of Patrol Officers," *American Journal of Police*, Vol. 15, No. 2 (1996), pp. 51–92.

70. Bryan Vila et al., *Evaluating the Effects of Fatigue on Police Patrol Officers: Final Report* (Washington, DC: National Institute of Justice, 2000).

71. Bryan Vila and Dennis Jay Kenney, "Tired Cops: The Prevalence and Potential Consequences of Police Fatigue," *NIJ Journal*, No. 248 (2002), p. 19.

72. Bryan Vila and Erik Y. Taiji, "Fatigue and Police Officer Performance," paper presented at the annual meeting of the American Society of Criminology, Chicago, 1996.

73. John Simerman, "Mayor Landrieu Fails in Bid to Halt Pending NOPD Reform Deal," *The Times-Picayune*, January 11, 2013, http://www.nola.com/crime/index.ssf/2013/01/mayor_landrieu _calls_halt_to_p.html#incart_m-rpt-2 (accessed March 11, 2013).

74. Civil Rights Division, U.S. Department of Justice, *Investigation of the New Orleans Police Department* (Washington, DC: USDOJ, 2011).

75. Some of the material in this section is adapted or derived from National Institute of Justice, *Use of Force by Police: Overview of National and Local Data* (Washington, DC: NIJ, 1999).

76. Matthew R. Durose, Erica L. Smith, and Patrick A. Langan, *Contacts between Police and the Public, 2005* (Washington, DC: Bureau of Justice Statistics, 2007).

77. Ibid, p. 10.

78. Not all studies agree on this point, and in 2005, researchers who examined the use of force by male and female officers in the Montgomery County Police Department in Maryland found that male and female officers were relatively comparable in their use of force. See Peter B. Hoffman and Edward R. Hickey, "Use of Force by Female Police Officers," *Journal of Criminal Justice*, Vol. 33, No. 2 (2005), p. 142.

79. International Association of Chiefs of Police, *Police Use of Force in America, 2001* (Alexandria, VA: IACP, 2001), p. 1.

80. Kenneth Adams, "What We Know about Police Use of Force," in National Institute of Justice, *Use of Force by Police: Overview of National and Local Data* (Washington, DC: NIJ, 1999), p. 4.

81. Geoffrey P. Alpert and Roger G. Dunham, *The Force Factor: Measuring Police Use of Force Relative to Suspect Resistance—A Final Report* (Washington, DC: National Institute of Justice, 2001).

82. Charlie Mesloh, Mark Henych, Ross Wolf, "Less Lethal Weapon Effectiveness, Use of Force, and Suspect & Officer Injuries: A Five-Year Analysis," Report to the National Institute of Justice, September, 2008, p. 9.

83. Samuel Walker, Geoffrey P. Alpert, and Dennis J. Kenney, *Responding to the Problem Police Officer: A National Study of Early Warning Systems* (Washington, DC: National Institute of Justice, 2000).

84. See Human Rights Watch, "The Christopher Commission Report," from which some of the wording in this paragraph is adapted, http://www.hrw.org/reports98/police/uspo73.htm (accessed March 30, 2007).

85. J. David Goodman, "Bratton Says New York Police Dept. Must Dismiss Bad Officers," *The New York Times*, October 2, 2014.

86. Sam W. Lathrop, "Reviewing Use of Force: A Systematic Approach," *FBI Law Enforcement Bulletin*, October 2000, p. 18.

87. *Tennessee v. Garner*, 471 U.S. 1 (1985).

88. *Graham v. Connor*, 490 U.S. 386, 396–397 (1989).

89. John C. Hall, "FBI Training on the New Federal Deadly Force Policy," *FBI Law Enforcement Bulletin*, April 1996, pp. 25–32.

90. James Fyfe, *Shots Fired: An Examination of New York City Police Firearms Discharges* (Ann Arbor, MI: University Microfilms, 1978).

91. James Fyfe, "Blind Justice? Police Shootings in Memphis," paper presented at the annual meeting of the Academy of Criminal Justice Sciences, Philadelphia, March 1981.

92. It is estimated that American police shoot *at* approximately 3,600 people every year. See William Geller, "Crime File: Deadly Force," a study guide (Washington, DC: National Institute of Justice, n.d.).

93. Anne Cohen, "I've Killed That Man Ten Thousand Times," *Police Magazine*, July 1980.

94. For more information, see Joe Auten, "When Police Shoot," *North Carolina Criminal Justice Today*, Vol. 4, No. 4 (summer 1986), pp. 9–14.

95. Details for this story come from Stephanie Slater, "Suicidal Man Killed by Police Fusillade," *Palm Beach Post*, March 11, 2005.

96. Rebecca Stincelli, *Suicide by Cop: Victims from Both Sides of the Badge* (Folsom, CA: Interviews and Interrogations Institute, 2004).

97. Quoted in Slater, "Suicidal Man Killed by Police Fusillade."

98. Anthony J. Pinizzotto, Edward F. Davis, and Charles E. Miller III, "Suicide by Cop: Defining a Devastating Dilemma," *FBI Law Enforcement Bulletin*, Vol. 74, No. 2 (February 2005), p. 15.

99. "Ten Percent of Police Shootings Found to Be 'Suicide by Cop,'" *Criminal Justice Newsletter*, September 1, 1998, pp. 1–2.

100. Robert J. Homant and Daniel B. Kennedy, "Suicide by Police: A Proposed Typology of Law Enforcement Officer-Assisted Suicide," *Policing: An International Journal of Police Strategies and Management*, Vol. 23, No. 3 (2000), pp. 339–355.

101. David W. Hayeslip and Alan Preszler, "NIJ Initiative on Less-Than-Lethal Weapons," National Institute of Justice Research in Brief (Washington, DC: NIJ, 1993).

102. Ibid.

103. Thomas Farragher and David Abel, "Postgame Police Projectile Kills an Emerson Student," *Boston Globe*, October 22, 2004, http://www.boston.com/sports/baseball/redsox/articles/2004/10/22/postgame_police_projectile_kills_an_emerson_student (accessed July 25, 2005).

104. *Bivens v. Six Unknown Federal Agents*, 403 U.S. 388 (1971).

105. *F.D.I.C. v. Meyer*, 510 U.S. 471 (1994).

106. U.S. Department of Justice, *Guidance for Federal Law Enforcement Agencies Regarding the Use of Race, Ethnicity, Gender, National Origin, Religion, Sexual Orientation, or Gender Identity* (Washington, DC: December 2014).

107. Ibid., pp. 1–2.

108. Adapted from Deborah Ramirez, Jack McDevitt, and Amy Farrell, *A Resource Guide on Racial Profiling Data Collection Systems: Promising Practices and Lessons Learned* (Washington, DC: U.S. Dept. of Justice, 2000), p. 3.

109. Sid Heal, "The ABC3s," *The Tactical Edge*, Fall 2004, pp. 36–39.

110. Ibid.

111. David Harris, *Driving While Black: Racial Profiling on Our Nation's Highways* (Washington, DC: American Civil Liberties Union, 1999).

112. "Justice Department Bars Race Profiling, with Exception for Terrorism," *Criminal Justice Newsletter*, July 15, 2003, pp. 6–7.

113. "Justice Department Issues Policy Guidance to Ban Racial Profiling," U.S. Department of Justice press release (No. 355), June 17, 2003.

114. Blaine Harden and Somini Sengupta, "Some Passengers Singled Out for Exclusion by Flight Crew," *New York Times*, September 22, 2001.

115. David Cole and John Lambreth, "The Fallacy of Racial Profiling," *New York Times*, May 13, 2001, http://college1.nytimes.com/buests/articles/2001/05/13/846196.xml (accessed August 28, 2009).

116. Rob Tillyer, "Opening the Black Box of Officer Decision-Making: An Examination of Race, Criminal History, and Discretionary Searches," *Justice Quarterly*, August 2012.

117. Amitai Etzioni, "Another Side of Racial Profiling," *USA Today*, May 21, 2001, p. 15A.

118. Gallup Poll Organization, *Racial Profiling Is Seen as Widespread, Particularly among Young Black Men* (Princeton, NJ: Gallup Poll Organization, December 9, 1999), p. 1.

119. Gallup Poll Organization, "Racial Profiling Seen as Pervasive, Unjust," July 20, 2004, http://www.gallup.com/poll/12406/Racial-Profiling-Seen-Pervasive-Unjust.aspx (accessed August 1, 2010).

120. Ramirez, McDevitt, and Farrell, *A Resource Guide on Racial Profiling Data Collection Systems*, p. 3.

121. Police Executive Research Forum, *Racially Biased Policing: A Principled Response* (Washington, DC: PERF, 2001).

122. Ibid., foreword.

123. Ibid., p. 39.

124. Ibid., p. 47.

125. Details for this story come from David Heinzmann, "Committee to Consider Settling Cop Misconduct Cases for Nearly $33 Million," *Chicago Tribune*, http://www.chicagotribune.com/news/local/breaking/chi-emanuel-seeks-to-settle-2-cop-misconduct-cases-for-nearly-33-million-20130114,0,4742395,full.story, January 15, 2013.

126. Charles R. Swanson, Leonard Territo, and Robert W. Taylor, *Police Administration: Structures, Processes, and Behavior*, 2nd ed. (New York: Macmillan, 1988).

127. *Malley v. Briggs*, 475 U.S. 335, 106 S.Ct. 1092 (1986).

128. Ibid., at 4246.

129. *Biscoe v. Arlington County*, 238 U.S. App. D.C. 206, 738 F.2d 1352, 1362 (1984). See also 738 F.2d 1352 (D.C. Cir. 1984), cert. denied; 469 U.S. 1159; and 105 S.Ct. 909, 83 L.E.2d 923 (1985).

130. John Hill, "High-Speed Police Pursuits: Dangers, Dynamics, and Risk Reduction," *FBI Law Enforcement Bulletin* (July 2002), pp. 14–18.

131. Civil Rights Division, U.S. Dept. of Justice, *Investigation of the New Orleans Police Department*, p. xii.

132. *City of Canton, Ohio v. Harris*, 489 U.S. 378 (1989).

133. Ibid., at 1204.

134. *Board of the County Commissioners of Bryan County, Oklahoma v. Brown*, 520 U.S. 397 (1997).

135. Jeffrey Bloomer, "Ex-cops Handed Tough Sentences for Katrina Shootings," *The Slatest*, April 4, 2012, http://slatest.slate.com/posts/2012/04/04/katrina_police_shootings_convicted_new_orleans_police_officers_handed_stiff_sentences_in_shootings.html (accessed May 20, 2012).

136. U.S. Code, Title 42, Section 1983.

137. *Bivens v. Six Unknown Federal Agents*, 403 U.S. 388 (1971).

138. See *F.D.I.C. v. Meyer*, 510 U.S. 471 (1994), in which the U.S. Supreme Court reiterated its ruling under *Bivens*, stating that only government employees and not government agencies can be sued.

139. *Wyler v. U.S.*, 725 F.2d 157 (2d Cir. 1983).

140. California Government Code, Section 818.

141. Federal Tort Claims Act, U.S. Code, Title 28, Section 1346(b), 2671–2680.

142. *Elder v. Holloway*, 114 S.Ct. 1019, 127 L.Ed.2d 344 (1994).

143. Ibid.

144. *Hunter v. Bryant*, 112 S.Ct. 534 (1991).

145. William U. McCormack, "Supreme Court Cases: 1991–1992 Term," *FBI Law Enforcement Bulletin*, November 1992, p. 30.

146. *Saucier v. Katz*, 533 U.S. 194 (2001).

147. See also *Brosseau v. Haugen*, 543 U.S. 194 (2004).

148. *Pearson v. Callahan*, 555 U.S. 223 (2009).

149. *Idaho v. Horiuchi*, 266 F.3d 979 (9th Cir. 2001).

150. For more information on police liability, see Daniel L. Schofield, "Legal Issues of Pursuit Driving," *FBI Law Enforcement Bulletin*, May 1988, pp. 23–29.

151. Michael S. Vaughn, Tab W. Cooper, and Rolando V. del Carmen, "Assessing Legal Liabilities in Law Enforcement: Police Chiefs' Views," *Crime and Delinquency*, Vol. 47, No. 1 (2001), p. 3.

PART

3

ADJUDICATION

Chapter 9
The Courts: Structure and Participants

Chapter 10
Pretrial Activities and the Criminal Trial

Chapter 11
Sentencing

RIGHTS OF THE ACCUSED BEFORE THE COURT

The accused has these common law, constitutional, statutory, and humanitarian rights:

- The right to a speedy trial
- The right to legal counsel
- The right against self-incrimination
- The right not to be tried twice for the same offense
- The right to know the charges
- The right to cross-examine witnesses
- The right against excessive bail

These individual rights must be effectively balanced against these community concerns:

- Conviction of the guilty
- Exoneration of the innocent
- The imposition of appropriate punishment
- The protection of society
- Efficient and cost-effective procedures
- Seeing justice done

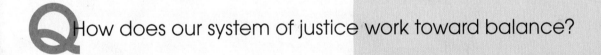

Q How does our system of justice work toward balance?

Equal Justice under the Law

The well-known British philosopher and statesman Benjamin Disraeli (1804–1881) once defined justice as "truth in action." The study of criminal case processing by courts at all levels provides perhaps the best opportunity available to us from within the criminal justice system to observe what should ideally be "truth in action." The courtroom search for truth, which is characteristic of criminal trials, pits the resources of the accused against those of the state. The ultimate outcome of such procedures, say advocates of our adversarial-based system of trial practice, should be both truth and justice.

Others are not so sure. British novelist William McIlvanney (1936–) once wrote, "Who thinks the law has anything to do with justice? It's what we have because we can't have justice." Indeed, many critics of the present system claim that courts at all levels have become so concerned with procedure and with sets of formalized rules that they have lost sight of the truth. The chapters that make up this section of *Criminal Justice Today* provide an overview of American courts, including their history and present structure, and examine the multifaceted roles played by both professional and lay courtroom participants. Sentencing—the practice whereby juries recommend and judges impose sanctions on convicted offenders—is covered in the concluding chapter of this section. Whether American courts routinely uncover truth and therefore dispense justice, or whether they are merely locked into a pattern of hollow procedure that does little other than mock the justice ideal, will be for you to decide.

© Konstantin L/Fotolia

9

THE COURTS: STRUCTURE AND PARTICIPANTS

OUTLINE

- Introduction
- History and Structure of the American Court System
- The State Court System
- The Federal Court System
- The Courtroom Work Group
- Professional Courtroom Participants
- Outsiders: Nonprofessional Courtroom Participants

LEARNING OBJECTIVES

After reading this chapter, you should be able to

- Summarize the development of American courts, including the concept of the dual-court system.
- Describe a typical state court system, including some of the differences between the state and federal court systems.
- Describe the structure of the federal court system, including the various types of federal courts.
- Identify all typical job titles of the courtroom work group members.
- Describe the roles of professional members of the courtroom work group.
- Describe the roles of outsiders, or nonprofessional courtroom participants.

The criminal court is the central, crucial institution in the criminal justice system.... It is the institution around which the rest of the system has developed.

PRESIDENT'S COMMISSION ON LAW ENFORCEMENT AND ADMINISTRATION OF JUSTICE

■ **lecture note**   Explain the differences between state and federal courts, and provide a brief overview of how our country's system of separate state and federal courts developed.

■ **federal court system**   The three-tiered structure of federal courts, comprising U.S. district courts, U.S. courts of appeal, and the U.S. Supreme Court.

■ **state court system**   A state judicial structure. Most states have at least three court levels: trial courts, appellate courts, and a state supreme court.

Introduction

In 2014, former TSA employee Dennis Marx of Cummings, Georgia, walked into the Forsyth County Courthouse and opened fire, injuring a deputy sheriff.[1] The 48-year-old Marx, who was armed with an assault rifle and a number of improvised explosive devices, was known to locals as a self-proclaimed "sovereign citizen." Officials said that he planned to "take the courthouse hostage." Marx had been due to appear in court on drug and gun charges. The local SWAT team, which was rushing to answer another call, arrived on the scene within 37 seconds of Marx's attack, and shot him dead before he could inflict further damage.[2]

Incidents like the Georgia courthouse attack highlight the critical role that our nation's courts and the personnel who staff them play in the American system of justice. Without courts to decide guilt or innocence and to impose sentences on those convicted of crimes, the activities of law enforcement officials would become meaningless.

There are many different levels of courts in the United States, but they all dispense justice and help ensure that officials in the justice system work within the law when carrying out their duties. At many points in this textbook and in three specific chapters (Chapters 7, 12, and 13), we take a close look at court precedents that have defined the legality of enforcement efforts and correctional action. In Chapter 4, we explored the law-making function of courts. This chapter provides a picture of how courts work by describing the American court system at both the state and federal levels. We will look at the roles of courtroom actors—from attorneys to victims and from jurors to judges. Then in Chapter 10, we will discuss pretrial activities and examine each of the steps in a criminal trial.

History and Structure of the American Court System

Two types of courts function within the American criminal justice system: (1) state courts and (2) federal courts. Figure 9-1 outlines the structure of today's **federal court system**, and Figure 9-2 diagrams shows variation among **state court systems**. This dual-court system is the result of general agreement among the nation's founders about the need for individual states to retain significant legislative authority and judicial autonomy separate from federal control. Under this concept, the United States developed as a relatively loose federation of semi-independent provinces. New states joining the union were assured of limited federal intervention in local affairs. State legislatures were free to create laws, and state court systems were needed to hear cases in which violations of those laws occurred.

The Forsyth County Courthouse in Cummings, Georgia. In 2014, the courthouse became the target of an attack by a "sovereign citizen" who had planned to take it over. What role do the courts play in the American criminal justice system?

© Tami Chappell/Reuters

Junior high school children posing in the pillory in Williamsburg, Virginia. Just as criminal punishments have changed throughout the centuries, so too have criminal courts, which today provide civilized forums for exploring conflicting claims about guilt and innocence. How might our courts continue to evolve?

Jeff Greenberg/PhotoEdit Inc.

■ Follow the author's tweets about the latest crime and justice news @schmalleger.

■ **jurisdiction** The territory, subject matter, or people over which a court or other justice agency may exercise lawful authority, as determined by statute or constitution.

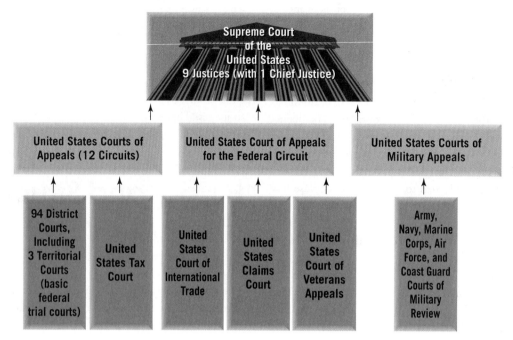

FIGURE 9-1 | The Structure of the Federal Courts

Source: Pearson Education, Inc.

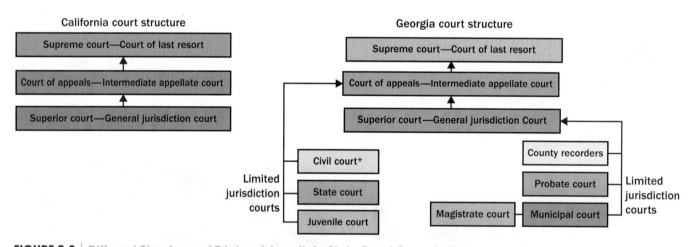

FIGURE 9-2 | Different Structures of Trial and Appellate State Court Organization

Source: Ron Malega and Thomas H. Cohen, *State Court Organization*, 2011 (Washington, DC: BJS, November 2013), p. 2.

In the last 200 years, states' rights have gradually waned relative to the power of the federal government, but the dual-court system still exists. Even today, state courts do not hear cases involving alleged violations of federal law, nor do federal courts get involved in deciding issues of state law unless there is a conflict between local or state statutes and federal constitutional guarantees. When such conflicts arise, claimed violations of federal due process guarantees—especially those found in the Bill of Rights—can provide the basis for appeals made to federal courts by offenders convicted in state court systems. Learn more about the dual-court system in America at **http://public .findlaw.com/abaflg/flg-2-2a-1.html**.

This chapter describes both federal and state court systems in terms of their historical development, **jurisdiction**, and current structure. Because it is within state courts that the large majority of criminal cases originate, we turn our attention first to them.

■ **original jurisdiction**   The lawful authority of a court to hear or to act on a case from its beginning and to pass judgment on the law and the facts. The authority may be over a specific geographic area or over particular types of cases.
■ **appellate jurisdiction**   The lawful authority of a court to review a decision made by a lower court.

The State Court System

The Development of State Courts

Each of the original American colonies had its own court system for resolving disputes, both civil and criminal. As early as 1629, the Massachusetts Bay Colony created a General Court, composed of the governor, his deputy, 18 assistants, and 118 elected officials. The General Court was a combined legislature and court that made laws, held trials, and imposed sentences.[3] By 1776, all of the American colonies had established fully functioning court systems.

Following the American Revolution, state court systems, were anything but uniform. Initially, most states made no distinction between **original jurisdiction**, the lawful authority of a court to hear cases that arise within a specified geographic area or that involve particular kinds of law violations, and **appellate jurisdiction**, the lawful authority of a court to review a decision made by a lower court. Many, in fact, had no provisions for appeal. Delaware, for example, did not allow appeals in criminal cases until 1897. States that did permit appeals often lacked any established appellate courts and sometimes used state legislatures for that purpose.

By the late nineteenth century, a dramatic increase in population, growing urbanization, the settlement of the West, and other far-reaching changes in the American way of life led to a tremendous increase in civil litigation and criminal arrests. Legislatures tried to keep pace with the rising tide of cases. States created a number of courts at the trial, appellate, and supreme court levels, calling them by a variety of names and assigning them functions that sometimes were completely different from those of similarly named courts in neighboring states. City courts, which were limited in their jurisdiction by community boundaries, arose to handle the special problems of urban life, such as disorderly conduct, property disputes, and the enforcement of restrictive and regulatory ordinances. Other tribunals, such as juvenile courts, developed to handle special kinds of problems or special clients. Some, like magistrate's courts or small-claims courts, handled only minor law violations and petty disputes. Still others, like traffic courts, were very narrow in focus. The result was a patchwork quilt of hearing bodies, some only vaguely resembling modern notions of a trial court.

State court systems developed by following several models. One was the New York State Field Code of 1848, which

An attorney making a closing argument to a jury. Why are courts sometimes called "the fulcrum of the criminal justice system"?

■ **courts of limited jurisdiction**   Courts of law that have jurisdiction on a restricted range of cases, primarily lesser criminal and civil matters, including misdemeanors, small claims, traffic, parking, and civil infractions. Such courts are also called inferior courts or lower courts. They can also handle the preliminary stages of felony cases in some states.

■ **courts of general jurisdiction**   Courts of law with primary jurisdiction on all issues not delegated to lower courts. Most often called major trial courts, they often hear serious criminal or civil cases. Cases are also designated to courts of general jurisdiction based on the severity of the punishment or allegation or on the dollar value of the case.

■ **lecture note**   Explain that most state judicial structures encompass courts at three levels: trial, appellate, and supreme. Mention that a state supreme court is also called a *court of last resort.*

■ **theme**   Why do most states have two levels of trial courts, those with limited jurisdiction and those with general jurisdiction?

■ **trial *de novo***   Literally, "new trial." The term is applied to cases that are retried on appeal, as opposed to those that are simply reviewed on the record.

clarified jurisdictional claims and specified matters of court procedure. While many states copied the plan of the Field Code, it was later amended so extensively that its usefulness as a model dissolved. The federal Judiciary Act of 1789 and later the federal Reorganization Act of 1801 provided other models for state court systems. States that followed the federal model developed a three-tiered structure of (1) trial courts of limited jurisdiction, (2) trial courts of general jurisdiction, and (3) appellate courts.

State Court Systems Today

The three-tiered federal model was far from perfect, however. Within the structure it provided, many local and specialized courts proliferated. Traffic courts, magistrate's courts, municipal courts, recorder's courts, probate courts, and courts held by justices of the peace were but a few that functioned at the lower levels. In the early twentieth century, the American Bar Association (ABA) and the American Judicature Society led the movement toward simplification of state court structures. Proponents of state court reform sought to unify redundant courts that held overlapping jurisdictions. Most reformers suggested a uniform model for all states that would build on (1) a centralized court structure composed of a clear hierarchy of trial and appellate courts, (2) the consolidation of numerous lower-level courts with overlapping jurisdictions, and (3) a centralized state court authority that would be responsible for budgeting, financing, and managing all courts within a state.

The court reform movement continues today. Although reformers have made substantial progress in many states, there are still many differences between and among state court systems (as Figure 9-2 shows). Reform states, like California, which early on embraced the reform movement, are now characterized by streamlined judicial systems consisting of precisely conceived trial courts of limited and general jurisdiction, supplemented by one or two appellate court levels. Nonreform, or traditional states (like Georgia), retain judicial systems that are a conglomeration of multilevel and sometimes redundant courts with poorly defined jurisdictions. Even in nonreform states, however, most criminal courts can be classified within the three-tiered structure of two trial court echelons and an appellate tier.

State Trial Courts

Trial courts are where criminal cases begin. The trial court conducts arraignments, sets bail, takes pleas, and conducts trials. (We will discuss each of these functions in more depth in the next chapter.) If the defendant pleads guilty or is found guilty, the trial court imposes sentence. Trial courts of limited, or special, jurisdiction are also called *lower courts.* Lower courts are authorized to hear only less serious criminal cases, usually involving misdemeanors, or to hear special types of cases, such as traffic violations, family disputes, and small claims. **Courts of limited jurisdiction**, which are depicted on TV shows like *Judge Judy* and *Judge Joe Brown*, rarely hold jury trials, depending instead on the hearing judge to make determinations of both fact and law. At the lower-court level, a detailed record of the proceedings is not maintained. Case files will include only information on the charge, the plea, the finding of the court, and the sentence. All but six of the states make use of trial courts of limited jurisdiction.[4] These lower courts are much less formal than **courts of general jurisdiction**.

Trial courts of general jurisdiction—variously called *high courts, circuit courts,* or *superior courts*—are authorized to hear any criminal case. In many states, they also provide the first appellate level for courts of limited jurisdiction. In most cases, superior courts offer defendants whose cases originated in lower courts the chance for a new trial instead of a review of the record of the earlier hearing. When a new trial is held, it is referred to as **trial *de novo.***

Trial courts of general jurisdiction operate within a fact-finding framework called the *adversarial process.* That process pits the interests of the state, represented by prosecutors, against the professional skills and abilities of defense attorneys. The adversarial process is not a free-for-all; rather, it is constrained by procedural rules specified in law and sustained through tradition.

State Appellate Courts

Most states today have an appellate division where people can appeal a decision against them. The appellate division generally consists of an intermediate appellate court (often called the *court of appeals*) and a high-level appellate court (generally termed the *state supreme court*). High-level appellate courts are referred to as

■ **court of last resort** The court authorized by law to hear the final appeal on a matter.
■ **appeal** Generally, the request that a court with appellate jurisdiction review the judgment, decision, or order of a lower court and set it aside (reverse it) or modify it.
■ **state court administrator** A coordinator who assists with case-flow management, operating funds budgeting, and court docket administration.

■ **lecture note** Explain that the function of appellate courts is to review decisions made by lower courts within their jurisdiction. Note that defendants convicted in a lower court generally have a right to appeal and that most convictions are confirmed upon appeal.
■ **lecture note** Describe the high workloads facing many criminal courts today. Discuss the fact that many simple disputes, even some involving minor crimes, may not need formal resolution before a formal court of law.
■ **lecture note** Describe the relatively recent evolution of dispute resolution centers as informal mechanisms for the mediation of conflicts. Use the example of a dispute over a parking space on a crowded residential street leading to a minor act of vandalism, such as a broken car antenna or a punctured tire, to illustrate the type of disagreement that might benefit more from mediation than from formal intervention by a court of law.
■ **theme** What are the goals of specialized court programs? How are they different from other criminal courts?

courts of last resort, indicating that a defendant can go no further with an appeal within the state court system once the high court rules on a case. All states have supreme courts, although only 39 have intermediate appellate courts.[5]

An **appeal** by a convicted defendant asks that a higher court review the actions of a lower court. Once they agree to review a decision, or accept an appeal, courts within the appellate division do not conduct a new trial. Instead, they review the case on the record, examining the written transcript of lower-court hearings to ensure that those proceedings were carried out fairly and in accordance with proper procedure and state law. These courts may also allow attorneys for both sides to make brief oral arguments and will generally consider other briefs or information filed by the appellant (the party initiating the appeal) or the appellee (the side opposed to the appeal). State statutes generally require that sentences of death or life imprisonment be automatically reviewed by the state supreme court.

Most convictions are affirmed on appeal. Occasionally, however, an appellate court will determine that the trial court erred in allowing certain kinds of evidence to be heard, that it failed to properly interpret the significance of a relevant statute, or that some other impropriety occurred. When that happens, the verdict of the trial court will be reversed, and the case may be sent back for a new trial, or *remanded*. When a conviction is overturned by an appellate court because of constitutional issues or when a statute is determined to be invalid, the state usually has recourse to the state supreme court or, when an issue of federal law is involved, as when a state court has ruled a federal law unconstitutional, to the U.S. Supreme Court.

Defendants who are not satisfied with the resolution of their case within the state court system may attempt an appeal to the U.S. Supreme Court. For such an appeal to have any chance of being heard, it must be based on claimed violations of the defendant's rights, as guaranteed under federal law or the U.S. Constitution. Under certain circumstances, federal district courts, which we will look at later in the chapter, may also provide a path of relief for state defendants who can show that their federal constitutional rights were violated. However, in the 1992 case of *Keeney* v. *Tamayo-Reyes*, the U.S. Supreme Court ruled that a "respondent is entitled to a federal evidentiary hearing [only] if he can show cause for his failure to develop the facts in the state-court proceedings and actual prejudice resulting from that failure, or if he can show that a fundamental miscarriage of justice would result from failure to hold such a hearing."[6] Justice Byron White, writing for the Court, said, "It is hardly a good use of scarce judicial resources to duplicate fact-finding in federal court merely because a petitioner has negligently failed to take advantage of opportunities in state-court proceedings."

Likewise, in *Herrera* v. *Collins* (1993),[7] the Court ruled that new evidence of innocence is no reason for a federal court to order a new state trial if constitutional grounds are lacking. The *Keeney* and *Herrera* decisions have severely limited access by state defendants to federal courts.

State Court Administration

To function efficiently, courts require uninterrupted funding, adequate staffing, trained support personnel, a well-managed case flow, and coordination between levels and among jurisdictions. To oversee these and other aspects of judicial management, every state has its own mechanism for court administration. Most have **state court administrators** who manage these operational functions.

State court administrators can receive assistance from the National Center for State Courts (NCSC) in Williamsburg, Virginia. The NCSC is an independent nonprofit organization dedicated to the improvement of the American court system. It was founded in 1971 at the behest of Chief Justice Warren E. Burger. You can visit the National Center for State Courts at **http://www.ncsc.org**.

At the federal level, the court system is administered by the Administrative Office of the United States Courts (AOUSC), in Washington, D.C. The AOUSC, created by Congress in 1939, prepares the budget and legislative agenda for federal courts. It also performs audits of court accounts, manages funds for the operation of federal courts, compiles and publishes statistics on the volume and type of business conducted by the courts, and recommends plans and strategies to efficiently manage court business. You can visit the Administrative Office of the United States Courts via **http://www.uscourts.gov/Home.aspx**.

■ **dispute-resolution center** An informal hearing place designed to mediate interpersonal disputes without resorting to the more formal arrangements of a criminal trial court.

■ **community court** A low-level court that focuses on quality-of-life crimes that erode a neighborhood's morale. Community courts emphasize problem solving rather than punishment and build on restorative principles such as community service and restitution.

Dispute-Resolution Centers and Specialized Courts

It is often possible to resolve minor disputes (in which minor criminal offenses might otherwise be charged) without a formal court hearing. Some communities have **dispute-resolution centers**, which hear victims' claims of minor wrongs such as passing bad checks, trespassing, shoplifting, and petty theft. Today, more than 200 centers throughout the country,[8] frequently staffed by volunteer mediators, work to resolve disagreements without assigning blame. Dispute-resolution programs began in the early 1970s, with the earliest being the Community Assistance Project in Chester, Pennsylvania; the Night Prosecutor Program in Columbus, Ohio; and the Arbitration as an Alternative Program in Rochester, New York. Following the lead of these programs, the U.S. Department of Justice helped promote the development of three experimental Neighborhood Justice Centers in Los Angeles; Kansas City, Missouri; and Atlanta. Each center accepted both minor civil and criminal cases.

Mediation centers are often closely integrated with the formal criminal justice process and may substantially reduce the caseload of lower-level courts. Some centers are, in fact, run by the courts and work only with court-ordered referrals. Others are semiautonomous but may be dependent on courts for endorsement of their decisions; others function with complete autonomy. Rarely, however, do dispute-resolution programs entirely supplant the formal criminal justice mechanism, and defendants who appear before a community mediator may later be charged with a crime. Community mediation programs have become a central feature of today's restorative justice movement (discussed in more detail in Chapter 11).

Unlike dispute-resolution centers, **community courts** are always *official* components of the formal justice system and can hand down sentences, including fines and jail time, without the need for further judicial review. Community courts began as grassroots movements undertaken by community residents and local organizations seeking to build confidence in the way offenders are handled for less serious offenses. A distinguishing feature of community courts is their focus on quality-of-life crimes that erode a neighborhood's morale. Like dispute-resolution centers they emphasize problem solving rather than punishment, and build on restorative principles such as community

A small claims court mediation session in progress. Staffed largely by volunteers, dispute-resolution centers facilitate cooperative solutions to relatively low-level disputes in which minor criminal offenses might otherwise be charged. How do dispute-resolution centers help relieve some of the pressures facing our criminal courts?

© ZUMA Press, Inc./Alamy

■ **specialized court** A low-level court that focuses on relatively minor offenses and handles special populations or addresses special issues such as reentry. Specialized courts are often a form of community courts.

■ **lecture note** Discuss the rise of federal courts by referring to Article III, Section I, of the U.S. Constitution, which outlines the specific structure of federal courts.

service and restitution. Other authors note that "The basic premise behind the problem-solving court model is the idea that instead of merely adjudicating legal questions or punishing criminal behavior after the fact, courts should seek to prevent crime by directly addressing its underlying causes."[9]

Community courts generally sentence convicted offenders to work within the community, "where neighbors can see what they are doing."[10] A recent study of the Red Hook Community Justice Center in Red Hook, New York, found that defendants considered the community court to be more fair than traditional courts.[11] According to the study, perceptions of fairness were primarily related to the more personal role played by community court judges, who dispense with much of the formality of traditional courts and who often offer support and praise to defendants who work within the parameters set by the court. Finally, a 2013 National Center for State Courts' study found the Red Hook center to be effective in reducing recidivism, noting that "RHCJC defendants were significantly less likely than downtown defendants to be re-arrested...."[12]

Recently, the community justice movement has led to the creation of innovative low-level courts in some parts of the country. These **specialized courts** focus on relatively minor offenses, and handle special populations or address special issues. Some hear only cases involving veterans, others focus on the needs of the mentally ill or the homeless. Still others handle only sex offenders charged with lessor offenses. The Brooklyn Mental Health Court provides an example of a specialized court that, in its own words, "seeks to craft a meaningful response to the problems posed by defendants with mental illness in the criminal justice system."[13] The Brooklyn court attempts to address both the needs of defendants with mental illness and public safety concerns. It uses the authority of the court to provide counseling and treatment for defendants with identified serious and persistent mental illnesses in lieu of jail or prison time. The court employs on-site clinical teams to assess the degree of mental illness from which a defendant suffers, and to gauge the risk that the defendant represents to the community were he or she to be released into a community-based supervision program.

Specialized courts that deal with specific offenses include gun courts, domestic violence courts, driving while intoxicated (DWI) or driving under the influence (DUI) courts, and drug courts. Other specialized courts, called reentry courts, utilize the drug court model to facilitate the reintegration of drug-involved offenders paroled into the community after being released from prison. Using the authority of the court to apply graduated sanctions and positive reinforcement, reentry courts

marshal resources to support positive reintegration by the returning offender. Reentry courts are discussed in more detail in Chapter 12.

Most specialized court programs are motivated by two sets of goals: (1) case management, in which the court works to expedite case processing and reduce caseloads, as well as to reduce time to disposition (thus increasing trial capacity for more serious crimes); and (2) therapeutic jurisprudence, in which the court works to reduce criminal offending through therapeutic and interdisciplinary approaches that address addiction and other underlying issues without jeopardizing public safety and due process.[14]

Specialized courts can be distinguished from other criminal courts by the fact that they operate according to a problem-solving model, rather than a retributive one—meaning that they seek to address the root causes of law violation, whether they lie within the individual, the community, or the larger culture.[15] Their purpose is not only to make justice more efficient, but more effective, as well.

The Federal Court System

Whereas state courts evolved from early colonial arrangements, federal courts were created by the U.S. Constitution. Article III, Section 1, of the Constitution provides for the establishment of "one supreme Court, and ... such inferior Courts as the Congress may from time to time ordain and establish." Article III, Section 2, specifies that such courts are to have jurisdiction over cases arising under the Constitution, federal laws, and treaties. Federal courts are also to settle disputes between states and to have jurisdiction in cases where one of the parties is a state.

Today's federal court system represents the culmination of a series of congressional mandates that have expanded the federal judicial infrastructure so that it can continue to carry out the duties envisioned by the Constitution. Notable federal statutes that have contributed to the present structure of the federal court system include the Judiciary Act of 1789, the Judiciary Act of 1925, and the Magistrate's Act of 1968.

As a result of constitutional mandates, congressional actions, and other historical developments, today's federal judiciary consists of three levels: (1) U.S. district courts, (2) U.S. courts of appeals, and (3) the U.S. Supreme Court. Each is described in turn in the following sections.

CJ | NEWS
America's Judiciary: Courting Disaster

Newscom

The Schenectady (New York) County Courthouse. How might state budget shortfalls impact the important role of courts?

As states slash budgets to get through a still-sluggish economy, the courts under their jurisdiction are feeling the pain in the form of fewer personnel, shorter hours of operation and backed-up caseloads. In 2014, for example, Kansas Chief Justice Lawton Nuss said in his annual State of the Judiciary speech that he anticipated a coming shutdown of courts statewide unless the Kansas legislature appropriated more money for the judiciary.

After years of cuts for courts, "we are now at the point where funding failures are not merely causing inconvenience, annoyances and burdens," said David Boies, co-chairman of an American Bar Association (ABA) commission looking into the problem. Altogether, 42 states cut judicial funding in 2011, according to the National Center for State Courts.

Covering 95% of all litigation, state-financed court systems are essential for prosecuting criminals, resolving personal conflicts, straightening out household finances, and getting business done. This work includes county-based trial courts that try criminal and civil cases, as well as special courts to address traffic accidents, small claims, family matters, and other issues.

Services are being cut at a time when case volumes are often on the rise due to the same economic forces driving the cuts. In tough economic times, courts tend to deal with increased foreclosures, bankruptcies, contract claims and embezzlement cases, the ABA reports.

Between 2005 and 2010, the state of Maine, for example, experienced a 50% increase in civil cases.

Generally, when courts cut their budgets, criminal cases are least affected. Many jurisdictions have to meet mandated time limits on the period between arrest and arraignment, and the case may be thrown out if the limits are violated. Citing the time limit, Georgia courts recently dismissed indictments against several suspects accused of violent crimes.

The focus on meeting criminal time limits means the brunt of the cuts goes to civil cases, including foreclosures, divorces, traffic violations and civil disputes. According to the New York Bar Association, for example, it often takes a year to begin a civil trial in Ulster County, New York.

Even as the economy improves, many states are still struggling with their budgets and continue to cut back court services:

- In California, the Los Angeles County Superior Court system plans to lay off about 350 employees in June due to cuts in spending for courts across the state. California justices have warned that it may take up to five years to resolve civil cases.

- In Florida, the 2013 state budget included a 7% cut for court clerks, who are essential to efficient court operation. Clerks say the cuts could lead to 40-day delays in the processing of documents.

- In New York, judges have begun to cut hours, usually stopping court at 4:30 p.m., even when testimony is ongoing or a jury is deliberating, the state bar association reports.

Recently, at least 15 states reported reduced hours of court operations in, the National Center for State Courts reported.

Budget-cutting tactics such as sending staff home in "furlough closures," however, just make the problem worse, said New Mexico Chief Justice Charles W. Daniels. "It's not like a furlough closure of a museum or a park or a tourist train, where you can actually save money by cutting services to the public on a given day," he said. "The work of busy courts just gets even more backed up and still takes the same resources, the same employee time, the same expense to process."

The ABA reports that state cuts for the judiciary started well before the recession and can be proportionately larger than cuts for other state-funded agencies. Back when state legislators were predominantly lawyers, Boies said they understood the courts' needs and routinely approved judicial funding, but fewer legislators are lawyers now.

Resources: "Task Force Finds Court Underfunding Still a Crisis, Business Partnership an Opportunity," *ABA Now*, February 6, 2012, http://www.abanow.org/2012/02/task-force-finds-court-underfunding-still-a-crisis-business-partnership-an-opportunity/; "Budget Cuts Clog Criminal Justice System," *Daily Herald*, October 27, 2011, http://www.heraldextra.com/news/national/article_9f1459ac-fb78-5a41-bd5e-8d930a28281b.html; and "Cuts Could Stall Sluggish Courts at Every Turn," *New York Times*, May 15, 2011, http://www.nytimes.com/2011/05/16/nyregion/budget-cuts-for-new-york-courts-likely-to-mean-delays.html?pagewanted=all; Andy Marso, "Nuss: Courts Will Shut Down without More Funds," *The Topeka Capital-Journal*, January 22, 2014, http://cjonline.com/news/2014-01-22/nuss-courts-will-shut-down-without-more-funds.

U.S. District Courts

The U.S. district courts are the trial courts of the federal court system.[16] Within limits set by Congress and the Constitution, the district courts have jurisdiction to hear nearly all categories of federal cases, including both civil and criminal matters. There are 94 federal judicial districts, including at least one district in each state (some states, such as New York and California, have

as many as four), the District of Columbia, and Puerto Rico. Each district includes a U.S. bankruptcy court as a unit of the district court. Three territories of the United States—the Virgin Islands, Guam, and the Northern Mariana Islands—have district courts that hear federal cases, including bankruptcy cases. There are two special trial courts that have nationwide jurisdiction over certain types of cases. The Court of International Trade addresses cases involving international trade and customs issues.

■ **lecture note** Tell the class that there are 94 federal district courts. Explain that federal district courts have original jurisdiction over all cases involving alleged violations of federal statutes.

■ **activity** Invite a magistrate judge to speak to the class. Have them prepare questions in advance about the challenges of the magistrate's role in the criminal justice process.
■ **lecture note** Refer to Figure 9-3 to describe the geographic boundaries of federal judicial circuits. Allude to the Judiciary Act of 1789, which created the U.S. Supreme Court and the federal court system.

The U.S. Court of Federal Claims has jurisdiction over most claims for monetary damages against the United States, disputes over federal contracts, unlawful "takings" of private property by the federal government, and a variety of other claims against the United States.

Federal district courts have original jurisdiction over all cases involving alleged violations of federal statutes. A district may be divided into divisions and may have several places where the court hears cases. District courts were first authorized by Congress through the Judiciary Act of 1789, which allocated one federal court to each state. Because of population increases over the years, new courts have been added in many states.

Nearly 650 district court judges staff federal district courts. Because some courts are much busier than others, the number of district court judges varies from a low of two in some jurisdictions to a high of 27 in others. District court judges are appointed by the president and confirmed by the Senate, and they serve for life. An additional 369 full-time and 110 part-time magistrate judges (referred to as *U.S. magistrates* before 1990) serve the district court system and assist the federal judges. Magistrate judges have the power to conduct arraignments and may set bail, issue warrants, and try minor offenders.

U.S. district courts handle tens of thousands of cases per year. During 2013, for example, 68,918 criminal cases[17] and 284,605 civil cases[18] were filed in U.S. district courts. Drug prosecution and the prosecution of illegal immigrants, especially in federal courts located close to the U.S.–Mexican border, has led to considerable growth in the number of cases filed. Federal drug prosecutions in the border states of California, Arizona, New Mexico, and Texas more than doubled between 1994 and 2000, from 2,864 to 6,116, and immigration prosecutions increased more than sevenfold, from 1,056 to 7,613.[19] During the past 20 years, the number of cases handled by the entire federal district court system has grown exponentially. The hiring of new judges and the creation of new courtroom facilities have not kept pace with the increase in caseload, and questions persist as to the quality of justice that overworked judges can deliver.

In 2011, in response to rapidly growing caseloads, Roslyn O. Silver, a federal judge in the Ninth Circuit's Tucson division, declared a federal court emergency in Arizona. The emergency declaration came in response to the rising number of illegal immigration and drug smuggling cases handled by federal courts in the state. In fact, federal criminal caseloads in Arizona rose 65% from 2008 to 2011 after the Department of Homeland Security established a policy of criminal prosecution for anyone caught crossing the border illegally.[20] Under the emergency declaration, federal courts can avoid certain Speedy Trial Act requirements and push the time limit for a trial to begin to 180 days (up from the 70 days normally required by the legislation).

Another pressing issue facing district court judges is the fact that their pay, which at around $200,000 in early 2015[21] placed them in the top 1% of income-earning Americans, is low compared to what most could earn in private practice. Recently, U.S. Supreme Court Justice John Roberts noted that because of relatively low pay, "judges effectively serve for a term dictated by their financial position rather than for life."[22] Learn more about the federal courts at **http://www.justicestudies.com/pubs/fedcourts.pdf**.

U.S. Courts of Appeals

The 94 judicial districts are organized into 13 regional circuits, each of which has a U.S. court of appeals.[23] A court of appeals hears appeals from the district courts located within its circuit, as well as appeals from decisions of federal administrative agencies. The Court of Appeals for the Federal Circuit has nationwide jurisdiction to hear appeals in special cases, such as those involving patent laws and cases decided by the Court of International Trade and the U.S. Court of Federal Claims.

The U.S. Court of Appeals for the Federal Circuit and the 12 regional courts of appeals are often referred to as *circuit courts*. Early in the nation's history, the judges of the first courts of appeals visited each of the courts in one region in a particular sequence, traveling by horseback and riding the "circuit." Today, the regional courts of appeals review matters from the district courts of their geographic regions, from the U.S. Tax Court, and from certain federal administrative agencies. A disappointed party in a district court usually has the right to have the case reviewed in the court of appeals for the circuit. The First through Eleventh Circuits all include three or more states, as illustrated in Figure 9-3.

Each court of appeals consists of six or more judges, depending on the caseload of the court. Circuit court judges are appointed for life by the president with the advice and consent of the Senate. The judge who has served on the court the longest and who is under 65 years of age is designated as the chief judge and performs administrative duties in addition to hearing cases. The chief judge serves for a maximum term of seven years. There are 167 judges on the 12 regional courts of appeals.

Circuit court judges are appointed for life by the president with the advice and consent of the Senate.

FIGURE 9-3 | Geographic Boundaries of the U.S. Courts of Appeals

Source: Pearson Education, Inc.

The U.S. Court of Appeals for the District of Columbia, which is often called the Twelfth Circuit, hears cases arising in the District of Columbia and has appellate jurisdiction assigned by Congress in legislation concerning many departments of the federal government. The U.S. Court of Appeals for the Federal Circuit (in effect, the Thirteenth Circuit) was created in 1982 by the merging of the U.S. Court of Claims and the U.S. Court of Customs and Patent Appeals. The court hears appeals in cases from the U.S. Court of Federal Claims, the U.S. Court of International Trade, the U.S. Court of Veterans Appeals, the International Trade Commission, the Board of Contract Appeals, the Patent and Trademark Office, and the Merit Systems Protection Board. The Federal Circuit Court also hears appeals from certain decisions of the secretaries of the Department of Agriculture and the Department of Commerce and cases from district courts involving patents and minor claims against the federal government.

Almost all appeals from federal district courts go to the court of appeals serving the circuit in which the case was first heard. Federal appellate courts have mandatory jurisdiction over the decisions of district courts within their circuits. *Mandatory jurisdiction* means that U.S. courts of appeals are required to hear the cases brought to them. Criminal appeals from federal district courts are usually heard by panels of three judges sitting on a court of appeals rather than by all the judges of each circuit. A defendant's right to appeal, however, has been interpreted to mean the right to one appeal. Hence the U.S. Supreme Court need not necessarily hear the appeals of defendants who are dissatisfied with the decision of a federal appellate court.

Federal appellate courts operate under the Federal Rules of Appellate Procedure, although each has also created its own separate Local Rules. Local Rules may mean that one circuit, such as

the Second, will depend heavily on oral arguments, while others may substitute written summary depositions in their place. Appeals generally fall into one of three categories: (1) frivolous appeals, which have little substance, raise no significant new issues, and are generally disposed of quickly; (2) ritualistic appeals, which are brought primarily because of the demands of litigants, even though the probability of reversal is negligible; and (3) nonconsensual appeals, which entail major questions of law and policy and on which there is considerable professional disagreement among the courts and within the legal profession.[24] The probability of reversal is highest in the case of nonconsensual appeals.

In 2013, the Judicial Conference of the United States, the primary policymaking arm of the federal courts, urged Congress to create 70 permanent new federal judgeships in appellate and district courts.[25] The conference cited a need for 5 new appeals court judges and 65 new federal judges at the district court level.

The U.S. Supreme Court

At the apex of the federal court system stands the U.S. Supreme Court. The Supreme Court is located in Washington, D.C., across the street from the U.S. Capitol. The Court consists of nine justices, eight of whom are associate justices. The ninth presides over the Court as the chief justice of the United States. Supreme Court justices are nominated by the president, are confirmed by the Senate, and serve for life. Lengthy terms of service are a tradition among justices. One of the earliest chief justices, John Marshall, served the Court for 34 years, from 1801 to 1835. The same was true of Justice Stephen J. Field, who sat on the bench between 1863 and 1897. Justice Hugo Black passed the 34-year record, serving an additional month, before

■ **lecture note**   Highlight the case of *Marbury* v. *Madison* (1803) as significant because it was through this case that the U.S. Supreme Court first asserted its power and laid claim to its continuing role as the ultimate arbitrator
of constitutional issues.

■ **activity**   Have the class research the congressional confirmation hearings of selected Supreme Court nominees, including John Roberts, Robert
Bork, David Souter, Clarence Thomas, Ruth Bader Ginsburg, and Stephen
Breyer. Ask them to identify the issues raised by both sides in the debates
over these candidates. Which of these candidates would probably be the favorite of individual-rights advocates? Of public-order advocates? Why?

■ **lecture note**   Explain that the U.S. Supreme Court wields immense
judicial power by virtue of its role as interpreter of constitutional mandates.

■ **judicial review**   The power of a court to review actions
and decisions made by other agencies of government.

he retired in 1971. Justice William O. Douglas set a record for
longevity on the bench, retiring in 1975 after 36 years and six
months of service. You can view the biographies of today's
Supreme Court justices via **http://www.supremecourt.gov/
about/biographies.aspx**.

The Supreme Court of the United States wields immense
power. The Court's greatest authority lies in its capacity for
judicial review of lower-court decisions and state and federal statutes. By exercising its power of judicial review, the
Court decides what laws and lower-court decisions keep with
the intent of the U.S. Constitution. The power of judicial review is not explicit in the Constitution but was anticipated by
its framers. In the *Federalist-Papers*, which urged adoption of
the Constitution, Alexander Hamilton wrote that through the
practice of judicial review, the Court would ensure that "the
will of the whole people," as grounded in the Constitution,
would be supreme over the "will of the legislature," which
might be subject to temporary whims.[26] It was not until 1803,
however, that the Court forcefully asserted its power of judicial
review. In an opinion written for the case of *Marbury* v. *Madison*

(1803),[27] Chief Justice John Marshall established the Court's
authority as final interpreter of the U.S. Constitution, declaring, "It is emphatically the province of the judicial department
to say what the law is."

The Supreme Court Today

The Supreme Court reviews the decisions of lower courts and
may accept cases both from U.S. courts of appeals and from state
supreme courts. It has limited original jurisdiction and does not
conduct trials except in disputes between states and in some
cases of attorney disbarment. For a case to be heard, at least
four justices must vote in favor of a hearing. When the Court
agrees to hear a case, it will issue a writ of *certiorari* to a lower
court, ordering it to send the records of the case forward for
review. Once having granted *certiorari*, the justices can revoke the
decision. In such cases, a writ is dismissed by ruling that it was
improvidently granted.

The U.S. Supreme Court may review any decision appealed
to it that it decides is worthy of review. In fact, however, the
Court elects to review only cases that involve a substantial federal

Julie Bernstein/Alamy

Demonstrators in support of a 2012 ruling by the Ninth Circuit Court of Appeals affirming a decision by U.S. District Court Judge Vaughn
R. Walker that overturned California's ban on gay marriages. The Ninth Circuit also held that the fact that Walker is gay was immaterial.
Do judges' personal perspectives influence their decisions? Should they?

SAUL LOEB/Getty Images

U.S. Supreme Court Justice Sonia Sotomayor (center) being applauded by President Barack Obama and Vice President Joe Biden at her 2009 nomination to the Court. Do you think that a justice's personal values and beliefs might influence his or her decisions on important matters that come before the court—or are such decisions always a matter of impersonal application of relevant law?

The U.S. Supreme Court may review any decision appealed to it that it decides is worthy of review. question. Of approximately 5,000 requests for review received by the Court yearly, only about 200 are heard.

A term of the Supreme Court begins, by statute, on the first Monday in October and lasts until early July. The term is divided among sittings, when cases will be heard, and time for the writing and delivering of opinions. Between 22 and 24 cases are heard at each sitting (which may last days), with each side allotted 30 minutes for arguments before the justices. Intervening recesses allow justices time to study arguments and supporting documentation and to work on their opinions.

Decisions rendered by the Supreme Court are rarely unanimous. Instead, the opinion that a majority of the Court's justices agree on becomes the judgment of the Court. Justices who agree with the Court's judgment write concurring opinions if they agree for a different reason or if they feel that they have some new light to shed on a legal issue in the case. Justices who do not agree with the decision of the Court write dissenting opinions, which may offer new possibilities for successful appeals of future cases. Visit the U.S. Supreme Court via **http://www.supremecourt.gov**.

The Courtroom Work Group

On May 24, 2011, following an extended period of jury selection, the first-degree murder trial of 23-year-old Casey Anthony began at the Orange County courthouse in Orlando, Florida.

Prosecutors told a packed courtroom that Casey was responsible for the death of her two-year-old daughter, Caylee Marie Anthony. Caylee had been reported missing on June 15, 2008, by her grandmother—a month after her mother said she had disappeared.[29] According to law enforcement officials, Casey told a string of lies about her daughter's disappearance, and in October 2008, she was charged with first-degree murder. Prosecutors also charged Casey with aggravated child abuse, aggravated manslaughter, and providing false information to law enforcement officers. Soon after, a utility worker found Caylee's remains among cloth laundry and plastic trash bags near her home. Glittery pink letters that spelled out the phrase "Big Trouble Comes Small" were found on the shirt that Caylee was wearing at the time of her death.

After a trial that lasted 36 days, Casey was acquitted of all of the serious charges that had been brought against her. The jury did, however, find her guilty of the relatively minor crime of lying to a law enforcement officer. Dozens of people were involved in the Anthony trial—including jurors, attorneys, witnesses, and courtroom security personnel. Also present were hundreds of media representatives and courtroom spectators. Millions of people watched the trial unfold on cable TV.

Professional Courtroom Participants

To the public eye, criminal trials frequently appear to be well-managed events even though they may entail quite a bit of drama. Like plays on a stage, trials involve many participants,

■ **theme**   What two subgroups constitute the courtroom work group? Is one more important than the other? Why or why not?

■ **lecture note**   Discuss the roles of the various professional courtroom actors, including the judge, prosecutor, defense attorney, bailiff, local court administrator, court reporter, clerk, and expert witness. Use a well-known case as an example.

■ **courtroom work group**   The professional courtroom actors, including judges, prosecuting attorneys, defense attorneys, public defenders, and others who earn a living serving the court.

paying for it

Cost-Efficient Courts

It might seem strange to spend money in order to save it. Yet, that's just what the Washington, D.C.–based Justice Policy Institute recommended in 2011 with publication of its report System Overload. The Institute pointed out that nearly four out of five people charged with a crime in the United States are eligible for assistance from court-appointed counsel; yet the funding allocated to public defender's offices has historically been so poor in many areas that they have been in a state of "chronic crisis" for decades. It's only by upping the quality of America's public defense system, the Institute says, that innocent people can be prevented from being convicted and going to prison—which would ultimately cost taxpayers far more than funding quality public defender programs.

Special-purpose courts, which divert nonviolent offenders from prison, can also serve taxpayers effectively. In Champaign County, Illinois, for example, felony drug offenders are routinely adjudicated in the area's special drug court. If found guilty, most offenders are placed on probation and ordered to undergo treatment at county expense, especially when judged not to be a danger to themselves or to the community. Some of the money spent on treatment can be recouped when offenders are also ordered to participate in mandatory community service programs and to pay restitution. Experts estimate that imprisonment in Illinois costs the state $21,500 per year for every offender kept behind bars. In contrast, probation, combined with drug treatment, costs approximately $4,000.

Drug courts, like many other special-purpose courts, effectively divert nonviolent defendants not only from prison, but from the more elaborate, and far more expensive, formal processing of trial courts.

Treatment courts, which serve mentally ill populations, are another recent innovation, designed to divert offenders with mental issues from prison and place them into treatment programs. In 2012, the state of Michigan ran eight mental health courts, serving nearly 700 people per year. Typical defendants seen by Michigan's treatment court have gotten into trouble with the law for relatively minor offenses, but because of their frequently lengthy arrest records, they might have ended up in jail or prison when handled by traditional criminal courts. Instead, Michigan's treatment courts work with community-based non-profit organizations, such as the Detroit Central City Community Mental Health agency, and order psychotherapy, medication, and even residential treatment for the most serious cases. The cost savings are obvious: In Detroit, community treatment costs about $10,000 per year, versus around $35,000 for incarceration.

Moreover, special-purpose courts hold the promise of breaking the revolving door of imprisonment. Many drug-involved and mentally ill offenders are bound to a vicious cycle of crime commission and, without the treatment options offered by these special courts, would keep the revolving door of prison spinning.

Special-purpose courts are not the only way that money can be saved in the court system. In 2012, the National Center for State Courts (NCSC) performed an analysis on the use of e-filings versus paper documents in selected courthouses. The NCSC found that effective e-filing systems could cut the costs of document intake and storage to as little as 11 cents per page compared with 69 cents per page for costs of paper intake and storage. Moreover, said the Center, "courthouses are incredibly expensive storage spaces."[28] A small file room measuring 20 by 60 feet, said the Center, "would cost $360,000 to construct and at 5% per year, cost $18,000 per year to heat/cool and maintain." A typical computer hard drive, which could contain all of that digitized data in that room, might be purchased for as little as $300, although backup and associated computer costs would raise the costs somewhat. Learn more about using technology to achieve greater efficiency in courtroom operation from the NCSC at **http://www.ncsc.org**.

Oscar Hidalgo/The New York Times/Redux Pictures

Arthur J. Jones (right), who quit his job as a public defender in Miami because of low pay and a huge workload. Jones was afraid that his huge client load could lead to mistakes. How might an effective public defender system be funded?

References: Champaign County Drug Court, "General Information," http://www.co.champaign.il.us/circt/DrugCourt/Info.htm (accessed August 1, 2012); Jeff Gerritt, "Salvaging Lives, Saving Money: Eight Pilot Courts That Divert Mentally Ill Offenders from Prison," *Detroit Free Press*, March 4, 2012, http://www.freep.com/article/20120304 (accessed August 1, 2012); and James E. McMillan, Carole D. Pettijohn, and Jennifer K. Berg, "Calculating an E-Court Return on Investment (ROI)," *Court Technology Bulletin*, February 16, 2012, http://courttech bulletin.blogspot.com/2012/02/calculating-e-court-return-on.html (accessed August 2, 2013).

■ **lecture note**   Explain the general responsibilities of the trial judge by referring to the American Bar Association's *Standards for Criminal Justice*. Stress the judge's role as mediator within an adversarial setting.

■ **activity**   Invite a criminal court judge to speak with the class. Have him or her outline the responsibilities of a judge and discuss the adversarial process. Ask the judge to discuss the greatest challenges he or she faces.

■ **judge**   An elected or appointed public official who presides over a court of law and who is authorized to hear and sometimes to decide cases and to conduct trials.

Casey Anthony in a Florida courtroom in 2011. After a six-week trial, Anthony was found guilty on charges that she had lied to police, but was found not guilty of first-degree murder and other serious charges. Why did some people feel that the verdict was unfair?

each of whom has a different role to fill. Unlike such plays, however, they are real-life events, and the impact that a trial's outcome has on people's lives can be far-reaching.

Participants in a criminal trial can be divided into two categories (Figure 9-4): professionals and outsiders. The professionals are the official courtroom actors; they are well versed in criminal trial practice and set the stage for and conduct the business of the court. Judges, prosecuting attorneys, defense attorneys, public defenders, and others who earn a living serving the court fall into this category. Professional courtroom actors are also called the **courtroom work group**. Some writers have pointed out that aside from statutory requirements and ethical considerations, courtroom interaction among professionals involves an implicit recognition of informal rules of civility, cooperation, and shared goals.[30] Hence even within the adversarial framework of a criminal trial, the courtroom work group is dedicated to bringing the procedure to a successful close.[31]

In contrast, outsiders—those trial participants who are only temporarily involved with the court—are generally unfamiliar with courtroom organization and trial procedure. Outsiders, or nonjudicial personnel, include jurors and witnesses as well as defendants and victims. Although in this chapter we refer to these people as nonprofessional courtroom actors, they may have a greater personal investment in the outcome of the trial than anyone else.

The Judge

The trial **judge** has the primary duty of ensuring justice. The American Bar Association's *Standards for Criminal Justice* describes the duties of the trial judge as follows: "The trial judge has the responsibility for safeguarding both the rights of the accused and the interests of the public in the administration of criminal justice ... . The purpose of a criminal trial is to determine whether the prosecution has established the guilt of the accused as required by law, and the trial judge should not allow the proceedings to be used for any other purpose."[32]

> The trial judge has the primary duty of ensuring justice.

In the courtroom, the judge holds ultimate authority, ruling on matters of law, weighing objections from both sides, deciding on the admissibility of evidence, and disciplining anyone who challenges the order of the court. In most jurisdictions, judges also sentence offenders after a verdict has been returned; in some states, judges serve to decide guilt or innocence for defendants who waive a jury trial.

Most state jurisdictions have a chief judge who, besides serving as a trial judge, must also manage the court system. Management includes hiring staff, scheduling sessions of court, ensuring the adequate training of subordinate judges, and coordinating activities with other courtroom actors. Chief judges usually assume their position by virtue of seniority and rarely have any formal training in management. Hence the managerial effectiveness of a chief judge is often a matter of personality and dedication more than anything else.

Judicial Selection

As mentioned earlier, judges at the federal level are nominated by the president of the United States and take their place on the bench only after confirmation by the Senate. At the state level, things work somewhat differently. Depending on the jurisdiction, state judgeships are won either through popular election or by political (usually gubernatorial) appointment. The process of judicial selection at the state level is set by law.

Both judicial election and appointment have been criticized for allowing politics to enter the judicial arena, although in somewhat different ways. Under the election system, judicial candidates must receive the endorsement of their parties, generate contributions,

> Both judicial election and appointment have been criticized for allowing politics to enter the judicial arena.

■ **theme**   This chapter describes three systems of judicial selection. Which of the three do you think would be most favored by public-order advocates? By individual-rights advocates? Why?

■ **lecture note**   Explain the various kinds of processes used in different jurisdictions for the selection of judges. Describe the problems associated with both political appointment and popular election, including the fact that appointed judges may unfairly represent the interests of those who appoint them.

■ **theme**   Throughout the Reagan–Bush era, the U.S. Supreme Court was characterized by an ideological shift toward the right. Many feel that that shift is still affecting the work of the Court. How might the daily activities of police officers, lower-court functionaries, and prison administrators be affected by the Court's conservatism? How do you feel about the High Court's ideology?

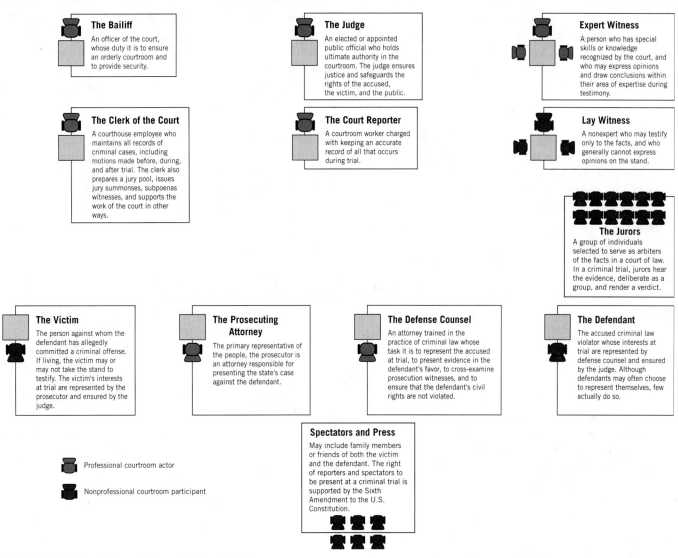

FIGURE 9-4 | Participants in a Criminal Trial

Source: Pearson Education, Inc.

and manage an effective campaign. Under the appointment system, judicial hopefuls must be in favor with incumbent politicians to receive appointments. Because partisan politics plays a role in both systems, critics have claimed that sitting judges can rarely be as neutral as they should be. They carry to the bench with them campaign promises, personal indebtedness, and possible political agendas.

To counter some of these problems, a number of states have adopted the Missouri Plan (or the Missouri Bar Plan) for judicial selection,[33] which combines elements of both election and appointment. It requires candidates for judicial vacancies to undergo screening by a nonpartisan state judicial nominating committee. Candidates selected by the committee are reviewed by an

arm of the governor's office, which selects a final list of names for appointment. Incumbent judges must face the electorate after a specified term in office. They then run unopposed in nonpartisan elections in which only their records may be considered. Voters have the choice of allowing a judge to continue in office or asking that another be appointed to take his or her place. Because the Missouri Plan provides for periodic public review of judicial performance, it is also called the *merit plan of judicial selection*.

Judicial Qualifications

A few decades ago, many states did not require any special training, education, or other qualifications for judges. Anyone (even

■ **lecture note**   Explain the role of the prosecuting attorney as the primary representative of the state or the people. Stress the fact that within the adversarial context of a criminal trial, the prosecuting attorney is expected to argue the state's case effectively.

■ **lecture note**   Discuss the prosecutor's law enforcement role and the need for close cooperation and communication with the police.

■ **prosecutor**   An attorney whose official duty is to conduct criminal proceedings on behalf of the state or the people against those accused of having committed criminal offenses.

someone without a law degree) who won election or was appointed could assume a judgeship. Today, however, almost all states require that judges in general jurisdiction and appellate courts hold a law degree, be a licensed attorney, and be a member of their state bar association. Many states also require newly elected judges to attend state-sponsored training sessions on subjects like courtroom procedure, evidence, dispute resolution, judicial writing, administrative record keeping, and ethics.

While most states provide instruction to meet the needs of trial judges, some organizations also provide specialized training. The National Judicial College (NJC), located on the campus of the University of Nevada at Reno, is one such institution. It was established in 1963 by the Joint Committee for the Effective Administration of Justice, chaired by Justice Tom C. Clark of the U.S. Supreme Court.[34] More than 3,000 judges enroll annually in courses offered by NJC, and many courses are offered online. The NJC, in collaboration with the National Council of Juvenile and Family Court Judges and the University of Nevada at Reno, offers the nation's only advanced judicial degree programs, leading to a master's degree and PhD in judicial studies.[35] Visit the National Judicial College via **http://www.judges.org**.

In some parts of the United States, lower-court judges, such as justices of the peace, local magistrates, and "district" court judges, may still be elected without educational and other professional requirements. Today, in 43 states, some 1,300 nonlawyer judges are serving in mostly rural courts of limited jurisdiction.[36] In New York, for example, of the 3,511 judges in the state's unified court system, approximately 2,250 are part-time town or village justices, and about 80% of town and village justices are not lawyers.[37] The majority of cases that come before New York lay judges involve alleged traffic violations, although they may also include misdemeanors, small-claims actions, and civil cases of up to $3,000.

Even though some have defended lay judges as being closer to the citizenry in their understanding of justice,[38] in most jurisdictions, the number of lay judges is declining. States that continue to use lay judges in lower courts do require that candidates for judgeships not have criminal records, and most states require that they attend special training sessions if elected.

Judicial Misconduct

Most judges are highly professional in and out of the courtroom. Occasionally, however, a judge oversteps the limits of his or her authority; some unprofessional judicial behavior may even violate the law. In April 2011, for example, 67-year-old senior U.S. District Court Judge Jack Tarpley Camp was sentenced to 30 days in federal prison for committing a series of crimes with an exotic dancer.[39] The sentencing judge, U.S. District Judge

Thomas Hogan, read the oath of office that Camp had taken 22 years earlier when he was sworn in, and said that Camp had disgraced his office. "He has denigrated the federal judiciary," said Hogan. "He has encouraged disrespect for the law." Camp's downfall came when he was arrested in 2010 for unlawful possession of controlled substances after paying an undercover law enforcement officer money for cocaine and a nonprescribed narcotic pain reliever. Authorities said that the judge intended to use the illegal drugs while partying with a stripper that he had befriended at the Goldrush Showbar in Atlanta, Georgia.[40] Evidence against Camp showed that he had had an ongoing affair with the woman, and had also given her his government-issued laptop computer—resulting in his conviction on a charge of unlawful conversion of government property.[41]

At the federal level, the Judicial Councils Reform and Judicial Conduct and Disability Act, passed by Congress in 1980, specifies the procedures necessary to register complaints against federal judges and, in serious cases, to begin the process of impeachment, or forced removal from the bench. Similarly, most states have their own commissions on judicial misconduct, while the Brenan Center for Justice at the New York University School of Law works to hold judges accountable for their conduct on the bench.

The Prosecuting Attorney

The **prosecutor**—called variously the *district attorney*, *state's attorney*, *county attorney*, *commonwealth attorney*, or *solicitor*—is responsible for presenting the state's case against the defendant.

> The prosecutor is responsible for presenting the state's case against the defendant.

The prosecuting attorney is the primary representative of the people by virtue of the belief that violations of the criminal law are an affront to the public. Except for federal prosecutors (called *U.S. attorneys*) and solicitors in five states, prosecutors are elected and generally serve four-year terms with the possibility of continuing reelection.[42] Widespread criminal conspiracies, whether they involve government officials or private citizens, may require the services of a special prosecutor whose office can spend the time and resources needed for efficient prosecution.[43]

In many jurisdictions, because the job of prosecutor entails too many duties for one person to handle, prosecutors supervise a staff of assistant district attorneys who do most in-court work. Assistants are trained attorneys, usually hired directly by the chief prosecutor and licensed to practice law in the state in which they work. Approximately 2,300 chief prosecutors, assisted by 24,000 deputy attorneys, serve the nation's counties and independent cities.[44]

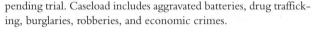

CJ | CAREERS
Assistant District Attorney

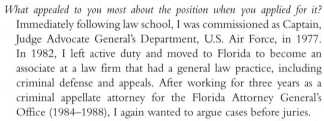

Name. Robert S. Jaegers

Position. Assistant State Attorney, Palm Beach County, Florida

Colleges attended. Ohio Northern University Pettit College of Law, Ada, Ohio; Pennsylvania State University

Majors. English and law

Year hired. Joined the State Attorney's Office in Palm Beach County, Florida, in 1988

Please give a brief description of your job. Currently Felony Division Trial Prosecutor with over 200 cases pending trial. Caseload includes aggravated batteries, drug trafficking, burglaries, robberies, and economic crimes.

What appealed to you most about the position when you applied for it? Immediately following law school, I was commissioned as Captain, Judge Advocate General's Department, U.S. Air Force, in 1977. In 1982, I left active duty and moved to Florida to become an associate at a law firm that had a general law practice, including criminal defense and appeals. After working for three years as a criminal appellate attorney for the Florida Attorney General's Office (1984–1988), I again wanted to argue cases before juries.

How would you describe the interview process? The current state attorney interview process involves an interview with three experienced prosecutors, then an interview with two of the three chief assistants, then an interview with the elected state attorney. The process has varied over the years, depending upon the wishes of the elected state attorney, from a single interview with the state attorney to the current process but without an interview with the state attorney. Law school internship experience is a plus, as is any prior experience as an attorney or legal support person.

What is a typical day like? A "typical" day begins at 8:30 a.m. with a morning-long session of short hearings (around 120 cases with sometimes as many different defendants), with four regularly assigned division prosecutors and as many as six specialty division prosecutors, and four public defender attorneys regularly assigned to the division, plus varying numbers of privately retained attorneys. All discuss arraignments, plea offers, demands for discovery from both sides, scheduling of trials, scheduling of motion hearings, scheduling of plea conferences, conducting plea conferences, demands by defendants to represent themselves, restitution hearings, requests to enter appearances by private attorneys, requests to withdraw from representation by private attorneys, requests to continue, demands for speedy trial, and so on. In short, we conduct all the proceedings necessary to move cases to conclusion, either by plea or by trial. If this is all concluded by 10 or 11 a.m., the judge may call for a jury pool and commence a trial. Following a lunch break, there are trials, or motions to suppress or dismiss with evidentiary hearings, or more lengthy hearings specially set by the parties and the judge.

What qualities/characteristics are most helpful for this job? The ability to be flexible in preparation, articulate in English, able to read opposing motions, and conduct research on legal opinions is paramount. Next is an ability to speak to groups of people from all backgrounds and abilities, and select a group of fair and impartial jurors to be your factfinders. You must be able to communicate your arguments, and help your witnesses convey the evidence they have to present to the factfinders in a readily understandable manner. Preparation is key. You must be able to work with and cooperate with your support staff of secretaries, investigators, information managers, judges' secretaries, clerks, and opposing counsel's secretaries, and do this even with opposing counsel. You must also be willing to devote the time to prepare for each trial and each hearing, even while knowing that the opposing side may decide at the last moment to concede and enter a plea. If you aren't prepared, the defense will sense that, and use it against you.

What is a typical starting salary? Starting salary as of 2012 is $40,000 per year. This is accompanied by medical benefits, retirement benefits, travel reimbursements, and continuing legal education opportunities.

What is the salary potential as you move up into higher-level jobs? The statutory maximum salary of the state attorney is $150,000 per year. Assistants are not usually compensated above this level.

What career advice would you give someone in college beginning studies in criminal justice? If you are contemplating a career as a prosecuting attorney, take every opportunity to study creative writing, English literature, psychology, public speaking and debate, and dramatics, and make sure to keep yourself physically fit. You may find yourself in many stressful situations, some physical and some mental, and a sound mind in a sound body gives you an advantage.

Source: Reprinted with permission of Robert S. Jaegers. Photo courtesy of Robert S. Jaegers. Logo courtesy of the Palm Beach County, Florida, State Attorney's Office.

Another prosecutorial role has traditionally been that of quasi-legal adviser to local police departments. Because prosecutors are sensitive to the kinds of information needed for conviction, they may help guide police investigations and will exhort detectives to identify credible witnesses, uncover additional evidence, and the like. This role is limited, however. Police departments are independent of the administrative authority of the prosecutor, and cooperation between them, although based on the common goal of conviction, is purely voluntary. Moreover, close cooperation between prosecutors and police may not always be legal. A 1998 federal law known as the McDade-Murtha Law,[45] for example, requires that federal prosecutors abide by all state bar ethics rules. In late 2000, in a reflection of the federal sentiment, the Oregon Supreme Court temporarily ended police–prosecutor collaboration in that state in instances involving potential deception by law enforcement officers.[46] The court, ruling in the Oregon State Bar disciplinary case of *In re Gatti*,[47] held that all lawyers within the state, including government prosecutors overseeing organized crime, child pornography, and narcotics cases, must abide by the Oregon State Bar's strictures against dishonesty, fraud, deceit, and misrepresentation.[48] Under the court's ruling, a prosecutor in Oregon who encourages an

■ **prosecutorial discretion**   The decision-making power of prosecutors, based on the wide range of choices available to them, in the handling of criminal defendants, the scheduling of cases for trial, the acceptance of negotiated pleas, and so on. The most important form of prosecutorial discretion lies in the power to charge, or not to charge, a person with an offense.

■ **lecture note**   Discuss prosecutorial discretion. Explain that the discretionary decision of a prosecutor as to whether a suspect should be charged with a crime makes the prosecutor one of the most powerful actors in the criminal justice system.

■ **exculpatory evidence**   Any information having a tendency to clear a person of guilt or blame.

undercover officer or an informant to misrepresent himself or herself could be disbarred and prohibited from practicing law. As a result of the highly controversial ruling, the FBI and the Drug Enforcement Administration ended all big undercover operations in Oregon, and local police departments cancelled many ongoing investigations. In 2002, the Oregon Supreme Court accepted an amendment to the state bar association's disciplinary rules to allow a lawyer to advise and to supervise otherwise lawful undercover investigations of violations of civil law, criminal law, or constitutional rights as long as the lawyer "in good faith believes there is a reasonable possibility that unlawful activity has taken place, is taking place or will take place in the foreseeable future."[49]

Once a trial begins, the job of the prosecutor is to vigorously present the state's case against the defendant. Prosecutors introduce evidence against the accused, steer the testimony of witnesses "for the people," and argue in favor of conviction. Because defendants are presumed innocent until proven guilty, the burden of demonstrating guilt beyond a reasonable doubt rests with the prosecutor.

Prosecutorial Discretion

American prosecutors occupy a unique position in the nation's criminal justice system by virtue of the considerable **prosecutorial discretion** they exercise. As U.S. Supreme Court Justice Robert H. Jackson noted in 1940, "The prosecutor has more control over life, liberty, and reputation than any other person in America."[50] Before a case comes to trial, the prosecutor may decide to accept a plea bargain, divert the suspect to a public or private social service agency, ask the suspect to seek counseling, or dismiss the case entirely for lack of evidence or for a variety of other reasons. Studies have found that the prosecution dismisses from one-third to one-half of all felony cases before trial or before a plea bargain is made.[51] Prosecutors also play a significant role before grand juries. States that use the grand jury system depend on prosecutors to bring evidence before the grand jury and to be effective in seeing indictments returned against suspects.

In preparation for trial, the prosecutor decides what charges are to be brought against the defendant, examines the strength of the incriminating evidence, and decides which witnesses to call. Two important U.S. Supreme Court decisions have held that it is the duty of prosecutors to make available any evidence in their possession to, in effect, help the defense build its case. In the first case, *Brady* v. *Maryland* (1963),[52] the Court held that the prosecution is required to disclose to the defense evidence

that directly relates to claims of either guilt or innocence. The second and more recent case is that of *U.S.* v. *Bagley*,[53] decided in 1985. In *Bagley*, the Court ruled that the prosecution must disclose any evidence that the defense requests. The Court reasoned that to withhold evidence, even when it does not relate directly to issues of guilt or innocence, may mislead the defense into thinking that such evidence does not exist.

In 2004, in a decision predicated upon *Brady*, the U.S. Supreme Court intervened to stop the execution of 45-year-old Texan Delma Banks ten minutes before it was scheduled to begin. In finding that prosecutors had withheld vital **exculpatory evidence**, or information that might have cleared Banks of blame, during his trial for the 1980 shooting death of a 16-year-old boy, the Court said that "a rule declaring 'prosecutor may hide, defendant must seek,' is not tenable in a system constitutionally bound to accord defendants due process."[54] Banks had spent 24 years on death row.

One special decision that the prosecutor makes concerns the filing of separate or multiple charges. The decision to try a defendant simultaneously on multiple charges allows for the presentation of a considerable amount of evidence and permits an in-court demonstration of a complete sequence of criminal events. This strategy has additional practical advantages: It saves time and money by substituting one trial for what might otherwise be a number of trials if each charge were to be brought separately before the court. From the prosecutor's point of view, however, trying the charges one at a time carries the advantage of allowing for another trial on a new charge if a "not guilty" verdict is returned.

The activities of the prosecutor do not end with a finding of guilt or innocence. Following conviction, prosecutors are usually allowed to make sentencing recommendations to the judge. For example, they can argue that aggravating factors (discussed in Chapter 11), prior criminal record, or the especially heinous nature of the offense calls for strict punishment. When a convicted defendant appeals, prosecutors may need to defend their own actions and, in briefs filed with appellate courts, to argue that the conviction was properly obtained. Most jurisdictions also allow prosecutors to make recommendations when defendants they have convicted are being considered for parole or for early release from prison.

Until relatively recently, prosecutors generally enjoyed much of the same kind of immunity against liability in the exercise of their official duties that judges do. The 1976 Supreme Court case *Imbler* v. *Pachtman*[55] provided the basis for immunity with its ruling that "state prosecutors are absolutely immune from

■ **theme**   How might prosecutors abuse their discretion? What types of discretionary decisions are inappropriate? How is prosecutorial misconduct addressed?

■ **lecture note**   List and explain the three major categories of criminal defense attorneys: private attorneys, court-appointed counsel, and public defenders.

■ **defense counsel**   A licensed trial lawyer hired or appointed to conduct the legal defense of a person accused of a crime and to represent him or her before a court of law.

liability … for their conduct in initiating a prosecution and in presenting the State's case." However, in the 1991 case of *Burns v. Reed*,[56] the Court held that "[a] state prosecuting attorney is absolutely immune from liability for damages…for participating in a probable cause hearing, but not for giving legal advice to the police."

> Until relatively recently, prosecutors generally enjoyed much of the same kind of immunity against liability in the exercise of their official duties that judges do.

The *Burns* case involved Cathy Burns of Muncie, Indiana, who shot her sleeping sons while laboring under a multiple personality disorder. To explore the possibility of multiple personality further, the police asked the prosecuting attorney if it would be appropriate for them to hypnotize the defendant. The prosecutor agreed that hypnosis would be a permissible avenue for investigation, and the suspect confessed to the murders while hypnotized. She later alleged in her complaint to the Supreme Court "that [the prosecuting attorney] knew or should have known that hypnotically induced testimony was inadmissible" at trial.[57]

Finally, in 2009, in the case of *Van de Kamp v. Goldstein*,[58] the U.S. Supreme Court reaffirmed its holding in *Imbler* and found that a prosecutor's absolute immunity from Section 1983 claims (discussed in the last chapter) extends to (1) a failure to properly train prosecutors, (2) a failure to properly supervise prosecutors, and (3) a failure to establish an information system containing potential impeachment material about informants. In the words of the justices, a prosecutor is absolutely immune from liability in civil suits when his or her actions are "intimately associated with the judicial phase of the criminal process" and the prosecutor is serving as "an officer of the court."

The Abuse of Discretion

Because prosecutors have so much discretion in their decision making, there is considerable potential for abuse. Many types of discretionary decisions are always inappropriate. Examples include accepting guilty pleas to drastically reduced charges for personal considerations, deciding not to prosecute friends or political cronies, and being overzealous in prosecuting to support political ambitions.

Administrative decisions such as case scheduling, which can wreak havoc with the personal lives of defendants and the professional lives of defense attorneys, can also be used by prosecutors to harass defendants into pleading guilty. Some forms of abuse may be unconscious. At least one study suggests that some prosecutors tend toward leniency where female defendants are concerned and tend to discriminate against minorities when deciding whether to prosecute.[59]

Although the electorate is the final authority to which prosecutors must answer, gross misconduct by prosecutors may be addressed by the state supreme court or by the state attorney general's office. Short of addressing *criminal* misconduct, however, the options available to the court and to the attorney general are limited.

In 2011, in an effort to deter prosecutorial misconduct at the federal level, the U.S. Department of Justice created a new internal watchdog office to oversee the actions of federal prosecutors. Called the Professional Misconduct Review Unit, the office is responsible for disciplining federal prosecutors who engage in intentional or reckless misconduct.[60]

The Prosecutor's Professional Responsibility

As members of the legal profession, prosecutors are expected to abide by various standards of professional responsibility, such as those found in the Model Rules of Professional Conduct of the American Bar Association (ABA). Most state bar associations have adopted their own versions of the ABA rules and expect their members to respect those standards. Consequently, serious violations of the rules may result in a prosecutor's being disbarred from the practice of law. Official ABA commentary on Rule 3.8, *Special Responsibilities of the Prosecutor*, says that "a prosecutor has the responsibility of a minister of justice and not simply that of an advocate; the prosecutor's duty is to seek justice, not merely to convict. This responsibility carries with it specific obligations to see that the defendant is accorded procedural justice and that guilt is decided upon the basis of sufficient evidence."[61] Hence prosecutors are barred by the standards of the legal profession from advocating any fact or position that they know is untrue. Prosecutors have a voice in influencing public policy affecting the safety of America's communities through the National District Attorneys Association (NDAA). Visit the NDAA via **http://www.ndaa.org**.

The Defense Counsel

The **defense counsel** is a trained lawyer who may specialize in the practice of criminal law. The task of the defense counsel is to represent the accused as soon as possible after arrest and to ensure that the defendant's civil rights are not violated during processing by the criminal justice system. Other duties of the defense counsel include testing the strength of the prosecution's

■ **lecture note**   Explain that as a result of the Supreme Court decision in the case of *Gideon* v. *Wainwright* (1963), criminal defendants are now entitled to have a lawyer to represent them in court. Ask students what impact the *Gideon* decision has had on the legal profession in this country.

■ **theme**   There are three systems used by states to deliver legal services to indigent defendants. What are the pros and cons of each? Which system do you prefer and why?

case, taking part in plea negotiations, and preparing an adequate defense to be used at trial. In the preparation of a defense, criminal lawyers may enlist private detectives, experts, witnesses to the crime, and character witnesses. Some lawyers perform aspects of the role of private detective or investigator themselves. Defense attorneys also review relevant court precedents to identify the best defense strategy.

Defense preparation often entails conversations between lawyer and defendant. Such discussions are recognized as privileged communications protected under the umbrella of attorney–client confidentiality.

> Lawyers cannot be compelled to reveal information that their clients have confided to them.

In other words, lawyers cannot be compelled to reveal information that their clients have confided to them.[62]

If the defendant is found guilty, the defense attorney will be involved in arguments at sentencing, may be asked to file an appeal, and may counsel the defendant and the defendant's family about any civil matters (payment of debts, release from contractual obligations, and so on) that must be arranged after sentence is imposed. Hence the work of the defense attorney encompasses many roles, including attorney, negotiator, investigator, confidant, family and personal counselor, social worker, and, as we shall see, bill collector.

The Criminal Lawyer

Three major categories of defense attorneys assist criminal defendants in the United States: (1) private attorneys, usually referred to as *retained counsel*; (2) *court-appointed counsel*; and (3) *public defenders*.

Private attorneys either have their own legal practices or work for law firms in which they are partners or employees. Private attorneys' fees can be high; most privately retained criminal lawyers charge from $100 to $250 per hour. Included in their bill is the time it takes to prepare for a case, as well as time spent in the courtroom. High-powered criminal defense attorneys who have a reputation for successfully defending their clients can be far more expensive. Fees charged by famous criminal defense attorneys can run into the hundreds of thousands of dollars—and sometimes exceed $1 million—for handling just one case!

Few law students choose to specialize in criminal law, even though the job of a criminal lawyer may appear glamorous. One reason may be that the collection of fees can be a significant source of difficulty for many defense attorneys. Most defendants are poor. Those who aren't are often reluctant to pay what they believe is an exorbitant fee, and woe be it to the defense attorney whose client is convicted before the fee has been paid!

Visit the National Association of Criminal Defense Lawyers (NACDL) via **http://www.nacdl.org** and the Association of Federal Defense Attorneys (AFDA) website **(http://afda.org)** to learn more about the practice of criminal law.

Court-Appointed Counsel

The Sixth Amendment to the U.S. Constitution guarantees criminal defendants the effective assistance of counsel. A series of U.S. Supreme Court decisions has established that defendants who are unable to pay for private criminal defense attorneys will receive adequate representation at all stages of criminal justice processing. In *Powell* v. *Alabama* (1932),[63] the Court held that the Fourteenth Amendment requires state courts to appoint counsel for defendants in capital cases who are unable to afford their own. In 1938, in *Johnson* v. *Zerbst*,[64] the Court overturned the conviction of an indigent federal inmate, holding that his Sixth Amendment due process right to counsel had been violated. The Court declared, "If the accused … is not represented by counsel and has not competently and intelligently waived his constitutional right, the Sixth Amendment stands as a jurisdictional bar to a valid conviction and sentence depriving him of his life or his liberty." The decision established the right of indigent defendants to receive the assistance of appointed counsel in all criminal proceedings in federal courts. The 1963 case of *Gideon* v. *Wainwright*[65] extended the right to appointed counsel to all indigent defendants charged with a felony in state courts. In *Argersinger* v. *Hamlin* (1972),[66] the Court required adequate legal representation for anyone facing a potential sentence of imprisonment. Juveniles charged with delinquent acts were granted the right to appointed counsel in the case of *In re Gault* (1967).[67]

> The Sixth Amendment to the U.S. Constitution guarantees criminal defendants the effective assistance of counsel.

In 2002, a closely divided U.S. Supreme Court expanded the Sixth Amendment right to counsel, ruling that defendants in state courts who are facing relatively minor charges must be provided with an attorney at government expense even when they face only the slightest chance of incarceration. The case, *Alabama* v. *Shelton*,[68] involved defendant LeReed Shelton, who was convicted of third-degree assault after taking part in a fistfight with another motorist following a minor traffic accident. Shelton had been advised of his right to have an attorney represent him at trial, and the judge who heard his case repeatedly suggested that he should hire an attorney and warned him of the dangers of serving as his own attorney, but at no time did the judge offer Shelton assistance of counsel. Unable to afford an

■ **public defender** An attorney employed by a government agency or subagency, or by a private organization under contract to a government body, for the purpose of providing defense services to indigents, or an attorney who has volunteered such service.

attorney, Shelton proceeded to represent himself and was convicted and sentenced to 30 days in the county jail. The sentence was suspended, and he was placed on two years of unsupervised probation, fined $500, and ordered to make restitution and to pay the costs of court. Shelton soon appealed on Sixth Amendment grounds, however, and the Alabama Supreme Court ruled in his favor, reasoning that a suspended sentence constitutes a "term of imprisonment" no matter how unlikely it is that the term will ever be served. On appeal by the state of Alabama, the case made its way to the U.S. Supreme Court, which agreed that "[a] suspended sentence is a prison term" and requires appointed counsel when an indigent defendant desires legal representation.

States have responded to the federal mandate for indigent defense in a number of ways. Most now use one of three systems to deliver legal services to criminal defendants who are unable to afford their own: (1) court-appointed counsel, (2) public defenders, and (3) contractual arrangements. Most systems are administered at the county level, although funding arrangements may involve state, county, and municipal monies—as well as federal grants and court fees.

Assigned Counsel

Assigned counsel, also known as *court-appointed defense attorneys*, are usually drawn from a roster of all practicing criminal attorneys within the jurisdiction of the trial court. Their fees are paid at a rate set by the state or local government. These fees are typically low, however, and may affect the amount of effort an assigned attorney puts into a case. In 2001, for example, New York's court-appointed attorneys were paid only $25 per hour for out-of-court preparation time and $40 an hour for time spent in the courtroom—a rate of pay that is 10 to 20 times less than what they normally earn for a private case.[69] So, although most attorneys assigned by the court to indigent defense take their jobs seriously, some feel only a loose commitment to their clients. Paying clients, in their eyes, deserve better representation.

Public Defenders

A **public defender** is a state-employed lawyer defending indigent defendants. A public defender program relies on full-time salaried staff. Staff members include defense attorneys, defense investigators, and office personnel. Defense investigators gather information in support of the defense effort. They may interview friends, family members, and employers of the accused, with an eye toward effective defense. Public defender programs have become popular in recent years, and a 2014 report by the Bureau of Justice Statistics (BJS) found that 49 states and the District of Columbia use

public defenders to provide legal representation for some or all indigent defendants.[70] Maine is the only state that does not have a publicly funded public defender office. The BJS noted that in 27 states and the District of Columbia, counties or local jurisdictions funded and administered public defender offices. In the remaining 22 states, one office oversaw indigent defense operations throughout the state. County-based public defender offices employ 71% of the nation's 15,026 public defenders. The 10,705 attorneys in county-based offices serve a total population of approximately 167 million residents. County-based public defender offices receive about 4 million cases per year, with a median of about 2,500 cases per office.

An earlier report by the BJS found that a public defender system is the primary method used to provide indigent counsel for criminal defendants and that 28% of state jurisdictions nationwide use public defender programs exclusively to provide indigent defense.[71] Critics charge that public defenders, because they are government employees, are not sufficiently independent from prosecutors and judges. For the same reason, clients may be suspicious of public defenders, viewing them as state functionaries. Finally, because of the huge caseloads typical of public defender's offices, there is pressure to use plea bargaining excessively. Learn more about system overload in public defenders offices via **http://tinyurl.com/4yywlrt**.

> Critics charge that public defenders, because they are government employees, are not sufficiently independent from prosecutors and judges.

Contractual Arrangements

Through a third type of indigent defense, contract attorney programs, county and state officials arrange with local criminal lawyers to provide for indigent defense on a contractual basis. Individual attorneys, local bar associations, and multipartner law firms may all be tapped to provide services. Contract defense programs are the least widely used form of indigent defense at present, although their popularity is growing.

Critics of the current system of indigent defense point out that the system is woefully underfunded. As a consequence of limited funding, many public defender's offices employ what critics call a "plead 'em and speed 'em through" strategy, which can often mean that attorneys meet their clients for the first time in courtrooms as trials are about to begin and use plea bargaining to move cases along. Mary Broderick of the National Legal Aid and Defender Association says, "We aren't being given the same weapons.... It's like trying to deal with smart bombs when all you've got is a couple of cap pistols."[72]

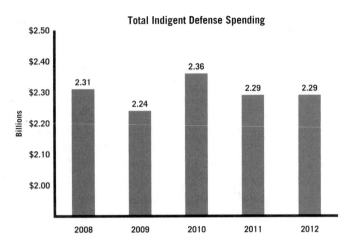

Total Indigent Defense Spending

FIGURE 9-5 | State Government Indigent Defense Expenditures, 2008–2012

Source: Erin Herberman and Tracey Kyckelhahn, *State Government Indigent Defense Expenditures, FY 2008–2012—Updated* (Washington, DC: BJS, 2014). *Note:* Indigent defense spending includes all of the operational expenditures for all spending on indigent defense, including contract attorneys, assigned counsel, and public defender office expenditures.

Proposed enhancements to indigent defense systems are offered by the National Legal Aid and Defender Association (NLADA). You can visit the NLADA via **http://www.nlada100years .org**. A 200-page report by the National Symposium on Indigent Defense, showing what individual states spend on indigent defense, is available at **http://www.justicestudies.com/pubs/cjindig .pdf**. Total moneys spent on indigent defense by the states between 2008 and 2012 are shown in Figure 9-5.

Although state indigent defense services are sometimes significantly underfunded, the same is not true of the federal system. The defense of indigent Oklahoma City bomber Timothy McVeigh, for example, cost taxpayers an estimated $13.8 million—which doesn't include the cost of his appeal or execution. McVeigh's expenses included $6.7 million for attorneys, $2 million for investigators, $3 million for expert witnesses, and approximately $1.4 million for office rent and secretarial assistance.[73]

Of course, defendants need not be represented by any counsel at all. Defendants may waive their right to an attorney and undertake their own defense—a right held by the U.S. Supreme Court to be inherent in the Sixth Amendment in the 1975 case of *Faretta* v. *California*.[74] Self-representation is uncommon, however, and only 1% of federal inmates and 3% of state inmates report having represented themselves.[75] Some famous instances of self-representation include the 1995 trial of Long Island Rail Road commuter train shooter Colin Ferguson, the 1999 assisted suicide trial of Dr. Jack Kevorkian, and the 2002 federal competency hearings of Zacarias Moussaoui.

Defendants who are not pleased with the lawyer appointed to defend them are in a somewhat different situation. They may request, through the court, that a new lawyer be assigned to represent them, as Timothy McVeigh did following his conviction and death sentence in the Oklahoma City bombing case. However, unless there is clear reason for reassignment, such as

an obvious personality conflict between defendant and attorney, few judges are likely to honor a request of this sort. Short of obvious difficulties, most judges will trust in the professionalism of appointed counsel.

State-supported indigent defense systems may also be called on to provide representation for clients upon appeal. An attorney who is appointed to represent an indigent defendant on appeal, however, may conclude that an appeal would be frivolous. If so, he or she may request that the appellate court allow him or her to withdraw from the case or that the court dispose of the case without requiring the attorney to file a brief arguing the merits of the appeal. In 1967, in the case of *Anders* v. *California*,[76] the U.S. Supreme Court found that to protect a defendant's constitutional right to appellate counsel, appellate courts must safeguard against the risk of accepting an attorney's negative assessment of a case where an appeal is not actually frivolous. The Court also found California's existing procedure for evaluating such requests to be inadequate, and the justices set forth an acceptable procedure. In 1979, in the case of *People* v. *Wende*,[77] the state of California adopted a new standardized procedure that, although not the same as the one put forth in *Anders*, was designed to protect the right of a criminal defendant to appeal.

The *Wende* standard was put to the test in the 2000 case of *Smith* v. *Robbins*.[78] The case began when convicted California murderer Lee Robbins told his court-appointed counsel that he wanted to file an appeal. His attorney concluded that the appeal would be frivolous and filed a brief with the state court of appeals to that effect. The court agreed with the attorney's assessment, and the appeal was not heard. The California Supreme Court denied further review of the case. After exhausting his state postconviction remedies, Robbins appealed to the federal courts, arguing that he had been denied effective assistance of appellate counsel because his counsel's brief did not comply with one of the requirements in *Anders*—specifically, the requirement that the brief must mention "anything in the record that might arguably support the appeal." A federal district court agreed, concluding that there were at least two issues that might have supported Robbins's appeal. The court found that the failure to include them in the brief deviated from the *Anders* procedure and thus amounted to deficient performance by counsel. The Ninth Circuit Court agreed, concluding that *Anders* established a mandatory procedure as a standard against which the performance of appointed counsel could be assessed. When the case finally reached the U.S. Supreme Court, the justices held that the *Anders* procedure is only one method of satisfying the Constitution's requirements for indigent criminal appeals and that the states are free to adopt different procedures as long as those procedures adequately safeguard a defendant's right to appellate counsel.

Finally, in 2001, in the case of *Texas* v. *Cobb*,[79] the Supreme Court ruled that the Sixth Amendment right to counsel is "offense specific" and applies only to the offense with which a

CJ | ISSUES
Gideon v. Wainwright and Indigent Defense

Today, about three-fourths of state-level criminal defendants and one-half of federal defendants are represented in court by publicly funded counsel.[1] As recently as 40 years ago, however, the practice of publicly funded indigent defense was uncommon. That changed in 1963 when, in the case of *Gideon* v. *Wainwright*,[2] the U.S. Supreme Court extended the right to legal counsel to indigent defendants charged with a criminal offense. The reasoning of the Court is well summarized in this excerpt from the majority opinion written by Justice Hugo Black:

> Governments, both state and federal, quite properly spend vast sums of money to establish machinery to try defendants accused of crime. Lawyers to prosecute are everywhere deemed essential to protect the public's interest in an orderly society. Similarly, there are few defendants charged with crime, few indeed, who fail to

hire the best lawyers they can get to prepare and present their defenses. That government hires lawyers to prosecute and defendants who have the money hire lawyers to defend are the strongest indications of the widespread belief that lawyers in criminal courts are necessities, not luxuries. The right of one charged with crime to counsel may not be deemed fundamental and essential to fair trials in some countries, but it is in ours. From the very beginning, our state and national constitutions and laws have laid great emphasis on procedural and substantive safeguards designed to assure fair trials before impartial tribunals in which every defendant stands equal before the law. This noble ideal cannot be realized if the poor man charged with crime has to face his accusers without a lawyer to assist him.

[1] Steven K. Smith and Carol J. DeFrances, *Indigent Defense* (Washington, DC: Bureau of Justice Statistics, 1996).
[2] *Gideon* v. *Wainwright*, 372 U.S. 335 (1963).

---

defendant is charged—and not to other offenses, even if they are factually related to the charged offense.

The Ethics of Defense

The job of defense counsel, as we have already mentioned, is to prepare and offer a vigorous defense on behalf of the accused at trial and to appeal cases that have merit. A proper defense at trial often involves the presentation of evidence and the examination of witnesses, both of which require careful thought and planning. Good attorneys may become emotionally committed to the outcomes of trials in which they are involved. Some lawyers, however, cross the line when they lose their professional objectivity and embrace the wider cause of their clients. That's what happened to Lynne Stewart, 65, who was convicted in 2005 of smuggling messages from her jailed client, the radical Egyptian sheik Omar Abdel-Rahman (also known as the "blind sheik"), to his terrorist followers outside of prison.[80] Abdel-Rahman is serving life behind bars for his role in an unsuccessful 1993 plot to bomb New York City landmarks. Stewart, a 1960s-era radical, has often chosen to represent the most contemptible clients, believing that justice requires that everyone receive a vigorous defense. She was arrested after she issued a public statement on behalf of the sheik expressing her client's withdrawal of support for a cease-fire involving his supporters in Egypt. Stewart had known in advance that making the statement violated an order to restrict the sheik's communications, but she later testified that she believed that violence is sometimes necessary to achieve justice. Other evidence showed that she had facilitated forbidden communications between Abdel-Rahman and a translator by using prearranged cues such as tapping on a table, shaking a water bottle, and uttering key terms like "chocolate" and "heart attack" during prison visits. In 2006, she was sentenced to serve 28 months in prison; but in 2010 a federal court ordered that

Stephen Chernin/AP Wide World Photos

Defense attorney Lynne Stewart, who was sentenced to prison in 2006 (and resentenced in 2010) for smuggling messages from her jailed client, the radical Egyptian sheik Omar Abdel-Rahman (aka the "blind sheik"), to his terrorist followers outside of prison. Our adversarial system requires that attorneys sometimes defend unpopular clients, but the defense role is carefully prescribed by ethical and procedural standards. How did Stewart's actions violate those standards?

she be resentenced due to new revelations about perjury and increased her sentence to ten years and a month.[81] Her appeal to the federal Court of Appeals for the Second Circuit was turned down in 2012.[82] She was released in 2014 on compassionate grounds, after physicians said she was dying of cancer.

The nature of the adversarial process, fed by the emotions of the participants combined with the often privileged and extensive knowledge that defense attorneys have about their cases, is enough to tempt the professional ethics of some counselors. Because the defense counsel may often know more about the guilt or innocence of the defendant than anyone else prior

■ **lecture note**   Describe the various ethical concerns of the trial lawyer (refer to the "ethics and professionalism box which highlights the American Bar Association's Model Rules of Professional Conduct). Ask students what features of the court process and the job of the defense attorney (e.g., the adversarial model and the win-lose mindset) might tempt defense attorneys to violate these standards.

■ **bailiff**   The court officer whose duties are to keep order in the courtroom and to maintain physical custody of the jury.
■ **activity**   Invite a prosecutor and a defense attorney to speak with the class. Ask them to describe their respective roles and to comment on what they believe are the pros and cons of the adversarial process in criminal trials.

to trial, the defense role is carefully prescribed by ethical and procedural considerations. Attorneys violate both law and the standards of their profession if they knowingly misrepresent themselves or their clients. As Michael Ratner, president of the Center for Constitutional Rights, put it when commenting on the *Stewart* case, "lawyers need to be advocates, but they don't need to be accomplices."[83]

To help attorneys understand what is expected of them, and what the appropriate limits of a vigorous defense might be, the American Bar Association provides significant guidance in the areas of legal ethics and professional responsibility. (See the "Ethics and Professionalism" box in this chapter.) Even so, some attorney–client interactions remain especially tricky. Defense attorneys, for example, are under no obligation to reveal information obtained from a client without the client's permission. However, all states permit defense lawyers to violate a client's confidentiality without fear of reprisal if they reasonably believe that doing so could prevent serious injury or death to another person. In 2004, with passage of a new evidence law broadening the state's evidence code, California joined the other 49 states in freeing attorneys to violate client confidentiality in such cases. California law makes disclosure discretionary, not mandatory. Kevin Mohr, a professor at Western State University College of Law in Fullerton, California, noted that the new law provides the first exception to the attorney–client privilege in California in more than 130 years. "A lawyer can now take action and intervene and prevent [a] criminal act from occurring," said Mohr.[84]

The California changes had been presaged by an action of the American Bar Association, which eased its secrecy rules surrounding attorney–client relationships in 2001.[85] Prior to that time, ABA rules permitted criminal defense attorneys to disclose incriminating information about a client only to prevent imminent death or substantial bodily harm. The 2001 rule change dispensed with the word *imminent*, allowing attorneys to reveal clients' secrets in order to stop future deaths or to prevent substantial bodily harm.

Somewhat earlier, the 1986 U.S. Supreme Court case of *Nix* v. *Whiteside*[86] clarified the duty of lawyers to reveal known instances of client perjury. The *Nix* case came to the Court upon the complaint of the defendant, Whiteside, who claimed that he was deprived of the assistance of effective counsel during his murder trial because his lawyer would not allow him to testify untruthfully. Whiteside wanted to testify that he had seen a gun or something metallic in his victim's hand before killing him. Before trial, however, Whiteside admitted to his lawyer that he had actually seen no weapon, but he believed that to testify to the truth would result in his conviction. The lawyer told Whiteside that, as a professional counselor, he would be forced to challenge Whiteside's false testimony if it occurred and to explain to the court the facts as he knew them. On the stand, Whiteside said only that he thought the victim was reaching for a gun but did not claim to have seen one. He was found guilty of second-degree murder and appealed to the Supreme Court on the claim of inadequate representation. The Court, recounting the development of ethical codes in the legal profession, held that a lawyer's duty to a client "is limited to legitimate, lawful conduct compatible with the very nature of a trial as a search for truth…. Counsel is precluded from taking steps or in any way assisting the client in presenting false evidence or otherwise violating the law."[87]

The Bailiff

The **bailiff**, another member of the professional courtroom work group, is usually an armed law enforcement officer. The job of the bailiff, also called a *court officer*, is to ensure order in the courtroom, to announce the judge's entry into the courtroom, to call witnesses, and to prevent the escape of the accused (if the accused has not been released on bond). The bailiff also supervises the jury when it is sequestered and controls public and media access to jury members. Bailiffs in federal courtrooms are deputy U.S. marshals.

Courtrooms can be dangerous places, and bailiffs play a critical role in courtroom security. In an event that led to tightened courtroom security nationwide, George Lott opened fire in a courtroom in Tarrant County, Texas, in 1992, killing two lawyers and injuring three other people.[88] Lott, an attorney, was frustrated by the court's handling of his divorce and by child molestation charges that had been filed against him by his ex-wife. Lott was sentenced to die in 1993. Following the Lott incident and others like it, most courts began using metal detectors, and many now require visitors to leave packages, cellular phones, and objects that might conceal weapons in lockers or to check them with personnel before entering the courtroom.

A comprehensive courthouse security plan must, of course, extend beyond individual courtrooms. In 2005, the National Center for State Courts released a comprehensive plan for improving security in state courthouses.[89] The plan contained a list of ten essential elements for court safety that included the need to (1) assess existing and potential threats, (2) identify physical strengths and weaknesses of existing courts, (3) develop a comprehensive emergency response plan, (4) be aware of the latest technologies in court security, and (5) build strong and effective partnerships among state courts, law enforcement agencies, and county commissioners.

ethics and professionalism

American Bar Association's Model Rules of Professional Conduct

To help attorneys understand what is expected of them, the American Bar Association (ABA) has provided significant guidance in the areas of legal ethics and professional responsibility. Specifically, the ABA has developed professional standards intended to serve as models for state bar associations and to guide legislative bodies focused on ensuring ethical behavior among attorneys.

The ABA's first major foray into the area of ethical guidelines resulted in the adoption of its original Canons of Professional Ethics on August 27, 1908. In 1913, in an effort to keep the association informed about state and local bar activities concerning professional ethics, the ABA established its Standing Committee on Professional Ethics. The name of the group was changed to the Committee on Ethics and Professional Responsibility in 1971, and the committee continues to function under that name today.

In 1969, the committee's Model Code of Professional Responsibility was formally adopted by the ABA. Eventually, the majority of state and federal jurisdictions adopted their own versions of the Model Code.

In 1977, the ABA Commission on Evaluation of Professional Standards was created and charged with rethinking the ethical problems of the legal profession. Over the next six years, the Commission drafted the Model Rules of Professional Conduct, which the ABA adopted on August 2, 1983. The Model Rules effectively supplanted the Model Code of Professional Responsibility, and today most state and federal jurisdictions have adapted the Model Rules to their own particular circumstances.

The Model Rules have been periodically amended—most significantly in 2002—but continue to provide the touchstone ethical standards of the American legal profession today. Visit the American Bar Association on the Internet at **http://www .americanbar.org**, and learn about its Center for Professional Responsibility at **http://www.americanbar.org/groups/ professional_responsibility.html**.

Thinking about Ethics

1. Should a defense attorney represent a client whom he or she knows to be guilty? Explain.

2. Would it be unethical for an attorney to refuse to represent such a client? Why or why not?

Reference: American Bar Association, *Model Rules of Professional Conduct—Preface*, http://www.abanet.org/cpr/mrpc/preface.html (accessed May 17, 2011).

Source: Pearson Education, Inc.

Trial Court Administrators

Many states now employ local court administrators whose job is to facilitate the smooth functioning of courts in a judicial district or area. A major impetus for the hiring of local court administrators came from the 1967 President's Commission on Law Enforcement and Administration of Justice. Examining state courts, the commission found "a system that treats defendants who are charged with minor offenses with less dignity and consideration than it treats those who are charged with serious crimes."[90] A few years later, the National Advisory Commission on Criminal Justice Standards and Goals recommended that all courts with five or more judges create the position of trial court administrator.[91]

Court administrators provide uniform court management, assuming many of the duties previously performed by chief judges, prosecutors, and court clerks. Where court administrators operate, the ultimate authority for running the court still rests with the chief judge. Administrators, however, are able to relieve the judge of many routine and repetitive tasks, such as record keeping, scheduling, case-flow analysis, personnel administration, space utilization, facilities planning, and budget management. They may also take the minutes at meetings of judges and their committees.

> Where court administrators operate, the ultimate authority for running the court still rests with the chief judge.

Juror management is another area in which trial court administrators are becoming increasingly involved. Juror utilization studies can identify problems such as the overselection of citizens for the jury pool and the reasons for excessive requests to be excused from jury service. They can also suggest ways to reduce the time jurors waste waiting to be called or impaneled.

Effective court administrators are able to track lengthy cases and identify bottlenecks in court processing. They then suggest strategies to make the administration of justice more efficient for courtroom professionals and more humane for lay participants.

The Court Reporter

The role of the court reporter (also called the *court stenographer* or *court recorder*) is to create a record of all that occurs during a trial. Accurate records are very important in criminal trial courts because appeals may be based entirely on what went on in the courtroom. Especially significant are all verbal comments made in the courtroom, including testimony, objections, the judge's rulings, the judge's instructions to the jury, arguments made by lawyers, and the results of conferences between the lawyers and the judge. The official trial record, often taken on a stenotype machine or an audio recorder, may later be transcribed in manuscript form and will become the basis for any appellate review of the trial.

■ **expert witness**   A person who has special knowledge and skills recognized by the court as relevant to the determination of guilt or innocence. Unlike lay witnesses, expert witnesses may express opinions or draw conclusions in their testimony.

■ ***Daubert* standard**   A test of scientific acceptability applicable to the gathering of evidence in criminal cases.

■ **lecture note**   Describe an expert witness as someone who is recognized as having special knowledge and skills in an area of concern to the court. Explain that expert witnesses, unlike lay witnesses, may express opinions and draw conclusions in their areas of expertise.

■ **theme**   Most authorities agree that jurors usually view expert testimony as more trustworthy than other forms of evidence. What are the implications of this? How might this affect how the prosecutor and defense attorney approach a case?

Today's court stenographers often employ computer-aided transcription (CAT) software, which translates typed stenographic shorthand into complete and readable transcripts. Court reporters may be members of the National Court Reporters Association, the United States Court Reporters Association, or the Association of Legal Administrators—all of which support the activities of these professionals. You can visit the National Court Reporters Association via **http://www.ncraonline.org**.

The Clerk of Court

The duties of the clerk of court (also known as the *county clerk*) extend beyond the courtroom. The clerk maintains all records of criminal cases, including all pleas and motions made both before and after the actual trial. The clerk also prepares a jury pool, issues jury summonses, and subpoenas witnesses for both the prosecution and the defense. During the trial, the clerk (or an assistant) marks physical evidence for identification as instructed by the judge and maintains custody of that evidence. The clerk also swears in witnesses and performs other functions as the judge directs. Some states allow the clerk limited judicial duties, such as the power to issue warrants, to handle certain matters relating to individuals declared mentally incompetent,[92] and to serve as judge of probate—overseeing wills and the administration of estates.

Expert Witnesses

Most of the "insiders" we've talked about so far either are employees of the state or have ongoing professional relationships with the court (as in the case of defense counsel). **Expert witnesses**, however, may not have that kind of status, although some do. Expert witnesses are recognized as having specialized skills and knowledge in an established profession or technical area. They must demonstrate their expertise through education, work experience, publications, and awards. Their testimony at trial provides an effective way of introducing scientific evidence in such areas as medicine, psychology, ballistics, crime scene analysis, photography, and many other disciplines. Expert witnesses, like the other courtroom actors described in this chapter, are generally paid professionals. And like all other witnesses, they are subject to cross-examination. Unlike lay witnesses, they are allowed to express opinions and to draw conclusions, but only within their particular area of expertise.

In the 1993 civil case of *Daubert* v. *Merrell Dow Pharmaceuticals*,[93] the U.S. Supreme Court established that the

A ballistics expert testifying on the witness stand in a criminal trial as jurors view evidence on nearby computer displays. Expert witnesses may express opinions and draw conclusions in their area of expertise; they need not limit their testimony to facts alone. Why are expert witnesses permitted such leeway?

Corbis Images

test for the admissibility of scientific expert testimony is for the trial judge to decide "at the outset … whether the expert is proposing to testify to (1) scientific knowledge that (2) will assist the trier of fact to understand or determine a fact in issue." The Court concluded that the task of the trial judge is one of "ensuring that an expert's testimony both rests on a reliable foundation and is relevant to the task at hand. Pertinent evidence based on scientifically valid principles," said the Court, "will satisfy those demands." The ***Daubert* standard** eased the criteria for the introduction of scientific evidence at both civil and criminal trials, effectively clearing the way for the use of DNA evidence in the courtroom.[94]

In 2010, in the case of *Melendez-Diaz* v. *Massachusetts*,[95] the Court further defined the role of forensic analysts, deciding that they are "witnesses" and their reports are "testimonial"—meaning that, under the Constitution's Confrontation Clause, they must personally testify at trial unless the defendant waives his or her right to cross-examine them. Similarly, in the 2011 U.S. Supreme Court case of *Bullcoming* v. *New Mexico*,[96] the Court found that the Confrontation Clause does not permit the introduction into evidence during trial of a forensic laboratory report through the in-court testimony of an analyst who did not sign the document or personally observe the test it describes. In

CJ | NEWS
DNA Sampling Solves Some of the Toughest Cases

For two decades, Francisco Acevedo managed to elude detection for three killings committed outside New York City from 1989 through 1996.

He slipped past dedicated investigators because he did not fit the profile of a serial killer: a middle-aged white man with a high IQ. But when he submitted a DNA sample as part of a drunken-driving arrest, it inextricably linked him to DNA found at the crime scenes. He was convicted of homicide in January 2012, essentially on the strength of the DNA alone.

DNA seems to have become the premier crime evidence of the twenty-first century, even supplanting fingerprints. It can easily be collected from potential suspects by swabbing the inside of the mouth. And as long as the sample from the crime scenes is not damaged, chances of identifying the wrong person are thought to be one in 1.1 million.

The effectiveness of DNA evidence was further enhanced when the FBI created the Combined DNA Index System in 1998. Through CODIS, federal, state, and local law enforcement officials can share DNA profiles and evidence. The FBI says the database contains more than 10 million DNA samples and has been used in 171,800 matches.

Encouraged by added convictions using DNA evidence, Congress and the states have been progressively widening the kinds of people who are required to undergo DNA collection. In the 1990s, collection mandates covered only convicted sex offenders. Then they were expanded to include people convicted of violent crimes and then people convicted of felonies. More recently, the federal government and more than half the states have added anyone who is arrested, without waiting for them to be convicted.

As a result, the number of profiles added to CODIS each year grew 15-fold from 75,000 in 2008 to an estimated 1.2 million in 2012, according to the Justice Department. Such a huge expansion in volume has often overwhelmed crime labs, which have to convert each DNA sample into a numeric sequence for the database. Backlogs have

A detained criminal suspect provides a DNA swab for analysis. The story in this box describes Francisco Acevdeo, 43, who was sentenced to 75 years in prison in 2012 for the cold-case murders of three women in New York more than 20 years ago. He was arrested after a DNA sample that he voluntarily provided following an arrest for driving under the influence (DUI) matched genetic material found at the crime scenes. Should everyone who is arrested be required to provide DNA samples?

built up, slowing the pace of court cases, and pressures to get samples processed has led some labs to erroneously identify DNA sequences, prompting faulty convictions that were discovered later. This happened in Houston, Las Vegas, and Tulsa, according to a report by the American Constitution Society for Law and Policy.

To alleviate the backlogs, the federal government gave $785 million in grants to state and local DNA labs from 2006 to 2012, and the FBI announced in September 2011 that it had effectively eliminated its own backlog. But in April 2012, the Alabama Department of Forensics reported that budget cuts required the elimination of 15% of its workforce, resulting in a backlog of 1,000 DNA cases.

References: *Maryland* v. *King,* U.S. Supreme Court, No. 12-207 (decided June 3, 2013); "Federal Court: If You're Arrested, Officials Can Take a DNA Sample," *Christian Science Monitor,* July 25, 2011, http://news.yahoo.com/federal-court-youre-arrested-officials-dna-sample-235110510.html; "A New Era of DNA Collections: At What Cost to Civil Liberties?" American Constitution Society for Law and Policy, September 2007, http://www.councilforresponsiblegenetics.org/pageDocuments/PG6T8WPI4A.pdf; and "Suspect in Yonkers Serial Killings Flew under the Radar," *The Journal News,* December 19, 2010, http://murderpedia.org/male.A/a/acevedo-francisco.htm.

---

effect, the Court held that a forensic analyst who testifies at a criminal trial must be the one who performed or witnessed the lab tests being described.

One difficulty with expert testimony is that it can be confusing to the jury. Sometimes the trouble is due to the nature of the subject matter and sometimes to disagreements between the experts themselves. Often, however, it arises from the strict interpretation given to expert testimony by procedural requirements. The difference between medical and legal definitions of insanity, for example, points to a divergence in both history and purpose between the law and science. Courts that attempt to apply criteria like the M'Naghten rule (discussed in Chapter 4) in deciding claims of "insanity" are often faced with the testimony of psychiatric experts who refuse to even recognize the word. Such experts may prefer, instead, to speak in terms of *psychosis* and *neurosis*—words that have no

> One difficulty with expert testimony is that it can be confusing to the jury.

place in legal jargon. Because of the uncertainties they create, legal requirements may pit experts against one another and may confound the jury.

Even so, most authorities agree that expert testimony is usually viewed by jurors as more trustworthy than other forms of evidence. In a study of scientific evidence, one prosecutor commented that if he had to choose between presenting a fingerprint or an eyewitness at trial, he would always go with the fingerprint.[97] As a consequence of the effectiveness of scientific evidence, the National Institute of Justice recommends that "prosecutors consider the potential utility of such information in all cases where such evidence is available."[98]

Some expert witnesses traverse the country and earn very high fees by testifying at trials. DNA specialist John Gerdes, for example, was paid $100 per hour for his work in support of the defense in the 1995 O. J. Simpson criminal trial, and New York forensic pathologist Michael Baden charged $1,500 per day for time spent working for Simpson in Los Angeles. Baden billed

■ **lay witness**   An eyewitness, character witness, or other person called on to testify who is not considered an expert. Lay witnesses must testify to facts only and may not draw conclusions or express opinions.

■ **subpoena**   A written order issued by a judicial officer or grand jury requiring an individual to appear in court and to give testimony or to bring material to be used as evidence. Some subpoenas mandate that books, papers, and other items be surrendered to the court.

Simpson more than $100,000, and the laboratory for which Gerdes worked received more than $30,000 from Simpson's defense attorneys.[99] In 2008, Simpson was convicted by a Las Vegas jury on 12 felony counts stemming from a confrontation in a hotel room in 2007. The convictions came 13 years to the day after his 1995 acquittal.

Outsiders: Nonprofessional Courtroom Participants

Defendants, victims, jurors, and most witnesses are usually unwilling or inadvertent participants in criminal trials. Although they are outsiders who lack the status of paid professional participants, these are precisely the people who provide the grist for the judicial mill. The press, a willing player in many criminal trials, makes up another group of outsiders. Let's look now at each of these courtroom actors.

Lay Witnesses

Nonexpert witnesses, also known as **lay witnesses**, may be called to testify by either the prosecution or the defense. Lay witnesses may be eyewitnesses who saw the crime being committed or who came upon the crime scene shortly after the crime occurred. Another type of lay witness is the character witness, who frequently provides information about the personality, family life, business acumen, and so on of the defendant in an effort to show that this is not the kind of person who would commit the crime with which he or she is charged. Of course, the victim may also be a witness, providing detailed and sometimes lengthy testimony about the defendant and the crime.

A written document called a **subpoena** officially notifies witnesses that they are to appear in court to testify. Subpoenas are generally served by an officer of the court or by a police officer, though they are sometimes mailed. Both sides in a criminal case may subpoena witnesses and might ask that individuals called to testify bring with them books, papers, photographs, videotapes, or other forms of physical evidence. Witnesses who fail to appear when summoned may face contempt-of-court charges.

The job of a witness is to provide accurate testimony concerning only those things of which he or she has direct knowledge. Normally, witnesses are not allowed to repeat things that others have told them unless they must do so to account for certain actions of their own. Because few witnesses are familiar with courtroom procedure, the task of testifying is fraught with uncertainty and can be traumatizing.

Everyone who testifies in a criminal trial must do so under oath, in which some reference to God is made, or after affirmation,[100] which is a pledge to tell the truth used by those who find either swearing or a reference to God objectionable.

> Lay witnesses may be surprised to find that cross-examination can force them to defend their personal and moral integrity.

All witnesses are subject to cross-examination, a process that will be discussed in the next chapter. Lay witnesses may be surprised to find that cross-examination can force them to defend their personal and moral integrity. A cross-examiner may question a witness about past vicious, criminal, or immoral acts, even when such matters have never been the subject of a criminal proceeding.[101] As long as the intent of such questions is to demonstrate to the jury that the witness is not credible, the judge will normally permit them.

Witnesses have traditionally been shortchanged by the judicial process. Subpoenaed to attend court, they have often suffered from frequent and unannounced changes in trial dates. A witness who promptly responds to a summons to appear may find that legal maneuvering has resulted in unanticipated delays. Strategic changes by either side may make the testimony of some witnesses entirely unnecessary, and people who have prepared themselves for the psychological rigors of testifying often experience an emotional letdown.

To compensate witnesses for their time and to make up for lost income, many states pay witnesses for each day that they spend in court. Payments range from $5 to $40 per day,[102] although some states pay nothing at all. Juror pay is also quite low. In a 2004 Chicago murder case in which Oprah Winfrey served as a juror, for example, all jurors, including Winfrey—a billionaire—were paid $17.20 a day for their services.[103] The 1991 U.S. Supreme Court case of *Demarest* v. *Manspeaker et al.*[104] held that federal prisoners subpoenaed to testify are entitled to witness fees just as nonincarcerated witnesses would be.

■ **victims' assistance program**   An organized program that offers services to victims of crime in the areas of crisis intervention and follow-up counseling and that helps victims secure their rights under the law.

■ **juror**   A member of a trial or grand jury who has been selected for jury duty and is required to serve as an arbiter of the facts in a court of law. Jurors are expected to render verdicts of "guilty" or "not guilty" as to the charges brought against the accused, although they sometimes fail to do so (as in the case of a hung jury).

■ **lecture note**   Point out that today, jury duty is the one way remaining in which members of the public can be involved in the judicial process today.

■ **theme**   What constitutes a jury of one's peers? Who are *your* peers? If you were to face trial on a criminal charge, would you want your peers on the jury? Explain.

■ **theme**   How well does our jury system serve individual-rights and public-order needs? Explain.

■ **lecture note**   Explain that one of the biggest challenges for jurors is to remain objective and to avoid making up their minds about guilt or innocence until all evidence has been heard.

■ **lecture note**   Define a peer jury as a jury composed of a representative cross section of the community

In an effort to make the job of witnesses less onerous, 39 states and the federal government have laws or guidelines requiring that witnesses be notified of scheduling changes and cancellations in criminal proceedings.[105] In 1982, Congress passed the Victim and Witness Protection Act, which required the U.S. attorney general to develop guidelines to assist victims and witnesses in meeting the demands placed on them by the justice system. A number of **victims' assistance programs** (also called *victim/witness-assistance programs*) have also taken up a call for the rights of witnesses and are working to make the courtroom experience more manageable.

Jurors

The Cook County, Illinois, jury on which television host Oprah Winfrey served convicted a man of first-degree murder in 2004. "It was an eye-opener for all of us," Winfrey said after the three-day trial ended. "It was not an easy decision to make."[106]

Article III of the U.S. Constitution requires that "[t]he trial of all crimes … shall be by jury." States have the authority to determine the size of criminal trial juries. Most states use juries composed of 12 people and one or two alternates designated to fill in for **jurors** who are unable to continue due to accident, illness, or personal emergency. Some states allow for juries of fewer than 12, and juries with as few as six members have survived Supreme Court scrutiny.[107]

Jury duty is regarded as a responsibility of citizenship. Other than juveniles and people in certain occupations, such as police personnel, physicians, members of the armed services on active duty, and emergency services workers, those who are called for jury duty must serve unless they can convince a judge that they should be excused for overriding reasons. Aliens, convicted felons, and citizens who have served on a jury within the past two years are excluded from jury service in most jurisdictions.

The names of prospective jurors are often gathered from the tax register, motor vehicle records, or voter registration rolls of a county or municipality. Minimum qualifications for jury service include adulthood, a basic command of spoken English, citizenship,

> Ideally, the jury should be a microcosm of society, reflecting the values, rationality, and common sense of the average person.

"ordinary intelligence," and local residency. Jurors are also expected to possess their "natural faculties," meaning that they should be able to hear, speak, see, move, and so forth. Some jurisdictions have recently allowed people with physical disabilities to serve as jurors, although the nature of the evidence to be presented in a case may preclude people with certain kinds of disabilities from serving.

Ideally, the jury should be a microcosm of society, reflecting the values, rationality, and common sense of the average person. The U.S. Supreme Court has held that criminal defendants have a right to have their cases heard before a jury of their peers.[108] Peer juries are those composed of a representative cross section of the community in which the alleged crime occurred and where the trial is to be held. The idea of a peer jury stems from the Magna Carta's original guarantee of jury trials for "freemen." Freemen in England during the thirteenth century, however, were more likely to be of similar mind than is a cross section of Americans today. Hence, although the duty of the jury is to deliberate on the evidence and, ultimately, to determine guilt or innocence, social dynamics may play just as great a role in jury verdicts as do the facts of a case.

In a 1945 case, *Thiel v. Southern Pacific Co.*,[109] the Supreme Court clarified the concept of a "jury of one's peers" by noting that although it is not necessary for every jury to contain representatives of every conceivable racial, ethnic, religious, gender, and economic group in the community, court officials may not systematically and intentionally exclude any juror solely because of his or her social characteristics.

In 2005, the American Bar Association released a set of 19 principles intended to guide jury reform.[110] ABA President Robert J. Grey, Jr., said that the principles were aimed at improving the courts' treatment of jurors and to "move jury service into the 21st Century." Some of the principles sounded like a juror's bill of rights and included provisions to protect jurors' privacy and personal information, to inform jurors of trial schedules, and to "vigorously promote juror understanding of the facts and the law." Courts should instruct jurors "in plain and understandable language," the ABA report said. When trials conclude, the report continued, jurors should be advised by judges that they have the right to talk to anyone, including members of the press, and that they also have the right to refuse to talk to anyone about their jury service. Practical recommendations included

■ **lecture note**   Point out that the victim's role in court processing (trial and sentencing) is much more limited today than in the past, and that many victims today have little if any input or involvement.
■ **theme**   How can the court processes potentially cause harm to victims of crime? In what ways might the courts work to reduce this harm, which is also known as "secondary injury?"

■ **lecture note**   Describe the role of the defendant in the criminal trial. Highlight the choices the defendant makes as the trial proceeds, including the selection of an attorney, the choice of a plea, and the decision about whether to testify.
■ **lecture note**   Point out that the defendant has considerably more influence over the court process than the victim does. Ask students whether they agree with this or if they believe victims should have more input.

allowing jurors to take notes, educating jurors regarding the essential aspects of a jury trial, and providing them with identical notebooks containing the court's preliminary instructions and selected exhibits that have been ruled admissible. Read the ABA's entire report, *Principles for Juries and Jury Trials*, at **http://tinyurl.com/43hzc8x**.

The Victim

Not all crimes have clearly identifiable victims, and in a murder case, the victim does not survive. Where there is an identifiable surviving victim, however, he or she is often one of the most forgotten people in the courtroom. Although the victim may have been profoundly affected by the crime itself and is often emotionally committed to the proceedings and trial outcome, he or she may not even be permitted to participate directly in the trial process. Although a powerful movement to recognize the interests of victims is in full swing in this country, it is still not unusual for crime victims to be totally unaware of the final outcome of a case that intimately concerns them.[111]

> Not all crimes have clearly identifiable victims.

Hundreds of years ago, the situation surrounding victims was far different. During the early Middle Ages in much of Europe, victims or their survivors routinely played a central role in trial proceedings and in sentencing decisions. They testified, examined witnesses, challenged defense contentions, and pleaded with the judge or jury for justice, honor, and often revenge. Sometimes they were even expected to carry out the sentence of the court by flogging the offender or by releasing the trapdoor used for hangings. This "golden age" of the victim ended with the consolidation of power into the hands of monarchs, who declared that vengeance was theirs alone.

Today, victims, like witnesses, experience many hardships as they participate in the criminal court process. These are a few of the rigors they endure:

- Uncertainty as to their role in the criminal justice process
- A general lack of knowledge about the criminal justice system, courtroom procedure, and legal issues
- Trial delays that result in frequent travel, missed work, and wasted time
- Fear of the defendant or of retaliation from the defendant's associates
- The trauma of testifying and of cross-examination

The trial process itself can make for a bitter experience. If victims take the stand, defense attorneys may test their memory, challenge their veracity, or even suggest that they were somehow responsible for their own victimization. After enduring cross-examination, some victims report feeling as though they, and not the offender, were portrayed as the criminal to the jury. The difficulties encountered by victims have been compared to a second victimization at the hands of the criminal justice system.

> After enduring cross-examination, some victims report feeling as though they, and not the offender, were portrayed as the criminal to the jury.

The Defendant

Generally, defendants must be present at their trials. The Federal Rules of Criminal Procedure, like state rules, require that a defendant must be present at every stage of a trial, except that a defendant who is initially present may be voluntarily absent after the trial has commenced.[112] In *Crosby* v. *U.S.* (1993),[113] the U.S. Supreme Court held that a defendant may not be tried in absentia, even if he or she was present at the beginning of a trial, if his or her absence is due to escape or failure to appear. In *Zafiro* v. *U.S.* (1993),[114] the justices held that, at least in federal courts, defendants charged with similar or related offenses may be tried together, even when their defenses differ substantially.

The majority of criminal defendants are poor, uneducated, and often alienated from the philosophy that undergirds the American justice system. Many are relatively powerless and are at the mercy of judicial mechanisms. However, experienced defendants, notably those who are career offenders, may be well versed in courtroom demeanor. As we discussed earlier, defendants in criminal trials may even choose to represent themselves, though such a choice may not be in their best interests.

> The majority of criminal defendants are poor, uneducated, and often alienated from the philosophy that undergirds the American justice system.

Even without self-representation, every defendant who chooses to do so can substantially influence events in the courtroom. Defendants exercise choice in (1) selecting and retaining counsel, (2) planning a defense strategy in coordination with their attorney, (3) deciding what information to provide to (or withhold from) the defense team, (4) deciding what plea to enter, (5) deciding whether to testify personally, and (6) determining whether to file an appeal if convicted.

■ **change of venue** The movement of a trial or lawsuit from one jurisdiction to another or from one location to another within the same jurisdiction. A change of venue may be made in a criminal case to ensure that the defendant receives a fair trial.

■ **theme** In what ways might pretrial news coverage be damaging to the objective outcome of a criminal trial? Given the emphasis that our society places on freedom of the press and freedom of speech, do you agree that judges should be allowed to issue gag rules restricting the ability of trial participants to discuss a case outside of court?
■ **theme** Do you think video cameras should be permitted in criminal courtrooms? Why or why not?

Nevertheless, even the most active defendants suffer from a number of disadvantages. One is the tendency of others to assume that anyone on trial must be guilty. Although a criminal defendant is "innocent until proven guilty," the very fact that the defendant is accused of an offense casts a shadow of suspicion that may foster biases in the minds of jurors and other courtroom actors. Another disadvantage lies in the often-substantial social and cultural differences that separate the offender from the professional courtroom staff. Whereas lawyers and judges tend to identify with upper-middle-class values and lifestyles, few offenders do. The consequences of such a gap between defendant and courtroom staff may be insidious and far-reaching.

Spectators and the Press

Spectators and the press are often overlooked because they do not have an official role in courtroom proceedings. Both spectators and media representatives may be present in large numbers at any trial. Spectators include members of the families of both victim and defendant, friends of either side, and curious onlookers—some of whom are avocational court watchers. Journalists, TV reporters, and other members of the press are apt to be present at "spectacular" trials (those involving an especially gruesome crime or a famous personality) and at those in which there is a great deal of community interest. The right of reporters and spectators to be present at a criminal trial is supported by the Sixth Amendment's requirement of a public trial.

Press reports at all stages of a criminal investigation and trial often create problems for the justice system. Significant pretrial publicity about a case may make it difficult to find jurors who have not already formed an opinion as to the guilt or innocence of the defendant. News reports from the courtroom may influence or confuse nonsequestered jurors who hear them, especially when they contain information brought to the bench but not heard by the jury.

In the 1976 case of *Nebraska Press Association v. Stuart*,[115] the U.S. Supreme Court ruled that trial court judges could not legitimately issue gag orders preventing the pretrial publication of information about a criminal case, as long as the defendant's right to a fair trial and an impartial jury could be ensured by traditional means.[116] These means include (1) a **change of venue**, whereby the trial is moved to another jurisdiction less likely to have been exposed to the publicity; (2) trial postponement, which would allow for memories to fade and emotions to cool; and (3) jury selection and screening to eliminate biased people from the jury pool. In 1986, the Court extended press access to preliminary hearings, which it said are "sufficiently like a trial

to require public access."[117] In 1993, in the case of *Caribbean International News Corporation v. Puerto Rico*,[118] the Court effectively applied that requirement to territories under U.S. control.

Today, members of the press and their video, television, and still cameras are allowed into most state courtrooms. New York is one significant exception, and in 2004, a state court upheld the constitutionality of a 51-year-old law[119] prohibiting the use of cameras in that state's courts.[120] Forty-two states specifically allow cameras at most criminal trials,[121] although most require that permission be obtained from the judge before filming begins. Most states also impose restrictions on certain kinds of recording—of jurors or of juveniles, for example, or of conferences between an attorney and the defendant or between an attorney and the judge—although most states allow the filming of such proceedings without audio pickup. Only a few states ban television or video cameras outright. Indiana, Maryland, Mississippi, Nebraska, and Utah all prohibit audiovisual coverage of criminal trials. The District of Columbia prohibits cameras at trials and at appellate hearings.[122]

> Forty-two states specifically allow cameras at most criminal trials.

The U.S. Supreme Court has been far less favorably disposed to television coverage than have most state courts. In 1981, a Florida defendant appealed his burglary conviction to the Supreme Court,[123] arguing that the presence of television cameras at his trial had turned the court into a circus for attorneys and made the proceedings more a sideshow than a trial. The Supreme Court, recognizing that television cameras have an untoward effect on many people, found in favor of the defendant. In the words of the Court, "Trial courts must be especially vigilant to guard against any impairment of the defendant's right to a verdict based solely upon the evidence and the relevant law."

Cameras of all kinds have been prohibited in all federal district criminal proceedings since 1946 by Rule 53 of the Federal Rules of Criminal Procedure.[124] In 1972, the Judicial Conference of the United States adopted a policy opposing broadcast of civil proceedings in district courts, and that policy was incorporated into the Code of Conduct for United States Judges. Nonetheless, some district courts have local rules that allow photographs and filming during selected proceedings.

A three-year pilot project that allowed television cameras into six U.S. district courts and two appeals courts closed on December 31, 1994, when the Judicial Conference voted to end the project. Conference members expressed concerns that cameras were a distracting influence and were having a "negative impact on jurors [and] witnesses"[125] by exposing them to possible harm by revealing their identities. Still, some federal appellate courts have created their own policy on the use of cameras and broadcast equipment in the courtroom. The official policy of the U.S. Court of Appeals for the Ninth Circuit, for example, permits cameras and media broadcasts that meet certain rules. The policy stipulates, "Three business days advance notice is required from the media of a request to be present to broadcast, televise, record electronically, or take photographs at a particular session. Such requests must be submitted to the Clerk of Court." The policy adds, "The presiding judge of the panel may limit or terminate media coverage, or direct the removal of camera coverage personnel when necessary to protect the rights of the parties or to assure the orderly conduct of the proceedings."[126]

Today's new personal technologies, however, which include cellular telephones with digital camera capabilities, streaming Web-based video, and miniaturized recording devices, all threaten courtroom privacy in fact, in 2014, members of an advocacy group smuggled a miniature camera into a session of the U.S. Supreme Court and recorded oral arguments in a case about campaign finance reform. The video was later posted to YouTube as part of a protest over the issue.[127]

SUMMARY

- In the United States, there are two judicial systems. One is a state system made up of state and local courts established under the authority of state governments. The other is the federal court system, created by Congress under the authority of the U.S. Constitution. This dual-court system is the result of a general agreement among the nation's founders about the need for individual states to retain significant legislative authority and judicial autonomy separate from federal control.

- A typical state court system consists of trial courts of limited jurisdiction, trial courts of general jurisdiction, and appellate courts—usually including a state supreme court. State courts have virtually unlimited power to decide nearly every type of case, subject only to the limitations of the U.S. Constitution, their own state constitutions, and state law. It is within state courts that the large majority of criminal cases originate.

- The federal court system consists of three levels: U.S. district courts, U.S. courts of appeals, and the U.S. Supreme Court. U.S. district courts are the trial courts of the federal system and are located principally in larger cities. They decide only those cases over which the Constitution gives them authority. The highest federal court, the U.S. Supreme Court, is located in Washington, D.C., and hears cases only on appeal from lower courts.

- The courtroom work group comprises professional courtroom personnel, including the judge, the prosecuting attorney, the defense counsel, the bailiff, the local court administrator, the court reporter, the clerk of court, and expert witnesses. Also present in the courtroom for a trial are "outsiders"—nonprofessional courtroom participants like witnesses and jurors.

- The courtroom work group is guided by statutory requirements and ethical considerations, and its members are generally dedicated to bringing the criminal trial and other courtroom procedures to a successful close. This chapter describes the role that each professional participant plays in the courtroom. The judge, for example, has the primary duty of ensuring a fair trial—in short, seeing that justice prevails.

- Nonprofessional courtroom participants include lay witnesses, jurors, the victim, the defendant, and spectators and members of the press. Nonjudicial courtroom personnel, or outsiders, may be unwilling or inadvertent participants in a criminal trial.

KEY TERMS

appeal, 283	judge, 292
appellate jurisdiction, 281	judicial review, 289
bailiff, 302	jurisdiction, 280
change of venue, 309	juror, 307
community court, 284	lay witness, 306
court of last resort, 283	original jurisdiction, 281
courts of limited jurisdiction, 282	prosecutor, 294
courts of general jurisdiction, 282	prosecutorial discretion, 296
courtroom work group, 292	public defender, 299
Daubert standard, 304	specialized courts, 285
defense counsel, 297	state court administrator, 283
dispute-resolution center, 284	state court system, 279
exculpatory evidence, 296	subpoena, 306
expert witness, 304	trial *de novo*, 282
federal court system, 279	victims' assistance program, 307

KEY CASES

Argersinger v. *Hamlin*, 298	*Herrera* v. *Collins*, 283
Burns v. *Reed*, 297	*Imbler* v. *Pachtman*, 296
Crosby v. *U.S.*, 308	*Keeney* v. *Tamayo-Reyes*, 283
Daubert v. *Merrell Dow Pharmaceuticals*, 304	*Marbury* v. *Madison*, 289
	Melendez-Diaz v. *Massachusetts*, 304
Demarest v. *Manspeaker et al.*, 306	*Van de Kamp* v. *Goldstein*, 297
Gideon v. *Wainwright*, 298	*Zafiro* v. *U.S.*, 308

QUESTIONS FOR REVIEW

1. How did the American court system develop? What is the dual-court system? Why do we have a dual-court system in America?

2. What is a typical state court system like? What are some of the differences between the state and federal court systems?

3. How is the federal court system structured? What are the various types of federal courts?

4. What is meant by the *courtroom work group*?

5. Who are the professional members of the courtroom work group, and what are their roles?

6. Who are the nonprofessional courtroom participants, and what are their roles?

QUESTIONS FOR REFLECTION

1. What are the three forms of indigent defense used in the United States? Why might defendants prefer private attorneys over public counsel?

2. What is an expert witness? What is a lay witness? How might their testimony differ? What are some of the issues involved in deciding whether a person is an expert for purposes of testimony?

3. How do the professional and nonprofessional courtroom participants work together to bring most criminal trials to a successful close? What do you think a "successful close" might mean to the judge? To the defense attorney? To the prosecutor? To the jury? To the defendant? To the victim?

NOTES

1. Catherine Beck, "Details Emerge about Courthouse Shooting Suspect," *WXIA-TV,* June 6, 2014, http://www.11alive.com/story/news/local/cumming/2014/06/06/dennis-marx-courthouse-shooting/10104641/ (accessed January 7, 2015).

2. Patrik Jonsson, "Forsyth County Courthouse Shooting: Dennis Marx Plotted 'Sovereign Citizen' Attack," June 7, 2014, http://www.csmonitor.com/USA/2014/0607/Forsyth-County-Courthouse-shooting-Dennis-Marx-plotted-sovereign-citizen-attack-video (accessed January 7, 2015).

3. Law Enforcement Assistance Administration, *Two Hundred Years of American Criminal Justice* (Washington, DC: U.S. Government Printing Office, 1976), p. 31.

4. David B. Rottman and Shauna M. Strickland, *State Court Organization, 2004* (Washington, DC: Bureau of Justice Statistics, 2006), p. 7.

5. In 1957, only 13 states had permanent intermediate appellate courts. Now, all but 10 states have these courts. See Rottman and Strickland, *State Court Organization, 2004*, pp. 9–10.

6. *Keeney, Superintendent, Oregon State Penitentiary v. Tamayo-Reyes*, 113 S.Ct. 853, 122 L.Ed.2d 203 (1992).

7. *Herrera v. Collins*, 113 S.Ct. 853, 122 L.Ed.2d 203 (1993).

8. Martin Wright, *Justice for Victims and Offenders* (Bristol, PA: Open University Press, 1991), p. 56.

9. Greg Berman and John Feinblatt, *Good Courts* (New York: The New Press, 2005).

10. "Bridging the Gap between Communities and Courts," http://www.communityjustice.org (accessed November 22, 2009).

11. M. Somjen Frazer, *The Impact of the Community Court Model on Defendant Perceptions of Fairness: A Case Study at the Red Hook Community Justice Center* (New York: Center for Court Innovation, 2006).

12. Cynthia G. Lee, Fred L. Cheesman II, David B. Rottman, Rachel Swaner, Survi Lambson, Mike Rempel, and Ric Curtis, *A Community Court Grows in Brooklyn: A Comprehensive Evaluation of the Red Hook Community Justice Center* (Williamsburg, VA: National Center for State Courts, 2013).

13. Center for Court Innovation, "Brooklyn Mental Health Court," http://www.courtinnovation.org/project/brooklyn-mental-health-court (accessed March 5, 2013).

14. Adapted from National Institute of Justice, "Specialized Courts," http://www.nij.gov/topics/courts/specialized-courts.htm (accessed March 3, 2013).

15. Rekha Mirchandani, "What's So Special about Specialized Courts? The State and Social Change in Salt Lake City's Domestic Violence Court," *Law and Society Review*, Vol. 39, No. 2 (2005), p. 379.

16. Most of the information and some of the wording in this section come from Administrative Office of the U.S. Courts, "Understanding the Federal Courts," http://www.uscourts.gov/UFC99.pdf (accessed April 2, 2009).

17. Administrative Office of the U.S. Courts, "U.S. District Courts—Criminal Cases Commenced, Terminated, and Pending" http://www.uscourts.gov/uscourts/Statistics/JudicialFactsAndFigures/2013/Table501.pdf (accessed January 30, 2015).

18. Administrative Office of the U.S. Courts, "U.S. District Courts—Civil Cases Filed, Terminated, and Pending," http://www.uscourts.gov/uscourts/Statistics/JudicialFactsAndFigures/2013/Table401.pdf (accessed January 30, 2015).

19. Administrative Office of the U.S. Courts, "U.S. District Courts—Judicial Caseload Profile."

20. John R. Emshwiller and Alexandra Beerzon, "Decree in Arizona Eases Trial Limit," *Wall Street Journal*, January 28, 2011, http://online.wsj.com/article/SB1000142405274870401360457610451 0607653374.html (accessed June 2, 2011).

21. Administrative Office of the United States Court, "Judicial Salaries Since 1968," http://www.uscourts.gov/JudgesAndJudgeships/JudicialCompensation/judicial-salaries-since-1968.aspx (accessed February 3, 2015).

22. Linda Greenhouse, "A New Justice, An Old Plea: More Money for the Bench," *The New York Times*, January 1, 2006, http://query.nytimes.com/gst/fullpage.html?res=9D07E3DA1030F932 A35752C0A9609C8B63 (accessed January 2, 2015).

23. Much of the information and some of the wording in this section come from Administrative Office of the U.S. Courts, "About the Federal Courts," http://www.uscourts.gov/about.html (accessed October 4, 2007).

24. Stephen L. Wasby, *The Supreme Court in the Federal Judicial System*, 3rd ed. (Chicago: Nelson-Hall, 1988), p. 58.

25. Judicial Conference of the United States, "Judicial Conference Judgeship Recommendations, March 2013," http://www.uscourts.gov/FederalCourts/JudicialConference/JudgeshipRecommendations.aspx (accessed January 10, 2015).

26. *The Supreme Court of the United States* (Washington, DC: U.S. Government Printing Office, no date), p. 4.

27. *Marbury v. Madison*, 1 Cranch 137 (1803).

28. National Center for State Courts, "Court Technology Bulletin," February 16, 2012, http://courttechbulletin.blogspot.com/2012/02/calculating-e-court-return-on.html (accessed July 26, 2012).

29. Many of the details for this story come from CBS News. See, for example, Mike Ballou, "Caylee Anthony Autopsy Reveals Grim Details But Sheds Little Light on Mystery," June 22, 2009, http://www.cbsnews.com/8301-504083_162-5103384-504083 .html (accessed May 20, 2010).

30. See, for example, Jeffrey T. Ulmer, *Social Worlds of Sentencing: Court Communities under Sentencing Guidelines* (Ithaca: State University of New York Press, 1997); and Roy B. Flemming, Peter F. Nardulli, and James Eisenstein, *The Craft of Justice: Politics and Work in Criminal Court Communities* (Philadelphia: University of Pennsylvania Press, 1993).

31. See, for example, Edward J. Clynch and David W. Neubauer, "Trial Courts as Organizations," *Law and Policy Quarterly*, Vol. 3 (1981), pp. 69–94.

32. American Bar Association, *ABA Standards for Criminal Justice*, 2nd ed. (Chicago: ABA, 1980).

33. In 1940, Missouri became the first state to adopt a plan for the "merit selection" of judges based on periodic public review.

34. National Judicial College, "About the NJC," http://www.judges .org/about (accessed February 2, 2009).

35. See National Judicial College, "National Impact," 2006, http:// www.judges.org/downloads/general_information/national _impact06 (accessed May 22, 2008).

36. Doris Marie Provine, *Judging Credentials: Nonlawyer Judges and the Politics of Professionalism* (Chicago: University of Chicago Press, 1986).

37. Town and village justices in New York State serve part-time and may or may not be lawyers; judges of all other courts must be lawyers, whether or not they serve full-time. From New York State Commission on Judicial Conduct, "2011 Annual Report," http://http://www.cjc.ny.gov/Publications/AnnualReports/ nyscjc.2011annualreport.pdf (accessed March 10, 2013).

38. Ibid.

39. Bill Rankin, "Ex-judge Camp Sentenced to 30 Days in Prison," *Atlanta Journal-Constitution*, March 11, 2011, http://www.ajc .com/news/atlanta/ex-judge-camp-sentenced-867817.html (accessed June 2, 2011).

40. West Virginia Justice Watch, "Former Circuit Court Judge Joseph Troisi Made State and National Headlines for Biting the Nose of a Defendant (1997)," http://www.wvjusticewatch.org/ ethics/bite_nose.htm (accessed July 5, 2005).

41. U.S. Department of Justice, Office of Public Affairs, Press Release, "Former Senior U.S. District Judge Sentenced to One Month in Prison for Misuse of Government Property and Drug Offenses," March 11, 2011, http://www.justice.gov/opa/ pr/2011/March/11-crm-315.html (accessed June 1, 2011).

42. Bureau of Justice Statistics, *Report to the Nation on Crime and Justice: The Data* (Washington, DC: U.S. Dept. of Justice, 1983).

43. For a discussion of the resource limitations that district attorneys face in combating corporate crime, see Michael L. Benson et al., "District Attorneys and Corporate Crime: Surveying the Prosecutorial Gatekeepers," *Criminology*, Vol. 26, No. 3 (August 1988), pp. 505–517.

44. Carol J. DeFrances and Greg W. Steadman, *Prosecutors in State Courts, 1996* (Washington, DC: Bureau of Justice Statistics, 1998).

45. U.S. Code, Title 28, Section 530A.

46. Some of the wording in this paragraph is adapted from Kim Murphy, "Prosecutors in Oregon Find 'Truth' Ruling a Real Hindrance," *Los Angeles Times*, August 5, 2001.

47. *In re Gatti*, S45801, Oregon Supreme Court, August 17, 2000.

48. The ruling was based on Disciplinary Rule 1-102 of the Oregon State Bar, which says, in part, that it is professional misconduct for a lawyer to "engage in conduct involving dishonesty, fraud, deceit or misrepresentation." The rule also prohibits a lawyer from violating this dishonesty provision through the acts of another. Also at issue was Disciplinary Rule 7-102, which prohibits a lawyer from "knowingly making a false statement of law or fact."

49. Most of the information and some of the wording in this section come from Administrative Office of the U.S. Courts, "Understanding the Federal Courts," http://www.uscourts.gov/ UFC99.pdf (accessed April 2, 2004).

50. Kenneth Culp Davis, *Discretionary Justice* (Baton Rouge: Louisiana State University Press, 1969), p. 190.

51. Barbara Borland, *The Prosecution of Felony Arrests* (Washington, DC: Bureau of Justice Statistics, 1983).

52. *Brady* v. *Maryland*, 373 U.S. 83 (1963).

53. *U.S.* v. *Bagley*, 473 U.S. 667 (1985).

54. *Banks* v. *Dretke*, 124 S.Ct. 1256, 1280 (2004).

55. *Imbler* v. *Pachtman*, 424 U.S. 409 (1976).

56. *Burns* v. *Reed*, 500 U.S. 478 (1991).

57. Ibid., complaint, p. 29.

58. *Van de Kamp* v. *Goldstein*, U.S. Supreme Court, No. 07-854 (decided January 26, 2009).

59. Cassia Spohn, John Gruhl, and Susan Welch, "The Impact of the Ethnicity and Gender of Defendants on the Decision to Reject or Dismiss Felony Charges," *Criminology*, Vol. 25, No. 1 (1987), pp. 175–191.

60. Brad Heath and Kevin McCoy, "Justice Dept. Office to Punish Prosecutors' Misconduct," *USA Today*, January 19, 2011, p. 1A.

61. American Bar Association Center for Professional Responsibility, *Model Rules of Professional Conduct* (Chicago: ABA, 2003), p. 87.

62. The same is true under federal law, and in almost all of the states, of communications between defendants and members of the clergy, psychiatrists and psychologists, medical doctors, and licensed social workers in the course of psychotherapy. See, for example, *Jaffee* v. *Redmond*, 116 S.Ct. 1923 (1996).

63. *Powell* v. *Alabama*, 287 U.S. 45 (1932).

64. *Johnson* v. *Zerbst*, 304 U.S. 458 (1938).

65. *Gideon* v. *Wainwright*, 372 U.S. 335 (1963).

66. *Argersinger* v. *Hamlin*, 407 U.S. 25 (1972).

67. *In re Gault*, 387 U.S. 1 (1967).

68. *Alabama* v. *Shelton*, 535 U.S. 654 (2002).

69. Jane Fritsch, "Pataki Rethinks Promise of a Pay Raise for Lawyers to the Indigent," *New York Times*, December 24, 2001.

70. Erinn Herberman and Tracey Kyckelhahn, *Sate Government Indigent Defense Expenditures, FY 2008–2012—Updated* (Washington, DC: October 24, 2014).

71. Ibid.

72. Carol J. DeFrances, *State-Funded Indigent Defense Services, 1999* (Washington, DC: National Institute of Justice, 2001).

73. "Nationline: McVeigh's Defense Cost Taxpayers $13.8 Million," *USA Today*, July 3, 2001.

74. *Faretta* v. *California*, 422 U.S. 806 (1975).

75. Smith and DeFrances, *Indigent Defense*, pp. 2–3.

76. *Anders* v. *California*, 386 U.S. 738 (1967).

77. *People* v. *Wende*, 25 Cal.3d 436, 600 P.2d 1071 (1979).

78. *Smith* v. *Robbins*, 528 U.S. 259 (2000).

79. *Texas* v. *Cobb*, 532 U.S. 162 (2001).

80. Details for this story come from Chisun Lee, "Punishing Mmes. Stewart: The Parallel Universes of Martha and Lynne," *Village*

Voice, February 15, 2005, http://www.refuseandresist.org/article-print.php?aid51757 (accessed January 5, 2006).

81. Scott Shifrel and James Fanelli, "Lynn Stewart, 70-year-old Radical Lawyer, Sentenced to 10 years in Prison for Aiding Bomb Plotter," *Daily News*, July 16, 2010, http://www.nydailynews.com/new-york/lynn-stewart-70-year-old-radical-lawyer-sentenced-10-years-prison-aiding-bomb-plotter-article-1.466192 (accessed July 31, 2013).

82. "Justice for Lynne Stewart," http://lynnestewart.org (accessed May 12, 2013).

83. "Lawyer Convicted of Terrorist Support," *USA Today*, February 11, 2005, p. 3A.

84. Mike McKee, "California State Bar to Allow Lawyers to Break Confidentiality," *Recorder*, May 17, 2004, http://www.law.com/jsp/article.jsp?id51084316038367 (accessed August 25, 2007).

85. "ABA Eases Secrecy Rules in Lawyer-Client Relationship," *USA Today*, August 7, 2001.

86. *Nix* v. *Whiteside*, 475 U.S. 157 (1986).

87. Ibid.

88. "Courtroom Killings Verdict," *USA Today*, February 15, 1993.

89. National Center for State Courts, "Improving Security in State Courthouses: Ten Essential Elements for Court Safety," http://www.ncsconline.org/whatsNew/TenPointPlan.htm (accessed October 20, 2007).

90. President's Commission on Law Enforcement and Administration of Justice, *The Challenge of Crime in a Free Society* (Washington, DC: U.S. Government Printing Office, 1967), p. 129.

91. National Advisory Commission on Criminal Justice Standards and Goals, *Courts* (Washington, DC: U.S. Government Printing Office, 1973), Standard 9.3.

92. See, for example, Joan G. Brannon, *The Judicial System in North Carolina* (Raleigh, NC: Administrative Office of the United States Courts, 1984), p. 14.

93. *Daubert* v. *Merrell Dow Pharmaceuticals, Inc.*, 509 U.S. 579, 113 S.Ct. 2786 (1993).

94. For the application of *Daubert* to DNA technology, see Barry Sheck, "DNA and *Daubert*," *Cardozo Law Review*, Vol. 15 (1994), p. 1959.

95. *Melendez-Diaz* v. *Massachusetts*, 557 U.S. 305 (2009).

96. *Bullcoming* v. *New Mexico*, U.S. Supreme Court, No. 09-10876 (decided June 23, 2011).

97. Joseph L. Peterson, "Use of Forensic Evidence by the Police and Courts," *National Institute of Justice Research in Brief* (Washington, DC: NIJ, 1987), p. 3.

98. Ibid., p. 6.

99. Jennifer Bowles, "Simpson-Paid Experts," *Associated Press*, August 12, 1995.

100. *California* v. *Green*, 399 U.S. 149 (1970).

101. Patrick L. McCloskey and Ronald L. Schoenberg, *Criminal Law Deskbook* (New York: Matthew Bender, 1988), Section 17, p. 123.

102. United States District Court, District of Massachusetts, "Additional Federal Jury Duty Information," http://www.mad.uscourts.gov/jurors/federal-information-more.htm (accessed May 22, 2012).

103. Anna Johnson, "Jury with Oprah Winfrey Convicts Man of Murder," *Associated Press*, August 19, 2004.

104. *Demarest* v. *Manspeaker et al.*, 498 U.S. 184, 111 S.Ct. 599, 112 L.Ed.2d 608 (1991).

105. Bureau of Justice Statistics, *Report to the Nation on Crime and Justice*, p. 82.

106. Johnson, "Jury with Oprah Winfrey Convicts Man of Murder."

107. *Williams* v. *Florida*, 399 U.S. 78, 90 S.Ct. 1893, 26 L.Ed.2d 446 (1970).

108. *Smith* v. *Texas*, 311 U.S. 128 (1940). That right does not apply when the defendants are facing the possibility of a prison sentence of less than six months in length or even when the potential aggregate sentence for multiple petty offenses exceeds six months (see *Lewis* v. *U.S.*, 518 U.S. 322 [1996]).

109. *Thiel* v. *Southern Pacific Co.*, 328 U.S. 217 (1945).

110. American Bar Association, *Principles for Juries and Jury Trials* (Chicago: ABA, 2005).

111. The author was himself the victim of a felony some years ago. His car was stolen in Columbus, Ohio, and recovered a year later in Cleveland. He was informed that the person who had taken it was in custody, but he never heard what happened to him, nor could he learn where or whether a trial was to be held.

112. Federal Rules of Criminal Procedure, Rule 43.

113. *Crosby* v. *U.S.*, 113 S.Ct. 748, 122 L.Ed.2d 25 (1993).

114. *Zafiro* v. *U.S.*, 113 S.Ct. 933, 122 L.Ed.2d 317 (1993).

115. *Nebraska Press Association* v. *Stuart*, 427 U.S. 539 (1976).

116. However, it is generally accepted that trial judges may issue limited gag orders aimed at trial participants.

117. *Press Enterprise Company* v. *Superior Court of California, Riverside County*, 478 U.S. 1 (1986).

118. *Caribbean International News Corporation* v. *Puerto Rico*, 508 U.S. 147 (1993).

119. N.Y. Civil Rights Law, Section 52.

120. Tom Perrotta, "New York Law Banning Cameras in State Courts Found Constitutional," *New York Law Journal*, May 23, 2004.

121. Charles L. Babcock et al., "Fifty-State Survey of the Law Governing Audio-Visual Coverage of Court Proceedings," http://www.jw.com/articles/details.cfm?articlenum5120 (accessed October 10, 2005).

122. See Radio-Television News Directors Association, "Summary of State Camera Coverage Rules," http://www.rtnda.org/issues/camerassummary.htm (accessed February 9, 2000).

123. *Chandler* v. *Florida*, 499 U.S. 560 (1981).

124. Rule 53 of the Federal Rules of Criminal Procedure reads, "The taking of photographs in the court room during the progress of judicial proceedings or radio broadcasting of judicial proceedings from the court room shall not be permitted by the court."

125. Harry F. Rosenthal, "Courts-TV," *Associated Press*, September 21, 1991. See also "Judicial Conference Rejects Cameras in Federal Courts," *Criminal Justice Newsletter*, September 15, 1994, p. 6.

126. Policy, U.S. Court of Appeals for the Ninth Circuit, http://www.ce9.uscourts.gov/web/OCELibra.nsf/504ca249c786e20f85256284006da7ab/ba060a3e537d2866882569760067ac8e?OpnDocument (accessed September 16, 2007).

127. Bill Mears, "Supreme Court Secretly Recorded on Camera," CNN, http://www.cnn.com/2014/02/27/politics/supreme-court-video/index.html (accessed February 10, 2015).

10

PRETRIAL ACTIVITIES AND THE CRIMINAL TRIAL

OUTLINE

- Introduction
- Pretrial Activities
- The Criminal Trial
- Stages in a Criminal Trial
- Improving the Adjudication Process

LEARNING OBJECTIVES

After reading this chapter, you should be able to

- Describe the pretrial steps and activities.
- State the purpose of the criminal trial.
- Describe the criminal trial process.
- Describe three approaches to improving the adjudication process.

Society asks much of the criminal court. The court is expected to meet society's demand that serious offenders be convicted and punished, and at the same time it is expected to insure that the innocent and unfortunate are not oppressed.

THE PRESIDENT'S COMMISSION ON LAW ENFORCEMENT AND ADMINISTRATION OF JUSTICE

■ **first appearance**   An appearance before a magistrate during which the legality of the defendant's arrest is initially assessed and the defendant is informed of the charges on which he or she is being held. At this stage in the criminal justice process, bail may be set or pretrial release arranged.

Introduction

On May 8, 2013, Arizona jurors found 32-year-old Jodi Arias guilty of first-degree murder in the brutal killing of her former boyfriend, Travis Alexander. Arias, who admitted shooting and stabbing her then-30-year-old lover at his home in 2008, claimed that she had been trying to defend herself from emotional, physical, and sexual abuse. Arias appeared as a petite and demure woman during her widely-televised trial, and dressed like a schoolgirl while on the stand. Although her appearance might have been unremarkable, Arias's trial captured the attention of the nation and the world as it wound through five months of testimony, cross-examination, and jury debate. *USA Today* described it this way, "the Jodi Arias trial, which would ordinarily be a run-of-the-mill domestic murder case," drew a media circus that fed a large following of TV viewers who watched the trial unfold.[1] They were captivated by its intimate details of "love, lies, sex, and dirty secrets." At one point, an audio recording was played during the trail in which Alexander said that he wanted to tie Arias to a tree and commit deviant sex acts on her.

Alexander's body was found in the shower of his Mesa, Arizona, home. He had been shot in the face, stabbed 30 times, and his throat had been cut from ear to ear. Court testimony revealed that Arias was a jilted lover who turned into a stalker, even though Alexander continued to invite her to his house and have sex with her while he saw other women.

Pretrial Activities

In this chapter, we will describe the criminal trial process, highlighting each important stage in the procedure. First, however, we look at the court-related activities that routinely take place *before* trial can begin. These activities (as well as the names given to them) vary among jurisdictions. They are described generally in the pages that follow (see Figure 10-1).

The First Appearance

Following arrest, most defendants do not come into contact with an officer of the court until their **first appearance** before a magistrate or a lower-court judge.[2] A first appearance, sometimes called an *initial appearance* or *magistrate's review*, occurs when defendants are brought before a judge (1) to be given formal notice of the charges against them, (2) to be advised of their rights, (3) to be given the opportunity to retain a lawyer or to have one appointed to represent them, and (4) perhaps to be afforded the opportunity for bail.

According to the procedural rules of all jurisdictions, defendants who have been taken into custody must be offered an in-court appearance before a magistrate "without unnecessary delay." The 1943 U.S. Supreme Court case of *McNabb* v. *U.S.*[3] established that any unreasonable delay in an initial court appearance would make confessions inadmissible if interrogating officers obtained them during the delay. Based on the *McNabb* decision, 48 hours following arrest became the standard maximum time by which a first appearance should be held.

> Defendants who have been taken into custody must be offered an in-court appearance before a magistrate "without unnecessary delay."

The first appearance may also involve a probable cause hearing, although such hearings may be held separately because they do not require the defendant's presence. (In some jurisdictions, a probable cause hearing may be combined with the preliminary hearing, which we will look at later in this chapter.) Probable cause hearings are necessary when arrests are made without a

Rob Schumacher/UPI/Newscom

Jodi Arias, convicted of the brutal murder of her boy-friend, Travis Alexander. Arias escaped the death penalty when the judge declared a mistrial in the sentencing phase of her trial in 2015. Why did her televised trial draw such a large audience?

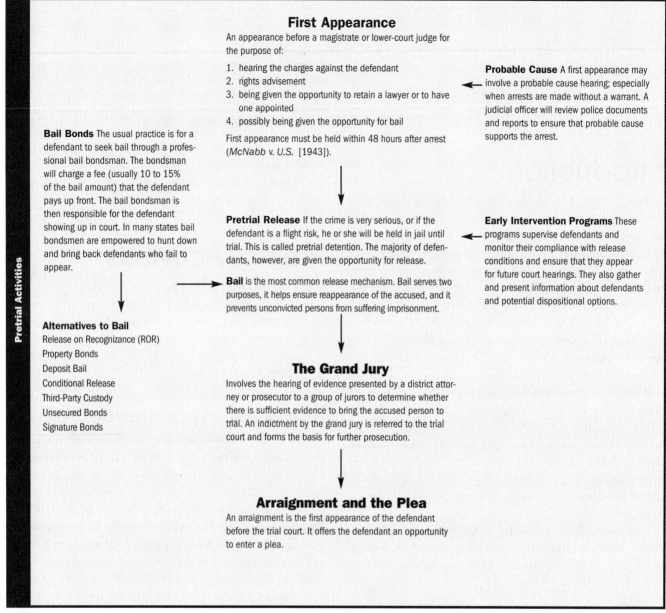

Pretrial Activities

First Appearance

An appearance before a magistrate or lower-court judge for the purpose of:

1. hearing the charges against the defendant
2. rights advisement
3. being given the opportunity to retain a lawyer or to have one appointed
4. possibly being given the opportunity for bail

First appearance must be held within 48 hours after arrest (*McNabb* v. *U.S.* [1943]).

Probable Cause A first appearance may involve a probable cause hearing; especially when arrests are made without a warrant. A judicial officer will review police documents and reports to ensure that probable cause supports the arrest.

Bail Bonds The usual practice is for a defendant to seek bail through a professional bail bondsman. The bondsman will charge a fee (usually 10 to 15% of the bail amount) that the defendant pays up front. The bail bondsman is then responsible for the defendant showing up in court. In many states bail bondsmen are empowered to hunt down and bring back defendants who fail to appear.

Pretrial Release If the crime is very serious, or if the defendant is a flight risk, he or she will be held in jail until trial. This is called pretrial detention. The majority of defendants, however, are given the opportunity for release.

Bail is the most common release mechanism. Bail serves two purposes, it helps ensure reappearance of the accused, and it prevents unconvicted persons from suffering imprisonment.

Early Intervention Programs These programs supervise defendants and monitor their compliance with release conditions and ensure that they appear for future court hearings. They also gather and present information about defendants and potential dispositional options.

Alternatives to Bail
Release on Recognizance (ROR)
Property Bonds
Deposit Bail
Conditional Release
Third-Party Custody
Unsecured Bonds
Signature Bonds

The Grand Jury

Involves the hearing of evidence presented by a district attorney or prosecutor to a group of jurors to determine whether there is sufficient evidence to bring the accused person to trial. An indictment by the grand jury is referred to the trial court and forms the basis for further prosecution.

Arraignment and the Plea

An arraignment is the first appearance of the defendant before the trial court. It offers the defendant an opportunity to enter a plea.

Figure 10-1 | Pretrial Activities

Source: Pearson Education, Inc.

warrant.[4] During a probable cause hearing, also called a *probable cause determination*, a judicial officer will review police documents and reports to ensure that probable cause supported the arrest. The review of the arrest proceeds in a relatively informal fashion, with the judge seeking to decide whether, at the time of apprehension, the arresting officer had reason to believe both (1) that a crime had been or was being committed and (2) that the defendant was the person who committed it. Most of the evidence presented to the judge comes either from the arresting officer or from the victim. If probable cause is not found, the suspect is released. As with a first appearance, a probable cause hearing should take place within 48 hours.

In 1991, in a class-action suit titled *County of Riverside* v. *McLaughlin*,[5] the U.S. Supreme Court imposed a promptness requirement on probable cause determinations for in-custody arrestees. The Court held that "a jurisdiction that provides judicial determinations of probable cause within 48 hours of arrest will, as a general matter, comply with the promptness requirement." The Court specified, however, that weekends and holidays could not be excluded from the 48-hour requirement (as they had been in Riverside County, California) and that, depending on the specifics of the case, delays of fewer than two days may still be unreasonable.

During a first appearance, the suspect is not given an opportunity to present evidence, although the U.S. Supreme Court has held that defendants are entitled to representation by counsel at their first appearance[6] and that an indigent person is entitled to have an attorney appointed for him or her at the initial appearance.[7] Following a reading of the charges and an advisement of rights, counsel may be appointed to represent indigent

■ **pretrial release** The release of an accused person from custody, for all or part of the time before or during prosecution, on his or her promise to appear in court when required.

■ **bail bond** A document guaranteeing the appearance of a defendant in court as required and recording the pledge of money or property to be paid to the court if he or she does not appear, which is signed by the person to be released and anyone else acting on his or her behalf.

A bail hearing in progress. Standing before the judge are Julie Barnes and Thomas Levesque, a homeless pair accused of accidentally starting a warehouse blaze that led to the deaths of six Worcester, Massachusetts, firefighters. Levesque's bail was set at $250,000 cash, or $2.5 million with surety; Barnes's bail was set at $75,000 cash, or $750,000 with surety. In 2002, the two agreed to a plea agreement, and each was sentenced to five years of probation for involuntary manslaughter. What purpose does bail serve?

defendants and proceedings may be adjourned until counsel can be obtained. In cases where a suspect is unruly, intoxicated, or uncooperative, a judicial review may take place without the suspect's presence.

Some states waive a first appearance and proceed directly to arraignment (discussed later), especially when the defendant has been arrested on a warrant. In states that move directly to arraignment, the procedures undertaken to obtain a warrant are regarded as sufficient to demonstrate a basis for detention before arraignment.

Pretrial Release

A significant aspect of the first appearance hearing is the consideration of **pretrial release**. Defendants charged with very serious crimes, or those who are thought likely to escape or to injure others, are usually held in jail until trial. Such a practice is called *pretrial detention*. Most defendants, however, are afforded the opportunity for release. Many jurisdictions make use of pretrial service programs, which may also be called *early-intervention programs*.[8] Such programs, which are typically funded by the states or by individual counties, perform two critical functions: (1) They gather and present information about newly arrested defendants and about available release options for use by judicial

officers in deciding what (if any) conditions are to be set for the defendants' release prior to trial, and (2) they supervise defendants who are released from custody during the pretrial period by monitoring their compliance with release conditions and by helping ensure that they appear for scheduled court events. Learn more about pretrial services at **http://www.justicestudies .com/pubs/pretrial.pdf**.

The initial pretrial release–detention decision is usually made by a judicial officer or by a specially appointed hearing officer who considers background information provided by the pretrial service program, along with the representations made by the prosecutor and the defense attorney. In making this decision, judicial officers are concerned about two types of risk: (1) the risk of flight or nonappearance for scheduled court appearances and (2) the risk to public safety.

Bail

Bail is the most common release–detention decision-making mechanism in American courts. Bail serves two purposes: (1) It helps ensure reappearance of the accused, and (2) it prevents unconvicted individuals from suffering imprisonment unnecessarily.

Bail involves the posting of a bond as a pledge that the accused will return for further hearings. **Bail bonds** usually involve cash deposits but may be based on property or other valuables. A fully secured bond requires the defendant to post the full amount of bail set by the court. The usual practice, however, is for a defendant to seek privately secured bail through the services of a professional bail agent. The agent will assess a percentage (usually 10 to 15%) of the required bond as a fee, which the defendant will have to pay up front. Those who "skip bail" by hiding or fleeing will sometimes be ordered by the court to forfeit their bail. Forfeiture hearings must be held before a bond can be taken, and most courts will not order bail forfeited unless it appears that the defendant intends to avoid prosecution permanently. Bail forfeiture will often be reversed if the defendant later appears willingly to stand trial.

In many states, bail bond agents are empowered to hunt down and bring back defendants who have fled. In some jurisdictions, bail bond agents hold virtually unlimited powers and have been permitted by courts to pursue, arrest, and forcibly extradite their charges from foreign jurisdictions without concern

In many states, bail bond agents are empowered to hunt down and bring back defendants who have fled.

CJ | CAREERS
Surety Agent

Name: Anya Pulai

Position: Bail Bond Agent/Bail Enforcement Agent, Good To Go Bail Bonds, Denver, Colorado

Colleges attended: Associate of Arts in Criminal Justice from University of Phoenix (2007); currently attending Regis University pursuing a bachelor's degree in criminology.

Year hired: 2008 to present, Bail Enforcement Agent; 2009 to present, Surety Agent, Sun Surety Insurance Company

Please give a brief description of your job: Bail bond amounts are set by a judge or magistrate during the intake process or a bail hearing. The judge will consider a variety of factors, including the severity of the crime, previous convictions, the defendant's ties to the community, family, and whether or not the defendant has steady employment. Typically, a family member or associate or the defendant will contact a surety agent or bond agent to arrange for release. These calls are accepted 24/7/365 by the surety office, which then begins a risk assessment process. In Colorado, a surety agent may charge no more than 15% of the bond amount. Once terms are agreed upon, and all the various collateral documentation including indemnity agreements, statements of collateral taken, rate deviation forms, and applications are completed, the bail bond is posted at the detention facility holding the defendant. In the event the defendant fails to appear (FTA) at a scheduled appearance date or time, warrants and mug shots must be obtained and efforts to apprehend the defendant and bring him or her into custody begin.

What appealed most about the position when you applied for it? This is not a "desk job." This career involves elements of customer service, sales, computer skills, area travel, and being physically fit. Understanding various criminal behavior models as well as supporting every citizen's right to defend himself without detention appealed to me.

How would you describe the interview process? Demonstrating the physical presence and ability to apprehend a suspected fugitive was critical. During my interview process, a female defendant was to be remanded back into custody for violations of the terms and conditions of her bond. The defendant fled the site and I was required

Anya Pulai
Courtesy of Anya Pulai

to pursue. A two-block sprint and apprehension ensued. Shortly thereafter, I obtained certification as a surety agent and began writing bail bonds as well.

What is a typical day like? We receive calls on a wide spectrum of bail bond needs. After verifying the detention facility, the amount of the bond, and the ability of the idemnitor to cosign for the bond, we will meet to complete the required documentation. I must then travel to the detaining facility to post the bond. Using various computer-based tools, I monitor my clients court schedules. If a failure to appear is identified, the bail enforcement process begins in a passive mode. This includes contacting the cosigner, family, employer, and associates of the defendant. Based on the specific scenario, several activities may be required, including rescheduling an appearance date or time, locating the defendant, motioning the court, or apprehension of the defendant, all the while accepting new clients.

What qualities/characteristics are most helpful for this job? Computer skills are required for database management and various tool sets used in locating fugitive defendants. Knowledge of area demographics greatly assists both the determination of risk management and the bail enforcement efforts. Understanding the educational background and emotional state of the client(s) is helpful. Having a basic understanding of the court and law enforcement process and ongoing physical conditioning are all helpful, as well.

What is a typical starting salary? New agents tend to work for established bail bond companies, and they are usually paid based on commission, or a percentage of the amount of bail written. About $25,000 to $40,000 year.

What is the salary potential as you move up into higher-level jobs? More experienced bail bond agent can make between $45,000 and $150,000 per year.

What career advice would you give someone in college beginning studies in criminal justice? There are many career opportunities in the criminal justice system, so career paths are not always clear for students entering college. My advice would be to research various career areas. Be wise. Ask questions. Study what you would like to pursue and don't settle for a job that you are not passionate about.

Source: Anya Pulai/Pearson Education, Inc.

---

for the due process considerations or statutory limitations that apply to law enforcement officers.[9] Recently, however, some states have enacted laws that eliminate for-profit bail bond businesses, replacing them instead with state-operated pretrial service agencies. Visit the Professional Bail Agents of the United States via **http://www.pbus.com** to learn more about the job of bail bond agents and to view the group's code of ethics.

Alternatives to Bail

The Eighth Amendment to the U.S. Constitution does not guarantee the opportunity for bail but does state that "[e]xcessive

bail shall not be required." Some studies, however, have found that many defendants who are offered the opportunity for bail are unable to raise the money. Thirty years ago, a report by the National Advisory Commission on Criminal Justice Standards and Goals found that as many as 93% of felony defendants in some jurisdictions were unable to make bail.[10]

To extend the opportunity for pretrial release to a greater number of nondangerous arrestees, many states and the federal government now offer various alternatives to the cash bond system, such as (1) release on recognizance, (2) property bond, (3) deposit bail, (4) conditional release, (5) third-party custody, (6) unsecured bond, and (7) signature bond.

■ **release on recognizance (ROR)** The pretrial release of a criminal defendant on his or her written promise to appear in court as required. No cash or property bond is required.
■ **property bond** The setting of bail in the form of land, houses, stocks, or other tangible property. In the event that the defendant absconds prior to trial, the bond becomes the property of the court.

■ **conditional release** The release by executive decision of a prisoner from a federal or state correctional facility who has not served his or her full sentence and whose freedom is contingent on obeying specified rules of behavior.

Courtesy of Anya Pulai

Denver area bail bond agent, Anya Pulai. Pulai is highlighted in a careers box in this chapter. What is the job of a bail bond agent?

Release on Recognizance (ROR) **Release on recognizance (ROR)** involves no cash bond, requiring as a guarantee only that the defendant agree in writing to return for further hearings as specified by the court. Release on recognizance was tested during the 1960s in a social experiment called the Manhattan Bail Project.[11] In the experiment, those arrested for serious crimes, including murder, rape, and robbery, and those with extensive prior criminal records were excluded from participating in the project. The rest of the defendants were scored and categorized according to a number of "ideal" criteria used as indicators of both dangerousness and the likelihood of pretrial flight. Criteria included (1) no previous convictions, (2) residential stability, and (3) a good employment record. Those likely to flee were not released.

Studies of the bail project revealed that it released four times as many defendants before trial as had been freed under the traditional cash bond system,[12] and that only 1% of those released fled from prosecution—the same percentage as for those set free on cash bond.[13] Later studies, however, were unclear as to the effectiveness of release on recognizance, with some finding a no-show rate as high as 12%.[14]

Property Bond **Property bonds** substitute other items of value in place of cash. Land, houses, automobiles, stocks, and so on may be consigned to the court as collateral against pretrial flight.

Deposit Bail Deposit bail is an alternative form of cash bond available in some jurisdictions. Deposit bail places the court in the role of the bail bond agent, allowing the defendant to post a percentage of the full bail with the court. Unlike private bail bond agents, court-run deposit bail programs usually return the amount of the deposit except for a small administrative fee (perhaps 1%). If the defendant fails to appear for court, the entire amount of court-ordered bail is forfeited.

Conditional Release **Conditional release** imposes requirements on the defendant, such as participating in a drug-treatment program; staying away from specified others, such as potential witnesses; and working at a regular job. *Release under supervision* is similar to conditional release but adds the stipulation that defendants report to an officer of the court or to a police officer at designated times.

Third-Party Custody Third-party custody is a bail bond alternative that assigns custody of the defendant to an individual or agency promising to ensure his or her later appearance in court.[15] Some pretrial release programs allow attorneys to assume responsibility for their clients in this fashion. If a defendant fails to appear, the attorney's privilege to participate in the program may be ended.

Unsecured Bonds An unsecured bond is based on a court-determined dollar amount of bail. Like a credit contract, it requires no monetary deposit with the court. The defendant agrees in writing that failure to appear will result in forfeiture of the entire amount of the bond, which might then be taken in the seizure of land, personal property, bank accounts, and so on.

Signature Bonds Signature bonds allow release based on the defendant's written promise to appear. Signature bonds involve no particular assessment of the defendant's dangerousness or likelihood of later appearance in court. They are used only in cases of minor offenses like traffic-law violations and some petty drug-law violations. Signature bonds may be issued by the arresting officer acting on behalf of the court.

Pretrial Release and Public Safety

Pretrial release is common practice. Approximately 57% of all state-level felony criminal defendants[16] and 66% of all federal felony defendants[17] are released before trial. At the state level, 43% of all defendants are detained until the court disposes of

■ **danger law**   A law intended to prevent the pretrial release of criminal defendants judged to represent a danger to others in the community.

their case. Murder defendants (88%) are the most likely to be detained. A majority of defendants charged with motor vehicle theft (61%), robbery (58%), or burglary (54%) are also detained until case disposition. Defendants on parole (83%) are more likely to be detained.

A growing movement, arguing that defendants released before trial may be dangerous to themselves or to others, seeks to reduce the number of defendants released under any conditions. Advocates of this conservative policy cite a number of studies documenting crimes committed by defendants released on bond. One study found that 16% of defendants released before trial were rearrested; of those, 30% were arrested more than once.[18] Another study determined that as many as 41% of those released before trial for serious crimes, such as rape and robbery, were rearrested before their trial date.[19] Not surprisingly, such studies generally find that the longer the time spent free on bail prior to trial, the greater the likelihood of misconduct.

In response to findings like these, some states have enacted **danger laws**, which limit the right to bail to certain kinds of offenders.[20] Other states, including Arizona, California, Colorado, Florida, and Illinois, have approved constitutional amendments restricting the use of bail.[21] Most such provisions exclude defendants charged with certain crimes from being eligible for bail and demand that other defendants being considered for bail meet stringent conditions. Some states combine these strictures with tough release conditions designed to keep close control over defendants before trial.

The 1984 federal Bail Reform Act allows federal judges to assess the danger of an accused to the community and to deny bail to defendants who are thought to be dangerous. In the words of the act, a suspect held in pretrial custody on federal criminal charges must be detained if "after a hearing … he is found to pose a risk of flight and a danger to others or the community and if no condition of release can give reasonable assurances against these contingencies."[22] Defendants seeking bail must demonstrate a high likelihood of later court appearance. The act also requires that a defendant have a speedy first appearance and, if he or she is to be detained, that a *detention hearing* be held together with the initial appearance.

In the 1990 case of *U.S. v. Montalvo-Murillo*,[23] however, a defendant who was not provided with a detention hearing at the time of his first appearance and was subsequently released by an appeals court was found to have no "right" to freedom because of this "minor" statutory violation. The Supreme Court held that "unless it has a substantial influence on the outcome of the

proceedings … failure to comply with the Act's prompt hearing provision does not require release of a person who should otherwise be detained" because "[a]utomatic release contravenes the statutory purpose of providing fair bail procedures while protecting the public's safety and assuring a defendant's appearance at trial."[24]

Court challenges to the constitutionality of pretrial detention legislation have not met with much success. The U.S. Supreme Court case of *U.S. v. Hazzard* (1984),[25] decided only a few months after enactment of federal bail reform, held that Congress was justified in providing for denial of bail to offenders who represent a danger to the community. Later cases have supported the presumption of flight, which federal law presupposes for certain types of defendants.[26]

The Grand Jury

The federal government and about half of the states use grand juries as part of the pretrial process. Grand juries comprise private citizens (ranging in number from 5 to 23, depending on the state and the grand jury's purpose) who hear evidence presented by the prosecution. Grand juries serve primarily as filters to eliminate cases for which there is not sufficient evidence for further processing.

In early times, grand juries served a far different purpose. The grand jury system began in England in 1166 as a way of identifying law violators. Lacking a law enforcement agency with investigative authority, the government looked to the grand jury as a source of information on criminal activity in the community. Even today, grand juries in most jurisdictions may initiate prosecution independently of the prosecutor, although they rarely do.

Grand jury hearings are held in secret, and the defendant is generally not afforded the opportunity to appear.[27] Similarly, the defense has no opportunity to cross-examine prosecution witnesses. Grand juries have the power to subpoena witnesses and to mandate a review of books, records, and other documents crucial to their investigation.

After hearing the evidence, the grand jury votes on the indictment presented to it by the prosecution. The indictment is a formal listing of proposed charges. If the majority of grand jury members agree to forward the indictment to the trial court, it becomes a "true bill" on which further prosecution will turn.

The United States is one of only a few countries in which grand juries are still used. In 2014, a grand jury in St. Louis

■ **competent to stand trial** A finding by a court that the defendant has sufficient present ability to consult with his or her attorney with a reasonable degree of rational understanding and that the defendant has a rational as well as factual understanding of the proceedings against him or her.

A grand jury in action. Grand jury proceedings are generally very informal, as this picture shows. What is the grand jury's job?

County, Missouri, grabbed the nation's attention when it refused to indict Ferguson police officer Darren Wilson. Wilson shot and killed 18-year-old Michael Brown during a street-stop that turned violent. The grand jury's decision led to nights of protest in cities across the nation by those who felt that the killing of the young black man was unjustified.

The Preliminary Hearing

States that do not use grand juries rely instead on a preliminary hearing "for charging defendants in a fashion that is less cumbersome and arguably more protective of the innocent."[28] In these jurisdictions, the prosecutor files an accusatory document called an *information*, or complaint, against the accused. A preliminary hearing is then held to determine whether there is probable cause to hold the defendant for trial. A few states, notably Tennessee and Georgia, use both the grand jury mechanism and a preliminary hearing as a "double check against the possibility of unwarranted prosecution."[29]

Although the preliminary hearing is not nearly as elaborate as a criminal trial, it has many of the same characteristics. The defendant is taken before a lower-court judge who summarizes the charges and reviews the rights to which all criminal defendants are entitled. The prosecution may present witnesses and will offer evidence in support of the complaint. The defendant is afforded the right to testify and may also call witnesses.

The primary purpose of the preliminary hearing is to give the defendant an opportunity to challenge the legal basis for his or her detention. At this point, defendants who appear to be or claim to be mentally incompetent may be ordered to undergo further evaluation to determine whether they are **competent to stand trial**. Competence to stand trial, which was briefly discussed in Chapter 4, may become an issue when a defendant appears to be incapable of understanding the proceedings or is unable to assist in his or her own defense due to mental disease or defect.

In 2003, the U.S. Supreme Court placed strict limits on the government's power to forcibly medicate some mentally ill defendants to make them competent to stand trial.[30] In the case of *Sell* v. *U.S.*,[31] the Court ruled that the use of antipsychotic drugs on a nonviolent pretrial defendant who does not represent a danger while institutionalized must be in the defendant's best medical interest and must be "substantially unlikely" to cause side effects that might compromise the fairness of the trial.

Barring a finding of mental incompetence, all that is required for the wheels of justice to move forward is a demonstration "sufficient to justify a prudent man's belief that the suspect has committed or was committing an offense" within the jurisdiction of the court.[32] If the magistrate finds enough evidence to justify a trial, the defendant is bound over to the grand jury. In states that do not require grand jury review, the defendant is sent directly to the trial court. If the complaint against the defendant cannot be substantiated, he or she is released. A release

■ **plea**   In criminal proceedings, the defendant's formal answer in court to the charge contained in a complaint, information, or indictment that he or she is guilty of the offense charged, is not guilty of the offense charged, or does not contest the charge.

■ *nolo contendere*   A plea of "no contest." A no-contest plea is used when the defendant does not wish to contest conviction. Because the plea does not admit guilt, however, it cannot provide the basis for later civil suits that might follow a criminal conviction.

■ **plea bargaining**   The process of negotiating an agreement among the defendant, the prosecutor, and the court as to an appropriate plea and associated sentence in a given case. Plea bargaining circumvents the trial process and dramatically reduces the time required for the resolution of a criminal case.

is not a bar to further prosecution, however, and the defendant may be rearrested if further evidence comes to light.

Arraignment and the Plea

Once an indictment has been returned or an information has been filed, the accused will be formally arraigned. Arraignment is "the first appearance of the defendant before the court that has the authority to conduct a trial."[33] Arraignment is generally a brief process with two purposes: (1) to once again inform the defendant of the specific charges against him or her and (2) to allow the defendant to enter a **plea**. The Federal Rules of Criminal Procedure allow for one of three types of pleas to be entered: guilty, not guilty, and *nolo contendere*. A *nolo contendere* (no-contest) plea is much the same as a guilty plea. A defendant who pleads "no contest" is immediately convicted and may be sentenced just as though he or she had pleaded guilty. A no-contest plea, however, is not an admission of guilt and provides one major advantage to defendants: It may not be used later as a basis for civil proceedings that seek monetary or other damages against the defendant.

Some defendants refuse to enter any plea and are said to "stand mute." Standing mute is a defense strategy that is rarely employed. Defendants who choose this alternative simply do not answer the request for a plea. However, for procedural purposes, a defendant who stands mute is considered to have entered a plea of not guilty.

Plea Bargaining

In 2012, 53-yerar-old Kenneth Kassab, of Marquette, Michigan, was on the verge of pleading guilty to federal charges of illegally transporting thousands of pounds of explosives, but changed his mind at the last minute and decided to go to trial.[34] Kassab, who always maintained his innocence, was arrested after his employer had ordered him to use a truck to move a large number of 50-pound bags of fertilizer similar to those that had been used in the 1995 bombing of the Alfred P. Murrah federal building in Oklahoma City, Oklahoma. Kassab had thought of accepting a plea deal offered by prosecutors in order to avoid what might have been a lengthy prison sentence—which a judge could have

imposed had he been convicted at trial. Instead, a week after deciding to reject the plea arrangement, a federal jury found him not guilty and he was set free. Kassab's case is unusual because 97% of all federal criminal defendants agree to plead guilty rather than going to trial—a significant increase from the 84% who made that choice in 1990.[35]

Guilty pleas are often not straightforward and are typically arrived at only after complex negotiations known as *plea bargaining*. **Plea bargaining** is a process of negotiation that usually involves the defendant, the prosecutor, and the defense counsel. It is founded on the mutual interests of all involved. Defense attorneys and their clients will agree to a plea of guilty when they are unsure of their ability to win acquittal at trial. Prosecutors may be willing to bargain because the evidence they have against the defendant is weaker than they would like it to be. Plea bargaining offers prosecutors the additional advantage of a quick conviction without the need to commit the time and resources necessary for trial. Benefits to the accused include the possibility of reduced or combined charges, lower defense costs, and a shorter sentence than might otherwise be anticipated.

The U.S. Supreme Court has held that a guilty plea constitutes conviction.[36] To validate the conviction, negotiated pleas require judicial consent. Judges often accept pleas that are the result of a bargaining process because such pleas reduce the court's workload. Although few judges are willing to guarantee a sentence before a plea is entered, most prosecutors and criminal trial lawyers know what sentences to expect from typical pleas.

Bargained pleas are commonplace in both federal and state courts. Surveys have found that 94% of state criminal cases are eventually resolved through a negotiated plea.[37] In a study of 37 big-city prosecutors, the Bureau of Justice Statistics found that for every 100 adults arrested on a felony charge, half were eventually convicted of either a felony or a misdemeanor.[38] Of all convictions, fully 94% were the result of a plea. Only 6% of convictions were the result of a criminal trial. After a guilty plea has been entered, it may be withdrawn with the consent of the court.

Some Supreme Court decisions, however, have enhanced the prosecutor's authority in the bargaining process by declaring that defendants cannot capriciously withdraw negotiated pleas.[39] Other rulings have supported discretionary actions by

CJ | ISSUES
Nonjudicial Pretrial Release Decisions

In most American jurisdictions, judicial officers decide whether an arrested person will be detained or released. Some jurisdictions, however, allow others to make that decision. Some observers argue that the critical issue is not whether the decision maker is a judge, but whether there are clear and appropriate criteria for making the decision, whether the decision maker has adequate information, and whether he or she has been well trained in pretrial release–detention decision making.

Nonjudicial decision makers and release–detention mechanisms include the following:

- *Police officers and desk appearance tickets.* Desk appearance tickets, or citations, are summonses given to defendants at the police station, usually for petty offenses or misdemeanor charges. The tickets can greatly reduce the use of pretrial detention and can save the court system a great deal of time by avoiding initial pretrial release or bail hearings in minor cases. However, because they are typically based only on the current charge (and sometimes on a computer search to check for outstanding warrants), high-risk defendants could be released without supervision or monitoring. As computerized access to criminal history information becomes more readily available, enabling rapid identification of individuals with prior records who pose a risk to the community, desk appearance tickets may be more widely used.

- *Jail administrators.* In many jurisdictions, jail officials have the authority to release (or to refuse to book into jail) arrestees who meet certain criteria. In some localities, jail officials exercise this authority pursuant to a court order that specifies priorities with respect to the categories of defendants who can be admitted to the jail and those who are to be released when the jail population exceeds a court-imposed ceiling. The "automatic release" approach helps minimize jail crowding, but it does so at the risk of releasing some defendants who pose a high risk of becoming fugitives or committing criminal acts. To help minimize these risks, some sheriffs and jail administrators have developed their own pretrial services or "release on recognizance" units with staff who conduct risk assessments based on interviews with arrestees, information from references, and criminal history checks.

- *Bail schedules.* These predetermined schedules set levels of bail (from release on recognizance to amounts of surety bond) based solely on the offense charged. Depending on local practices, release pursuant to a bail schedule may take place at a police station, at the local jail, or at court. This practice saves time for judicial officers and allows rapid release of defendants who can afford to post the bail amount. However, release determinations based solely on the current charge are of dubious value because there is no proven relationship between a particular charge and risk of flight or subsequent crime. Release pursuant to a bail schedule depends simply on the defendant's ability to post the amount of the bond. Moreover, when a defendant is released by posting bond, there is generally no procedure for supervision to minimize the risks of nonappearance and subsequent crime.

- *Bail bond agents.* When a judicial officer sets the amount of bond that a defendant must produce to be released, or when bond is set mechanically on the basis of a bail schedule, the real decision makers are often the surety bail bond agents. If no bail bond agent will offer bond, the defendant without other sources of money will remain in jail. The defendant's ability to pay a bail bond agent the 10% fee (and sometimes to post collateral) bears no relationship to his or her risk of flight or danger to the community.

- *Pretrial service agencies.* In some jurisdictions, pretrial service agencies have the authority to release certain categories of defendants. The authority is usually limited to relatively minor cases, although agencies in a few jurisdictions can release some categories of felony defendants. Because the pretrial service agency can obtain information about the defendant's prior record, community ties, and other pending charges, its decision to release or detain is based on more extensive information and criteria than when the decision is based on a bail schedule. However, because these programs lack the independence that judicial officers are allowed, they are susceptible to political and public pressure.

Reference: Adapted from Barry Mahoney et al., *Pretrial Services Programs: Responsibilities and Potential* (Washington, DC: National Institute of Justice, 2001).

---

prosecutors in which sentencing recommendations were retracted even after bargains had been struck.[40] Some lower-court cases have upheld the government's authority to withdraw from a negotiated plea when the defendant fails to live up to certain conditions.[41] Conditions may include requiring the defendant to provide information on other criminals, criminal cartels, and smuggling activities.

In 2012, in two decisions that expanded the authority of judges in the plea bargaining process, the U.S. Supreme Court held that the Sixth Amendment right to effective assistance of counsel applies to all critical states of criminal proceedings, including that of plea bargaining.[42] The Court also held that, "as a general rule, defense counsel has the duty to communicate formal prosecution offers to accept a plea on terms and conditions that may be favorable to the accused." Failure to communicate such offers to the defendant may be the basis for later appeal, but only where the defendant can demonstrate a reasonable probability that those offers would have been accepted and that the plea would have been entered without the prosecution's canceling it, or the trial court's refusing to accept it.

Although it is generally agreed that bargained pleas should relate in some way to the original charge, they are not always related. Entered pleas may be chosen for the punishments likely to be associated with them rather than for their accuracy in describing the criminal offense in which the defendant was involved.[43] This is especially true when the defendant wants to minimize the socially stigmatizing impact of the offense. A charge of indecent liberties, for example, in which the defendant is accused of sexual misconduct, may be pleaded out as assault. Such a plea, which takes advantage of the fact that indecent liberties can be considered a form of sexual assault, would effectively disguise the true nature of the offense.

■ **rules of evidence**   Court rules that govern the admissibility of evidence at criminal hearings and trials.

■ **adversarial system**   The two-sided structure under which American criminal trial courts operate. The adversarial system pits the prosecution against the defense. In theory, justice is done when the most effective adversary is able to convince the judge or jury that his or her perspective on the case is the correct one.

> Even though the Supreme Court has endorsed plea bargaining and protected suspects' rights during the process, the public sometimes views it suspiciously.

Even though the Supreme Court has endorsed plea bargaining and protected suspects' rights during the process, the public sometimes views it suspiciously. Law-and-order advocates, who generally favor harsh punishments and long jail terms, claim that plea bargaining results in unjustifiably light sentences. As a consequence, prosecutors, almost all of whom regularly engage in the practice, rarely advertise it. Plea bargaining can be a powerful prosecutorial tool, but this power carries with it the potential for misuse. Because they circumvent the trial process, plea bargains can be abused by prosecutors and defense attorneys who are more interested in the speedy resolution of cases than they are in seeing justice done. Carried to the extreme, plea bargaining may result in defendants being convicted of crimes they did not commit. Although it is rare, innocent defendants (especially those with prior criminal records) who think a jury will convict them—for whatever reason—may plead guilty to reduced charges to avoid a trial. In an effort to protect defendants against hastily arranged pleas, the Federal Rules of Criminal Procedure require judges to (1) inform the defendant of the various rights he or she is surrendering by pleading guilty, (2) determine that the plea is voluntary, (3) require disclosure of any plea agreements, and (4) make sufficient inquiry to ensure there is a factual basis for the plea.[44]

The Criminal Trial

From arrest through sentencing, the criminal justice process is carefully choreographed. Arresting officers must follow proper procedure when gathering evidence and arresting and questioning suspects. Magistrates, prosecutors, jailers, and prison officials are all subject to their own strictures. Nowhere, however, is the criminal justice process more closely circumscribed than it is at the criminal trial.

Procedures in a modern courtroom are highly formalized. **Rules of evidence**, which govern the admissibility of evidence, and other procedural guidelines determine the course of a criminal hearing and trial. Although rules of evidence are partially based on tradition, all U.S. jurisdictions have formalized, written

rules of evidence. Criminal trials at the federal level generally adhere to the requirements of the Federal Rules of Evidence.

Trials are also circumscribed by informal rules and professional expectations. An important component of law school education is the teaching of rules that structure and define appropriate courtroom demeanor. In addition to statutory rules, law students are thoroughly exposed to the ethical standards of their profession, as found in the American Bar Association standards and other writings.

Nature and Purpose of the Criminal Trial

In the remainder of this chapter, we will describe the chronology of a criminal trial and will explore some of the widely accepted rules of criminal procedure. Before we begin, however, it is good to keep two points in mind. One is that the primary purpose of any criminal trial is the determination of the defendant's guilt or innocence. In this regard, it is important to recognize the crucial distinction that scholars make between factual guilt and legal guilt. Factual guilt deals with the issue of whether the defendant is actually responsible for the crime of which he or she stands accused. If the defendant did it, then he or she is, in fact, guilty. Legal guilt is not as clear. Legal guilt is established only when the prosecutor presents sufficient evidence to convince the judge (where the judge determines the verdict) or the jury that the defendant is guilty as charged. The distinction between factual guilt and legal guilt is crucial because it points to the fact that the burden of proof rests with the prosecution, and it indicates the possibility that guilty defendants may nonetheless be found "not guilty."

The second point to remember is that criminal trials under our system of justice are built around an **adversarial system** and that central to this system is the advocacy model. Participating in the adversarial system are advocates for the state (the prosecutor or the district attorney) and for the defendant (the defense counsel, the public defender, and so on). The philosophy behind the adversarial system is that the greatest number of just resolutions in criminal trials will occur when both sides are allowed to argue their cases effectively and vociferously before a fair and impartial jury. The system requires that advocates for both sides do their utmost, within the boundaries set by law and

paying for it

Cost-Efficient Courts

In 2013, California Supreme Court Chief Justice Tani Cantil-Sakauye reportedly remarked, "I hear people on television all the time saying, 'We'll have our day in court; and I nudge my husband and say, 'Don't they know there aren't any courts anymore?'" Cantil-Sakauye's tongue-in-cheek remarks were a reaction to severe state budget cuts that have drastically reduced the number of courtrooms and court resources throughout the cash-strapped state. By the end of 2012, California's Judicial Council, the policymaking body of the California court system, had already shuttered 60 courtrooms in Los Angeles County alone, and was planning to close ten more courthouses, lay off additional courtroom staff, and halt construction on all new courts in ten of the state's counties. In 2013, the Council withdrew its proposal to create 50 new judgeships due to the state's failure to fund positions that had previously been recommended. The Council estimates that 264 additional judges are needed to effectively handle growing caseloads throughout the state.

One significant casualty of budget cuts was the California Case Management System (CCMS), a paperless computerized network that was once touted to potentially increase the efficiency of courts throughout the state by linking them electronically. The CCMS, which would have made court records easily available to judicial personnel throughout the state's court system, was opposed by court workers and unions due to their belief that jobs would be lost through automation. Estimates are that around half a billion dollars had been spent developing the system, and that it's full implementation would have cost the state an additional $120 million over the next two years.

Even Judge Lance Ito, the famous jurist who presided over O. J. Simpson's California murder trial in the 1990s, now finds himself shuttling between judicial chambers where much of the furniture has been stripped away and the heat is off to save money. Ito, who faces retirement in a few years, and whose former courtroom was closed because of cutbacks, observes:

"This has been a slow-motion train wreck since 2008 .... I have no staff, no bailiff, no court reporter and I have to persuade friendly clerks to enter minute orders."

Fortunately, not all states have had to cut back on court funding to the same degree as California. And even in that state, progress is being made to restore fiscal liquidity. In the late fall of 2012, for example, California's voters approved Proposition 30, increasing the state's sales tax and hiking income taxes on those earning over $250,000. That money has not yet made its way into state coffers, however, and in an effort to cover shortfalls in the state's judicial budget, Governor Jerry Brown announced an austerity plan for state courts that was scheduled to take effect in 2014. Many of the governor's proposals called for a doubling of court fees, including charging one dollar per page for every copy of a court record distributed to the public or to attorneys (the current rate is 50 cents per page). Other planned savings would accrue from not destroying dated public records or records relating to marijuana possession, and providing transcripts of preliminary hearings only in homicide cases.

Another effort to raise money for the state is a one-time amnesty program for persons who have failed to pay motor vehicle fines. The program permits violators to voluntarily pay 50% of unpaid fines that were imposed prior to January 1, 2009, in lieu of the full amount, without risking contempt-of-court citations or other criminal penalties. Other suggestions to raise money have included allowing a percentage of all criminal fines imposed to be used for court administration, and allowing a greater percentage of delinquent fines for criminal infractions to go to the courts. Estimates show that about $7.5 billion in delinquent court-ordered debt remains unpaid. One member of California's Administrative Office of the Courts notes that "if courts were receiving the money directly, they may have more of an incentive to collect." Critics fear, however, that such a move would only encourage judges to impose stiff fines more frequently than they have in the past.

References: California Vehicle Code, Section 42008.7, Infractions: One-Time Amnesty Program, http://www.dmv.ca.gov/pubs/vctop/d18/vc42008_7.htm (accessed March 3, 2013); Kendall Taggart, "Billions in Court-Ordered Debt Goes Uncollected," California Watch, June 5, http://californiawatch.org/dailyreport/billions-court-ordered-debt-goes-uncollected-16459 (accessed March 3, 2013); "California Judicial Council Halts Court Case Management System," The Sacramento Bee, http://blogs.sacbee.com/capitolalertlatest/2012/03/california-judicial-council-halts-controversial-court-case-management-system.html (accessed March 6, 2013); "Brown Looks to Fee Hikes to Fund Courts," The Los Angeles Times, January 15, 2013, http://latimesblogs.latimes.com/california-politics/2013/01/brown-looks-to-fee-hikes-to-fund-courts.html (accessed March 16, 2013); "State's Judicial Council Puts New Courthouses on Ice," The Los Angeles Times, http://latimesblogs.latimes.com/california-politics/2013/01/council-puts-new-courthouses-on-ice.html (accessed March 5, 2013); and "Judges Say Courts under Siege from Budget Cuts," Associated Press, January 20, 2013, http://www.appeal-democrat.com/news/judges-122737-say-angeles.html (accessed March 5, 2013).

professional ethics, to protect and advance the interests of their clients (i.e., the defendant and the state). The advocacy model makes clear that it is not the job of the defense attorney or the prosecution to decide the guilt of any defendant. Hence, even defense attorneys who are convinced that their clients are guilty are still exhorted to offer the best possible defense and to counsel their clients as effectively as possible.

The adversarial system has been criticized by some thinkers who point to fundamental differences between law and science in the way the search for truth is conducted.[45] Whereas proponents of traditional legal procedure accept the belief that truth can best be uncovered through an adversarial process, scientists adhere to a painstaking process of research and replication to acquire knowledge. Most of us would agree that scientific

■ **Speedy Trial Act** A 1974 federal law requiring that proceedings against a defendant in a federal criminal case begin within a specified period of time, such as 70 working days after indictment. Some states also have speedy trial requirements.

At least 328 convictions have been overturned using DNA evidence since 1989. advances in recent years may have made factual issues less difficult to ascertain. For example, some of the new scientific techniques in evidence analysis, such as DNA fingerprinting, can now unequivocally link a suspect to criminal activity or even show that someone who was once thought guilty is actually innocent. At least 328 convictions have been overturned using DNA evidence since 1989, when Gary Dotson of Illinois became the first person convicted of a crime to be exonerated through the use of such evidence.[46] According to Samuel Gross and colleagues at the University of Michigan Law School, who published a comprehensive study of exonerations in 2004, those 328 people "had spent more than 3400 years in prison for crimes for which they never should have been convicted."[47] Exonerations occur most frequently in cases where DNA evidence is relatively easy to acquire, such as rape and murder cases. False conviction rates for other crimes, such as robbery, are much more difficult to assess using DNA. Hence, says Gross, "the clearest and most important lesson from the recent spike in rape exonerations is that false convictions that come to light are the tip of the iceberg."[48]

Whether scientific findings should continue to serve a subservient role to the adversarial process is a question widely discussed. The answer will be determined by the results the two processes are able to produce. If the adversarial model results in the acquittal of too many demonstrably guilty people because of legal "technicalities," or if the scientific approach identifies too many suspects inaccurately, either could be restricted.

Stages in a Criminal Trial

We turn now to a discussion of the steps in a criminal trial. As Figure 10-2 shows, trial chronology consists of eight stages:

1. Trial initiation
2. Jury selection
3. Opening statements
4. Presentation of evidence
5. Closing arguments
6. Judge's charge to the jury
7. Jury deliberations
8. Verdict

Jury deliberations and the verdict are discussed jointly. If the defendant is found guilty, a sentence is imposed by the judge at the conclusion of the trial. Sentencing is discussed in the next chapter.

Trial Initiation: The Speedy Trial Act

In 2005, a Louisiana state appeals court threw out murder charges against James Thomas and ordered him released. Thomas, an impoverished day laborer, had been arrested in 1996 and had spent eight and a half years in jail waiting for a trial that never came. The ruling by the appeals court was widely seen as an indictment of Louisiana's understaffed and underfunded public defender system; the public defenders had simply been too busy to work on Thomas's case. A private attorney managed to get Thomas set free after his mother scraped together $500 to pay his fee.

The U.S. Constitution contains a speedy trial provision in its Sixth Amendment. The U.S. Constitution contains a speedy trial provision in its Sixth Amendment, which guarantees that "[i]n all criminal prosecutions, the accused shall enjoy the right to a speedy and public trial." Clogged court calendars, limited judicial resources, and general inefficiency, however, often combine to produce what appears to many to be unreasonable delays in trial initiation. The attention of the U.S. Supreme Court was brought to bear on trial delays in three precedent-setting cases: *Klopfer* v. *North Carolina* (1967),[49] *Barker* v. *Wingo* (1972),[50] and *Strunk* v. *U.S.* (1973).[51] The *Klopfer* case involved a Duke University professor who had engaged in civil disobedience to protest segregated facilities. In ruling on Klopfer's long-delayed trial, the Court asserted that the right to a speedy trial is a fundamental guarantee of the Constitution. In the *Barker* case, the Court held that Sixth Amendment guarantees to a quick trial could be illegally violated even in cases where the accused did not explicitly object to delays. In *Strunk*, it found that the denial of a speedy trial should result in the dismissal of all charges.

In 1974, against the advice of the Justice Department, the U.S. Congress passed the federal **Speedy Trial Act**.[52] The act, which was phased in gradually and became fully effective in 1980, allows for the dismissal of federal criminal charges in cases in which the prosecution does not seek an indictment or information within 30 days of arrest (a 30-day extension is granted when the grand jury is not in session) or where a trial does not begin within 70 working days after indictment for defendants who plead "not guilty." If a defendant is not available for trial, or

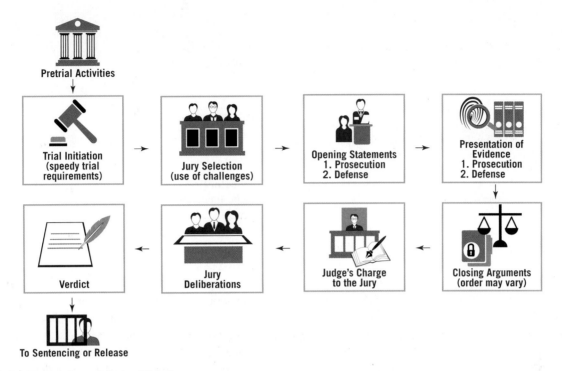

Figure 10-2 | Stages in a Criminal Trial
Source: Pearson Education, Inc.

James Thomas, who was charged with murder in 1996 and was freed in April 2005 after spending eight and a half years in a Louisiana jail waiting for his case to go to trial. A Louisiana state appeals court ruled that the state had taken too long to try him. Why does our system of justice require speedy trials?

Bill Feig/AP Wide World Photos

if witnesses cannot be called within the 70-day limit, the period may be extended up to 180 days. Delays brought about by the defendant, through requests for a continuance or because of escape, are not counted in the specified time periods.

In an important 1988 decision, *U.S.* v. *Taylor*,[53] the U.S. Supreme Court applied the requirements of the Speedy Trial Act to the case of a drug defendant who had escaped following arrest. The Court made it clear that trial delays that derive from the willful actions of the defendant do not apply to the 70-day period. The Court also held that trial delays, even when they result from government action, do not necessarily provide

grounds for dismissal if they occur "without prejudice." Delays without prejudice are those that are due to circumstances beyond the control of criminal justice agencies.

In 1993, an Indiana prisoner, William Fex, appealed a Michigan conviction on armed robbery and attempted murder charges, claiming that he had to wait 196 days after submitting a request to Indiana prison authorities for his Michigan trial to commence. In *Fex* v. *Michigan* (1993),[54] the U.S. Supreme Court ruled that "common sense compel[s] the conclusion that the 180-day period does not commence until the prisoner's disposition request has actually been delivered to the court and prosecutor of the jurisdiction that lodged the detainer against him." In Fex's case, Indiana authorities had taken 22 days to forward his request to Michigan.

However, in a 1992 case, *Doggett* v. *U.S.*,[55] the Court held that a delay of eight and a half years violated speedy trial provisions because it resulted from government negligence. In *Doggett*, the defendant was indicted on a drug charge in 1980 but left the country for Panama, where he lived until 1982, when he reentered the United States. He lived openly in the United States until 1988, when a credit check revealed him to authorities. He was arrested, tried, and convicted of federal drug charges stemming from his 1980 indictment. In overturning his conviction, the U.S. Supreme Court ruled, "[E]ven delay occasioned by the Government's negligence creates prejudice that compounds over time, and at some point, as here, becomes intolerable."[56]

In 2006, the Court refused to hear an appeal by dirty bomb conspiracy suspect Jose Padilla, letting stand a lower court's decision that said the president could order a U.S. citizen who was arrested in this country for suspected ties to

■ **peremptory challenge**   The right to challenge a potential juror without disclosing the reason for the challenge. Prosecutors and defense attorneys routinely use peremptory challenges to eliminate from juries individuals who, although they express no obvious bias, are thought to be capable of swaying the jury in an undesirable direction.

■ **jury selection**   The process whereby, according to law and precedent, members of a trial jury are chosen.

terrorism to be held indefinitely without charges and without going to trial.[57] Padilla, who was arrested in 2002, had been held for four years in a Navy brig without being charged with a crime. Shortly before Padilla's case was to come before the Court, however, he was transferred from military custody to a civilian jail, indicted on terrorism charges, and scheduled to go to trial—rendering his appeal moot. Although there was no official ruling in the case, Justice Anthony Kennedy, writing for himself, Justice John Paul Stevens, and Chief Justice John Roberts, observed that the federal district court scheduled to hear the case would now "be obliged to afford him the protection, including the right to a speedy trial, guaranteed to all federal criminal defendants."[58]

The federal Speedy Trial Act is applicable only to federal courts. However, the *Klopfer* case effectively made constitutional guarantees of a speedy trial applicable to state courts. In keeping with the trend toward reduced delays, many states have since enacted their own speedy trial legislation. Most state legislation sets a limit of 90 or 120 days as a reasonable period of time for a trial to commence.

Jury Selection

The Sixth Amendment guarantees the right to an impartial jury. An impartial jury is not necessarily an ignorant one. In other words, potential jurors will not always be excused from service on a jury if they have some knowledge of the case before them.[59] However, candidates who have already formed an opinion as to the guilt or innocence of the defendant are likely to be excused.

Some prospective jurors *try* to get excused, whereas others who would like to serve are excused because they are not judged to be suitable. Prosecution and defense attorneys use challenges to ensure the impartiality of the jury being impaneled. Three types of challenges are recognized in criminal courts: (1) challenges to the array, (2) challenges for cause, and (3) **peremptory challenges**.

Challenges to the array signify the belief, generally by the defense attorney, that the pool from which potential jurors are to be selected is not representative of the community or is biased in some significant way. A challenge to the array is argued before the hearing judge before **jury selection** begins.

During jury selection, both prosecution and defense attorneys question potential jurors in a process known as *voir dire* examination. Jurors are expected to be unbiased and free of preconceived notions of guilt or innocence. Challenges for cause, which may arise during *voir dire* examination, make the claim that an individual juror cannot be fair or impartial. A special issue of juror objectivity that has concerned the U.S. Supreme Court is whether jurors with philosophical opposition to the death penalty should be excluded from juries whose decisions might result in the imposition of capital punishment. In the case of *Witherspoon* v. *Illinois* (1968),[60] the Court ruled that a juror opposed to the death penalty could be excluded from such juries if it were shown that (1) the juror would automatically vote against conviction without regard to the evidence or (2) the juror's philosophical orientation would prevent an objective consideration of the evidence. The *Witherspoon* case left a number of issues unresolved, among them the concern that it is difficult to demonstrate how a juror would automatically vote, a fact that might not even be known to the juror before trial begins.

Another area of concern that the Supreme Court has addressed involves the potential that jurors could be influenced by pretrial news stories. In 1991, for example, the Court decided the case of *Mu'Min* v. *Virginia*.[61] Dawud Majud Mu'Min was a Virginia inmate who was serving time for first-degree murder. While accompanying a work detail outside the prison, he committed another murder. At the ensuing trial, 8 of the 12 jurors who were seated admitted that they had heard or read something about the case, although none indicated that he or she had formed an opinion in advance as to Mu'Min's guilt or innocence. Following his conviction, Mu'Min appealed to the Supreme Court, claiming that his right to a fair trial had been denied due to pretrial publicity. The Court disagreed and upheld his conviction, citing the jurors' claim not to be biased.

The third kind of challenge, the peremptory challenge, allows attorneys to remove potential jurors without having to give a reason. Peremptory challenges, used by both the prosecution and the defense, are limited in number. Federal courts allow each side up to 20 peremptory challenges in capital cases and as

■ **scientific jury selection** The use of correlational techniques from the social sciences to gauge the likelihood that potential jurors will vote for conviction or for acquittal.

■ **sequestered jury** A jury that is isolated from the public during the course of a trial and throughout the deliberation process.

few as 3 in minor criminal cases.[62] States vary as to the number of peremptory challenges they permit.

A developing field that seeks to take advantage of peremptory challenges is **scientific jury selection**. Scientific jury selection uses correlational techniques from the social sciences to gauge the likelihood that a potential juror will vote for conviction or acquittal. It makes predictions based on the economic, ethnic, and other personal and social characteristics of each member of the juror pool. Such techniques generally remove potential jurors who have any knowledge or opinions about the case to be tried. Also removed are people who have been trained in the law or in criminal justice. Anyone working for a criminal justice agency or anyone who has a family member working for such an agency or for a defense attorney will likely be dismissed through peremptory challenges on the chance that they may be biased in favor of one side or the other. Additionally, scientific jury selection techniques may result in the dismissal of highly educated or professionally successful individuals to eliminate the possibility of such individuals exercising undue control over jury deliberations.

Critics of the jury-selection process charge that the end result is a jury composed of people who are uneducated, uninformed, and generally inexperienced at making any type of well-considered decision. Some jurors may not understand the charges against the defendant or may not comprehend what is required for a finding of guilt or innocence. Likewise, some may not even possess the attention span needed to hear all the testimony that will be offered in a case. As a consequence, critics say, decisions rendered by such a jury may be based more on emotion than on findings of fact.

Another emerging technique is the use of "shadow juries" to assess the impact of a defense attorney's arguments. Shadow jurors are hired court observers who sit in the courtroom and listen to what both sides in a criminal trial have to say. They hear evidence as it is presented and listen as witnesses are examined and cross-examined. Unlike professional legal experts, shadow jurors are laypeople who are expected to give defense attorneys a feel for what the "real" jurors are thinking and feeling as a case progresses, allowing for ongoing modifications in defense strategy. After wrangling over jury selection has run its course, the jury is sworn in, and alternate jurors are selected. Alternates may be called to replace jurors taken ill or dismissed from the jury because they don't conform to the requirements of jury service once trial has begun. At this point, the judge will decide whether the jury is to be sequestered during the trial. Members of **sequestered juries** are not permitted to have contact with the public and are often housed in a motel or hotel until the trial ends. Anyone who attempts to contact a sequestered jury or to influence members of a nonsequestered jury may be held

accountable for jury tampering. Following jury selection, the stage is set for opening arguments[63] to begin.[64]

Jury Selection and Race

Race alone cannot provide the basis for jury selection, and juries may not be intentionally selected for racial balance. As long ago as 1880, the U.S. Supreme Court held that "a statute barring blacks from service on grand or petit juries denied equal protection of the laws to a black man convicted of murder by an all-white jury."[65] Even so, peremptory challenges continued to be used to strike racial imbalance on juries. In 1965, for example, a black defendant in Alabama was convicted of rape by an all-white jury. The local prosecutor had used his peremptory challenges to exclude blacks from the jury. The case eventually reached the Supreme Court, where the conviction was upheld.[66] At that time, the Court refused to limit the practice of peremptory challenges, reasoning that to do so would place these challenges under the same judicial scrutiny as challenges for cause.

However, in the 1986 case of *Batson* v. *Kentucky*,[67] following what many claimed was widespread abuse of peremptory challenges by prosecution and defense alike, the Supreme Court was forced to overrule its earlier decision. Batson, an African American man, had been convicted of second-degree burglary and other offenses by an all-white jury. The prosecutor had used his peremptory challenges to remove all blacks from jury service at the trial. The Court agreed that the use of peremptory challenges for purposeful discrimination constitutes a violation of the defendant's right to an impartial jury.

The *Batson* decision laid out the requirements that defendants must prove when seeking to establish the discriminatory use of peremptory challenges. They include the need to prove that the defendant is a member of a recognized racial group that was intentionally excluded from the jury and the need to raise a reasonable suspicion that the prosecutor used peremptory challenges in a discriminatory manner. Justice Thurgood Marshall, writing a concurring opinion in *Batson*, presaged what was to come: "The inherent potential of peremptory challenges to destroy the jury process by permitting the exclusion of jurors on racial grounds should ideally lead the Court to ban them entirely from the criminal justice system."

A few years later, in *Ford* v. *Georgia* (1991),[68] the Court moved much closer to Justice Marshall's position when it remanded a case for a new trial because the prosecutor had misused peremptory challenges. The prosecutor had used nine of the ten peremptory challenges available under Georgia law to eliminate black prospective jurors. Following his conviction on charges of kidnapping, raping, and murdering a white woman, the African American defendant James Ford argued that the prosecutor had demonstrated a systematic racial bias in other cases as well as his

■ **opening statement**   The initial statement of the prosecutor or the defense attorney, made in a court of law to a judge or jury, describing the facts that he or she intends to present during trial to prove the case.

own. Specifically, Ford argued that his Sixth Amendment right to an impartial jury had been violated by the prosecutor's racially based method of jury selection. His appeal to the Supreme Court claimed that "the exclusion of members of the black race in the jury when a black accused is being tried is done in order that the accused will receive excessive punishment if found guilty, or to inject racial prejudice into the fact finding process of the jury." Although the Court did not find a basis for such a Sixth Amendment claim, it did determine that the civil rights of the jurors themselves had been violated under the Fourteenth Amendment due to a pattern of discrimination based on race.

In another 1991 case, *Powers* v. *Ohio*,[69] the Court found in favor of a white defendant who claimed that his constitutional rights had been violated by the intentional exclusion of blacks from his jury through the use of peremptory challenges. In *Powers*, the Court held that "[a]lthough an individual juror does not have the right to sit on any particular petit jury, he or she does possess the right not to be excluded from one on account of race."

In *Edmonson* v. *Leesville Concrete Co., Inc.* (1991),[70] a civil case with significance for the criminal justice system, the Court held that peremptory challenges in *civil* suits were not acceptable if based on race. Justice Anthony Kennedy, writing for the majority, said that race-based juror exclusions are forbidden in civil lawsuits because jury selection is a "unique governmental function delegated to private litigants" in a public courtroom.

In the 1992 case of *Georgia* v. *McCollum*,[71] the Court barred *criminal* defendants and their attorneys from using peremptory challenges to exclude potential jurors on the basis of race. In *McCollum*, Justice Harry Blackmun, writing for the majority, said, "Be it at the hands of the state or defense, if a court allows jurors to be excluded because of group bias, it is a willing participant in a scheme that could only undermine the very foundation of our system of justice—our citizens' confidence in it."

Soon thereafter, peremptory challenges based on gender were similarly restricted (*J.E.B.* v. *Alabama*, 1994),[72] although the Court has refused to ban peremptory challenges that exclude jurors because of religious or sexual orientation.[73] Also, in 1996, the Court refused to review "whether potential jurors can be stricken from a trial panel because they are too fat."[74] The case involved Luis Santiago-Martinez, a drug defendant whose lawyer objected to the prosecution's use of peremptory challenges "because the government," he said, "had used such strikes to discriminate against the handicapped, specifically the obese."

The attorney, who was himself obese, claimed that thin jurors might have been unfairly biased against his arguments.

In the 1998 case of *Campbell* v. *Louisiana*,[75] the Court held that a white criminal defendant can raise equal protection and due process objections to discrimination against blacks in the selection of grand jurors. Attorneys for Terry Campbell, who was white, objected to an apparent pattern of discrimination in the selection of grand jury foremen. The foreman of the Evangeline Parish, Louisiana, grand jury that heard second-degree murder charges against him (in the killing of another white man) was white, as had been all such foremen for the last 16 years. The Supreme Court reasoned that "regardless of skin color, an accused suffers a significant 'injury in fact' when the grand jury's composition is tainted by racial discrimination." The Court also said, "The integrity of the body's decisions depends on the integrity of the process used to select the grand jurors."

In the 2003 case of *Miller-El* v. *Cockrell*,[76] the Court found that a convicted capital defendant's constitutional rights had been violated by Dallas County, Texas, prosecutors who engaged in intentional efforts to remove eligible blacks from the pool of potential jurors. Ten out of 11 eligible blacks were excluded through the use of peremptory strikes. The Court said, "In this case, debate as to whether the prosecution acted with a race-based reason when striking prospective jurors was raised by the statistical evidence demonstrating that 91% of the eligible African Americans were excluded … ; and by the fact that three of the State's proffered race-neutral rationales for striking African Americans—ambivalence about the death penalty, hesitancy to vote to execute defendants capable of being rehabilitated, and the jurors' own family history of criminality—pertained just as well to some white jurors who were not challenged and who did serve on the jury."[77] The decision was reaffirmed in the 2005 U.S. Supreme Court case of *Miller-El* v. *Dretke*,[78] and again in the 2008 case of *Snyder* v. *Louisiana*.[79] The Court's decision in *Snyder* v. *Louisiana*, which provides a good summary of its position on the use of peremptory strikes to eliminate black prospective jurors, is available at **http://tinyurl.com/3zgqtjf**.

Opening Statements

The presentation of information to the jury begins with **opening statements** made by the prosecution and the defense. The purpose of opening statements is to advise the jury of what the attorneys intend to prove and to describe how such proof will be offered. Evidence is not offered during opening statements.

■ **evidence** Anything useful to a judge or jury in deciding the facts of a case. Evidence may take the form of witness testimony, written documents, videotapes, magnetic media, photographs, physical objects, and so on.

■ **direct evidence** Evidence that, if believed, directly proves a fact. Eyewitness testimony and videotaped documentation account for the majority of all direct evidence heard in the criminal courtroom.

■ **circumstantial evidence** Evidence that requires interpretation or that requires a judge or jury to reach a conclusion based on what the evidence indicates. From the proximity of the defendant to a smoking gun, for example, the jury might conclude that he or she pulled the trigger.

■ **real evidence** Evidence that consists of physical material or traces of physical activity.

Eventually, however, the jury will have to weigh the evidence presented during the trial and decide which side made the more effective arguments. When a defendant has little evidence to present, the main job of the defense attorney will be to dispute the veracity of the prosecution's version of the facts. Under such circumstances, defense attorneys may choose not to present any evidence or testimony at all, focusing instead on the burden-of-proof requirement facing the prosecution. Such plans will generally be made clear during opening statements. At this time, the defense attorney is also likely to stress the human qualities of the defendant and to remind jurors of the awesome significance of their task.

Lawyers for both sides are bound by a "good-faith" ethical requirement in their opening statements. Attorneys may mention only the evidence that they believe actually can and will be presented as the trial progresses. Allusions to evidence that an attorney has no intention of offering are regarded as unprofessional and have been defined by the U.S. Supreme Court as "professional misconduct."[80] When material alluded to in an opening statement cannot, for whatever reason, later be presented in court, opposing counsel gains an opportunity to discredit the other side.

The Presentation of Evidence

The crux of the criminal trial is the presentation of evidence. First, the state is given the opportunity to present evidence intended to prove the defendant's guilt. After prosecutors have rested their case, the defense is afforded the opportunity to provide evidence favorable to the defendant.

Types of Evidence

Evidence can be either direct or circumstantial. **Direct evidence**, if believed, proves a fact without requiring the judge or jury to draw inferences. For example, direct evidence may consist of the information contained in a photograph or a videotape. It might also consist of testimonial evidence provided by a witness on the stand. A straightforward statement by a witness ("I saw him do it!") is a form of direct evidence.

Circumstantial evidence is indirect. It requires the judge or jury to make inferences and to draw conclusions. At a murder trial, for example, a person who heard gunshots and moments later saw someone run by with a smoking gun in hand might testify to those facts. Even without an eyewitness to the actual homicide, the jury might conclude that the person seen with the gun was the one who pulled the trigger and committed the crime. Circumstantial evidence is sufficient to produce a conviction in a criminal trial. In fact, some prosecuting attorneys prefer to work entirely with circumstantial evidence, weaving a tapestry of the criminal act into their arguments to the jury.

Real evidence, which may be either direct or circumstantial, consists of physical material or traces of physical activity. Weapons, tire tracks, ransom notes, and fingerprints all fall into the category of real evidence. Real evidence, sometimes called *physical evidence*, is introduced in the trial by means of exhibits. *Exhibits* are objects or displays that, after having been formally accepted as evidence by the judge, may be shown to members of the jury. *Documentary evidence*, one type of real evidence, includes written evidence like business records, journals, written confessions, and letters. Documentary evidence can extend beyond paper and ink to include stored computer data and video and audio recordings.

The Evaluation of Evidence

One of the most significant decisions a trial court judge makes is which evidence can be presented to the jury. To make this determination, judges examine the relevance of the evidence to the case at hand. Relevant evidence has a bearing on the facts at issue. For example, decades ago, it was not unusual for a woman's sexual history to be brought out in rape trials. Under "rape shield statutes," most states today will not allow this practice, recognizing that these details have no bearing on the case. Rape shield statutes have been strengthened by recent U.S. Supreme Court decisions, including the 1991 case of *Michigan v. Lucas*.[81]

Colorado's rape shield law played a prominent role in the 2004 case of Kobe Bryant, a basketball superstar who was accused of sexually assaulting a 19-year-old Vail-area resort employee. Bryant admitted to having a sexual encounter with the woman but claimed it was consensual. Defense attorneys sought to have the Colorado law declared unconstitutional in an effort to show that injuries to the woman were the result of her having had sexual intercourse with multiple partners before and after her encounter with Bryant. The woman later dropped the

■ **testimony**   Oral evidence offered by a sworn witness on the witness stand during a criminal trial.

■ **probative value**   The degree to which a particular item of evidence is useful in, and relevant to, proving something important in a trial.

criminal case against Bryant and settled a civil suit against him in 2005.[82] The terms of the suit were not disclosed.

In evaluating evidence, judges must also weigh the **probative value** of an item of evidence against its potential inflammatory or prejudicial qualities. Evidence has probative value when it is useful and relevant, but even useful evidence may unduly bias a jury if it is exceptionally gruesome or is presented in such a way as to imply guilt. For example, gory color photographs may be withheld from the jury's eyes. In one recent case, a new trial was ordered when photos of the crime scene were projected on a wall over the head of the defendant as he sat in the courtroom. An appellate court found the presentation to have prejudiced the jury.

Sometimes evidence is found to have only limited admissibility. This means that the evidence can be used for a specific purpose but that it might not be accurate in other details. Photographs, for example, may be admitted as evidence for the narrow purpose of showing spatial relationships between objects under discussion, even if the photographs were taken under conditions that did not exist when the offense was committed (such as daylight).

When judges allow the use of evidence that may have been illegally or unconstitutionally gathered, there may be grounds for a later appeal if the trial concludes with a "guilty" verdict. Even when evidence is improperly introduced at trial, however, certain Supreme Court decisions[83] have held that there may be no grounds for an effective appeal unless such introduction "had substantial and injurious effect or influence in determining the jury's verdict."[84] Called the *harmless error rule*, this standard places the burden on the prosecution to show that the jury's decision would most likely have been the same even in the absence of the inappropriate evidence. The rule is not applicable when a defendant's constitutional guarantees are violated by "structural defects in the constitution of the trial mechanism" itself[85]—as when a judge gives constitutionally improper instructions to a jury. (We'll discuss those instructions later in this chapter.)

The Testimony of Witnesses

Witness **testimony** is generally the chief means by which evidence is introduced at trial. Witnesses may include victims, police officers, the defendant, specialists in recognized fields, and others with useful information to provide. Some of these witnesses may have been present during the commission of the offense, whereas most will have had only a later opportunity to investigate the situation or to analyze evidence.

Oscar Pistorius, the South African Paralympic athlete, shown at his 2014 trial. He was convicted of the shooting death of his girlfriend and model, Reeva Steenkamp. What is the primary purpose of a criminal trial?

■ **perjury** The intentional making of a false statement as part of the testimony by a sworn witness in a judicial proceeding on a matter relevant to the case at hand.

Before a witness is allowed to testify to any fact, the questioning attorney must establish the person's competence. Competence to testify requires that witnesses have personal knowledge of the information they will discuss and that they understand their duty to tell the truth.

One of the defense attorney's most critical decisions is whether to put the defendant on the stand. Defendants have a Fifth Amendment right to remain silent and to refuse to testify. In the precedent-setting case of *Griffin* v. *California* (1965),[86] the U.S. Supreme Court declared that if a defendant refuses to testify, prosecutors and judges are enjoined from even commenting on this fact, although the judge should instruct the jury that such a failure cannot be held to indicate guilt. In the 2001 case of *Ohio* v. *Reiner*,[87] the U.S. Supreme Court extended Fifth Amendment protections to witnesses who deny any and all guilt in association with a crime for which another person is being prosecuted.

Direct examination of a witness takes place when a witness is first called to the stand. If the prosecutor calls the witness, the witness is referred to as a *witness for the prosecution*. If the direct examiner is a defense attorney, the witness is a *witness for the defense*.

The direct examiner may ask questions that require a "yes" or "no" answer or may ask narrative questions that allow the witness to tell a story in his or her own words. During direct examination, courts generally prohibit the use of leading questions or those that suggest answers to the witness.[88]

Cross-examination is the questioning of a witness by someone other than the direct examiner. Anyone who offers testimony in a criminal court has the duty to submit to cross-examination.[89] The purpose of cross-examination is to test the credibility and the memory of the witness.

Most states and the federal government restrict the scope of cross-examination to material covered during direct examination. Questions about other matters, even though they may relate to the case before the court, are not allowed in most states, although a few states allow the cross-examiner to raise any issue as long as the court deems it relevant. Leading questions, generally disallowed in direct examination, are regarded as the mainstay of cross-examination. Such questions allow for a concise restatement of testimony that has already been offered and serve to focus efficiently on potential problems that the cross-examiner seeks to address.

Some witnesses commit **perjury**—that is, they make statements that they know are untrue. Reasons for perjured testimony vary, but most witnesses who lie on the stand do so in an effort to help friends accused of crimes. Witnesses who perjure themselves are subject to impeachment, in which either the defense or the prosecution demonstrates that a witness has intentionally offered false testimony. For example, previous statements made by the witness may be shown to be at odds with more recent declarations. When it can be demonstrated that a witness has offered inaccurate or false testimony, the witness has been effectively impeached. Perjury is a serious offense in its own right, and dishonest witnesses may face fines or jail time.

At the conclusion of the cross-examination, the direct examiner may again question the witness. This procedure is called *redirect examination* and may be followed by a recross-examination and so on, until both sides are satisfied that they have exhausted fruitful lines of questioning.

Children as Witnesses

An area of special concern is the use of children as witnesses in a criminal trial, especially when the children are also victims. Currently, in an effort to avoid what may be traumatizing direct confrontations between child witnesses and the accused, 37 states allow the use of videotaped testimony in criminal courtrooms, and 32 permit the use of closed-circuit television, which allows the child to testify out of the presence of the defendant. In 1988, however, in the case of *Coy* v. *Iowa*,[90] the U.S. Supreme Court ruled that a courtroom screen, used to shield child witnesses from visual confrontation with a defendant in a child sex-abuse case, had violated the confrontation clause of the Constitution (found in the Sixth Amendment).

On the other hand, in the 1990 case of *Maryland* v. *Craig*,[91] the Court upheld the use of closed-circuit television to shield children who testify in criminal courts. The Court's decision was partially based on the realization that "a significant majority of States have enacted statutes to protect child witnesses from the trauma of giving testimony in child-abuse cases … [which] attests to the widespread belief in the importance of such a policy."

Although a face-to-face confrontation with a child victim may not be necessary in the courtroom, until 1992 the Supreme Court had been reluctant to allow into evidence descriptions of abuse and other statements made by children, even to child-care professionals, when those statements were made outside the courtroom. In *Idaho* v. *Wright* (1990),[92] the Court reasoned that such "statements [are] fraught with the dangers of unreliability which the Confrontation Clause is designed to highlight and obviate."

However, in *White* v. *Illinois* (1992),[93] the Court reversed its stance, ruling that in-court testimony provided by a medical provider and the child's babysitter, which repeated what the child had said to them concerning White's sexually abusive behavior, was permissible. The Court rejected White's claim that out-of-court statements should be admissible only when the witness is unavailable to testify at trial, saying instead, "A finding of unavailability of an out-of-court declarant is necessary only if the

CJ | ISSUES
Pretrial and Post-Trial Motions

A *motion* is "an oral or written request made to a court at any time before, during, or after court proceedings, asking the court to make a specified finding, decision, or order." Written motions are called *petitions*. The following are the most common motions made by both sides in a criminal case before and after trial.

Motion for Discovery

A motion for discovery, filed by the defense, asks the court to allow the defendant's lawyers to view the evidence that the prosecution intends to present at trial. Physical evidence, lists of witnesses, documents, photographs, and so on that the prosecution plans to introduce in court are usually made available to the defense as a result of a motion for discovery.

Motion to Suppress Evidence

The defense may file a motion to suppress evidence if it learns, in the preliminary hearing or through pretrial discovery, of evidence that it believes to have been unlawfully acquired.

Motion to Dismiss Charges

A variety of circumstances may result in the filing of a motion to dismiss charges. They include (1) an opinion, by defense counsel, that the indictment or information is not sound; (2) violations of speedy trial legislation; (3) a plea bargain with the defendant, which may require testimony against codefendants; (4) the death of an important witness or the destruction or disappearance of necessary evidence; (5) the confession, by a supposed victim, that the facts in the case were fabricated; and (6) the success of a motion to suppress evidence that effectively eliminates the prosecution's case.

Motion for Continuance

This motion seeks a delay in the start of the trial. Defense motions for continuance are often based on an inability to locate important witnesses, the illness of the defendant, or a change in defense counsel immediately prior to trial.

Motion for Change of Venue

In well-known cases, pretrial publicity may lessen the opportunity for a case to be tried before an unbiased jury. A motion for a change in venue asks that the trial be moved to some other area where prejudice against the defendant is less likely to exist.

Motion for Severance of Offenses

Defendants charged with a number of crimes may ask to be tried separately on all or some of the charges. Although consolidating charges for trial saves time and money, some defendants believe that it is more likely to make them appear guilty.

Motion for Severance of Defendants

This request asks the court to try the accused separately from any codefendants. Motions for severance are likely to be filed when the defendant believes that the jury may be prejudiced against him or her by evidence applicable only to other defendants.

Motion to Determine Present Sanity

A lack of "present sanity," even though it may be no defense against the criminal charge, can delay trial. A person cannot be tried, sentenced, or punished while insane. If a defendant is insane at the time a trial is to begin, this motion may halt the proceedings until treatment can be arranged.

Motion for a Bill of Particulars

This motion asks the court to order the prosecutor to provide detailed information about the charges that the defendant will be facing in court. Defendants charged with a number of offenses, or with a number of counts of the same offense, may make such a motion. They may, for example, seek to learn which alleged instances of an offense will become the basis for prosecution or which specific items of contraband allegedly found in their possession are held to violate the law.

Motion for a Mistrial

A mistrial may be declared at any time, and a motion for a mistrial may be made by either side. Mistrials are likely to be declared in cases in which highly prejudicial comments are made by either attorney. Defense motions for a mistrial do not provide grounds for a later claim of double jeopardy.

Motion for Arrest of Judgment

After the verdict of the jury has been announced, but before sentencing, the defense may make a motion for arrest of judgment. With this motion, the defense asserts that some legally acceptable reason exists as to why sentencing should not occur. Defendants who are seriously ill, who are hospitalized, or who have gone insane prior to judgment being imposed may file such a motion.

Motion for a New Trial

After a jury has returned a guilty verdict, the court may entertain a defense motion for a new trial. Acceptance of such a motion is usually based on the discovery of new evidence that is of significant benefit to the defense and that will set aside the conviction.

Reference: U.S. Department of Justice, *Dictionary of Criminal Justice Data Terminology*, 2nd ed. (Washington, DC: U.S. Government Printing Office, 1982).

■ **hearsay**   Something that is not based on the personal knowledge of a witness. Witnesses who testify about something they have heard, for example, are offering hearsay by repeating information about a matter of which they have no direct knowledge.

■ **hearsay rule**   The long-standing precedent that hearsay cannot be used in American courtrooms. Rather than accepting testimony based on hearsay, the court will ask that the person who was the original source of the hearsay information be brought in to be questioned and cross-examined. Exceptions to the hearsay rule may occur when the person with direct knowledge is dead or is otherwise unable to testify.

■ **closing argument**   An oral summation of a case presented to a judge, or to a judge and jury, by the prosecution or by the defense in a criminal trial.

out-of-court statement was made at a prior judicial proceeding." Placing *White* within the context of generally established exceptions, the Court declared, "A statement that has been offered in a moment of excitement—without the opportunity to reflect on the consequences of one's exclamation—may justifiably carry more weight with a trier of fact than a similar statement offered in the relative calm of the courtroom. Similarly, a statement made in the course of procuring medical services, where the declarant knows that a false statement may cause misdiagnosis or mistreatment, carries special guarantees of credibility that a trier of fact may not think replicated by courtroom testimony."

The Hearsay Rule

Hearsay is anything not based on the personal knowledge of a witness. A witness may say, for example, "John told me that Fred did it!" Such a witness becomes a hearsay declarant, and following a likely objection by counsel, the trial judge will have to decide whether the witness's statement will be allowed to stand as evidence. In most cases, the judge will instruct the jury to disregard the witness's comment, thereby enforcing the **hearsay rule**, which prohibits the use of "secondhand evidence."

Exceptions to the hearsay rule have been established by both precedent and tradition. One exception is the dying declaration. A dying declaration is a statement made by a person who is about to die. When heard by a second party, it may usually be repeated in court, provided that certain conditions have been met. A dying declaration is generally a valid exception to the hearsay rule when it is made by someone who knows that he or she is about to die and when the statement made relates to the cause and circumstances of the impending death.

Spontaneous statements provide another exception to the hearsay rule. A statement is considered spontaneous when it is made in the heat of excitement before the person has had time to make it up. For example, a defendant who was injured and is just regaining consciousness following a crime may say something that could later be repeated in court by those who heard it.

Out-of-court statements, especially if they were recorded during a time of great excitement or while a person was under considerable stress, may also become exceptions to the hearsay rule. Many states, for example, permit juries to hear 9-1-1

tape recordings or to read police transcripts of victim interviews without requiring that the people who made them appear in court. In two recent cases, however, the U.S. Supreme Court barred admission of tape-recorded 9-1-1 calls when the people making them were alive and in good health but not available for cross-examination. In *Crawford* v. *Washington*,[94] a 2004 case, the Court disallowed a woman's tape-recorded eyewitness account of a fight in which her husband stabbed another man, holding that the Constitution bars admission of testimonial statements of a witness who did not appear at trial unless he or she was unable to testify and the defendant had a prior opportunity for cross-examination. In *Davis* v. *Washington*,[95] decided in 2006, the Court held that a 9-1-1 call made by a woman who said that her former boyfriend was beating her had been improperly introduced as testimonial evidence. The woman had been subpoenaed but failed to appear in court. The keyword in both cases is *testimonial*, and the Court indicated that "statements are nontestimonial when made in the course of police interrogation under circumstances objectively indicating that the primary purpose of interrogation is to enable police assistance to meet an ongoing emergency."[96]

The use of other out-of-court statements, such as writings or routine video or audio recordings, usually requires the witness to testify that the statements or depictions were accurate at the time they were made. Witnesses who so testify may be subject to cross-examination by the defendant's attorney. Nonetheless, this "past recollection recorded" exception to the hearsay rule is especially useful in drawn-out court proceedings that occur long after the crime. Under such circumstances, witnesses may no longer remember the details of an event. Their earlier statements to authorities, however, can be introduced into evidence as past recollection recorded.

Closing Arguments

At the conclusion of a criminal trial, both sides have the opportunity for a final narrative presentation to the jury in the form of a **closing argument**. This summation provides a review and analysis of the evidence. Its purpose is to persuade the jury to draw a conclusion favorable to the presenter. Testimony can be quoted, exhibits referred to, and attention drawn to inconsistencies in the evidence presented by the other side.

■ **reasonable doubt**   In legal proceedings, an actual and substantial doubt arising from the evidence, from the facts or circumstances shown by the evidence, or from the lack of evidence.[108] Also, the state of a case such that, after the comparison and consideration of all the evidence, jurors cannot say they feel an abiding conviction of the truth of the charge.[109,110]

■ **reasonable doubt standard**   The standard of proof necessary for conviction in criminal trials.

■ **verdict**   The decision of the jury in a jury trial or of a judicial officer in a nonjury trial.

States vary as to the order of closing arguments. Nearly all allow the defense attorney to speak to the jury before the prosecution makes its final points. A few permit the prosecutor the first opportunity for summation. Some jurisdictions and the Federal Rules of Criminal Procedure[97] authorize a defense rebuttal. A rebuttal is a response to the closing argument of the other side.

Some specific issues may need to be addressed during summation. If, for example, the defendant has not taken the stand during the trial, the defense attorney's closing argument will inevitably stress that this failure to testify cannot be regarded as indicating guilt. Where the prosecution's case rests entirely on circumstantial evidence, the defense can be expected to stress the lack of any direct proof, and the prosecutor is likely to argue that circumstantial evidence can be stronger than direct evidence, as it is not as easily affected by human error or false testimony.

The Judge's Charge to the Jury

After closing arguments, the judge charges the jury to "retire," select one of its number as a foreman, and deliberate on the evidence that has been presented until it has reached a verdict. The words of the judge's "charge" vary somewhat between jurisdictions and among judges, but all judges will remind members of the jury of their duty to consider objectively only the evidence that has been presented and of the need for impartiality. Most judges also remind jury members of the statutory elements of the alleged offense, of the burden of proof that rests on the prosecution, and of the need for the prosecution to have proved the defendant's guilt beyond a **reasonable doubt** before the jury can return a guilty verdict. The **reasonable doubt standard** is the single most important criterion for determining the level of proof necessary for conviction in criminal trials. If the prosecutor fails to prove a defendant's guilt beyond a reasonable doubt, then the jury must return a not-guilty verdict.

In their charge, many judges also provide a summary of the evidence presented, usually from notes they took during the trial, as a means of refreshing the jurors' memories of events. About half of all the states allow judges the freedom to express their own views as to the credibility of witnesses and the significance of evidence. Other states only permit judges to summarize the evidence in an objective and impartial manner.

Recently, as the "CJ News" box in this section shows, the plethora of digital communications devices now available has made it difficult for courts to control jurors' access to out-of-court information. Read a set of jury instructions designed for federal courts to use in alleviating this problem at **http://www .justicestudies.com/pubs/electronic_instructions.pdf.**

Following the charge, the jury is removed from the courtroom and is permitted to begin its deliberations. In the absence of the jury, defense attorneys may choose to challenge portions of the judge's charge. If they feel that some oversight has occurred in the original charge, they may ask the judge to provide the jury with additional instructions or information. Such objections, if denied by the judge, often become the basis for an appeal when a conviction is returned.

Jury Deliberations and the Verdict

In cases in which the evidence is either very clear or very weak, jury deliberations may be brief, lasting only a matter of hours or even minutes. Some juries, however, deliberate days or sometimes weeks, carefully weighing all the nuances of the evidence they have seen and heard. Many jurisdictions require that juries reach a unanimous **verdict**, although the U.S. Supreme Court has ruled that unanimous verdicts are not required in noncapital cases.[98] Even so, some juries are unable to agree on any verdict. When a jury is deadlocked, it is said to be a *hung jury*. When a unanimous decision is required, juries may be deadlocked by the strong opposition of several members or of only one member to a verdict agreed on by all the others.

In some states, judges are allowed to add a boost to nearly hung juries by recharging them under a set of instructions that the Supreme Court put forth in the 1896 case of *Allen* v. *U.S.*[99] The *Allen* charge, as it is known, urges the jury to vigorous deliberations and suggests to obstinate jurors that their objections may be ill founded if they make no impression on the other jurors.

Problems with the Jury System

Judge Harold J. Rothwax, a well-known critic of today's jury system, tells the tale of a rather startling 1991 case over which he presided. The case involved a murder defendant, a handsome young man who had been fired by a New York company that serviced ATMs. After being fired, the defendant intentionally

CJ | NEWS

Social Media Pose New Threats to Keeping Jurors Isolated during Trials

A young man uses an iPad. Digital devices are commonplace today. How might jurors' unauthorized use of modern technology influence their deliberations?

Growing use of the Internet and social media has made it much easier for jurors to violate age-old prohibitions against conversing with outsiders about a case, conducting outside research, and contacting plaintiffs or defendants.

The rise of Facebook, Twitter, and Wikipedia, combined with widespread use of smartphones, seems to have blurred the traditional line between jurors and the outside world. "This is a generational change, and I don't know if the legal system is ready for it," said Thaddeus Hoffmeister, a professor at the University of Dayton Law School who specializes in jury issues.

Violations that once took some effort, such as going to a library to look up a term or just making a phone call to a friend, now can be done with a few keystrokes. Research suggests very few violators are caught. But when they are, the courts take the matter very seriously. They may throw out the verdict, cite jurors for contempt, and even jail them.

A 2011 study by Reuters Legal found that Internet-related juror misconduct had led to 21 overturned verdicts or new trials since January 2009. Because violations can occur away from the courthouse and jurors' online use is rarely monitored, courts have identified very few violators. A national survey of federal judges by the Federal Judicial Center, found that just 6% were aware of social media used during deliberations, but 79% admitted they would have no way of knowing about violations.

Jurors' use of Facebook can be easy to spot. In a few high-profile cases, jurors have improperly "friended" plaintiffs, defendants, and even each other in the period before jurors can get together to deliberate. One juror who friended the plaintiff in an auto accident case was sentenced to three days in jail.

In a Twitter violation in Arkansas, a murder conviction was thrown out on appeal in December 2011 because the juror tweeted after being asked to stop, and one of his tweets revealed the verdict before it was announced. The court ordered a new trial, but it did not punish the juror.

Although jurors have never been allowed to conduct outside research, Internet-based research is so second-nature that it may not occur to jurors they are violating the rules. In 2014, a Florida juror, who happened to be a criminology student at a local college, was found in contempt of court and jailed after Web research he conducted revealed that he and fellow jurors were participating in a retrial that had been ordered after an earlier jury had been unable to decide on a verdict. In jailing the juror, the judge noted that implicit instructions had been given not to research the case on social media.

To prevent violations, experts say jury instructions should specify each kind of prohibited Internet use, explain the reasoning behind the ban, and show how the legal process could be damaged. For example, even when nothing is revealed on a juror's blog or a posting on Facebook, just reading the comments to the posts might improperly influence jury members.

Experts also recommend that candidates in the jury-selection process be asked about their own online activities and whether they'd be comfortable stopping them for the duration of the trial. Some potential jurors who said they could not stop have withdrawn voluntarily. It has also been proposed that the courts ask jurors to name frequently used sites and to provide the passwords for them, so that they can be monitored during the trial.

In 2012, the federal Judicial Conference's Committee on Court Administration and Case Management (CACM) admonished federal judges to repeatedly warn jurors not to discuss cases that they are deliberating on social media or the Internet. The Committee's proposed model jury instructions can be accessed at **http://www.justicestudies.com/modelinst.pdf.**

Resources: "Jurors' Use of Social Media during Trials Leading to Mistrials," Martindale-Hubble, March 22 2012, http://blog.martindale.com/jurors-use-of-social-media-during-trials-leading-to-mistrials; "Jurors' Use of Social Media during Trials and Deliberations," Federal Judicial Center, November 22, 2011, http://www.fjc.gov/public/pdf.nsf/lookup/dunnjuror.pdf/$file/dunnjuror.pdf; and "Friend or Foe? Social Media, the Jury and You," The Jury Expert, September 26, 2011, http://www.thejuryexpert.com/2011/09/friend-or-foe-social-media-the-jury-and-you/; Terri Parker, "Jailed Goodman Juror Apologizes, Pleads Not Guilty to Contempt," WPBF TV, October 10, 2014, http://www.wpbf.com/news/jailed-goodman-juror-apologizes-pleads-not-guilty-to-contempt/29049970.

caused a machine in a remote area to malfunction. When two former colleagues arrived to fix it, he robbed them, stole the money inside the ATM, and shot both men repeatedly. One of the men survived long enough to identify his former coworker as the shooter. The man was arrested, and a trial ensued, but after three weeks of hearing the case, the jury deadlocked. Judge Rothwax later learned that the jury had voted 11 to 1 to convict the defendant, but the one holdout just couldn't believe that "someone so good-looking could … commit such a crime."[100]

Many routine cases as well as some highly publicized cases, like the murder trial of O. J. Simpson, have called into question the ability of the American jury system to do its job—that is, to sort through the evidence and to accurately determine the defendant's guilt or innocence. In a televised 1995 trial, Simpson was acquitted of the charge that he murdered his ex-wife Nicole Brown and her friend Ronald Goldman outside Brown's home in 1994. Many people believed that strong evidence tied Simpson to the crimes, and the criminal trial left many people feeling unsatisfied with the criminal justice system and with the criminal trial process. Later, a civil jury ordered Simpson to pay $33.5 million to the Goldman family and to Nicole Brown's estate.

Because jurors are drawn from all walks of life, many cannot be expected to understand modern legal complexities and to appreciate all the nuances of trial court practice. It is likely that even the best-intentioned jurors cannot understand and rarely observe some jury instructions.[101] In highly charged cases, emotions are often difficult to separate from fact, and during deliberations, some juries are dominated by one or two members with forceful personalities.

Jurors may be less than effective in cases where they fear personal retaliation. In the state-level trial of the police officers accused in the infamous 1991 Rodney King beating, for example, jurors reported being afraid for their lives due to the riots in Los Angeles that broke out after their not-guilty verdict was announced. Some slept with weapons by their side, and others sent their children away to safe locations.[102] Because of the potential for harm that jurors faced in the 1993 federal trial of the same officers, U.S. District Judge John G. Davies ruled that the names of the jurors be forever kept secret. Members of the press called the secrecy order "an unprecedented infringement of the public's right of access to the justice system."[103] Similarly, in the 1993 trial of three black men charged with the beating of white truck driver Reginald Denny during the Los Angeles riots that followed the Rodney King verdict, Los Angeles Superior Court Judge John Ouderkirk ordered that the identities of the jurors not be released.

> Opponents of the jury system have argued that it should be replaced by a panel of judges who would both render a verdict and impose sentence.

Opponents of the jury system have argued that it should be replaced by a panel of judges who would both render a verdict and impose sentence. Regardless of how well considered such a suggestion may be, such a change could not occur without modification of the Constitution's Sixth Amendment right to trial by jury.

An alternative suggestion for improving the process of trial by jury has been the call for professional jurors. Professional jurors would be paid by the government, as are judges, prosecutors, and public defenders. They would be expected to have the expertise to sit on any jury. Professional jurors would be trained to listen objectively and would be taught the kinds of decision-making skills they would need to function effectively within an adversarial context. They would hear one case after another, perhaps moving between jurisdictions in cases of highly publicized crimes.

A professional jury system offers these advantages:

1. *Dependability.* Professional jurors could be expected to report to the courtroom in a timely fashion and to be good listeners, as both would be required by the nature of the job.

2. *Knowledge.* Professional jurors would be trained in the law, would understand what a finding of guilt requires, and would know what to expect from the other professionals in the courtroom.

3. *Equity.* Professional jurors would understand the requirements of due process and would be less likely to be swayed by the emotional content of a case, having been schooled in the need to separate matters of fact from personal feelings.

A professional jury system would not be without difficulties. Jurors under such a system might become jaded, deciding cases out of hand as routines lead to boredom. They might categorize defendants according to whether they "fit the type" for guilt or innocence based on the jurors' previous experiences. Job requirements for professional jurors would be difficult to establish without infringing on the jurors' freedom to decide cases as they understand them. For the same reason, any evaluation of the job performance of professional jurors would be a difficult call. Finally, professional jurors might not truly be peer jurors, as their social characteristics might be skewed by education, residence, and politics.

Improving the Adjudication Process

Courts today are coming under increasing scrutiny, and well-publicized trials, like those of Casey Anthony, Drew Peterson, Jodi Arias, Michael Jackson, O. J. Simpson, and John Allen Muhammad, have heightened awareness of problems with the American court system. One of today's most important issues is reducing the number of jurisdictions by unifying courts. The current multiplicity of jurisdictions frequently leads to what many critics believe are avoidable conflicts and overlaps in the handling of criminal defendants. In some states, problems are exacerbated by the lack of any centralized judicial authority that might resolve jurisdictional and procedural disputes.[104] Proponents of unification suggest eliminating overlapping jurisdictions, creating special-purpose courts, and establishing administrative offices to achieve economies of scale.[105]

The number of court-watch citizens' groups is also rapidly growing. Such organizations focus on the trial court level, but they are part of a general movement seeking greater openness in government decision making at all levels.[106] Court-watch groups regularly monitor court proceedings and attempt to document and often publicize inadequacies. They frequently focus on the handling of indigents, fairness in the scheduling of cases for trial, unnecessary court delays, the reduction of waiting time, the treatment of witnesses and jurors, and the adequacy of rights advisements for defendants throughout judicial proceedings.

CJ | ISSUES
Courtrooms of the Future

In the mid-1990s, the College of William and Mary, in conjunction with the National Center for State Courts (NCSC), unveiled Courtroom 21. At the time, it was the most technologically advanced courtroom in the United States. Courtroom 21, which has since changed its name to the Center for Legal and Court Technology (CLCT), is located in the McGlothlin Courtroom of the College of William and Mary. It offers a glimpse at what American courtrooms might be like in the mid-twenty-first century. The CLCT includes the following integrated capabilities:

1. *Automatic video recording of the proceedings, using ceiling-mounted cameras with voice-initiated switching.* A sophisticated voice-activation system directs cameras to record the person speaking and to record evidence as it is being presented.

2. *Recorded and televised evidence display with optical disk storage.* Documentary or real evidence can be presented to the judge and the jury through the use of a video "presenter," which also makes a video record of the evidence as it is being presented, so it can be used later.

3. *Remote two-way television.* The two-way television arrangement allows video and audio signals to be sent from the judge's bench to areas throughout the courtroom, including the jury box.

4. *Text-, graphics-, and video-capable jury computers.* The CLCT's jury box contains computers for information display and animation so that jury members can easily view documents, live or prerecorded video, and graphics, such as charts, diagrams, and pictures. Video-capable jury computers also allow for the remote appearance of witnesses and for the display of crime scene reenactments via computer animation.

5. *Access to online legal research databases for the judge and for counsel on both sides.* Available databases contain an extensive selection of state and federal statutes, case law, and other precedents.

6. *Built-in video playback facilities for out-of-court testimony.* Video depositions can be played on courtroom monitors to present expert witness testimony or to impeach a witness.

7. *Information storage with software search capabilities.* Integrated software programs provide text-searching capabilities for courtroom participants.

The technology demonstrated by the CLCT suggests many possibilities. For one thing, attorneys could use court video equipment for filing remote motions and for other types of hearings. As one of the CLCT designers puts it, "Imagine the productivity gains if lawyers no longer need to travel across a city or county for a ten-minute appearance."

An even more intriguing vision of courtrooms of the future is offered by the Technology of Justice Task Force in its draft report to the Pennsylvania Futures Commission on Justice in the 21st Century. The task force predicted that by the year 2020, "there will be 'virtual courtrooms,' where appropriate, to provide hearings without the need for people to come to a physical courthouse." The task force envisions trials via teleconferencing, public Internet access to many court documents, and payment of fines by credit card. Visit the Center for Legal and Court Technology on the Web at **http://www.legaltechcenter.net**.

Discussion Questions

1. Do you think that technologies like those discussed in this box might affect the outcome of criminal trials? Explain.

2. Are there any types of criminal trials in which the use of high-technology courtrooms might not be appropriate? If so, describe them.

Reference: National Center for State Courts website, http://www.ncsc.us (accessed October 11, 2007), from which some of the material in this box is taken; Courtroom 21 website, http://www.courtroom21.net (accessed October 11, 2007); and "The Courtroom 21 Project: A Light at the End of the Legal Technology Tunnel," http://technology.findlaw.com/modern-law-practice/the-courtroom-21-project-a-light-at-the-end-of-the-legal.html (accessed January 4, 2015).

Fred Lederer, director of the Center for Legal and Court Technology (formerly the Courtroom 21 Project) at the College of William and Mary Law School in Williamsburg, Virginia, acting as a bailiff as he swears in a witness via the Internet. What limits do you think might be applied to "virtual courtrooms" of the future?

Gary C. Knapp/AP Wide World Photos

CJ | ISSUES
The Bilingual Courtroom

One of the central multicultural issues facing the criminal justice system today is the need for clear communication with recent immigrants and subcultural groups that have not been fully acculturated. Many such groups hold to traditions and values that differ from those held by the majority of Americans. Such differences influence the interpretation of things seen and heard. Even more basic, however, are language differences that might prevent effective communication with criminal justice system personnel.

Techniques that law enforcement officers can use in overcoming language differences were discussed in Chapter 8. This box focuses on the use of courtroom interpreters to facilitate effective and accurate communication. The role of the courtroom interpreter is to present neutral verbatim, or word-for-word, translations. Interpreters must provide true, accurate, and complete interpretation of the exact statements made by non-English-speaking defendants, victims, and witnesses—whether on the stand, in writing, or in court-related conferences. The Court Interpreters and Translators Association also requires, through its code of professional ethics, that translators remember their "absolute responsibility to keep all oral and written information gained completely confidential."

Although most court interpreters are actually present in the courtroom at the time of the trial, telephone interpreting provides an alternative for courts that have trouble locating qualified interpreters. Today, state court administrative offices in Florida, Idaho, New Jersey, and Washington sponsor programs through which qualified interpreters in metropolitan counties are made available to courts in rural counties by telephone.

The federal Court Interpreters Act of 1978[1] specifically provides for the use of interpreters in federal courts. It applies to both criminal and civil trials and hearings. The act reads, in part, as follows:[2]

> The presiding judicial officers ... shall utilize [an interpreter] ... in judicial proceedings instituted by the United States, if the presiding judicial officer determines on such officer's own motion or on the motion of a party that such party (including the defendant in a criminal case), or a witness who may present testimony in such judicial proceedings—
> (A) speaks only or primarily a language other than English; or
> (B) suffers from a hearing impairment ... so as to inhibit such party's comprehension of the proceedings or communication with counsel or the

presiding officer, or so as to inhibit such witness's comprehension of questions and the presentation of such testimony.

As this extract from the statute shows, translators are also required for individuals with hearing impairments who communicate primarily through American Sign Language. The act does not require that an interpreter be appointed when a person has a speech impairment that is not accompanied by a hearing impairment. A court is not prohibited, however, from providing assistance to that person if it will aid in the efficient administration of justice.

Because it is a federal law, the Court Interpreters Act does not apply to state courts. Nonetheless, most states have enacted similar legislation. A few states are starting to introduce high-standard testing for court interpreters, although most states currently conduct little or no interpreter screening. The federal government and states with high standards for court interpreters generally require interpreter certification. To become certified, an interpreter must pass an oral examination, such as the federal court interpreter's examination or an examination administered by a state court or by a recognized international agency, such as the United Nations.

There is growing recognition among professional court interpreters of the need for standardized interstate testing and certification programs. To meet that need, the National Center for State Courts created the Consortium for State Court Interpreter Certification. The consortium works to pool state resources for developing and administering court interpreter testing and training programs. The consortium's founding states were Minnesota, New Jersey, Oregon, and Washington, and many other states have since joined.

Because certified interpreters are not always available, even by telephone, most states have created a special category of "language-skilled interpreters." To qualify as a language-skilled interpreter, a person must demonstrate to the court's satisfaction his or her ability to interpret court proceedings from English to a designated language and from that language to English. Many states require sign language interpreters to hold a Legal Specialist Certificate, or its equivalent, from the Registry of Interpreters for the Deaf, showing that they are certified in American Sign Language. Learn more about language interpretation in the courts from the National Association of Judiciary Interpreters and Translators via **http://www.najit.org**.

[1]U.S. Code, Title 28, Section 1827.
[2]Ibid., at Section 1827(d)(1).
Sources: The National Association of Judiciary Interpreters and Translators website, http://www.najit.org (accessed October 11, 2007); Madelynn Herman and Anne Endress Skove, "State Court Rules for Language Interpreters," memorandum no. IS 99.1242, National Center for State Courts, Knowledge Management Office, September 8, 1999; Madelynn Herman and Dot Bryant, "Language Interpreting in the Courts," National Center for State Courts, http://www.ncsc.dni.us/KMO/Projects/Trends/99-00/articles/CtInterpreters.htm (accessed October 11, 2007); and National Crime Prevention Council, Building and Crossing Bridges: Refugees and Law Enforcement Working Together (Washington, DC: NCPC, 1994).

The statistical measurement of court performance is another area that is receiving increased attention. Research has looked at the efficiency with which prosecutors schedule cases for trial, the speed with which judges resolve issues, the amount of time judges spend on the bench, and the economic and other costs to defendants, witnesses, and communities involved in the judicial process.[107] Statistical studies of this type often attempt to measure elements of court performance as diverse as sentence variation, charging accuracy, fairness in plea bargaining, evenhandedness, delays, and attitudes toward the court by lay participants. Visit **http://www.justicestudies.com/pubs/tcps.pdf** for more information on standards and measures in court performance.

SUMMARY

- This chapter describes the criminal trial process and the court-related activities that take place before the trial begins. Pretrial activities include the first appearance, which involves appointment of counsel for indigent defendants and consideration of pretrial release; the preliminary hearing to determine whether there is probable cause to hold the defendant; the filing of an information by the prosecutor or the return of an indictment by the grand jury; and arraignment, at which the defendant may enter a plea. Guilty pleas, when they are made, are often not as straightforward as they might seem and are typically arrived at only after complex negotiations known as *plea bargaining*.

- The criminal trial involves an adversarial process that pits the prosecution against the defense. Trials are peer-based fact-finding processes intended to protect the rights of the accused while disputed issues of guilt or innocence are resolved. The primary purpose of a criminal trial is to determine whether a defendant, through his or her behavior, violated the criminal law of the jurisdiction in which the court has authority.

- A criminal trial has eight stages: trial initiation, jury selection, opening statements, the presentation of evidence, closing arguments, the judge's charge to the jury, jury deliberations, and the verdict. Each is described in detail in this chapter. At least a few experts have suggested the training and use of a cadre of professional jurors, versed in the law and in trial practice, who could insulate themselves from media portrayals of famous defendants and who would resolve questions of guilt or innocence more on the basis of reason than emotion.

- The American court system has been called into question by some well-publicized trials of the last two decades, which have demonstrated apparent weaknesses in the trial process. Some people suggest that court unification might help address a number of today's problems by reducing the number of jurisdictions, resulting in more uniform procedures.

KEY TERMS

adversarial system, 324	opening statement, 330
bail bond, 317	peremptory challenge, 328
circumstantial evidence, 331	perjury, 333
closing argument, 335	plea, 322
competent to stand trial, 321	plea bargaining, 322
conditional release, 319	pretrial release, 317
danger law, 320	probative value, 332
direct evidence, 331	property bond, 319
evidence, 331	real evidence, 331
first appearance, 315	reasonable doubt, 336
hearsay, 335	reasonable doubt standard, 336
hearsay rule, 335	release on recognizance (ROR), 319
jury selection, 328	
nolo contendere, 322	rules of evidence, 324

scientific jury selection, 329   testimony, 332
sequestered jury, 329   verdict, 336
Speedy Trial Act, 326

KEY CASES

County of Riverside v. *McLaughlin*, 316	*Maryland* v. *Craig*, 333
Coy v. *Iowa*, 333	*McNabb* v. *U.S.*, 315
Doggett v. *U.S.*, 327	*Michigan* v. *Lucas*, 331
Edmonson v. *Leesville Concrete Co., Inc.*, 330	*Miller-El* v. *Cockrell*, 330
	Mu'Min v. *Virginia*, 328
Fex v. *Michigan*, 327	*Powers* v. *Ohio*, 330
Georgia v. *McCollum*, 330	*U.S.* v. *Montalvo-Murillo*, 320
Idaho v. *Wright*, 333	*White* v. *Illinois*, 333

QUESTIONS FOR REVIEW

1. What activities are typically undertaken during the pretrial period (i.e., before the start of a criminal trial)?
2. What is the purpose of a criminal trial? What is the difference between factual guilt and legal guilt? What do we mean by the term *adversarial system*?
3. What are the various stages of a criminal trial? Describe each one.
4. How might the adjudication process be improved?

QUESTIONS FOR REFLECTION

1. Before trial, courts may act to shield the accused from the punitive power of the state through the use of pretrial release. In doing so, how can they balance the rights of the defendant against the potential for future harm that he or she may represent?
2. A significant issue facing pretrial decision makers is how to ensure that all defendants, rich and poor, black and white, male and female, are afforded the same degree of protection from unfair processing by the criminal justice system. How can that be achieved?
3. What is plea bargaining, and what is its function? To what kinds of cases is it most suited?
4. What purpose does plea bargaining serve for the defense? For the prosecution? Given the criticisms leveled against plea bargaining, do you believe that it's an acceptable practice? Explain.
5. Might recent advances in technology, such as DNA fingerprinting, possibly supplant the role of advocacy in the fact-finding process that is today regarded as central to criminal trials? If so, how? If not, why not?
6. What exceptions to the hearsay rule have courts recognized? Describe the reasoning behind these exceptions.
7. Do you think the present jury system is outmoded? Why? How might a professional jury system be more effective than the present system of peer jurors?

NOTES

1. Michelle Washington, "Five Things to Get You Up to Speed in Jodi Arias Trial," *USA Today*, May 6, 2013, http://m.usatoday.com/article/news/nation/2138823 (accessed July 8, 2013).

2. *Arraignment* is another term used to describe an initial appearance, although we will reserve use of that word to describe a later court appearance following the defendant's indictment by a grand jury or the filing of an information by the prosecutor.

3. *McNabb* v. *U.S.*, 318 U.S. 332 (1943).

4. This is the case because such arrests do not involve judicial determination of probable cause.

5. *County of Riverside* v. *McLaughlin*, 500 U.S. 44 (1991).

6. *White* v. *Maryland*, 373 U.S. 59 (1963).

7. *Rothgery* v. *Gillespie County, Texas*, 554 U.S. 191 (2008).

8. Much of the information in this section comes from Barry Mahoney et al., *Pretrial Services Programs: Responsibilities and Potential* (Washington, DC: National Institute of Justice, 2001).

9. *Taylor* v. *Taintor*, 83 U.S. 66 (1873).

10. National Advisory Commission on Criminal Justice Standards and Goals, *The Courts* (Washington, DC: U.S. Government Printing Office, 1973), p. 37.

11. C. Ares, A. Rankin, and H. Sturz, "The Manhattan Bail Project: An Interim Report on the Use of Pre-trial Parole," *New York University Law Review*, Vol. 38 (January 1963), pp. 68–95.

12. H. Zeisel, "Bail Revisited," *American Bar Foundation Research Journal*, Vol. 4 (1979), pp. 769–789.

13. Ibid.

14. "Twelve Percent of Those Freed on Low Bail Fail to Appear," *New York Times*, December 2, 1983, p. 1.

15. Bureau of Justice Statistics (BJS), *Report to the Nation on Crime and Justice*, 2nd ed. (Washington, DC: U.S. Dept. of Justice, 1988), p. 76.

16. See Tracey Kyckelhahn and Thomas H. Cohen, *Felony Defendants in Large Urban Counties, 2004* (Washington, DC: Bureau of Justice Statistics, 2008), p. iv.

17. John Scalia, *Federal Pretrial Release and Detention, 1996* (Washington, DC: Bureau of Justice Statistics, 1999), p. 1, http://www.ojp.usdoj.gov/bjs/pub/pdf/fprd96.pdf (accessed January 25, 2007).

18. Donald E. Pryor and Walter F. Smith, "Significant Research Findings Concerning Pretrial Release," *Pretrial Issues*, Vol. 4, No. 1 (Washington, DC: Pretrial Services Resource Center, February 1982). See also the Pretrial Services Resource Center website at http://www.pretrial.org/mainpage.htm (accessed July 15, 2009).

19. BJS, *Report to the Nation on Crime and Justice*, p. 77.

20. According to Joseph B. Vaughn and Victor E. Kappeler, the first such legislation was the 1970 District of Columbia Court Reform and Criminal Procedure Act. See Vaughn and Kappeler, "The Denial of Bail: Pre-Trial Preventive Detention," *Criminal Justice Research Bulletin*, Vol. 3, No. 6 (Huntsville, TX: Sam Houston State University, 1987), p. 1.

21. Ibid.

22. Bail Reform Act of 1984, U.S. Code, Title 18, Section 3142(e).

23. *U.S.* v. *Montalvo-Murillo*, 495 U.S. 711 (1990).

24. Ibid., syllabus.

25. *U.S.* v. *Hazzard*, 35 CrL. 2217 (1984).

26. See, for example, *U.S.* v. *Motamedi*, 37 CrL. 2394, CA 9 (1985).

27. A few states now have laws that permit the defendant to appear before the grand jury.

28. John M. Scheb and John M. Scheb II, *American Criminal Law* (St. Paul, MN: West, 1996), p. 31.

29. Ibid.

30. The information in this paragraph is adapted from Linda Greenhouse, "Supreme Court Limits Forced Medication of Some for Trial," *New York Times*, June 16, 2003, http://www.nytimes.com/2003/06/17/politics/17DRUG.html (accessed June 17, 2005).

31. *Sell* v. *U.S.*, 539 U.S. 166 (2003).

32. Federal Rules of Criminal Procedure, 5.1(a).

33. Scheb and Scheb, *American Criminal Law*, p. 32.

34. Gary Fields and John R. Emshwiller, "Federal Guilty Pleas Soar as Bargains Trump Trials," *Wall Street Journal*, September 23, 2012, http://online.wsj.com/article/SB1000087239639044358930457763761009720680.html (accessed April 1, 2013).

35. Ibid.

36. *Kercheval* v. *U.S.*, 274 U.S. 220, 223, 47 S.Ct. 582, 583 (1927); *Boykin* v. *Alabama*, 395 U.S. 238 (1969); and *Dickerson* v. *New Banner Institute, Inc.*, 460 U.S. 103 (1983).

37. Ronald F. Wright and Paul Hofer, analysis of Bureau of Justice Statistics data from: Erica Goode, "Stronger Hand for Judges in the 'Bazaar' of Plea Deals," *New York Times*, March 22, 2012, http://www.nytimes.com/2012/03/23/us/stronger-hand-for-judges-after-rulings-on-plea-deals.html?_r=2&ref=us (accessed March 23, 2012).

38. Barbara Boland et al., *The Prosecution of Felony Arrests, 1987* (Washington, DC: U.S. Government Printing Office, 1990).

39. *Santobello* v. *New York*, 404 U.S. 257 (1971).

40. *Mabry* v. *Johnson*, 467 U.S. 504 (1984).

41. *U.S.* v. *Baldacchino*, 762 F.2d 170 (1st Cir. 1985); *U.S.* v. *Reardon*, 787 F.2d 512 (10th Cir. 1986); and *U.S.* v. *Donahey*, 529 F.2d 831 (11th Cir. 1976).

42. *Missouri* v. *Frye*, U.S. Supreme Court, No. 10-444 (decided March 21, 2012), and *Lafler* v. *Cooper*, U.S. Supreme Court, No. 10-209 (decided March 21, 2012).

43. For a classic discussion of such considerations, see David Sudnow, "Normal Crimes: Sociological Features of the Penal Code in a Public Defender Office," *Social Problems*, Vol. 123, No. 3 (winter 1965), p. 255.

44. Federal Rules of Criminal Procedure, No. 11.

45. Marc G. Gertz and Edmond J. True, "Social Scientists in the Courtroom: The Frustrations of Two Expert Witnesses," in Susette M. Talarico, ed., *Courts and Criminal Justice: Emerging Issues* (Beverly Hills, CA: Sage, 1985), pp. 81–91.

46. Dotson was the first person convicted of a crime (rape) to be exonerated by DNA evidence. Kirk Bloodsworth, whose case is discussed in a "CJ News" box in the next chapter, was the first death row inmate to be exonerated through the use of DNA analysis. Richard Buckland, a 17-year-old English teenager with learning disabilities, was likely the first person whose innocence was demonstrated through the use of DNA analysis. Although Buckland was a suspect in two rape cases, he had not been convicted at the time DNA evidence proved his innocence.

47. Samuel R. Gross et al., "Exonerations in the United States, 1989 through 2003," April 4, 2004, http://www.mindfully.org/Reform/2004/Prison-Exonerations-Gross19apr04.htm (accessed May 28, 2009).

48. Ibid.

49. *Klopfer* v. *North Carolina*, 386 U.S. 213 (1967).

50. *Barker* v. *Wingo*, 407 U.S. 514 (1972).

51. *Strunk* v. *U.S.*, 412 U.S. 434 (1973).

52. Speedy Trial Act, U.S. Code, Title 18, Section 3161 (1974).

53. *U.S.* v. *Taylor*, 487 U.S. 326, 108 S.Ct. 2413, 101 L.Ed.2d 297 (1988).

54. *Fex* v. *Michigan*, 113 S.Ct. 1085, 122 L.Ed.2d 406 (1993).

55. *Doggett* v. *U.S.*, 112 S.Ct. 2686 (1992).

56. William U. McCormack, "Supreme Court Cases: 1991–1992 Term," *FBI Law Enforcement Bulletin*, November 1992, pp. 28–29.

57. *Padilla* v. *Hanft*, No. 05-533, cert. denied.

58. Ibid.

59. See, for example, the U.S. Supreme Court's decision in the case of *Murphy* v. *Florida*, 410 U.S. 525 (1973).

60. *Witherspoon* v. *Illinois*, 391 U.S. 510 (1968).

61. *Mu'Min* v. *Virginia*, 500 U.S. 415 (1991).

62. Federal Rules of Criminal Procedure, Rule 24(6).

63. Although the words *argument* and *statement* are sometimes used interchangeably to refer to opening remarks, defense attorneys are enjoined from drawing conclusions or "arguing" to the jury at this stage in the trial. Their task, as described in the section that follows, is simply to explain to the jury how the defense will be conducted.

64. Learn more about shadow juries from Molly McDonough, "Me and My Shadow: Shadow Juries Are Helping Litigators Shape Their Cases during Trial," *National Law Journal*, May 17, 2001.

65. Supreme Court majority opinion in *Powers* v. *Ohio*, 499 U.S. 400 (1991), citing *Strauder* v. *West Virginia*, 100 U.S. 303 (1880).

66. *Swain* v. *Alabama*, 380 U.S. 202 (1965).

67. *Batson* v. *Kentucky*, 476 U.S. 79 (1986).

68. *Ford* v. *Georgia*, 498 U.S. 411 (1991), footnote 2.

69. *Powers* v. *Ohio*, 499 U.S. 400 (1991).

70. *Edmonson* v. *Leesville Concrete Co., Inc.*, 500 U.S. 614 (1991).

71. *Georgia* v. *McCollum*, 505 U.S. 42 (1992).

72. *J.E.B.* v. *Alabama*, ex rel. T. B., 511 U.S. 127 (1994).

73. See, for example, *Davis* v. *Minnesota*, 511 U.S. 1115 (1994).

74. Michael Kirkland, "Court Rejects Fat Jurors Case," United Press International, January 8, 1996. The case was *Santiago-Martinez* v. *U.S.*, No. 95-567 (1996).

75. *Campbell* v. *Louisiana*, 523 U.S. 392 (1998).

76. *Miller-El* v. *Cockrell*, 537 U.S. 322 (2003).

77. Ibid., syllabus.

78. *Miller-El* v. *Dretke*, 545 U.S. 231 (2005).

79. *Snyder* v. *Louisiana*, 552 U.S. 472 (2008).

80. *U.S.* v. *Dinitz*, 424 U.S. 600, 612 (1976).

81. *Michigan* v. *Lucas*, 500 U.S. 145 (1991).

82. Associated Press, "Suit Settlement Ends Bryant Saga," March 3, 2005, http://msnbc.msn.com/id/7019659 (accessed July 12, 2010).

83. *Kotteakos* v. *U.S.*, 328 U.S. 750 (1946); *Brecht* v. *Abrahamson*, 113 S.Ct. 1710, 123 L.Ed.2d 353 (1993); and *Arizona* v. *Fulminante*, 111 S.Ct. 1246 (1991).

84. The Court, citing *Kotteakos* v. *U.S.* (1946), in *Brecht* v. *Abrahamson*, 113 S.Ct. 1710, 123 L.Ed.2d 353 (1993).

85. *Sullivan* v. *Louisiana*, 113 S.Ct. 2078, 124 L.Ed.2d 182 (1993).

86. *Griffin* v. *California*, 380 U.S. 609 (1965).

87. *Ohio* v. *Reiner*, 123 S.Ct. 1252, 532 U.S. 17 (2001).

88. Leading questions may, in fact, be permitted for certain purposes, including refreshing a witness's memory, impeaching a hostile witness, introducing undisputed material, and helping a witness with impaired faculties.

89. *In re Oliver*, 333 U.S. 257 (1948).

90. *Coy* v. *Iowa*, 487 U.S. 1012 (1988).

91. *Maryland* v. *Craig*, 497 U.S. 836, 845-847 (1990).

92. *Idaho* v. *Wright*, 497 U.S. 805 (1990).

93. *White* v. *Illinois*, 112 S.Ct. 736 (1992).

94. *Crawford* v. *Washington*, 541 U.S. 36 (2004).

95. *Davis* v. *Washington*, 547 U.S. 813 (2006). See also *Hammon* v. *Indiana*, U.S. Supreme Court, 547 U.S. 813 (2006).

96. *Davis* v. *Washington*, syllabus.

97. Federal Rules of Criminal Procedure, Rule 29.1.

98. See *Johnson* v. *Louisiana*, 406 U.S. 356 (1972); and *Apodaca* v. *Oregon*, 406 U.S. 404 (1972).

99. *Allen* v. *U.S.*, 164 U.S. 492 (1896).

100. Judge Harold J. Rothwax, *Guilty: The Collapse of Criminal Justice* (New York: Random House, 1996).

101. Amiram Elwork, Bruce D. Sales, and James Alfini, *Making Jury Instructions Understandable* (Charlottesville, VA: Michie, 1982).

102. "King Jury Lives in Fear from Unpopular Verdict," *Fayetteville (NC) Observer-Times*, May 10, 1992.

103. "Los Angeles Trials Spark Debate over Anonymous Juries," *Criminal Justice Newsletter*, February 16, 1993, pp. 3–4.

104. Some states have centralized offices called Administrative Offices of the Courts or something similar. Such offices, however, are often primarily data-gathering agencies with little or no authority over the day-to-day functioning of state or local courts.

105. See, for example, Larry Berkson and Susan Carbon, *Court Unification: Its History, Politics, and Implementation* (Washington, DC: U.S. Government Printing Office, 1978); and Thomas Henderson et al., *The Significance of Judicial Structure: The Effect of Unification on Trial Court Operators* (Alexandria, VA: Institute for Economic and Policy Studies, 1984).

106. See, for example, Thomas J. Cook et al., *Basic Issues in Court Performance* (Washington, DC: National Institute of Justice, 1982).

107. See, for example, Sorrel Wildhorn et al., *Indicators of Justice: Measuring the Performance of Prosecutors, Defense, and Court Agencies Involved in Felony Proceedings* (Lexington, MA: Lexington Books, 1977).

108. Irving Stone, *Clarence Darrow for the Defense* (New York: Doubleday, 1941).

109. *Victor* v. *Nebraska*, 114 S.Ct. 1239, 127 L.Ed.2d 583 (1994).

110. As found in the California jury instructions.

Rich Legg/Getty Images

11

SENTENCING

OUTLINE

- Introduction
- The Philosophy and Goals of Criminal Sentencing
- Indeterminate Sentencing
- Structured Sentencing
- Sentencing and Today's Prison Crisis
- Innovations in Sentencing
- The Presentence Investigation
- The Victim—Forgotten No Longer
- Modern Sentencing Options
- Death: The Ultimate Sanction
- Opposition to Capital Punishment

LEARNING OBJECTIVES

After reading this chapter, you should be able to

- Describe the five goals of contemporary criminal sentencing.
- Define *indeterminate sentencing*, including its purpose.
- Describe structured sentencing models that became so popular during the late 20th century, using the federal model as an example.
- Tell how get-tough sentencing practices led to significant prison overcrowding in the United States.
- Describe alternative sentences, fines, diversion, and offender registries.
- Explain the purpose of presentence investigations, presentence investigation reports, and presentencing hearings.
- Describe the history of victims' rights and services, including the growing role of the victim in criminal justice proceedings today.
- List the four traditional sentencing options.
- State the arguments for and against capital punishment.

Excessive bail shall not be required, nor excessive fines imposed, nor cruel and unusual punishments inflicted.

EIGHTH AMENDMENT TO THE U.S. CONSTITUTION

■ **lecture note** Describe the various goals of criminal sentencing, including retribution, incapacitation, deterrence, rehabilitation, and restoration.

■ **sentencing**   The imposition of a criminal sanction by a judicial authority.

■ Follow the author's tweets about the latest crime and justice news @schmalleger.

Introduction

On June 25, 2013, Oregon became the third state to adopt racial impact legislation.[1] The other two states with similar laws are Connecticut and Iowa. Racial impact laws require policymakers to conduct racial-impact studies and to prepare racial-impact statements for any proposed policy changes affecting criminal **sentencing**, probation, or parole. Oregon's law was passed after research showed that black Oregonians make up only 2% of the state's population, yet constitute 9% of its prisoners. About the same time as the Oregon legislation became law, however, North Carolina, which had been one of the first states to require racial-impact studies, repealed its Racial Justice Act, noting that an unintended consequence of the legislation had been to effectively block executions in the state.[2]

Marc Mauer, head of the Washington, D.C.-based Sentencing Project, says, "The premise behind racial impact statements is that policies often have unintended consequences that would be best addressed prior to adoption of new initiatives."[3] One example Mauer gives is that of enhanced criminal penalties associated with drug sales near school grounds—a law, he says, more likely to be violated by minorities because they tend to live in areas with greater proximity to schools. Studies of the racial impact of sentencing practices, Mauer says, force us to examine twin problems in the justice system: (1) the need for policies and practices that can work effectively to promote public safety, and (2) the need to reduce disproportionate rates of minority incarceration when feasible. "These are not competing goals," says Mauer. "If we are successful in addressing crime in a proactive way, we will be able to reduce high imprisonment rates; conversely, by promoting racial justice we will increase confidence in the criminal justice system and thereby aid public safety efforts."

Under an organized system of criminal justice, sentencing is the imposition of a penalty on a person convicted of a crime. Sentencing follows what is intended to be an impartial judicial proceeding during which criminal responsibility is ascertained.

> Sentencing is the imposition of a penalty on a person convicted of a crime.

Most sentencing decisions are made by judges, although in some cases, especially where a death sentence is possible, juries may be involved in a special sentencing phase of courtroom proceedings. The sentencing decision is one of the most difficult made by any judge or jury. Not only does it affect the future of the defendant—and at times it is a decision about his or her life or death—but society looks to sentencing to achieve a diversity of goals, some of which are not fully compatible with others.

This chapter examines sentencing in terms of both philosophy and practice. We will describe the goals of sentencing as well as the historical development of various sentencing models in the United States. Consequences of various sentencing philosophies will be explained. This chapter also contains a detailed overview of victimization and victims' rights in general, especially as they relate to courtroom procedure and to sentencing practice. Federal sentencing guidelines and the significance of presentence investigations are also described. For an overview of sentencing issues, visit the Sentencing Project via **http://www .sentencingproject.org**.

The Philosophy and Goals of Criminal Sentencing

Traditional sentencing options have included imprisonment, fines, probation, and—for very serious offenses—death. Limits on the range of options available to sentencing authorities are generally specified by law. Historically, those limits have shifted as understandings of crime and the goals of sentencing have changed. Sentencing philosophies, or the justifications on which various sentencing strategies are based, are manifestly intertwined with issues of religion, morals, values, and emotions.[4] Philosophies that gained ascendancy at a particular point in history usually reflected more deeply held social values. Centuries ago, for example, it was thought that crime was due to sin and that suffering was the culprit's due. Judges were expected to be harsh. Capital punishment, torture, and painful physical penalties served this view of criminal behavior.

> Sentencing philosophies are intertwined with issues of religion, morals, values, and emotions.

An emphasis on equitable punishments became prevalent around the time of the American and French Revolutions, brought about in part by Enlightenment philosophies. Offenders came to be seen as highly rational beings who intentionally and somewhat carefully chose their course of action. Sentencing philosophies of the period stressed the need for sanctions that outweighed the benefits to be derived from criminal activity. The severity of punishment became less important than quick and certain penalties.

Recent thinking has emphasized the need to limit offenders' potential for future harm by separating them from society. We also still believe that offenders deserve to be punished, and we have not

■ **lecture note** Explain that retribution is similar to the notion of "an eye for an eye, a tooth for a tooth." Add that during Old Testament times, "an eye for an eye" often reduced the punishment offenders experienced.

■ **theme** What is the just deserts model of sentencing? Do you agree with this model? Why or why not?

■ **lecture note** Explain incapacitation as society's interest in making the offender incapable of immediately committing other crimes.

■ **retribution**   The act of taking revenge on a criminal perpetrator.

■ **just deserts**   A model of criminal sentencing that holds that criminal offenders deserve the punishment they receive at the hands of the law and that punishments should be appropriate to the type and severity of the crime committed.

■ **incapacitation**   The use of imprisonment or other means to reduce the likelihood that an offender will commit future offenses.

A courtroom drawing showing Rosemary Dillard, whose husband was killed on September 11, 2001, speaking to Zacarias Moussaoui, as family members of other 9/11 victims listen. The scene took place in U.S. District Court in Alexandria, Virginia, during the sentencing hearing for the convicted al-Qaeda conspirator. On May 4, 2006, federal Judge Leonie M. Brinkema sentenced Moussaoui to life in prison with no possibility of release. What was Moussaoui's crime? Do you think that his sentence was just and fair? Might it deter other would-be terrorists?

Dana Verkouteren/AP Wide World Photos

TABLE 11-1 | Sentencing—Goals and Purposes

SENTENCING GOAL	PURPOSE
Retribution	A just deserts perspective that emphasizes taking revenge on a criminal perpetrator or group of offenders.
Incapacitation	The use of imprisonment or other means to reduce the likelihood that a particular offender will commit more crime.
Deterrence	A sentencing rationale that seeks to inhibit criminal behavior through punishment or the fear of punishment.
General deterrence	Seeks to prevent future crimes like the one for which the sentence is being imposed.
Specific deterrence	Seeks to prevent a *particular* offender from engaging in repeat criminality.
Rehabilitation	The attempt to reform a criminal offender.
Restoration	A goal of sentencing that seeks to make the victim "whole again."

entirely abandoned hope for their rehabilitation. Modern sentencing practices are influenced by five goals, which weave their way through widely disseminated professional and legal models, continuing public calls for sentencing reform, and everyday sentencing practice. Each goal represents a quasi-independent sentencing philosophy, as each makes distinctive assumptions about human nature and holds implications for sentencing practice. Table 11-1 shows the five general goals of contemporary sentencing.

Retribution

Retribution is a call for punishment based on a perceived need for vengeance. Retribution is the earliest known rationale for punishment. Most early societies punished all offenders who were caught. Early punishments were immediate—often without the benefit of a hearing—and they were often extreme, with little thought given to whether the punishment "fit" the crime. Death and exile, for example, were commonly imposed, even for relatively minor offenses. The Old Testament dictum of "an eye for an eye, a tooth for a tooth"—often cited as an ancient justification for retribution—was actually intended to reduce the severity of punishment for relatively minor crimes.

Today, retribution corresponds to the **just deserts** model of sentencing, which holds that offenders are responsible for their crimes. When they are convicted and punished, they are said to have gotten their "just deserts." Retribution sees punishment as deserved, justified, and even required[5] by the offender's behavior. The primary sentencing tool of the just deserts model is imprisonment, but in extreme cases capital punishment (i.e., death) becomes the ultimate retribution. Both in the public's view and in political policymaking, retribution is still a primary goal of criminal sentencing.

Incapacitation

Incapacitation, the second goal of criminal sentencing, seeks to protect innocent members of society from offenders who might harm them if not prevented from doing so. In ancient times, mutilation and amputation of the extremities were sometimes used to prevent offenders from repeating their crimes. Modern incapacitation strategies separate offenders from the community to reduce opportunities for further criminality. Incapacitation, sometimes called the "lock 'em up approach," forms the basis for the modern movement toward prison "warehousing." Unlike retribution, incapacitation requires only restraint—and not punishment.

■ **lecture note**   Explain deterrence as an attempt to convince someone (either the offender being sentenced or someone else) that criminal activity is not worthwhile. Discuss how deterrence might be measured or studied.

■ **theme**   What is the difference between general deterrence and specific deterrence? Are they equally important? If both cannot be achieved to the same level, which should take priority and why?

■ **lecture note**   Explain rehabilitation as an attempt to change the offender into a law-abiding citizen. Discuss how rehabilitation might be measured or studied.

■ **deterrence**   A goal of criminal sentencing that seeks to inhibit criminal behavior through the fear of punishment.

■ **specific deterrence**   A goal of criminal sentencing that seeks to prevent a particular offender from engaging in repeat criminality.

■ **recidivism**   The act of relapsing into a problem or criminal behavior during or after receiving sanctions, or while undergoing an intervention due to a previous behavior or crime. In criminal justice settings, recidivism is often measured by criminal acts that result in rearrest, reconviction, or return to prison.

■ **lecture note**   Explain restoration as an attempt to make victims "whole again," insofar as possible. Discuss how restoration might be measured or studied.

■ **theme**   What is restorative justice? How does it differ from retributive justice? Do you think that restorative justice can occur in a system that emphasizes retributive justice?

■ **general deterrence**   A goal of criminal sentencing that seeks to prevent others from committing crimes similar to the one for which a particular offender is being sentenced by making an example of the person sentenced.

■ **rehabilitation**   The attempt to reform a criminal offender. Also, the state in which a reformed offender is said to be.

■ **recidivism rate**   A measure of the rate of reoffending (usually defined by arrest) for a given population of released prisoners, or for a group of criminally sanctioned offenders, over time. Rates of recidivism are generally calculated over a three- or a five-year time period.

Deterrence

Deterrence uses the example or threat of punishment to convince people that criminal activity is not worthwhile. Its overall goal is crime prevention. **Specific deterrence** seeks to reduce the likelihood of **recidivism** (repeat offenses) by convicted offenders, whereas **general deterrence** strives to influence the future behavior of people who have not yet been arrested and who may be tempted to turn to crime. Deterrence is one of the more "rational" goals of sentencing because it is an easily articulated goal and because it is possible to investigate objectively the amount of punishment required to deter.

Deterrence is compatible with the goal of incapacitation, as at least specific deterrence can be achieved through incapacitating offenders. Tufts University Professor Hugo Adam Bedau, however, points to significant differences between retribution and deterrence.[6] Retribution is oriented toward the past, says Bedau. It seeks to redress wrongs already committed. Deterrence, in contrast, is a strategy for the future. It aims to prevent new crimes.

Rehabilitation

Rehabilitation seeks to bring about fundamental changes in offenders and their behavior. As in the case of deterrence, the ultimate goal of rehabilitation is a reduction in the number of criminal offenses. Whereas deterrence depends on a fear of the consequences of violating the law, rehabilitation generally works through education and psychological treatment to reduce the likelihood of future criminality.

The term *rehabilitation*, however, is a misnomer for the kinds of changes that its supporters seek. Rehabilitation literally means to return a person to his or her previous condition; however, it is likely that in most cases restoring criminals to their previous state will result in nothing but a more youthful type of criminality.

> The ultimate goal of rehabilitation is a reduction in the number of criminal offenses.

In the late 1970s, the rehabilitative goal in sentencing fell victim to the "nothing-works doctrine." The nothing-works doctrine was based on studies of **recidivism rates** that consistently showed that rehabilitation was more an ideal than a reality.[7] With as many as 90% of former convicted offenders returning to lives of crime following release from prison-based treatment programs, public sentiments in favor of incapacitation grew. Although the rehabilitation ideal has clearly suffered in the public arena, emerging evidence has begun to suggest that effective treatment programs do exist and may be growing in number.[8]

Restoration

Victims of crime and their families are frequently traumatized by their experiences. Some victims are killed, and others receive lasting physical or emotional injuries. For many, the world is never

© Drew Crawford/The Image Works

Female inmates being trained to work with fiber optics at the Federal Correctional Institution in Danbury, Connecticut. Skills acquired through such prison programs might translate into productive, noncriminal careers for ex-convicts. Rehabilitation is an important, but infrequently voiced, goal of modern sentencing practices. What are some other sentencing goals identified in this chapter?

■ **theme** With which of the goals of criminal sentencing do you most agree? Why?

■ **theme** Which of the goals of criminal sentencing do you think individual-rights advocates would most likely find attractive? Which would public-order advocates favor? Why?

■ **restoration** A goal of criminal sentencing that attempts to make the victim "whole again."

■ **theme** Are the goals of criminal sentencing compatible? Could a sentence that is designed to achieve one goal negatively affect attempts to achieve another goal? How?

■ **activity** Place students in groups and ask them to consider the five goals of criminal sentencing. Have them rank them in order of importance and identify which goals are compatible and which are contradictory.

■ **restorative justice (RJ)** A sentencing model that builds on restitution and community participation in an attempt to make the victim "whole again."

the same. The victimized may live in constant fear, be reduced in personal vigor, and be unable to form trusting relationships. **Restoration** is a sentencing goal that seeks to address this damage by making the victim and the community "whole again."

A U.S. Department of Justice report explains restoration this way: "Crime was once defined as a 'violation of the State.' This remains the case today, but we now recognize that crime is far more. It is—among other things—a violation of one person by another. While retributive justice may address the first type of violation adequately, restorative justice is required to effectively address the latter.... Thus [through restorative justice] we seek to attain a balance between the legitimate needs of the community, the ... offender, and the victim."[9] The "healing" of all parties has many aspects, ranging from victims' assistance initiatives to legislation supporting victims' compensation.

Restorative justice (RJ) is also referred to as *balanced and restorative justice*. Conceptually, "balance" is achieved by giving equal consideration to community safety and offender accountability. Restorative justice focuses on "crime as harm, and justice as repairing the harm."[10] The community safety dimension of the RJ philosophy recognizes that the justice system has a responsibility to protect the public from crime and from offenders.[11] It also recognizes that the community can participate in ensuring its own

safety. The accountability element defines criminal conduct in terms of obligations incurred by the offender, both to the victim and to the community.[12] RJ also has what some describe as a competency development element, which holds that offenders who enter the justice system should leave it more capable of participating successfully in the wider society than when they entered. In essence, RJ is community-focused; its primary goal is improving the quality of life for all members of the community. See Table 11-2 for a comparison of retributive and restorative justice.

> In essence, restorative justice is community-focused.

Sentencing options that seek to restore the victim have focused primarily on restitution payments that offenders are ordered to make, either to their victims or to a general fund, which may then reimburse victims for suffering, lost wages, and medical expenses. In support of these goals, the 1984 Federal Comprehensive Crime Control Act specifically requires that "[i]f sentenced to probation, the defendant must also be ordered to pay a fine, make restitution, and/or work in community service."[13]

Some advocates of the restoration philosophy of sentencing point out that restitution payments and work programs that benefit the victim can also have the added benefit of rehabilitating the offender. The hope is that such sentences will teach

TABLE 11-2 | Differences between Retributive and Restorative Justice

RETRIBUTIVE JUSTICE	RESTORATIVE JUSTICE
Crime is an act against the state, a violation of a law, an abstract idea.	Crime is an act against another person or the community.
The criminal justice system controls crime.	Crime control lies primarily with the community.
Offender accountability is defined as taking punishment.	Offender accountability is defined as assuming responsibility and taking action to repair harm.
Crime is an individual act with individual responsibility.	Crime has both individual and social dimensions of responsibility.
Victims are peripheral to the process of resolving a crime.	Victims are central to the process of resolving a crime.
The offender is defined by deficits.	The offender is defined by the capacity to make reparation.
The emphasis is on adversarial relationships.	The emphasis is on dialogue and negotiation.
Pain is imposed to punish, deter, and prevent.	Restitution is a means of restoring both parties; the goal is reconciliation.
The community is on the sidelines, represented abstractly by the state.	The community is the facilitator in the restorative process.
The response is focused on the offender's past behavior.	The response is focused on harmful consequences of the offender's behavior; the emphasis is on the future and on reparation.
There is dependence on proxy professionals.	Both the offender and the victim are directly involved.

Source: Adapted from Gordon Bazemore and Mark S. Umbreit, *Balanced and Restorative Justice: Program Summary* (Washington, DC: Office of Juvenile Justice and Delinquency Prevention, 1994), p. 7.

■ **theme** What is indeterminate sentencing? What were the reasons behind the development of this model of sentencing?

■ **lecture note** Explain that the indeterminate sentencing model, the most common model in the United States for most of the twentieth century, assumed that sentenced offenders would take part in their own rehabilitation if offered the chance at early freedom. Ask students what assumptions about human behavior this model makes.

■ **indeterminate sentencing** A model of criminal punishment that encourages rehabilitation through the use of general and relatively unspecific sentences (such as a term of imprisonment of from one to ten years).

■ **lecture note** Discuss the problems with the indeterminate sentencing model. Explain that most states no longer use this model and review the reasons why this is the case.

offenders personal responsibility through structured financial obligations, job requirements, and regularly scheduled payments. Learn more about restorative justice at **http://www.ojjdp.gov/pubs/implementing**.

Indeterminate Sentencing

Whereas the *philosophy* of criminal sentencing is reflected in the goals of sentencing we have just discussed, different sentencing *practices* have been linked to each goal. During most of the twentieth century, for example, the rehabilitation goal was influential. Because rehabilitation requires that individual offenders' personal characteristics be closely considered in defining effective treatment strategies, judges were generally permitted wide discretion in choosing from among sentencing options. Although incapacitation is increasingly becoming the sentencing strategy of choice today, many state criminal codes still allow judges to impose fines, probation, or widely varying prison terms, all for the same offense. These sentencing practices, characterized primarily by vast judicial choice, constitute an **indeterminate sentencing** model.

Indeterminate sentencing has both a historical and a philosophical basis in the belief that convicted offenders are more likely to participate in their own rehabilitation if participation will reduce the amount of time they have to spend in prison. Inmates exhibiting good behavior will be released early, while recalcitrant inmates will remain in prison until the end of their terms. For that reason, parole generally plays a significant role in states that employ the indeterminate sentencing model.

Indeterminate sentencing relies heavily on judges' discretion to choose among types of sanctions and to set upper and lower limits on the length of prison stays. Indeterminate sentences are typically imposed with wording like this: "The defendant shall serve not less than five and not more than twenty-five years in the state's prison, under the supervision of the state department of correction." Judicial discretion under the indeterminate model also extends to the imposition of concurrent or consecutive sentences when the offender is convicted on more than one charge. Consecutive sentences are served one after the other, whereas concurrent sentences expire simultaneously.

> Indeterminate sentencing relies heavily on judges' discretion.

The indeterminate model was also created to take into consideration detailed differences in degrees of guilt. Under this model, judges can weigh minute differences among cases, situations, and offenders. Under the indeterminate sentencing model, the inmate's behavior while incarcerated is the primary determinant of the amount of time served. State parole boards wield great discretion under this model, acting as the final arbiters of the actual sentence served.

A few states employ a partially indeterminate sentencing model. They allow judges to specify only the maximum amount of time to be served. Some minimum is generally implied by law but is not under the control of the sentencing authority. General practice is to set one year as a minimum for all felonies, although a few jurisdictions assume no minimum time at all, making offenders eligible for immediate parole.

Critiques of Indeterminate Sentencing

Indeterminate sentencing is still the rule in many jurisdictions, including Georgia, Hawaii, Iowa, Kentucky, Massachusetts, Michigan, Nevada, New York, North Dakota, Oklahoma, Rhode Island, South Carolina, South Dakota, Texas, Utah, Vermont, West Virginia, and Wyoming.[14] Beginning in the 1970s, however, the model came under fire for contributing to inequality in sentencing. Critics claimed that the indeterminate model allows judges' personalities and personal philosophies to produce too wide a range of sentencing practices, from very lenient to very strict. The indeterminate model was also criticized for perpetuating a system under which offenders might be sentenced, at least by some judges, more on the basis of personal and social characteristics, such as race, gender, and social class, than on culpability.

Because of the personal nature of judicial decisions under the indeterminate model, offenders often depend on the advice and ploys of their attorneys to appear before a judge who is thought to be a good sentencing risk. Requests for delays are a common defense strategy in indeterminate sentencing states, where they are used to try to manipulate the selection of the judge involved in the sentencing decision.

Another charge leveled against indeterminate sentencing is that it tends to produce "dishonesty" in sentencing. Because of sentence cutbacks for good behavior and involvement in work and study programs, time served in prison is generally far less

■ **lecture note**   Describe the differences between indeterminate and structured sentencing, alluding to the fact that the structured approach generally sets a predetermined term in prison, whereas the indeterminate model sets only minimums and maximums.

■ **lecture note**   Review the various models of structured sentencing discussed in the chapter (determinate sentencing, voluntary/advisory sentencing guidelines, and presumptive sentencing). Discuss which (if any) is used in your state. In a distance learning environment, consider asking students to identify the sentencing model used in their home state.

■ **gain time**   The amount of time deducted from time to be served in prison on a given sentence as a consequence of participation in special projects or programs.

■ **good time**   The amount of time deducted from time to be served in prison on a given sentence as a consequence of good behavior.

■ **proportionality**   A sentencing principle that holds that the severity of sanctions should bear a direct relationship to the seriousness of the crime committed.

■ **equity**   A sentencing principle, based on concerns with social equality, that holds that similar crimes should be punished with the same degree of severity, regardless of the social or personal characteristics of the offenders.

■ **social debt**   A sentencing principle that holds that an offender's criminal history should objectively be taken into account in sentencing decisions.

■ **structured sentencing**   A model of criminal punishment that includes determinate and commission-created presumptive sentencing schemes, as well as voluntary/advisory sentencing guidelines.

■ **determinate sentencing**   A model of criminal punishment in which an offender is given a fixed term of imprisonment that may be reduced by good time or gain time. Under the model, for example, all offenders convicted of the same degree of burglary would be sentenced to the same length of time behind bars.

TABLE 11-3 | Percentage of Sentence Served in State Prison by Offense and Race

OFFENSE TYPE	PERCENTAGE OF SENTENCE SERVED	
	WHITE INMATES	BLACK INMATES
Violent	57.3	60.9
Property	37.0	41.5
Drug	31.7	36.1
Public-order	40.4	49.0
Average for all offenses	42.6	48.5

Source: Thomas P. Bonczar, "First Releases from State Prison, 2009: Sentence Length and Time Served in Prison, by Offense and Race," *National Corrections Reporting Program*, http://bjs.ojp.usdoj.gov/content/data/ncrpt09.zip (accessed October 25, 2013).

than sentences would seem to indicate. An inmate sentenced to five to ten years, for example, might actually be released in a couple of years after all **gain time**, **good time**, and other special allowances have been calculated. (Some of the same charges can be leveled against determinate sentencing schemes under which corrections officials can administratively reduce the time served by an inmate.) A survey by the Bureau of Justice Statistics found that even violent offenders released from state prisons during the study period had served, on average, only 51% of the sentences they originally received.[15] Nonviolent offenders had served even smaller portions of their sentences. Table 11-3 shows the percentage of an imposed sentence that an offender released from state prison had actually served.

To ensure long prison terms in indeterminate jurisdictions, some court officials have gone to extremes. In 1994, for example, Oklahoma Judge Dan Owens set a record that stands to this day when he sentenced convicted child molester Charles Scott Robinson to 30,000 years in prison.[16] Judge Owens, complying with the jury's efforts to ensure that Robinson would spend the rest of his life behind bars, sentenced him to serve six consecutive 5,000-year sentences. Robinson had 14 previous felony convictions.

Structured Sentencing

Until the 1970s, all 50 states used some form of indeterminate (or partially indeterminate) sentencing. Eventually, however, calls for equity and proportionality in sentencing, heightened by claims of racial disparity in the sentencing practices of some judges,[17] led many states to move toward greater control over their sentencing systems.

Critics of the indeterminate model called for the recognition of three fundamental sentencing principles: **proportionality**, **equity**, and **social debt**. Proportionality refers to the belief that the severity of sanctions should bear a direct relationship to the seriousness of the crime committed. Equity means that similar crimes should be punished with the same degree of severity, regardless of the social or personal characteristics of offenders. According to the principle of equity, for example, two bank robbers in different parts of the country, who use the same techniques and weapons, with the same degree of implied threat, should receive roughly the same sentence even though they are tried under separate circumstances and in different jurisdictions. The equity principle needs to be balanced, however, against the notion of social debt. In the case of the bank robbers, the offender who has a prior criminal record can be said to have a higher level of social debt than the first-time robber, where all else is equal. Greater social debt, of course, suggests a more severe punishment or a greater need for treatment.

Beginning in the 1970s, a number of states addressed these concerns by developing a different model of sentencing, known as **structured sentencing**. One form of structured sentencing, called **determinate sentencing**, requires that a convicted offender be sentenced to a fixed term that may be reduced by good time (time off for good behavior) or earned time (time off in recognition of special efforts on the part of the inmate). Determinate sentencing states eliminated the use of traditional parole and created explicit standards to specify the amount of punishment appropriate for a given offense. Determinate

■ **lecture note** Discuss the role of aggravating and mitigating circumstances in criminal sentencing. Use the "CJ Issues" box "Aggravating and Mitigating Circumstances" to provide examples of such sentencing considerations.

■ **lecture note** Explain that the determinate model of criminal sentencing establishes fixed terms of confinement, with dramatically reduced possibilities for parole.

■ **theme** Do you favor the indeterminate model or the structured model of criminal sentencing? Why?

■ **theme** What aggravating circumstances, if any, might you add to the list in the "CJ Issues" box titled "Aggravating and Mitigating Circumstances"? What mitigating circumstances, if any, might you add? Would you delete any? If so, why?

■ **lecture note** Describe the federal government's adoption of determinate sentencing under the 1984 Comprehensive Crime Control Act.

■ **theme** What is truth in sentencing? Why has it become an important issue?

■ **voluntary/advisory sentencing guidelines**
Recommended sentencing policies that are not required by law.

■ **presumptive sentencing** A model of criminal punishment that meets the following conditions: (1) The appropriate sentence for an offender convicted of a specific charge is presumed to fall within a range of sentences authorized by sentencing guidelines that are adopted by a legislatively created sentencing body, usually a sentencing commission. (2) Sentencing judges are expected to sentence within the range or to provide written justification for failing to do so. (3) There is a mechanism for review, usually appellate, of any departure from the guidelines.

■ **aggravating circumstances** Circumstances relating to the commission of a crime that make it more grave than the average instance of that crime.

■ **mitigating circumstances** Circumstances relating to the commission of a crime that may be considered to reduce the blameworthiness of the defendant.

■ **truth in sentencing** A close correspondence between the sentence imposed on an offender and the time actually served in prison.

sentencing practices also specify an anticipated release date for each sentenced offender.

In a report that traced the historical development of determinate sentencing, the National Council on Crime and Delinquency (NCCD) observed that "the term 'determinate sentencing' is generally used to refer to the sentencing reforms of the late 1970s." At that time, the legislatures of California, Illinois, Indiana, and Maine abolished the parole release decision and replaced indeterminate penalties with fixed (or flat) sentences that could be reduced by good-time provisions. In response to the then-growing determinate sentencing movement, a few states developed **voluntary/advisory sentencing guidelines** during the 1980s. These guidelines consisted of recommended sentencing policies that were not required by law but served as guides to judges. Voluntary/advisory sentencing guidelines are usually based on past sentencing practices and may build on either determinate or indeterminate sentencing structures. Florida, Maryland, Massachusetts, Michigan, Rhode Island, Utah, and Wisconsin all experimented with voluntary/advisory guidelines during the 1980s. Voluntary/advisory guidelines constitute a second form of structured sentencing.

A third model of structured sentencing employs what the NCCD calls "commission-based presumptive sentencing guidelines." **Presumptive sentencing** became common in the 1980s as states began to experiment with sentencing guidelines developed by sentencing commissions. These models differed from both determinate and voluntary/advisory guidelines in three respects. First, presumptive sentencing guidelines were not developed by the state legislature but by a sentencing commission that often represented a diverse array of criminal justice and sometimes private interests. Second, presumptive sentencing guidelines were explicit and highly structured, typically relying on a quantitative scoring instrument to classify the offense for which a person was to be sentenced. Third, the guidelines were

not voluntary in that judges had to adhere to the sentencing system or provide a written rationale for departing from it.

By 2010, the federal government and 16 states had established commission-created sentencing guidelines. Ten of the 16 states used presumptive sentencing guidelines; the remaining 6 relied on voluntary/advisory guidelines. As a consequence, sentencing guidelines authored by legislatively created sentencing commissions have become the most popular form of structured sentencing.

Guideline jurisdictions, which specified a presumptive sentence for a given offense, generally allowed for "aggravating" or "mitigating" circumstances—indicating a greater or lesser degree of culpability—which judges could take into consideration when imposing a sentence somewhat at variance from the presumptive term. **Aggravating circumstances** call for a tougher sentence and may include especially heinous behavior, cruelty, injury to more than one person, and so on. **Mitigating circumstances**, which indicate that a lesser sentence is called for, are generally similar to legal defenses, although in this case they only reduce criminal responsibility, not eliminate it. Mitigating circumstances include such things as cooperation with the investigating authority, surrender, and good character. Common aggravating and mitigating circumstances are listed in the "CJ Issues" box.

Federal Sentencing Guidelines

In 1984, with the passage of the Comprehensive Crime Control Act, the federal government adopted presumptive sentencing for nearly all federal offenders.[18] The act also addressed the issue of **truth in sentencing**. Under the old federal system, on average, good-time credits and parole reduced time served to about one-third of the actual sentence.[19] At the time, the sentencing practices of most states reflected the federal model. Although

■ **lecture note**   Explain that structured sentencing can result in sentences that mislead the public because inmates in some jurisdictions are still released early for good behavior and other reasons.

■ **lecture note**   Explain how federal sentencing guidelines focus on two main components: the offense level and the offender's criminal history. Give examples of various offense levels and criminal history categories to give students a clear sense of how this model works.

CJ | ISSUES
Aggravating and Mitigating Circumstances

Listed here are typical aggravating and mitigating circumstances that judges may consider in arriving at sentencing decisions in presumptive sentencing jurisdictions.

Aggravating Circumstances

- The defendant induced others to participate in the commission of the offense.
- The offense was especially heinous, atrocious, or cruel.
- The defendant was armed with or used a deadly weapon during the crime.
- The defendant committed the offense to avoid or prevent a lawful arrest or to escape from custody.
- The offense was committed for hire.
- The offense was committed against a current or former law enforcement or corrections officer while engaged in the performance of official duties or because of the past exercise of official duties.
- The defendant took advantage of a position of trust or confidence to commit the offense.

Mitigating Circumstances

- The defendant has no record of criminal convictions punishable by more than 60 days of imprisonment.
- The defendant has made substantial or full restitution.
- The defendant has been a person of good character or has had a good reputation in the community.
- The defendant aided in the apprehension of another felon or testified truthfully on behalf of the prosecution.
- The defendant acted under strong provocation, or the victim was a voluntary participant in the criminal activity or otherwise consented to it.
- The offense was committed under duress, coercion, threat, or compulsion that was insufficient to constitute a defense but that significantly reduced the defendant's culpability.
- At the time of the offense, the defendant was suffering from a mental or physical condition that was insufficient to constitute a defense but that significantly reduced the defendant's culpability.

Note: Recent U.S. Supreme Court rulings have held that facts influencing sentencing enhancements, other than prior record or admissions made by a defendant, must be determined by a jury, not by a judge.

---

sentence reductions may have benefited offenders, they often outraged victims, who felt betrayed by the sentencing process. The 1984 act nearly eliminated good-time credits[20] and began the process of phasing out federal parole and eliminating the U.S. Parole Commission (read more about the commission in Chapter 12).[21] The emphasis on truth in sentencing created, in effect, a sentencing environment of "what you get is what you serve." Truth in sentencing, described as "a close correspondence between the sentence imposed upon those sent to prison and the time actually served prior to prison release,"[22] has become an important policy focus of many state legislatures and the U.S. Congress. The Violent Crime Control and Law Enforcement Act of 1994 set aside $4 billion in federal prison construction funds (called Truth in Sentencing Incentive Funds) for states that adopt truth-in-sentencing laws and are able to guarantee that certain violent offenders will serve 85% of their sentences.

Title II of the Comprehensive Crime Control Act, called the Sentencing Reform Act of 1984,[23] established the nine-member U.S. Sentencing Commission. The commission, which continues to function today, comprises presidential appointees, including three federal judges. The Sentencing Reform Act limited the discretion of federal judges by mandating the creation of federal sentencing guidelines, which federal judges were required to follow. The sentencing commission was given the task of developing structured sentencing guidelines to reduce disparity, promote consistency and uniformity, and increase fairness and equity in sentencing.

The guidelines established by the commission took effect in November 1987 but quickly became embroiled in a series of legal disputes, some of which challenged Congress's authority to form the Sentencing Commission. In January 1989, in the case of **Mistretta v. U.S.**,[24] the U.S. Supreme Court held that Congress had acted appropriately in establishing the Sentencing Commission and that the guidelines developed by the commission could be applied in federal cases nationwide. The federal Sentencing Commission continues to meet at least once a year to review the effectiveness of the guidelines it created. Visit the U.S. Sentencing Commission via **http://www.ussc.gov**.

Federal Guideline Provisions

As originally established, federal sentencing guidelines specified a sentencing range from which judges had to choose. If a particular case had "atypical features," judges were allowed to depart from the guidelines. Departures were generally expected only

■ **lecture note**   Mention that plea bargains, which account for most of the criminal sentences handed down in federal courts, remain relatively unaffected by the structured sentencing guidelines adopted in 1984.

in the presence of aggravating or mitigating circumstances—a number of which are specified in the guidelines.[25] Aggravating circumstances may include the possession of a weapon during the commission of a crime, the degree of criminal involvement (whether the defendant was a leader or a follower in the criminal activity), and extreme psychological injury to the victim. Punishments also increase when a defendant violates a position of public or private trust, uses special skills to commit or conceal offenses, or has a criminal history. Defendants who express remorse, cooperate with authorities, or willingly make restitution may have their sentences reduced under the guidelines. Any departure from the guidelines may, however, become the basis for appellate review concerning the reasonableness of the sentence imposed, and judges who deviate from the guidelines were originally required to provide written reasons for doing so.

Federal sentencing guidelines are built around a table containing 43 rows, each corresponding to one offense level. The

> Federal sentencing guidelines are built around a table containing 43 rows, each corresponding to one offense level.

penalties associated with each level overlap those of the levels above and below to discourage unnecessary litigation. A person convicted of a crime involving $11,000, for example, and sentenced under the guidelines, is unlikely to receive a penalty substantially greater than if the amount had been somewhat less than $10,000. A change of six levels roughly doubles the sentence imposed under the guidelines, regardless of the level at which one starts. Because of their matrix-like quality, federal sentencing provisions have been referred to as *structured*. The federal sentencing table is available at **http://www.justicestudies.com/pubs/sentable.pdf**.

The sentencing table also contains six rows corresponding to the criminal history category into which an offender falls. Criminal history categories are determined on a point basis. Offenders earn points for previous convictions. Each prior sentence of imprisonment for more than one year and one month counts as three points. Two points are assigned for each prior prison sentence over six months or if the defendant committed the offense while on probation, parole, or work release. The system also assigns points for other types of previous convictions and for offenses committed less than two years after release from imprisonment. Points are added to determine the criminal history category into which an offender falls. Thirteen points or more are required for the highest category. At each offense level, sentences in the highest criminal history category are generally two to three times as severe as for the lowest category. The types of offenses for which federal offenders are sentenced, and how the proportion of those types have changed over time, can be seen in Figure 11-1.

Defendants may also move into the highest criminal history category by virtue of being designated a career offender. Under the sentencing guidelines, a defendant is a career offender if "(1) the defendant was at least 18 years old at the time of the…offense, (2) the…offense is a crime of violence or trafficking in a controlled substance, and (3) the defendant has at least two prior felony convictions of either a crime of violence or a controlled substance offense."[26]

According to the U.S. Supreme Court, an offender may be adjudged a career offender in a single hearing, even when previous convictions are lacking.

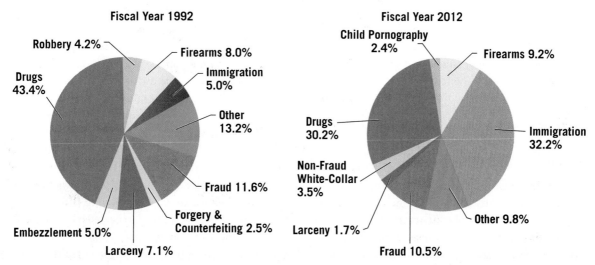

FIGURE 11-1 | Distribution of Federal Offenders in Each Primary Offense Category, Fiscal Years 1992 and 2012

Sources: U.S. Sentencing Commission, 2012 Datafile, USSC FY11; and the 1992 Datafile, USSC FY92.

■ **lecture note**   Discuss the impact that the adoption of structured sentencing has had on federal prison populations and on other aspects of the federal criminal justice system. Explain how federal sentencing has recently changed as a result of U.S. Supreme Court decisions.

Plea Bargaining under the Guidelines

Plea bargaining plays a major role in the federal judicial system. Approximately 90% of all federal sentences are the result of guilty pleas,[27] and the large majority of those stem from plea negotiations. In the words of former Sentencing Commission Chairman William W. Wilkins, Jr., "With respect to plea bargaining, the Commission has proceeded cautiously.... The Commission did not believe it wise to stand the federal criminal justice system on its head by making too drastic and too sudden a change in these practices."[28]

> Plea bargaining plays a major role in the federal judicial system.

Although the commission allowed plea bargaining to continue, it required that the agreement (1) be fully disclosed in the record of the court (unless there is an overriding and demonstrable reason why it should not be) and (2) detail the actual conduct of the offense. Under these requirements, defendants are unable to hide the actual nature of their offense behind a substitute plea. Information on the decision-making process itself is available to victims, the media, and the public.

In 1996, in the case of *Melendez* v. *U.S.*,[29] the U.S. Supreme Court held that a government motion requesting that a trial judge deviate from the federal sentencing guidelines as part of a cooperative plea agreement does not permit imposition of a sentence below a statutory minimum specified by law. In other words, under *Melendez*, although federal judges could depart from the guidelines, they could not accept plea bargains that would have resulted in sentences lower than the minimum required by law for a particular type of offense.

The Legal Environment of Structured Sentencing

A crucial critique of aggravating factors and their use in presumptive sentencing schemes was offered by the U.S. Supreme Court in 2000 in the case of **Apprendi v. New Jersey**.[30] In Apprendi, the Court questioned the fact-finding authority of judges in making sentencing decisions, ruling that other than the fact of a prior conviction, any fact that increases the penalty for a crime beyond the prescribed statutory *maximum* is, in effect, an element of the crime, which must be submitted to a jury and proved beyond a reasonable doubt. The case involved Charles Apprendi, a New Jersey defendant who pleaded guilty to unlawfully possessing a firearm—an offense that carried a

> In *Apprendi*, the Court questioned the fact-finding authority of judges in making sentencing decisions.

prison term of five to ten years under state law. Before sentence was imposed, however, the judge found that Apprendi had fired a number of shots into the home of an African American family living in his neighborhood and concluded that he had done so to frighten the family and convince them to move. The judge held that statements made by Apprendi allowed the offense to be classified as a hate crime, which required a longer prison term under the sentencing enhancement provision of New Jersey's hate-crime statute than did the weapons offense to which Apprendi had confessed. The Supreme Court, in overturning the judge's finding and sentence, took issue with the fact that after Apprendi pleaded guilty, an enhanced sentence was imposed without the benefit of a jury-based fact-finding process. The high court ruled that "under the Due Process Clause of the Fifth Amendment and the notice and jury trial guarantees of the Sixth Amendment, any fact (other than prior conviction) that increases the maximum penalty for a crime must be charged in an indictment, submitted to a jury, and proven beyond a reasonable doubt."

The *Apprendi* case essentially says that *requiring* sentencing judges to consider facts not proven to a jury violates the federal Constitution. It raised the question of whether judges anywhere could legitimately deviate from established sentencing guidelines or apply sentence enhancements based solely on judicial determinations of aggravating factors—especially when such determinations involve findings of fact that might otherwise be made by a jury.[31]

Since *Apprendi*, the Court has expanded the number and types of facts that must be decided by a jury. In 2010, for example, in the case of *U.S.* v. *O'Brien*,[32] the Court held that a determination that a firearm was a machinegun, as described by relevant law, is an element to be proved to a jury beyond a reasonable doubt, not a sentencing factor to be proved to a sentencing judge. The finding impacted a sentencing requirement that a 30-year minimum term of imprisonment be imposed for convictions involving the use of a fully automatic firearm during the commission of a crime.

The *O'Brien* case built upon the important 2004 case of **Blakely v. Washington**,[33] in which the U.S. Supreme Court effectively invalidated any state sentencing schema that allows judges rather than juries to determine any factor that increases a criminal sentence, except for prior convictions. The Court found that because the facts supporting Blakely's increased sentence were neither admitted by the defendant himself nor found by a jury, the sentence violated the Sixth Amendment right to trial by jury. The *Blakely* decision required that the sentencing laws of eight states be rewritten. Washington state legislators responded quickly and created a model law for other legislatures to emulate. The Washington law mandates that "the facts supporting aggravating circumstances shall be proved to a jury beyond a reasonable doubt," or, "if a jury is waived, proof shall be to the court beyond a reasonable doubt."

In 2007, in the case of *Cunningham* v. *California*,[34] the Supreme Court applied its reasoning in *Blakely* to California's determinate sentencing law, finding the law invalid because it placed sentence-elevating fact-finding within the judge's purview. As in *Blakely*, the California law was found to violate a defendant's Sixth Amendment right to trial by jury.

In 2005, in the combined cases of **U.S. v. Booker** [35] and *U.S.* v. *Fanfan*,[36] attention turned to the constitutionality of federal sentencing practices that relied on extra-verdict determinations of fact in the application of sentencing enhancements. In *Booker*, the U.S. Supreme Court issued what some have called an "extraordinary opinion,"[37] which actually encompasses two separate decisions. The combined cases brought two issues before the Court: (1) whether fact-finding done by judges under federal sentencing guidelines violates the Sixth Amendment right to trial by jury; and (2) if so, whether the guidelines are themselves unconstitutional. As in the preceding cases discussed in this section, the Court found that, on the first question, defendant Freddie Booker's drug-trafficking sentence had been improperly enhanced under the guidelines on the basis of facts found solely by a judge. In the view of the Court, the Sixth Amendment right to trial by jury is violated where, under a mandatory guidelines system, a sentence is increased because of an enhancement based on facts found by the judge that were not found by a jury nor admitted by the defendant.[38] Consequently, Booker's sentence was ruled unconstitutional and invalidated. On the second question, the Court reached a compromise and did not strike down the federal guidelines as many thought it would. Instead, it held that the guidelines could be *considered* by federal judges during sentencing but that they were no longer mandatory.

In effect, the decision in *Booker* and *Fanfan* turned the federal sentencing guidelines on their head, making them merely advisory and giving federal judges wide latitude in imposing punishments. While federal judges must still take the guidelines into consideration in reaching sentencing decisions, they do not have to follow them.

In 2007, in a continued clarification of *Booker*, the Supreme Court ruled that federal appeals courts that hear challenges from defendants about prison time may presume that federal criminal sentences are reasonable if they fall within U.S. Sentencing Guidelines. In that case, *Rita* v. *U.S.*,[39] the Court held that "even if the presumption increases the likelihood that the judge, not the jury, will find 'sentencing facts,' it does not violate the Sixth Amendment." The justices reasoned that "a nonbinding appellate reasonableness presumption for Guidelines sentences does not *require* the sentencing judge to impose a Guidelines sentence."

In another 2007 case, *Gall* v. *United States*,[40] the Court clarified its position on appellate review of sentencing decisions by lower courts when it held that "because the Guidelines are now advisory, appellate review of sentencing decisions is limited to determining whether they are 'reasonable.'"

In 2013, in the case of *Alleyne* v. *U.S.*, the Court ruled that any fact that increases the mandatory minimum sentence is an "element" that must be submitted to the jury.[41] In this case, a federal judge had increased an offender's sentence after investigating his prior convictions and finding that he had been convicted of multiple crimes.[42] The *Alleyne* court held that "*Apprendi*'s principle applies with equal force to facts increasing the mandatory minimum, for a fact triggering a mandatory minimum alters the prescribed range of sentences to which a criminal defendant is exposed." The justices also wrote, however, that: "This ruling does not mean that any fact that influences judicial discretion must be found by a jury." Nonetheless, the *Alleyne* decision makes it more difficult for the government to use the fact of a defendant's prior conviction to enhance a federal criminal sentence.

A recent report submitted to Congress by the U.S. Sentencing Commission found that "the sentencing guidelines remain the essential starting point for determining all federal sentences and continue to exert significant influence on federal sentencing trends over time."[43] The commission found that "the rate at which courts impose sentences within the applicable guideline range [stood] at 53.9 percent during the most recent time period studied."[44]

In light of the Court's decisions, it is now up to Congress to reconsider federal sentencing law following *Booker*—a process that has been under way for the past few years. In 2011, the U.S. Sentencing Commission called upon Congress "to exercise its power to direct sentencing policy by enacting [new] mandatory minimum penalties" in modified format.[45] Read the Commission's 2013 congressional report about the impact of *U.S.* v. *Booker* on federal sentencing at **http://www.justicestudies.com/pdf/sentencing2013.pdf.**

Three-Strikes Laws

In the spring of 1994, California legislators passed the state's now-famous "three strikes and you're out" bill. Amid much fanfare, Governor Pete Wilson signed the "three-strikes" measure into law, calling it "the toughest and most sweeping crime bill in California history."[46]

California's original three-strikes law, which was retroactive in that it counts offenses committed before the date the legislation was signed, required a sentence of 25 years to life for three-time felons with convictions for two or more serious or violent prior offenses. Criminal offenders facing a "second strike" could receive up to double the normal sentence for their most recent offense. Parole consideration was not available until at least 80% of the sentence had been served.

Today, about half of the states have passed three-strikes legislation. At the federal level, the Violent Crime Control and Law Enforcement Act of 1994 contains a three-strikes provision that mandates life imprisonment for federal criminals convicted of three violent felonies or drug offenses.

Questions remain, however, about the effectiveness of three-strikes legislation, and many people are concerned about its impact on the justice system. A 2001 study of the original California legislation and its consequences concluded that three-strikes laws are overrated.[47] According to the study, which was conducted by the Washington, D.C.-based Sentencing Project, "California's three-strikes law has increased the number and severity of sentences for nonviolent offenders—and contributed to the aging of the prison population—but has had no significant effect on the state's decline in crime."

A 2012 review of three-strikes legislation found that 16 states had modified such laws in response to difficult economic conditions; this means that the high cost of imprisonment is leading legislatures to rethink long prison terms. Modifications have included giving judges more discretion in sentencing and narrowing the types of crimes that count as a "strike."

Practically speaking, California's three-strikes law has had a dramatic impact on the state's criminal justice system. "'Three strikes and you're out' sounds great to a lot of people," says Alan Schuman, president of the American Probation and Parole Association. "But no one will cop a plea when it gets to the third time around. We will have more trials, and this whole country works on plea bargaining and pleading guilty, not jury trials," Schuman said at a meeting of the association. In an early study conducted by RAND, it was estimated that full enforcement of the law could cost as much as $5.5 billion annually—or $300 per California taxpayer per year.

In 2003, in two separate cases, the U.S. Supreme Court upheld the three-strikes California convictions of Gary Ewing and Leandro Andrade in California.[48] Ewing, who had four prior felony convictions, had received a 25-years-to-life sentence following his conviction for felony grand theft of three golf clubs. Andrade, who also had a long record, was sentenced to 50 years in prison for two petty theft convictions.[49] In writing for the Court in the *Ewing* case, Justice Sandra Day O'Connor noted that states should be able to decide when repeat offenders "must be isolated from society…to protect the public safety," even when nonserious crimes trigger the lengthy sentence. In deciding these two cases, both of which were based on Eighth Amendment claims, the Court found that it is not cruel and unusual punishment to impose a possible life term for a nonviolent felony when the defendant has a history of serious or violent convictions.

In November, 2012, California voters overwhelmingly approved a change to their state's three-strikes law.[50] The changes mean that now only two categories of offenders can be sentenced as three-strikers: (1) those who commit new "serious or violent" felonies as their third offense, and (2) previously released murderers, rapists, or child molesters who are convicted of a new third strike, even if it is not a "serious or violent" felony. Another California ballot initiative, Proposition 47, passed in 2014 and changed many crime from felonies to misdemeanors. Consequently, most instances of drug possession and all property crimes involving amounts of less than $950 are no longer felonies in California. Both the 2012 and 2014 changes allow inmates who were sentenced under older laws to petition for release. Estimates are that at least 10,000 inmates imprisoned in the state at the time of the propositions' passage are now eligible for release.[51]

Mandatory Sentencing

Mandatory sentencing, another form of structured sentencing, deserves special mention.[52] Mandatory sentencing is just what its name implies: a structured sentencing scheme that mandates clearly enumerated punishments for specific offenses or for habitual offenders convicted of a series of crimes. Mandatory sentencing, because it is truly *mandatory*, differs from presumptive sentencing, which allows at least a limited amount of judicial discretion within ranges established by published guidelines. Some mandatory sentencing laws require only modest mandatory prison terms (e.g., three years for armed robbery), whereas others are much more far-reaching.

Typical of far-reaching mandatory sentencing schemes are the "three-strikes" laws just described. Three-strikes laws (and, in some jurisdictions, two-strikes laws) require mandatory sentences (sometimes life in prison without the possibility of parole) for offenders

> Three-strikes laws require mandatory sentences for offenders convicted of a third serious felony.

■ diversion   The official suspension of criminal or juve-nile proceedings against an alleged offender at any point after a recorded justice system intake, but before the entering of a

judgment, and referral of that person to a treatment or care program administered by a nonjustice or private agency. Also, release without referral.

Noise offenders in Fort Lupton, Colorado, were recently ordered to endure an hour of unpopular music. The music, selected by a judge who wanted to punish them for disturbing the tranquility of the community, included songs by Bing Crosby and Willie Nelson. Will alter-native sentences like this deter others from committing similar offenses?

convicted of a third (or second) serious felony. Such mandatory sentencing enhancements are aimed at deterring known and po-tentially violent offenders and are intended to incapacitate con-victed criminals through long-term incarceration.

Three-strikes laws impose longer prison terms than most earlier mandatory minimum sentencing laws. California's origi-nal three-strikes law, for example, required that offenders who were convicted of a violent crime and who had two prior con-victions serve a minimum of 25 years in prison. The law dou-bled prison terms for offenders convicted of a second violent felony.[53] Three-strikes laws also vary in breadth. The laws of some jurisdictions stipulate that both of the prior convictions and the current one be for violent felonies; others require only that the prior convictions be for violent felonies. Some three-strikes laws count only prior adult convictions, whereas others permit consideration of juvenile crimes. As noted, California's 2012 and 2014 revisions of its three-strikes laws reduce their ap-plication to only two categories of offenders.

By passing mandatory sentencing laws, legislators con-veyed the message that certain crimes are deemed espe-cially grave and that people who commit them deserve, and should expect, harsh sanctions. These laws were often passed in response to public outcries following heinous or well-publicized crimes.

Research findings on the impact of mandatory sentencing laws on the criminal justice system have been summarized by British criminologist Michael Tonry.[54] Tonry found that under mandatory sentencing, officials tend to make earlier and more selective arrest, charging, and **diversion** decisions. They also tend to bargain less and to bring more cases to trial.

In an analysis of federal sentencing guidelines, other re-searchers found that blacks received longer sentences than whites, not because they received differential treatment by judges but because they constitute the large majority of those convicted of trafficking in crack cocaine (versus powdered cocaine)[55]—a crime that Congress had at one time singled out for especially harsh mandatory penalties. In 2006, for example, 82% of those sentenced under federal crack cocaine laws were black, and only 8.8% were white, even though more than two-thirds of people who used crack cocaine were white.[56] This seeming disparity led the U.S. Congress to eliminate the distinction between crack and regular cocaine for purposes of sentencing, and in 2010 President Barack Obama signed the federal Fair Sentencing Act (FSA)[57] into law. The act reduced a previous disparity in the amounts of powder cocaine and crack cocaine specified by the federal sentencing guidelines and eliminated what had been a mandatory minimum sentence under federal law for simple pos-session of crack cocaine. As a result of the FSA, a first conviction

■ **lecture note**   Discuss the impact of get-tough-on-crime policies, including various sentencing policies, on the prison population today. Point out that while crime rates are decreasing, incarceration rates are increasing. Ask students whether they think that the increasing rates of incarceration

may have caused the reduced crime rates and explain why this may not actually be the case (for example, point out that many offenders currently are being incarcerated for violations of drug laws, rather than violent or property crimes).

for simple possession of any amount of crack cocaine, like simple possession of powder cocaine, is subject to a penalty range of zero to one year of imprisonment regardless of quantity.

In 2014, in an effort to modernize drug sentencing policy and to focus the resources of the criminal justice system squarely on violent offenders and public safety risks, Senator Dick Durbin (R-Illinois) introduced legislation in the U.S. Senate called the Smarter Sentencing Act. If passed into law, the act would adjust federal mandatory sentencing guidelines for a variety of crimes. The intent is to reduce the size of the federal prison population and costs associated with it. The proposed law reduces mandatory sentences for drug offenses and expands the ability of nonviolent offenders to reduce their sentences under the federal Fair Sentencing Act of 2010.[58]

Sentencing and Today's Prison Crisis

Over the past thirty years, mandatory sentencing, three-strikes laws, and other get-tough on crime and criminals policies have dramatically increased the use of incarceration as a sentencing option. Although crime rates began to fall throughout the nation

beginning in the mid-1990s (see Chapter 2), more and more convicted offenders were sent to prison. Some people have argued that increasing rates of imprisonment produced lower crime rates, but it is noteworthy that many new prison admissions came from drug convictions and were largely the result of the nation's "war on drugs" (discussed in more detail in Chapter 15), not the consequence of violent or property crimes. As you'll recall from Chapter 2, drug crimes are excluded from the calculations used by the FBI and BJS in determining crime rates. Figure 11-2 contrasts combined rates of major violent and property crimes with the growth of incarceration between 1978 and 2012. As can be seen, while crime rates dipped by more than 30%, the number of persons sent to prison increased by almost 300%.

Rising incarceration rates have led to significantly overcrowded prisons, and have reached the point where they are imposing huge financial burdens on both state and federal governments. In 2014, the Washington, D.C.-based Center on Budget and Policy Priorities found that sentencing policies, not crime rates, are the

> Rising incarceration rates have reached the point where they are imposing huge financial burdens on both state and federal governments.

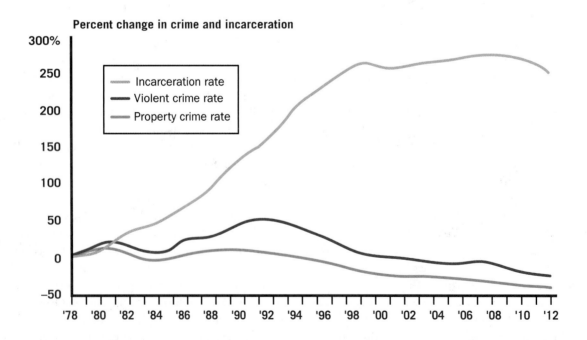

Percent change in crime and incarceration

FIGURE 11-2 | Incarceration Rates vs. Crime Rates in the United States, 1978–2012.

Source: U.S. Department of Justice, Bureau of Justice Statistics; FBI, Uniform Crime Reports; and Center on Budget and Policy Priorities.

CJ | CAREERS
Medicolegal Death Investigator

Name. Leracia Blalock

Position. Medicolegal Death Investigator, Office of the Coroner for Adams and Broomfield Counties, Brighton, Colorado

Colleges attended. The Ohio State University

Major. Bachelor of Science in Forensic Biology

Year hired. 2014

Leracia Blalock

Please give a brief description of your job.
The term "medicolegal" pertains to medicine and the law. A medicolegal death investigator works in the combined field of medicine and law, and is commonly referred to as a "coroner investigator" or a "death investigator." As a death investigator, I am responsible for establishing a differential diagnosis of the cause and manner of death by conducting a competent and thorough investigation of the circumstances surrounding death; I also determine the decedent's identity and notify the next-of-kin that the death has occurred. In Adams and Broomfield Counties (Colorado), all deaths are reported to the Office of the Coroner. It is my responsibility to determine when the circumstances of a death require further investigation in accordance with Colorado Revised Statutes. A coroner's office is responsible for accurately determining the cause and manner of death. The cause of death refers to the injury or disease that brought about the death. The manner of death refers to the circumstances surrounding the cause of death. In Colorado, the manner of death is classified into one of five categories: natural, accident, homicide, suicide, and undetermined. Most deaths are natural and occur under the attendance of a physician, such as in a hospital. A death investigator will spend the majority of his/her time liaising with physicians to establish the manner and cause of death. If a death is unattended, such as a residential death, a death investigator will liaise with other law enforcement officials, crime scene investigators, families, and witnesses in order to conduct a competent investigation of the circumstances surrounding the death. It is imperative that the scene investigation is thorough so that the cause and manner of death can be accurately determined. Despite how media depicts scene investigations, a death investigator is responsible for completing a forensic examination of the scene and the deceased; documenting things such as trauma, injuries, identifying marks, postmortem changes, and indications of disease processes and exposure to toxins. After the scene investigation is complete, a death investigator will either release the body to a mortuary or transport the body to the coroner's office for further investigation, such as an autopsy. Other major job duties include collecting and inventorying the decedent's medications, securing the decedent's property, identifying and collecting evidence, reviewing medical records, assisting in autopsies, and testifying in court.

What appealed to you most about the position when you applied for it? I have always had an interest in a law enforcement career. However, my passion was for forensic death investigations. I wanted a career that had a primary emphasis on death investigations in addition to liaising with other law enforcement agencies. Once I obtained relative experience in the field of forensics and death investigation, I knew that this career path was meant for me.

How would you describe the interview process? The interview process, qualifications, and background investigation vary by counties and districts. At the location in which I was hired, the interview process started with a ten-hour job "shadow." During this time I observed the shift of a death investigator employee and I was able to see what a typical work day is like for a death investigator. This helped to determine if the job was right for me. After the shadow experience, I underwent an interview with the Chief Coroner, Chief Deputy Coroner, Operations Manager, and a representative from Human Resources. Following this, I had to pass an extensive criminal background check including a polygraph test, a psychological evaluation, a medical examination, and a drug screening. Lastly, a written test was administered to determine my knowledge in death investigations. Typical candidates have a degree or prior experience in law enforcement, forensic science, pharmaceuticals, biology, chemistry, anthropology, or death investigations.

Prior to being hired, I was a volunteer in the Medicolegal Death Investigator Reserve Academy at the Office of the Coroner for Adams and Broomfield Counties. During this program I assisted death investigators by collecting and logging property and medications, photographing forensic evidence, and completing forensic external examinations.

What is a typical day like? Our office has a total of eight death investigators. We operate on a rotating schedule in order to provide 24/7 coverage; therefore, one investigator will be assigned per shift, with a two-hour overlap period between shifts. The primary objective, when you arrive at work, is to brief with the previous shift and load up the van for any scenes you may need to attend to. You have to be prepared to leave for a scene at any minute during your shift. The morning shift typically consists of assisting other investigators with any follow-up, such as contacting a physician during normal business hours, whereas the night shift typically consists of logging medications and property, etc. In general, every investigator is responsible for assisting with any tasks that need to be completed, in addition to handling any calls, death reports, or scene responses in a timely manner and completing the paperwork. If law enforcement officials request a coroner's response to a scene, then you are responsible for documenting the scene with photographs and notes; interviewing family members, friends, and witnesses; completing a forensic examination on the decedent; and making death notifications to the next-of-kin.

What qualities/characteristics are most helpful for this job? Helpful characteristics include empathy, compassion, energy, and the ability to adapt. This job requires you to constantly keep an open mind and to think on your feet. In addition, you have be able to effectively work independently and with others.

What is a typical starting salary? In general, the average starting wage for a death investigator in the United States is approximately $20.00 per hour.

What is the salary potential as you move up into higher-level jobs? There are multiple career opportunities within the field of forensics. The increase in salary potential varies.

What advice would you give someone in college beginning studies in criminal justice? There are many career-oriented opportunities available for college students. Obtain career-oriented internships and classes to get your foot in the door, and network accordingly. Lastly, don't be afraid to take a risk—you never know what opportunities will result from it.

■ **alternative sentencing**   The use of court-ordered community service, home detention, day reporting, drug treatment, psychological counseling, victim–offender programming, or intensive supervision in lieu of other, more traditional sanctions such as imprisonment and fines.

■ **justice reinvestment**   A concept that prioritizes the use of alternatives to incarceration for persons convicted of eligible nonviolent offenses, standardizes the use of risk assessment instruments in pretrial detention, authorizes the use of early-release mechanisms for prisoners who meet eligibility requirements, and reinvests savings from such initiatives into effective crime-prevention programs.

biggest drivers of rising incarceration rates. The center also noted that:

- Seen historically, crime rates have risen and fallen independently of incarceration rates.
- The proportion of criminal offenders sent to prison has climbed dramatically over time.
- Lengths of prison stays have significantly increased for all types of crime.
- High levels of incarceration impose significant human economic costs without necessarily making society any safer.
- High incarceration rates present mounting financial challenges to governments at all levels.[59]

Innovations in Sentencing

In an ever-growing number of cases, innovative judges in certain jurisdictions are using discretionary sentencing to impose truly unique punishments.

Faced with prison overcrowding, high incarceration costs, and continued public calls for retribution, some judges have used shaming strategies to deter wrongdoers. At least one Florida court ordered those convicted of drunk driving to put a "Convicted DUI" sticker on their license plates. Similarly, a few years ago, Boston courts began ordering men convicted of sexual solicitation to spend time sweeping streets in Chinatown, an area known for prostitution. The public was invited to watch men sentenced to the city's "John Sweep" program clean up streets and alleyways littered with used condoms and sexual paraphernalia. In still other examples, an Arkansas judge made shoplifters walk in front of the stores they stole from, carrying signs describing their crimes, and in California, a purse snatcher was ordered to wear noisy tap dancing shoes whenever he went out in public.[60]

There is considerable support in criminal justice field for shaming as a crime-reduction strategy. Australian criminologist John Braithwaite, for example, found shaming to be a particularly effective strategy because, he said, it holds the potential to enhance moral awareness among offenders, thereby building conscience and increasing inner control.[61] Dan Kahan, a professor at the University of Chicago Law School, points out that "shame supplies the main motive why people obey the law, not so much because they're afraid of formal sanctions, but because they care what people think about them."[62]

Whether public shaming will grow in popularity as an **alternative sentencing** strategy is unclear. What is clear, however, is that the American public and an ever-growing number of judicial officials are now looking for workable alternatives to traditional sentencing options.

Questions about Alternative Sanctions

Alternative sanctions include the use of court-ordered community service, home detention, day reporting, drug treatment, psychological counseling, victim–offender programming, or intensive supervision in lieu of other, more traditional, sanctions like imprisonment and fines. Many of these strategies are discussed in more detail in the next chapter.

It is important to note here, however, that a new framework, known as justice reinvestment, is starting to make a significant impact on sentencing authorities. **Justice reinvestment** is a concept that prioritizes the use of alternatives to incarceration for persons convicted of eligible nonviolent offenses, standardizes the use of risk assessments instruments in pretrial detention, authorizes the use of early-release mechanisms for prisoners who meet eligibility requirements, and reinvests savings from such initiatives into effective crime-prevention programs.[63] In general, justice reinvestment strategies included efforts to scale back certain harsh sentencing provisions and to reduce returns to prison for probation and parole violators.

> Justice reinvestment prioritizes the use of alternatives to incarceration for persons convicted of eligible nonviolent offenses.

As the term itself indicates, some recent legislative measures associated with the strategy also include statutory mechanisms for reinvesting savings that have been achieved through reducing prison populations into other aspects of the criminal justice system—including evidence-based in-prison treatment programs and local law enforcement efforts designed to deter crime.[64] One of those legislative initiatives, North Carolina's 2011 Justice Reinvestment Act, expands post-release supervision to all felons and limits the authority of parole officials and judges to revoke post-release supervision. The law also requires supervision agencies to concentrate resources on high-risk individuals and empowers probation officers to employ sanctions to increase accountability in a manner that is both cost-effective and proven to have a greater impact on reducing recidivism.[65]

■ **presentence investigation (PSI)**   The examination of a convicted offender's background prior to sentencing.

Presentence examinations are generally conducted by probation or parole officers and are submitted to sentencing authorities.

Finally, the North Carolina law ensures that treatment programs are targeted to people who have the greatest treatment needs and are most likely to reoffend.

A report by the Sentencing Project identified Georgia, Hawaii, Kansas, Missouri, Oklahoma, and Pennsylvania as leaders in the justice reinvestment movement.[66] Texas might be added to the list, as a 2013 study by the Council of State Governments determined, for example, that Texas saved almost $2 billion over five years by focusing on justice reinvestment efforts, including savings of $1.5 billion on prison constructions and more than $340 million in averted annual operations costs of confinement facilities. By 2013, more than half of the states had implemented comprehensive justice reinvestment programs designed to shift resources from incarceration toward treatment and prevention.

As prison populations continue to rise, alternative strategies are likely to become even more attractive. A number of questions must be answered, however, before most alternative sanctions can be employed with confidence, including whether alternative sentencing programs increase the threat to public safety, whether alternative sanctions are cost-effective, and how program outcomes should be judged.[67] Learn more about the Justice Reinvestment Initiative, a project of the Council of State Governments and the Bureau of Justice Assistance, at **http://www.justicereinvestment.org.**

The Presentence Investigation

Before imposing sentence, a judge may request information on the background of a convicted defendant. This is especially true in indeterminate sentencing jurisdictions, where judges retain considerable discretion in selecting sanctions. One of the drivers behind many sentencing decisions today is offender risk and needs assessment (RNA). In one report, the National Center for State Courts identified certain factors that increase the likelihood of reoffending, the presence of which suggest that prison terms and removal from the community are better sentencing options than probation.[68] High-risk factors identified include (1) antisocial personality patterns (impulsiveness, pleasure seeking, aggressive and irritable traits), (2) procriminal attitudes (negative attitudes toward the law), (3) social supports for crime (criminal friends), (4) substance abuse, (5) family and marital problems, (6) poor school or work performance, and (7) a lack of involvement in prosocial recreational and leisure activities.[69] Factors that are likely to increase the chances for rehabilitation, and which might indicate that probation or reduced prison

terms are appropriate, include a good job record, satisfactory educational attainment, strong family ties, church attendance, no prior arrests for violent offenses, and psychological stability.

Information about a defendant's background often comes to the judge in the form of a **presentence investigation (PSI)** report. The task of preparing presentence reports usually falls to a probation or parole office. Presentence reports take one of three forms: (1) a detailed written report on the defendant's personal and criminal history, including an assessment of present conditions in the defendant's life (often called the *long form*);

> Information about a defendant's background often comes to the judge in the form of a presentence investigation.

(2) an abbreviated written report summarizing the information most likely to be useful in a sentencing decision (the *short form*); and (3) a verbal report to the court made by the investigating officer based on field notes but structured according to established categories. A presentence report is much like a résumé, except that it focuses on what might be regarded as negative as well as positive life experiences.

The data on which a presentence report is based come from a variety of sources. The Federal Bureau of Investigation's National Crime Information Center (NCIC), begun in 1967, contains computerized information on people wanted for criminal offenses throughout the United States. Individual jurisdictions also maintain criminal records repositories that can provide comprehensive files on the criminal history of those who have been processed by the justice system.

Sometimes the defendant provides much of the information in the presentence report. In this case, efforts must be made to corroborate the defendant's information. Unconfirmed data are generally marked on the report as "defendant-supplied data" or simply "unconfirmed."

In a presentence report, almost all third-party data are subject to ethical and legal considerations. The official records of almost all agencies and organizations, though often an ideal source of information, are protected by state and federal privacy requirements. In particular, the federal Privacy Act of 1974[70] may limit access to these records. Investigators must first check on the legal availability of all records before requesting them and must receive in writing the defendant's permission to access the records. Other public laws, among them the federal Freedom of Information Act,[71] may make the presentence report available to the defendant, although courts and court officers have generally been held to be exempt from the provision of such statutes.

The final section of a presentence report is usually devoted to the investigating officer's recommendations. A recommendation may be made in favor of probation, split sentencing, a term

■ **lecture note**   Describe the usefulness of presentence reports in assisting judges in determining the appropriate kind and length of sentence for
convicted offenders.

■ **theme**   What are the three forms that presentence reports may take?
Do you think written or verbal reports are better? Which type do you think
would have the most influence on the judge's sentencing decision?

■ **lecture note**   Discuss the growing victims' rights movement, and draw
students' attention to the demand for a victims' Constitutional amendment.

of imprisonment, or any other sentencing option available in the jurisdiction. Participation in community service programs or in drug- or substance-abuse programs may be recommended for probationers. Most judges are willing to accept the report writer's recommendation because they recognize the professionalism of the presentence investigator and because they know that the investigator may be assigned to supervise the defendant if he or she is sentenced to a community alternative.

Jurisdictions vary in their use of presentence reports. Federal law mandates presentence reports in federal criminal courts and specifies 15 topical areas that each report must cover. The 1984 federal Determinate Sentencing Act directs report writers to include information on the classification of the offense and of the defendant under the offense-level and criminal history categories established by the statute. Some states require presentence reports only in felony cases, and others require them in cases where the defendant faces the possibility of incarceration for six months or more. Other states have no requirement for presentence reports beyond those ordered by a judge.

Report writing, rarely anyone's favorite task, may seriously tax the limited resources of probation agencies. In September 2004, officers from the New York City Department of Probation wrote 2,414 presentence investigation reports for adult offenders and 461 reports for juvenile offenders, averaging about 10 reports per probation officer per month.[72]

victims in the filing of civil suits to recoup financial losses directly from the offender.

About the same time, voters in California approved Proposition 8, a resolution that called for changes in the state's constitution to reflect concern for victims. A continuing goal of victims' advocacy groups is an amendment to the U.S. Constitution, which such groups say is needed to provide the same kind of fairness to victims that is routinely accorded to defendants. In the past, for example, the National Victims' Constitutional Amendment Passage (NVCAP) has sought to add a phrase to the Sixth Amendment: "likewise, the victim, in every criminal prosecution, shall have the right to be present and to be heard at all critical stages of judicial proceedings." The NVCAP now advocates the addition of a new amendment to the U.S. Constitution. Visit the NVCAP via **http://www.nvcap.org**.

In September 1996, a victims' rights constitutional amendment—Senate Joint Resolution 65—was proposed by a bipartisan committee in the U.S. Congress,[76] but problems of wording and terminology prevented its passage. A revised amendment was

> A continuing goal of victims' advocacy groups is an amendment to the U.S. Constitution.

The Victim—Forgotten No Longer

Thanks to a grassroots resurgence of concern for the plight of victims that began in this country in the early 1970s, the sentencing process now frequently includes consideration of the needs of victims and their survivors.[73] In times past, although victims might testify at trial, the criminal justice system frequently downplayed a victim's experience, including the psychological trauma engendered both by having been a victim and by having to endure the criminal proceedings that bring the criminal to justice. That changed in 1982, when the President's Task Force on Victims of Crime gave focus to a burgeoning victims' rights movement and urged the widespread expansion of victims' assistance programs during what was then their formative period.[74] Victims' assistance programs today offer services in the areas of crisis intervention and follow-up counseling and help victims secure their rights under the law.[75] Following successful prosecution, some victims' assistance programs also advise

U.S. Attorney General Eric H. Holder, Jr., speaking at the 2009 Office for Victims of Crime Candlelight Ceremony. What more can the justice system do for crime victims? What more *should* it do?

■ **theme** Do you support a constitutional amendment setting forth the rights of victims in a criminal proceeding? If so, what provisions should the amendment contain? If not, why not?

■ **theme** If the rights of the victim and the rights of the suspect conflict in some way, whose rights should have a higher priority and why? What if the rights of the victim conflict with the rights of a convicted offender (as opposed to an unconvicted suspect)?

proposed in 1998,[77] but its wording was too restrictive for it to gain endorsement from victims' organizations.[78] The next year, a new amendment was proposed by the Senate Judiciary Committee's Subcommittee on the Constitution, Federalism, and Property, but it did not make it to the Senate floor. The U.S. Department of Justice, which had previously supported the measure, reversed its position due to a provision in the proposed amendment that gives crime victims the right to be notified of any state or federal grant of clemency. The U.S. attorney general apparently believed that the provision would impede the power of the president. The legislation also lacked the support of then–President Bill Clinton and was officially withdrawn by its sponsors in 2000.

Although a victims' rights amendment to the federal Constitution may not yet be a reality, more than 30 states have passed their own victims' rights amendments.[79] According to the NVCAP, California Proposition 9, or the Victims' Rights and Protection Act of 2008 (also known as Marsy's Law), is the most comprehensive victims' bill of rights of any state in the nation.[80] Proposition 9, which appeared on the November 4, 2008, ballot in California, passed with 53.8% of the vote. It amended the California Constitution by adding new provisions that provide victims in California with a number of specifically enforceable rights (see the "CJ Issues" box).

At the federal level, the 1982 Victim and Witness Protection Act (VWPA)[81] requires judges to consider victim-impact statements at federal sentencing hearings and places responsibility for their creation on federal probation officers. In 1984, the federal Victims of Crime Act (VOCA) was enacted with substantial bipartisan support. VOCA authorized federal funding to help states establish victims' assistance and victims' compensation programs. Under VOCA, the U.S. Department of Justice's Office for Victims of Crime provides a significant source of both funding and information for victims' assistance programs. The rights of victims were further strengthened under the Violent Crime Control and Law Enforcement Act of 1994, which created a federal right of allocution, or right to speak, for victims of violent and sex crimes. This gave victims the right to speak at the sentencing of their assailants. The 1994 law also requires sex offenders and child molesters convicted under federal law to pay restitution to their victims and prohibits the diversion of federal victims' funds to other programs. Other provisions of the 1994 law provide civil rights remedies for victims of felonies motivated by gender bias and extend "rape shield law" protections to civil cases and to all criminal cases, prohibiting inquiries into a victim's sexual history. A significant feature of the 1994 law can be found in a subsection titled the Violence against Women Act (VAWA). The VAWA, which provides financial support for police, prosecutors, and victims' services in cases involving sexual violence or domestic abuse, is discussed in greater detail in Chapter 2.

Much of the philosophical basis of today's victims' movement can be found in the restorative justice model, which was discussed briefly earlier in this chapter. Restorative justice emphasizes offender accountability and victim reparation. Restorative justice also provides the basis for victims' compensation programs, which are another means of recognizing the needs of crime victims. Today, all 50 states have passed legislation providing for monetary payments to victims of crime. Such payments are primarily designed to compensate victims for medical expenses and lost wages. All existing programs require that applicants meet certain eligibility criteria, and most set limits on the maximum amount of compensation that can be received.

> Today, all 50 states have passed legislation providing for monetary payments to victims of crime.

Generally disallowed are claims from victims who are significantly responsible for their own victimization, such as those who are injured in fights they provoke. In 2002, California's victims' compensation program, the largest in the nation, provided $117 million to more than 50,000 victims for crime-related expenses.

In 2001, the USA PATRIOT Act amended the Victims of Crime Act of 1984 to make victims of terrorism and their families eligible for victims' compensation payments.[82] It also created an antiterrorism emergency reserve fund to help provide compensation to victims of terrorism. A year earlier, in November 2000, the federal Office for Victims of Crime (OVC) created the Terrorism and International Victims Unit (TIVU) to develop and manage programs and initiatives that help victims of domestic and international terrorism, mass violence, and crimes that have transnational dimensions.[83]

In 2004, the U.S. Senate passed the Crime Victims' Rights Act[84] as part of the Justice for All Act. Some saw the legislation as at least a partial statutory alternative to a constitutional victims' rights amendment. The Crime Victims' Rights Act establishes statutory rights for victims of federal crimes and gives them the necessary legal authority to assert those rights in federal court. The act grants the following rights to victims of federal crimes:[85]

1. The right to be reasonably protected from the accused
2. The right to reasonable, accurate, and timely notice of any public proceeding involving the crime or of any release or escape of the accused
3. The right to be included in any such public proceeding
4. The right to be reasonably heard at any public proceeding involving release, plea, or sentencing

■ **lecture note**   Discuss the purpose of victim-impact statements and the role they play during a sentencing hearing.

■ **victim-impact statement**   The in-court use of victim- or survivor-supplied information by sentencing authorities seeking to make an informed sentencing decision.

CJ | ISSUES
Victims' Rights in California

In order to preserve and protect a victim's rights to justice and due process, a victim shall be entitled to the following rights:

1. To be treated with fairness and respect for his or her privacy and dignity, and to be free from intimidation, harassment, and abuse, throughout the criminal or juvenile justice process.

2. To be reasonably protected from the defendant and persons acting on behalf of the defendant.

3. To have the safety of the victim and the victim's family considered in fixing the amount of bail and release conditions for the defendant.

4. To prevent the disclosure of confidential information or records to the defendant, the defendant's attorney, or any other person acting on behalf of the defendant, which could be used to locate or harass the victim or the victim's family or which disclose confidential communications made in the course of medical or counseling treatment, or which are otherwise privileged or confidential by law.

5. To refuse an interview, deposition, or discovery request by the defendant, the defendant's attorney, or any other person acting on behalf of the defendant, and to set reasonable conditions on the conduct of any such interview to which the victim consents.

6. To reasonable notice of and to reasonably confer with the prosecuting agency, upon request, regarding the arrest of the defendant if known by the prosecutor, the charges filed, the determination whether to extradite the defendant, and, upon request, to be notified of and informed before any pretrial disposition of the case.

7. To reasonable notice of all public proceedings, including delinquency proceedings, upon request, at which the defendant and the prosecutor are entitled to be present and of all parole or other post-conviction release proceedings, and to be present at all such proceedings.

8. To be heard, upon request, at any proceeding, including any delinquency proceeding, involving a post-arrest release decision, plea, sentencing, post-conviction release decision, or any proceeding in which a right of the victim is at issue.

9. To a speedy trial and a prompt and final conclusion of the case and any related post-judgment proceedings.

10. To provide information to a probation department official conducting a pre-sentence investigation concerning the impact of the offense on the victim and the victim's family and any sentencing recommendations before the sentencing of the defendant.

11. To receive, upon request, the pre-sentence report when available to the defendant, except for those portions made confidential by law.

12. To be informed, upon request, of the conviction, sentence, place and time of incarceration, or other disposition of the defendant, the scheduled release date of the defendant, and the release of or the escape by the defendant from custody.

13. To restitution.

14. To the prompt return of property when no longer needed as evidence.

15. To be informed of all parole procedures, to participate in the parole process, to provide information to the parole authority to be considered before the parole of the offender, and to be notified, upon request, of the parole or other release of the offender.

16. To have the safety of the victim, the victim's family, and the general public considered before any parole or other post-judgment release decision is made.

17. To be informed of the rights enumerated in paragraphs (1) through (16).

Reference: Section 28(e) of Article I of the California Constitution.

---

5. The right to confer with the federal prosecutor handling the case
6. The right to full and timely restitution as provided by law
7. The right to proceedings free from unreasonable delay
8. The right to be treated with fairness and with respect for the victim's dignity and privacy

In addition to establishing these rights, the legislation expressly requires federal courts to ensure that they are afforded to victims. In like manner, federal law enforcement officials are required to make their "best efforts to see that crime victims are notified of, and accorded," these rights. To teach citizens about the rights of victims of crime, the federal government created a website that you can access via **http://www.crimevictims.gov**.

It includes an online directory of crime victims' services, which can be searched locally, nationally, and internationally. A user-friendly database of victims' rights laws can be found online at **http://www.victimlaw.info**.

Victim-Impact Statements

Another consequence of the national victims' rights movement has been a call for the use of **victim-impact statements** before sentencing. A victim-impact statement is generally a written document describing the losses, suffering, and trauma experienced by the crime victim or by the victim's survivors. Judges are expected to consider such statements in arriving at an appropriate sanction for the offender.

The drive to mandate inclusion of victim-impact statements in sentencing decisions, already required in federal courts by the 1982 Victim and Witness Protection Act, was substantially enhanced by the "right-of-allocution" provision of the Violent Crime Control and Law Enforcement Act of 1994. Victim-impact statements played a prominent role in the sentencing of Timothy McVeigh, who was convicted of the 1995 bombing of the Murrah Federal Building in Oklahoma City and was executed in 2001. Some states, however, have gone further than the federal government. In 1984, the state of California, for example, passed legislation giving victims a right to attend and participate in sentencing and parole hearings.[86] Approximately 20 states now have laws requiring citizen involvement in sentencing, and all 50 states and the District of Columbia "allow for some form of submission of a victim-impact statement either at the time of sentencing or to be contained in the presentence investigation reports" made by court officers.[87] Where written victim-impact statements are not available, courts may invite the victim to testify directly at sentencing.

An alternative to written impact statements and to the appearance of victims at sentencing hearings is the victim-impact video. Some contemporary victim-impact videos display photo montages of the victim and are set to music and narrated. In 2008, for example, the U.S. Supreme Court rejected an appeal from a death row inmate wanting to exclude just such a digitized narrative set to music by Enya that had been played to the jury during the sentencing phase of his trial.[88]

One study of the efficacy of victim-impact statements found that sentencing decisions are rarely affected by them. The authors concluded that victim-impact statements have little effect on courts because judges and other officials "have established ways of making decisions which do not call for explicit information about the impact of crime on victims."[89] Learn more about the rights of crime victims and the history of the victims' movement at **http://www.justicestudies.com/pubs/victimrights.pdf**. You can read the 2013 Office for Victims of Crime report, *Vision 21: Transforming Victim Services*, at **http://www.justicestudies.com/pubs/vision21.pdf.** The thrust of the report is that victim services should be based on evidence of what works and what doesn't.[90]

Modern Sentencing Options

Sentencing is fundamentally a risk-management strategy designed to protect the public while serving the ends of retribution, incapacitation, deterrence, rehabilitation, and restoration. Because the goals of sentencing are difficult to agree on, so too are sanctions. Lengthy prison terms do little for rehabilitation, and community-release programs can hardly protect the innocent from offenders bent on continuing criminality.

Assorted sentencing philosophies continue to permeate state-level judicial systems. Each state has its own sentencing laws, and frequent revisions of those statutes are not uncommon. Because of huge variation from one state to another in the laws and procedures that control the imposition of criminal sanctions, sentencing has been called "the most diversified part of the Nation's criminal justice process."[91]

There is at least one common ground, however. It can be found in the four traditional sanctions that continue to dominate the thinking of most legislators and judges: fines, probation, imprisonment, and death (Figure 11-3). Fines and the death penalty are discussed in this chapter, probation is described in Chapter 12, and imprisonment is covered in Chapters 13 and 14.

In jurisdictions that employ indeterminate sentencing, fines, probation, and imprisonment are widely available to judges. The option selected generally depends on the severity of the offense and the judge's best guess as to the likelihood of the defendant's future criminal involvement. Sometimes two or more options are combined, such as when an offender is fined and sentenced to prison or placed on probation and fined in support of restitution payments.

Jurisdictions that operate under presumptive sentencing guidelines generally limit the judge's choice to only one option and often specify the extent to which that option can be applied. Dollar amounts of fines, for example, are rigidly set, and prison terms are specified for each type of offense. The death penalty remains an option in a fair number of jurisdictions, but only for a highly select group of offenders.

■ **lecture note**   Discuss Figure 11-3. Ask the class to identify likely reasons for the increase in court-ordered prison commitments during the last 40 years.

■ **lecture note**   Review the usefulness of monetary fines as criminal sanctions in terms of the various advantages identified in this section.

Capital punishment

Fines

Imprisonment

Probation

FIGURE 11-3 | Four Traditional Sentencing Options

State trial courts convict approximately 1,100,000 felons each year; and another 65,000 or so felony convictions occur each year in federal courts.[92] One recent report found that for felons convicted in state courts (Figure 11-4):

- About 41% were sentenced to active prison terms; another 28% received jail sentences involving less than one year's confinement.
- The average sentence length for those sent to state prisons has decreased since 1990 (from 6 to 4 years and 11 months).
- Felons sentenced today are likely to serve more of their sentence before release (50%) than those sentenced in 1990 (33%).
- Of the total, 27% were sentenced to probation, with no jail or prison time to serve.
- The average probation sentence was 38 months.
- The largest category for which state felons were sent to prison was drug offenses.

Although the percentage of felons who receive active sentences may seem low, the number of criminal defendants receiving active prison time has increased dramatically. Figure 11-5 shows that the number of court-ordered prison commitments has increased nearly eightfold in the past 40 years. The number

of new prison commitments peaked around 2010–2011 and has recently shown a small decline. *The Justice Atlas of Sentencing and Corrections*, an interactive online tool showing the residential distribution of people sent to prison, reentering communities, and the populations of people under probation and parole supervision, can be found at **http://www.justiceatlas.org**.

Fines

Although the fine is one of the oldest forms of punishment, the use of fines as criminal sanctions suffers from built-in inequities and a widespread failure to collect them. Inequities arise when offenders with vastly different financial resources are fined similar amounts. A fine of $100, for example, can place a painful economic burden on a poor defendant but is negligible when imposed on a wealthy offender.

Nonetheless, fines are once again receiving attention as a serious sentencing alternative. One reason for the renewed interest is the stress placed on state resources by burgeoning prison populations. The extensive imposition of fines not only results in less crowded prisons but can contribute to state and local coffers and can lower the tax burden of law-abiding citizens. There are other advantages:

- Fines can deprive offenders of the proceeds of criminal activity.
- Fines can promote rehabilitation by enforcing economic responsibility.
- Fines can be collected by existing criminal justice agencies and are relatively inexpensive to administer.
- Fines can be made proportionate to both the severity of the offense and the ability of the offender to pay.

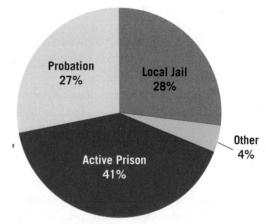

FIGURE 11-4 | The Sentencing of Convicted Felons in State Courts, by Type of Sentence

Source: Data from Sean Rosenmerkel, Matthew Durose, and Donald Farole, Jr., *Felony Sentences in State Courts, 2006* (Washington, DC: Bureau of Justice Statistics, December 2009).

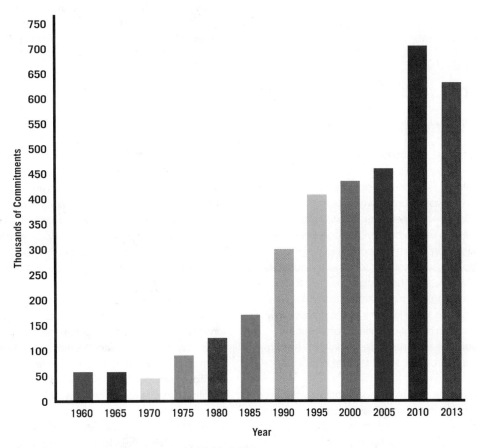

FIGURE 11-5 | Court-Ordered Prison Commitments, 1960–2013

Source: Data from Sean Rosenmerkel, Matthew Durose, and Donald Farole, Jr., *Felony Sentences in State Courts, 2006* (Washington, DC: Bureau of Justice Statistics, December 2009) and other years; and E. Ann Carson, *Prisoners in 2013* (Washington, DC: Bureau of Justice Statistics, 2014), p. 9, and other years.

A National Institute of Justice (NIJ) survey found that an average of 86% of convicted defendants in courts of limited jurisdiction receive fines as sentences, some in combination with another penalty.[93] Fines are also widely used in courts of general jurisdiction, where the NIJ study found judges imposing fines in 42% of all cases that came before them for sentencing. Some studies estimate that more than $1 billion in fines are collected nationwide each year.[94]

Fines are often imposed for relatively minor law violations, such as driving while intoxicated, reckless driving, disturbing the peace, disorderly conduct, public drunkenness, and vandalism. Judges in many courts, however, report the use of fines for relatively serious violations of the law, including assault, auto theft, embezzlement, fraud, and the sale and possession of various controlled substances. Fines are most likely to be imposed where the offender has both a clean record and the ability to pay.[95]

Studies have found that courts of limited jurisdiction, which are the most likely to impose fines, are also the least likely to have adequate information on offenders' financial status.[96] Perhaps as a consequence, judges are sometimes reluctant to impose fines. Two of the most widely cited objections by judges to the use of fines are (1) that fines allow more affluent offenders to "buy their way out" and (2) that poor offenders cannot pay fines.[97]

A solution to both objections can be found in the Scandinavian system of day fines. The day-fine system is based on the idea that fines should be proportionate to the severity of the offense but also need to take into account the financial resources of the offender. Day fines are computed by first assessing the seriousness of the offense, the defendant's degree of culpability, and his or her prior record as measured in "days." The use of days as a benchmark of seriousness is related to the fact that, without fines, the offender could be sentenced to a number of days (or months or years) in jail or prison. The number of days an offender is assessed is then multiplied by the daily wages that person earns. Hence, if two people are sentenced to a five-day fine, but one earns only $20 per day and the other $200 per day, the first would pay a $100 fine and the second $1,000.

In 2010, a Swiss court fined a multimillionaire, whose name was not released to the press, $290,000 for driving his Ferrari through a 35-mph speed limit zone at 85 mph.[98] The court calculated the fine based on the speeder's wealth (said to total $22.7 million) and his record of past offenses.

■ **theme**   What are the four traditional sentencing options identified in this chapter? What kinds of crimes, or sets of circumstances, are most appropriate for the imposition of each of these sentences?

■ **activity**   Assign each student a state that permits the use of the death penalty and have them research current statistics on capital punishment in that state. Have them obtain information on the types of crimes punishable by death in that state, the method(s) of imposing death used, the number of offenders on death row, the demographics of death row inmates, and so on.

■ **Discuss**   What factors help determine whether someone deserves the death penalty? What assumptions about mental or physical disabilities might affect the application of the death penalty?

■ **capital punishment**   The death penalty. Capital punishment is the most extreme of all sentencing options.

■ **capital offense**   A criminal offense punishable by death.

paying for it

Cost-Efficient Corrections and Sentencing

Since the early 1970s, the use of incarceration as a criminal sentencing option had been growing steadily, primarily as a result of the enactment of "get-tough-on-crime" legislation, like two- and three-strikes laws, and the war on drugs, which accounted for a huge number of our nation's prisoners—especially at the federal level. Faced, however, with severe budget shortfalls and rapidly rising prison populations, states were forced to find ways to save money and began looking at alternative sentencing practices and programs to lower the cost of handling convicted felons.

Four types of sentencing reforms, instituted in various ways by 28 states, have helped to lower justice systems costs by lowering prison populations in a number of jurisdictions over the past few years: (1) sentence modifications, (2) drug-law reform, (3) probation revocation reforms, and (4) reforms in juvenile sentencing.

The first of these reforms, sentence modifications, effectively diverts many nonviolent offenders from prison, makes wider use of alternative sentencing options, and shifts inmates who would normally be incarcerated in state facilities to local jails or privately run facilities. The second, drug-law reform, makes wider use of drug courts and drug treatment as alternatives to imprisonment, and has also resulted in the reformation of drug statutes, shortening periods of confinement and making wider use of supervised early release into the community. The third strategy, probation revocation reforms, allows selected probation violators to remain free in the community under more intense supervision, and subsequently requires additional rule violation for probation revocation. Depending on the offense, some probation violators are now deemed ineligible for imprisonment through changes in the law, but face tougher lifestyle restrictions if they violate the conditions of their probation. Finally, reforms in juvenile sentencing give judges greater leeway in the handling of delinquents and mean that fewer young people will spend time confined in state-run facilities.

The use of local jails to hold inmates who would otherwise be sent to state facilities and contracts with private correctional services companies to house inmates needing confinement are other ways that states are attempting to lower the cost of confinement. In Tennessee, for example, the cost to house an inmate in a county jail averages around $35 per day, and moving that inmate to a state-run facility ups the cost to almost $65 per day. Private companies, which bid for state contracts, can often be more efficient than state-run departments of corrections, at least in dealing with certain types of inmates, resulting in significant cost savings. Some government officials also claim that private prisons shelter states from at least some forms of civil liability that may arise from lawsuits brought by prisoners. Finally, one way of alleviating the high cost of incarceration is being tried in Riverside, California, where county officials have begun charging jail inmates $142.42 for every night they spend locked up.

References: Steve Ahillen, "Explore Cost-Effective Alternatives to Prison," *Tennessee News Sentinel*, March 10, 2012, http://www.politifact.com/tennessee/promises/haslam-o-meter/promise/1072/explore-cost-effective-alternatives-to-prison (accessed May 30, 2013); Nicole D. Porter, *The State of Sentencing, 2011: Developments in Policy and Practice* (Washington, DC: The Sentencing Project, 2013); and Jennifer Medina, "In California, a Plan to Charge Inmates for Their Stay," *New York Times*, December 11, 2011.

Death: The Ultimate Sanction

Some crimes are especially heinous and seem to cry out for extreme punishment. In 2008, for example, a 28-year-old grocery store stock clerk named Kevin Ray Underwood was sentenced to death in the atrocious murder of a ten-year-old girl in what authorities said was an elaborate plan to cannibalize the girl's flesh.[99] Underwood had been the girl's neighbor in Purcell, Oklahoma, and her mutilated body was discovered in his apartment covered with deep saw marks. Investigators told reporters that Underwood had sexually assaulted the little girl and planned to eat her corpse using the meat tenderizer and barbecue skewers that they confiscated from his kitchen. "In my 24 years as a prosecutor, this ranks as one of the most heinous and atrocious cases I've ever been involved with," said McClain County Prosecutor Tim Kuykendall.

Many states today have statutory provisions that provide for a sentence of **capital punishment** for especially repugnant crimes (known as **capital offenses**). Estimates are that more than 18,800 legal executions have been carried out in the United States since 1608, when records began to be kept on capital punishment.[100] Although capital punishment was widely used throughout the eighteenth and nineteenth centuries, the mid-twentieth century offered a brief respite in the number of offenders legally executed

Kevin Ray Underwood, whom some have called the "poster boy" for capital punishment. Underwood, of Purcell, Oklahoma, was sentenced to death in 2008 in the atrocious murder of a ten-year-old girl in an elaborate plan to cannibalize her flesh. After sexually abusing and killing the girl, Underwood mutilated her body and planned to eat her corpse using meat tenderizer and barbecue skewers. What would be an appropriate sentence for Underwood?

in this country. Between 1930 and 1967, the year when the U.S. Supreme Court ordered a nationwide stay of pending executions, nearly 3,800 people were put to death. The peak years were 1935 and 1936, with nearly 200 legal killings each year. Executions declined substantially every year thereafter. Between 1967 and 1977, a *de facto* moratorium existed, with no executions carried out in any U.S. jurisdiction. Following the lifting of the moratorium, executions resumed (Figure 11-6). In 1983, only 5 offenders were put to death, whereas 39 were executed nationwide in 2013.[101] A modern record for executions was set in 1999, with 98 executions—35 in Texas alone.[102]

Today, the federal government and 34 of the 50 states[103] permit execution for first-degree murder, and treason, kidnapping, aggravated rape, the murder of a police or corrections officer, and murder while under a life sentence are punishable by death in some jurisdictions.[104] Illinois, which up until recently was among states with a death penalty, repealed its capital punishment statute in 2011, replacing it with a sentence of life in prison without possibility of parole. In 2012, Connecticut took capital punishment off of its books, although the 11 men on death row at the time of repeal are still slated to be executed. Another state to abolish the death penalty is Maryland, which repealed its death penalty statute in 2013. Finally, in 2015, Nebraska legislators overroad their governor's veto and abolished capital punishment.

The United States is not the only country to make use of capital punishment. On January 15, 2015, for example, Saudi Arabia beheaded Laila Basim, a young woman who had been convicted in a Shia court of killing her seven-year-old stepdaughter.[105] The court ordered that Basim be executed by the

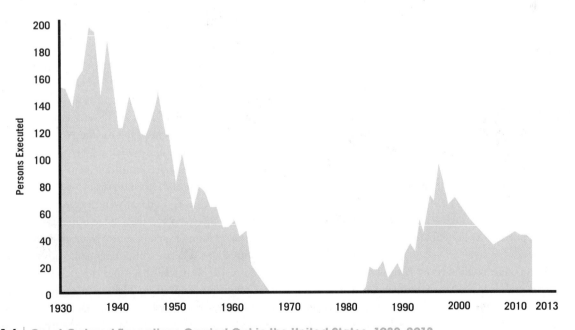

FIGURE 11-6 | Court-Ordered Executions Carried Out in the United States, 1930–2013

Note: Excludes executions ordered by military authority.

Sources: Tracy L. Snell, *Capital Punishment,* 2013—Statistical Tables (Washington, DC: Bureau of Justice Statistics, December 2014); and Death Penalty Information Center, "Executions by Year," http://www.deathpenaltyinfo.org/executions-year (accessed May 20, 2015).

■ **lecture note**   Explain that a period of 12 years and 9 months typically
elapses between the time a sentence of death is imposed and the time it is
carried out. Discuss why the delay is so lengthy. Ask whether that is too long
and how it might be reduced.

■ **writ of *habeas corpus***   A writ that directs the person detaining a prisoner to bring him or her before a judicial officer to
determine the lawfulness of the imprisonment.

sword and "in the most painful manner"—meaning that she was
not given tranquilizers or painkillers before facing the executioner. Four policemen held her down as she screamed "I did not
kill." It took three strikes with the sword to sever her neck. In
2014, Saudi Arabia executed 87 people, up from 78 in 2013.[106]
Japan hung 3 criminals in the first two months of 2013,[107] and
China, the world's most populous country, is reported to routinely execute more than 1,700 people annually—meaning that
more people are executed in China than in the rest of the world
combined. According to Amnesty International, at least 778
people were executed worldwide in 2013, excluding thousands
of people put to death in China where records are not released.
Amnesty International says that tens of thousands are on death
rows around the world.[108]

The list of crimes punishable by death under federal jurisdiction in the United States increased dramatically with passage
of the Violent Crime Control and Law Enforcement Act of 1994
and was expanded still further by the 2001 USA PATRIOT Act.
The list now includes a total of about 60 offenses. State legislators have also worked to expand the types of crimes for which
a death sentence can be imposed. In 1997, for example, the
Louisiana Supreme Court upheld the state's year-old child rape
statute, which allows for the imposition of a capital sentence
when the victim is younger than 12 years of age. The case involved an AIDS-infected father who raped his three daughters,
ages five, eight, and nine. In upholding the father's death sentence, the Louisiana court ruled that child rape is "like no other
crime."[109] In 2008, however, in the case of *Kennedy* v. *Louisiana*,
the U.S. Supreme Court ruled that the Eighth Amendment bars
Louisiana (and other states) from imposing the death penalty for
the rape of a child where the crime did not result, and was not
intended to result, in the victim's death.[110]

A total of 3,035 offenders were under sentence of death
throughout the United States on October 1, 2014.[111] The latest statistics show that 98.2% of those on death row are male,
approximately 56% are white, 14% are Hispanic, 42% are
African American, and the remainder consists of other races
(mostly Native American and Pacific Islander).[112] Statistics
on race have been less meaningful recently, as classification
depends on self-reports, and individuals may report being of
more than one race.

Methods of imposing death vary by state. The majority of
death penalty states authorize execution through lethal injection.
Electrocution is the second most common means, whereas hanging,
the gas chamber, and firing squads have survived, at least as options
available to the condemned, in a few states. For the most current
statistical information on capital punishment, visit the Death Penalty
Information Center via **http://www.deathpenaltyinfo.org**.

Habeas Corpus Review

The legal process through which a capital sentence is carried
to conclusion is fraught with problems. One serious difficulty
centers on the fact that automatic review of all death sentences
by appellate courts and constant legal maneuvering by defense
counsel often lead to a dramatic delay between the time the
sentence is handed down and the time it is carried out. Today,
an average of 12 years and 9 months passes between the imposition of a death sentence and execution.[113] Such lengthy delays,
compounded by uncertainty over whether an execution will
ever occur, directly contravene the generally accepted notion
that punishment should be swift and certain.

Even death row inmates can undergo life-altering changes.
When that happens, long-delayed executions can become highly
questionable events. The case of Stanley "Tookie" Williams, who
was executed at California's San Quentin Prison in 2005 at age
51, is illustrative.[114] Williams, self-described cofounder of the infamous Crips street gang in the early 1970s, was sentenced to die
for the brutal shotgun murders of four people during a robbery
26 years earlier. In 1993, however, he experienced what he called
a "reawakening" and began working from prison as an antigang
crusader. Williams found a sympathetic publisher and wrote a series
of children's books titled *Tookie Speaks Out against Gang Violence*.
The series was intended to help urban youth reject the lure of gang
membership and embrace traditional values. He also wrote *Life in
Prison*, an autobiography describing the isolation and despair experienced by death row inmates. In his final years, Williams worked
with his editor, Barbara Cottman Becnel, to create the Internet
Project for Street Peace, a demonstration project linking teens from
the rough-and-tumble streets of Richmond, California, to peers in
Switzerland in an effort to help them avoid street violence. In 2001,
Williams was nominated for the Nobel Peace Prize by a member of the Swiss Parliament and for the Nobel Prize in Literature
by a number of college professors. Pleas to spare his life, which
came from Jesse Jackson, anti–death penalty activist Sister Helen
Prejean, the National Association for the Advancement of Colored
People (NAACP), and others, were rejected by Governor Arnold
Schwarzenegger who said that "there is no reason to second-guess
the jury's decision of guilt or raise significant doubts or serious reservations about Williams' convictions and death sentence."[115]

In a speech before the American Bar Association in 1989,
then-Chief Justice William Rehnquist called for reforms of the
federal *habeas corpus* system, which, at the time, allowed condemned prisoners virtually limitless opportunities for appeal.
Writs of *habeas corpus* (Latin for "you have the body"), which
require that a prisoner be brought into court to determine if
he or she is being legally held, form the basis for many federal

■ **theme** question Former U.S. Supreme Court Justice William Brennan has said that the death penalty will be abolished one day in the United States. Do you agree? Explain.

appeals made by prisoners on state death rows. In 1968, Chief Justice Earl Warren called the right to file *habeas* petitions, as guaranteed under the U.S. Constitution, the "symbol and guardian of individual liberty." Twenty years later, however, Rehnquist claimed that writs of *habeas corpus* were being used indiscriminately by death row inmates seeking to delay executions even where grounds for delay did not exist. "The capital defendant does not need to prevail on the merits in order to accomplish his purpose," said Rehnquist. "He wins temporary victories by postponing a final adjudication."[116]

> Chief Justice Earl Warren called the right to file *habeas* petitions the "symbol and guardian of individual liberty."

In a move to reduce delays in the conduct of executions, the U.S. Supreme Court, in the case of **McCleskey v. Zant** (1991),[117] limited the number of appeals a condemned person may lodge with the courts. Saying that repeated filing for the sole purpose of delay promotes "disrespect for the finality of convictions" and "disparages the entire criminal justice system," the Court established a two-pronged criterion for future appeals. According to *McCleskey*, in any petition beyond the first filed with the federal court, a capital defendant must (1) demonstrate good cause why the claim now being made was not included in the first filing and (2) explain how the absence of that claim may have harmed the petitioner's ability to mount an effective defense. Two months later, the Court reinforced *McCleskey* when it ruled, in **Coleman v. Thompson** (1991),[118] that state prisoners could not cite "procedural default," such as a defense attorney's failure to meet a state's filing deadline for appeals, as the basis for an appeal to federal court.

In 1995, in the case of **Schlup v. Delo**,[119] the Court continued to define standards for further appeals from death-row inmates, ruling that before appeals based on claims of new evidence could be heard, "a petitioner must show that, in light of the new evidence, it is more likely than not that no reasonable juror would have found him guilty beyond a reasonable doubt." A "reasonable juror" was defined as one who "would consider fairly all of the evidence presented and would conscientiously obey the trial court's instructions requiring proof beyond a reasonable doubt."

Opportunities for federal appeals by death row inmates were further limited by the Antiterrorism and Effective Death Penalty Act (AEDPA) of 1996,[120] which sets a one-year postconviction deadline for state inmates filing federal *habeas corpus* appeals. The deadline is six months for state death-row inmates who were provided a lawyer for *habeas* appeals at the state level. The act also requires federal courts to presume that the factual findings of state courts are correct, does not permit the claim of state court misinterpretations of the U.S. Constitution as a basis for *habeas* relief unless those misinterpretations are "unreasonable," and requires that all petitioners must show, prior to obtaining a hearing, facts sufficient to establish by clear and convincing evidence that but for constitutional error, no reasonable fact-finder would have found the petitioner guilty. The act also requires approval by a three-judge panel before an inmate can file a second federal appeal raising newly discovered evidence of innocence. In 1996, in the case of *Felker* v. *Turpin*,[121] the U.S. Supreme Court ruled that limitations on the authority of federal courts to consider successive *habeas corpus* petitions imposed by AEDPA are permissible since they do not deprive the U.S. Supreme Court of its original jurisdiction over such petitions. Finally, in the 2013 case of *McQuiggin* v. *Perkins*, the Court held that actual innocence, if proved, "serves as a gateway through which a petitioner may pass whether the impediment is a procedural bar....or expiration of the AEDPA statute of limitations." In *McQuiggin*, the justices wrote, a "fundamental miscarriage of justice exception" creates a "sensitivity to the injustice of incarcerating an innocent individual."[122]

Some recent statements by Supreme Court justices have indicated that long delays caused by the government in carrying out executions may render the punishment unconstitutionally cruel and unusual. One example comes from the 1998 case of *Elledge* v. *Florida*,[123] where the execution of William D. Elledge had been delayed for 23 years. Although the full Court refused to hear the case, Justice Stephen Breyer observed that "[t]wenty-three years under sentence of death is unusual—whether one takes as a measuring rod current practice or the practice in this country and in England at the time our Constitution was written." Moreover, wrote Breyer, execution after such a long delay could be considered cruel because Elledge "has experienced that delay because of the State's own faulty procedures and not because of frivolous appeals on his own part." Elledge died on death row at the Union Correctional Institution in Florida in 2008. He had been under sentence of death for 34 years; at the time of his death from asthma, he was 57 years old.

> Long delays caused by the government in carrying out executions may render the punishment unconstitutionally cruel and unusual.

Opposition to Capital Punishment

Thirty years ago, David Magris, who was celebrating his 21st birthday with a crime spree, shot Dennis Tapp in the back during a holdup, leaving Tapp a paraplegic. Tapp had been working a late-night shift, tending his father's quick-serve gas station.

Magris went on to commit more robberies that night, killing 20-year-old Steven Tompkins in a similar crime. Although Magris was sentenced to death by a California court, the U.S. Supreme Court overturned the state's death-penalty law in 1972, opening the door for Magris to be paroled in 1985. Long before Magris was freed from prison, however, Tapp had already forgiven him. A few minutes after the shooting happened, Tapp regained consciousness, dragged himself to a telephone, and called for help. The next thing he did was ask "God to forgive the man who did this to me."[124] Today, the men—both staunch death penalty opponents—are friends, and Magris is president of the Northern California Coalition to Abolish the Death Penalty. "Don't get me wrong," says Tapp, "What [David] did was wrong.... He did something stupid and he paid for it."[125]

Because the death penalty is such an emotional issue, attempts have been made to abolish capital punishment since the founding of the United States. The first recorded effort to eliminate the death penalty occurred at the home of Benjamin Franklin in 1787.[126] At a meeting there on March 9 of that year, Dr. Benjamin Rush, a signer of the Declaration of Independence and a leading medical pioneer, read a paper against capital punishment to a small but influential audience. Although his immediate efforts came to naught, his arguments laid the groundwork for many debates that followed. Michigan, widely regarded as the first abolitionist state, joined the Union in 1837 without a death penalty. A number of other states, including Alaska, Hawaii, Massachusetts, Minnesota, New York, New Jersey, New Mexico, West Virginia, and Wisconsin, have since spurned death as a possible sanction for criminal acts. As noted earlier, capital punishment remains a viable sentencing option in 33 of the states and in all federal jurisdictions, while arguments continue to rage over its value.

Today, six main rationales for abolishing capital punishment are heard, as shown in Table 11-4.

TABLE 11-4 | **Capital Punishment: Retentionist and Abolitionist Rationales**

REASONS TO ABOLISH	REASONS TO KEEP
Innocent People Have Been Executed Claim: The death penalty can be and has been inflicted on innocent people. Counterclaim: Although it has been shown that some innocent people have been condemned to death, and although it can be assumed that a number of innocent people remain on death row, it has not been demonstrated that innocent people have actually been executed.	**Just Deserts** Claim: Some people deserve to die for what they have done. Death is justly deserved; anything less cannot suffice as a sanction for the most heinous crimes. Counterclaim: Capital punishment is a holdover from primitive times; contemporary standards of human decency mandate alternatives such as life imprisonment.
Lack of Proven Deterrence Claim: The death penalty is not an effective deterrent, and numerous studies have shown the truth of that assertion. Counterclaim: If capital punishment were imposed with both certainty and swiftness, then it would be effective as a deterrent. It is our system of appeals and lengthy delays that make it ineffective.	**Revenge/Retribution** Claim: Capital punishment can be seen as revenge for the pain and suffering that the criminal inflicted on the victim. In *Gregg v. Georgia*, the justices of the U.S. Supreme Court wrote that "(t)he instinct for retribution is part of the nature of man." Hence, sentencing a capital offender to death can provide closure to a victim's family members. Counterclaim: Forgiveness and rehabilitation are higher goals than revenge and retribution.
Arbitrariness Claim: The imposition of the death penalty is, by the very nature of our legal system, arbitrary. Effective legal representation and access to the courts is differentially available to people with varying financial and other resources. Counterclaim: Many safeguards exist at all levels of criminal justice processing to protect the innocent and to ensure that only the guilty are actually put to death.	**Protection** Claim: Executed offenders cannot commit further crimes; and execution serves as an example to other would-be wrongdoers of the fate that awaits them. Moreover, society has a duty to act in defense of others, and to protect its innocent members. Counterclaim: Societal interests in protection can be met in other ways, such as incarceration or life imprisonment.
Discrimination Claim: The death penalty discriminates against certain ethnic and racial groups. Counterclaim: Any examination of disproportionality must go beyond simple comparisons and must measure both frequency and seriousness of capital crimes between and within racial groups. The Supreme Court, in the 1987 case of *McCleskey v. Kemp*, held that a simple showing of racial discrepancies in the application of the death penalty does not constitute a constitutional violation. Members of underrepresented groups were more likely to be sentenced to death, but only because they were more likely to be arrested on facts that could support a capital charge, not because the justice system acts in a discriminatory fashion.	

REASONS TO ABOLISH	REASONS TO KEEP
Expense Claim: Because of all the appeals involved in death penalty cases, the cost to a state can run into the millions of dollars for each execution. Counterclaim: Although official costs associated with capital punishment are high, no cost is *too* high if it achieves justice.	
Human Life Is Sacred Claim: Killing at the hands of the state is not a righteous act but instead lowers all of us to the same moral level as the crimes committed by the condemned. Counterclaim: If life is sacred, then the taking of life demands revenge.	
For additional perspectives: The National Coalition to Abolish the Death Penalty, http://www.ncadp.org.	*For additional perspectives:* Pro-Death http://Penalty.com, http://www.prodeathpenalty.com.

freedom OR safety? YOU decide

What Are the Limits of Genetic Privacy?

By mid-2013, 28 states and the federal government had enacted arrestee DNA collection laws, which authorize the collection of suspect DNA following arrest or charging. The federal law, the DNA Fingerprint Act of 2005, requires that any adult arrested for a federal crime must provide a DNA sample. The law also mandates DNA collection from persons detained under the authority of the United States who are not U.S. citizens or are not lawfully in the country. Some states, however, limit preconviction DNA collection to violent offenses or sex crimes, whereas other states include all felonies, and some extend the requirement to misdemeanors as well. Figure 11-7 shows states that have enacted arrestee DNA collection laws. In 2013, in the case of *Maryland* v. *King*, the U.S. Supreme Court upheld Maryland's practice of collecting and testing DNA from arrested felons without the use of a warrant. Writing for the majority in that case, Justice Kennedy said, "When officers make an arrest supported by probable cause to hold for a serious offense and bring the suspect to the station to be detained in custody, taking and analyzing a cheek swab of the arrestee's DNA is, like fingerprinting and photographing, a legitimate police booking procedure that is reasonable under the Fourth Amendment."

Forensic DNA can be a powerful tool in the hands of investigators. In 2005, for example, police in Truro, Massachusetts, charged Christopher M. McCowen, a garbageman with a long rap sheet, with the murder of 46-year-old Christa Worthington, a fashion writer who had been raped and stabbed to death in the kitchen of her isolated home in 2002. The case, which had baffled authorities for three years, drew national interest when Truro authorities asked the town's 790 male residents to voluntarily submit saliva-swab DNA samples for analysis. Investigators were hoping to use genetic testing to match semen recovered from the murder scene to the killer. "We're trying to find the person who has something to hide," said Sergeant David Perry of the Truro Police Department. Although McCowen voluntarily submitted a DNA sample from a cheek swab in early 2004, it took the state crime lab more than a year to analyze it.

DNA profiling has been used in criminal investigations for only about 20 years. The first well-known DNA forensic analysis occurred in 1986, when British police sought the help of Alec Jeffreys, a geneticist at the University of Leicester who is widely regarded as the father of "DNA fingerprinting." The police were trying to solve the vicious rape and murder of two young schoolgirls. At the center of their investigation was a young man who worked at a mental institution close to where the girls' bodies had been found. Soon after he was questioned, the man confessed to the crimes and was arrested, but police were uncertain of the suspect's state of mind and wanted to be sure that they had the right person.

Jeffreys compared the suspect's DNA to DNA taken from semen samples found on the victims. The samples did not match, leading to a wider police investigation. Lacking any clear leads, the authorities requested that all males living in the area of the killings voluntarily submit to DNA testing so that they might be excluded as suspects. By the fall of 1987, the number of men tested had exceeded 4,500, but the murderer still hadn't been found. Then, however, investigators received an unexpected tip. They learned that a local baker named Colin Pitchfork had convinced another man to provide a DNA sample in his place. Pitchfork was picked up and questioned. He soon confessed, providing details about the crime that only the perpetrator could know. Pitchfork became the 4,583rd man to undergo DNA testing, and his DNA proved a perfect match with that of the killer.

(continues)

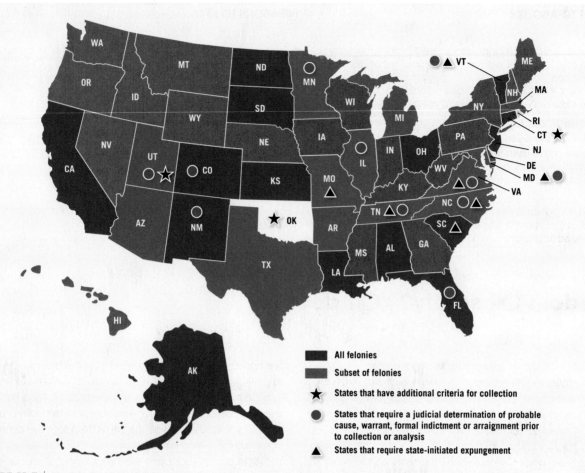

FIGURE 11-7 | States That Have Enacted Arrestee DNA Collection Laws

Source: National Institute of Justice, "DNA Sample Collection from Arrestees," http://nij.gov/topics/forensics/evidence/dna/collection-from-arrestees.htm (accessed June 1, 2015).

In the last 20 years, the use of DNA testing by police departments has come a long way. Today, the Combined DNA Index System (CODIS) database of the Federal Bureau of Investigation (FBI) makes use of computerized records to match the DNA of individuals previously convicted of certain crimes with forensic samples gathered at crime scenes across the country. A recent federal law allows the FBI and other federal law enforcement agencies to include preconviction DNA in their databases. Fifteen states also allow the collection of DNA samples from people awaiting trial.

Advocates of genetic privacy, however, question whether anyone—even those convicted of crimes—should be sampled against their wishes and have their genetic profiles added to government databases. The Truro case, in which the American Civil Liberties Union (ACLU) sent letters to the town's police chief and Cape Cod prosecutor calling for an end to the "DNA dragnet," highlights what many fear—especially when local police announced that they would pay close attention

to those who refused to cooperate. One commentator noted that it's "a very old trap" to say, "If you have nothing to hide, then why not cooperate?"

European courts, it would seem, agree. In 2008, the European Court of Human Rights ruled unanimously that British officials had to destroy nearly 1 million DNA samples and fingerprints taken from people without criminal records. Keeping the samples, the court said, was a violation of the right to privacy established under the European Human Rights Convention, to which the United Kingdom is a signatory.

You Decide

What degree of "genetic privacy" should an individual be entitled to? Should the government require routine genetic testing of nonoffenders for identification purposes? Should it require it of arrestees who have not been convicted? How might such information be used in the event of a terrorist attack?

References: Paisley Dodds, "European Court Makes Landmark Ruling on DNA Rights," AP Worldstream, December 5, 2008; Anna Gorman, "U.S. to Collect DNA Samples of Arrested Immigrants," *Los Angeles Times*, January 9, 2009; "Man Charged with 2002 Murder of Cape Cod Writer," *USA Today*, April 15, 2005, http://www.usatoday.com/news/nation/2005-04-15-cape-cod-murder_x.htm (accessed July 4, 2006); "ACLU Slams Mass DNA Collection," http://CBSNews.com, January 10, 2005, http://www.cbsnews.com/stories/2005/01/10/national/main665938.shtml (accessed July 4, 2006); and Howard C. Coleman and Eric D. Swenson, *DNA in the Courtroom: A Trial Watcher's Guide* (Seattle: Genelex Corporation, 2000), http://www.genelex.com/paternitytesting/paternitybook.html (accessed July 4, 2008).

The Death Penalty and Innocent People

The Death Penalty Information Center claims that 142 people in 26 states were freed from death row between 1973 and late 2012 after it was determined that they were innocent of the capital crimes of which they had been convicted (Figure 11-8).[127] One study of felony convictions that used analysis of DNA to provide postconviction evidence of guilt or innocence found 28 cases in which defendants had been wrongly convicted and sentenced to lengthy prison terms. The study, *Convicted by Juries, Exonerated by Science*, effectively demonstrated that the judicial process can be flawed.[128] DNA testing can play a critical role in identifying wrongful convictions because, as Barry Scheck and Peter Neufeld, cofounders of the Innocence Project at the Benjamin N. Cardozo School of Law, point out, "Unlike witnesses who disappear or whose recollections fade over time, DNA in biological samples can be reliably extracted decades after the commission of the crime. The results of such testing have invariably been found to have a scientific certainty that easily outweighs the eyewitness identification testimony or other direct or circumstantial proof that led to the original conviction."[129] "Very simply," say Scheck and Neufeld, "DNA testing has demonstrated that far more wrongful convictions occur than even the most cynical and jaded scholars had suspected."[130]

A 2000 study by Columbia Law School Professor James Liebman and colleagues examined 4,578 death penalty cases in state and federal courts from 1973 to 1995.[132] They found that appellate courts overturned the conviction or reduced the sentence in 68% of the cases examined. In 82% of the successful appeals, defendants were found to be deserving of a lesser sentence, and convictions were overturned in 7% of such appeals. According to the study's authors, "Our 23 years worth of findings reveal a capital punishment system collapsing under the weight of its own mistakes." You can read the Liebman report in its entirety at **http://www.justicestudies.com/pubs/liebman.pdf**.

A recent NIJ-funded study found 10 factors that can lead to a wrongful conviction of an innocent defendant instead of a dismal or acquittal.[133] Those factors are shown in Figure 11-9. The NIJ study also distinguished between cases in which erroneous convictions are returned and near misses, or cases in which innocent defendants came close to being convicted but were eventually acquitted. Cases that lead to erroneous convictions and those that lead to near misses were found to share many of the same characteristics, including false confession, official misconduct, eyewitness misidentification, or an incorrect tip to the police. Factors that lead to an erroneous conviction included a punitive state culture (a just deserts mind-set in which prosecutors seek convictions at all costs), forensic error (either incorrect or failed crime scene or crime laboratory analysis), weak facts still pressed by the prosecution, or a mistaken or lying eyewitness. Factors that led to a near miss included, but were not limited to, an older defendant with no criminal history, a strong defense, or prosecutorial disclosure of critical evidence.

Claims of innocence are being partially addressed today by recently passed state laws that mandate DNA testing of all death row inmates in situations where DNA testing might help establish guilt or innocence (i.e., in cases where blood or semen from the perpetrator is available for testing).[134]

In 2004, in recognition of the potential of DNA testing to exonerate the innocent, President George W. Bush signed the Innocence Protection Act[135] into law. The Innocence Protection Act provides federal funds to eliminate the backlog of unanalyzed DNA samples in the nation's crime laboratories[136] and sets aside money to improve the capacity of federal, state, and local crime laboratories to conduct DNA analyses.[137] The act also facilitates access to postconviction DNA testing for those serving time in state[138] or federal prisons or on death row and sets forth conditions under which a federal prisoner asserting innocence may obtain postconviction DNA testing of specific evidence. Similarly, the legislation requires

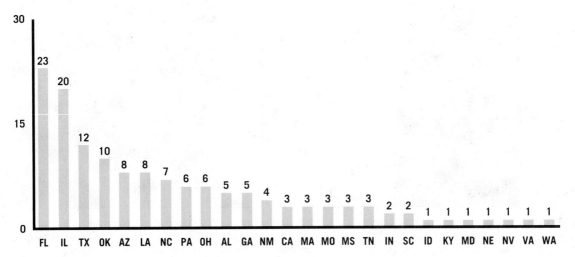

FIGURE 11-8 | Exonerations by State, 1988–2012

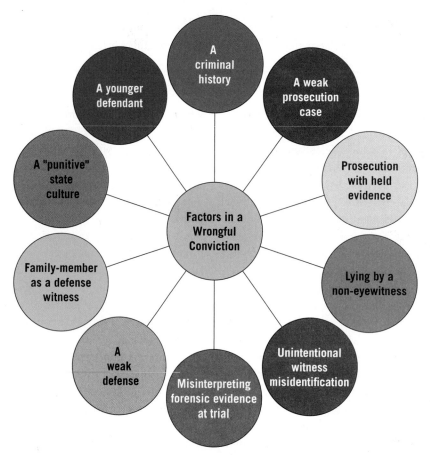

FIGURE 11-9 | Ten Factors that Can Lead to a Wrongful Conviction

Source: Adapted from Jon B. Gould, Julia Carrano, Richard Leo, and Joseph Young, "Predicting Erroneous Convictions: A Social Science Approach to Miscarriages of Justice—Final Report to the National Institute of Justice, February 2013," https://www.ncjrs.gov/pdffiles1/nij/grants/241389.pdf.

Death penalty opponent Mark Bherand sitting outside San Quentin Prison holding a sign as he awaits the execution of convicted killer Stanley "Tookie" Williams on December 13, 2005. Williams, reputed cofounder of the Crips street gang, had been convicted of four murders that occurred in 1979. He was denied clemency by California's then-Governor Arnold Schwartzenegger. What arguments can be made in favor of and against capital punishment? Which arguments do you find most compelling?

■ **activity** Ask the class to undertake an inquiry into opinions about the death penalty. Have students construct a survey instrument and conduct personal interviews to gauge the degree of opposition to or support for the death penalty. Have students use different offender characteristics (for example, race and gender) as well as different offenses (for example, rape, murder, terrorism, and school shootings) in the survey to see how support varies.

the preservation of biological evidence by federal law enforcement agencies for any defendant under a sentence of imprisonment or death.

In 2006, in the only state action of its kind to date, the North Carolina General Assembly established the North Carolina Innocence Inquiry Commission, and charged it with investigating and evaluating postconviction claims of factual innocence.[139] The commission, which comprises eight members selected by the chief justice of the North Carolina Supreme Court and the chief judge of the North Carolina Court of Appeals, examines only new evidence that was not considered at trial. As of mid-2010, the commission had considered 756 cases, resulting in one exoneration.[140] By mid-2012, 44 states had innocence projects, many of them private initiatives based at law schools or universities, devoted to helping identify and release innocent prisoners.[141] One 2014 study estimated that around 4.1% of all death row inmates are probably falsely convicted and could be exonerated, although only very few false convictions are actually ever discovered and overturned.[142]

Not all claims of innocence are supported by DNA tests or by other forms of inquiry, however. In 2006, for example, DNA test results confirmed the guilt of Roger Keith Coleman, a Virginia coal miner who had steadfastly maintained his innocence until he was executed in 1992. Coleman, executed for the 1981 rape and murder of his sister-in-law, Wanda McCoy, died declaring his innocence and proclaiming that he would one day be exonerated. His case became a cause célèbre for death penalty opponents, who convinced Virginia Governor Mark Warner to order DNA tests on surviving evidence. Coleman's supporters claimed that the tests would provide the first scientific proof that an innocent man had been executed in the United States. Results from the tests, however, conclusively showed that blood and semen found at the crime scene had come from Coleman. Recent studies have confirmed the convictions of about 42% of inmates whose cases are selected for DNA testing through the Innocence Project.[143] About 43% are exonerated by the tests. Because strong doubts about guilt already exist in cases where inmates are selected for testing, however, the percentage of confirmed convictions seems surprising.

Finally, in 2010 the U.S. Supreme Court ruled, in the case of *District Attorney's Office* v. *Osborne*,[144] that there is no fundamental constitutional right to access DNA-testable evidence long after a criminal conviction is final. Learn more about DNA testing and how it can help determine guilt or innocence from the federal government's DNA Initiative, whose motto is "advancing criminal justice through DNA technology," via **http://www.dna.gov**.

The Death Penalty and Deterrence

During the 1970s and 1980s, the deterrent effect of the death penalty became a favorite subject for debate in academic circles.[145] Studies of states that had eliminated the death penalty failed to show any increase in homicide rates.[146] Similar studies of neighboring states, in which jurisdictions retaining capital punishment were compared with those that had abandoned it, also failed to demonstrate any significant differences.[147] Although death penalty advocates remain numerous, few still argue for the penalty based on its deterrent effects. One study that has found support for use of the death penalty as a deterrent was reported in 2001 by Hashem Dezhbakhsh and his colleagues at Emory University.[148] According to the researchers, "Our results suggest that capital punishment has a strong deterrent effect.... In particular, each execution results, on average, in 18 fewer murders."[149] They note that most other studies in the area have not only been methodologically flawed but have failed to consider the fact that a number of states sentence select offenders to death but do not carry out executions. They write, "If criminals know that the justice system issues many death sentences but the executions are not carried out, then they may not be deterred by an increase in probability of a death sentence."[150]

> Although death penalty advocates remain numerous, few argue for the penalty based on its deterrent effects.

In 2012, however, in a succinct summary of studies on the deterrent effect of the death penalty, the Committee on Law and Justice of the National Academy of Sciences released *Deterrence and the Death Penalty,* a publication that included a detailed analysis of previous death penalty research.[151] The committee found that "research to date is not informative about whether capital punishment decreases, increases, or has no effect on homicide rates." It concluded that "claims that research demonstrates that capital punishment decreases or increases the homicide rate or has no effect on it should not influence policy judgments about capital punishment." Read the entire National Academy of Sciences report at **http://www.justicestudies.com/pdf/deathpenaltynas.pdf**.

The Death Penalty and Discrimination

The claim that the death penalty is discriminatory is hard to investigate. Although past evidence suggests that blacks and other minorities in the United States have been disproportionately sentenced to death,[152] more recent evidence is not as clear. At first glance, disproportionality seems apparent: 45 of the 98 prisoners executed between January 1977 and May 1988 were African American or

CJ | NEWS
High Costs Lead to Reconsideration of Death Penalty

Judges, prosecutors, and legislators are reconsidering use of the death penalty, and the crippling cost of obtaining such convictions is a key factor.

"Death by execution is excessively expensive," wrote Florida Judge Charles M. Harris in an April 2012 opinion piece. "Most people who support the death penalty believe it is more cost-effective than life in prison. Perhaps at one time, when executions were swift and sure, this may have been the case. It is not now."

Countless studies support this argument. The state of Indiana, for example, found that the average death penalty case cost ten times more than a case involving a sentence of life without parole. Similarly, a recent Urban Institute study determined that the average capital case in Maryland cost almost $1 million more than a comparable non-death-penalty case.

Much of the cost goes into preparing for trial. The prosecution of Scott Peterson, the Californian accused of murdering his pregnant wife, Laci, for example, required more than 20,000 hours of staff time, costing $3.2 million. Peterson was sentenced to death in 2005, but he

A session of the California legislature. States like California are considering the cost of capital punishment, along with public sentiment and moral aspects of court-ordered executions, in weighing the future of the death penalty in their states. What role, if any, should cost play in capital punishment decisions?

Max Whittaker/Getty Images.

is appealing, usually a long process that takes even longer in California. The California Supreme Court spends more than half its time reviewing death penalty cases.

The extra expenses can be traced back to a U.S. Supreme Court decision in 1976, four years after the High Court reinstated the death penalty, requiring additional precautions in death penalty cases. Jury selection, for example, takes three to four weeks longer and costs $200,000 more than in life-without-parole cases, according to a California study.

In the sentencing phase of a death penalty case, defendants have the right to present mitigating factors, requiring expensive expert testimony. After conviction, it can take years to exhaust appeals, which adds to both court and incarceration costs. According to a 2011 report, California death row inmates require solitary cells and extra guards, costing the state $100,663 more per inmate per year than regular confinement.

County governments typically pick up the tab for criminal trials, resulting in tax increases or service cuts. The Peterson trial, for example, forced Stanislaus County to redistribute legal cases and cut its consumer fraud protection unit. And counties can't easily avoid this obligation. When commissioners of Lincoln County, Georgia, for example, refused to allocate funds for a new trial ordered for death row inmate Johnny Lee Jones, they were put in jail.

But despite punishing costs, the expansive legal rights of defendants facing death have not been rolled back—perhaps in part due to disturbing reports of wrongful convictions exposed by DNA evidence, recanted testimony, and other factors. "When innocent people are executed, those mistakes cannot be remedied," observes the ACLU.

Whatever the reason, Americans seem to be losing interest in execution. According to Gallup polls, support for the death penalty has fallen from a high of 80% in 1994 to 61% in 2011. The number of death sentences handed out nationwide declined from 284 in 1999 to 111 in 2008, according to the Associated Press.

For states struggling with crippling deficits, savings from abolishing capital punishment are very tempting. North Carolina estimated potential savings at $11 million per year, Florida estimated $51 million in savings per year, and a California study said the state could immediately save $1 billion by eliminating the death penalty.

Currently 15 states have no death penalty. The latest to join the list is Maryland, which ended the death penalty in 2012.

Resources: "Fight against Death Penalty Gains Momentum in States," *Los Angeles Times*, April 14, 2012, http://articles.latimes.com/2012/apr/14/nation/la-na-death-penalty-20120415; "Just or Not, Cost of Death Penalty Is a Killer for State Budgets," Fox News, March 27, 2012, http://www.foxnews.com/us/2010/03/27/just-cost-death-penalty-killer-state-budgets/; and "Death Penalty Costs California $184 Million a Year, Study Says," *Los Angeles Times*, June 20, 2011, http://articles.latimes.com/2011/jun/20/local/la-me-adv-death-penalty-costs-20110620.

Hispanic, and 84 of the 98 had been convicted of killing whites.[153] A 1996 Kentucky study found that blacks accused of killing whites in that state between 1976 and 1991 had a higher-than-average

> *McCleskey v. Kemp* held that a simple showing of racial discrepancies in the application of the death penalty does not constitute a constitutional violation.

probability of being charged with a capital crime and of being sentenced to die than did homicide offenders of other races.[154] For an accurate appraisal to be made, however, any claims of disproportionality must go beyond simple comparisons with racial representation in the larger population and must somehow measure both frequency and seriousness of capital crimes between and

within racial groups. Following that line of reasoning, the Supreme Court, in the 1987 case of *McCleskey* v. *Kemp*,[155] held that a simple showing of racial discrepancies in the application of the death penalty does not constitute a constitutional violation. A 2001 study of racial and ethnic fairness in federal capital punishment sentences attempted to go beyond mere percentages in its analysis of the role played by race and ethnicity in capital punishment sentencing decisions.[156] Although the study, which closely reviewed 950 capital punishment cases, found that approximately 80% of federal death row inmates are African American, researchers found "no intentional racial or ethnic bias in how capital punishment was administered in federal cases."[157] Underrepresented groups were more likely to be sentenced to death, "but only because they are

■ **lecture note** Review the key Supreme Court decisions regarding the death penalty and related issues. Explain the impact that *Furman v. Georgia* and *Gregg v. Georgia* had on death penalty statutes around the country.

more likely to be arrested on facts that could support a capital charge, not because the justice system acts in a discriminatory fashion," the report said.[158] Read the entire report at **http://www .justice.gov/dag/pubdoc/deathpenaltystudy.htm**.

Another 2001 study, this one by New Jersey Supreme Court Special Master David Baime, found no evidence of bias against African American defendants in capital cases in New Jersey during the period studied (August 1982 through May 2000). The study concluded, "Simply stated, we discern no sound basis from the statistical evidence to conclude that the race or ethnicity of the defendant is a factor in determining which cases advance to a penalty trial and which defendants are ultimately sentenced to death. The statistical evidence abounds the other way—it strongly suggests that there are no racial or ethnic disparities in capital murder prosecution and death sentencing rates."[159]

Evidence of socioeconomic discrimination in the imposition of the death penalty in Nebraska between 1973 and 1999 was found in a 2001 study of more than 700 homicide cases in that state. The study, which had been mandated by the state legislature, found that whereas race did not appear to influence death penalty decisions, killers of victims with high socioeconomic status received the death penalty four times as often as would otherwise be expected. According to the study, "The data document significant statewide disparities in charging and sentencing outcomes based on the socio-economic status of the victim."[160]

Justifications for Capital Punishment

On February 11, 2004, 47-year-old Edward Lewis Lagrone was executed by lethal injection in Huntsville, Texas, for the murder of three people in their home. Earlier, Lagrone had molested and impregnated one of the victims, a ten-year-old child, whom he shot in the head as she was trying to protect her 19-month-old sister.[161] Lagrone also killed two of the child's great-aunts who were in the house at the time of the attack. One of the women, 76-year-old Caola Lloyd, was deaf, blind, and bedridden with cancer. Prior to the killings, Lagrone had served 7 years of a 20-year prison sentence for another murder and was on parole. "He's a poster child to justify the death penalty," said David Montague, the Tarrant County assistant district attorney who prosecuted Lagrone.

Like many others today, Montague feels that "cold-blooded murder" justifies a sentence of death. Justifications for the death penalty are collectively referred to as the *retentionist position*. The three retentionist arguments are (1) just deserts, (2) revenge, and (3) protection.

The just deserts argument makes the simple and straightforward claim that some people deserve to die for what they have done. Death is justly deserved; anything less cannot suffice as a sanction for the most heinous crimes. As U.S. Supreme Court Justice Potter Stewart once wrote, "The decision that capital punishment may be the appropriate sanction in extreme cases is an expression of the community's belief that certain crimes are themselves so grievous an affront to humanity that the only adequate response may be the penalty of death."[162]

> The just deserts argument makes the claim that some people deserve to die for what they have done.

Those who justify capital punishment as revenge attempt to appeal to the idea that survivors, victims, and the state are entitled to "closure." Only after execution of the criminal perpetrator, they say, can the psychological and social wounds engendered by the offense begin to heal.

The retentionist claim of protection asserts that offenders, once executed, can commit no further crimes. Clearly the least emotional of the retentionist claims, the protectionist argument may also be the weakest, as societal interests in protection can also be met in other ways, such as incarceration. In addition, various studies have shown that there is little likelihood of repeat offenses among people convicted of murder and later released.[163] One reason for such results, however, may be that murderers generally serve lengthy prison sentences prior to release and may have lost whatever youthful propensity for criminality they previously possessed. For an intriguing debate over the constitutionality of the death penalty, see **http://debatepedia .idebate.org/en/index.php/Debate:_Death_penalty**.

The Courts and the Death Penalty

The U.S. Supreme Court has for some time served as a sounding board for issues surrounding the death penalty. One of the Court's earliest cases in this area was *Wilkerson v. Utah* (1878),[164] which questioned shooting as a method of execution and raised Eighth Amendment claims that firing squads constituted a form of cruel and unusual punishment. The Court disagreed, however, contrasting the relatively civilized nature of firing squads with the various forms of torture often associated with capital punishment around the time the Bill of Rights was written.

Similarly, the Court supported electrocution as a permissible form of execution in *In re Kemmler* (1890).[165] In *Kemmler*, the Court defined cruel and unusual methods of execution as follows: "Punishments are cruel when they involve torture or a lingering death; but the punishment of death is not cruel, within the meaning of that word as used in the Constitution. It implies there is something inhuman and barbarous, something more than the mere extinguishing of

The Supreme Court supported electrocution as a permissible form of execution in *In re Kemmler*. life."[166] Almost 60 years later, the Court ruled that a second attempt at the electrocution of a convicted person, when the first did not work, did not violate the Eighth Amendment.[167] The Court reasoned that the initial failure was the consequence of accident or unforeseen circumstances and not the result of an effort on the part of executioners to be intentionally cruel.

It was not until 1972, however, in the landmark case of **Furman v. Georgia**,[168] that the Court recognized "evolving standards of decency"[169] that might necessitate a reconsideration of Eighth Amendment guarantees. In a 5–4 ruling, the *Furman* decision invalidated Georgia's death penalty statute on the basis that it allowed a jury unguided discretion in the imposition of a capital sentence. The majority of justices concluded that the Georgia statute, which permitted a jury to decide issues of guilt or innocence while it weighed sentencing options, allowed for an arbitrary and capricious application of the death penalty.

Many other states with statutes similar to Georgia's were affected by the *Furman* ruling but moved quickly to modify their procedures. What evolved was the two-step procedure used today in capital cases. In the first stage, guilt or innocence is decided; if the defendant is convicted of a crime for which execution is possible or if he pleads guilty to such an offense, a second (or penalty) phase ensues. The penalty phase, a kind of mini-trial, generally permits the introduction of new evidence that may have been irrelevant to the question of guilt but that may be relevant to punishment, such as drug use or childhood abuse. In most death penalty jurisdictions, juries determine the punishment. However, in Arizona, Idaho, Montana, and Nebraska, the trial judge sets the sentence in the second phase of capital murder trials, and Alabama, Delaware, Florida, and Indiana allow juries only to recommend a sentence to the judge. The Supreme Court formally approved the two-step trial procedure in **Gregg v. Georgia** (1976).[170] Post-*Gregg* decisions set limits on the use of death as a penalty for all but the most severe crimes. Other important U.S. Supreme Court decisions of relevance to the death penalty are shown in Table 11-5.

TABLE 11-5 | **The Courts and the Death Penalty**

YEAR	U.S. SUPREME COURT CASE	RULING
2014	*Hall* v. *Florida*	States cannot rely solely on an IQ score of above 70 to bar an inmate from claiming mental disability in the face of execution. Doing so creates an "unacceptable risk" that inmates with intellectual disabilities might be executed in violation of the Constitution.
2008	*Kennedy* v. *Louisiana*	The Eighth Amendment bars states from imposing the death penalty for the rape of a child where the crime did not result, and was not intended to result, in the victim's death.
2008	*Baze* v. *Rees*	The capital punishment protocol of lethal injection involving a three-drug "cocktail" used by Kentucky does not violate the Eighth Amendment because it does not create a substantial risk of wanton and unnecessary infliction of pain, torture, or lingering death.
2005	*Deck* v. *Missouri*	The Constitution forbids the use of visible shackles during a capital trial's penalty phase, as it does during the guilt phase, unless that use is "justified by an essential state interest"—such as courtroom security—specific to the defendant on trial.
2005	*Roper* v. *Simmons*	The Eighth and Fourteenth Amendments forbid imposition of the death penalty on offenders who were under the age of 18 when their crimes were committed.
2004	*Schriro* v. *Summerlin*	The rule established in *Apprendi* and *Ring* cannot be applied retroactively to sentences already imposed because it is merely a new procedural rule and not a substantive change.
2002	*Atkins* v. *Virginia*	Executing mentally retarded people violates the Constitution's ban on cruel and unusual punishments.
2002	*Ring* v. *Arizona*	Juries—not judges—must decide the facts, including those relating to aggravating circumstances that may lead to a death sentence.
1977	*Coker* v. *Georgia*	Struck down a Georgia law imposing the death penalty for the rape of an adult woman; the Court concluded that capital punishment under such circumstances is "grossly disproportionate" to the crime.
1976	*Gregg* v. *Georgia*	Upheld a new two-stage (bifurcated) procedural requirement of Georgia's revised capital punishment statute. The law requires guilt or innocence to be determined in the first stage of a bifurcated trial. Upon a guilty verdict, a presentencing hearing is held where the judge or jury hears additional aggravating and mitigating evidence. At least 1 of 10 specified aggravating circumstances must be found to exist beyond a reasonable doubt before a death sentence can be imposed.
1976	*Woodson* v. *North Carolina*	A state law requiring mandatory application of the death penalty for all first-degree murders was found to be unconstitutional.
1972	*Furman* v. *Georgia*	Recognized "evolving standards of decency" in invalidating Georgia's death penalty statute because it allowed a jury unguided discretion in the imposition of a capital sentence. The Georgia statute, which permitted a jury to decide issues of guilt or innocence while simultaneously weighing sentencing options, was found to allow for an arbitrary and capricious application of the death penalty.

Although questions may arise about sentencing practices, the majority of justices on today's High Court seem largely convinced of the fundamental constitutionality of a sentence of death. Open to debate, however, is the constitutionality of *methods* for execution. In a 1993 hearing, *Poyner* v. *Murray*,[174] the U.S. Supreme Court hinted at the possibility of revisiting questions first raised in *Kemmler*. The case challenged Virginia's use of the electric chair, calling it a form of cruel and unusual punishment. Syvasky Lafayette Poyner, who originally brought the case before the Court, lost his bid for a stay of execution and was electrocuted in March 1993. Nonetheless, in *Poyner*, Justices David H. Souter, Harry A. Blackmun, and John Paul Stevens wrote, "The Court has not spoken squarely on the underlying issue since *In re Kemmler*...and the holding of that case does not constitute a dispositive response to litigation of the issue in light of modern knowledge about the method of execution in question."

In a still more recent ruling, members of the Court questioned the constitutionality of hanging, suggesting that it too may be a form of cruel and unusual punishment. In that case, *Campbell* v. *Wood* (1994),[175] the defendant, Charles Campbell, raped a woman, was released from prison at the completion of his sentence, and then went back and murdered her. His request for a stay of execution was denied since the law of Washington State, where the murder occurred, offered Campbell a choice of various methods of execution and therefore an alternative to hanging. Similarly, in 1996, the Court upheld California's death penalty statute, which provides for lethal injection as the primary method of capital punishment in that state.[176] The constitutionality of the statute had been challenged by two death row inmates who claimed that a provision in the law that permitted condemned prisoners the choice of lethal gas in lieu of injection brought the statute within the realm of allowing cruel and unusual punishments.

Questions about the constitutionality of electrocution as a means of execution again came to the fore in 1997, when flames shot from the head and the leather mask covering the face of Pedro Medina during his Florida execution. Similarly, in 1999, blood poured from behind the mask covering Allen Lee "Tiny" Davis's face as he was put to death in Florida's electric chair. State officials claimed that the 344-pound Davis suffered a nosebleed brought on by hypertension and the blood-thinning medication that he had been taking. Photographs of Davis taken during and immediately after the execution showed him grimacing while bleeding profusely onto his chest and neck. In 2001, the Georgia Supreme Court declared electrocution to be unconstitutional, ending its use in that state.[177] The Georgia court cited testimony from lower-court records showing that electrocution may not result in a quick death or in an immediate cessation of consciousness. By the time of the court's decision, however, the Georgia legislature had already passed a law establishing lethal injection as the state's sole method of punishment for capital crimes.[178]

Timothy Ring, the Arizona death row inmate who won a 2002 U.S. Supreme Court case that could potentially invalidate the death sentences of at least 150 other prisoners. In that case, *Ring* v. *Arizona*, the Court held that defendants have a Sixth Amendment right to have a jury, and not just a judge, determine the existence of aggravating factors justifying the death penalty. What other decisions made by the Court since then have further refined the *Ring* ruling?

> *Ring* v. *Arizona* established that juries, not judges, must decide the facts that lead to a death sentence.

Following *Apprendi* v. *New Jersey* (discussed earlier in this chapter), attorneys for an Arizona death row inmate successfully challenged that state's practice of allowing judges, sitting without a jury, to make factual determinations necessary for imposition of the death penalty. In **Ring v. Arizona** (2002),[171] a jury had found Timothy Stuart Ring guilty of felony murder occurring in the course of an armed robbery for the killing of an armored car driver in 1994, but it deadlocked on the charge of premeditated murder. Under Arizona law, Ring could not be sentenced to death, the statutory maximum penalty for first-degree murder, unless a judge made further findings in a separate sentencing hearing. The death penalty could be imposed only if the judge found the existence of at least one aggravating circumstance specified by law that was not offset by mitigating circumstances. During such a hearing, the judge listened to an accomplice who said that Ring planned the robbery and shot the guard. The judge then determined that Ring was the actual killer and found that the killing was committed for financial gain (an aggravating factor). Following the hearing, Ring was sentenced to death. His attorneys appealed, claiming that, by the standards set forth in *Apprendi*, Arizona's sentencing scheme violated the Sixth Amendment's guarantee of a jury trial because it entrusted a judge with fact-finding powers that allowed Ring's sentence to be raised above what would otherwise have been the statutory maximum. The U.S. Supreme Court agreed and overturned Ring's sentence, finding that "Arizona's enumerated aggravating factors operate as the functional equivalent of an element of a greater offense." *Ring* established that juries, not judges, must decide the facts that lead to a death sentence. The *Ring* ruling called into question at least 150 judge-imposed death sentences[172] in at least five states (Arizona, Colorado, Idaho, Montana, and Nebraska).[173]

■ **lecture note**   List and explain the various arguments for and against the death penalty as a form of criminal sentencing. Engage the class in a discussion as to the relative merits of each of these arguments.

CJ | NEWS

Death-Row Exonerations Based on DNA Expose Flaws in Legal System

At last count, DNA testing has exonerated almost 60 people convicted of murder, and 17 of them were death row inmates, according to the Innocence Project.

The group, dedicated to freeing wrongly accused prisoners, says DNA testing has "opened a window into wrongful convictions so that we may study the causes and propose remedies that may minimize the chances that more innocent people are convicted."

Miscarriages of justice exposed by DNA testing include erroneous reports by witnesses, misidentification of evidence, biased jailhouse informants, and false confessions obtained by overzealous prosecutors.

Kirk Bloodsworth was the first death row inmate exonerated by DNA. He was found guilty in 1985 of raping and strangling a nine-year-old girl in Rosedale, Maryland, based on the testimony of five eyewitnesses. After learning that DNA testing was used to convict a man for murder, Bloodsworth asked to use it to un-convict him. The $15,000 test, which his attorney financed out-of-pocket, ruled him out, and he was released in 1993.

Speaking in 2013, to an audience of anti-capital-punishment supporters, Bloodsworth said "I was accused of the most brutal murder

Kirk Bloodsworth, the first death row inmate exonerated through the use of DNA evidence. Bloodsworth had been found guilty in 1985 of raping and strangling a nine-year-old Rosedale, Maryland, girl based on the testimony of five eyewitnesses. Later DNA testing absolved him of guilt, and he was released in 1993.

MLADEN ANTONOV/AFP/Getty Images/Newscom

in Maryland history.... It [only] took the jury two and a half hours to send me to the gas chamber."

In an even more serious miscarriage of justice, Claude Jones was executed in Texas in 2000 for murdering the owner of a Texas liquor store. Jones's conviction was largely based on a strand of hair at the crime scene that purportedly was his. But DNA tests ten years after the execution showed that it actually belonged to the storeowner.

In another example of the power of DNA testing, Michael Blair had a prior sex crime conviction on his record when he was picked up in 1993 for the murder of a seven-year-old girl in Plano, Texas. Three eyewitnesses said they saw him near the crime scene, even though the police had found him 17 miles away that day. Hairs in Blair's car were falsely linked to the victim. Blair was sentenced to death for the crime, but DNA testing eight years later excluded him and identified two other men. He was released.

Although Juan Rivera was never sentenced to death, he was convicted three times for the 1992 rape and murder of an 11-year-old babysitter in Waukegan, Illinois. On the night of the murder, he had been confined to his home by an electronic leg monitor for stealing a car stereo, but after many hours of interrogation he confessed to the crime. His confession allegedly contained details that only the killer would know, and three jailhouse informants also implicated him.

Before Rivera's third trial, tests showed his DNA did not match semen from the crime scene, but the prosecutor argued it could have come from an unidentified lover of the 11-year-old. "We don't quaver because somebody holds up three letters: DNA," he said. And Rivera was found guilty again. But in December 2011, an appeals court reversed the conviction and barred any more retrials, saying the evidence had been insufficient to convince any "rational trier of fact" of Rivera's guilt. Rivera was freed after spending nearly 20 years in prison.

The Innocence Project, founded in 1992 at the Cardozo School of Law at Yeshiva University in New York City, receives 3,000 requests for help every year and is evaluating 6,000 to 8,000 potential cases at any given time. It now has 61 affiliated chapters across the country.

A similar group, the Center on Wrongful Convictions at Northwestern University Law School in Chicago, Illinois, has been instrumental in 48 exonerations, including cases pursued by its lawyers before the center was founded. Thirteen of those prisoners had been sentenced to death, and 26 of the cases involved DNA testing.

In addition, the Death Penalty Information Center in Washington, D.C., provides analysis and information on issues about capital punishment, including wrongful convictions.

Resources: "230 Exonerated in U.S. by DNA Testing, 17 Were Sentenced to Die," The Innocence Project http://www.dadychery.org/2012/02/01/230-exonerated-by-dna-17-were-sentenced-to-die/; "1st Death Row Inmate Exonerated by DNA to Speak at UM," The Missoulian, October 11, 2011, http://missoulian.com/news/local/article_1c836748-f3b2-11e0-b14b-001cc4c002e0.html; "Never Think a Person in Prison Is Lost,' Juan Rivera Tells Law Students," The Chicago Tribune, April 4, 2012, http://www.chicagotribune.com/news/local/ct-met-juan-rivera-judge-20120404,0,1540689.story; and Scott Shane, "A Death Penalty Fight Comes Home," New York Times, February 5, 2013, http://www.nytimes.com/2013/02/06/us/exonerated-inmate-seeks-end-to-maryland-death-penalty.html?_r=0.

In 2006, questions were raised about lethal injections as constituting cruel and unusual punishment. Those questions originated with eyewitness accounts, postmortem blood testing, and execution logs that seemed to show that some of those executed remained conscious but paralyzed and experienced excruciating pain before dying.[179] Such claims focused on the composition of the chemical cocktail used in executions, which contains one drug (sodium thiopental, a short-acting barbiturate) to induce sleep, another (pancuronium bromide) to paralyze the muscles (but which does not cause unconsciousness), and a third (potassium chloride) to stop the heart. If the first chemical is improperly administered, the condemned person remains conscious, and the procedure can cause severe pain and discomfort.

Complicating matters is the fact that the ethical codes of most professional medical organizations forbid medical practitioners to take life—meaning that although the codes are not legally binding, medi-

> Medical professionals are largely excluded from taking part in executions, other than to verify the fact that death has occurred.

cal professionals are largely excluded from taking part in executions, other than to verify the fact that death has occurred. To counter fears that lethal injections cause pain, some states have begun using medical monitoring devices that show brain activity and can ensure that sleep is occurring.[180]

Finally, in 2014, in the case of *Hall* v. *Florida*, the Supreme Court held that states cannot rely solely on an IQ score of above 70 to bar an inmate from claiming mental disability in the face of execution.[181] Doing so, the Court ruled, creates an "unacceptable risk" that inmates with intellectual disabilities might be executed in violation of the Constitution.

In 2008, the Court took up this issue in the case of *Baze* v. *Rees*,[182] which had been brought by prisoners on Kentucky's death row. The Court held that the capital punishment protocol used by Kentucky does not violate the Eighth Amendment because it does not create a substantial risk of wanton and unnecessary infliction of pain, torture, or lingering death. "Because some risk of pain is inherent in even the most humane execution method," wrote the justices, "the Constitution does not demand the avoidance of all risk of pain."

The Future of the Death Penalty

Support for the death penalty varies considerably from state to state and from one region of the country to another. Short of renewed Supreme Court intervention, the future of capital punishment may depend more on popular opinion. A 2015 national poll of

> Ultimately, public opinion about the death penalty may turn on the issue of whether innocent people have been executed.

registered voters found that 56% were in favor of capital punishment for murder.[183] Support for the death penalty has, for the most part, consistently declined since 1994, when 80% were in favor of the punishment. Support has increased, however, for death penalty alternatives, including life with no possibility of parole, or life with the possibility of parole.

Ultimately, public opinion about the death penalty may turn on the issue of whether innocent people have been executed. According to a number of recent studies, Americans from all walks of life are less likely to support capital punishment if they believe that innocent people have been put to death at the hands of the justice system or if they think that the death penalty is being applied unfairly.[184]

SUMMARY

- The goals of criminal sentencing include retribution, incapacitation, deterrence, rehabilitation, and restoration. Retribution corresponds to the just deserts model of sentencing, which holds that offenders are responsible for their crimes. Incapacitation seeks to protect innocent members of society from offenders who might harm them if not prevented from doing so. The goal of deterrence is to prevent future criminal activity through the example or threat of punishment. Rehabilitation seeks to bring about fundamental changes in offenders and their behavior to reduce the likelihood of future criminality. Restoration seeks to address the damage done by crime by making the victim and the community "whole again."

- The indeterminate sentencing model is characterized primarily by vast judicial choice. It builds on the belief that convicted offenders are more likely to participate in their own rehabilitation if such participation will reduce the amount of time that they have to spend in prison.

- Structured sentencing is largely a child of the just deserts philosophy. It grew out of concerns with proportionality, equity, and social debt—all of which this chapter discusses. Numerous different types of structured sentencing models have been created, including determinate sentencing, which requires that a convicted offender be sentenced to a fixed term that may be reduced by good time or gain time, and a voluntary/advisory sentencing model under which guidelines consist of recommended sentencing policies that are not required by law, are usually based on past sentencing practices, and are meant to serve as guides to judges. Mandatory sentencing, another form of structured sentencing, mandates clearly enumerated punishments for specific offenses or for habitual offenders convicted of a series of crimes. The applicability of structured sentencing guidelines has been called into question by recent U.S. Supreme Court decisions.

- Just deserts and get tough on crime policies have increased prison populations to the point of overflowing, adding to budget crises that both the federal and state governments have been facing for the past couple of decades. Prison population in the United States have grown far faster than rates of serious violent and property crime, leading to calls for changes in some laws and for the implementation of alternative forms of criminal sentencing.

- Alternative sanctions include the use of court-ordered community service, home detention, day reporting, drug treatment, psychological counseling, victim–offender mediation, and intensive supervision in lieu of other, more traditional sanctions such as imprisonment and fines. Numerous questions have been raised about alternative sentences, including questions about their impact on public safety, the cost-effectiveness of such sanctions, and the long-term effects of community sanctions on people assigned to alternative programs.

- Probation and parole officers routinely conduct background investigations to provide information that judges may use in deciding on the appropriate kind or length of sentence for convicted offenders.

- Historically, criminal courts have often allowed victims to testify at trial but have otherwise downplayed the experience of victimization and the suffering it causes. A new interest in the experience of victims, beginning in the 1970s in this country, has led to a greater legal recognition of victims' rights, including a right to allocution (the right to be heard during criminal proceedings). Many states have passed victims' rights amendments to their constitutions, although a federal victims' rights amendment has yet to be enacted. The Crime Victims' Rights Act of 2004 established statutory rights for victims of federal crimes and gives them the necessary legal authority to assert those rights in federal court.

- The four traditional sentencing options identified in this chapter are fines, probation, imprisonment, and—in cases of especially horrific offenses—death. The appropriateness of each sentencing option for various kinds of crimes was discussed, and the pros and cons of each were examined.

- Arguments for capital punishment identified in this chapter include revenge, just deserts, and the protection of society. The revenge argument builds upon the need for personal and communal closure. The just deserts argument makes the straightforward claim that some people deserve to die for what they have done. Societal protection is couched in terms of deterrence, as those who are executed cannot commit future crimes, and execution serves as an example to other would-be criminals. Arguments against capital punishment include findings that death sentences have been imposed on innocent people, that the death penalty has not been found to be an effective deterrent, that it is often arbitrarily imposed, that it tends to discriminate against powerless groups and individuals, and that it is very expensive because of the numerous court appeals involved. Opponents also argue that the state should recognize the sanctity of human life.

KEY TERMS

aggravating circumstances, 351
alternative sentencing, 360
capital offense, 368
capital punishment, 368
determinate sentencing, 350
deterrence, 347
diversion, 357
equity, 350
gain time, 350
general deterrence, 347

good time, 350
incapacitation, 346
indeterminate sentencing, 349
just deserts, 346
justice reinvestment, 360
mandatory sentencing, 356
mitigating circumstances, 351
presentence investigation (PSI), 361
presumptive sentencing, 351

proportionality, 350
recidivism, 347
recidivism rates, 347
rehabilitation, 347
restoration, 348
restorative justice (RJ), 348
retribution, 346
sentencing, 345

social debt, 350
specific deterrence, 347
structured sentencing, 350
truth in sentencing, 351
victim-impact statement, 364
voluntary/advisory sentencing guidelines, 351
writ of *habeas corpus*, 371

KEY CASES

Apprendi v. *New Jersey*, 354
Blakely v. *Washington*, 354
Coleman v. *Thompson*, 371
Furman v. *Georgia*, 380
Gregg v. *Georgia*, 380
In re Kemmler, 379

McCleskey v. *Zant*, 371
Mistretta v. *U.S.*, 352
Ring v. *Arizona*, 381
Schlup v. *Delo*, 371
U.S. v. *Booker*, 355
Wilkerson v. *Utah*, 379

QUESTIONS FOR REVIEW

1. Describe the five goals of contemporary criminal sentencing discussed in this chapter. Which of these goals do you think ought to be the primary goal of sentencing? How might your choice vary with the type of offense committed? In what circumstances might your choice be less acceptable?

2. Illustrate the nature of indeterminate sentencing, and explain its positive aspects. What led some states to abandon indeterminate sentencing?

3. What is structured sentencing? What is the status of the federal structured sentencing model today?

4. How did get-tough sentencing policies lead to the overcrowding that we see in our prisons today?

5. What are alternative sanctions? Give some examples of alternative sanctions, and offer an assessment of how effective they might be.

6. What is a presentence investigation? How do presentence investigations contribute to the contents of presentence reports? How are presentence reports used?

7. Describe the history of victims' rights and services in this country. What role does the victim play in criminal justice proceedings today?

8. What are the four traditional sentencing options? Under what circumstances might each be appropriate?

9. Outline the major arguments on both sides of the capital punishment debate.

QUESTIONS FOR REFLECTION

1. Of the different kinds of sentencing practices described in this chapter, which do you think makes the most sense? Why?

2. If you could set sentencing practices in your state and had to choose between a determinate and an indeterminate scheme, which would you select? Why?

3. What is truth in sentencing? Do you agree that it is an important concept? Why or why not?

4. Explain the development of federal sentencing guidelines. What have recent court decisions said about the applicability of those guidelines?

5. Is there a way to be tough on crime without further increasing prison populations?

NOTES

1. The Sentencing Project, "Oregon Passes Racial Impact Statement Legislation," *Race and Justice News*, June 28, 2013.

2. Matt Smith, "'Racial Justice Act' Repealed in North Carolina," CNN, June 21, 2013, http://www.cnn.com/2013/06/20/justice/north-carolina-death-penalty (accessed August 2, 2013).

3. Marc Mauer, "Racial Impact Statements: Changing Policies to Address Disparities," *Criminal Justice*, Vol. 23, No. 4 (winter 2009).

4. For a thorough discussion of the philosophy of punishment and sentencing, see David Garland, *Punishment and Modern Society: A Study in Social Theory* (Chicago: University of Chicago Press, 1990). See also Ralph D. Ellis and Carol S. Ellis, *Theories of Criminal Justice: A Critical Reappraisal* (Wolfeboro, NH: Longwood Academic, 1989); and Colin Summer, *Censure, Politics, and Criminal Justice* (Bristol, PA: Open University Press, 1990).

5. Punishment is said to be required because social order (and the laws that represent it) could not exist for long if transgressions went unsanctioned.

6. Hugo Adam Bedau, "Retributivism and the Theory of Punishment," *Journal of Philosophy*, Vol. 75 (November 1978), pp. 601–620.

7. The definitive study during this period was Douglas Lipton, Robert Martinson, and J. Woks, *The Effectiveness of Correctional Treatment: A Survey of Treatment Valuation Studies* (New York: Praeger Press, 1975).

8. See, for example, Lawrence W. Sherman et al., *Preventing Crime: What Works, What Doesn't, What's Promising* (Washington, DC: National Institute of Justice, 1997).

9. Gordon Bazemore and Mark S. Umbreit, foreword to *Balanced and Restorative Justice: Program Summary* (Washington, DC: Office of Juvenile Justice and Delinquency Prevention, 1994).

10. Shay Bilchik, *Balanced and Restorative Justice for Juveniles: A Framework for Juvenile Justice in the 21st Century* (Washington, DC: Office of Juvenile Justice and Delinquency Prevention, 1997), p. ii.

11. Ibid., p. 14.

12. Ibid.

13. U.S. Code, Title 18, Section 3563(a)(2).

14. Donna Hunzeker, "State Sentencing Systems and 'Truth in Sentencing,'" *State Legislative Report*, Vol. 20, No. 3 (Denver, CO: National Conference of State Legislatures, 1995).

15. Paula M. Ditton and Doris James Wilson, *Truth in Sentencing in State Prisons* (Washington, DC: Bureau of Justice Statistics, 1999).

16. "Oklahoma Rapist Gets 30,000 Years," *United Press International*, southwest edition, December 23, 1994.

17. For a historical consideration of alleged disparities, see G. Kleck, "Racial Discrimination in Criminal Sentencing: A Critical Evaluation of the Evidence with Additional Evidence on the Death Penalty," *American Sociological Review*, No. 46 (1981), pp. 783–805; and G. Kleck, "Life Support for Ailing Hypotheses: Modes of Summarizing the Evidence for Racial Discrimination in Sentencing," *Law and Human Behavior*, No. 9 (1985), pp. 271–285.

18. As discussed later in this chapter, federal sentencing guidelines did not become effective until 1987 and still had to meet many court challenges.

19. U.S. Sentencing Commission, *Federal Sentencing Guidelines Manual* (Washington, DC: U.S. Government Printing Office, 1987), p. 2.

20. Inmates can still earn a maximum of 54 days per year of good-time credit.

21. The Parole Commission Phaseout Act of 1996 requires the attorney general to report to Congress yearly as to whether it is cost-effective for the U.S. Parole Commission to remain a separate agency or whether its functions (and personnel) should be assigned elsewhere. Under the law, if the attorney general recommends assigning the commission's functions to another component of the Department of Justice, federal parole will continue as long as necessary.

22. Lawrence A. Greenfeld, *Prison Sentences and Time Served for Violence* (Washington, DC: Bureau of Justice Statistics, April 1995).

23. For an excellent review of the act and its implications, see Gregory D. Lee, "U.S. Sentencing Guidelines: Their Impact on Federal Drug Offenders," *FBI Law Enforcement Bulletin*, May 1995, pp. 17–21.

24. *Mistretta v. U.S.*, 488 U.S. 361, 371 (1989).

25. For an engaging overview of how mitigating factors might be applied under the guidelines, see *Koon v. U.S.*, 116 S.Ct. 2035, 135 L.Ed.2d 392 (1996).

26. U.S. Sentencing Commission, *Federal Sentencing Guidelines Manual*, p. 207.

27. Ibid., p. 8.

28. National Institute of Justice, *Sentencing Commission Chairman Wilkins Answers Questions on the Guidelines*, National Institute of Justice Research in Action Series (Washington, DC: NIJ, 1987), p. 7.

29. *Melendez v. U.S.*, 117 S.Ct. 383, 136 L.Ed.2d 301 (1996).

30. *Apprendi v. New Jersey*, 120 S.Ct. 2348 (2000).

31. See, for example, Alexandra A. E. Shapiro and Jonathan P. Bach, "Applying 'Apprendi' to Federal Sentencing Rules," *New York Law Journal*, March 23, 2001, http://www.lw.com/pubs/articles/pdf/applyingApprendi.pdf (accessed June 30, 2008); and Freya Russell, "Limiting the Use of Acquitted and Uncharged Conduct at Sentencing: *Apprendi v. New Jersey* and Its Effect on the Relevant Conduct Provision of the United States Sentencing Guidelines," *California Law Review*, Vol. 89 (July 2001), p. 1199.

32. *U.S. v. O'Brien*, U.S. Supreme Court, No. 08-1569 (decided May 24, 2010).

33. *Blakely v. Washington*, 542 U.S. 296 (2004).

34. *Cunningham v. California*, 549 U.S. 270 (2007).

35. *U.S. v. Booker*, 543 U.S. 220 (2005).

36. Combined with *U.S. v. Booker* (2005).

37. Stanley E. Adelman, "Supreme Court Invalidates Federal Sentencing Guidelines...to an Extent," *On the Line, the Newsletter of the American Correctional Association*, May 2005, p. 1.

38. See *United States v. Rodriguez*, 398 F.3d 1291, 1297 (11th Cir. 2005).

39. *Rita v. U.S.*, 551 U.S. 338 (2007).

40. *Gall v. U.S.*, 552 U.S. 38 (2007).

41. *Alleyne v. U.S.*, U.S. Supreme Court, No. 11-9335 (decided June 17, 2013).

42. The *Alleyne* case overturned the Court's earlier ruling in *Harris v. U.S.* (2002), which held that "judicial factfinding that increases

the mandatory minimum sentence for a crime is permissible under the Sixth Amendment."

43. U.S. Sentencing Commission, News Release, "Sentencing Commission Issues Comprehensive Report on the Continuing Impact of *United States* v. *Booker* on Federal Sentencing," January 30, 2013.

44. Ibid.

45. United States Sentencing Commission, "Report to Congress: Mandatory Minimum Penalties in the Federal Criminal Justice System," October 2011, http://www.ussc.gov/Legislative _and_Public_Affairs/Congressional_Testimony_and_Reports/ Mandatory_Minimum_Penalties/20111031_RtC_Mandatory _Minimum.cfm (accessed November 24, 2011).

46. Michael Miller, "California Gets 'Three Strikes' Anti-Crime Bill," Reuters, March 7, 1994.

47. Tamar Lewin, "Three-Strikes Law Is Overrated in California, Study Finds," *New York Times*, August 23, 2001, http://query. nytimes.com/gst/fullpage.html?res59505E7DB1531F930A1575B C0A9679C8B63 (accessed September 2, 2009).

48. *Ewing* v. *California*, 538 U.S. 11 (2003); and *Lockyer* v. *Andrade*, 538 U.S. 63 (2003).

49. Under California law, a person who commits petty theft can be charged with a felony if he or she has prior felony convictions. The charge is known as "petty theft with prior convictions." Andrade's actual sentence was two 25-year prison terms to be served consecutively.

50. Tracey Kaplan, "Proposition 36: Voters Overwhelmingly Ease Three Strikes Law," *Mercury News*, November 7, 2012.

51. Barry Krisberg, "Prop 47: As California Goes, So Goes the Nation?" *The Crime Report*, November 5, 2014.

52. Much of the material in this section is derived from Dale Parent et al., *Mandatory Sentencing*, National Institute of Justice Research in Action Series (Washington, DC: NIJ, 1997).

53. In mid-1996, the California Supreme Court ruled the state's three-strikes law an undue intrusion on judges' sentencing discretion, and California judges now use their own discretion in evaluating which offenses "fit" within the meaning of the law.

54. Michael Tonry, *Sentencing Reform Impacts* (Washington, DC: National Institute of Justice, 1987).

55. D. C. McDonald and K. E. Carlson, *Sentencing in the Courts: Does Race Matter? The Transition to Sentencing Guidelines, 1986–90* (Washington, DC: Bureau of Justice Statistics, 1993).

56. U.S. Sentencing Commission, *Special Report to Congress: Cocaine and Federal Sentencing Policy* (Washington, DC: U.S. Sentencing Commission, May 2007).

57. Fair Sentencing Act of 2010, Pub. L. 111-122.

58. S. 1410: Smarter Sentencing Act of 2014, GovTrack Bill Summary, https://www.govtrack.us/congress/bills/113/ s1410#summary/oursummary (accessed January 30, 2015).

59. Michael Mitchell and Michael Leachman, *Changing Priorities: State Criminal Justice Reforms and Investments in Education* (Washington, D.C.: Center on Budget and Policy Priorities, 2014).

60. Richard Willing, "Thief Challenges Dose of Shame as Punishment," *USA Today*, August 18, 2004, p. 3A.

61. John Braithwaite, *Crime, Shame, and Reintegration* (Cambridge, England: Cambridge University Press, 1989).

62. Such evidence does, in fact, exist. See, for example, Harold G. Grasmick, Robert J. Bursik, Jr., and Bruce J. Arneklev, "Reduction in Drunk Driving as a Response to Increased Threats of Shame, Embarrassment, and Legal Sanctions," *Criminology*, Vol. 31, No. 1 (1993), pp. 41–67.

63. Council of State Governments, Lessons from the States, *Reducing Recidivism and Curbing Corrections Costs through Justice Reinvestment* (Council of State Governments, 2013).

64. Ibid.

65. Ibid., p. 4, from which some of the wording in these sentences is adapted.

66. Nicole D. Porter, *The State of Sentencing 2012* (Washington, DC: The Sentencing Project, 2013).

67. Joan Petersilia, *House Arrest*, National Institute of Justice Crime File Study Guide (Washington, DC: NIJ, 1988).

68. The Center adapted a number of these principles from James Andrews and D. A. Bonta, "Risk-Need-Responsivity Model for Offender Assessment and Rehabilitation," http://www .publicsafety.gc.ca/res/cor/rep/_fl/Risk_Need_2007-06 _e.pdf (accessed March 2, 2013).

69. Pamela M. Casey, Roger K. Warren, and Jennifer K. Elek, *Using Offender Risk and Needs Assessment Information at Sentencing: Guidance for Courts from a National Working Group* (National Center for State Courts, 2011).

70. Privacy Act of 1974, 5 U.S.C.A. 522a, 88 Statute 1897, Pub. L. 93-579, December 31, 1974.

71. Freedom of Information Act, U.S. Code, Title 5, Section 522, and amendments. The status of presentence investigative reports has not yet been clarified under this act to the satisfaction of all legal scholars.

72. City of New York, Citywide Accountability Program, S.T.A.R.S. (Statistical Tracking, Analysis, and Reporting System), http://www.nyc.gov/html/prob/pdf/stars_92005.pdf (accessed May 13, 2007).

73. For a good review of the issues involved, see Robert C. Davis, Arthur J. Lurigio, and Wesley G. Skogan, *Victims of Crime*, 2nd ed. (Thousand Oaks, CA: Sage, 1997); and Leslie Sebba, *Third Parties: Victims and the Criminal Justice System* (Columbus: Ohio State University Press, 1996).

74. President's Task Force on Victims of Crime, *Final Report* (Washington, DC: U.S. Government Printing Office, 1982).

75. Peter Finn and Beverly N. W. Lee, *Establishing and Expanding Victim-Witness Assistance Programs* (Washington, DC: National Institute of Justice, 1988).

76. Senate Joint Resolution (SJR) 65 is a major revision of an initial proposal, SJR 52, which Senators Kyl and Feinstein introduced on April 22, 1996. Representative Henry Hyde introduced House Joint Resolution 174, a companion to SJR 52, and a similar proposal, House Joint Resolution 173, on April 22, 1996.

77. Senate Joint Resolution 44, 105th Congress.

78. See the National Center for Victims of Crime's critique of the 1998 amendment at http://www.ncvc.org/law/Ncvca.htm (accessed January 10, 2000).

79. See the National Victims' Constitutional Amendment Network news page, http://www.nvcan.org/news.htm (accessed January 10, 2007).

80. National Victims' Constitutional Amendment Passage, http://www.nvcap.org (accessed June 9, 2009).

81. Pub. L. 97-291.

82. USA PATRIOT Act of 2001, Section 624.

83. Office for Victims of Crime, *Report to the Nation, 2003* (Washington, DC: OVC, 2003).

84. 18 U.S.C. § 3771.

85. U.S. Senate, Republican Policy Committee, Legislative Notice No. 63, April 22, 2004.

86. Proposition 8, California's Victim's Bill of Rights.

87. National Victim Center, Mothers against Drunk Driving, and American Prosecutors Research Institute, *Impact Statements:*

A Victim's Right to Speak; A Nation's Responsibility to Listen (Washington, DC: Office for Victims of Crime, July 1994).

88. *Kelly v. California*, 555 U.S. 1020 (2008).

89. Robert C. Davis and Barbara E. Smith, "The Effects of Victim Impact Statements on Sentencing Decisions: A Test in an Urban Setting," *Justice Quarterly*, Vol. 11, No. 3 (September 1994), pp. 453–469.

90. Office for Victims of Crime, *Vision 21: Transforming Victim Services—Final Report* (Washington, DC: USDOJ, May 2013).

91. Bureau of Justice Statistics, *Report to the Nation on Crime and Justice*, 2nd ed. (Washington, DC: U.S. Government Printing Office, 1988), p. 90.

92. Sean Rosenmerkel, Matthew Durose, and Donald Farole, Jr., *Felony Sentences in State Courts, 2006* (Washington, DC: Bureau of Justice Statistics, December 2009). Data for 1990 come from Matthew R. Durose, David J. Levin, and Patrick A. Langan, *Felony Sentences in State Courts, 1998* (Washington, DC: Bureau of Justice Statistics, 2001).

93. Matthew R. Durose and Patrick A. Langan, *Felony Sentences in State Courts, 2002* (Washington, DC: Bureau of Justice Statistics, 2004), p. 2.

94. Sally T. Hillsman, Joyce L. Sichel, and Barry Mahoney, *Fines in Sentencing* (New York: Vera Institute of Justice, 1983).

95. Ibid., p. 2.

96. Ibid., p. 4.

97. Ibid.

98. "Swiss Speeder Fined a Record $290,000," *USA Today*, January 7, 2010, http://content.usatoday.com/communities/ondeadline/post/2010/01/swiss-speeder-fined-a-record-290000/1 (accessed July 5, 2010).

99. James S. Tyree and Tony Thornton, "Judge Sentences Underwood to Die," *Oklahoman*, April 3, 2008, http://newsok.com/article/3224954/1207252268 (accessed May 28, 2009).

100. Death Penalty Information Center, "State-by-State Death Penalty Information," http://www.deathpenaltyinfo.org/FactSheet.pdf (accessed July 12, 2009).

101. Death Penalty Information Center, "Executions by Year," http://www.deathpenaltyinfo.org/executions-year (accessed May 20, 2015).

102. Statistics in this paragraph from "State-by-State Death Penalty Information."

103. Tracy L. Snell, *Capital Punishment, 2013—Statistical Tables* (Washington, DC: BJS, 2014).

104. Tracy L. Snell, *Capital Punishment*, 2013.

105. Johnlee Varghese, "Saudi Arabia Publicly Beheads Burmese Woman by Sword; Woman Shouts 'I Did Not Kill, I Did Not Kill,'" *International Business Times*, January 16, 2015, http://www.ibtimes.co.in/saudi-arabia-publicly-beheads-burmese-woman-by-sword-woman-shouts-i-did-not-kill-i-did-not-kill-620619 (accessed March 5, 2015).

106. "Saudi Beheadings Spiked in 2014 Amid Kingdom's Fears of Dissent," Fox News, January 5, 2015, http://www.foxnews.com/world/2015/01/05/saudi-beheadings-spiked-in-14-amid-kingdom-fears-dissent (accessed March 5, 2015).

107. Justin McCurry, "Japan Executions Resume with Three Hangings," *The Guardian*, http://www.guardian.co.uk/world/2013/feb/21/japan-executions-resume-three-hangings (accessed April 4, 2013).

108. Amnesty International, "The Death Penalty in 2013," http://amnesty.org/en/death-penalty/death-sentences-and-executions-in-2013 (accessed May 1, 2015).

109. Richard Willing, "Expansion of Death Penalty to Nonmurders Faces Challenges," *USA Today*, May 14, 1997.

110. *Kennedy v. Louisiana*, 554 U.S. 407(2008).

111. Death Penalty Information Center, "Death Row Inmates by State," http://www.deathpenaltyinfo.org/death-row-inmates-state-and-size-death-row-year (accessed April 20, 2015).

112. Tracy L. Snell, *Capital Punishment*, 2013.

113. Ibid., Table 11.

114. Details for this story come from Jenifer Warren and Maura Dolan, "Tookie Williams Is Executed," *Los Angeles Times*, December 13, 2005, http://www.latimes.com/news/local/la-me-execution13dec13,0,799154.story?coll=la-home-headlines (accessed May 20, 2006).

115. "Warden: Williams Frustrated at End," http://CNN.com, December 13, 2005, http://www.cnn.com/2005/LAW/12/13/williams.execution (accessed July 2, 2006).

116. "Chief Justice Calls for Limits on Death Row Habeas Appeals," *Criminal Justice Newsletter*, February 15, 1989, pp. 6–7.

117. *McCleskey v. Zant*, 499 U.S. 467, 493–494 (1991).

118. *Coleman v. Thompson*, 501 U.S. 722 (1991).

119. *Schlup v. Delo*, 115 S.Ct. 851, 130 L.Ed.2d 808 (1995).

120. Pub. L. 103-322.

121. *Felker v. Turpin*, 117 S.Ct. 30, 135 L.Ed.2d 1123 (1996).

122. *McQuiggin v. Perkins*, U.S. Supreme Court, No. 12-126 (decided May 28, 2013).

123. *Elledge v. Florida*, 525 U.S. 944 (1998).

124. Michelle Locke, "Victim Forgives," Associated Press wire service, May 19, 1996.

125. Ibid.

126. Arthur Koestler, *Reflections on Hanging* (New York: Macmillan, 1956), p. xii.

127. Death Penalty Information Center, "Innocence: List of Those Freed from Death Row," http://www.deathpenaltyinfo.org/innocence-list-those-freed-death-row (accessed July 1, 2013).

128. Edward Connors et al., *Convicted by Juries, Exonerated by Science: Case Studies in the Use of DNA Evidence to Establish Innocence after Trial* (Washington, DC: National Institute of Justice, 1996).

129. Barry Scheck and Peter Neufeld, "DNA and Innocence Scholarship," in Saundra D. Westervelt and John A. Humphrey, *Wrongly Convicted: Perspectives on Failed Justice* (New Brunswick, NJ: Rutgers University Press, 2001), pp. 248–249.

130. Ibid., p. 246.

131. *Maryland v. King*, U.S. Supreme Court, No. 12-207 (decided June 3, 2013).

132. James S. Liebman, Jeffrey Fagan, and Simon H. Rifkind, *A Broken System: Error Rates in Capital Cases, 1973–1995* (New York: Columbia University School of Law, 2000), http://justice.policy.net/jpreport/finrep.PDF (accessed March 3, 2008).

133. Jon B. Gould, Julia Carrano, Richard Leo, and Joseph Young, "Predicting Erroneous Convictions: A Social Science Approach to Miscarriages of Justice—Final Report to the National Institute of Justice, February 2013," https://www.ncjrs.gov/pdffiles1/nij/grants/241389.pdf.

134. See, for example, Jim Yardley, "Texas Retooling Criminal Justice in Wake of Furor on Death Penalty," *New York Times*, June 1, 2001.

135. Title IV of the Justice for All Act of 2004.

136. At the time the legislation was enacted, Congress estimated that 300,000 rape kits remained unanalyzed in police department evidence lockers across the country.

137. The act also provides funding for the DNA Sexual Assault Justice Act (Title III of the Justice for All Act of 2004) and the Rape Kits and DNA Evidence Backlog Elimination Act of 2000 (U.S. Code, Title 42, Section 14135), authorizing more than $500

million for programs to improve the capacity of crime labs to conduct DNA analysis, reduce non-DNA backlogs, train evidence examiners, support sexual assault forensic examiner programs, and promote the use of DNA to identify missing persons.

138. In those states that accept federal monies under the legislation.

139. See N.C. G.S. § 15A-1460-75.

140. North Carolina Innocence Inquiry Commission, "Case Statistics," http://www.innocencecommission-nc.gov/statistics. htm (accessed June 20, 2010).

141. The Innocence Project, "Other Projects around the World," http://www.innocenceproject.org/about/Other-Projects.php (accessed April 30, 2012).

142. Samuel R. Gross, Barbara O'Brien, Chen Hu, and Edward H. Kennedy, "Rate of False Conviction of Criminal Defendants Who Are Sentenced to Death," *Proceedings of the National Academy of Sciences*, Vol. 111., No. 20 (March 25, 2014) http://www.pnas.org/cgi/doi/10.1073/pnas.1306417111 (accessed May 4, 2015).

143. Laura Bauer, "DNA Tests on Inmates Sometimes Proved They Were Guilty," *Kansas City Star*, April 7, 2009.

144. *District Attorney's Office* v. *Osborne*, 129 S.Ct. 2308 (2009).

145. Studies include S. Decker and C. Kohfeld, "A Deterrence Study of the Death Penalty in Illinois: 1933–1980," *Journal of Criminal Justice*, Vol. 12, No. 4 (1984), pp. 367–379; and S. Decker and C. Kohfeld, "An Empirical Analysis of the Effect of the Death Penalty in Missouri," *Journal of Crime and Justice*, Vol. 10, No. 1 (1987), pp. 23–46.

146. See, especially, W. C. Bailey, "Deterrence and the Death Penalty for Murders in Utah: A Time Series Analysis," *Journal of Contemporary Law*, Vol. 5, No. 1 (1978), pp. 1–20; and W. C. Bailey, "An Analysis of the Deterrent Effect of the Death Penalty for Murder in California," *Southern California Law Review*, Vol. 52, No. 3 (1979), pp. 743–764.

147. B. E. Forst, "The Deterrent Effect of Capital Punishment: A Cross-State Analysis of the 1960's," *Minnesota Law Review*, Vol. 61, No. 5 (1977), pp. 743–767.

148. Hashem Dezhbakhsh, Paul Rubin, and Joanna Mehlhop Shepherd, "Does Capital Punishment Have a Deterrent Effect? New Evidence from Post-Moratorium Panel Data," Emory University, January 2001, http://userwww.service.emory.edu/~cozden/ Dezhbakhsh_01_01_paper.pdf (accessed November 13, 2001).

149. Ibid., abstract.

150. Ibid., p. 19.

151. Committee on Law and Justice, *Deterrence and the Death Penalty* (Washington, DC: National Academy of Sciences, 2012).

152. As some of the evidence presented before the Supreme Court in *Furman* v. *Georgia*, 408 U.S. 238 (1972), suggested.

153. *USA Today*, April 27, 1989.

154. Thomas J. Keil and Gennaro F. Vito, "Race and the Death Penalty in Kentucky Murder Trials: 1976–1991," *American Journal of Criminal Justice*, Vol. 20, No. 1 (1995), pp. 17–36.

155. McCleskey v. Kemp, 481 U.S. 279, 107 S.Ct. 1756, 95 L.Ed.2d 262 (1987).

156. Department of Justice, *The Federal Death Penalty System: Supplementary Data, Analysis and Revised Protocols for Capital Case Review* (Washington, DC: Department of Justice, 2001).

157. David Stout, "Attorney General Says Report Shows No Racial and Ethnic Bias in Federal Death Sentences," *New York Times*, June 7, 2001, http://college1.nytimes.com/guests/articles /2001/06/07/850513.xml (accessed May 20, 2007).

158. "Expanded Study Shows No Bias in Death Penalty, Ashcroft Says," *Criminal Justice Newsletter*, Vol. 31, No. 13 (June 18, 2001), p. 4.

159. Mary P. Gallagher, "Race Found to Have No Effect on Capital Sentencing in New Jersey," *New Jersey Law Journal* (August 21, 2001), p. 1.

160. "Nebraska Death Penalty System Given Mixed Review in a State Study," *Criminal Justice Newsletter*, Vol. 31, No. 16 (August 2001), pp. 4–5.

161. Details for this story come from Michael Graczyk, "Killer of Pregnant Ten-Year-Old Set to Die Tonight," *Associated Press*, February 10, 2004; and Texas Execution Information Center, "Edward Lagrone," http://www.txexecutions.org/reports/318. asp (accessed May 15, 2004).

162. Justice Potter Stewart, as quoted in *USA Today*, April 27, 1989, p. 12A.

163. Koestler, *Reflections on Hanging*, pp. 147–148; and Gennaro F. Vito and Deborah G. Wilson, "Back from the Dead: Tracking the Progress of Kentucky's Furman-Commuted Death Row Population," *Justice Quarterly*, Vol. 5, No. 1 (1988), pp. 101–111.

164. *Wilkerson* v. *Utah*, 99 U.S. 130 (1878).

165. *In re Kemmler*, 136 U.S. 436 (1890).

166. Ibid., p. 447.

167. *Louisiana ex rel. Francis* v. *Resweber*, 329 U.S. 459 (1947).

168. *Furman* v. *Georgia*, 408 U.S. 238 (1972).

169. A position first adopted in *Trop* v. *Dulles*, 356 U.S. 86 (1958).

170. *Gregg* v. *Georgia*, 428 U.S. 153 (1976).

171. *Ring* v. *Arizona*, 536 U.S. 584 (2002).

172. "Dozens of Death Sentences Overturned," *Associated Press*, June 24, 2002.

173. The ruling could also affect Florida, Alabama, Indiana, and Delaware, where juries recommend sentences in capital cases but judges have the final say.

174. *Poyner* v. *Murray*, 113 S.Ct. 1573, 123 L.Ed.2d 142 (1993).

175. *Campbell* v. *Wood*, 114 S.Ct. 1337, 127 L.Ed.2d 685 (1994).

176. *Director Gomez, et al.* v. *Fierro and Ruiz*, 117 S.Ct. 285 (1996).

177. The court issued its decision after reviewing two cases: *Dawson* v. *State* and *Moore* v. *State*.

178. "Georgia Court Finds Electrocution Unconstitutional," *Criminal Justice Newsletter*, Vol. 31, No. 18 (October 15, 2001), pp. 3–4.

179. Adam Liptak, "Judges Set Hurdles for Lethal Injection," *New York Times*, April 12, 2006.

180. "North Carolina, Using Medical Monitoring Device, Executes Killer," *Associated Press*, April 22, 2006.

181. *Hall* v. *Florida*, 572 U.S. ____ (2014).

182. *Baze* v. *Rees*, 553 U.S. 35 (2008).

183. "Less Support for Death Penalty, Especially Among Democrats," Pew Research Center, April 16, 2015.

184. James D. Unnever and Francis T. Cullen, "Executing the Innocent and Support for Capital Punishment," *Criminology and Public Policy*, Vol. 4, No. 1 (2005), p. 3.

PART 4

CORRECTIONS

RIGHTS OF THE CONVICTED AND IMPRISONED

The convicted and imprisoned have these common law, constitutional, statutory, and humanitarian rights:

- A right against cruel or unusual punishment
- A right to protection from physical harm
- A right to sanitary and healthy conditions of confinement
- A limited right to legal assistance while imprisoned
- A limited right to religious freedom while imprisoned
- A limited right to freedom of speech while imprisoned
- A limited right to due process prior to denial of privileges

These individual rights must be effectively balanced against these public-order concerns:

- Punishment of the guilty
- Safe communities
- The reduction of recidivism
- Secure prisons
- Control over convicts
- The prevention of escape
- Rehabilitation
- Affordable prisons

How does our system of justice work toward balance?

Punishment—Justice for the Unjust?

The great Christian writer C. S. Lewis (1898–1963) once remarked that if satisfying justice is to be the ultimate goal of Western criminal justice, then the fate of offenders cannot be dictated merely by practical considerations. "The concept of just desert is the only connecting link between punishment and justice," Lewis wrote. "It is only as deserved or undeserved that a sentence can be just or unjust," he concluded.

Once a person has been arrested, tried, and sentenced, the correctional process begins. Unlike Lewis's exhortation, however, the contemporary American correctional system—which includes probation, parole, jails, prisons, capital punishment, and a variety of innovative alternatives to traditional sentences—is tasked with far more than merely carrying out sentences. We also ask of our correctional system that it ensure the safety of law-abiding citizens, that it select the best alternative from among the many available for handling each offender, that it protect

those under its charge, and that it guarantee fairness in the handling of all with whom it comes into contact.

This section of *Criminal Justice Today* details the development of probation, parole, community corrections, and imprisonment as corrections philosophies; describes the nuances of prison and jail life; discusses special issues in contemporary corrections (including AIDS, geriatric offenders, and female inmates); and summarizes the legal environment that both surrounds and infuses the modern-day practice of corrections. As you read through this section, encountering descriptions of various kinds of criminal sanctions, you might ask yourself, "When would a punishment of this sort be deserved?" In doing so, remember to couple that thought with another question: "What are the ultimate consequences (for society and for the offender) of the kind of correctional program we are discussing here?" Unlike Lewis, you may also want to ask, "Can we afford it?"

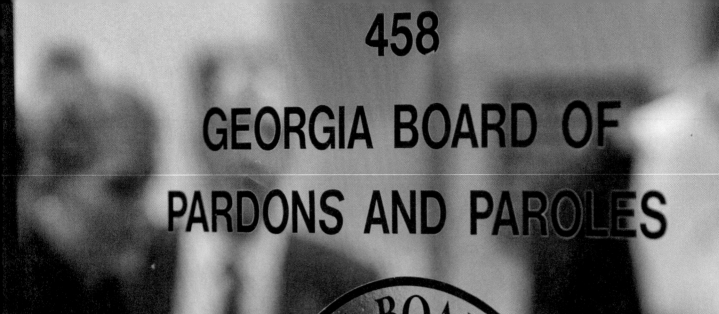

Newscom

12 PROBATION, PAROLE, AND INTERMEDIATE SANCTIONS

OUTLINE

LEARNING OBJECTIVES

After reading this chapter, you should be able to

- Describe the history, purpose, and characteristics of probation.
- Describe the history, purpose, and characteristics of parole.
- Compare the advantages and disadvantages of probation and parole.
- Identify significant court cases affecting probation and parole.
- Compare and contrast the work of probation officers and parole officers.
- Describe various intermediate sanctions.
- Describe the likely future of probation and parole.

The responsibility for community treatment and supervision has been entrusted mainly to probation and parole services.

PRESIDENT'S COMMISSION ON LAW ENFORCEMENT AND ADMINISTRATION OF JUSTICE.[1]

■ **community corrections** The use of a variety of officially ordered program-based sanctions that permit convicted offenders to remain in the community under conditional supervision as an alternative to an active prison sentence.

■ **probation** A sentence of imprisonment that is suspended. Also, the conditional freedom granted by a judicial officer to a convicted offender, as long as the person meets certain conditions of behavior.

Introduction

In 2015, former CIA Director David Petraeus became the most famous person in recent times to be placed on probation.[2] Petraeus, a highly decorated Army General and former commander of the multinational force in Iraq, pled guilty to giving classified information to his former mistress and biographer, Paula Broadwell. He avoided going to prison, but was sentenced to serve two years on probation and fined $100,000.[3]

This chapter takes a close look at the realities behind the practice of what we call **community corrections**. Community corrections, also termed *community-based corrections*, is a sentencing style that depends less on traditional confinement options and more on correctional resources available in the community. Its goal is to enhance desistance from crime and to reduce the likelihood of recidivism.[4] Community corrections includes a wide variety of sentencing options, such as probation, parole, home confinement, the electronic monitoring of offenders, and other new and developing programs—all of which are covered in this chapter. Learn more about community corrections by visiting the International Community Corrections Association via **http://www.iccaweb.org**.

Former CIA Director David Petraeus leaves the federal courthouse in Charlotte, N.C., in 2015 after pleading guilty to sharing top government secrets with his biographer, Paula Broadwell. Petraeus, whose career was destroyed by an extramarital affair with Broadwell, was sentenced to two years' probation and fined $100,000. What's the difference between probation and parole?

What Is Probation?

Probation, one aspect of community corrections, is "a sentence served while under supervision in the community."[5] Like other sentencing options, probation is a court-ordered sanction. Its goal is to retain some control over criminal offenders while using community programs to help rehabilitate them. Most of the alternative sanctions discussed later in this chapter are, in fact, predicated on probationary sentences in which the offender is ordered to abide by certain conditions—such as participation in a specified program—while remaining free in the community. Although the court in many jurisdictions can impose probation directly, most probationers are sentenced first to confinement but then immediately have their sentences suspended and are remanded into the custody of an officer of the court—the probation officer.

Probation has a long history. By the fourteenth century, English courts had established the practice of "binding over for good behavior,"[6] in which offenders could be entrusted into the custody of willing citizens. American John Augustus (1784–1859)

> American John Augustus (1784–1859) is generally recognized as the world's first probation officer.

is generally recognized as the world's first probation officer. Augustus, a Boston shoemaker, attended sessions of criminal court in the 1850s and offered to take carefully selected offenders into his home as an alternative to imprisonment.[7] At first, he supervised only drunkards, but by 1857 Augustus was accepting many kinds of offenders and was devoting all his time to the service of the court.[8] Augustus died in 1859, having bailed out more than 2,000 convicts. In 1878, the Massachusetts legislature enacted a statute that authorized the city of Boston to hire a salaried probation officer. Missouri followed suit in 1897, along with Vermont (1898) and Rhode Island (1899).[9] Before the end of the nineteenth century, probation had become an accepted and widely used form of community-based supervision. By 1925, all 48 states had adopted probation legislation. In that same year, the federal government enacted legislation enabling federal district court judges to appoint paid probation officers and to impose probationary terms.[10]

■ **lecture note**   Referring to Figure 12-1, describe the percentages of individuals under the various types of correctional supervision in the United States. Ask why probation is such a commonly used alternative.

■ **lecture note**   Ask the class to discuss the merits of granting probation to violent offenders. Explain that probation may result when the prosecutor's evidence is especially weak (making him or her more likely to deal) or when a plea bargain is accepted in lieu of a jury trial.

■ **lecture note**   Discuss the various conditions of probation that may be imposed by the court. Explain that general conditions apply to all probationers in the jurisdiction while special conditions may be imposed on individual probationers at the discretion of the sentencing judge.

■ **probation revocation**   A court order taking away a convicted offender's probationary status and usually withdrawing the conditional freedom associated with that status in response to a violation of the conditions of probation.

The Extent of Probation

Today, probation is the most common form of criminal sentencing in the United States. Between 20% and 60% of those found guilty of crimes are sentenced to some form of probation. Figure 12-1 shows that 56% of all offenders under correctional supervision in the United States as of January 1, 2013, were on probation.[11] The rest were either in jail, in prison, or on parole, or under some other form of supervised or unsupervised release. Figure 12-2 shows that the number of offenders under any type of correctional supervision increased dramatically between 1980 and 2013, but that the annual rate of increase has been steadily falling during that period, and has finally turned negative. In terms of absolute numbers, persons supervised yearly on probation has increased from slightly more than 1 million in 1980 to around 4 million today—a 400% increase.[12]

Even violent offenders stand about a one in five chance of receiving a probationary term. A Bureau of Justice Statistics study of felony sentences found that 5% of people convicted of homicide were placed on probation, as were 21% of convicted sex offenders.[13] Twelve percent of convicted robbers and 30% of those committing aggravated assault were similarly sentenced to probation rather than active prison time. In one example, 47-year-old Carrie Mote of Vernon, Connecticut, was sentenced to probation for shooting her fiancé in the chest with a .38-caliber handgun after he called off their wedding.[14] Mote,

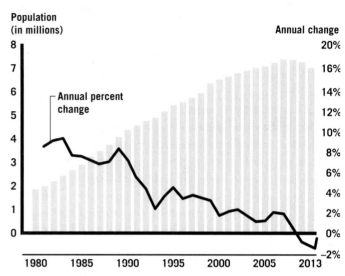

FIGURE 12-2 | Estimated Number of Adults under Some Form of Correctional Supervision and Annual Percent Change, 1980–2013

Source: Lauren E. Glaze and Danielle Kaeble, *Correctional Populations in the United States*, 2013 (Washington, DC: Bureau of Justice Statistics, December 2014), p. 1.

who faced a maximum of 20 years in prison, claimed to be suffering from diminished psychological capacity at the time of the shooting because of the emotional stress brought on by the canceled wedding.

At the beginning of 2014, a total of 3,910,600 adults were on probation throughout the nation.[15] Individual states, however, make greater or lesser use of probation. North Dakota authorities, with the smallest probationary population, supervise only 4,398 people, while Georgia reports 514,477 offenders on probation. Sixty-six percent of the 2.1 million adults discharged from probation in 2013 had successfully met the conditions of their supervision. Approximately 15% of those discharged from supervision, however, were incarcerated because of a rule violation or because they committed a new offense. Another 3% absconded, and 11% had their probation sentence revoked without being ordered to serve time.[16]

Probation Conditions

Those sentenced to probation must agree to abide by court-mandated conditions of probation. A violation of conditions can lead to **probation revocation**. Conditions are of two types: general and specific. General conditions apply to all probationers

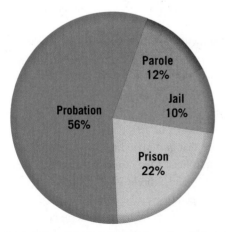

FIGURE 12-1 | Offenders under Correctional Supervision in the United States, by Type of Supervision

Source: Bureau of Justice Statistics, Correctional Surveys.

■ **Follow the author's tweets about the latest crime and justice news @schmalleger.**

A violation of conditions can lead to probation revocation.

in a given jurisdiction and usually require that the probationer obey all laws, maintain employment, remain within the jurisdiction of the court, possess no firearms, allow the probation officer to visit at home or at work, and so forth. As a general condition of probation, many probationers are also required to pay a fine to the court, usually in a series of installments. The fine is designed to reimburse victims for damages and to pay lawyers' fees and other court costs.

Special conditions may be mandated by a judge who feels that the probationer is in need of particular guidance or control. Depending on the nature of the offense, a judge may require that the offender surrender his or her driver's license; submit at reasonable times to warrantless and unannounced searches by a probation officer; supply breath, urine, or blood samples as needed for drug or alcohol testing; complete a specified number of hours of community service; or pass the general equivalency diploma (GED) test within a specified time. The judge may also dictate special conditions tailored to the probationer's situation. Such individualized conditions may prohibit the offender from associating with named others (a codefendant, for example), they may require that the probationer be at home after dark, or they may demand that the offender complete a particular treatment program within a set time.

Federal Probation

The federal probation system is more than 80 years old.[17] In 1916, in the *Killets* case,[18] the U.S. Supreme Court ruled that federal judges did not have the authority to suspend sentences and to order probation. After a vigorous campaign by the National Probation Association, Congress passed the National Probation Act in 1925, authorizing the use of probation in federal courts. The bill came just in time to save a burgeoning federal prison system from serious overcrowding. The prostitution-fighting Mann Act, Prohibition legislation, and the growth of organized crime all led to increased arrests and a dramatic growth in the number of federal probationers in the early years of the system.

Although the 1925 act authorized one probation officer per federal judge, it allocated only a total of $25,000 for officers' salaries. As a consequence, only eight officers were hired to serve 132 judges, and the system came to rely heavily on voluntary probation officers. Some sources indicate that as many as 40,000 probationers were under the supervision of volunteers at the peak of the system.[19] By 1930, however, Congress provided adequate funding, and a corps of salaried professionals began to provide probation services to the U.S. courts. Today, approximately 7,750 federal probation officers (also known as *community corrections officers*), whose services are administered through the

freedom OR safety? YOU decide

Special Conditions of Probation

In 2008, Texas judge Charlie Baird sentenced 22-year-old Felicia Salazar to a probationary term of ten years for injury to a child. Salazar's offense was actually one of omission, because she had failed to protect her 19-month-old child from a brutal beating by the child's father. The judge found especially problematic the fact that Salazar had failed to seek medical care for the child after the beating, even though the child had suffered a number of broken bones. In a surprising move, Judge Baird added an unusual condition to the other, more ordinary probation conditions that he imposed on Salazar: She was ordered not to conceive and bear a child during the probationary period. Following Judge Baird's probation order, some people questioned whether the special condition he imposed on Salazar unconstitutionally infringed on her fundamental right to procreate.

A similar story comes from Wisconsin, where Circuit Court Judge Tim Boyle ordered 44-year-old Corey Curtis to stop

procreating until he could support his nine children whom he had fathered with six different women. The judge imposed the requirement on Curtis in 2012 as a condition of a three-year probationary term, citing the fact that he owed more than $90,000 in back child support.

Critics of both the *Salazar* and *Curtis* cases point to the 1942 case of *Skinner* v. *Oklahoma*, which overturned Oklahoma's Habitual Criminal Sterilization Act and established procreation as a fundamental constitutional right.

You Decide

Did Judge Baird go too far in requiring that Salazar not become pregnant while on probation? What other special conditions of probation might he have imposed on Salazar that might have been more acceptable to critics?

References: *Skinner* v. *Oklahoma*, 316 U.S. 535 (1942); Sherry F. Colb, "A Judge Orders a Woman Not to Have Children while on Probation: Did He Violate Her Rights?" *FindLaw,* November 26, 2008, http://writ.lp.findlaw.com/colb/20081126.html?=features (accessed May 25, 2013); and "Wisconsin Judge Orders Deadbeat Dad of Nine (with Six Women) to Stop Procreating," *The Smoking Gun,* http://www.thesmokinggun.com/buster/wisconsin/judicial-procreation-ban-647901 (accessed June 2, 2013).

■ **lecture note**   Explain parole as supervised early release from prison. Note that, as with probation, offenders who violate the terms of parole may be returned to prison to complete the remaining portions of their sentences.

■ **theme**   What is the difference between probation and parole? How are they similar?

■ **lecture note**   Discuss the current movement away from discretionary parole release and ask students whether they agree with this. Explain the increasing use of statutory release and point out that, like parole, it also involve post-release supervision.

■ **theme**   Why do you think medical parole is on the increase? Do you agree with this trend? Explain.

■ **parole**   The status of a convicted offender who has been conditionally released from prison by a paroling authority before the expiration of his or her sentence, is placed under the supervision of a parole agency, and is required to observe the conditions of parole.

■ **reentry**   The managed return to the community of an individual released from prison. Also, the successful transitioning of a released inmate back into the community.

■ **parole board**   A state paroling authority. Most states have parole boards that decide when an incarcerated offender is ready for conditional release. Some boards also function as revocation hearing panels.

■ **discretionary release**   The release of an inmate from prison to supervision that is decided by a parole board or other authority.

Administrative Office of the U.S. Courts, serve the 94 federal judicial districts in more than 500 locations across the country.[20] At any given time, they supervise approximately 151,000 offenders—a number that has increased annually throughout the past decade.

Federal probation and pretrial services officers are federal law enforcement officers. They have statutory authority to arrest or detain individuals suspected or convicted of federal offenses, as well as the authority to arrest probationers for a violation of the conditions of probation. Under existing policy, however, they are encouraged to obtain an arrest warrant from a court, and the warrant is to be executed by the U.S. Marshals Service. Most federal probation officers may carry a firearm for defensive purposes while on duty. Before doing so, however, they must complete rigorous training and certification requirements, provide objective justification for doing so, and be approved to do so on an individual basis. Some federal districts do not allow any probation officers to carry firearms in the performance of their official duties; these include the Eastern and Western districts of Wisconsin, Eastern Virginia, Eastern Virgin Islands, Middle Tennessee, Massachusetts, Connecticut, and Central California.[21]

Federal officials have implemented a results-based management and decision-making framework for the federal probation and pretrial services system. The Probation and Pretrial Services Automated Case Tracking System (PACTS) collects records from the electronic files of thousands of probation officers in all 94 federal districts and stores those records in a single data warehouse called the National PACTS Reporting (NPR) System.[22] The data are then fed into the federal Decision Support System (DSS), which combines data from NPR with data from other judiciary systems, the United States Sentencing Commission, the Federal Bureau of Investigation (FBI), the Federal Bureau of Prisons, and the Bureau of the Census. Because of how it works, DSS provides a valuable evidence-based initiative at the federal level, and federal probation officials are using it to test underlying assumptions about

the relationship between probation supervision practices and supervision outcomes.

What Is Parole?

Parole is the supervised early release of inmates from correctional confinement. It is a prisoner **reentry** strategy that differs from probation in both purpose and implementation. Whereas probationers generally avoid serving time in prison, parolees have already been incarcerated. Although probation is a sentencing option available to a judge who determines the form probation will take, parole results from an administrative decision by a legally designated paroling authority. Probation is a sentencing strategy, but parole is a corrections strategy whose primary purpose is to return offenders gradually to productive lives. By making early release possible, parole can also act as a stimulus for positive behavioral change.

Parole was a much-heralded tool of nineteenth-century corrections. Its advocates had been looking for a behavioral incentive to motivate youthful offenders to reform. Parole, through its promise of earned early release, seemed the ideal innovation. The use of parole in this country began with New York's Elmira Reformatory in 1876. Indeterminate sentences were then a key part of the rehabilitation philosophy, and they remain so today.

States differ as to the type of parole decision-making mechanism they use, as well as the level at which it operates. Two major models prevail: (1) **Parole boards** grant parole based on their judgment and assessment. The parole board's decisions are termed *discretionary parole*. (2) Statutory decrees produce *mandatory parole*, with release dates usually set near the completion of the inmate's prison sentence, minus time off for good behavior and other special considerations. Fifteen states have entirely abolished **discretionary release** from prison by a parole board for all offenders. Another five states have abolished discretionary parole for certain violent offenses or other crimes against a

■ **medical parole**   An early-release option under which an inmate who is deemed "low risk" due to a serious physical or mental health condition is released from prison earlier than he or she might have been under normal circumstances.

■ **mandatory release**   The release of an inmate from prison that is determined by statute or sentencing guidelines and is not decided by a parole board or other authority.

■ **parole (probation) violation**   An act or a failure to act by a parolee (or a probationer) that does not conform to the conditions of his or her parole (or probation).

■ **lecture note**   Discuss the conditions of parole that may be imposed and compare them to those imposed on probationers.

■ **conditions of parole (probation)**   The general and special limits imposed on an offender who is released on parole (or probation). General conditions tend to be fixed by state statute, whereas special conditions are mandated by the sentencing authority (court or board) and take into consideration the background of the offender and the circumstances of the offense.

person. As a result of the movement away from release by parole boards, statutory release, usually involving a brief mandatory period of post-release supervision, has become the most common method of release from prison.[23]

One form of discretionary parole that *is* on the increase, it should be noted, is medical parole. **Medical parole** is an early release option available in some states under which an inmate who is deemed "low risk" due to a serious physical or mental health condition is released from prison earlier than he or she might have been under normal circumstances.[24]

States that do not utilize discretionary parole can still have substantial reentry populations, and everyone who is released from prison faces the challenges of reentering society. California, for example, one of the states that no longer uses parole boards for most release decisions, has traditionally had one of the largest reentry populations in the country.[25] Although it does not have a parole board, California has a Board of Parole Hearings (BPH), which determines when the state's most serious offenders are ready for release from prison. California's 2011 Criminal Justice Realignment Act,[26] however, shifted the supervision of most parolees under what the state calls the Post-Release Community Supervision program, from state parole officers to county probation officers. The BPH continues to hold parole hearings for persons sentenced to life in prison, persons applying for medical parole, mentally disordered offenders, and sexually violent predators held at the state level.[27] Other inmates, sentenced after the realignment legislation went into effect, must be released without any restrictions or supervision, meaning that California has effectively eliminated parole supervision for all but its most serious offenders.

The Extent of Parole

Parolees make up one of the smallest of the correctional categories shown in Figure 12-1. While most states are working to lower their prison populations, the growing reluctance to use parole today seems to be due to the realization that correctional routines have generally been ineffective at producing any substantial reformation among many offenders before their release back into the community. The abandonment of the rehabilitation goal, combined with a return to determinate sentencing in many jurisdictions—including the federal judicial system—has substantially reduced the amount of time the average corrections client spends on supervised parole.

Although discretionary parole releases are far less common than they used to be, about 25% of inmates who are freed from prison are still paroled by a paroling authority, such as a parole board.[28] States operating under determinate sentencing guidelines, however, often require that inmates serve a short period of time, such as 90 days, on what some jurisdictions term *reentry parole*—a form of supervised **mandatory release**. Mandatory parole releases have increased 91% since 1990,[29] even though they typically involve either a very small amount of time on parole or no time at all. As a result, determinate sentencing schemes have changed the face of parole in America, resulting in a dramatic reduction in the average time spent under postprison supervision. They have, however, had little or no impact on the actual number of offenders released from prison.

At the beginning of 2014, approximately 853,215 people were under parole supervision throughout the United States.[30] As with probation, states vary considerably in the use they make of parole, influenced as they are by the legislative requirements of sentencing schemes. For example, on January 1, 2014, Maine, a state that is phasing out parole, reported only 21 people under parole supervision (the lowest of all the states), and Rhode Island had only 459. Texas (the highest of all) had a parole population in excess of 111,300, and Pennsylvania officials were busy supervising 103,802 parolees.

Of those who exited parole in 2013, approximately 61% successfully completed parole, whereas about 19% are returned to prison for **parole violations**, and another 9% go back to prison for new offenses during their parole period. (Others may be transferred to new jurisdictions, may abscond and not be caught, or may die—bringing the total to 100%.)[31] An interesting parole decision-making tool is available on the Web at: **http://www.insideprison.com/parole_decision_making.asp#.UWr9O6t4bYg.**

Parole Conditions

In those jurisdictions that retain discretionary parole, the **conditions of parole** remain very similar to the conditions agreed to by probationers. General conditions of parole usually include agreement not to leave the state as well as to obey extradition requests from other jurisdictions. Parolees must also periodically report to parole officers, and parole officers may visit parolees at their homes and places of business, often arriving unannounced.

■ **parole revocation**   The administrative action of a paroling authority removing a person from parole status in response to a violation of lawfully required conditions of parole, including the prohibition against committing a new offense. Parole revocation usually results in the offender's return to prison.

■ **restitution**   A court requirement that an accused or convicted offender pay money or provide services to the victim of the crime or provide services to the community.

CJ | ISSUES
Culturally Skilled Probation Officers

A recent article by Robert Shearer and Patricia King in the journal *Federal Probation* describes the characteristics of "good therapeutic relationships" in probation work and says that "one of the major impediments to building an effective relationship may be found in cross-cultural barriers."

According to Shearer and King, probation officers who work with immigrants or with those whose cultures differ substantially from that of mainstream America must realize that a client's culture has to be taken into consideration. Doing so can make officers far more effective as both counselors and supervisors.

That's because differences in culture can lead to difficulties in developing the rapport that is necessary to build a helping relationship between an offender and a probation officer. Consequently, effective probation officers work to understand the values, norms, lifestyles, roles, and methods of communicating that characterize their clients.

Culturally skilled probation officers, say the authors, are aware of and sensitive to their own cultural heritage, and they value and respect differences as long as they do not lead to continued law violation. Culturally skilled officers are also aware of their own preconceived notions, biases, prejudicial attitudes, feelings, and beliefs. They avoid stereotyping and labeling. Skilled officers are comfortable with the cultural differences that exist between themselves and their clients, and they willingly refer clients to someone who may be better qualified to help.

Developing multicultural awareness is the first step to becoming culturally skilled, say Shearer and King. Developing awareness is an ongoing process that culminates in cultural empathy—the ability to understand a client's worldview.

According to the authors, developing cultural empathy involves six steps:

- The counselor must understand and accept the context of family and community for clients from different cultural backgrounds.

This is especially important when working with Hispanic clients, who highly value relationships within the extended family.

- Counselors should incorporate indigenous healing practices from the client's culture whenever they can. For example, this might be possible when working with Native Americans.
- Counselors must become knowledgeable about the historical and sociopolitical background of clients, especially when clients have fled from repressive regimes in their home countries and might still fear authority figures.
- They must become knowledgeable of the psychosocial adjustment that must be made by clients who have moved from one environment to another. This includes the sense of loneliness and separation that some immigrants feel on arrival in their adopted country.
- They must be sensitive to the oppression, discrimination, and racism previously encountered by many clients, such as the Kurdish people who suffered discrimination and experienced genocide under Saddam Hussein.
- Counselors must facilitate empowerment for those clients who feel underprivileged and devalued (e.g., immigrants who may feel forced to accept menial jobs even though they worked in prestigious occupations in their native countries).

Shearer and King conclude that developing cultural awareness provides the probation officer with an effective approach that actively draws the probationer into the therapeutic relationship and that increases the likelihood of a successful outcome.

Reference: Robert A. Shearer and Patricia Ann King, "Multicultural Competencies in Probation: Issues and Challenges," *Federal Probation*, Vol. 68, No. 1 (June 2004).

The successful and continued employment of parolees is one of the major concerns of parole boards and their officers, and studies have found that successful employment is a major factor in reducing the likelihood of repeat offenses.[32] Hence, the importance of continued employment is typically stressed on parole agreement forms, with the condition that failure to find employment within 30 days may result in **parole revocation**. As with probationers, parolees who are working can be ordered to pay fines and penalties. A provision for making **restitution** payments is also frequently included as a condition of parole.

As with probation, special parole conditions may be added by the judge and might require the parolee to pay a "parole supervisory fee" (often around $15 to $20 per month). This

relatively new innovation shifts some of the expense of community corrections to the offender.

Federal Parole

Federal parole decisions are made by the U.S. Parole Commission (USPC).

Federal parole decisions are made by the U.S. Parole Commission (USPC), located in Chevy Chase, Maryland. The Commission uses hearing examiners to visit federal prisons. Examiners typically ask inmates to describe why, in their opinion, they are ready for parole. The inmate's job readiness, home plans, past record, accomplishments while in prison, good

■ **theme**   How well do the terms imposed on probationers and parolees serve the rights of individuals? How well do they serve the needs of the community? What issues or needs are not addressed but should be?

■ **lecture note**   List and discuss each of the advantages of probation and parole, such as lower costs versus imprisonment, the opportunity for restitution, and the reduced risk of criminal socialization.

behavior, and previous experiences on probation or parole form the basis for the examiners' report to the parole commission. The 1984 Comprehensive Crime Control Act, which mandated federal fixed sentencing and abolished parole for offenses committed after November 1, 1978, began a planned phaseout of the U.S. Parole Commission. Under the act, the commission was to be abolished by 1992. Various federal legislation has since extended the life of the commission, and it continues to have jurisdiction over all federal offenders who committed their crimes before November 1, 1987, state probationers and parolees in the Federal Witness Protection Program, persons sentenced under the criminal code of the District of Columbia, and U.S. citizens convicted in foreign countries who have elected to serve their sentences in this country. The federal budget for fiscal year 2014 included a total of $13 million, for 85 positions, including 7 attorneys, at the USPC.[33] Visit the commission's website via **http://www.justice.gov/uspc**.

Probation and Parole: The Pluses and Minuses

Probation is used to meet the needs of offenders who require some correctional supervision short of imprisonment while providing a reasonable degree of security to the community. Parole, which is essentially a reentry program, fulfills a similar purpose for offenders released from prison.

Advantages of Probation and Parole

Both probation and parole provide a number of advantages over imprisonment.

Both probation and parole provide a number of advantages over imprisonment, including these:

- *Lower cost.* Imprisonment is expensive. Incarcerating a single offender in Georgia, for example, costs approximately $18,700 per year, whereas the cost of parole is as little as $1,577 per parolee.[34] The expense of imprisonment in some other states may be more than three times as high as it is in Georgia.
- *Increased employment.* Few people in prison have the opportunity for productive employment. Work-release programs, correctional industries, and inmate labor programs operate in most states, but they usually provide only low-paying jobs and require few skills. At best, such programs include only a small portion of the inmates in any given facility. Probation and parole, on the other hand, make it possible for offenders under correctional supervision to work full-time at jobs in the "free" economy. Offenders can contribute to their own and their families' support, stimulate the local economy by spending their wages, and support the government through the taxes they pay.
- *Restitution.* Offenders who are able to work are candidates for court-ordered restitution. Society's interest in restitution may be better served by a probationary sentence or parole than by imprisonment. Restitution payments to victims may help restore their standard of living and personal confidence while teaching the offender responsibility.
- *Community support.* The decision to release a prisoner on parole or to sentence a convicted offender to probation is often partially based on considerations of family and other social ties. Such decisions are made in the belief that offenders will be more subject to control in the community if they participate in a web of positive social relationships. An advantage of both probation and parole is that they allow the offender to continue personal and social relationships. Probation avoids splitting up families, and parole may reunite family members separated from each other by a prison sentence.
- *Reduced risk of criminal socialization.* Criminal values permeate prisons; prison has been called a "school in crime." Probation insulates adjudicated offenders, at least to some degree, from these kinds of values. Parole, by virtue of the fact that it follows time served in prison, is less successful than probation in reducing the risk of criminal socialization.
- *Increased use of community services.* Probationers and parolees can take advantage of services offered through the community, including psychological therapy, substance-abuse counseling, financial services, support groups, church outreach programs, and social services. Although a few similar opportunities may be available in prison, the community environment itself can enhance the effectiveness of treatment programs by reducing the stigmatization of the offender and by allowing the offender to participate in a more "normal" environment.
- *Increased opportunity for rehabilitation.* Probation and parole can both be useful behavioral management tools. They reward cooperative offenders with freedom and allow for the opportunity to shape the behavior of offenders who may be difficult to reach through other programs.

■ **lecture note**   List and discuss the disadvantages of probation and parole, including the relatively low degree of punishment inherent in both options.

■ **theme**   Do communities have the right to be informed when exconvicts are released from prison? Do victims? How can we as a society balance the community's right to self-protection with individuals' right to live where they choose, even in the case of exconvicts?

■ **theme**   Who would be more likely to favor parole as a sentencing option, public-order advocates or individual-rights advocates? What about probation? Why?

■ **theme**   Consider the diverse sentencing goals identified in Chapter 11. Which of the goals identified there are most likely to be met through the use of probation? Which through parole? Why?

■ **lecture note**   Describe probation and parole revocation. Explain that, in most cases, revocation orders can be issued only after a hearing in front of a neutral body and that certain procedures must be followed.

■ **lecture note**   Explain that the courts have not held probation and parole officers to the same standards as police officers in the gathering of evidence. Discuss the fact that probation and parole officers may turn incriminating statements made by clients over to prosecutors and that officers may enter a client's home without a warrant.

■ **revocation hearing**   A hearing held before a legally constituted hearing body (such as a parole board) to determine whether a parolee or probationer has violated the conditions and requirements of his or her parole or probation.

■ **conditional release**   The release of an inmate from prison to community supervision under a set of conditions for remaining on parole. If a condition is violated, the individual might be returned to prison or might face another sanction in the community.[i]

Disadvantages of Probation and Parole

Any honest appraisal of probation and parole must recognize that they share a number of strategic drawbacks, including these:

- *Relative lack of punishment.* The just deserts model of criminal sentencing insists that punishment should be a central theme of the justice process. Although rehabilitation and treatment are recognized as worthwhile goals, the model suggests that punishment serves both society's need for protection and the victim's need for revenge. Many view probation, however, as practically no punishment at all. Parole is likewise accused of unhinging the scales of justice because (1) it releases some offenders early, even when they have been convicted of serious crimes, while some relatively minor offenders remain in prison, and (2) it is misleading to those harmed by crime because it does not require completion of the offender's entire sentence behind bars.

- *Increased risk to the community.* Probation and parole are strategies designed to deal with convicted criminal offenders. The release into the community of such offenders increases the risk that they will commit additional offenses. Community supervision can never be so complete as to eliminate such a possibility, and evaluations of parole have pointed out that an accurate assessment of offender dangerousness is beyond our present capability.[35]

- *Increased social costs.* Some offenders placed on probation and parole will effectively and responsibly discharge their obligations. Others, however, will become social liabilities. In addition to the increased risk of new crimes, probation and parole increase the chance that added expenses will accrue to the community in the form of child support, welfare costs, housing expenses, legal aid, indigent health care, and the like.

- *Discriminatory and unequal effects.* Some experts argue that reentry programs are unfair to women because female inmates undergoing the reentry experience find themselves qualitatively disadvantaged in their search for jobs and shelter, in reobtaining custody of their children, in successfully finding programs to help them abstain from drugs, and so on.[36] Some say, for example, that a man leaving prison "has better opportunities for securing a sufficient income-producing and legal job by virtue of his gender alone."[37]

The Legal Environment

Eleven especially significant U.S. Supreme Court decisions provide the legal framework for probation and parole supervision. Among those cases, that of *Griffin* v. *Wisconsin* (1987)[38] may be the most significant. In *Griffin*, the Supreme Court ruled that probation officers may conduct searches of a probationer's residence without either a search warrant or probable cause. According to the Court, "A probationer's home, like anyone else's, is protected by the Fourth Amendment's requirement that searches be 'reasonable.'" However, "[a] State's operation of a probation system . . . presents 'special needs' beyond normal law enforcement that may justify departures from the usual warrant and probable cause requirements." Probation, the Court concluded, is similar to imprisonment because it is a "form of criminal sanction imposed upon an offender after a determination of guilt." Similarly, in the 1998 case of *Pennsylvania Board of Probation and Parole* v. *Scott*,[39] the Court declined to extend the exclusionary rule to apply to searches by parole officers, even where such searches yield evidence of parole violations. See Table 12-1 for an overview of these and other significant cases in the field of probation and parole.

Other court cases focus on the conduct of parole or probation **revocation hearings**. Revocation is a common procedure. Annually, about 20% of adults on parole as well as 26% of those on probation throughout the United States have their **conditional release** revoked.[40] The supervising officer may request that probation or parole be revoked

> Annually, about 20% of adults on parole as well as 26% of those on probation throughout the United States have their conditional release revoked.

TABLE 12-1 | U.S. Supreme Court Decisions of Special Significance for Probation and Parole

IN THIS CASE	THE COURT HELD THAT
Samson v. California (2006)	Police officers may conduct a warrantless search of a person who is subject to a parole search condition, even when there is no suspicion of criminal wrongdoing and even when the sole reason for the search is that the person is on parole.
U.S. v. Knights (2001)	The warrantless search authority normally reserved for probation and parole officers extends to police officers when supported by reasonable suspicion and authorized by the conditions of probation.
Pennsylvania Board of Probation and Parole v. Scott (1998)	The exclusionary rule does not apply to searches by parole officers, even where such searches yield evidence of parole violations.
Griffin v. Wisconsin (1987)	Probation officers may conduct searches of a probationer's residence without the need for a search warrant or probable cause.
Minnesota v. Murphy (1984)	A probationer's incriminating statements to a probation officer may be used as evidence against him or her if the probationer does not specifically claim a right against self-incrimination.
Bearden v. Georgia (1983)	Probation cannot be revoked for failure to pay a fine and make restitution if it can't be shown that the defendant was responsible for the failure. Moreover, if a defendant lacks the capacity to pay a fine or make restitution, then the hearing authority must consider any viable alternatives to incarceration before imposing a prison sentence.
Greenholtz v. Nebraska Penal Inmates (1979)	Parole boards do not have to specify the evidence or reasoning used in deciding to deny parole.
Gagnon v. Scarpelli (1973)	The safeguards identified in Morrissey v. Brewer were extended to probationers.
Morrissey v. Brewer (1972)	Procedural safeguards are necessary in revocation hearings involving parolees. They include (a) written notice of the claimed violations of parole; (b) disclosure to the parolee of evidence against him or her; (c) opportunity to be heard in person and to present witnesses and documentary evidence; (d) the right to confront and cross-examine adverse witnesses (unless the hearing officer specifically finds good cause for not allowing confrontation); (e) a "neutral and detached" hearing body such as a traditional parole board, members of which need not be judicial officers or lawyers; and (f) a written statement.
Mempa v. Rhay (1967)	Both notice and a hearing are required before probation revocation, and the probationer should have the opportunity for representation by counsel before a deferred prison sentence is imposed.
Escoe v. Zerbst (1935)	Probation "comes as an act of grace to one convicted of a crime" and the revocation of probation without hearing or notice to the probationer is permissible. This decision has since been greatly modified by other decisions in this table.

if a client has violated the conditions of community release or has committed a new crime. The most frequent violations for which revocation occurs are (1) failure to report as required to a probation or parole officer, (2) failure to participate in a stipulated treatment program, and (3) alcohol or drug abuse while under supervision.[41] Revocation hearings may result in an order that a probationer's suspended sentence be made "active" or that a parolee return to prison to complete his or her sentence in confinement.

In 2010, a new law went into effect in California authorizing the placement of parolees into non-revocable parole (NRP).[42] Widely regarded as a correctional innovation, NRP is an effort to safely reduce state prison populations. NRP prohibits the California Department of Corrections and Rehabilitation (CDCR) from returning certain parolees to prison, placing a parole hold on those parolees, or reporting

those parolees to the Board of Parole Hearings for a violation of parole. Sex offenders, validated gang members, serious felons, and prisoners found guilty of serious disciplinary offenses are not eligible for NRP. Furthermore, only persons evaluated by the CDCR using a risk assessment tool and not determined to pose a high risk of reoffending can be assigned to NRP. The parole period under NRP generally lasts for one year, during which time parolees are not required to report to a parole officer. They are, however, subject to being searched by any law enforcement officer at any time.

Another important legal issue surrounds the potential liability of probation officers and parole boards for the criminal actions of offenders they supervise or whom they have released. Some courts have held that officers are generally immune from suit because they are performing a judicial function on behalf of the state.[43] Other courts, however, have indicated that parole board members

■ **theme**   What competing needs and rights must parole boards weigh? Whose rights or needs should be given the greatest consideration?

■ **lecture note**   Tell the class that members of parole boards have generally been immune to lawsuits arising from "bad" release decisions. Ask students whether they think parole decision makers should be held personally liable for the decisions they make.

■ **activity**   Invite a probation or parole officer to speak with the class, either in person or through virtual conferencing. Have students prepare questions to ask the speaker about the use of alternative sentencing options in the local area and about the rewards and difficulties associated with his or her job.

paying for it

Cost-Efficient Parole

By 2015, the state of Georgia had closed most of its parole offices and changed the style of supervision used by its parole officers. Today, almost all parolees in Georgia are tracked by "parole officer-friendly remote technology," providing a huge savings in leased office space statewide. "The day of the parolee reporting to a parole office is long gone," says Michael Nail, Georgia's executive director of the Board of Pardons and Paroles. Instead, two-person parole teams use vehicles as "virtual offices" to visit the communities where parolees live and work. "It's no longer parolees coming to where the parole officer works," says Nail.

Some of the new technologies used by Georgia's parole officers are facilitated through the Google Apps for Government platform, and consist of a voice-recognition system teamed with GPS technologies that allow officers to verify a parolee's location at any time. Parolees deemed at higher risk of reoffending are supervised under an enhanced house arrest monitoring system, which uses cell phones and voice-recognition technology to track parolee's locations. The hardware, provided by AnyTrax, costs the state about $7 per month per enrolled parolee—a fee paid by the parolees themselves. That cost is substantially below the expenses associated with GPS bracelets and the monitoring systems they require.

To use the AnyTrax system, offenders employ a cell phone to call a toll-free number and interact with an automated system through a series of questions and answers. Every contact is documented and offender identity is verified by voiceprint biometrics. The AnyTrax system conducts an automated interview for every caller and reports the results to the officer assigned to that parolee. GPS technology, called CellTrax, reveals the location of the caller. Officers are able to quickly review interview results through a computerized system that alerts them to problems that may require more direct intervention.

Typically, the states spends about $53 million per year on parole supervision, but these innovations have allowed the parole board to reduce expenditures beyond the state's mandated 3% cuts and have saved the state about $2 million per year in office-related expenses.

Georgia parole officers supervise around 23,000 parolees—a number which has not changed substantially since the new system was implemented. Parolees assigned to the voice-recognition system show high rates of desistance, with only 1.7% of them returning to prison.

References: "The Virtual Office," *Georgia State Board of Pardons and Paroles*, https://pap.georgia.gov/virtual-office (accessed May 5, 2015); Mike Klein, "End of an Era: Georgia Begins to Close Parole Offices," *Georgia Public Policy Foundation*, November 30, 2012, http://www.georgiapolicy.org/end-of-an-era-georgia-begins-to-close-parole-offices/ (accessed May 5, 2015); and "Self-Report," *AnyTrax.com*, http://www.anytrax.com/our-services/self-report (accessed May 5, 2015).

who do not carefully consider mandated criteria for judging parole eligibility could be liable for injurious actions committed by parolees.[44] In general, however, most experts agree that parole board members cannot be successfully sued unless release decisions are made in a grossly negligent or wantonly reckless manner.[45] Discretionary decisions of individual probation and parole officers that result in harm to members of the public, however, may be more actionable under civil law, especially where their decisions were not reviewed by judicial authority.[46]

The Job of Probation and Parole Officers

The tasks performed by probation and parole officers are often quite similar. Some jurisdictions combine the roles of both into one job. This section describes the duties of probation and parole officers, whether separate or performed by the same individuals. Probation/

Supervision of sentenced probationers or released parolees is the most active stage of the probation/parole process.

parole work consists primarily of four functions: (1) intake procedures, (2) diagnosis and needs assessment, (3) client supervision, and (4) presentence investigations.

Where probation is a possibility, intake procedures may include a presentence investigation, which examines the offender's background to provide the sentencing judge with facts needed to make an informed sentencing decision. Intake procedures may also involve a dispute-settlement process during which the probation officer works with the defendant and the victim to resolve the complaint before sentencing. Intake duties tend to be more common for juvenile offenders than they are for adults, but all officers may eventually have to recommend to the judge the best sentencing alternative for a particular case.

Diagnosis, the psychological inventorying of the probation or parole client, may be done either formally with written tests

Hotel heiress Paris Hilton arriving at Pure Nightclub in Las Vegas for her sister Nicky's 25th birthday party. One year earlier, Paris pleaded "no contest" to an alcohol-related reckless driving offense in Los Angeles and was sentenced to three years' probation. She was also fined $1,500 plus court costs and ordered to participate in an alcohol education program. In 2010, she was arrested for possession of a controlled substance after cocaine was found in her purse by Las Vegas police during a vehicle stop. Apparently probation wasn't enough to deter Paris. Why not?

The Challenges of the Job

One of the biggest challenges that probation and parole officers face is the need to balance two conflicting sets of duties—one of which is to provide quasi–social work services and the other is to handle custodial responsibilities. In effect, two inconsistent models of the officer's role coexist. The social work model stresses an officer's service role and views probationers and parolees as clients. In this model, officers are caregivers whose goals are to accurately assess the needs of their clients and to match clients with community resources, such as job placement, indigent medical care, family therapy, and psychological and substance-abuse counseling. The social work model depicts probation/parole as a "helping profession" wherein officers assist their clients in meeting the conditions imposed on them by their sentence. The other model for officers is correctional. In this model, probation and parole clients are "wards" whom officers are expected to control. This model emphasizes community protection, which officers are supposed to achieve through careful and close supervision. Custodial supervision means that officers will periodically visit their charges at work and at home,

Kelly Sott, 33, girlfriend of Cameron Douglas (son of actor Michael Douglas) is photographed at federal court in Manhattan immediately after leaving a federal lockup, where she spent seven months for attempting to smuggle heroin packed in an electric toothbrush to Cameron while he was under house arrest for drug dealing. How might court-ordered community supervision benefit Sott?

administered by certified psychologists or through informal arrangements, which typically depend on the observational skills of the officer. Needs assessment, another area of officer responsibility, extends beyond the psychological needs of the client to a cataloging of the services necessary for a successful experience on probation or parole. Supervision of sentenced probationers or released parolees is the most active stage of the probation/parole process, involving months (and sometimes years) of periodic meetings between the officer and the client and an ongoing assessment of the success of the probation/parole endeavor in each case.

All probation and parole officers must keep confidential the details of the presentence investigation, including psychological tests, needs assessment, conversations between the officer and the client, and so on. On the other hand, courts have generally held that communications between the officer and the client are not privileged, as they might be between a doctor and a patient or between a social worker and his or her client.[47] Hence officers can share with the appropriate authorities any incriminating evidence that a client relates.

■ **theme**   Contrast the intermediate sentencing options described in this chapter with the goals of sentencing identified in Chapter 11. Which option is most likely to achieve each goal? Why?

■ **caseload**   The number of probation or parole clients assigned to one probation or parole officer for supervision.

■ **intermediate sanctions**   The use of split sentencing, shock probation or parole, shock incarceration, community service, intensive supervision, or home confinement in lieu of other, more traditional sanctions such as imprisonment and fines.

Georgia probation officers preparing to excavate a site at the Tri-State Crematory in Noble, Georgia, in 2002. Officials found the remains of hundreds of corpses on the crematory's 16-acre grounds. The crematory's operator, Ray Brent Marsh, was charged with 787 felony counts, including theft by deception, abuse of a corpse, and burial service fraud. He was also charged with 47 counts of making false statements to authorities. Convicted on many of the charges, he was sentenced to 12 years in prison in 2005. A probation officer's job can involve a wide variety of duties. What are the usual duties of a probation officer?

Mark Humphrey/AP Wide World Photos

often arriving unannounced. It also means that they must be willing to report clients for new offenses and for violations of the conditions of their release.

Most officers, by virtue of their personalities and experiences, identify more with one model than with the other. They consider themselves primarily caregivers or corrections officers. Regardless of the emphasis that each individual officer chooses, however, the demands of the job are bound to generate role conflict at one time or another.

A second challenge of probation and parole work is large **caseloads**. Back in 1973, the President's Commission on Law Enforcement and Administration of Justice recommended that probation and parole caseloads average around 35 clients per officer.[48] However, caseloads of 250 clients are common in some jurisdictions today, and Internet-facilitated remote supervision (discussed in a box in this chapter) can lead to higher caseloads still. Large caseloads combined with limited training and the time constraints imposed by administrative demands culminate in stopgap

supervisory measures. "Postcard probation," in which clients mail in a letter or card once a month to report on their whereabouts and circumstances, is an example of one stopgap measure that harried agencies with large caseloads use to keep track of their wards. A comprehensive review of state parole practices in California found that 65% of the state's parolees saw their parole officer no more than twice every three months, and 23% saw their officers only once every three months. Parolees with the highest level of supervision, including high-risk sex offenders, averaged two face-to-face meetings with their parole officer each month.[49]

Another difficulty with probation and parole work is the frequent lack of opportunity for career mobility within the profession. Probation and parole officers are generally assigned to small agencies serving limited geographic areas, under the leadership of one or two chief probation officers. Unless retirement or death claims a supervisor, there is little chance for other officers to advance.

A recent report by the National Institute of Justice (NIJ) found that, like law enforcement officers, probation and parole officers experienced a lot of stress.[50] The major sources of stress for probation and parole officers were found to be high caseloads, excess paperwork, and pressures associated with deadlines. Stress levels have also increased in recent years because offenders who are sentenced to probation and released on parole today have committed more serious crimes than in the past, and more offenders have serious drug-abuse histories and show less hesitation in using violence.[51] The NIJ study found that officers typically cope by requesting transfers, retiring early, or taking "mental health days" off from work. The report says, however, that "physical exercise is the method of choice for coping with the stress."[52] Learn more about working as a probation or parole officer at the American Probation and Parole Association's website via **http://www.appa-net.org/eweb**.

Intermediate Sanctions

As noted in Chapter 11, significant new alternative sentencing options have become available to judges. Many such options are called **intermediate sanctions** because they employ sentencing alternatives that fall somewhere between outright imprisonment and simple probationary release back into the community. They are also sometimes termed *alternative sentencing strategies*. Michael J. Russell, former director of the National Institute of Justice, says that "intermediate punishments are intended to provide prosecutors, judges, and corrections officials with sentencing options that permit them to apply appropriate punishments to convicted offenders while not being constrained by the traditional choice between prison and probation. Rather than substituting for prison

■ **lecture note** Explain that intermediate sanctions resulted from the desire to improve the effectiveness of rehabilitative efforts.

CJ | CAREERS
Probation Officer

Name. Stephanie Drury

Position. Probation officer, Pontiac, Michigan

College attended. Wayne State University (BS, criminal justice; MS, criminal justice)

Year hired. 2009

Please give a brief description of your job. I am a probation officer for approximately 110 men. The Adult Treatment Court is a specialty court for offenders with severe substance-abuse problems, and many of them also have a mental health diagnosis. My role there is to provide intensive supervision. I attend court with them every two weeks to inform the judge of their progress. Additionally, I see each of them at least once a week in order to ensure they are complying with all conditions of the program and maintaining their sobriety.

What appealed to you most about the position when you applied for it? I completed an internship with the federal probation department in Detroit and thoroughly enjoyed probation work, so I applied for the state probation job. The Adult Treatment Court position was appealing because I work directly with the judge and am able to provide intensive supervision to my probationers.

How would you describe the interview process? The interview consisted of a panel of three members of the Michigan Department of Corrections followed by a written test. Questions were based on my academic experience, along with any professional experience I had that would make me a perfect candidate. Also, real-life situations and scenarios were discussed in order to show the panel how I might deal with a particular situation.

What is a typical day like? I monitor the daily development of the females of the Adult Treatment Court, which includes probation supervision and making sure they are taking their medication, going to therapy, and attending programs such as Narcotics Anonymous. With the men on general supervision, I complete presentence investigations, field work, jail visits, and court appearances.

What qualities/characteristics are most helpful for this job? You have to be strong and in control at all times. If you don't have a backbone, the offenders will walk all over you and not take you seriously. It is a demanding job, and you have to be very organized to successfully supervise so many individuals on your caseload. You can exercise a lot of discretion and be your own boss, yet you also have a supervisor who will assist you in times of need.

What is a typical starting salary? $16.54 per hour, with benefits.

What is the salary potential as you move up into higher-level jobs? A probation officer with six years or more of experience will earn approximately $28.00 per hour or more, depending on his or her classification.

What advice would you give someone in college beginning studies in criminal justice? Find internships to gain experience in specific areas in the field of criminal justice. Engage yourself in as much real-life experience as possible, and network with as many professionals as possible, as these two methods will set you apart from other job candidates.

Source: Reprinted with permission of Stephanie Drury. Photo courtesy of Stephanie Drury.

---

or probation, however, these sanctions, which include intensive supervision, house arrest with electronic monitoring (also referred to as *remote location monitoring*), and shock incarceration—programs that stress a highly structured and regimented routine, considerable physical work and exercise, and at times intensive substance-abuse treatment—bridge the gap between those options and provide innovative ways to ensure swift and certain punishment."[53]

Numerous citizen groups and special-interest organizations are working to widen the use of sentencing alternatives. One organization of special note is the Sentencing Project. The organization, based in Washington, D.C., is dedicated to promoting a greater use of alternatives to incarceration. It provides technical assistance to public defenders, court officials, and other community organizations.

The Sentencing Project and other groups like it have contributed to the development of more than 100 locally based alternative sentencing service programs. Most alternative sentencing services work in conjunction with defense attorneys to develop written sentencing plans. Such plans are basically well-considered citizen suggestions as to appropriate sentencing in a given instance. Plans are often quite detailed and may include letters of support from employers, family members, the defendant, and even victims. Sentencing plans may be used in plea bargaining sessions or may be presented to judges following trial and conviction. Some years ago, for example, lawyers for country-and-western singer Willie Nelson successfully proposed to tax court officials an alternative option that allowed the singer to pay huge past tax liabilities by performing in concerts for that purpose. Lacking such an alternative, the tax court might have seized Nelson's property or even ordered the singer to be confined to a federal facility. About the same time, former NBA player DeShawn Stevenson was sentenced to two years of probation and was ordered to perform 100 hours of community service for the statutory rape of a 14-year-old girl whom he had plied with brandy.[54] Stevenson, who played for the Utah Jazz at the time of the offense, fulfilled the terms of his sentence by delivering motivational speeches at boys' clubs in California and New York.

■ **split sentence**   A sentence explicitly requiring the convicted offender to serve a period of confinement in a local, state, or federal facility, followed by a period of probation.

■ **shock probation**   The practice of sentencing offenders to prison, allowing them to apply for probationary release, and surprisingly permitting such release. Offenders who receive shock probation may not be aware that they will be released on probation and may expect to spend a much longer time behind bars.

■ **shock incarceration**   A sentencing option that makes use of "boot camp"–type prisons to impress on convicted offenders the realities of prison life.

The basic philosophy behind intermediate sanctions is this: When judges are offered well-planned alternatives to imprisonment for offenders who appear to represent little or no continuing threat to the community, the likelihood of a prison sentence is reduced. An analysis of alternative sentencing plans like those sponsored by the Sentencing Project shows that judges accept them in up to 80% of the cases in which they are recommended and that as many as two-thirds of offenders who receive intermediate sentences successfully complete them.[55]

Intermediate sanctions have three distinct advantages: (1) They are less expensive to operate per offender than imprisonment; (2) they are "socially cost-effective" because they keep the offender in the community, thus avoiding both the breakup of the family and the stigmatization that accompanies imprisonment; and (3) they provide flexibility in terms of resources, time of involvement, and place of service.[56] Some of these new sentencing options are described in the paragraphs that follow.

Split Sentencing

In jurisdictions where **split sentences** are an option, judges may impose a combination of a brief period of imprisonment and probation. Defendants who are given split sentences are often ordered to serve time in a local jail rather than in a long-term confinement facility. Ninety days in jail, followed by two years of supervised probation, is a typical split sentence. Split sentences are frequently given to minor drug offenders and serve notice that continued law violations may result in imprisonment for much longer periods.

Shock Probation and Shock Parole

Shock probation strongly resembles split sentencing. The offender serves a relatively short period of time in custody (usually in a prison rather than a jail) and is released on probation by court order. The difference is that shock probation clients must *apply* for probationary release from confinement and cannot be certain of the judge's decision. In shock probation, the court in effect makes a resentencing decision. Probation is only a statutory possibility and often little more than an aspiration for the offender as imprisonment begins. If probationary release is ordered, it may well come as a "shock" to the offender. The hope is that the unexpected reprieve will cause the offender to steer clear of future criminal involvement. Shock probation was begun in Ohio in 1965[57] and is

A New Mexico boot camp staff member conducting a push-up drill with young offenders. Boot camps use military-style discipline in an attempt to lessen the likelihood of recidivism among young and first-time offenders. How successful have boot camps been in reducing recidivism?

Vladimir Chaloupka/Las Cruces Sun-News/AP Wide World Photos

used today in about half of the United States.[58] Shock probation lowers the cost of confinement, maintains community and family ties, and may be an effective rehabilitative tool.[59]

Shock parole is similar to shock probation. Whereas shock probation is ordered by judicial authority, shock parole is an administrative decision made by a paroling authority. Parole boards or their representatives may order an inmate's early release, hoping that the brief exposure to prison has reoriented the offender's life in a positive direction.

Shock Incarceration

Shock incarceration programs, which became popular during the 1990s, utilized military-style "boot camp" prison settings to provide highly regimented environments involving strict discipline, physical training, and hard labor.[60] Shock incarceration

■ **mixed sentence**   A sentence that requires that a convicted offender serve weekends (or other specified periods of time) in a confinement facility (usually a jail) while undergoing probationary supervision in the community.

■ **theme**   How does community service relate to the basic concepts of restorative justice?

■ **community service**   A sentencing alternative that requires offenders to spend at least part of their time working for a community agency.

programs were designed primarily for young first offenders and are of short duration, generally lasting for only 90 to 180 days. Offenders who successfully completed these programs were typically returned to the community under some form of supervision. Program "failures" were usually moved into the general prison population for longer terms of confinement.

Georgia established the first shock incarceration program in 1983.[61] Following Georgia's lead, more than 30 other states began their own programs.[62] About half of the states provided for voluntary entry into the program, and a few allowed inmates to voluntarily quit the program.

One of the most comprehensive studies of boot camp prison programs that was ever conducted focused on eight states: Florida, Georgia, Illinois, Louisiana, New York, Oklahoma, South Carolina, and Texas. The report found that boot camp programs have been popular because "they are ... perceived as being tough on crime" and "have been enthusiastically embraced as a viable correctional option."[63] The report concluded, however, that "the impact of boot camp programs on offender recidivism is at best negligible."

In recent years, boot camp programs have fallen into disfavor and have largely been discontinued. In 2005, the Bureau of Prisons announced plans to eliminate its boot camp programs (known as "intensive confinement"), hoping to save more than $1 million a year on programs that hadn't proven their worth;[64] and in 2006, Florida Governor Jeb Bush signed legislation ending state-run boot camps in that state following the death of a 14-year-old participant. Two of the last states to continue to operate boot camps are Wyoming and Nevada. Nevada runs a "program of regimental discipline" at its Three Lakes Valley facility. The facility has a capacity of 75 youthful detainees, and accepts only nonviolent offenders who have committed relatively minor crimes.[65] The Wyoming Boot Camp, which can house up to 56 inmates, is located in the Wyoming Honor Conservation Camp at Newcastle, Wyoming.[66] It accepts young offenders under the age of 25 who have been court recommended, and sessions last for 180 days.

epa european pressphoto agency b.v./Alamy

Actress Lindsay Lohan listens to the judge during a probation hearing in Los Angeles, California, on March 29, 2012. In May 2011, following a plea deal on charges of felony grand theft involving a $2,500 necklace stolen from a jewelry store, Lohan was placed under house arrest and ordered to wear an electronic monitor on her ankle. Why is remote location monitoring becoming a popular alternative to imprisonment?

Mixed Sentencing and Community Service

Some **mixed sentences** require that offenders serve weekends in jail and receive probation supervision during the week. Other types of mixed sentencing require offenders to participate in treatment or community-service programs while on probation. Community-service programs began in Minnesota in 1972 with the Minnesota Restitution Program, which gave property offenders the opportunity to work and turn over part of their pay as restitution to their victims.[67] Courts throughout the nation quickly adopted the idea and began to build restitution orders into suspended-sentence agreements.

Community service is more an adjunct to, rather than a type of, correctional sentence. Community service is compatible with most other forms of innovation in probation and parole. Even with home confinement (discussed later in the chapter), offenders can be sentenced to community-service activities that

■ **lecture note**   Explain the difference between standard probation and intensive probation supervision. Ask students what goals of sentencing (if any) might be more effectively met by IPS as compared to incarceration?

■ **intensive probation supervision (IPS)**   A form of probation supervision involving frequent face-to-face contact between the probationer and the probation officer.

ethics and professionalism

American Probation and Parole Association Code of Ethics

- I will render professional service to the justice system and the community at large in effecting the social adjustment of the offender.
- I will uphold the law with dignity, displaying an awareness of my responsibility to offenders while recognizing the right of the public to be safeguarded from criminal activity.
- I will strive to be objective in the performance of my duties, recognizing the inalienable right of all persons, appreciating the inherent worth of the individual, and respecting those confidences which can be reposed in me.
- I will conduct my personal life with decorum, neither accepting nor granting favors in connection with my office.
- I will cooperate with my co-workers and related agencies and will continually strive to improve my professional competence through the seeking and sharing of knowledge and understanding.
- I will distinguish clearly, in public, between my statements and actions as an individual and as a representative of my profession.

- I will encourage policy, procedures and personnel practices, which will enable others to conduct themselves in accordance with the values, goals and objectives of the American Probation and Parole Association.
- I recognize my office as a symbol of public faith and I accept it as a public trust to be held as long as I am true to the ethics of the American Probation and Parole Association.
- I will constantly strive to achieve these objectives and ideals, dedicating myself to my chosen profession.

Thinking about Ethics

1. Which of the ethical principles enumerated here might also apply to corrections officers working in prisons and jails?

2. Which might apply to law enforcement officers?

3. Which might apply to prosecutors and criminal defense attorneys?

Source: American Probation and Parole Association. Reprinted with permission.

are performed in the home or at a job site during the hours they are permitted to be away from their homes. Washing police cars, cleaning school buses, refurbishing public facilities, and assisting in local government offices are typical forms of community service. Some authors have linked the development of community-service sentences to the notion that work and service to others are good for the spirit.[68] Community-service participants are usually minor criminals, drunk drivers, and youthful offenders.

One problem with community-service sentences is that authorities rarely agree on what they are supposed to accomplish. Most people admit that offenders who work in the community are able to reduce the costs of their own supervision. There is little agreement, however, on whether such sentences reduce recidivism, act as a deterrent, or serve to rehabilitate offenders.

Intensive Probation Supervision

Intensive probation supervision (IPS) has been described as the "strictest form of probation for adults in the United States."[69] IPS is designed to achieve control in a community setting over offenders who would otherwise go to prison. Some

states have extended intensive supervision to parolees, allowing the early release of some who would otherwise serve longer prison terms.

Georgia was the first state to implement IPS, beginning its program in 1982. The Georgia program involves a minimum of five face-to-face contacts between the probationer and the supervising officer per week, mandatory curfew, required employment, a weekly check of local arrest records, routine and unannounced alcohol and drug testing, 132 hours of community service, and automatic notification of probation officers via the State Crime Information Network when an IPS client is arrested.[70] The caseloads of probation officers involved in IPS are much lower than the national average. Georgia officers work as a team, with one probation officer and two surveillance officers supervising about 40 probationers.[71]

One published study showed that IPS programs can be effective at reducing recidivism, especially if the programs are well planned and fully implemented.[72] The study, which examined programs in California's Contra Costa and Ventura Counties, found that the programs worked because, among other things, they used team approaches in their supervision activities and had clear missions and goals.

■ **home confinement** House arrest. Individuals ordered confined to their homes are sometimes monitored electronically to ensure they do not leave during the hours of confinement. Absence from the home during working hours is often permitted.

■ **remote location monitoring** A supervision strategy that uses electronic technology to track offenders who have been sentenced to house arrest or who have been ordered to limit their movements while completing a sentence involving probation or parole.

Home Confinement and Remote Location Monitoring

Home confinement, also referred to as *house arrest*, can be defined as "a sentence imposed by the court in which offenders are legally ordered to remain confined in their own residences."[73] Home confinement usually makes use of a system of **remote location monitoring**. Remote location monitoring is typically performed via a computerized system of electronic bracelets. Participants wear a waterproof, shock-resistant transmitting device around the ankle 24 hours a day. The transmitter continuously emits a radio-frequency signal, which is detected by a receiving unit connected to the home telephone. Older systems use random telephone calls that require the offender to insert a computer chip worn in a wristband into a specially installed modem in the home, verifying his or her presence. Some use voice recognition technology and require the offender to verify his or her presence in the home by answering computerized calls. Modern electronic monitoring systems alert the officer when a participant leaves a specific location or tampers with the electronic monitoring equipment, and some systems even make it possible to record the time a supervised person enters or leaves the home.

Much of the electronic monitoring equipment in use today indicates only when participants enter or leave the equipment's range—not where they have gone or how far they have traveled. Newer satellite-supported and cellular systems, however, are capable of continuously monitoring the location of offenders and tracking them as they move from place to place (Figure 12-3). Such systems can alert the officer when participants venture into geographically excluded locations or when they fail to present themselves at required locations at specific times.[74]

Most remotely monitored offenders on home confinement may leave home only to go to their jobs, attend to medical emergencies, or buy household essentials. Because of the strict limits it imposes on offender movements, house arrest has been cited as offering a valuable alternative to prison for offenders with special needs. Pregnant women, geriatric convicts, offenders with disabilities, seriously or terminally ill offenders, and offenders who have intellectual disabilities may all be better supervised through home confinement than through traditional incarceration.

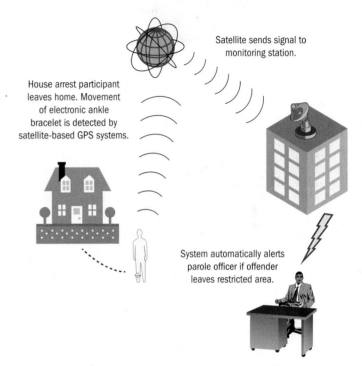

Satellite sends signal to monitoring station.

House arrest participant leaves home. Movement of electronic ankle bracelet is detected by satellite-based GPS systems.

System automatically alerts parole officer if offender leaves restricted area.

FIGURE 12-3 | Remote Location Monitoring—How It Works

One of the best-known people to be placed recently under house arrest using a remote location monitoring system was actress Lindsay Lohan. In 2011, Lohan was placed under house arrest and ordered to wear an electronic monitor on her ankle following a plea of no contest to charges that she had stolen an expensive necklace from a Los Angeles jewelry store.[75]

The Community Justice Assistance Division of the Texas Department of Criminal Justice runs one of the most ambitious home confinement programs in the country. In 1997, nearly 3.5% of the state's probationers were being electronically monitored on probation.[76] By 2011, parole offices throughout the state had adopted electronic monitoring, and 3,312 offenders were under electronic monitoring surveillance.[77]

The electronic monitoring of offenders has substantially increased across the nation during the past 20 years. A survey by the National Institute of Justice in 1987, as the use of electronic monitoring was just beginning, showed only 826 offenders being

CJ | NEWS
How GPS Technology Keeps Track of Sex Offenders

Paul Bersebach/Newscom

An ankle bracelet with a built-in global positioning system (GPS). The bracelet can be placed on parolees and used by parole officers to monitor individuals under house arrest, or to follow the movements of those permitted by the court to move throughout the community while under supervision. What do you see as the advantages and disadvantages of this technology? How would individual-rights and public-safety advocates see GPS technology when used this way?

In 2006, when 23 states had adopted global positioning systems (GPSs) to monitor sex offenders, the approach was hailed as a promising technique to control habitual predators.

GPS monitors, strapped to the ankle, were seen as a less costly way to protect against sex offenders than prison or frequent parole officer visits. Advocates of home confinement thought that the use of monitors might even discourage recidivism, because offenders would be aware that authorities were watching their every move.

Today, however, the number of participating states has reportedly not grown and authorities seem less enthusiastic. "GPS technology is far more limited than anticipated and should be viewed as a tool rather than depended upon as a control mechanism," says Gaylene Armstrong, a professor of criminal justice at Sam Houston State University.

In a two-year study of GPS monitoring of sex offenders in Phoenix, published in the *Journal of Criminal Justice* in 2011, Armstrong discovered that considerable numbers of alerts from the devices were due to harmless events such as equipment failure. Research on whether GPS monitors deter crimes has also been inconclusive, and many offenders have been cutting off the devices or trying to find other ways of fooling them.

False alerts are a particular problem because they obscure actual trouble spots. The 274 parole officers working GPS caseloads in California, the largest user of GPS monitors for sex offenders, received almost a million alerts in 2009, according to a state report. Each alert

shows up as a dot on a computer screen. "We are just drowning in dots," said Robert Coombs, chair of the state's Sex Offender Management Board. "What happens is the more broadly we use it, the more difficult it becomes in identifying the meaningful data."

California's information overload has led to some colossal failures. One paroled sex offender in the state's GPS program was Phillip Garrido, who kidnapped 11-year-old Jaycee Lee Dugard and was keeping her in a shed behind his house for 18 years. After Garrido was arrested in 2009, a state inquiry determined officers failed to respond to hundreds of alerts from his monitor, and the state subsequently paid Dugard $20 million in a settlement. Garrido, who fathered two children with Dugard, is now serving a 431-year sentence.

Some states, however, are less overwhelmed. In Washington, each parole officer is assigned between 20 and 30 offenders, and tracks each offender's GPS movements several times a day. Michigan has created a central monitoring center to weed out false alarms, and Florida has hired a private company to sort through alerts.

But effective monitoring can be costly. The reported cost of monitoring one person ranges from $5 to as much as $33 per day, and California spent $60 million to track just 6,500 parolees in 2010. Also, when parole officers devote a lot of time to GPS monitoring, it means less face-to-face and telephone time with parolees—alternative supervision strategies that are considered to be more effective. Innovative jurisdictions have been experimenting with cost reductions. In 2015, a few areas were experimenting with using the GPS technology built into offenders' personal cell phones as a way to reduce cost while providing reliable monitoring. Probationers, who are called randomly at different times of the day, are expected to answer calls from their supervising officers who can then use GPS to determine their client's whereabouts. Voice-recognition technology plays an important role in identifying probationers who receive such calls.

GPS may be useful in locating an offender when a child is missing, but many law enforcement officials now say the chief advantage of GPS tracking is not stopping a crime, but gathering evidence after a crime has been committed. "Essentially, a GPS bracelet allows you to make a case after the fact," said Gerard Leone, a Massachusetts district attorney. "And that is why I stress it is not an appropriate substitution for incarceration."

Six states have authorized lifetime GPS tracking for sex offenders, extending beyond parole. Critics say this is a violation of the Fourth Amendment ban on search and seizure and of the *ex post facto* clause prohibiting retroactively adding punishment to an offender's sentence. However, the North Carolina Supreme Court rejected the *ex post facto* argument in 2010. It is yet to be tested in federal court.

Resources: "GPS Monitoring of Sex Offenders Should Be Used as Tool, Not Control Mechanism, Researchers Find," *Science Daily*, August 8, 2011, http://www.sciencedaily.com/releases/2011/08/110808152417.htm; "Calif. to Change Sex-Offender Tracking," *Associated Press*, May 26, 2011, http://abcnews.go.com/US/wireStory?id=13696574#.T5lkxRxvYzA; "Tracking Sex Offenders Is No Easy Fix," *The Bay Citizen*, July 20, 2010, http://www.baycitizen.org/crime/story/gps-tracking-sex-offenders-imperfect; "Georgia Touts Technology Use to Cut Parole Revocations, Recidivism," The Crime Report, May 1, 2014, http://www.thecrimereport.org/news/crime-and-justice-news/2014-05-technology-and-probation-parole (accessed May 5, 2015).

monitored electronically nationwide.[78] By 2000, however, more than 16,000 defendants and offenders under the supervision of U.S. probation and pretrial services officers were on home confinement—most under electronic monitoring programs.[79] A 2012 estimate put the number of persons in the United States under

electronic monitoring at around 200,000—including 27,000 people awaiting deportation.[80]

In 1999, South Carolina became one of the first states to use satellites to track felons recently freed from state prisons. The satellite-tracking plan, which made use of 21 satellites in the

■ **theme**   Discuss the value of each of the intermediate sanctions described in this chapter. Which of these options are, in your opinion, the most fair? Why?

■ **theme**   How might parole change in the future? How should it change? Why?

global positioning system (GPS), allowed the state's Probation and Parole Department to track every move made by convicts wearing electronic bracelets.[81] The system, which also notified law enforcement officers when a bracelet-wearing offender left his or her assigned area, could electronically alert anyone holding a restraining order whenever the offender came within two miles of them. Over the past 15 years, GPS tracking of parolees has become commonplace and is now used across the country.

The home confinement program in the federal court system has three components, or levels of restriction.[82] *Curfew* requires program participants to remain at home every day during certain times, usually in the evening. With *home detention*, the participant remains at home at all times except for preapproved and scheduled absences, such as for work, school, treatment, church, attorney's appointments, court appearances, and other court-ordered obligations. *Home incarceration*, the highest level of restriction, calls for 24-hour-a-day "lockdown" at home, except for medical appointments, court appearances, and other activities that the court specifically approves.

Many states and the federal government view house arrest as a cost-effective response to the high cost of imprisonment. Georgia, for example, estimates that home confinement costs approximately $1,130 per year per supervised probationer and $1,577 per supervised parolee.[83] Incarceration costs are much higher, running around $18,700 per year per Georgia inmate, with another $43,756 needed to build each cell.[84] Advocates of house arrest argue that it is also socially cost-effective[85] because it substantially decreases the opportunity for the kinds of negative socialization that occur in prison. Opponents, however, have pointed out that house arrest may endanger the public and that it may provide little or no actual punishment. Critics of Michael Vick's home confinement, for example, complained that the sentence was more of a reward than a punishment. Vick's home, a five-bedroom, 3,538-square-foot brick house, lacks few amenities, and the conditions imposed on Vick allowed him to do pretty much as he pleased while in the house.

> Many states and the federal government view house arrest as a cost-effective response to the high cost of imprisonment.

A large study funded by the NIJ of more than 5,000 Florida offenders placed on GPS monitoring found that electronic monitoring significantly reduced the likelihood of failure under community supervision.[86] The risk of failure was found to be about 31% less than that of offenders placed on other forms of community supervision. Similarly, a recent NIJ study that compared a group of GPS-monitored California sex offenders over a one-year period found that "a clear pattern" success for those being monitored versus a control group who received traditional parole supervision.[87] Study authors noted that the chance for both parole revocation and any return-to-custody event was about 38% higher among the subjects who received traditional parole supervision. The NIJ study also examined costs and benefits associated with electronic monitoring, and concluded that "the GPS program costs roughly $35.96 per day per parolee, while the cost of traditional supervision is $27.45 per day per parolee—a difference of $8.51. However, the results favor the GPS group in terms of both noncompliance and recidivism. In other words, the GPS monitoring program is more expensive but more effective."

The Future of Probation and Parole

Parole was widely criticized during the 1980s and 1990s by citizen groups that claimed it unfairly reduces prison sentences imposed on serious offenders. Official attacks on parole came from some powerful corners. Senator Edward Kennedy called for the abolition of parole, as did former Attorney General Griffin Bell and former U.S. Bureau of Prisons Director Norman Carlson.[88] Academics chimed in, alleging that parole programs provide no assurance that criminals will not commit further crimes. The media joined the fray, condemning parole for its failure to curb recidivism and highlighting the so-called revolving prison door as representative of the failure of parole.

These criticisms are not without value. Today, around 688,000 former prisoners—almost 2,000 per day—are released annually from state and federal prisons and returned to society, most of them on some form of supervised release.[89] Although statistics on the 2010 cohort are not yet fully available, estimates are that over half of them will have been reincarcerated within three years (and some of them will have successfully completed parole prior to their return to prison).[90] Figure 12-4 shows recidivism rates within three years of release for prisoners in 15 states.

Parole violators account for more than half of prison admissions in many states, and 70% of parole violators sent to in prison were arrested or were convicted of a new offense *while* on parole.[91] Many of these offenses involved drugs. In 2013, for example, a study by the Kentucky-based Council of State Governments found that one in five arrests in four of California's largest cities involved individuals under probation or parole supervision at the time of their arrest.[92] The study also found that persons under supervision were involved in one in six arrests for violent crime and one in three of all arrests for drug crime. Had the study also sought to identify persons arrested who had *previously* been on probation or parole, as well as those *currently* being supervised, the results would likely have been much higher.

> Parole violators account for more than half of prison admissions in many states.

■ **desistance**   The cessation of offending or other antisocial behavior.

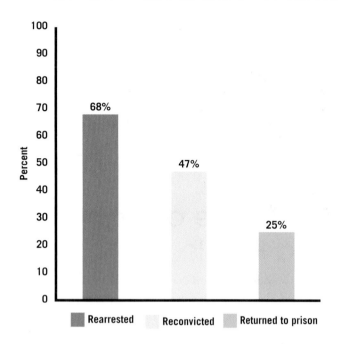

FIGURE 12-4 | Three-Year Recidivism Rates of Prisoners Released from Prison in 15 States

Source: Jeremy Travis, Ronald Davis, and Sarah Lawrence, *Exploring the Role of the Police in Prisoner Reentry*, New Perspectives in Policing Bulletin (Washington, DC: U.S. Department of Justice, National Institute of Justice, 2012).

Critics say that numbers like these are indicative of poor reintegration of prisoners into the community and are associated with wide-ranging social costs, including decreased public safety and weakened family and community ties.[93] Adequate reintegration efforts have also suffered in the face of today's budget shortfalls. In California, for example, the 2011 Realignment Legislation mentioned earlier in this chapter stipulated that any parolee (other than those originally sentenced to life in prison) whose parole is revoked will serve a term no longer than 180 days in the county jail.[94] The bill also provides that parolees who do not incur any infractions will be released from parole supervision in six months. Under the law, California's Board of Parole Hearings discontinued parole revocation hearings in mid-2013, and that responsibility was moved to local criminal court judges. Although thorough assessments of California's experiment with realignment have yet to be made, one report by a Los Angeles County advisory board found that responsibility for a large number of high-risk offenders, many with mental illness, has been shifted to counties that may be ill-prepared to deal adequately with those offenders.[95]

Even some prisoners have challenged the fairness of parole, saying it is sometimes arbitrarily granted, which creates an undue

> Some prisoners have challenged the fairness of parole, saying it is sometimes arbitrarily granted.

amount of uncertainty and frustration for inmates. Parolees have complained about the unpredictable nature of the parole experience, citing their powerlessness in the parole contract.

Against the pressure of attacks like these, parole advocates struggled to clarify and communicate the value of supervised release in the corrections process. As more and more states moved toward the elimination of parole, advocates called for moderation. One report by the American Probation and Parole Association (APPA), for example, concluded that states that have eliminated parole "have jeopardized public safety and wasted tax dollars." The researchers wrote, "Getting rid of parole dismantles an accountable system of releasing prisoners back into the community and replaces it with a system that bases release decisions solely on whether a prison term has been completed."[96]

Changes in Reentry Policies

By the close of the twentieth century, criticisms of parole had begun to wane, and numerous reports supported well-considered offender reentry and post-release supervision programs that were able to demonstrate **desistance** from crime. In 2005, for example, the Re-entry Policy Council, a bipartisan assembly of almost 100 leading elected officials, policymakers, corrections leaders, and practitioners from community-based organizations around the country, released a report on offender reentry titled *Charting the Safe and Successful Return of Prisoners to the Community*. The 500-page document pointed out that virtually every person incarcerated in a jail in this country, as well as 97% of those incarcerated in prisons, will eventually be released back into society. This, said the report, results in nearly 650,000 people being released from prisons, and more than 7 million individuals being released from jails throughout the United States each year—many of them without any form of post-release supervision.[97]

As the report noted, almost two out of every three people released from prison are rearrested within three years of their release.[98] Report authors also noted that although the number of people reentering society has increased fourfold in the past 20 years, and spending on corrections has increased nearly sevenfold during that time, the likelihood of a former prisoner succeeding in the community upon release has not improved.

A host of complex issues create barriers to successful reentry. Three-quarters of those released from prison and jail, for example, have a history of substance abuse; two-thirds have no high school diploma; nearly half of those leaving jail earned less than $600 per month immediately prior to their incarceration; and they leave jail with significantly diminished opportunities for employment. Moreover, said the report, more than a third of jail inmates are saddled with a physical or mental disability, and the rate of serious mental illness among released inmates is

■ **reentry courts** "Specialized courts that help reduce recidivism and improve public safety through the use of judicial oversight to apply graduated sanctions and positive reinforcement, to marshal resources to support the prisoner's reintegration, and to promote positive behavior by the returning prisoners."[ii] Also, specialized courts that are based on the drug-court model, and which function to rapidly place drug-affected defendants into appropriate treatment programs with close supervision by a single judge familiar with both the treatment and the offenders.

at least three times higher than the rate of mental illness among the general population.[99]

According to the report, "the multi-faceted—and costly—needs of people returning to their families and communities require a re-inventing of reentry akin to the reinvention of welfare in the 90s." It requires, the report continued, "a multi-system, collaborative approach that takes into account all aspects of [the] problem." In other words, "the problems faced by re-entering adults are not merely the problems of corrections or community corrections, but also of public health workers, housing providers, state legislators, workforce development staff, and others."

To guide states and local jurisdictions in the creation of successful offender reentry programs, the report provides 35 policy statements, each of which is supported by a series of research highlights. The report can be read in its entirety at **http://csgjusticecenter.org/reentry/publications/the-report-of-the-re-entry-policy-council-charting-the-safe-and-successful-return-of-prisoners-to-the-community/**.

In 2003, the U.S. Department of Justice, in conjunction with other federal agencies, initiated funding for 89 reentry sites across the country under the Serious and Violent Offender Reentry Initiative (SVORI).[100] SVORI programs were geared toward serious and violent offenders, particularly adults released from prison, as well as juveniles released from correctional facilities. The goal of the SVORI initiative was to reduce the likelihood of reincarceration by providing tailored supervision and services to improve the odds for a successful transition to the community. SVORI services included employment assistance, education and skills training, substance-abuse counseling, and help with post-release housing.

SVORI programs also tried to enhance desistance by closely monitoring participant noncompliance, reoffending, rearrest, reconviction, and reincarceration. The initiative's priorities included providing services both to those adults and juveniles who were most likely to pose a risk to the community upon release and to those who faced multiple challenges upon returning to the community. SVORI funding supported the creation of a three-phase continuum of services that (1) begins in prison, (2) moves to a structured reentry phase before and during the early months of release, and (3) continues for several years as released prisoners take on increasingly productive roles in the community.[101]

In 2012, after SVORI funding ended, the NIJ published a 560-page final report evaluating results of the SVORI program.[102] The study found encouraging results for the effect of the SVORI program participation on arrest and, to a lesser extent, incarceration outcomes. The effect of SVORI program participation was found to have been associated with longer times to arrest and with fewer arrests during followup periods. Results were weaker for the effects of the SVORI program on post-release reincarceration, however. For adult males, SVORI program participation was associated with a longer time to reincarceration and also fewer reincarcerations. For the adult females, the results were mixed and not significant. The final SVORI report can be read in its entirety at **http://www.justicestudies.com/pubs/final_svori.pdf**.

In response to the high post-release failure rates and the overwhelming needs of individuals returning from incarceration, many reentry-type programs designed to facilitate the transition from incarceration to the community have been implemented over the past several decades.[103] Not all of them fall under the SVORI model. Among the most significant alternatives are **reentry courts** (also discussed in Chapter 9), which combine intensive judicial oversight with rehabilitative services, and arose as part of a broader national movement toward the development and implementation of specialized "problem-solving courts," such as drug, mental health, domestic violence, and community courts, as an approach for addressing specific problems among criminal justice populations.

Reentry courts are mostly based on the drug-court model, begun in Miami in 1989, which functions to rapidly place drug-affected defendants into appropriate treatment programs with close supervision by a single judge familiar with both the treatment and the offenders.[104] Similarly, under the reentry court concept, reentry court judges oversee an offender's supervised release into the community.[105] Hence, reentry courts address the critical needs of returning prisoners—particularly in the period immediately following release—through the combination of judicial oversight and a collaborative case management process. According to the Bureau of Justice Assistance, "the underlying goal of reentry courts is to establish a seamless system of offender accountability and support services throughout the reentry process."[106]

The typical reentry court offers an array of reintegration services to which participants can be referred and provides continual oversight using a preestablished set of graduated sanctions and rewards. Throughout the reentry period, a reentry case-management team makes continual recommendations to the reentry court judge.

The National Reentry Resource Center—a joint effort by the Urban Institute, the American Probation and Parole Association, the Center of Juvenile Justice Reform at Georgetown University, the Association of State Correctional Administrators, and the Council of State Governments' Justice Center—can be visited on the Web at **http://www.national reentryresourcecenter.org**. Read an NIJ-sponsored study of the effectiveness of reentry courts at **http://www.justice studies.com/pubs/reentrycourts.pdf.**

In March 2008, in an effort to help the more than 600,000 people leaving prison each year, the U.S. Congress passed the Second Chance Act.[107] The bill was signed into law by President George W. Bush shortly afterward. The law's purpose is to reduce the number of people being returned to prison after parole release due to state-run "hair-trigger" parole systems that send large numbers of people back to prison not for new crimes, but for technical violations or other relatively minor reasons.

The act authorized the expenditure of approximately $400 million in federal funds to "break the cycle of criminal recidivism

> The Second Chance Act was intended to break the cycle of criminal recidivism by assisting offenders reentering the community from incarceration to establish a self-sustaining and law-abiding life.

[by assisting] offenders reentering the community from incarceration to establish a self-sustaining and law-abiding life."[108] The legislation funds prison-to-community transition services and programs through grants to nonprofit organizations. Such services and programs include the following:

- Reentry courts
- Education and job training while in prison
- Mentoring programs for adults and juveniles leaving confinement
- Drug treatment (including family-based treatment) for incarcerated parents during and after incarceration
- Alternatives to incarceration for parents convicted of nonviolent drug offenses

David Duke, the former Ku Klux Klan leader whose case raised eyebrows when he was released on federal parole in 2004. Duke, who served a year in federal prison on fraud charges, was released to a halfway house in Baton Rouge, Louisiana, and met the work requirements of his release by performing duties for the "white civil rights group" that he heads. Might a more suitable placement have been found for Duke?

Nick Ut/AP Wide World Photos

CJ | ISSUES
Remote Reporting Probation

Recently, a number of Internet-based interactive probation services, including ProbationComm (created by Circle Seven Software) and PoCheck software, have been adopted by states seeking to lower the costs of probation supervision. Both ProbationComm and PoCheck, along with similar other services, allow low-risk probationers to keep in touch with their probation officers through an Internet reporting service. These online services allow for easy communication between client and officers through e-mail, Web-based forms, and instant messaging. Probationers participating in Internet supervision can access the service from home, or through public computers such as those available at local libraries. Clients are generally assessed a small fee, usually in the range of $10 to $20, for participation in the program.

Remote reporting systems typically allow probation officers to send mass e-mailings to their entire caseload of clients, or to target individual probationers in their communications. Through the use of easy-to-complete online forms, clients are able to report changes in status (such as changes in jobs, hiring, or health issues) to the probation officer, and the system notifies officers of upcoming events, such as pending discharges from supervision. It can also flag probationers who report losing jobs, changing marital status, or a change in place of residence. With links to law enforcement agencies and automated databases, Internet-based systems alerts probation officers of arrests, citations, and other law enforcement contacts with clients.

One major advantage of remote reporting programs is that they allow significantly increased caseloads. A Texas study, for example, showed that Internet reporting makes it possible for one probation officer to supervise up to 500 probationers—more than twice the normal number—without increasing the number of hours of work required over traditional supervision. This significant increase in supervisory capacity can be very important for jurisdictions seeking to make the most efficient use of limited resources.

Although Web-hosted interactive probation services are relatively new (the first went online in 2002), some jurisdictions still use interactive probation kiosks, similar to ATM machines. In 1997, for example, probation authorities in New York City began the use of probation kiosks designed to lower probation officer caseloads. Fifteen electronic kiosks, similar in design to ATMs, were scattered throughout the city,

allowing probationers to check in with probation officers by placing their palms on a specially designed surface and by answering questions presented on a flashing screen.

The kiosks, which some jurisdictions still use, identify probationers by the shape and size of their hands, which were previously scanned into the system. Probationers using the kiosk system are prompted to press "yes" or "no" in response to questions like these: "Have you moved recently?" "Have you been arrested again?" "Do you need to see a probation officer?" Meetings with officers can be scheduled directly from the kiosk. By analyzing data submitted through kiosks, probation officers can zero in on individual probationers who are having problems, prompting more personal attention.

Some jurisdictions, however, may have been too quick to jump on the remote reporting bandwagon. In 2005, for example, Dallas, Texas, temporarily suspended the use of kiosks after finding that not all program participants had been properly screened. Although participation in the program required an assessment for readiness through face-to-face meetings with probation officers, some participants had undetected problems, including drug dependence and mental illness. As one critic of the Dallas program pointed out, "Inappropriate use of probation automation risks saving money in the short run while increasing long-term costs through higher recidivism rates."

Critics charge that high-tech supervision of probationers, whether online or through the use of kiosks, Internet services, or dial-in telephone numbers (often enhanced through the use of voice-recognition technologies), carries unacceptable risk. Without personal supervision, those critics say, probationers are more likely to reoffend—an assertion that is essentially untested. Other opponents say remote reporting services are far removed from meaningful "punishment," and that offenders deserve stricter treatment. Supporters, on the other hand, say that high-tech probation supervision will have to become commonplace as probation and parole budges are strained. "New York City had no choice; it had to do something like that," says Todd Clear, professor of criminal justice at New York's John Jay College. Clear assisted the city in restructuring its probation program. "No one wants probationers reporting to kiosks, but the alternative was even more unthinkable—a system in which nobody receives quality service," said Clear.

References: PoCheck, "Probation and Parole Report-in System," http://www.pocheck.com; ProbationComm, "Introducing ProbationComm," http://www.probationcomm.com/docs/ProbationComm_Introduction.pdf (accessed March 1, 2013); and Marc A. Levin, "Salvation in Probation Automation?" *Conservative Voice*, September 27, 2005, http://www.theconservativevoice.com/articles/article.html?id=8585 (accessed May 1, 2011); Cathaleen Qiao Chen, "Lawmakers Urged to Reform Parole with Technology," *The Texas Tribune*, April 29, 2014, http://www.texastribune.org/2014/04/29/lawmakers-urged-reform-criminal-justice-technology (accessed May 5, 2015).

- Supportive programming for children of incarcerated parents
- Early release for certain elderly prisoners convicted of nonviolent offenses
- Reentry research through research awards to study parole and postsupervision revocation and related community safety issues

The legislation also allocates funding for Federal Bureau of Prisons programs that do the following:

1. Provide prisoners nearing the completion of their sentences with information concerning health care, nutrition, employment opportunities, money management, and availability of government assistance

2. Allow certain nonviolent prisoners over 60 years of age to be placed in home detention for the duration of their sentences

3. Educate juvenile offenders on the consequences of drug use and criminal activity

The Second Chance Act seems to be having its desired effect, as a nationwide study of 500,000 parolees who left supervision showed that only 30% were sent back to confinement in 2013 versus a 36% recidivism rate in 2008.[109]

The Reinvention of Probation and Evidence-Based Practices

Although probation has generally fared better than parole, it too has its critics. The primary purpose of probation has always been rehabilitation. Probation is a powerful rehabilitative tool because, at least in theory, it allows the resources of a community to be focused on the offender. Unfortunately for advocates of probation, however, the rehabilitative ideal is less popular today than it has been in the past. Because it has been too frequently and inappropriately used with repeat or relatively serious offenders, the image of probation has been tarnished. Probation advocates have been forced to admit that it is not a very powerful deterrent because it is far less punishing than a term of imprisonment.

A few years ago, the Public Safety Performance Project of the Pew Center on the States released a report outlining strategies for successful probation supervision and parole reentry. The report, titled *Putting Public Safety First*, outlined 13 strategies that the center says "can reduce recidivism and hold offenders accountable for their actions while also cutting substance abuse and unemployment, and restoring family bonds."[110] Primary among the strategies is defining the success of probation and parole in terms of recidivism reduction. The entire report can be accessed at **http://www.pewtrusts.org/our_work_report_detail.aspx?id=46570**.

In an effort to assess the degree to which the Pew Center's 13 strategies were being implemented, the Justice Policy Center of the Urban Institute published a lengthy review of parole practices across the country.[111] While the review found that few agencies were using all of the 13 strategies, it did find that most agencies are moving in the direction of implementing many of them. Although 93% of survey respondents reported that their offices have the goal of reducing recidivism, only 75% said that recidivism rates of current paroles were being tracked; and an amazingly low 13% of offices said that they continued to track recidivism rates of parolees who have completed parole. Moreover, definitions of recidivism varied considerably between agencies, and included "reincarceration," "reconviction," "new arrest," and "technical violation."[112] One positive result from the survey showed that awareness and use of evidence-based practices among parole agencies has become relatively widespread. This, say the report's authors, "suggests that a consensus on the value of the general concept is emerging." Nonetheless, the review also found that "there is considerable uncertainty on what evidence-based practice means in parole."[113] Nonetheless, the evidence-based movement in probation and parole is gaining steam, and in 2009, the California legislature enacted a law creating the California Community Corrections Performance Incentive Program, which promotes the use of evidence-based strategies for reducing the rate of failure on probation.[114]

Recently, the National Institute of Corrections published a report showing that, among programs studied, treatment-oriented intense supervision of offenders in the community had the largest impact on reducing recidivism (Figure 12-5).[115] That report, entitled "Evidence-Based Policy, Practice and Decisionmaking," can be accessed at **http://www.justicestudies.com/pubs/ppdecisionmaking.pdf**.

Finally, in 2012, the NIJ funded studies of Hawaii's HOPE program, a highly successful probation initiative that addresses

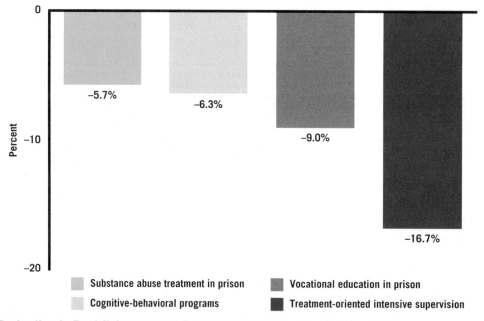

FIGURE 12-5 | Reduction in Recidivism among Released Offenders, by Program Type

Source: National Institute of Corrections, *Evidence-Based Policy, Practice, and Decisionmaking: Implications for Paroling Authorities* (Washington, DC: U.S. Department of Justice, 2011).

probation violations in a swift, certain, and proportionate manner. HOPE, which stands for Hawaii's Opportunity Probation with Enforcement, when compared with traditional probation programs results in (1) a 55% reduction in arrests for new crimes, (2) a 72% reduction in the likelihood of drug use, (3) a 61% reduction in skipped appointments with probation supervisors, and (4) a 53% reduction in probation revocation.[116]

HOPE begins with a direct, formal warning delivered by a judge in court to offenders enrolled in the program. The warning explicitly states that any future probation violations will result in an immediate, brief jail stay. Probationers with drug issues are assigned a color code at the warning hearing and are required to call the HOPE hotline each weekday morning to find out which color has been chosen for that day. Probationers whose color is selected must appear at the probation office before 2 p.m. the same day for a drug test. Non-drug-involved offenders must comply with their conditions of probation and may be required to attend treatment.

When probationers violate the conditions of probation, they are arrested or an arrest warrant is issued. As soon as a probation officer detects a violation, he or she completes a "Motion to Modify Probation" form and sends it to the judge, who promptly holds a violation hearing. A probationer found to have violated the terms of probation is sentenced to a short jail stay. Upon release, the probationer reports to his or her probation officer and resumes participation in HOPE. Each successive violation is met with an escalated response (i.e., longer jail stays). Learn more about the HOPE program, including efforts to replicate it elsewhere, at **http://www.justicestudies.com/pubs/hope.pdf**.

SUMMARY

- Probation, simply put, is a sentence of imprisonment that is suspended. Its goal is to retain some control over criminal offenders while using community programs to help rehabilitate them. Probation, a court-ordered sanction, is one form of community corrections (also termed *community-based corrections*)—that is, a sentencing style that depends less on traditional confinement options and more on correctional resources available in the community. John Augustus, a Boston shoemaker, is generally recognized as the world's first probation officer. By 1925, all 48 states had adopted probation legislation. In that same year, the federal government enacted legislation enabling federal district court judges to appoint paid probation officers and to impose probationary terms.

- Parole is the conditional early release of a convicted offender from prison. It is a corrections strategy with a primary purpose of returning offenders gradually to productive lives. Parole differs from probation in that parolees, unlike probationers, have been incarcerated. Parole supported the concept of indeterminate sentencing, which held that a prisoner could earn early release through good behavior and self-improvement.

- Both probation and parole provide opportunities for the reintegration of offenders into the community through the use of resources not readily available in institutional settings. They are far less expensive than imprisonment, lead to increased employment among program participants, make possible restitution payments, and increase opportunities for rehabilitation. Unfortunately, however, increased freedom for criminal offenders also means some degree of increased risk for other members of society and increased social costs.

- Eleven especially significant U.S. Supreme Court decisions, each of which was discussed in this chapter, provide the legal framework for probation and parole supervision. The 1987 case of *Griffin* v. *Wisconsin* may be the most significant. In *Griffin*, the Supreme Court ruled that probation officers may conduct searches of a probationer's residence without either a search warrant or probable cause. Other important court decisions include the 1998 case of *Pennsylvania Board of Probation and Parole* v. *Scott*, in which the Court declined to extend the exclusionary rule to apply to searches by parole officers, and the 2001 case of *U.S.* v. *Knights*, which expanded the search authority normally reserved for probation and parole officers to police officers under certain circumstances.

- Probation/parole work consists primarily of four functions: (1) presentence investigations, (2) other intake procedures, (3) diagnosis and needs assessment, and (4) client supervision. The tasks performed by probation and parole officers are often quite similar, and some jurisdictions combine the roles of both into one job.

- Intermediate sanctions, which are sometimes termed *alternative sentencing strategies*, employ sentencing alternatives that fall somewhere between outright imprisonment and simple probationary release back into the community. These sanctions include shock incarceration, intensive supervision, and home confinement with electronic monitoring (also referred to as *remote location monitoring*). Intermediate sanctions have three distinct advantages: (1) They are less expensive than imprisonment; (2) they are "socially cost-effective" because they keep the offender in the community; and (3) they provide flexibility in terms of resources, time of involvement, and place of service.

- In recent years, parole and sometimes probation have been criticized for increasing the risk of community victimization by known offenders. In response, many states eliminated or significantly curtailed parole opportunities. Now, however, as jurisdictions seek to reduce prison populations, reentry programs are once again seen as the best hope for successfully transitioning released inmates back into the community.

KEY TERMS

KEY CASES

QUESTIONS FOR REVIEW

1. What is probation? How did it develop? What purpose does it serve?
2. What is parole? How do probation and parole differ? How are they alike?
3. List and explain the advantages and disadvantages of probation and parole.
4. Describe significant court cases that have had an impact on the practice of probation and parole.
5. What do probation and parole officers do? What role do probation officers play in the sentencing of convicted offenders?
6. What are intermediate sanctions? How do they differ from more traditional forms of sentencing? What advantages do they offer?
7. How are probation and parole changing? What does the future hold for them?

QUESTIONS FOR REFLECTION

1. What significance does the contemporary concept of prisoner reentry hold for today's corrections administrators? For society? How do the terms *reentry* and *parole* differ?
2. What corrections philosophy originally supported the idea of indeterminate sentencing and parole? Does that philosophy still have merit today? Why or why not?
3. Do you believe, as some do, that traditional parole has been a failure? Explain.

NOTES

i. Jeremy Travis and Sarah Lawrence, *Beyond the Prison Gates: The State of Parole in America* (Washington, DC: Urban Institute Press, 2002), p. 3.
ii. Debbie Dawes, *The National Institute of Justice's Evaluation of Second Chance Act Adult Reentry Courts: Program Characteristics and Preliminary Themes from Year 1* (Washington, DC: Bureau of Justice Assistance, 2013).

1. President's Commission on Law Enforcement and Administration of Justice, *The Challenge of Crime in a Free Society* (Washington, DC: 1967, USGPO), p. 164.
2. Mitch Weiss, "Petraeus Sentenced to 2 Years' Probation for Military Leak," Associated Press, April 26, 2015.
3. Michael S. Schmidt and Matt Apuzzo, "David Petraeus Is Sentenced to Probation in Leak Investigation," *New York Times*, April 23, 2015.
4. "Desistance" is defined later in this chapter.
5. James M. Byrne, *Probation*, National Institute of Justice Crime File Series Study Guide (Washington, DC: NIJ, 1988), p. 1.
6. Alexander B. Smith and Louis Berlin, *Introduction to Probation and Parole* (St. Paul, MN: West, 1976), p. 75.
7. John Augustus, *First Probation Officer: John Augustus' Original Report on His Labors—1852* (Montclair, NJ: Patterson-Smith, 1972).
8. Smith and Berlin, *Introduction to Probation and Parole*, p. 77.
9. Ibid., p. 80.
10. George C. Killinger, Hazel B. Kerper, and Paul F. Cromwell, Jr., *Probation and Parole in the Criminal Justice System* (St. Paul, MN: West, 1976), p. 25.
11. Lauren E. Glaze and Danielle Kaeble, *Correctional Populations in the United States, 2013* (Washington, DC: Bureau of Justice Statistics, December 2014).
12. Thomas Bonczar, Erinn Herberman, *Probation and Parole in the United States, 2013* (Washington, DC: Bureau of Justice Statistics, October 2014), p.1.
13. Jodi M. Brown and Patrick A. Langan, *Felony Sentences in the United States, 1996* (Washington, DC: Bureau of Justice Statistics, 1999).
14. "Woman Gets Probation for Shooting Fiancé," Associated Press, April 16, 1992, p. 9A.
15. Bonczar and Herberman, *Probation and Parole in the United States, 2013* (Washington, DC: Bureau of Justice Statistics, October 2014), p. 5.
16. Ibid.
17. This section owes much to Sanford Bates, "The Establishment and Early Years of the Federal Probation System," *Federal Probation* (June 1987), pp. 4–9.
18. *Ex parte United States*, 242 U.S. 27 (1916).
19. Bates, "The Establishment and Early Years of the Federal Probation System," p. 6.
20. U.S. Probation and Pretrial Services System, *Year-in-Review Report: Fiscal Year 2004* (Washington, DC: U.S. Probation and Pretrial Services System, 2005).
21. See Brian A. Reaves and Timothy C. Hart, *Federal Law Enforcement Officers, 2000* (Washington, DC: Bureau of Justice Statistics, 2002), p. 4, from which some of the wording in this paragraph has been adapted.
22. John M. Hughes, "We're Back on Track: Preparing for the Next 50 Years," *Federal Probation*, Vol. 75, No. 2 (September

2011), http://www.uscourts.gov/uscourts/FederalCourts/PPS/Fedprob/2011-09/back_on_track.html (accessed August 28, 2013).

23. Adapted from Timothy A. Hughes, Doris James Wilson, and Allen J. Beck, *Trends in State Parole, 1990–2000* (Washington, DC: Bureau of Justice Statistics, 2001), p. 1.

24. Justice Policy Institute, "How to Safely Reduce Prison Populations and Support People Returning to Their Communities," June 2010, p. 4.

25. Hughes, Wilson, and Beck, *Trends in State Parole, 1990–2000*.

26. California Assembly Bill 109.

27. California Department of Corrections and Rehabilitation, "Parole Revocations," http://www.cdcr.ca.gov/realignment/Parole-Revocations.html (accessed February 15, 2015).

28. Ibid.

29. Ibid.

30. Herberman and Bonczar, *Probation and Parole in the United States, 2013*.

31. Ibid., Table 6.

32. "The Effectiveness of Felony Probation: Results from an Eastern State," *Justice Quarterly* (December 1991), pp. 525–543.

33. United States Parole Commission, *FY 2014 Performance Budget* (Washington, DC: USPC, April 2013).

34. State of Georgia, Board of Pardons and Paroles, "Parole Supervision," http://pap.georgia.gov/parole-supervision (accessed February 14, 2015).

35. See Andrew von Hirsch and Kathleen J. Hanrahan, *Abolish Parole?* (Washington, DC: Law Enforcement Assistance Administration, 1978).

36. Theresa A. Severance, "Preparing for Re-entry: Challenges and Strategies," *Women, Girls & Criminal Justice*, Vol. 8, No. 3 (April/May 2007), p. 1.

37. P. O'Brien, *Making It in the "Free World": Women in Transition from Prison* (Albany: State University of New York Press, 2001).

38. *Griffin* v. *Wisconsin*, 483 U.S. 868, 107 S.Ct. 3164 (1987).

39. *Pennsylvania Board of Probation and Parole* v. *Scott*, 524 U.S. 357 (1998).

40. Herberman and Bonczar, *Probation and Parole in the United States, 2013*, Table 4 and 6.

41. Robyn L. Cohen, *Probation and Parole Violators in State Prison, 1991* (Washington, DC: Bureau of Justice Statistics, 1995).

42. California Department of Corrections and Rehabilitation, Division of Adult Parole Operations, "Non-Revocable Parole," http://www.cdcr.ca.gov/Parole/Non_Revocable_Parole/index.html (accessed February 22, 2015).

43. *Harlow* v. *Clatterbuick*, 30 CrL. 2364 (VA S.Ct. 1986); *Santangelo* v. *State*, 426 N.Y.S.2d 931 (1980); *Welch* v. *State*, 424 N.Y.S.2d 774 (1980); and *Thompson* v. *County of Alameda*, 614 P.2d 728 (1980).

44. *Tarter* v. *State of New York*, 38 CrL. 2364 (NY S.Ct. 1986); *Grimm* v. *Arizona Board of Pardons and Paroles*, 115 Arizona 260, 564 P.2d 1227 (1977); and *Payton* v. *U.S.*, 636 F.2d 132 (5th Cir. 1981).

45. Rolando del Carmen, *Potential Liabilities of Probation and Parole Officers* (Cincinnati, OH: Anderson, 1986), p. 89.

46. See, for example, *Semler* v. *Psychiatric Institute*, 538 F.2d 121 (4th Cir. 1976).

47. *Minnesota* v. *Murphy*, 465 U.S. 420 (1984).

48. National Advisory Commission on Criminal Justice Standards and Goals, *Task Force Report: Corrections* (Washington, DC: U.S. Government Printing Office, 1973).

49. Council of State Governments Justice Center, *The Impact of Probation and Parole Populations on Arrests in Four California Cities* (New York, 2013).

50. National Institute of Justice, *Stress among Probation and Parole Officers and What Can Be Done about It* (Washington, DC: NIJ, 2005).

51. Ibid., p. 1.

52. Ibid., p. ii.

53. From the introduction to James Austin, Michael Jones, and Melissa Bolyard, *The Growing Use of Jail Boot Camps: The Current State of the Art* (Washington, DC: National Institute of Justice, 1993), p. 1.

54. Michael McCarthy and Jodi Upton, "Athletes Lightly Punished after Their Day in Court," *USA Today*, May 4, 2006.

55. Sentencing Project, *Changing the Terms of Sentencing: Defense Counsel and Alternative Sentencing Services* (Washington, DC: Sentencing Project, no date).

56. Joan Petersilia, *Expanding Options for Criminal Sentencing* (Santa Monica, CA: RAND Corporation, 1987).

57. Ohio Revised Code, Section 2946.06.1 (July 1965).

58. Lawrence Greenfeld, *Probation and Parole, 1984* (Washington, DC: U.S. Government Printing Office, 1986).

59. Harry Allen et al., *Probation and Parole in America* (New York: Free Press, 1985), p. 88.

60. For a good overview of such programs, especially as they apply to juvenile corrections, see Doris Layton MacKenzie et al., *A National Study Comparing the Environments of Boot Camps with Traditional Facilities for Juvenile Offenders* (Washington, DC: National Institute of Justice, 2001).

61. Doris Layton MacKenzie and Deanna Bellew Ballow, "Shock Incarceration Programs in State Correctional Jurisdictions—An Update," *NIJ Reports* (May/June 1989), pp. 9–10.

62. "Shock Incarceration Marks a Decade of Expansion," *Corrections Compendium* (September 1996), pp. 10–28.

63. National Institute of Justice, *Multisite Evaluation of Shock Incarceration* (Washington, DC: NIJ, 1995).

64. Richard Willing, "U.S. Prisons to End Boot-Camp Program," *USA Today*, February 3, 2005, http://usatoday30.usatoday.com/news/nation/2005-02-03-boot-camps_x.htm (accessed February 23, 2015).

65. See, Nevada Department of Corrections, "Three Lakes Valley Boot Camp," http://www.doc.nv.gov/?q=node/36 (accessed July 5, 2013).

66. Wyoming Department of Corrections, "Youthful Offender Program (Wyoming Boot Camp), http://doc.state.wy.us/institutions/whcc/boot_camp_whcc.html (accessed February 24, 2015).

67. Douglas C. McDonald, *Restitution and Community Service*, National Institute of Justice Crime File Series Study Guide (Washington, DC: NIJ, 1988).

68. Richard J. Maher and Henry E. Dufour, "Experimenting with Community Service: A Punitive Alternative to Imprisonment," *Federal Probation* (September 1987), pp. 22–27.

69. James P. Levine, Michael C. Musheno, and Dennis J. Palumbo, *Criminal Justice in America: Law in Action* (New York: John Wiley, 1986), p. 549.

70. Billie S. Erwin and Lawrence A. Bennett, "New Dimensions in Probation: Georgia's Experience with Intensive Probation Supervision," National Institute of Justice Research in Brief (Washington, DC: NIJ, 1987).

71. Probation Division, State of Georgia, "Intensive and Specialized Probation Supervision," http://www.dcor.state.ga.us/Probation Division/html (accessed March 2, 2009).

72. Crystal A. Garcia, "Using Palmer's Global Approach to Evaluate Intensive Supervision Programs: Implications for Practice," *Corrections Management Quarterly*, Vol. 4, No. 4 (2000), pp. 60–69.

73. Joan Petersilia, *House Arrest*, National Institute of Justice Crime File Series Study Guide (Washington, DC: NIJ, 1988).

74. Darren Gowen, "Remote Location Monitoring: A Supervision Strategy to Enhance Risk Control," *Federal Probation*, Vol. 65, No. 2 (September 2001), p. 39.

75. Alan Duke, "Lindsay Lohan Sentenced in Theft Case," CNN, May 11, 2011, http://edition.cnn.com/2011/SHOWBIZ/celebrity.news.gossip/05/11/lohan.sentence (Accessed June 1, 2011).

76. *Electronic Monitoring*, TDCJ-CJAD Agency Brief (Austin: Texas Department of Criminal Justice, March 1999).

77. Texas Department of Criminal Justice, *Agency Strategic Plan: Fiscal Years 2013–2017*, July 6, 2012, https://www.tdcj.state.tx.us/documents/finance/Agency_Strategic_Plan_FY2013-17.pdf (accessed May 4, 2015).

78. Marc Renzema and David T. Skelton, *The Use of Electronic Monitoring by Criminal Justice Agencies, 1989* (Washington, DC: National Institute of Justice, 1990).

79. U.S. Probation and Pretrial Services, *Court and Community* (Washington, DC: Administrative Office of the U.S. Courts, 2000).

80. James Kilgore, "The Rise of Electronic Monitoring in Criminal Justice," *Counter Punch*, April 30, 2012.

81. "Satellites Tracking People on Parole," Associated Press, April 13, 1999.

82. U.S. Probation and Pretrial Services, "Home Confinement," http://www.uscourts.gov/misc/cchome.pdf (accessed March 22, 2009).

83. State of Georgia Board of Pardons and Paroles, "Parole Supervision," http://pap.georgia.gov/parole-supervision (accessed February 25, 2015).

84. Construction costs are for cells classified as "medium security."

85. "BI Home Escort: Electronic Monitoring System," advertising brochure (Boulder, CO: BI Inc., no date).

86. William Bales, et al., *A Quantitative and Qualitative Assessment of Electronic Monitoring* (Washington, DC: National Institute of Justice, U.S. Department of Justice, May 2010), http://www.ncjrs.gov/pdffiles1/nij/grants/230530.pdf (accessed May 20, 2013).

87. Stephen V. Gies, et al., *Monitoring High-Risk Sex Offenders with GPS Technology: An Evaluation of the California Supervision Program, Final Report* (Washington, DC: National Institute of Justice, 2012).

88. James A. Inciardi, *Criminal Justice*, 2nd ed. (New York: Harcourt Brace Jovanovich, 1987), p. 664.

89. E. Ann Carson, *Prisoners in 2013* (Washington, DC: Bureau of Justice Statistics, 2014).

90. Patrick A. Langan and David J. Levin, *National Recidivism Study of Released Prisoners: Recidivism of Prisoners Released in 1994* (Washington, DC: Bureau of Justice Statistics, 2002).

91. Bureau of Justice Statistics, "Forty-Two Percent of State Parole Discharges Were Successful," October 3, 2001, http://www.ojp.usdoj.gov/newsroom/2001/bjs01181.html (accessed July 3, 2007).

92. Council of States Government Justice Center, *The Impact of Probation and Parole Populations on Arrests in Four California Cities* (Lexington, KY: CSG, 2013).

93. Urban Institute and RTI International, *National Portrait of SVORI* (Washington, DC: Urban Institute Press, 2004).

94. California Assembly Bill 109.

95. Abby Sewell, "L.A. County Seeing High-Risk Offenders Entering Its Probation System," *Los Angeles Times*, November 30, 2012, http://articles.latimes.com/2012/nov/30/local/la-me-realignment-20121130 (accessed December 21, 2014).

96. American Probation and Parole Association and the Association of Paroling Authorities International, *Abolishing Parole: Why the Emperor Has No Clothes* (Lexington, KY: APPA, 1995).

97. Much of this information is taken from Re-entry Policy Council, *Report of the Re-entry Policy Council: Charting the Safe and Successful Return of Prisoners to the Community—Executive Summary* (New York: Council of State Governments, 2005), http://www.reentrypolicy.org/executivesummary.html (accessed July 10, 2009).

98. Langan and Levin, *National Recidivism Study of Released Prisoners*; and *Does Parole Work? Analyzing the Impact of Postprison Supervision on Rearrest Outcomes* (Washington, DC: Urban Institute, 2005).

99. Esther Griswold, Jessica Pearson, and Lanae Davis, *Testing a Modification Process for Incarcerated Parents* (Denver, CO: Center for Policy Research), pp. 11–12.

100. Urban Institute and RTI International, *National Portrait of SVORI*, from which some of the wording in this section is adapted.

101. See Laura Winterfield and Susan Brumbaugh, *The Multi-Site Evaluation of the Serious and Violent Offender Reentry Initiative* (Washington, DC: Urban Institute Press, 2005).

102. Pamela K. Lattimore, et al., *Prisoner Reentry Services: What Worked for SVORI Evaluation Participants?* (Washington, DC: National Institute of Justice, 2012).

103. Wording in this paragraph is adapted from Debbie Dawes, *The National Institute of Justice's Evaluation of Second Chance Act Adult Reentry Courts: Program Characteristics and Preliminary Themes from Year 1* (Washington, DC: Bureau of Justice Assistance, 2013).

104. Lane County (Oregon) Circuit Court, "Drug Court," http://www.ojd.state.or.us/lan/drugcrt/index.htm (accessed May 29, 2009).

105. See, for example, Jeremy Travis, *But They All Come Back: Facing the Challenges of Prisoner Reentry* (Washington, DC: Urban Institute Press, 2005).

106. Bureau of Justice Assistance, *Second Chance Act State, Local, and Tribal Reentry Courts FY2010 Competitive Grant Announcement* (Washington, DC: U.S. Department of Justice, Office of Justice Programs, 2010), http://www.ojp.usdoj.gov/BJA/grant/10SecondChanceCourtsSol.pdf (accessed May 3, 2013).

107. Public Law 110–199.

108. Congressional Budget Office, "Cost Estimate: S. 1060, Second Chance Act of 2007," p. 4, http://www.cbo.gov/ftpdocs/86xx/doc8620/s1060.pdf (accessed August 28, 2008).

109. Herberman and Bonczar, *Probation and Parole in the United States, 2013*, Table 6.

110. Public Safety Performance Project, *Putting Public Safety First: 13 Strategies for Successful Supervision and Reentry* (Washington, DC: Pew Center on the States, 2008).

111. Jesse Jannetta, Brian Elderbroom, Amy Solomon, Megan Cahill, and Barbara Parthasarthy, *An Evolving Field: Findings from the 2008 Parole Practices Survey* (Washington, DC: Urban Institute, 2009).

112. Ibid., p. 22.

113. Ibid., p. 2.

114. California Senate Bill 678 (2009).

115. National Institute of Corrections, *Evidence-Based Policy, Practice, and Decisionmaking: Implications for Paroling Authorities* (Washington, DC: U.S. Department of Justice, 2011).

116. Kevin McEvoy, "Hope: A Swift and Certain Process for Probationers," *National Institute of Justice Journal*, No. 269 (March 2012), pp. 16–17, from which some of the wording in the next two paragraphs is taken.

© Kletr/Fotolia

13 PRISONS AND JAILS

LEARNING OBJECTIVES

After reading this chapter, you should be able to

- Describe the history of punishment, concluding with its impact on the modern philosophy of corrections.
- List major milestones in the historical development of prisons.
- Describe the purpose and major characteristics of today's prisons.
- Summarize the role jails currently play in American corrections and issues jail administrators face.
- Describe the current and likely future roles of private prisons.

Everybody wants to send people to prison, (but) nobody wants to pay for it.
CALIFORNIA GOVERNOR JERRY BROWN[1]

■ **prison**   A state or federal confinement facility that has custodial authority over adults sentenced to confinement.

■ *lex talionis*   The law of retaliation, often expressed as "an eye for an eye" or "like for like."

Introduction

Five years ago, a two-person panel of the California Board of Parole Hearings denied medical parole to 42-year-old Steven Martinez, a convicted rapist.[2] Martinez, a quadriplegic, was the first inmate to be considered for medical parole under a new law intended to save the state money by releasing inmates who are permanently incapacitated. Paralyzed during a prison knife attack that severed his spinal cord ten years ago, Martinez was serving a 157-year sentence for numerous felonies that he committed during the violent rape of a woman in 1998. The medical care he needs had been costing the state $625,000 per year.[3] In deciding to deny Martinez's parole, parole commissioner John Peck stated, "This panel finds that he is a violent person who can use other people to carry out threats and would be a public safety threat to those attending to him outside prison walls." Even so, more than a year later, the U.S. Court of Appeals for the Fourth Circuit ordered that Martinez be released. His parents, who are still living, agreed to care for him in their San Diego home.[4]

Martinez's case illustrates the tension that exists today between the need to cut correctional costs and the concern over public safety. The fact that Martinez was denied parole seemed especially surprising to some observers because the denial came almost immediately after the U.S. Supreme Court found that California's prisons are dangerously overcrowded and upheld an earlier order by a three-judge federal panel that state officials must find a way to reduce the current 143,335-inmate population by roughly 33,000.[5] That order, originally issued in 2001, was based on a determination that overcrowding in California's prisons had led to conditions so egregious that they violated the Constitution's Eighth Amendment ban on cruel and unusual punishment.[6] In 2011, the High Court agreed that prison overcrowding left the state unable to deliver minimal care to prisoners with serious medical and mental health problems and produced "needless suffering and death." The court gave California officials two years to comply with the order to reduce prison populations. In 2014, federal judges, finding that California had not met the original mandate for prison population reduction, ordered parole officials in that state to implement a plan by 2015 to free all nonviolent second-strike offenders (except sex offenders) on parole after serving half of their sentences.[7] California's booming prisons, which seriously undermined the state's financial situation, were the result of get-tough on crime policies that had permeated the national scene since the 1970s.

Early Punishments

The use of **prisons** as places where convicted offenders serve time as punishment for breaking the law is a relatively new development in the handling of offenders. In fact, the emphasis on *time served* as the essence of criminal punishment is scarcely 200 years old.

Before the development of prisons, early punishments were often cruel and torturous. An example is the graphic and unsettling description of a man broken on the rack in 1721, which is provided by Camden Pelham in his *Chronicles of Crime*.[8] The offender, Nathaniel Hawes, a domestic servant in the household of a wealthy nobleman, had stolen a sheep. When the overseer of the household discovered the offense, Hawes "shot him dead." This is Pelham's description of what happened next: "For these offences, of course, he was sentenced to be broken alive upon the rack, without the benefit of the *coup de grâce*, or mercy-stroke. Informed of the dreadful sentence, he composedly laid himself down upon his back on a strong cross, on which, with his arms and legs extended, he was fastened by ropes. The executioner, having by now with a hatchet chopped off his left hand, next took up a heavy iron bar, with which, by repeated blows, he broke his bones to shivers, till the marrow, blood, and splinters flew about the field; but the prisoner never uttered a groan nor a sigh! The ropes being next unlashed, I imagined him dead ... till ... he writhed himself from the cross. When he fell on the grass ... he rested his head on part of the timbar, and asked the by-standers for a pipe of tobacco, which was infamously answered by kicking and spitting on him. He then begged his head might be chopped off, but to no purpose." Pelham goes on to relate how the condemned man then engaged in conversation with onlookers, recounting details of his trial. At one point he asked one of those present to repay money he had loaned him, saying, "Don't you perceive, I am to be kept alive." After six hours, Pelham says, Hawes was put out of his misery by a soldier assigned to guard the proceedings. "He was knocked on the head by the ... sentinel; and having been raised upon a gallows, the vultures were busy picking out the eyes of the mangled corpse, in the skull of which was clearly discernible the mark of the soldier's musket."

This gruesome tale may seem foreign to modern readers—as though it describes an event that happened in a barbarous time long ago or in a place far away. However, a mere 200 years ago, before the emergence of imprisonment, convicted offenders were routinely subjected to physical punishment that often resulted in death. Although fines were sometimes levied, corporal punishments were the most common form of criminal punishment and generally fit the doctrine of *lex talionis* (the law of retaliation). Under *lex talionis*, the convicted offender was sentenced to suffer a punishment that closely approximated the original injury. This rule of "an eye for an eye, a tooth for a tooth," generally duplicated the offense. Hence, if a person blinded another, he was blinded in return. Murderers were executed, sometimes in a way tailored to approximate the method they had used in committing the crime.

Flogging

Historically, the most widely used of physical punishment was flogging.[9] The Bible mentions instances of whipping, and Christ himself was scourged. Whipping was widely used in England throughout the Middle Ages, and some offenders were said to have been beaten as they ran through the streets, hands tied behind their backs. American colonists carried the practice of flogging with them to the New World.

The last officially sanctioned flogging of a criminal offender in the United States was in Delaware on June 16, 1952, when a burglar received 20 lashes,[10] but the practice of whipping continues in other parts of the world. Amnesty International reports its use in various countries for political and other prisoners. In 1994, the flogging in Singapore of Michael Fay, an American teenager convicted of spray-painting parked cars, caused an international outcry from opponents of corporal punishment. But in parts of the United States some people reacted in just the opposite way. After the Fay flogging (called *caning* in Singapore because it was carried out with a bamboo rod), eight states entertained legislation to endorse whipping or paddling as a criminal sanction. For example, Mississippi legislators proposed paddling graffitists and petty thieves; Tennessee lawmakers considered punishing vandals and burglars by public caning on courthouse steps; and Louisiana looked into the possibility of ordering parents (or a corrections officer if the parents refused) to spank their children in judicial chambers.[11] None of the proposals made it into law.

Mutilation

Whereas flogging is a painful punishment whose memory might deter repeat offenses, mutilation is primarily a strategy of specific deterrence that makes it difficult or impossible for individuals to commit future crimes. Throughout history, various societies have amputated the hands of thieves and robbers, blinded spies, and castrated rapists. Blasphemers had their tongues ripped out, and pickpockets suffered broken fingers. Extensive mutilation, which included cutting off the ears and ripping out the tongue, was instituted in eleventh-century Britain and imposed on hunters who poached on royal lands.[12]

Today, some countries in the Arab world, including Iran and Saudi Arabia, still rely on a limited use of mutilation as a penalty to incapacitate selected offenders. Mutilation also creates a general deterrent by providing potential offenders with walking examples of the consequences of crime.

Branding

Before modern technology and the advent of mechanized record keeping, branding was used to readily identify convicted offenders and to warn others with whom they might come in contact of their dangerous potential.

The Romans, Greeks, French, British, and many others have all used branding at one time or another. Harry Barnes and Negley Teeters, early writers on the history of the criminal justice system, report that branding in the American colonies was customary for certain crimes, with first offenders being branded on the hand and repeat offenders receiving an identifying mark on the forehead.[13] Women were rarely marked physically, although they may have been shamed and forced to wear marked clothing. Nathaniel Hawthorne's *The Scarlet Letter* is a report on that practice, where the central figure is required to wear a red letter *A* embroidered on her dress, signifying adultery.

Public Humiliation

Many early punishments were designed to humiliate offenders in public and to allow members of the community an opportunity for vengeance. The stocks and pillory were two such punishments. The pillory closed over the head and hands and held the offender in a standing position, while the stocks kept the person sitting with the head free. A few hundred years ago, each European town had its own stocks or pillory, usually located in some central square or alongside a major thoroughfare.

Offenders sent to the stocks or pillory could expect to be heckled and spit on by passersby. Other citizens might gather to throw tomatoes or rotten eggs. On occasion, citizens who were particularly outraged by the magnitude or nature of the offense would throw rocks at the offender, ending his life. Retribution remained a community prerogative, and citizens wielded the power of final sentencing. The pillory was still used in Delaware as late as 1905.[14]

The ducking stool, used in colonial times to punish gossips, provided another form of public humiliation. The offender was tied to it and lowered into a river or lake, turning nearly upside down like a duck searching for food underwater.

Workhouses

Sixteenth-century Europe suffered severe economic upheaval, caused partly by wars and partly by the approach of the Industrial Revolution, which was soon to sweep the continent. By 1550,

■ **workhouse**　An early form of imprisonment whose purpose was to instill habits of industry in the idle.

2005 Getty Images

A man undergoing public punishment for a transgression of the Islamic code in Tehran, Iran. Other than the death penalty, corporal punishment for crime has been abolished in the United States, but it remains common in some Muslim nations. Might similar corporal punishments ever again have a place in Western criminal justice? Why or why not?

thousands of unemployed and vagrant people were scouring towns and villages seeking food and shelter. It was not long before they depleted the economic reserves of churches, which were the primary social relief agencies of the time.

In the belief that poverty was caused by laziness, governments were quick to create **workhouses** designed to instill "habits of industry" in the unemployed. The first workhouse in Europe opened in 1557 and taught work habits, not specific skills. Inmates were made to fashion their own furniture, build additions to the facility, and raise gardens. When the number of inmates exceeded the volume of useful work to be done, make-work projects, including treadmills and cranks, were invented to keep them busy.

Workhouses were judged successful, if only because they were constantly filled. By 1576, Parliament decreed that every county in England should build a workhouse. Although workhouses were forerunners of our modern prisons, they did not incarcerate criminal offenders—only vagrants and the destitute. Nor were they designed to punish, but served instead to reinforce the value of hard work.

Exile

Many societies have banished criminals. The French sent criminal offenders to Devil's Island, and the Russians used Siberia for centuries for the same purpose. England sent convicts to the

American colonies beginning in 1618. The British program of exile, known as *transportation*, served the dual purpose of providing a captive labor force for development of the colonies while assuaging growing English sentiments opposing corporal punishments. In 1776, however, the American Revolution forced the practice to end, and British penology shifted to the use of aging ships, called *hulks*, as temporary prisons. Hulks were anchored in harbors throughout England and served as floating confinement facilities even after transportation (to other parts of the globe) resumed.

In 1787, only 17 years after Captain Cook had discovered the continent, Australia became the new port of call for English prisoners. The name of Captain William Bligh, governor of the New South Wales penal colony, survives today as a symbol of the difficult conditions and the rough men and women of those times.

The Emergence of Prisons

The identity of the world's first true prison is unknown, but at some point, penalties for crime came to include incarceration. During the Middle Ages, "punitive imprisonment appears to have been introduced into Europe ... by the Christian Church in the incarceration of certain offenders against canon law."[15] Similarly, debtors' prisons existed throughout Europe during the fifteenth and sixteenth centuries, although they housed inmates who had violated the civil law rather than criminals. John Howard, an early prison reformer, mentions prisons housing criminal offenders in Hamburg, Germany; Bern, Switzerland; and Florence, Italy, in his 1777 book, *State of Prisons*.[16] Early efforts to imprison offenders led to the founding of the Hospice of San Michele, a papal prison that opened in 1704, and the Maison de Force, begun at Ghent, Belgium, in 1773. The Hospice was actually a residential school for delinquent boys and housed 60 youngsters at its opening. Both facilities stressed reformation over punishment and became early alternatives to the use of physical and public punishments.

Near the end of the eighteenth century, the concept of imprisonment as punishment for crime reached its fullest expression in the United States. Imprisonment *as* punishment differs significantly from the concept of imprisonment *for* punishment, and embodiment of this concept in American penal institutions represented the beginning of a new chapter in corrections reform. Soon after they opened, U.S. prisons came to serve as models for European reformers searching for ways to humanize criminal punishment. For that reason, and to better appreciate how today's prisons operate, it is important to understand the historical development of the prison movement in the United States. Figure 13-1 depicts the stages through which American prisons progressed following the introduction around 1790 of the concept of incarceration as a punishment for crime. Each historical era is discussed in the pages that follow.

The Penitentiary Era (1790–1825)

In 1790, Philadelphia's Walnut Street Jail was converted into a penitentiary by the Pennsylvania Quakers. The Quakers viewed incarceration as an opportunity for penance and saw prisons as places wherein offenders might make amends with society and accept responsibility for their misdeeds. The philosophy of imprisonment begun by the Quakers, heavily imbued with elements of rehabilitation and deterrence, carries over to the present day.[17]

Inmates of the Philadelphia Penitentiary were expected to wrestle alone with the evils they harbored. Penance was the primary vehicle through which rehabilitation was anticipated, and a study of the Bible was strongly encouraged. Solitary confinement

MPI/Getty Images

The Walnut Street Jail, America's first "true" prison, circa 1800. What philosophical principles were behind the Quaker penitentiary concept?

was the rule, and the penitentiary was architecturally designed to minimize contact between inmates and between inmates and staff. Exercise was allowed in small high-walled yards attached to each cell. Eventually, handicrafts were introduced into the prison setting, permitting prisoners to work in their cells.

Fashioned after the Philadelphia model, the Western Penitentiary opened in Pittsburgh in 1826, and the Eastern Penitentiary opened in Cherry Hill, Pennsylvania, three years later. Solitary confinement and individual cells, supported by a massive physical structure with impenetrable walls, became synonymous with the Pennsylvania system of imprisonment. Supporters heralded the **Pennsylvania system** as one that was humane and provided inmates with the opportunity for rehabilitation. Many well-known figures of the day spoke out in support of the Pennsylvania system, among them Benjamin Franklin and Benjamin Rush—both of whom were influential members of the Philadelphia Society for Alleviating the Miseries of Public Prisons.[18]

The Mass Prison Era (1825–1876)

Vermont, Massachusetts, Maryland, and New York all built institutions modeled after Pennsylvania's penitentiaries. As prison populations began to grow, however, solitary confinement

Prison Era

	The Penitentiary Era	The Mass (Congregate) Prison Era	The Reformatory Era	The Industrial Era	The Punitive Era	The Treatment Era	The Community-Based (Decarceration) Era	The Warehousing Era	The Just Deserts Era	The Evidence-Based Era
Year	1790	1825	1876	1890	1935	1945	1967	1980	1995	2012
Philosophy	Rehabilitation, Deterrence	Incapacitation, Deterrence	Rehabilitation	Incapacitation, Restoration	Retribution	Rehabilitation	Restoration, Rehabilitation	Incapacitation	Retribution, Incapacitation, Deterrence	Cost-Effective Workable Solutions
Representative Institutions	Philadelphia Penitentiary; Eastern Penitentiary (Cherry Hill, PA); Western Penitentiary (Pittsburgh)	New York State Prison (Auburn, NY)	Elmira Reformatory (Elmira, NY)	Auburn (NY); Sing Sing (NY); Stateville (IL); San Quentin (CA); Attica (NY)	Alcatraz (CA)	Marion (IL)	Massachusetts Youth Services; Halfway Houses	Many State and Federal Prisons	Continues to Influence Many Prisons Today	A New and Growing Emphasis on "What Works" in an Era of Economic Retrenchment

FIGURE 13-1 | Stages of Prison Development in the United States

■ **Auburn system**   A form of imprisonment developed in New York State around 1820 that depended on mass prisons, where prisoners were held in congregate fashion and required to remain silent. This style of imprisonment was a primary competitor with the Pennsylvania system.

■ **reformatory style**   A late-nineteenth-century correctional model based on the use of the indeterminate sentence and a belief in the possibility of rehabilitation, especially for youthful offenders. The reformatory concept faded with the emergence of industrial prisons around the start of the twentieth century.

became prohibitively expensive. One of the first large prisons to abandon the Pennsylvania model was the New York State Prison at Auburn. Auburn introduced the congregate but silent system, under which inmates lived, ate, and worked together in enforced silence. This style of imprisonment, which came to be known as the **Auburn system**, featured group workshops rather than solitary handicrafts and reintroduced corporal punishments into the handling of offenders. Whereas isolation and enforced idleness were inherent punishments under the early Pennsylvania system, Auburn depended on whipping and hard labor to maintain the rule of silence.[19]

The Auburn prison was the site of an experiment in solitary confinement, which was the basis of the Pennsylvania system. Eighty-three men were placed in small solitary cells on Christmas Day of 1821 and were released in 1823 and 1824. Five of the 83 died, one went insane, another attempted suicide, and the others became "seriously demoralized."[20] Although the Auburn experiment did not accurately simulate the conditions in Pennsylvania (it allowed for no exercise, placed prisoners in tiny cells, and shunned handicrafts—which had been introduced into Pennsylvania's prisons by the time the experiment began), it did provide an effective basis for condemnation of the Pennsylvania system. Partly as a result of the experiment, the Reverend Louis Dwight, an influential prison reformer of the time and the leader of the prestigious Prison Discipline Society of Boston, became an advocate of the Auburn system, citing its lower cost[21] and more humane conditions.[22] The lower cost resulted from the simpler facilities required by mass imprisonment and from group workshops that provided economies of scale unachievable under solitary confinement. Dwight also believed that the Pennsylvania style of imprisonment was unconscionable and inhumane. As a consequence of criticisms fielded by Dwight and others, most American prisons built after 1825 followed the Auburn architectural style and system of prison discipline.

About the same time, however, a number of European governments sent representatives to study the virtues of the two American systems. Interestingly, most concluded that the Pennsylvania system was more conducive to reformation than the Auburn system, and many European prisons adopted a strict separation of inmates. Two French visitors, Gustave de Beaumont and Alexis de Tocqueville, stressed the dangers of

Eastern State Penitentiary in Philadelphia. Built in the 1820s, construction costs totaled $780,000, making it the most expensive public building at that time. Although the penitentiary building today serves only as a tourist attraction, its early-nineteenth-century builders hoped that just the sight of its 30-foot-high, 12-foot-thick walls would be enough to instill fear in the hearts of would-be lawbreakers. Did they achieve their goal?

what they called "contamination," whereby prisoners housed in Auburn-like prisons could negatively influence one another.[23]

The Reformatory Era (1876–1890)

With the tension between the Auburn and Pennsylvania systems, American penology existed in an unsettled state for a half century. That tension was resolved in 1876 with the emergence of the **reformatory style**, which grew out of practices innovated by two especially noteworthy corrections leaders of the mid-1880s: Captain Alexander Maconochie and Sir Walter Crofton.

Captain Alexander Maconochie and Norfolk Island

During the early 1840s, Captain Alexander Maconochie served as the warden of Norfolk Island, a prison off the coast of Australia for "doubly condemned" inmates. English prisoners sent to Australia who committed other crimes while they were taken to Norfolk to be segregated from less recalcitrant

■ **lecture note**   Explain that Sir Walter Crofton's program was the first rehabilitative approach that included progressive stages to move prisoners back toward being productive members of the community.

■ **lecture note**   Discuss the development of the Elmira Reformatory as an alternative to both the Pennsylvania and the Auburn systems. Tell how the reformatory concept depended on the idea of earned early release inherent in indeterminate sentencing, which assumed that an inmate could "reform" himself.

CJ | ISSUES

Chaplain James Finley's Letter from the Ohio Penitentiary, 1850

It is true, there are yet two systems of prison discipline still in use, but both claim to have the two parties—the criminal and society—equally in view. The congregate system, going on the supposition that habits of labor and moral character are the chief desiderata among this class of men, set them to work at those trades for which their physical and mental powers, together with the consideration of their former occupations, may more especially adapt them; religious instruction is also given them by men appointed expressly for the purpose; and they are permitted to labor in large communities, where they can see but not converse with each other, as the friends of this system imagine that social intercourse, of some kind and to some extent, is almost as necessary to

man as food. The separate system, on the other hand, looking upon all intercourse between criminals as only evil in its tendency, by which one rogue becomes the instructor or accomplice of another, secludes the convicts from each other but, to atone for this defect, it encourages the visits of good men to the cells of the prisoners; and the officers of these prisons make it a particular point of duty to visit the inmates very frequently themselves. The physical habits of the imprisoned are provided for by such trades as can be carried on by individual industry; a teacher is employed to lead them on in the study of useful branches of education; while the Gospel is regularly taught to them, not only by sermons on the Sabbath, but by private efforts of the chaplain in his daily rounds.

Source: James Finley, *Memorials of Prison Life* (Cincinnati: Swormstedt and Poe, 1855).

---

offenders. Prior to Maconochie's arrival, conditions at Norfolk had been atrocious. Disease and unsanitary conditions were rampant on the island, fights among inmates left many dead and more injured, and the physical facilities were not conducive to good supervision. Maconochie immediately set out to reform the island prison by providing incentives for prisoners to participate in their own reformation.

Maconochie developed a system of marks through which prisoners could earn enough credits to buy their freedom. Bad behavior removed marks from the inmate's ledger, and acceptable behavior added marks. The mark system made possible early release and led to a recognition of the indeterminate sentence as a useful tool in the reformation of offenders. Before Maconochie, inmates had been sentenced to determinate sentences specifying a fixed number of years they had to serve before release. The mark system placed responsibility for winning an early release squarely on the inmate. Because of the system's similarity to the later practice of parole, it won for Maconochie the title "father of parole."

Opinion leaders in England, however, saw Maconochie's methods as too lenient. Many pointed out that the indeterminate sentence made possible new lives for criminals in a world of vast opportunity (the Australian continent) at the expense of the British Empire. Amid charges that he coddled inmates, Maconochie was relieved of his duties as warden in 1844.

Sir Walter Crofton and the Irish System

Maconochie's innovations soon came to the attention of Sir Walter Crofton, head of the Irish prison system. Crofton

adapted the idea of early release to his program of progressive stages. Inmates who entered Irish prisons had to work their way through four stages. The first, or entry level, involved solitary confinement and dull work. Most prisoners in the first level were housed at Mountjoy Prison in Dublin. The second stage assigned prisoners to Spike Island, where they worked on fortifications. The third stage placed prisoners in field units, which worked directly in the community on public-service projects. Unarmed guards supervised the prisoners. The fourth stage depended on what Crofton called the "ticket of leave." The ticket of leave allowed prisoners to live and work in the community under the occasional supervision of a "moral instructor." It could be revoked at any time up until the expiration of the offender's original sentence.

Crofton was convinced that convicts could not be rehabilitated without successful reintegration into the community. His innovations were closely watched by reformers across Europe. But in 1862, a wave of violent robberies swept England and led to the passage of the 1863 Garotters Act, which mandated whipping for robberies involving violence and longer prison sentences for many other crimes, effectively rolling back the clock on Crofton's innovations, at least in Europe.

The Elmira Reformatory and the Birth of Parole in the United States

In 1865, Gaylord B. Hubbell, warden of Sing Sing Prison in New York, visited Great Britain and studied prisons there. He returned to the United States greatly impressed by the Irish system and recommended that indeterminate sentences be used in American

■ **industrial prison** A correctional model intended to capitalize on the labor of convicts sentenced to confinement.

CJ | ISSUES
An Early Texas Prison

In 1860, an unknown writer described conditions in the Texas Penitentiary at Huntsville as follows:

> By a special enactment of the Legislature, the front of the cell of any prisoner sentenced to solitary confinement for life, is painted black, and his name and sentence distinctly marked thereon. The object would seem to be to infuse a salutary dread into the minds of the other prisoners. Upon the only black-painted cell in the prison was the following inscription, in distinct white letters: William Brown, aged twenty-four years, convicted for murder in Grimes County, spring term, 1858, for which he is now suffering solitary confinement for life. Brown himself, however, was in fact at work in the factory with the other convicts! He entered the Penitentiary in May, 1859, and had been kept in close confinement in his cell, without labor, never being permitted to leave it for any purpose, until about the first of October, when his health was found to have suffered so much that, to preserve his life, he was, under a discretionary power vested in the Directors, released from the rigor of his sentence, and subjected to only the ordinary confinement of the prison. His health has since greatly improved. It is not to be wondered at that his health should decline under the strict enforcement of such a sentence. The cell in which he was confined was the same as to size, ventilation, and light as the rest; and being one of the lower tier of cells, the top of the doorway was some feet below the lower edge of the window upon the opposite side of the corridor in the outside wall. He had even less chance for fresh air than if his cell had been in almost any other location. It is the sight and knowledge of such instances of solitary unemployed confinement as this, and a willful neglect or refusal to inform themselves upon, and recognize, the very wide distinction between the terms separate and solitary, that renders many persons so violently prejudiced against, and opposed to the "Separate System."

Source: *The Journal of Prison Discipline and Philanthropy*, Vol. 15, No. 1 (January 1860), pp. 7–17.

---

prisons. The New York Prison Association supported Hubbell and called for the creation of a "reformatory" based on the concept of an earned early release if the inmate reformed himself.

When the new National Prison Association held its first conference in 1870 in Cincinnati, it adopted a 37-paragraph Declaration of Principles that called for reformation to replace punishment as the goal of imprisonment. The most significant result of the conference, however, was the move to embody those principles in a reformatory built on American soil.

In 1876, the Elmira Reformatory opened in Elmira, New York, under the direction of Zebulon Brockway, a leading advocate of indeterminate sentencing and the former superintendent of the Detroit House of Correction. The state of New York had passed an indeterminate sentencing bill that made possible early release for inmates who earned it. However, because reformation was thought most likely among younger people, the Elmira Reformatory accepted only first offenders between the ages of 16 and 30. A system of graded stages required inmates to meet educational, behavioral, and other goals. Schooling was mandatory, and trade training was available in telegraphy, tailoring, plumbing, carpentry, and other areas.

Because reformation was thought most likely among younger people, the Elmira Reformatory accepted only first offenders between the ages of 16 and 30.

Unfortunately, the reformatory "proved a relative failure and disappointment."[24] Many inmates reentered lives of crime following their release, which called the success of the reformatory ideal into question. Some authors attributed the failure of the reformatory to "the ever-present jailing psychosis"[25] of the prison staff or to an overemphasis on confinement and institutional security rather than reformation, which made it difficult to implement many of the ideals on which the reformatory had been based.

Even though the reformatory was not a success, the principles it established remain important today. Thus, indeterminate sentencing, parole, trade training, education, and the primacy of reformation over punishment all serve as a foundation for ongoing debates about the purpose of imprisonment.

The Industrial Era (1890–1935)

With the failure of the reformatory style of prison, concerns over security and discipline became dominant in American prisons. Inmate populations rose, costs soared, and states began to study practical alternatives. An especially attractive option was found in the potential profitability of inmate labor, and the era of the **industrial prison** in America was born.

■ **state-use system** A form of inmate labor in which items produced by inmates may be sold by or to only state offices. Items that only the state can sell include such things as license plates and hunting licenses, while items sold only to state offices include furniture and cleaning supplies.

■ **Ashurst-Sumners Act** Federal legislation of 1935 that effectively ended the industrial prison era by restricting interstate commerce in prison-made goods.

Industrial prisons in the northern United States were characterized by thick, high walls; stone or brick buildings; guard towers; and smokestacks rising from within the walls. These prisons smelted steel, manufactured cabinets, molded tires, and turned out many other goods for the open market. Prisons in the South, which had been devastated by the Civil War, tended more toward farm labor and public-works projects. The South, with its labor-intensive agricultural practices, used inmates to replace slaves who had been freed during the war.

The following six systems of inmate labor were in use by the early twentieth century:[26]

- *Contract system*. Private businesses paid to use inmate labor. They provided the raw materials and supervised the manufacturing process inside prison facilities.
- *Piece-price system*. Goods were produced for private businesses under the supervision of prison authorities. Prisons were paid according to the number and quality of the goods manufactured.
- *Lease system*. Prisoners were taken to the work site under the supervision of armed guards. Once there, they were turned over to the private contractor, who employed them and maintained discipline.
- *Public-account system*. This system eliminated the use of private contractors. Industries were entirely prison owned, and prison authorities managed the manufacturing process from beginning to end. Goods were sold on the free market.
- *State-use system*. Prisoners manufactured only goods that could be sold by or to other state offices, or they provided labor to assist other state agencies.
- *Public-works system*. Prisoners maintained roads and highways, cleaned public parks and recreational facilities, and maintained and restored public buildings.

Large prisons that were built or converted to industrialization included San Quentin in California, Sing Sing and Auburn in New York, and the Illinois State Penitentiary at Stateville. Many prison industries were quite profitable and contributed significantly to state treasuries. Reports from 1932 show that 82,276 prisoners were involved in various forms of prison labor that year, producing products with a total value of $75,369,471—a huge amount considering the worth of the dollar 80 years

ago.[27] Beginning as early as the 1830s, however, workers began to complain of being forced to compete with cheap prison labor. In 1834, mechanics in New York filed a petition with the state legislature asking that prison industries paying extremely low wages be eliminated. Labor unions became very well organized and powerful by the early part of the twentieth century, and the Great Depression of the 1930s, during which jobs were scarce, brought with it a call for an end to prison industries.

In 1929, union influence led Congress to pass the Hawes-Cooper Act, which required prison-made goods to conform to the regulations of the states through which they were shipped. Hence states that outlawed the manufacture of free-market goods in their own prisons were effectively protected from prison-made goods that might be imported from other states. The death blow to prison industries, however, came in 1935 with the passage of the **Ashurst-Sumners Act**, which specifically prohibited the interstate transportation and sale of prison goods where state laws forbade them. In consort with the Ashurst-Sumners legislation, and because of economic pressures brought on by the Depression, most states soon passed statutes that curtailed prison manufacturing within their borders, and the industrial era in American corrections came to a close.

Prison Industries Today

Although still hampered by some federal and state laws, prison industries began making a comeback in the latter part of the twentieth century. Under the state-use philosophy, most states still permit the prison manufacture of goods that will be used exclusively by the prison system itself or by other state agencies or that only the state can legitimately sell on the open market. An example of the latter is license plates, the sale of which is a state monopoly. North Carolina provides a good example of a modern state-use system. Its Correction Enterprises operates around 20 inmate-staffed businesses, each of which is self-supporting. North Carolina inmates manufacture prison clothing; raise vegetables and farm animals to

> Under the state-use philosophy, most states still permit the prison manufacture of goods that will be used exclusively by the prison system itself or by other state agencies or that only the state can legitimately sell on the open market.

Warden T. M. Osborne and correctional officers stand in a cellblock at Sing Sing Prison at Ossining, New York, in 1915. How have prisons changed in the last 100 years?

feed inmates throughout the state; operate an oil refinery, a forestry service, and a cannery; and manufacture soap, license plates, and some office furniture. All manufactured goods other than license plates are for use within the prison system or by other state agencies. North Carolina's Correction Enterprises pays 5% of its profits to the state's crime victims' compensation fund.[28]

The federal government also operates a kind of state-use system in its institutions through a government-owned corporation called Federal Prison Industries, Inc. (also called UNICOR).[29] The corporation was established in 1934 to retain some employment programs for federal inmates in anticipation of the elimination of free-market prison industries. Critics of UNICOR charge that inmates are paid very low wages and are trained for jobs that do not exist in the free economy.[30] Even so, a long-term study published in 1994 found that federal inmates who participated in UNICOR "showed better adjustment, were less likely to be revoked at the end of their first year back in the community, and were more likely to find employment in the halfway house and community."[31] The study also found that inmates "earned slightly more money in the community than inmates who had similar background characteristics, but who did not participate in work and vocational training programs."

Free-market moneymaking prison industries also staged a comeback in the late 1990s and into the early years of the twenty-first century. Some were funded by private-sector investment. In 1981, under the Prison Rehabilitative Industries

and Diversified Enterprises, Inc., legislation, commonly called the PRIDE Act, Florida became the first state to experiment with the wholesale transfer of its correctional industry program from public to private control.[32] PRIDE industries include sugarcane processing, construction, and automotive repair. Other states followed suit.

Today, the Prison Industry Enhancement Certification Program (PIECP),[33] administered by the Bureau of Justice Assistance (BJA), exempts certified state and local departments of corrections from normal federal restrictions on the sale of inmate-made goods in interstate commerce.[34] In addition, the program lifts restrictions on certified corrections departments, permitting them to sell inmate-made goods to the federal government in amounts exceeding the $10,000 maximum normally imposed on such transactions. The PIECP also allows private industry to establish joint ventures with state and local correctional agencies to produce goods using inmate labor. Today, 45 correctional industry programs are certified to operate under the PIECP and employ 4,666 inmates.[35]

Some local community leaders fear that inmate jobs will lower employment opportunities for citizens of small towns and cities that are close to correctional facilities. The economically lean times brought about by the Great Recession of the early part of the twenty-first century have led to cost cutting by prison administrators who are sensitive to both their own budgetary needs and to the needs of civilian workers whose jobs

■ **theme** How did the trend toward a punitive approach in imprisonment reflect social trends? How did the balance between individual rights and public order shift during that historical period?

■ **lecture note** Explain the impact of the moratorium on prison industries on prisons and how this contributed to the move to a more punitive prison environment.

■ **medical model** A therapeutic perspective on correctional treatment that applies the diagnostic perspective of medical science to the handling of criminal offenders.

Alcatraz Federal Penitentiary. The island prison closed in 1963, a victim of changing attitudes toward corrections. It survives today as a San Francisco tourist attraction. What security levels characterize most American prisons today?

might be threatened by inmate labor programs.[36] Learn more about the history of federal prison industries at **http://www.justicestudies.com/pubs/fedindust.pdf**. Visit the National Correctional Industries Association at **http://www.nationalcia.org** to see additional information about the PIECP.

The Punitive Era (1935–1945)

The moratorium on free-market prison industries initiated by the Ashurst-Sumners Act was to last for more than half a century. Prison administrators, left with few ready alternatives, seized on custody and institutional security as the long-lost central purposes of the correctional enterprise. The punitive era that resulted was characterized by the belief that prisoners owed a debt to society that only a rigorous period of confinement could repay. Writers of the period termed such beliefs the *convict bogey* and the *lock psychosis*,[37] referring to the fact that convicts were to be both shunned and securely locked away from society. Large maximum-security institutions flourished, and the prisoner's daily routine became one of monotony and frustration. The punitive era was a lackluster time in American corrections. Innovations were rare, and a philosophy of "out of sight, out of mind" characterized American attitudes toward inmates. The

term *stir-crazy* grew out of the experience of many prisoners with the punitive era's lack of educational, treatment, and work programs. In response, inmates created their own diversions, frequently attempting to escape or inciting riots. One especially secure and still notorious facility of the punitive era was the federal penitentiary on Alcatraz Island, which is described in some detail at **http://www.alcatrazhistory.com/rs2.htm**.

The Treatment Era (1945–1967)

In the late 1940s, the mood of the nation was euphoric. Memories of World War II were dimming, industries were productive beyond the best hopes of most economic forecasters, and America's position of world leadership was fundamentally unchallenged. Nothing seemed impossible. Amid the bounty of a postwar boom economy, politicians and the public accorded themselves the luxury of restructuring the nation's prisons. A new interest in "corrections" and reformation, combined with the latest in behavioral techniques, ushered in a new era. The treatment era was based on a **medical model** of corrections—one that implied that the offender was sick and that rehabilitation was only a matter of finding the right treatment. Inmates came to be seen more as "clients" or "patients" than as offenders, and terms like *resident* and *group member* replaced *inmate*.

Therapy during the period took a number of forms, many of which are still used today. Most therapeutic models assumed that inmates needed help to mature psychologically and had to be taught to assume responsibility for their lives. Prisons built their programs around both individual treatment and group therapy approaches. In individual treatment, the offender and the therapist develop a face-to-face relationship. Group therapy relies on the sharing of insights, gleaned by members of the therapeutic group, to facilitate the growth process, often by first making clear to offenders the emotional basis of their criminal behavior. Other forms of therapy used in prisons have included behavior therapy, drug therapy, neurosurgery, sensory deprivation, and aversion therapy.

Inmates have not always been happy with the treatment model. In 1972, a group of prisoners at the Marion, Illinois, federal prison joined together and demanded a right to refuse treatment.[38] The National Prison Project of the American Civil Liberties Union (ACLU) supported the inmates' right to refuse personality-altering treatment techniques.[39] Other suits followed. Worried about potential liability, the Law Enforcement Assistance Administration (LEAA) banned the expenditure of LEAA funds to support any prison programs utilizing psychosurgery, medical research, chemotherapy, or behavior modification.[40]

The treatment era also suffered from attacks on the medical model on which it was based. Academics and legal scholars pointed to a lack of evidence in support of the model[41] and began to stress individual responsibility rather than treatment in the handling of offenders. Indeterminate sentencing statutes, designed to reward inmates for improved behavior, fell before the swelling drive to replace treatment with punishment.

Any honest evaluation of the treatment era would conclude that, in practice, treatment was more an ideal than a reality. Many treatment programs existed, some of them quite intensive. Unfortunately, the correctional system in America was never capable of providing any consistent or widespread treatment because the majority of its guards and administrators were oriented primarily toward custody and were not trained to provide treatment. However, although we have identified 1967 as the end of the treatment era, many correctional rehabilitation programs survive to the present day, and new ones are continually being developed.

The Community-Based Era (1967–1980)

Beginning in the 1960s, the realities of prison overcrowding combined with a renewed faith in humanity and the treatment era's

Advocates of community corrections portrayed prisons as dehumanizing, claiming that they further victimized offenders who had already been negatively labeled by society.

belief in the possibility of behavioral change to inspire a movement away from institutionalized corrections and toward the creation of opportunities for reformation within local communities. The transition to community corrections (also called *deinstitutionalization, diversion,* and *decarceration*) was based on the premise that rehabilitation could not occur in isolation from the free social world to which inmates must eventually return.[42] Advocates of community corrections portrayed prisons as dehumanizing, claiming that they further victimized offenders who had already been negatively labeled by society. Some states strongly embraced the movement toward decarceration. In 1972, for example, Massachusetts drew national attention when it closed all of its reform schools and replaced them with group homes.[43]

Decarceration, which built on many of the intermediate sanctions discussed in the previous chapter, used a variety of programs to keep offenders in contact with the community and out of prison. Among them were halfway houses, work-release programs, and open institutions. Halfway houses have sometimes been called *halfway-in* or *halfway-out houses,* depending on whether offenders were being given a second chance before incarceration or were in the process of gradual release from prison. Boston had halfway houses as early as the 1920s, but they operated for only a few years.[44] It was not until 1961 that the Federal Bureau of Prisons opened a few experimental residential centers in support of its new prerelease programs focusing on juveniles and youthful offenders. Called *prerelease guidance centers,* the first of these facilities were based in Los Angeles and Chicago.[45]

Halfway houses and work-release programs still operate in many parts of the country. A typical residential treatment facility today houses 15 to 20 residents and operates under the supervision of a director, supported by a handful of counselors. The environment is nonthreatening, and residents are generally free to come and go during the workday. The building looks more like a motel or a house than it does a prison. Fences and walls are nonexistent. Transportation is provided to and from work or educational sites, and the facility retains a portion of the resident's wages to pay the costs of room and board. Residents are expected to return to the facility after work, and some group therapy may be provided.

Today's work-release programs house offenders in traditional correctional environments—usually minimum-security prisons—but permit them to work at jobs in the community during the

■ **lecture note**   Explain warehousing as a correctional strategy that developed during the 1980s when sentencing authorities, disillusioned with high rates of recidivism, turned to a "lock-'em-up" approach to reducing crime.

■ **work release**   A prison program through which inmates are temporarily released into the community to meet job responsibilities.

■ **lecture note**   Discuss the work of Robert Martinson, who formulated the nothing-works doctrine. Explain that Martinson's impact on sentencing strategies was significant because he was able to show that no correctional programs could consistently and significantly reduce the rate of repeat criminality.

■ **warehousing**   An imprisonment strategy that is based on the desire to prevent recurrent crime and that has abandoned all hope of rehabilitation.

day and to return to the prison at night. Inmates are usually required to pay a token amount for their room and board in the institution. The first work-release law was passed by Wisconsin in 1913, but it was not until 1957 that a comprehensive program created by North Carolina spurred the development of work-release programs nationwide.[46] **Work release** for federal prisoners was authorized by the federal Prisoner Rehabilitation Act of 1965.[47] As work-release programs grew, study release—whereby inmates attend local colleges and technical schools—was initiated in most jurisdictions as an adjunct to work release.

Work-release programs are still very much a part of modern corrections. Almost all states have them, and many inmates work in the community as they approach the end of their sentence. Unfortunately, work-release programs are not without their social costs. Some inmates commit new crimes while in the community, and others use the opportunity to escape.

The community-based format led to innovations in the use of volunteers and to the extension of inmate privileges. "Open institutions" routinely provided inmates with a number of opportunities for community involvement and encouraged the community to participate in the prison environment. Some open institutions allowed weekend passes or extended visits by family members and friends, while a few experimented with conjugal visitation and with prisons that housed both men and women ("coeducational incarceration"). In 1968, the California Correctional Institute at Tehachapi initiated conjugal visits, in which inmates who were about to begin parole were permitted to live with their families for three days per month in apartments on the prison grounds. By the late 1960s, conjugal visitation was under consideration in many other states, and the National Advisory Commission on Criminal Justice Standards and Goals recommended that correctional authorities should make "provisions for family visits in private surroundings conducive to maintaining and strengthening family ties."[48] In 1995, however, California, which then allowed about 26,000 conjugal visits a year, eliminated this privilege for those sentenced to death or to life without parole and for those without a parole date. Rapists, sex offenders, and recently disciplined inmates were also denied conjugal privileges.

The Warehousing Era (1980–1995)

In the history of criminal justice, the three decades from 1980 to 2010 will likely be remembered as a time of mass imprisonment. In the 1980s, as concerns with community protection reached a near crescendo, and as stiff drug laws and strict repeat offender statutes put more and more people behind bars, rates of imprisonment reached previously unheralded levels.

About the same time, public disappointment in our nation's corrections system resulted at least partially from media reports of high recidivism,[49] coupled with descriptions of institutions where inmates lounged in relative luxury, enjoyed regular visits from spouses and lovers, and took frequent weekend passes—all of which created the image of "prison country clubs." The failure of the rehabilitative ideal in community-based corrections, however, was due as much to changes in the individual sentencing decisions of judges as it was to citizen outrage and restrictive legislative action. Evidence shows that many judges came to regard rehabilitation programs as failures and decided to implement the just deserts model[50] of criminal sentencing. The just deserts model, discussed earlier, built on a renewed belief that offenders should "get what's coming to them." It quickly led to a policy of **warehousing** serious offenders for the avowed purpose of protecting society—and led also to a rapid decline of the decarceration initiative.

Recidivism rates were widely quoted in support of the drive to warehouse offenders. One study, for example, showed that nearly 70% of young adults paroled from prison in 22 states during 1978 were rearrested for serious crimes one or more times within six years of their release.[51] The study group was estimated to have committed 36,000 new felonies within the six years following their release, including 324 murders, 231 rapes, 2,291 robberies, and 3,053 violent assaults.[52] Worse still, observed the study's authors, was the fact that 46% of recidivists would have been in prison at the time of their readmission to prison if they had served the maximum term to which they had originally been sentenced.[53]

The failure of the rehabilitative model in corrections had already been proclaimed emphatically by Robert Martinson in 1974.[54] Martinson and his colleagues had surveyed 231 research studies conducted to evaluate correctional treatments between 1945 and 1967. They were unable to identify any treatment program that substantially reduced recidivism. Although Martinson argued for fixed sentences, a portion of which would be served in the community, his findings were often interpreted to mean that lengthy prison terms were necessary to incapacitate offenders who could not be reformed. About the same time, the prestigious National Academy of Sciences released a report in support of Martinson, saying, "We do not now know of any program or method of rehabilitation that could be guaranteed to reduce the

■ **nothing-works doctrine**   The belief, popularized by Robert Martinson in the 1970s, that correctional treatment programs have had little success in rehabilitating offenders.

criminal activity of released offenders."[55] This combined attack on the treatment model led to the **nothing-works doctrine**, which, beginning in the late 1970s, cast a pall of doubt over the previously dominant treatment philosophy.

The nothing-works philosophy contributed to new sentencing schemes, such as mandatory minimum sentencing provisions and truth-in-sentencing requirements. Together with the growing popularity of "three-strikes-and-you're-out" laws, these sentencing rules affected prison populations by substantially increasing the average time served by offenders before release. In the 1990s, prison populations continued to grow substantially because of a rise in the number of parole violators returned to prison; a drop in the annual release rates of inmates; a small number of inmates who would serve long terms or who would never be released; and enhanced punishments for drug offenders.[56] Average time served continues to increase. In 1990, for example, murderers served, on average, 92 months before release. Today, a person convicted of murder can expect to serve 106 months in prison before being released—a 15% increase. During the same period, actual time served in prison for the crime of rape increased 27%, and drug offenders spent 35% more time behind bars.[57]

American prison populations grew dramatically during the warehousing era (Figures 13-2 and 13-3)—and the increase is only now beginning to drop off. Between 1980 and 2014, state and federal prison populations more than quadrupled, from 329,000 inmates to around 1.6 million.[58] Much of the rise in prison populations can be attributed directly to changes in sentencing laws aimed at taking drug offenders off the streets and to the resulting rapid growth in the number of incarcerated drug felons and, more recently, immigration law violators. A warehousing era report by the American Bar Association, for example, directly attributed the huge growth in the number of inmates to what it saw as a system-wide overemphasis on drug-related offenses—an emphasis that tended to imprison mostly poor, undereducated African American youths who were rarely dangerous.[59] The report pointed out that while the per capita *rate of reported crime* dropped 2.2% across the nation during the 1980s, "the *incarceration rate* increased more than 110 percent."[60]

Warehousing also contributed to numerous administrative difficulties, many of which continue to affect prison systems throughout the nation today. By 1992, when the warehousing era was in full swing, institutions in 40 states and the District of Columbia

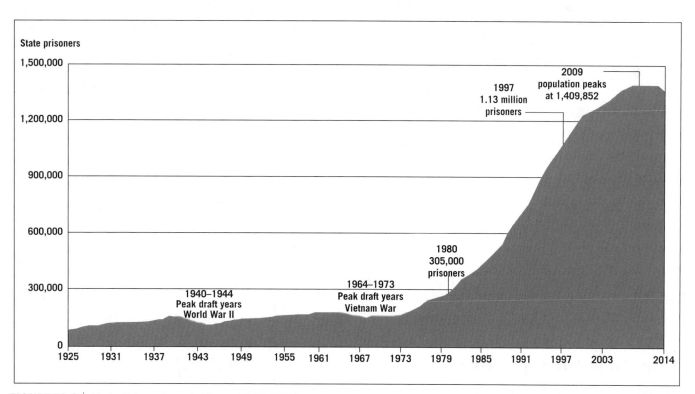

FIGURE 13-2 | State Prison Populations, 1925–2014

Note: Numbers may not reflect the actual number of persons sentenced to incarceration because some states, like California, have begun to house substantial numbers of inmates in local jails rather than in state prison facilities.

Source: Bureau of Justice Statistics, *Crime and Justice Atlas 2000* (Washington, DC: BJS, 2001), pp. 42–43; and Bureau of Justice Statistics, *Prisoners in 2014* (Washington, DC: BJS, 2015); and other years.

■ **lecture note**   Refer to Figures 13-2 and 13-3. Ask students what factors have contributed to the huge increase in prison populations during recent decades.

■ **theme**   The just deserts era continued the emphasis on incarceration that began during the warehousing era. How did the two eras differ?

■ **justice model**   A contemporary model of imprisonment based on the principle of just deserts.

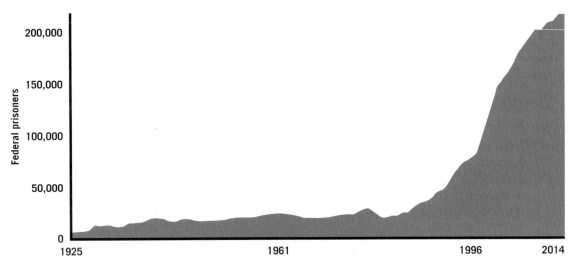

FIGURE 13-3 | Federal Prison Populations, 1925–2014

Source: Bureau of Justice Statistics and the Federal Bureau of Prisons.

were operating under court orders to alleviate overcrowding.[61] Entire prison systems in nine states—Alaska, Florida, Kansas, Louisiana, Mississippi, Nevada, Rhode Island, South Carolina, and Texas—had come under court control because overcrowded conditions made it impossible for prison administrators to meet court-supported constitutional requirements related to inmate safety. Today, even more state corrections systems have become subject to federal oversight or are operating under federal consent decrees.[62]

To meet the housing needs of burgeoning prison populations during the 1980s and 1990s, some states constructed "temporary" tent cities within prison yards. Others moved more beds into already packed dormitories, often stacking prisoners three high in triple bunk beds. A few states declared a policy of early release for less dangerous inmates and instituted mandatory diversion programs for first-time nonviolent offenders. Others used sentence rollbacks to reduce the sentences of selected inmates by a fixed amount, usually 90 days. Early parole was similarly employed by numerous states to reduce overcrowded conditions. Most states shifted some of their correctional burden to local jails, and by 2000, 34 states, the District of Columbia, and the federal government were sending some prisoners to jails because of overcrowding at their own long-term institutions.[63]

The Just Deserts Era (1995–2012)

Warehousing and prison overcrowding were primarily the result of both public and official frustration with rehabilitative efforts. In a sense, however, they were also consequences of a strategy

> Warehousing and prison overcrowding were primarily the result of both public and official frustration with rehabilitative efforts.

> The era of just deserts represented a kind of return to the root purpose of incarceration: punishment.

without a clear-cut philosophy. Because rehabilitation didn't seem to work, early advocates of warehousing—not knowing what else to do—assumed a pragmatic stance and advocated separating criminals from society by keeping them locked up for as long as possible. Their avowed goal was the protection of law-abiding citizens. Consequently, by the early 2000s, prison populations approached the breaking point, requiring the construction of many new facilities.

In the midst of a prison construction boom, a new philosophy based on the second prong of the **justice model**—that is, an emphasis on individual responsibility—became the operative principle underlying many correctional initiatives. The new philosophy was grounded squarely on the concept of just deserts, in which imprisonment is seen as a fully deserved and proper consequence of criminal and irresponsible behavior rather than just the end result of a bankrupt system unable to reform its charges. Unlike previous correctional eras, which layered other purposes on the correctional experience (the reformatory era, for example, was concerned with reformation, and the industrial era sought economic gain), the era of just deserts represented a kind of return to the root purpose of incarceration: punishment.

At the start of the just deserts era, state legislatures, encouraged in large part by their constituencies, scrambled to limit inmate

■ **lecture note** Discuss how new styles of prisons are often created out of perceptions that an earlier style failed to achieve the goals of punishment. What are the implications of such an observation?

privileges and to increase the pains of imprisonment. As with any other era, the exact beginning of the just deserts era is difficult to pinpoint. Noted corrections expert Jeanne Stinchcomb says, "The justice model gained momentum throughout the 1980s and 1990s, fueled by political conservatism, media sensationalism, an all-out 'war on drugs,' and public attitudes expressed in 'zero-tolerance' terms."[64] It is safe to say, however, that the just deserts model of criminal punishments was firmly in place by 1995. In that year, Alabama became the first state in modern times to reestablish chain gangs.[65] Under the Alabama system, shotgun-armed guards oversaw prisoners who were chained together by the ankles while they worked the state's roadsides—picking up trash, clearing brush, and filling ditches. The system, intended primarily for parole violators, was tough and unforgiving. Inmates served up to 90 days on chain gangs, during which they worked 12-hour shifts and remained chained even while using portable toilet facilities.

A few months later, Arizona became the second state to field prison chain gangs. Florida jumped on the chain gang bandwagon soon afterward.[66] Alabama chain gangs, which had expanded to include female prisoners, were discontinued in 1996 following a lawsuit against the state, and other state departments of correction have discontinued their use. The few chain gangs that still exist today are run mostly by county sheriffs and are populated by jail inmates. Brevard County, Florida, for example, operates jail chain gangs, and Arizona sheriff Joe Arpaio instituted chain gangs for both male and female inmates in the jail facilities in his jurisdiction.[67]

In another example of the move toward greater punishment indicative of the just deserts era, Virginia abolished parole in 1995, increased sentences for certain violent crimes by as much as 700%, and announced that it would build a dozen new prisons.[68] Changes in Virginia law were intended to move the state further in the direction of truth–sentencing and to appease the state's voters, who—reflecting public opinion nationwide—demanded a "get-tough" stance toward criminals.

"Get-tough" initiatives were reflected in the "three-strikes-and-you're-out" laws that swept through state legislatures in the late 1990s.[69] Three-strikes legislation, which is discussed in more detail in Chapter 11, generally mandates lengthy prison terms for criminal offenders convicted of a third violent crime or felony. Three-strikes laws have been enacted in almost 30 states and by the federal government. Critics of such laws, however, say that they do not prevent crime.[70] Jerome Skolnick, of the University of California at Berkeley, for example, criticizes three-strikes legislation because, he says, such practices almost certainly do not reduce the risk of victimization—especially the risk of becoming a victim of random violence. That is so, says Skolnick, because most violent crimes are committed by young men between the ages of 13 and 23. "It follows," according to

Skolnick, "that if we jail them for life after their third conviction, we will get them in the twilight of their careers, and other young offenders will take their place."[71]

Criticisms of three-strikes laws, however, failed to appreciate the sentiments supporting the just deserts era. Proponents of "get-tough" policies, although no doubt interested in personal safety, lower crime rates, and balanced state and federal budgets, were keenly focused on retribution. And where retribution fuels a correctional policy, deterrence, reformation, and economic considerations play only secondary roles. As more and more states enacted three-strikes and other "get-tough" legislation, prison populations across the nation continued to swell, eclipsing even those of the warehousing era. The impact of the just deserts era remains with us today, leaving the United States with one of the highest rates of imprisonment in the world.[72] Learn more about the impact of the just deserts model on corrections via **http://www.sentencingproject.org/doc/publications/inc_lessonsofgettough.pdf.**

The Evidence-Based Era (2012–Present)

Although the just deserts philosophy provided what became for many an acceptable rationale for continued prison expansion, it soon ran up against the very practical fiscal needs imposed by the Great Recession of the early twenty-first century. The recession made it necessary for states to save money and to cut their budgets, leading to an end of the just deserts era around 2012. In the grip of newfound motivation predicated upon forced financial austerity, many state legislatures began to question the wisdom of locking up nonviolent, elderly, and seriously ill offenders for long periods of time, and prison populations started to finally decline. The new era in corrections, the evidence-based era, is built around the need to employ cost-effective solutions to correctional issues.

The evidence-based era was ushered in by a number of federal, academic, and state studies focused on the effectiveness of imprisonment and on the difficulties associated with the high costs of incarceration. One 500-page report by the National Academy of Sciences in 2014 summed up the philosophy of the new era, saying, "Given the small crime prevention effects of long prison sentences and the possibly high financial, social, and human costs of incarceration, federal and state policy makers should revise current criminal justice policies to significantly reduce the rate of incarceration in the United States. In particular, they should reexamine policies regarding mandatory minimum sentences and long sentences."[73] The report is available as a free download from the National Research Council at https://download.nap.edu/login.php?record_id=18613. Learn more

CJ | ISSUES
Evidence-Based Corrections

The National Institute of Corrections (NIC) says that "in corrections, evidence-based practice is the breadth of research and knowledge around processes and tools which can improve correctional outcomes, such as reduced recidivism."[1] The NIC has been promoting the use of evidence-based practice (EBP) for a number of years, and in June 2008 the NIC partnered with the Center for Effective Public Policy to build an EBP framework that is intended to be relevant to the entire criminal justice system. The system-wide framework that the NIC is developing focuses on justice system events from arrest through final disposition and discharge. When fully implemented, the framework should result in more collaborative evidence-based decision making throughout the criminal justice system nationwide. According to the NIC, the purpose of the EBP decision-making initiative "is to equip criminal justice policymakers in local communities with the information, processes, and tools that will result in measurable reductions of pretrial misconduct and post-conviction reoffending."

There are three phases in the NIC initiative. Phase I, which has already been completed, produced the framework itself, which is outlined in the NIC publication A Framework for Evidence-Based Decision Making in Local Criminal Justice Systems. That publication, available at the NIC website (**http://nicic.gov**), describes key criminal justice decision points and provides an overview of evidence-based knowledge about effective justice practices. It defines risk and harm reduction as key goals of the criminal justice system and lays out practical local-level strategies for applying these principles and techniques.

In the second phase of its initiative, the NIC—along with its collaborating partner, the federal Office of Justice Programs (OJP)—selected seven seed sites from across the country that were interested in piloting principles included within the framework. Fifty key representatives from the selected seed sites attended a kickoff workshop in Bethesda, Maryland, in October 2010. The workshop clarified expectations for Phase II implementation, and established a working network among the selected sites.

Seed sites are now participating in an initiative evaluation, which is being administered by the Urban Institute and is designed to assess each site's readiness to implement the full framework in Phase III. During Phase III, selected sites will be expected to fully implement the NIC-established framework and to participate in a long-term outcome evaluation to measure the impact of implementing the principles contained within the framework.

[1]National Institute of Corrections, "Evidence-Based Practices," http://nicic.gov/EvidenceBasedPractices (accessed November 7, 2015).

Sources: National Institute of Corrections, "Evidence-Based Practices," http://nicic.gov/EvidenceBasedPractices (accessed November 7, 2015); and National Institute of Corrections, "Evidence-Based Decision Making," http://nicic.gov/EBDM (accessed November 7, 2015).

---

about evidence-based practices in corrections in the "CJ Issues" box in this chapter.

Prisons Today

As mentioned earlier in this chapter, prisons developed near the end of the eighteenth century to facilitate the use of incarceration as punishment for crime. In the remainder of this chapter, we examine the nature of American prisons today. As you read through the material that follows, you would be well served to ask whether prisons in America today are still true to the ideal that led to their creation.

There are approximately 1,720 state prisons and 119 federal prisons in operation across the country today.[74] Recently, however, the rate of new prison construction has slowed—and even stopped in many states—as budget issues at both the state and federal level have led to a new fiscal conservatism. Likewise, the growth of America's prison population has recently been slowing, and numbers in some states (most notably California) have begun to show a decrease as state budgetary concerns have led to fiscal conservatism (see the "CJ Issues" box discussing California's Public Safety Realignment program).

On January 1, 2015, the nation's state and federal prisons held 1,561,500 inmates, of which 1,508,600 were serving sentences of a year or more.[75] Slightly more than 7% (or 112,961) of those imprisoned were women.[76] The incarceration rate for state and federal prisoners sentenced to more than a year stood at 471 prisoners for every 100,000 U.S. residents in 2014. In that year, males had an imprisonment rate (1,169 per 100,000 U.S. male residents) that was 14 times higher than the rate for females (65 per 100,000).[77] If today's incarceration rates remain unchanged, 6.6% of U.S. residents born in 2001 will go to prison at some point during their lifetime.[78]

Statistics tell us quite a bit about those in our prisons (Figures 13-5 and 13-6). Most people sentenced to state prisons are convicted of violent crimes (53%), whereas property crimes

CJ | NEWS
California's Governor Wants Federal Oversight of Prisons to End

ZUMA Press, Inc./Alamy

California Governor Jerry Brown addresses members of the media in 2013, describing his plans to regain control over the state's prison system and end its control by the federal government. What problems did the U.S. Supreme Court find with the running of California's prisons?

California's broken and overcrowded prison system shows what can happen when the public demands tough sentencing provisions but not enough cells are built to deal with the ensuing flood of inmates.

A few years ago, federal judges assumed oversight of the beleaguered California prison system, ordering the state to significantly reduce its inmate population to a specified target by June 2013. But Governor Jerry Brown, grappling with a tight state budget, said the target would be too costly to meet. In January 2013, he filed a court challenge to regain state control of the prison system.

"Let those judges give us our prisons back," Brown declared. "We can run our own prisons." The historical roots of the ongoing court battle can be traced back to the 1980s and 1990s, an era of high crime rates, when Californians clamored for strict sentencing laws to lock up felons and, in some cases, actually throw away the key. In 1994, voters passed the three-strikes law, requiring a life sentence after three felony convictions. From 1982 to 2000, California's prison population swelled five-fold and the state built 23 new prisons.

In the 2000s, however, circumstances changed. Crime rates plummeted, state funds contracted, and California could no longer afford new prisons or even adequate space and health care for the inmates it already had. Tough sentencing laws, however, were still on the books, and flooding the prisons with new inmates at a cost to the state of $55,500 per prisoner per year.

With conditions deteriorating, California's inmates were being packed into three-tier bunks in prison gymnasiums and classrooms. That's when federal judges took action and found that prison overcrowding in California was so extensive that it violated the U.S. Constitution's ban on cruel and unusual punishment.

In 2006, the judges seized control of the prison health-care system and turned it over to an independent agency, which led to an increase in state spending. And in 2009, all three judges ordered the state to cut the number of inmates to a targeted level and set June 2013 as the deadline.

The state appealed the judges' order to the U.S. Supreme Court, but it lost in May 2011. To meet the mandate, more than 30,000 inmates were removed from the system through the state's "realignment initiative"—which meant shifting low-level offenders to county jails and sending some inmates to private prisons in other states. Although the state will help counties offset the cost of housing convicted offenders, estimates show that the state will save $486 million annually by sharing the burden for housing less serious offenders in county jails. Meanwhile, counties will be left holding at least some the bill for expanding their jails. One year after realignment began, some California counties, including Kern, Fresno, Sierra, and Yolo, saw their jail populations more than double—and more inmates are coming.

In April 2012, prison officials reported that they had run out of new ways to significantly reduce the prison population, short of letting felons back out on the streets, which they vowed not to do. Predicting it would fall short of the 2013 target, the state asked the judges to lower the target level, and in exchange it would improve rehabilitative and health-care services. But the judges refused, which prompted Brown to file his court challenge. It was later rejected by federal judges. In the meantime, Californians have lost their zeal for the tough sentencing laws that overcrowded their prisons in the first place.

In a proposition on the November 2012 ballot, California voters opted to pare back the three-strikes law by ending the life-in-prison requirement for third-strike offenders who haven't committed serious and violent crimes. Again, in 2014, the state's voters approved Proposition 47, a measure to change many felonies (especially those involving possession of small amounts of drugs and minor property crimes) to misdemeanors. Both measures are likely to lead to the release of over ten thousand inmates from California's prisons and to keep thousands of newly sentenced offenders out of prison.

Resources: Howard Mintz, "Governor: Drop California Prisons from Court Orders to Shed Inmates," *Mercury News*, January 8, 2013, http://www.mercurynews.com/crime-courts/ci_22331595/governor-argues-california-prisons-should-be-removed-from; Mac Taylor, "Providing Constitutional and Cost-Effective Inmate Medical Care," Legislative Analyst's Office, April 19, 2012, http://www.lao.ca.gov/reports/2012/crim/inmate-medical-care/inmate-medical-care-041912.pdf; Solomon Moore, "Court Orders California to Cut Prison Population," *New York Times*, February 9, 2009, http://www.nytimes.com/2009/02/10/us/10prison.html; Matthew Green, "Shouldering the Burden: California's New Jail Boom," KQED, http://blogs.kqed.org/lowdown/2012/08/16/shouldering-the-burden-californias-new-jail-boom-interactive-map/ (accessed March 2, 2013); Henry K. Lee, "Highest Court Thwarts Governor on Prison Crowding," SFGate, October 15, 2013 (accessed January 10, 2015); and Sasha Abramsky, "How California Voters Got So Smart on Crime," *The Nation*, March 26, 2015.

CJ | ISSUES
California's Public Safety Realignment (PSR) Program

In 2011, the California legislature passed the Criminal Justice Realignment Act and initiated the state's Public Safety Realignment (PSR) program. The program, which was implemented in response to a federal court order that required California to reduce overcrowding, places offenders convicted of less serious crimes in local jails rather than in state prisons (see the "CJ News" box earlier in the chapter).

California's PSR legislation has been called the most significant change in the California Penal Code since the state's Determinate Sentencing Law was passed in 1977. The most important aspect of the new law is that it shifts control over thousands of prisoners from the state to the county level. Specifically, the new law does three things. First, it mandates that low-level felons sentenced to one to a few years in prison (who in the past would normally have served their time in state-run prisons) will now be sent to county jails instead. Second, the supervision of most parolees will become the responsibility of county probation officials instead of state parole officers. Third, parolees supervised at the county level and who have their parole revoked will serve time for violations in county jails instead of state prisons, and the amount of time they serve will be limited to 180 days.

The PSR program effectively divides the state's felon population into two categories: (1) those legally defined as violent, serious, and/or sex offenders (who continue to be sent to state prison and who are supervised by state parole officers upon release), and (2) lower-level offenders who were formerly housed in state prisons or managed by the state parole system (but who are now being managed by local justice systems and are housed in county jails or managed by county probation officers).

The bill also provides that parolees who do not incur any infractions will be released from parole supervision in six months. Under the law, California's Board of Parole Hearings discontinued parole revocation hearings in mid-2013, and that responsibility was moved to local trial court judges.

California's realignment legislation effectively shifts much of the burden of paying for correctional services from the state to the counties. Serious questions, however, remain about the adequacy of funding and local capacity to manage the changes mandated by the law. The realignment statute provided a one-time appropriation to cover costs associated with hiring and training new personnel and the costs of construction of needed facilities. A dedicated and permanent revenue stream is intended to flow to the counties through allocation of a portion of both state vehicle license fees and the state sales tax (which was raised in 2012 through a state-wide referendum). It is still too early to tell whether the shift of resources between state and county levels will be sufficient to sustain the dual goals of safety and rehabilitation in California corrections. Figure 13-4 shows the impact of realignment on California's prison population through 2015.

Consequently, although the imprisonment rate in states like California may appear to be falling when reported in national statistics, realignment strategies merely shift the responsibility for housing state prisoners to county governments and tend to disguise the actual number of people being confined. Seventy percent of the recent nationwide decrease in prison populations reported by the Bureau of Justice Statistics, for example, was due to California's Public Safety Realignment program.

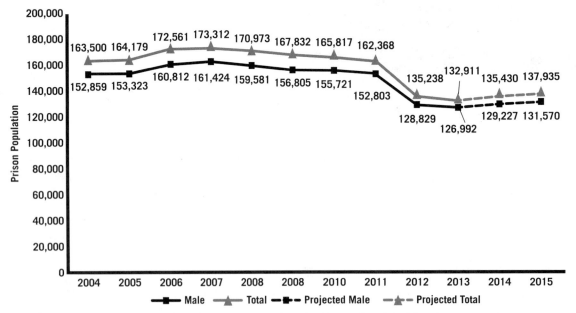

FIGURE 13-4 | Impact of Realignment on Prison Populations in the State of California

Source: California Department of Corrections and Rehabilitation, Office of Research, "Spring 2014 Population Projections," June 2014, http://www.cdcr.ca.gov/Reports_Research/Offender_Information_Services_Branch/Projections/S14Pub.pdf (accessed November 7, 2015).

Who's in Prison and Why?

In federal prisons, more than half (50.1%) of all inmates are serving time for drug offenses, whereas slightly more than a third (36%) are incarcerated for public-order crimes.

In state prisons, approximately 53% of prisoners are serving time for violent offenses, 19% are serving sentences for property offenses, and 16% are serving sentences for drug crimes. Eleven percent are convicted of public-order crimes.

Robbery is the most common violent crime for which males are imprisoned (14%), followed by murder (13%) and assault (10%).

Males comprise 93% of people in prison; 7% are female.

The percentage of females serving time for murder (11% of all sentenced females) is similar to that of males (13%).

Of federal prisoners, 41% are age 40 or older.

Most inmates (36%) are black; 34% are white and 22% are Hispanic.

Black and Hispanic prisoners are both younger and imprisoned at higher rates than white inmates.

The incarceration rate for black women is 2.9 times higher than the rate for white women; the rate for Hispanic women is 1.5 times higher than for white women.

Immigration offenders now account for 9% of all federal prisoners, but their numbers are falling.

Only 73.5% of federal prisoners are U.S. citizens, and more than 18% of persons confined in federal prisons hold Mexican citizenship,

Federal prisons have custody of 30% of all non-U.S. citizen inmates, and California, Florida, and Texas incarcerate 35% of prisoners who are non-U.S. citizens.

How Many People Are in Prison?

At the start of 2015, the number of state and federal prisoners sentenced to more than one year totaled 1,508,600.

At the start of 2015, 612 out of every 100,000 U.S. residents were sentenced to more than one year in prison.

The U.S. incarceration rate is among the highest in the world.*

The number of people incarcerated in state and federal prisons increased by 15% from 1,316,333 to 1,518,104 between 2000 and 2010.

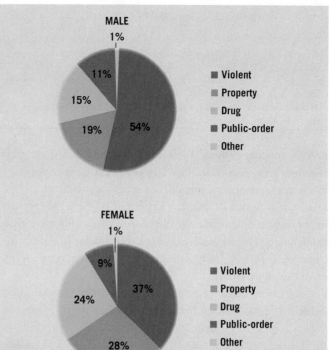

FIGURE 13-5 | State Prisoners by Gender and Type of Crime, 2014

Source: E. Ann Carson *Prisoners in 2014* (Washington, DC: Bureau of Justice Statistics, September 2015).

For the first time in more than 40 years, prison populations declined in 2011 by nearly 1% over the previous year.

Seventy percent of the recent nationwide decrease in prison populations is due to California's Public Safety Realignment program, which shifted the responsibility for confining most lower-level offenders to the state's counties.

The percentage of all prisoners housed in private prison facilities is 8.4%, with states housing 7% of inmates in private facilities and the Federal Bureau of Prisons holding 19% of its population in private facilities.

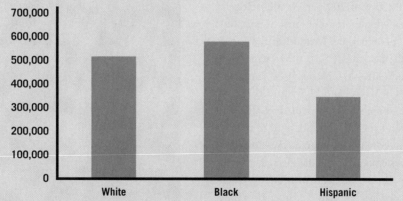

FIGURE 13-6 | Numbers of State and Federal Prisoners by Race, 2014

Source: E. Ann Carson, *Prisoners in 2014* (Washington, DC: 2015).

*International comparisons are based on the number of people held in prisons and jails.

Sources: Federal Bureau of Prisons, "Quick Facts about the Bureau of Prisons," January 4, 2015, http://www.bop.gov/news/quick.jsp#4 (accessed November 7, 2015); and Roy Walmsley, World Prison Population List, 9th ed. (Essex University: International Center for Prison Studies, 2013).

(19%) and drug crimes (16%) are the second and third most common type of offenses for which offenders are imprisoned.[79] In contrast, prisoners sentenced for drug-law violations are the single largest group of federal inmates (50.1%), and the increase in the imprisonment of drug offenders accounts for more than three-quarters of the total growth in the number of federal inmates since 1980.[80] Immigration offenders now account for 9% of all federal prisoners.[81]

An examination of imprisonment statistics by race highlights the huge disparity between blacks and whites in prison. Whereas only an estimated 958 white men are imprisoned in the United States for every 100,000 white men in their late 20s, figures show an incarceration rate of 5,434 black men for every 100,000 black men of the same age—six times greater than the figure for whites.[82] Almost 17% of adult black men in the United States have served time in prison—a rate over twice as high as that for adult Hispanic males (7.7%) and over six times as high as that for adult white males (2.6%).[83] According to the Bureau of Justice Statistics (BJS), a black male living in America today has a 32.3% lifetime chance of going to prison, and a black female has a 5.6% lifetime chance of imprisonment. That contrasts sharply with the lifetime chances of imprisonment for white males (5.9%) and white females (0.9%).[84]

The use of imprisonment varies considerably between states. Although the average rate of imprisonment in the United States at the start of 2015 was 471 per every 100,000 people in the population,[85] some state rates were nearly double that figure.[86] Louisiana, for example, was holding 816 out of every 100,000 of its citizens in prison at the start of 2015, while Oklahoma was second with an incarceration rate of 700 per 100,000 citizens. Texas, a state with traditionally high rates of imprisonment, held 584 prisoners per every 100,000 people. Maine had the lowest rate of imprisonment of all the states (153); other states with low rates were Rhode Island (178), Minnesota (194), and New Hampshire (219). As the "CJ News" and "CJ Issues" boxes in this chapter show, however, some states, particularly California, have found novel ways of reducing the official count of prisoners being held at the state level. In California's case, a strategy of realignment has been implemented to shift selected nonviolent prisoners out of state-run prisons and into county lockups. Consequently, when comparing state incarceration rates and when examining national statistics on imprisonment, it may make more sense to talk about the number of criminal offenders sentenced to confinement, rather than merely counting those held in state prisons.

The size of prison facilities varies greatly. One out of every four state institutions is a large maximum-security prison, with a population approaching 1,000 inmates. A few exceed that figure, but the typical state prison is small, with an inmate population of less than 500. Community-based facilities average around 50 residents. The typical prison system in relatively populous states consists of[87]

- One high-security prison for long-term, high-risk offenders
- One or more medium-security institutions for offenders who are not high risks
- One institution for adult women
- One or two institutions for young adults (generally under age 25)
- One or two specialized mental-hospital-type security prisons for prisoners who are mentally ill
- One or more open-type institutions for low-risk, nonviolent inmates

Incarceration costs average around $62 per inmate per day at the state level, and $77.50 per inmate per day at the federal level, when all types of adult correctional facilities are averaged together.[88] Imprisonment is especially costly in some states, like California, where citizens pay over $150 per day to house each inmate (Figure 13-7). Prison systems across the nation face spiraling costs as the number of inmates grows and as the age of the inmate population increases. According to a 2014 BJS report, the cost of running the nation's correctional facilities and related programs exceeds $83, of which more than half, or $48 billion, went to run state prisons.[89]

Inmates making collect phone calls at the Davidson County Prison in Tennessee. There are approximately 1,325 state prisons and 84 federal prisons in operation across the country today. Together, they hold over 1.6 million inmates. The prison shown here is run by Corrections Corporation of America. Are we likely to see a greater use of privately run correctional facilities in the future? Why or why not?

A. Ramey/PhotoEdit Inc.

■ **prison capacity**   The size of the correctional population an institution can effectively hold.[i] There are three types of prison capacity: rated, operational, and design.

■ **rated capacity**   The number of inmates a prison can handle according to the judgment of experts.

■ **operational capacity**   The number of inmates a prison can effectively accommodate based on management considerations.

■ **design capacity**   The number of inmates a prison was intended to hold when it was built or modified.

paying for it

California's Public Safety Realignment

This chapter began with the story of a paralyzed California inmate who had been denied release under the state's medical parole program. That story highlighted the high cost of confining prisoners who are in need of comprehensive medical care—in this case at a cost of $625,000 per year to the state's taxpayers.

In an effort to address budget shortfalls, however, some states have embraced cost-savings measures that have resulted in fewer people being confined to prison. One of the most significant of those measures, in terms of its impact on national prison statistics, is California's Public Safety Realignment (PSR) initiative, under which offenders convicted of less serious offenses are confined in local jails rather than in state prisons. The PSR program is discussed in the "CJ News" and "CJ Issues" boxes in this chapter.

Another way to reduce costs and to achieve savings in corrections is to ensure that offenders receive only the degree of supervision that they need in order to protect society and to facilitate their rehabilitation. As a consequence, states today have begun using risk-measuring instruments (questionnaires or survey instruments completed by prison staff, probation officers, or specially designated evaluators) to assess the potential future risk posed to society by offenders facing sentencing, and by imprisoned offenders who might otherwise be released. In order to make the maximum use of such a strategy, many states are changing their sentencing standards in order to allow those convicted of minor offenses—especially those with no history of violence or sex crimes—to be placed on probation or to be confined under living arrangements that provide alternatives to imprisonment, such as home confinement or halfway houses.

Resources: Barry Krisberg and Eleanor Taylor-Nicholson, *Criminal Justice Realignment: A Bold New Era in California Corrections* (Berkeley, CA: University of California, Berkeley Law School, 2011); and California Department of Corrections and Rehabilitation, "Funding of Realignment," http://www.cdcr.ca.gov/realignment/Funding-Realignment.html (accessed November 7, 2015).

Overcrowding

The just deserts philosophy led to substantial and continued increases in the American prison population even as crime rates were dropping. In 1990, for example, the U.S. rate of imprisonment stood at 292 prisoners per every 100,000 residents. By 1995, it had reached 399, and by 2015 it was 471. Beginning in 2009, however, the rate of growth finally began to decline, at least in prisons run by the states.[90]

Even though many new prisons have been built throughout the nation during the past 20 years to accommodate the growing number of inmates, prison overcrowding is still a reality in many jurisdictions (Figure 13-8). Some of the most crowded prisons are those in the federal system: The crowding rate in federal prisons (which are not included in Figure 13-8) recently stood at 40% over capacity.[91] A recent report by the Government Accounting Office (GAO) found that "BOP projects an additional 15% increase in its inmate population by 2020."[92]

Prison overcrowding can be measured along a number of dimensions, including these:[93]

- Space available per inmate (such as square feet of floor space)
- How long inmates are confined in cells or housing units (versus time spent in recreation and other activities)
- Living arrangements (e.g., single versus double bunks)
- Type of housing (such as use of segregation facilities, tents, and so on in place of general housing)

Further complicating the picture is the fact that prison officials have developed three definitions of **prison capacity**. **Rated capacity** refers to the size of the inmate population that a facility can handle according to the judgment of experts. **Operational capacity** is the number of inmates that a facility can effectively accommodate based on an appraisal of the institution's staff, programs, and services. **Design capacity** refers to the inmate population that the institution was originally built to handle. Rated capacity estimates usually yield the largest inmate capacities, whereas design capacity (on which observations in this chapter are based) typically shows the highest amount of overcrowding.

Overcrowding by itself is not cruel and unusual punishment, according to the U.S. Supreme Court in *Rhodes* v. *Chapman* (1981),[94] which considered the issue of double bunking along with other alleged forms of "deprivation" at the Southern Ohio Correctional Facility.

> Overcrowding by itself is not cruel and unusual punishment, according to the U.S. Supreme Court in *Rhodes* v. *Chapman* (1981).

The Court, reasoning that overcrowding is not necessarily dangerous if other prison services are adequate, held that prison housing

Approximate Annual Costs to Incarcerate an Inmate in Prison

Type of Expenditure	2013–14 (Actual)	2014–15 (Estimated)	2015–16 (Projected)
Security	$ 28,571	$ 31,512	$ 30,861
Inmate Health Care	$ 17,227	$ 18,923	$ 19,477
Medical care	$ 12,285	$ 13,415	$ 13,864
Psychiatric services	2,399	2,912	3,096
Pharmaceuticals/Ancillary	1,376	1,385	1,324
Dental care	1,167	1,211	1,193
Facility Operations and Records	$ 6,208	$ 6,530	$ 6,679
Facility operations (maintenance, utilities, etc.)	$ 3,809	$ 4,009	$ 4,163
Classification services	1,584	1,649	1,660
Maintenance of inmate records	681	712	696
Reception and Diagnosis	113	136	136
Transportation	21	24	24
Administration	$ 3,603	$ 3,731	$ 3,828
Inmate Support	$ 3,149	$ 3,329	$ 3,354
Food	$ 1,963	$ 2,010	$ 2,001
Inmate activities	99	100	100
Inmate employment	217	218	305
Clothing	342	349	340
Religious activities	85	110	110
Canteen	443	542	497
Rehabilitation Programs	$ 1,909	$ 1,859	$ 2,004
Academic education	$ 1,044	$ 1,112	$ 1,102
Vocational training	499	291	318
Substance abuse programs	366	456	585
Miscellaneous	$ 56	$ 91	$ 91
Total	$ 60,723	$ 65,977	$ 66,294

Totals do not include in-state and out-of-state contracted facilities.

FIGURE 13-7 | Annual Costs to Incarcerate an Inmate in Prison in California, 2013–2016
Source: The California Legislative Analyst's Office.

conditions may be "restrictive and even harsh," for they are part of the penalty that offenders pay for their crimes.

However, overcrowding combined with other negative conditions may lead to a finding against the prison system, as was the case with the 2011 U.S. Supreme Court case of *Brown v. Plata*, with which this chapter opened. The American Correctional Association (ACA) notes that a totality-of-conditions approach has led courts to assess the overall quality of prison life while viewing overcrowded conditions in combination with

- the prison's ability to meet basic human needs,
- the adequacy of the facility's staff,
- the program opportunities available to inmates, and
- the quality and strength of the prison management.

■ **theme**   What is selective incapacitation and what is the main goal? Do you agree with the concept of selective incapacitation? Can the criminal justice system accurately identify potentially dangerous offenders or is the "false positive" problem too great?

■ **selective incapacitation**   A policy that seeks to protect society by incarcerating individuals deemed to be the most dangerous.

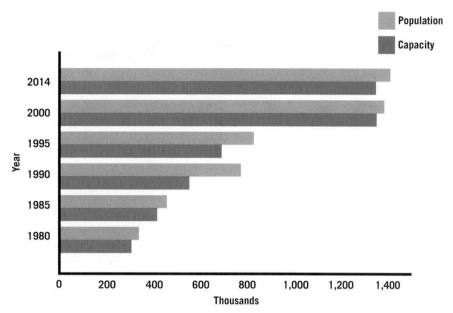

FIGURE 13-8 | State Prison Populations, Inmates versus Capacity, 1980–2014

Source: Bureau of Justice Statistics, *Correctional Populations in the United States* (Washington, DC: BJS, various years).

Selective Incapacitation: A Contemporary Strategy to Reduce Prison Populations

Some authors have identified the central issue of imprisonment as one of collective versus **selective incapacitation**.[95] Collective incapacitation, a strategy that would imprison almost all serious offenders, is still found in jurisdictions that rely largely on predetermined, or fixed, sentences for given offenses or for a series of specified kinds of offenses (as in the case of some forms of three-strikes legislation). Collective incapacitation is, however, prohibitively expensive as well as unnecessary, in the opinion of many experts. Not all offenders need to be imprisoned because not all represent a continuing threat to society, but those who do are difficult to identify.[96]

Selective incapacitation seeks to identify the most dangerous criminals, with the goal of removing them from society.

> Selective incapacitation seeks to identify the most dangerous criminals, with the goal of removing them from society.

Consequently, the assessment of dangerousness (see Chapter 3) is central to today's contemporary strategy of selective incapacitation. Repeat offenders with records of serious and violent crimes are the most likely candidates for imprisonment—as are child sex offenders given their especially negative status in the public eye.

In support of selective incapacitation, many states have enacted career-offender statutes that attempt to identify potentially dangerous offenders out of known criminal populations. Selective incapacitation efforts, however, have been criticized for yielding a rate of "false positives" of over 60%,[97] and some authors have called selective incapacitation a "strategy of failure."[98] Nevertheless, in an analysis of recidivism studies, Canadians Paul Gendreau, Tracy Little, and Claire Goggin found that criminal history, a history of preadult antisocial behavior, and "criminogenic needs"—which were defined as measurable antisocial thoughts, values, and behaviors—were all dependable predictors of recidivism.[99]

Many states today, facing budgetary challenges, have had to scramble in an attempt to implement selective incarceration principles. A recent report by the Sentencing Project, for example, found that four states—Kansas, Michigan, New Jersey, and New York—announced the closing of a combined number of 20 prisons in 2012, reducing prison capacity by over 14,100 beds.[100] The Project also reported that 13 states eliminated 15,500 additional prison beds in 2011. Savings due to the 2012 closing were estimated to total more than $337 million. The largest of the closures is the planned shuttering of the California Rehabilitation Center at Norco by June 2016. California expects to eliminate 3,900 beds and to save $125 million annually in operating costs.[101]

The state reductions came about by limiting the length of mandatory minimum sentences for drug offenses, diverting defendants with low-level convictions from incarceration, enhancing release programs, and reducing parole revocations. Recently, for example, Connecticut Governor Dannel P. Malloy signed into law a hotly debated piece of legislation that gave inmates in

■ **lecture note**   Review the various levels of security and explain that the same facility may combine multiple custody levels.

that state sentence-reduction credits if they participate in various kinds of prison-run self-improvement programs. Connecticut House Majority Leader Brendan Sharkey explained the new law this way: "If this is about being soft on crime, I say 'baloney.' This is about being smart on crime."[102]

As state budget problems continue, the just deserts model has relinquished ground to selective incapacitation. As more and more states embrace the evidence-based correctional model, it is likely that we will see the continued sentencing of violent criminals to lengthy prison stays, combined with the early release of offenders deemed unlikely to reoffend, and the increased use of less expensive alternative sanctions and diversion for minor offenders.

Security Levels

Maximum-custody (or maximum-security) prisons tend to be massive old buildings with large inmate populations. However, some, like Central Prison in Raleigh, North Carolina, are much newer and incorporate advances in prison architecture to provide tight security without sacrificing building aesthetics. Such institutions provide a high level of security characterized by tall fences, thick walls, secure cells, gun towers, and armed prison guards. Maximum-custody prisons tend to locate cells and other inmate living facilities at the center of the institution and place a variety of barriers between the living area and the institution's outer perimeter. Technological innovations, such as electric perimeters, laser motion detectors, electronic and pneumatic locking systems, metal detectors, X-ray machines, television surveillance, radio communications, and computer information systems, are frequently used today to reinforce the more traditional maximum-security strategies. These technologies have helped lower the cost of new prison construction. However, some people argue that prisons may rely too heavily on electronic detection devices that have not yet been adequately tested.[103] Death row inmates are all maximum-security prisoners, although the level of security on death row exceeds even that experienced by most prisoners held in maximum custody. Prisoners on death row must spend much of the day in single cells and are often permitted a brief shower only once a week under close supervision.

Most states today have one large, centrally located maximum-security institution. Some of these prisons combine more than one custody level and may be both maximum- and medium-security facilities. Medium security is a custody level that in many ways resembles maximum security. Medium-security prisoners are generally permitted more freedom to associate with one another and can go to the prison yard, exercise room, library, and shower and bathroom facilities under less intense supervision. An important security tool in medium-security prisons is the count, which is a head count of inmates

taken at regular intervals. Counts may be taken four times a day and usually require inmates to report to designated areas to be counted. Until the count has been "cleared," all other inmate activity must cease. Medium-security prisons tend to be smaller than maximum-security institutions and often have barbed-wire-topped chain-link fences instead of the more secure stone or concrete block walls found in many of the older maximum-security facilities. Cells and living quarters tend to have more windows and are often located closer to the perimeter of the institution than in maximum-security facilities. Dormitory-style housing, where prisoners live together in ward-like arrangements, is sometimes found in medium-security facilities. There are generally more opportunities for inmates to participate in recreational and other prison programs than in maximum-custody facilities.

In minimum-security institutions, inmates are generally housed in dormitory-like settings and are free to walk the yard and to visit most of the prison facilities. Some newer prisons provide minimum-security inmates with private rooms, which they can decorate (within limits) according to their tastes. Inmates usually have free access to a canteen that sells items like cigarettes, toothpaste, and candy bars. Minimum-security inmates often wear uniforms of a different color from those of inmates in higher custody levels, and in some institutions they may wear civilian clothes. They work under only general supervision and usually have access to recreational, educational, and skills-training programs on the prison grounds. Guards are unarmed, gun towers do not exist, and fences, if they are present at all, are usually low and gates are sometimes even unlocked. Many minimum-security prisoners participate in some sort of work- or study-release program, and some have extensive visitation and furlough privileges. Counts may be taken, although most minimum-security institutions keep track of inmates through daily administrative work schedules. The primary "force" holding inmates in minimum-security institutions is their own restraint. Inmates live with the knowledge that minimum-security institutions are one step removed from close correctional supervision and that if they fail to meet the expectations of administrators, they will be transferred into more secure institutions, which will probably delay their release. Inmates returning from assignments in the community may be frisked for contraband, but body-cavity searches are rare in minimum custody, being reserved primarily for inmates suspected of smuggling.

The typical American prison today is medium or minimum custody. Some states have as many as 80 or 90 small institutions, which may originally have been located in every county to serve the needs of public works and highway maintenance. Medium- and minimum-security institutions house the bulk of the country's prison population and offer a number of programs and services designed to assist with the rehabilitation of offenders

■ **classification system** A system used by prison administrators to assign inmates to custody levels based on offense history, assessed dangerousness, perceived risk of escape, and other factors.

and to create the conditions necessary for the successful reentry of the inmate into society. Most prisons offer psychiatric services, academic education, vocational education, substance-abuse treatment, health care, counseling, recreation, library services, religious programs, and industrial and agricultural training.[104] Learn more about all aspects of contemporary prisons from the Corrections Connection via **http://www.corrections.com**.

Prison Classification Systems

Most states use a **classification system** to assign new prisoners to initial custody levels based on their perceived dangerousness, escape risk, and type of offense. A prisoner might be assigned to a minimum-, medium-, or maximum-custody institution. Inmates move through custody levels according to the progress they are judged to have made in self-control and demonstrated responsibility. Serious violent criminals who begin their prison careers with lengthy sentences in maximum custody have the opportunity in most states to work their way up to minimum security, although the process usually takes a number of years. Those who represent continual disciplinary problems are returned to closer custody levels. Minimum-security prisons, as a result, house inmates convicted of all types of criminal offenses.

Once an inmate has been assigned to a custody level, he or she may be reassessed for living and work assignments within the institution. Just as initial (or external) custody classification systems determine security levels, internal classification systems are designed to help determine appropriate housing plans and program interventions within a particular facility for inmates who share a common custody level. In short, initial classification determines the institution in which an inmate is placed, and internal classification determines placement and program assignment within that institution.[105]

Objective prison classification systems were adopted by many states in the 1980s, but it wasn't until the late 1990s that such systems were refined and validated. Fueled by litigation and overcrowding, classification systems are now viewed as the principal management tool for allocating scarce prison resources efficiently and for minimizing the potential for violence or escape. Classification systems are also expected to provide greater accountability and to forecast future prison bed-space needs. A properly functioning classification system is the "brain" of prison management, governing and influencing many important decisions, including such fiscal matters as staffing levels, bed space, and programming.[106]

One of the best-known internal classification systems in use today is the adult internal management system (AIMS). AIMS was developed more than 20 years ago to reduce institutional predatory behavior by identifying potential predators

Inmates flashing gang signs for the camera. If you were a warden, what changes would you make to improve the management of a prison like this one?

It is important to recognize that the criteria used to classify prisoners must be relevant to the legitimate security needs of the institution.

and separating them from vulnerable inmates. AIMS assesses an inmate's predatory potential by quantifying aspects of his or her (1) record of misconduct, (2) ability to follow staff directions, and (3) level of aggression toward other inmates.

Before concluding this discussion of classification, it is important to recognize that the criteria used to classify prisoners must be relevant to the legitimate security needs of the institution. In 2005, for example, the U.S. Supreme Court, in the case of *Johnson* v. *California*,[107] invalidated the California Department of Corrections and Rehabilitation's (CDCR) unwritten policy of racially segregating prisoners in double cells for up to 60 days each time they entered a new correctional facility. The policy had been based on a claim that it prevented violence caused by racial gangs. The Court, however, held that the California policy was "immediately suspect" as an "express racial classification" and found that the CDCR was unable to demonstrate that the practice served a compelling state interest.

The Federal Prison System

In 1895, the federal government opened a prison at Leavenworth, Kansas, for civilians convicted of violating federal law. Leavenworth had been a military prison, and control over the facility was transferred from the Department of the Army to the Department of Justice. By 1906, the Leavenworth facility had been expanded to a capacity of 1,200 inmates, and another federal prison—in Atlanta, Georgia—was built. McNeil Island Prison in Washington State was also functioning by the early 1900s. The first federal prison for women opened in 1927 in Alderson, West Virginia. With the increasing complexity of the federal criminal code, the number of federal prisoners grew.[108]

On May 14, 1930, the Federal Bureau of Prisons (BOP) was created under the direction of Sanford Bates. The BOP was charged with providing progressive and humane care for federal inmates, professionalizing the federal prison service, and ensuring consistent and centralized administration of the 11 federal prisons in operation at the time.[109] The bureau inherited a system that was dramatically overcrowded. Many federal prisoners were among the most notorious criminals in the nation, and ideals of humane treatment and rehabilitation were all but lacking in the facilities of the 1920s. Bates began a program of improvements to relieve overcrowding and to increase the treatment capacity of the system. In 1933, the Medical Center for Federal Prisoners opened in Springfield, Missouri, with a capacity of around 1,000 inmates. Alcatraz Island began operations in 1934. Following Bates, James V. Bennett ran the BOP from 1937–1964, and worked to humanize prison conditions in the federal system. Because of his long tenure, Bennett left a mark on the system that remains today in its striving to set a standard for well-run institutions.

Most of the federal prison system's growth since the mid-1980s has been the result of the Sentencing Reform Act of 1984 (which established determinate sentencing, abolished parole, and reduced good time) and federal mandatory-minimum-sentencing laws enacted in 1986, 1988, and 1990. From 1980 to 1989, the federal inmate population more than doubled, from just over 24,000 to almost 58,000. During the 1990s, the population more than doubled again, and it continued to grow throughout the early years of the twenty-first century, reaching approximately 217,800 prisoners (or 33% over capacity) by 2015.[110] According to the Washington, D.C.–based Urban Institute, "the increase in expected time served by drug offenders was the single greatest contributor to growth in the federal prison population beginning in 1998 (Figure 13-10).[111]

Today, the federal prison system consists of 119 institutions, six regional offices, the Central Office (headquarters), two staff-training centers, and 22 residential reentry management offices (which were previously known as community corrections offices).[112] The regional offices and the Central Office provide administrative oversight and support to the institutions and to the residential reentry management offices, which oversee community corrections centers and home-confinement programs. The federal correctional workforce is one of the fastest growing in the country, and at mid-2014, the BOP employed about 39,000 people.[113]

The BOP classifies its institutions according to five security levels (Figure 13-9): (1) administrative maximum (**ADMAX**), (2) high security, (3) medium security, (4) low security, and (5) minimum

security. High-security facilities are called *U.S. penitentiaries* (USPs), medium- and low-security institutions are both called *federal correctional institutions* (FCIs), and minimum-security prisons are termed *federal prison camps* (FPCs).[114] Minimum-security facilities (e.g., Eglin Air Force Base, Florida, and Maxwell Air Force Base, Alabama) are essentially honor-type camps with barracks-type housing and no fencing. Low-security facilities in the federal prison system are surrounded by double chain-link fencing and employ vehicle patrols around their perimeters to enhance security. Medium-security facilities (like those in Terminal Island, California; Lompoc, California; and Seagoville, Texas) make use of similar fencing and patrols but supplement them with electronic monitoring of the grounds and perimeter areas. High-security facilities (USPs like those in Atlanta, Georgia; Lewisburg, Pennsylvania; Terre Haute, Indiana; and Leavenworth, Kansas) are architecturally designed to prevent escapes and to contain disturbances. They also make use of armed patrols and intense electronic surveillance. Combination facilities within the BOP, which include institutions with different missions and security levels, are called Federal Correctional Complexes (FCCs).

A separate federal prison category is that of administrative facilities, consisting of institutions with special missions that are designed to house all types of inmates. Most administrative facilities are metropolitan detention centers (MDCs). MDCs, which are generally located in large cities close to federal courthouses, are the jails of the federal correctional system and hold defendants awaiting trial in federal court. Another five administrative facilities, medical centers for federal prisoners (MCFPs), function as hospitals.

Federal correctional facilities exist either as single institutions or as federal correctional complexes—that is, sites consisting of more than one type of correctional institution (Figure 13-11). The federal correctional complex at Allenwood, Pennsylvania, for example, consists of a U.S. penitentiary, a federal prison camp, and two federal correctional institutions (one low and one medium security), each with its own warden. Federal institutions can be classified by type as follows: 55 are federal prison camps (holding 35% of all federal prisoners), 17 are low-security facilities (28%), 26 are medium-security facilities (23%), eight are high-security prisons (13%), and one is an ADMAX facility (1%).

> Most administrative facilities are metropolitan detention centers (MDCs).

The federal system's only ADMAX unit, the $60 million ultra-high-security prison at Florence, Colorado, is a relatively recent addition to the federal system. Dubbed "the Alcatraz of the Rockies," the 575-bed facility was designed to be the most secure prison ever built by the government.[115] Opened in 1995, it holds mob bosses, spies, terrorists, murderers, and escape artists. Dangerous inmates

Federal Bureau of Prisons: Institutional Security Levels and Terminology

The federal Bureau of Prisons (BOP) operates institutions at five different security levels (minimum, low, medium, high, and administrative). Security levels are distinguished based upon such features as the type of inmate housing within the institution; the presence of external patrols, towers, security barriers, or detection devices; internal security features; and staff-to-inmate ratio.

Minimum Security Federal Prison Camps (FPCs): Feature dormitory housing, limited or no perimeter fencing, and a relatively low staff-to-inmate ratio. Some are located next to military bases, making it possible for inmates to help serve the labor needs of the base. Many BOP facilities have a small, minimum-security camp adjacent to the main facility. These satellite prison camps provide inmate labor to the main institution and to off-site work programs.

Low Security Federal Correctional Institutions (FCIs): Feature double-fenced perimeters with electronic detection systems, mostly dormitory or cubicle housing, and a staff-to-inmate ratio that is somewhat higher than that of FPCs.

Medium Security Federal Correctional Institutions (FCIs): Have strengthened (double-fenced with electronic detection systems) perimeters, mostly cell-type housing, a higher staff-to-inmate ratio than low security FCIs, and greater internal controls.

High Security United States Penitentiaries (USPs): Have highly secured perimeters featuring walls or reinforced fences, multiple- and single-occupant cell housing, the highest staff-to-inmate ratio, and close control of inmate movement.

Administrative Facilities: Have special missions—for example, detaining pretrial offenders; treating inmates with serious or chronic medical problems; or containing extremely dangerous, violent, or escape-prone inmates. They include Metropolitan Correctional Centers (MCCs), Metropolitan Detention Centers (MDCs), Federal Detention Centers (FDCs), Federal Medical Centers (FMCs), the Medical Center for Federal Prisoners (MCFP), the Federal Transfer Center (FTC), and the Administrative-Maximum USP (ADX).

Federal Correctional Complexes (FCCs): Contain institutions with different missions and security levels located in close proximity, allowing them to gain cost efficiencies through shared services, enable staff to gain experience at various security levels, and enhance emergency preparedness by having additional resources readily available.

FIGURE 13-9 | Federal Bureau of Prisons: Institutional Security Levels and Terminology

Source: Adapted from Federal Bureau of Prisons, *State of the Bureau 2010* (Washington, DC; U.S. Dept. of Justice, 2011), p. 2.

■ **lecture note** Describe jails as temporary confinement facilities originally intended to hold defendants awaiting trial or to house convicted offenders awaiting sentencing. Explain that many jurisdictions now use jails in
lieu of prisons for offenders sentenced to short terms of imprisonment.

■ **lecture note** Review the various purposes of jails and discuss the possible problems inherent in placing so many responsibilities on one institution.

■ **theme** What unique qualities do jails have (because of inmate profiles,
sentences, location, etc.) that prisons do not? How might jail administrators
capitalize on those qualities?

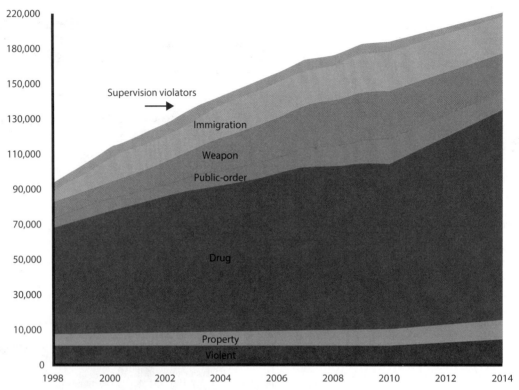

FIGURE 13-10 | Federal Prisons Populations at Yearend, by Offense, 1998–2014
Source: Bureau of Justice Statistics, Correctional Reporting Program.

are confined to their cells 23 hours per day and are not allowed to
see or associate with other inmates. Electronically controlled doors
throughout the institution channel inmates to individual exercise
sessions, and educational courses, religious services, and administrative matters are conducted via closed-circuit television piped directly into the prisoners' cells. Remote-controlled heavy steel doors
within the prison allow correctional staff to section off the institution in the event of rioting, and the system can be controlled from
outside if the entire prison is compromised.

In an effort to combat rising expenses associated with a rapidly growing federal prison population, the U.S. Congress passed
legislation in 1992 that imposes a "user fee" on federal inmates
who are able to pay the costs associated with their incarceration.[116]
Under the law, inmates may be assessed a dollar amount up to
the cost of a year's incarceration—currently around $22,600.[117]
The statute, which was designed so as not to impose hardships on
poor offenders or their dependents, directs that collected funds,
estimated to total $48 million per year, are to be used to improve
alcohol- and drug-abuse programs within federal prisons. Visit
the Federal Bureau of Prisons website at **http://www.bop.gov**.

Recent Improvements

In the midst of frequent lawsuits, court-ordered changes in
prison administration, and overcrowded conditions, outstanding prison facilities are being recognized through the accreditation program of the American Correctional Association (ACA).
The ACA Commission on Accreditation has developed a set of
standards that correctional institutions can use for conducting
self-evaluations. Institutions that meet the standards can apply
for accreditation under the program.

Another avenue toward improvement of the nation's prisons can be found in the National Academy of Corrections, the
training arm of the National Institute of Corrections. The academy, located in Colorado, offers seminars, videoconferencing,
and training sessions for state and local corrections managers,
trainers, personnel directors, sheriffs, and state legislators.[118]
Issues covered include strategies to control overcrowding,
community corrections program management, prison programs, gangs and disturbances, security, and public and media
relations.[119]

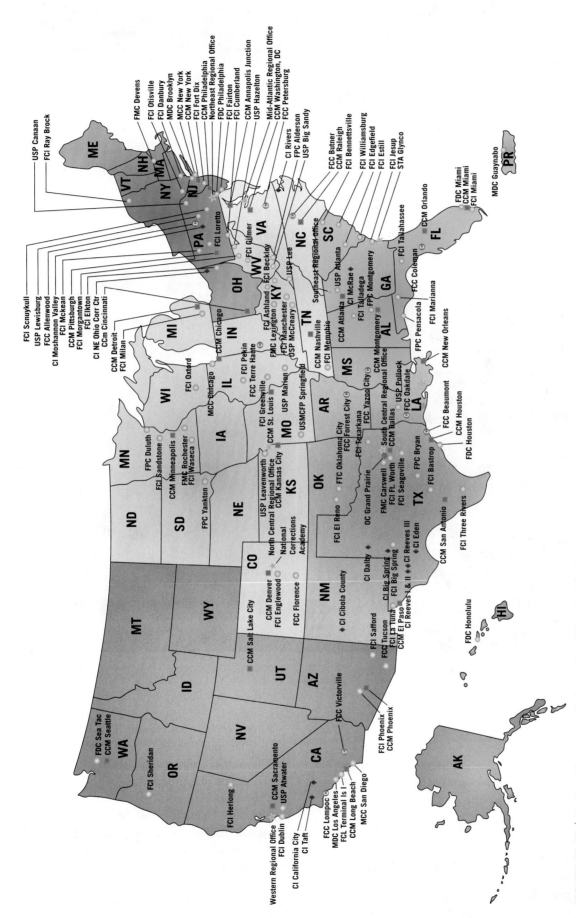

FIGURE 13-11 | Federal Bureau of Prisons Facilities by Region

Source: Federal Bureau of Prisons, http://www.bop.gov/locations/locationmap.jsp.

449

■ **jail**   A confinement facility administered by an agency of local government, typically a law enforcement agency, intended for adults but sometimes also containing juveniles, which holds people detained pending adjudication or committed after adjudication, usually those sentenced to a year or less.

The Federal Bureau of Prisons ADMAX facility in Florence, Colorado, which opened in 1995. It is the only ultra-high-security institution in the federal system. What kinds of inmates are held here?

Jails

Jails are locally operated short-term confinement facilities originally built to hold suspects following arrest and pending trial. Today's jails also serve these purposes:[120]

- They receive individuals pending arraignment and hold them awaiting trial, conviction, or sentencing.
- They readmit probation, parole, and bail-bond violators and absconders.
- They temporarily detain juveniles, inmates who are mentally ill, and others pending transfer to appropriate facilities.
- They hold individuals for the military, for protective custody, for contempt, and for the courts as witnesses.
- They release convicted inmates to the community upon completion of their sentence.
- They transfer inmates to federal, state, or other authorities.
- They house inmates for federal, state, or other authorities because of overcrowding in their facilities.
- They operate community-based programs with day reporting, home detention, electronic monitoring, and other types of supervision.
- They hold inmates sentenced to short terms (generally less than one year).

■ **lecture note**   Tell students that the proportion of women in jails across the nation has risen steadily during the past two decades. Ask students to name some of the reasons for that increase.

Los Angeles County's Twin Towers Correctional Facility. The $373 million jail opened in 1997 and is one of the world's largest jails. What are the differences between a prison and a jail?

A recent report by the BJS found that the nation's jails held 744,600 inmates—15% of whom were women.[121] Juveniles held in local jails numbered around 4,200.[122] More than half of jail inmates have been convicted of a crime, a quarter are being detained while awaiting arraignment or trial, and a sixth are being held on a prior sentence but are also awaiting arraignment or trial on a new charge.[123] Jail authorities also supervised an additional 63,478 men and women in the community under programs that included the following: electronic monitoring (14,223), home detention without electronic monitoring (646), day reporting (4,413), community service (14,331), and weekend programs (9,698).[124]

A total of 3,283 jails operate throughout the United States, staffed by approximately 234,000 jail employees—the equivalent of about one employee for every three jail inmates.[125] Overall, the nation's jail budget is huge, and facilities are overflowing. State and local governments spend $10 billion every year to operate the nation's jails,[126] with more than $1 billion in additional monies earmarked for new jail construction and for renovation. On average, the housing of one jail inmate costs more than $14,500 per year.[127]

More than 11 million people are admitted (or readmitted) to the nation's jails each year.[128] Some jail inmates stay for as little as one day, whereas others serve extended periods of time. Significantly, one of the fastest-growing sectors of today's jail population consists of sentenced offenders serving time in local jails because overcrowded prisons cannot accept them.

Most people processed through the country's jails are members of minority groups, with 35% of jail inmates classifying themselves as African American, 15% as Hispanic, and 3% as other minorities. Less than 1% report being of more than one race, and 47% of jail inmates classify themselves as white.

Slightly more than 85% are male.[129] The typical jail inmate is an unmarried black male between 25 and 34 years of age who reports having had some high school education. Typical charges include drug trafficking (12.1%), assault (11.7%), drug possession (10.8%), and larceny (7%).[130]

According to the BJS, about 6% of jail facilities house almost half of all jail inmates in the nation.[131] So, although most jails are small—many were built to house 50 or fewer inmates—most people who spend time in jail do so in larger institutions. Across the country, a handful of "megajails" house thousands of inmates each. The largest such facilities are in Los Angeles; New York City; Cook County, Illinois; Harris County, Texas; and Maricopa County, Arizona. Los Angeles County's 4,000-bed Twin Towers Correctional Facility cost $373 million to build and opened in 1997.[132] The city of Los Angeles' 512-bed Metropolitan Detention Center, although not nearly as large, opened in 2011 and cost the city $84 million to build. The largest employer among huge jails is Cook County's, with more than 1,200 personnel on its payroll.[133] The nation's 50 largest jail jurisdictions hold 29.5% of all jail inmates.[134] The two jurisdictions with the most jail inmates, Los Angeles County and New York City, together hold approximately 31,085 inmates, or 4.2% of the national total.[135]

Women and Jail

Although women number only 15% of the country's jail population, they are the largest growth group in jails nationwide.[136] Jailed women face a number of special problems. Only 25.7% of the nation's jails report having a classification system specifically designed to evaluate female inmates,[137] and although many jurisdictions have plans "to build facilities geared to the female offender,"[138] not all jurisdictions today even provide separate housing areas for women. Educational levels are very low among jailed women, and fewer than half are high school graduates.[139] Drug abuse is another significant source of difficulty for jailed women. More than 30% of women who are admitted to jail have a substance-abuse problem at the time of admission, and in some parts of the country, that figure may be as high as 70%.[140]

Pregnancy is another problem. Nationally, 4% of female inmates are pregnant when they enter jail,[141] but in urban areas, as much as 10% of the female jail population is reported to be pregnant on any given day.[142] As a consequence, a few hundred children are born in jails each year. However,

> Although women number only 15% of the country's jail population, they are the largest growth group in jails nationwide.

■ **lecture note**   Discuss the problem of jail overcrowding and ask students how the prison overcrowding problem may affect jail populations.

substantive medical programs for female inmates, such as obstetrics and gynecological care, are often lacking. In planning future medical services for female inmates, some writers have advised jail administrators to expect to see an increasingly common kind of inmate: "an opiate-addicted female who is pregnant with no prior prenatal care having one or more sexually transmitted diseases, and fitting a high-risk category for AIDS (prostitution, IV drug use)."[143]

Not only are jailed mothers separated from their children, but they may have to pay for their support. Twelve percent of all jails in one study reported requiring employed female inmates to contribute to the support of their dependent children.

When we consider women and jails, female inmates are only half the story. Women who work in corrections are the other half. In one study, Linda Zupan, a member of a new generation of jail scholars, found that women made up 22% of the corrections officer force in jails across the nation.[144] The deployment of female personnel, however, was disproportionately skewed toward jobs in the lower ranks. Although 60% of all support staff (secretaries, cooks, and janitors) were women, only one in every ten chief administrators was female. Even so, Zupan did find that female corrections employees were significantly committed to their careers and that the attitudes of male workers toward female coworkers in jails were generally positive. Zupan's study uncovered 626 jails in which over 50% of the corrections officer force consisted of women. However, 954 of the nation's 3,316 jails operating at the time of the study had no female officers.[145] Zupan noted that "an obvious problem associated with the lack of female officers in jails housing females concerns the potential for abuse and exploitation of women inmates by male staff."[146]

Jails that do hire women generally accord them equal footing with male staffers. Although cross-gender privacy is a potential area of legal liability, in three-quarters of the jails studied by Zupan, female officers were assigned to supervise male housing areas. Only one in four jails that employed women restricted their access to unscreened shower and toilet facilities used by men or to other areas, such as sexual offender units.

The Growth of Jails

Jails have been called the "shame of the criminal justice system." Many are old, poorly funded, scantily staffed by underpaid and poorly trained employees, and given low priority in local budgets. By the end of the 1980s, many of our nation's jails had become seriously overcrowded, and court-ordered caps were sometimes placed on jail populations. One of the first such caps was imposed on the Harris County Jail in Houston, Texas, in 1990. In that year, the jail was forced to release 250 inmates after missing a deadline for reducing its resident population of 6,100 people.[147] A nationwide survey by the BJS, undertaken around the same time, found that 46% of all jails had been built more than 25 years earlier, and of that percentage, over half were more than 50 years old.[148]

A 1983 national census revealed that jails were operating at 85% of their rated capacity (Table 13-1).[149] In 1990, however, the nation's jails were running at 104% of capacity, and new jails could be found on drawing boards and under construction across the country. By 2015, jail capacity had increased substantially, and overall jail occupancy was reported at 83% of rated capacity. Some individual facilities, however, were still desperately overcrowded.[150] Jail jurisdictions with the largest average daily populations also reported the highest occupancy rates.

Although jail overcrowding is not the issue it was a decade or two ago, it is still a problem. Overcrowded prisons have taken a toll on jails. Today, approximately 82,000 inmates are being held in local jails because of overcrowding in state and federal prisons.[151] Also, the practice of giving jail sentences to offenders who are unable or unwilling to make restitution, alimony, or child-support payments has added to jail occupancy and has made the local lockup, at least partially, a debtors' prison. Symptomatic of problems brought on by huge jail populations, 314 suicides were reported in jails across the nation during a recent year.[152] Jail deaths from all causes total about 980 annually. Other factors conspire to keep jail populations high, including the inability of jail inmates to make bond, delays between arrest

TABLE 13-1 | Jail Facts

	1983	1988	1993	2000	2014
Number of jails	3,338	3,316	3,304	3,365	3,283[a]
Number of jail inmates	223,551	343,569	459,804	621,149	744,600
Rated capacity of jails	261,556	339,949	475,224	677,787	890,500
Percentage of capacity occupied	85%	101%	97%	92%	84%

[a]Estimate based on earlier data.

Sources: Todd D. Minton and Daniela Golinelli, *Jail Inmates at Midyear 2014—Statistical Tables* (Washington, DC: Bureau of Justice Statistics, 2015).

freedom OR safety? YOU decide

To What Degree Should the Personal Values of Workers in the Criminal Justice System Influence Job Performance?

In 2009, a "conscience-protection rule" was published in the Federal Register—having been enacted by the administration of George W. Bush just before he left office. The rule, meant mainly to apply to the health-care industry, gives doctors, hospitals, receptionists, and other workers and volunteers the right to refuse to participate in any medical care that they find morally objectionable. In particular, the rule "protects the rights of medical providers to care for their patients in accord with their conscience," said outgoing Health and Human Services Secretary Mike Leavitt.

The rule came too late to apply to a 2007 incident in which a 21-year-old college student who was visiting Tampa, Florida, was attacked and raped while walking back to her car. The story of the woman, who was attending the annual Gasparilla festival, a pirate-themed parade, took an interesting twist. Investigating officers first took her to a nearby rape crisis center, where she was physically examined and given an initial emergency post-coital contraception pill, also known as a *morning-after pill*, to prevent unwanted pregnancy.

Officers then drove the victim through the area where the attack allegedly took place in an effort to find the rapist and to pinpoint the scene of the crime. As they drove, officers entered the woman's identifying information into their car's computer system and discovered that a juvenile warrant that had been issued against her in 2003 for unpaid restitution in a theft case was still outstanding. Once they discovered the warrant, officers promptly arrested, booked, and jailed the woman. She remained behind bars for two days until her family was able to hire an attorney who arranged for her release.

During the time she was jailed, the victim said, a jail health-care worker refused to administer a second—and required—dose of the morning-after medication. The medicine's manufacturer specifies that two doses, administered 20 hours apart, are needed to prevent pregnancy. Some members of the local media, which accused the police department of insensitivity to the needs of crime victims, reported that the jail worker felt compelled to deny the woman the medication due to personal religious beliefs against use of the pill.

Vic Moore, the jailed woman's attorney, told reporters that he was "Shocked. Stunned. Outraged. I don't have words to describe it," he said. "She is not a victim of any one person. She is a victim of the system. There's just got to be some humanity involved when it's a victim of rape."

The Tampa Police Department, which was stung by media reports in the case, has since initiated a policy advising officers not to arrest a crime victim who has suffered injury or mental trauma whenever reasonably possible.

You Decide

To what extent (if at all) should the values of workers within the criminal justice system be allowed to influence their performance of job-related tasks? Do you feel that the jail worker referenced in this story was within her "rights" by denying a second dose of the morning-after pill to the victim of an alleged rape? Why or why not?

References: David G. Savage, "Health Providers' 'Conscience' Rule to Take Effect," *Los Angeles Times,* December 19, 2008; and Phil Davis, "Rape Victim Is Jailed on Old Warrant," Associated Press, January 31, 2007.

and case disposition, an overburdened criminal justice system, and what some have called "unproductive statutes" requiring that specified nonviolent offenders be jailed.[153]

Some innovative jurisdictions have successfully contained the growth of jail populations by diverting arrestees to community-based programs. San Diego, California, for example, uses a privately operated detoxification reception program to divert many inebriates from the "drunk tank."[154] Officials in Galveston County, Texas, routinely divert arrestees who are mentally ill directly to a mental health facility.[155] Other areas use pretrial services and magistrates' offices, which are open 24 hours a day, for setting bail, making release possible.

New-Generation Jails

Some suggest that the problems found in many jails stem from "mismanagement, lack of fiscal support, heterogeneous inmate populations, overuse and misuse of detention, overemphasis on custodial goals, and political and public apathy."[156] Others propose that environmental and organizational aspects of traditional jail architecture and staffing have led to many difficulties.[157] Traditional jails, say these observers, were built on the assumption that inmates are inherently violent and potentially destructive. Through the use of thick walls, bars, and other architectural barriers, jails were constructed to give staff maximum control and to restrict inmates' movements. Such institutions, however, also limit the correctional staff's visibility and access to confinement areas. As a consequence, they tend to encourage just the kinds of inmate behavior that jails were meant to control. Today, efficient hallway patrols and expensive video technology help in overcoming the limits that old jail architecture places on supervision.

In an effort to solve many of the problems that dogged jails in the past, a new jail-management strategy emerged during the 1970s. Prison architects developed a new style of jail architecture in which modern designs were used to improve communications between inmates and staff, allowing for enhanced supervision.

■ **new-generation jail**   A temporary confinement facility that eliminates many of the traditional barriers between inmates and correctional personnel. Also called *podular jail, direct-supervision jail,* and *indirect-supervision jail.*
■ **regional jail**   A jail that is built and run using the combined resources of a variety of local jurisdictions.

■ **theme**   What are direct-supervision jails? How do they differ from traditional jails? Advocates of direct-supervision jails make many arguments in support of them. Do you believe that such jails are superior to their predecessors? Why or why not?
■ **theme**   How does the AJA code of ethics (see the "Ethics and Professionalism" box in this chapter) seek to balance individual rights (of inmates and guards) with public-order concerns?

These **new-generation jails**, also known as podular jails, allow for continuous observation of inmates. New-generation jails are of two types: direct-supervision and indirect-supervision jails.[158] *Direct-supervision jails* cluster cells around a central living area or "pod," which contains tables, chairs, and televisions. A correctional officer is stationed within each pod and is able to observe inmate interaction and can relate to inmates on a personal level. During the day, inmates stay in the open area (dayroom) and are typically not permitted to go to their rooms except with permission of the officer in charge. *Indirect-supervision jails* are similar in construction to direct-supervision facilities, but they place the correctional officer's station inside of a secure room. Officers are able to communicate with inmates through the use of microphones, and speakers with built-in microphones are placed inside living areas.

New-generation jails help eliminate the old physical barriers that separated staff and inmates in traditional facilities. In a number of new-generation jails, large reinforced Plexiglas panels supplanted walls and serve to separate activity areas, such as classrooms and dining halls, from one another. Soft furniture is the rule throughout such institutions, and individual rooms take the place of cells, allowing inmates at least a modicum of personal privacy. In today's new-generation jails, 16 to 46 inmates typically live in one pod, with correctional staffers present among the inmate population around the clock.

New-generation jails have been touted for their tendency to reduce inmate dissatisfaction and for their ability to deter rape and violence among the inmate population. By eliminating many architectural barriers to staff–inmate interaction, new-generation facilities are said to place officers back in control of institutions. Numerous studies have demonstrated the success of such jails in reducing the likelihood of inmate victimization. One such study also found that staff morale in direct-supervision jails was far higher than in traditional institutions, that inmates reported reduced stress levels, and that fewer inmate-on-inmate and inmate-on-staff assaults occurred.[159] Similarly, sexual assault, jail rape, suicide, and escape have all been found to occur far less frequently in direct-supervision facilities than in traditional institutions.[160] Significantly, new-generation jails appear to be substantially less susceptible to lawsuits brought by inmates and to adverse court-ordered judgments against jail administrators.

Jails and the Future

In contrast to more visible issues confronting the justice system— such as the death penalty, gun control, terrorism, and big-city gangs—jails have received relatively little attention from the media

and have generally escaped close public scrutiny.[161] National efforts are under way, however, to improve the quality of jail life. Some changes involve adding crucial programs for inmates. An American Jail Association (AJA) study of drug-treatment programs in jails, for example, found that "a small fraction (perhaps fewer than 10%) of inmates needing drug treatment actually receive these services."[162]

Jail industries are another growing programmatic area. The best of them serve the community while training inmates in marketable skills.[163] In an exemplary effort to humanize its megajails, for example, the Los Angeles County Sheriff's Department opened an inmate telephone-answering service.[164] Many callers contact the sheriff's department daily, requesting information about the county's 22,000 jail inmates. These requests for information were becoming increasingly difficult to handle due to the growing fiscal constraints facing local government. To handle the huge number of calls effectively without tying up sworn law enforcement personnel, the department began using inmates specially trained to handle incoming calls. Eighty inmates were assigned to the project, with groups of different sizes covering shifts throughout the day. Each inmate staffer went through a training program to learn proper telephone procedures and how to run computer terminals containing routine data on the department's inmates. The system now handles 4,000 telephone inquiries a day. The time needed to answer a call and to begin to provide information has dropped from 30 minutes under the old system to a remarkable 10 seconds today.

Capturing much recent attention are **regional jails**—that is, jails that are built and run using the combined resources of a variety of local jurisdictions. Regional jails have begun to replace smaller and often antiquated local jails in at least a few locations. One example of a regional jail is the Western Tidewater Regional Jail, serving the cities of Suffolk and Franklin and the county of Isle of Wright in Virginia.[165] Regional jails, which are just beginning to come into their own, may develop quickly in Virginia, where the state, recognizing the economies of consolidation, offers to reimburse localities up to 50% of the cost of building regional jails.

The emergence of state standards has become an increasingly important area in jail management. Thirty-two states have set standards for municipal and county jails.[166] In 25 states, those standards are mandatory. The purpose of jail standards is to identify basic minimum conditions necessary for inmate health and safety. On the national level, the Commission on Accreditation for Corrections, operated jointly by the American Correctional Association and the federal government, has developed its own set of jail standards,[167] as has the National Sheriff's Association. Both sets of standards are designed to ensure a minimal level of

■ **theme**   Do you agree with the movement towards privatization of prisons or do you believe prisons should remain under the direct control of the government? Explain.

■ **lecture note**   Describe prisons and the privatization movement. Explain the advantages and disadvantages of private prisons.

■ **privatization**   The movement toward the wider use of private prisons.

■ **private prison**   A correctional institution operated by a private firm on behalf of local, state, or federal government.

Inmates playing cards at the Los Angeles North County Correctional Facility in Saugus, California. The Los Angeles County jail system is the largest in the world, housing more than 20,000 inmates on a given day. What are direct-supervision jails?

comfort and safety in local lockups. Increased standards, though, are costly. Local jurisdictions, already hard-pressed to meet other budgetary demands, will probably be slow to upgrade their jails to meet such external guidelines unless forced to do so. In a study of 61 jails that was designed to test compliance with the National Sheriff's Association guidelines, Ken Kerle discovered that in many standards areas—especially those of tool control, armory planning, community resources, release preparation, and riot planning—the majority of jails were badly out of compliance.[168] Lack of a written plan was the most commonly cited reason for failing to meet the standards.

One final element in the unfolding saga of jail development deserves special mention: the expansion of jails throughout California to accommodate inmates who have been reassigned under that state's realignment strategy (discussed earlier in this chapter). According to the California Board of State and Community Corrections, the state's jail population has been rising significantly as more and more inmates are sent to jail in lieu of state prison, and jail administrators are looking to increase jail capacity.[169] In Fresno County, for example, jail floors that had been closed have now been reopened, and the county is looking for additional places to house inmates.[170] Learn more about jails by visiting the American Jail Association via **http://www.aja.org**.

Private Prisons

State-run prison systems have always contracted with private industries for food, psychological testing, training, and recreational and other services, and it is estimated that more than three dozen states today rely on private businesses to serve a variety of correctional needs. It follows, then, that states have now turned to private industry for the provision of prison space. The **privatization** movement, which began in the early 1980s, was slow to catch on, but it has since grown at a rapid pace. In 1986, only 2,620 prisoners could be found in privately run confinement facilities.[171] But by 2015, privately operated correctional facilities serving as prisons and jails held over 131,300 state and federal prisoners across 30 states and the District of Columbia.[172]

Private prisons held 7% of all state prisoners and 19% of federal prisoners at the start of 2015. New Mexico is the state that uses private prisons the most, with 44% of its inmates held there. One source says that the overall growth rate of the private prison industry has been around 35% annually[173]—comparable to the highest growth rates anywhere in the corporate sector.

Privately run prisons are operated by Corrections Corporation of America (CCA), GEO Group (formerly, Wackenhut Corrections Corporation), Management & Training, LCS Correctional Services,

ethics and professionalism

American Jail Association Code of Ethics for Jail Officers

As an officer employed in a detention/correctional capacity, I swear (or affirm) to be a good citizen and a credit to my community, state, and nation at all times. I will abstain from all questionable behavior which might bring disrepute to the agency for which I work, my family, my community, and my associates. My lifestyle will be above and beyond reproach and I will constantly strive to set an example of a professional who performs his/her duties according to the laws of our country, state, and community and the policies, procedures, written and verbal orders, and regulations of the agency for which I work.

On the job I promise to:

Keep	The institution secure so as to safeguard my community and the lives of the staff, inmates, and visitors on the premises.
Work	With each individual firmly and fairly without regard to rank, status, or condition.
Maintain	A positive demeanor when confronted with stressful situations of scorn, ridicule, danger, and/or chaos.
Report	Either in writing or by word of mouth to the proper authorities those things which should be reported, and keep silent about matters which are to remain confidential according to the laws and rules of the agency and government.
Manage	And supervise the inmates in an even-handed and courteous manner.
Refrain	At all times from becoming personally involved in the lives of the inmates and their families.
Treat	All visitors to the jail with politeness and respect and do my utmost to ensure that they observe the jail regulations.
Take	Advantage of all education and training opportunities designed to assist me to become a more competent officer.
Communicate	With people in or outside of the jail, whether by phone, written word, or word of mouth, in such a way so as not to reflect in a negative manner upon my agency.
Contribute	To a jail environment which will keep the inmate involved in activities designed to improve his/her attitude and character.
Support	All activities of a professional nature through membership and participation that will continue to elevate the status of those who operate our nation's jails. Do my best through word and deed to present an image to the public at large of a jail professional, committed to progress for an improved and enlightened criminal justice system.

Do my best through word and deed to present an image to the public at large of a jail professional, committed to progress for an improved and enlightened criminal justice system.

Thinking about Ethics

1. Why does this code of ethics require jail officers to "take advantage of all education and training opportunities designed to assist (them) to become a more competent officer"? What does education have to do with ethics?

2. Are there any elements that you might add to this code? Are there any that you might delete?

Source: American Jail Association, *Code of Ethics for Jail Officers*, adopted January 10, 1991. Revised May 19, 1993. Web available: https://members.aja.org/ethics.aspx. American Jail Association, copyright 2013. Reprinted with permission.

Emerald Corrections, and numerous other smaller companies. The CCA, the largest of the private prison contractors, houses more than 75,000 inmates at 66 facilities.[174] Most states that use private firms to supplement their prison resources contract with such companies to provide a full range of custodial and other correctional services. State corrections administrators use private companies to reduce overcrowding, lower operating expenses, and avoid lawsuits targeted at state officials and employees.[175] But some studies have shown that private prisons may not bring the kinds of cost savings that had been anticipated.[176] One study by the U.S. General Accounting Office,[177] for example, found "neither cost savings nor substantial differences in the quality of services" between private and publicly run prisons.[178] Similar findings emerged in a report by the Bureau of Justice Assistance. That report, titled *Emerging Issues on Privatized Prisons*, found that "private prisons offer only modest cost savings, which are basically a result of moderate reductions in staffing patterns, fringe benefits, and other labor-related costs."[179]

Many hurdles remain before the privatization movement can effectively provide large-scale custodial supervision. Among the most significant barriers to privatization are old state laws that prohibit private involvement in correctional management. Other practical hurdles exist as well. States that do contract with private firms may face the specter of strikes by corrections officers who do not come under state laws restricting the ability of public employees to strike. Moreover, because responsibility for the protection of inmate rights still lies with the states, their liability will not transfer to private corrections.[180] In today's legal climate, it is unclear whether a state can shield itself or its employees through private prison contracting, but it appears that the courts are unlikely to recognize such shielding. To limit their own liability, states will probably have to oversee private operations as well as set standards for training and custody. In 1997, in the case of *Richardson* v. *McKnight*,[181] the U.S. Supreme Court made it clear that corrections officers employed

CJ | ISSUES
Arguments for and against the Privatization of Prisons

Reasons to Privatize

1. Private companies can provide construction financing options that allow the government to pay only for capacity as needed in lieu of accumulating long-term debt.

2. Private companies offer modern state-of-the-art correctional facility designs that are more efficient to operate and built based upon value engineering specifications.

3. Private operators typically design and construct a new correctional facility in half the time of a comparable government construction project.

4. Private vendors provide government clients with the convenience and accountability of one entity for all compliance issues.

5. Private correctional management companies are able to mobilize rapidly and to specialize in unique facility missions.

6. Private companies provide economic development opportunities by hiring locally and, to the extent possible, purchasing locally.

7. Government can reduce or share its liability exposure through effective contracts with private correctional companies.

8. Government can retain flexibility by limiting the contract duration and by specifying facility missions.

9. Adding other service providers injects competition among both public and private organizations.

Reasons Not to Privatize

1. There are certain responsibilities that only the government should undertake, such as public safety and environmental protection. To provide incarceration or detention, the government has legal, political, and moral obligations. Major constitutional competition among both public and private issues revolves around the deprivation of liberty, discipline, and preserving the constitutional rights of the detained. Related issues include use of force, loss of time credit, and segregation.

2. Few private companies are available from which to choose.

3. Private operators may be inexperienced with key correctional and detention issues.

4. Private companies may become monopolies through political ingratiation, favoritism, etc.

5. Government may lose the ability to perform and properly oversee detention functions over time.

6. The profit motive will inhibit the proper performance of duties. Private companies have financial incentives to cut corners.

7. Procurement process is slow, inefficient, and open to risks.

8. Creating a good, clear contract with effective quality assurance mechanisms and accountability is a daunting task.

9. Lack of enforcement remedies in contracts along with the lack of willingness to utilize available remedies leaves only termination or lawsuits as recourse.

Source: Dennis Cunningham from presentation entitled "Public Strategies for Private Prisons," Department of Homeland Security Immigration and Customs Enforcement Detention Services Manager's Conference, August 10-12, 2012, Dallas, Texas.

---

by a private firm are not entitled to qualified immunity from suits by prisoners charging a violation of Section 1983 of Title 42 of the U.S. Code. (See Chapter 8 for more information on Section 1983 lawsuits.) However, in the 2011 case of *Minneci v. Pollard*, the Court held that a *Bivens* action (a liability action directed specifically at federal officials or enforcement agents) against employees of a privately run federal prison in California could not proceed because state tort law already "authorizes adequate alternative damages actions."[182] In 2001, in the case of *Correctional Services Corporation v. Malesko*,[183] the Court found that private corporations acting under color of federal law cannot be held responsible in a *Bivens* action because the purpose of *Bivens* (which was discussed in Chapter 8) "is to deter individual federal officers from committing Constitutional violations."[184]

Perhaps the most serious legal issues confront states that contract to hold inmates outside of their own jurisdiction. More than a decade ago, for example, two inmates escaped from a 240-man sex-offender unit run by the Corrections Corporation of America (CCA) under contract with the state of Oregon. Problems immediately arose because the CCA unit was located near Houston, Texas—not in Oregon, where the men had originally been sentenced to confinement. Following the escape, Texas officials were unsure whether they even had arrest power over the former prisoners, as their escape was not a crime in Texas. Although prison escape *is* a crime under Texas

law, the law applies to only state-run facilities, not to private facilities where correctional personnel are not employed by the state or empowered in any official capacity by state law. Harris County (Texas) Prosecutor John Holmes explained the situation this way: "They have not committed the offense of escape under Texas law ... and the only reason at all that they're subject to being arrested and were arrested was because during their leaving the facility, they assaulted a guard and took his motor vehicle. That we can charge them with and have."[185]

Opponents of the movement toward privatization cite these and many other issues. They claim that, aside from legal concerns, cost reductions via the use of private facilities can be achieved only by lowering standards. They fear a return to the inhumane conditions of early jails, as private firms seek to turn prisons into profit-making operations. For states that do choose to contract with private firms, the National Institute of Justice (NIJ) recommends a "regular and systematic sampling" of former inmates to appraise prison conditions, as well as annual on-site inspections of each privately run institution. State personnel serving as monitors should be stationed in large facilities, says the NIJ, and a "meticulous review" of all services should be conducted before the contract renewal date.[186] Finally, some fear that private prisons skim prisoners who are the "best of the worst" and leave the "worst of the worst" in public-run institutions, making *those* populations even more difficult to manage.

Reed Saxon/AP Wide World Photos

The 2,300-bed California City Correctional Center in the Mojave Desert town of California City. The facility, which opened in December 1999, was built by the Corrections Corporation of America (CCA) to provide medium-security correctional services under a contract with the Federal Bureau of Prisons. The Nashville-based CCA says that it can run prisons as efficiently as the government, and its supporters claim that private prisons are the way of the future. Do you agree? Why or why not?

SUMMARY

- Before the development of prisons in the late eighteenth and early nineteenth centuries, early criminal punishments were frequently cruel and torturous. Flogging, mutilation, branding, and public humiliation were some of the physical punishments imposed on offenders before the development of prisons.

- In an important historical development, around the year 1800, imprisonment *as* punishment replaced the notion of imprisonment *for* punishment. The state of today's prisons is largely the result of historical efforts to humanize the treatment of offenders, coupled with recent attempts to have the prison experience reflect prevailing social attitudes toward crime and punishment. Early workhouses, which flourished in Europe a few hundred years ago and housed the noncriminal poor and destitute, provided a model for efforts to institutionalize those whom society perceived as burdensome. Imprisonment in the United States began with the penitentiary philosophy of the Pennsylvania Quakers, who believed that solitary confinement and meditation on one's transgressions could lead to reformation. Soon, however, the mass-prison philosophy, represented by prisons like Auburn Prison in New York, won the day, and the contemporary system of imprisonment—in which relatively large numbers of people are confined together and often allowed to interact closely—emerged.

- Prisons today are largely classified according to security level, such as maximum, medium, and minimum security. Most contemporary American correctional facilities are medium or minimum security. Although the goals of recidivism and deterrence are still important in the minds of corrections administrators, today's prisons tend to warehouse inmates awaiting release. Public disappointment with high rates of recidivism has produced a prison system today that is focused on the concept of just deserts and that is only beginning to emerge from the strong influence of the nothing-works doctrine discussed in this chapter. Overcrowded facilities are still the norm in many jurisdictions, although a nationwide effort is now underway to reduce the size of prison populations everywhere.

- In contrast to prisons, which are long-time confinement facilities designed to hold those who have been sentenced to serve time for committing crime, jails are short-term confinement facilities whose traditional purpose has been to hold those awaiting trial or sentencing. Inmates who have been tried and sentenced may also be held at jails until their transfer to a prison facility, and today's jails sometimes hold inmates serving short sentences of confinement. Recently, the emergence of direct-supervision jails, in which traditional barriers between inmates and staff have been mostly eliminated, seems to have reduced the incidence of jail violence and can be credited with improving the conditions of jailed inmates in jurisdictions where such facilities operate.

- Privately run correctional facilities, or private prisons, have grown in number over the past few decades as the movement toward the privatization of correctional facilities has gained steam. Private prisons, operated by for-profit corporations, hold inmates on behalf of state governments or the federal government and provide for their care and security. A number of questions remain as to the role such facilities will play in the future, including whether they can be cost-effective and whether they can somehow reduce the legal liability of state governments and government employees that is often associated with confinement.

KEY TERMS

ADMAX, 446
Ashurst-Sumners Act, 428
Auburn system, 425
classification system, 445
design capacity, 441
industrial prison, 427
jail, 450
justice model, 434
lex talionis, 420
medical model, 430
new-generation jail, 454
nothing-works doctrine, 433
operational capacity, 441

Pennsylvania system, 423
prison, 420
prison capacity, 441
private prison, 455
privatization, 455
rated capacity, 441
reformatory style, 425
regional jail, 454
selective incapacitation, 443
state-use system, 428
warehousing, 432
work release, 432
workhouse, 422

KEY NAMES

Zebulon Brockway, 427
Sir Walter Crofton, 425
Alexander Maconochie, 425

Robert Martinson, 432
Alexis de Tocqueville, 425

QUESTIONS FOR REVIEW

1. What types of criminal punishments were used before the advent of imprisonment as a criminal sanction? How have early punishments influenced modern correctional philosophy?
2. Trace the historical development of prisons in the United States, beginning with the Pennsylvania system. How has correctional practice in America changed over time? What changes do you predict for the future?
3. What are today's prisons like? What purposes do they serve?
4. What role do jails play in American corrections? What are some of the issues that jail administrators currently face?
5. What is the role of private prisons today?

QUESTIONS FOR REFLECTION

1. What are the demographics (social characteristics) of today's prisoners? What gender and racial disparities, if any, exist in today's prison population?
2. What is the just deserts model of corrections? Explain the pros and cons of this model. How did it lead to an increased use of imprisonment and to prison overcrowding?
3. What is the relationship, if any, between changes in the rate of criminal offending and changes in the rate of imprisonment in America during the last decade? What is the reason for that relationship?
4. What will be the state of private prisons two or three decades from now?

NOTES

i. Bureau of Justice Statistics, *Prisoners in 1998* (Washington, DC: BJS, 1999), p. 7.
1. Dan Walters, "With California Prison Overcrowding, Jerry Brown Still Traversing a Minefield," *The Sacramento Bee*, January 9, 2013, http://www.sacbee.com/2013/01/09/5101509/dan-walters-with-california-prison.html#storylink=cpy (accessed March 3, 2013).
2. "Steven Martinez, Quadriplegic Rapist, Will Be Freed from California Prison," Huffington Post, http://www.huffingtonpost.com/2012/11/16/steven-martinez-quadriplegic-rapist-_n_2145339.html (accessed October 15, 2013).
3. Rob Quinn, "Quadriplegic Rapist Denied Parole," *Newser*, May 25, 2011, http://www.newser.com/story/119382/quadriplegic-rapist-denied-parole.html (accessed June 1, 2011).
4. Lauren Steussy and Chris Chan, "Quadriplegic Rapist to Be Released from Prison," NBC San Diego, http://www.nbcsandiego.com/news/local/Quadriplegic-Rapist-to-be-Released-from-Prison-179722421.html (accessed March 3, 2013).
5. *Brown v. Plata*, 563 U.S. ____ (2011).
6. David G. Savage and Patrick McGreevy, "U.S. Supreme Court Orders Massive Inmate Release to Relieve California's Crowded Prisons," *Los Angeles Times*, May 24, 2011, http://articles.latimes.com/2011/may/24/local/la-me-court-prisons-20110524 (accessed June 1, 2011).
7. *Plata v. Brown*, U.S. Court of Appeals for the Ninth Circuit, No. 13-15466 (decided May 28, 2014).
8. Camden Pelham, *Chronicles of Crime: A Series of Memoirs and Anecdotes of Notorious Characters* (London: T. Miles, 1887), pp. 28–30.
9. This section owes much to Harry Elmer Barnes and Negley K. Teeters, *New Horizons in Criminology*, 3rd ed. (Upper Saddle River, NJ: Prentice Hall, 1959).
10. Ibid., p. 290.
11. Ann O'Hanlon, "New Interest in Corporal Punishment: Several States Weigh Get-Tough Measures," *Washington Post* wire service, March 5, 1995.
12. Barnes and Teeters, *New Horizons in Criminology*, p. 292.
13. Ibid.
14. Ibid., p. 293.
15. Arthur Evans Wood and John Barker Waite, *Crime and Its Treatment: Social and Legal Aspects of Criminology* (New York: American Book Company, 1941), p. 488.
16. John Howard, *State of Prisons* (London, 1777; reprint, New York: E. P. Dutton, 1929).
17. Although some writers hold that the Quakers originated the concept of solitary confinement for prisoners, there is evidence that the practice already existed in England before 1789. John Howard, for example, described solitary confinement in use at Reading Bridewell in the 1780s.
18. Vergil L. Williams, *Dictionary of American Penology: An Introduction* (Westport, CT: Greenwood Press, 1979), p. 200.
19. Barnes and Teeters, *New Horizons in Criminology*, p. 348.
20. Williams, *Dictionary of American Penology*, p. 29.
21. With regard to cost, supporters of the Pennsylvania system argued that it was actually less expensive than the Auburn style of imprisonment because it led more quickly to reformation.
22. Williams, *Dictionary of American Penology*, p. 30.
23. Gustave de Beaumont and Alexis de Tocqueville, *On the Penitentiary System in the United States, and Its Application in France* (Philadelphia: Carey, Lea and Blanchard, 1833).

24. Barnes and Teeters, *New Horizons in Criminology,* p. 428.

25. Ibid.

26. Ibid.

27. Wood and Waite, *Crime and Its Treatment,* p. 555, citing U.S. Bureau of Labor Statistics.

28. See North Carolina Department of Corrections, Correction Enterprises website, http://www.doc.state.nc.us/eprise (accessed October 20, 2011).

29. See U.S. Department of Justice, Federal Prison Industries, Inc., website, http://www.unicor.gov.

30. Robert Mintz, "Federal Prison Industry—The Green Monster, Part One: History and Background," *Crime and Social Justice,* Vol. 6 (fall/winter 1976), pp. 41–48.

31. William G. Saylor and Gerald G. Gaes, "PREP Study Links UNICOR Work Experience with Successful Post-Release Outcome," *Corrections Compendium* (October 1994), pp. 5–6, 8.

32. Criminal Justice Associates, *Private Sector Involvement in Prison-Based Businesses: A National Assessment* (Washington, DC: U.S. Government Printing Office, 1985). See also National Institute of Justice, *Corrections and the Private Sector* (Washington, DC: U.S. Government Printing Office, 1985).

33. The PIECP was first authorized under the Justice System Improvement Act of 1979 (Public Law 96-157, Sec. 827) and later expanded under the Justice Assistance Act of 1984 (Public Law 98-473, Sec. 819). The Crime Control Act of 1990 (Public Law 101-647) authorizes continuation of the program indefinitely.

34. Domingo S. Herraiz, *Prison Industry Enhancement Certification Program* (Washington, DC: Bureau of Justice Assistance, 2004).

35. National Correctional Industries Association, "PIECP: First Quarter 2013 Statistical Data Report," http://www.nationalcia.org/wp-content/uploads/Quarter-1-2013-Statistical-Report.pdf (accessed September 4, 2013).

36. Kevin Pieper, "States Stop Funding Prison Work Crews," *USA Today,* September 14, 2011, p. 3A.

37. Barnes and Teeters, *New Horizons in Criminology,* p. 355.

38. Williams, *Dictionary of American Penology,* p. 225.

39. Ibid., p. 64.

40. Ibid., p. 227.

41. Donal E. J. MacNamara, "Medical Model in Corrections: Requiescat in Pacis," in Fred Montanino, ed., *Incarceration: The Sociology of Imprisonment* (Beverly Hills, CA: Sage, 1978).

42. For a description of the community-based format in its heyday, see Andrew T. Scull, *Decarceration: Community Treatment and the Deviant—A Radical View* (Upper Saddle River, NJ: Prentice Hall, 1977).

43. Ibid., p. 51.

44. Williams, *Dictionary of American Penology,* p. 45.

45. Ibid.

46. Clemens Bartollas, *Introduction to Corrections* (New York: Harper and Row, 1981), pp. 166–167.

47. The act also established home furloughs and community treatment centers.

48. National Advisory Commission on Criminal Justice Standards and Goals, Standard 2.17, Part 2c.

49. *Recidivism* can be defined in various ways according to the purpose the term is intended to serve in a particular study or report. Recidivism is usually defined as rearrest (versus reconviction) and generally includes a time span of five years, although some Bureau of Justice Statistics studies have used six years, and other studies one or two years, as definitional criteria.

50. Various advocates of the just deserts, or justice, model can be identified. For a detailed description of rehabilitation and just deserts, see Michael A. Pizzi, Jr., "The Medical Model and the 100 Years War," *Law Enforcement News,* July 7, 1986, pp. 8, 13; and MacNamara, "Medical Model in Corrections."

51. Bureau of Justice Statistics, *Annual Report, 1987* (Washington, DC: BJS, 1988), p. 70.

52. Ibid.

53. Ibid.

54. Robert Martinson, "What Works: Questions and Answers about Prison Reform," *Public Interest,* No. 35 (1974), pp. 22–54. See also Douglas Lipton, Robert M. Martinson, and Judith Wilkes, *The Effectiveness of Correctional Treatment: A Survey of Treatment Evaluation Studies* (New York: Praeger, 1975).

55. L. Sechrest, S. White, and E. Brown, eds., *The Rehabilitation of Criminal Offenders: Problems and Prospects* (Washington, DC: National Academy of Sciences, 1979).

56. U.S. Department of Justice, *Office of Justice Programs Fiscal Year 2000 Program Plan: Resources for the Field* (Washington, DC: Office of Juvenile Justice and Delinquency Prevention, 1999).

57. Timothy A. Hughes, Doris James Wilson, and Allen J. Beck, *Trends in State Parole, 1990–2000* (Washington, DC: Bureau of Justice Statistics, 2001).

58. E. Ann Carson, *Prisoners in 2014* (Washington, D.C.: Bureau of Justice Statistics, 2015).

59. Lynn S. Branham, *The Use of Incarceration in the United States: A Look at the Present and the Future* (Washington, DC: American Bar Association, 1992).

60. "Reliance on Prisons Is Costly But Ineffective, ABA Panel Says," *Criminal Justice Newsletter,* April 15, 1992, p. 7.

61. *Criminal Justice Newsletter,* February 3, 1992, p. 8.

62. American Correctional Association, *Vital Statistics in Corrections* (Laurel, MD: ACA, 2000).

63. Allen J. Beck and Paige M. Harrison, *Prisoners in 2004* (Washington, DC: Bureau of Justice Statistics, 2005).

64. Jeanne B. Stinchcomb, "From Rehabilitation to Retribution: Examining Public Policy Paradigms and Personnel Education Patterns in Corrections," *American Journal of Criminal Justice,* Vol. 27, No. 1 (2002), p. 3.

65. Although many other states require inmates to work on road maintenance, and although the inmates are typically supervised by armed guards, Alabama became the first state in modern times to shackle prisoners on work crews.

66. See "Back on the Chain Gang: Florida Becomes Third State to Resurrect Forced Labor," Associated Press wire service, November 22, 1995.

67. Andrew Ford, "Brevard County Sheriff Chain Gang," *USA Today,* May 2, 2013, http://www.usatoday.com/story/news/nation/2013/05/02/brevard-county-sheriff-chain-gang/2130335/ (accessed August 9, 2013).

68. See Debra L. Dailey, "Summary of the 1998 Annual Conference of the National Association of Sentencing Commissions," http://www.ussc.gov/states/dailefsr.pdf (accessed October 30, 2006).

69. The state of Washington is generally credited with having been the first state to pass a three-strikes law by voter initiative (in 1993).

70. For a good overview of the topic, see David Shichor and Dale K. Sechrest, *Three Strikes and You're Out: Vengeance as Public Policy* (Thousand Oaks, CA: Sage, 1996).

71. David S. Broder, "When Tough Isn't Smart," *Washington Post* wire service, March 24, 1994.

72. Roy Walmsley, *World Prison Population List* (Essex, England: International Center for Prison Studies, 2013).

73. Jeremy Travis, Bruce Western, and Steve Redburn, eds., *The Growth of Incarceration in the United States: Exploring Causes and Consequences* (Washington, DC: National Academies Press, 2014), p. 343.

74. James J. Stephan, *Census of State and Federal Correctional Facilities, 2005* (Washington, DC: Bureau of Justice Statistics, 2008).

75. E. Ann Carson, *Prisoners in 2014* (Washington, D.C.: Bureau of Justice Statistics, 2015), All other statistics in this section refer to inmates sentenced to a year or more in prison.

76. Ibid.

77. Ibid.

78. Thomas P. Bonczar, *Prevalence of Imprisonment in the U.S. Population, 1974–2001* (Washington, DC: Bureau of Justice Statistics, 2003), p. 1.

79. Carson, *Prisoners in 2014.*

80. Federal Bureau of Prisons, "Statistics," http://www.bop.gov/about/statistics/population_statistics.jsp (accessed July 31, 2015).

81. Ibid.

82. Carson, *Prisoners in 2014.*

83. Bonczar, *Prevalence of Imprisonment in the U.S. Population, 1974–2001*, p. 1.

84. Ibid., p. 8.

85. Carson, *Prisoners in 2014.*

86. Ibid.

87. Robert M. Carter, Richard A. McGee, and E. Kim Nelson, *Corrections in America* (Philadelphia: J. B. Lippincott, 1975), pp. 122–123.

88. James J. Stephan, *State Prison Expenditures, 2001* (Washington, DC: Bureau of Justice Statistics, 2004); and Administrative Office of the United States Courts, "Newly Available: Costs of Incarceration and Supervision in FY 2010," June 23, 2011, http://www.uscourts.gov/News/NewsView/11-06-23/Newly_Available_Costs_of_Incarceration_and_Supervision_in_FY_2010.aspx (accessed May 21, 2012).

89. Tracey Kyckelhahn, *Justice Expenditures and Employment Extracts Program 2010,* (Washington, DC: Bureau of Justice Statistics, July 2014).

90. Carson, *Prisoners in 2014.* Much of the decline in state prison populations, however, can be accounted for the way in which incarcerated felons are counted—especially in the state of California, where a strategy of realignment has shifted state prisoners to county jails.

91. Julie Samuels, Nancy La Vigne, Samuel Taxy, *Stemming the Tide: Strategies to Reduce the Growth and Cut the Cost of the Federal Prison System* (Washington, DC: November 2013), p.1.

92. United States Government Accountability Office, Bureau of Prisons: *Growing Inmate Crowding Negatively Affects Inmates, Staff, and Infrastructure* (Washington, DC: GAO, September 2012).

93. Carson, *Prisoners in 2014.*

94. *Rhodes v. Chapman,* 452 U.S. 337 (1981).

95. D. Greenberg, "The Incapacitative Effect of Imprisonment, Some Estimates," *Law and Society Review,* Vol. 9 (1975), pp. 541–580. See also Jacqueline Cohen, "Incapacitating Criminals: Recent Research Findings," National Institute of Justice, *Research in Brief* (Washington, DC: NIJ, December 1983).

96. For information on identifying dangerous repeat offenders, see M. Chaiken and J. Chaiken, *Selecting Career Criminals for Priority Prosecution,* final report (Cambridge, MA: Abt Associates, 1987).

97. J. Monahan, *Predicting Violent Behavior: An Assessment of Clinical Techniques* (Beverly Hills, CA: Sage, 1981).

98. S. Van Dine, J. P. Conrad, and S. Dinitz, *Restraining the Wicked: The Incapacitation of the Dangerous Offender* (Lexington, MA: Lexington Books, 1979).

99. Paul Gendreau, Tracy Little, and Claire Goggin, "A Meta-analysis of the Predictors of Adult Offender Recidivism: What Works!" *Criminology,* Vol. 34, No. 4 (November 1996), pp. 575–607.

100. Nicole D. Porter, *On the Chopping Block 2012: State Prison Closings* (Washington, DC: The Sentencing Project, December 2012).

101. California Department of Corrections and Rehabilitation, *The Future of California Corrections* (Sacramento, CA: California Department of Corrections and Rehabilitation, 2012), http://www.cdcr.ca.gov/2012plan/docs/plan/complete.pdf (accessed November 8, 2015).

102. Jon Lender, "Prisoner Release Bill Wins Final Approval," *The Hartford Courant,* May 31, 2001, http://www.ctnow.com/news/hc-house-prisoners-program-0601-20110531,0,6846758.story (accessed June 4, 2011).

103. George Camp and Camille Camp, "Stopping Escapes: Perimeter Security," *Prison Construction Bulletin* (Washington, DC: National Institute of Justice, 1987).

104. Adapted from G. A. Grizzle and A. D. Witte, "Efficiency in Collections Agencies," in Gordon P. Whitaker and Charles D. Phillips, eds., *Evaluating the Performance of Criminal Justice Agencies* (Washington, DC: National Institute of Justice, 1983).

105. Patricia L. Hardyman et al., *Internal Prison Classification Systems: Case Studies in Their Development and Implementation* (Washington, DC: National Institute of Corrections, 2002), from which some of the wording in this section is taken.

106. Ibid.

107. *Johnson v. California,* 543 U.S. 499 (2005).

108. U.S. Bureau of Prisons, "Facilities," http://www.bop.gov/map.html (accessed February 2, 2005).

109. Some of the information in this section is derived from Federal Bureau of Prisons, *About the Federal Bureau of Prisons* (Washington, DC: BOP, 2001).

110. Federal Bureau of Prisons, *Monday Morning Highlights,* May 30, 2013.

111. Kamala Malli-Kane, Barbara Parthasarathy, and William Adams, *Examining Growth in the Federal Prison Population, 1998 to 2010* (Washington, DC: Urban Institute, 2012), p. 3.

112. Federal Bureau of Prisons, "About the Bureau of Prisons," http://www.bop.gov/about/index.jsp (accessed November 7, 2015).

113. Federal Bureau of Prisons, "Quick Facts," http://www.bop.gov/about/facts.jsp (accessed July 5, 2013).

114. Ibid.

115. For additional information, see Dennis Cauchon, "The Alcatraz of the Rockies," *USA Today,* November 16, 1994.

116. "Congress OKs Inmate Fees to Offset Costs of Prison," *Criminal Justice Newsletter,* October 15, 1992, p. 6.

117. Stephan, *State Prison Expenditures, 2001,* p. 3.

118. National Institute of Corrections website, http://www.nicic.org (accessed November 7, 2015).

119. Ibid.

120. Doris J. James, *Profile of Jail Inmates, 2002* (Washington, DC: Bureau of Justice Statistics, 2004), p. 2.

121. Todd D. Minton and Zhen Zeng, *Jail Inmates at Midyear 2014—Statistical Tables* (Washington, DC: Bureau of Justice Statistics, 2015), p. 1.

122. Ibid.

123. James, *Profile of Jail Inmates, 2002,* p. 1.

124. BJS, *Jail Inmates at Midyear 2014,* p. 9.

125. James Stephan, *Census of Jail Facilities, 2006* (Washington, DC: Bureau of Justice Statistics, 2011), p. 1.

126. Ibid.

127. Ibid.

128. BJS, *Jail Inmates at Midyear 2014,* p. 9.

129. Ibid., p. 3.

130. James, *Profile of Jail Inmates, 2002,* p. 2.

131. Stephan, *Census of Jails, 1999.*

132. See Gale Holland, "L.A. Jail Makes Delayed Debut," *USA Today,* January 27, 1997, p. 3A.

133. See Dale Stockton, "Cook County Illinois Sheriff's Office," *Police,* October 1996, pp. 40–43. The Cook County Department of Correction operates ten separate jails, which house approximately 9,000 inmates. The department employs more than 2,800 correctional officers.

134. William J. Sabol and Todd D. Minton, *Jail Inmates at Midyear 2007* (Washington, DC: Bureau of Justice Statistics, 2008), p. 3.

135. Todd D. Minton and Daniela Golinelli, *Jail Inmates at Midyear 2013–Statistical Tables* (Washington, DC: Bureau of Justice Statistics, 2013), p. 10.

136. Ibid., p. 7.

137. William Reginald Mills and Heather Barrett, "Meeting the Special Challenge of Providing Health Care to Women Inmates in the '90's," *American Jails,* Vol. 4, No. 3 (September/October 1990), p. 55.

138. Ibid., p. 21.

139. Ibid.

140. Ibid., p. 55.

141. American Correctional Association, *Vital Statistics in Corrections.*

142. Mills and Barrett, "Providing Health Care to Women Inmates," p. 55.

143. Ibid.

144. Linda L. Zupan, "Women Corrections Officers in the Nation's Largest Jails," *American Jails* (January/February 1991), pp. 59–62.

145. Linda L. Zupan, "Women Corrections Officers in Local Jails," paper presented at the annual meeting of the Academy of Criminal Justice Sciences, Nashville, TN, March 1991.

146. Ibid., p. 6.

147. "Jail Overcrowding in Houston Results in Release of Inmates," *Criminal Justice Newsletter,* October 15, 1990, p. 5.

148. Bureau of Justice Statistics, *Census of Local Jails, 1988* (Washington, DC: BJS, 1991), p. 31.

149. Kathleen Maguire and Ann L. Pastore, *Sourcebook of Criminal Justice Statistics, 1994* (Washington, DC: U.S. Government Printing Office, 1995).

150. BJS, *Jail Inmates at Midyear 2014,* p. 6.

151. Carson, *Prisoners in 2014.*

152. Christopher J. Mumola, *Suicide and Homicide in State Prisons and Local Jails* (Washington, DC: Bureau of Justice Statistics, 2005), p. 1.

153. George P. Wilson and Harvey L. McMurray, "System Assessment of Jail Overcrowding Assumptions," paper presented at the annual meeting of the Academy of Criminal Justice Sciences, Nashville, TN, March 1991.

154. Andy Hall, *Systemwide Strategies to Alleviate Jail Crowding* (Washington, DC: National Institute of Justice, 1987).

155. Ibid.

156. Linda L. Zupan and Ben A. Menke, "The New Generation Jail: An Overview," in Joel A. Thompson and G. Larry Mays, eds., *American Jails: Public Policy Issues* (Chicago: Nelson-Hall, 1991), p. 180.

157. Ibid.

158. Herbert R. Sigurdson, Billy Wayson, and Gail Funke, "Empowering Middle Managers of Direct Supervision Jails," *American Jails* (winter 1990), p. 52.

159. Byron Johnson, "Exploring Direct Supervision: A Research Note," *American Jails* (March/April 1994), pp. 63–64.

160. H. Sigurdson, *The Manhattan House of Detention: A Study of Podular Direct Supervision* (Washington, DC: National Institute of Corrections, 1985). For similar conclusions, see Robert Conroy, Wantland J. Smith, and Linda L. Zupan, "Officer Stress in the Direct Supervision Jail: A Preliminary Case Study," *American Jails* (November/December 1991), p. 36.

161. For a good review of the future of American jails, see Ron Carroll, "Jails and the Criminal Justice System in the Twenty-First Century," *American Jails* (March/April 1997), pp. 26–31.

162. Robert L. May II, Roger H. Peters, and William D. Kearns, "The Extent of Drug Treatment Programs in Jails: A Summary Report," *American Jails* (September/October 1990), pp. 32–34.

163. See, for example, John W. Dietler, "Jail Industries: The Best Thing That Can Happen to a Sheriff," *American Jails* (July/August 1990), pp. 80–83.

164. Robert Osborne, "Los Angeles County Sheriff Opens New Inmate Answering Service," *American Jails* (July/August 1990), pp. 61–62.

165. See J. R. Dewan, "Regional Jail—The New Kid on the Block," *American Jails* (May/June 1995), pp. 70–72.

166. Tom Rosazza, "Jail Standards: Focus on Change," *American Jails* (November/December 1990), pp. 84–87.

167. American Correctional Association, *Manual of Standards for Adult Local Detention Facilities,* 3rd ed. (College Park, MD: ACA, 1991).

168. Ken Kerle, "National Sheriff's Association Jail Audit Review," *American Jails* (spring 1987), pp. 13–21.

169. Norimitsu Onishi, "In California, County Jails Face Bigger Loads," *New York Times,* August 5, 2012, http://www.nytimes.com/2012/08/06/us/in-california-prison-overhaul-county-jails-face-bigger-load.html (accessed March 3, 2013).

170. Ibid.

171. Beck and Harrison, *Prisoners in 2000,* p. 7.

172. Carson, *Prisoners in 2014.*

173. Eric Bates, "Private Prisons: Over the Next Five Years Analysts Expect the Private Share of the Prison 'Market' to More Than Double," *The Nation,* Vol. 266, No. 1 (1998), pp. 11–18.

174. Mason, *Too Good to Be True,* p. 2.

175. Gary Fields, "Privatized Prisons Pose Problems," *USA Today,* November 11, 1996, p. 3A.

176. Dale K. Sechrest and David Shichor, "Private Jails: Locking Down the Issues," *American Jails,* March/April 1997, pp. 9–18.

177. U.S. General Accounting Office, *Private and Public Prisons: Studies Comparing Operational Costs and/or Quality of Service* (Washington, DC: U.S. Government Printing Office, 1996).

178. Sechrest and Shichor, "Private Jails," p. 10.

179. James Austin and Garry Coventry, *Emerging Issues on Privatized Prisons* (Washington, DC: Bureau of Justice Statistics, 2001), p. ix.

180. For a more detailed discussion of this issue, see Austin and Coventry, *Emerging Issues on Privatized Prisons.*

181. *Richardson* v. *McKnight,* 521 U.S. 399 (1997).

182. *Minneci* v. *Pollard,* 565 U.S. ____ (2012).

183. *Correctional Services Corporation* v. *Malesko,* 122 S.Ct. 515 (2001).

184. Ibid.

185. Quoted in Bates, "Private Prisons."

186. Judith C. Hackett et al., "Contracting for the Operation of Prisons and Jails," National Institute of Justice Research in Brief (Washington, DC: NIJ, June 1987), p. 6.

© Image Source/Alamy.

14

PRISON LIFE

LEARNING OBJECTIVES

After reading this chapter, you should be able to

- Describe the realities of prison life and prison subculture from the inmate's point of view.
- Differentiate between men's and women's prisons.
- Describe prison life from the corrections officer's point of view.
- Describe the nature of security threat groups and summarize the causes and stages of prison riots.
- Discuss the legal aspects of prisoners' rights, including the consequences of related precedent-setting U.S. Supreme Court cases.
- Describe the major issues that prisons face today.

Prison walls do not form a barrier separating prison inmates from the protections of the Constitution.

TURNER V. SAFLEY, 482 U.S. 78 (1987)

■ **theme**   What are total institutions? What are the positive and negative qualities of total institutions? Would prisons be better at rehabilitating inmates if they were more open to the outside world?

■ **lecture note**   Describe total institutions as enclosed places where residents share all aspects of their daily lives. Explain that inhabitants of total institutions work, recreate, worship, eat, and sleep together.

■ **total institution**   An enclosed facility separated from society both socially and physically, where the inhabitants share all aspects of their daily lives.

■ **Follow the author's tweets about the latest crime and justice news @schmalleger.**

Introduction

Recently, 23-year-old Laura Kaeppeler, Miss America 2012, dedicated the year of her reign to the theme "Circles of Support: Mentoring Children of Incarcerated Parents."[1] Kaeppeler said, "It's everyday life for millions of children, and it allows me to connect with people on a level they don't expect a pageant contestant to connect with them. This is a real problem people can relate to." Kaeppeler's father had been imprisoned when she was 17 for a white-collar crime.

For many years, prisons and prison life could be described by the phrase "out of sight, out of mind." Very few citizens cared about prison conditions, and those unfortunate enough to be locked away were regarded as lost to the world. By the mid-twentieth century, however, this attitude started to change. Concerned citizens began to offer their services to prison administrators, neighborhoods began accepting work-release prisoners and halfway houses, and social scientists initiated a serious study of prison life. Today, as shows like *Prison Break* make clear, prisons and prison life have entered the American mainstream. Part of the reason for this is that prisons today hold more people than ever before, and incarceration impacts not only those imprisoned but also family members, friends, and victims on the outside.

This chapter describes the realities of prison life today, including prisoner lifestyles, prison subcultures, sexuality in prison, prison violence, and prisoners' rights and grievance procedures. We will discuss both the inmate world and the staff world. A separate section on women in prison details the social structure of women's prisons, daily life in those facilities, and the various types of female inmates. We begin with a brief overview of early research on prison life.

Research on Prison Life—Total Institutions

In 1935, Hans Reimer, who was then chair of the Department of Sociology at Indiana University, set the tone for studies of prison life when he voluntarily served three months in prison as an incognito participant-observer.[2] Reimer reported the results of his studies to the American Prison Association, stimulating many other, albeit less spectacular, efforts to examine prison life. Other early studies include Donald Clemmer's *The Prison Community* (1940),[3] Gresham Sykes's *The Society of Captives* (1958),[4] Richard Cloward and Donald Cressey's *Theoretical*

James Atoa/Alamy

Laura Kaeppeler, Miss America 2012. Kaeppeler dedicated the year of her reign to mentoring the children of incarcerated parents. What do most Americans think of prisons and prisoners?

Studies in Social Organization of the Prison (1960),[5] and Cressey's edited volume, *The Prison* (1961).[6]

These studies and others focused primarily on maximum-security prisons for men. They treated correctional institutions as formal or complex organizations and employed the analytic techniques of organizational sociology, industrial psychology, and administrative science.[7] As modern writers on prisons have observed, "The prison was compared to a primitive society, isolated from the outside world, functionally integrated by a delicate system of mechanisms, which kept it precariously balanced between anarchy and accommodation."[8]

Another approach to the study of prison life was developed by Erving Goffman, who coined the term **total institution** in a 1961 study of prisons and mental hospitals.[9] Goffman described total institutions as places where the same people work, recreate, worship, eat, and sleep together daily. Such places include prisons, concentration camps, mental hospitals, seminaries, and other facilities in which residents are cut off from the larger society either forcibly or willingly. Total institutions are small societies. They evolve their own distinctive values and styles of life and pressure residents to fulfill rigidly prescribed behavioral roles.

■ **theme**   What similarities and differences do you notice between prison society, as described in this chapter, and free society? What might account for the similarities and differences you observe?
■ **lecture note**   Describe prison subculture as a lifestyle that reflects criminal values and behavior patterns characteristic of incarcerated offenders. Note that prison subculture shows amazing consistency among prisons across the United States.
■ **lecture note**   Define prisonization as the socialization of new inmates into prison subculture. Use the five elements of the prison code discussed in the text to describe the realities of that subculture.

■ **prison subculture**   The values and behavioral patterns characteristic of prison inmates. Prison subculture has been found to be surprisingly consistent across the country.
■ **prisonization**   The process whereby newly institutionalized offenders come to accept prison lifestyles and criminal values. Although many inmates begin their prison experience with only a few values that support criminal behavior, the socialization experience they undergo while incarcerated leads to a much greater acceptance of such values.

Generally speaking, the work of prison researchers built on findings of other social scientists who discovered that any group with similar characteristics confined in the same place at the same time develops its own subculture. Prison subcultures, described in the next section, also provide the medium through which prison values are communicated and expectations are made known.

The Male Inmate's World

Two social realities coexist in prison settings. One is the official structure of rules and procedures put in place by the wider society and enforced by prison staff. The other is the more informal but decidedly more powerful inmate world.[10] The inmate world, best described by how closely it touches the lives of inmates, is controlled by **prison subculture**. The realities of prison life—including a large and often densely packed inmate population that must look to the prison environment for all its needs—mean that prison subculture develops independently of the plans of prison administrators and is not easily subjected to the control of prison authorities.

Inmates entering prison discover a whole new social world in which they must participate or face consequences ranging from dangerous ostracism to physical violence and homicide.[11] The socialization of new inmates into the prison subculture has been described as a process of **prisonization**[12]—the new prisoner's learning of convict values, attitudes, roles, and even language. By the time this process is complete, new inmates have become "cons." Gresham Sykes and Sheldon Messinger recognized five elements of the prison code in 1960:[13]

1. Don't interfere with the interests of other inmates. Never rat on a con.
2. Don't lose your head. Play it cool and do your own time.

A corrections officer escorts a prison inmate through a high-security area. Custody and control remain the primary concerns of prison staff throughout the country. Is the emphasis on custody and control justified?

Halfdark/Getty Images

■ **prison argot**   The slang characteristic of prison subcultures and prison life.

■ **lecture note**   Use the "CJ Issues" box titled "Prison Argot: The Language of Confinement" to explain prison argot, the slang used by inmates. Relate it to the slang used by other groups, such as the language used to describe activities on the Internet.

■ **lecture note**   Describe the evolution of prison subculture as new generations of convicts arrive. Explore some of the differences between traditional and emerging subcultural values.

■ **theme**   What are the main subcultures in prisons? How can they all co-exist?

3. Don't exploit inmates. Don't steal. Don't break your word. Be right.
4. Don't whine. Be a man.
5. Don't be a sucker. Don't trust the guards or staff.

Some criminologists have suggested that the prison code is simply a reflection of general criminal values. If so, these values are brought to the institution rather than created there. Either way, the power and pervasiveness of the prison code require convicts to conform to the worldview held by the majority of prisoners.

Stanton Wheeler, Ford Foundation Professor of Law and Social Sciences at the University of Washington, closely examined the concept of prisonization in an early study of the Washington State Reformatory.[14] Wheeler found that the degree of prisonization experienced by inmates tends to vary over time. He described changing levels of inmate commitment to prison norms and values by way of a U-shaped curve. When an inmate first enters prison, Wheeler said, the conventional values of outside society are of paramount importance. As time passes, inmates adopt the lifestyle of the prison. However, within the half year prior to release, most inmates begin to demonstrate a renewed appreciation of conventional values.

Different prisons share aspects of a common inmate culture.[15] **Prison argot**, or language, provides one example of how widespread prison subculture can be. The terms used to describe inmate roles in one institution are generally understood in others. The word *rat*, for example, is prison slang for an informer. Popularized by crime movies of the 1950s, the term is understood today by members of the wider society. Recent research into prison language suggests that argot in prison reflects and reinforces "the organization, language, and status hierarchy of...prison subculture."[16] Researchers suggest that correctional administrators and staff must learn the language of prison in order to maximize staff efficiency, and to ensure the safety of staff and inmates.[17] Words common to prison argot are shown in the nearby "CJ Issues" box.

The Evolution of Prison Subcultures

Prison subcultures change constantly. Like any other American subculture, they evolve to reflect the concerns and experiences of the wider culture, reacting to new crime-control strategies and embracing novel opportunities for crime. The AIDS epidemic of the 1970s and 1980s, for example, brought about changes in prison sexual behavior, at least for a segment of the inmate population, and the emergence of a high-tech criminal group has further differentiated convict types. Because of such changes, John Irwin, as he was completing his classic study titled *The Felon*[18] (1970), expressed worry that his book was already obsolete.[19] *The Felon*, for all its insights into prison subcultures, follows in the descriptive tradition of works by Clemmer and Reimer. Irwin recognized that by 1970, prison subcultures had begun to reflect the cultural changes sweeping America. A decade later, other investigators of prison subcultures were able to write, "It was no longer meaningful to speak of a single inmate culture or even subculture. By the time we began our field research...it was clear that the unified, oppositional convict culture, found in the sociological literature on prisons, no longer existed."[20]

Charles Stastny and Gabrielle Tyrnauer, describing prison life at Washington State Penitentiary in 1982, discovered four clearly distinguishable subcultures: (1) official, (2) traditional, (3) reform, and (4) revolutionary.[21] Official culture was promoted by the staff and by the administrative rules of the institution. Enthusiastic participants in official culture were mostly corrections officers and other staff members, although inmates were also well aware of the normative expectations that official culture imposed on them. Official culture affected the lives of inmates primarily through the creation of a prisoner hierarchy based on sentence length, prison jobs, and the "perks" that cooperation with the dictates of official culture could produce. Traditional prison culture, described by early writers on the subject, still existed, but its participants spent much of their time lamenting the decline of the convict code among younger prisoners. Reform culture was unique at Washington State Penitentiary. It was the result of a brief experiment with inmate self-government during the early 1970s. Some elements of prison life that evolved during the experimental period survived the termination of self-government and were eventually institutionalized in what Stastny and Tyrnauer called "reform culture." They included inmate participation in civic-style clubs, citizen involvement in the daily activities of the prison, banquets, and inmate speaking tours. Revolutionary culture built on the radical political rhetoric of the disenfranchised and found a ready audience among minority prisoners who saw themselves as victims of society's basic unfairness. Although they did not participate in it, revolutionary inmates understood traditional prison culture and generally avoided running afoul of its rules.

The Functions of Prison Subcultures

How do social scientists and criminologists explain the existence of prison subcultures? Although people around the world live in groups and create their own cultures, in few cases does the intensity of human interaction approach the level found in prisons. As we discussed in Chapter 13, many of today's prisons are densely crowded places where inmates can find no retreat from the constant demands of staff and the pressures of fellow prisoners. Prison subcultures, according to some authors, are fundamentally an adaptation to deprivation and confinement. In *The Society of Captives*, Sykes called these deprivations the "pains of imprisonment."[22] The pains of imprisonment—the frustrations induced by the rigors of confinement—form the nexus of a deprivation model of prison subculture. Sykes said that prisoners are deprived of (1) liberty, (2) goods and services, (3) heterosexual relationships, (4) autonomy, and (5) personal security—and that these deprivations lead to the development of subcultures intended to ameliorate the personal pains that accompany deprivation.

Prison subcultures, according to some authors, are fundamentally an adaptation to deprivation and confinement.

In contrast to the deprivation model, the importation model of prison subculture suggests that inmates bring with them values, roles, and behavior patterns from the outside world. Such external values, second nature as they are to career offenders, depend substantially on the criminal worldview. When offenders are confined, these external elements shape the social world of inmates.

The social structure of the prison—the accepted and relatively permanent social arrangements—is another element that shapes prison subculture. Clemmer's early prison study recognized nine structural dimensions of inmate society. He said that prison society could be described in terms of the following:[23]

- Prisoner–staff dichotomy
- Three general classes of prisoners
- Work gangs and cell-house groups
- Racial groups
- Type of offense
- Power of inmate "politicians"
- Degree of sexual abnormality
- Record of repeat offenses
- Personality differences due to preprison socialization

Clemmer's nine structural dimensions still describe prison life today. When applied to individuals, they designate an inmate's position in the prison "pecking order" and create expectations of the appropriate role for that person. Prison roles serve to satisfy the needs of inmates for power, sexual performance, material possessions, individuality, and personal pleasure and to define the status of one prisoner relative to another. For example, inmate leaders, sometimes referred to as "real men" or "toughs" by prisoners in early studies, offer protection to those who live by the rules. They also provide for a redistribution of wealth inside prison and see to it that the rules of the complex prison-derived economic system—based on barter, gambling, and sexual favors—are observed. For an intimate multimedia portrait of life behind bars, visit **http://www.npr.org/programs/atc/prisondiaries**.

Prison roles serve to satisfy the needs of inmates for power, sexual performance, material possessions, individuality, and personal pleasure and to define the status of one prisoner relative to another.

Prison Lifestyles and Inmate Types

Prison society is strict and often unforgiving. Even so, inmates are able to express some individuality through the choice of a prison lifestyle. John Irwin viewed these lifestyles (like the subcultures of which they are a part) as adaptations to the prison environment.[24] Other writers have since elaborated on these coping mechanisms. Following are some of the types of prisoners that researchers have described.

- *The mean dude.* Some inmates adjust to prison by being violent. Other inmates know that these prisoners are best left alone. The mean dude is frequently written up and spends much time in solitary confinement. This role is most common in male institutions and in maximum-security prisons. For some prisoners, the role of mean dude in prison is similar to the role they played in their life prior to being incarcerated. Certain personality types, such as the psychopath, may feel a natural attraction to this role. Prison culture supports violence in two ways: (1) by expecting inmates to be tough and (2) through the prevalence of the idea that only the strong survive inside prison.

- *The hedonist.* Some inmates build their lives around the limited pleasures available within the confines of prison.

CJ | ISSUES
Prison Argot: The Language of Confinement

Writers who have studied prison life often comment on prisoners' use of a special language or slang termed *prison argot*. This language generally describes prison activities and the roles assigned by prison culture to types of inmates. This box lists a few of the many words and phrases identified in studies by different authors. The first group includes words that are characteristic of men's prisons; the second group includes words used in women's prisons.

Men's Prison Slang

Ace duce: A best friend

Badge (or bull, hack, the man, or screw): A corrections officer

Banger (or burner, shank, or sticker): A knife

Billy: A white man

Boneyard: The conjugal visiting area

Cat-J (or J-cat): A prisoner in need of psychological or psychiatric therapy or medication

Cellie: A cell mate

Chester: A child molester

Dog: A homeboy or friend

Fag: A male inmate who is believed to be a "natural" or "born" homosexual

Featherwood: A white prisoner's woman

Fish: A newly arrived inmate

Gorilla: An inmate who uses force to take what he wants from others

Homeboy: A prisoner from one's hometown or neighborhood

Ink: Tattoos

Lemon squeezer: An inmate who masturbates frequently

Man walking: A phrase used to signal that a guard is coming

Merchant (or peddler): One who sells when he should give

Peckerwood (or wood): A white prisoner

Punk: A male inmate who is forced into a submissive role during homosexual relations

Rat (or snitch): An inmate who squeals (provides information about other inmates to the prison administration)

Schooled: Knowledgeable in the ways of prison life

Shakedown: A search of a cell or of a work area

Teddy bear: Nonaggressive wolves

Tree jumper: A rapist

Turn out: To rape or make into a punk

Wolf: A male inmate who assumes the dominant role during homosexual relations

Women's Prison Slang

Cherry (or cherrie): A female inmate who has not yet been introduced to lesbian activities

Fay broad: A white female inmate

Femme (or mommy): A female inmate who plays the female role during lesbian relations

Safe: The vagina, especially when used for hiding contraband

Stud broad (or daddy): A female inmate who assumes the male role during lesbian relations

References: Gresham Sykes, *The Society of Captives* (Princeton, NJ: Princeton University Press, 1958); Rose Giallombardo, *Society of Women: A Study of a Woman's Prison* (New York: John Wiley, 1966); and Richard A. Cloward et al., *Theoretical Studies in Social Organization of the Prison* (New York: Social Science Research Council, 1960). For a more contemporary listing of prison slang terms, see Reinhold Aman, *Hillary Clinton's Pen Pal: A Guide to Life and Lingo in Federal Prison* (Santa Rosa, CA: Maledicta Press, 1996); Jerome Washington, *Iron House: Stories from the Yard* (Ann Arbor, MI: QED Press, 1994); Morrie Camhi, *The Prison Experience* (Boston: Charles Tuttle, 1989); and Harold Long, *Survival in Prison* (Port Townsend, WA: Loompanics, 1990).

The smuggling of contraband, homosexuality, gambling, drug running, and other officially condemned activities provide the center of interest for prison hedonists. Hedonists generally have an abbreviated view of the future, living only for the "now."

- *The opportunist.* The opportunist takes advantage of the positive experiences prison has to offer. Schooling, trade training, counseling, and other self-improvement activities are the focal points of the opportunist's life in prison. Opportunists are generally well liked by prison staff, but other prisoners shun and mistrust them because they come closest to accepting the role that the staff defines as "model prisoner."
- *The retreatist.* Prison life is rigorous and demanding. Badgering by the staff and actual or feared assaults by other inmates may cause some prisoners to attempt psychological retreat from the realities of imprisonment. Such inmates may experience neurotic or psychotic episodes, become heavily involved in drug and alcohol abuse through the illicit prison economy, or even attempt suicide. Depression and mental illness are the hallmarks of the retreatist personality in prison.
- *The legalist.* The legalist is the "jailhouse lawyer." Convicts facing long sentences, with little possibility for early release through the correctional system, are most likely to turn to the courts in their battle against confinement.
- *The radical.* Radical inmates view themselves as political prisoners. They see society and the successful conformists who populate it as oppressors who have forced criminality on many "good people" through the creation of a system that distributes wealth and power inequitably. The inmate who takes on the radical role is unlikely to receive much sympathy from prison staff.
- *The colonizer.* Some inmates think of prison as their home and don't look forward to leaving. They "know the ropes," have many "friends" inside, and may feel more

■ **lecture note** Discuss homosexuality in prison, and ask why it is so common. Describe the difference between homosexual behavior in prison and homosexual behavior in the free society as the contrast between limited opportunity and free choice. Note that relatively few offenders involved in homosexual activities in prison will continue them upon release.

■ **lecture note** Discuss the problem of prison rape and explain the characteristics of offenders. What effects can sexual assault in prison have on victims?

comfortable institutionalized than on the streets. They typically hold positions of power or respect among the inmate population. Once released, some colonizers commit new crimes to return to prison.

- *The religious.* Some prisoners profess a strong religious faith. They may be born-again Christians, committed Muslims, or even Satanists or witches. Religious inmates frequently attend services, may form prayer groups, and sometimes ask the prison administration to allocate meeting facilities or to create special diets to accommodate their claimed spiritual needs. Although it is certainly true that some inmates have a strong religious faith, staff members are apt to be suspicious of the overly religious prisoner.

- *The gang-banger.* Gang-bangers are affiliated with prison gangs and depend upon the gang for defense and protection. They display gang signs, sport gang-related tattoos, and use their gang membership as a channel for the procurement of desired goods and services both inside and outside of prison.

- *The realist.* The realist sees confinement as a natural consequence of criminal activity and as an unfortunate cost of doing business. This stoic attitude toward incarceration generally leads the realist to "pull his (or her) own time" and to make the best of it. Realists tend to know the inmate code, are able to avoid trouble, and continue in lives of crime once released.

Homosexuality and Sexual Victimization in Prison

Sexual behavior inside prisons is both constrained and encouraged by prison subculture. Sykes's early study of prison argot found many words describing homosexual activity. Among them were the terms *wolf*, *punk*, and *fag*. Wolves were aggressive men who assumed the masculine role in homosexual relations. Punks were forced into submitting to the female role. The term *fag* described a special category of men who had a natural proclivity toward homosexual activity and effeminate mannerisms. Whereas both wolves and punks were fiercely committed to their heterosexual identity and participated in homosexuality only because of prison conditions, fags generally engaged in homosexual lifestyles before their entry into prison and continued to emulate feminine mannerisms and styles of dress once incarcerated.

STR/AFP/Getty Images

Transvestite and ex-inmate Diana Acuna Talquenca (R) and prison inmate Osvaldo Martin Torres, shown on the day of their marriage at Almafuerte prison in Argentina. Homosexuality is common in both men's and women's prisons. How does it differ between the two? Why do Talquenca and Torres provide an exception to the "rule" of male prison homosexuality?

■ **lecture note**   Use Figure 14–1 to discuss the relative proportions of ethnic groups in the nation's prison population. How do students account for the fact that the pie charts shown in the figure do not even approximate the proportions of racial and ethnic groups in the wider society? Should society strive to create a more racially and ethnically "balanced" prison population? If so, how?

Prison homosexuality depends to a considerable degree on the naiveté of young inmates experiencing prison for the first time. Even when newly arrived inmates are protected from fights, older prisoners looking for homosexual liaisons may ingratiate themselves by offering cigarettes, money, drugs, food, or protection. At some future time, these "loans" will be called in, with payoffs demanded in sexual favors. Because the inmate code requires the repayment of favors, the "fish" who tries to resist may quickly find himself face to face with the brute force of inmate society.

Prison rape, which is generally considered to involve physical assault, represents a special category of sexual victimization behind bars. In 2003, Congress mandated the collection of statistics on prison rape as part of the Prison Rape Elimination Act (PREA).[25] The PREA requires the Bureau of Justice Statistics (BJS) to collect data in federal and state prisons, county and city jails, and juvenile institutions, with the U.S. Census Bureau acting as the official repository for collected data.

In 2013, the BJS published the results of its third annual National Inmate Survey (NIS).[26] The survey was conducted in 233 state and federal prisons, 358 local jails, and 15 special confinement facilities operated by Immigration and Customs Enforcement (ICE). A total of 92,449 inmates participated. The survey was also administered to 527 juveniles ages 16 to 17 held in state prisons and 1,211 juveniles of the same age held in local jails. Among the findings:

- An estimated 4.0% of state and federal prison inmates and 3.2% of jail inmates reported experiencing one or more incidents of sexual victimization by another inmate or facility staff in the past 12 months.
- Among state and federal prison inmates, 2.0% (or an estimated 29,300 prisoners) reported an incident involving another inmate, 2.4% (34,100) reported an incident involving facility staff, and 0.4% (5,500) reported both an incident by another inmate and staff.
- About 1.6% of jail inmates (11,900) reported an incident with another inmate, 1.8% (13,200) reported an incident with staff, and 0.2% (2,400) reported both an incident by another inmate and staff.
- An estimated 1.8% of juveniles ages 16 to 17 held in adult prisons and jails reported being victimized by another inmate, compared to 2.0% of adults in prisons and 1.6% of adults in jails; an estimated 3.2% of juveniles ages 16 to 17 held in adult prisons and jails reported experiencing staff sexual misconduct.

- Inmates who reported their sexual orientation as gay, lesbian, bisexual, or other were among those with the highest rates of sexual victimization. Among non-heterosexual inmates, 12.2% of prisoners and 8.5% of jail inmates reported being sexually victimized by another inmate; 5.4% of prisoners and 4.3% of jail inmates reported being victimized by staff.

The PREA survey is only a first step in understanding and eliminating prison rape. As the BJS notes, "Due to fear of reprisal from perpetrators, a code of silence among inmates, personal embarrassment, and lack of trust in staff, victims are often reluctant to report incidents to correctional authorities."[27] Learn more about the PREA and read new survey results as they become available via **http://nicic.gov/prea**.

Humbolt State University sociologist Lee H. Bowker, reviewing studies of sexual violence in prison, provides the following summary observations:[28]

- Most sexual aggressors do not consider themselves homosexuals.
- Sexual release is not the primary motivation for sexual attack.
- Many aggressors must continue to participate in gang rapes to avoid becoming victims themselves.
- The aggressors have themselves suffered much damage to their masculinity in the past.

As in cases of heterosexual rape, sexual assaults in prison are likely to leave psychological scars on the victim long after the physical event is over.[29] Victims of prison rape live in fear, may feel constantly threatened, and can turn to self-destructive activities.[30] Many victims question their masculinity and undergo a personal devaluation. Some victims of prison sexual assault become violent, attacking and sometimes killing the person who raped them. The Human Rights Watch researchers found that prisoners "fitting any part of the following description" are more likely to become rape victims: "young, small in size, physically weak, white, gay, first offender, possessing 'feminine' characteristics such as long hair or a high voice; being unassertive, unaggressive, shy, intellectual, not street-smart, or 'passive'; or having been convicted of a sexual offense against a minor." The researchers also noted that "prisoners with several overlapping characteristics are much more likely than other prisoners to be targeted for abuse."

The report concluded that to reduce the incidence of prison rape, "prison officials should take considerably more care in matching cell mates, and that, as a general rule, double-celling should be avoided."

■ **theme** Figure 14-1 shows that women account for only 7% of all prisoners and that African Americans make up 38% of our nation's prison population. How do you account for the huge disparity between these figures and the percentages of women (about 52%) and African Americans (about 12%) in American society?

■ **lecture note** Use Figure 14-2 to discuss the proportion of underrepresented groups in prison. Ask why the proportion of women in prison is so small and why it continues to grow. Should society strive to achieve a more "equitable" representation of women among the inmate population?

■ **lecture note** Explain that the vast majority of women in prison are parents, and most are custodial parents. Discuss the economic impact this may have on society. Point out that many children of female inmates never visit their mothers during the period of incarceration, explain the various reasons for this, and ask students how they think having an incarcerated parent may affect children.

The Female Inmate's World

As Chapter 13 showed, around 112,961 women were imprisoned in state and federal correctional institutions throughout the United States at the start of 2015, accounting for about 7% of all prison inmates.[31] Texas had the largest number of female prisoners (14,326), exceeded only by the federal government (at 13,999).[32] Figure 14-1 provides a breakdown of the total American prison population by gender and ethnicity. While there are still far more men imprisoned across the nation than women (approximately 13 men for every woman), the number of female inmates is rising.[33] In 1981, women made up only 4% of the nation's overall prison population, but the number of female inmates nearly tripled during the 1980s and is continuing to grow at a rate greater than that of male inmates.

In 2003, the National Institute of Corrections (NIC) published the results of its three-year project on female offenders in adult correctional settings.[34] Findings from the study produced the national profile of incarcerated women that is shown in Table 14-1. Figures 14-2 and 14-3 provide additional details. The NIC says that "women involved in the criminal justice system represent a population marginalized by race, class, and gender."[35] Black women, for example, are overrepresented in correctional populations. White women comprise 50% of the nation's female prison population compared to 21% for black females. However,

Table 14-1 | National Profile of Female Offenders

A profile based on national data for female offenders reveals the following characteristics:

- Disproportionately women of color
- In their early to mid-30s
- Most likely to have been convicted of a drug-related offense
- From fragmented families that include other family members who have been involved with the criminal justice system
- Survivors of physical and/or sexual abuse as children and adults
- Individuals with significant substance-abuse problems
- Individuals with multiple physical and mental health problems
- Unmarried mothers of minor children
- Individuals with a high school or general equivalency diploma (GED) but limited vocational training and sporadic work histories

Source: Barbara Bloom, Barbara Owen, and Stephanie Covington, *Gender-Responsive Strategies: Research, Practice, and Guiding Principles for Women Offenders* (Washington, DC: National Institute of Corrections, 2003).

the imprisonment rate for black females (109 per 100,000) is twice the rate of white females (53 per 100,000).[36]

According to the NIC, women face life circumstances that tend to be specific to their gender, such as sexual abuse, sexual assault, domestic violence, and the responsibility of being the primary caregiver for dependent children. Research shows that female offenders differ significantly from their male counterparts regarding personal histories and pathways to crime.[37] A female offender, for example, is more likely to have been the primary caretaker of young children at the time of her arrest, more likely to have experienced physical and/or sexual abuse, and more likely to have distinctive physical and mental health needs. Women's most common pathways to crime, said the NIC, involve survival strategies that result from physical and sexual abuse, poverty, and substance abuse (Figure 14-4).

Parents in Prison

Eighty percent of women entering prison are mothers, and 85% of those women had custody of their children at the time of admission. Approximately 70% of all women under correctional supervision have at least one child younger than age 18. Two-thirds of incarcerated women

Statistically speaking, 1 out of every 43 American children has a parent in prison today, and ethnic variation in the numbers is striking.

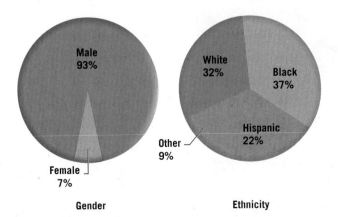

Figure 14-1 | Prison Inmates by Gender and Ethnicity in State and Federal Prisons, 2014

Male 93%
Female 7%
Gender

White 32%
Black 37%
Hispanic 22%
Other 9%
Ethnicity

Source: E. Ann Carson, *Prisoners in 2014* (Washington, DC: Bureau of Justice Statistics, September 2015).

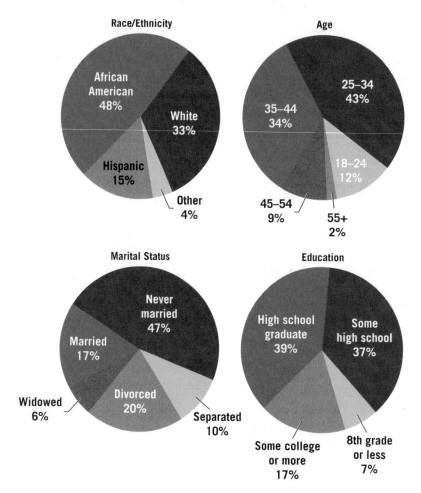

Figure 14-2 | Women State Prison Inmates: Features and Characteristics

Source: Lawrence A. Greenfeld and Tracy L. Snell, *Women Offenders* (Washington, DC: Bureau of Justice Statistics, October 2000).

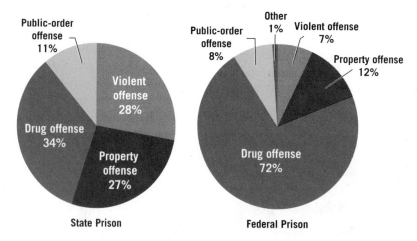

Figure 14-3 | Most Serious Offenses of Women in State and Federal Prisons

Source: Lawrence A. Greenfeld and Tracy L. Snell, *Women Offenders* (Washington, DC: Bureau of Justice Statistics, October 2000).

have minor children; about two-thirds of women in state prisons and half of women in federal prisons had lived with their young children before entering prison. One out of four women entering prison has either recently given birth or is pregnant. Pregnant inmates, many of whom are drug users, malnourished, or sick,

often receive little prenatal care—a situation that risks additional complications.

More than 1.7 million American children have a parent in prison.[38] The number of mothers who are incarcerated has more than doubled, from 29,500 in 1991 to 65,600 in 2007.

■ **gender responsiveness** The process of understanding and taking into account the differences in characteristics and life experiences that women and men bring to the criminal justice system, and adjusting strategies and practices in ways that appropriately respond to those conditions.

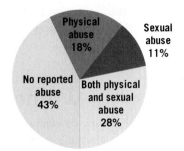

Figure 14-4 | Women State Prison Inmates: Physical and Sexual Abuse History

Source: Lawrence A. Greenfeld and Tracy L. Snell, *Women Offenders* (Washington, DC: Bureau of Justice Statistics, October 2000).

Statistically speaking, 1 out of every 43 American children has a parent in prison today, and ethnic variation in the numbers is striking. Whereas only 1 out of every 111 white children has experienced the imprisonment of a parent, 1 out of every 15 black children has had that experience.

> More than half of the children of female prisoners never visit their mothers during the period of incarceration.

More than half of the children of female prisoners never visit their mothers during the period of incarceration.[39] The lack of visits is due primarily to the remote location of prisons, a lack of transportation, and the inability of caregivers to arrange visitation.

According to one report on the children of incarcerated parents, "The pain of losing a parent to a prison sentence matches, in many respects, the trauma of losing a parent to death or divorce."[40] That report, *Children on the Outside*, prepared by Brooklyn-based Justice Strategies, recommends that states reduce what the report's authors see as overreliance on incarceration as a crime-fighting strategy—especially for nonviolent and many drug offenders. Such a reduction would return many parents to the community and reunite them with their children. Until such a policy is more fully implemented, however, the organization recommends (1) improving the sense of stability and safety that the children of imprisoned parents experience through individual counseling and educational workshops in schools; (2) enhancing the economic security of those children by providing financial support to relatives who are acting as caregivers; (3) supporting the children's sense of connectedness and worthiness by facilitating their ability to maintain regular contact with their incarcerated parent; (4) facilitating those children's social attachment and ability to trust by developing stable and consistent alternative home environments into which they can be placed; and (5) fostering a strong sense

of having an important place in the world among those children through supportive counseling and prioritized placement of children with family members.

Separation from their children is a significant deprivation for many parents, and helping incarcerated parents is just as important as helping their children. Consequently, some states offer parenting classes for female inmates with children. In a national survey of prisons for women, 36 states responded that they provide parenting programs that deal with caretaking, reducing violence toward children, visitation problems, and related issues.[41] Some offer play areas furnished with toys, whereas others attempt to alleviate difficulties in mother–child visits. The typical program studied meets for two hours per week and lasts from four to nine weeks.

> Separation from their children is a significant deprivation for many parents, and helping incarcerated parents is just as important as helping their children.

Gender Responsiveness

Critics have long charged that female inmates face a prison system designed for male inmates and run by men. Consequently, meaningful prison programs for women are often lacking, and the ones that are in place were originally adapted from programs in men's prisons or were based on traditional views of female roles that leave little room for employment opportunities in the contemporary world. Many trade-training programs still emphasize low-paying jobs, such as cook, beautician, or laundry machine operator, and classes in homemaking are not uncommon.

Gender responsiveness means "understanding and taking account of the differences in characteristics and life experiences that women and men bring to the criminal justice system, and adjusting strategies and practices in ways that appropriately respond to those conditions."[42] A recent NIC report concluded with a call for recognition of the behavioral and social differences between female and male offenders—especially those that have specific implications for gender-responsive policies and practices. Among the report's recommendations are the following:[43]

- The creation of an effective system for female offenders that is structured differently from a system for male offenders
- The development of gender-responsive policies and practices targeting women's pathways to criminality in order to provide effective interventions that address the intersecting issues of substance abuse, trauma, mental health needs, and economic marginality

■ **activity**   Invite a corrections administrator (warden, program director, shift supervisor, and so on) to speak with the class either in person or via virtual conferencing. Ask him or her to comment on the ideas discussed in this chapter, such as the types of inmates identified in the text. Does the speaker believe that these concepts adequately describe prison reality as he or she has experienced it? Ask about prison argot in the administrator's facility.

■ **lecture note**   Direct students' attention to the recommendations of the Task Force on the Female Offender. Ask students to identify the rationale behind each recommendation.

- The modification of criminal justice sanctions and interventions to recognize the low risk to public safety represented by the typical female offender
- The consideration of women's relationships, especially those with their children, and women's roles in the community in deciding appropriate correctional sanctions

The NIC study concluded that gender-responsive correctional practices can improve outcomes for female offenders by considering their histories, behaviors, and life circumstances. It also suggested that investments in gender-responsive policy and procedures will likely produce long-term dividends for the criminal justice system and the community as well as for female offenders and their families.

One example of gender responsiveness can be found in a relatively new program in operation at the Decatur (Illinois) Correctional Center. The program allows newborn infants to live with their mothers in a special wing called the Mom and Babies Unit, where each mother has her own room and access to large, brightly colored dayrooms decorated with painted murals. The dayrooms are equipped with toys and children's books, and lead to outdoor patios that provide additional play space for the children. The wing looks much like a typical day-care center. The Decatur program is designed to facilitate the needs of women who are likely to be released by the time their children reach two years of age. The success of the program, which has been in operation for a few years, can be measured in reduced recidivism. "Of the 25 offenders that have gone through this program none...have returned to...prison," says Michael Randle, director of the Illinois

Photo Courtesy of Oregon Department of Corrections

Colette Peters, director of Oregon's Department of Corrections. Appointed in 2012, she is the department's first female head. Do you believe that the appointment of women to higher-level positions in corrections will increase gender responsiveness throughout the system?

Department of Corrections.[44] Similarly, the federal Bureau of Prisons operate the Mothers and Infants Together program, which allows eligible women to live in a community correctional setting with their infants for up to 18 months after giving birth.[45]

Institutions for Women

Most female inmates are housed in centralized state facilities known as women's prisons, which are dedicated exclusively to incarcerating female felons. Some states, however, particularly those with small populations, continue to keep female prisoners in special wings of what are otherwise institutions for men. Although there is not a typical prison for women, the American Correctional Association's 1990 report by the Task Force on the Female Offender found that the institutions that house female inmates could be generally described as follows:[46]

- Most prisons for women are located in towns with fewer than 25,000 inhabitants.
- Significant numbers of facilities were not designed to house female inmates.
- Some facilities that house female inmates also house men.
- Few facilities for women have programs especially designed for female offenders.
- Few major disturbances or escapes are reported among female inmates.
- Substance abuse among female inmates is very high.
- Few work assignments are available to female inmates.

Social Structure in Women's Prisons

"Aside from sharing the experience of being incarcerated," says Professor Marsha Clowers of the John Jay College of Criminal Justice, "female prisoners have much in common."[47] Because so many female inmates share social characteristics such as a lack of education and a history of abuse, they often also share similar values and behaviors. Early prison researchers found that many female inmates construct organized pseudofamilies. Typical of such studies are D. Ward and G. Kassebaum's *Women's Prison* (1966),[48] Esther Heffernan's *Making It in Prison* (1972),[49] and Rose Giallombardo's *Society of Women* (1966).[50]

Giallombardo, for example, examined the Federal Reformatory for Women at Alderson, West Virginia, spending a year gathering data in the early 1960s. Focusing closely on the social formation of families among female inmates, she titled one of her chapters "The Homosexual Alliance as a Marriage Unit." In it she described in great detail the sexual identities

■ **lecture note**   Explain the "family" structures so frequently found in prisons for women. Note that "families" are found cross-culturally and nationwide in women's institutions. Ask the class to explain the phenomenon.

■ **theme**   Why is sexual misconduct between staff and inmates more commonly found in women's prisons than in men's prisons? What might be done to prevent it?

CJ | ISSUES
The Bangkok Rules on the Treatment of Female Prisoners

In December 2010, the United Nations General Assembly formally adopted the *Rules for the Treatment of Female Prisoners and Non-Custodial Measures for Women Offenders*, commonly known as the Bangkok Rules. The Rules, which were approved by the unanimous vote of all 193 member nations, address the special needs that women prisoners have and are the first international standards to address the needs of the children of confined mothers. Many of the rules also concern women's special roles as mothers.

Although the Rules do not carry the weight of law in the United States, they reflect a world consensus concerning the treatment of incarcerated women, and any imprisonment policies or practices that are in conflict with them are likely to be challenged on the grounds that they violate human rights. The 70 rules that comprise the UN resolution are too numerous to list here in their entirety, but some of the most important are provided here in abbreviated form:

- Prior to or on admission, women with caretaking responsibilities for children shall be permitted to make arrangements for those children, including the possibility of a reasonable suspension of detention, taking into account the best interests of the children.

- Women prisoners shall be allocated, to the extent possible, to prisons close to their home or place of social rehabilitation, taking account of their caretaking responsibilities, as well as the individual woman's preference and the availability of appropriate programs and services.

- Gender-specific health-care services at least equivalent to those available in the community shall be provided to women prisoners.

- If the existence of sexual abuse or other forms of violence before or during detention is diagnosed, the woman prisoner shall be [fully] informed of her right to seek recourse from judicial authorities.

- Non-custodial sentences for pregnant women and women with dependent children shall be preferred where possible and appropriate, with custodial sentences being considered when the offence is serious or violent or the woman represents a continuing danger, and after taking into account the best interests of the child or children, while ensuring that appropriate provision has been made for the care of such children.

- Instruments of restraint shall never be used on women during labor, during birth and immediately after birth.

- Particular efforts shall be made to provide appropriate programs for pregnant women, nursing mothers and women with children in prison.

- Women prisoners shall not be discouraged from breastfeeding their children, unless there are specific health reasons to do so.

- Decisions to allow children to stay with their mothers in prison shall be based on the best interests of the children. Children in prison with their mothers shall never be treated as prisoners.

- Women prisoners whose children are in prison with them shall be provided with the maximum possible opportunities to spend time with their children.

- The environment provided for such children's upbringing shall be as close as possible to that of a child outside prison.

- Effective measures shall be taken to ensure that women prisoners "dignity and respect are protected during personal searches, which shall only be carried out by women staff who have been properly trained in appropriate searching methods and in accordance with established procedures.

United Nations officials note that the Bangkok Rules "do not in any way replace the Standard Minimum Rules for the Treatment of Prisoners or the Tokyo Rules and, therefore, all relevant provisions contained in those two sets of rules continue to apply to all prisoners and offenders without discrimination." The Tokyo Rules (adopted in 1990) are officially known as the United Nations Standard Minimum Rules for Non-custodial Measures and focus on alternatives to imprisonment, including staff training, diversion, treatment, linkages with relevant agencies, and the use of volunteers.

The Bangkok Rules can be read online in their entirety at http://www.un.org/en/ecosoc/docs/2010/res%202010-16.pdf. The United Nations Standard Minimum Rules for the Treatment of Prisoners can be found at http://www.unodc.org/pdf/criminal_justice/UN_Standard_Minimum_Rules_for_the_Treatment_of_Prisoners.pdf; and the United Nations Standard Minimum Rules for Non-Custodial Measures can be accessed at http://www.un.org/documents/ga/res/45/a45r110.htm.

References: Myrna Raeder, *Pregnancy- and Child-Related Legal and Policy Issues Concerning Justice-Involved Women* (Washington, DC: National Institute of Corrections, December, 2013); United Nations General Assembly, *Rules for the Treatment of Female Prisoners and Non-Custodial Measures for Women Offenders*.

assumed by women at Alderson and the symbols they chose to communicate those roles. Hairstyle, dress, language, and mannerisms were all used to signify "maleness" or "femaleness." Giallombardo detailed "the anatomy of the marriage relationship from courtship to 'fall out,' that is, from inception to the parting of the ways, or divorce."[51] Romantic love at Alderson was of central importance to any relationship between inmates,

and all homosexual relationships were described as voluntary. Through marriage, the "stud broad" became the husband and the "femme" the wife.

Studies attempting to document how many inmates are part of prison "families" have produced varying results. Some found as many as 71% of female prisoners involved in the phenomenon, while others found none.[52] The kinship systems described by

■ **theme** How do the types of female inmates described in this chapter compare to the types of male inmates? In what ways do they reflect or not reflect male and female roles in the larger society?

Giallombardo and others, however, extend beyond simple "family" ties to the formation of large, intricately related groups that include many nonsexual relationships. In these groups, the roles of "children," "in-laws," "grandparents," and so on may be explicitly recognized. Even "birth order" within a family can become an issue for kinship groups.[53] Kinship groups sometimes occupy a common household—usually a prison cottage or a dormitory area. The descriptions of women's prisons provided by authors like Giallombardo show a closed society in which all aspects of social interaction—including expectations, normative forms of behavior, and emotional ties—are regulated by an inventive system of artificial relationships that mirror those of the outside world.

Many studies of female prisoners have shown that incarcerated women suffer intensely from the loss of affectional relationships once they enter prison and that they form homosexual liaisons to compensate for such losses.[54] Those liaisons then become the foundation of prison social organization.

A decade ago, Barbara Owen, professor of criminology at California State University, Fresno, conducted a study of female inmates at the Central California Women's Facility (the largest prison for women in the world). Her book, *"In the Mix": Struggle and Survival in a Women's Prison*,[55] describes the daily life of the inmates, with an emphasis on prison social structure. Owen found that prison culture for women is tied directly to the roles that women normally assume in free society as well as to other factors shaped by the conditions of women's lives in prison and in the free world. Like Heffernan's work, *"In the Mix"* describes the lives of women before prison and suggests that those lifestyles shape women's adaptation to prison culture. Owen found that preexisting economic marginalization, self-destructive behaviors, and personal histories of physical, sexual, and substance abuse may be important defining features of inmates' lives before they enter prison.[56] She also discovered that the sentences that women have to serve, along with their work and housing assignments, effectively pattern their daily lives and relationships. Owen describes "the mix" as that aspect of prison culture that supports the rule-breaking behavior that propels women into crime and causes them to enter prison. Owen concludes that prison subcultures for women are very different from the violent and predatory structure of contemporary male prisons.[57] Like men, women experience "pains of imprisonment," but their prison culture offers them other ways to survive and adapt to these deprivations.

A study of a women's correctional facility in the southeastern United States found that female inmates asked about their preincarceration sexual orientation gave answers that were quite different than when they were asked about their sexual orientation while incarcerated.[58] In general, before being incarcerated, 64% of inmates interviewed reported being exclusively heterosexual, 28% said they were bisexual, and 8% said that they were lesbians. In contrast, while incarcerated, these same women reported sexual orientations of 55% heterosexual, 31% bisexual, and 13% lesbian. Researchers found that same-sex sexual behavior within the institution was more likely to occur in the lives of young inmates who had had such experiences before entering prison. The study also found that female inmates tended to take part in lesbian behavior the longer they were incarcerated.

Finally, a significant aspect of sexual activity far more commonly found in women's prisons than in men's prisons is sexual misconduct between staff and inmates. Although a fair amount of such behavior is attributed to the exploitation of female inmates by male corrections officers acting from positions of power, some studies suggest that female inmates may sometimes attempt to manipulate unsuspecting male officers into illicit relationships in order to gain favors.[59]

Types of Female Inmates

As in institutions for men, the subculture of women's prisons is multidimensional. Esther Heffernan, for example, found that three terms used by the female prisoners she studied—the *square*, the *cool*, and the *life*—were indicative of three styles of adaptation to prison life.[60] Square inmates had few early experiences with criminal lifestyles and tended to sympathize with the values and attitudes of conventional society. Cool prisoners were more likely to be career offenders. They tended to keep to themselves and generally supported inmate values. Women who participated in the life subculture were quite familiar with lives of crime. Many had been arrested repeatedly for prostitution, drug use, theft, and so on. They were full participants in the economic, social, and familial arrangements of the prison. Heffernan believed that the life offered an alternative lifestyle to women who had experienced early consistent rejection by conventional society. Within the life, women could establish relationships, achieve status, and find meaning in their lives. The square, the cool, and the life represented subcultures to Heffernan because individuals with similar adaptive choices tended to relate closely to one another and to support the lifestyle characteristic of that type.

The social structure of women's prisons was altered about 20 years ago by the arrival of cocaine-addicted "crack kids," as they were called in prison argot. Crack kids, whose existence highlighted generational differences among female offenders, were streetwise young women with little respect for traditional prison values, for their elders, or even for their own children. Known for frequent fights and for their lack of even simple

■ **activity** If you did not do so while discussing Chapter 13, now would be a good time to schedule a tour of a local prison. Ask to see as many facilities as possible, including dormitories, workshops, cafeterias, segregation units, religious assembly areas, and the like. If possible, schedule time to hear from inmates about the challenges of prison life. Ask if there are any positive aspects to "being on the inside."

■ **lecture note** Describe the jobs and roles prison staff members fulfill. Explain that one staffer may wear many different hats.

■ **theme** How are correctional officers socialized into the work word of the prison? What factors influence staff culture?

Jack Kurtz/The Image Works

Female inmates in Sheriff Joe Arpaio's "equal opportunity jail" in Maricopa County, Arizona, being inspected by a corrections officer before leaving for chain gang duty. Not all states make use of chain gangs, and only a few use female inmates on chain gangs. Should jail chain gangs be more widely used?

domestic skills, these young women quickly estranged many older inmates, some of whom call them "animalescents."

Violence in Women's Prisons

Some authors suggest that violence in women's prisons is less frequent than it is in institutions for men. Lee Bowker observes that "except for the behavior of a few 'guerrillas,' it appears that violence is only used in women's prisons to settle questions of dominance and subordination when other manipulative strategies fail to achieve the desired effect."[61] It appears that few homosexual liaisons are forced, perhaps representing a general aversion among women to such victimization in wider society. At least one study, however, has shown the use of sexual violence in women's prisons as a form of revenge against inmates who are overly vocal in their condemnation of lesbian practices among other prisoners.[62]

To address the problems of imprisoned women, including violence, the Task Force on the Female Offender recommended a number of changes in the administration of prisons for women.[63] Among those recommendations were:

- Substance-abuse programs should be available to female inmates.
- Female inmates need to acquire greater literacy skills, and literacy programs should form the basis on which other programs are built.
- Female offenders should be housed in buildings without male inmates.

- Institutions for women should develop programs for keeping children in the facility in order to "fortify the bond between mother and child."
- To ensure equal access to assistance, institutions should be built to accommodate programs for female offenders.

The Staff World

The flip side of inmate society can be found in the world of the prison staff, which includes many people working in various professions. Staff roles encompass those of warden, psychologist, counselor, area supervisor, program director, instructor, corrections officer, and—in some large prisons—physician and therapist.

According to the federal government, approximately 748,000 people are employed in corrections,[64] with the majority performing direct custodial tasks in state institutions: 62% of corrections employees work for state governments, followed by 33% at the local level and 5% at the federal level.[65] On a per capita basis, the District of Columbia has the most state and local corrections employees (53.3 per every 10,000 residents), followed by Texas (43.8).[66] Across the nation, 70% of corrections officers are Caucasian, 22% are African American, and slightly more than 5% are Hispanic.[67] Women account for 20% of all corrections officers, with the proportion of female officers increasing at around 19% per year. The American Correctional Association (ACA) encourages correctional agencies to "ensure that recruitment, selection, and promotion opportunities are open to women."[68]

Corrections officers, generally considered to be at the bottom of the staff hierarchy, may be divided into cell-block guards and tower guards; others are assigned to administrative offices, where they perform clerical tasks. The inmate-to-staff ratio in state prisons averages around 4.1 inmates for each corrections officer.[69]

Like prisoners, corrections officers undergo a socialization process that helps them function by the official and unofficial rules of staff society. In a classic study, Lucien Lombardo described the process by which officers are socialized into the prison work world.[70] Lombardo interviewed 359 corrections personnel at New York's Auburn Prison and found that rookie officers quickly had to abandon preconceptions of both inmates and other staff members. According to Lombardo, new officers learn that inmates are not the "monsters" much of the public makes them out to be. On the other hand, rookies may be seriously disappointed in their experienced colleagues when they realize that the ideals of professionalism, often emphasized during early training, rarely translate into reality. The pressures of the institutional work environment,

■ **lecture note**   Explain that custody and control are still the major concerns of corrections staffers—just as they have been since the inception of imprisonment.

■ **lecture note**   Discuss how the ACA's code of ethics is designed to uphold both the standards of the profession and the values of society. Ask students what social values the code embodies.

A correctional official oversees the segregation unit for violent prisoners at a California facility. The job of a corrections officer centers largely on the custody and control of inmates, but growing professionalism is enhancing both personal opportunities and job satisfaction among officers. Why is professionalism important to job satisfaction?

© Marmaduke St. John / Alamy

however, soon force most corrections personnel to adopt a united front when relating to inmates.

One of the leading formative influences on staff culture is the potential threat that inmates pose. Inmates far outnumber corrections personnel in every institution, and the hostility they feel for guards is only barely hidden even at the best of times. Corrections personnel know that however friendly inmates may appear, a sudden change in the institutional climate—from a simple disturbance in the yard to a full-blown riot—can quickly and violently unmask deep-rooted feelings of mistrust and hatred.

As in years past, prison staffers are still most concerned with custody and control. Society, especially under the just deserts philosophy of criminal sentencing, expects corrections staff to keep inmates in custody; this is the basic prerequisite of successful job performance. Custody is necessary before any other correctional activities, such as instruction or counseling, can be undertaken. Control, the other major staff concern, ensures order, and an orderly prison is thought to be safe and secure. In routine daily activities, control over almost all aspects of inmate behavior becomes paramount in the minds of most corrections officers. It is the twin interests of custody and control that lead to institutionalized procedures for ensuring security in most facilities. The enforcement of strict rules; body and cell searches; counts; unannounced shakedowns; the control of dangerous items, materials, and contraband; and the extensive use of bars, locks, fencing, cameras, and alarms all support the staff's vigilance in maintaining security.

The Professionalization of Corrections Officers

Corrections officers have generally been accorded low occupational status. Historically, the role of prison guard required minimal formal education and held few opportunities for professional growth and career advancement. Such jobs were typically low paying, frustrating, and often boring. Growing problems in our nation's prisons, including emerging issues of legal liability, however, increasingly require a well-trained and adequately equipped force of professionals. As corrections personnel have become better trained and more proficient, the old concept of guard has been supplanted by that of corrections officer. The ACA's code of ethics for correctional officers is reproduced in the "Ethics and Professionalism" box in this chapter.

Many states and a growing number of large-city correctional systems try to eliminate individuals with potentially harmful personality characteristics from corrections officer applicant pools. New Jersey, New York, Ohio, Pennsylvania, and Rhode Island, for example, have all used some form of psychological screening in assessing candidates for prison jobs.[71]

Although only a few states utilize psychological screening, all have training programs intended to prepare successful applicants for prison work. New York, for example, requires trainees to complete six weeks of classroom-based instruction, 40 hours of rifle range practice, and six weeks of on-the-job training. Training days begin around 5 a.m. with a mile run and conclude after dark with study halls for students who need extra help. To keep pace with rising inmate populations, the state has often had to run a number of simultaneous training academies.[72] Anyone interested in working in the field of corrections should visit the website Discover Corrections. Funded by the Bureau of Justice Assistance, an arm of the U.S. Department of Justice, the site can be reached at **http://www.discover corrections.com.**

Security Threat Groups and Prison Riots

On February 19, 2012, a riot broke out in a desperately overcrowded Mexican prison in the town of Apodaca, close to the Mexican city of Monterrey.[73] By the time the fighting was over, 44 inmates had been killed and the prison was in shambles. Officials called the riot a "feud" between members of rival drug cartels, and claimed that all of the deaths had occurred at the hands of other inmates. Only a month earlier, 30 inmates died

■ **lecture note**   Comment that the 1970s were once called the "explosive decade" of prison riots. Suggest that the frequency of riots in prison may reflect the frequency of public protests in the wider society of which prisons are a part.

in a similar altercation in a prison in Tamaulipas, located just across the border from the U.S. city of Brownsville, Texas.

Unlike prisons in Mexico, today's American prisons are relatively calm, but the ten years between 1970 and 1980 have been called the "explosive decade" of prison riots.[74] The decade began with a massive uprising at Attica Prison in New York State in September 1971, which resulted in 43 deaths and left more than 80 men wounded. The decade ended in 1980 in Santa Fe, New Mexico. There, in a riot at the New Mexico Penitentiary, 33 inmates died, the victims of vengeful prisoners out to eliminate rats and informants. Many of the deaths involved mutilation and torture. More than 200 other inmates were beaten and sexually assaulted, and the prison was virtually destroyed.

Although the number of prison riots decreased after the 1970s, they did continue. For 11 days in 1987, the federal penitentiary in Atlanta, Georgia, was under the control of inmates. The institution was heavily damaged, and inmates had to be temporarily relocated while it was rebuilt. The Atlanta riot followed on the heels of a similar, but less intense, disturbance at the federal detention center in Oakdale, Louisiana. Both outbreaks were attributed to the dissatisfaction of Cuban inmates, most of whom had arrived in the mass exodus known as the *Mariel boatlift*.[75]

Easter Sunday 1993 marked the beginning of an 11-day rebellion at the 1,800-inmate Southern Ohio Correctional Facility in Lucasville, Ohio—one of the country's toughest maximum-security prisons. When the riot ended, nine inmates and one corrections officer were dead. The officer had been hung.[76]

Riots related to inmate grievances over perceived disparities in federal drug-sentencing policies and the possible loss of weight-lifting equipment occurred throughout the federal prison system in October 1995. Within a few days, the unrest led to a nationwide lockdown of 73 federal prisons. Although fires were set and a number of inmates and guards were injured, no deaths resulted. In February 2000, a riot between 200 black and Hispanic prisoners in California's Pelican Bay State Prison resulted in the death of one inmate. Fifteen other inmates were wounded. Then, in November 2000, 32 inmates took a dozen corrections officers hostage at the privately run Torrance County Detention Facility in Estancia, New Mexico. Two of the officers were stabbed and seriously injured, while another eight were beaten. The riot was finally quelled after an emergency-response team threw tear-gas canisters into the area where the prisoners had barricaded themselves.[77]

In 2004, a disturbance took place at the medium- to high-security Arizona State Prison Complex at Lewis. Two corrections officers and a staff member were injured in a fight that broke out during breakfast preparations, and two other officers were captured and held hostage for 15 days in a watchtower. Officials were able to keep disorder from spreading to the rest of the facility, and the incident ended when inmates released the officers and surrendered.

In 2005, 42 inmates were injured when a ruckus broke out during breakfast between Hispanic and white prisoners at California's San Quentin State Prison. The riot occurred in a section of the prison housing about 900 inmates who were under lockdown because of previous fighting between the groups.[78] In

The Arizona State Prison Complex at Lewis, where two inmates held two corrections officers hostage in a watchtower in 2004. One officer, a female, was raped. On April 30, 2004, inmate Steven Coy was sentenced to seven consecutive life sentences for his part in the hostage crisis. How can the safety of corrections workers be improved?

Tom Hood/AP Wide World Photos.

■ **lecture note**   Explore the causes of prison riots. Discuss the importance of informal controls within prison subculture in keeping order and preventing riots.

■ **theme**   What are security threat groups (STGs) and how do their presence affect the risk of disorder and violence within a prison facility? How might correctional officials deal with the threat of STGs?

ethics and professionalism

American Correctional Association Code of Ethics

Preamble

The American Correctional Association expects of its members unfailing honesty, respect for the dignity and individuality of human beings, and a commitment to professional and compassionate service. To this end, we subscribe to the following principles:

- Members shall respect and protect the civil and legal rights of all individuals.
- Members shall treat every professional situation with concern for the welfare of the individuals involved and with no intent to personal gain.
- Members shall maintain relationships with colleagues to promote mutual respect within the profession and improve the quality of service.
- Members shall make public criticisms of their colleagues or their agencies only when warranted, verifiable, and constructive.
- Members shall respect the importance of all disciplines within the criminal justice system and work to improve cooperation with each segment.
- Members shall honor the public's right to information and share information with the public to the extent permitted by law subject to individuals' right to privacy.
- Members shall respect and protect the right of the public to be safeguarded from criminal activity.
- Members shall refrain from using their positions to secure personal privileges or advantages.
- Members shall refrain from allowing personal interest to impair objectivity in the performance of duty while acting in an official capacity.
- Members shall refrain from entering into any formal or informal activity or agreement which presents a conflict of interest or is inconsistent with the conscientious performance of duties.
- Members shall refrain from accepting any gifts, service, or favor that is or appears to be improper or implies an obligation inconsistent with the free and objective exercise of professional duties.
- Members shall clearly differentiate between personal views/statements and views/statements/positions made on behalf of the agency or association.
- Members shall report to appropriate authorities any corrupt or unethical behaviors in which there is sufficient evidence to justify review.
- Members shall refrain from discriminating against any individual because of race, gender, creed, national origin, religious affiliation, age, disability, or any other type of prohibited discrimination.
- Members shall preserve the integrity of private information; they shall refrain from seeking information on individuals beyond that which is necessary to implement responsibilities and perform their duties; members shall refrain from revealing nonpublic information unless expressly authorized to do so.
- Members shall make all appointments, promotions, and dismissals in accordance with established civil service rules, applicable contract agreements, and individual merit, and not in furtherance of partisan interests.
- Members shall respect, promote, and contribute to a workplace that is safe, healthy, and free of harassment in any form.

Adopted August 1975 at the 105th Congress of Correction. Revised August 1990 at the 120th Congress of Correction. Revised August 1994 at the 124th Congress of Correction.

Thinking about Ethics

1. How does the American Correctional Association's Code of Ethics differ from the American Jail Association's Code of Ethics found in Chapter 13? How is it similar?

2. Do you think that one code of ethics should cover corrections officers working in both jails and prisons? Why or why not?

Source: American Correctional Association. Reprinted with permission. Visit the American Correctional Association at http://www.aca.org.

2008, the federal correctional institution in Three Rivers, Texas, was locked down following two gang-related fights that killed one inmate and injured 22.[79]

In 2009, four prisoners were hospitalized and about 700 had to be relocated after inmates set fire to the medium-security Northpoint Training Center in Kentucky.[80] About the same time, 200 inmates were injured in a riot at the California Institution for Men in Chino, California, when rioting at the institution left at least one building ablaze.[81] The Chino facility is home to more than 5,900 inmates, many of whom are housed in old military-style barracks.

Although riots are difficult to predict in specific institutions, some state prison systems appear ripe for disorder. The Texas prison system, for example, is home to a number of

■ **theme** What is the hands-off doctrine? Do you believe we should return to a hands-off policy? Explain. Would the hands-off doctrine be more likely to appeal to public-order advocates or to individual-rights advocates? Why?

■ **security threat group (STG)** An inmate group, gang, or organization whose members act together to pose a threat to the safety of corrections staff or the public, who prey upon other inmates, or who threaten the secure and orderly operation of a correctional institution.

■ **lecture note** Explain the hands-off doctrine as a nonintervention policy that American courts assumed with regard to prisons before the late 1960s. Explain that widespread abuses of power by correctional staff, combined with an increasingly sensitive Supreme Court, led to many decisions concerning correctional administration during the past three decades.
■ **lecture note** Explain the concept of civil death and discuss those aspects that still exist in the modern correctional system today.

AP Photo/Houston Chronicle, Cody Duty

Assistant Attorney General Lanny Breuer speaks to media representatives in Houston, Texas, announcing the arrest of dozens of alleged members of the white supremacist Aryan Brotherhood of Texas security threat group in 2013 on federal racketeering and other charges. The gang is suspected of involvement in the shooting deaths of Tom Clements, the head of Colorado prisons, and two Texas prosecutors.

gangs—referred to by corrections personnel as **security threat groups (STGs)**—among whom turf violations can easily lead to widespread disorder. Gang membership among inmates in the Texas prison system, practically nonexistent in 1983, was estimated at more than 1,200 just nine years later.[82] The Texas Syndicate, the Aryan Brotherhood of Texas, and the Mexican Mafia (sometimes known as *La Eme*, Spanish for the letter *M*) are thought to be the largest gangs functioning in the Texas prison system today. Each has around 300 members.[83] Other gangs known to operate in prisons across the country are shown in Table 14–2.

Gangs in Texas grew rapidly in part because of the power vacuum created when a court ruling ended the "building tender" system.[84] Building tenders were tough inmates who were given almost free rein by prison administrators in keeping other inmates in line, especially in many of the state's worst prisons. The end of the building tender system dramatically increased demands on the Texas Department of Criminal Justice for increased

> Gangs in Texas grew rapidly in part because of the power vacuum created when a court ruling ended the "building tender" system.

abilities and professionalism among its guards and other prison staff. Today, prison gangs have developed into criminal organizations whose reach may extend far beyond prison walls. In 2013, for example, Colorado prison chief Tom Clements was gunned down by a former inmate and gang member as he answered the front door of his home. Authorities believe that the killing was ordered by imprisoned gang leaders known as *shot callers*. Similar killings of two district attorneys in 2013 may have been related to security threat groups in Texas prisons. Terry Pelz, a former Texas prison warden, observes that "The gangs [have gone] from protecting themselves in prison on racial lines to evolving into criminal enterprises."[85]

Prisoners' Rights

In May 1995, Limestone Prison inmate Larry Hope was handcuffed to a hitching post after arguing with another inmate while working on a chain gang near an interstate highway in Alabama.[86] Hope was released two hours later, after a supervising officer determined that Hope had not instigated the altercation. During the two hours that he was coupled to the post, Hope was periodically offered drinking water and bathroom breaks, and his responses to those offers were recorded on an activity log. Because of the height of the hitching post, however, his arms grew tired, and it was later determined that whenever he tried moving his arms to improve his circulation, the handcuffs cut into his wrists, causing pain.

One month later, Hope was punished more severely after he had taken a nap during the morning bus ride to the chain gang's work site. When the bus arrived, he was slow in responding to an order to exit the vehicle. A shouting match soon led to a scuffle with an officer, and four other guards intervened and subdued Hope, handcuffing him and placing him in leg irons for transportation back to the prison. When he arrived at the facility, officers made him take off his shirt and again put him on the hitching post. He stood in the sun for approximately seven hours, sustaining a sunburn. Hope was given water only once or twice during that time and was provided with no bathroom breaks. At one point, an officer taunted him about his thirst. According to Hope: "[The guard] first gave water to some dogs, then brought the water cooler closer to me, removed its lid, and kicked the cooler over, spilling the water onto the ground."

Eventually, Hope filed a civil suit against three officers, claiming that he experienced "unnecessary pain" and that the "wanton infliction of pain...constitutes cruel and unusual punishment forbidden by the Eighth Amendment." His case eventually reached the U.S. Supreme Court, and on June 27, 2002, the Court found that Hope's treatment was "totally without penological justification" and constituted an Eighth Amendment violation. The Court ruled that "Despite the clear lack of emergency, respondents knowingly subjected [Hope] to a substantial risk of physical harm, unnecessary pain, unnecessary exposure to the sun, prolonged thirst and taunting, and a deprivation of bathroom breaks that created a risk of particular discomfort and humiliation."

Table 14-2 | Ten Most Influential Security Threat Groups in American Prisons

Security threat groups, or prison gangs, are self-perpetuating criminal organizations that have significant influence beyond the penal system. Prison gangs are structured along racial or ethnic lines, and consist of a select group of inmates who participate in an organizational hierarchy and are governed by a shared code of conduct. Prison gangs vary in both organization and composition, from highly structured gangs such as the Aryan Brotherhood and Nuestra Familia to gangs with a less formal structure such as the Mexican Mafia (La Eme).

	ARYAN BROTHERHOOD	BARRIO AZTECA	BLACK GUERRILLA FAMILY	DEAD MAN INCORPORATED	TEXAS SYNDICATE	NETA	HERMANOS DE PISTOLEROS LATINOS	PUBLIC ENEMY NUMBER ONE	MEXICAN MAFIA AKA LA EME	NAZI LOW RIDERS	MEXIKANEMI AKA TEXAS MEXICAN MAFIA	LA NUESTRA FAMILIA
Estimated Numbers	20,000	2,000	1,000 plus associates	370 and thousands of associates	1,300 plus 10,000 associates	12,000	1,000	500	400 plus 1,000 associates	Up to 5,000 members	2,000	250 and thousands of associates
Racial Composition	White	Mexican Nationals or Mexican/ Americans	African-American	White	Mexican-American Hispanic	Puerto Rican	Mexican and Mexican-American	White	Mexican-American/Hispanic	White	Mexican nationals and Mexican-Americans	Mexican-American Hispanic
Location	Concentrated in the Western U.S.	South-western U.S.	California and Maryland	Maryland and Virginia	California, Texas, New Mexico, Arizona	Puerto Rico and North-east U.S.	Texas and South-western U.S.	Eastern and Western U.S.	California	Pacific Coast and South-western U.S.	Texas and the Southwest	California

References: Michael Kelley, "America's 11 Most Powerful Prison Gangs." *Business Insider Australia*, http://www.businessinsider.com.au/most-dangerous-prison-gangs-in-the-us-2014-2; David Skarbek, *The Social Order of the Underworld: How Prison Gangs Govern the American Penal System* (Oxford Univ. Press); "Prison in America: Protection Rackets," *The Economist*. August 30, 2014, http://www.economist.com/news/books-and-arts/21614090-prison-gangs-are-rational-solution-growing-problem-protection-rackets; U.S. Department of Justice, Organized Crime and Gang Section, "Prison Gangs," http://www.justice.gov/criminal/ocgs/gangs/prison.html; and Florida Department of Corrections, "Major Prison Gangs," http://www.dc.state.fl.us/pub/gangs/la.html.

paying for it

The Cost-Benefit Knowledge Bank for Criminal Justice

Throughout this book, you will find a number of boxes like this one. They all examine criminal justice system costs and raise questions about providing cost-effective services in the justice arena. We've explored the issue of cost-efficiency in policing, courts, and corrections.

In this box, we take a look at the Cost-Benefit Knowledge Bank for Criminal Justice (CBKB), a recently developed online resource sponsored by the Vera Institute of Justice with funding from the federal Bureau of Justice Assistance. The CBKB, which can be reached at http://cbkb.org, works to "help practitioners and jurisdictions build their capacity to conduct cost-benefit studies and apply cost-benefit analysis to policymaking." It supports practitioners in building the "capacity to promote, use, and interpret cost-benefit analysis in criminal justice settings."

The CBKB website offers webinars on topics such as budget and finance in criminal justice, victim costs, reading cost–benefit reports, and step-by-step guides to cost–benefit analysis for justice policy. New webinars are added continuously, and an archive of past webinars enables interested parties to review those that have already been conducted.

The site also offers a library of cost–benefit studies relative to the justice area. Topics of some of the available documents include "evidence-based programs," "a cost-benefit analysis of county diversion programs," and "can drug courts save money?" CBKB materials are available in the areas of courts, crime prevention, information technology, law enforcement, probation and parole, reentry, sentencing and corrections, substance use and mental health, and victimization.

Finally, the CBKB website offers its New Perspectives Tool, which allows justice planners and program administrators to capture the costs and benefits of anticipated and ongoing programs from the point of view of multiple affected parties. The tool provides methods to quantify costs to (1) taxpayers, (2) crime victims (including tangible and intangible costs), (3) program participants, (4) justice agencies and personnel, and (5) businesses and neighborhoods. In the reentry area, for example, the tool encourages planners to examine both benefits (such as conferring skills on participants that result in better-paying jobs and wider work prospects) and costs (such as staff salaries, transportation expenses, and lost wages that might have been earned if participants were employed instead of enrolled in the program). The tool also encourages the consideration of benefits to the children of offenders reentering society and to businesses and neighborhoods that can benefit from increased commercial activities as well as increased property values resulting from reduced crime. "Which perspectives are included in—or excluded from—a CBA (cost–benefit analysis) can affect the bottom line," says the CBKB. Table 14-3 provides an example of the kinds of useful information available through the CBKB.

The CBKB is available on Facebook (http://www.facebook.com/costbenefit) and on Twitter (@CBKBank). It also has its own YouTube channel (http://www.youtube.com/user/CBKBank). Perhaps the best way to keep up with activities and sponsored events at the CBKB, however, is through its blog at http://cbkb.org/blog. You can also subscribe to an e-mail newsletter that will keep you updated on CBKB activities.

Table 14-3 | **Financial Benefits of Programs for Adult Offenders**

PROGRAMS FOR ADULT OFFENDERS	PERCENT CHANGE IN CRIME	TO CRIME VICTIMS	TO TAXPAYER	PROGRAM COSTS PER PARTICIPANT	COST/ BENEFIT PER PARTICIPANT[a]
Vocational education in prison	−9.0	$8,114	$6,806	$1,182	$13,738
Intensive supervision: treatment-oriented programs	−16.7	9,318	9,369	7,124	11,563
General education in prison (basic education or postsecondary)	−7.0	6,325	5,306	962	10,669
Cognitive-behavioral therapy in prison or community	−6.3	5,658	4,764	105	10,299
Drug treatment in community	−9.3	5,133	5,495	574	10,054
Correctional industries in prison	−5.9	5,360	4,496	417	9,439
Drug treatment in prison (therapeutic communities or outpatient)	−5.7	5,133	4,306	1,604	7,835
Employment and job training in the community	−4.3	2,373	2,386	400	4,359

[a]Positive numbers indicate system savings.
Source: National Institute of Corrections, *Evidence-Based Policy, Practice, and Decisionmaking: Implications for Paroling Authorities* (Washington, DC: NIC, 2011; updated 2013).

References: Cost-Benefit Knowledge Bank for Criminal Justice, "Featured Content," http://cbkb.org (accessed August 21, 2013).

■ **hands-off doctrine**   A policy of nonintervention with regard to prison management that U.S. courts tended to follow until the late 1960s. For the past 40 years, the doctrine has languished as judicial intervention in prison administration dramatically increased, although there is now some evidence that a new hands-off era is approaching.

■ **civil death**   The legal status of prisoners in some jurisdictions who are denied the opportunity to vote, hold public office, marry, or enter into contracts by virtue of their status as incarcerated felons. Although civil death is primarily of historical interest, some jurisdictions still limit the contractual opportunities available to inmates.

■ **balancing test**   A principle, developed by the courts and applied to the corrections arena by *Pell* v. *Procunier* (1974), that attempts to weigh the rights of an individual, as guaranteed by the Constitution, against the authority of states to make laws or to otherwise restrict a person's freedom in order to protect the state's interests and its citizens.

▤ **theme**   Describe the conditional rights of prisoners as identified by various court decisions. Which of the rights listed in this chapter do you agree should apply to incarcerated individuals? Why? Which, in your opinion, should not? Why not?

In deciding the *Hope* case, the Court built on almost 40 years of precedent-setting decisions in the area of prisoners' rights. Before the 1960s, American courts had taken a neutral approach—commonly called the **hands-off doctrine**—toward the running of prisons. Judges assumed that prison administrators were sufficiently professional in the performance of their duties to balance institutional needs with humane considerations. The hands-off doctrine rested on the belief that defendants lost most of their rights upon conviction, suffering a kind of **civil death**. Many states defined the concept of civil death through legislation that denied inmates the right to vote, to hold public office, and even to marry. Some states made incarceration for a felony a basis for uncontested divorce at the request of the noncriminal spouse. Aspects of the old notion of civil death are still a reality in a number of jurisdictions today, and the Sentencing Project says that 3.9 million American citizens across the nation are barred from voting because of previous felony convictions.[87]

Although the concept of civil death has not entirely disappeared, the hands-off doctrine ended in 1970, when a federal court declared the entire Arkansas prison system to be unconstitutional after hearing arguments that it represented a form of cruel and unusual punishment.[88] The court's decision resulted from what it judged to be pervasive overcrowding and primitive living conditions. Longtime inmates claimed that over the years, a number of inmates had been beaten or shot to death by guards and buried in unmarked graves on prison property. An investigation did unearth some skeletons in old graves, but their origin was never determined.

Detailed media coverage of the Arkansas prison system gave rise to suspicions about correctional institutions everywhere. Within a few years, federal courts intervened in the running of prisons in Florida, Louisiana, Mississippi, New York City, and Virginia.[89] In 1975, in a precedent-setting decision, U.S. District Court Judge Frank M. Johnson issued an order banning the Alabama Board of Corrections from accepting any more inmates. Citing a population that was more than double the capacity of the state's system, Judge Johnson enumerated 44 standards to be met before additional inmates could be admitted to prison. Included in the requirements were specific guidelines on living space, staff-to-inmate ratios, visiting privileges, the racial makeup of staff, and food-service modifications.[90]

The Legal Basis of Prisoners' Rights

In 1974, the U.S. Supreme Court case of *Pell* v. *Procunier*[91] established a "balancing test" that, although originally addressing only the First Amendment rights, eventually served as a general guideline for all prison operations. In *Pell*, the Court ruled that the "prison inmate retains those First Amendment rights that are not inconsistent with his status as a prisoner or with the legitimate penological objectives of the corrections system."[92] In other words, inmates have rights, much the same as people who are not incarcerated, provided that the legitimate needs of the prison for security, custody, and safety are not compromised. Other courts have declared that order maintenance, security, and rehabilitation are all legitimate concerns of prison administration but that financial exigency and convenience are not. As the **balancing test** makes clear, we see reflected in prisoners' rights a microcosm of the dilemma of "individual rights versus public order" found in wider society.

Further enforcing the legal rights of prisoners is the Civil Rights of Institutionalized Persons Act (CRIPA) of 1980.[93] The law, which has been amended over time, applies to all adult and juvenile state and local jails, detention centers, prisons, mental hospitals, and other care facilities (such as those operated by a state, county, or city for individuals who are physically disabled or chronically ill). Another federal law, the Religious Land Use and Institutionalized Persons Act of 2000 (RLUIPA), has particular relevance to prison programs and activities that are at least partially supported with federal monies. RLUIPA states:

> No government shall impose a substantial burden on the religious exercise of a person residing in or confined to an institution even if the burden results from a rule of general applicability, unless the government demonstrates that imposition of the burden on that person (1) is in furtherance of a compelling governmental interest; and (2) is the least restrictive means of furthering that compelling governmental interest.

Significantly, the most recent version of CRIPA states:[94]

> No action shall be brought with respect to prison conditions under section 1983 of this title, or any other Federal law, by a prisoner confined in any jail, prison, or other correctional facility until such administrative remedies as are available are exhausted.

Prisoners' rights, because they are constrained by the legitimate needs of imprisonment, can be thought of as conditional rights rather than absolute rights. The Second Amendment to the U.S. Constitution, for example, grants citizens the right to bear arms. The right to arms is, however, necessarily compromised by the need for order and security in prison, and we would not expect a court to rule that inmates have a right to weapons. Prisoners' rights must be balanced against the security, order-maintenance, and treatment needs of correctional institutions.

> Prisoners' rights must be balanced against the security, order-maintenance, and treatment needs of correctional institutions.

Conditional rights, because they are subject to the exigencies of imprisonment, bear a strong resemblance to privileges, which is not surprising because "privileges" were all that inmates officially had until the modern era. The practical difference between a privilege and a conditional right is that privileges exist only at the convenience of granting institutions and can be revoked at any time for any reason. The rights of prisoners, on the other hand, have a basis in the Constitution and in law external to the institution. Although the institution may restrict such rights for legitimate correctional reasons, those rights may not be infringed without cause that can be demonstrated in a court of law. Mere institutional convenience does not provide a sufficient legal basis for the denial of rights.

The past few decades have seen many lawsuits brought by prisoners challenging the constitutionality of some aspect of confinement. As mentioned in Chapter 11, suits filed by prisoners with the courts are generally called writs of *habeas corpus* and formally request that the person detaining a prisoner bring him or her before a judicial officer to determine the lawfulness of the imprisonment. The American Correctional Association says that most prisoner lawsuits are based on "1. the Eighth Amendment prohibition against cruel and unusual punishment; 2. the Fourteenth Amendment prohibition against the taking of life, liberty, or property without due process of law; and 3. the Fourteenth Amendment provision requiring equal protection of the laws."[95] Aside from appeals by inmates that question the propriety of their convictions and sentences, such constitutional challenges represent the bulk of legal action initiated by the imprisoned. State statutes and federal legislation, however, including Section 1983 of the Civil Rights Act of 1871, provide other bases for challenges to the legality of specific prison conditions and procedures. The U.S. Supreme Court has not yet spoken with finality on a number of prisoners' rights questions. Nonetheless, High Court decisions of the last few decades and a number of lower-court findings can be interpreted to identify the existing conditional rights of prisoners, as shown in Table 14-4. Table 14-5 shows a number of important U.S. Supreme Court cases involving prisoners' rights claims.

Table 14-4 | The Conditional Rights of Inmates[1]

Communications and Visitation

A right to receive publications directly from the publisher
A right to meet with members of the press[2]
A right to communicate with nonprisoners

Religious Freedom

A right of assembly for religious services and groups
A right to attend services of other religious groups
A right to receive visits from ministers
A right to correspond with religious leaders
A right to observe religious dietary laws
A right to wear religious insignia

Access to the Courts and Legal Assistance

A right to have access to the courts[3]
A right to visits from attorneys
A right to have mail communications with lawyers[4]
A right to communicate with legal assistance organizations
A right to consult jailhouse lawyers[5]
A right to assistance in filing legal papers, which should include one of the following:
• Access to an adequate law library (prison libraries today are increasingly digital)
• Paid attorneys
• Paralegal personnel or law students

Medical Care

A right to sanitary and healthy conditions
A right to medical attention for serious physical problems
A right to required medications
A right to treatment in accordance with "doctor's orders"

Protection from Harm

A right to food, water, and shelter
A right to protection from foreseeable attack
A right to protection from predictable sexual abuse
A right to protection against suicide

Institutional Punishment and Discipline

An absolute right against corporal punishments (unless sentenced to such punishments)
A limited right to due process before punishment, including the following:
• A notice of charges
• A fair and impartial hearing
• An opportunity for defense
• A right to present witnesses
• A written decision

[1] All "rights" listed are provisional in that they may be constrained by the legitimate needs of imprisonment.
[2] But not beyond the opportunities afforded for inmates to meet with members of the general public.
[3] As restricted by the Prison Litigation Reform Act of 1996.
[4] Mail communications are generally designated as privileged or nonprivileged. Privileged communications include those between inmates and their lawyers or court officials and cannot legitimately be read by prison officials. Nonprivileged communications include most other written communications.
[5] Jailhouse lawyers are inmates with experience in the law, usually gained from filing legal briefs on their own behalf or on the behalf of others. Consultation with jailhouse lawyers was ruled permissible in the Supreme Court case of *Johnson v. Avery*, 393 U.S. 483 (1968), unless inmates are provided with paid legal assistance.

Table 14-5 | Important U.S. Supreme Court Cases Involving Prisoners' Rights Claims, by Year of Decision

CASE NAME	YEAR DECIDED	CONSTITUTIONAL BASIS	FINDING
Holt v. Hobbs	2015		The Court supported the Religious Land Use and Institutionalized Persons Act of 2000, which provides that no government shall impose a substantial burden on the religious exercise of a prisoner unless it can show that the baurden "is the least restrictive means of furthering a compelling governmental interest."
Howes v. Fields	2012	Fifth Amendment	Inmates facing questioning by law enforcement officers while incarcerated need not be advised of their *Miranda* rights.
Florence v. Burlington County	2012	Fourth Amendment	Officials may strip search those arrested for any offense, including minor ones, before admitting them to jail.
Brown v. Plata	2011	Eighth Amendment	Overcrowded conditions in California's prisons were so egregious that the state was unable to deliver minimal care to prisoners with serious medical and mental health problems, requiring a forced reduction in prison populations.
U.S. v. Georgia	2006		Under the Americans with Disabilities Act, a state may be liable for rights deprivations suffered by inmates held in its prisons who are disabled.
Johnson v. California	2005		A California Department of Corrections and Rehabilitation's unwritten policy of racially segregating prisoners in double cells each time they entered a new correctional facility was invalidated.
Wilkinson v. Austin	2005		Upheld an Ohio policy allowing the most dangerous offenders to be held in "supermax" cells following several levels of review prior to transfer.
Overton v. Bazzetta	2003		A visitation regulation that denies most visits to prisoners who commit two substance-abuse violations while incarcerated was upheld.
Porter v. Nussle	2002	Eighth Amendment	The Prison Litigation Reform Act of 1995 (PLRA) "exhaustion requirement" applies to all inmate suits about prison life, whether they involve general circumstances or particular episodes and whether they allege excessive force or some other wrong.
Hope v. Pelzer	2002	Eighth Amendment	The Court found a constitutional violation in the case of a prisoner who was subjected to unnecessary pain, humiliation, and risk of physical harm.
Booth v. Churner	2001	Eighth Amendment	The Prison Litigation Reform Act's requirement that state inmates must "exhaust such administrative remedies as are available" before filing a suit over prison conditions was upheld.
Lewis v. Casey	1996		Inmates need not be given the wherewithal to file any and every type of legal claim. All that is required is "that they be provided with the tools to attack their sentences."
Sandin v. Conner	1995	Fourteenth Amendment	Rejected the argument that disciplining inmates is a deprivation of constitutional due process rights.
Helling v. McKinney	1993	Eighth Amendment	Environmental conditions of prison life, including secondhand cigarette smoke, that pose a threat to inmate health have to be corrected.
Wilson v. Seiter	1991	Eighth Amendment	Clarified the totality of conditions concept by holding that some conditions of confinement, taken "in combination," may violate prisoners' rights when each would not do so alone.
Washington v. Harper	1990	Eighth Amendment	A mentally ill inmate who is a danger to self or others may be forcibly treated with psychoactive drugs.

Table 14-5 (*continued*)

CASE NAME	YEAR DECIDED	CONSTITUTIONAL BASIS	FINDING
Turner v. *Safley*	1987	First Amendment	A ban on correspondence between Missouri inmates was upheld as "reasonably related to legitimate penological interests."
O'Lone v. *Estate of Shabazz*	1987	First Amendment	An inmate's right to religious practice was not violated by prison officials who refused to alter his work schedule so that he could attend Friday afternoon services.
Whitley v. *Albers*	1986	Eighth Amendment	The shooting and wounding of an inmate was not a violation of that inmate's rights, because "the shooting was part and parcel of a good-faith effort to restore prison security."
Ponte v. *Real*	1985		Inmates are entitled to certain rights in disciplinary hearings.
Hudson v. *Palmer*	1984	Fourth Amendment	Prisoners have no reasonable expectation of privacy in their prison cells and no protections against what would otherwise be "unreasonable searches."
Block v. *Rutherford*	1984	First Amendment	State regulations may prohibit meetings of inmate unions as well as the use of the mail to deliver union information within the prison; also, prisoners do not have a right to be present during cell searches.
Rhodes v. *Chapman*	1981	Eighth Amendment	Double-celling of inmates is not in itself cruel and unusual punishment.
Ruiz v. *Estelle*	1980	Eighth Amendment	Unconstitutional conditions were found to exist within the Texas prison system—including overcrowding, understaffing, brutality, and substandard medical care.
Cooper v. *Morin*	1980		Neither inconvenience nor cost is an acceptable excuse for treating female inmates differently from male inmates.
Bell v. *Wolfish*	1979	Fourth Amendment	Pretrial detainees and other prisoners may be strip searched, to include body-cavity searches, as needed, regardless of the reason for their incarceration.
Jones v. *North Carolina-Prisoners' Labor Union, Inc.*	1977	First Amendment	Inmates have no inherent right to publish newspapers or newsletters for use by other inmates.
Bounds v. *Smith*	1977		Resulted in the creation of law libraries in many prisons.
Estelle v. *Gamble*	1976	Eighth Amendment	Prison officials have a duty to provide proper inmate medical care.
Ruiz v. *Estelle*	1975	Eighth Amendment	Conditions of confinement within the Texas prison system were found to be unconstitutional.
Wolff v. *McDonnell*	1974	Fourteenth Amendment	Sanctions cannot be levied against inmates without appropriate due process.
Procunier v. *Martinez*	1974	First Amendment	Censorship of inmate mail is acceptable only when necessary to protect legitimate governmental interests.
Pell v. *Procunier*	1974	First Amendment	Inmates retain First Amendment rights that are not inconsistent with their status as prisoners or with the legitimate penological objectives of the corrections system.
U.S. v. *Hitchcock*	1972	Fourth Amendment	A warrantless cell search is not unreasonable.
Cruz v. *Beto*	1972	First Amendment	Inmates have to be given a "reasonable opportunity" to pursue their religious faiths; also, visits can be banned if such visits constitute threats to security.
Johnson v. *Avery*	1968		Inmates have a right to consult "jailhouse lawyers" when trained legal assistance is not available.
Monroe v. *Pape*	1961		Inmates have a right to bring action in federal court when deprived of their rights by state officers acting under color of state law.

■ **lecture note**   Review the grievance procedures used in the prisons in your state. In a distance learning environment, consider having students research the procedures in their home states.

■ **grievance procedure**   A formalized arrangement, usually involving a neutral hearing board, whereby institutionalized individuals have the opportunity to register complaints about the conditions of their confinement.

A "jailhouse lawyer" works in a prison law library. Such inmates, although they rarely have any formal legal training, help other inmates prepare legal writs and represent them in in-house disciplinary actions. Why are jailhouse lawyers important to today's prisons?

bikeriderlondon/Shutterstock

Grievance Procedures

Today, all sizable prisons have established **grievance procedures** whereby an inmate files a complaint with local authorities and receives a mandated response. Modern grievance procedures range from the use of a hearing board composed of staff members and

inmates to a single staff appointee charged with the resolution of complaints. Inmates who are dissatisfied with the handling of their grievance can generally appeal beyond the local prison.

Disciplinary actions by prison authorities may also require a formalized hearing process, especially when staff members bring charges of rule violations against inmates that might result in some form of punishment being imposed on them. In a precedent-setting decision in the case of *Wolff* v. *McDonnell* (1974),[96] the Supreme Court decided that sanctions could not be levied against inmates without appropriate due process. The *Wolff* case involved an inmate who had been deprived of previously earned good-time credits because of misbehavior. The Court established that good-time credits were a form of "state-created right(s)," which, once created, could not be "arbitrarily abrogated."[97] *Wolff* was especially significant because it began an era of court scrutiny into what came to be called *state-created liberty interests*. State-created liberty interests were based on the language used in published prison regulations and were held, in effect, to confer due process guarantees on prisoners. Hence, if a prison regulation said that a disciplinary hearing should be held before a prisoner could be sent to solitary confinement and that the hearing should permit a discussion of the evidence for and against the prisoner, courts interpreted that regulation to mean that the prisoner had a state-created right to a hearing and

© ZUMA Press, Inc./Alamy

New Port Richey, Florida, USA—A group of inmates pray during a jailhouse bible study at the New Port Richey jail. Faith-based prison programs are sponsored by religious organizations and supplement government-sponsored training and rehabilitation programs. What special roles might such programs play?

■ **lecture note** Comment on the observation made in the text that the U.S. Supreme Court may have signaled at least a partial return to the hands-off doctrine. Use the case of *Wilson* v. *Seiter* (1991) as the basis for a discussion of the issue.

■ **lecture note** Explain that the Eighth Amendment (against cruel and unusual punishment) and the Fourteenth Amendment (requiring equal protection of the laws) have been used as the basis for most inmate suits against the conditions of confinement.

■ **deliberate indifference** A wanton disregard by corrections personnel for the well-being of inmates. Deliberate indifference requires both actual knowledge that a harm is occurring and disregard of the risk of harm. A prison official may be held liable under the Eighth Amendment for acting with deliberate indifference to inmate health or safety only if he or she knows that inmates face a substantial risk of serious harm and disregards that risk by failing to take reasonable measures to abate it.

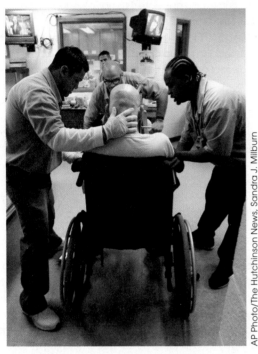

Hutchinson Correctional Facility (Kansas) inmate hospice volunteers Carlos Ballesteros, left, Chad Engro, and Robert Shanklin, right, help a patient in the prison's infirmary. Court decisions over the years have established a firm set of inmate rights. Among them is the right to necessary health care. What other rights do inmates have?

that sending him or her to solitary confinement in violation of the regulation was a violation of a state-created liberty interest. In later court decisions, state-created rights and privileges were called *protected liberties* and were interpreted to include any significant change in a prisoner's status.

In the interest of due process, and especially where written prison regulations governing the hearing process exist, courts have generally held that inmates going before disciplinary hearing boards are entitled to (1) a notice of the charges brought against them, (2) the chance to organize a defense, (3) an impartial hearing, and (4) the opportunity to present witnesses and evidence in their behalf. A written statement of the hearing board's conclusions should be provided to the inmate.[98] In the case of *Ponte* v. *Real* (1985),[99] the Supreme Court held that prison officials must provide an explanation to inmates who are denied the opportunity to have a desired witness at their hearing. The case of *Vitek* v. *Jones* (1980)[100] extended the requirement of due process to inmates about to be transferred from prisons to mental hospitals.

So that inmates will know what is expected of them as they enter prison, the American Correctional Association recommends that "a rulebook that contains all chargeable offenses, ranges of penalties and disciplinary procedures [be] posted in a conspicuous and accessible area; [and] a copy...given to each inmate and staff member."[101]

A Return to the Hands-Off Doctrine?

Many state-created rights and protected liberties may soon be a thing of the past. In June 1991, an increasingly conservative U.S. Supreme Court signaled what seemed like the beginning of a new hands-off era. The case, *Wilson* v. *Seiter et al.*,[102] involved a Section 1983 suit brought against Richard P. Seiter, director of the Ohio Department of Rehabilitation and Correction, and Carl Humphreys, warden of the Hocking Correctional Facility (HCF) in Nelsonville, Ohio. In the suit, Pearly L. Wilson, a felon incarcerated at HCF, alleged that a number of the conditions of his confinement constituted cruel and unusual punishment in violation of the Eighth and Fourteenth Amendments. Specifically, Wilson cited overcrowding, excessive noise, insufficient locker storage space, inadequate heating and cooling, improper ventilation, unclean and inadequate restrooms, unsanitary dining facilities and food preparation, and housing with mentally and physically ill inmates. Wilson asked for a change in prison conditions and sought $900,000 from prison officials in compensatory and punitive damages.

Both the federal district court in which Wilson first filed affidavits and the Sixth Circuit Court of Appeals held that no constitutional violations existed because the conditions cited by Wilson were not the result of malicious intent on the part of officials. The U.S. Supreme Court agreed, noting that the **deliberate indifference** standard applied in *Estelle* v. *Gamble* (1976)[103] to claims involving medical care is similarly applicable to other cases in which prisoners challenge the conditions of their confinement. In effect, the Court created a standard that effectively means that all future challenges to prison conditions by inmates, which are brought under the Eighth Amendment, must show deliberate indifference by the officials responsible for the existence of those conditions before the Court will hear the complaint.

The written opinion of the Court in *Wilson* v. *Seiter* is telling. Writing for the majority, Justice Antonin Scalia observed that "if a prison boiler malfunctions accidentally during a cold winter, an inmate would have no basis for an Eighth Amendment

freedom OR safety? YOU decide

Should Prison Libraries Limit Access to Potentially Inflammatory Literature?

In mid-2007, the Federal Bureau of Prisons (BOP) ordered chaplains at BOP facilities nationwide to remove potentially inflammatory literature from the shelves of chapel libraries. The move came in response to a report by the U.S. Justice Department's Office of the Inspector General, which recommended that prisons take steps to avoid becoming recruiting grounds for militant Islamists and other radical groups.

Thousands of books were soon removed under what the BOP called the Standardized Chapel Library Project, which it admitted was an effort to bar inmate access to literature that the BOP felt could "discriminate, disparage, advocate violence or radicalize." In identifying materials for removal, the BOP relied on the advice of experts who were asked to identify up to 150 book titles and 150 multimedia resources for each of 20 religious categories ranging from Bahaism to Yoruba. Prayer books were explicitly excluded from the list of materials targeted for removal.

Soon after the project was made public, however, members of Congress and a number of religious leaders urged the BOP to reverse its stance and return the books to chapel shelves.

In fall 2007, the Republican Study Committee, a group of conservative Republicans in the House of Representatives, sent a letter to BOP Director Harley G. Lappin saying, "We must ensure that in America the federal government is not the undue arbiter of what may or may not be read by our citizens."

Representative Jeb Hensarling of Texas, who heads the Republican Study Committee, explained that "anything that impinges upon the religious liberties of American citizens, be they incarcerated or not, is something that's going to cause...great concern." For its part, the BOP countered that it has a legitimate interest in screening out and removing items from inside of its facilities that could incite violence.

The controversy appeared to have ended in 2008 with passage of the Second Chance Act (Public Law 110-199), federal legislation that funded a number of reentry initiatives for people leaving prison and that required the director of the BOP "to discontinue the Standardized Chapel Library project or any other project that limits prisoner access to reading and other educational material." (The Second Chance Act is discussed in more detail in Chapter 12.) In 2009, however, the BOP revived its plan to limit prison chapel books and proposed a rule that would exclude materials from chapel libraries "that could incite, promote, or otherwise suggest the commission of violence or criminal activity." The proposed new rule targeted only literature encouraging violence, but critics said that it would still result in the banning of many religious texts.

You Decide

Should prison libraries be permitted to limit access to library literature that might incite violence or endanger the safety of inmates and staff? Would it matter if that literature is religious in nature? How might the BOP meet the concerns of the Republican Study Committee, religious leaders, and authors of the Second Chance Act while still accomplishing its objective of removing literature that it believes might incite violence?

References: Solomon Moore, "Plan Would Limit Prison Chapel Books," *New York Times*, March 18, 2009; Laurie Goodstein, "Prisons Purging Books on Faith from Libraries," *New York Times*, September 10, 2007; Laurie Goodstein, "Critics Right and Left Protest Book Removals," *New York Times*, September 21, 2007; and Neela Banerjee, "Prisons to Restore Purged Religious Books," *New York Times*, September 27, 2007.

---

claim, even if he suffers objectively significant harm. If a guard accidentally stepped on a prisoner's toe and broke it, this would not be punishment in anything remotely like the accepted meaning of the word." At the time that the *Wilson* decision was handed down, critics voiced concerns that the decision could effectively excuse prison authorities from the need to improve living conditions within institutions on the basis of simple budgetary constraints.

In the 1995 case of *Sandin* v. *Conner*,[104] the U.S. Supreme Court took a much more definitive stance in favor of a new type of hands-off doctrine and voted 5 to 4 to reject the argument that any state action taken for a punitive reason encroaches on a prisoner's constitutional due process right to be free from the deprivation of liberty. In *Sandin*, Demont Conner, an inmate at the Halawa Correctional Facility in Hawaii, was serving an indeterminate sentence of 30 years to life for numerous crimes, including murder, kidnapping, robbery, and burglary. In

a lawsuit in federal court, Conner alleged that prison officials had deprived him of procedural due process when a hearing committee refused to allow him to present witnesses during a disciplinary hearing and then sentenced him to segregation for alleged misconduct. An appellate court agreed with Conner, concluding that an existing prison regulation that instructed the hearing committee to find guilt in cases where a misconduct charge is supported by substantial evidence meant that the committee could not impose segregation if it did not look at all the evidence available to it.

The Supreme Court, however, reversed the decision of the appellate court, holding that while "such a conclusion may be entirely sensible in the ordinary task of construing a statute defining rights and remedies available to the general public, [i]t is a good deal less sensible in the case of a prison regulation primarily designed to guide correctional officials in the administration of a prison." The Court concluded that "such regulations [are] not designed to confer rights on inmates" but are meant only to provide guidelines to prison staff members.

In *Sandin*, the Court effectively set aside substantial portions of earlier decisions, such as *Wolff* v. *McDonnell* (1974)[105] and *Hewitt* v. *Helms* (1983),[106] which, wrote the justices, focused more on procedural issues than on those of "real substance." As a consequence, the majority opinion held, past cases like these have "impermissibly shifted the focus" away from the nature of a due process deprivation to one based on the language of a particular state or prison regulation. "The *Hewitt* approach," wrote the majority in *Sandin*, "has run counter to the view expressed in several of our cases that federal courts ought to afford appropriate deference and flexibility to state officials trying to manage a volatile environment.... The time has come," said the Court, "to return to those due process principles that were correctly established and applied" in earlier times. In short, *Sandin* made it much more difficult for inmates to effectively challenge the administrative regulations and procedures imposed on them by prison officials, even when stated procedures are not explicitly followed.

A more recent case whose findings support the action of federal corrections officers is that of *Ali* v. *Federal Bureau of Prisons*. The case, decided by the U.S. Supreme Court in 2008,[107] involved a federal prisoner, Abdus-Shahid M. S. Ali, who claimed that some of his personal belongings disappeared when he was transferred from one federal prison to another. The missing items, which were to have been shipped in two duffle bags belonging to Ali, included copies of the Koran, a prayer rug, and a number of religious magazines. Ali filed suit against the BOP under the Federal Tort Claims Act (FTCA),[108] which authorizes "claims against the United States for money damages...for injury or loss of property...caused by the negligent or wrongful act or omission of any employee in the government while acting within the scope of his office or employment." In denying Ali's claim, the Court found that the law specifically provides immunity for federal law enforcement officers and determined that federal corrections personnel are "law enforcement officers" within the meaning of the law. Similarly, in 2013, in the case of *Millbrook* v. *United States*, the court again found that the FTCA excepts "law enforcement officers' [including correctional officers] acts or omissions that arise within the scope of their employment, regardless of whether the officers are engaged in investigative or law enforcement activity, or are executing a search, seizing evidence, or making an arrest."[109]

Finally, in two cases from 2012, the U.S. Supreme Court ruled firmly in favor of correctional officials in limiting the rights of inmates. In the first case, *Howes* v. *Fields* (2012), the Court found that inmates who face questioning by law enforcement officers while they are incarcerated need not be advised of their *Miranda* rights prior to the start of interrogation.[110] In the second case, *Florence* v. *Burlington County* (2012), the Court ruled that officials had the power to strip search persons who had been arrested prior to admission to a jail or other detention facility, even if the offense for which they were arrested was a minor one.[111] In that case, Justice Kennedy, writing for the majority, noted that "maintaining safety and order at detention centers requires the expertise of correctional officials, who must have substantial discretion to devise reasonable solutions to problems." He went on to write that "the term 'jail' is used here in a broad sense to include prisons and other detention facilities."

The Prison Litigation Reform Act of 1996

Only about 2,000 petitions per year concerning inmate problems were filed with the courts in 1961, but by 1975 the number of filings had increased to around 17,000, and in 1996 prisoners filed 68,235 civil rights lawsuits in federal courts nationwide.[112] Some inmate-originated suits seemed patently ludicrous and became the subject of much media coverage in the mid-1990s. One such suit involved Robert Procup, a Florida State Prison inmate serving time for the murder of his business partner. Procup repeatedly sued Florida prison officials—once because he got only one roll with his dinner, again because he didn't get a luncheon salad, a third time because prison-provided TV dinners didn't come with a drink, and a fourth time because his cell had no television. Two other well-publicized cases involved an inmate who went to court asking to be allowed to exercise religious freedom by attending prison chapel services in the nude and an inmate who, thinking he could become pregnant via homosexual relations, sued prison doctors who wouldn't provide him with birth-control pills. An infamous example of seemingly frivolous inmate lawsuits was one brought by inmates claiming religious freedoms and demanding that members of the Church of the New Song, or CONS, be provided steak and Harvey's Bristol Cream every Friday in order to celebrate communion. The CONS suit stayed in various courts for ten years before finally being thrown out.[113]

The PLRA was a legislative effort to restrict inmate filings to worthwhile cases and to reduce the number of suits brought by state prisoners in federal courts. The huge number of inmate-originated lawsuits in the mid-1990s created a backlog of cases in many federal courts and was targeted by the media and by some citizens' groups as an

■ **lecture note**   Identify some of the major issues facing prisons today, including AIDS, geriatric offenders, and mentally ill inmates. Ask students whether they can envision any similar kinds of issues that might be on the horizon, waiting to emerge.

■ **lecture note**   Review the problem of HIV/AIDS in prison and explain the two types of strategies corrections administrators can use to reduce the transmission of AIDS.

unnecessary waste of taxpayers' money. The National Association of Attorneys General, which supports efforts to restrict frivolous inmate lawsuits, estimated that lawsuits filed by prisoners cost states more than $81 million a year in legal fees alone.[114]

In 1996, the federal Prison Litigation Reform Act (PLRA) became law.[115] The PLRA was a legislative effort to restrict inmate filings to worthwhile cases and to reduce the number of suits brought by state prisoners in federal courts. The PLRA

- Requires inmates to exhaust their prison's grievance procedure before filing a lawsuit.
- Requires judges to screen all inmate complaints against the federal government and to immediately dismiss those deemed frivolous or without merit.
- Prohibits prisoners from filing a lawsuit for mental or emotional injury unless they can also show there has been physical injury.
- Requires inmates to pay court filing fees. Prisoners who don't have the needed funds can pay the filing fee over a period of time through deductions from their prison commissary accounts.
- Limits the award of attorneys' fees in successful lawsuits brought by inmates.
- Revokes the credits earned by federal prisoners toward early release if they file a malicious lawsuit.
- Mandates that court orders affecting prison administration cannot go any further than necessary to correct a violation of a particular inmate's civil rights.
- Makes it possible for state officials to have court orders lifted after two years unless there is a new finding of a continuing violation of federally guaranteed civil rights.
- Mandates that any court order requiring the release of prisoners due to overcrowding be approved by a three-member court before it can become effective.

The U.S. Supreme Court has upheld provisions of the PLRA on a number of occasions. According to one BJS study, the PLRA has been effective in reducing the number of frivolous lawsuits filed by inmates alleging unconstitutional prison conditions.[116] The study found that the filing rate of inmates' civil rights petitions in federal courts had been cut in half four years after passage of the act. A similar study by the National Center for State Courts, whose

> According to one BJS study, the PLRA has been effective in reducing the number of frivolous lawsuits filed by inmates alleging unconstitutional prison conditions.

results were published in 2004, found that the act "produced a statistically significant decrease in both the volume and trend of lawsuits…nationally and in every [federal court] circuit."[117]

Opponents of the PLRA fear that it is stifling the filing of meritorious suits by inmates facing real deprivations. According to the American Civil Liberties Union (ACLU), for example, "The Prison Litigation Reform Act…attempts to slam the courthouse door on society's most vulnerable members. It seeks to strip the federal courts of much of their power to correct even the most egregious prison conditions by altering the basic rules which have always governed prison reform litigation. The PLRA also makes it difficult to settle prison cases by consent decree, and limits the life span of any court judgment."[118]

Issues Facing Prisons Today

Prisons are society's answer to a number of social problems. They house outcasts, misfits, and some highly dangerous people. Although prisons provide a part of the answer to the question of crime control, they also face problems of their own. A few of those special problems are described here.

AIDS

Chapter 8 discussed the steps that police agencies are taking Police agencies are taking steps to deal with health threats from acquired immunodeficiency syndrome (AIDS). In 2012, the BJS reported finding that 20,093 state and federal inmates were infected with HIV (human immunodeficiency virus), the virus that causes AIDS.[119] The BJS report found that the rate of HIV/AIDS among state and federal prison inmates declined from 194 cases per 10,000 inmates in 2001 to 146 per 10,000 at year-end 2010. The size of the decline is shown in Figure 14-5.

California, Florida, New York, and Texas each hold more than 1,000 inmates with HIV/AIDS; in combination, these states hold 51% (9,492) of all state prisoners with HIV/AIDS. Among state and federal inmates with HIV/AIDS at yearend 2010, 18,337 were male and 1,756 were female.

Some years ago, AIDS was the leading cause of death among prison inmates.[120] Today, however, the number of inmates who die from AIDS (or, more precisely, from AIDS-related complications like pneumonia or Kaposi's sarcoma) is much lower. The introduction of drugs like protease inhibitors and useful combinations of antiretroviral therapies have significantly reduced inmate deaths from AIDS.[121] The BJS reported that AIDS-related

■ **theme**   Discuss the factors leading to a higher incidence of geriatric offenders. How does this situation affect prisoners' rights to medical treatment, which was discussed earlier in this chapter?

■ **theme**   Do you think geriatric inmates incarcerated for nonviolent crimes should be released to the community? Why or why not?

■ **lecture note**   Discuss the problems that geriatric inmates create for prisons. In additional to the cost of medical care, problems include prison structures, which generally are not designed for disabled individuals; security risks due to the use of canes and crutches, which could also be used as weapons; and the stress that caring for elderly inmates may place on corrections staff.

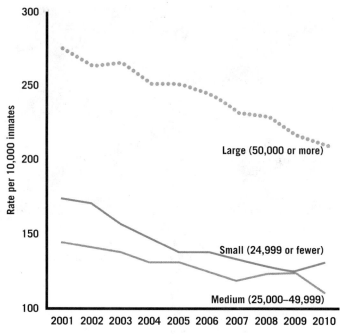

Figure 14-5 | Rate of HIV/AIDS Cases per 10,000 Inmates, by Size of State Prison Custody Population, 2001–2010

Source: Laura M. Maruschak, HIV in Prisons, 2001–2010 (Washington, DC: Bureau of Justice Statistics, September 2012), p. 2.

deaths among all state and federal prison inmates declined by an average of 16% per year between 2001 and 2010, from 24 deaths per 100,000 inmates in 2001 to 5 per 100,000 in 2010.

Most infected inmates brought the HIV virus into prison with them, and one study found that fewer than 10% of HIV-positive inmates acquired the virus while in prison.[122] Nonetheless, the virus can be spread behind bars through homosexual activity (including rape), intravenous drug use, and the sharing of tainted tattoo and hypodermic needles. Inmates who were infected before entering prison are likely to have had histories of high-risk behavior, especially intravenous drug use.

A report by the National Institute of Justice (NIJ) suggests that corrections administrators can use two types of strategies to reduce the transmission of AIDS.[123] One strategy relies on medical technology to identify seropositive inmates and to segregate them from the rest of the prison population. Mass screening and inmate segregation, however, may be prohibitively expensive. They may also be illegal. Some states specifically prohibit HIV-antibody testing without the informed consent of the person tested.[124] The related issue of confidentiality may be difficult to manage, especially when the purpose of testing is to segregate infected inmates from others. In addition, civil liability may result if inmates are falsely labeled as infected or if inmates

known to be infected are not prevented from spreading the disease. Only Alabama and South Carolina still segregate all known HIV-infected inmates,[125] but more limited forms of separation are practiced elsewhere. Many state prison systems have denied HIV-positive inmates jobs, educational opportunities, visitation privileges, conjugal visits, and home furloughs, causing some researchers to conclude that "inmates with HIV and AIDS are routinely discriminated against and denied equal treatment in ways that have no accepted medical basis."[126] In 1994, for example, a federal appeals court upheld a California prison policy that bars HIV-positive inmates from working in food-service jobs.[127] In contrast, in 2001, the Mississippi Department of Correction ended its policy of segregating HIV-positive prisoners from other inmates in educational and vocational programs.

The second strategy is prevention through education. Educational programs teach both inmates and staff members about the dangers of high-risk behavior and suggest ways to avoid HIV infection. An NIJ model program recommends the use of simple, straightforward messages presented by knowledgeable and approachable trainers.[128] Alarmism, says the NIJ, should be avoided. One survey found that 98% of state and federal prisons provide some form of AIDS/HIV education and that 90% of jails do as well—although most such training is oriented toward corrections staff rather than inmates.[129] Learn more about HIV in prisons at **http://www.justicestudies.com/pubs/hiv.pdf**.

Geriatric Offenders

In 2013, 89-year-old Anthony Marshall, the frail and wheelchair-bound son of the late philanthropist and socialite Brooke Astor, became the oldest person ever sent to a New York prison for a nonviolent crime.[130] Marshall, who depends on an oxygen tank to breathe, had been convicted of plundering his mother's huge fortune and was sentenced to one to three years behind bars.

Crimes committed by elderly people, especially violent crimes, have recently been on the decline. Nonetheless, the significant expansion of America's retiree population has led to an increase in the number of elderly people who are behind bars. In fact, crimes of violence are what bring most older people into the correctional system. According to one early study, 52% of inmates who were over the age of 50 when they entered prison had committed violent crimes, compared with 41% of younger inmates.[131] An ACLU survey found that there were 8,853 state and federal prisoners age 55 and older scattered throughout America's prisons in 1981.[132] Today, that number stands at 124,900, and experts project that by 2030 there will be over 400,000 such inmates. Thus, it is expected that the elderly

■ **lecture note**   Link the situation of inmates with mental illness and intellectual disabilities to that of geriatric inmates and point out that most correctional institutions do not have the ability to care properly for inmates with serious mental illnesses.

prison population United States will increase by 4,400% over this 50-year span. Similarly, the per capita rate of incarceration for inmates age 55 and over now stands at more than 642 per 100,000 U.S. residents of like age.[133]

Not all of today's elderly inmates were old when they entered prison. Because of harsh sentencing laws passed throughout the country in the 1990s, a small but growing number of inmates (10%) will serve 20 years or more in prison, and 5% will never be released.[134] This means that many inmates who enter prison when they are young will grow old behind bars. The "graying" of America's prison population has a number of causes: "(1) the general aging of the American population, which is reflected inside prisons; (2) new sentencing policies such as 'three strikes,' 'truth-in-sentencing,' and 'mandatory minimum' laws that send more criminals to prison for longer stretches; (3) a massive prison building boom that took place in the 1980s and 1990s, and which has provided space for more inmates, reducing the need to release prisoners to alleviate overcrowding; and (4) significant changes in parole philosophies and practices,"[135] with state and federal authorities phasing out or canceling parole programs, thereby forcing jailers to hold inmates with life sentences until they die.

Long-termers and geriatric inmates have special needs. They tend to suffer from physical disabilities and illnesses not generally encountered among their more youthful counterparts. Unfortunately, few prisons are equipped to deal adequately with the medical needs of aging offenders. Some large facilities have begun to set aside special sections to care for elderly inmates with "typical" disorders, such as Alzheimer's disease, cancer, or heart disease. Unfortunately, such efforts have barely kept pace with the problems that geriatric offenders present. The number of inmates requiring around-the-clock care is expected to increase dramatically during the next two decades.[136]

> Unfortunately, few prisons are equipped to deal adequately with the medical needs of aging offenders.

Incarcerating people into old age is costly and may be counterproductive. Research has consistently shown that "by age 50 most people have significantly outlived the years in which they are most likely to commit crimes."[137] Moreover, most aging prisoners are not incarcerated for serious or violent offenses, and could probably be allowed to reenter the community with little danger to others. In Texas, for example, 65% of elderly prisoners are confined for nonviolent drug crimes, property crimes, and other nonviolent offenses. Because of rising medical expenses, the costs of confining a prisoner over age 50 jumps to an average of $68,270, whereas housing and other associated costs of keeping an inmate below that age behind bars is only $34,135.[138]

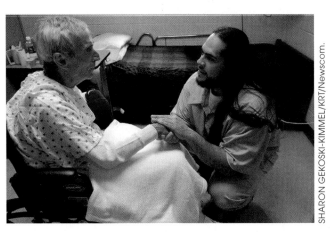

Salvatore LoGiudice, left, 78, is assisted by fellow inmate Dennis Galan, in the hospice section at South Woods State Prison in Bridgeton, New Jersey. Why is the proportion of geriatric inmates increasing? What special needs do they have?

Finally the idea of rehabilitation takes on a new meaning where geriatric offenders are concerned. What kinds of programs are most useful in providing older inmates with the tools needed for success on the outside? Which counseling strategies hold the greatest promise for introducing socially acceptable behavior patterns into the long-established lifestyles of elderly offenders about to be released? There are few easy answers to such questions.

Inmates with Mental Illness and Intellectual Disabilities

Inmates with mental illness make up another group with special needs. Some of these inmates are neurotic or have personality problems, which increases tensions in prison. Others have serious psychological disorders that may have escaped diagnosis at trial or that did not provide a legal basis for the reduction of criminal responsibility. Other offenders develop psychiatric symptoms while in prison.

Inmates suffering from significant mental illnesses account for a substantial number of those imprisoned. One study by the BJS found that the nation's prisons and jails hold an estimated 1.25 million inmates with mental illness (56% of those confined) and that more incarcerated women (73%) than men (55%) are mentally ill.[139] A second government study found that 40% of these inmates receive no treatment at all. Finally, a 2014 report by the Virginia-based Treatment Advocacy Center found 356,268 inmates with *severe* mental illness in prisons nationally—a number ten times greater than people being treated for similar conditions in state psychiatric hospitals.[140]

■ **theme**   What role can corrections personnel play in preventing future attacks of terrorism?

■ **theme**   What kinds of terrorist activity might occur in prison? What steps can corrections personnel take to reduce the threat of terrorist activity in their facilities?

A 2000 BJS survey of public and private state-level adult correctional facilities (excluding jails) found that 51% of such institutions provide 24-hour mental health care, and 71% provide therapy and counseling by trained mental health professionals as needed.[141] A large majority of prisons distribute psychotropic medications (when such medications are ordered by a physician), and 66% have programs to help released inmates obtain community mental health services. According to BJS, 13% of state prisoners were receiving some type of mental health therapy at the time of the survey, and 10% were receiving psychotropic medications, including antidepressants, stimulants, sedatives, and tranquilizers.

Unfortunately, few state-run correctional institutions have any substantial capacity for the in-depth psychiatric treatment of inmates who have serious mental illnesses. Numerous states, however, do operate facilities that specialize in psychiatric confinement of convicted criminals. The BJS reports that state governments throughout the nation operate 12 facilities devoted exclusively to the care of inmates with mental illness and that another 143 prisons report psychiatric confinement as one specialty among other functions that they perform. As mentioned previously, the U.S. Supreme Court has ruled that inmates who are mentally ill can be required to take antipsychotic drugs, even against their wishes.[142]

Inmates with intellectual disabilities constitute still another group with special needs. Some studies estimate the proportion of these inmates at about 10%.[143] Inmates with low IQs are less likely than other inmates to complete training and rehabilitative programs successfully. They also evidence difficulty in adjusting to the routines of prison life. As a consequence, they are likely to exceed the averages in proportion of sentence served.[144] Only seven states report special facilities or programs for inmates with intellectual disabilities.[145] Other state systems "mainstream" such inmates, making them participate in regular activities with other inmates.

Terrorism and Corrections

Today's antiterrorism efforts have brought to light the important role that corrections personnel can play in preventing future attacks against America and in averting crises that could arise in correctional institutions as a result of terrorist action. Some years after the attacks of 911, former New York City Police Commissioner Bernard B. Kerik told participants at the ACA's winter conference that corrections officers can help in the fight against terrorism through effective intelligence gathering and intelligence sharing. "Intelligence—that's the key to the success of this battle," Kerik said.[146] "You have to be part of that, because when we take the people off the streets in this country that go to jail, they communicate and they talk, they work with other criminals, organized

A woman talks with her husband through a video visitation system at the DeSoto County Jail in Jernando, Mississippi. What are the benefits of such a system? The drawbacks?

gangs, organized units. You've got to collect that information, you have to get it back to the authorities that need it."

Prison administrators must also be concerned about the potential impact of outside terrorist activity on their facility's inmate and staff populations. Of particular concern to today's prison administrators is the possibility of bioterrorism. A concentrated population like that of a prison or jail is highly susceptible to the rapid transmission of biological agents.[147]

The threat of a terrorist act being undertaken by inmates within a prison or jail can be an important consideration in facility planning and management, especially because inmates may be particularly vulnerable to recruitment by terrorist organizations. According to Chip Ellis, research and program coordinator for the National Memorial Institute for the Prevention of Terrorism, "Prisoners are a captive audience, and they usually have a diminished sense of self or a need for identity and protection. They're usually a disenchanted or disenfranchised group of people, [and] terrorists can sometimes capitalize on that situation."[148] Inmates can be radicalized in many ways, including exposure to other radical inmates, the distribution of extremist literature, and anti-U.S. sermons heard during religious services.

Recently, the Institute for the Study of Violent Groups (ISVG), located at Sam Houston State University, charged that the most radical form of Islam, Wahhabism, was being spread in American prisons by clerics approved by the Islamic Society of North America, one of two organizations chosen by the Federal Bureau of Prisons to select prison chaplains.[149] "Proselytizing in prisons," said the ISVG, "can produce new recruits with American citizenship." An example of such activity can be found in the story of accused terrorist Kevin James, 32, who was sentenced in federal court in Santa Ana, California, in 2009 to 16 years in prison. James had pleaded guilty in 2007 to conspiracy

CJ │ ISSUES
Technocorrections

The technological forces that have made cell phones commonplace are beginning to converge with the ongoing efforts of correctional administrators to create what some have called *technocorrections*. Members of the correctional establishment—the managers of the jail, prison, probation, and parole systems and their sponsors in elected office—are seeking more cost-effective ways to increase public safety and to meet the needs of correctional administrators as the number of people under correctional supervision continues to grow. Technocorrections is an emerging field being defined by a correctional establishment that seeks to take advantage of the potential offered by new technologies to reduce the costs of supervising criminal offenders and to minimize the risk they pose to society.

Emerging technologies in four areas will soon be central elements of technocorrections: electronic tracking and location systems, pharmacological treatments, genetic and neurobiological risk assessments, and enhanced communications both inside and outside of correctional facilities. Although these technologies may significantly increase public safety and lessen the pains of imprisonment, we must also be mindful of the threats they pose to democratic principles. The critical challenge will be to learn how to take advantage of new technological opportunities applicable to the corrections field while minimizing their threats.

Tracking and Location Systems

Electronic tracking and location systems are the technology that is perhaps most familiar to correctional practitioners today. Most states use electronic monitoring—either with the older bracelets that communicate through a device connected to telephone lines or with more modern versions based on cellular or satellite tracking.

Tiny cameras might also be integrated into tracking devices to provide live video of offenders' locations and activities. Miniature electronic devices implanted in the body to signal the location of offenders at all times, to create unique identifiers that trigger alarms, and to monitor key bodily functions that affect unwanted behaviors are under development and are close to becoming reality.[1]

Pharmacological Treatments

Pharmacological breakthroughs—new "wonder drugs" being developed to control behavior in correctional and noncorrectional settings—will also be a part of technocorrections. Corrections officials are already familiar with some of these drugs, which are currently used to treat offenders who are mentally ill. Yet these drugs could also be used to control mental conditions affecting undesirable behaviors even for offenders who are not mentally ill.

It is only a matter of time before research findings in this area lead to the development of drugs to control neurobiological processes. These drugs could become correctional tools to manage violent offenders and perhaps even to prevent violence. Such advances are related to the third area of technology that will affect corrections: genetic and neurobiological risk-assessment technologies.

Risk-Assessment Technologies

Corrections officials today are familiar with the DNA profiling of offenders, particularly sex offenders. This is just the beginning of the correctional application of gene-related technologies, however. The Human Genome Project, supported by the National Institutes of Health and the Department of Energy, began in 1990 and was completed in 2003. The goal of the Human Genome Project was to create a map of the 3 billion chemical bases that make up human DNA. The map was constructed by high-powered "sequencer" machines that can analyze human DNA faster than any human researcher can.[2] Emerging as a powerhouse of the high-tech economy, the biotechnology industry will drive developments in DNA-based risk assessment.

Neurobiological research is taking the same path, although thus far no neurobiological patterns specific enough to be reliable biological markers for violent behavior have been uncovered. Is it possible that breakthroughs in these areas will lead to the development of risk-assessment tools that use genetic or neurobiological profiles to identify children who have a propensity toward addiction or violence? We may soon be able to link genetic and neurobiological traits with social and environmental factors to reliably predict who is at risk for addiction, sex offending, violent behavior, or crime in general.

Attempts will surely be made to develop genetic or neurobiological tests for assessing risks posed by individuals. This is already done for the risk of contracting certain diseases. Demand for risk assessments of individuals will come from corrections officials under pressure to prevent violent recidivism.

"Preventive incarceration" is already a reality for some convicted sex offenders. More than a dozen states commit certain sex offenders to special "civil commitment" facilities after they have served their prison sentences because of a behavioral or mental abnormality that makes them dangerous.[3] This happens today with no clear understanding of the nature of the abnormality. It is not difficult to imagine what might be done to justify preventive incarceration if this "abnormal" or criminal behavior could be explained and predicted by genetic or neurobiological profiling.

Enhanced Communications

In 2012, a Sentencing Project study of video visitation programs found that "at least 20 states already have video capability or have plans to adopt the technology."[4] The Project noted that the benefits of video visitation for correctional facilities include reducing the risk of contraband entering facilities, cost savings associated with fewer staff needed to oversee visits, and increased revenues from fees paid by inmates or virtual visitors. The Project also said that video visitation could be of significant benefit to the children of incarcerated parents, who might not otherwise have an opportunity for face-to-face communication with their parent.

[1] "Microchip Implants Closer to Reality," *Futurist*, Vol. 33, No. 8 (October 1999), p. 9.

[2] Walter Isaacson, "The Biotech Century," *Time*, January 11, 1999, p. 42; and Michael D. Lemonick and Dick Thompson, "Racing to Map Our DNA," *Time*, January 11, 1999, p. 44.

[3] See *Kansas v. Hendricks*, 521 U.S. 346 (1997), in which the Court approved such a practice. In the case of *Kansas v. Crane* (122 S.Ct. 867 (2002)), however, the U.S. Supreme Court ruled that the Constitution does not permit commitment of certain types of dangerous sexual offenders without a "lack-of-control determination."

[4] Susan D. Phillips, *Video Visits for Children Whose Parents Are Incarcerated: In Whose Best Interests?* (Washington, DC: The Sentencing Project, 2012), p. 3.

Sources: Adapted from Tony Fabelo, *"Technocorrections": The Promises, the Uncertain Threats* (Washington, DC: National Institute of Justice, 2000); and U.S. Department of Energy, "Human Genome Project Information," http://www.ornl.gov/TechResources/Human_Genome/home.html (accessed July 30, 2010).

CJ | NEWS
Radical Islam, Terrorism, and U.S. Prisons

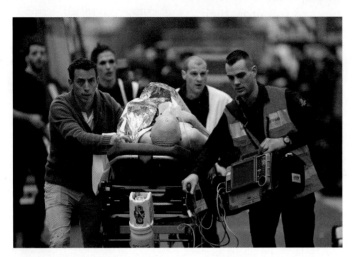

A seriously wounded staffer is removed from the offices of *Charlie Hebdo*, the French newspaper that came under attack from Islamic militants in 2015. At least one of the two attackers had been radicalized during the three years he spent in a French prison. How might American correctional officers help in the nation's fight against terrorism in this country?

In 2015, two heavily armed terrorists, later found to be brothers, attacked the Paris offices of *Charlie Hebdo*, a newspaper famous for printing caricatures of the Prophet Muhammad. During the attack, the terrorists, who killed 12 of the newspaper's staff and wounded others, could be heard yelling "Allahu Akbar" (Arabic for "God is Great"), and "We have avenged the Prophet Muhammad."

Authorities later determined that at least one of the terrorist brothers, Cherif Kouachi, had become radicalized during the three years he spent in the French prison, Fleury-Mérogis.

Even before the attacks, a report by French police intelligence identified 95 prisoners as having become radicalized and classified them as "dangerous." Another 105 were said to "merit attention," with the report's authors noting that they could become "time bombs" once released.

American experts, however, seem to think the situation is different in this country. "The claim that U.S. prisons will generate scores of terrorists spilling out onto the streets of our cities appears to be false or, at least, much overstated," Bert Useem, PhD, a sociology professor at Purdue University, told a U.S. House panel studying the matter in June 2011. Useem noted that of 178 Muslim Americans involved in terrorism-related violence, only 12 showed any connection to radicalization behind bars.

Experts attribute this positive outcome, more than a decade after the September 11, 2001, terrorist attacks, as much to U.S. prisoners'

lack of interest in Middle Eastern causes as to the steps prison authorities have taken to make sure inmates do not go down this path. The federal BOP and state systems have improved monitoring of Muslim prisoners and reduced their access to radical Islamist literature, and authorities such as the FBI have kept track of some prisoners after release.

In a country that is less than 1% Muslim, reportedly 10% of U.S. prisoners have embraced Islam. "The primary motivation I found was spiritual 'searching'— seeking religious meaning to interpret and resolve discontent," wrote Mark Hamm, PhD, a professor of criminology at Indiana State University. His two-year study of prisoner radicalization appeared in the *National Institute of Justice Journal* in October 2008.

Although that spiritual quest is quite different from the path to jihad, Hamm warned that "the potential for ideologically inspired criminality" still exists. He noted that a few terrorist plots had been uncovered in Florida and California prisons. In California's New Folsom Prison in 2005, several Muslim convicts led by Kevin James plotted terrorist acts against the National Guard, synagogues, and the Israeli consulate. When several members of the group were paroled, they committed a string of bank heists to finance their plan, but they were caught before they could commit it.

Middle Eastern interests have reached out to U.S. prisons. In 2003, the *Wall Street Journal* reported that Saudi Arabia "ships out hundreds of copies of the Quran each month, as well as religious pamphlets and videos, to prison chaplains and Islamic groups who then pass them along to inmates."

Many U.S. prisoners and their Islamic chaplains have embraced the Saudis' Wahhabi Salafist sect, with its Islamic-supremacist interpretation of the Quran. Warith Deen Umar, a Wahhabi Salafist who was head Muslim chaplain of the New York prisons until 2000, told the *Wall Street Journal* that prison "is the perfect recruitment and training grounds for radicalism and the Islamic religion."

The *Wall Street Journal*'s revelations prompted a review by the Office of the Inspector General (OIG) of the use of Muslim chaplains and Islamic literature in the BOP. The OIG's 2004 report issued 16 recommendations, including requiring imams (Muslim religious leaders) to work closely with security staff, closely monitoring volunteer imams, and screening prayer books. Many state prisons took up the recommendations as well.

In addition, longstanding prohibitions against using the Internet have barred prisoners' access to radical sites, although some have smuggled in smartphones. As a further precaution, the BOP in 2006 began isolating a few dozen radical Islamist prisoners in two communication management units (CMUs) that severely restrict visitation rights and monitor all telephone calls and mail. The CMU at the U.S. Penitentiary in Marion, Illinois, houses 18 Muslims, including Kevin James.

Resources: Bert Useem, "Testimony for the Committee on Homeland Security," June 15, 2011, http://homeland.house.gov/sites/homeland.house.gov/files/Testimony%20Useem.pdf; "Imams Reject Talk That Islam Radicalizes Inmates," *New York Times*, May 23, 2009, http://www.nytimes.com/2009/05/24/nyregion/24convert.html?_r=1&ref=us; and "Prisoner Radicalization: Assessing the Threat in U.S. Correctional Institutions," *National Institute of Justice Journal*, October 2008, http://www.nij.gov/journals/261/prisoner-radicalization.htm; Jim Yardley, "Jihadism Born in a Paris Park and Fueled in the Prison Yard, *The New York Times*, January 11, 2015, http://www.nytimes.com/2015/01/12/world/europe/jihadism-born-in-a-paris-park-and-fueled-in-the-prison-yard.html.

to wage war against the United States[150] and was accused of plotting terrorist attacks on Jewish and military targets throughout California while imprisoned. Among his targets were the Los Angeles International Airport, the Israeli Consulate, and U.S. Army recruiting centers (Read more about James in the CJ Issues box in this chapter.).

In response to the terrorist threat, the BOP implemented a number of practices, and today it coordinates with other federal agencies to share intelligence information about suspected or known terrorists in its inmate population. The BOP closely tracks inmates with known or suspected terrorist ties and monitors their correspondence and other communications. The BOP

> The BOP closely tracks inmates with known or suspected terrorist ties and monitors their correspondence and other communications.

also trains staff members to recognize terrorist-related activity and to effectively manage convicted terrorists within the correctional environment. A BOP program to counter radicalization efforts among inmates has been in place for the past twelve years.[151] Learn more about prison radicalization from the Federal Bureau of Investigation (FBI) at **http://www.justicestudies.com/pubs/racial.pdf**, and read more about prison issues of all kinds from the Prison Policy Initiative via **http://www.prisonpolicy.org**.

freedom OR safety? YOU decide

Censoring Prison Communications

While concerns over the terrorist attacks of 911 were still high, NBC News announced that it had learned that Arab terrorists in federal maximum-security prisons had been sending letters to extremists on the outside, exhorting them to attack Western interests. The terrorists included Mohammed Salameh, a follower of radical sheik Omar Abdel-Rahman. Salameh had been sentenced to more than 100 years in prison for his part in the 1993 bombing attack on New York's World Trade Center. That attack, which killed 6 and injured more than 1,000, blew a huge hole in the basement parking garage of one of the towers but failed to topple the buildings.

NBC News revealed that the men, while being held in the federal ADMAX facility in Florence, Colorado—the country's most secure federal prison—sent at least 14 letters to a Spanish terror cell, praised Osama bin Laden in Arabic newspapers, and advocated additional terror attacks. In July 2002, Salameh, a Palestinian with a degree in Islamic law from a Jordanian university, sent a letter to the Al-Quds Arabic daily newspaper proclaiming that "Osama Bin Laden is my hero of this generation."

Andy McCarthy, a former federal prosecutor who worked to send the terrorists to prison, said that Salameh's letters were "exhorting acts of terrorism and helping recruit would-be terrorists for the Jihad." Michael Macko, who lost his father in the Trade Center bombing, posed this question: "If they are

encouraging acts of terrorism internationally, how do we know they're not encouraging acts of terrorism right here on U.S. soil?"

Prison officials told reporters that communications involving the imprisoned bombers had not been closely censored because the men hadn't been considered very dangerous. The letters didn't contain any plans for attacks, nor did they name any specific targets. One Justice Department official said that Salameh was "a low level guy" who was not under any special restrictions and that his letters were seen as "generic stuff" and "no cause for concern."

Rights advocates suggested that inmates should have the right to free speech—even those imprisoned for acts of terrorism—and that advocating terrorism is not the same thing as planning it or carrying it out. After all, they said, calls for a holy war, however repugnant they may be in the current international context, are merely political statements—and politics is not against the law.

You Decide

What kinds of prison communications, if any, should be monitored or restricted (letters, telephone calls, e-mail)? Do you believe that communications containing statements like those described here should be confiscated? What kinds of political statements, if any, should be permitted?

References: Lisa Myers, "Imprisoned Terrorists Still Advocating Terror," *NBC Nightly News*, February 28, 2005, http://www.msnbc.msn.com/id/7046691 (accessed August 28, 2005); and Lisa Myers, "Bureau of Prisons under Fire for Jihad Letters," http://MSNBC.com, March 1, 2005, http://www.msnbc.msn.com/id/7053165 (accessed August 28, 2005).

SUMMARY

- Prisons are small, self-contained societies that are sometimes described as *total institutions*. Studies of prison life have detailed the existence of prison subcultures, or inmate worlds, replete with inmate values, social roles, and lifestyles. New inmates who are socialized into prison subculture are said to undergo the process of prisonization. Prison subcultures are very influential, and both inmates and staff must reckon with them. Today's prisons are miniature societies, reflecting the problems and challenges that exist in the larger society of which they are a part.

- Female inmates represent a small but growing proportion of the nation's prison population. Many female inmates have histories of physical and sexual abuse. Although they are likely to have dependent children, their parenting skills may be limited. Most female inmates are housed in centralized state facilities known as women's prisons, which are dedicated exclusively to incarcerating female felons. Some states, however, particularly those with small populations, continue to keep female prisoners in special wings of what are otherwise institutions for men. Few facilities for women have programs especially designed for female offenders.

- Like prisoners, corrections officers undergo a socialization process that helps them function by the official and unofficial rules of staff society. Prison staffers are most concerned with custody and control. The enforcement of strict rules; body and cell searches; counts; unannounced shakedowns; the control of dangerous items, materials, and contraband; and the extensive use of bars, locks, fencing, cameras, and alarms all support the staff's vigilance in maintaining security. Although concerns with security still command center stage, professionalism is playing an increasing role in corrections today, and today's corrections personnel are better trained and more proficient than ever before.

- For many years, courts throughout the nation assumed a hands-off approach to prisons, rarely intervening in the day-to-day administration of prison facilities. That changed in the late 1960s, when the U.S. Supreme Court began to identify inmates' rights mandated by the Constitution. Rights identified by the Court include the right to physical integrity, an absolute right to be free from unwarranted corporal punishments, certain religious rights, and procedural rights, such as those involving access to attorneys and to the courts. The conditional rights of prisoners, which have repeatedly been supported by the Court, mandate professionalism among prison administrators and require vigilance in the provision of correctional services. High Court decisions have generally established that prison inmates retain those constitutional rights that are not inconsistent with their status as prisoners or with the legitimate penological objectives of the correctional system. In other words, inmates have rights, much the same as people who are not incarcerated, provided that the legitimate needs of the prison for security, custody, and safety are not compromised. The era of prisoners' rights was sharply curtailed in 1996 with the passage of the Prison Litigation Reform Act, spurred on by a growing recognition of the legal morass resulting from the unregulated access to federal courts by inmates across the nation.

- The major problems and issues facing prisons today include (1) the need to deal with a growing geriatric offender population, which is the result of longer sentences and the aging of the American population; (2) a sizable number of inmates who are mentally ill and have intellectual disabilities; and (3) a concern over inmates with terrorist leanings and those who have been incarcerated for terrorism-related crimes.

KEY TERMS

balancing test, 484	prison argot, 466
civil death, 484	prison subculture, 465
deliberate indifference, 489	prisonization, 465
gender responsiveness, 473	security threat group
grievance procedure, 488	(STG), 481
hands-off doctrine, 484	total institution, 464

KEY CASES

Block v. *Rutherford*, 487	*Jones* v. *North Carolina Prisoners'*
Brown v. *Plata*, 486	*Labor Union*, 487
Bounds v. *Smith*, 487	*Overton* v. *Bazzetta*, 486
Cruz v. *Beto*, 487	*Pell* v. *Procunier*, 487
Estelle v. *Gamble*, 487	*Ruiz* v. *Estelle*, 487
Helling v. *McKinney*, 486	*Sandin* v. *Conner*, 486
Hudson v. *Palmer*, 487	*Wolff* v. *McDonnell*, 487
Johnson v. *Avery*, 487	

QUESTIONS FOR REVIEW

1. What are prison subcultures, and how do they influence prison life? How do they develop, and what purpose do they serve?

2. How do women's prisons differ from men's? Why have women's prisons been studied less often than institutions for men?

3. What are the primary concerns of prison staff? What other goals do staff members focus on?

4. What are the commonly accepted rights of prisoners in the United States today? Where do these rights come from? What U.S. Supreme Court cases are especially significant in the area of prisoners' rights?

5. What are some of the major issues that prisons face today? What new issues might the future bring?

QUESTIONS FOR REFLECTION

1. What does *prisonization* mean? Describe the U-shaped curve developed by Stanton Wheeler to illustrate the concept of prisonization. How can an understanding of Wheeler's U-shaped curve help prevent recidivism?

2. What is the hands-off doctrine? What is the status of that doctrine today? What is its likely future?

3. Explain the balancing test established by the Supreme Court in deciding issues of prisoners' rights. How might such a test apply to the emerging area of inmate privacy?

4. What does the term *state-created rights* mean within the context of corrections? What do you predict for the future of state-created rights?

NOTES

1. "Miss Wisconsin Makes Father's Prison Time a Miss America Platform," CBS News, January 15, 2012, http://www.cbsnews.com/8301-31749_162-57359505-10391698/miss-wisconsin-makes-fathers-prison-time-a-miss-america-platform (accessed May 18, 2012).

2. Hans Reimer, "Socialization in the Prison Community," *Proceedings of the American Prison Association, 1937* (New York: American Prison Association, 1937), pp. 151–155.

3. Donald Clemmer, *The Prison Community* (Boston: Holt, Rinehart and Winston, 1940).

4. Gresham M. Sykes, *The Society of Captives: A Study of a Maximum Security Prison* (Princeton, NJ: Princeton University Press, 1958).

5. Richard A. Cloward et al., *Theoretical Studies in Social Organization of the Prison* (New York: Social Science Research Council, 1960).

6. Donald R. Cressey, ed., *The Prison: Studies in Institutional Organization and Change* (New York: Holt, Rinehart and Winston, 1961).

7. Lawrence Hazelrigg, ed., *Prison within Society: A Reader in Penology* (Garden City, NY: Anchor, 1969), preface.

8. Charles Stastny and Gabrielle Tyrnauer, *Who Rules the Joint? The Changing Political Culture of Maximum-Security Prisons in America* (Lexington, MA: Lexington Books, 1982), p. 131.

9. Erving Goffman, *Asylums: Essays on the Social Situation of Mental Patients and Other Inmates* (Garden City, NY: Anchor, 1961).

10. For a firsthand account of the prison experience, see Victor Hassine, *Life without Parole: Living in Prison Today* (Los Angeles: Roxbury, 1996); and W. Rideau and R. Wikberg, *Life Sentences: Rage and Survival behind Prison Bars* (New York: Times Books, 1992).

11. Gresham M. Sykes and Sheldon L. Messinger, "The Inmate Social System," in Richard A. Cloward et al., eds., *Theoretical Studies in Social Organization of the Prison* (New York: Social Science Research Council, 1960), pp. 5–19.

12. The concept of prisonization is generally attributed to Clemmer, *The Prison Community*, although Quaker penologists of the late eighteenth century were actively concerned with preventing "contamination" (the spread of criminal values) among prisoners.

13. Sykes and Messinger, "The Inmate Social System," p. 5.

14. Stanton Wheeler, "Socialization in Correctional Communities," *American Sociological Review*, Vol. 26 (October 1961), pp. 697–712.

15. Sykes, *The Society of Captives*, p. xiii.

16. Christopher Hensley, Jeremy Wright, Richard Tewksbury, and Tammy Castle, "The Evolving Nature of Prison Argot and Sexual Hierarchies," *The Prison Journal*, Vol. 83 (2003), pp. 289–300.

17. Ibid., p. 298.

18. John Irwin, *The Felon* (Upper Saddle River, NJ: Prentice Hall, 1970).

19. Stastny and Tyrnauer, *Who Rules the Joint?* p. 135.

20. Ibid.

21. Ibid.

22. Sykes, *The Society of Captives*.

23. Clemmer, *The Prison Community*, pp. 294–296.

24. Irwin, *The Felon*.

25. Public Law 108–79.

26. Office of Justice Programs, *PREA Data Collection Activities, 2013* (Washington, DC: Bureau of Justice Statistics, June 2013).

27. Dee Halley, "The Prison Rape Elimination Act of 2003: Addressing Sexual Assault in Correctional Settings," *Corrections Today* (June 2005), pp. 30, 100.

28. Lee H. Bowker, *Prison Victimization* (New York: Elsevier, 1980), p. 42.

29. Halley, "The Prison Rape Elimination Act of 2003," p. 1.

30. Hans Toch, *Living in Prison: The Ecology of Survival* (New York: Free Press, 1977), p. 151.

31. E. Ann Carson, *Prisoners in 2014*, (Washington, DC: Bureau of Justice Statistics, September 2015).

32. Ibid., p.3.

33. Ibid.

34. Much of the information and some of the wording in this section come from Barbara Bloom, Barbara Owen, and Stephanie Covington, *Gender-Responsive Strategies: Research, Practice, and Guiding Principles for Women Offenders* (Washington, DC: National Institute of Corrections, 2003).

35. Ibid.

36. *Prisoners in 2014*, p. 15.

37. Joanne Belknap, *The Invisible Woman: Gender, Crime, and Justice* (Belmont, CA: Wadsworth, 2001).

38. Data in this paragraph come from L. E. Glaze and L. M. Maruschak, *Parents in Prison and Their Minor Children* (Washington, DC: Bureau of Justice Statistics, 2008).

39. B. Bloom and D. Steinhart, *Why Punish the Children? A Reappraisal of the Children of Incarcerated Mothers in America* (San Francisco: National Council on Crime and Delinquency, 1993).

40. Patricia Allard and Judith Greene, *Children on the Outside: Voicing the Pain and Human Costs of Parental Incarceration* (New York: Justice Strategies, 2011), pp. 4–5.

41. Mary Jeanette Clement, "National Survey of Programs for Incarcerated Women," paper presented at the annual meeting of the Academy of Criminal Justice Sciences, Nashville, TN, March 1991, pp. 8–9.

42. Barbara Bloom, Barbara Owen and Stephanie Covington, *Gender-Responsive Strategies: Research, Practice, and Guiding Principles for Women Offenders* (National Institute of Corrections, 2002)

43. Barbara Bloom and Stephanie Covington, *Research, Practice, and Guiding Principles for Women Offenders* (Washington, DC: U.S. Department of Justice, 2003).

44. Huey Freeman, "Illinois Program Guides New Mothers," *Pantagraph*, April 12, 2010, http://www.pantagraph.com/news/state-and-regional/illinois/article_ab1d5106-4631-11df-97d4-001cc4c002e0.html (accessed June 7, 2011).

45. Myrna Raeder, *Pregnancy- and Child-Related Legal and Policy Issues Concerning Justice-Involved Women* (Washington, DC: National Institute of Corrections: December, 2013).

46. American Correctional Association, *The Female Offender.*

47. Marsha Clowers, "Dykes, Gangs, and Danger: Debunking Popular Myths about Maximum Security Life," *Journal of Criminal Justice and Popular Culture*, Vol. 9, No. 1 (2001), pp. 22–30.

48. D. Ward and G. Kassebaum, *Women's Prison: Sex and Social Structure* (London: Weidenfeld and Nicolson, 1966).

49. Esther Heffernan, *Making It in Prison: The Square, the Cool, and the Life* (London: Wiley-Interscience, 1972).

50. Rose Giallombardo, *Society of Women: A Study of Women's Prisons* (New York: John Wiley, 1966).

51. Ibid., p. 136.

52. For a summary of such studies (including some previously unpublished), see Lee H. Bowker, *Prisoner Subcultures* (Lexington, MA: Lexington Books, 1977), p. 86.

53. Giallombardo, *Society of Women*, p. 162.

54. David Ward and Gene Kassebaum, *Women's Prison: Sex and Social Structure* (Piscataway, NJ: Aldine Transaction, 2008).

55. Barbara Owen, *"In the Mix": Struggle and Survival in a Women's Prison* (Albany: State University of New York Press, 1998).

56. Barbara Owen, "Prisons: Prisons for Women—Prison Subcultures," available online at http://law.jrank.org/pages/1802/Prisons-Prisons-Women-Prison-subcultures.html.

57. See Joanne Belknap, book review of Barbara Owen's *"In the Mix": Struggle and Survival in a Women's Prison*, in *Western Criminology Review* (1999), http://wcr.sonoma.edu/v1n2/belknap.html (accessed April 11, 2009).

58. Mary Koscheski and Christopher Hensley, "Inmate Homosexual Behavior in a Southern Female Correctional Facility," *American Journal of Criminal Justice*, Vol. 25, No. 2 (2001), pp. 269–277.

59. See, for example, Margie J. Phelps, "Sexual Misconduct between Staff and Inmates," *Corrections Technology and Management*, Vol. 12 (1999).

60. Heffernan, *Making It in Prison.*

61. Bowker, *Prison Victimization*, p. 53.

62. Giallombardo, *Society of Women.*

63. American Correctional Association, *The Female Offender*, p. 39.

64. Kristen A. Hughes, *Justice Expenditure and Employment in the United States, 2003* (Washington, DC: Bureau of Justice Statistics, 2006), p. 7.

65. Ibid., p. 6.

66. Ibid., Table 5: "Justice System Employment and Percent Distribution of Full-Time Equivalent Employment, by State and Types of Government."

67. American Correctional Association, "Correctional Officers in Adult Systems," in *Vital Statistics in Corrections* (Laurel, MD: ACA, 2000). "Other" minorities round out the percentages to a total of 100%.

68. Ibid.

69. American Correctional Association, "Correctional Officers in Adult Systems."

70. Lucien X. Lombardo, *Guards Imprisoned: Correctional Officers at Work* (New York: Elsevier, 1981), pp. 22–36.

71. Leonard Morgenbesser, "NY State Law Prescribes Psychological Screening for CO Job Applicants," *Correctional Training* (winter 1983), p. 1.

72. "A Sophisticated Approach to Training Prison Guards," *Newsday*, August 12, 1982.

73. Jose de Cordoba, "Mexico Prison Riot Leaves 44 Dead," *Wall Street Journal*, February 20, 2012, http://online.wsj.com/article/SB10001424052970203358704577233192848519360.html(accessed April 4, 2012).

74. Stastny and Tyrnauer, *Who Rules the Joint?* p. 1.

75. See Frederick Talbott, "Reporting from behind the Walls: Do It before the Siren Wails," *Quill* (February 1988), pp. 16–21.

76. "Ohio Prison Rebellion Is Ended," *USA Today*, April 22, 1993.

77. "Guards Hurt in Prison Riot," Associated Press, November 11, 2000.

78. "San Quentin Prison Riot Leaves 42 Injured," *USA Today*, August 9, 2005.

79. Ralph Blumenthal, "Gang Fights in Prison Injure 22 and Kill One," *New York Times*, March 29, 2008.

80. Jeffrey McMurray, "Four Kentucky Inmates Still Hospitalized after Prison Riot," Associated Press, August 22, 2009, http://news.yahoo.com/s/ap/20090822/ap_on_re_us/us_ky_prison_melee (accessed September 4, 2009).

81. John Asbury, "Chino Prison Rioting Spurs Call for Changes," *The Press Enterprise*, August 9, 2009, http://www.pe.com/localnews/sbcounty/stories/PE_News_Local_S_riot10.2abdafb.html (accessed September 5, 2009).

82. Robert S. Fong, Ronald E. Vogel, and S. Buentello, "Prison Gang Dynamics: A Look inside the Texas Department of Corrections," in A. V. Merlo and P. Menekos, eds., *Dilemmas and Directions in Corrections* (Cincinnati, OH: Anderson, 1992).

83. Ibid.

84. *Ruiz v. Estelle*, 503 F. Supp. 1265 (S.D. Tex., 1980).

85. Alan Greenblatt, "Experts: Prison Gang Reach Increasingly Extends into Streets," NPR, April 5, 2013, http://www.npr.org/2013/04/02/176035798/experts-prison-gang-reach-increasingly-extends-into-streets (accessed April 10, 2013).

86. The facts in this story are taken from *Hope v. Pelzer*, 122 S.Ct. 2508, 153 L.Ed.2d 666 (2002).

87. "Convictions Bar 3.9 Million from Voting," Associated Press wire service, September 22, 2000.

88. *Holt v. Sarver*, 309 F.Supp. 362 (E.D. Ark. 1970).

89. Vergil L. Williams, *Dictionary of American Penology: An Introduction* (Westport, CT: Greenwood Press, 1979), pp. 6–7.

90. Joint order issued in *McCray v. Sullivan*, Civ. Action 5620-69-H; *McCray v. Sullivan*, Civ. Action 6091-70-H; *White v. Commissioner of Alabama Board of Corrections*, Civ. Action 7094-72-H; *Pugh v. Sullivan, et al.*, Civ. Action 74-57N; and *James v. Wallace, et al.*, Civ. Action 74-203-N.

91. *Pell v. Procunier*, 417 U.S. 817, 822 (1974).

92. Ibid.

93. Title 42 U.S.C.A. 1997, Public Law 104-150.

94. Section 1997e.

95. American Correctional Association, *Legal Responsibility and Authority of Correctional Officers: A Handbook on Courts, Judicial Decisions and Constitutional Requirements* (College Park, MD: ACA, 1987), p. 8.

96. *Wolff v. McDonnell*, 94 S.Ct. 2963 (1974).

97. Ibid.

98. Ibid.

99. *Ponte v. Real*, 471 U.S. 491, 105 S.Ct. 2192, 85 L.Ed.2d 553 (1985).

100. *Vitek v. Jones*, 445 U.S. 480 (1980).

101. American Correctional Association, Standard 2-4346. See ACA, *Legal Responsibility and Authority of Correctional Officers*, p. 49.

102. *Wilson v. Seiter et al.*, 501 U.S. 294 (1991).

103. *Estelle v. Gamble*, 429 U.S. 97, 106 (1976).

104. *Sandin v. Conner*, 63 U.S.L.W. 4601 (1995).

105. *Wolff v. McDonnell*, 94 S.Ct. 2963 (1974).

106. *Hewitt* v. *Helms*, 459 U.S. 460 (1983).

107. *Ali* v. *Federal Bureau of Prisons*, 552 U.S. 214 (2008).

108. 28 U.S.C. Section 1346(b)(1).

109. *Milbrook* v. *U.S.*, U.S. Supreme Court (decided March 27, 2013).

110. *Howes* v. *Fields*, 566 U.S. _____ (2012).

111. *Florence* v. *Burlington County*, 566 U.S. _____ (2012).

112. Laurie Asseo, "Inmate Lawsuits," Associated Press wire service, May 24, 1996; and Bureau of Justice Statistics, "State and Federal Prisoners Filed 68,235 Petitions in U.S. Courts in 1996," press release, October 29, 1997.

113. *Theriault* v. *Carlson,* 495 F.2d 390.

114. Asseo, "Inmate Lawsuits."

115. Public Law 104-134. Although the PLRA was signed into law on April 26, 1996, and is frequently referred to as the Prison Litigation Reform Act of 1996, the official name of the act is the Prison Litigation Reform Act of 1995.

116. John Scalia, *Prisoner Petitions Filed in U.S. District Courts, 2000, with Trends, 1980–2000* (Washington, DC: Bureau of Justice Statistics, 2002).

117. F. Cheesman, R. Hanson, and B. Ostrom, *A Tale of Two Laws Revisited: Investigating the Impact of the Prison Litigation Reform Act and the Antiterrorism and Effective Death Penalty Act* (Williamsburg, VA: National Center for State Courts, 2004).

118. ACLU, "ACLU Position Paper: Prisoners' Rights," 1999, http://www.aclu.org/files/FilesPDFs/prisonerrights.pdf (accessed August 11, 2013); see also ACLU, "Prisoners' Rights," http://www.aclu.org/prisoners-rights (accessed May 10, 2015).

119. Laura M. Maruschak, *HIV in Prisons, 2001–2010* (Washington, DC: Bureau of Justice Statistics, 2012), p. 1.

120. Dennis Cauchon, "AIDS in Prison: Locked Up and Locked Out," *USA Today*, March 31, 1995, p. 6A.

121. Laura M. Maruschak, *HIV in Prisons, 2005* (Washington, DC: Bureau of Justice Statistics, 2007), p. 16.

122. Centers for Disease Control and Prevention, "HIV Transmission among Male Inmates in a State Prison System: Georgia, 1992–2005," *Morbidity and Mortality Weekly Report*, Vol. 55, No. 15 (April 21, 2006), pp. 421–426.

123. Theodore M. Hammett, *AIDS in Correctional Facilities: Issues and Options*, 3rd ed. (Washington, DC: National Institute of Justice, 1988), p. 37.

124. At the time of this writing, California, Massachusetts, New York, Wisconsin, and the District of Columbia were among those jurisdictions.

125. "Mississippi Eases Policy of Separating Inmates with HIV," *Corrections Journal*, Vol. 5, No. 6 (2001), p. 5.

126. Cauchon, "AIDS in Prison."

127. See "Court Allows Restriction on HIV-Positive Inmates," *Criminal Justice Newsletter*, Vol. 25, No. 23 (December 1, 1994), pp. 2–3.

128. Ibid.

129. Darrell Bryan, "Inmates, HIV, and the Constitutional Right to Privacy: AIDS in Prison Facilities," *Corrections Compendium*, Vol. 19, No. 9 (September 1994), pp. 1–3.

130. "Anthony Marshall Surrenders, Sent to Prison in Astor Theft Case," Associated Press, June 21, 2013, http://www.nypost.com/p/news/local/manhattan/anthony_marshall_surrenders_sent_KWMFREobNwOfPdnXZSV74I (accessed May 10, 2015).

131. Lincoln J. Fry, "The Older Prison Inmate: A Profile," *Justice Professional*, Vol. 2, No. 1 (spring 1987), pp. 1–12.

132. American Civil Liberties Union, *The Mass Incarceration of the Elderly* (New York: ACLU, June 2012).

133. *Prisoners in 2014*, p. 15.

134. Bureau of Justice Statistics, "The Nation's Prison Population Grew by 60,000 Inmates Last Year," press release, August 15, 1999.

135. Jim Krane, "Demographic Revolution Rocks U.S. Prisons," APB Online, April 12, 1999, http://www.apbonline.com/safestreets/oldprisoners/mainpris0412.html (accessed January 5, 2006).

136. Ronald Wikbert and Burk Foster, "The Long-Termers: Louisiana's Longest Serving Inmates and Why They've Stayed So Long," paper presented at the annual meeting of the Academy of Criminal Justice Sciences, Washington, DC, 1989, p. 51.

137. American Civil Liberties Union, *The Mass Incarceration of the Elderly*, p. vi.

138. Ibid., p. vii.

139. Doris J. James and Lauren E. Glaze, *Mental Health Problems of Prison and Jail Inmates* (Washington, DC: Bureau of Justice Statistics, 2006).

140. Stephanie Mencimer, "There Are 10 Times More Mentally Ill People Behind Bars Than in State Hospitals," *Mother Jones*, April 8, 2014.

141. Allen J. Beck and Laura M. Maruschak, *Mental Health Treatment in State Prisons, 2000*, Bureau of Justice Statistics Special Report (Washington, DC: BJS, 2001), p. 1, from which most of the information in this paragraph and the next is derived.

142. *Washington* v. *Harper*, 494 U.S. 210 (1990).

143. Robert O. Lampert, "The Mentally Retarded Offender in Prison," *Justice Professional*, Vol. 2, No. 1 (spring 1987), p. 61.

144. Ibid., 64.

145. George C. Denkowski and Kathryn M. Denkowski, "The Mentally Retarded Offender in the State Prison System: Identification, Prevalence, Adjustment, and Rehabilitation," *Criminal Justice and Behavior*, Vol. 12 (1985), pp. 55–75.

146. "Opening Session: Kerik Emphasizes the Importance of Corrections' Protective Role for the Country," http://www.aca.org/conferences/Winter05/updates05.asp (accessed July 22, 2008).

147. Keith Martin, "Corrections Prepares for Terrorism," Corrections Connection News Network, January 21, 2002, http://www.corrections.com (accessed June 15, 2010).

148. Quoted in Meghan Mandeville, "Information Sharing Becomes Crucial to Battling Terrorism behind Bars," http://Corrections.com, December 8, 2003, http://database.corrections.com/news/results2.asp?ID_8988 (accessed July 11, 2005).

149. Institute for the Study of Violent Groups, "Land of Wahhabism," *Crime and Justice International*, March/April 2005, p. 43.

150. "Man behind U.S. Terrorism Plot Gets 16 Years," *International Herald Tribune*, March 6, 2009, http://www.iht.com/articles/ap/2009/03/06/america/NA-US-Terrorism-Probe.php (accessed March 27, 2011).

151. Federal Bureau of Prisons, *State of the Bureau, 2004* (Washington, DC: BOP, 2005).

ISSUES FOR THE FUTURE

The accused has these common law, constitutional, statutory, and humanitarian rights that may be threatened by technological advances and other developments:

- A right to privacy
- A right to be assumed innocent
- A right against self-incrimination
- A right to equal protection of the laws
- A right against cruel and unusual punishment

These individual rights must be effectively balanced against the following present and emerging community concerns:

- Continuing drug abuse among youth
- The threat of juvenile crime
- Urban gang violence
- High-technology, computer, and Internet crime (cybercrime)
- Terrorism and narcoterrorism
- Occupational and white-collar crime

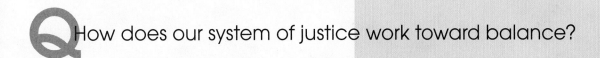

Q How does our system of justice work toward balance?

The Future Comes One Day at a Time

No one can truly say what the future holds. Will the supporters of individual rights or the advocates of public order ultimately claim the day? We cannot say for sure. This much is certain, however: Things change. The future system of American criminal justice will not be quite the same system we know today. Many of the coming changes, however, are now discernible—and hints of what is to come appear on the horizon with increasing frequency and growing clarity. Some of the more obvious of the coming changes are already upon us. They include (1) the need for increased trust of the police and other justice agencies by minority and disadvantaged communities; (2) a restructuring of the juvenile justice system in the face of growing knowledge about human development and concerns about cost efficiency; (3) the increased

bankruptcy of a war against drugs whose promises now seem increasingly hollow; (4) a growing recognition of America's international role as both victim and purveyor of worldwide criminal activity; (5) the "war on terrorism," including its substantial potential consequences for individual rights in America; and (6) the quickly unfolding potential of cybercrimes, those that both employ high technology in their commission and target the fruits of such technology.

This last part of *Criminal Justice Today* discusses most of these issues in the chapters that follow. It also draws your attention back to the bedrock underlying the American system of justice: the Constitution, the Bill of Rights, and the demands of due process, all of which will continue to structure the American justice system well into the future.

AP Wide World Photos

15

JUVENILE JUSTICE

LEARNING OBJECTIVES

After reading this chapter, you should be able to

- Describe how the juvenile justice system has evolved in the Western world.
- Describe important U.S. Supreme Court decisions relating to juvenile justice, including their impact on the handling of juveniles by the system.
- Compare juvenile and adult legal rights and their respective systems of justice.
- Briefly describe possible future directions in juvenile justice.

It is with young people that prevention efforts are most needed and hold the greatest promise.

PRESIDENT'S COMMISSION ON LAW ENFORCEMENT AND ADMINISTRATION OF JUSTICE[1]

■ **lecture note**   Discuss Figure 15-1. Explain that although juveniles make up only a relatively small proportion of the entire U.S. population, they account for a seemingly large proportion of all offenses. Ask the class to suggest reasons for this phenomenon.

Introduction

In 2010, in the case of *Graham* v. *Florida*, the U.S. Supreme Court formally recognized fundamental differences between the brains of juveniles and adults. The justices wrote that "developments in psychology and brain science continue to show fundamental differences between juvenile and adult minds." They went on to give examples, saying that "parts of the brain involved in behavior control continue to mature through late adolescence," and that "[j]uveniles are more capable of change than are adults, and their actions are less likely to be evidence of 'irretrievably depraved character' than are the actions of adults."[2] Consequently, in *Graham*, the Court abolished life imprisonment without the possibility of parole for persons who commit serious crimes (other than homicide) as teenagers. Two years later, in 2012, the Court reinforced its view of adolescent development by holding, in the case of *Miller* v. *Alabama*, that "mandatory life without parole for a juvenile precludes consideration of his chronological age and its hallmark features—among them, immaturity, impetuosity, and failure to appreciate risks and consequences."[3] While we will discuss both of these cases later in this chapter, the written opinions that support them provide important evidence that understandings of adolescent behavior are changing and that those changes are now impacting the juvenile justice system in significant new ways.[4]

A key finding of the Office of Juvenile Justice and Delinquency Prevention's Study Group on Serious and Violent Juvenile Offenders is that most chronic juvenile offenders begin their delinquency careers before age 12, and some as early as age 10.[5] The most recent national data show that in 2014 police arrested 54,834 children ages 12 and younger.[6] These very young offenders (known as *child delinquents*) represent almost 7% of the total number of juvenile arrestees (those up to age 18).

Although states vary as to the age at which a person legally enters adulthood, statistics on crime make it clear that young people are disproportionately involved in certain offenses. A recent report, for example, found that nearly 16% of all violent crimes and 26% of all property crimes are committed by people younger than 18, although this age group makes up only 26% of the population of the United States.[7] On average, about 17% of all arrests in any year are of juveniles,[8] and people younger than 18 have a higher likelihood of being arrested for robbery and other property crimes than do people in any other age group. Figure 15-1 shows Uniform Crime Report/NIBRS statistics on juvenile arrests for selected offense categories.

The Office of Juvenile Justice and Delinquency Prevention (OJJDP) is a primary source of information on juvenile justice in the United States. A sweeping OJJDP overview of juvenile crime and the juvenile justice system in America reveals the following:[9]

- About one million juveniles (under 18) are arrested annually in America.
- Violent crime by juveniles is decreasing.
- Younger juveniles account for a substantial proportion of juvenile arrests and the juvenile court caseload.
- Relative to male delinquency, female delinquency has grown substantially.
- Greater percentages of females than males are in placement for status offenses and assaults.
- Both girls and boys who are in the juvenile justice system usually have problems at home and school that have put them at risk for delinquency—including maltreatment, poverty, or both—and these factors also may have a negative impact on their adjustment to young adulthood.
- Minority juveniles are greatly overrepresented in the custody population.
- Crowding is a serious problem in juvenile facilities.

Recent data from a seven-year collaborative, multidisciplinary project, called the Pathways to Desistance Study, reveal that:[10]

- Most youth who commit felonies greatly reduce their offending over time, regardless of the intervention or treatment they receive.
- Longer stays in juvenile institutions do not reduce recidivism.

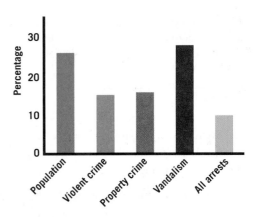

FIGURE 15-1 | Juvenile Involvement in Crime versus System Totals, 2014

Note: The term juvenile refers to people younger than 18 years of age.

Source: Federal Bureau of Investigation, Crime in the United States, 2014 (Washington, DC: U.S. Dept. of Justice, 2015).

■ **lecture note**　Explain the historical treatment of juveniles as small adults. Underscore the fact that in past centuries, juveniles who committed crimes were treated much the same as adults. Discuss whether that might happen again.

■ **delinquency**　In the broadest usage, juvenile actions or conduct in violation of criminal law, juvenile status offenses, and other juvenile misbehavior.

■ **juvenile justice system**　The aggregate of the government agencies that function to investigate, supervise, adjudicate, care for, or confine youthful offenders and other children subject to the jurisdiction of the juvenile court.

■ *parens patriae*　A common law principle that allows the state to assume a parental role and to take custody of a child when he or she becomes delinquent, is abandoned, or is in need of care that the natural parents are unable or unwilling to provide.

- Community-based supervision as a component of aftercare is effective for youth who have committed serious crimes.
- Substance-abuse treatment reduces both substance use and criminal offending.

The Pathways to Desistance Study, funded by the OJJDP, followed 1,354 serious juvenile offenders ages 14 through 18 for seven years after their conviction. The study looked at the factors that lead youth who have committed serious offenses to continue or to desist from offending, including individual maturation, life changes, and involvement with the criminal justice system. Learn more about the OJJDP via **http://www.ojjdp.gov**, and read its recently launched *Journal of Juvenile Justice* at **http://www.journalofjuvjustice.org**. Additional information about the Pathways to Desistance Study can be found at **http://www.pathwaysstudy.pitt.edu/index.html**.

This chapter has four purposes. First, we will briefly look at the history of the **juvenile justice system**. The juvenile justice system has its roots in the adult system. In the juvenile system, however, we find a more uniform philosophical base and a generally clear agreement about the system's purpose. These differences may be due to the system's relative newness and to the fact that society generally agrees that young people who have gone wrong are worth salvaging. However, the philosophy that underlies the juvenile justice system in America is increasingly being questioned by "get-tough" advocates of law and order, many of whom are fed up with violent juvenile crime.

> The philosophy that underlies the juvenile justice system in America is being questioned by "get-tough" advocates of law and order, many of whom are fed up with violent juvenile crime.

Our second purpose is to compare the juvenile and adult systems as they currently operate. The reasoning behind the juvenile justice system has led to administrative and other procedures that, in many jurisdictions, are not found in the adult system. The juvenile justice process, for example, is frequently not as open as the adult system. Hearings may be held in secret, the names of offenders are not published, and records of juvenile proceedings may later be destroyed.[11]

Our third purpose is to describe the agencies, processes, and problems of the juvenile justice system itself. Although each state may have variations, they all share a common system structure.

Near the end of this chapter, we will turn to our fourth focus and will consider some of the issues raised by critics of the current system. As conservative attitudes brought changes in the adult criminal justice system over the past few decades, the juvenile justice system remained relatively unchanged. Based on premises quite different from those of the adult system, juvenile justice has long been a separate decision-making arena in which the best interests of the child have been accorded great importance. As we will see, substantial changes are now afoot.

Juvenile Justice throughout History

Before the modern era, children who committed crimes in the Western world received no preferential treatment because of their youth. They were adjudicated and punished alongside adults, and a number of recorded cases have come down through history of children as young as six being hung or burned at the stake.[12]

Earliest Times

Similarly, little distinction was made between criminality and **delinquency** or other kinds of undesirable behavior.

Early philosophy in dealing with juveniles derived from a Roman principle called *patria potestas*. Under Roman law (circa 753 b.c.), children were members of their family, but the father had absolute control over children, and they in turn had an absolute responsibility to obey his wishes. Roman understanding of the social role of children strongly influenced English culture and eventually led to the development of the legal principle of *parens patriae* in Western law, which allowed the king, or the English state, to take the place of parents in dealing with children who broke the law.

By the end of the eighteenth century, social conditions in Europe and America had begun to change, and the Enlightenment, a highly significant intellectual and social movement, emphasized human potential. In this new age, children were recognized as the only true heirs to the future, and society became increasingly concerned about their well-being.

By the middle of the nineteenth century, large-scale immigration to America was under way. Unfortunately, some immigrant families fell victims of the cities that drew them, settling in squalor

Columbine (Colorado) High School shooters Eric Harris (left) and Dylan Klebold examining a sawed-off shotgun in a still image taken from a videotape made at a makeshift shooting range in 1999. About six weeks after the video was made, Klebold (17) and Harris (18) shot and killed 15 people and injured 20 more at the school. How might such disasters be averted in the future?

in hastily formed ghettos. Many children, abandoned by families that were unable to support them, were forced into lives on the streets, where they formed tattered gangs—surviving off the refuse of the cities. An 1823 report by the Society for the Prevention of Pauperism in the city of New York called for the development of "houses of refuge" to save children from lives of crime and poverty, and in 1824, the first house of refuge opened in New York City.[13] It sheltered mostly young thieves, vagrants, and runaways. Other children, especially those with more severe delinquency problems, were placed in adult prisons and jails. Houses of refuge became popular in New York, and other cities quickly copied them. It was not long, however, before they became overcrowded and living conditions deteriorated.

Not long afterward, the American child-savers movement began. Child savers espoused a philosophy of productivity and eschewed idleness and unprincipled behavior.

One product of the child-savers movement was the reform school—a place for delinquent juveniles that embodied the atmosphere of a Christian home. By the middle of the nineteenth century, the reform school approach to handling juveniles led to the creation of the Chicago Reform School, which opened in the 1860s.

> One product of the child-savers movement was the reform school—a place for delinquent juveniles that embodied the atmosphere of a Christian home.

Reform schools focused primarily on predelinquent youth who showed tendencies toward more serious criminal involvement, and attempted to emulate wholesome family environments.

The Juvenile Court Era

In 1870, an expanding recognition of children's needs led Massachusetts to enact legislation that required separate hearings for juveniles.[14] New York followed with a similar law in 1877,[15] which also prohibited contact between juvenile and adult offenders. Rhode Island enacted juvenile court legislation in 1898, and in 1899 the Colorado School Law became the first comprehensive legislation designed to address the adjudication of problem children.[16] It was, however, the 1899 codification of Illinois juvenile law that became the model for juvenile court statutes throughout the nation.

The Illinois Juvenile Court Act created a juvenile court, separate in form and function from adult criminal courts. To avoid the lasting stigma of criminality, the law applied the term *delinquent* rather than *criminal* to young adjudicated offenders. The act specified that the best interests of the child were to guide juvenile court judges in their deliberations. In effect, judges were to serve as advocates for juveniles, guiding their development. Determining guilt or innocence took second place

■ **delinquent child**   A child who has engaged in activity that would be considered a crime if the child were an adult. The term *delinquent* is used to avoid the stigma associated with the term *criminal*.
■ **undisciplined child**   A child who is beyond parental control, as evidenced by his or her refusal to obey legitimate authorities, such as school officials and teachers.
■ **dependent child**   A child who has no parents or whose parents are unable to care for him or her.

■ **neglected child**   A child who is not receiving the proper level of physical or psychological care from his or her parents or guardians or who has been placed up for adoption in violation of the law.
■ **abused child**   A child who has been physically, sexually, or mentally abused. Most states also consider a child who is forced into delinquent activity by a parent or guardian to be abused.
■ **status offender**   A child who commits an act that is contrary to the law by virtue of the offender's status as a child. Purchasing cigarettes, buying alcohol, and being truant are examples of such behavior.

to the betterment of the child. The law abandoned a strict adherence to the due process requirements of adult prosecutions, allowing informal procedures designed to scrutinize the child's situation. By sheltering the juvenile from the punishment philosophy of the adult system, the Illinois Juvenile Court emphasized reformation in place of retribution.[17]

In 1938, the federal government passed the Juvenile Court Act, which embodied many of the features of the Illinois statute. By 1945, every state had enacted special legislation focusing on the handling of juveniles, and the juvenile court movement became well established.[18]

The juvenile court movement was based on five philosophical principles that can be summarized as follows:[19]

- The state is the "higher or ultimate parent" of all the children within its borders.
- Children are worth saving, and nonpunitive procedures should be used to save the child.
- Children should be nurtured. While the nurturing process is under way, they should be protected from the stigmatizing impact of formal adjudicatory procedures.
- To accomplish the goal of reformation, justice needs to be individualized; that is, each child is different, and the needs, aspirations, living conditions, and so on of each

child must be known in their individual particulars if the court is to be helpful.
- Noncriminal procedures are necessary to give primary consideration to the needs of the child. The denial of due process can be justified in the face of constitutional challenges because the court acts not to punish, but to help.

Learn more about the history of juvenile justice and the juvenile court at **http://www.justicestudies.com/pubs/juvenile.pdf**.

Categories of Children in the Juvenile Justice System

By the time of the Great Depression, most states had expanded juvenile statutes to include the following six categories of children. These categories are still used today in most jurisdictions to describe the variety of children subject to juvenile court jurisdiction.

- **Delinquent children** are those who violate the criminal law. If they were adults, the word *criminal* would be applied to them.
- **Undisciplined children** are said to be beyond parental control, as evidenced by their refusal to obey legitimate authorities, such as school officials and teachers. They need state protection.
- **Dependent children** typically have no parents or guardians to care for them. Their parents are deceased, they were placed for adoption, or they were abandoned in violation of the law.
- **Neglected children** are those who do not receive proper care from their parents or guardians. They may suffer from malnutrition or may not be provided with adequate shelter.
- **Abused children** are those who suffer physical abuse at the hands of their custodians. This category was later expanded to include emotional and sexual abuse.
- **Status offender** is a special category that embraces children who violate laws written only for them. In some states, status offenders are referred to as persons in need of supervision (PINS).

A group of teenagers. American juveniles have many opportunities but also face numerous challenges. What are the six categories of children that state juvenile justice statutes usually describe as subject to juvenile court jurisdiction?

Michael Newman/PhotoEdit Inc.

■ **status offense**   An act or conduct that is declared by statute to be an offense, but only when committed by or engaged in by a juvenile, and that can be adjudicated only by a juvenile court.

■ **lecture note**   Discuss the various legal categories most states apply to children within their jurisdiction. Refer to the definitions provided in the text to be sure students understand the differences between each category.
■ **theme**   What are the different categories of children? Should there be other categories? If so, which?

Status offenses include behavior such as truancy, vagrancy, running away from home, and incorrigibility. The youthful "status" of juveniles is a necessary element in such offenses. Adults, for example, may "run away from home" and not violate any law. Runaway children, however, are subject to apprehension and juvenile court processing because state laws require that they be subject to parental control.

> Status offenses include behavior such as truancy, vagrancy, running away from home, and incorrigibility.

Status offenses were a natural outgrowth of juvenile court philosophy. As a consequence, however, juveniles in need of help often faced procedural dispositions that treated them as though they were delinquent. Rather than lowering the rate of juvenile

CJ | NEWS
Schools Are Taking Bullying Seriously

AlexandreNunes/Shutterstock

A younger boy being physically threatened and bullied by an older one. What can be done to prevent bullying in schools? In the community?

In an age when students socialize online, bad behavior has moved from the stairwell and locker room to Facebook and Twitter. This so-called cyberbullying complicates the issue because it doesn't occur on school grounds, and many parents and teachers aren't involved in social media.

States passed the first state anti-bullying laws after the 1999 shootings at Columbine High School in suburban Denver, which were blamed in part on bullying. Suicides of some taunted students, often outed for being gay, also prompted these laws. By March 2012, every state except Montana had an anti-bullying statute.

The laws vary widely, but in general, they include requiring schools to establish anti-bullying policies, track incidents, create training and prevention programs for teachers and students, and establish sanctions such as suspension, reassignment, or expulsion. In addition, states have amended laws to cover cyberbullying and subtler kinds of harassment, such as ostracizing.

So far, the laws have stood up in the courts. When a West Virginia high school senior was suspended from school for creating a fake Internet profile of another student, calling here a "slut who had herpes," her parents sued the school on free speech grounds, but a federal appeals court threw out their lawsuit.

Even revered high school athletics programs aren't immune from angry parents citing the new laws. A few years ago, for example, three stars of the Carmel, Indiana, high school basketball team were suspended for five days for bullying two freshmen team members on the bus ride home from a game.

In many cases, however, the laws are spottily enforced. In Georgia, the first state to pass an anti-bullying law in 1999, Atlanta area schools reported more than 1,900 bullying incidents in the 2009–2010 school year, but only 30 expulsions or reassignments as a result, and a whole suburban county reported no incidents at all.

Furthermore, school policies may not deter bullying. A Massachusetts school with a suicide due to bullying had an anti-bullying policy in place.

There is a lot of bad behavior in schools, but what constitutes bullying? The test, one New York judge wrote, is whether the conduct is "sufficiently severe, persistent or pervasive that it creates a hostile environment" that "deprives a student of substantial educational opportunities."

Bullying in schools, once thought to be just part of growing up, is now widely seen as a root cause of poor learning, school violence, and suicide—a revised view that has set off an avalanche of state anti-bullying laws and major adjustments in school policies.

Experts say anywhere from 20 to 50% of students are bullied at some point, and 10% are regularly victimized. The harmful effects have been documented in several U.S. studies. Some 160,000 children stay home from school each day to avoid bullying, and 4.1% of victims have brought weapons to school in response. Victims are 5.6 times more likely to contemplate suicide.

But until recently, many school authorities did nothing. The National Association of School Psychologists reports that nearly 25% of teachers do not believe intervention in bullying is necessary.

Resources: "Schools, Parents Try to Keep Pace with Cyber-bullying Tactics," *Baltimore Sun*, April 22 2012, http://articles.baltimoresun.com/2012-04-22/news/bs-md-ho-cyber-reader-20120422_1_cyber-bullying-anti-bullying-laws-rutgers-university-freshman; "Analysis of State Bullying Laws and Policies," U.S. Department of Education, December 2011, http://www2.ed.gov/rschstat/eval/bullying/state-bullying-laws/state-bullying-laws.pdf; and "Law Firmer against Bullies," *Atlanta Journal-Constitution*, November 20, 2010, http://www.ajc.com/news/atlanta/law-firmer-against-bullies-748057.html.

■ **lecture note**   Describe the hands-off approach to juvenile justice that the U.S. Supreme Court followed until the 1960s. Then discuss the precedent setting cases that have been decided since then.

■ **lecture note**   Spotlight the 1967 *Gault* decision, which is often considered the most significant of all the court precedents relating to the handling of juveniles. Explain that this decision extended many of the rights of adult defendants to juveniles.

incarceration, the juvenile court movement led to its increase. Critics of the juvenile court movement quickly focused on the abandonment of due process rights, especially in the case of status offenders, as a major source of problems. Detention and incarceration, they argued, were inappropriate options where children had not committed crimes.

The Legal Environment

Throughout the first half of the twentieth century, the U.S. Supreme Court followed a hands-off approach to juvenile justice, much like its early approach to prisons.

Throughout the first half of the twentieth century, the U.S. Supreme Court followed a hands-off approach to juvenile justice, much like its early approach to prisons (see Chapter 14). The adjudication and further processing of juveniles by the system were left mostly to specialized juvenile courts or to local appeals courts. Although one or two early Supreme Court decisions[20] dealt with issues of juvenile justice, it was not until the 1960s that the Court began close legal scrutiny of the principles underlying the system itself. Some of the most important U.S. Supreme Court cases relating to juvenile justice are shown in Figure 15-2.

In the 1967 case known as *In re Gault,* the U.S. Supreme Court held, in part, as follows:[21]

> [T]he Juvenile Court Judge's exercise of the power of the state as *parens patriae* [is] not unlimited…. Notice, to comply with due process requirements, must be given sufficiently in advance of scheduled court proceedings so that reasonable opportunity to prepare will be afforded…. The probation officer cannot act as counsel for the child. His role in the adjudicatory hearing, by statute and in fact, is as arresting officer and witness against the child. There is no material difference in this respect between adult and juvenile proceedings of the sort here involved…. A proceeding where the issue

is whether the child will be found to be "delinquent" and subjected to the loss of his liberty for years is comparable in seriousness to a felony prosecution. The juvenile needs the assistance of counsel to cope with the problems of law, to make skilled inquiry into the facts, to insist upon regularity of the proceedings, and to ascertain whether he has a defense and to prepare and submit it.

In that 1967 case, however, the Court did not agree with another contention of Gault's lawyers: that transcripts of juvenile hearings should be maintained. Transcripts are not necessary, the Court said, because (1) there is no constitutional right to a transcript, and (2) no transcripts are produced in the trials of most adult misdemeanants.

Today, the impact of *Gault* is widely felt throughout the juvenile justice system. Juveniles are now guaranteed many of the same procedural rights as adults. Most precedent-setting

Juveniles are now guaranteed many of the same procedural rights as adults.

Supreme Court decisions that followed *Gault* further clarified the rights of juveniles, focusing primarily on those few issues of due process that it had not explicitly addressed. One of these was the 1970 case of *In re Winship,* which centered on the standard of evidence needed in juvenile hearings. Winship's attorney had argued that the guilt of a juvenile facing a hearing should have to be proved beyond a reasonable doubt—the evidentiary standard of adult criminal trials. In its ruling the Court agreed, saying:[22]

> The constitutional safeguard of proof beyond a reasonable doubt is as much required during the adjudicatory stage of a delinquency proceeding as are those constitutional guards applied in *Gault*…. We therefore hold…that where a 12 year old child is charged with an act of stealing which renders him liable to confinement for as long as six years, then, as a matter of due process…the case against him must be proved beyond a reasonable doubt.

As a consequence of *Winship,* allegations of delinquency today must be established beyond a reasonable doubt. The Court

1966 ►	1967 ►	1970 ►	1971 ►	1975 ►
Kent v. United States	**In re Gault**	**In re Winship**	**Mckeiver v. Pennsylvania**	**Breed v. Jones**
Courts must provide the "essentials of due process" in juvenile proceedings. This important case signaled the beginning of systematic U.S. Supreme Court review of lower-court practices in delinquency hearings.	In hearings that could result in commitment to an institution juveniles have four basic rights: Notice of charges Right to counsel Right to confront and to cross-examine witnesses Protection against self-incrimination	In delinquency matters the state must prove its case beyond a reasonable doubt. Prior to Winship, a lower standard of evidence had been required by juvenile courts in some states—a mere preponderance of the evidence.	Jury trials are not constitutionally required in juvenile cases. At the same time the Court established that jury trials are not prohibited for juveniles. Today, 12 states allow for jury trials in serious cases involving juveniles.	Severely restricted the conditions under which transfers from juvenile to adult courts may occur. In this case Jones was adjudicated delinquent in juvenile court and then transferred to adult court resulting in double jeopardy. Today, transfers to adult court, if they are to occur, must be made before an adjudicatory hearing in juvenile court.

FIGURE 15-2 | The Legal Environment of Juvenile Justice

allowed, however, the continued use of the lower evidentiary standard in adjudicating juveniles charged with status offenses. Even though both standards continue to exist, most jurisdictions have chosen to use the stricter burden-of-proof requirement for all delinquency proceedings.

Cases like *Winship* and *Gault* have not extended all adult procedural rights to juveniles charged with delinquency. The 1971 case of *McKeiver v. Pennsylvania*,[23] for example, reiterated what earlier cases had established—specifically that juveniles do not have the constitutional right to trial by a jury of their peers. It is important to note, however, that the *McKeiver* decision did not specifically prohibit jury trials for juveniles. As a consequence, approximately 12 states today allow the option of jury trials for juveniles.

In 1975, in the case of *Breed v. Jones,* the Court severely restricted the conditions under which transfers from juvenile to adult courts may occur by mandating that such transfers that do occur must be made before any adjudicatory hearing in juvenile court. In 1984, in the case of *Schall v. Martin*, the U.S. Supreme Court upheld the constitutionality of a New York state statute, ruling that pretrial detention of juveniles based on "serious risk" does not violate the principle of fundamental fairness required by due process.[24] In so holding, the Court recognized that states have a legitimate interest in preventing future delinquency by juveniles thought to be dangerous.

Although the *Schall* decision upheld the practice of preventive detention, the Court seized on the opportunity provided by the case to impose procedural requirements on the detaining authority. Consequently, preventive detention today cannot be imposed without (1) prior notice, (2) an equitable detention hearing, and (3) a statement by the judge setting forth the reason or reasons for detention.

In 1988, in the case of *Thompson v. Oklahoma*,[25] the U.S. Supreme Court determined that national standards of decency did not permit the execution of any offender who was under age 16 at the time of the crime. In 2005, in the case of *Roper v. Simmons*,[26] the Court set a new standard when it ruled that age *is* a bar to execution when the offender commits a capital crime when younger than 18. The *Roper* case involved Christopher Simmons, a high school junior who, at 17, planned and committed a callous capital murder of a woman whom he bound with duct tape and electrical wire, terrorized, and threw off a bridge. About nine months later, after he had turned 18, he was

tried and sentenced to death. Regardless of the heinous nature of Simmons's crime, the justices reasoned that "juveniles' susceptibility to immature and irresponsible behavior means their irresponsible conduct is not as morally reprehensible as that of an adult…[and] their own vulnerability and comparative lack of control over their immediate surroundings mean juveniles have a greater claim than adults to be forgiven for failing to escape negative influences in their whole environment." The fact, said the Court, "that juveniles still struggle to define their identity means it is less supportable to conclude that even a heinous crime committed by a juvenile is evidence of irretrievably depraved character." The *Roper* ruling invalidated the capital sentences of 72 death row inmates in 12 states.[27]

In 2010, the Court, in the case of *Graham v. Florida*,[28] interpreted the cruel and unusual punishment clause of the U.S. Constitution to mean that a juvenile offender cannot be sentenced to life in prison without parole for a crime not involving homicide. Its ruling, said the Court, "gives the juvenile offender a chance to demonstrate maturity and reform." Finally, in 2012, in *Miller v. Alabama*, the Court held that *mandatory* life-without-parole sentences for individuals 17 or younger convicted of homicide violate the Eighth Amendment.

Legislation Concerning Juveniles and Justice

In response to the rapidly increasing crime rates of the late 1960s, Congress passed the Omnibus Crime Control and Safe Streets Act of 1968. The act provided money and technical assistance for states and municipalities seeking to modernize their justice systems. The Safe Streets Act provided funding for youth services bureaus, which had been recommended by the 1967 presidential commission report *The Challenge of Crime in a Free Society*. These bureaus were available to police, juvenile courts, and probation departments and acted as a centralized community resource for handling delinquents and status offenders. Youth services bureaus also handled juveniles referred by schools and young people who referred themselves. Unfortunately, within a decade after their establishment, most youth services bureaus succumbed to a lack of continued federal funding.

1984	▶	1988–1989	▶	2005	▶	2010	▶	2011	▶	2012
Schall v. Martin		**Thompson v. Oklahoma and Stanford v. Kentucky**		**Roper v. Simmons**		**Graham v. Florida**		**J.D.B. v. North Carolina**		**Miller v. Alabama**
The Court overturned lower court decisions banning the pretrial detention of juveniles, and held that such detention may be necessary for the protection of the child and of others.		Minimum age for the death penalty is set at 16.		The U.S. Supreme Court ruled that age is a bar to execution when the offender commits a capital crime when he is younger than age 18. The Court held that "even a heinous crime committed by a juvenile" is not "evidence of irretrievably depraved character." Roper invalidated the capital sentences of 72 death-row inmates in 12 states.		The Eighth Amendment's ban on cruel and unusual punishments prohibits the imprisonment of a juvenile for life without the possibility of parole as punishment for a crime not involving homicide.		The age of suspects must be considered when determining whether they would feel free not to respond to police questioning.		Mandatory life-without-parole sentences for individuals 17 or younger convicted of homicide violate the Eighth Amendment.

■ **lecture note**   Discuss the various federal Acts that Congress has passed that specifically relate to juveniles and the juvenile justice system.

■ **theme**   What are the rights of juveniles who appear before a juvenile court? How did these rights come to be recognized?

In 1974, recognizing the special needs of juveniles, Congress passed the Juvenile Justice and Delinquency Prevention (JJDP) Act. Employing much the same strategy as the 1968 law, the JJDP Act provided federal grants to states and cities seeking to improve their handling and disposition of delinquents and status offenders. Nearly all the states chose to accept federal funds through the JJDP Act. Participating states had to meet two conditions within five years:

- They had to agree to a "sight and sound separation mandate," under which juveniles would not be held in institutions where they might come into regular contact with adult prisoners.
- Status offenders had to be deinstitutionalized, with most being released into the community or placed in foster homes.

Within a few years, institutional populations were cut by more than half, and community alternatives to juvenile institutionalization were rapidly being developed. Jailed juveniles were housed in separate wings of adult facilities or were removed from adult jails entirely.

When the JJDP Act was reauthorized for funding in 1980, the separation mandate was expanded to require that separate juvenile jails be constructed by the states. Studies supporting reauthorization of the JJDP Act in 1984 and 1988, however, found that nearly half the states had failed to come into "substantial compliance" with the new jail and lockup mandate. As a consequence, Congress modified the requirements of the act, continuing funding for states making "meaningful progress" toward removing juveniles from adult jails.[29] The 1988 reauthorizing legislation added a "disproportionate minority confinement" (DMC) requirement under which states seeking federal monies in support of their juvenile justice systems had to agree to ameliorate conditions leading to the disproportionate confinement of minority juveniles.[30]

In 1996, in the face of pressures toward punishment and away from treatment for violent juvenile offenders, the Office of Juvenile Justice and Delinquency Prevention proposed new rules for jailing juveniles. The new rules allow an adjudicated delinquent to be detained for up to 12 hours in an adult jail before a court appearance and make it easier for states to house juveniles in separate wings of adult jails.[31] The most recent JJDP Act reauthorization occurred in 2002[32] and expanded the DMC concept to include all aspects of the juvenile justice process. Consequently, DMC has come to mean "disproportionate minority contact" under today's law.[33] By 2005, 56 of 57 eligible states and U.S. territories had agreed to all of the act's requirements and were receiving federal funding under the legislation.[34]

In 2003, Congress passed child-protection legislation in what is commonly called the "Amber Alert" law. Officially known as the PROTECT Act of 2003 (Prosecutorial Remedies and Other Tools to End the Exploitation of Children Today), the law provides federal funding to the states to ensure the creation of a national Amber network (America's Missing: Broadcast Emergency Response) to facilitate rapid law enforcement and community response to kidnapped or abducted children. The law also established the position of a federal Amber Alert coordinator and set uniform standards for the use of Amber Alerts across our country. Another provision of the law provides for the prosecution of anyone engaged in pandering of child pornography, and it contains an extraterritorial clause that makes possible the federal prosecution of U.S. citizens who travel outside of the country to engage in child sex tourism.[35] The federal government's Amber Alert website can be accessed via **http://www.amberalert.gov**.

The Legal Rights of Juveniles

Most jurisdictions today have statutes designed to extend the *Miranda* provisions to juveniles. Many police officers routinely offer *Miranda* warnings to juveniles in their custody before questioning them. It is unclear, however, whether juveniles can legally waive their *Miranda* rights. A 1979 U.S. Supreme Court ruling held that juveniles should be accorded the opportunity for a knowing waiver when they are old enough and sufficiently educated to understand the consequences of a waiver.[36] A later High Court ruling upheld the murder conviction of a juvenile who had been advised of his rights and waived them in the presence of his mother.[37]

One important area of juvenile rights centers on investigative procedures. In 1985, for example, the U.S. Supreme Court ruled in *New Jersey* v. *T.L.O.*[38] that schoolchildren have a reasonable expectation of privacy in their personal property. The case involved a 14-year-old girl who was accused of violating school rules by smoking in a high school bathroom. A vice principal searched the girl's purse and found evidence of marijuana use. Juvenile officers were called, and the girl was eventually adjudicated in juvenile court and found delinquent.

On appeal to the New Jersey Supreme Court, the girl's lawyers were successful in having her conviction reversed on the grounds that the search of her purse, as an item of personal property, had been unreasonable. The state's appeal to the U.S. Supreme Court resulted in a ruling that prohibited school officials from engaging in unreasonable searches of students or their property. A reading of the Court's decision leads to the conclusion that a search could be considered reasonable if it (1) is based on a logical suspicion of rule-breaking actions; (2) is required to maintain order, discipline, and safety among students; and (3) does not exceed the scope of the original suspicion.

Finally, in 2011, the U.S. Supreme Court held that the age of suspects must be considered when determining whether they would feel free not to respond to police questioning. In writing for the majority in *J.D.B.* v. *North Carolina,* [39] Justice Sonia Sotomayor wrote, "It is beyond dispute that children will often feel bound to submit to police questioning when an adult in the same circumstances would feel free to leave."

The Juvenile Justice Process Today

Juvenile court jurisdiction rests on the offender's age and conduct. The majority of states today define a child subject to juvenile court jurisdiction as a person who has not yet turned 18. A few states set the age at 16, and several use 17. Figure 15–3 shows the upper ages of children subject to juvenile court jurisdiction in delinquency matters, by state. When they reach their 18th birthday, children in most states become subject to the jurisdiction of adult criminal courts.

In 2014, the OJJDP reported that U.S. courts with juvenile jurisdiction annually handle slightly more than 1.2 million delinquency cases.[40] Depending on the laws of the state and the behavior involved, the jurisdiction of the juvenile court may be exclusive. *Exclusive jurisdiction* applies when the juvenile court is the only court that has statutory authority to deal with children for specified infractions. For example, status offenses such as truancy normally fall within the exclusive jurisdiction of juvenile courts. Delinquency, which involves violation of the criminal law, however, is often not within the juvenile court's exclusive jurisdiction. All 50 states, the District of Columbia, and the federal government have provisions that allow juveniles who commit serious crimes to be bound over to criminal court. Forty-six states give juvenile court judges the power to waive jurisdiction over cases involving juveniles so that they can be transferred to criminal court.[41] Fifteen states have "direct file" provisions that authorize the prosecutor to decide whether to file certain kinds of cases in juvenile or criminal court. Juveniles who commit

> The majority of states today define a child subject to juvenile court jurisdiction as a person who has not yet turned 18.

CJ | ISSUES

The Juvenile Justice System versus Criminal Case Processing

Criminal Proceedings	Juvenile Proceedings
Focus on criminality	Focus on delinquency and a special category of "status offenses"
Comprehensive rights against unreasonable searches of person, home, and possessions	Limited rights against unreasonable searches
A right against self-incrimination; a knowing waiver is possible	A right against self-incrimination; waivers are questionable
Assumed innocent until proven guilty	Guilt and innocence are not primary issues; the system focuses on the interests of the child
Adversarial setting	Helping context
Arrest warrants form the basis for most arrests	Petitions or complaints legitimize apprehension
Right to an attorney	Right to an attorney
Public trial	Closed hearing; no right to a jury trial
System goals are punishment and reformation	System goals are protection and treatment
No right to treatment	Specific right to treatment
Possibility of bail or release on recognizance	Release into parental custody
Public record of trial and judgment	Sealed records; sometimes destroyed by a specified age
Possible incarceration in adult correctional facility	Separate facilities at all levels

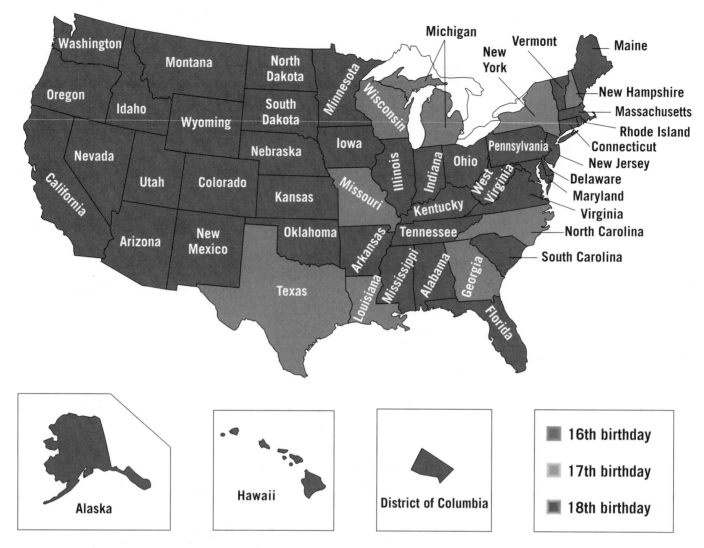

FIGURE 15-3 | Maximum Age of Juvenile Court Jurisdiction over Young Offenders, by State

Note: Wisconsin places 17-year-olds in juvenile courts for misdemeanor charges, but in adult criminal courts for felony charges.

Source: Office of Juvenile Justice and Delinquency Prevention.

violent crimes or who have prior records are among the most likely to be transferred to adult courts.[42]

Where juvenile court authority is not exclusive, the jurisdiction of the court may be original or concurrent. Original jurisdiction means that a particular offense must originate, or begin, with juvenile court authorities. Juvenile courts have original jurisdiction over most delinquency petitions and all status offenses. Concurrent jurisdiction exists where other courts have equal statutory authority to originate proceedings. If a juvenile has committed a homicide, rape, or other serious crime, for example, an arrest warrant may be issued by the adult court.

Some states specify that juvenile courts have no jurisdiction over certain excluded offenses. Delaware, Louisiana, and Nevada, for example, allow no juvenile court jurisdiction over children charged with first-degree murder. Twenty-nine states

have statutes that exclude certain serious, violent, or repeat offenders from the juvenile court's jurisdiction.

Adult and Juvenile Justice Compared

The court cases of relevance to the juvenile justice system that we have identified in this chapter have two common characteristics: They all turn on due process guarantees specified by the Bill of Rights, and they all make the claim that adult due process should serve as a model for juvenile proceedings. Due process guarantees, as interpreted by the U.S. Supreme Court, are clearly designed to ensure that juvenile proceedings are fair and that the interests of juveniles are protected. However, the Court's interpretations do not offer any pretense of providing juveniles with the same kinds of protections guaranteed to adult

■ **lecture note** Describe the juvenile justice system as being built around the processes of intake, adjudication, disposition, and post adjudicatory review. Compare this to the adult court process.

■ **juvenile petition** A document filed in juvenile court alleging that a juvenile is a delinquent, a status offender, or a dependent and asking that the court assume jurisdiction over the juvenile or that an alleged delinquent be transferred to a criminal court for prosecution as an adult.

■ **lecture note** Explain the differences between adult and juvenile intake procedures, and highlight the wide variety of options available in the juvenile justice system.

■ **lecture note** Describe the various types of intake hearings, including detention hearing, preliminary hearing, and transfer hearing.

■ **lecture note** Explain the purpose of the preliminary hearing in the juvenile justice system.

defendants. Although the High Court has tended to agree that juveniles are entitled to due process protection, it has refrained from declaring that juveniles have a right to all the aspects of due process afforded adult defendants.

Juvenile court philosophy brings with it other differences from the adult system. Among them are (1) a reduced concern with legal issues of guilt or innocence and an emphasis on the child's best interests; (2) an emphasis on treatment rather than punishment; (3) privacy and protection from public scrutiny through the use of sealed records, laws against publishing the names of juvenile offenders, and so forth; (4) the use of the techniques of social science in dispositional decision making rather than sentences determined by a perceived need for punishment; (5) no long-term confinement, with most juveniles being released from institutions by their 21st birthday, regardless of offense; (6) separate facilities for juveniles; and (7) broad discretionary alternatives at all points in the process.[43] This combination of court philosophy and due process requirements has created a unique justice system for juveniles that takes into consideration the special needs of young people while attempting to offer reasonable protection to society. The juvenile justice system is diagrammed in Figure 15-4.

How the System Works

The juvenile justice system can be viewed as a process that, when carried to completion, moves through four stages: intake, adjudication, disposition, and postadjudicatory review. Although organizationally similar to the adult criminal justice process, the juvenile system is far more likely to maximize the use of discretion and to employ diversion from further formal processing at every point in the process. Each stage is discussed in the pages that follow.

Intake and Detention Hearings

Delinquent juveniles may come to the attention of the police or juvenile court authorities either through arrest or through the filing of a **juvenile petition** by an aggrieved party. Juvenile petitions are much like criminal complaints in that they allege illegal behavior. They are most often filed by teachers, school administrators, neighbors, store managers, or

others who have frequent contact with juveniles. Parents who are unable to control the behavior of their teenage children are the source of many other petitions. Crimes in progress bring other juveniles to the attention of the police; three-quarters of all referrals to juvenile court come directly from law enforcement authorities.[44]

Many police departments have juvenile officers who are specially trained in dealing with juveniles. Because of the emphasis on rehabilitation that characterizes the juvenile justice process, juvenile officers can usually choose from a number of discretionary alternatives in the form of special programs, especially in the handling of nonviolent offenders. In Delaware County, Pennsylvania, for example, police departments participate in "youth aid panels." These panels are composed of private citizens who volunteer their services to provide an alternative to the formal juvenile court process. Youngsters who are referred to a panel and agree to abide by the decision of the group are diverted from the juvenile court.

Real justice conferencing (RJC) is another example of a diversionary program. Started in Bethlehem, Pennsylvania, in 1995, RJC is said to be a cost-effective approach to juvenile crime, school misconduct, and violence prevention. The Bethlehem program has served as a model for programs in other cities. It makes use of family group conferences (sometimes called *community conferences*) in lieu of school disciplinary or judicial processes or as a supplement to them. The family group conference, built around a restorative justice model, allows young offenders to tell what they did, to hear from those they affected, and to help decide how to repair the harm their actions caused. Successful RJC participants avoid the more formal mechanisms of the juvenile justice process.

However, even youth who are eventually diverted from the system may spend some time in custody. One juvenile case in five involves detention before adjudication.[45] Unlike the adult system, where jail is seen as the primary custodial alternative for people awaiting a first appearance, the use of secure detention for juveniles is acceptable only as a last resort. Detention hearings investigate whether

> Unlike the adult system, where jail is seen as the primary custodial alternative for people awaiting a first appearance, the use of secure detention for juveniles is acceptable only as a last resort.

THE JUVENILE JUSTICE SYSTEM

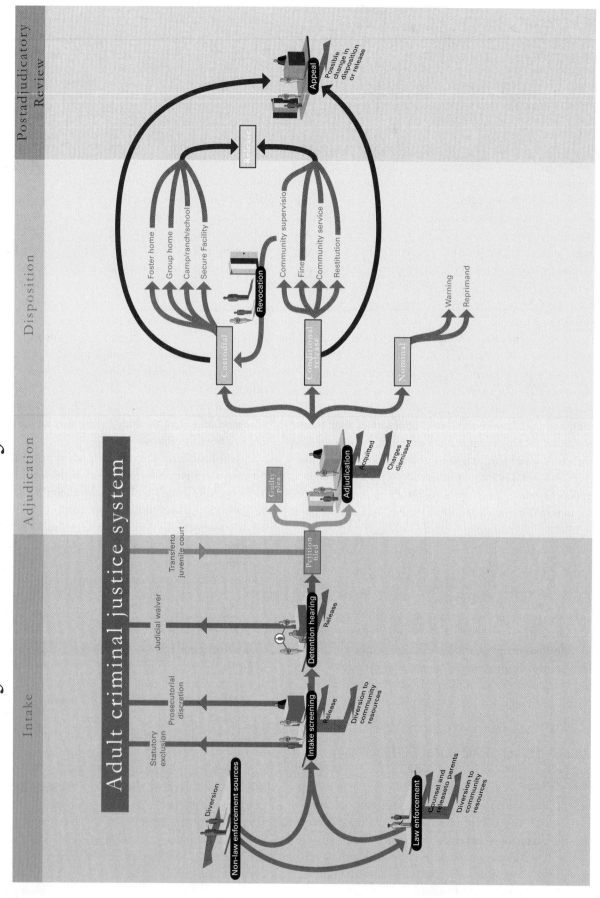

FIGURE 15-4 | The Juvenile Justice System

516

■ **intake** The first step in decision making regarding a juvenile whose behavior or alleged behavior is in violation of the law or could otherwise cause a juvenile court to assume jurisdiction.

candidates for confinement represent a "clear and immediate danger to themselves and/or to others." This judgment is normally rendered within 24 hours of apprehension. Runaways, because they are often not dangerous, are especially difficult to confine. Juveniles who are not detained are generally released into the custody of their parents or guardians or into a supervised temporary shelter, such as a group home.

Detention Hearing Detention hearings are conducted by the juvenile court judge or by an officer of the court, such as a juvenile probation officer who has been given the authority to make **intake** decisions. Intake officers, like their police counterparts, have substantial discretion. Along with detention, they can choose diversion and outright dismissal of some or all of the charges against the juvenile. Diverted juveniles may be sent to job-training programs, mental health facilities, drug-treatment programs, educational counseling, or other community service agencies. When caring parents are present who can afford private counseling or therapy, intake officers may release the juvenile into their custody with the understanding that they will provide for treatment. The National Center for Juvenile Justice estimates that more than half of all juvenile cases disposed of at intake are handled informally, without a petition, and are dismissed or diverted to a social service agency.[46]

Preliminary Hearing A preliminary hearing may be held in conjunction with the detention hearing. The purpose of the preliminary hearing is to determine whether there is probable cause to believe that the juvenile committed the alleged act. At the hearing, the juvenile, along with the child's parents or guardians, will be advised of his or her rights as established by state legislation and court precedent. If probable cause is established, the juvenile may still be offered diversionary options, such as an "improvement period" or "probation with adjudication." These alternatives usually provide a one-year period during which the juvenile must avoid legal difficulties, attend school, and obey his or her parents. Charges may be dropped at the end of this informal probationary period if the juvenile has met the conditions specified.

Richard Hutchings/PhotoEdit Inc.

Juvenile court in action. Juvenile courts are expected to act in the best interests of the children who come before them. Should that rule apply to all juveniles who come before the court, regardless of their offense?

■ **adjudicatory hearing** The fact-finding process by which the juvenile court determines whether there is sufficient evidence to sustain the allegations in a petition.

■ **teen court** An alternative approach to juvenile justice in which alleged offenders are judged and sentenced by a jury of their peers.

Transfer Hearing When a serious offense is involved, statutory provisions may allow for transfer of the case to adult court at the prosecuting attorney's request. Transfer hearings are held in juvenile court and focus on (1) the applicability of transfer statutes to the case under consideration and (2) whether the juvenile is amenable to treatment through the resources available to the juvenile justice system. Exceptions exist where statutes mandate transfer (as is sometimes the case with first-degree murder).

Adjudication

Adjudicatory hearings for juveniles are similar to adult trials, with some notable exceptions. Similarities derive from the fact that the due process rights of children and adults are essentially the same. Differences include the following:

- *Emphasis on privacy.* An important distinctive characteristic of the juvenile system is its concern with privacy. Juvenile hearings are not open to the public or to the media. Witnesses are permitted to be present only to offer testimony and may not stay for the rest of the hearing. No transcript of the proceedings is created. One purpose of the emphasis on privacy is to prevent juveniles from being negatively labeled by the community.
- *Informality.* Whereas the adult criminal trial is highly structured, the juvenile hearing is more informal and less adversarial. The juvenile court judge takes an active role in the fact-finding process rather than serving as arbitrator between prosecution and defense.
- *Speed.* Informality, the lack of a jury, and the absence of an adversarial environment promote speed. Whereas the adult trial may run into weeks or even months, the juvenile hearing is normally completed in a matter of hours or days.
- *Evidentiary standard.* On completion of the hearing, the juvenile court judge must weigh the evidence. If the charge involves a status offense, the judge may adjudicate the juvenile as a status offender upon finding that a preponderance of the evidence supports this finding. A preponderance of the evidence exists when evidence of an offense is more convincing than evidence offered to the contrary. If the charge involves a criminal-type offense, the evidentiary standard rises to the level of reasonable doubt.
- *Philosophy of the court.* Even in the face of strong evidence pointing to the offender's guilt, the judge may decide that it is not in the juvenile's best interests to be adjudicated delinquent. The judge also has the power, even after the evidence is presented, to divert the juvenile from the system. Juvenile court statistics indicate that only about half of all cases disposed of by juvenile courts are processed formally.[47] Formal processing involves the filing of a petition requesting an adjudicatory or transfer hearing. Informal cases, on the other hand, are handled without a petition. Among informally handled (nonpetitioned) delinquency cases, 40% are dismissed by the court. Most of the remainder result in voluntary probation (23%) or other dispositions (37%), but a small number (less than 1%) involve voluntary out-of-home placements.[48] Residential treatment is ordered 24% of the time in cases where the youth was adjudicated delinquent.[49]
- *No right to trial by jury.* As referred to earlier, the U.S. Supreme Court case of *McKeiver* v. *Pennsylvania*,[50] juveniles do not have a constitutional right to trial by jury, and most states do not provide juveniles with a statutory opportunity for jury trial.[51]

Some jurisdictions, however, allow juveniles to be tried by their peers. The juvenile court in Columbus County, Georgia, for example, began experimenting with peer juries in 1980.[52] In Georgia, peer juries are composed of youths under the age of 17 who receive special training by the court. Jurors are required to be successful in school and may not be under the supervision of the court or have juvenile petitions pending against them. Training consists of classroom exposure to the philosophy of the juvenile court system, Georgia's juvenile code, and Supreme Court decisions affecting juvenile justice.[53] The county's youthful jurors are used only in the dispositional (or sentencing) stage of the court process, and then only when adjudicated youths volunteer to go before the jury.

Today, hundreds of **teen court** programs are in operation across the country. The OJJDP notes that teen courts are "an effective intervention in many jurisdictions where enforcement of misdemeanor charges is sometimes given low priority because of heavy caseloads and the need to focus on more serious offenders."[54] Teen courts, says the OJJDP, "present communities with opportunities to teach young people valuable life and coping skills and promote positive peer influence for youth who are defendants and for volunteer youth who play a variety of roles in the teen court process." Learn more about teen courts via **http://www.justicestudies.com/pubs/teen courts.pdf**.

■ **dispositional hearing** The final stage in the processing of adjudicated juveniles in which a decision is made on the form of treatment or penalty that should be imposed on the child.
■ **juvenile disposition** The decision of a juvenile court, concluding a dispositional hearing, that an adjudicated juvenile be committed to a juvenile correctional facility; be placed in a juvenile residence, shelter, or care or treatment program; be required to meet certain standards of conduct; or be released.

Disposition

Once a juvenile has been found delinquent, the judge will set a **dispositional hearing**, which is similar to an adult sentencing hearing. Dispositional hearings are used to decide what action the court should take relative to the juvenile. As in adult courts, the judge may order a presentence investigation before making a dispositional decision. These investigations are conducted by special court personnel, sometimes called *juvenile court counselors*, who are, in effect, juvenile probation officers. Attorneys on both sides of the issue will also have the opportunity to make recommendations concerning dispositional alternatives.

The juvenile justice system typically gives the judge a much wider range of sentencing alternatives than does the adult system. Two major classes of **juvenile disposition** exist to confine or not to confine. Because rehabilitation is still the primary objective of the juvenile court, the judge is likely to select the least restrictive alternative that meets the needs of the juvenile while recognizing the legitimate concerns of society for protection.

Most judges decide not to confine juveniles. Statistics indicate that in nearly two-thirds (64%) of all adjudicated

A young in-custody female being led to a detention holding cell by a female deputy sheriff in Saline County, Nebraska. Although institutionalized juveniles are housed separately from adult offenders, juvenile institutions share many of the problems of adult facilities. What changes have recently occurred in the handling of juvenile offenders?

© Mikael Karlsson/Alamy

delinquency cases, juveniles are placed on formal probation.[55] Probationary disposition usually means that juveniles will be released into the custody of a parent or guardian and ordered to undergo some form of training, education, or counseling. As in the adult system, juveniles placed on probation may be ordered to pay fines or to make restitution. In 12% of adjudicated delinquency cases, courts order juveniles to pay restitution or a fine, to participate in some form of community service, or to enter a treatment or counseling program—dispositions that require minimal continuing supervision by probation staff.[56] Because juveniles rarely have financial resources or jobs, most economic sanctions take the form of court-ordered work programs, as in refurbishing schools or cleaning school buses.

Of course, not all juveniles who are adjudicated delinquent receive probation. About one-quarter of adjudicated cases result in the youth being placed outside the home in a residential facility. In a smaller number of cases (12%), the juvenile was adjudicated delinquent, but the case was then dismissed or the youth was otherwise released.[57]

Secure Institutions for Juveniles Juveniles who demonstrate the potential for serious new offenses may be ordered to participate in rehabilitative programs within a secure environment, such as a youth center or a training school. As of January 2014, approximately 54,150 young people were being held under custodial supervision in the United States.[58] Of these, 37% were being held for crimes against persons like murder, rape, or robbery; 24% were being held for property crimes; 7% were locked up for drug offenses; 2% were held for public-order offenses (including weapons offenses); 16% were held for technical violations of the conditions of their release; and 4% were held for status offenses.[59]

Most confined juveniles are held in semisecure facilities designed to look less like prisons and more like residential high school campuses. Most states, however, operate at least one secure facility for juveniles that is intended as a home for the most recalcitrant youthful offenders. Halfway houses, "boot camps,"[60] ranches, forestry camps, wilderness programs, group homes, and state-hired private facilities also hold some of the juveniles reported to be under confinement. Children placed in group homes continue to attend school and live in a family-like environment in the company of other adjudicated children, shepherded

CJ | ISSUES
Juvenile Courts versus Adult Courts

The language used in juvenile courts is less harsh than that used in adult courts. For example, juvenile courts

- Accept "petitions of delinquency" rather than criminal complaints
- Conduct "hearings," not trials

- "Adjudicate" juveniles to be "delinquent" rather than find them guilty of a crime
- Order one of a number of available "dispositions" rather than sentences

---

by "house parents." Learn more about the juvenile justice systems of each state from the National Center for Juvenile Justice's State Juvenile Justice Profiles via **http://www.ncjj.org/Research_Resources/State_Profiles.aspx**.

The operative philosophy of custodial programs for juveniles focuses squarely on the rehabilitative ideal. Juveniles are usually committed to secure facilities for indeterminate periods of time, with the typical stay being less than one year. Release is often timed to coincide with the beginning or the end of the school year.

Most juvenile facilities are small, with 82% designed to hold 50 residents or fewer.[61] Many institutionalized juveniles are held in the thousand or so homelike facilities across the nation that are limited to ten residents or fewer.[62] At the other end of the scale are the nation's 30 large juvenile institutions, each designed to hold more than 200 hard-core delinquents.[63] Residential facilities for juveniles are intensively staffed. One study found that staff members outnumber residents ten to nine on the average in state-run institutions, and by an even greater ratio in privately run facilities.[64]

Jurisdictions vary widely in their use of secure detention for juveniles. Juvenile custody populations range from a low of 27 in Vermont to a high of 8,094 in California.[65] This variance reflects population differences as well as economic realities and philosophical beliefs. Some jurisdictions, like California, have shifted detention costs to the state's counties. Hence, California shows a higher rate of institutionalization than many other states. Similarly, some states have more firmly embraced the reformation ideal and are more likely to use diversionary options for juveniles.

Characteristics of Juveniles in Confinement
Institutionalized juveniles are a small but special category of young people with serious problems. A recent report on institutionalized youth by the OJJDP found five striking characteristics:[66]

- 86.4% were male.
- 40% were black, 32.4% were white, and 22.7% were Hispanic.
- 3.6% were institutionalized for having committed a status offense, such as being truant, running away, or violating curfew.

- 61% were in residential facilities for a serious person or property offense.
- 1.3% were charged with homicide.

Overcrowding in Juvenile Facilities
As in adult prisons, overcrowding exists in many juvenile institutions. In one recent government survey, 31% of facilities surveyed said that the number of residents they held put them at or over capacity.[67]

A national study of the conditions of confinement in juvenile detention facilities conducted by the OJJDP found that "there are several areas in which problems in juvenile facilities are substantial and widespread—most notably living space, health care, security, and control of suicidal behavior."[68] Using a variety of evaluative criteria, the study found that 47% of juveniles were confined in facilities whose populations exceeded their reported design capacity and that 33% of residents had to sleep "in rooms that were smaller than required by nationally recognized standards." To address the problem, the authors of the study recommended the use of alternative placement options so that only juveniles judged to be the most dangerous to their communities would be confined in secure facilities. Similarly, because it found that injuries to residents were most likely to occur within large dormitory-like settings, the OJJDP study recommended that "large dormitories be eliminated from juvenile facilities." Finally, the study recommended that "all juveniles be screened for risk of suicidal behavior immediately upon their admission to confinement" and that initial health screenings be "carried out promptly at admission." Other problems that the OJJDP found "important enough to warrant attention" included education and treatment services. Further study of both areas is needed, the OJJDP said.

Numerous states use private facilities. Surveys show that 68% of juveniles are held in public facilities, with the remaining 32% housed in private facilities.[69] In the past few years, admissions to private facilities (comprised primarily of halfway houses, group homes, shelters, ranches, camps, and farms) have increased by more than 100%, compared with an increase of only about 10% for public facilities (mostly detention centers and training schools).[70] The fastest-growing category of detained juveniles is drug and alcohol offenders. Approximately 7% of all juvenile detainees are being held because of alcohol- and drug-related

CJ | NEWS
Delinquent Girls

In the 1990s, a surge of girls' arrests brought female juvenile crime to the country's attention. Girls' rates of arrest for some crimes increased faster than boys' rates of arrest. By 2004, girls accounted for 30% of all juvenile arrests, but delinquency experts did not know whether these trends reflected changes in girls' behavior or changes in arrest patterns. The juvenile justice field struggled to understand how best to respond to the needs of the girls entering the system.

Consequently, in 2004, the OJJDP convened the Girls Study Group (GSG) to establish a research-based foundation to guide the development, testing, and dissemination of strategies to reduce or prevent girls' involvement in delinquency and violence. Fiscal year 2008 saw the beginning of the OJJDP's dissemination of the GSG's findings. The study group sponsored a one-day preconference session at the March 2008 Blueprints for Violence Prevention conference in Denver, Colorado. The focus of the preconference session was to convey findings and discuss the evidence base for girls' programming and needs. In addition, GSG members presented some of the group's findings to the Coordinating Council on Juvenile Justice and Delinquency Prevention.

In June 2008, the OJJDP launched a Girls' Delinquency web page and began producing a series of bulletins that present the study group's findings on such issues as patterns of offending among adolescents and how they differ for girls and boys; risk and protective factors associated with delinquency, including gender differences; and the causes and correlates of girls' delinquency.

Finally, in 2012, the Georgetown Center on Poverty, Inequality, and Public Policy released a report on improving the juvenile justice system for girls. The report noted that the existing juvenile justice system was originally designed for delinquent boys, and doesn't adequately recognize the needs of girls. The Center also examined the challenges facing girls in the juvenile justice system and offered suggestions for gender-responsive reform at the local, state, and federal levels. In the words of the report:

> The typical girl in the system is a non-violent offender, who is very often low-risk, but high-need, meaning the girl poses little risk to the public but she enters the system with significant and pressing personal needs. The set of challenges that girls often face as they enter the juvenile justice system include trauma, violence, neglect, mental and physical problems, family conflict, pregnancy, residential and academic instability, and school failure. The juvenile justice system only exacerbates these problems by failing to provide girls with services at the time when they need them most.

The Center concluded its report with a number of policy recommendations that it hopes will be enacted at the federal level. They include:

- Conduct research on programs for girls, particularly regarding best practices in gender-responsive programming, and conditions of confinement for girls.

- Mandate a comprehensive effort by the U.S. Department of Justice to improve training and technical assistance for better recognition of the unique needs of marginalized girls among judges, law enforcement, and juvenile justice staff.

- Allocate federal funding and encourage states to apply for federal funding for gender-specific programming.

- Close the loophole that currently allows states to detain youths for technical violations of court orders—a practice that has a disproportionate impact on girls.

- Encourage the development of national standards for gender-responsive programming.

- Promote policies to keep girls out of the adult criminal justice system.

See the Girls' Delinquency page at the Office of Juvenile Justice and Delinquency Prevention at **http://www.ojjdp.gov/programs/girlsdelinquency.html**.

Bob Daemmrich/Alamy

A female delinquent appears before a judge in juvenile court. How does the delinquency of girls differ from that of boys?

Note: Detailed information about the GSG can be found at the Girls Study Group website at http://www.girlsstudygroup.rti.org.

Sources: *Girls Study Group: Understanding and Responding to Girls' Delinquency* (Washington, DC: OJJDP, 2010); and Liz Watson and Peter Edelman, *Improving the Juvenile Justice System for Girls: Lessons from the States* (Washington, DC: Georgetown Center on Poverty, Inequality and Public Policy, October 2012).

---

offenses.[71] Reflecting widespread socioeconomic disparities, an OJJDP report found that "a juvenile held in a public facility . . . was most likely to be black, male, between 14 and 17 years of age, and held for a delinquent offense such as a property crime or a crime against a person. On the other hand, a juvenile held in custody in a private facility…was most likely to be white, male, 14 to 17 years of age, and held for a nondelinquent offense such as running away, truancy, or incorrigibility."[72] The report also noted that "juvenile corrections has become increasingly privatized."

CAREER | PROFILE
Juvenile Justice Professional

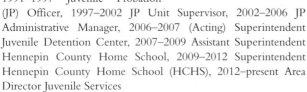

Name. Fred Bryan

Position. Director, Juvenile Service Division, Hennepin County Department of Community Corrections and Rehabilitation

Colleges attended. University of Northern Iowa (BA)

Majors. Social Work; Corrections minor

Year hired. 1984–1990 Juvenile Correctional Officer, 1990–1991 Juvenile Corrections Supervisor, 1991–1997 Juvenile Probation (JP) Officer, 1997–2002 JP Unit Supervisor, 2002–2006 JP Administrative Manager, 2006–2007 (Acting) Superintendent Juvenile Detention Center, 2007–2009 Assistant Superintendent Hennepin County Home School, 2009–2012 Superintendent Hennepin County Home School (HCHS), 2012–present Area Director Juvenile Services

Please give a brief description of your job. As the Area Director of Juvenile Services, I am responsible for oversight of our three juvenile services areas—our Juvenile Probation Department, our Juvenile Detention Center, and our juvenile residential treatment center (Hennepin County Home School).

What appealed to you most about the position when you applied for it? In Hennepin County we have committed ourselves to providing juvenile services that are evidenced-based practices and to making decisions regarding program changes based on data collected internally and from other jurisdictions. Thus, I was at a point in my career where I wanted to be in a position that afforded me the opportunity to make policy decisions involving the implementation of evidenced-based programs that have system-wide impacts. By being in this position, I am able to work with system stakeholders and partners to implement program changes that affect how we deal with youth on a county-wide level.

How would you describe the interview process? Interviewing for a job at this level requires knowledge of not only the intricacies of the specific areas in juvenile services that are reporting to me, but also requires knowledge and understanding of how juvenile services fit into the larger picture of our department as well as the structure of the county as a whole. During the interview process, I had to articulate how I would be able to work with system partners and stakeholders

such as the County Board and Administration, the Juvenile Court, the Human Services Department, and community stakeholders in such a manner that addressed the needs of youth while being able to foresee how a decision in the juvenile services area may impact another aspect of our department or the community at large.

What is a typical day like? A typical day for me may require that I spend time in each area of juvenile services addressing such needs as programming, budget, staffing, or disciplinary issues. Each area has a manager who is responsible for the day-to-day operations, and these managers and I work closely together to ensure each area has the resources and support needed to continue to provide effective evidenced-based practices for youth. I am also part of our department's administrative team, which requires me to work with our other Area Directors and Department Directors to address department-wide issues. Additionally, on any given day I may be working with our juvenile judges, County Administration, the Human Services Department, or community-based organizations.

What qualities/characteristics are most helpful for this job? The ability to work with a broad range of professionals who all may have their own agenda is essential. Political acumen is also a highly useful skill, as often the decisions made or not made have impact on other areas within the broader system or may be in conflict with the status quo. This job also requires the ability to assimilate a broad range of information and apply what is relevant.

What is a typical starting salary? The salary range is $95,000–$131,000 per year.

What is the salary potential as you move up into higher-level jobs? The highest step in our department would be the Department Director, which has a salary range of $117,000–$176,000 per year.

What career advice would you give someone in college beginning studies in criminal justice? My advice would be to focus on what the research is saying in regard to the relevant and effective current practices in criminal justice. For example, in the juvenile justice field the research tells us that only the high-risk juveniles should be removed from the community and placed out of their homes—that low- to moderate-risk youth are better served with a community-based approach and that to remove these youth from their homes and communities unnecessarily will in fact make them worse. Additionally, spend time researching or volunteering in different areas within the criminal justice field that interest you. You will acquire a broader perspective, which will aid you in determining an eventual career path.

Postadjudicatory Review

The detrimental effects of institutionalization on young offenders may make the opportunity for appellate review more critical for juveniles than it is for adults. However, federal court precedents have yet to establish a clear right to appeal from juvenile court. Even so, most states do have statutory provisions that make such appeals possible.[73]

From a practical point of view, however, juvenile appeals may not be as consequential as are appeals of adult criminal

> Most juvenile complaints are handled informally, and only relatively low numbers of adjudicated delinquents are placed outside the family.

convictions. Most juvenile complaints are handled informally, and only relatively low numbers of adjudicated delinquents are placed outside the family.

Moreover, because sentence lengths are short for most confined juveniles, appellate courts hardly have time to complete the review process before the juvenile is released.

■ **theme**   Why are juvenile appeals less consequential than appeals of adult criminal convictions? Do you think the federal courts need to establish a clear right to appeal from juvenile court? Why or why not?

■ **blended sentence**   A juvenile court disposition that imposes both a juvenile sanction and an adult criminal sentence upon an adjudicated delinquent. The adult sentence is suspended if the juvenile offender successfully completes the term of the juvenile disposition and refrains from committing any new offense.[i]

■ **lecture note**   Review the major developments that took place in many states during the past 25 years. Ask the class what changes they think may be forthcoming.

■ **theme**   What changes seem to be on the horizon for the American system of juvenile justice? Will they be in keeping with the philosophy of the juvenile court movement, now more than 100 years old, or will they likely overturn important components of that system?

The Post–Juvenile Court Era

In the late twentieth century, and extending into the early years of the twenty-first, cases of serious juvenile offending, combined with extensive media coverage of violent juvenile crime across the United States to fuel public misperceptions that violence committed by teenagers had reached epidemic proportions and that no community was immune to random acts of youth violence. At the same time, the apparent "professionalization" of delinquency, the hallmark of which is the repeated and often violent criminal involvement of juveniles in drug-related gang activity, came to be viewed as a major challenge to the idealism of the juvenile justice system. Consequently, by the turn of the twenty-first century, the issue of youth violence was at or near the top of nearly every state's agenda. Most states took some form of legislative or executive action to stem what was seen as an escalating level of dangerous crime by juveniles. As the OJJDP observed, "This level of [legislative and executive] activity has occurred only three other times in our nation's history: at the outset of the juvenile court movement at the turn of the [twentieth] century; following the U.S. Supreme Court's *Gault* decision in 1967; and with the enactment of the Juvenile Justice and Delinquency Prevention Act in 1974."[74] The OJJDP identified five significant developments that took place in many states during the past quarter century:[75]

1. *Transfer provisions.* New transfer provisions made it easier to move juvenile offenders from the juvenile justice system to the criminal justice system.
2. *Sentencing authority.* New laws on sentencing gave criminal and juvenile courts the authority to use expanded sentencing options such as the **blended sentence** (the combination of a juvenile disposition followed by a suspended adult sentence if the former is carried out successfully) in cases involving juveniles.
3. *Confidentiality changes.* Modifications were made to laws containing court confidentiality provisions in order to make juvenile records and proceedings more open.
4. *Victims' rights.* Laws were passed that increased the role of victims of juvenile crime in the juvenile justice process.
5. *Correctional programming.* New correctional programs in adult and juvenile facilities were developed to handle juveniles sentenced as adults or as violent juvenile offenders.

Changes like these prompted juvenile justice experts Jeffrey Butts and Ojmarrh Mitchell, members of the Program on Law and Behavior at the Urban Institute in Washington, D.C., to say that "policymakers throughout the United States have greatly dissolved the border between juvenile and criminal justice."[76] As evidence, they noted that juvenile courts across the United States are becoming increasingly similar to criminal courts in the methods they use to reach conclusions and to process cases, as well as in the general atmosphere that characterizes them.

Following these changes, some claimed that many states had substantially "criminalized" juvenile courts. In March 2000, for example, California voters endorsed sweeping changes in the state's juvenile justice system by passing Proposition 21, the Gang Violence and Juvenile Crime Prevention Act. The law reduced confidentiality in the juvenile court, limited the use of probation for young offenders, and increased the power of prosecutors to send juveniles to adult court and to put them in adult prisons. Public support for the measure was undiminished by projections that it would increase operational costs in the California juvenile justice system by $500 million annually.[77] Because of laws like California's Proposition 21, a leading expert on juvenile justice noted that "the similarities of juvenile and adult courts are becoming greater than the differences between them."[78]

> Because of laws like California's Proposition 21, leading experts on juvenile justice note that the similarities of juvenile and adult courts are becoming greater than the differences between them.

Cindy Lederman, presiding judge of the Miami-Dade Juvenile Court, referred to such changes as the "adultification" of the juvenile justice system.[79] The juvenile court, said Lederman, has undergone significant change since it was created. In the early twentieth century, the juvenile court focused on social welfare and was primarily concerned with acting in a child's best interest. By the mid-twentieth century, it had seized on the issue of children's due process rights as an important guiding principle. By the start of the twenty-first century, said Lederman, it had turned its focus to accountability and punishment.

At the federal level, the Department of Justice Authorization Act for Fiscal Year 2003[80] set dramatic new accountability standards for federally funded programs for juveniles who violate the law.[81] The law built on the premise that young people who violate criminal laws should be held accountable for their offenses through the swift and consistent application of sanctions that are proportionate to the offense.[82] Lawmakers made it clear that it was their belief that enhanced accountability and swift sanctions were both a matter of basic justice and a way to combat delinquency and improve the quality of life in our nation's communities.

It now seems, however, that in recent years the pendulum has begun to swing back toward the original principles of the juvenile court. In an age of shrinking state budgets and lack of faith in the ability of residential placement to accomplish reformation, a number of states are moving to reestablish such principles. In 2011, for example, Texas—a state normally known for its conservative approach to criminal and juvenile justice—enacted legislation consolidating the former Texas Youth Commission with the Texas Juvenile Probation Commission into one agency: the Texas Juvenile Justice Department.[83] The legislation tasked the newly created Texas Juvenile Justice Department with evaluating the effectiveness of county and state programs and services for youth, and with developing outcome measures appropriate to such an evaluation. The department was also directed to make full use of community-based programs as alternatives to residential placement. The Texas legislature closed 3 of 10 youth prisons in the states, and shifted a substantial amount of state money to local rehabilitation programs. One important feature of the new approach in Texas is the funding of county probation departments throughout Texas to provide mental health services for juvenile offenders kept in the community.[84] Similarly, in 2007, the Rhode Island General Assembly reversed the governor's recommendation to decrease the age of juvenile jurisdiction from 18 to 17, and restored the age of juvenile jurisdiction to 18; and that same year, Connecticut raised the age of juvenile court jurisdiction from 16 to 18.[85] In 2010, Virginia allowed juveniles transferred to or charged in criminal courts to remain in juvenile, rather than adult, detention facilities.[86]

By 2012, the National Conference on State Legislatures was able to note that research distinguishing adolescents from adults is contributing to an important and growing trend among states to reestablish boundaries between the adult and juvenile justice systems. One of the more prominent shifts in juvenile justice policy, said the Conference, has been the focus on juveniles' developmental needs.[87] In keeping with that focus, a recent report by the National Academy of Sciences (NAS) found that "adolescents differ from adults and children in three important ways that contribute to differences in behavior."[88] NAS researchers found that, because of significant differences in developing adolescent brains, young people (1) have less capacity for self-regulation in emotionally charged contexts; (2) have a heightened sensitivity to proximal external influences, such as peer pressure and immediate incentives; and (3) show less ability than adults to make judgments and decisions that require future orientation. According to the NAS report, "the combination of these three cognitive patterns accounts for the tendency of adolescents to prefer and engage in risky behaviors that have a high probability of immediate reward but can have harmful consequences."[89]

In 2013, as further evidence of a move away from severe punishments for juveniles, the Washington, D.C.–based Justice Policy Institute (JPI) reported findings from five states that showed a significant move away from the use of juvenile confinement.[90] Those states, Connecticut, Tennessee, Louisiana, Minnesota, and Arizona, achieved a greater than 50% drop in juvenile residential placement populations between the years 2001 and 2010.[91] The experience in the states studied was similar to that of the nation as a whole, where juvenile incarceration rates declined from 335 per 100,000 in 2001 to 225 by 2010.[92] For all states and the District of Columbia, the number of youth in residential placement dropped steadily from its high of 107,493 in 1999 to 54,150 in January 2014 (Figure 15-5).[93] Declines in residential populations were mostly the result of decreases in confinement for property offenses, and a move away from holding youth for drug offenses. In the states studied, the JPI found that "state leaders recommitted their systems to a holistic juvenile justice ideal that acknowledges that youthful behavior is inherently different than adult behavior and that it requires different interventions and services."[94]

Proposals for further change abound. Recently, New York's John Jay College of Criminal Justice released a comprehensive study of strategies for changing the juvenile justice system.[95] The study's authors noted that "Placing youth in large, group confinement facilities does not seem to be justified from the perspective of treatment effectiveness or the prevention of future recidivism." According to the study, recent models for reform adopted by a number of states can be categorized into three groups according to the kinds of influences that have led to their development. The three models are: (1) *resolution strategies* (involving direct managerial changes brought about by the efforts of administrators, policymakers,

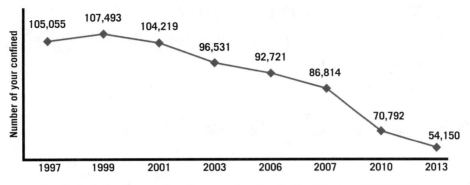

FIGURE 15-5 | Number of Youth Held in Secure Confinement in the United States, 1997–2013

Source: Office of Juvenile Justice and Delinquency Prevention, OJJDP, "Easy Access to the Census of Juveniles in Residential Placement" (1997–2013). http://www.ojjdp.gov/ojstatbb/ezacjrp/asp/State_Adj.asp (accessed November 10, 2015).

and elected officials), (2) *reinvestment strategies* (the use of financial incentives to encourage state and local governments to reduce spending on confinement and to invest in community-based programs), and (3) *realignment strategies* (permanent organizational and structural modifications intended to alter the juvenile justice system, including the closing of facilities and the elimination of agencies). The study found that "reform strategies in juvenile justice are sustainable when they cannot be easily reversed by future policymakers facing different budgetary conditions and changing political environments." Consequently, the study authors noted that realignment strategies may be the best choice for sustaining reform over the long term. Access the John Jay report at **http://tinyurl.com/6bpx98x**.

Finally, over the last few years, the state of California moved to complete a strategy of juvenile justice "realignment." Under the strategy, the state's counties will assume full responsibility for managing all of the state's juvenile offenders. Even before the implementation of the realignment strategy, California law allowed only juveniles who had been adjudicated for a serious, violent, or sex offense to be sent to state facilities. Consequently, 99% of the state's juvenile offenders are now housed or supervised in county-run facilities.[96] To finalize the realignment strategy, California Governor Jerry Brown announced that he would stop new admissions to the state's Division of Juvenile Justice (DJJ) facilities. Brown offered to provide counties with the funding needed to manage juvenile offenders at the local level. The realignment strategy was proposed as an effort to offer correctional intervention "at the point where the offender is most likely to return."[97] Even so, the strategy was largely based on economic necessity. As a report by the California-based Center on Juvenile and Criminal Justice noted, "the state of California can no longer afford to operate a dual juvenile justice system."[98]

Today, evidence-based practices in the juvenile justice arena (see the CJ Issues box in this chapter) are helping to establish a set of best-practice guidelines, providing state policymakers and juvenile justice administrators insight into what works best to control juvenile crime and to rehabilitate youthful offenders. In 2010, for example, the National Center for Youth in Custody (NC4YC) was launched by the OJJDP to support, improve, and reform youth detention and correction facilities and adult facilities housing youthful offenders. The objectives of NC4YC are to advance the field of juvenile justice by providing training and technical assistance and by disseminating effective practices and approaches to the justice community. The center will strive to serve the range of facilities in which juveniles are placed, including adult facilities that confine juvenile offenders. The center emphasizes the rehabilitative goals of the juvenile justice system and has four central objectives:

- To deliver strategic, targeted, and measurable training and technical assistance directly to facilities that detain or confine youth.
- To identify, document, and promote effective, evidence-based approaches to working with youth in custody.
- To expand the knowledge base and research on juvenile justice and best practices in detaining and confining youth.
- To create a resource community for juvenile justice practitioners, youth in custody, and families.

Necessitated by budgetary concerns at both the state and federal level, the tide is now shifting to evidence-based models that demonstrate effectiveness in the handling of juvenile offenders. Consequently, the flood of recent federal and state legislation, mandated by surging public demand for greater responsibility among adolescents, has come up against recent implementation of the evidence-based cost-saving model. As a result, the juvenile justice system of the mid-twenty-first century may in many respects be quite different than the one we have known.

CJ | ISSUES
Evidence-Based Juvenile Justice

Evidence-based research permits the identification of effective strategies through the evaluation and analysis of ongoing programs. In 2012, the Committee on Assessing Juvenile Justice Reform of the National Academies of Sciences released a report on reforming juvenile justice.[1] The Committee found that "a harsh system of punishing troubled youth can make things worse, while a scientifically based juvenile justice system can make an enduring difference in the lives of many youth who most need the structure and services it can provide." The Committee recommended that the goals, design, and operation of the juvenile justice system "should be informed by the growing body of knowledge about adolescent development. If designed and implemented in a developmentally informed way," the Committee said, "procedures for holding adolescents accountable for their offending, and the services provided to them, can promote positive legal socialization, reinforce a prosocial identity, and reduce reoffending." The Committee warned, however, that "if the goals, design, and operation of the juvenile justice system are not informed by this growing body of knowledge, the outcome is likely to be negative interactions between youth and justice system officials, increased disrespect for the law and legal authority, and the reinforcement of a deviant identity and social disaffection."

Two of today's best-known evidence-based initiatives in the area of juvenile justice are (1) the Blueprints for Violence Prevention program developed by the Center for the Study and Prevention of Violence (CSPV) at the University of Colorado–Boulder, and (2) the OJJDP's Model Programs Guide (MPG). The Blueprints study, one of the earliest research efforts to focus on evidence-based delinquency programs, began as an effort to identify model violence-prevention initiatives and implement them within the state of Colorado.[2] The OJJDP soon became an active supporter of the Blueprints project and provided additional funding to the CSPV to sponsor and evaluate program replications in sites across the United States. As a result, Blueprints has evolved into a large-scale prevention initiative, both identifying model programs and providing technical support to help sites choose and implement those programs that have been proven to be effective. After reviewing more than 600 programs to date, the Blueprints study has identified 11 model programs and 21 promising programs that prevent violence and drug use and treat youth with problem behaviors.[3]

The MPG, also developed with support from the OJJDP, is intended to assist communities in implementing evidence-based prevention and intervention programs that can make a difference in the lives of children.[4] The MPG database consists of over 200 evidence-based programs that cover the continuum of youth services, from prevention through sanctions to reentry. It is used by juvenile justice practitioners, administrators, and researchers to initiate programs that have already proven their ability to enhance accountability, ensure public safety, and reduce recidivism. The OJJDP offers the MPG in the form of an easy-to-use online database that address a range of issues, including substance abuse, mental health, and education programs. The MPG database contains summary information on many evidence-based delinquency programs. Programs are categorized into exemplary, effective, and promising, based on an established set of methodological criteria and the strength of the findings. The MPG database can be queried through an online search tool at http://www.ojjdp.gov/mpg/search.aspx.

[1] National Research Council, Reforming Juvenile Justice: A Developmental Approach, Committee on Assessing Juvenile Justice Reform, Richard J. Bonnie, Robert L. Johnson, Betty M. Chemers, and Julie A. Schuck, eds. Committee on Law and Justice, Division of Behavioral and Social Sciences and Education (Washington, DC: The National Academies Press, 2012).

[2] Sharon Mihalic, Abigail Fagan, Katherine Irwin, Diane Ballard, and Delbert Elliott, Blueprints for Violence Prevention (Washington, DC: OJJDP, July 2004).

[3] Ibid.

[4] OJJDP, "OJJDP Model Programs Guide," http://www.ojjdp.gov/mpg/Default.aspx (accessed March 10, 2015).

SUMMARY

- Under today's laws, children occupy a special status that is tied closely to cultural advances that occurred in the Western world during the past 200 years. Before the modern era, children who committed crimes received no preferential treatment. They were adjudicated, punished, and imprisoned alongside adults. Beginning a few hundred years ago, England, from which we derive many of our legal traditions, adapted the principle of *parens patriae*. That principle allowed the government to take the place of parents in dealing with children who broke the law. Around the middle of the nineteenth century, the child-savers movement began in the United States. Child savers espoused a philosophy of productivity and eschewed idleness and unprincipled behavior. Not long afterward, the 1899 codification of Illinois juvenile law became the model for juvenile court statutes throughout the United States. It created a juvenile court separate in form and function from adult criminal courts and based on the principle of *parens patriae*. To avoid the lasting stigma of criminality, the term *delinquent*, rather than *criminal*, began to be applied to young adjudicated offenders. Soon, juvenile courts across the country focused primarily on the best interests of the child as a guide in their deliberations.

- Important U.S. Supreme Court decisions of special relevance to the handling of juveniles by the justice system include (1) *Kent* v. *U.S.* (1966), which established minimal due process standards for juvenile hearings; (2) *In re Gault* (1967), in which the Court found that a child has many of the same due process rights as an adult; (3) *In re Winship* (1970), which held that the constitutional safeguard of proof beyond a reasonable doubt is required during the adjudicatory stage of a delinquency proceeding; (4) *McKeiver* v. *Pennsylvania* (1971), which held that jury trials were not required in delinquency cases; (5) *Breed* v. *Jones* (1975), which restricted the conditions under which transfers from juvenile to adult court may occur; (6) *Schall* v. *Martin* (1984), in which the Court held that pretrial detention of juveniles based on "serious risk" does not violate due process, although prior notice, an equitable detention hearing, and a statement by the juvenile court judge explaining the reasons for detention are required; (7) *Roper* v. *Simmons* (2005), which held that age *is* a bar to capital punishment when the offender commits a capital crime when he or she is younger than 18; (8) *Graham* v. *Florida* (2010), in which the Court found that the Constitution does not permit a juvenile offender to be sentenced to life in prison without parole for a nonhomicide crime; (9) *J.D.B.* v. *North Carolina* (2011), which held that the age of suspects must be considered when determining whether they would feel free not to respond to police questioning; and (10) *Miller* v. *Alabama* (2012), in which the Court held that *mandatory* life-without-parole sentences for individuals 17 or younger convicted of homicide violate the Eighth Amendment.

- Due process guarantees, as interpreted by the U.S. Supreme Court, are designed to ensure that juvenile proceedings are fair and that the interests of juveniles are protected. Although the Court has established that juveniles are entitled to fundamental due process protections, it has refrained from declaring that juveniles have a right to all aspects of due process afforded adult defendants. The juvenile justice system differs in other ways from the adult system. For example, the juvenile system (1) is less concerned with legal issues of guilt or innocence and focuses on the child's best interests; (2) emphasizes treatment rather than punishment; (3) ensures privacy and protection from public scrutiny through the use of sealed records and laws against publishing the names of juvenile offenders; (4) uses the techniques of social science in dispositional decision making rather than sentences determined by a perceived need for punishment; (5) does not order long-term confinement, with most juveniles being released from institutions by their 21st birthday; (6) has separate facilities for juveniles; and (7) allows broad discretionary alternatives at all points in the process.

- The "professionalization" of delinquency, the hallmark of which is the repeated and often violent criminal involvement of juveniles in drug-related gang activity, presented a major challenge to the idealism of the juvenile justice system in the latter part of the twentieth century. Consequently, the juvenile justice system's commitment to a philosophy of protection and restoration, expressed in the juvenile court movement of the late nineteenth and early twentieth centuries began to dissipate. However, necessitated by budgetary concerns at both the state and federal level, the tide has now shifted to evidence-based models that demonstrate effectiveness in the handling of juvenile offenders. The present juvenile justice system, for the most part, continues to differ substantially from the adult system in the multitude of

opportunities it provides for diversion and in the emphasis it places on rehabilitation rather than punishment.

KEY TERMS

abused child, 508	juvenile justice system, 506
adjudicatory hearing, 518	juvenile petition, 515
blended sentence, 523	neglected child, 508
delinquency, 506	*parens patriae*, 506
delinquent child, 508	status offender, 508
dependent child, 508	status offense, 509
dispositional hearing, 519	teen court, 518
intake, 517	undisciplined child, 508
juvenile disposition, 519	

KEY CASES

Breed v. *Jones*, 511	*McKeiver* v. *Pennsylvania*, 511
Graham v. *Florida*, 511	*Miller* v. *Alabama*, 511
In re Gault, 510	*Roper* v. *Simmons*, 511
In re Winship, 510	*Schall* v. *Martin*, 511
Kent v. *U.S.*, 526	

QUESTIONS FOR REVIEW

1. Describe the history and evolution of the juvenile justice system in the Western world, and list the six categories of children recognized by the laws of most states.
2. What was the impact of the *Gault* decision on juvenile justice in America? What adult rights were not accorded to juveniles by *Gault*? What other U.S. Supreme Court decisions have had a substantial impact on the handling of juvenile offenders by the justice system?
3. What are the major similarities and differences between the juvenile and adult justice systems?
4. In your opinion, should juveniles continue to receive what many regard as preferential treatment from the courts? Why or why not?

QUESTIONS FOR REFLECTION

1. This chapter pointed out that substantial changes are now afoot in the area of juvenile justice. What are some of those changes? With which of those changes do you agree? Are there any with which you don't agree? Explain.
2. This chapter discussed California's Proposition 21, which voters in that state passed in 2000. What was the intent of Proposition 21? Were the changes that it brought about needed, or do you think that the state would have been better off if the proposition had failed to pass? Why?
3. What is meant by the "adultification" of the juvenile justice system? Is adultification a good idea? Explain.

NOTES

i. Howard N. Snyder and Melissa Sickmund, *Juvenile Offenders and Victims: 2006 National Report* (Washington, DC: Office of Juvenile Justice and Delinquency Prevention, 2006).

1. President's Commission on Law Enforcement and Administration of Justice, *The Challenge of Crime in A Free Society* (Washington, DC: 1967, USGPO), p. 58.
2. President's Commission on Law Enforcement and Administration of Justice, *The Challenge of Crime in A Free Society* (Washington, DC: 1967, USGPO), p. 58.
3. *Miller* v. *Alabama,* 132 S.Ct. 2455 (2012).
4. Greg Miller, "Brain Science a Factor in Supreme Court Decision on Juvenile Crimes," *Science Magazine,* May 2010, http://news.sciencemag.org/2010/05/ brain-science-factor-supreme-court-decision-juvenile-crimes (accessed May 21, 2014).
5. Office of Juvenile Justice and Delinquency Prevention, *OJJDP Research, 2000* (Washington, DC: OJJDP, 2001).
6. Federal Bureau of Investigation, *Crime in the United States, 2014* (Washington, DC: U.S. Dept. of Justice, 2015).
7. Ibid.; and U.S. Census Bureau, *Age, 2000: A Census 2000 Brief* (Washington, DC: U.S. Census Bureau, 2001), http://www.census.gov/prod/2001pubs/c2kbr01-12.pdf (accessed January 2, 2011).
8. The term *juvenile* refers to people younger than 18 years of age.
9. H. Snyder, C. Puzzanchera, and W. Kang, *Easy Access to FBI Arrest Statistics, 1994–2002* (Washington, DC: Office of Juvenile Justice and Delinquency Prevention, 2005), http://ojjdp.ncjrs.org/ojstatbb/ezaucr (accessed November 11, 2012); Andrea J. Sedlak and Carol Bruce, *Youth's Characteristics and Backgrounds: Findings from the Survey of Youth in Residential Placement* (Washington, DC: OJJDP, 2010); and C. L. Bright, et al., "Young Adult Outcomes of Girls Involved in the Juvenile Justice System: Distinct Patterns of Risk and Protection," *Corrections and Mental Health,* Vol. 1, No. 3 (2013).
10. Edward P. Mulvey, *Highlights from Pathways to Desistance: A Longitudinal Study of Serious Adolescent Offenders* (Washington, DC: OJJDP).
11. A reform movement, now under way, may soon lead to changes in the way juvenile records are handled.
12. For an excellent review of the handling of juveniles throughout history, see Wiley B. Sanders, ed., *Juvenile Offenders for a Thousand Years* (Chapel Hill: University of North Carolina Press, 1970).
13. See Sanford Fox, "Juvenile Justice Reform: An Historical Perspective," in Sanford Fox, ed., *Modern Juvenile Justice: Cases and Materials* (St. Paul, MN: West, 1972), pp. 15–48.
14. Johnson, *Introduction to the Juvenile Justice System,* p. 3.
15. Ibid.
16. Ibid.
17. Fox, "Juvenile Justice Reform," p. 47.
18. Ibid., p. 5.
19. Principles adapted from Robert G. Caldwell, "The Juvenile Court: Its Development and Some Major Problems," in Rose Giallombardo, ed., *Juvenile Delinquency: A Book of Readings* (New York: John Wiley, 1966), p. 358.
20. See, for example, *Haley* v. *Ohio,* 332 U.S. 596 (1948).
21. *In re Gault,* 387 U.S. 1 (1967).
22. *In re Winship,* 397 U.S. 358 (1970).
23. *McKeiver* v. *Pennsylvania,* 403 U.S. 528 (1971).
24. *Schall* v. *Martin,* 467 U.S. 253 (1984).
25. *Thompson* v. *Oklahoma,* 487 U.S. 815, 818–838 (1988).

26. *Roper* v. *Simmons,* 543 U.S. 551 (2005).
27. Death Penalty Information Center, "Juvenile Offenders Currently on Death Row, or Executed, by State," http://www.deathpenaltyinfo.org/article.php?scid527&did5882 (accessed September 10, 2011).
28. *Graham* v. *Florida,* No. 08–7412. Decided May 17, 2010.
29. "Drug Bill Includes Extension of OJJDP, with Many Changes," *Criminal Justice Newsletter,* Vol. 19, No. 22 (November 15, 1988), p. 4.
30. The Formula Grants Program supports state and local delinquency prevention and intervention efforts and juvenile justice system improvements. Through this program, the OJJDP provides funds directly to states, territories, and the District of Columbia to help them implement comprehensive state juvenile justice plans based on detailed studies of needs in their jurisdictions. The Formula Grants Program is authorized under the JJDP Act of 2002 (U.S. Code, Title 42, Section 5601, *et seq.*).
31. See "OJJDP Eases Rules on Juvenile Confinement," *Corrections Compendium* (November 1996), p. 25.
32. The Juvenile Justice and Delinquency Prevention Act of 2002 (Public Law 107-273).
33. Howard N. Snyder and Melissa Sickmund, *Juvenile Offenders and Victims: 2006 National Report* (Washington, DC: Office of Juvenile Justice and Delinquency Prevention, 2006).
34. Ibid., p. 97.
35. See, for example, *United States* v. *Williams,* U.S. Supreme Court, 2008 (No. 06-694), which upheld the law's provision criminalizing the possession and distribution of material pandered as child pornography; and U.S. Department of State, *Trafficking in Persons Report* (Washington, DC: U.S. Department of State, June 2007), p. 72.
36. *Fare* v. *Michael C.,* 442 U.S. 707 (1979).
37. *California* v. *Prysock,* 453 U.S. 355 (1981).
38. *New Jersey* v. *T.L.O.,* 105 S.Ct. 733 (1985).
39. *J.D.B.* v. *North Carolina,* U.S. Supreme Court, No. 09-11121 (decided June 16, 2011).
40. Office of Juvenile Justice and Delinquency Prevention, "Juvenile Court Cases," *Statistical Briefing Book,* http://ojjdp.ncjrs.gov/ojstatbb/court/qa06201.asp (accessed August 12, 2014).
41. National Center for Juvenile Justice, "State Juvenile Justice Profiles," http://www.ncjj.org/stateprofiles (accessed August 10, 2011).
42. Charles M. Puzzanchera, *Delinquency Cases Waived to Criminal Court, 1990–1999* (Washington, DC: Office of Juvenile Justice and Delinquency Prevention, 2003).
43. Adapted from Peter Greenwood, *Juvenile Offenders,* National Institute of Justice Crime File Series Study Guide (Washington, DC: NIJ, n.d.).
44. Bureau of Justice Statistics, *Report to the Nation on Crime and Justice,* 2nd ed. (Washington, DC: U.S. Government Printing Office, 1988), p. 78.
45. Ibid.
46. Ibid.
47. Sarah Hockenberry and Charles Puzzanchera, *Juvenile Court Statistics, 2013* (Pittsburgh, PA: National Center for Juvenile Justice, 2015).
48. Ibid., p. 52.
49. Ibid.
50. *McKeiver* v. *Pennsylvania,* 403 U.S. 528 (1971).
51. Some states, such as West Virginia, do provide juveniles with a statutory right to trial.

52. Other early peer juries in juvenile courts began operating in Denver, Colorado; Duluth, Minnesota; Deerfield, Illinois; Thompkins County, New York; and Spanish Fork City, Utah, at about the same time. See Philip Reichel and Carole Seyfrit, "A Peer Jury in the Juvenile Court," *Crime and Delinquency*, Vol. 30, No. 3 (July 1984), pp. 423–438.

53. Ibid.

54. Tracy M. Godwin, *A Guide for Implementing Teen Court Programs* (Washington, DC: Office of Juvenile Justice and Delinquency Prevention, 1996).

55. Sarah Hockenberry and Charles Puzzanchera, *Juvenile Court Statistics 2013* (Pittsburgh, PA: National Center for Juvenile Justice, 2015).

56. Ibid., p. 52.

57. Ibid., p. 52.

58. Office of Juvenile Justice and Delinquency Prevention, "Easy Access to the Census of Juveniles in Residential Placement," http://www.ojjdp.gov/ojstatbb/ezacjrp (accessed August 8, 2015).

59. Ibid.

60. See, for example, Blair B. Bourque et al., *Boot Camps for Juvenile Offenders: An Implementation Evaluation of Three Demonstration Programs*, National Institute of Justice Research in Brief (Washington, DC: NIJ, 1996).

61. OJJDP, *Statistical Briefing Book,* http://www.ojjdp.gov/ojstatbb/default.asp (accessed November 10, 2015).

62. Ibid.

63. Ibid.

64. Ibid.

65. OJJDP, "Easy Access to the Census of Juveniles in Residential Placement" (1997-2013). http://www.ojjdp.gov/ojstatbb/ezacjrp/asp/State_Adj.asp (accessed November 10, 2015).

66. "Easy Access to the Census of Juveniles in Residential Placement: 1997-2013, http://www.ojjdp.gov/ojstatbb/ezacjrp/asp/State_Offense.asp (accessed November 8, 2015).

67. Sarah Hockenberry, Melissa Sickmund, and Anthony Sladky, *Juvenile Residential Facility Census, 2012* (Washington, DC: OJJDP, 2015).

68. Dale G. Parent et al., *Conditions of Confinement: Juvenile Detention and Corrections Facilities* (Washington, DC: Office of Juvenile Justice and Delinquency Prevention, 1994).

69. OJJDP, "Juveniles in Residential Placement" (1997-2013). http://www.ojjdp.gov/ojstatbb/ezacjrp/asp/Offense_Facility.asp?state=0&topic=Offense_Facility&year=2013&percent=row

70. *Corrections Compendium* (December 1993), p. 14.

71. Sickmund et al., "Easy Access to the Census of Juveniles in Residential Placement," 2013, http://www.ojjdp.gov/ojstatbb/ezacjrp/ (accessed, November 10, 2015).

72. Office of Juvenile Justice and Delinquency Prevention, *National Juvenile Custody Trends, 1978–1989* (Washington, DC: U.S. Dept. of Justice, 1992), p. 2.

73. Section 59 of the Uniform Juvenile Court Act recommends the granting of a right to appeal for juveniles (National Conference of Commissioners on Uniform State Laws, Uniform Juvenile Court Act, 1968).

74. Patricia Torbet et al., *State Responses to Serious and Violent Juvenile Crime* (Washington, DC: Office of Juvenile Justice and Delinquency Prevention, 1996).

75. Snyder and Sickmund, *Juvenile Offenders and Victims: 2006 National Report*, pp. 96–97.

76. Jeffrey A. Butts and Ojmarrh Mitchell, "Brick by Brick: Dismantling the Border between Juvenile and Adult Justice," in Phyllis McDonald and Janice Munsterman, eds., *Criminal Justice 2000, Vol. 2: Boundary Changes in Criminal Justice Organizations* (Washington, DC: National Institute of Justice, 2000), p. 207.

77. Ibid., pp. 167–213.

78. Barry C. Feld, "Abolish the Juvenile Court: Youthfulness, Criminal Responsibility, and Sentencing Policy," *Journal of Criminal Law and Criminology* (winter 1998).

79. Cindy S. Lederman, "The Juvenile Court: Putting Research to Work for Prevention," *Juvenile Justice Bulletin*, Vol. 6, No. 2 (Washington, DC: Office of Juvenile Justice and Delinquency Prevention, 1999), p. 23.

80. Public Law 107-273.

81. Activities funded under the legislation fall under Juvenile Accountability Block Grants (JABG) program.

82. See Cheryl Andrews and Lynn Marble, "Changes to OJJDP's Juvenile Accountability Program," *Juvenile Justice Bulletin* (Washington, DC: Office of Juvenile Justice and Delinquency Prevention, 2003).

83. SB 653.

84. Patricia Kilday Hart, "Lawmakers in Lockstep on Juvenile-Justice Bills," *The Houston Chronicle*, May 21, 2011, http://www.chron.com/disp/story.mpl/metropolitan/7575646.html (accessed June 7, 2011).

85. Sarah Alice Brown, *Trends in Juvenile Justice State Legislation: 2001–2011* (Washington, DC: National Conference of State Legislatures, 2012).

86. Ibid.

87. Ibid., p. 3.

88. Richard J. Bonnie, et al, *Reforming Juvenile Justice: A Developmental Approach* (Washington, DC: National Academies Press, 2012).

89. Ibid.

90. Justice Policy Institute, "Common Ground: Lessons Learned from Five States That Reduced Juvenile Confinement by More Than Half," February 2013, http://www.justicepolicy.org/uploads/justicepolicy/documents/commonground_online.pdf (accessed May 10, 2013).

91. Part of the decline in juvenile justice populations held in detention in Connecticut came about as a result of that state's raising its age of juvenile court jurisdiction to include people who are 17 years old.

92. "Common Ground: Lessons Learned from Five States".

93. OJJDP, "Easy Access to the Census of Juveniles in Residential Placement" (1997-2013). http://www.ojjdp.gov/ojstatbb/ezacjrp/asp/State_Adj.asp (accessed November 10, 2015).

94. "Common Ground: Lessons Learned from Five States".

95. Jeffrey A. Butts and Douglas N. Evans, *Resolution, Reinvestment, and Realignment: Three Strategies for Changing Juvenile Justice* (New York: John College of Criminal Justice, 2011).

96. Legislative Analyst's Office, "The 2012–13 Budget: Completing Juvenile Justice Realignment," February 15, 2002, http://www.lao.ca.gov/analysis/2012/crim_justice/juvenile-justice-021512.aspx (accessed May 3, 2012).

97. Brian Heller de Leon and Selena Teji, "Juvenile Justice Realignment in 2012," a Center on Juvenile and Criminal Justice Policy Brief, January 12, 2012.

98. Ibid.

© berc/Fotolia

16 DRUGS AND CRIME

LEARNING OBJECTIVES

After reading this chapter, you should be able to

- Explain the nature of illegal drugs and the role social convention plays in deciding what constitutes an illegal drug.
- Discuss the history of drug abuse and antidrug legislation in America.
- Describe the categories and effects of each major type of illegal and abused drugs.
- Explain the link between drugs and other social problems.
- Summarize various efforts to respond to the drug problem, including your assessment of each effort's effectiveness.

This Administration remains committed to a balanced public health and public safety approach to drug policy. This approach is based on science, not ideology—and scientific research suggests that we have made real progress.

PRESIDENT BARACK OBAMA[1]

■ **lecture note**   Discuss the impact of drug crimes on the American criminal justice system.

■ **Follow the author's tweets about the latest crime and justice news @schmalleger**

■ **drug abuse**   Illicit drug use that results in social, economic, psychological, or legal problems for the user.[i]

Introduction

In 2015 the U.S. government requested that Mexico extradite drug kingpin Joaquin "El Chapo" Guzman. Guzman had been arrested months earlier, but became well known in this country when the Chicago Crime Commission named him "public enemy number one" in 2013. Al Capone held that title back in the 1930s. Guzman, who later made a spectacular escape from prison, is the leader of the powerful Sinaloa drug cartel, which federal agents believe supplies the bulk of narcotics that are sold in Chicago and other American cities. Jack Riley, head of the Drug Enforcement Administration's Chicago office, says that Guzman's cartel used Chicago as a distribution hub for the rest

Kelley McCall/AP Images

A package of K2, which has been described as "a concoction of dried herbs sprayed with chemicals." In 2011, the federal government outlawed five chemicals used in herbal blends and sold over the Internet to a growing number of teens and young adults. Do you agree that people who buy and sell substances like K2 should be subject to criminal sanctions?

of the United States. "This is where Guzman turns his drugs into money," he said.[2] The federal government offered a $5 million reward for Guzman's capture, and *Forbes* magazine estimates that the drug lord controls a personal fortune worth over $1 billion. Following his escape from prison, Guzman is also Mexico's most-wanted man.[3]

Drug Abuse: More Than an Individual Choice

Drug abuse is pervasive in American society. A recent Police Foundation survey of 300 police chiefs across the country found that drug abuse is the most serious law enforcement problem facing communities today.[4] Sixty-three percent of the chiefs, who represented cities and towns of all sizes, cited drug abuse as an "extremely serious" or "very serious" problem. Other serious problems that the chiefs identified were domestic violence (50%), property crime (48%), violent crime (18%), and the threat of terrorism (17%).

The resulting impact of drug crimes on the American criminal justice system over the past four or five decades has been nothing less than phenomenal. In some parts of the country, court dockets became so clogged with drug cases that criminal case processing almost ground to a halt. Prison populations also reflect the huge increase in drug crimes (Table 16-1). Three-quarters of the growth in the number of federal prison inmates between 1980 and 2010 was due to drug crimes,[5] and about 49% of all offenders in federal prisons today are serving drug

PUBLIC ENEMY NUMBER ONE
Joaquín Guzmán Loera
"El Chapo"

ALIASES:	El Chapo, Chapo Guzman, El Rapido
DOB:	April 4, 1957
ALT. DOB:	December 25, 1954
POB:	Sinaloa, Mexico
NATIONALITY:	Mexican
CITIZENSHIP:	Mexico
HEIGHT:	5 feet 8 inches
WEIGHT:	165 pounds
HAIR COLOR:	Black
EYE COLOR:	Brown

Joaquín Archivaldo Guzmán Loera, aka "El Chapo", is wanted in Chicago on charges for participating in international drug trafficking conspiracies in collaboration with 35 other defendants. El Chapo is the leader of the notorious Sinaloa drug cartel, and had helped manage part of his operation in Chicago, where allegedly 1,500 to 2,000 kilograms of cocaine were handled per month. The Northern District of Illinois seeks the forfeiture of more than $1.8 billion in cash proceeds in the indictments against him. He is known to be frequently travelling throughout Mexico to evade capture with the help of the members of the notorious Sinaloa Cartel.

chicago
crime
commission
Combating Crime Since 1919

M. Spencer Green/AP Images

Drug lord Joaquin Guzman, aka "El Chapo," shown in a 2013 wanted poster displayed by the Chicago Crime Commission. El Chapo was named as Chicago's "Public Enemy Number 1" because of allegations that he controls much of the cocaine flowing into the city from Mexico. He was arrested by Mexican authorities in 2014, but escaped from prison in 2015. How would you address America's drug problems?

■ **lecture note**   Discuss social-order offenses. Ask whether individuals should be entitled to choose to use drugs without government intervention, and if there is such a thing as "responsible drug use."

■ **theme**   Besides those given in the text, what other reasons can you think of for limiting or controlling social-order offenses? For not limiting and controlling them?

■ **lecture note**   Discuss the personal and social costs of drug abuse. Be sure to mention the social disruption that can follow from official corruption generated by drug money.

TABLE 16-1 | **Federal Prisoners, by Type of Offense**

OFFENSE TYPE	NUMBER OF PRISONERS	PERCENTAGE OF INMATE POPULATION
Drug Offenses	96,544	48.7
Weapons, Explosives, Arson	31,813	16.0
Immigration	19,802	10.0
Robbery	7,359	3.7
Burglary, Larceny, Property Offenses	7,886	4.0
Extortion, Fraud, Bribery	12,166	6.1
Homicide, Aggravated Assault, and Kidnapping Offenses	5,728	2.9
Miscellaneous	1,549	0.8
Sex Offenses	13,520	6.8
Banking and Insurance, Counterfeit, Embezzlement	730	0.4
Continuing Criminal Enterprise	454	0.2
National Security	75	0.0

Note: Data calculated only for those with offense-specific information available.
Sources: Federal Bureau of Prisons, "Quick Facts," http://www.bop.gov/about/statistics/statistics_inmate_offenses.jsp (accessed July 2, 2015).

sentences.[6] This is also true of 85% of the noncitizens and 66% of women who are imprisoned. Yet drug offenders are rarely violent. More than half (55.7%) of federal prisoners sentenced for a drug offense fall into the lowest criminal history category of the federal sentencing guidelines, and in 87% of cases no weapon was involved in their crime.[7]

Although drug crimes account for only about 20% of state prison populations, the number of men held in state prisons as a result of drug crimes has increased by almost 50% since 1990, whereas the number of women incarcerated for drug crimes has risen by almost 200%.[8] Even though state governments are making efforts to reduce prison populations and to divert nonviolent offenders from lengthy prison stays, the number of drug offenders still confined remains astonishingly high—due in large part to antiquated laws, long sentences that were handed out in the past, and repeat offending by those attracted to illicit drugs.

Drug Crime

Whereas in many textbooks drug-related crime is looked at briefly as one of several social-order or victimless crimes, in this text we take an in-depth look at drug crime because of its pervasive and far-reaching impact, not only on the criminal justice system but on all aspects of society. Drug abuse accounts for a large proportion of present-day law violations. It contributes to other types of criminal activity, such as smuggling, theft, robbery,

and murder, and leads to a huge number of arrests, clogged courtrooms, and overcrowded prisons. As a consequence, drug abuse places tremendous strain on the criminal justice system, and the fight against it is one of the most expensive activities ever undertaken by federal, state, and local governments.

Because drug abuse is one of a great number of social-order offenses, it shares many characteristics with "victimless" crimes, such as prostitution and gambling. A hallmark of such crimes is that they involve willing participants. In the case of drug-law violations, buyers, sellers, and users willingly purchase, sell, and consume illegal drugs. They do not complain to the authorities of criminal injuries to themselves or to others resulting from the illegal use of drugs. Few so-called victimless crimes, however, are truly without an injured party. Even where the criminal participant does not perceive an immediate or personal injury, the behavior frequently affects the legitimate interests of nonparticipants. In many so-called victimless crimes, it is society that is the ultimate victim. Prostitution, for example, lowers property values in areas where it regularly occurs, degrades the status of women, and may victimize the customers and their families through the spread of AIDS and other sexually transmitted diseases.

Drug abuse has many of its own destructive consequences, including lost productivity, an inequitable distribution of economic resources among the poorest members of society, disease, wasted human potential, fragmented families, violence, and other crimes. Some evidence has also linked drug trafficking to international terrorism and to efforts to overthrow the democratic

■ **controlled substance** A specifically defined bioactive or psychoactive chemical substance proscribed by law.
■ **drug** Any chemical substance defined by social convention as bioactive or psychoactive.
■ **recreational drug user** A person who uses drugs relatively infrequently, primarily with friends, and in social contexts that define drug use as pleasurable. Most addicts begin as recreational users.
■ **psychoactive substance** A chemical substance that affects cognition, feeling, or awareness.

governments of the West. Each of these consequences will be discussed in some detail in this chapter. We begin now with an analysis of what constitutes a drug, explore the history of drug abuse in America, and then describe the various categories of major **controlled substances.** Finally, we will look at the link between drugs and other forms of crime and will describe possible solutions to the problem of drug abuse. See **http://www.justicestudies.com/pubs/drugabuse.pdf** to learn more about drugs and crime.

What Is a Drug?

Before we begin any comprehensive discussion of drugs, we must first grapple with the concept of what a drug is. In common usage, a **drug** may be any chemical substance that has a noticeable effect on the mind or body. Drugs may enter the body via injection, inhalation, swallowing, or even direct absorption through the skin or mucous membranes. Some drugs, like penicillin and tranquilizers, are useful in medical treatment, whereas others, like heroin and cocaine, are attractive almost exclusively to **recreational drug users**[9] or to those who are addicted to them.[10]

In determining which substances should be called "drugs," it is important to recognize the role that social definitions of any phenomenon play in our understanding of it. Hence what Americans today consider to be a drug depends more on social convention or agreed-on definitions than it does on any inherent property of the substance itself. The history of marijuana provides a case in point. Before the early twentieth century, marijuana was freely available in the United States. Although alcohol was the recreational drug of choice at the time, marijuana found a following among some artists and musicians. Marijuana was also occasionally used for medical purposes to "calm the nerves" and to treat hysteria. Howard Becker, in his classic study of the early Federal Bureau of Narcotics (forerunner of the Drug Enforcement Administration, or DEA), demonstrates how federal agencies worked to outlaw marijuana in order to increase their power.[11] Federally funded publications voiced calls for laws against the substance, and movies like *Reefer Madness* led the drive toward classifying marijuana as a dangerous drug. The 1939 Marijuana Tax Act was the result, and marijuana has been

thought of as a drug worthy of federal and local enforcement efforts ever since.

Both the law and social convention make strong distinctions between drugs that are socially acceptable and those that are not. Some substances with profound effects on the mind and body are not even thought of as drugs. Gasoline fumes, chemical vapors of many kinds, perfumes, certain vitamins, sugar-rich foods, and toxic chemicals may all have profound effects. Even so, most people do not think of these substances as drugs, and they are rarely regulated by criminal law.

Changing social awareness has reclassified alcohol, caffeine, and nicotine as "drugs," although before the 1960s it is doubtful that most Americans would have applied that word to these three substances. Even today, alcohol, caffeine, and nicotine are readily available throughout the country, with only minimal controls on their manufacture and distribution. As a result, these three drugs continue to enjoy favored status in both our law and culture. Nonetheless, alcohol abuse and addiction are commonplace in American society, and anyone who has tried to quit smoking knows the power that nicotine can wield.

Occupying a middle ground on the continuum between acceptability and illegality are substances that have a legitimate medical use and are usually available only with a prescription. Antibiotics, diet pills, and, in particular, tranquilizers, stimulants, and mood-altering chemicals (like the popular drug Prozac) are culturally acceptable but typically can be attained legally only with a physician's prescription. The majority of Americans clearly recognize these substances as drugs, albeit useful ones.

Powerful drugs, those with the ability to produce substantially altered states of consciousness and with a high potential for addiction, occupy the forefront in social and legal condemnation. Among them are **psychoactive substances** like heroin, peyote, mescaline, LSD, and cocaine. Even here, however, legitimate uses for such drugs may exist. Cocaine is used in the treatment of certain medical conditions and can be applied as a topical anesthetic during medical interventions. LSD has been employed experimentally to investigate the nature of human consciousness, and peyote and mescaline may be used legally by members of the Native American Church in religious services. Even heroin has been advocated as beneficial in relieving the suffering associated with some forms of terminal illness. Hence, answers to the question of "What is a drug?" depend to a large

■ **lecture note**   Discuss with the class the effects that alcohol produces that cause it to be associated with such a large number of crimes.

■ **theme**   Give a few examples of how changes in social awareness can result in significant alterations in society's official position with regard to specific drugs and concomitant legislation.

extent on the social definitions and conventions operating at a given time and in a given place. Some of the clearest definitional statements relating to controlled substances can be found in the law, although informal strictures and definitions guide much of everyday drug use.

Alcohol Abuse

Although the abuse of alcohol is rarely described in the same terms as the illegal use of controlled substances, alcohol misuse can lead to serious problems with grim consequences. Fifteen years ago, for example, a pickup truck driven by Gallardo Bermudes, 35, rear-ended a car carrying 11 people—two adults and nine children—near Beaumont, California.[12] Most of the children in the car were the sons and daughters of Jose Luis Rodriquez and Mercedes Diaz. Eight of the children burned to death when the car flipped over and caught fire after being hit. Bermudes, who fled from the scene, had been convicted of drunk driving on three previous occasions. He later told police investigators that he had consumed 10 to 15 beers before the crash.

Most states define a blood-alcohol level of 0.08% as intoxication and hold that anyone who drives with that amount of alcohol in his or her blood is driving under the influence (DUI) of alcohol;[13] and in October 2000, an amendment to a federal highway construction bill[14] required that states lower their blood-alcohol limits for drunk driving to 0.08% or lose a substantial percentage of the federal highway construction funds allocated to them.[15]

Drunk driving has been a major social concern for some time. Groups like Mothers Against Drunk Driving (MADD) and Remove Intoxicated Drivers (RID) have given impetus to enforcement efforts to curb drunk drivers. Today, approximately 1.2 million drunk-driving arrests are made annually—more than for any offense other than drug abuse.[16] The average driver arrested for DUI is substantially impaired. Studies show that he or she has consumed an average of six ounces of pure alcohol (the equivalent of a dozen bottles of beer) in the four hours preceding arrest.[17] Twenty-six percent of arrestees have consumed nearly twice that amount Approximately 22% of all vehicle crashes resulting in death are alcohol related.[18] The National Highway Traffic Safety Administration estimates that alcohol causes around 12,000 traffic fatalities annually.[19]

Another offense directly related to alcohol consumption is public drunkenness. During the late 1960s and early 1970s, some groups fought to decriminalize drunkenness and to treat it as a health problem. Although the number of arrests for public drunkenness reached more than 530,000 in 2012,[20] law enforcement officers retain a great deal of discretion in handling these offenders. Many people who are drunk in public, unless they are assaultive or involved in other crimes, are likely to receive an "official escort" home rather than face arrest.

The use of alcohol may also lead to the commission of other, very serious crimes. Some experts have found that alcohol use lowers inhibitions and increases the likelihood of aggression.[21] A report by the National Institute of Justice (NIJ) concluded that "of all psychoactive substances, alcohol is the only one whose consumption has been shown to commonly increase aggression."[22] Approximately 37% of offenders consume alcohol immediately before committing a crime.[23] In cases of violent crime, the percentage of offenders under the influence of alcohol at the time of the crime jumps to 42%—and is highest for murder (44.6%).[24]

> Approximately 37% of offenders consume alcohol immediately before committing a crime.

Lawmakers appear willing to deal with the problems caused by alcohol only indirectly. The American experience with Prohibition is not one that legislators are anxious to repeat. In all likelihood, future efforts to reduce the damaging effects of alcohol will continue to take the form of educational programs, legislation to raise the drinking age, and enforcement efforts designed to deter the most visible forms of abuse. Struggles in other areas may also have some impact. For example, lawsuits claiming civil damages are now being brought against some liquor companies and taverns on behalf of accident victims, cirrhosis patients, and others. We can anticipate, however, that although concern over alcohol abuse will continue, few sweeping changes in either law or social custom will occur anytime soon.

A History of Drug Abuse in America

Alcohol is but one example of the many conflicting images of drug use prevalent in contemporary American society. The "war on drugs," initiated during the latter part of the twentieth century, portrayed an America fighting for its very existence against the scourge of drug abuse. Although many of the negative images of drugs that emanated from the "war" period may be correct, they have not always been a part of the American worldview.

Opium and its derivatives, for example, were widely available in patent medicines of the nineteenth and early twentieth centuries. Corner drugstores stocked mixtures of opium and alcohol, and traveling road shows extolled the virtues of these magical curatives. These elixirs, purported to offer relief from almost every malady, did indeed bring about feelings of well-being in most users. Although no one is certain just how

■ **lecture note** Explain that many drugs that today are viewed as dangerous were at one time widely available to the general public.

■ **lecture note** Discuss Sigmund Freud's book *The Cocaine Papers*. Ask students whether Freud was wrong about cocaine. Why did he believe what he did?

widespread opium use was in the United States a hundred years ago, some authors have observed that baby formulas containing opium were fed to infants born to addicted mothers.[25]

Opium was also widely used by Chinese immigrants who came to the West Coast in the nineteenth century, often to work on the railroads. Opium dens—in which the drug was smoked—flourished, and the use of opium quickly spread to other ethnic groups throughout the West. Some of the more affluent denizens of West Coast cities ate the substance, and avant-garde poetry was written extolling the virtues of the drug.

Morphine, an opium derivative, has a similar history. Although it was legally available in this country almost since its invention, its use as a painkiller on the battlefields of the Civil War dramatically heightened public awareness of the drug.[26] In the late nineteenth century, morphine was widely prescribed by physicians and dentists, many of whom abused the substance themselves. By 1896, per capita morphine consumption peaked, and addiction to the substance throughout the United States was apparently widespread.[27]

> Heroin, the most potent derivative of opium ever created, was invented as a substitute for morphine in 1874.

Heroin, the most potent derivative of opium ever created, was invented as a substitute for morphine in 1874. It was commercially marketed as a new pain remedy and cough suppressant beginning in 1898.[28] When it was first introduced, heroin's addictive properties were unknown, and it was said to be useful in treating morphine addiction.[29]

Marijuana, which is considerably less potent than heroin, has a relatively short history in this country. Imported by Mexican immigrants around the turn of the twentieth century, the drug quickly became associated with nonmainstream groups. By 1930, most of the states in the Southwest had passed legislation outlawing marijuana, and some authors have suggested that antimarijuana laws were primarily targeted at Spanish-speaking immigrants who were beginning to challenge whites in the economic sector.[30] As mentioned earlier, other writers have suggested that the rapidly growing use of marijuana throughout the 1920s and 1930s provided a rationale for the development of drug legislation and the concomitant expansion of drug enforcement agencies.[31] By the 1960s, public attitudes regarding marijuana had begun to change. The hippie generation popularized the drug, touting its "mellowing" effects on users. In a short time, marijuana use became epidemic across the country, and books on marijuana cultivation and preparation flourished. Today, recreational use of marijuana is legal in a handful of states, and it is expected that a number of other jurisdictions will soon join the movement to legalize or decriminalize the drug.

Another drug that found adherents among some youthful idealists of the 1960s and 1970s was LSD. LSD, whose

Tito Herrera/Ap Images

U.S. Coast Guard officers guard 19.4 metric tons of cocaine confiscated from the cargo ship *Gatun* on March 22, 2007. The seizure proved to be one of the biggest maritime cocaine hauls on record. What other kinds of crime are linked to drug crime?

chemical name is lysergic acid diethylamide, was first synthesized in Switzerland in 1938 and was used occasionally in this country in the 1950s for the treatment of psychiatric disorders.

Many drugs, when first "discovered," were touted for their powerful analgesic or therapeutic effects. Cocaine was one of them. An early leading proponent of cocaine use, for example, was Sigmund Freud, who prescribed it for a variety of psychological disorders. Freud was himself a user and wrote a book, *The Cocaine Papers*, describing the many benefits of the drug. The cocaine bandwagon reached the United States in the late nineteenth century, and various medicines and beverages containing cocaine were offered to the American public. Although the manufacturer denies it today, some claim that Coca-Cola originally contained seltzer water, sugar, and cocaine in what was then advertised as a real "pick-me-up." Historians say cocaine was removed from Coca-Cola in 1910 but continued to be used by jazz musicians and artists. Beginning in the 1970s, cocaine became associated with exclusive parties, the well-to-do, and the jet set. It was not long before an extensive drug underworld developed, catering to the demands of affluent users. Crack cocaine, a derivative of powdered cocaine that is smoked, became popular in the 1980s and is sold today in the form of "rocks," "cookies," or "biscuits" (large pieces of crack).

Drug Use and Social Awareness

Although drugs have long been a part of American society, there
have been dramatic changes during the last century in the form
drug use takes and in the social consequences associated with
drug involvement. Specifically, six elements have emerged that
today cast drug use in a far different light than in the past:

- The conceptualization of addiction as a physical condition
- The understanding that drug use is associated with other
  kinds of criminal activity
- Generally widespread social condemnation of drug use as
  a waste of economic resources and human lives
- Comprehensive and detailed federal and state laws regulating the use or availability of drugs
- A large and perhaps still-growing involvement with illicit
  drugs among the urban poor and the socially disenfranchised, both as an escape from the conditions of life and
  as a path to monetary gain
- The view that drug abuse is a law enforcement issue
  rather than primarily a medical problem

In an insightful work that clarifies the ideational basis of
modern antidrug sentiments, criminologists Franklin Zimring
and Gordon Hawkins examine three schools of thought that,
they say, form the basis for current drug policy in the United
States.[32] The first is "public health generalism," a perspective
that holds that all controlled substances are potentially harmful
and that drug abusers are victimized by the disease of addiction.
This approach views drugs as medically harmful and argues that
effective drug control is necessary as a matter of public health.
The second approach, "cost–benefit specifism," proposes that
drug policy be built around a balancing of the social costs of
drug abuse (crime, broken families, drug-related killings, and
so on) with the costs of enforcement. The third approach, the

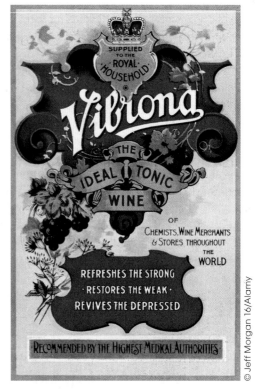

A 1907 advertisement for cocaine-laced wine. Cocaine, a
controlled substance today, was commonly found in late-
nineteenth-century medicines and consumer products. Why did
the federal government enact legislation outlawing the use of
psychoactive substances like marijuana and cocaine?

"legalist," suggests that drug-control policies are necessary to prevent the collapse of public order and of society itself. Advocates
of the legalist perspective say that drug use is "defiance of lawful authority that threatens the social fabric."[33] According
to Zimring and Hawkins, all recent and contemporary antidrug policies have been based on one of these three schools of
thought. Unfortunately, say these authors, it may not be possible
to base successful antidrug policy on such beliefs because they

TABLE 16-2 | Timeline of Federal Drug Control Legislation

1906	1914	1937	1938	1956
Food and Drugs Act	Harrison Narcotics Act	Marijuana Tax Act	Food, Drug and Cosmetic Act	Narcotics Control Act
Required the proper and accurate labeling of "patent medicines"	Taxed and regulated the use of "narcotics" including coca and cocaine	Regulated the buying and selling of cannabis	Required that new drugs be proven safe before marketing	Increased penalties for drug law violations

■ **lecture note** Review the early antidrug legislation in the U.S. and explain how these laws affected social views of drugs and drug users.

■ **Harrison Narcotics Act** The first major piece of federal antidrug legislation, passed in 1914.

■ **Controlled Substances Act (CSA)** Title II of the Comprehensive Drug Abuse Prevention and Control Act of 1970, which established schedules classifying psychoactive drugs according to their degree of psychoactivity.

do not necessarily recognize the everyday realities of drug use. Nonetheless, antidrug legislation and activities undertaken in the United States today are accorded political and ideational legitimacy via all three perspectives. Learn more about addiction from the National Institute of Drug Abuse at **http://www.nida.nih. gov/scienceofaddiction/sciofaddiction.pdf**.

Antidrug Legislation

Antidrug legislation in the United States dates back to around 1875, when the city of San Francisco enacted a statute prohibiting the smoking of opium.[34] A number of western states quickly followed the city's lead. The San Francisco law and many that followed it, however, clearly targeted Chinese immigrants and were rarely applied to other ethnic groups involved in the practice.

The first major piece of federal antidrug legislation came in 1914, with the enactment of the **Harrison Narcotics Act** (Table 16-2). The Harrison Act required anyone dealing in opium, morphine, heroin, cocaine, and specified derivatives of these drugs to register with the federal government and to pay a tax of $1 per year. The only people permitted to register were physicians, pharmacists, and other members of the medical profession. Nonregistered drug traffickers faced a maximum fine of $2,000 and up to five years in prison.

Because the Harrison Act allowed physicians to prescribe controlled drugs for the purpose of medical treatment, heroin addicts and other drug users could still legally purchase the drugs they needed. All the law required was a physician's prescription. By 1920, however, court rulings had established that drug "maintenance" only prolonged addiction and did not qualify as "treatment."[35] The era of legally available heroin had ended.

Marijuana was not included in the Harrison Act because it was not considered a dangerous drug.[36] By the 1930s, however,

government attention became riveted on marijuana. At the urging of the Federal Bureau of Narcotics, Congress passed the Marijuana Tax Act in 1937. As the title of the law indicates, the Act simply placed a tax of $100 per ounce on cannabis. Those who did not pay the tax were subject to prosecution. With the passage of the Boggs Act in 1951, however, marijuana, along with a number of other drugs, entered the class of federally prohibited controlled substances. The Boggs Act also removed heroin from the list of medically useful substances and required the removal, within 120 days, of any medicines containing heroin from pharmacies across the country.[37]

The Narcotic Control Act of 1956 increased penalties for drug trafficking and possession and made the sale of heroin to anyone under age 18 a capital offense. However, on the eve of the massive explosion in drug use that was to begin in the mid-1960s, the Kennedy administration began a shift in emphasis from the strict punishment of drug traffickers and users to rehabilitation. A 1963 presidential commission recommended the elimination of the Federal Bureau of Narcotics, recommended shorter prison terms for drug offenders, and stressed the need for research and social programs in dealing with the drug problem.[38]

The Comprehensive Drug Abuse Prevention and Control Act of 1970

By 1970, America's drug problem was clear, and legislators were anxious to return to a more punitive approach to controlling drug abuse. Under President Richard Nixon, legislation designed to encompass all aspects of drug abuse and to permit federal intervention at all levels of use was enacted. Termed the Comprehensive Drug Abuse Prevention and Control Act of 1970, the legislation still forms the basis of federal enforcement efforts today. Title II of the law is the **Controlled Substances Act (CSA).** The CSA sets up five schedules that classify

1970	1973	1984	1988	1996	2006
Comprehensive Drug Abuse Prevention and Control Act	Heroin Trafficking Act	Analogue Act	Anti-Drug Abuse Act	Comprehensive Methamphetamine Control Act	Combat Methamphetamine Epidemic Act
Created federal drug schedules and associated penalties	Increased criminal penalties for the distribution of heroin	Criminalized designer drugs	Established the Office of National Drug Control Policy and increased penalties for recreational drug use	Restricted access to chemicals and equipment used in the manufacture of methamphetamine	Made it harder to obtain pseudoephedrine, ephedrine, and phenylpropanolamine (chemicals used in the manufacture of methamphetamine)

■ **lecture note**   *Enumerate the various categories of controlled substances, as defined by the federal Controlled Substances Act, and list the drugs that fall into each category. Ask students whether they are surprised at any of the classifications. If so, what does that say about their own understanding of drug abuse?*

■ **theme**   *What are anabolic steroids? What effects do they have on the body? What are their legal and illegal uses? Into what federal enforcement category do they fall?*

■ **lecture note**   *Describe the relatively recent addition of anabolic steroids to Schedule III of the Controlled Substances Act. Discuss both the legitimate and illegitimate uses of steroids by referring to Table 16-2.*

■ **psychological dependence**   A craving for a specific drug that results from long-term substance abuse. Psychological dependence on drugs is marked by the belief that drugs are needed to achieve a feeling of well-being.[ii]

■ **physical dependence**   A biologically based craving for a specific drug that results from frequent use of the substance. Physical dependence on drugs is marked by a growing tolerance of a drug's effects, so that increased amounts of the drug are needed to obtain the desired effect, and by the onset of withdrawal symptoms over periods of prolonged abstinence.[iii]

psychoactive drugs according to their degree of psychoactivity and abuse potential:[39]

- Schedule I controlled substances have no established medical usage, cannot be used safely, and have great potential for abuse.[40] Federal law requires that any research employing Schedule I substances be fully documented and that the substances themselves be stored in secure vaults. Included under this category are heroin, LSD, mescaline, peyote, methaqualone (Quaaludes), psilocybin, marijuana,[41] and hashish, as well as other specified hallucinogens. Penalties for first-offense possession and sale of Schedule I controlled substances under the federal Narcotic Penalties and Enforcement Act of 1986 include up to life imprisonment and a $10 million fine. Penalties increase for subsequent offenses.

- Schedule II controlled substances are drugs with high abuse potential for which there is a currently accepted pharmacological or medical use. Most Schedule II substances are also considered to be addictive.[42] Drugs that fall into this category include opium, morphine, codeine, cocaine, phencyclidine (PCP), and their derivatives. Certain other stimulants, such as methylphenidate (Ritalin) and phenmetrazine (Preludin), and a few barbiturates with high abuse potential also come under Schedule II. Legal access to Schedule II substances requires written nonrefillable prescriptions, vault storage, and thorough record keeping by vendors. Penalties for first-offense possession and sale of Schedule II controlled substances include up to 20 years' imprisonment and a $5 million fine under the federal Narcotic Penalties and Enforcement Act. Penalties increase for subsequent offenses.

- Schedule III controlled substances have lower abuse potential than do those in Schedules I and II. They are drugs with an accepted medical use but that may lead to a high level of **psychological dependence** or to moderate or low **physical dependence**.[43] Schedule III substances include many of the drugs found in Schedule II but in derivative or diluted form. Common low-dosage antidiarrheals, such as opium-containing paregoric, and cold medicines and pain relievers with low concentrations of codeine fall into this category. Anabolic steroids,

whose abuse by professional athletes has been subject to scrutiny, were added to the list of Schedule III controlled substances in 1991. Legitimate access to Schedule III drugs is through a doctor's prescription (written or oral), with refills authorized in the same manner. Maximum penalties associated with first-offense possession and sale of Schedule III controlled substances under federal law include five years' imprisonment and fines of up to $1 million.

- Schedule IV controlled substances have a relatively low potential for abuse (when compared to those in higher schedules), are useful in established medical treatments, and involve only a limited risk of psychological or physical dependence.[44] Depressants, certain sleep aids, and minor tranquilizers such as Valium, Librium, and Equanil fall into this category, as do some stimulants. Schedule IV substances are medically available in the same fashion as Schedule III drugs. Maximum penalties associated with first-offense possession and sale of Schedule IV substances under federal law include three years in prison and fines of up to $1 million.

- Schedule V controlled substances are prescription drugs with a low potential for abuse and with only a very limited possibility of psychological or physical dependence.[45] Cough medicines (antitussives) and antidiarrheals containing small amounts of opium, morphine, or codeine are found in Schedule V. A number of Schedule V medicines may be purchased through retail vendors with only minimal controls or upon the signature of the buyer (with some form of identification required). Maximum federal penalties for first-offense possession and sale of Schedule V substances include one year in prison and a $250,000 fine.

Pharmacologists, chemists, and botanists regularly create new drugs. Likewise, street-corner "chemists" in clandestine laboratories churn out inexpensive designer drugs—laboratory-created psychoactive substances with widely varying effects and abuse potential. Designer drugs include substances with names like Ecstasy (MDMA), GHB (gamma-hydroxybutyrate), K2, ketamine, MDPV (methylenedioxypyrovalerone), and meth (methamphetamine), which will be discussed in greater detail later in this chapter. The Controlled Substances Act (CSA) includes provisions for determining which new drugs should be controlled

■ **drug czar** The popular name for the head of the Office of National Drug Control Policy (ONDCP), a federal position that was created during the Reagan presidency to organize federal drug-fighting efforts.

Cyclist Lance Armstrong, who was forced to give up seven Tour de France titles after he admitted to "doping." Anabolic steroids were added to the list of Schedule III controlled substances in 1991. Why did the federal government outlaw the nonmedical use of most steroidal compounds?

and into which schedule they should be placed (Table 16-3). Under the CSA, criteria for assigning a new drug to one of the existing schedules include (1) the drug's actual or relative potential for abuse; (2) scientific evidence of the drug's pharmacological effects; (3) the state of current scientific knowledge regarding the substance; (4) its history and current pattern of abuse; (5) the scope, duration, and significance of abuse; (6) risk, if any, to the public health; (7) the drug's psychic or physiological dependence liability; and (8) whether the substance is an immediate precursor of a substance already controlled.[46] Proceedings to add a new chemical substance to the list of those controlled by law or to delete or change the schedule of an existing drug may be initiated by the chief administrator of the Drug Enforcement Administration, by the Department of Health and Human Services, or by a petition from any interested party, including manufacturers, medical societies, or public-interest groups.[47] Read the text of the CSA at **http://www.justice.gov/dea/pubs/csa.html**.

The Anti-Drug Abuse Act of 1988

In 1988, the country's Republican leadership, under President Ronald Reagan, capitalized on the public's frustration with rampant drug abuse and stepped up the "war on drugs." The president created a new cabinet-level post, naming a **drug czar** to be in charge of federal drug-fighting initiatives through the Office of National Drug Control Policy (ONDCP). William Bennett, a former secretary of education, was appointed to fill the post. At the same time, Congress passed the Anti-Drug Abuse Act. The overly optimistic tenor of the Act is clear from its preamble, which reads, "It is the declared policy of the United States Government to create a Drug-Free America by 1995."[48] That goal, which reflected far more political rhetoric than realistic planning, was incredibly naïve.

Even so, the Anti-Drug Abuse Act of 1988 carries much weight. Under the law, penalties for "recreational" drug users increased substantially,[49] and weapons purchases by suspected drug dealers became more difficult. The law also denies federal benefits, ranging from loans (including student loans) to contracts and licenses, to convicted drug offenders.[50] Earned benefits, such as Social Security, retirement, and health and disability benefits, are not affected by the legislation, nor are welfare payments or existing public-housing arrangements (although separate legislation does provide for termination of public-housing tenancy for drug offenses[51]). Under the law, civil penalties of up to $10,000 may be assessed against convicted "recreational" users for possession of even small amounts of drugs.

> Under the Anti-Drug Abuse Act of 1988, penalties for "recreational" drug users increased substantially.

Aflo Editorial/Aflo Co., Ltd/Alamy

■ **lecture note**   Review other key federal antidrug legislation and ask students whether these laws reflect general social views on drugs and drug abuse.

TABLE 16-3 | Major Controlled Substances under the Federal Controlled Substances Act

SCHEDULE	DESCRIPTION OF SCHEDULE	DRUGS IN SCHEDULE	STREET NAMES
I	• high potential for abuse • no currently accepted medical use in the United States • lacks accepted safety standards for use under medical supervision	marijuana,ⁱ heroin, opioids, hallucinogenic substances, peyote, mescaline, gamma-hydroxybutyric acid (GHB), and others	pot, weed, grass, reefer, joint, angel dust, horse
II	• high potential for abuse • currently accepted for medical use • may lead to severe psychological or physical dependence	cocaine, opium, oxycodone, methadone, morphine, Seconal, methamphetamine, Adderall and other amphetamines	snow, crack, coke, meth, speed, uppers
III	• potential for abuse less than the drugs or other substances in Schedules I and II • currently accepted for medical use • may lead to moderate or low physical dependence or high psychological dependence	anabolic steroids, ketamine, hydrocodone, and a number of barbiturates and sedatives	downers, goof balls, yellow jackets
IV	• lower potential for abuse relative to the drugs or other substances in Schedule III • currently accepted for medical use • may lead to limited physical dependence or psychological dependence relative to the rugs or other substances in Schedule III	some antidiarrheal drugs; some partial opioid analgesics; some sleeping pills such as Lunesta (eszopiclone) and Ambien (zolpidem); long-acting barbiturates; and benzodiazepines such as Xanax, Librium, and Valium	blues, peaches, bars, zombie pills, no-go pills, A-minus
V	• low potential for abuse relative to the drugs or other substances in Schedule IV • currently accepted for medical use • may lead to limited physical dependence or psychological dependence relative to the drugs or other substances in Schedule IV	some cough suppressants, anticonvulsants, and selected prescription pain pills	

Note: The Controlled Substances Act (CSA) is Title II of the Comprehensive Drug Abuse Prevention and Control Act of 1970.
ⁱAt the request of the FDA, the DEA is reviewing marijuana's status as a Category I controlled substance.

The legislation also allows capital punishment for drug-related murders. The killing of a police officer by an offender seeking to avoid apprehension or prosecution is specifically cited as carrying a possible sentence of death, although other murders by major drug dealers also fall under the capital punishment provision.[52] In May 1991, 37-year-old David Chandler, an Alabama marijuana kingpin, became the first person to be sentenced to die under the law.[53] Chandler was convicted of ordering the murder of a police informant in 1990.

One especially interesting aspect of the Anti-Drug Abuse Act is its provision for designating selected areas as high-intensity drug-trafficking areas (HIDTAs), making them eligible for federal drug-fighting assistance so that joint interagency operations can be implemented to reduce drug problems. Using the law, former drug czar William Bennett declared Washington, D.C., a "drug zone" in 1989. His designation was based in part on what was then the city's reputation as the murder capital of the country. At the time of the declaration, more than 60% of Washington's murders were said to be drug related,[54] and legislators and tourists were clamoring for action. Bennett's plan called for more federal investigators and prosecutors and for specially built prisons to handle convicted drug dealers. Visit ONDCP at **http://www.whitehousedrugpolicy.gov**.

Other Federal Antidrug Legislation

Other significant federal antidrug legislation exists in the form of the Crime Control Act of 1990, the Violent Crime Control and Law Enforcement Act of 1994, the Drug-Free Communities Act of 1997, and the reauthorization of the USA PATRIOT Act in 2006.[55] The Crime Control Act of 1990 (1) doubled the appropriations authorized for drug-law enforcement grants to states and local communities; (2) enhanced drug-control and drug-education programs aimed at the nation's schools; (3) expanded specific drug enforcement assistance to rural states; (4) expanded regulation of precursor chemicals used in the manufacture of illegal drugs; (5) sanctioned anabolic steroids under the Controlled Substances Act; (6) included provisions to enhance control over international money laundering; (7) created "drug-free school zones" by enhancing penalties for drug offenses occurring in proximity to schools; and (8) enhanced the

■ **curtilage** In legal usage, the area surrounding a residence that can reasonably be said to be a part of the residence for Fourth Amendment purposes.

ability of federal agents to seize property used in drug transactions or purchased with drug proceeds.

The Violent Crime Control and Law Enforcement Act of 1994 provided $245 million for rural anticrime and antidrug efforts; set aside $1.6 billion for direct funding to localities around the country for anticrime efforts, including drug-treatment programs; budgeted $383 million for drug-treatment programs for state and federal prisoners; created a treatment schedule for all drug-addicted federal prisoners; required postconviction drug testing of all federal prisoners upon release; allocated $1 billion for drug-court programs for nonviolent offenders with substance-abuse problems; and mandated new stiff penalties for drug crimes committed by gangs. The Act also tripled penalties for using children to deal drugs and enhanced penalties for drug dealing in drug-free zones near playgrounds, schoolyards, video arcades, and youth centers. Finally, the law also expanded the federal death penalty to cover offenders involved in large-scale drug trafficking and mandated life imprisonment for criminals convicted of three violent felonies or drug offenses.

The Drug-Free Communities Act of 1997 provided support to local communities to reduce substance abuse among youth. It helped enhance broad-based community antidrug coalitions, which were previously shown to be successful at driving down casual drug use. Under the law, neighborhoods with successful anti drug programs became eligible to apply for federal grants to assist in their continued development.

More recently, the congressional reauthorization of the USA PATRIOT Act in 2006 led to enactment of a provision in that legislation known as the Combat Methamphetamine Epidemic Act. That legislation makes it harder to obtain pseudo-ephedrine, ephedrine, and phenylpropanolamine—ingredients in some over-the-counter cold medicines that can be used in the manufacture of methamphetamine.[56] The legislation requires medicines containing these chemicals to be kept behind store counters or in locked cabinets and limits the amount of those substances that a person can purchase to 3.6 grams per day, or up to 9 grams per month. Under the legislation, customers purchasing pseudoephedrine, ephedrine, or phenylpropanolamine are required to show photo identification and to sign a store log. The PATRIOT Act renewal also authorized $99 million per year for the federal Meth Hot Spots program, which was intended to train state and local law enforcement officers in

The 2006 Combat Methamphetamine Epidemic Act made it harder to obtain pseudoephedrine, ephedrine, and phenylpropanolamine—ingredients in some over-the-counter cold medicines that can be used in the manufacture of methamphetamine.

how to investigate methamphetamine offenses and to provide personnel and equipment for enforcement and prosecution.

The Investigation of Drug Abuse and Manufacturing

Investigation of the illegal production, transportation, sale, and use of controlled substances is a major police activity. Investigation of drug-manufacturing activities has given rise to an area of case law that supplements the plain-view doctrine discussed in Chapter 7. Two legal concepts, abandonment and curtilage, have taken on special significance in drug investigations.

Abandonment refers to the fact that property, once it has been clearly thrown away or discarded, ceases to fall under Fourth Amendment protections against unreasonable search and seizure. The U.S. Supreme Court case of *California* v. *Greenwood* (1988)[57] began when Officer Jenny Stracner of the Laguna Beach (California) Police Department arranged with a neighborhood trash collector to receive garbage collected at a suspect's residence. The refuse was later found to include items "indicative of narcotics use."[58] Based on this evidence, Stracner applied for a search warrant, which was used in a search of the defendant's home. The search uncovered controlled substances, including cocaine and hashish. The defendant, Billy Greenwood, was arrested. Upon conviction, Greenwood appealed, arguing that the trash had been placed in opaque bags and could reasonably be expected to remain unopened until it was collected and disposed of. His appeal emphasized his right to privacy with respect to his trash.

The Supreme Court disagreed, saying that "[a]n expectation of privacy does not give rise to Fourth Amendment protection unless society is prepared to accept that expectation as objectively reasonable. . . . [I]t is common knowledge that plastic garbage bags left on or at the side of a public street are readily accessible to animals, children, scavengers, snoops, and other members of the public." Hence, the Court concluded, the property in question had been abandoned, and no reasonable expectation of privacy can attach to trash left for collection "in an area accessible to the public." The concept of abandonment extends beyond trash that is actively discarded. In *Abel* v. *U.S.* (1960),[59] for example, the Court found that the warrantless search of a motel room by a Federal Bureau of Investigation (FBI) agent immediately after it had been vacated was acceptable.

Curtilage, a concept that the Supreme Court clearly recognized in the case of *Oliver* v. *U.S.* (1984),[60] refers to the fact that household activity generally extends beyond the walls of a residence. People living in a house, for example, spend some of their time in their yard. Property within the curtilage of a residence has

■ **lecture note**   Link the dual concepts of abandonment and curtilage to drug investigations. Explain that personal items that have been clearly abandoned may be searched without a warrant but that the idea of curtilage restricts law enforcement authority for most searches to property beyond the area of normal household activity.

■ **lecture note**   Explain that two major classes of drug-abusing offenders can be identified: adult offenders and juvenile offenders. Ask why this distinction is useful.

■ **theme**   What is your view of current drug use on campus overall? Of specific types of drugs, such as marijuana or cocaine? How does your view compare with the data presented here? What factors might account for any differences?

generally been accorded the same Fourth Amendment guarantees against search and seizure as areas within the walls of a house or an apartment. But just how far does the curtilage of a residence extend? Does it vary according to the type or location of the residence? Is it necessary for an area to be fenced for it to fall within residential curtilage?

A collateral area of concern is that of activity conducted in fields. The open-fields doctrine began with the case of *Hester* v. *U.S.* (1924),[61] in which the Supreme Court held that law enforcement officers could search an open field without a warrant. The *Oliver* case extended that authority to include secluded and fenced fields posted with "No Trespassing" signs.

In *U.S.* v. *Dunn* (1987),[62] the U.S. Supreme Court considered a Houston-area defendant's claim that the space surrounding a barn, which was located approximately 50 yards from the edge of a fence surrounding a farmhouse, was protected against intrusion by the Fourth Amendment. The Court rejected the defendant's arguments and concluded that even though an area may be fenced, it is not within the curtilage of a residence if it is sufficiently distant from the area of household activity that attends the residence.

Other related decisions have supported seizures based on warrantless aerial observation of marijuana plants growing in the backyard of a defendant's home[63] and those based on naked-eye sightings from helicopters of the contents of a greenhouse.[64] The Court's reasoning in such cases is that flights within navigable airspace are common. Where no comprehensive efforts to secure privacy have been made, there can be no reasonable expectation of privacy—even within areas that might normally be considered curtilage. Were sophisticated surveillance techniques to be employed by law enforcement authorities, however—such as the use of drone aircraft, satellite, or infrared photography—the Court's decision would be in doubt because such devices extend beyond the realm of "normal flight."

> According to the courts, where no comprehensive efforts to secure privacy have been made, there can be no reasonable expectation of privacy.

The Most Common Drugs—And Who Is Using Them

The *National Survey on Drug Use and Health* (NSDUH), an annual publication of the federal Substance Abuse and Mental Health Services Administration (SAMHSA), estimates that

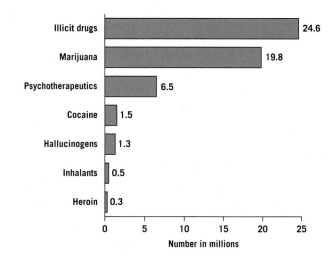

FIGURE 16-1 | Current Illicit Drug Use among Persons Age 12 or Older in the United States, 2013

Source: Substance Abuse and Mental Health Services Administration, *National Survey on Drug Use and Health* (Rockville, MD: Office of Applied Studies, NHSDA, 2014).

24.6 million Americans age 12 and older are "current" users of illegal drugs—defined as those who have used an illicit drug in the month preceding the survey[65] (Figure 16-1). Nearly 19.8 million people are estimated to be using marijuana, and an estimated 1.5 million people are current cocaine users. Hallucinogens are used by more than 1.3 million people. There are an estimated 439,000 current methamphetamine users and 289,000 current heroin users. An estimated 6.1 million Americans are current nonmedical users of prescription-type psychotherapeutic drugs. This includes 4.5 million using pain relievers, 2 million using tranquilizers, 1.1 million using stimulants, and nearly 374,000 using sedatives. Close to a half-million regular users of inhalants were also identified.

These figures represent a considerable decline from 1979, the year in which the highest levels of drug abuse in the United States were reported, although figures for recent years have shown a gradual increase in drug use (especially "occasional use"). As the Office of National Drug Control Policy (ONDCP) points out, however, federal studies typically underestimate the number of hardcore drug abusers in the country because they fail to survey the homeless, prisoners, people living at colleges, active-duty military personnel, and those in mental and other institutions. ONDCP estimates that there are 2.1 million hardcore cocaine addicts and up to 1 million heroin addicts in the country[66]—figures well above those reported by the survey.

Rates of drug use show substantial variation by age. In 2013, for example, 3.3% of American youths age 12 or 13 reported current illicit drug use compared with 9.2% of youths

■ **lecture note** Use the "CJ Issues" box titled "Drugs: What's in a Name" to illustrate the differences between brand names, generic names, and street names for drugs.

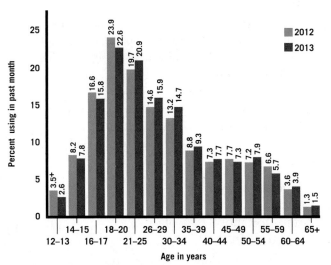

FIGURE 16-2 | Current Illicit Drug Use by Age in the United States, 2012 and 2013

Source: Substance Abuse and Mental Health Services Administration, *National Survey on Drug Use and Health* (Rockville, MD: Office of Applied Studies, NHSDA, 2014).

age 14 or 15 and 17.2% of youths age 16 or 17 (Figure 16-2). As in other years, illicit drug use in 2013 tended to increase with age among young people, peaking among 18- to 20-year-olds (23.8%) and declining steadily after that point with increasing

In 2013, 22.4 million adults age 18 or older currently used illicit drugs.

age. Current employment status is also highly correlated with rates of current illicit drug use. An estimated 17.2% of unemployed adults age 18 or older were current illicit drug users in the United States in 2013, compared with 8.0% of those employed full-time and 11.6% of those employed part-time. Although the rate of drug use was higher among the unemployed compared with those from other employment groups, most drug users were employed. Of the 22.4 million illicit drug users age 18 or older in 2013, 13.1 million were employed either full- or part-time. The use of drugs is also more prevalent in some parts of the country than in others.

Drug Trafficking

A number of agencies report on the amount and types of illicit drugs that enter the country or are produced here. The federal General Counterdrug Intelligence Plan,[67] implemented in February 2000, designated the National Drug Intelligence Center (NDIC) as the nation's principal center for strategic domestic counterdrug intelligence and planning.[68] Prior to 2012, when the office was closed, the NDIC published the National

CJ | ISSUES
Drugs: What's in a Name?

Drug names have been a source of confusion for many people who have attempted to grapple with the drug problem. A single drug may have a dozen or more names. Drugs may be identified according to brand name, generic name, street name, or psychoactive category.

Brand Name

The name given to a chemical substance by its manufacturer is the brand name. Brand names are registered and are often associated with trademarks. They identify a drug in the pharmaceutical marketplace may not be used by other manufacturers. Psychoactive substances with no known medical application or experimental use are not produced by legitimate companies and have no brand name.

Generic Name

The chemical or other identifying name of a drug is the generic name. Generic names are often used by physicians in writing prescriptions because generic drugs are often less costly than brand-name drugs. Generic names are also used in most drug-abuse legislation at the federal and state levels to specify controlled substances. Generic names are sometimes applicable only to the psychoactive chemical substances in

drugs and not to the drugs themselves. With marijuana, for example, the chemical tetrahydrocannabinol, or THC, is the active substance.

Street Name

Street names are slang terms. Many of them originated with the pop culture of the 1960s, and others continue to be produced by modern-day drug subculture. For example, street names for cocaine include coke, flake, and snow; heroin is known as horse, smack, or H.

Psychoactive Category

Psychoactive drugs are categorized according to the effects they produce on the human mind. Narcotics, stimulants, depressants, and hallucinogens are typical psychoactive categories.

An Example

PCP and angel dust are the street names for a veterinary anesthetic marketed under the brand name Sernylan. Sernylan contains the psychoactive chemical phencyclidine, which is classified as a depressant under the Controlled Substances Act.

■ **drug trafficking**   Trading or dealing in controlled substances, including the transporting, storage, importing, exporting, or sale of a controlled substance.

■ **lecture note**   Discuss how the laws relating to marijuana have changed over time. Ask students how the laws reflect social views of marijuana use.

Drug Threat Assessment, a comprehensive annual report on **drug trafficking** and abuse trends within the United States. The assessment identified the most serious drug threats, monitored fluctuations in national consumption levels, tracked drug availability by geographic area, and analyzed trafficking and distribution patterns. The report also included information on illicit drug availability, demand, production, cultivation, transportation, and distribution, as well as the effects of particular drugs on abusers and society as a whole. With the NDIC's closure, responsibility for gathering and disseminating data on drug trafficking was transferred to the DEA. Learn more about the DEA via **http://www.justice.gov/dea**.

Marijuana

Marijuana, whose botanical name is *Cannabis sativa* L., grows wild throughout most of the tropic and temperate regions of the world.[69] Marijuana commonly comes in loose form, as the ground leaves and seeds of the hemp plant. Also available to street-level users are stronger forms of the drug, such as sinsemilla (the flowers and the leaves of the female cannabis plant), hashish (the resinous secretions of the hemp plant), and hash oil (a chemically concentrated form of delta-9-tetrahydrocannabinol, or THC, the psychotropic agent in marijuana).

Marijuana is usually smoked, although it may be eaten or made into a "tea." Low doses of marijuana create restlessness and an increasing sense of well-being, followed by dreamy relaxation and a frequent craving for sweets. Sensory perceptions may be heightened by the drug, whereas memory and rational thought are impaired. Marijuana's effects begin within a few minutes following use and may last for two to three hours.

Although marijuana has no officially sanctioned medical use, it may sometimes serve as a supplemental medication in cases of ongoing chemotherapy (where it often reduces nausea), glaucoma (where it may reduce pressure within the eye), anorexia and "AIDS wasting" (where it may increase appetite and lead to weight gain), and sleep disorders.[70] To support such use, voters in California and Arizona passed ballot initiatives in 1996 legalizing the use of marijuana for medical purposes when approved or prescribed by a doctor. California's medical marijuana law was overturned, however, by a unanimous U.S. Supreme Court in the 2001 case of *U.S.* v. *Oakland Cannabis Buyers' Cooperative*.[71] In that case, the Court found that the activities of the Oakland (California) Cannabis Buyers' Cooperative, which distributed marijuana to qualified patients for medical purposes, were in violation of the U.S. Controlled Substances Act—regardless of what state law said. The Court also held that there is no medical necessity exception to the federal Act's prohibitions on manufacturing and distributing marijuana.[72] In 2005,

in the case of *Gonzales* v. *Raich*,[73] the Court reinforced its earlier holding, ruling that Congress holds the final authority, under the commerce clause of the U.S. Constitution, to prohibit the cultivation and use of marijuana. Even so, outgoing White House drug czar Gil Kerlikowske announced in 2009 that federal authorities would no longer raid medical-marijuana providers in states where voters have made medical marijuana legal.[74]

Most marijuana users, however, do not use cannabis for medical purposes. The majority of users are young people, many younger than 20 years old. In 2013, for example, the National Institute on Drug Abuse reported that past-year use of marijuana was 13% for 8th graders, 30% for 10h graders, and 36% for 12th graders.[75]

> Intelligence shows that domestic production accounts for about 19% of all marijuana in the United States.

Intelligence shows that domestic production accounts for about 19% of all marijuana in the United States. Most marijuana brought into the United States comes from Mexico, Jamaica, and Colombia.[76] Of all the marijuana entering the country or produced domestically, approximately one-quarter, or 4,000 metric tons, is seized or lost in transit.[77]

Cocaine

Cocaine (cocaine hydrochloride [HCL]) is the most potent central nervous system stimulant of natural origin.[78] Cocaine is extracted from the leaves of the coca plant (whose botanical name is *Erythroxylon coca*). Since ancient times, the drug has been used by native Indians throughout the highlands of Central and South America, who chew the leaves of the coca plant to overcome altitude sickness and to sustain the high levels of physical energy needed for strenuous mountain farming.

Cocaine has some medical value as a topical anesthetic for use on sensitive tissues, such as the eyes and mucous membranes. Throughout the early twentieth century, physicians valued cocaine for its ability to anesthetize tissue while simultaneously constricting blood vessels and reducing bleeding. Recently, more effective products have replaced cocaine in many medical applications.

A report by the ONDCP classifies cocaine users into three groups: "(1) the younger, often minority crack user; (2) the older injector who is combining cocaine HCL with heroin in a speedball; and (3) the older, more affluent user who is snorting cocaine HCL."[79] Cocaine generally reaches the United States in the form of a

> Cocaine is often diluted with a variety of other ingredients, allowing sellers to reap high profits from small amounts of the drug.

much-processed white crystalline powder. It is often diluted with a variety of other ingredients, including sugar and anesthetics like lidocaine. Dilution allows sellers to reap high profits from small amounts of the drug.

Cocaine produces intense psychological effects, including a sense of exhilaration, superabundant energy, hyperactivity, and extended wakefulness.[80] Irritability and apprehension may be unwanted side effects. Excessive doses may cause seizures and death from heart failure, cerebral hemorrhage, and respiratory collapse. Some studies show that repeated use of cocaine may heighten sensitivity to these toxic side effects of the drug.[81]

Federal data indicate that cocaine has become the country's most dangerous commonly used drug. During a recent year, nearly 100,000 hospital emergencies involving cocaine abuse were reported across the country.[82] The Federal Drug Seizure System reported the seizure of around 137,000 pounds of cocaine throughout the United States in 2010.[83]

Most cocaine enters the United States from Peru, Bolivia, or Colombia. Together, these three countries have an estimated annual production capability of around 555 tons of pure cocaine.[84] During the 1980s, most cocaine coming into the United States was controlled by the Medellín Cartel, based in Medellín, Colombia. Multinational counterdrug efforts had crippled the cartel by the start of the 1990s, however, and the Cali Cartel (based in Cali, Colombia), a loose organization of five semi-independent trafficking organizations, took over as the major illegal supplier of cocaine to this country. Arrests of the Cali Cartel's top leaders, Gilberto Rodriguez and his brother, Miguel,

however, sounded the death knell for what may have been the world's most successful drug-trafficking organization ever.[85] By 2013, however, Mexican drug gangs had largely replaced Columbian cartels as major drug suppliers to the United States and Canada. In that same year, Mexican officials announced the arrest of Miguel Angel Trevino Morales, one of Mexico's most-wanted drug lords and leader of the Zetas cartel, and Mario Armando Ramirez Trevino, a top leader of the Gulf Cartel.[86]

Heroin

Classified as a narcotic, heroin is a derivative of opium—itself the product of the milky fluid found in the flowering poppy plant (*Papaver somniferum*). Opium poppies have been grown in the Mediterranean region since 300 b.c.[87] and are now produced in many other parts of the world as well. Although heroin is not used medicinally in this country, many of the substances to which it is chemically related—such as morphine, codeine, hydrocodone, naloxone, and oxymorphone—do have important medical uses as pain relievers.

Heroin is a highly seductive and addictive drug that produces euphoria when smoked, injected underneath the skin ("skin popping"), or shot directly into the bloodstream ("mainlining"). Because tolerance for the drug increases with use, larger and larger doses of heroin must be taken to achieve the pleasurable effects desired by addicts. Heroin deprivation causes withdrawal symptoms that initially include watery eyes, runny nose, yawning, and perspiration. Further deprivation results in

© Blaine Harrington III/Alamy

A scene from Denver's 2015 Cannabis Cup celebration. The annual event, hosted by *High Times Magazine*, draws thousands of people who are able to sample the wares of marijuana vendors. See Chapter 1 for a discussion of recent events surrounding marijuana legalization in this country. Do you think that the possession of small amounts of marijuana for personal recreational use should be legal?

restlessness, irritability, insomnia, tremors, nausea, and vomiting. Stomach cramps, diarrhea, chills, and other flulike symptoms are also common. Most withdrawal symptoms disappear within seven to ten days[88] or when the drug is readministered.

Street-level heroin varies widely in purity. It is often cut with powdered milk, food coloring, cocoa, or brown sugar. Most heroin sold in the United States is only 5% pure.[89] Because of dosage uncertainties, overdosing is common. Mild overdoses produce lethargy and stupor, whereas larger doses may cause convulsions, coma, and death. Other risks, including infectious hepatitis and AIDS, are associated with using contaminated needles from other users. The Centers for Disease Control and Prevention (CDC) estimates that almost one-third of AIDS cases are associated with intravenous drug use.[90]

Heroin abuse has remained fairly constant during the past few decades. Some indicators point to an increased availability of heroin in the last few years.[91] Street-level heroin prices have declined in recent years, and nationwide heroin-related emergency room admissions have reached almost 40,000 per year.

Most heroin in the United States comes from South America, Southwest Asia (Afghanistan, Pakistan, and Iran), Southeast Asia (Burma, Laos, and Thailand), and Mexico. According to data from the Heroin Signature Program (HSP), which uses chemical analysis of the trace elements in heroin supplies to identify source countries, 65% of all heroin entering the United States comes from South America.[92] The Federal Drug Seizure System reports the seizure of approximately 5,510 pounds of heroin throughout the United States annually.[93]

Evidence indicates that the heroin abuse picture is changing. Although older users still dominate heroin markets in all parts of the country,[94] increasing numbers of non-inner-city young users (under 30 years of age) are turning to the drug. Additionally, because high-purity powdered heroin is widely available in most parts of the country, new users seem to be experimenting with heroin inhalation, which often appears to lead to injection as addiction progresses. Treatment programs report that the typical heroin user is male, is over 30 years old, and has been in treatment previously.[95] Alcohol, cocaine, and marijuana remain concurrent problems for heroin users in treatment.

Methamphetamine

Known on the street as speed, chalk, meth, ice, crystal, and glass, methamphetamine is a stimulant drug chemically related to other amphetamines (like MDMA) but with stronger effects on the central nervous system. Methamphetamine is taken in pill form or is used in powdered form by snorting or injecting.[96] Crystallized methamphetamine (known as ice, crystal, or glass) is a smokable and even more powerful form of the drug. Effects of methamphetamine use include increased heart rate and blood pressure, increased wakefulness, insomnia, increased physical activity, decreased appetite, and anxiety, paranoia, or violent behavior. The drug is easily made in simple home "laboratories"

An Afghan farmer works in a poppy field in Nangarhar province of eastern Afghanistan. Despite U.S. efforts to curtail poppy cultivation in the country, Afghanistan remains the world's largest producer of heroin. Much of the money that's spent on heroin comes from the United States, where the sale of illicit drugs constitutes a multibillion-dollar industry. Why haven't U.S. efforts to stop poppy cultivation worked?

("meth labs") from readily available chemicals, and recipes describing how to produce the substance circulate on the Internet. Methamphetamine appeals to the abuser because it increases the body's metabolism, produces euphoria and alertness, and gives the user a sense of increased energy. An increasingly popular drug at raves, it is not physically addictive but can be psychologically addictive. High doses or chronic use of the drug increases nervousness, irritability, and paranoia.

Methamphetamine use increases the release of very high levels of the neurotransmitter dopamine, which stimulates brain cells, enhancing mood and body movement.[97] Chronic methamphetamine abuse significantly changes how the brain functions. Animal research going back more than 30 years shows that high doses of methamphetamine can damage neuron cell endings. Dopamine- and serotonin-containing neurons do not die after methamphetamine use, but their nerve endings ("terminals") are stunted, and regrowth appears to be limited. Noninvasive human-brain-imaging studies have shown alterations in the activity of the dopamine system with regular methamphetamine use. These alterations are associated with reduced motor speed and impaired verbal learning. Recent studies in chronic methamphetamine abusers have also revealed significant structural and functional changes in areas of the brain associated with emotion and memory, which may account for many of the emotional and cognitive problems observed in chronic methamphetamine abusers.

Recently, the DEA reported the emergence of candy-flavored methamphetamine around the country, leading to fears that methamphetamine manufacturers were targeting especially young users. Police departments in Nevada, California, Washington, Idaho, Texas, and New Mexico reported finding bags of what users call "Strawberry Quick"—a flavored form of methamphetamine meant to be snorted or sold illegally as a powerful energy drink.[98]

■ **theme** What are club drugs? Why are they used? Should they be illegal? Explain.

■ **club drug** A synthetic psychoactive substance often found at nightclubs, bars, "raves," and dance parties. Club drugs include MDMA (Ecstasy), ketamine, methamphetamine (meth), GBL, PCP, GHB, and Rohypnol.

Club Drugs

In 1997, DEA officials recommended that the "date rape drug" Rohypnol (also discussed in Chapters 2 and 4) be added to the list of Schedule I controlled substances. Rohypnol is a powerful sedative manufactured by Hoffmann-LaRoche Pharmaceuticals.[99]

Rohypnol is among the "club drugs" that became popular in the mid- to late 1990s. **Club drug** is a general term used to refer primarily to synthetic psychoactive substances often found at nightclubs, bars, and "raves" (all-night dance parties). In addition to Rohypnol, club drugs include GHB, GBL (gamma-butyrolactone), MDMA (Ecstasy), ketamine, methamphetamine (meth), and PCP.

CJ | NEWS
"Bath Salts" Drugs: Very Potent, Hard to Target

Chris Knight/The Patriot-News/AP Images

Bath salts displayed on a store counter in Pennsylvania. Bath salts are synthetic stimulants that mimic the effects of traditional drugs like cocaine and methamphetamine, but a recent law banned more than two dozen of the most common chemicals used to make the drugs.

When a naked Florida man tried to chew off the face of a homeless man in May 2012, police initially reported he was high on "bath salts." It turned out the rampaging man—shot dead by police—only had marijuana in his system. But his bizarre behavior seemed to fit the profile of people high on bath salts, a relatively cheap but extremely potent new drug.

After initially giving users a quick high, bath salts can plunge them into agitation, paranoia, hallucinations, extreme violence, and suicide. An emergency room doctor reported that one user had been running for more than 24 hours, convinced that the devil was chasing him with an ax.

Bath salts have little in common with soap, although they come in a powder that resembles Epsom salts—a non-drug that is put into bathwater to relieve aches and pains. Rather than being one specific drug, this new narcotic is actually a family of drugs, first developed in makeshift laboratories about a decade ago.

After bath salts overran Europe, U.S. poison control centers began registering overdoses from them in 2009. The drugs, often imported from China or India, proved to be particularly popular in the American South. When they were initially not outlawed in the United States, they were openly sold in head shops, adult book shops, and convenience stores for as little as $15 a packet. Each packet, wrapped in foil or plastic, holds 200 to 500 milligrams of powder.

These potent packets have been sold as fake plant food, stain remover, toilet bowl cleaner, and hookah cleaner, in addition to bath salts. They are usually labeled "Not for Human Consumption," in an attempt to protect purveyors from prosecution. When a drug is not specifically outlawed, federal law stipulates that law enforcement officials must show it was intended for human use before targeting purveyors.

The enforcement situation changed in October 2011, however, when the U.S. Food and Drug Administration (FDA) took action. Citing an "imminent threat to public safety," the FDA placed a temporary federal ban on three of the most common drugs used for bath salts: mephedrone, methylenedioxypyrovalerone (MDPV), and methylone.

Many states have also banned the drug. West Virginia, for instance, made it a misdemeanor to sell, buy, or possess the drug, with a maximum sentence of six months in jail and a $1,000 fine.

In 2012, the federal ban became permanent and was widened to more than two dozen of the most common bath salt drugs. But even with the full federal ban, bath salts remain difficult for law enforcement to identify. Many of these substances are too new to show up on standard drug tests, and new variations come out constantly. According to the United Nations Office of Drugs and Crime, 42% of testing laboratories in 48 countries reported new substances in 2011 alone. One designer drug that is also proving a problem for law enforcement is Flakka, and its use is now spreading throughout the country.

Enforcement will continue to be difficult, because the changing chemistry of the drugs will require new laws to ban them and changes in standard drug tests to identify them. "The moment you start to regulate one of them, they'll come out with a variant that sometimes is even more potent," said Dr. Nora Volkow, director of the National Institute on Drug Abuse. Learn more about bath salts at **http://justicestudies.com/pubs/salts.pdf.**

Resources: Matthew Perrone, "Bath Salts Laws: Officials Struggle to Regulate New Recipes for Synthetic Drugs," Associated Press, July 25, 2012, http://www.huffingtonpost.com/2012/07/25/bath-salts-laws_n_1701339.html; United Nations Office of Drugs and Crime, "Tracking Designer Drugs, Legal Highs and Bath Salts," November 1, 2012, https://www.unodc.org/unodc/en/frontpage/2012/November/tracking-designer-drugs-legal-highs-and-bath-salts.html; Matt McMillan, "Bath Salts' Drug Trend: Expert Q&A," WebMD, no date, http://www.webmd.com/mental-health/features/bath-salts-drug-dangers; and Robert Glatter, "Flakka: The New Designer Drug You Need to Know About," Forbes, April 4, 2015.

A few years ago, the growing use of Rohypnol at fraternity parties, raves, bars, and dance clubs gave rise to the phrase *chemically assisted date rape*, a term applied to rapes in which sexual predators use drugs to incapacitate unsuspecting victims. Rohypnol (a brand name for flunitrazepam) is a member of the benzodiazepine family of depressants and is legally prescribed in 64 countries for insomnia and as a preoperative anesthetic. Seven to ten times more powerful than Valium, Rohypnol has become popular with some college students and with "young men [who] put doses of Rohypnol in women's drinks without their consent in order to lower their inhibitions."[100] Available on the black market, it dissolves easily in drinks and can leave anyone who unknowingly consumes it unconscious for hours, making them vulnerable to sexual assault. The drug is variously known as roples, roche, ruffles, roofies, and rophies on the street.

Penalties for trafficking in flunitrazepam were increased under the Drug-Induced Rape Prevention and Punishment Act of 1996,[101] effectively placing it into a Schedule I category for sentencing purposes. Under the Act, it is a crime to give someone a controlled substance without the person's knowledge and with intent to commit a violent crime.

GHB, another "date rape drug," has effects similar to those of Rohypnol. GHB, a central nervous system depressant, is now designated as a Schedule I drug but was once sold in health food stores as a performance enhancer for use by bodybuilders. Rumors that GHB stimulates muscle growth were never proven. The intoxicating effects of GHB, however, soon became obvious. In 1990, the Food and Drug Administration (FDA) banned the use of GHB except under the supervision of a physician. In 2001, federal sentencing guideline changes removed the upper limit, or cap, on GHB sentences in cases where large amounts of the drug were sold or distributed.[102]

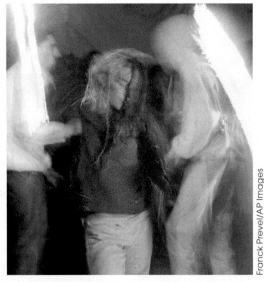

A fire juggler lighting up the night at a rave attended by thousands in the French village of Paule. Raves typically involve abundant drugs, particularly the designer drug Ecstasy. What are some other club drugs?

Franck Prevel/AP Images

GBL is a chemical used in many industrial cleaners and is the precursor chemical for the manufacture of GHB. Several Internet businesses offer kits that contain GBL and the proper amount of sodium hydroxide or potassium hydroxide, along with litmus paper and directions for the manufacture of GHB. The process is quite simple and does not require complex laboratory equipment. Like GHB, GBL can be added to water and is nearly undetectable. GBL is synthesized by the body to produce GHB. As a consequence, some users drink small quantities of unmodified GBL. This often causes a severe physical reaction, usually vomiting. GBL increases the effects of alcohol and can cause respiratory distress, seizure, coma, and death.

MDMA (Ecstasy), the most popular of the club drugs, is primarily manufactured in and trafficked from Europe. DEA reports indicate widespread abuse of this drug within virtually every city in the United States. Estimates from the Drug Abuse Warning Network (DAWN) show that hospital emergency department mentions for MDMA quadrupled over three years, from 1,143 in 1998 to 4,511 in 2000.[103] A redesigned DAWN survey, known as the New DAWN, found that 21,836 MDMA-related emergency department visits were reported in 2010.[104] Although MDMA is primarily found in urban settings, abuse of this substance has also been noted in rural communities. Prices in the United States generally range from $20 to $30 per dosage unit; however, prices as high as $50 per dosage unit have been reported in Miami. MDMA (3, 4-methylenedioxymethamphetamine) is a synthetic psychoactive substance possessing stimulant and mild hallucinogenic properties. Known as the "hug drug" or the "feel-good drug," it reduces inhibitions, produces feelings of empathy for others, eliminates anxiety, and produces extreme relaxation. In addition to chemical stimulation, the drug reportedly suppresses the need to eat, drink, or sleep. This enables club goers to endure all-night and sometimes two- to three-day parties. MDMA is taken orally, usually in tablet form, and its effects last approximately four to six hours. Often taken in conjunction with alcohol, the drug destroys both dopamine and serotonin cells in the brain. When taken at raves, the drug often leads to severe dehydration and heatstroke, as it has the effect of "short-circuiting" the body's temperature signals to the brain. An MDMA overdose is characterized by a rapid heartbeat, high blood pressure, faintness, muscle cramping, panic attacks, and, in more severe cases, seizures or loss of consciousness. Side effects of the drug are jaw muscle tension and teeth grinding. As a consequence, MDMA users will often use pacifiers to help relieve the tension. The most critical life-threatening response to MDMA is hyperthermia, or excessive body heat. Many rave clubs now have cooling centers or cold showers designed to allow participants to lower their body temperatures. MDMA is a Schedule I drug under the Controlled Substances Act.

The Ecstasy Anti-Proliferation Act of 2000[105] directed the U.S. Sentencing Commission to increase penalties for the manufacture, importation, exportation, and trafficking of MDMA. Under resulting emergency amendments to the U.S. sentencing

■ **activity** Invite a pharmacist to speak with the class. Ask the speaker to describe the legal requirements associated with prescription drugs and the processes through which pharmaceutical diversion can occur. Ask him or her to describe the effects of the various controlled substances that are illegally available through pharmaceutical diversion.

■ **lecture note** Explain the difference between direct and indirect costs and give examples of each.

■ **lecture note** Review the three main areas of indirect costs resulting from illicit drug use.

■ **theme** What is the relationship between drug abuse and other forms of criminal activity? Why does this relationship exist? Do you think that the legalization of drugs would reduce drug-related crimes? Explain.

■ **pharmaceutical diversion** The transfer of prescription medicines controlled by the Controlled Substances Act by theft, deception, and/or fraudulent means for other than their intended legitimate therapeutic purposes.

guidelines, MDMA trafficking became a crime with serious consequences. As a result of this penalty enhancement, which became permanent in 2001, a violator convicted of trafficking 200 grams of MDMA (approximately 800 tablets) can receive a five-year prison sentence.

Ketamine (known as K, special K, and cat Valium) produces effects that include mild intoxication, hallucinations, delirium, catatonia, and amnesia. Low doses of the drug create an experience called K-Land, a mellow, colorful "wonder world." Higher doses produce an effect referred to as K-Hole, an "out-of-body" or "near-death" experience. Use of the drug can cause delirium, amnesia, depression, long-term memory and cognitive difficulties, and fatal respiratory problems.[106]

Marketed as a dissociative general anesthetic for human and veterinary use, the only known street source of ketamine is **pharmaceutical diversion.** Significant numbers of veterinary clinics have been robbed specifically for their ketamine stock. Ketamine liquid can be injected, applied to smokable material, or consumed in drinks. The powdered form is made by allowing the solvent to evaporate, leaving a white or slightly off-white powder that, once pulverized, looks very similar to cocaine. The powder can be put into drinks, smoked, or injected. Pharmaceutical diversion and illicit Internet pharmacies are major sources of supply for pharming parties, which have been called "the newest venue for teenage prescription-drug abuse."[107]

Finally, in 2011, the DEA used its emergency scheduling authority to temporarily control methylenedioxypyrovalerone and two other synthetic stimulants, mephedrone and methylone.[108] The drugs, which can be snorted or taken orally, are also known as psychoactive bath salts (PBAs), and go by names such as Flakka, Ivory Wave and Vanilla Sky. They act as central nervous system stimulants.

The Costs of Abuse

The societal costs of drug abuse can be categorized as direct and indirect. Direct costs are those costs immediately associated with drug crimes themselves, such as the dollar losses incurred by a homeowner from a burglary committed to support a drug habit. The value of stolen property, damage to the dwelling, and the costs of cleanup and repair figure into any calculation of direct costs. Indirect costs, which are harder to measure, include such things as the homeowner's lost wages from time off at work

needed to deal with the burglary's aftermath, the value of time spent filling out police reports, going to court, and so on. Other indirect costs, such as the mental stress and feelings of violation and personal insecurity that often linger in the wake of criminal victimization are much harder to measure.

The Indirect Costs of Abuse

A recent report by the U.S. Department of Justice's National Drug Intelligence Center (NDIC), entitled *The Economic Impact of Illicit Drug Use on American Society* [109] placed the annual national cost of illicit drug use in the United States at a staggering $193 billion. That total includes costs from three areas: (1) justice system expenditures needed to deal with the consequences of illegal drug use, (2) health care, and (3) lost productivity.

The first area, justice system expenditures, includes three component costs: criminal justice–system costs (estimated to be $56,373,000), direct costs to crime victims ($1,455,000), and a catchall category of other crime costs ($3,547,885). The three subcategories together total $61,376,694. Justice system–related expenses include money spent on incarcerating drug offenders, on state and local drug abuse–related police protection, on jails for holding drug offenders prior to trial, and on the adjudication of drug offenders. Much of the justice system cost comes in the form of private legal defense attributable to drug abuse.

Health-care costs include money spent on emergency room care, ongoing medical treatment for drug abuse–related illnesses and dependence, psychiatric institutionalization, and hospitalization. A major component of health-care costs related to drug abuse consists of spending on care for HIV/AIDS patients and hepatitis patients whose infections are directly attributable to drug-related activities (for example, the sharing of needles). Also included are expenses stemming from the annual estimated 23,500 drug-related deaths from overdose, poisoning, and homicide. The costs associated with this second category total $11,416,232.

Finally, costs of lost productivity include six components: labor participation costs ($49,237,777), specialty treatment costs for services provided at the state level ($2,828,207), specialty treatment costs for services provided at the federal level ($44,830), hospitalization costs ($287,260), costs of incarceration ($48,121,949), and premature mortality costs ($16,005,008). These categories total $120,304,004.

As the NDIC report points out, the largest proportion of indirect costs comes from lost worker productivity. In contrast to

■ **lecture note**   Summarize the impact of drugs on felony convictions, and trace their impact throughout the criminal justice system.

the other indirect costs of drug abuse (which entail expenditures for goods and services), this value reflects a loss of potential—specifically, lost work in the labor market and in household production that was never performed but could reasonably be expected to have been performed in the absence of drug abuse. Estimates of lost worker productivity are based on premature death from drug use, lost time at work due to criminal victimization, and institutionalization for drug treatment and dependence also enter the totals. Other studies have found that the legitimate U.S. economy loses about 1 million person years of effort every 12 months as the result of drug-related crimes.[110]

Drug-Related Crime

The direct costs of drug-related crime have at least three dimensions: (1) economic losses from crimes committed by drug users to obtain money for drugs or from crimes committed by users whose judgment is altered by drugs; (2) the costs associated with drug transactions themselves (for example, what people spend to buy drugs); and (3) economic losses due to organized criminal activities in support of the drug trade (including money laundering).

The Office of National Drug Control Policy says that about 382,000 individuals suffer drug abuse–attributable violent crimes

every year and that about 5.2% of all homicides are related to narcotic drug-law violations.[111] Additionally, an estimated 5 million property offenses are committed annually in order to pay for illicit drugs. The ONDCP estimates that more than a quarter of the total number of property offenses in any given year are directly attributable to drug abuse.[112] Other crimes committed by those seeking to pay for drugs include prostitution, identity theft, fraud, and robbery. As Figure 16-3 shows, approximately 1.6 million people were arrested for drug-law violations (excluding alcohol) in the United States in 2014.[113]

Crimes committed by drug-dependent offenders can run the gamut from serious to relatively minor. A National Institute of Justice study of 201 heroin users in Central and East Harlem (New York City), for example, found that each daily user committed on average about 1,400 crimes per year. Of these offenses, 1,116 were directly drug related, involving primarily drug sales and use.[114] Another 75 were relatively minor crimes, such as shoplifting, but the remaining 209 offenses committed by each user involved relatively serious violations of the law, such as robbery, burglary, theft, forgery, fraud, and the fencing of stolen goods. Another study, which examined the daily activities of 354 Baltimore heroin addicts over a nine-year period, found that they had committed a total of nearly 750,000

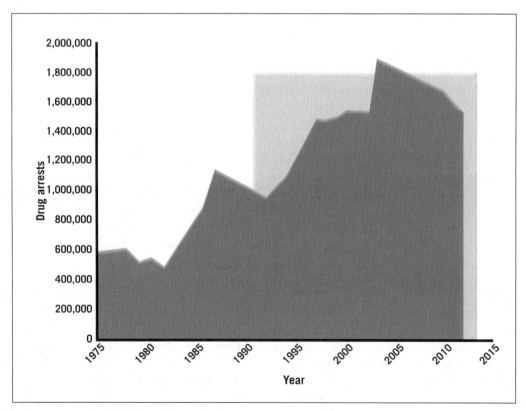

FIGURE 16-3 | Drug Arrests in the United States, 1975-2014

Source: Federal Bureau of Investigation, *Crime in the United States*, various years.

■ **lecture note** Describe money laundering as a financial scheme to disguise ill-gotten gains. Refer to the federal banking requirement that financial institutions report all deposits in excess of $10,000. Ask students whether they think this requirement effectively thwarts money-laundering schemes.

■ **money laundering** The process by which criminals or criminal organizations seek to disguise the illicit nature of their proceeds by introducing them into the stream of legitimate commerce and finance.[iv]

criminal offenses.[115] Learn more about the dynamics of the drug–crime relationship at **http://www.justicestudies.com/ pubs/dynamics.pdf,** and see a summary of national findings from the 2013 National Survey on Drug Use and Health at **http:// justicestudies.com/pubs/nsduh2013.**

The sale of illegal drugs is a $57 billion industry in the United States; that's the amount that the ONDCP estimates that Americans spend annually on illicit drugs.[116] Some perspective on this figure can be gained by recognizing that each year Americans spend approximately $44 billion on alcohol products and another $37 billion on tobacco products.[117]

Organized criminal activities in support of the drug trade represent a third area of direct costs. Cash can flow into the hands of dealers in such huge amounts that it can be difficult for them to spend it. Few people buy houses, cars, and other big-ticket items with cash, and cash transactions arouse suspicion. **Money laundering** is the name given to the process used by drug dealers to hide the source of their revenues, to avoid taxes, and to disguise the financial evidence of drug dealing. Drug profits are laundered by converting them into other assets, such as real estate, stocks and bonds, racehorses, jewels, gold, and other valuables. The Bureau of Justice Statistics says that many millions of dollars in drug money are laundered through commercial banks and other financial institutions each year.[118] Under the federal Money Laundering Strategy Act of 1998,[119] particular regions have been designated as high-intensity financial crimes areas (HIFCAs). HIFCAs can be found in Chicago, New York, New Jersey, San Juan, Los Angeles, San Francisco, and the southwestern border region, including Arizona and Texas. During 2001, more than 1,400 defendants were charged in U.S. district courts with money laundering as their most serious offense.[120]

In an effort to catch money launderers, U.S. banking law requires financial institutions to report deposits in excess of $10,000.[121] Traffickers attempt to avoid the law through two techniques known as smurfing and structuring.[122] Smurfers repeatedly purchase bank checks in denominations of less than $10,000, which are then sent to accomplices in other parts of the country, who deposit them in existing accounts.

> In an effort to catch money launderers, U.S. banking law requires financial institutions to report deposits in excess of $10,000.

Once the checks have cleared, the funds are transferred to other banks or moved out of the country. Structuring is very similar and involves cash deposits to bank accounts in amounts of less than $10,000 at a time. After accounts are established, the money is withdrawn and deposited in increments elsewhere, making it difficult to trace. Countries that have secrecy laws protecting depositors are favorites for drug traffickers. Among them are Switzerland, Panama, Hong Kong, the United Arab Emirates, and the Bahamas.[123] Recent action by the U.S. government, however, has forced Swiss banks to reveal the identities of American depositors who may have used the country's laws to avoid scrutiny.[124]

In 1994, in the case of *Ratzlaf* v. *U.S.*,[125] the U.S. Supreme Court made the task of catching money launderers more difficult. The Court ruled that no one can be convicted of trying to evade bank-reporting requirements unless authorities can prove that offenders knew they were violating the law.

In 2001, in an effort to enhance the amount of information received by federal regulators from banks about potential money-laundering activities, Congress passed the International Money Laundering Abatement and Anti-Terrorist Financing Act of 2001, which is Title III of the USA PATRIOT Act.[126] The law requires banks to make considerable effort in determining the source of money held in individual overseas accounts and provides for sanctions to be placed on nations that hinder this reporting.

Although federal law prohibits the laundering of money, relatively few states have had strict laws against the practice. As a consequence, many local enforcement agencies were reluctant to investigate money-laundering activities in their jurisdictions. To counteract this reluctance and to facilitate interagency cooperation, the federal government created the Financial Crimes Enforcement Network (FINCEN). Partially as a result of FINCEN leadership, 36 states have adopted money-laundering legislation, and more are likely to do so.[127] You can access the FINCEN website via **http://www.fincen.gov.**

Solving the Drug Problem

American drug-control strategies seem caught in a kind of limbo between conservative approaches, advocating supply reduction through strict enforcement and interdiction, and innovative strategies, proposing demand reduction through education, treatment, and counseling. In 2014, the Office of Control Policy (ONDCP) released its annual publication, *National Drug Control Strategy*,[128] offering a balanced public-health and public-safety approach to drug policy. Strategy authors said that the document represented a new approach to drug control "based on science, not ideology." In fact, the 2014 *National Drug Control Strategy* recognizes that substance-use

■ **theme**   This chapter identifies various strategies for controlling drug abuse. List each of the strategies, and order the list according to your evaluation of each strategy's chance for success. Give reasons to support the order you've chosen. Which of these strategies do you think would appeal most to public-order advocates? To individual-rights advocates? Why?

disorders "are medical conditions, and reducing the stigma surrounding these medical conditions is a particularly important component of drug policy reform." The *National Drug Control Strategy* recognizes that "the United States cannot arrest or incarcerate its way out of the drug problem," and emphasizes prevention over incarceration. Significantly, the publication also acknowledges that "drug issues are a truly global challenge requiring shared solutions," and seeks to expand global drug-prevention and drug-treatment initiatives through cooperation with other countries and the United Nations.

In developing the 2014 *National Drug Control Strategy*, officials at the ONDCP drew upon the *Principles of Modern Drug Policy* that were released by the Global Commission on Drug Policy at the Third World Forum Against Drugs, a gathering of international drug policy leaders hosted in Stockholm by the government of Sweden. The *Principles* document addresses the drug problem as a shared responsibility among nations, reaffirming support for the three United Nations drug conventions and calling for international cooperation to counter transnational organized crime and protect citizen security. Among the ten principles identified by the international conference, a number are especially important because they inform the ONDCP's strategy. They include:

1. *Ensure Balanced, Compassionate, and Humane Drug Policies.* Modern drug policies must acknowledge that drug addiction is a chronic disease of the brain that can be prevented and treated. Public health and public safety initiatives are complementary and equally vital to achieving reductions in drug use and its consequences. The challenge lies in combining cost-effective, evidence-based approaches that protect public health and safety.

2. *Integrate Prevention, Treatment, and Recovery Support Services into Public-Health Systems.* Public-health approaches, such as evidenced-based prevention, screening, and brief interventions in health-care settings, drug treatment programs, and recovery support services, are vital components of an effective drug-control strategy.

3. *Protect Human Rights.* Respect for human rights is an integral part of drug policy. Citizens, especially children, have the right to be safe from illegal drug use and associated crime, violence, and other consequences—whether in their family or the community. Drug-involved offenders who have contact with the criminal justice system deserve to be supervised with respect for their basic human rights and to be provided with services to treat their underlying substance-use disorder.

4. *Support and Expand Access to Medication-Assisted Therapies.* Recent innovations in medication-assisted therapies have demonstrated increasing effectiveness in reducing drug use and its consequences. These medications should be further studied to identify new therapies and best practices in program implementation.

5. *Reform Criminal Justice Systems to Support Both Public Health and Public Safety.* Criminal justice systems play a vital role in breaking the cycle of drug use, crime, incarceration, and rearrest. Although individuals should be held responsible for breaking the law, the criminal justice system should help bring them into contact with treatment services if they are suffering from a substance-use disorder. This includes providing treatment services in correctional facilities, providing alternatives to incarceration such as drug courts for nonviolent drug-involved offenders, and using monitoring, drug testing, and other means to ensure recovery from illegal drug use.

6. *Disrupt Drug Trafficking.* Transnational criminal organizations should be targeted, with a focus on the arrest, prosecution, and incarceration of drug traffickers; the seizure of illegal assets; the disruption of drug production networks; the control of precursor chemicals; and the eradication of illegal drug crops. International cooperation on information exchange, extradition, and training and technical assistance should be strengthened to eliminate safe harbors for transnational criminal organizations.

7. *Address the Drug Problem as a Shared Responsibility.* Drug use, production, and trafficking are increasingly globalized problems and pose challenges to all nations. Because of the global nature of today's drug markets, international cooperation is essential to protect public health and safety.[129]

Read the 2014 *National Drug Control Strategy* in its entirety at **http://justicestudies.com/pubs/ndcs_2014.pdf.**

Politics aside, six general types of strategies can be identified among the many methods proposed for attacking the drug problem: (1) strict domestic law enforcement, (2) asset forfeiture, (3) interdiction, (4) domestic and international crop control, (5) prevention and treatment, and (6) legalization and decriminalization. Each of these strategies is discussed in the following pages, and the amount of money spent by the federal government on enforcement, prevention and treatment, and interdiction is shown in Figure 16-4.

■ **forfeiture** The authorized seizure of money, negotiable instruments, securities, or other things of value. Under federal antidrug laws, judicial representatives are authorized to seize all cash, negotiable instruments, securities, or other things of value furnished or intended to be furnished by any person in exchange for a controlled substance, as well as all proceeds traceable to such an exchange.

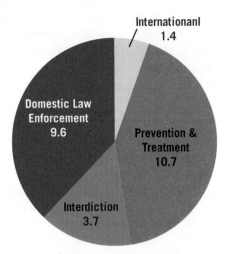

FIGURE 16-4 | Federal Drug Control Spending, 2014

Source: Office of National Drug Control Policy, *National Drug Control Budget, FY 2014.*

Sergeant Jeff Yurkiewicz of the Pennsylvania State Police K-9 Unit leading his dog, Jake, through a search for drugs and contraband at the Allegheny County Jail in Pittsburgh. More than 20 dogs were brought in to search the entire jail for drugs. Strict enforcement of antidrug laws is one of six strategies discussed in this chapter for attacking the drug problem. What are the other five?

Strict Law Enforcement

Trafficking in controlled substances is, of course, an illegal activity in the United States—and has been for a long time. Conservative politicians generally opt for a strict program of antidrug law enforcement and costly drug sentences, with the goal of removing dealers from the streets, disrupting supply lines, and eliminating sources of supply. Unfortunately, legal prohibitions appear to have done little to discourage widespread drug abuse. Those who look to strict law enforcement as a primary drug-control strategy usually stress the need for secure borders, drug testing to identify users, and stiff penalties to discourage others from drug involvement. The U.S. Coast Guard policy of "zero tolerance," for example, which was highly touted in the late 1980s, led to widely publicized seizures of multimillion-dollar vessels when even small amounts of drugs (probably carried aboard by members of the crew) were found.

But strict enforcement measures may eventually lead to greater long-term problems. As James Q. Wilson observes, "It is not clear that enforcing the laws against drug use would reduce crime. On the contrary, crime may be caused by such enforcement because it keeps drug prices higher than they would otherwise be."[130]

Some U.S. enforcement strategies attempt to enlist the help of foreign officials. However, because drug exports represent extremely lucrative sources of revenue and may even be thought of as valuable "foreign trade" by the governments of some nations, effective international antidrug cooperation is hard to come by. In 1991, for example, partly in response to pressures from cocaine-producing cartels within the country, Colombia outlawed the extradition of Colombian citizens for any purpose—making the extradition and trial of Colombian cocaine kingpins impossible.

A number of international drug-control treaties do, however, exist. In 2005, in actions supported by such treaties, the DEA announced that its Operation Cyber Chase, which had targeted Internet traffickers who used more than 200 websites to illicitly distribute pharmaceutical controlled substances, had led to more than 20 arrests in the United States, Australia, Costa Rica, and India.[131] Among the substances being sold by the cybertraffickers through illegal pharmaceutical websites were the drugs Vicodin, Xanax, and OxyContin. International cooperation resulted in the forfeiture of 41 bank accounts that were linked to the storefronts and worth over $6 million.[132] One important group concerned with ensuring compliance with United Nations drug-control conventions is the International Narcotics Control Board (INCB). Visit the INCB via **http://www.incb.org.**

Asset Forfeiture

Forfeiture, an enforcement strategy that federal statutes and some state laws support, bears special mention. Antidrug forfeiture statutes authorize judges to seize "all monies, negotiable instruments, securities, or other things of value furnished

■ **Racketeer Influenced and Corrupt Organizations
(RICO)** A federal statute that allows for the federal seizure of
assets derived from illegal enterprise.

The new St. Louis, Missouri, police headquarters. The building,
which is seven stories tall, was purchased using money seized from
criminal activities. What are the pros and cons of forfeiture laws?

or intended to be furnished by any person in exchange for a
controlled substance ... [and] all proceeds traceable to such an
exchange."[133] Forfeiture statutes are based on the relation-back
doctrine. This doctrine assumes that because the government's
right to illicit proceeds relates back to the time they are generated, anything acquired through the expenditure of those proceeds also belongs to the government.[134]

The first federal laws to authorize forfeiture as a criminal sanction were passed in 1970. They were the Continuing
Criminal Enterprise (CCE) statute and the Organized Crime
Control Act. A section of the Organized Crime Control
Act known as the **Racketeer Influenced and Corrupt
Organizations (RICO)** statute was designed to prevent criminal infiltration of legitimate businesses and has been extensively
applied in federal drug-smuggling cases. In 1978, Congress authorized civil forfeiture of any assets acquired through narcotics
trafficking in violation of federal law. Many states modeled their
own legislation after federal law and now have similar statutes.

The newer civil statutes have the advantage of being relatively easy to enforce. Civil forfeiture requires proof only by a
preponderance of the evidence, rather than proof beyond a reasonable doubt, as in criminal prosecution. In civil proceedings
based on federal statutes, there is no need to trace the proceeds in question to a particular narcotics transaction. It is enough to link them to narcotics trafficking generally.[135]

Forfeiture amounts can be huge. In one 15-month period, for example, the South Florida–Caribbean

> In a single investigation
> involving two brothers
> convicted of heroin
> smuggling, the federal
> government seized a
> shopping center, three
> gasoline stations, and seven
> homes worth more than
> $20 million in New York
> City.

Task Force, composed of police agencies from the federal, state, and
local levels, seized $47 million in airplanes, vehicles, weapons, cash,
and real estate.[136] In a single investigation involving two brothers
convicted of heroin smuggling, the federal government seized a
shopping center, three gasoline stations, and seven homes worth
more than $20 million in New York City.[137]

Although all states now have forfeiture statutes, prosecutions built on them have met with less success than prosecutions
based on federal law. The Police Executive Research Forum
(PERF) attributes the difference to three causes: (1) the fact that
federal law is more favorable to prosecutors than most state laws
are (2) the greater resources of the federal government, and (3)
the difficulties imposed by statutory requirements that illegal
proceeds be traced to narcotics trafficking.[138]

In 1993, in *U.S. v. 92 Buena Vista Ave.*,[139] the U.S. Supreme
Court established an "innocent owner defense" in forfeiture
cases, whereby the government is prohibited from seizing drug-
transaction assets that were later acquired by a new and innocent
owner. In the same year, in the case of *Austin v. U.S.*,[140] the
Court placed limits on the government's authority to use forfeiture laws against drug criminals, finding that seizures of property must not be excessive when compared to the seriousness of
the offense charged. Otherwise, the justices wrote, the Eighth
Amendment's ban on excessive fines could be contravened. The
justices, however, refused to establish a rule by which excessive
fines could be judged. The *Austin* ruling was supported by two
other 1993 cases, *Alexander v. U.S.* and *U.S. v. James Daniel Good
Real Property*.[141] In *Alexander*, the Court found that forfeitures
under the RICO statute must be limited according to the rules
established in *Austin*, and in *Good*, the Court held that "absent
exigent circumstances, the Due Process Clause requires the
Government to afford notice and a meaningful opportunity to
be heard before seizing real property subject to civil forfeiture."

In 1996, the U.S. Supreme Court upheld the seizure of private property used in the commission of a crime, even though
the property belonged to an innocent owner not involved in
the crime. The case, *Bennis v. Michigan*,[142] involved the government's taking of a car that had been used by the owner's husband
when procuring the services of a prostitute. In effect, the justices
ruled, an innocent owner is not protected from property forfeiture related to criminal conviction.

Also in 1996, in the case of *U.S. v. Ursery*,[143] the Supreme
Court rejected claims that civil forfeiture laws constitute a form
of double jeopardy. In *Ursery*, the defendant's house had been
seized by federal officials who claimed that it had been used to
facilitate drug transactions. The government later seized other
personal items owned by Guy Jerome Ursery, saying that they
had been purchased with the proceeds of drug sales and that
Ursery had engaged in money-laundering activities to hide the

■ **lecture note**   Describe the various agencies involved in drug-interdiction activities. Ask students if interdiction is still a worthwhile strategy, given the monumental task of controlling U.S. orders.

■ **interdiction**   The interception of drug traffic at the nation's borders. Interdiction is one of the many strategies used to stem the flow of illegal drugs into the United States.

source of his illegal income. The court of appeals, however, reversed Ursery's drug conviction and the forfeiture judgment, holding that the double jeopardy clause of the U.S. Constitution prohibits the government from both punishing a defendant for a criminal offense and forfeiting his or her property for that same offense in a separate civil proceeding. In reaffirming Ursery's conviction, however, the U.S. Supreme Court concluded that "civil forfeitures are neither 'punishment' nor criminal for purposes of the Double Jeopardy Clause." In distinguishing civil forfeitures and criminal punishments, the majority opinion held that "Congress has long authorized the Government to bring parallel criminal actions and . . . civil forfeiture proceedings based upon the same underlying events . . ., and this Court consistently has concluded that the Double Jeopardy Clause does not apply to such forfeitures because they do not impose punishment."

Civil forfeiture laws have come under considerable fire recently as being fundamentally unfair. More than 200 forfeiture laws have been enacted across the country in recent years, many requiring only mere suspicion before items of value can be seized by government agents. Once property has been seized, getting it back can be a nightmare, even when no crime was committed. A few years ago, U.S. Representative Henry Hyde of Illinois reported that 80% of people whose property was seized by the federal government under drug laws were never formally charged with any crime.[144]

To address problems with federal forfeiture provisions, Congress passed the Civil Asset Forfeiture Reform Act of 2000. Under the law, federal prosecutors must meet a burden-of-proof standard in forfeiture cases. They are required to establish by a preponderance of the evidence that the property in question was subject to forfeiture. The property owner has five years in which to make a claim on the property after the government has seized it,

but a claimant's status as a fugitive from justice is grounds for dismissal of the case contesting the forfeiture of the property. Under the new law, it is a crime to remove or destroy property to prevent seizure for forfeiture. In 2015, in a continuing effort to address the abuse of forfeiture powers by some law enforcement agencies, U.S. Attorney General Eric H. Holder, Jr., barred the use of federal law by enforcement agencies at any level to seize cash, cars, or other property without evidence that a crime has occurred. Holder's action was "the most sweeping check on police power to confiscate personal property since the seizures began three decades ago . . ."[145]

Interdiction

Annual seizures of cocaine in the United States total about 140 tons. In 2007, however, officials were surprised at the amount of cocaine seized when the U.S. Coast Guard cutter *Sherman* stopped the Panamanian cargo ship *Gatun* about 20 miles off the California coast.[146] Twenty tons of cocaine, with an estimated street value of $600 million, was discovered and transported to the Coast Guard facility in Alameda to be destroyed. The 14 crew members aboard the *Gatun* were Panamanians and Mexicans who were not armed and offered no resistance when stopped. It was not immediately clear if any of them knew what cargo they were carrying. Prior to the 2007 Coast Guard seizure, other large caches had vied for size records, including 9 tons of cocaine found in a house in Harlingen, Texas; 6 tons discovered on a ship in the Gulf of Mexico; and more than 5 tons hidden in barrels of lye in New York City.[147] A 2001 seizure by the Coast Guard of 13 tons of cocaine aboard a Belize-registered fishing boat south of San Diego, California, had held the previous record as the biggest cocaine seizure in U.S. maritime history.[148]

Interdiction involves efforts aimed at stopping drugs from entering the United States. The Coast Guard, the Border Patrol, and U.S. Customs agents have played the most visible roles in interdiction efforts during the last few decades. Interdiction strategies in the fight against drugs, however, are almost doomed to failure by the sheer size of the task. Although most enforcement efforts are focused on international airports and major harbors, the international boundary of the United States extends over 12,000 miles. Rough coastline, sparsely populated desert, and dense forests provide natural barriers to easy observation and make detection of controlled substances entering the country very difficult. Add to this the fact that more than 420 billion tons of goods and more than 270 million people cross over the American border annually, and the job of interdiction becomes more complicated still.[149] Because most drugs can be highly

> Interdiction strategies in the fight against drugs are almost doomed to failure by the sheer size of the task.

U.S. Customs and Border Protection canine officer Steve Fischer works with his dog, Hex, while examining a cargo container looking for illegal drugs at the Port of Long Beach, California. Where do most illegal drugs come from?

© Tim Rue/Corbis

potent in even minute quantities, the interdiction strategy suffers from the proverbial "needle in the haystack" predicament.

Crop Control

Crop control strategies attempt to limit the amount of drugs available for the illicit market by targeting foreign producers. Crop control in source countries generally takes one of two forms. In the first, government subsidies (often with U.S. support) are made available to farmers to induce them to grow other kinds of crops. Sometimes illegal crops are bought and destroyed. The second form of control involves aerial spraying or ground-level crop destruction.

Source country crop control suffers from two major drawbacks.[150] First, the potentially large profits that can be made from illegal acreage encourage farmers in unaffected areas to take up the production of crops that have been destroyed elsewhere. Second, it can be difficult to get foreign governments to cooperate in eradication efforts. In some parts of the world, opium and coca are major cash crops, and local governments are reluctant to undertake any action directed against them.

Prevention and Treatment

As the population of incarcerated drug offenders swelled, state legislatures began to question the necessity of imprisoning nonviolent substance abusers who were not involved in drug sale or distribution. In 1996, as a consequence of such thinking, Arizona voters approved Proposition 200, the Drug Medicalization, Prevention, and Control Act. A central purpose of the Act was to expand drug-treatment and drug-education services for drug offenders and to utilize probation for nonviolent drug offenders, thereby potentially diverting many arrested drug abusers from prison. To fund the program, the Arizona law established the state's Drug Treatment and Education Fund, administered by Arizona's Office of the Courts; the fund draws revenues from the state's luxury tax on liquor.

A study by Arizona's Administrative Office of the Courts concluded that the Arizona law is "resulting in safer communities and more substance abusing probationers in recovery."[151] Moreover, said the report, the law has saved the state millions of dollars and has helped more than 75% of program participants to remain drug free.[152] In 2000, the state of California followed Arizona's lead when voters approved Proposition 36 (the California Substance Abuse and Crime Prevention Act of 2000), a sweeping initiative requiring treatment instead of imprisonment for nonviolent drug users throughout the state.[153] Similar

French customs officers check the luggage of a passenger arriving from Istanbul, Turkey. Drug interdiction, which involves efforts aimed at stopping drugs from entering a country illegally, is an international strategy. Are U.S. interdiction efforts working?

Frank Schmalleger

legislation became law in Kansas in 2003 when Governor Kathleen Sebelius signed Senate Bill 123, the First Time Non-Violent Drug Offenders Act. The law requires Kansas judges to place nonviolent offenders convicted of nothing more than drug possession in community-based or faith-based drug-treatment programs for up to 18 months.[154]

Many different kinds of prevention and treatment programs are available for drug offenders. Michael Goodstadt of the Addiction Research Foundation groups drug-prevention and drug-treatment programs into three categories: (1) those that provide factual information about drugs; (2) those that address feelings, values, and attitudes; and (3) those that focus directly on behavior.[155] Most modern programs contain elements of all three approaches, and most experts agree that drug-prevention programs, if they are to be successful, must include a wide array of programs including components for individuals, families, schools, the media, health-care providers, law enforcement officials, and other community agencies and organizations.[156]

> Most experts agree that drug-prevention programs, if they are to be successful, must include a wide array of programs, including components for individuals, families, schools, the media, health-care providers, law enforcement officials, and other community agencies and organizations.

Antidrug education programs can be found in schools, churches, and youth groups and may be provided by police departments, social service agencies, hospitals, and private citizens' groups. Project DARE (the Drug Abuse Resistance Education

■ **lecture note** Discuss the history and development of drug courts, and the research into drug court effectiveness.

■ **activity** Invite a drug court judge to visit the class. Ask the judge to describe the drug court program and the various stages through which participants must pass. Include a discussion of what happens if a participant fails to complete the program successfully. Have students ask the judge for information regarding the success rate of the program.

■ **drug court** A special state, county, or municipal court that offers first-time substance-abuse offenders judicially mandated and court-supervised treatment alternatives to prison.

program) falls into Goodstadt's second category. DARE, which for many years had been the nation's most visible school-based antidrug education program, began as a cooperative effort between the Los Angeles Police Department and the Los Angeles Unified School District in 1983. Using uniformed law enforcement officers to conduct classes in elementary schools, the program focused on decision-making skills, peer pressure, and alternatives to drug use.

A 1994 study cast the effectiveness of the DARE program into doubt, and officials in the Clinton administration were charged with refusing to recognize the study's results. The study, published in the *American Journal of Public Health*, reviewed DARE programs in six states and British Columbia and found that "the popular drug prevention program does not work well and is less effective than other drug prevention efforts targeted at students."[157] Defending the DARE program, Justice Department officials questioned the study's methodology and published their own version of the study's results, which showed that "user satisfaction" with the DARE program is high. The study, according to Justice Department interpreters, found substantial grassroots support for the DARE program and led to the conclusion that DARE "has been extremely successful at placing substance abuse education in the nation's schools."[158]

Later studies again questioned DARE's effectiveness. A 1997 review of numerous DARE studies concluded that the program's "effects on drug use, except for tobacco use, are non-significant."[159] A 1999 University of Kentucky study tracked more than 1,000 midwestern students who participated in Project DARE in the sixth grade in order to see if the level of drug abuse among them differed from those who had not been exposed to the program.[160] The study found no difference in actual drug use immediately following exposure to the program or ten years later, when most of the former students were 20 years old. In 2001, the U.S. Surgeon General categorized DARE programs as "ineffective," and in 2007 the DARE program appeared on a list of treatments that have the potential to harm clients published by the Association for Psychological Science.[161] Even so, the program survives into the present day and has grown internationally—with programs in Europe as well as the United States.

Other studies also show that there is little evidence to support the belief that school-based antisubstance-abuse education will produce the desired effect on problem drug users or those at risk of beginning drug use.[162] Studies analyzing state-by-state spending on school-based drug education, for example, show little relationship between the amount of money spent on drug education and the number of hardcore cocaine users.[163] To be

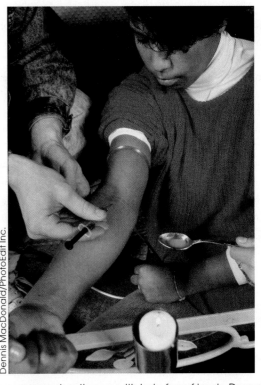

Dennis MacDonald/PhotoEdit Inc.

A young woman shooting up with help from friends. Drug abuse extends to all social groups and can be found among all ages. Why does illicit drug use persist in the United States after decades of efforts to curtail it?

effective, programs will probably have to acknowledge the perceived positive aspects of the drug experience, as well as cultural messages that encourage drug use.[164] Until they do, many participants in today's antidrug programs may discount them as conflicting with personal experience.

Other kinds of drug-education programs may be effective, however. A study by the RAND Corporation's Drug Policy Research Center (DPRC), for example, found education to be the most efficacious alternative for dealing with drug abuse.[165] DPRC researchers focused on the use of alternative strategies for reducing cocaine abuse. Visit RAND's DPRC via **http://www.rand.org/multi/dprc**.

Drug Courts

One of the most widely accepted antidrug programs operating today is the **drug court.** Drug courts focus on promoting public safety and employ a nonadversarial approach that provides defendants with easy access to a range of alcohol-, drug-, and other related treatment and rehabilitation services. Drug courts also monitor abstinence from the use of drugs on an individual basis through frequent alcohol and other drug testing. Failing to comply with court-ordered treatment, or returning to drug use, may result in harsher punishments, including imprisonment.

Modern drug courts are modeled after a Dade County, Florida, innovation that became known as the Miami Drug Court model. An early evaluation of Miami's drug court found a high rate of success: Few clients were rearrested, incarceration rates were lowered, and the burden on the criminal justice system was lessened.[166] The success of the drug-court model led to $1 billion worth of funding under the Violent Crime Control and Law Enforcement Act of 1994 for the establishment of similar courts throughout the nation. Since then, the growth in the number of drug courts serving the nation has been huge. Today, the National Association of Drug Court Professionals (NADCP) reports that more than 2,700 drug courts are operating in the United States.[167]

A recent NIJ Multisite Adult Drug Court Evaluation[168] found that drug-court participants reported less criminal activity (40% vs. 53%) and had fewer rearrests (52% vs. 62%) than comparable offenders who were not handled by specialized courts. The study also found that drug-court participants reported less drug use (56% vs. 76%) and were less likely to test positive (29% vs. 46%) than comparable offenders. Finally, the study found that treatment investment costs were higher for participants, but because of lowered recidivism, drug courts averaged an overall savings of $5,680 to $6,208 per offender.

There are special drug courts for juveniles and for drunk drivers (sometimes called DUI courts). The National Drug Court Institute, in conjunction with the NADCP, provides training for judges and professional courtroom staff interested in today's drug-court movement. Learn more about drug courts via **http://www.ndci.org/ndci-home**.

Legalization and Decriminalization

According to a recent report by the Global Commission on Drug Policy, that was mentioned earlier in this chapter, "political leaders and public figures should have the courage to articulate publicly what many of them acknowledge privately: that the evidence overwhelmingly demonstrates that repressive strategies will not solve the drug problem."[169]

Two years before that report was issued, Gil Kerlikowske, the then-newly appointed Obama administration director of the Office of National Drug Control Policy, said that he wanted to scrap the idea that the United States is fighting "a war on drugs," noting that the war analogy has created an unnecessary barrier to dealing with real problems. "Regardless of how you try to explain to people it's a 'war on drugs' or a 'war on a product,' people see a war as a war on them," Kerlikowske said. "We're not at war with people in this country."[170]

Also, in mid-2011, the Global Commission on Drug Policy, a prestigious group of internationally recognized political and scientific leaders, released a detailed report calling the war on

Martin Mejia/AP Images

Venezuelan Norlyn Mota (left) and Margarita Andrea of the Dominican Republic, prepare to participate in the annual beauty pageant for inmates at the Santa Monica Women's Prison in Lima, Peru. Most women incarcerated at the Peruvian penitentiary worked as drug "mules" and were caught trying to smuggle cocaine out of Peru. How can we solve the drug problem?

drugs a failure. The commission recommended ending "the criminalization, marginalization, and stigmatization of people who use drugs but who do no harm to others." It also encouraged governments around the world to regulate drugs without unnecessary criminalization, and to undermine the power of organized crime groups that depend upon drug moneys to threaten the social order in many parts of the world. The commission explained that it wanted to "bring to the international level an informed, science-based discussion about humane and effective ways to reduce the harm caused by drugs to people and societies." The full report, *War on Drugs: Report of the Global Commission on Drug Policy*, is available for viewing at the commission's website (**http://www.globalcommissionondrugs.org**).

> The Global Commission on Drug Policy recommended ending "the criminalization, marginalization, and stigmatization of people who use drugs but who do no harm to others."

■ **theme**   What is the difference between legalization and decriminaliza-tion? Which strategy do you think is the better approach to the problem of cocaine abuse? Why? To the problem of marijuana abuse? Why?

■ **lecture note**   Discuss the arguments for and against legalization and decriminalization of drugs. Ask students which arguments in each group they find most and least persuasive.

■ **legalization**   Elimination of the laws and criminal penalties associated with certain behaviors—usually the production, sale, distribution, and possession of a controlled substance.

■ **lecture note**   Discuss the difference between legalization and decrimi-nalization by comparing it to the difference between using a crosswalk and jaywalking. Point out that although neither is criminal, one is ticketable as a minor offense.

■ **decriminalization**   The redefinition of certain previously criminal behaviors into regulated activities that become "ticket-able" rather than "arrestable."

Realizations like those reached by former Drug Czar Gil Kerlikowske and the Global Commission on Drug Policy have led a number of well-meaning people to question the wisdom of current laws and to seek alternatives to existing U.S. drug-control policies. For them, it has become clear that the fight against drug abuse through the application of strict criminal justice sanctions is bound to fail. Arrest, incarceration, and a national prison system filled with drug-law violators do not seem to hold the answer to winning the drug-control battle.

More than one-third (37%) of the police chiefs who partici-pated in the Police Foundation survey mentioned near the start of this chapter say that our nation's drug policy needs a fundamental overhaul, and 47% think that it needs major changes. Only 2% of responding chiefs said that they would maintain the status quo.[171]

Often regarded as the most "radical" approach to solv-ing the drug problem, legalization and decriminalization have been proposed repeatedly, and in recent years, these ideas seem to be gaining at least a modicum of respectability. Although the words *legalization* and *decriminalization* are often used in-terchangeably, there is a significant difference. **Legalization** refers to the removal of all legal strictures from the use or pos-session of the drug in question. Manufacture and distribution might still be regulated. **Decriminalization,** on the other hand, substantially reduces penalties associated with drug use but may not eliminate them entirely. Hence decriminalization

A Mexican police officer responds to street violence initiated by drug gangs in Acapulco. Earlier, 15 decapitated bodies were discovered in front of a popular shopping area. Is the legalization or decriminalization of controlled substances a realistic option for Mexico? For the United States?

of a controlled substance might mean that the drug "would re-main illegal but the offense of possession would be treated like a traffic violation, with no loss of liberty involved for the trans-gressor."[172] A number of states, including Colorado, Oregon, Alaska, and Washington, recently legalized possession of small amounts of marijuana for personal use, although laws in those jurisdictions bar public use of the drug, and driving while using marijuana still violates DUI laws.[173]

In response to state action, in 2013 the U.S. Department of Justice issued a memorandum to all federal prosecutors provid-ing guidance on enforcement of the Controlled Substances Act in those jurisdictions. The memorandum took a "hands-off" approach and established federal enforcement priorities with regard to marijuana distribution and use in states that have le-galized the drug. Those priorities include preventing the distri-bution of marijuana to minors and preventing marijuana sales revenue from going to criminal enterprises and cartels.[174]

Various arguments have been offered in support of both legalization and decriminalization. They say that if drugs were legal or decriminalized, they:[175]

- would be easy to track and control. The involvement of organized criminal cartels in the drug-distribution net-work could be substantially curtailed.
- could be taxed, generating huge revenues.
- would be cheap, significantly reducing the number of drug-related crimes committed to feed expensive drug habits.
- might decline in attractiveness, as some people find ex-citement in violating the law.
- would enhance civil liberties and reduce political turmoil.

Advocates of legalization are primarily motivated by cost–benefit considerations, weighing the social costs of prohibition against its results.[176] The results, they say, have been meager at best, whereas the costs have been almost more than society can bear.

Opponents of legalization argue from both a moral and a practical stance. Some, like former New York City Mayor Rudolph Giuliani, believe that legalization would only condone a behavior that is fundamentally immoral.[177] Others argue that under legalization, drug use would increase, causing more wide-spread drug-related social problems than exist today. Robert DuPont, former head of the National Institute on Drug Abuse, for example, estimates that up to ten times the number of people

■ **lecture note**   List each of the potential solutions to the problem of
drug abuse that the text explores. Ask students which of the solutions they
think would be most effective. Do solutions differ depending on the drug in
question?

■ **lecture notes**   Review the *Principles of Modern Drug Policy* listed in the
text and discuss why they are important.

who now use cocaine would turn to the substance if it were
legal.[178] Read the original memorandum at **http://www.
justicestudies.com/pubs/marijuana_memo.pdf**.

A compromise approach has been suggested in what some
writers call the limitation model. The limitation model "would
make drugs legally available, but with clearly defined limits as to
which institutions and professions could distribute the drugs."[179]
Hence, under such a model, doctors, pharmacists, and perhaps
licensed drug counselors could prescribe controlled substances
under appropriate circumstances, and the drugs themselves
might be taxed. Some claim that a more extreme form of the
limitation model might be workable. Under that model, drugs
would be sold through designated "drugstores" with distribution systems structured much like those of liquor stores today.
Controlled substances would be sold to those of suitable age but
taxed substantially, and the use of such substances under certain
circumstances (when driving, for example) might still be illegal.
The regulation and taxation of controlled substances would correspond to today's handling of alcoholic beverages.

Another example of the limitation model, already tried in
some countries, is the two-market system.[180] The two-market
approach would allow inexpensive and legitimate access to
controlled substances for registered addicts. Only maintenance
amounts (the amounts needed to forestall symptoms of drug
withdrawal) of the needed drugs, however, would be available. The two-market approach would purportedly reduce the
massive profits available to criminal drug cartels while simultaneously discouraging new drug use among those who are not
addicted. Great Britain provides an example of the two-market
system. During the 1960s and 1970s, British heroin addicts who

registered with the government received prescriptions for limited
amounts of heroin, which was dispensed through medical clinics.
Because of concern about system abuses, clinics in the late 1970s
began to dispense reduced amounts of heroin, hoping to wean
addicts away from the drug.[181] By 1980, heroin was replaced by
methadone,[182] a synthetic drug designed to prevent the physical symptoms of heroin withdrawal. Methadone, in amounts
sufficient to prevent withdrawal, does not produce a heroin-like
high. Recent studies, however, show that methadone can build
up in the body to a toxic level if taken too often.[183]

It is doubtful that the two-market system will be adopted in
the United States anytime soon. American cultural condemnation of major mind-altering drugs has created a reluctance to
accept the legitimacy of drug treatment using controlled substances. In addition, cocaine is much more of a problem in the
United States than heroin is. The large number of drug abusers
in the country, combined with the difficulty of defining and
measuring addiction to drugs like cocaine, would make any
maintenance program impractical.

One group advocating for a change in current drug laws,
including the possible decriminalization of some controlled substances, is Law Enforcement Against Prohibition (LEAP). LEAP,
whose members are current and former law enforcement officers, describes itself as "an organization made up of former drug
warriors speaking out about the excesses and abuses of current
drug policy and the utter failure of the war on drugs." The group
originated with Peter Christ, a retired police captain living in
New York City. Christ believed that an organization like LEAP
would catch the attention of the media and appeal to other law
enforcement officers. Visit LEAP at **http://www.leap.cc**.

SUMMARY

- In determining which substances should be called drugs, it is
important to recognize the role of social convention. Hence,
what Americans today consider to be a drug depends more on
agreed-on understandings than it does on any inherent property
of the chemical substance itself. Powerful drugs, those with the
ability to produce substantially altered states of consciousness
and with a high potential for addiction, occupy the forefront in
social and legal condemnation. Among them are psychoactive
substances like heroin, peyote, mescaline, LSD, and cocaine.
Changes in thinking that took place during the 1960s and
1970s led to the inclusion of far less powerful substances, such
as alcohol and nicotine, in the "drug" category.

- Many of today's controlled substances were once unregulated
by law. Even heroin, cocaine, and opium, were once freely
available and contained in widely used medicines. The first
major piece of federal antidrug legislation was the Harrison
Narcotics Act of 1914. It required anyone dealing in opium,
morphine, heroin, cocaine, and specified derivatives of these
drugs to register with the federal government and to pay a tax.
In 1937, Congress passed the Marijuana Tax Act, which simply
placed a tax on cannabis; those who did not pay the tax were
subject to prosecution. The passage of the Boggs Act in 1951
made marijuana, along with a number of other drugs, a federally prohibited controlled substance. The Narcotic Control
Act of 1956 increased penalties for drug trafficking and possession and made the sale of heroin to anyone under age 18 a

capital offense. The Comprehensive Drug Abuse Prevention and Control Act, passed in 1970, is the basis of federal enforcement efforts today. Title II of the law is the Controlled Substances Act (CSA). The CSA sets up five schedules that classify psychoactive drugs according to their degree of psychoactivity and abuse potential. The Anti-Drug Abuse Act of 1988 increased penalties for "recreational" drug users and made weapons purchases by suspected drug dealers more difficult. The law also denies federal benefits, ranging from loans to contracts and licenses, to convicted drug offenders and allows capital punishment for drug-related murders.

- The use of illicit drugs is widespread in the United States. One of the best sources of data on the use of illegal drugs and the characteristics of drug users is the federal *National Survey on Drug Use and Health* (NSDUH), an annual publication of the Substance Abuse and Mental Health Services Administration. NSDUH data for 2013 showed that 24.6 million Americans age 12 and older were "current" users of illegal drugs. Over 19.8 million people were estimated to be using marijuana, and an estimated 1.5 million people were current cocaine users. An estimated 6.5 million Americans were current nonmedical users of prescription-type psychotherapeutic drugs. Although the numbers may seem large, these figures represent a considerable decline from 1979, the year in which the highest levels of drug abuse in the United States were reported. Nonetheless, figures for recent years show a gradual increase in drug use (especially "occasional use"). As this chapter points out, rates of drug use vary considerably by age, and adolescents and people in their 20s tend to show the highest rates of illicit drug use.

- Drug crimes and drug-related crimes account for a substantial proportion of all crimes committed in this country. Although the manufacture, importation, sale, and use of illegal drugs account for many law violations, many others are also linked to drug use. Among them are thefts of all kinds, burglary, assault, and murder. Similarly, many criminal enterprises are supported by the street-level demand for drugs. The high cost of drugs forces many users, some of whom have little legitimate income, to commit property crimes to make money to continue their drug habit. On the other hand, users of illicit drugs who have substantial legitimate incomes may indirectly shift the cost of drug use to society through lowered job productivity, psychological or family problems, and medical expenses.

- Six general types of strategies are among the many methods proposed for attacking the drug problem: (1) strict domestic law enforcement, (2) asset forfeiture, (3) interdiction, (4) crop control, (5) prevention and treatment, and (6) legalization and decriminalization. Recently, some states, including Oregon, Colorado, Alaska, and Washington, have legalized the possession and use of small amounts of marijuana for private recreational purposes. A number of other state legislatures are considering implementing similar policies.

KEY TERMS

club drug, 547
controlled substance, 533
Controlled Substances Act (CSA), 537
curtilage, 541
decriminalization, 559
drug, 533
drug abuse, 531
drug court, 557
drug czar, 539
drug trafficking, 544
forfeiture, 553

Harrison Narcotics Act, 537
interdiction, 555
legalization, 559
money laundering, 551
pharmaceutical diversion, 549
physical dependence, 538
psychoactive substance, 533
psychological dependence, 538
Racketeer Influenced and Corrupt Organizations (RICO), 554
recreational drug user, 533

KEY CASES

Alexander v. U.S., 554
Austin v. U.S., 554
California v. Greenwood, 541
Oliver v. U.S., 541
Ratzlaf v. U.S., 551

U.S. v. Dunn, 542
U.S. v. 92 Buena Vista Ave., 554
U.S. v. Oakland Cannabis Buyers' Cooperative, 544
U.S. v. Ursery, 554

QUESTIONS FOR REVIEW

1. What constitutes a drug for purposes of the criminal law? What role does social convention play in deciding what constitutes a controlled substance?
2. How long have substances that today would be considered illicit been used in the United States? For what purposes? List and describe some of the most important pieces of federal drug-control legislation.
3. What are the major types of drugs that are illegally used in this country? Describe the effects and legal classification of each.
4. What is the relationship between drug use and other social problems? What kinds of crimes might be linked to drug use?
5. What strategies have been used or suggested as ways of responding to the drug problem? Which of these strategies seem to hold the most potential?

QUESTIONS FOR REFLECTION

1. How successful have government efforts to curtail illicit drug use been? Why haven't they met with greater success?
2. What is meant by the decriminalization of illicit drugs? How does decriminalization differ from legalization?
3. Would you be in favor of the decriminalization of any drugs that are currently considered to be federally controlled substances? Legalization? If so, which ones and why?

NOTES

i. Bureau of Justice Statistics, *Drugs, Crime, and the Justice System* (Washington, DC: BJS, 1992), p. 20.

ii. Ibid., p. 21.

iii. Ibid.

iv. U.S. Department of Treasury, *2000–2005 Strategic Plan* (Washington, DC: U.S. Government Printing Office, 2000), p. 1.

1. Office of National Drug Control Policy, *Fact Sheet: A 21st Century Drug Policy* (Washington, DC: ONDCP, 2013), p. 1.

2. Michael Tarm, "Chicago Gets First 'Public Enemy No. 1' Since Al Capone: Mexican Cartel Kingpin," NBCnews.com, February 14, 2013, usnews.nbcnews.com/_news/2013/02/14/16961063-chicago-gets-first-public-enemy-no-1-since-al-capone-mexican-cartel-kingpin (accessed May 2, 2013).

3. "The World's Most Powerful People," *Forbes*, http://www.forbes.com/lists/2009/20/power-09_Joaquin-Guzman_NQB6.html (accessed May 20, 2013).

4. Peter D. Hart Research Associates, *Drugs and Crime across America: Police Chiefs Speak Out—A National Survey among Chiefs of Police* (Washington, DC: Police Foundation, December 2004).

5. National Association of Drug Court Professionals, *The Facts: Facts on Drug Courts* (Alexandria, VA: NADCP, 2001).

6. Federal Bureau of Prisons, "Statistics: Offenses," http://www.bop.gov/about/statistics/statistics_inmate_offenses.jsp (accessed June 1, 2015).

7. Sentencing Project, *The Federal Prison Population: A Statistical Analysis* (Washington, DC: Sentencing Project, 2005).

8. Bureau of Justice Statistics, "Data Analysis Tool," http://www.bjs.gov/content/dtdata.cfm#corrections (accessed May 30, 2013).

9. The term *recreational user* is well established in the literature of drug abuse. Unfortunately, it tends to minimize the seriousness of drug abuse by according the abuse of even hard drugs the status of a hobby.

10. Cocaine has some legitimate medical uses, and can be a valuable anesthetic and vasoconstricting agent.

11. Howard Becker, *Outsiders: Studies in the Sociology of Deviance* (New York: Free Press, 1963).

12. Jay Tokasz, "Eight of 11 People in Car Die in Crash," *USA Today*, June 20, 1995.

13. In most states, individuals may also be arrested for driving under the influence of other drugs and controlled substances, including prescription medicines.

14. Fiscal year 2001 Transportation Appropriations Bill (H.R. 4475), signed by the president on October 23, 2000.

15. "Drunk Driving Limit Lowered," *Lawyers Weekly USA*, October 16, 2000.

16. Federal Bureau of Investigation, *Crime in the United States, 2014* (Washington, DC: U.S. Dept. of Justice, 2015).

17. James B. Jacobs, *Drinking and Crime, National Institute of Justice Crime File Series Study Guide* (Washington, DC: NIJ, n.d.).

18. *Traffic Safety Facts: 2008 Data* (Washington, DC: National Highway Traffic Safety Administration, 2008), http://www.nrd.nhtsa.dot.gov/Pubs/811155.PDF (accessed October 10, 2011).

19. National Highway Traffic Safety Administration, http://www.nhtsa.gov (accessed May 20, 2013)

20. FBI, *Crime in the United States, 2014.*

21. Bureau of Justice Statistics, *Report to the Nation on Crime and Justice*, 2nd ed. (Washington, DC: U.S. Government Printing Office, 1988), p. 50.

22. Jeffrey A. Roth, "Psychoactive Substances and Violence," *National Institute of Justice Research in Brief* (Washington, DC: NIJ, February 1994), p. 1.

23. Christopher J. Mumola, *Substance Abuse and Treatment, State and Federal Prisoners, 1997* (Washington, DC: Bureau of Justice Statistics, 1999).

24. Ibid.

25. Howard Abadinsky, *Drug Abuse: An Introduction* (Chicago: Nelson-Hall, 1989), p. 32.

26. Charles E. Terry and Mildred Pellens, *The Opium Problem* (New York: Committee on Drug Addiction, 1928).

27. Ibid.

28. Office of National Drug Control Policy, *Heroin, ONDCP Fact Sheet* (Washington, DC: ONDCP, 2003), p. 1.

29. Terry and Pellens, *The Opium Problem*, p. 76.

30. David Musto, *The American Disease: Origins of Narcotic Control* (New Haven, CT: Yale University Press, 1973).

31. Becker, Outsiders.

32. Franklin E. Zimring and Gordon Hawkins, *The Search for Rational Drug Control* (New York: Cambridge University Press, 1992).

33. Ibid., p. 9.

34. President's Commission on Organized Crime, *Organized Crime Today* (Washington, DC: U.S. Government Printing Office, 1986).

35. *Webb v. U.S.*, 249 U.S. 96 (1919).

36. Michael D. Lyman and Gary W. Potter, *Drugs in Society: Causes, Concepts, and Control* (Cincinnati, OH: Anderson, 1991), p. 359.

37. Drug Enforcement Administration, *Drug Enforcement: The Early Years* (Washington, DC: DEA, 1980), p. 41.

38. White House Conference on Drug Abuse, *Commission Report* (Washington, DC: U.S. Government Printing Office, 1963).

39. For a good summary of the law, see Drug Enforcement Administration, *Drugs of Abuse* (Washington, DC: U.S. Government Printing Office, 1997).

40. Drug Enforcement Administration, *Drug Enforcement Briefing Book* (Washington, DC: DEA, n.d.), p. 3.

41. A number of states now recognize that marijuana may be useful in the treatment of nausea associated with cancer chemotherapy, glaucoma, and other medical conditions.

42. DEA, *Drug Enforcement Briefing Book*, p. 3.

43. Ibid.

44. Ibid., p. 4.

45. Ibid.

46. DEA, *Drugs of Abuse.*

47. Ibid.

48. Anti-Drug Abuse Act of 1988, Public Law 100-690, Section 5251.

49. This provision became effective on September 1, 1989.

50. "Congress Gives Final OK to Major Antidrug Bill," *Criminal Justice Newsletter*, Vol. 19, No. 21 (November 1, 1988), pp. 1–4.

51. The U.S. Supreme Court upheld that legislation in the 2002 case of *Department of Housing and Urban Development* v. *Rucker*, 122 S.Ct. 1230, 152 L.Ed.2d 258 (2002).

52. "Congress Gives Final OK to Major Antidrug Bill," p. 2.

53. "Drug Lord Sentenced to Death," *USA Today*, May 15, 1991, p. 3A.

54. Ibid.

55. Public Laws 101–647, 103–322, 105–20, and 109–177.

56. USA PATRIOT Improvement and Reauthorization Act of 2005 (Public Law 109–177). The act was signed into law by President George W. Bush on March 9, 2006.

57. *California v. Greenwood*, 486 U.S. 35 (1988).

58. Ibid.

59. *Abel v. U.S.*, 363 U.S. 217 (1960).

60. *Oliver v. U.S.*, 466 U.S. 170 (1984).

61. *Hester v. U.S.*, 265 U.S. 57 (1924).

62. *U.S. v. Dunn*, 480 U.S. 294 (1987).

63. *California v. Ciraolo*, 476 U.S. 207 (1986).

64. *Florida v. Riley*, 488 U.S. 445, (1989).

65. Substance Abuse and Mental Health Services Administration, *National Survey on Drug Use and Health* (Rockville, MD: Office of Applied Studies, NHSDA, 2014).

66. ONDCP, *Heroin*, p. 1.

67. Office of National Drug Control Policy, *General Counterdrug Intelligence Plan* (Washington, DC: ONDCP, 2000), http://www.fas.org/irp/ops/le/docs/gcip/index.html.

68. Information in this section comes from the National Drug Intelligence Center, http://www.usdoj.gov/ndic.

69. Office of National Drug Control Policy, *Pulse Check: National Trends in Drug Abuse—Marijuana* (Washington, DC: ONDCP, 2002), http://www.whitehousedrugpolicy.gov/publications/drugfact/pulsechk/nov02/marijuana.html (accessed August 4, 2003).

70. See Anita Manning and Andrea Stone, "How States Will Face Regulating Marijuana as Medicine," *USA Today*, November 7, 1996.

71. *U.S. v. Oakland Cannabis Buyers' Cooperative*, 532 U.S. 483 (2001).

72. Ibid., syllabus.

73. *Gonzales v. Raich*, 545 U.S. 1 (2005).

74. Gary Fields, "White House Czar Calls for End to 'War on Drugs,'" *Wall Street Journal*, May 14, 2009, http://online.wsj.com/article/SB124225891527617397.html (accessed June 5, 2011).

75. National Institute on Drug Abuse, *Monitoring the Future: National Results on Adolescent Drug Use* (Ann Arbor, MI: Institute for Social Research, 2014), Table 4-1b.

76. National Narcotics Intelligence Consumers Committee, *The NNICC Report, 1998* (Washington, DC: Drug Enforcement Administration, 2000), preface.

77. Ibid.

78. Ibid.

79. ONDCP, *Pulse Check*.

80. NNICC, *The NNICC Report, 1998*.

81. Ibid.

82. Ibid.

83. U.S. Census Bureau, "Federal Drug Arrests and Seizures by Type of Drug," http://www.census.gov/compendia/statab/2012/tables/12s0328.xls (accessed August 10, 2013).

84. NNICC, *The NNICC Report, 1998*.

85. Sam Vincent Meddis, "Arrests 'Last Rites' for Cali Cartel," *USA Today*, August 7, 1995.

86. Jessica King, "Mexico Arrests Alleged Leader of Gulf Cartel Near U.S. Border," CNN, August 20, 2013, http://www.cnn.com/2013/08/18/world/americas/mexico-cartel-arrest (accessed August 21, 2013).

87. DEA, *Drugs of Abuse*, p. 14.

88. Ibid., p. 12.

89. Ibid., p. 15.

90. Office of National Drug Control Policy, *The National Drug Control Strategy: Executive Summary* (Washington, DC: ONDCP, 1995), p. 13.

91. DEA, *Drugs of Abuse*.

92. NNICC, *The NNICC Report, 1998*.

93. U.S. Drug Enforcement Administration, *Drug Trafficking in the United States* (Washington, DC: DEA, 2004), http://www.policyalmanac.org/crime/archive/drug_trafficking.shtml (accessed December 3, 2011).

94. ONDCP, *Pulse Check*.

95. Ibid.

96. Much of the information in this section comes from the National Institute on Drug Abuse's website at http://www.nida.nih.gov (accessed July 4, 2011).

97. National Institute on Drug Abuse, "NIDA InfoFacts: Methamphetamine," http://www.nida.nih.gov/Infofacts/methamphetamine.html (accessed May 9, 2011).

98. Donna Leinwand, "DEA Sees Flavored Meth Use," *USA Today*, March 26, 2007.

99. Much of the information on club drugs in this section comes from Drug Enforcement Administration, "An Overview of Club Drugs," *Drug Intelligence Brief*, February 2000, http://www.usdoj.gov/dea/pubs/intel/20005intellbrief.pdf (accessed March 2, 2010).

100. "'Rophies' Reported Spreading Quickly throughout the South," *Drug Enforcement Report*, June 23, 1995, pp. 1–5.

101. Public Law 104-305.

102. Sentencing enhancement information in this section comes from the congressional testimony of Asa Hutchinson, administrator of the Drug Enforcement Agency, before the Senate Caucus on International Narcotics Control, December 4, 2001, http://www.usdoj.gov/dea/pubs/cngrtest/ct120401.html (accessed February 3, 2009).

103. Substance Abuse and Mental Health Services Administration, *The DAWN Report*, http://www.samhsa.gov/oas/dawn.htm (accessed March 10, 2010).

104. Substance Abuse and Mental Health Services Administration, *Drug Abuse Warning Network, 2010: National Estimates of Drug-Related Emergency Department Visits* (Washington, DC: U.S. Dept. of Health and Human Services, September, 2012), http://www.samhsa.gov/data/2k13/DAWN2k10ED/DAWN2k10ED.htm (accessed August 11, 2013).

105. Public Law 106-310.

106. DEA, "An Overview of Club Drugs," from which some of the wording in this section is taken.

107. Carolyn Banta, "Trading for a High: An Inside Look at a 'Pharming Party,'" *Time*, August 1, 2005, p. 35.

108. Fran Lowry, "DEA Moves to Make 'Bath Salts' Illegal as Overdoses Rise," *Medscape Medical News*, September 7, 2011.

109. National Drug Intelligence Center, *The Economic Impact of Illicit Drug Use on American Society* (Washington, DC: U.S. Department of Justice, 2011).

110. Office of National Drug Control Policy, *The Economic Costs of Drug Abuse in the United States, 1992–2002* (Washington, DC: ONDCP, December 2004).

111. Office of National Drug Control Policy, *The National Drug Control Strategy 2003: Executive Summary* (Washington, DC: ONDCP, 2003), p. 12.

112. Material in this paragraph is taken from ONDCP, *The Economic Costs of Drug Abuse in the United States, 1992–2002*, pp. iii–18.

113. FBI, *Crime in the United States*, 2014 Washington, DC: U.S. Dept. of Justice, 2015).

114. Bernard A. Gropper, "Probing the Links between Drugs and Crime," *National Institute of Justice Research in Brief* (Washington, DC: NIJ, February 1985), p. 4.

115. J. C. Ball, J. W. Shaffer, and D. N. Nurco, *Day to Day Criminality of Heroin Addicts in Baltimore: A Study in the Continuity of Offense Rates* (Washington, DC: National Institute of Justice, 1983).

116. "ONDCP Finds Americans Spent $57 Billion in One Year on Illegal Drugs," Office of National Drug Control Policy press release, 1997.

117. Office of National Drug Control Policy, *What America's Users Spend on Illegal Drugs* (Washington, DC: ONDCP, 1991), p. 4.

118. Mark Motivans, *Money Laundering Offenders, 1994–2001* (Washington, DC: Bureau of Justice Statistics, 2003).

119. Public Law 105-310.

120. Motivans, *Money Laundering Offenders*, p. 1.

121. U.S. Code, Title 18, Section 1957.

122. NNICC, *The NNICC Report, 1998.*

123. Ibid.

124. "Swiss Banking," Swissprivacy.com, http://www.swissprivacy.com/swiss-banking (accessed August 20, 2013).

125. *Ratzlaf v. U.S.*, 114 S.Ct. 655, 126 L.Ed.2d 615 (1994).

126. Public Law 107-56.

127. Motivans, *Money Laundering Offenders*, p. 10.

128. ONDCP, *The National Drug Control Strategy, 2013.*

129. Office of National Drug Control Policy, "Principles of Modern Drug Policy," http://www.whitehouse.gov/ondcp/policy-and-research/principles-of-modern-drug-policy (accessed August 20, 2015).

130. James Q. Wilson, "Drugs and Crime," in Michael Tonry and James Q. Wilson, eds., *Drugs and Crime* (Chicago: University of Chicago Press, 1990), p. 522.

131. Drug Enforcement Administration, "DEA Announces Major Takedown of Online Drug Dealers," April 20, 2005, http://www.pushingback.com/archives/042005_2.html (accessed July 4, 2007).

132. "Twenty Arrested in Crackdown on Internet Pharmacies," CNN.com, April 20, 2005, http://www.cnn.com/2005/LAW/04/20/internet.drugs.ap (accessed July 4, 2007).

133. U.S. Code, Title 21, Section 881(a)(6).

134. Michael Goldsmith, *Civil Forfeiture: Tracing the Proceeds of Narcotics Trafficking* (Washington, DC: Police Executive Research Forum, 1988), p. 3.

135. *U.S. v. $4,255,625.39 in Currency*, 762 F.2d 895, 904 (1982).

136. Bureau of Justice Assistance, *Asset Forfeiture Bulletin*, October 1988, p. 2.

137. Ibid.

138. Goldsmith, *Civil Forfeiture.*

139. *U.S. v. 92 Buena Vista Ave.*, 113 S.Ct. 1126, 122 L.Ed.2d 469 (1993).

140. *Austin v. U.S.*, 113 S.Ct. 2801, 15 L.Ed.2d 448 (1993).

141. *Alexander v. U.S.*, 113 S.Ct. 2766, 125 L.Ed.2d 441 (1993); and *U.S. v. James Daniel Good Real Property*, 114 S.Ct. 492, 126 L.Ed.2d 490 (1993).

142. *Bennis v. Michigan*, 116 S.Ct. 1560, 134 L.Ed.2d 661 (1996).

143. *U.S. v. Ursery*, 116 S.Ct. 2135, 135 L.Ed.2d 549 (1996).

144. Statement by the Honorable Henry J. Hyde, "Civil Asset Forfeiture Reform Act," http://www.house.gov/judiciary/161.htm (accessed March 10, 2010).

145. "Holder Severely Limits Federal Civil Asset Forfeiture Program," *Police Magazine*, January 16, 2015, http://www.policemag.com/channel/patrol/news/2015/01/16/holder-severely-limits-federal-civil-asset-forfeiture-program.aspx (accessed May 2, 2015).

146. National Briefing: "Largest Drug Seizure at Sea," *New York Times*, April 24, 2007, http://query.nytimes.com/gst/fullpage.html?res59801EEDD143EF937A15757C0A9619C8B63 (accessed May 10, 2010).

147. "Cocaine Found Packed in Toxic Chemical Drums," *Fayetteville (NC) Observer-Times*, November 5, 1989.

148. "Raid on Boat in Pacific Seizes 13 Tons of Cocaine," Associated Press, May 15, 2001.

149. Mark Moore, *Drug Trafficking, National Institute of Justice Crime File Series Study Guide* (Washington, DC: NIJ, 1988), p. 3.

150. Ibid.

151. Ibid.

152. Ibid.

153. In 2003, a California appellate court ruled that Proposition 36 does not apply to inmates in the state's correctional system. See *People v. Ponce*, Court of Appeals of California, First Appellate District, Division Five, No. A096707, March 7, 2003.

154. "Governor Signs Final Round of Bills," Kansas Governor's Office, April 21, 2003, http://www.ksgovernor.org/news/docs/news_rel042103.html (accessed August 3, 2006).

155. Michael S. Goodstadt, *Drug Education, National Institute of Justice Crime File Series Study Guide* (Washington, DC: NIJ, n.d.), p. 1.

156. See Federal Advisory Committee, *Methamphetamine Interagency Task Force: Final Report* (Washington, DC: Office of National Drug Control Policy, 2000), p. 5, from which some of the wording in this paragraph is adapted.

157. "DARE Not Effective in Reducing Drug Abuse, Study Finds," *Criminal Justice Newsletter*, October 3, 1994, pp. 6–7.

158. The government version of the study was first reported as *The DARE Program: A Review of Prevalence, User Satisfaction, and Effectiveness, National Institute of Justice Update* (Washington, DC: NIJ, October 1994). The full study, as published by the NIJ, is Christopher L. Ringwalt et al., *Past and Future Directions of the DARE Program: An Evaluation Review* (Washington, DC: National Institute of Justice, 1995).

159. Fox Butterfield, no headline, *New York Times* wire service, April 16, 1997, citing Office of Justice Programs, *Preventing Crime: What Works, What Doesn't, What's Promising* (Washington, DC: U.S. Dept. of Justice, 1997).

160. Donald R. Lynam et al., "Project DARE: No Effects at Ten-Year Follow-Up," *Journal of Consulting and Clinical Psychology*, Vol. 67, No. 4 (1999).

161. S. O. Lilienfeld, "Psychological Treatments That Cause Harm," *Perspectives on Psychological Science*, Vol. 2 (2007), pp. 53–70.

162. Goodstadt, *Drug Education*, p. 3.

163. *USA Today*, September 6, 1990, citing a report by the U.S. Senate Judiciary Committee.

164. Ibid.

165. RAND Corporation, *Drug Policy Research Center: Are Mandatory Minimum Drug Sentences Cost-Effective?* (Santa Monica, CA: RAND, 1997).

166. John S. Goldkamp and Doris Weiland, "Assessing the Impact of Dade County's Felony Drug Court," *National Institute of Justice Research in Brief* (Washington, DC: NIJ, December 1993).

167. National Institute of Justice, *Drug Courts* (Washington, DC: NIJ, April 2013).

168. National Institute of Justice, "Multisite Adult Drug Court Evaluation," http://www.nij.gov/nij/topics/courts/drug-courts/madce.htm (accessed August 20, 2013).

169. The Global Commission on Drug Policy, "War on Drugs: Report of the Global Commission on Drug Policy," 2011,

http://www.globalcommissionondrugs.org/Report (accessed June 8, 2013), p. 10.

170. Fields, "White House Czar Calls for End to 'War on Drugs.'"

171. Peter D. Hart Research Associates, *Drugs and Crime across America*, p. 5.

172. Arnold S. Trebach, "Thinking through Models of Drug Legalization," *Drug Policy Letter* (July/August 1994), p. 10.

173. In mid-2013, Colorado lawmakers sets limits on levels of delta-9-tetrahydrocannabinol, or THC, at five nanograms or more per milliliter of blood, for drivers. Those found with THC at that amount or more are considered to be under the influence by juries during court proceedings.

174. U.S. Dept. of Justice, Memorandum for all United States Attorneys, "Guidance Regarding Marijuana Enforcement," August 29, 2013.

175. For a more thorough discussion of some of these arguments, see Ronald Hamowy, ed., *Dealing with Drugs: Consequences of Government Control* (Lexington, MA: Lexington Books, 1987).

176. "Should Drugs Be Legal?" *Newsweek*, May 30, 1988, p. 36.

177. Ibid., p. 37.

178. Ibid., pp. 37–38.

179. Trebach, "Thinking through Models of Drug Legalization," p. 10.

180. For a more detailed discussion of the two-market system, see John Kaplan, *Heroin, National Institute of Justice Crime File Series Study Guide* (Washington, DC: NIJ, n.d.).

181. Ibid., p. 3.

182. Ibid., p. 4.

183. Donna Leinwand, "Deadly Abuse of Methadone Tops Other Prescription Drugs," *USA Today*, February 13, 2007, citing a representative of the Food and Drug Administration.

Stephen Chernin/Getty Images

17 TERRORISM, MULTINATIONAL CRIMINAL JUSTICE, AND GLOBAL ISSUES

LEARNING OBJECTIVES

After reading this chapter, you should be able to

- Describe the principles that form the basis of Islamic law.
- List five important international criminal justice organizations, and summarize their collective role in fighting international crime.
- Explain globalization and its possible relationship to crime and terrorism.
- Distinguish between human smuggling and human trafficking, and describe the extent of both problems today.
- Define the four major types of terrorism.

In the twenty-first century, Americans have come to appreciate that they are part of a global society and that criminal transgressions within and beyond our Nation's borders have worldwide ramifications.

OFFICE FOR VICTIMS OF CRIME[1]

■ **theme** What is comparative criminal justice (or comparative criminology) and why is it an important field of study for criminologists today?

■ **Follow the author's tweets about the latest crime and justice news @schmalleger.**

■ **comparative criminologist** One who studies crime and criminal justice on a cross-national level.

■ **ethnocentric** Holding a belief in the superiority of one's own social or ethnic group and culture.

Introduction

In January 2015, 20-year-old Christopher Lee Cornell of Cincinnati, Ohio, was arrested by the FBI and charged with plotting a terrorist attack on the U.S. Capitol using pipe bombs and rifles.[2] Some saw Cornell as the perfect example of a "lone wolf" terrorist—one who is inspired by an ideology of hatred and motivated to carry out attacks in the name of an organization with which he is only loosely affiliated. About a year preceding his arrest, Cornell had converted to Islam and taken on the name of Raheel Mahrus Ubaydah. Soon after that, he allegedly posted support for violent jihad and the Islamic State on his Twitter account.

The case of Christopher Cornell is not unusual. In 2013, Quazi Mohammad Rezwanul Ahsan Nafis, a Bangladeshi citizen, pled guilty in federal court to terrorism charges for attempting to blow up the Federal Reserve Bank of New York, located in Lower Manhattan.[3] Nafis, then 21, had been tracked by undercover agents after they had learned that he wanted to attack an important financial center in an effort to destroy the American economy. In earlier recorded conversations with undercover agents, Nafis said, "I just want something big. Something very big. Very very very very big, that will shake the whole country."

Also, in 2015, Shelton Thomas Bell, 21, of Jacksonville, Florida, was sentenced to 20 years in federal prison for attempting to provide material support to terrorists. According to prosecutors, Bell conspired to train and prepare as a combatant for overseas violent Jihad. Once overseas, his plan was to receive further training and weapons from the terrorist group, Ansar al-Sharia in Yemen. He was arrested, however, before he could leave the country.[4]

These stories show how vital it is for American criminal justice and other government organizations to appreciate the ideology, culture, and means of communications linking criminals and potential terrorists in this country to those overseas and around the world.

Criminologists who study crime and criminal justice on a cross-national level are referred to as **comparative criminologists,** and their field is called *comparative criminal justice, comparative criminology,* or *cross-national criminal justice.* Comparative criminal justice is becoming increasingly valued for the insights it provides. By contrasting native institutions of justice with similar institutions in other countries, procedures and problems in one system can be reevaluated in the light of world experience. As technological advances effectively "shrink" the world, we are able to learn firsthand about the criminal justice systems of other countries and to use that information to improve our own.

Accused "lone wolf" would-be terrorist Christopher Lee Cornell of Cincinnati, Ohio. Cornell, 20, was arrested in 2015 by the FBI and charged with plotting a terrorist attack on the U.S. Capitol using pipe bombs and rifles. Are Americans likely to see more lone-wolf terrorist attacks in the future, or fewer?

This chapter explains the value of comparative criminal justice, points to the problems that arise in comparing data from different nations, and explains international terrorism within the context of cross-national crime. By way of example, this chapter also briefly examines criminal justice systems based on Islamic principles. International police agencies are described, and the role of the United Nations (UN) in the worldwide fight against crime and terrorism is discussed. Additional information on the justice systems of many countries can be found in the *World Factbook of Criminal Justice Systems,* available at **http://bjs.ojp.usdoj.gov/content/pub/html/wfcj.cfm.** Another place to visit for international criminal justice information is the National Institute of Justice's International Center, which is accessible via **http://www.nij.gov/international.**

Ethnocentrism and the Study of Criminal Justice

The study of criminal justice in the United States has been largely **ethnocentric.** Because people are socialized from birth into a particular culture, they tend to prefer their own culture's way of doing things over that of any other. Native patterns of behavior are seen as somehow "natural" and therefore better than foreign ones. The same is true for values, beliefs, and customs. People tend to think that their religion holds a spiritual edge over other religions, that their values and ethical sense are superior to those of others, and that the fashions they wear, the language they speak, and the rituals of daily life in which they participate are somehow better than comparable practices

■ **theme**   What is ethnocentrism? Why can ethnocentrism be problematic for the study of criminal justice? How can ethnocentrism be overcome?

■ **lecture note**   Explain ethnocentrism as culture-centeredness. Discuss how ethnocentrism can be a limiting factor in the study of international criminal justice.

■ **activity**   If your university has study abroad programs, invite a member of the Study Abroad Office staff to address the class either in person or virtually. Ask the staff member to describe how they deal with the issue of ethnocentrism among students participating in study abroad programs.

■ **activity**   Ask members of the class to identify foreign students whom they know. Select a small group of foreign students to invite to address the class either in person or virtually. Ask each speaker to describe the criminal justice system in his or her home country. Ask class members how they can best keep their ethnocentrism in perspective during this activity. If the class includes foreign students, they may be invited to speak as well. Additionally, point out that ethnocentrism is not limited to the United States and may be experienced by foreign students studying American criminal justice.

Karim Kadim/AP Images

An Iraqi man holding a picture of top Shiite cleric Ayatollah Ali Sistani during a protest in support of an Islamic constitution. The traditions and legal systems of many Middle Eastern countries are strongly influenced by Islamic law, which is based on the teachings of the Koran and the sayings of the Prophet Muhammad. How does Islamic law differ from the laws of most Western nations?

elsewhere. Ethnocentric individuals do not consider that people elsewhere in the world cling to their own values, beliefs, and standards of behavior with just as much fervor as they do.

Only in recent years have American students of criminal justice begun to examine the justice systems of other cultures. Unfortunately, not all societies are equally open, and it is not always easy to explore them. In some societies, even the *study* of criminal justice is taboo. As a result, data-gathering strategies taken for granted in Western societies may not be well received elsewhere. One author, for example, has observed that in China, "the seeking of criminal justice information through face-to-face questioning takes on a different meaning in Chinese officialdom than it does generally in the Western world. While we accept this method of inquiry because we prize thinking on our feet and quick replies, it is rather offensive in China because it shows lack of respect and appreciation for the information given through the preferred means of prepared questions and formal briefings."[5] Hence, most of the information available about Chinese criminal justice comes by way of bureaucracy, and routine Western social science practices like door-to-door

interviews, participant observation, and random surveys would produce substantial problems for researchers who attempt to use these techniques in China.

Problems with Data

Similar difficulties arise in the comparison of crime rates from one country to another. The crime rates of different nations are difficult to compare because of (1) differences in the way a specific crime is defined, (2) diverse crime reporting practices, (3) political and other influences on the reporting of statistics to international agencies, (4) social, cultural, and economic differences.[6]

Definitional differences create what may be the biggest problem. For cross-national comparisons of crime data to be meaningful, it is essential that the reported data share conceptual similarities. Unfortunately, that is rarely the case. Nations report offenses according to the legal criteria by which arrests are made and under which prosecution can occur. Switzerland, for example, includes bicycle thefts in its reported data on what we call "auto theft" because Swiss data gathering focuses more

For cross-national comparisons of crime data to be meaningful, it is essential that the reported data share conceptual similarities.

on the concept of personal transportation than it does on the type of vehicle stolen. The Netherlands has no crime category for robberies, counting them as thefts. Japan classifies an assault that results in death as an assault or an aggravated assault, not as a homicide. Greek rape statistics include crimes of sodomy, "lewdness," seduction of a child, incest, and prostitution. China reports only robberies and thefts that involve the property of citizens; crimes against state-owned property fall into a separate category.

Social, cultural, and economic differences among countries compound these difficulties. Auto theft statistics, for example, when compared between countries like the United States and China, need to be placed in an economic as well as demographic context. Whereas the United States has two automobiles for every three people, Bangladesh has only one car per every 2,600 of its citizens.[7] For the auto theft rate in Bangladesh to equal that of the United States, every automobile in the country would have to be stolen over 100 times each year!

Reporting practices vary substantially between nations. The International Criminal Police Organization (Interpol) and the UN are the only international organizations that regularly collect crime statistics from a large number of countries.[8] Both agencies can only request data and have no way of checking on the accuracy of the data reported to them. Many countries do not disclose the requested information, and those that do often make only partial reports. In general, small countries are more likely to report than are large ones, and nonsocialist countries are more likely to report than are socialist countries.[9]

International reports of crime are often delayed. Complete up-to-date data are rare because the information made available to agencies like the UN and Interpol is reported at different times and according to schedules that vary from nation to nation. In addition, official UN world crime surveys are conducted infrequently. To date, only ten such surveys have been undertaken.[10]

Crime statistics also reflect political biases and national values. Some nations do not accurately admit to the frequency of certain kinds of culturally reprehensible crimes. Communist countries, for example, appear loathe to report crimes like theft, burglary, and robbery because the very existence of such offenses demonstrates felt inequities within the communist system.

After the breakup of the Soviet Union, Alexander Larin, a criminal justice scholar who worked as a Russian investigator during the 1950s and 1960s, revealed that "inside the state security bureaucracy, where statistics were collected and circulated, falsification of crime figures was the rule, not the exception. The practice was self-perpetuating.... Supervisors in the provinces were under pressure to provide Moscow with declining crime rates. And no self-respecting investigator wanted to look worse than his neighbor.... From the top to the bottom, the bosses depended on their employees not to make them look bad with high crime statistics."[11]

On the other hand, observers in democratic societies showed similar biases in their interpretation of statistics following the end of the cold war. Some Western analysts, for example, reporting on declines in the prison populations of Eastern and Central Europe during that period, attributed the decline to lessened frustration and lowered crime rates brought about by democratization. In one country, Hungary, prison populations declined from 240 inmates per 100,000 residents in 1986 to 130 per 100,000 in 1993, with similar decreases in other nations.[12] The more likely explanation, however, is the wholesale post-Soviet release of political dissidents from prisons formerly run by communist regimes. Learn more about world crime via the UN's Global Report on Crime and Justice, which is available at **http://www.uncjin.org/Special/GlobalReport.html.**

Islamic Criminal Justice

Islamic law has been the subject of much discussion in the United States since the September 11, 2001, terrorist attacks on the World Trade Center and the Pentagon. It is important for American students of criminal justice to recognize, however, that Islamic law refers to legal ideas (and sometimes entire legal systems) based on the teachings of Islam and that it bears no intrinsic relationship to acts of terrorism committed by misguided zealots with Islamic backgrounds. Similarly, Islamic law is by no means the same thing as jihad (Islamic holy war) or Islamic fundamentalism. Although Americans are now much better informed about the concept of Islamic law than they were in the past, some may not be aware that various interpretations of Islam still form the basis of laws in many countries and that the entire legal systems of some nations are based on Islamic principles.

■ **lecture note**   Introduce the concept of Islamic law (*Shari'ah*). Describe *Hudud* offenses as crimes against God and *Tazir* offenses as crimes against society. Describe how the Western distinction between *mala in se* offenses and *mala prohibita* offenses parallels the Islamic offense categories.

■ **Islamic law**   A system of laws, operative in some Arab countries, based on the Muslim religion and especially the holy book of Islam, the Koran.

■ **lecture note**   Compare and contrast the structure and process of Islamic courts to those of the United States. Point out the differential treatment of men and women and the strict limits placed on appeals.

■ ***Hudud* crime**   A serious violation of Islamic law that is regarded as an offense against God. *Hudud* crimes include such behavior as theft, adultery, sodomy, alcohol consumption, and robbery.

Islamic law holds considerable sway in a large number of countries, including Syria, Iran, Iraq (where a new constitution was voted on and approved in 2005), Pakistan, Afghanistan, Yemen, Saudi Arabia, Kuwait, the United Arab Emirates, Bahrain, Algeria, Jordan, Lebanon, Libya, Ethiopia, Gambia, Nigeria, Oman, Qatar, Senegal, Tunisia, Tajikistan, Uzbekistan, and Turkey (which practices official separation of church and state).

Islamic law descends directly from the teachings of the Prophet Muhammad, whom the *Cambridge Encyclopedia of Islam* describes as a "prophet-lawyer."[13] Muhammad rose to fame in the city of Mecca (in what is now Saudi Arabia) as a religious reformer. Later, however, he traveled to Medina, where he became the ruler and lawgiver of a newly formed religious society. In his role as lawgiver, Muhammad enacted legislation whose aim was to teach men what to do and how to behave in order to achieve salvation. As a consequence, Islamic law today is a system of duties and rituals founded on legal and moral obligations—all of which are ultimately sanctioned by the authority of a religious leader (or leaders) who may issue commands (known as *fatwas* or *fatwahs*) that the faithful are bound to obey.

Criminal justice professor Sam Souryal and his coauthors describe four aspects of justice in Arab philosophy and religion. Islamic justice, they say, means the following:[14]

- A sacred trust, a duty imposed on humans to be discharged sincerely and honestly. As such, these authors say, "justice is the quality of being morally responsible and merciful in giving everyone his or her due."
- A mutual respect of one human being by another. From this perspective, a just society is one that offers equal respect for individuals through social arrangements made in the common interest of all members.
- An aspect of the social bond that holds society together and transforms it into a brotherhood in which everyone becomes a keeper of everyone else and each is held accountable for the welfare of all.
- A command from God. Whoever violates God's commands should be subject to strict punishments according to Islamic tradition and belief.
- "The third and fourth meanings of justice are probably the ones most commonly invoked in Islamic jurisprudence" and form the basis of criminal justice practice in many Middle Eastern countries.

Saudi Arabian blogger Raif Badawi. In 2015 Badawi was sentenced by an Islamic court to receive 1,000 lashes for criticizing the country's clerics. His punishment was to include 20 weekly sets of 50 lashes and a quarter-million dollar fine. The teachings of Islam underpins the legal systems of many nations in the Middle East and elsewhere. What kinds of offenses does it prohibit? What punishments does it specify?

© Jenny Matthews/Alamy

The *Hudud* Crimes

Islamic law forms the basis of theocratic judicial systems in Kuwait, Saudi Arabia, the Sudan, Iran, and Algeria. Other Arabic nations, such as Egypt, Syria, and Jordan, recognize substantial elements of Islamic law in their criminal justice systems but also make wide use of Western and nontheocratic legal principles. Islamic law is based on four sources. In order of importance, these sources are (1) the Koran (also spelled *Quran* and *Qur'an*), or Holy Book of Islam, which Muslims believe is the word of God, or Allah; (2) the teachings of the Prophet Muhammad; (3) a consensus of the clergy in cases where neither the Koran nor the prophet directly addresses an issue; and (4) reason or logic, which should be used when no solution can be found in the other three sources.[15]

Islamic law is sometimes also referred to as *Sharia* law (or *Shari'ah* in Arabic). The Arabic word *Sharia* means "path of God" and can be more fully described as "a process through which Muslim scholars and jurists determine God's will and moral guidance as they apply to every aspect of a Muslim's life."[16]

Islamic law recognizes seven **Hudud crimes**—or crimes based on religious strictures. *Hudud* (sometimes called *Hodood* or *Huddud*) crimes are essentially violations of "natural law" as interpreted by Arab culture. Divine displeasure is thought to be the basis of crimes defined as *Hudud*, and *Hudud* crimes are often said to be crimes against God (or, more specifically, God's rights). The Koran specifies punishments for four of the seven *Hudud* crimes: (1) making war on Allah and His messengers, (2) theft, (3) adultery or fornication, and (4) false accusation of fornication or adultery. The three other *Hudud* offenses are mentioned by the Koran, but no punishment is specified: (1) "corruption on earth," (2) drinking alcohol, and (3) highway robbery—and the punishments for these crimes are determined by tradition.[17] The *Hudud* offenses and associated typical punishments are shown in Table 17-1. "Corruption on earth" is a general category of religious offense, not well understood in the West, that includes activities such as embezzlement, revolution against lawful authority, fraud, and "weakening the society of God." In 2011, for example, American pastor Terry Jones was sentenced to death by an Egyptian court for his role in burning the Koran shown in an anti-Islamic film.[18] Jones, the head of the Dove World Outreach church in Florida, was tried and sentenced in absentia, but authorities have warned that he could be executed if he ever sets foot in to Egypt.

Islamic law mandates strict punishment of moral failure. Sexual offenders, even those who engage in what would be considered essentially victimless crimes in Western societies, are subject to especially harsh treatment. The Islamic penalty for sexual intercourse outside of marriage, for example, is 100 lashes. Men are stripped to the waist, women have their clothes bound tightly, and flogging is carried out with a leather whip. Adultery carries a much more severe penalty: flogging and stoning to death.

> The Islamic penalty for sexual intercourse outside of marriage is 100 lashes; adultery carries a much more severe penalty: flogging and stoning to death.

Under Islamic law, even property crimes are firmly punished. Thieves who are undeterred by less serious punishments may eventually suffer amputation of the right hand. In a reputedly humane move, Iranian officials recently began to use an electric guillotine, specially made for the purpose, which can sever a hand at the wrist in one-tenth of a second. For amputation to be imposed, the item stolen must have value in Islam. Pork and alcohol, for example, are regarded as being without value, and their theft is not subject to punishment. Islamic legal codes also establish a minimum value for stolen items that could result in a sentence of amputation. Likewise, offenders who have stolen because they are hungry or are in need are exempt from the punishment of amputation and receive fines or prison terms.

Slander and the consumption of alcohol are both punished by 80 lashes. Legal codes in strict Islamic nations also specify whipping for the crimes of pimping, lesbianism, kissing by an unmarried couple, cursing, and failure of a woman to wear a veil. Islamic law provides for the execution, sometimes through crucifixion, of robbers. Laws stipulate that

TABLE 17-1 | Crime and Punishment in Islamic Law

Islamic law looks to the Koran and to the teachings of the Prophet Muhammad to determine which acts should be classified as crimes. The Koran and tradition specify punishments to be applied to designated offenses, as the following verse from the Koran demonstrates: "The only reward of those who make war upon Allah and His messenger and strive after corruption in the land will be that they will be killed or crucified, or have their hands and feet on alternate sides cut off, or will be expelled out of the land" (*Surah* V, Verse 33). Other crimes and punishments include the following:

OFFENSE	PUNISHMENT
Theft	Amputation of the hand
Adultery	Stoning to death
Fornication	One hundred lashes
False accusation (of fornication or adultery)	Eighty lashes
Corruption on earth	Death by the sword or by burning
Drinking alcohol	Eighty lashes; death if repeated three times
Robbery	Cutting off of hands and feet on alternate sides, exile, or execution

Sources: For more information, see Sam S. Souryal, Dennis W. Potts, and Abdullah I. Alobied, "The Penalty of Hand Amputation for Theft in Islamic Justice," *Journal of Criminal Justice*, Vol. 22, No. 3 (1994), pp. 249–265; and Parviz Saney, "Iran," in Elmer H. Johnson, ed., *International Handbook of Contemporary Developments in Criminology* (Westport, CT: Greenwood Press, 1983), pp. 356–369.

■ *Tazir* **crime**   A minor violation of Islamic law that is regarded as an offense against society, not God.

anyone who survives three days on the cross may be spared. Depending on the circumstances of the robbery, however, the offender may suffer the amputation of opposite hands and feet or may be exiled.

Rebellion, or revolt against a legitimate political leader or established economic order, which is considered an aspect of "corruption on earth," is punishable by death. The offender may be killed outright in a military or police action or, later, by sentence of the court. The last of the *Hudud* crimes is rejection of Islam. The penalty, once again, is death and can be imposed for denying the existence of God or angels, denying any of the prophets of Islam, or rejecting any part of the Koran.

Souryal and coauthors observe that *Hudud* crimes can be severely punished because "punishment serves a three-tiered obligation: (1) the fulfillment of worship, (2) the purification of society, and (3) the redemption of the individual." However, they add, the interests of the individual are the least valuable component of this triad and may have to be sacrificed "for the wholesomeness and integrity of the encompassing justice system."[19]

The *Tazir* Crimes

All crimes other than *Hudud* crimes fall into an offense category called *tazirat*. **Tazir** crimes are regarded as any actions not considered acceptable in a spiritual society. They include crimes against society and against individuals, but not against God. *Tazir* crimes may call for *quesas* (retribution) or *diya* (compensation or fines). Crimes requiring *quesas* are based on the Arabic principle of "an eye for an eye" and generally require physical punishments up to and including death. *Quesas* offenses may include murder, manslaughter, assault, and maiming. Under Islamic law, such crimes may require the victim or his representative to serve as prosecutor. The state plays a role only in providing the forum for the trial and in imposing punishment. Sometimes victims' representatives dole out punishment. In 1997, for example, 28-year-old taxi driver Ali Reza Khoshruy, nicknamed "The Vampire" because he stalked, raped, and killed women at night after picking them up in his cab, was hung from a yellow crane in the middle of Tehran, the Iranian capital.[20] Before the hanging, prison officials and male relatives of the victims cursed Khoshruy and whipped him with thick leather belts as he lay tied to a metal bed. The whipping was part of a 214-lash sentence.

Unlike statutory law in the West, Islamic law is not codified—meaning that judges are empowered to interpret the law based on their readings of the holy texts, precedent, and their own personal judgment. In some countries governed by Sharia law, however, the law of criminal procedure can be found in written form, similar to its counterpart in the West.

Islamic Courts

Islamic courts typically exist on three levels.[21] The first level hears cases involving the potential for serious punishments, including death, amputation, and exile. The second level deals with relatively minor matters, such as traffic offenses and violations of city ordinances. Special courts, especially in Iran, may hear cases involving crimes against the government, narcotics offenses, state security, and corruption. Appeals within the Islamic court system are only possible under rare circumstances and are by no means routine. A decision rendered by second-level courts will generally stand without intervention by higher judicial authorities.

Under Islamic law, men and women are treated very differently. Testimony provided by a man, for example, can be heard in court. The same evidence, however, can be provided only by two virtuous women; one female witness is not sufficient.

Although Islamic law may seem archaic or even barbaric to many Westerners, Islamic officials defend their system by pointing to low crime rates at home and by pointing to what they consider near anarchy in Western nations. An early criticism of Islamic law, however, was offered by Max Weber at the start of the twentieth century.[22] Weber said that Islamic justice is based more on the moral conceptions of individual judges than on any rational and predictable code of laws. He found that the personality of each judge, what he called "charisma," was more important in reaching a final legal result than was the written law. Weber's conclusion was that a modern society could not develop under Islamic law because enforcement of the law was too unpredictable. Complex social organizations, he argued, could only be based on a rational and codified law that is relatively unchanging from place to place and over time.[23]

More recent observers have agreed that "Islamic justice is based on philosophical principles that are considered alien, if not unconscionable, to the Western observer." However, these same writers note, strict punishments such as hand amputation "may not be inconsistent with the fundamentals of natural law or Judeo-Christian doctrine. The imposition of the penalty in

> Weber said that Islamic justice is based more on the moral conceptions of individual judges than on any rational and predictable code of laws.

specific cases and under rigorous rules of evidence—as the principle requires—may be indeed justifiable, and even necessary, in the Islamic context of sustaining a spiritual...society."[24]

International Criminal Justice Organizations

The first international conference on criminology and criminal justice met in London in 1872.[25] It evolved out of emerging humanitarian concerns about the treatment of prisoners. Human rights, the elimination of corporal punishment, and debates over capital punishment occupied the conference participants. Although other meetings were held from time to time, little agreement could be reached among the international community on criminal etiology, justice paradigms, or the philosophical and practical bases for criminal punishment and rehabilitation. Finally, in 1938, the International Society for Criminology (ISC) was formed to bring together people from diverse cultural backgrounds who shared an interest in social policies relating to crime and justice. In its early years, membership in the ISC consisted mostly of national officials and academics with close government ties.[26] As a consequence, many of the first conferences (called *international congresses*) sponsored by the ISC strongly supported the status quo and were devoid of any significant recommendations for change or growth.

Throughout the 1960s and 1970s, the ISC was strongly influenced by a growing worldwide awareness of human rights. About the same time, a number of international organizations began to press for an understanding of the political and legal processes through which deviance and crime come to be defined. Among them were the Scandinavian Research Council for Criminology (formed in 1962), the Criminological Research Council (created in 1962 by the Council of Europe), and other regional associations concerned with justice issues.

Many contemporary organizations and publications continue to focus world attention on criminal justice issues. Perhaps the best-known modern center for the academic study of cross-national criminal justice is the International Center of Comparative Criminology at the University of Montreal. Established in 1969, the center serves as a locus of study for criminal justice professionals from around the world and maintains an excellent library of international criminal justice information. The International Police Executive Symposium (IPES) was founded in 1994 to bring international police researchers and practitioners together and to facilitate cross-cultural and

international exchanges between criminal justice experts around the world. A number of journals publish content covering international issues in criminal justice, including the *International Journal for Crime, Justice and Social Democracy*, and the *International Journal of Law, Crime and Justice*.

The UN Crime and Justice Information Network (UNCJIN) holds much promise as an online provider of international criminal justice information. Visit the UNCJIN via **http://www.uncjin .org.** Finally, the UN Center for International Crime Prevention, in conjunction with the World Society of Victimology, sponsors the International Victimology website, available at http:**//www .worldsocietyofvictimology.org.**

The Role of the United Nations in Criminal Justice

The United Nations, composed of 185 member states and based in New York City, is the largest and most inclusive international body in the world. From its inception in 1945, the UN has been very interested in international crime prevention and world criminal justice systems. A UN resolution titled the International Bill of Human Rights supports the rights and dignity of everyone who comes into contact with a criminal justice system.

One of the best-known specific UN recommendations on criminal justice is its Standard Minimum Rules for the Treatment of Prisoners. The rules call for the fair treatment of prisoners, including recognition of the basic humanity of all inmates, and set specific standards for housing, nutrition, exercise, and medical care. Follow-up surveys conducted by the UN have shown that the rules have had a considerable influence on national legislation and prison regulations throughout the world.[27] Although the rules do not have the weight of law unless adopted and enacted into local legislation, they carry the strong weight of tradition, and at least one expert claims that "there are indeed those who argue that the rules have entered the *corpus* of generally customary human rights law, or that they are binding...as an authoritative interpretation of the human rights provisions of the UN charter."[28]

A more recent and potentially significant set of recommendations can be found in the UN Code of Conduct for Law Enforcement Officials. The code calls on law enforcement officers throughout the world to be cognizant of human rights in the performance of their duties. It specifically proscribes the use of torture and other abuses.

The UN World Crime Surveys, which report official crime statistics from nearly 100 countries, provide a global portrait of criminal activity. Seen historically, the surveys have shown that

■ **International Criminal Police Organization (Interpol)**   An international law enforcement support organization that began operations in 1946 and today has 190 member nations.

crimes against property are most characteristic of nations with developed economies (where they constitute approximately 82% of all reported crime), whereas crimes against the person occur much more frequently in developing countries (where they account for 43% of all crime).[29] Complementing the official statistics of the World Crime Surveys are data from the International Crime Victim Survey (ICVS), which is conducted in approximately 50 countries. To date, twelve surveys have been conducted—beginning in 1989.

Through its Office for Drug Control and Crime Prevention (UNDOC), the UN continues to advance the cause of crime prevention and to disseminate useful criminal justice information. The program provides forums for ongoing discussions of justice practices around the world. It has regional links throughout the world, sponsored by supportive national governments that have agreed to fund the program's work. The European Institute for Crime Prevention and Control (HEUNI), for example, provides the program's regional European link in a network of institutes operating throughout the world. Other network components include the UN Interregional Crime and Justice Research Institute (UNICRI) in Rome; an Asian regional institute (UNAFEI) in Tokyo; ILANUE, based in San Jose, Costa Rica, which focuses on crime problems in Latin America and the Caribbean; an African institute (UNAFRI) in Kampala, Uganda; Australia's AIC in Canberra; an Arabic institute (ASSTC) in Riyadh, Saudi Arabia; and other centers in Siracusa, Italy, and in Vancouver and Montreal, Canada.[30] Visit the UN Office for Drug Control and Crime Prevention via **http://www.unodc.org.**

In 1995, the United States signed an agreement with the UN Crime Prevention and Criminal Justice Branch that is intended to facilitate the international sharing of information and research findings.[31] Under the agreement, the National Institute of Justice joined 11 other criminal justice research organizations throughout the world as an associate UN institute.

Continuing a tradition begun in 1885 by the former International Penal and Penitentiary Commission, the UN holds an international congress on crime every five years. The first UN crime congress, the 1955 Congress on the Prevention of Crime and the Treatment of Offenders, met in Geneva, Switzerland. Crime congresses provide a forum through which member states can exchange information and experiences, compare criminal justice practices between countries, find solutions to crime, and take action at an international level. The 13th UN crime congress was held in Qatar in 2015. That meeting focused on developing strategies to promote the rule of law at national and international levels. A summary of declarations that were agreed upon at the 13th Congress can be read at **https://www.unodc. org/unodc/en/crime-congress/13-crime-congress.html.**

UN Crime Congresses frequently encourage international enforcement of the UN Protocol to Prevent, Suppress and Punish Trafficking in Persons, which was created in 2000, and supplements the UN Convention against Transnational Organized Crime (TOC).[32] Nations that are parties to the protocol must criminalize the offense of human trafficking, prevent trafficking, protect and assist victims of trafficking, and promote international cooperation to combat the problem of trafficking.[33] The UN reports that by 2008, 63% of the 155 countries that responded to a survey had adopted a statute specifically criminalizing trafficking in persons at least for the purposes of sexual exploitation and forced labor (Figure 17-1). Seventeen percent of responding countries said that they had a less-specific law that could be applied to trafficking in persons. Twenty percent of the countries covered, however, did not have a specific offense of trafficking in persons in their legislation. Read the U.S. Department of State's 2014 *Trafficking in Persons Report* at **http://www.state.gov/j/tip/rls/tiprpt/2014/index.htm.**

Interpol and Europol

The **International Criminal Police Organization (Interpol),** headquartered in Lyons, France, traces its origins back to the first International Criminal Police Congress of 1914, which met in Monaco.[34] The theme of that meeting was international cooperation in the investigation of crimes and the apprehension of fugitives. Interpol, however, did not officially begin operations until 1946, when the end of World War II brought about a new spirit of international harmony.

Today, 190 nations belong to Interpol.[35] The U.S. Interpol unit is called the U.S. National Central Bureau (USNCB) and

Young Vietnamese prostitutes detained by Cambodian police during a brothel raid in Phnom Penh. The 2003 federal Trafficking Victims Protection Reauthorization Act focuses on the illegal practice of sex trafficking and on the illegal "obtaining of a person for labor services." How common is human trafficking? In what parts of the world is it most prevalent?

Gary Way/Getty Images

■ **lecture note** Describe the theme of international police cooperation that characterizes Interpol. Ask what role students envision for Interpol in the twenty-first century.

■ **theme** What is Europol? Why was it established and what is its mission? What is its relationship with Interpol?

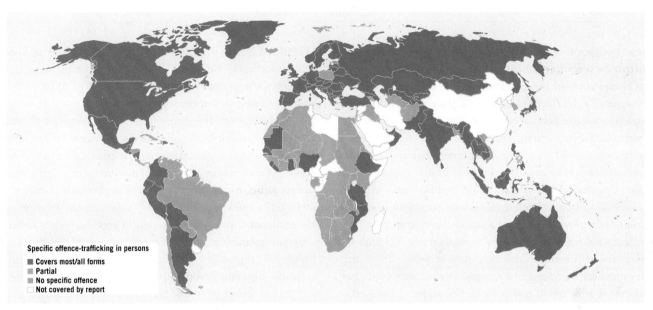

FIGURE 17-1 | Trafficking in Persons: Status of National Legislation, by Country
Source: United Nations Office on Drugs and Crime.

is a separate agency within the U.S. Department of Justice. USNCB is staffed with personnel from 12 federal agencies, including the Drug Enforcement Administration, the Secret Service, and the Federal Bureau of Investigation (FBI). Through the USNCB, Interpol is linked to all major U.S. computerized criminal records repositories, including the FBI's National Crime Information Index, the State Department's Advanced Visa Lookout System, and the Department of Homeland Security's Master Index.

Interpol's primary purpose is to act as a clearinghouse for information on offenses and suspects who are believed to operate across national boundaries. The organization is committed to promoting "the widest possible mutual assistance between all criminal police authorities within the limits of laws existing in…different countries and in the spirit of the Universal Declaration of Human Rights."[36] Historically, Interpol pledged itself not to intervene in religious, political, military, or racial disagreements in participant nations. As a consequence, numerous bombings and hostage situations that were related to these types of disagreements were not officially investigated until 1984, when Interpol officially entered the fight against international terrorism.

At Interpol's Eighty-Third General Assembly, held in Monaco in 2014, senior law enforcement officials from around the world discussed critical challenges facing police agencies in responding to current and developing criminal phenomena, and shared best practices based on national and international experience.[37] Today, Interpol continues to expand its activities. It is

The entrance hall of Interpol headquarters in Lyon, France. What does Interpol do?

in the process of developing a centralized international forensic DNA database and is creating an international framework for disaster victim identification.[38]

Interpol does not have its own field investigators. The agency has no powers of arrest or of search and seizure in member countries. Instead, Interpol's purpose is to facilitate, coordinate, and encourage police cooperation as a means of combating international crime. It draws on the willingness of local and national police forces to lend support to its activities. The headquarters staff of Interpol consists of about 250 individuals, many with prior police experience, who direct data-gathering efforts around the world and who serve to alert law enforcement organizations to the movement of suspected

■ **European Police Office (Europol)**   The integrated police intelligence-gathering and dissemination arm of the member nations of the European Union.

offenders within their jurisdiction. Visit Interpol headquarters via **http://www.interpol.int.**

The members of the European Union (EU) agreed to the establishment of the **European Police Office (Europol)** in the Maastricht Treaty of February 7, 1992. Based in The Hague, the Netherlands, Europol started limited operations in 1994 in the form of the Europol Drugs Unit. Over time, other important law enforcement activities were added to the Europol agenda. The Europol Convention was ratified by all member states in 1998, and Europol commenced full operations the next year. Europol's mission is to improve the effectiveness and cooperation of law enforcement agencies within the member states of the EU with the ultimate goal of preventing and combating terrorism, illegal drug trafficking, illicit trafficking in radioactive and nuclear substances, illegal money laundering, trafficking in human beings, and other serious forms of international organized crime. Europol is sometimes described as the "European Union police clearing house."[39] In 2013, the European Commission established a European Cybercrime Center (EC3) at Europol. The center has become the focal point in the European Union's fight against cybercrime.[40]

Europol and Interpol work together to develop information on international terrorism, drug trafficking, and trafficking in human beings.[41] Visit Europol on the Web at **http://www .europol.europa.eu.**

The International Criminal Court

On April 12, 2000, the International Criminal Court (ICC) was created under the auspices of the United Nations. The ICC is intended to be a permanent criminal court for trying individuals (not countries) who commit the most serious crimes of concern to the international community, such as genocide, war crimes, and crimes against humanity—including the wholesale murder of civilians, torture, and mass rape. The goal of the ICC is to be a global judicial institution with international jurisdiction complementing national legal systems around the world. Support for the ICC was developed through the UN, where more than 70 countries approved the court's creation by ratifying the Rome Statute of the International Criminal Court.

> The goal of the International Criminal Court is to be a global judicial institution with international jurisdiction complementing national legal systems around the world.

By 2015, 123 countries had ratified the statute, and another 16 were considering doing so.[42] The ICC's first prosecutor, Luis Moreno Ocampo of Argentina, was elected in April 2003, and was still serving in that capacity in 2015.[43]

The ICC initiative began after World War II, with unsuccessful efforts to establish an international tribunal to try individuals accused of genocide and other war crimes.[44] In lieu of such a court, military tribunals were held in Nuremberg, Germany, and Tokyo, Japan, to try those accused of war crimes. Although the 1948 UN Genocide Convention[45] called for the creation of an international criminal court to punish genocide-related offenses, efforts to establish a permanent court were delayed for decades by the cold war and by the refusal of some national governments to accept the court's proposed international legal jurisdiction.

In December 1948, the UN General Assembly adopted the Universal Declaration of Human Rights and the Convention on the Prevention and Punishment of the Crime of Genocide. It also called for criminals to be tried "by such international penal tribunals as may have jurisdiction." A number of member states soon asked the UN International Law Commission (ILC) to study the possibility of establishing an international criminal court.

Development of the ICC was delayed by the cold war that took place between the world's superpowers, which were not willing to subject their military personnel or commanders to international criminal jurisdiction in the event of a "hot" war. In 1981, however, the UN General Assembly asked the International Law Commission to consider creating an international Code of Crimes.

The 1992 war in Bosnia-Herzegovina, which involved clear violations of the Genocide and Geneva Conventions, heightened world interest in the establishment of a permanent ICC. A few years later, 160 countries participated in the Conference of Plenipotentiaries on the Establishment of an International Criminal Court,[46] which was held in Rome. At the end of that conference, member states voted overwhelmingly in favor of the Rome Statute,[47] calling for establishment of an ICC.

> In 2012, in the first verdict ever reached by the ICC, judges found Thomas Lubanga, a rebel leader in eastern Congo, guilty of conscripting child soldiers.

In 2012, in the first verdict ever reached by the ICC, judges found Thomas Lubanga, a rebel leader in eastern Congo, guilty of conscripting child soldiers.[48] His conviction was upheld by appeals judges at the ICC in 2014.[49] Learn more about this case and other activities of the

■ **globalization** The internationalization of trade, services, investment, information, and other forms of human social activity.

Iain Masterton/Alamy

The International Criminal Court (ICC) in the Hague, Netherlands. What is the jurisdiction of the ICC?

ICC by visiting the Coalition for an International Criminal Court via **http://www.iccnow.org.**

Before the ICC came into existence, Belgium made its courts available to the rest of the world for the prosecution of alleged crimes against humanity.[50] The country's legal system, in essence, took on the role of global prosecutor for these kinds of crimes. Under a 1993 Belgian law, which is regarded by many as the world's most expansive statute against genocide and other crimes against humanity, Belgian justices were called on to enforce substantial portions of the country's criminal laws on a global scale. Belgian courts also focused on enforcing the 1949 Geneva Convention governing the conduct of war and the treatment of refugees. Belgian law specifically provides for the criminal prosecution of individuals who are not Belgian citizens, and it provides no immunity to prosecution for foreign leaders. In 2001, for example, a Brussels jury convicted four people, including two Catholic nuns, of contributing to ethnic violence in the central African nation of Rwanda in 1994.

Belgian authorities have investigated more than a dozen complaints involving current and former state officials, including Ariel Sharon (former prime minister of Israel), Saddam Hussein (former Iraqi leader), Hissene Habre (former dictator of Chad), Hashemi Rafsanjani (former president of Iran), Driss Basri (former interior minister of Morocco), Denis Sassou Nguesso (president of Congo-Brazzaville), and Fidel Castro (former leader of Cuba). In the case of the Cuban leader, Cuban exiles charged Castro in Brussels's criminal court in October 2001 with false imprisonment, murder, torture, and other crimes against humanity. As a result of such investigations, Belgium has experienced strained relationships with a number of countries, and

some in the nation have questioned the wisdom of charging sitting heads of state with violations of the criminal law.

Globalization and Crime

Globalization refers to the internationalization of trade, services, investments, information, and other forms of human social activity, including crime. The process of globalization is fed by modern systems of transportation and communication, including air travel, television, and the Internet. Globalization contributes to growing similarities in the way people do things and in the beliefs and values that they hold. The lessening of differences brought about by globalization is highlighted by a definition from one authoritative source, which says that globalization is "a process of social homogenization by which the experiences of everyday life, marked by the diffusion of commodities and ideas, can foster a standardization of cultural expressions around the world."[51] The adoption of English as the *de facto* standard language on the Internet and of the global software community, for example, has exposed many around the world to literature and ideas that they might not otherwise have encountered and has influenced the way they think. Consequently, globalization is opposed in many parts of the world by those who would hold to traditional ways of thinking and acting. Instead of inevitably uniting humanity, as some had hoped, globalization has also made people aware of differences—and has led many people to reject cultures and ideas dissimilar to their own.

> Instead of inevitably uniting humanity, globalization has also made people aware of differences—and has led many people to reject cultures and ideas dissimilar to their own.

The first steps toward globalization occurred long before the modern era and were taken by nation-states seeking to expand their spheres of influence. The banner of globalization today is carried by multinational corporations whose operations span the globe. The synergistic effects of rapid travel, instantaneous communication, and national economies that are tied closely to one another have led to an increasingly rapid pace of the globalization process, which some refer to as *hyperglobalization*. Criminal entrepreneurs and terrorists are among those with a global vision, and at least some of them think and plan like the CEOs of multinational businesses. Today's international criminal community consists of terrorists, drug traffickers, pornography

■ **lecture note** Explain transnational organized crime as crime involving organized criminal groups that operate across national boundaries. Review the conditions that the UN has identified to determine if a crime can be considered transnational in nature. Link transnational organized crime and these international criminal groups to the concept of globalization.

■ **transnational organized crime** Unlawful activity undertaken and supported by organized criminal groups operating across national boundaries.

■ **lecture note** Explain some of the forms of transnational organized crime and explain the threat they may pose to the security of multiple countries around the world.

■ **extradition** The surrender by one state or jurisdiction to another of an individual accused or convicted of an offense in the second state or jurisdiction.

peddlers, identity thieves, copyright violators, and those who traffic in human beings, body parts, genetic material, and military weapons.

Transnational Organized Crime

In 2006, Cheng Chui Ping, known to her associates as the Snakehead Queen, was sentenced in U.S. District Court to 35 years in prison for having smuggled as many as 3,000 illegal immigrants into the United States from her native China. "Snakeheads" are human smugglers, and, prior to her arrest, Ping may have been the most active human smuggler in New York City. Her fees, which were partially determined by an immigrant's ability to pay, ranged up to $40,000 per person, and the FBI says that her illegal transnational activities may have netted her as much as $40 million.[52]

Transnational Organized Crime and the internationally organized criminal groups that support it are partly the result of an ongoing process of globalization. Transnational crime is unlawful activity undertaken and supported by organized criminal groups operating across national boundaries, and it promises to become one of the most pressing challenges of the twenty-first century for criminal justice professionals. In a recent conference in Seoul, Korea, then-U.S. Attorney General Laurie Robinson addressed the issue of transnational crime, saying, "The United States recognizes that we cannot confront crime in isolation.... It is clear crime does not respect international boundaries. It is clear crime is global. As recent economic trends demonstrate, what happens in one part of the world impacts all the rest. And crime problems and trends are no different."[53]

According to the United Nations, an offense can be considered transnational in nature if any of the following conditions are met:[54]

1. It is committed in more than one country.
2. It is committed in one country but a substantial part of its preparation, planning, direction, or control takes place in another country.
3. It is committed in one country but involves an organized criminal group that engages in criminal activities in more than one country.
4. It is committed in one country but has substantial effects in another country.

Transnational organized crime comes in many forms, including drug trafficking, money laundering, terrorism, alien smuggling, trafficking in weapons of mass destruction, human trafficking, fraud, and corrupt practices by government officials who have been paid by criminal organizations for their cooperation. Transnational organized crime threatens the national security of all countries; and some international criminal organizations work to replace legitimate governments with their own actors who can be manipulated through bribery and intimidation.[55]

The National Institute of Justice (NIJ) says that transnational crime groups have profited more from globalization than have legitimate businesses, which are subject to domestic and host country laws and regulations. The NIJ points out that transnational crime syndicates and networks, abetted by official corruption, blackmail, and intimidation, can use open markets and open societies to their full advantage.[56]

Worse still, entire nations may become rogue countries, or quasi-criminal regimes where criminal activity runs rampant and wields considerable influence over the national government (Figure 17-2). Russia, for example, may be approaching this status through an intertwining of the goals of organized criminal groups and official interests that run to the top levels of government. The number of organized criminal groups operating in Russia is estimated to be more than 12,000.[57] Emilio Viano, professor of criminology at American University and an expert on Russian organized crime, notes that "what we have is an immense country practically controlled by organized crime. These groups are getting stronger and stronger and using Russia as a base for their global ventures—taking over everything from drugs and prostitution to currency exchange and stealing World Bank and IMF [International Monetary Fund] loans."[58] Not long ago, for example, Russian organized crime hit men shot and killed Andrei Kozlov, the top deputy chairman of the Russian Central Bank.[59] Kozlov, who was gunned down as he left a soccer match in Moscow, had worked for four years to fight criminality and money laundering in Russia's banking system in an effort to draw foreign investments into the country.

One tool in the fight against transnational crime is **extradition.** Not all countries, however, are willing to extradite suspects wanted in the United States. Consequently, as Kevin Ryan of Vermont's Norwich University observes, "The globalization of United States law enforcement policy has also entailed the

> The number of organized criminal groups operating in Russia is estimated to be more than 12,000.

■ **sex trafficking** The recruitment, harboring, transportation, provision, or obtaining of a person for the purpose of a commercial sex act.

■ **lecture note** Suggest that the idea of terrorism centers on the commission of crimes (usually acts of violence) for political or ideological ends. Ask students whether they would expand that definition. Ask whether they believe that acts of terrorism will increase in frequency throughout the remainder of this century.

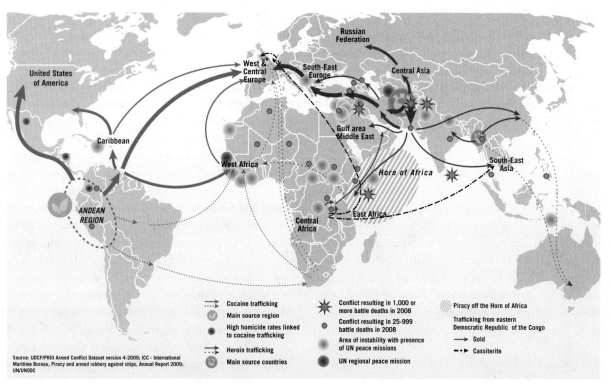

FIGURE 17-2 | Transnational Organized Crime and Political Instability
Source: United Nations Office on Drugs and Crime.

abduction of fugitives from abroad to stand trial when an asylum nation refuses an extradition request."[60] Although certainly not a common practice, the forcible removal of criminal suspects from foreign jurisdictions appears more likely with suspected terrorists than with other types of criminals. A special report on transnational organized crime and its impact on the United States is available at **http://justicestudies.com/pubs/toc.pdf.**

Human Smuggling and Trafficking

The recent globalization of crime and terrorism, which is sometimes called the *globalization of insecurity*, has necessitated enhanced coordination of law enforcement efforts in different parts of the world as well as the expansion of American law enforcement activities beyond national borders. In 2000, for example, the U.S. Congress passed the Trafficking Victims Protection Act (TVPA).[61] Trafficking offenses under the law, which is aimed primarily at international offenders, include (1) **sex trafficking,** in which a commercial sex act is induced by force, fraud, or coercion or in which the person induced to perform such act has not attained 18

years of age;[62] and (2) the recruitment, harboring, transportation, provision, or obtaining of a person for labor services, through the use of force, fraud, or coercion, for the purpose of subjection to involuntary servitude, peonage, debt bondage, or slavery. The TVPA also provides funds for training U.S. law enforcement personnel at international police academies, and U.S. police agencies routinely send agents to assist law enforcement officers in other countries who are involved in transnational investigations.

Under the TVPA, human trafficking does not require the crossing of an international border, nor does it even require the transportation of victims from one locale to another. That's because victims of severe forms of trafficking are not always illegal aliens; they may be U.S. citizens, legal residents, or visitors. Victims do not have to be women or children—they may also be adult males. The Trafficking Victims Protection Reauthorization Act (TVPRA) of 2003[63] added a new initiative to the original law to collect foreign data on trafficking investigations, prosecutions, convictions, and sentences. The TVPA was authorized again in 2005, 2008, and 2013.[64] Another piece of federal legislation, the Justice for Victims of Trafficking Act (JVTA) of 2015, enhanced criminal penalties for sex traffickers and made federal grant monies available to fight such crimes.

■ **human smuggling**   Illegal immigration in which an agent is paid to help a person cross a border clandestinely.
■ **trafficking in persons (TIP)**   The exploitation of unwilling or unwitting people through force, coercion, threat, or deception.

According to the United Nations,[65] trafficking in persons and human smuggling are some of the fastest-growing areas of international criminal activity today. There are important distinctions that must be made between these two forms of crime. Following federal law, the U.S. State Department defines **human smuggling** as "the facilitation, transportation, attempted transportation or illegal entry of a person(s) across an international border, in violation of one or more country's laws, either clandestinely or through deception, such as the use of fraudulent documents." In other words, human smuggling refers to illegal immigration in which an agent is paid to help a person cross a border clandestinely.[66] Human smuggling may be conducted to obtain financial or other benefits for the smuggler, although sometimes people engage in smuggling for other motives, such as to reunite their families. Human smuggling generally occurs with the consent of those being smuggled, and they often pay a smuggler for his or her services. Once in the country they've paid to enter, smuggled individuals rarely remain in contact with the smuggler. The State Department notes that the vast majority of people who are assisted in illegally entering the United States annually are smuggled, rather than trafficked.

Although smuggling might not involve active coercion, it can be deadly. In January 2007, for example, truck driver Tyrone Williams, 36, a Jamaican citizen living in Schenectady, New York, was sentenced to life in prison for causing the deaths of 19 illegal immigrants in the nation's deadliest known human smuggling attempt.[67] Williams locked more than 70 immigrants in a container truck during a 2003 trip from South Texas to Houston but abandoned the truck about 100 miles from its destination. The victims died from dehydration, overheating, and suffocation in the Texas heat before the truck was discovered and its doors opened.

In contrast to smuggling, **trafficking in persons (TIP)** can be compared to a modern-day form of slavery, prompting former Secretary of State Condoleezza Rice to say that "defeating human trafficking is a great moral calling of our day."[68] Trafficking involves the exploitation of unwilling or unwitting people through force, coercion, threat, or deception and includes human rights abuses such as debt bondage, deprivation of liberty, or lack of control over freedom and labor. Trafficking is often undertaken for purposes of sexual or labor exploitation.

U.S. government officials estimate that 800,000 to 900,000 victims are trafficked globally each year and that 17,500 to 18,500 are trafficked into the United States.[69] Women and children comprise the largest group of victims, and they are often physically and emotionally abused. Although TIP is often an international crime that involves the crossing of borders, it is important to note that TIP victims can be trafficked within their own countries and communities. Traffickers can move victims between locations within the same country and often sell them to other trafficking organizations.

The International Labor Organization, the UN agency charged with addressing labor standards, employment, and social protection issues, estimates that there are 12.3 million people in forced labor, bonded labor, forced child labor, and sexual servitude throughout the world today.[70] Other estimates range as high as 27 million.[71]

A recent study released by the National Institute of Justice found that the majority of human trafficking cases in the United States involve sex trafficking (85%), whereas a much smaller percentage of all investigated cases involve labor trafficking (11%).[72]

It is sometimes difficult to distinguish between smuggling and trafficking because trafficking often includes an element of smuggling (that is, the illegal crossing of a national border). Moreover, some trafficking victims may believe they are being smuggled when they are really being trafficked. This happens, for example, when women trafficked for sexual exploitation believe they are agreeing to work in legitimate industries for decent wages—part of which they may have agreed to pay to the trafficker who smuggled them. They don't know that upon arrival the traffickers would keep them in bondage, subject them to physical force or sexual violence, force them to work in the sex trade, and take most or all of their income. United Nations literature notes that Chinese syndicates are notorious for continuing to control the lives of migrants at their destination and that they discipline them by force and extract heavy payment for smuggling services—holding "their clients as virtual hostages until the fees have been paid."[73]

The U.S. Department of State's *Trafficking in Persons* report says that "human trafficking is a multi-dimensional threat. It deprives people of their human rights and freedoms, it increases global health risks, and it fuels the growth of organized crime."[74] At the individual level, the report notes, "human trafficking has a devastating impact on individual victims, who often suffer physical and emotional abuse, rape, threats against self and family, document theft, and even death."

The distinction between smuggling and trafficking is sometimes very subtle, but key components that generally distinguish trafficking from smuggling are the elements of fraud, force, or coercion. However, under U.S. law, if the person is under 18 and induced to perform a commercial sex act, then it is considered trafficking, regardless of whether fraud, force, or coercion is involved. Table 17-2 provides a guide to distinguishing human trafficking from smuggling.

■ **terrorism** A violent act or an act dangerous to human life, in violation of the criminal laws of the United States or of any state, that is committed to intimidate or coerce a government, the civilian population, or any segment thereof, in furtherance of political or social objectives.[i]

TABLE 17-2 | **Distinguishing between Human Trafficking and Smuggling**

TRAFFICKING	SMUGGLING
Must contain an element of force, fraud, or coercion (actual, perceived, or implied), unless victim under 18 years of age is involved in commercial sex acts.	The person being smuggled is generally cooperating.
Involves forced labor and/or exploitation.	Involves no forced labor or other exploitation.
Persons trafficked are victims.	Persons smuggled are violating the law. They are not victims.
Victims are enslaved, are subjected to limited movement or isolation, or have had documents confiscated.	Smuggled individuals are free to leave, change jobs, etc.
Need not involve the actual movement of the victim.	Facilitates the illegal entry of people from one country into another.
May or may not cross an international border.	Always crosses an international border.
Victim must be involved in labor/services or commercial sex acts (that is, must be "working").	Person must only be in country or attempting entry illegally.

Note: This table is meant to be conceptual and is not intended to provide precise legal distinctions between smuggling and trafficking.
Source: Adapted from U.S. Department of State, Bureau for International Narcotics and Law Enforcement Affairs, Human Smuggling and Trafficking Center, *Distinctions between Human Smuggling and Human Trafficking* (Washington, DC: January 1, 2005).

According to the United Nations, human smuggling and trafficking have become a worldwide industry that "employs" millions of people and leads to the annual turnover of billions of dollars.[75] The UN also says that many of the routes used by smugglers have become well established and are widely known. Routes from Mexico and Central America to the United States, for example; from West Asia through Greece and Turkey to Western Europe; and within East and Southeast Asia are regularly traveled. More often than not, the UN says, the ongoing existence of flourishing smuggling routes is facilitated by weak legislation, lax border controls, corrupt officials, and the power and influence of organized crime.

Although there are significant differences between TIP and human smuggling, the underlying conditions that give rise to both of these illegal activities are often similar. Extreme poverty, lack of economic opportunity, civil unrest, and political uncertainty are all factors that contribute to social environments in which human smuggling and trafficking in persons occurs.

Section 7202 of the Intelligence Reform and Terrorism Prevention Act of 2004 established the Human Smuggling and Trafficking Center within the U.S. State Department. The secretary of state, the secretary of homeland security, the attorney general, and members of the national intelligence community oversee the center. The center was created to achieve greater integration and overall effectiveness in the U.S. government's enforcement of issues related to human smuggling, trafficking in persons, and criminal support of clandestine terrorist travel. Visit the Human Smuggling and Trafficking Center via **http://www.state.gov/m/ds/hstcenter.** Learn more about the characteristics of suspected human trafficking incidents at **http://www.justicestudies.com/pubs/humtraffick.pdf,** and about human sex trafficking at **http://www.justicestudies.com/pubs/sextraffick.pdf.** Also, you can examine the 2013–2017 *Federal Strategic Action Plan on Services for Victims of Human Trafficking in the United States* at **http://www.justicestudies.com/pubs/antitrafficking_plan.pdf.**

Terrorism

Terrorism as a criminal activity and the prevention of further acts of terrorism became primary concerns of American political leaders and justice system officials following the September 11, 2001, terrorist attacks on the United States. There is, however, no single uniformly accepted definition of terrorism that is applicable to all places and all circumstances. Some definitions are statutory in nature, whereas others were created for such practical purposes as gauging success in the fight against terrorism. Still others relate to specific forms of terrorism, such as cyberterrorism (discussed later in this section), and many legislative sources speak only of "acts of terrorism" or "terrorist activity" rather than terrorism itself because the nature of Western jurisprudence is to legislate against acts rather than against concepts.

A widely accepted definition of the term can be found in the federal Foreign Relations Authorization Act,[76] which defines *terrorism* in terms of four primary elements. The Act says that terrorism is (1) premeditated, (2) politically motivated, (3) violent, (4) committed against noncombatant targets.[77] The FBI offers a nonstatutory working definition of terrorism as "a violent act or an act dangerous to human life in violation of the criminal laws of the United States or of any state to intimidate or coerce a government, the civilian population, or any segment thereof, in furtherance of political or

■ **theme** Examine Gwynn Nettler's characteristics of terrorism. How are terrorists like other criminals? How do they differ?

■ **lecture note** Describe the six characteristics of terrorism listed in the text. Use them to describe how acts of terrorism differ from acts of war.

■ **lecture note** Distinguish between domestic terrorism and international terrorism, and clarify the difference between international and foreign terrorism.

■ **lone wolf terrorist** A domestic terrorist who perpetrates political violence by acting alone; who does not belong to an organized terrorist group or network; who acts without the direct influence of a leader; and whose tactics and methods are self-directed.

CJ | ISSUES
Lone Wolf Terrorism and the Radicalization Process

In 2015, the U.S. Department of Justice released a report on lone wolf terrorism in America. **Lone wolf terrorists** are domestic terrorists who perpetrate political violence by acting alone; who do not belong to an organized terrorist group or network; who act without the direct influence of a leader; and whose tactics and methods are self-directed. Many, but not all, lone wolf terrorists are radicalized homegrown jihadists.

"Homegrown" is a term that describes terrorist activity or plots perpetrated within the United States or abroad by American citizens, legal permanent residents, or visitors radicalized largely within the United States. "Radicalization" describes the process of acquiring and holding extremist, or beliefs. The term "jihadist" describes radicalized individuals using Islam as an ideological and/or religious justification for their belief in the establishment of a global caliphate, or jurisdiction governed by a Muslim civil and religious leader known as a caliph.

The Justice Department report identified 45 lone wolves who committed 45 terrorist attacks in the United States between 2001 and 2013. Those attacks killed 55 people and injured another 126.

Individuals become lone wolf terrorists by radicalizing and then adopting violence as a tactic. Lone wolf terrorism generally begins with personal and political grievances which become the basis for an affinity with an extremist group. Group ideology is then adopted through a process of radicalization. Radicalization is not necessarily illegal because American law and values guarantee both free speech and free thought. Actions undertaken in violation of the law, however, are another matter. "Violent extremism" describes violent action taken on the basis of radical or extremist beliefs. In other words, when someone moves from simply believing in an ideology to illegally pursuing it via violent methods, he or she becomes a terrorist. Because the move from belief to violence is so individualized, there is no single path that individuals follow to become full-fledged terrorists.

Intermediaries, social networks, the Internet, and prisons have been cited as playing key roles in the radicalization process. Intermediaries—who are often charismatic individuals—frequently help persuade previously law-abiding citizens to radicalize. Social networks, virtual or actual, support and reinforce the decisions individuals make as they embrace violence, as does perusal of online materials. Although there has been much discussion regarding the powerful influence that online jihadist material may have on the formation of terrorists, no consensus has emerged regarding the Web and terrorism. Prisons, seen by some as potential hotbeds of radicalization, have not yet played a large role in producing homegrown jihadists.

To counter the plots of lone wolf terrorists U.S. law enforcement has employed at least one tactic that uses "agent provocateurs." In agent provocateur cases—often called sting operations—government undercover agents befriend suspects and offer to facilitate their activities. The use of these techniques has generated considerable public controversy and illustrates an issue facing law enforcement today. Enforcement agencies are expected to prevent homegrown terrorism, but their use of preemptive techniques spawns concern among community members and civil libertarians. In cases where sting operations are used, law enforcement officials must be careful to avoid enticing the terrorist plotter to engage in activities that he or she might not otherwise have undertaken. Should that happen, the plotter, if arrested and charged, might be acquitted under an entrapment defense (see Chapter 3).

Resource: Jerome P. Bjelopera, *American Jihadist Terrorism: Combating a Complex Threat* (Washington, DC: Congressional Research Service, 2013); and Mark Hamm and Ramon Spaaj, *Lone Wolf Terrorism in America* (Washington, DC: U.S. Dept. of Justice, 2015).

---

social objectives."[78] Among the laws that define certain forms of human *activity* as terrorism, the Immigration and Nationality Act provides one of the most comprehensive and widely used definitions. That definition is shown in the "CJ Issues" box.

According to criminologist Gwynn Nettler, all forms of terrorism share six characteristics:[79]

- *No rules.* There are no moral limitations on the type or degree of violence that terrorists can use.
- *No innocents.* No distinctions are made between soldiers and civilians. Children can be killed as well as adults.
- *Economy.* Kill one, frighten 10,000.
- *Publicity.* Terrorists seek publicity, and publicity encourages terrorism.

- *Meaning.* Terrorist acts give meaning and significance to the lives of terrorists.
- *No clarity.* Beyond the immediate aim of destructive acts, the long-term goals of terrorists are likely to be poorly conceived or impossible to implement.

Moreover, notes Nettler, "Terrorism that succeeds escalates."[80]

Types of Terrorism

It is important to distinguish between two major forms of terrorism: domestic and international. Distinctions between the two forms are made in terms of the origin, base of operations, and objectives of a terrorist organization. In the United States,

■ **domestic terrorism** The unlawful use of force or violence by an individual or a group that is based and operates entirely within the United States and its territories, acts without foreign direction, and directs its activities against elements of the U.S. government or population.[ii]

■ **lecture note** Highlight the growth of radical groups throughout America by pointing to the white supremacist and separatist organizations described in this chapter and in Chapter 2. Ask students whether they think such organizations will ever present a real threat to our nation's security.

domestic terrorism refers to the unlawful use of force or violence by an individual or a group that is based in and operates entirely within this country and its territories without foreign direction and whose acts are directed against elements of the U.S. government or population.[81] *International terrorism,* in contrast, is the unlawful use of force or violence by an individual or a group that has some connection to a foreign power, or whose activities transcend national boundaries, against people or property in order to intimidate or coerce a government, the civilian population, or any segment thereof, in furtherance of political or social objectives.[82] International terrorism is sometimes mistakenly called *foreign terrorism,* a term that, strictly speaking, refers only to acts of terrorism that occur outside of the United States. Another form of terrorism, cyberterrorism, can have a domestic or international origin and cuts across the two major categories discussed here. Narcoterrorism, which is defined and discussed later, is generally a form of international terrorism.

> It is important to distinguish between two major forms of terrorism: domestic and international.

Domestic Terrorism

Throughout the 1960s and 1970s, **domestic terrorism** in the United States required the expenditure of considerable criminal justice resources. The Weathermen, Students for a Democratic Society, the Symbionese Liberation Army, the Black Panthers, and other radical groups routinely challenged the authority of federal and local governments. Bombings, kidnappings, and shoot-outs peppered the national scene. As overt acts of domestic terrorism declined in frequency in the 1980s, international terrorism took their place. The war in Lebanon; terrorism in Israel; bombings in France, Italy, and Germany; and the many violent offshoots of the Iran-Iraq war and the first Gulf War occupied the attention of the media and of much of the rest of the world. Vigilance by the FBI, the Central Intelligence Agency (CIA), and other agencies largely prevented the spread of terrorism to the United States.

> Worrisome today are domestic underground survivalist and separatist groups and potentially violent special-interest groups, each with its own vision of a future America.

Worrisome today are domestic underground survivalist and separatist groups and potentially violent special-interest groups, each with its own vision of a future America. In 1993, for example, a confrontation between David Koresh's Branch Davidian followers and federal agents left 72 Davidians (including Koresh) and four federal agents dead in Waco, Texas.

Exactly two years to the day after the Davidian standoff ended in a horrific fire that destroyed the compound, a powerful truck bomb devastated the Alfred P. Murrah Federal Building in downtown Oklahoma City. One hundred sixty-eight people died, and hundreds more were wounded. The targeted nine-story building had housed offices of the Social Security Administration; the Drug Enforcement Administration; the Secret Service; the Bureau of Alcohol, Tobacco, Firearms and Explosives; and a day-care center called America's Kids. The fertilizer-and-diesel-fuel device used in the terrorist attack was estimated to have weighed about 1,200 pounds and had been left in a rental truck on the Fifth Street side of the building. The blast, which left a crater 30 feet wide and 8 feet deep and spread debris over a ten-block area, demonstrated just how vulnerable the United States is to terrorist attack.

In 1997, a federal jury found 29-year-old Timothy McVeigh guilty of 11 counts, ranging from conspiracy to first-degree murder, in the Oklahoma City bombing. Jurors concluded that McVeigh had conspired with Terry Nichols, a friend he had met in the U.S. Army, and with unknown others to destroy the Murrah Building. Prosecutors made clear their belief that the attack was intended to revenge the 1993 assault on the Branch Davidian compound. McVeigh was sentenced to death and was executed by lethal injection at the U.S. penitentiary in Terre Haute, Indiana, in 2001.[83] McVeigh was the first person under federal jurisdiction to be put to death since 1963. In 2004, Terry Nichols was convicted of 161 counts of first-degree murder by an Oklahoma jury and was sentenced to 161 life terms for his role in the bombings.[84] He had previously been convicted of various federal charges.

In 2005, 38-year-old Eric Robert Rudolph pleaded guilty to a string of bombing attacks in Alabama and Georgia, including a blast at Atlanta's Centennial Park during the 1996 Olympics in which one person died and 111 were injured.[85] Rudolph, an antiabortion and antigay extremist, was sentenced to life in prison without the possibility of parole after having eluded law enforcement officers for years.

Active fringe groups include the Sovereign Citizens (discussed in Chapter 1) and those espousing a nationwide "common law movement," under which the legitimacy of elected government officials is not recognized. An example is the Republic of Texas separatists who took neighbors hostage near Fort Davis, Texas, in 1997 to draw attention to their claims that Texas was illegally annexed by the United States in 1845. Although not necessarily bent on terrorism, such special-interest groups may turn to violence if thwarted in attempts to reach their goals.

CJ | ISSUES
What Is Terrorist Activity?

Federal law enforcement efforts directed against agents of foreign terrorist organizations derive their primary authority from the Immigration and Nationality Act, found in Title 8 of the U.S. Code. The Act defines terrorist activity as follows:

(ii) "Terrorist activity" defined

As used in this chapter, the term "terrorist activity" means any activity which is unlawful under the laws of the place where it is committed (or which, if committed in the United States, would be unlawful under the laws of the United States or any State) and which involves any of the following:

(I) The hijacking or sabotage of any conveyance (including an aircraft, vessel, or vehicle).
(II) The seizing or detaining, and threatening to kill, injure, or continue to detain, another individual in order to compel a third person (including a governmental organization) to do or abstain from doing any act as an explicit or implicit condition for the release of the individual seized or detained.
(III) A violent attack upon an internationally protected person (as defined in section 1116(b)(4) of title 18) or upon the liberty of such a person.
(IV) An assassination.
(V) The use of any—
(a) biological agent, chemical agent, or nuclear weapon or device, or
(b) explosive or firearm (other than for mere personal monetary gain), with intent to endanger, directly or indirectly,

the safety of one or more individuals or to cause substantial damage to property.
(c) A threat, attempt, or conspiracy to do any of the foregoing.

(iii) "Engage in terrorist activity" defined

As used in this chapter, the term "engage in terrorist activity" means to commit, in an individual capacity or as a member of an organization, an act of terrorist activity or an act which the actor knows, or reasonably should know, affords material support to any individual, organization, or government in conducting a terrorist activity at any time, including any of the following acts:

(I) The preparation or planning of a terrorist activity.
(II) The gathering of information on potential targets for terrorist activity.
(III) The providing of any type of material support, including a safe house, transportation, communications, funds, false documentation or identification, weapons, explosives, or training, to any individual the actor knows or has reason to believe has committed or plans to commit a terrorist activity.
(IV) The soliciting of funds or other things of value for terrorist activity or for any terrorist organization.
(V) The solicitation of any individual for membership in a terrorist organization, terrorist government, or to engage in a terrorist activity.

Nicolaus Czarnecki/ZUMA Press/Alamy

Crowds gather at the Boston Marathon bombing memorial on Boylston Street in Boston, Massachusetts, in May 2013, three weeks after the attacks. How does federal law define "terrorist activity"?

■ **international terrorism**   The unlawful use of force or violence by an individual or a group that has some connection to a foreign power, or whose activities transcend national boundaries, against people or property in order to intimidate or coerce a government, the civilian population, or any segment thereof, in furtherance of political or social objectives.[iii]

■ **activity**   Ask students to assemble a list of international terrorist incidents that have taken place around the globe during the past year. The U.S. Department of State publication *Patterns of Global Terrorism* might be a good place to start. Which countries experienced the largest number of international incidents of terrorism? Which countries had the fewest? How do rates of international terrorism within the United States compare to rates elsewhere?

Ron Edmonds/AP Images

President Barack Obama speaks in the East Room of the White House on May 29, 2009, about the need to secure America's digital infrastructure. What kinds of criminal opportunities does cyberspace provide?

Sometimes individuals can be as dangerous as organized groups. In 1996, for example, 52-year-old Theodore Kaczynski, a Lincoln, Montana, antitechnology recluse, was arrested and charged in the Unabomber case. The Unabomber (so called because the bomber's original targets were universities and airlines) had led police and FBI agents on a 17-year-long manhunt through a series of incidents that involved as many as 16 bombings, resulting in three deaths and 23 injuries. Kaczynski pleaded guilty to federal charges in 1998 and was sentenced to life in prison without possibility of parole.

In another bombing incident, two Chechen brothers, Dzhokhar and Tamerian Tsarnaev, set off two homemade pressure cooker bombs near the finish line of the 2013 Boston Marathon. Three people were killed and another 264 were injured. One brother was killed in an encounter with police shortly after the bombing, while the other was convicted of a number of federal charges including use of a weapon of mass destruction, and was sentenced to death by lethal injection.

International Terrorism

In 1988, Pan American's London–New York Flight 103 was destroyed over Scotland by a powerful two-stage bomb as it reached its cruising altitude of 30,000 feet, killing all of the 259 passengers and crew members aboard. Another 11 people on the ground were killed and many others injured as flaming debris from the airplane crashed down on the Scottish town of Lockerbie. It was the first time Americans were clearly the target of **international terrorism.** Any doubts that terrorists were

targeting U.S. citizens were dispelled by the 1996 truck bomb attack on U.S. military barracks in Dhahran, Saudi Arabia. Nineteen U.S. Air Force personnel were killed and more than 250 others were injured in the blast, which destroyed the Khobar Towers housing complex.

The 1993 bombing of the World Trade Center in New York City and the 1995 conviction of Sheik Omar Abdel-Rahman and eight other Islamic fundamentalists on charges of plotting to start a holy war and of conspiring to commit assassinations and bomb the United Nations indicated to many that the threat of international terrorism could soon become a part of daily life in America.[86] According to some terrorism experts, the 1993 explosion at the World Trade Center, which killed four people and created a 100-foot hole through four subfloors of concrete, ushered in an era of international terrorist activity in the United States. In 1999, the Second U.S. Circuit Court of Appeals upheld the convictions of the sheik and his co-conspirators. They remain in federal prison.[87]

In 2001, Islamic terrorist Osama bin Laden showed the world how terrorists can successfully strike at American interests on U.S. soil when members of his organization attacked the World Trade Center and the Pentagon using commandeered airliners, killing approximately 3,000 people. Earlier, in 1998, bin Laden's agents struck American embassies in Nairobi, Kenya, and Dares Salaam, Tanzania, killing 257 people, including 12 Americans. In 2003, a coordinated attack by Islamic extremists on a residential compound for foreigners in Riyadh, Saudi Arabia, killed 34 people (nine attackers died), including eight Americans, and wounded many more.[88] Similar attacks are continuing in the Middle East and elsewhere.

Some believe that the wars in Afghanistan and Iraq, as well as a coordinated international effort against al-Qaeda, may have substantially weakened that organization's ability to carry out future strikes outside of the Middle East. Those who study international terrorism, however, note that jihadism, or the Islamic holy war movement, survives independent of any one organization and appears to be gaining strength around the world.[89] Jihadist principles continue to serve as the organizing rationale for extremist groups in much of the Muslim world. In 2012, Brian Michael Jenkins, of the RAND Corporation, told Congress that jihadism is difficult to defeat because it "is many things at once—an ideology of violent jihad, a universe of like-minded fanatics, a global terrorist enterprise—and it operates on a number of fronts in both the physical and virtual worlds."[90] Learn more about the global threat from Islamic fundamentalism at **http://justicestudies.com/pubs/al_qae.da.pdf,** and about

■ **lecture note**   Define cyberterrorism and explain why the U.S. is so concerned about the need to secure cyberspace from possible terrorist threats.

■ **lecture note**   Define narcoterrorism as the political alliance between Terrorist organizations and drug-supplying cartels. Ask students how narco-terrorism might directly affect the United States.

■ **cyberterrorism**   A form of terrorism that makes use of high technology, especially computers and the Internet, in the planning and carrying out of terrorist attacks.

■ **infrastructure**   The basic facilities, services, and installations that a country needs to function. Transportation and communications systems, water and power lines, and institutions that serve the public, including banks, schools, post offices, and prisons, are all part of a country's infrastructure.[iv]

■ **narcoterrorism**   A political alliance between terrorist organizations and drug-supplying cartels. The cartels provide financing for the terrorists, who in turn provide quasi-military protection to the drug dealers.

how terrorism has evolved since 9/11 at **http://justicestudies.com/pubs/since911.pdf.**

Cyberterrorism

A relatively new kind of terrorism, called **cyberterrorism**, can be either of domestic or international origin. Cyberterrorism makes use of high technology, especially computers and the Internet, in the planning and carrying out of terrorist attacks. The term was coined in the 1980s by Barry Collin, a senior research fellow at the Institute for Security and Intelligence in California, who used it to refer to the convergence of cyberspace and terrorism.[91] It was later popularized by a 1996 RAND report that warned of an emerging "new terrorism" distinguished by how terrorist groups organize and by how they use technology. The report warned of a coming "netwar" or "infowar" consisting of coordinated cyberattacks on our nation's economic, business, and military **infrastructure**.[92] A year later, FBI agent Mark Pollitt offered a working definition of *cyberterrorism*, saying that it is "the premeditated, politically motivated attack against information, computer systems, computer programs, and data which results in violence against noncombatant targets by subnational groups or clandestine agents."[93]

Scenarios describing cyberterrorism possibilities are imaginative and diverse. Some have suggested that a successful cyberterrorist attack on the nation's air traffic control system might cause airplanes to collide in midair or that an attack on food- and cereal-processing plants that drastically altered the levels of certain nutritional supplements might sicken or kill a large number of our nation's children. Other such attacks might cause the country's power grid to collapse or could muddle the records and transactions of banks and stock exchanges. Possible targets in such attacks are almost endless.

In 1998, the Critical Infrastructure Assurance Office (CIAO) was created by a presidential directive to coordinate the federal government's initiatives on critical infrastructure protection and to provide a national focus for cyberspace security. In 2001, the White House formed the President's Critical Infrastructure Protection Board (PCIPB) and tasked it with recommending policies in support of critical infrastructure protection.[94] In February 2003, the PCIPB released an important document titled *The National Strategy to Secure Cyberspace*,[95] which is available at **http://www.justicestudies.com/pubs/cyberstrategy.pdf.**

In 2003, CIAO functions were transferred to the National Cyber Security Division (NCSD) of the Directorate of Information Analysis and Infrastructure Protection within the Department of Homeland Security (DHS). According to DHS, the creation of the NCSD improved protection of critical cyberassets by "maximizing and leveraging the resources" of previously separate offices.[96] The NCSD coordinates its activities with the U.S. Computer Emergency Response Team (US-CERT), which runs a National Cyber Alert System. Visit US-CERT, which is also a part of the Department of Homeland Security, at **http://www.us-cert.gov.** Another group, the Secret Service National Threat Assessment Center (NTAC), developed its Critical Systems Protection Initiative to offer advanced cybersecurity prevention and response capabilities to the nation's business community. Visit the NTAC at **http://www.secretservice.gov/ntac_ssi.shtml.**

In 2009, President Obama announced the creation of a new White House position: security "czar" for cyberspace. The president's announcement followed news that the Pentagon would create a new cybercommand in an effort to improve the protection of military computer networks and to coordinate both offensive and defensive cybermissions.[97] Today, Michael Daniels, former research assistant at the Southern Center for International Studies, heads the White House's office of cybersecurity. Visit the U.S. Army's cybercommand at **http://www.arcyber.army.mil.**

Narcoterrorism

Some authors have identified a link between major drug traffickers and terrorist groups.[98] In mid-2005, for example, Afghan drug lord Bashir Noorzai was arrested in New York and held without bond on charges that he tried to smuggle more than $50 million worth of heroin into the United States.[99] Noorzai, who was on the Drug Enforcement Administration's (DEA's) list of most wanted drug kingpins, had apparently operated with impunity under the protection of the Taliban between 1990 and 2004. According to the DEA, Noorzai's organization "provided demolitions, weapons and manpower to the Taliban." In exchange, the Taliban was said to have protected Noorzai's opium crops and transit routes through Afghanistan and Pakistan.

The link between drug traffickers and insurgents has been termed **narcoterrorism**.[100] Narcoterrorism, simply defined, is the involvement of terrorist organizations and insurgent groups in the trafficking of narcotics.[101] It is generally international in scope. The relationship that exists between terrorist organizations and drug traffickers is mutually beneficial. Insurgents derive financial benefits from their supporting role in drug trafficking, and the traffickers receive protection and benefit from the use of terrorist tactics against foes and competitors.

The first documented instance of an insurgent force financed at least in part with drug money came to light during an investigation of the virulent anti-Castro Omega 7 group in the early 1980s.[102] Clear-cut evidence of modern narcoterrorism, however, is difficult to obtain. Contemporary insurgent organizations with links to drug dealers probably include the 19th of April Movement (M-19) operating in Colombia, Sendero Luminoso (Shining Path) of Peru, the Revolutionary Armed Forces of Colombia, and the large Farabundo Marti National Liberation Front, which has long sought to overthrow the elected government of El Salvador.[103]

Narcoterrorism raises a number of questions. Drug researcher James Inciardi summarizes them as follows:[104]

- What is the full threat posed by narcoterrorism?
- How should narcoterrorism be dealt with?
- Is narcoterrorism a law enforcement problem or a military one?
- How might narcoterrorism be affected by changes in official U.S. policy toward drugs and drug use?
- Is the international drug trade being used as a tool by anti-U.S. and other interests to undermine Western democracies in a calculated way?

Unfortunately, in the opinion of some experts, the United States is ill prepared to combat this type of international organized crime. Testifying before the Senate's Foreign Relations Subcommittee on Terrorism, Narcotics, and International Operations, William J. Olson, a senior fellow at the National Strategy Information Center, told Congress that more than $1 trillion (equivalent to one-sixth of the U.S. gross national product) is generated yearly by organized criminal activities like those associated with narcoterrorism. "We must recognize that the rules of the crime game have changed," said Olson. "International criminal organizations are challenging governments, permeating societies. They're running roughshod over weak institutions and exploiting gaps in the U.S. and international response. They have the upper hand at the moment and they know it," he added.[105] Other experts testified that a comprehensive national strategy—one that goes far beyond law enforcement and criminal prosecution to include diplomacy and organized international efforts—is needed to combat international organized criminal enterprises before they can co-opt global markets and worldwide financial institutions.[106]

Even more potentially damaging are efforts being made by some criminal groups to wrest control of political institutions in various parts of the world. As transnational organized crime expert Emilio Viano points out, "Powerful drug constituencies influence the electoral process more and more, seeking to gain actual political representation and consequently weaken the rule of law in a number of countries."[107]

Causes of Terrorism

According to the U.S. government,[108] international terrorist organizations build on a process shown in Figure 17-3. The federal government's *National Strategy for Counterterrorism*[109] says that the *underlying conditions* that lead to terrorism include poverty, political corruption, religious and ideational conflict, and ethnic strife. Such conditions provide terrorists with the opportunity to legitimize their cause and to justify their actions. Feeding on the social disorganization fostered by these conditions, terrorists position themselves to demand political change.

The second level in Figure 17-3, the *international environment*, refers to the geopolitical boundaries within which terrorist organizations form and through which they operate. If international borders are free and open, then terrorist groups can readily establish safe havens, hone their capabilities, practice their techniques, and provide support and funding to distant members and collaborators. Either knowingly or unwittingly, nations (*states*) can provide the physical assets and bases needed for the terrorist *organization* to grow and function. Finally, the terrorist *leadership*, at the top of the pyramid, provides the overall direction and strategy that give life to the organization's terror campaign.

Combating Terrorism

Terrorism represents a difficult challenge to all societies. The open societies of the Western world, however, are potentially more vulnerable than are totalitarian regimes such as dictatorships. Western democratic ideals restrict police surveillance of likely terrorist groups and curtail luggage, vehicle, and airport searches. Press

FIGURE 17-3 | The Building Process for International Terrorist Organizations

Source: *National Strategy for Combating Terrorism* (Washington, DC: White House, 2003), p. 6.

coverage of acts of terrorism encourage copycat activities by other fringe groups and communicate information on workable techniques. Laws designed to limit terrorist access to technology, information, and physical locations are stopgap measures at best. The federal Terrorist Firearms Detection Act of 1988 is an example. Designed to prevent the development of plastic firearms by requiring handguns to contain at least 3.7 ounces of detectable metal,[110] it applies only to weapons manufactured within U.S. borders.

In 1996, the Antiterrorism and Effective Death Penalty Act (AEDPA) became law. The act includes a number of provisions:

- It bans fundraising and financial support within the United States for international terrorist organizations.
- It provides $1 billion for enhanced terrorism-fighting measures by federal and state authorities.
- It allows foreign terrorism suspects to be deported or to be kept out of the United States without the disclosure of classified evidence against them.
- It permits a death sentence to be imposed on anyone committing an international terrorist attack in the United States in which a death occurs.
- It makes it a federal crime to use the United States as a base for planning terrorist attacks overseas.
- It orders identifying chemical markers known as *taggants* to be added to plastic explosives during manufacture.
- It orders a feasibility study on marking other explosives (except gunpowder).

More than a year before the events of September 11, 2001, the National Commission on Terrorism released a report titled *Countering the Changing Threat of International Terrorism*.[111] The commission, created by House and Senate leaders in 1998 in response to the bombings of the U.S. embassies in Kenya and Tanzania, was led by former U.S. Ambassador-at-Large for Counter-Terrorism L. Paul Bremer. The commission's report, which we now see presaged the 2001 attacks on the World Trade Center and the Pentagon, began with these words: "International terrorism poses an increasingly dangerous and difficult threat to America." The report identified Afghanistan, Iran, Iraq, Sudan, and Syria as among state sponsors of terrorism and concluded that "the government must immediately take steps to reinvigorate the collection of intelligence about terrorists' plans, use all available legal avenues to disrupt and prosecute terrorist activities and private sources of support, convince other nations to cease all support for terrorists, and ensure that federal, state, and local officials are prepared for attacks that may result in mass casualties." A number of the commission's recommendations were implemented only *after* the terrorist attacks of 2001.

Following the 2001 attacks, Congress enacted and the president signed the USA PATRIOT Act. The act, which is discussed in detail in other chapters and which was reauthorized in 2006 with some amendments, and had certain expiring provisions extended again in 2011, created a number of new crimes, such as terrorist attacks against mass transportation and harboring or concealing terrorists. Those crimes were set forth in Title VIII of the Act, titled "Strengthening the Criminal Laws against Terrorism." Excerpts from Title VIII can be found in the "CJ Issues" box.

> Following the 2001 attacks, Congress enacted and the president signed the USA PATRIOT Act.

Antiterrorism Committees and Reports

Numerous important antiterrorism reports and studies have been released during the last seven or eight years by various groups, including the Advisory Panel to Assess Domestic Response Capabilities for Terrorism Involving Weapons of Mass Destruction (also known as the Gilmore Commission), the National Commission on Terrorism, the U.S. Commission on National Security in the Twenty-First Century, the New York–based Council on Foreign Relations (CFR), and the National Commission on Terrorist Attacks upon the United States (aka the *9/11 Commission*).

Some pre–September 11, 2001, reports offered valuable suggestions that, if followed, might have helped prevent the events that took place on that day. Some of the subsequent reports have been voices of reason in the rush to strengthen the nation's antiterrorism defenses at potentially high costs to individual freedoms. The 2002 CFR report, for example, notes that "systems such as those used in the aviation sector, which start from the assumption that every passenger and every bag of luggage poses an equal risk, must give way to more intelligence-driven and layered security approaches that emphasize prescreening and monitoring based on risk criteria."

The report of the 9/11 Commission, released on July 22, 2004, which many saw as especially valuable, said that the September 11, 2001, attacks should have come as no surprise because the U.S. government had received clear warnings that Islamic terrorists were planning to strike at targets within the United States. The report also said that the United States is still not properly prepared to deal adequately with terrorist threats and called for the creation of a new federal intelligence-gathering center to unify the more than a dozen federal agencies currently gathering terrorism-related intelligence at home and abroad. In December 2005, members of the 9/11 Commission held a final news conference in which they lambasted the lack of progress made by federal officials charged with implementing safeguards to prevent future terrorist attacks within the United States. Former Commission Chair Thomas Kean called it "shocking" that the nation remained so vulnerable. "We shouldn't need another wake-up call," said Kean. "We believe that the terrorists will strike again."[112]

■ **lecture note**   Discuss the creation of the Department of Homeland Security (DHS) and its composition. Explain why the FBI is not part of the DHS.

Palestinian boys holding toy rifles as a girl displays a poster of Osama bin Laden in Gaza City during a demonstration at Al Azhar University to honor suicide bombers. The school was organized by members of the Islamic Jihad. The 9/11 Commission report, released in 2004, pointed to the radical ideology underpinning international Islamic terrorism today and bemoaned the fact that too many Middle Eastern children are being socialized into a culture of terrorism. How can radical ideologies be combated?

In 2010, the Bipartisan Policy Center's National Security Preparedness Group released a wide-ranging report on the evolving nature of terrorism. The report, *Assessing the Terrorist Threat*, made clear that the biggest threat to American national security may no longer come from large international terrorist organizations—but may come instead from small groups of homegrown terrorists, or even loners, who have bought into the ideology of terrorism.[113]

Finally, in 2012, Brian Michael Jenkins, a senior advisor to the president of the RAND Corporation, testified before the U.S. Senate's Homeland Security and Governmental Affairs Committee, telling its members that "Al Qaeda finds fertile ground in failed or failing states where it can attach itself to local insurgencies. It may provide only modest material assistance and operational advice, but the diffusion of al Qaeda-affiliated and connected movements in the region demonstrates that its brand name still carries prestige."[114] Jenkins's testimony followed the "Arab Spring" uprisings of 2010–2013, in which a wave of antigovernment demonstrations, protests, and civil wars broke out in North African and Middle Eastern countries and led to the overthrow of a number of political leaders who were in power at the time.

Although it is impossible to discuss each of the reports mentioned here in detail in this chapter, most of them are available in their entirety at **http://justicestudies.com/terror_reports.**

The Department of Homeland Security

The Homeland Security Act of 2002, enacted to protect America against terrorism, created the federal Department of Homeland Security (DHS), which is charged with protecting the nation's critical infrastructure against terrorist attack. The department began operations on March 1, 2003, with former Pennsylvania Governor Tom Ridge as its first director. The director, whose official title is secretary of homeland security, is a member of the president's cabinet. On January 21, 2009, Janet Napolitano became the third secretary of homeland security, and continues to serve in that capacity as this book goes to press. A former Arizona governor, Napolitano also served as the U.S. attorney who led the investigation into the Oklahoma City bombing.

Experts say that the creation of DHS is the most significant transformation of the U.S. government since 1947, when President Harry S. Truman merged the various branches of the armed forces into the Department of Defense in an effort to better coordinate the nation's defense against military threats.[115] DHS coordinates the activities of 22 disparate domestic agencies, the largest of which are (1) U.S. Customs and Border Protection (CBP), (2) U.S. Citizenship and Immigration Services (CIS), (3) the U.S. Coast Guard (USCG), (4) the Federal Emergency Management Agency (FEMA), (5) U.S. Immigration and

CJ | ISSUES

The USA PATRIOT Act of 2001 (as Amended and Reauthorized)

Title VIII of the USA PATRIOT Act created two new federal crimes of terrorist activity: (1) terrorist attacks against mass transportation systems and (2) harboring or concealing terrorists. The following excerpts from the act describe these offenses.

Title VIII—Strengthening the Criminal Laws Against Terrorism

Sec. 801. Terrorist Attacks and Other Acts of Violence Against Mass Transportation Systems Chapter 97 of title 18, United States Code, is amended by adding at the end the following:

§ 1993. *Terrorist attacks and other acts of violence against mass transportation systems*

(a) GENERAL PROHIBITIONS.—Whoever willfully—

(1) wrecks, derails, sets fire to, or disables a mass transportation vehicle or ferry;

(2) places or causes to be placed any biological agent or toxin for use as a weapon, destructive substance, or destructive device in, upon, or near a mass transportation vehicle or ferry, without previously obtaining the permission of the mass transportation provider, and with intent to endanger the safety of any passenger or employee of the mass transportation provider, or with a reckless disregard for the safety of human life;

(3) sets fire to, or places any biological agent or toxin for use as a weapon, destructive substance, or destructive device in, upon, or near any garage, terminal, structure, supply, or facility used in the operation of, or in support of the operation of, a mass transportation vehicle or ferry, without previously obtaining the permission of the mass transportation provider, and knowing or having reason to know such activity would likely derail, disable, or wreck a mass transportation vehicle or ferry used, operated, or employed by the mass transportation provider;

(4) removes appurtenances from, damages, or otherwise impairs the operation of a mass transportation signal system, including a train control system, centralized dispatching system, or rail grade crossing warning signal without authorization from the mass transportation provider;

(5) interferes with, disables, or incapacitates any dispatcher, driver, captain, or person while they are employed in dispatching, operating, or maintaining a mass transportation vehicle or ferry, with intent to endanger the safety of any passenger or employee of the mass transportation provider, or with a reckless disregard for the safety of human life;

(6) commits an act, including the use of a dangerous weapon, with the intent to cause death or serious bodily injury to an employee or passenger of a mass transportation provider or any other person while any of the foregoing are on the property of a mass transportation provider;

(7) conveys or causes to be conveyed false information, knowing the information to be false, concerning an attempt or alleged attempt being made or to be made, to do any act which would be a crime prohibited by this subsection; or

(8) attempts, threatens, or conspires to do any of the aforesaid acts, shall be fined under this title or imprisoned not more than twenty years, or both, if such act is committed, or in the case of a threat or conspiracy such act would be committed, on, against, or affecting a mass transportation provider engaged in or affecting interstate or foreign commerce, or if in the course of committing such act, that person travels or communicates across a State line in order to commit such act, or transports materials across a State line in aid of the commission of such act.

(b) AGGRAVATED OFFENSE.—Whoever commits an offense under subsection (a) in a circumstance in which—

(1) the mass transportation vehicle or ferry was carrying a passenger at the time of the offense; or

(2) the offense has resulted in the death of any person, shall be guilty of an aggravated form of the offense and shall be fined under this title or imprisoned for a term of years or for life, or both. Sec. 803. Prohibition Against Harboring Terrorists

(a) IN GENERAL.—Chapter 113B of title 18, United States Code, is amended by adding after section 2338 the following new section:

§ 2339. *Harboring or concealing terrorists*

(a) Whoever harbors or conceals any person who he knows, or has reasonable grounds to believe, has committed, or is about to commit, an offense under section 32 (relating to destruction of aircraft or aircraft facilities), section 175 (relating to biological weapons), section 229 (relating to chemical weapons), section 831 (relating to nuclear materials), paragraph (2) or (3) of section 844(f) (relating to arson and bombing of government property risking or causing injury or death), section 1366(a) (relating to the destruction of an energy facility), section 2280 (relating to violence against maritime navigation), section 2332a (relating to weapons of mass destruction), or section 2332b (relating to acts of terrorism transcending national boundaries) of this title, section 236(a) (relating to sabotage of nuclear facilities or fuel) of the Atomic Energy Act of 1954 (42 U.S.C. 2284(a)), or section 46502 (relating to aircraft piracy) of title 49, shall be fined under this title or imprisoned not more than ten years, or both.

(b) A violation of this section may be prosecuted in any Federal judicial district in which the underlying offense was committed, or in any other Federal judicial district as provided by law.

(c) TECHNICAL AMENDMENT.—The chapter analysis for chapter 113B of title 18, United States Code, is amended by inserting after the item for section 2338 the following: "2339. Harboring or concealing terrorists."

Note: The USA PATRIOT Act was reauthorized by Congress in March 2006. Some subsections that had been subject to sunset provisions were extended in 2011.

Customs Enforcement (ICE), (6) the U.S. Secret Service (USSS), and (7) the Transportation Security Administration (TSA).

The *Bureau of Immigration and Customs Enforcement (ICE),* also known as U.S. Immigration and Customs Enforcement, is the largest investigative arm of the Department of Homeland Security. The ICE is responsible for identifying and eliminating vulnerabilities in the nation's border, economic, transportation, and infrastructure security. The *Bureau of Customs and Border Protection (CBP)* is the unified border-control agency of the United States, and has as its mission the protection of our country's borders and the American people. The *Bureau of Citizenship and Immigration Services (CIS),* also known as U.S. Citizenship and Immigration Services, or USCIS, dedicates its energies to providing efficient immigration services and easing the transition to American citizenship.

Immigration law enforcement is a major function of DHS and its component agencies. According to a 2015 DHS report,

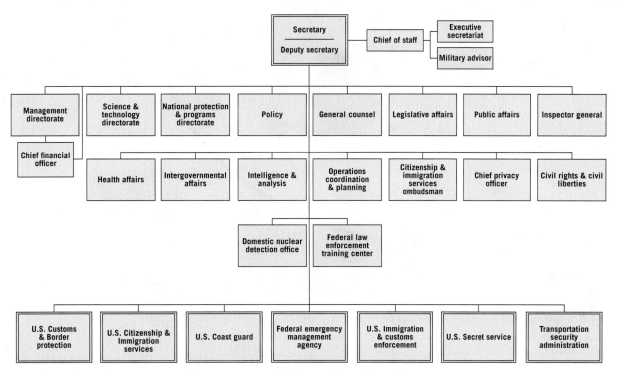

FIGURE 17-4 | Organizational Chart of the Department of Homeland Security

Source: Department of Homeland Security.

the department continues the Administration's focus on border security, travel and trade by supporting 21,370 Border Patrol agents and 25,775 CBP Officers at American ports of entry as well the continued deployment of proven, effective surveillance technology along the highest trafficked areas of the Southwest Border.[116] The total federal budget for DHS in 2015 was $60.9 billion, with immigration services receiving much of that money. In 2015, spending for the two main immigration enforcement agencies, the CBP and the ICE exceeded $18 billion.[117] The U.S. Coast Guard, which also plays an important role in securing the nation's ports of call, received more than $10 billion to fund continuing operations. Border apprehensions reached a peak in 2000, with 1.7 million arrests.[118] Only a year later, the number of arrests for border violations had declined to 340,252,[119] largely as the result of declining economic conditions in the United States that led to fewer attempts to gain access to the country by undocumented aliens.

The DHS organizational chart is shown in Figure 17-4, and you can visit DHS on the Web via **http://www.dhs.gov.**

The National Counterterrorism Strategy

In 2011, the White House released its official *National Strategy for Counterterrorism*.[120] The strategy maintained a focus on deterring Islamic-inspired terrorism and promised to pressure "al-Qa'ida's

core while emphasizing the need to build foreign partnerships and capacity...to strengthen our resilience." The authors of the strategy noted that it "augments our focus on confronting the al-Qa'ida-linked threats that continue to emerge from beyond its core safehaven in South Asia." The strategy makes it clear that "the preeminent security threat to the United States continues to be from *al-Qa'ida and its affiliate and adherents*."

The national strategy in the fight against terrorism includes a two-pronged approach: (1) reduce the scope of operations of terrorist organizations, and (2) reduce their capability (Figure 17-5). The July 2004 report of the 9/11 Commission proposed sweeping changes within the U.S. intelligence community, including the creation of the position of national intelligence director (NID). Soon afterward, the Intelligence Reform and Terrorism Prevention Act of 2004 facilitated the creation of the National Counterterrorism Center (NCTC) under the newly created position of NID.[121] The NID acts as the principal advisor to the president, the National Security Council, and the Homeland Security Council for intelligence matters related to national security. The NCTC serves as the primary organization in the U.S. government for integrating and analyzing all intelligence pertaining to terrorism and counterterrorism and for conducting strategic counterterrorism operational planning. Today's NCTC intelligence analysts have access to dozens of networks and information systems from across the intelligence, law enforcement,

■ **foreign terrorist organization (FTO)**   A foreign organization that engages in terrorist activity that threatens the security of U.S. nationals or the national security of the United States and that is so designated by the U.S. secretary of state.

■ **theme**   What are foreign terrorist organizations (FTOs)? What criteria must an organization meet to be designated an FTO? What are the consequences of an FTO designation for an organization?

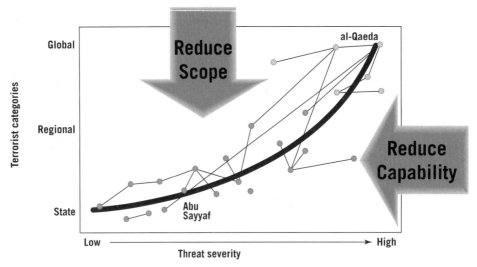

FIGURE 17-5 │ Reducing the Scope and Capability of Terrorist Organizations

Source: *National Strategy for Combating Terrorism* (Washington, DC: White House, 2003) p. 13.

military, and homeland security communities. These systems provide foreign and domestic information pertaining to international terrorism and sensitive law enforcement activities.[122] The *National Strategy* is available in its entirety at **http://www.justicestudies .com/pubs/counterterrorismstrategy.pdf.** Visit the National Counterterrorism Center at **http://www.nctc.gov.**

In 2015, the *National Security Strategy* was released by the White House, and includes the support of universal values at home and around the world, as well as the implementation of strong economic growth as a driver of international prosperity. Both principles are intended to decrease international conflict and the world-wide threat of terrorism.

Foreign Terrorist Organizations

The Immigration and Nationality Act[123] and the Intelligence Reform and Terrorism Prevention Act of 2004[124] provide the U.S. Department of State with the authority to designate any group outside the United States as a **foreign terrorist organization (FTO).** The process involves an exhaustive interagency review process in which all evidence of a group's activity, from both classified and open sources, is scrutinized. The State Department, working closely with the Justice and Treasury Departments and the intelligence community, prepares a detailed "administrative record" that documents the organization's terrorist activity.

An air traveler being screened by Transportation Security Administration employees in Chicago's O'Hare International Airport. The hijackings of four airplanes by Islamic terrorists on September 11, 2001, led to tightened security controls over air travel nationwide and abroad. How did the hijackings reduce freedoms that Americans had previously taken for granted?

Federal law requires that any organization considered for FTO designation must meet three criteria: (1) It must be foreign; (2) it must engage in terrorist activity as defined in Section 212 (a)(3)(B) of the Immigration and Nationality Act;[125] and (3) the organization's activities must threaten the security of U.S. nationals or the national security (national defense, foreign relations, or economic interests) of the United States. Table 17-3 lists 52 FTOs, as designated by the U.S. Department of State. The most

TABLE 17-3 | Designated Foreign Terrorist Organizations as of Mid-2015

Foreign terrorist organizations (FTOs) are foreign organizations that are designated by the secretary of state in accordance with Section 219 of the Immigration and Nationality Act (INA), as amended. FTO designations play a critical role in the fight against terrorism and are an effective means of curtailing support for terrorist activities and pressuring groups to get out of the terrorism business.

Abu Nidal Organization (ANO)	Jaish-e-Mohammed (JEM)
Abu Sayyaf Group (ASG)	Jemaah Islamiya (JI)
Al-Aqsa Martyrs Brigade (AAMB)	Jundallah
al-Mulathamun Battalion	Kahane ChaiKata'ib Hizballah (KH)
al-Nusrah Front	Kurdistan Workers' Party (PKK)
Ansaru	Lashkar e-Tayyiba (LT)
Ansar al-Islam (AAI)	Lashkar i Jhangvi (LJ)
Ansar Dine (AD)	Liberation Tigers of Tamil Eelam (LTTE)
Ansar al-Shari'a in Benghazi	Libyan Islamic Fighting Group (LIFG)
Ansar al-Shari'a in Darnah	Moroccan Islamic Combatant Group (GICM)
Ansar al-Shari'a in Tunisia	Mujahadin-e Khalq Organization (MEK)
Ansar Bayt al-Maqdis	Mujahidin Shura Council in the Environs of Jerusalem (MSC)
Army of Islam (AOI)	National Liberation Army (ELN)
Asbat al-Ansar (AAA)	Palestine Islamic Jihad—Shaqaqi Faction (PIJ)
Aum Shinrikyo (AUM)	Palestine Liberation Front—Abu Abbas Faction (PLF)
Basque Fatherland and Liberty (ETA)	Popular Front for the Liberation of Palestine (PFLP)
Boko Haram	Popular Front for the Liberation of Palestine-General Command (PFLP-GC)
Communist Party of Philippines/New People's Army (CPP/NPA)	Al-Qa'ida (AQ)
Continuity Irish Republican Army (CIRA)	Al-Qa'ida in the Arabian Peninsula (AQAP)
Gama'a al-Islamiyya (IG)	Al-Qa'ida in Iraq (AQI)
Hamas	Al-Qa'ida in the Islamic Maghreb (AQIM)
Haqqani Network	Real IRA (RIRA)
Harakat ul-Jihad-i-Islami (HUJI)	Revolutionary Armed Forces of Colombia (FARC)
Harakat ul-Jihad-i-Islami/Bangladesh (HUJI-B)	Revolutionary Organization 17 November (17N)
Harakat ul-Mujahideen (HUM)	Revolutionary People's Liberation Party/Front (DHKP/C)
Hizballah	Revolutionary Struggle (RS)
Indian Mujahideen (IM)	Al-Shabaab (AS)
Islamic Jihad Union (IJU)	Shining Path (SL)
Islamic Movement of Uzbekistan (IMU)	Tehrik-e Taliban Pakistan (TTP)
Jabhat al-Nusra	

Source: U.S. Department of State, Office of the Coordinator for Counterterrorism. Current as of February 20, 2015.

recent organization to be added to the list is the Mujahidin Shura Council in the Environs of Jerusalem (MSC), which was placed on the list in late 2014.[126] For more detailed descriptions of these organizations, see the latest State Department *Country Reports on Terrorism*, which can be accessed at **http://www.state.gov/j/ct/rls/crt/2013.**

Under federal law, FTO designations are subject to judicial review. In the event of a challenge to a group's FTO designation in federal court, the U.S. government relies on the administrative record to defend the designation decision. These administrative records contain intelligence information and are therefore classified. FTO designations expire in two years unless renewed.

Once an organization has been designated as an FTO, specific legal consequences follow. First, it becomes unlawful for a person in the United States or subject to the jurisdiction of the United States to provide funds or other material support to a designated FTO. Second, representatives and certain members of a designated FTO, if they are aliens, can be denied visas or kept from entering the United States. Finally, U.S. financial institutions must block funds of designated FTOs and their agents and must report the blockage to the Office of Foreign Assets Control within the U.S. Department of the Treasury.

The State Department also has the authority to designate selected foreign governments as state sponsors of international terrorism. In mid-2007, Cuba, Iran, North Korea, Sudan, and Syria were designated as state sponsors of international terrorism. The situation in Syria has changed since the Arab spring that began in 2010 and relations with Cuba have thawed (t was removed from the list in 2015). Iran, however, remains the most active state sponsor of terrorism, according to the State Department.[127] The State Department says that the Iranian government provides continuing support to numerous terrorist groups, including the Lebanese Hizballah, Hamas, and the Palestinian Islamic Jihad, all of which seek to undermine the Middle East peace process through the use of terrorism.

North Korea harbored several hijackers of a Japanese Airlines flight to North Korea in the 1970s and maintains links to terrorist groups. It also continues to sell ballistic missile technology to countries designated by the United States as state sponsors of terrorism.

Finally, Sudan continues to provide a safe haven for members of various terrorist groups, including the Lebanese Hizballah, Gama'a al-Islamiyya, Egyptian Islamic Jihad, the Palestinian Islamic Jihad, and Hamas, although it has been engaged in a counterterrorism dialogue with the United States since mid-2000.

aL-QAEDA
Global
ACTIVITIES
Funding, planning, and conducting terrorism
MEMBERS
Unknown
Founded by Osama bin Laden in the 1980s, al-Qaeda first supported the *mujahidin* fighting Soviets in Afghanistan. Today the group wages war on the world, through a global Islamist insurgency.

1. UNITED SELF-DEFENSE FORCES OF COLOMBIA
Colombia
ACTIVITIES
Massacres, narcotics
MEMBERS
12,000 to 15,000
This right-wing coalition of paramilitaries was formed to fight leftist insurgents but often targets civilians.

1. REVOLUTIONARY ARMED FORCES OF COLOMBIA (FARC)
Colombia
ACTIVITIES
Bombing, kidnapping, narcotics
MEMBERS
15,000 to 18,000
These communist insurgents use kidnapping and mass murder in their fight to overthrow the Colombian government and redistribute wealth.

1. NATIONAL LIBERATION ARMY (ELN)
Colombia
ACTIVITIES
Kidnapping, bombing, extortion
MEMBERS
3,000
This leftist group is one of the leading practitioners of kidnapping for ransom. It also attacks government oil pipelines and energy infrastructure.

2. ■ SALAFIST GROUP FOR CALL AND COMBAT
Algeria
ACTIVITIES
Attacks on government and military
MEMBERS
Several hundred
This newly powerful Islamist group aims to topple Algeria's secular government, expel foreign influences, and advance al-Qaeda's agenda in Africa and Europe.

3. ■ MOROCCAN ISLAMIC COMBATANT GROUP
Morocco
ACTIVITIES
Bombing, arms, forgery
MEMBERS
Unknown
This Moroccan Islamist group, reportedly linked to al-Qaeda, is accused of recent mass-casualty bombings in Madrid and Casablanca.

HOT SPOT
COLOMBIA

As communist insurgents battle right-wing militias—and each other—for territory and drug profits, locals are caught in the crossfire. The government is now fighting to regain control of the countryside.

The latest wave of international terrorism has focused the world's attention on a tactic that uses death and destruction as political tools. But terrorism itself, with roots deep in history and geography, is hardly new.

HOT SPOT
ISRAEL & THE OCCUPIED TERRITORIES

Fueled by nationalism and mistrust, the cycle continues: Palestinian insurgents use terrorism against Israeli troops, settlers, and civilians in the occupied territories and Israel—while Israeli forces target militants, often inflicting civilian casualties.

6. ISLAMIC RESISTANCE MOVEMENT (HAMAS)
Israel, West Bank, Gaza Strip
ACTIVITIES
Suicide attacks
MEMBERS
Several thousand
Seeking to destroy Israel and extend Muslim rule across the Middle East, Hamas has mounted dozens of suicide attacks against Israeli civilians.

6. PALESTINE ISLAMIC JIHAD
Israel, West Bank, Gaza Strip
ACTIVITIES
Suicide attacks
MEMBERS
Several dozen
Led by operatives based in Lebanon and Syria, this radical group aims to replace Israel with a Palestinian Islamic state.

6. AL AQSA MARTYRS' BRIGADES
Israel, West Bank, Gaza Strip
ACTIVITIES
Shootings, suicide attacks
MEMBERS
Unknown
This group, linked to Palestinian leader Yasser Arafat's Fatah movement, arose during a Palestinian intifada in 2000.

6. KACH AND KAHANE CHAI
Israel, West Bank
ACTIVITIES
Shootings, assaults
MEMBERS
Several dozen
Outlawed since the massacre of 29 Muslims at Hebron in 1994, these groups seek to expand Israel by driving Palestinians from the West Bank and Gaza Strip.

6. HEZBOLLAH
Lebanon
ACTIVITIES
Bombing, hijacking, suicide attacks
MEMBERS
Several hundred
Formed in 1982 after the Israeli invasion of Lebanon, this Iran-backed group claimed victory when Israel pulled out in 2000. Its goal: destruction of the Jewish state.

6. ■ ASBAT AL ANSAR
Lebanon
ACTIVITIES
Assassination, bombing
MEMBERS
About 300
These al-Qaeda-linked extremists attack both domestic and international targets within Lebanon.

FIGURE 17-6 | International Terrorist Groups and Areas of Operation

Source: Adapted from Walter Laqueur, "World of Terror" (National Geographic Maps), *National Geographic*, November 2004, pp. 72–74. Reprinted by permission.

4. BASQUE FATHERLAND AND LIBERTY (ETA)
Spain, France
ACTIVITIES
Assassination, bombing, extortion
MEMBERS
Dozens
Founded in 1959, this group has targeted Spanish officials and security forces in its fight for an independent Basque state in northern Spain and southwestern France.

5. REAL IRA
Northern Ireland
ACTIVITIES
Assassination, bombing, robbery
MEMBERS
100 to 200
An offshoot that formed after the Irish Republican Army declared a cease-fire in 1997, the RIRA has killed dozens in its fight for a united Ireland, free from British rule.

WHERE THEY ARE

This map shows a sample of the many groups that use terror to achieve their goals, attracting an array of nationalists, political ideologues, and religious zealots. Some groups are multifaceted, incorporating politics and social programs along with violence; others are purely brutal. Today one type of group—related to a movement called Islamism—has earned an especially high profile for its drive to impose theocracy on Muslim lands and excise "impure" Western influences. According to the CIA, the deadliest of these groups— al-Qaeda—operates in 68 countries worldwide.

HOT SPOT
INDIA & PAKISTAN

Nuclear rivals India and Pakistan duel over the region of Kashmir, a flash point for conflict between Indian troops and Pakistan-based terrorist groups. Attacks against the pro-U.S. government of Pakistan are also on the rise.

5. ULSTER DEFENCE ASSOCIATION
Northern Ireland
ACTIVITIES
Bombing, narcotics, shootings, intimidation
MEMBERS
Several hundred
Largest of the Protestant paramilitary groups that favor retaining British rule. Though bound by a cease-fire, the group often engages in violence against Catholics.

8. KURDISTAN WORKERS' PARTY (PKK)
Turkey
ACTIVITIES
Assassination, bombing
MEMBERS
More than 5,000
Also known as Kongra-Gel, this separatist group operates from northern Iraq and targets Turkish security forces and civilians in its fight for an independent Kurdish state.

9. ■ CHECHEN SEPARATISTS
Russia
ACTIVITIES
Bombing, kidnapping, murder
MEMBERS
Several thousand
Seeking independence from Russia, rebels have killed Moscow-backed Chechen officials, including Chechnya's president, and killed and kidnapped Russian civilians.

9. ■ ISLAMIC MOVEMENT OF UZBEKISTAN
Central Asia
ACTIVITIES
Bombing, kidnapping
MEMBERS
More than 1,000
This homegrown Islamist coalition seeks to replace Uzbekistan's secular regime and advance the regional goals of al-Qaeda.

10. ■ LASHKAR E-JHANGVI
Pakistan
ACTIVITIES
Massacres, bombing
MEMBERS
Fewer than a hundred
A small but brutally effective Sunni group, LEJ has attacked Shiite mosques and foreigners in a bid to destabilize Pakistan. Also linked to the 2002 murder of journalist Daniel Pearl.

HOT SPOT
INDONESIA & PHILIPPINES

Recent acts of terrorism have claimed hundreds of lives in Indonesia, prime target for indigenous groups like Jemaah Islamiyah that are now affiliated with al-Qaeda. In the Philippines, Muslim and Marxist rebels are an ongoing threat to stability.

10. ■ JAISH-E-MOHAMMED
Pakistan
ACTIVITIES
Massacres, bombing
MEMBERS
Several hundred
This Islamist group is blamed for the bombing of an Indian state legislature in Kashmir that killed 38. Now split into two factions, this group, like others, fights to make predominantly Muslim Kashmir part of Pakistan.

10. LASHKAR E-TAIBA
Pakistan
ACTIVITIES
Massacres, bombing
MEMBERS
Several hundred
With training camps in Afghanistan, LET specializes in daredevil missions with devastating results, directed mainly against Indian troops and civilians in Kashmir.

11. LIBERATION TIGERS OF TAMIL EELAM
Sri Lanka
ACTIVITIES
Assassination, bombing
MEMBERS
10,000 to 15,000
Favoring suicide attacks, members seek an independent Tamil state in Sri Lanka. A precarious cease-fire is now in place.

12. ■ JEMAAH ISLAMIYAH
Southeast Asia
ACTIVITIES
Bombing
MEMBERS
Unknown
Responsible for a series of deadly bombings across Southeast Asia— including the Bali nightclub attacks in 2002—al-Qaeda's local partner seeks an Islamic superstate spanning the region.

TAWHID W' AL JIHAD
Iraq
ACTIVITIES
Kidnapping, bombing
MEMBERS
Unknown
Jordanian Abu Musab al Zarqawi leads this loose network of jihadists, most of whom are Iraqi. Their common goal: to expel U.S. forces and create a Sunni Islamic state in Iraq. Many of its fighters are veterans of an older group, Ansar al Islam.

12. ABU SAYYAF
Philippines
ACTIVITIES
Kidnapping, bombing, piracy
MEMBERS
300 to 500
High-profile kidnappings of foreigners for ransom keep this group well financed—though the profit motive may be clouding Abu Sayyaf's founding vision of an Islamic state in the southern Philippines.

12. ■ MORO ISLAMIC LIBERATION FRONT
Philippines
ACTIVITIES
Bombing
MEMBERS
Around 12,000
Though it officially disavows terrorism, this insurgent group is linked to attacks on Philippine cities through its support for Jemaah Islamiyah. Now in peace talks with the government, the MILF aims for ethnic autonomy.

13. Boko Haram
ACTIVITIES
Massacres, kidnapping, bombing
MEMBERS
15,000-30,000
Officially known as Jama'atu Ahlus-Sunnah Lidda'Awati Wal Jihad, the group is an Islamic sect waging war in northern Nigeria.

LEGEND

■ Countries where al-Qaeda cells are known to be operating

■ Countries where al-Qaeda cells may be operating

■ Group affiliated with al-Qaeda

AUSTRALIA

PHILIPPINES

The Future of International Terrorism

Terrorist groups are active throughout the world (Figure 17-6), and the United States is not their only target. Terrorist groups operate in South America, Africa, the Middle East, Latin America, the Philippines, Japan, India, England, Nepal, and some of the now independent states of the former Soviet Union. The Central Intelligence Agency reports that "terrorist tactics will become increasingly sophisticated and designed to achieve mass casualties."[128] The CIA also notes that nations "with poor governance; ethnic, cultural, or religious tensions; weak economies; and porous borders will be prime breeding grounds for terrorism."[129]

In the area of Islamic terrorism, the CIA expects that "by 2020 Al-Qaeda will have been superseded by similarly inspired but more diffuse Islamic extremist groups," something that is already happening.[130]

The current situation leads many observers to conclude that the American justice system is not fully prepared to deal with the threat represented by domestic and international terrorism. Prior intelligence-gathering efforts that focused on such groups have largely failed or were not quickly acted on, leading to military intervention in places like Afghanistan and Iraq. Intelligence failures are at least partially understandable, given that many terrorist organizations are tight-knit and very difficult for intelligence operatives to penetrate.

SUMMARY

- Islamic law descends directly from the teachings of the Prophet Muhammad and looks to the Koran to determine which acts should be classified as crimes. Today's Islamic law is a system of duties and rituals founded on legal and moral obligations—all of which are ultimately sanctioned by the authority of religious leaders who may issue commands known as *fatwas*. Islamic law recognizes seven *Hudud* crimes—or crimes based on religious strictures. In Middle Eastern countries today, punishments for *Hudud* offenses are often physical and may include lashing, flogging, or even stoning. All other crimes fall into an offense category called *tazirat*. *Tazir* crimes are regarded as any actions not considered acceptable in a spiritual society. They include crimes against society and against individuals, but not those against God.

- The United Nations is the largest and most inclusive international body in the world. Since its inception in 1945, it has concerned itself with international crime prevention and world criminal justice systems, as illustrated by a number of important resolutions and documents, including the International Bill of Human Rights, which supports the rights and dignity of everyone who comes into contact with a criminal justice system; the Standard Minimum Rules for the Treatment of Prisoners; and the UN Code of Conduct for Law Enforcement Officials, which calls on law enforcement officers throughout the world to be cognizant of human rights in the performance of their duties. The World Crime Surveys, which report official crime statistics from nearly 100 countries, provide a periodic global portrait of criminal activity. Other significant international criminal justice organizations are the International Criminal Police Organization (Interpol), which acts as a clearinghouse for information on offenses and suspects who are believed to operate across national boundaries, and the European Police Office (Europol), which aims to improve the effectiveness and cooperation of law enforcement agencies within the member states of the European Union. Finally, the International Criminal Court (ICC) was created in 2000 under the auspices of the United Nations. The ICC is intended to be a permanent criminal court for trying individuals who commit the most serious crimes of concern to the international community, such as genocide, war crimes, and crimes against humanity—including the wholesale murder of civilians, torture, and mass rape.

- Globalization—the internationalization of trade, services, investment, information, and other forms of human social activity—has been occurring for a long time but has recently increased in pace due largely to advances in technology, such as new modes of transportation and communication. Transnational crime, which may be one of the most significant challenges of the twenty-first century, is a negative consequence of globalization. Transnational crime is unlawful activity undertaken and supported by organized criminal groups operating across national boundaries. Criminal opportunities for transnational groups have come about in part by globalization of the world's economy and by advances in communications, transportation, and other technologies. Today's organized international criminal cartels recognize no boundaries and engage in activities like drug trafficking, money laundering, human trafficking, counterfeiting of branded goods, and weapons smuggling.

- In 2000, the U.S. Congress passed the Trafficking Victims Protection Act (TVPA). Trafficking offenses under the law include (1) sex trafficking and (2) other forms of trafficking, defined as the recruitment, harboring, transportation, provision, or obtaining of a person for labor services, through the use of force, fraud, or coercion, for the purpose of subjection to involuntary servitude, peonage, debt bondage, or slavery. There are important legal differences between human trafficking and human smuggling. Under federal law human smuggling refers to illegal immigration in which an agent is paid to help a person cross a border clandestinely. Human smuggling generally occurs with the consent of those being smuggled, and they often pay a smuggler for his or her services.

- This chapter defines *terrorism* as a violent act or an act dangerous to human life, in violation of the criminal laws of the United States or of any state, that is committed to intimidate or coerce a government, the civilian population, or any segment thereof, in furtherance of political or social objectives. Terrorism, which today is the focus of significant criminal justice activity, brings with it the threat of massive destruction and large numbers of casualties. Domestic and international terrorism are the two main forms of terrorism with which law enforcement organizations concern themselves today. Specific forms of terrorist activity, such as cyberterrorism and attacks on information-management segments of our nation's critical infrastructure, could theoretically shut down or disable important infrastructure services such as electricity, food processing, military activity, and even state and federal governments. The vigilance required to prevent terrorism, both domestic and international, consumes a significant amount of law enforcement resources and has resulted in new laws that restrict a number of freedoms that many Americans have previously taken for granted.

KEY TERMS

comparative criminologist, 567	International Criminal Police
cyberterrorism, 586	Organization (Interpol), 574
domestic terrorism, 583	international terrorism, 585
ethnocentric, 567	Islamic law, 570
European Police Office	lone wolf terrorist, 582
(Europol), 576	narcoterrorism, 586
extradition, 578	sex trafficking, 579
foreign terrorist organization	*Tazir* crime, 572
(FTO), 592	terrorism, 581
globalization, 577	trafficking in persons (TIP), 580
Hudud crime, 571	transnational organized crime,
human smuggling, 580	578
infrastructure, 586	

QUESTIONS FOR REVIEW

1. What are the principles that inform Islamic law? How do these principles contribute to the structure and activities of the criminal justice systems of Muslim nations that follow Islamic law?

2. What important international criminal justice organizations does this chapter discuss? Describe the role of each in fighting international crime.

3. What is globalization, and how does it relate to transnational organized crime? What relationships might exist between transnational organized crime and terrorism?

4. What is human smuggling? Human trafficking? How do the two differ under the law?

5. What is terrorism? What are the two major types of terrorism discussed in this chapter?

QUESTIONS FOR REFLECTION

1. Why is terrorism a law enforcement concern? How is terrorism a crime? What can the American criminal justice system do to better prepare for future terrorist crimes?

2. What are the causes of terrorism? What efforts is the U.S. government making to prevent and control the spread of domestic terrorism and international terrorism?

3. What are the benefits of studying criminal justice systems in other countries? What problems are inherent in such study?

NOTES

i. Federal Bureau of Investigation, Counterterrorism Section, *Terrorism in the United States, 1987* (Washington, DC: FBI, 1987).

ii. Adapted from Federal Bureau of Investigation, "FBI Policy and Guidelines: Counterterrorism," http://www.fbi.gov/contact/fo/jackson/cntrterr.htm (accessed March 4, 2011).

iii. Ibid.

iv. Adapted from Dictionary.com, http://dictionary.reference.com/search?q5infrastructure (accessed January 10, 2011).

1. Office for Victims of Crime, *Report to the Nation, 2003* (Washington, DC: OVC, 2003), p. 83.

2. "Ohio Terror Defendant Scheduled Back in Court to Face New Charges from Federal Grand Jury," *Fox News*, January 22, 2015, http://www.foxnews.com/us/2015/01/22/ohio-terror-defendant-scheduled-back-in-court-to-face-new-charges-from-federal (accessed January 29, 2015).

3. Mosi Secret, "Bangladeshi Admits Trying to Blow Up Federal Bank," *New York Times*, February 7, 2013.

4. FBI, "Jacksonville Would-Be Terrorist Sentenced to 20 Years," *FBI press* release, January 14, 2015, http://www.fbi.gov/jacksonville/press-releases/2015/jacksonville-would-be-terrorist-sentenced-to-20-years (accessed May 1, 2015).

5. Robert Lilly, "Forks and Chopsticks: Understanding Criminal Justice in the PRC," *Criminal Justice International* (March/April 1986), p. 15.

6. Adapted from Carol B. Kalish, *International Crime Rates, Bureau of Justice Statistics Special Report* (Washington, DC: BJS, 1988).

7. "Which Country Has the Fewest Cars," Big Site of Amazing Facts, http://www.bigsiteofamazingfacts.com/which-country-has-the-fewest-cars (accessed July 2, 2013).

8. Kalish, *International Crime Rates*.

9. Ibid.

10. For information about the latest survey, see *The Twelfth United Nations Survey on Crime Trends and the Operations of Criminal Justice* (New York: United Nations, 2012), http://www.unodc.org/unodc/en/data-and-analysis/crimedata.html (accessed December 9, 2011).

11. As quoted in Lee Hockstader, "Russia's War on Crime: A Lopsided, Losing Battle," *Washington Post* wire service, February 27, 1995.

12. Roy Walmsley, *Developments in the Prison Systems of Central and Eastern Europe*, HEUNI papers No. 4 (Helsinki, 1995).

13. J. Schact, "Law and Justice," *The Cambridge Encyclopedia of Islam*, Vol. 2, p. 539, from which most of the information in this

paragraph comes. Available at http://www.fordham.edu/halsall/med/schacht.html (accessed July 1, 2011).

14. Sam S. Souryal, Dennis W. Potts, and Abdullah I. Alobied, "The Penalty of Hand Amputation for Theft in Islamic Justice," *Journal of Criminal Justice*, Vol. 22, No. 3 (1994), pp. 249–265.

15. Parviz Saney, "Iran," in Elmer H. Johnson, ed., *International Handbook of Contemporary Developments in Criminology* (Westport, CT: Greenwood Press, 1983), p. 359.

16. Amy Sullivan, "Sharia Myth Sweeps America," *USA Today*, June 13, 2011, p. 11A.

17. This section owes much to Matthew Lippman, "Iran: A Question of Justice?" *Criminal Justice International*, 1987, pp. 6–7.

18. Sarah El Deeb, "Terry Jones, Florida Pastor, Sentenced to Death in Egypt over Anti-Islam Film along with 7 Coptic Christians," *Huffington Post*, November 28, 2012 (accessed July 4, 2013).

19. Souryal, Potts, and Alobied, "The Penalty of Hand Amputation."

20. Afshin Valinejad, "Iran Flogs, Hangs Serial Killer Known as 'The Vampire,'" *USA Today*, August 14, 1997, p. 11A.

21. For additional information on Islamic law, see Adel Mohammed el Fikey, "Crimes and Penalties in Islamic Criminal Legislation," *Criminal Justice International*, 1986, pp. 13–14; and Sam S. Souryal, "Shariah Law in Saudi Arabia," *Journal for the Scientific Study of Religion*, Vol. 26, No. 4 (1987), pp. 429–449.

22. Max Weber, in Max Rheinstein, ed., *On Law in Economy and Society* (New York: Simon and Schuster, 1967), translated from the 1925 German edition.

23. Ibid.

24. Souryal, Potts, and Alobied, "The Penalty of Hand Amputation."

25. Paul Friday, "International Organization: An Introduction," in Elmer H. Johnson, ed., *International Handbook of Contemporary Developments in Criminology* (Westport, CT: Greenwood Press, 1983), p. 31.

26. Ibid., p. 32.

27. Gerhard O. W. Mueller, "The United Nations and Criminology," in Elmer H. Johnson, ed., *International Handbook of Contemporary Developments in Criminology* (Westport, CT: Greenwood Press, 1983), pp. 74–75.

28. Roger S. Clark, *The United Nations Crime Prevention and Criminal Justice Program: Formulation of Standards and Efforts at Their Implementation* (Philadelphia: University of Pennsylvania Press, 1994).

29. Ibid., pp. 71–72.

30. "International News," *Corrections Compendium*, June 1995, p. 25.

31. Khaled Dawoud, "U.N. Crime Meeting Wants Independent Jail Checks," Reuters, May 6, 1995.

32. "Protocol to Prevent, Suppress and Punish Trafficking in Persons, Especially Women and Children, Supplementing the United Nations Convention against Transnational Organized Crime," Report of the Ad Hoc Committee on the Elaboration of a Convention against Transnational Organized Crime on the Work of Its First to Eleventh Sessions, U.N. GAOR, 55th Sess., Agenda Item 105, U.N. Document Number A/55/383 (2000), Annex II.

33. For additional information, see Mohamed Y. Mattar, "Trafficking in Persons, Especially Women and Children, in Countries of the Middle East: The Scope of the Problem and the Appropriate Legislative Response," *Fordham International Law Journal*, Vol. 26 (March 2003), p. 721, http://209.190.246.239/article.pdf (accessed August 2, 2006).

34. See "Interpol: Extending Law Enforcement's Reach around the World," *FBI Law Enforcement Bulletin* (December 1998), pp. 10–16.

35. Interpol, "Member Countries," http://www.interpol.int/Member-countries/World (accessed April 21, 2013).

36. "Interpol at Forty," *Criminal Justice International*, November/December 1986, pp. 1, 22.

37. Interpol, "83rd INTERPOL General Assembly," http://www.interpol.int/News-and-media/Events/2014/83rd-INTERPOL-General-Assembly/83rd-INTERPOL-General-Assembly (accessed May 20, 2015).

38. Interpol General Secretariat, *Interpol at Work: 2003 Activity Report* (Lyons, France, 2004).

39. Marc Champion, Jeanne Whalen, and Jay Solomon, "Terror in London: Police Make One Arrest after Raids in North England," *Wall Street Journal*, July 12, 2005, http://online.wsj.com/article/0,SB112116092902883194,00.html?mod5djemTAR (accessed August 15, 2007).

40. European Cybercrime Center, "A Collective EU Response to Cybercrime," https://www.europol.europa.eu/ec3 (accessed June 1, 2015).

41. ICPO-Interpol General Assembly Resolution No. AG-2001-RES-07.

42. Coalition for the International Criminal Court, "Together for Justice," http://iccnow.org (accessed May 20, 2015).

43. See the Coalition for an International Criminal Court, "Building the Court," http://www.iccnow.org/buildingthecourt.html (accessed July 30, 2011).

44. Much of the information and some of the wording in this section are adapted from "The ICC International Criminal Court Home Page," http://www.icc-cpi.int/Menus/ICC (accessed July 4, 2011); and the ICC "Timeline," http://www.iccnow.org/html/timeline.htm (accessed April 12, 2009).

45. Convention on the Prevention and Punishment of the Crime of Genocide, adopted by Resolution 260 (III) A of the U.N. General Assembly on December 9, 1948, http://www.preventgenocide.org/law/convention/text.htm (accessed July 4, 2011).

46. Plenipotentiary is another word for "diplomat."

47. Rome Statute of the International Criminal Court, United Nations Diplomatic Conference of Plenipotentiaries on the Establishment of an International Criminal Court, Rome, Italy, June 15–July 16, 1998 U.N. Document Number A/CONF.183/9 (1998), art. 7, http://www.un.org/law/icc/statutw/romefra.htm (accessed July 4, 2009).

48. Roy Gutman, "Is International Criminal Court the Best Way to Stop War Crimes?" *McClatchy Newspapers*, April 27, 2012, http://www.kentucky.com/2012/04/26/2164351/is-international-criminal-court.html (accessed August 12, 2012).

49. "ICC Appeals Judges Uphold Conviction of Congolese Warlord Lubanga," December 1, 2014, http://blink.htcsense.com/web/articleweb.aspx?regionid=1&articleid=32624116 (accessed March 1, 2015).

50. Much of the information in this paragraph and the next comes from David J. Lynch, "Belgium Plays Global Prosecutor," *USA Today*, July 16, 2001; and Katie Nguyen, "Cubans Use Belgian Law to File Case against Castro," Reuters, October 4, 2001.

51. Adapted from "Globalization," *Encyclopedia Britannica*, http://www.britannica.com/eb/article?eu5369857 (accessed July 28, 2011).

52. Federal Bureau of Investigation, "The Case of the Snakehead Queen: Chinese Human Smuggler Gets 35 Years," March 17, 2006, http://www.fbi.gov/page2/march06/sisterping031706.htm (accessed May 11, 2009).

53. Laurie Robinson, address given at the Twelfth International Congress on Criminology, Seoul, Korea, August 28, 1998.

54. National Institute of Justice, *Asian Transnational Organized Crime and Its Impact on the United States* (Washington, DC: NIJ, 2007), p. 1.

55. Robert S. Gelbard, "Foreign Policy after the Cold War: The New Threat—Transnational Crime," address at St. Mary's University, San Antonio, TX, April 2, 1996.

56. NIJ, *Asian Transnational Organized Crime*, p. 1.

57. Barbara Starr, "A Gangster's Paradise," ABC News Online, September 14, 1998, http://more.abcnews.go.com/sections/world/dailynews/russiacrime980914.html (accessed January 24, 2004).

58. Ibid.

59. Raymond Bonner and Timothy L. O'Brien, "Activity at Bank Raises Suspicions of Russia Mob Tie," *New York Times*, August 19, 1999.

60. Kevin F. Ryan, "Globalizing the Problem: The United States and International Drug Control," in Eric L. Jensen and Jurg Gerber, eds., *The New War on Drugs: Symbolic Politics and Criminal Justice Policy* (Cincinnati, OH: Anderson, 1997).

61. Trafficking Victims Protection Act of 2000, Div. A of Public Law 106-386, Section 108, as amended.

62. Sex trafficking is defined separately under U.S. Code, Title 22, Section 7102 (8); (9); (14) as "the recruitment, harboring, transportation, provision, or obtaining of a person for the purpose of a commercial sex act."

63. Public Law 108-193.

64. President Obama signed into law the Trafficking Victims Protection Reauthorization Act (TVPRA) of 2005 on January 10, 2006, and the Trafficking Victims Protection Reauthorization Act of 2013 was part of the Violence Against Women Reauthorization Act of 2013.

65. Bureau for International Narcotics and Law Enforcement Affairs, Human Smuggling and Trafficking Center, *Distinctions between Human Smuggling and Human Trafficking* (Washington, DC: January 1, 2005).

66. Raimo Väyrynen, "Illegal Immigration, Human Trafficking, and Organized Crime," United Nations University/World Institute for Development Economics Research, Discussion Paper No. 2003/72 (October 2003), p. 16.

67. Details for this story come from "Immigrant Smuggler Faulted in 19 Deaths Sentenced to Life in Prison," *Associated Press*, January 18, 2007, http://www.usatoday.com/news/nation/2007-01-18-smuggler_x.htm (accessed September 9, 2009).

68. Office of the Under Secretary for Democracy and Global Affairs, *Trafficking in Persons Report* (Washington, DC: U.S. Dept. of State, June 2007).

69. Ibid., p. 8.

70. Ibid.

71. Ibid.

72. Amy Farrell, Jack McDevitt, Rebecca Pfeffer, Stephanie Fahy, Colleen Owens, Meredith Dank, and William Adams, *Identifying Challenges to Improve the Investigation and Prosecution of State and Local Human Trafficking Cases: Executive Summary* (Washington, DC: National Institute of Justice, 2012), p. 3.

73. Bureau for International Narcotics and Law Enforcement Affairs, *Human Smuggling and Trafficking Center, Distinctions between Human Smuggling and Human Trafficking*, p. 16.

74. Office of the Under Secretary for Democracy and Global Affairs, *Trafficking in Persons Report*, p. 5.

75. Ibid.

76. Foreign Relations Authorization Act, U.S. Code, Title 22, Section 2656 f(d)(2).

77. In the words of the act: "The term 'terrorism' means premeditated, politically motivated violence perpetrated against noncombatant targets by subnational groups or clandestine agents" U.S. Code, Title 22, Section 2656 f(d)(2).

78. Federal Bureau of Investigation, Counterterrorism Section, *Terrorism in the United States, 1987* (Washington, DC: FBI, 1987), in which the full definition offered here can be found. See also "FBI Policy and Guidelines: Counterterrorism," http://www.fbi.gov/contact/fo/jackson/cntrterr.htm (accessed January 15, 2008), which offers a somewhat less formal definition of the term.

79. Gwynn Nettler, *Killing One Another* (Cincinnati, OH: Anderson, 1982).

80. Ibid., p. 253.

81. Adapted from "FBI Policy and Guidelines."

82. Ibid.

83. The death penalty was imposed for the first-degree murders of eight federal law enforcement agents who were at work in the Murrah Building at the time of the bombing. Although all of the killings violated Oklahoma law, only the killings of the federal agents fell under federal law, which makes such murders capital offenses.

84. "Terry Nichols Receives Life Sentences for Each of 161 Victims in 1995 Oklahoma City Bombing," Associated Press, August 9, 2004.

85. "Rudolph Agrees to Plea Agreement," *CNN Law Center*, April 12, 2005, http://www.cnn.com/2005/LAW/04/08/rudolph.plea (accessed May 21, 2007).

86. Bruce Frankel, "Sheik Guilty in Terror Plot," *USA Today*, October 2, 1995, p. 1A. Sheik Abdel-Rahman and codefendant El Sayyid Nosair were both sentenced to life in prison. Other defendants received sentences of between 25 and 57 years in prison. See Sascha Brodsky, "Terror Verdicts Denounced," United Press International, January 17, 1996.

87. For recent updates on Abdel-Rahman, see the New York Times page at http://www.nytimes.com/topic/person/omar-abdel-rahman (accessed November 8, 2015).

88. "Qaeda Suspect Dead, Suicide Eyed," *CBSNews.com*, July 3, 2003, http://www.cbsnews.com/stories/2003/06/26/world/main560618.shtml (accessed July 10, 2003).

89. Philip Stephens, "All Nostalgia Is Futile at the Beginning of History," *Financial Times*, May 27, 2005, p. 13.

90. Brian Michael Jenkins, *New Challenges to U.S. Counterrorism Efforts: An Assessment of the Current Terrorist Threat*, testimony before the Committee on Homeland security and Governmental Affairs of the United States Senate, July 11, 2012 (Santa Monica, CA: Rand Corporation, 2012), http://www.rand.org/pubs/testimonies/CT377.html (accessed May 1, 2013).

91. See Barry Collin, "The Future of Cyberterrorism," *Crime and Justice International,* March 1997, pp. 15–18.

92. John Arquilla and David Ronfeldt, *The Advent of Netwar* (Santa Monica, CA: RAND Corporation, 1996).

93. Mark M. Pollitt, "Cyberterrorism: Fact or Fancy?" *Proceedings of the Twentieth National Information Systems Security Conference*, October 1997, pp. 285–289.

94. The White House Office of the Press Secretary, "Executive Order on Critical Infrastructure Protection," October 16, 2001, http://www.whitehouse.gov/news/releases/2001/10/20011016-12.html (accessed May 21, 2007).

95. President's Critical Infrastructure Protection Board, *The National Strategy to Secure Cyberspace* (Washington, DC: U.S. Government Printing Office, September 18, 2002).

96. Department of Homeland Security, "Ridge Creates New Division to Combat Cyber Threats," press release, June 6, 2003, http://www.dhs.gov/dhspublic/display?content5916 (accessed May 28, 2007).

97. Lolita C. Baldor and John Andrew Prime, "Obama Announces Cyber Security Office," *Associated Press*, http://www.shreveporttimes.com/article/20090530/NEWS01/905300321/1060/NEWS01 (accessed July 3, 2009).

98. Daniel Boyce, "Narco-terrorism," *FBI Law Enforcement Bulletin* (October 1987), p. 24; and James A. Inciardi, "Narcoterrorism: A Perspective and Commentary," in Robert O. Slater and Grant Wardlaw, eds., *International Narcotics* (London: Macmillan/St. Martins, 1989).

99. Details for this story come from "Alleged Afghan Drug Kingpin Arrested," *USA Today*, April 26, 2005.

100. The term narcoterrorism was reportedly invented by former Peruvian President Fernando Belaunde Terry; see James A. Inciardi, "Narcoterrorism," paper presented at the 1988 annual meeting of the Academy of Criminal Justice Sciences, San Francisco, CA, p. 8.

101. Boyce, "Narco-terrorism," p. 24.

102. Ibid., p. 25.

103. U.S. Department of State, *Terrorist Group Profiles* (Washington, DC: U.S. Government Printing Office, 1989).

104. Inciardi, "Narcoterrorism."

105. "U.S. Government Lacks Strategy to Neutralize International Crime," *Criminal Justice International*, Vol. 10, No. 5 (September/October 1994), p. 5.

106. *National Strategy for Combating Terrorism* (Washington, DC: White House, 2003).

107. Emilio C. Viano, Jose Magallanes, and Laurent Bridel, "Transnational Organized Crime: Myth, Power, and Profit," *Crime and Justice International*, May/June 2005, p. 23.

108. *National Strategy for Combating Terrorism*, p. 6.

109. *National Strategy for Counterterrorism* (Washington, DC: White House, 2011).

110. The actual language of the act sets a standard for metal detectors through the use of a "security exemplar" made of 3.7 ounces of stainless steel in the shape of a handgun. Weapons made of other substances might still pass the test provided that they could be detected by metal detectors adjusted to that level of sensitivity. See "Bill Is Signed Barring Sale or Manufacture of Plastic Guns," *Criminal Justice Newsletter*, Vol. 19, No. 23 (December 1, 1988), pp. 4–5.

111. National Commission on Terrorism, *Countering the Changing Threat of International Terrorism* (Washington, DC: U.S. Dept. of State, 2000).

112. Mimi Hall, "Report: USA Left Open to Attack," *USA Today*, December 6, 2005, p. 1A.

113. Peter Bergen and Bruce Hoffman, *Assessing the Terrorist Threat* (Washington, DC: National Security Preparedness Group, 2010).

114. Brian Michael Jenkins, *New Challenges to U.S. Counterterrorism Efforts*.

115. U.S. Department of Homeland Security, "DHS Organization: Building a Secure Homeland," http://www.dhs.gov/dhspublic/theme_home1.jsp (accessed August 28, 2007).

116. U.S. Department of Homeland Security, *Fiscal Year 2015, Budget in Brief* (Washington, DC: DHS, 2015), http://www.dhs.gov/sites/default/files/publications/FY15BIB.pdf (accessed May 21, 2015).

117. Ibid.

118. Doris Meissner, Donald M. Kerwin, Muzaffar Chishti, and Claire Bergeron, *Immigration Enforcement in the United States: The Rise of a Formidable Machinery* (Washington, DC: Migration Policy Institute, 2013).

119. Ibid., p. 3.

120. *National Strategy for Counterterrorism*.

121. The NCTC was established by executive order in 2004, although Congress codified the NCTC in the Intelligence Reform and Terrorism Prevention Act of 2004 and placed the NCTC within the Office of the Director of National Intelligence.

122. National Counterterrorism Center, *NCTC and Information Sharing* (Washington, DC: NCTC, 2006), p. i, from which some of the wording in this paragraph is taken.

123. U.S. Code, Title 8, Section 1-1599.

124. Public Law 108-408.

125. U.S. Code, Title 8, Section 219.

126. U.S. Department of State, "Foreign Terrorist Organizations," http://www.state.gov/j/ct/rls/other/des/123085.htm (accessed May 20, 2015).

127. Information in this paragraph comes from U.S. Department of State, "Patterns of Global Terrorism, 2002," http://www.state.gov/s/ct/rls/pgtrpt/2002/ (accessed August 2, 2007); and U.S. Department of State, "State Sponsors of Terrorism," http://www.state.gov/s/ct/c14151.htm (accessed July 2, 2008).

128. Central Intelligence Agency, *National Foreign Intelligence Council, Global Trends, 2015: A Dialogue about the Future with Nongovernment Experts* (Washington, DC: U.S. Government Printing Office, 2000).

129. Ibid.

130. Central Intelligence Agency, *National Foreign Intelligence Council, Mapping the Global Future: Report of the National Intelligence Council's 2020 Project* (Washington, DC: U.S. Government Printing Office, 2005).

Newscom

18

HIGH-TECHNOLOGY CRIMES

LEARNING OBJECTIVES

After reading this chapter, you should be able to

- Describe the historical relationship between technological advances and criminal activity.
- Describe the current and likely future roles of technology in both crime and in the fight against crime.
- Describe the field of criminalistics, including the contribution of evolving technology.

The rise of a new kind of America requires a new kind of law enforcement system.

ALVIN TOFFLER

■ **theme**   What opportunities and threats does the chapter suggest contemporary technology presents to the criminal justice system today?

Introduction

In late 2014, Sony Pictures became the victim of a cyberattack on the company's computer network.[1] The attack, which the FBI blamed on North Korea's government, led to cancellation of a movie slated for Christmas release, and revealed thousands of private emails and internal documents kept on the company's servers. Many of the messages proved embarrassing to Sony executives when they were found to contain numerous derogatory comments about well-known actors. FBI cybercrime experts reported that a "technical analysis of the data deletion malware used in this attack revealed links to other malware that the FBI knows North Korean actors previously developed."[2]

Just as police departments are making use of new technologies, so too are modern-day criminals—including rouge states and transnational criminal organizations—who use the Internet and other communications technologies because they provide novel criminal opportunities. Recently, for example, Phoenix police investigators discovered a DVD inside a suspect's car containing personal information about a number of undercover officers taken from Facebook and other websites. Phoenix authorities were forced to issue a "security alert," telling officers that they were being "targeted" on Facebook, and warning them that posting photographs and other personal information on social media sites "may create serious officer safety consequences."[3] Similarly, gang experts have discovered that gang members are using their cell phone cameras to provide real-time "surveillance" of police activities.

Because technology is one of the most important instruments of change in the modern world, this chapter focuses on the opportunities and threats that contemporary technology presents to the justice system.

Technology and Crime

Rapid advances in the biological sciences and electronic technologies during the past few decades, including genetic mapping, nanotechnology, computer networking, the Internet, wireless services of all kinds, artificial intelligence (AI), deep intelligence initiatives, and global positioning system (GPS) devices, have ushered in a wealth of new criminal opportunities.

Sony Pictures plaza in Culver City, California. In late 2014, the company became the victim of an embarrassing and expensive cyberattack. How does the attack illustrate the changing nature of criminal threats?

■ **lecture note**   Explain the concept of biocrime and describe some of the varied types of potentially possible biocrimes.

■ **technocrime**   A criminal offense that employs advanced or emerging technology in its commission.

■ **Follow the author's tweets about the latest crime and justice news @schmalleger.**

■ **theme**   In years past, human cloning met with congressional efforts to criminalize it. Should you have a right to clone your own cells?

■ **biocrime**   A criminal offense perpetrated through the use of biologically active substances, including chemicals and toxins, disease-causing organisms, altered genetic material, and organic tissues and organs. Biocrimes unlawfully affect the metabolic, biochemical, genetic, physiological, or anatomical status of living organisms.

Rapid advances in the biological sciences and electronic technologies during the past few decades have ushered in a wealth of new criminal opportunities.

Crimes that employ advanced or emerging technologies in their commission are referred to as **technocrimes.**

New York State Police Captain and law enforcement visionary Thomas Cowper says that "it is important for police officers and their agencies to understand emerging technologies" for three reasons:[4] (1) to anticipate their use by terrorists and criminals and thereby thwart their use against our nation and citizens, (2) to incorporate their use into police operations when necessary, and (3) to deal effectively with the social changes and cultural impact that inevitably result from technological advances. According to Cowper, "Continued police apathy and ignorance of nanotech, biotech and AI, and the potential changes they will bring to our communities and way of life, will only add to the turmoil, making law enforcement a part of the problem and not part of the solution."[5]

Biocrime

In 2005, the World Health Organization raised alarms when it said that some samples of a potentially dangerous influenza virus that had been sent to thousands of laboratories in 18 countries had been lost and could not be located. Bio-kits containing the influenza A (H2N2) virus, which caused the flu pandemic of 1957–1958, were sent to 4,614 laboratories for use in testing the labs' ability to identify flu viruses. Meridian Bioscience Inc. of Cleveland, Ohio, sent the kits on behalf of the College of American Pathologists and three other U.S. organizations that set testing standards for laboratories. Although most of the laboratories were in the United States, some were in Latin America, and a few were in the Arab world—raising fears that Islamic terrorists might use the viral material, against which most people living today have no immunity, to create a pandemic. The H2N2 scare ended on May 2, 2005, when the U.S. Centers for Disease Control and Prevention (CDC) issued a press release saying that the last remaining sample of the virus outside the United States had been found and destroyed at the American University of Beirut in Lebanon.[6] The Lebanese sample had been misplaced by a local delivery service but was discovered in a warehouse at the Beirut airport. Although the incident came to a successful conclusion, it heightened concerns about the spread of highly pathogenic avian influenza viruses and the possible appropriation by criminals of reverse-genetics research on the 1918 pandemic flu virus that killed millions worldwide.

Biological crime, or **biocrime,** is a criminal offense perpetrated through the use of biologically active substances, including chemicals and toxins, disease-causing organisms, altered genetic material, and organic tissues and organs. Biocrimes unlawfully affect the metabolic, biochemical, genetic, physiological, or anatomical status of living organisms. A major change in such status can, of course, produce death.

Biocrime is a high-technology offense that involves the use of purposefully altered genetic material or advanced bioscientific techniques.

Biocrimes can be committed with simple poisons, but the biocrimes of special concern today involve technologically sophisticated delivery and dispersal systems and include the use of substances that have been bioengineered to produce the desired effect. Biocrime becomes a high-technology offense when it involves the use of purposefully altered genetic material or advanced bioscientific techniques.

Although many people are aware of the dangers of terrorist-related biocrimes, including biological attacks on agricultural plants and animals (agroterrorism) and on human beings, many other kinds of potential biocrimes lurk on the horizon. They include the illegal harvesting of human organs for medical transplantation, human cloning, and the direct alteration of the DNA of living beings to produce a mixing of traits between species. Stem cell harvesting, another area that faces possible criminalization, is currently the subject of hot debate. The situation in the United States with regard to stem cell harvesting is one of funding restrictions, not legal or criminal restrictions. Although the federal government has yet to enact comprehensive legislation curtailing, regulating, or forbidding many of the kinds of activities mentioned here, there are a number of special interest groups that continue to lobby for such laws.

In 2004, Korean scientists became the first to announce that they had successfully cloned a human embryo and had extracted embryonic stem cells from it.[7] In 2005, those same scientists used the process to make stem cells tailored to match an individual patient, meaning that medical treatments for diseases like diabetes might be possible without fear of cellular rejection. Similarly, in 2005, British scientists working at Newcastle University in England disclosed that they had created a cloned human embryo.

■ **hacker**   A computer hobbyist or professional, generally with advanced programming skills. Today, the term *hacker* has taken on a sinister connotation, referring to hobbyists who are bent on illegally accessing the computers of others or who attempt to demonstrate their technological prowess through computerized acts of vandalism.

Cloning is a cellular reproductive process that does not require the joining of a sperm and an egg; it occurs when the nucleus of an egg is replaced with the nucleus of another cell.

President George W. Bush favored a ban on all research into human cloning in the United States[8] and threatened to veto proposed federal legislation in 2005 that would have provided federal support for cloning research.[9] Similarly, in 2003, the U.S. House of Representatives voted to criminalize all human cloning activities and research.[10] The proposed legislation, known as the Human Cloning Research Prohibition Act, would have made it a crime to transfer the nucleus of an ordinary human cell into an unfertilized human egg whose own nucleus had been removed.[11] It also would have made it a crime to "receive or import a cloned human embryo or any product derived from a cloned human embryo." The scientific technique targeted by the bill, known as *nuclear transfer*, is the process that was used to clone Dolly the sheep in 1996.[12] A similar bill, known as the Human Cloning Prohibition Act of 2005, was introduced by Senator Sam Brownback, a Republican from Kansas.[13] Although it didn't become law, the Human Cloning Prohibition Act of 2009, a similar bill, died in the House.[14] If passed, the bills would have prohibited both reproductive cloning and the use of cloning technology to derive stem cells. In other words, the legislation aimed to thwart not just reproductive cloning, in which a copy of a living organism might be made, but also therapeutic cloning.[15]

Therapeutic cloning is a healing technique in which a person's own cells are used to grow a new organ, such as a heart, liver, or lungs, to replace a diseased or damaged organ. Opponents feared that the proposed legislation, which specified punishments of up to a $1 million fine and ten years in prison, would have significantly retarded biomedical progress in the United States, relegating America to a kind of technological backwater in the world's burgeoning biotechnology industry.[16] In 2009, President Obama, in what many saw as an important step forward for the American scientific community, signed a presidential directive lifting restrictions on federal funding for embryonic stem cell research, but promised that the U.S. government would "never open the door" to human cloning.[17]

Cybercrime

The dark side of new technologies, as far as the justice system is concerned, is the potential they create for committing old crimes in new ways or for committing new crimes never before imagined. In 2014, for example, Russian national Aleksandry Andreevich Panin, pleaded guilty in U.S. federal court, to conspiracy to commit wire and bank fraud for his role as the primary developer and distributor of the malicious software known as Spyeye, which infected more than 1.4 million computers in the United States and abroad. Based on information received from the financial services industry, more than 10,000 bank accounts had been compromised by Spyeye infections.[18]

Similarly, a few years ago, technologically savvy scam artists replicated the website of the Massachusetts State Lottery Commission.[19] The scammers, believed to be operating out of Nigeria, sent thousands of e-mails and cell phone text messages telling people that they had won $30,000 in the Massachusetts State Lottery. People who received the messages were told to sign on to an official-looking website to claim their prize. The site required that users enter their Social Security and credit card numbers and pay a $100 processing fee before the winnings could be distributed.

A person's online activities occur in a virtual world comprised of bits and bytes. That's why we said in Chapter 2 that "true" computer criminals engage in behavior that goes beyond the theft of hardware. Cybercrime, or computer crime, focuses on the information stored in electronic media, which is why it is sometimes referred to as *information technology crime* or *infocrime*. Two decades ago, for example, the activities of computer expert Kevin Mitnick, then known as the Federal Bureau of Investigation's (FBI's) "most wanted **hacker**,"[20] alarmed security experts because of the potential for harm that Mitnick's electronic intrusions represented. The 31-year-old Mitnick broke into an Internet service provider's computer system and stole more than 20,000 credit card numbers. Tsutoma Shimomura, whose home computer Mitnick had also attacked, helped FBI experts track Mitnick through telephone lines and computer networks to the computer in his Raleigh, North Carolina, apartment, where he was arrested. In March 1999, Mitnick pleaded guilty to seven federal counts of computer and wire fraud. He was sentenced to 46 months in prison but was released on parole in January 2000. Under the terms of his release, Mitnick was barred from access to computer hardware and software and from any form of wireless communication for a period of three years.[21] In an interview after his release, Mitnick pointed out that "malicious hackers don't need to use stealth computer techniques to break into a network. … Often they just trick someone into giving them passwords and other information."[22] According to Mitnick, "People are the weakest link. … You can have the best technology, firewalls, intrusion-detection systems, biometric devices … and somebody can call an unsuspecting employee … [and] they [get] everything."

Neil Barrett, a digital crime expert at International Risk Management, a London-based security consultancy, agrees.

■ **lecture note** Summarize the federal and state statutes under which cybercriminals can be prosecuted. Ask which laws seem most effective and why.

■ **social engineering** A nontechnical kind of cyberintrusion that relies heavily on human interaction and often involves tricking people into breaking normal security procedures.

■ **lecture note** Discuss the types of cybercrime listed in the text. Contrast each with the techniques used to control it.

■ **activity** Ask students to assemble a library of computer-security programs, including those that deal with data encryption and virus protection. Use the documentation files available with the software to demonstrate the usefulness of such programs and to illustrate the kinds of threats facing computer users today. Be careful to use only software or applications from reputable sources. Note that some vendors require purchase for continued use of their products.

"The most likely way for bad guys to break into the system is through **social engineering.** This involves persuading administrators or telephonists to give details of passwords or other things by pretending to be staff, suppliers or trusted individuals—even police officers. They could be even masquerading as a computer repair man to get access to the premises."[23] Social engineering is a devastating security threat, says Barrett, because it targets and exploits a computer network's most vulnerable aspect—people.

Transnational Cybercrime

An especially important characteristic of cybercrime is that it can easily be cross-jurisdictional or transnational. A cybercriminal sitting at a keyboard in Australia, for example, can steal money from a bank in Russia and then transfer the digital cash to an account in Chile. For investigators, the question may be, "What laws were broken?" Complicating matters is the fact that Australia and Chile have fragmented cybercrime laws, and Russia[24] has laws that are particularly ineffective.

According to researchers at McConnell International, a consulting firm based in Washington, D.C., of 52 developing countries surveyed in 2000, only the Philippines had effective cybercrime legislation in effect.[25] The Philippines enacted a new cybercrime law in 2000 after the creator of the highly damaging "Love Bug" computer virus, a 23-year-old Filipino student named Onel de Guzman, could not be prosecuted under the country's existing cybercrime laws.[26] De Guzman was finally charged with theft and violation of a law that had been enacted to deter credit card fraud. The country's new cybercrime law could not be applied to him retroactively.

In an effort to enhance similarities in the cybercrime laws of different countries and to provide a model for national lawmaking bodies concerned with controlling cybercrimes, the 43-nation Council of Europe approved a cybercrime treaty in November 2001.[27] The treaty outlaws specific online activities, including fraud and child pornography, and outlines what law enforcement officials in member nations may and may not do in enforcing cybercrime laws. The goal of the treaty is to standardize both legal understandings of cybercrime and cybercrime laws in member nations. It also allows police officers to detain suspects wanted in other countries for cybercrimes and facilitates the gathering of information on such crimes across national borders. In addition to the council's member states, the treaty was also signed by the United States, Canada, Japan, and South Africa.[28]

Types of Cybercrime

In 2005, a novel form of cybercrime made its appearance in the form of computer ransomware that installs itself on users' computers through an insecure Internet connection and then encrypts the users' data files.[29] When the machines' owners try to access their own information, they are presented with a message telling them to provide their charge card number to a remote server, which then sends them an unlock code. According to the FBI, this high-tech form of extortion is still rare but on the rise. Particularly targeted are financial institutions and other businesses that stand to lose large amounts of money if their data is corrupted or irretrievable.[30]

> In 2005, a novel form of cybercrime made its appearance in the form of computer ransomware that installs itself on users' computers through an insecure Internet connection and then encrypts the users' data files.

Peter Grabosky of the Australian Institute of Criminology suggests that most cybercrimes fall into one of the following broad categories:[31] (1) theft of services, such as telephone or long-distance access; (2) communications in furtherance of criminal conspiracies—for example, the e-mail communications said to have taken place between members of Osama bin Laden's al-Qaeda terrorist network;[32] (3) information piracy and forgery—that is, the stealing of trade secrets or copyrighted information; (4) the dissemination of offensive materials such as child pornography, high volumes of unwanted commercial material such as bulk e-mail (spam), or extortion threats like those made against financial institutions by hackers claiming the ability to destroy a company's electronic records; (5) electronic money laundering and tax evasion (through electronic funds transfers that conceal the origin of financial proceeds); (6) electronic vandalism and terrorism, including computer viruses, worms, Trojan horses, and cyberterrorism (see Chapter 17); (7) telemarketing fraud (including investment fraud and illegitimate electronic auctions); (8) illegal interception of telecommunications—that is, illegal eavesdropping; and (9) fraud involving electronic funds transfer (specifically, the illegal interception and diversion of legitimate transactions).

A recent Computer Crime and Security Survey, conducted by the Computer Security Institute (CSI) and the FBI, found that the most expensive computer security incidents are those involving financial fraud.[33] Forty-six percent of the 351 information security professionals responding to the survey reported

■ **computer virus**   A computer program designed to secretly invade systems and either modify the way in which they operate or alter the information they store. Viruses are destructive software programs that may effectively vandalize computers of all types and sizes.

■ **malware**   Malicious computer programs such as viruses, worms, and Trojan horses.

that their companies or organizations had been subjected to at least one targeted attack during the survey period. "Targeted attacks" were defined as malware attacks aimed exclusively at the respondent's organization. Eighteen percent of respondents stated that they notified individuals whose personal information was breached. Sixteen percent said that as a result of attacks they provided new security services to users or customers. An overview of the Computer Security Institute's survey results can be found online at **http://gocsi.com/survey.**

Another source of data on Internet crime is the Internet Crime Complaint Center (IC3), a partnership between the FBI, BJA, and the White Collar Crime Center. In 2014, the IC3 published its *2013 Internet Crime Report*—the 14th annual compilation of information on complaints received and/or referred to the IC3 by law enforcement agencies for appropriate action.[34] In 2013, the IC3 received 262,813 complaints involving financial losses of more than $781 million. Nondelivery of merchandise ordered over the Internet, identity theft, overpayment fraud, advance-fee fraud, and fraudulent FBI-related scams (in which an individual poses as an FBI agent in an effort to defraud victims) were among the top types of fraud reported. The 2013 IC3 report, which provides a snapshot of the prevalence and impact of Internet fraud cases and describes the kinds of complaints that were filed, is available at **http://www.ic3.gov/media/annualreport/2013_IC3Report.pdf**.

Computer Viruses, Worms, and Trojan Horses
Computer viruses are a special concern of computer users everywhere. Computer viruses were first brought to public attention in 1988, when the Pakistani virus (or Pakistani brain virus) became widespread in personal and office computers across the United States.[35] The Pakistani virus was created by Amjad Farooq Alvi and his brother, Basit Farooq Alvi, two cut-rate computer software dealers in Lahore, Pakistan. The Alvi brothers made copies of costly software products and sold them at low prices, mostly to Western shoppers looking for a bargain. Motivated by convoluted logic, the brothers hid a virus on each disk they sold to punish buyers for seeking to evade copyright laws.

A more serious virus incident later that year affected sensitive machines in National Aeronautics and Space Administration (NASA) nuclear weapons labs, federal research centers, and universities across the United States.[36] The virus did not destroy data. Instead, it made copies of itself and multiplied so rapidly that it clogged and effectively shut down computers within hours after invading them. Robert Morris, creator of the virus,

Nick Ut/AP Images

Luis Mijangos, 32, of Santa Ana, California. Mijangos was sentenced to six years in prison in 2011 for sextortion (digital extortion) after he pleaded guilty to computer hacking and wiretapping. Mijangos used file-sharing networks to infect the computers of women and teenage girls, searching them for sexually explicit pictures. He'd then contact the victims demanding that they provide more photos or videos, or he'd post what he had on the Web. In some cases he was also able to turn on victims' computer microphones and cameras to record their personal activities. How can you tell if your computer is immune to attacks like those perpetrated by Mijangos?

was sentenced in 1990 to 400 hours of community service, three years' probation, and a fine of $10,000.[37] Since then, many other virus attacks have made headlines, including the infamous Michelangelo virus in 1992; the intentional distribution of infected software on an AIDS-related research CD-ROM distributed about the same time; the Kournikova virus in 2000; and the later Sircam, Nimda, W32, NastyBrew, Berbew, Mydoom, and Code Red worms.

Technically speaking, most of today's malicious software falls under the category of worms or Trojan horses—called **malware** by technophiles. Malware (also called *crimeware*) has become increasingly sophisticated. Although early viruses were

■ **software piracy** The unauthorized duplication of software or the illegal transfer of data from one storage medium to another. Software piracy is one of the most prevalent cybercrimes in the world.

■ **spam** Unsolicited commercial bulk e-mail whose primary purpose is the advertisement or promotion of a commercial product or service.

relatively easy to detect with hardware or software scanning devices that looked for virus "signatures," new malicious software using stealth and polymorphic computer codes changes form with each new "infection" and is much more difficult to locate and remove. Moreover, whereas older viruses infected only executable programs, or those that could be run, newer malware (such as the Word for Windows Macro virus, also called the *Concept virus*) attaches itself to word-processing documents and to computer codes that are routinely distributed via the World Wide Web (including Java and Active-X components used by Web browsers). In 1998, the world's first HTML virus was discovered. The virus, named HTML Internal, infects computers whose users are merely viewing Web pages.[38] Later that year, the first Java-based malware, named Strange Brew, made its appearance,[39] and in 2004 malware capable of infecting digital images using the Joint Photographic Experts Group (JPEG) format was discovered.[40] Evolving forms of malware are even able to infect cell phones and other wireless-enabled handheld devices.

Phishing

One form of cyber crime that relies primarily on social engineering to succeed is *phishing* (pronounced "fishing"). Phishing is a relatively new form of high-technology fraud that uses official-looking e-mail messages to elicit responses from victims, directing them to phony websites. Microsoft Corporation says that phishing is "the fastest-growing form of online fraud in the world today."[41] Phishing e-mails typically instruct recipients to validate or update account information before their accounts are canceled. Phishing schemes, which have targeted most major banks, the Federal Deposit Insurance Corporation, IBM, eBay, PayPal, and some major health-care providers, are designed to steal valuable information like credit card numbers, Social Security numbers, user IDs, and passwords. In late-2014, the Antiphishing Working Group found more than 128,000 existing phishing Web sites, and said that the United States continued to be the top country hosting phishing sites.[42]

> Phishing is a relatively new form of high-technology fraud that uses official-looking e-mail messages to elicit responses from victims, directing them to phony websites.

Software Piracy

Another form of cybercrime, the unauthorized copying of software programs, also called **software piracy,** is rampant. According to the Software and Information Industry Association (SIIA), global losses from software piracy total nearly $12.2 billion annually.[43] The SIIA says that 38% of all software in use in the world today has been copied illegally. Some countries have especially high rates of illegal use. Of all the computer software in use in Vietnam, for example, the SIIA estimates that 97% has been illegally copied, whereas 95% of the software used in China and 92% of the software used in Russia are thought to be pirated—resulting in a substantial loss in manufacturers' revenue.

In 2005, in the landmark case of *MGM v. Grokster*,[44] the U.S. Supreme Court found that online file-sharing services may be held liable for copyright infringement if they promote their services explicitly as a way for users to download copyrighted music and other content. The *Grokster* decision contrasts with the 1984 case of *Sony Corporation of America v. Universal City Studios, Inc.*, in which the Court held that a distributor/operator of a copying tool cannot be held liable for users' copyright infringements so long as the tool in question is capable of substantial noninfringing uses.[45]

Spam

Nearly a decade ago, federal legislators acted to criminalize the sending of unsolicited commercial e-mail, or **spam.** The federal CAN-SPAM Act (Controlling the Assault of Non-Solicited Pornography and Marketing), which took effect on January 1, 2004, regulates the sending of "commercial electronic mail messages."[46] The law, which applies equally to mass mailings and to individual e-mail messages, defines commercial electronic mail messages as electronic mail whose *primary purpose* is the "commercial advertisement or promotion of a commercial product or service." The CAN-SPAM law requires that a commercial e-mail message include the following three features: (1) a clear and conspicuous identification that the message is an advertisement or solicitation, (2) an opt-out feature, allowing recipients to opt out of future mailings, and (3) a valid physical address identifying the sender.

Some experts estimate that 80% of all e-mail today is spam,[47] and many states have enacted their own antispam laws. Virginia's 2003 antispam statute,[48] one of the first in the nation, imposes criminal penalties of from one to five years for anyone convicted of falsifying electronic mail transmission information or other routing information during the sending of unsolicited commercial bulk e-mail (UCBE). The law applies to anyone sending more than 10,000 UCBEs in a 24-hour period and to anyone who generates more than $1,000 in revenue from a UCBE transmission. The law also applies to anyone who uses fraudulent practices to send bulk e-mail to or from Virginia, a

■ **theme** Put yourself in the position of a futurist. What developments do you see on the horizon that might result in new technologies of potential service to future criminals? Describe the kinds of crimes that might result.

■ **lecture note** Explain that state-sponsored terrorist groups are becoming more technological sophisticated and taking advantage of new technologies to further their goals.

■ **weapon of mass destruction (WMD)** A chemical, biological, or nuclear weapon that has the potential to cause mass casualties.

■ **bioterrorism** The intentional or threatened use of viruses, bacteria, fungi, or toxins from living organisms to produce death or disease in humans, animals, or plants.[1]

state that is home to a number of large Internet service providers, including America Online. In 2005, in the nation's first felony prosecution of a spammer, Jeremy Jaynes, age 30, one of the world's most active spammers, received a nine-year prison sentence under Virginia's law after he was convicted of using false Internet addresses and aliases to send mass e-mailings to America Online subscribers. Prosecutors were able to prove that Jaynes, a Raleigh, North Carolina, resident, earned as much as $750,000 a month by sending as many as 10 million illegal messages a day using computers operating in Virginia.[49]

Terrorism and Technology

The technological sophistication of state-sponsored terrorist organizations is rapidly increasing. Handguns and even larger weapons are now being manufactured out of plastic polymers and ceramics. Capable of firing Teflon-coated armor-piercing hardened ceramic bullets, such weapons are extremely powerful and impossible to uncover with metal detectors. Some people have also raised concerns over the new technology represented by 3-D printers, capable of cranking out complex shapes that could be assembled into weapons—including handguns and other weapons; and in 2013, the State Department ordered the removal of what are believed to be the world's first printable gun blueprints from a website called Defense Distributed.[50] The do-it-yourself instructions had already been downloaded more than 100,000 times before the site was able to take them down.

Evidence points to the black market availability of other sinister items, including liquid metal embrittlement (LME), a chemical that slowly weakens any metal it contacts. LME could easily be applied with a felt-tipped pen to fuselage components in domestic aircraft, causing delayed structural failure.[51] Backpack-type electromagnetic pulse generators may soon be available to terrorists. Such devices could be carried into major cities, set up next to important computer installations, and activated to wipe out billions of items of financial, military, or other information now stored on magnetic media. International terrorists, along with the general public, have easy access to maps and other information that could be used to cripple the nation. The approximately 500 extremely-high-voltage (EHV) transformers on which the nation's electric grid depends, for example, are largely undefended and until recently were specified with extreme accuracy on easily available Web-based power network maps.

It is now clear that at least some terrorist organizations are seeking to obtain **weapons of mass destruction (WMDs)**,

involving possible chemical, biological, radiological, and nuclear threats. A Central Intelligence Agency (CIA) report recently made public warned that al-Qaeda's "end goal" is to use WMDs. The CIA noted that the group had "openly expressed its desire to produce nuclear weapons" and that sketches and documents recovered from an al-Qaeda facility in Afghanistan contained plans for a crude nuclear device.[52]

The collapse of the Soviet Union in the late 1980s led to very loose internal control over nuclear weapons and weapons-grade fissionable materials held in the former Soviet republics. Evidence of this continues to surface. In 2003, for example, a cab driver in the Eastern European nation of Georgia was arrested while transporting containers of cesium-137 and strontium-90, materials that could be used to make a "dirty" bomb (a radiological dispersal device, or RDD)[53] that would use conventional explosives to spread nuclear contamination over a wide area.[54] A month later, officials arrested a traveler in Bangkok, Thailand, who had a canister of cesium-137 in his possession. Although the Thai traveler told police that he had acquired the cesium in Laos, scientists were able to determine that it had originated in Russia.

A study by Harvard University researchers found that the United States and other countries were moving too slowly in efforts to help Russia and other former Soviet-bloc nations destroy poorly protected nuclear material and warheads left over from the cold war.[55] The study also warned that most civilian nuclear reactors in Eastern Europe are "dangerously insecure." Experts say the amount of plutonium needed to make one bomb can be smuggled out of a supposedly secure area in a briefcase or even in the pocket of an overcoat.

Biological weapons were banned by the 1975 international Biological Weapons Convention,[56] but biological terrorism (or bioterrorism), which seeks to disperse destructive or disease-producing biologically active agents among civilian or military populations, is of considerable concern today. **Bioterrorism,** one form of biocrime, is defined by the Centers for Disease Control and Prevention as the "intentional or threatened use of viruses, bacteria, fungi, or toxins from living organisms to produce death or disease in humans, animals, or plants."[57] The infamous anthrax letters mailed to at least four people in the United States in 2001 provide an example of a bioterrorism incident intended to create widespread fear among Americans. Five people, including mail handlers, died, and 23 others were infected.[58] Other possible bioterror agents include botulism toxin, brucellosis, cholera, glanders, plague, ricin, smallpox, tularemia Q fever, and a number of viral agents capable of producing diseases such as viral hemorrhagic fever and severe acute respiratory syndrome (SARS). As mentioned earlier, experts fear that technologically savvy terrorists could create their own novel bioweapons through bioengineering, a process that uses snippets of made-to-order DNA, the molecular code on which life is based.[59] Visit the Institute for Biosecurity at **http://www.bioterrorism.slu.edu**, and read the CDC's overview of bioterrorism at **http://www.justicestudies.com/pubs/biochemcdc.pdf**.

Technology and Crime Control

Technology, although it has increased criminal opportunity, has also been a boon to police investigators and other justice system personnel. In one recent example the 2015 Social Media, the Internet, and Law Enforcement conference (SMILECon) was held in Phoenix, Arizona to help train police in the use of social media. Conference organizers noted that police departments can both benefit as well as suffer from recent developments in social networking, and said that the adoption of social media by law enforcement agencies "is in a stage of exponential growth."[60]

In a practical example of the use of social media in policing, the Bergen County (New Jersey) Sheriff's Office recently launched "FaceCrook", which includes public information on outstanding warrants tied to a Google Maps app, including an anonymous tip feature that allows people to provide anonymous tips via computer and telephone (**http://www.facecrook.net**).[61]

In another example, the Dunwoody, Georgia, Police Department experimented with using Twitter to help the city's 46,000 residents better understand the nature of police work. For 24 hours the department tweeted about each significant activity undertaken by its officers—beginning with an early morning traffic stop and concluding the next morning with a 6 a.m. report of a suspicious person.

Other police departments are jumping on board the social media bandwagon. A few years ago, for example, the California Highway Patrol created Twitter pages—one for each of its divisions; and the Modesto, California, Police Department set up an active Twitter account to notify followers about major incidents and to provide links to ongoing investigations and newsworthy events. The department also uses Twitter to steer people away from accident sites, to coordinate the activities of searchers during Amber Alerts, and to warn people to stay inside during potentially dangerous situations. "It's a valuable tool that allows us to get our message out," says Stanislaus County Sheriff's Department spokesperson Deputy Luke Schwartz.[62] "You're going to see a lot more law enforcement agencies get on board with social networking sites like Twitter and Facebook," says Schwartz.

Schwartz points out, however, that social networking technologies don't always benefit the police. "The element of surprise is everything, and social media is taking away the element of surprise that we need to keep people safe when we have tactical situations," Schwartz said.[63]

One of the best examples of the use of social media in law enforcement today is TheDailyOfficer. Follow TheDailyOfficer on Twitter **@DailyOfficer**, from which you can access an ever-changing compilation of current police news and blogs from around the world. Concerned citizens can provide tips to law enforcement agencies via the Web-based Crime Stoppers International tipline at **http://www.facebook.com/CSI-World**. Another website, Connected Cops, describes itself as "law enforcement's partner on the social web," and can be visited at **http://connectedcops.net**. Connected Cops is international in scope, and provides a blog populated with messages from law enforcement social media visionaries on how to leverage technology in the service of law enforcement.

Similarly, access by law enforcement to high-technology investigative tools has produced enormous amounts of information on crimes and suspects, and the use of innovative investigative tools like DNA fingerprinting, keystroke captures, laser and night-vision technologies, digital imaging, and thermography are beginning to shape many of the practical aspects of the twenty-first-century criminal justice system. Today, some laptop computers and vehicles are programmed to contact police when they are stolen and provide satellite-based tracking information so authorities can determine their whereabouts. Many rental car companies, for example, now have cars equipped with systems that can send and receive from a central location. Security employees at those companies can send instructions to vehicles to prevent the car from starting and thus being stolen. The system can also track the car as it moves. Likewise, some police departments are using high-technology "bait cars" to catch auto thieves.[64] Bait cars can signal when stolen, send digitized images of perpetrators to investigators, radio their position to officers, be remotely immobilized, and lock their doors on command, trapping thieves inside.

The New York City Police Department's Real Time Crime Center, where police work can seem like science fiction. At the center, where about a dozen analysts work, information on suspects is displayed on huge screens and can be relayed to detectives' laptops instantly. What do you imagine the future of police work will be like?

Another crime-fighting technology making headway in the identification of stolen vehicles is automatic plate recognition (APR) technology. APR readers installed in police vehicles can read over 5,000 license plates an hour, and can alert officers of stolen vehicles, expired registrations, and the like. Some states, however, fearing privacy concerns, are starting to ban APR technology except in certain locals like toll plazas.[65]

Car thieves have made some technological advances of their own, including the "laundering" of vehicle identification numbers (VINs), which allows stolen cars to be sold as legitimate vehicles.[66] Stolen cars with "cloned" VINs are usually not discovered until an insurance claim is filed and investigators learn that there are two or more vehicles registered with the same VIN to people in different locations. As these stories indicate, the future will no doubt see a race between technologically sophisticated offenders and law enforcement authorities to determine who can wield the most advanced technical skills in the age-old battle between crime and justice.[67] Have a look at how the FBI sees crime fighting's future at **http://www.justicestudies.com/pubs/futuretech.pdf**.

One of the best examples of the use of contemporary technologies in the service of crime fighting can be found at New York City's Real Time Crime Center. The center is staffed by specially trained data analysts who pore over enormous multiple-screen monitors that feed streams of information to them from video cameras, human intelligence gatherers, detectives and police officers, and computer programs searching for links between diverse bits of information. The center has been described as "a round-the-clock computer-data warehouse that can digitally track down information, from a perpetrator's mug shot to

his second former mother-in-law's address." Kenneth Mekeel, a former captain of detectives, now runs the center. "It used to take us days to find a number or an address," Mekeel says. "Now we send stuff to detectives who are literally standing [at the crime scene]."[68]

Leading Technological Organizations in Criminal Justice

The National Law Enforcement and Corrections Technology Center (NLECTC) performs yearly assessments of key technological needs and opportunities facing the justice system. The center is responsible for helping identify, develop, manufacture, and adopt new products and technologies designed for law enforcement, corrections, and other criminal justice applications.[69] The NLECTC concentrates on four areas of advancing technology: (1) communications and electronics, (2) forensic science, (3) transportation and weapons, and (4) protective equipment.[70] Once NLECTC researchers have identified opportunities for improvement in any area, they make referrals to the Law Enforcement Standards Laboratory—a part of the National Bureau of Standards—for the testing of available hardware. The Justice Technology Information Network (JUSTNET), a service of the NLECTC, acts as an information gateway for law enforcement, corrections, and criminal justice technology and notifies the justice community of the latest technological advances. JUSTNET, accessible on the Web, lists the websites of technology providers and makes them easy to access. Visit the NLECTC at **justnet.org**.

■ **theme**   Ask students to imagine how police work was done before the technological innovations described in this chapter. How effective would the police techniques of decades ago be in solving today's crimes?

■ **lecture note**   Discuss the use of social media by the police. Ask students if they follow the Facebook pages or Twitter feeds of their local police department. What do students think about the police use of Twitter and other social media platforms?

■ **criminalistics**   The use of technology in the service of criminal investigation; the application of scientific techniques to the detection and evaluation of criminal evidence.

■ **criminalist**   A police crime-scene analyst or laboratory worker versed in criminalistics.

Also, in 2013, the U.S. Department of Justice in conjunction with the National Institute of Standards and Technology (NIST) established the National Commission on Forensic Science as part of a new initiative to strengthen and enhance the practice of forensic science (which is discussed in more detail in the section that follows).[71] The commission provides guidance for federal, state, and local forensic science laboratories and works to coordinate technical advances in forensic sciences across federal, state, and local department and agencies. It is also working to create uniform codes for professional responsibility and requirements for training and certification in the area of forensic sciences.

Another important organization is the Society of Police Futurists International (PFI). PFI members are a highly select group of forward-thinking international police professionals. The group employs prediction techniques developed by other futures researchers to make reasonable forecasts about the likely role of the criminal justice system in the future. Recently, the PFI and the FBI collaborated to form a futures working group (FWG) to examine and promote innovation in policing. Consisting of approximately 15 members from the PFI and staff members from the FBI Academy, the FWG has implemented a variety of projects in collaboration with other organizations and academic institutions engaged in futures research. The group intends to continue to pursue opportunities for further cooperative efforts between American and international law enforcement agencies and organizations like the Foresight Institute (a British-based futures think tank).

Keep abreast of technological, cultural, and other changes affecting justice systems worldwide by visiting the Society of Police Futurists International via **http://www.policefuturists. org** and the Foresight Institute at **http://www.foresight.org**.

Criminalistics: Past, Present, and Future

Technological advances throughout history have signaled both threats and opportunities for the justice field. By the turn of the twentieth century, for example, police call boxes were standard features in many cities, utilizing the new technology of telephonic communications to pass along information on crimes in progress or to describe suspects and their activities. A few years later, police departments across the nation adapted to the rapid growth in the number of private automobiles and the laws governing their use. Over the years, motorized patrol, VASCAR speed-measuring devices, radar, laser speed detectors, and police

helicopters and aircraft were all called into service to meet the need for a rapid response to criminal activity. Today's citizens band radios, often monitored by local police and highway patrol agencies, and cell phones with direct numbers to police dispatchers continue the trend of adapting advances in communications technology to police purposes. In-field computers (that is, laptop or handheld computers typically found in police vehicles) are commonplace, and many local police departments provide their officers with access to computer databases from the field.

The use of technology in the service of criminal investigation is a subfield of criminal justice referred to as **criminalistics**. Criminalistics applies scientific techniques to the detection and evaluation of criminal evidence. Police crime-scene analysts and laboratory personnel who use these techniques are referred to as **criminalists**. Modern criminalistics began with the need for the certain identification of individuals. Early methods of personal identification were notoriously inaccurate. In the nineteenth century, for instance, one day of the week was generally dedicated to a "parade" of newly arrested offenders; experienced investigators from distant jurisdictions would scrutinize the convicts, looking for recognizable faces.[72] By the 1840s, the Quetelet system of anthropometry was gaining in popularity.[73] The Quetelet system depended on precise measurements of various parts of the body to give an overall "picture" of a person for use in later identification.

The first "modern" system of personal identification was created by Alphonse Bertillon.[74] Bertillon was the director of the Bureau of Criminal Identification of the Paris Police Department during the late nineteenth century. The Bertillon system of identification was based on the idea that certain physical characteristics, such as eye color, skeletal size and shape, and ear form, did not change substantially after physical maturity. The system combined physical measurements with the emerging technology of photography. Although photography had been used previously in criminal identification, Bertillon standardized the technique by positioning measuring guides beside suspects so that their physical dimensions could be calculated from their photographs and by taking both front views and profiles.

Fingerprints, produced by contact with the ridge patterns in the skin on the fingertips, became the subject of intense scientific study in the mid-1840s. Although their importance in criminal investigation today seems obvious, it was not until the 1880s that scientists began to realize that each person's fingerprints are unique and unchangeable over a lifetime. Both discoveries appear to have come from the Englishmen William Herschel and Henry Faulds, who were working in Asia.[75] Some writers, observing

■ **lecture note**   Use the invention of fingerprinting techniques to illustrate the evolution of law enforcement technology. Ask students to name
technological changes that might have similar far-reaching effects on the
criminal justice system of the future.

■ **lecture note**   Review the new and emerging technologies in criminalistics, such as DNA profiling, online databases, computer-aided investigation,
and computer-based training.

■ **biometrics**   The science of recognizing people by physical
characteristics and personal traits.

that Asian lore about finger ridges and their significance extends
back to antiquity, suggest that Herschel and Faulds must have
been privy to such information.[76] As early as the Tang Dynasty
(A.D. 618–906), inked fingerprints were being used in China as
personal seals on important documents, and there is some evidence that the Chinese had classified patterns of the loops and
whorls found in fingerprints and were using them for the identification of criminals as far back as 1,000 years ago.[77]

The use of fingerprints in identifying offenders was popularized by Sir Francis Galton[78] and was officially adopted by
Scotland Yard in 1901. By the 1920s, fingerprint identification was being used in police departments everywhere, having
quickly replaced Bertillon's anthropometric system. Suspects
were fingerprinted, and their prints were compared with those
lifted from a crime scene. Those comparisons typically required
a great deal of time and a bit of luck to produce a match.

Over time, as fingerprint inventories in the United States
grew huge, including those of everyone in the armed services
and in certain branches of federal employment, researchers
looked for a rapid and efficient way to compare large numbers
of prints. Until the 1980s, most effective comparison schemes
depended on manual classification methods that automatically
eliminated large numbers of prints from consideration. As late as
1974, one author lamented, "Considering present levels of technology in other sciences … [the] classification of fingerprints
has profited little by technological advancements, particularly in
the computer sciences. [Fingerprint comparisons are] limited by
the laborious inspection by skilled technicians required to accurately classify and interpret prints. Automation of the classification and comparison process would open up fingerprinting to
its fullest potential."[79]

Within a decade, advances in computer hardware and software made possible CAL-ID, the automated fingerprint identification system (AFIS) of the California Department of Justice.
The system used optical scanning and software pattern matching
to compare suspects' fingerprints. Such computerized systems
have grown rapidly in capability, and links between systems operated by different agencies are now routine. Modern technology employs proprietary electro-optical scanning systems that
digitize live fingerprints, eliminating the need for traditional
inking and rolling techniques.[80] Other advances in fingerprint
identification and matching are also being made. The use of la-
sers in fingerprint lifting, for example, allowed the FBI to detect
a 50-year-old fingerprint of a Nazi war criminal on a postcard.[81]
Other advances, including a process known as surface-enhanced
Raman spectroscopy (SERS), now make it possible, in at least
some cases, to lift latent fingerprints from the skin of crime

victims and even from bodies that have been submerged underwater for considerable periods of time.[82]

Computerization and digitization have improved accuracy
and reduced the incidence of "false positives" in fingerprint
comparisons.[83] The Los Angeles Police Department (LAPD),
which uses an automated fingerprint identification system, estimates that fingerprint comparisons that in the past would have
taken as long as 60 years can now be performed in a single day
or less.[84] Computerized fingerprint identification systems took
a giant step forward in 1986 with the introduction of a new
electronic standard for fingerprint data exchange.[85] This standard makes it possible to exchange data between different automated fingerprint identification systems. Before its invention,
the comparison of fingerprint data among AFISs was often difficult or impossible. Using the standard, cities across the nation
can share and compare fingerprint information over the Internet
or over secure networks linking their AFISs.[86]

Some years ago, the FBI developed the Integrated Automated Fingerprint Identification System (IAFIS) as part of the
National Crime Information Center (NCIC) (see Chapter 5).
The IAFIS integrates state fingerprint databases and automates
search requests from police agencies throughout the country.
A few years ago, use of IAFIS led to the arrest of a convicted
murderer who was on parole in Reno, Nevada, and resulted
in his being charged with a beating death that took place in
Escondido, California, in 1977.[87] A smudged fingerprint found
at the scene of the 1977 killing couldn't be matched with suspects at the time of the murder, but a cross-check of state databases undertaken by a cold case squad more than 30 years later
took only 16 minutes to return a match. The suspect in the case
was extradited to San Diego, where he pleaded guilty to charges
in the 1977 crime. Learn more about IAFIS at **http://www.
fbi.gov/hq/cjisd/iafis.htm**.

Fingerprinting provides an example of an early form of
biometric technology used to positively identify individuals.
Modern **biometrics** typically employs hardware and software
to provide identity verification for specific purposes. Today's
biometric devices include retinal and iris scanners, facial recognition systems, keyboard rhythm recognition units, voice
authentication systems, hand geometry and digital fingerprint
readers, facial thermography, and body odor sniffers. Some
universities are now using hand geometry units to allow resident access to secure dormitories. In a significant adaptation
of biometric technology, the Liberian International Ship and
Corporate Registry, one of the largest shipping registries in the
world, announced in 2003 that it was implementing a digital
fingerprint recognition system to prevent known terrorists from

■ **ballistics** The analysis of firearms, ammunition, projectiles, bombs, and explosives.
■ **forensic anthropology** The use of anthropological principles and techniques in criminal investigation.
■ **forensic entomology** The study of insects to determine such matters as a person's time of death.

■ **theme** What coming social and technological changes can you foresee that will likely have a significant impact on the criminal justice system? What aspects of the system are likely to remain unchanged?
■ **lecture note** Describe DNA profiling as an investigative technique that analyzes cellular residue left at crime scenes. Refer to Figure 18-1 for a description of the stages involved in DNA analysis.

infiltrating the cargo ship industry.[88] Multimodal biometric systems utilize more than one physiological or behavioral characteristic for identification (preventing, for example, the use of a severed finger to gain access to a controlled area).

Modern criminalistics also depend heavily on **ballistics** to analyze weapons, ammunition, and projectiles; medical pathology to determine the cause of injury or death; **forensic anthropology** to reconstruct the likeness of a decomposed or dismembered body; **forensic entomology** to determine issues such as the time of death; forensic dentistry to help identify deceased victims and offenders; the photography of crime scenes (now often done with video or digital cameras); plaster and polymer castings of tire tracks, boot prints, and marks made by implements; polygraph (the "lie detector") and voiceprint identification (used by the Central Intelligence Agency and the National Security Agency to authenticate voice recordings made by known terrorists); as well as a plethora of other techniques. Many criminal investigative practices have been thoroughly tested and are now accepted by most courts for the evidence they offer. Polygraph[89] and voiceprint identification techniques are still being refined, however, and have not won the wide acceptance of the other techniques mentioned.

New Technologies in Criminalistics

New and emerging law enforcement technologies include the following:

- DNA profiling and new serological/tissue identification techniques, many of which have already received widespread acceptability
- Online databases for the sharing of in-depth and timely criminal justice information
- Computer-aided investigations
- Computer-based training

Brief descriptions of these technologies, including their current state of development and the implications they hold for the future, are provided in the paragraphs that follow.

DNA Identification

In March 2000, a man known only by his genetic makeup was indicted and charged with a series of sexual assaults in Manhattan.[90] Authorities said that it was the first indictment based solely on a DNA profile. The man, dubbed the "East Side Rapist" and named in the indictment as "John Doe, an unidentified male," followed

Forensic anthropologist Frank Bender explaining how he makes forensic models at his studio in Philadelphia. Bender, who describes himself as "the recomposer of the decomposed," has helped police identify dozens of murder victims and, in some cases, find their killers. Would you consider working as a forensic anthropologist?

CJ | NEWS
Kim Dotcom of Megaupload Arrested for Online Piracy

Megaupload founder Kim Dotcom poses in front of his New Zealand Mansion. Dotcom, whose given name is Kim Schmitz, was arrested in 2012 and charged with criminal copyright infringement for allegedly digitizing and stealing $500 million worth of music, film, and TV shows and making them available on his servers. Might Dotcom have avoided arrest if he lived in another country?

At 6-foot-6 and 322 pounds, Web entrepreneur Kim Dotcom has made a career of being larger than life, and his spectacular arrest on January 20, 2012, in his sprawling mansion in New Zealand lived up to that image.

New Zealand police cut through a series of locks to get to the 38-year-old native German, whose given name is Kim Schmitz. Though there were reports he had a shotgun handy, Dotcom, who had holed up in a safe room at his mansion when police arrived, surrendered peacefully.

Concurrent with the arrest, authorities in nine countries shut down worldwide operations of Megaupload, Dotcom's hugely popular file-sharing website. Executing 20 warrants, they seized hundreds of servers and closed 18 domain names.

U.S. prosecutors orchestrated the entire operation, executing an indictment against Dotcom and others at Megaupload for criminal copyright infringement. The company is accused of stealing $500 million worth of copyrighted material from music, film, and television rights holders over five years of operation.

The film and recording industries pushed to prosecute Dotcom, pointing to a disturbing erosion of their royalty income through unauthorized use on the Internet. The criminal investigation, begun two years prior to the arrest, was based on a lawsuit filed by the Motion Picture Association of America against the Megaupload website.

The indictment points to a new, gloves-off stage in the battle against unauthorized use of copyrighted material on the Internet. A decade ago, when copyright holders sued the file-sharing service Napster and shut it down, no criminal charges were filed, no one was arrested, and no one went to prison.

In addition to criminal copyright violations, Dotcom and his associates were charged with money laundering and racketeering, which alone could bring ten years in prison. Dotcom asserts that his site, Megaupload, is no different than YouTube, which escaped infringement charges in 2010. But Dotcom, who started his career as a hacker, had been previously convicted of insider trading and computer hacking in Germany.

Megaupload made its money by serving as a "digital locker" that stored users' files, which then could be accessed by anyone entering the site. At its peak, the site logged 50 million visits daily, making up 4% of all Internet traffic.

The company gave payments to locker-users whose content generated high traffic. Prosecutors allege this content was often pirated. For example, one copyright infringer allegedly uploaded nearly 17,000 videos to the site, which gleaned 334 million views as a result of that content.

Under the federal Digital Millennium Copyright Act, websites are protected from prosecution if they are unaware of pirated content and take down content when copyright holders inform them of violations. But prosecutors charge that Megaupload staff knew full well they were harboring pirated content and did not completely take down content when requested, leaving hundreds of copies still on the site, in some cases.

But some experts think prosecutors may be overreaching. James Grimmelmann of New York Law School said he hopes Dotcom is found guilty, but added that many of the activities in the indictment appear to be legitimate business strategies for Internet sites, such as offering premium subscriptions, running ads, and rewarding active users.

Jennifer Granick, an attorney blogging for Stanford's Center for Internet and Society, said it's going to be hard to win infringement charges based on users' content, rather than content directly pirated by Megaupload. She added that some legal arguments in the case are based on civil copyright law, which is not applicable to criminal copyright law.

New Zealand authorities were squeamish about cooperating too closely with U.S. officials. Over U.S. objections, a New Zealand judge granted Dotcom bail, requiring that he remain in the area and not use the Internet. U.S. officials continue to argue for his extradition.

In 2015, however, Dotcom positioned himself as an "Internet freedom fighter," and vowed to create a political party in the United States. His plan is to have candidates representing his party—called the Internet Party—run on a platform of internet freedom, free university education, and the decriminalization of cannabis.

Resources: "Megaupload Founder Launches New Sharing Site," USA Today, January 22, 2013, p. B1; "MegaUpload File Sharing Site Shut Down for Piracy by Feds," Los Angeles Times, January 19, 2012, http://latimesblogs.latimes.com/entertainmentnewsbuzz/2012/01/file-sharing-megaupload-shut-down-for-piracy-by-feds.html; "Why the Feds Smashed Megaupload," Ars Technica, February 8, 2012, http://arstechnica.com/tech-policy/news/2012/01/why-the-feds-smashed-megaupload.ars; and "Kim Dotcom's Wild Ride Hits Digital Piracy Wall," Newsday, February 27, 2012, http://www.newsday.com/business/technology/kim-dotcom-s-wild-ride-hits-digital-piracy-wall-1.3560434; Janko Roettgers, "Kim Docom Wants to Take His Internet Party to the U.S.," Gagaom, https://gigaom.com/2014/12/02/kim-dotcom-wants-to-take-his-internet-party-to-the-u-s/ (accessed January 15, 2015).

by his DNA profile, was charged with two sexual assaults in 1995 and one in 1997. He is alleged to have sexually attacked 16 women since 1994. No arrest has yet been made.

Three years later, New York City Mayor Michael Bloomberg announced that his city would begin using DNA to seek

hundreds of indictments in unsolved sexual attacks.[91] Bloomberg said that the DNA-based indictments would effectively "stop the clock" on the state's ten-year statute of limitations, which bars prosecution of even known felons if they have not been charged with the crime within ten years of its commission.

Max Gilbert/dpa/picture-alliance/Newscom

■ **DNA profiling** The use of biological residue, found at the scene of a crime, for genetic comparisons in aiding in the identification of criminal suspects.

DNA analysis is nearly infallible from a scientific point of view and is increasingly preferred by criminal justice experts as a method of identification.

DNA analysis (also discussed in Chapter 11) is nearly infallible from a scientific point of view and is increasingly preferred by criminal justice experts as a method of identification. It can prove innocence as well as demonstrate guilt. In December 2001, for example, Marvin Lamond Anderson, a Virginia parolee, was cleared of rape charges stemming from a 1982 crime for which he had served 15 years in prison.[92] Anderson received assistance from the Innocence Project, a volunteer organization specializing in the use of DNA technology to investigate and challenge what it regards as dubious convictions. A Virginia law passed in 2000, which allows felons to seek exoneration and expungement of their convictions on the basis of modern DNA testing, helped Anderson prove that he could not have committed the crime of which he had been convicted. DNA taken from a 19-year-old cotton swab was compared to the state's DNA database of more than 100,000 convicted felons and conclusively demonstrated that Anderson had not committed the crime. Learn more about the Innocence Project via **http://www.innocenceproject.org**.

The federal DNA Fingerprint Act of 2005[93] repealed an earlier provision found in the DNA Identification Act of 1994 that had prohibited including in the National DNA Index System (CODIS) any DNA profiles taken from arrestees who had not been charged with a crime. The 2005 law also requires the director of the FBI to expunge the DNA analysis record of a person from the system if the attorney general receives a certified copy of a final court order establishing that each charge serving as the basis on which the analysis was included has been dismissed, has resulted in an acquittal, or has not been filed within the applicable period. However, the law amended the DNA Analysis Background Elimination Act of 2000 to authorize the U.S. attorney general's office to (1) collect DNA samples from individuals who are arrested, or from non-U.S. residents who are detained under U.S. authority, and (2) to authorize any other federal agency that arrests or detains individuals or supervises individuals facing charges to collect DNA samples.[94]

The U.S. Department of Justice notes that "DNA evidence is playing a larger role than ever before in criminal cases throughout the country, both to convict the guilty and to exonerate those wrongly accused or convicted."[95] **DNA profiling,** also termed *DNA fingerprinting,* makes use of human DNA for purposes of identification. DNA (deoxyribonucleic acid) is a nucleic acid found in the center of cells. It is the principal component of chromosomes, the structures that transmit hereditary characteristics between generations. Each DNA molecule is a long two-stranded chain made up of subunits called *nucleotides,* coiled in the form of a double helix. Because genetic material is unique to each individual (except in the case of identical twins or clones), it can provide a highly reliable source of suspect identification. DNA profiling was originally used as a test for determining paternity.

DNA profiling requires only a few human cells for comparison. One drop of blood, a few hairs, a small amount of skin, or a trace of semen usually provides sufficient genetic material. Because the DNA molecule is very stable, genetic tests can be conducted on evidence taken from crime scenes long after fingerprints have disappeared. The process, diagrammed in Figure 18-1, involves the use of a highly technical procedure called *electrophoresis.* All 50 states and the Federal Bureau of Investigation now collect DNA samples from convicted offenders and retain the profiles generated from those samples in databases.[96]

All 50 states and the Federal Bureau of Investigation now collect DNA samples from convicted offenders and retain the profiles generated from those samples in databases.

Forensic use of DNA technology in criminal cases began in 1986 when British police asked Dr. Alec Jeffreys (who coined the term *DNA fingerprint*)[97] of Leicester University to verify a suspect's confession that he was responsible for two rapemurders in the English Midlands. DNA tests proved that the suspect could not have committed the crimes. Police then began obtaining blood samples from several thousand male inhabitants in the area in an attempt to identify a new suspect.[98]

In another British case the next year, 32-year-old Robert Melias became the first person ever convicted of a crime on the basis of DNA evidence.[99] Melias was convicted of raping a 43-year-old disabled woman, and the conviction came after genetic tests of semen left on the woman's clothes positively identified him as the perpetrator.[100]

In 1994, the DNA Identification Act[101] provided substantial funding to improve the quality and availability of DNA analyses for law enforcement identification. The act also provided for the establishment of the Combined DNA Index System (CODIS) for law enforcement purposes (see Chapter 5 for more information). The index, which held 1 million profiles by mid-2002,[102] allows investigators to produce quick matches with DNA samples already on file. The law limits accessibility of DNA samples to investigators, court officials, and personnel authorized to evaluate such samples for the purposes of criminal prosecution and defense.

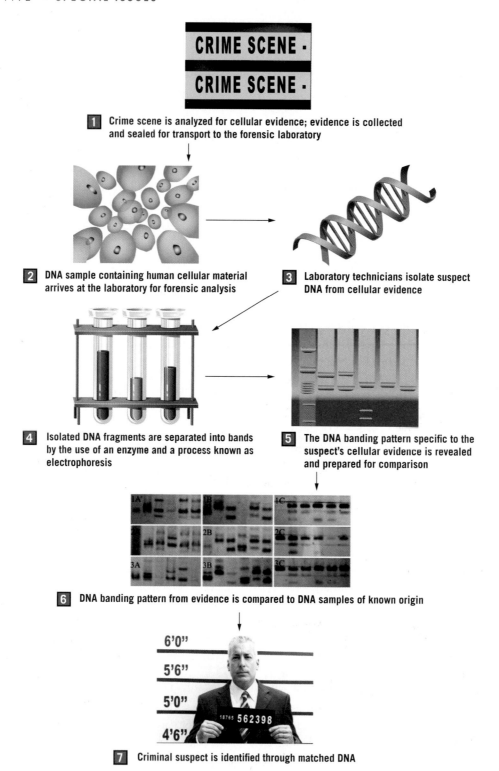

CRIME SCENE ·

CRIME SCENE ·

1 Crime scene is analyzed for cellular evidence; evidence is collected and sealed for transport to the forensic laboratory

2 DNA sample containing human cellular material arrives at the laboratory for forensic analysis

3 Laboratory technicians isolate suspect DNA from cellular evidence

4 Isolated DNA fragments are separated into bands by the use of an enzyme and a process known as electrophoresis

5 The DNA banding pattern specific to the suspect's cellular evidence is revealed and prepared for comparison

6 DNA banding pattern from evidence is compared to DNA samples of known origin

7 Criminal suspect is identified through matched DNA

Figure 18-1 | The DNA Fingerprinting Process.

In 1998, in an effort to enhance the use of DNA evidence as a law enforcement tool, the U.S. attorney general established the National Commission on the Future of DNA Evidence. The task of the commission was to submit recommendations to the U.S. Department of Justice to help ensure more effective use of DNA as a crime-fighting tool and to foster its use throughout the criminal justice system. The commission addressed issues in five specific areas: (1) the use of DNA in postconviction relief cases; (2) legal concerns, including *Daubert* challenges (see Chapter 9) and the scope of discovery in DNA cases; (3) criteria for training and technical assistance for criminal justice professionals involved in the identification, collection, and preservation of DNA evidence at the crime scene; (4) essential laboratory capabilities in the face of emerging technologies; and (5) the impact of future technological developments on the use of DNA in the criminal justice system. Each topic became the focus of in-depth analysis by separate working groups comprised of prominent professionals. The work of the commission culminated in the National Law Enforcement Summit on DNA Technology, held in Washington, D.C., on July 27–28, 2000. The proceedings of the summit, as well as transcripts of commission meetings, are available via **http://www.nij.gov/nij/topics/forensics/evidence/dna/commission/welcome.html**.

The commission's work led the White House to sponsor an *Advancing Justice through DNA Technology* initiative. The initiative culminated in passage of federal legislation designed to take advantage of the opportunities offered by DNA testing. That legislation, the DNA Sexual Assault Justice Act of 2004 and the Innocence Protection Act of 2004 (also discussed in Chapter 11)—both of which are parts of the Justice for All Act of 2004[103]—was signed into law by President George W. Bush on October 30, 2004. The Innocence Protection Act established new procedures for applications for DNA testing by inmates in the federal prison system. Those new procedures require a court to order DNA testing if (1) the inmate applicant asserts that he or she is actually innocent of a qualifying offense, (2) the proposed DNA testing would produce new material evidence that would support such an assertion, and (3) it would create a reasonable probability that the applicant did not commit the offense. The court must grant the applicant's motion for a new trial or resentencing if DNA testing indicates that a new trial would likely result in acquittal. The Act also seeks to preserve DNA evidence by prohibiting the destruction of biological evidence in a federal criminal case while a defendant remains incarcerated. The law established the Kirk Bloodsworth Post-Conviction DNA Testing Program, which provides millions of dollars in grants to states for postconviction DNA testing. It also provided money for states to train prosecutors in the appropriate use of DNA evidence and to train defense counsel to ensure effective representation in capital cases. A provision of the Innocence Protection Act increased the maximum amount of damages an individual may be awarded for being wrongfully imprisoned in the federal system from $5,000 to $50,000 per year in noncapital cases and $100,000 per year in capital cases.

The DNA Sexual Assault Justice Act authorized (1) $10 million per year for five years for grants to states and local governments to eliminate forensic science backlogs; (2) $12.5 million per year for five years to provide grants for training and education relating to the identification, collection, preservation, and analysis of DNA evidence for law enforcement officers, correctional personnel, and court officers; (3) $42.1 million in additional funds for the FBI to enhance its DNA programs, including the Combined DNA Index System; (4) $30 million per year for five years to create a grant program to provide training, technical assistance, education, equipment, and information to medical personnel relating to the identification, collection, preservation, analysis, and use of DNA evidence; and (5) $15

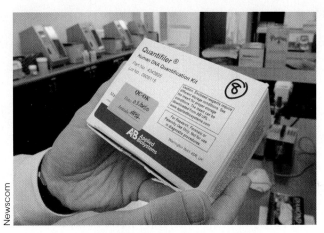

Newscom

A Human DNA Quantification Kit made by Applied Biosystems for use by law enforcement officers. What benefits can on-the-scene DNA collection and analysis provide to police agencies?

million per year for five years to establish a National Forensic Science Commission to be appointed by the attorney general to provide recommendations for maximizing the use of forensic science technology in the criminal justice system.

The Justice for All Act also amended the federal statute of limitations[104] by adding the following words to existing law: "In a case in which DNA testing implicates an identified person in the commission of a felony ... no statute of limitations that would otherwise preclude prosecution of the offense shall preclude such prosecution until a period of time following the implication of the person by DNA testing has elapsed that is equal to the otherwise applicable limitation period." The wording allows for prosecutions where DNA analysis reveals the identity of "cold case" perpetrators in investigations that might have otherwise been abandoned.

> The 2013 U.S. Supreme Court case of *Maryland* v. *King* upheld state and federal laws that permit law enforcement agencies to collect DNA samples from criminal suspects following arrest for serious offenses.

Finally, as mentioned in a previous chapter, the 2013 U.S. Supreme Court case of *Maryland* v. *King* upheld state and federal laws that permit law enforcement agencies to collect DNA samples from criminal suspects following arrest for serious offenses.[105] Learn more about the impact of forensic DNA on American criminal justice from the National Academy of Sciences via its recent report, *Strengthening Forensic Science in the United States: A Path Forward*, at **http://www.justicestudies.com/pubs/forensics.pdf**.

Online Databases

Computerized information systems and the personnel who operate them are an integral part of most police departments today. Police department computers assist with such routine tasks as

■ **theme** Law enforcement agencies are increasingly making criminal database information available to the public via the Internet. What are the pros and cons of doing this? Should this type of police data be made generally available? Why or why not?

■ **expert system** Computer hardware and software that attempt to duplicate the decision-making processes used by skilled investigators in the analysis of evidence and in the recognition of patterns that such evidence might represent.

word processing, filing, record keeping, report printing, and personnel, equipment, and facilities scheduling. Computers that serve as investigative tools, however, have the greatest potential to affect criminal justice in the near future. The automated fingerprint technology discussed earlier is but one example of information-based systems designed to help in identifying offenders and solving crimes. Others include the nationwide National Crime Information Center and the Violent Criminal Apprehension Program (ViCAP) databases; state-operated police identification networks; specialized services like METAPOL, an information-sharing network run by the Police Executive Research Forum; and the FBI's CODIS, which allows law enforcement agencies to compare DNA profiles in their possession with other DNA profiles that have been entered into local, state, and national databases in order to identify a suspect or to link serial crimes. NCIC and police information networks furnish a 24-hour channel with information on suspects, stolen vehicles, and other data that can be accessed through computers installed in patrol cars.

Increasingly, law enforcement agencies are making criminal database information available to the public via the Internet. Among the most common forms of information available are sex-offender registries, although the FBI's Most Wanted list and the Most Wanted lists of various states can also be viewed online. In 1998, Texas became the first state to make its entire criminal convictions database available on the Internet.[106] See the FBI's Most Wanted list via **http://www.fbi.gov/wanted/topten**.

Computer-Aided Investigations

Some police agencies use large computer databases that can cross-reference specific information about crimes to determine patterns and to identify suspects. One of the earliest of these programs was HITMAN, developed by the Hollywood (California) Police Department in 1985. HITMAN has since evolved into a department-wide database that helps detectives in the Los Angeles Police Department solve violent crimes. The LAPD uses a similar computer program to track a target population of approximately 60,000 gang members.[107]

The developing field of artificial intelligence uses computers to make inferences based on available information and to draw conclusions or to make recommendations to the system's operators. **Expert systems,** as these computer models are often called, depend on three components: (1) a user interface or terminal, (2) a knowledge base containing information on what is already known in the area of investigation, and (3) a computer program known as an *inference engine* that compares user input and stored information according to established decision-making rules.

Numerous expert systems exist today. One is used by the FBI's National Center for the Analysis of Violent Crime (NCAVC) in a project designed to profile violent serial criminals. The NCAVC system depends on computer models of criminal profiling to provide a theoretical basis for the development of investigative strategies. Other systems have been developed as well, including some that focus on serological (blood serum) analysis, narcotics interdiction, serial murder and rape, and counterterrorism.[108]

Similar to expert systems are relational databases, which permit fast and easy sorting of large numbers of records. Perhaps the best-known early criminal justice database of this sort was called Big Floyd. It was developed in the 1980s by the FBI in conjunction with the Institute for Defense Analyses. Big Floyd was designed to access the more than 3 million records in the FBI's Organized Crime Information System and to allow investigators to decide which federal statutes apply in a given situation and whether investigators have enough evidence for a successful prosecution.[109] In the years since Big Floyd, other "bad-guy" relational databases targeting malfeasants of various types have been created, including computer systems to track deadbeat parents and quack physicians. In 1996, President Bill Clinton ordered the Department of Justice to create a computerized national registry of sex offenders.[110] The national sex-offender registry, developed as part of an overhaul of the FBI's computer systems, went online in 1999. It provides a database of registered sex offenders that is available only to law enforcement personnel. A publically available resource, the Dru Sjodin National Sex Offender Public Website (NSOPW), which is named in memory of a 22-year-old college student who was kidnapped and murdered by a registered sex offender, provides information on thousands of sex offenders under the Sex Offender Registration and Notification Act (SORNA). It can be found on the Web at **http://www.nsopw.gov.**

Some systems are even more problem-specific. For example, ImAger, a product of Face Software, Inc., uses computer technology to artificially age photographs of missing children. The program has been used successfully to identify and recover a number of children. One of them was only six months old when he disappeared and was found after ImAger created a photo of what the child would look like at age five. The child was recognized by viewers who called police after the image was broadcast on television.[111] Another composite-imaging program, Compusketch by Visatex Corporation, is used by police artists to create simulated photographs of criminal suspects.[112]

The most advanced computer-aided investigation systems are being touted by agencies like NASA and the Defense

Advanced Research Projects Agency (DARPA) as having the ability to prevent crime. DARPA, for example, announced its new Total Information Awareness (TIA) Program in 2003.[113] The five-year development project used information-sorting and pattern-matching software to sift through vast numbers of existing business and government databases in an effort to identify possible terror threats. The software attempted to detect suspicious patterns of activity, identify the people involved, and locate them so that investigations could be conducted. Suspected insurgents might be identified with similar software when it detects a series of credit card, bank, and official transactions that form a pattern that resembles preparations for an insurgency attack. The process, which is known as *data mining,* generates computer models in an attempt to predict terrorists' actions. Privacy advocates have raised concerns about the DARPA software, but the agency has tried to defuse concerns by assuring the public that the project "is not an attempt to build a supercomputer to snoop into the private lives or track the everyday activities of American citizens." The agency claims that "all TIA research complies with all privacy laws, without exception."

Another DARPA project that could meet the needs of American law enforcement agencies but is currently being developed for military use overseas is called Combat Zones That See (CZTS).[114] The CZTS program will build a huge surveillance system by networking existing cameras from department stores, subway platforms, banks, airports, parking lots, and other points of surveillance and by feeding images to supercomputer-like processors capable of recognizing suspects by face, gait, and mannerisms as they move from one place to another. The data can be fed via satellite to remote locations across the globe, allowing the agency to track suspects on the move—either within cities or between countries. Vehicles could also be tracked. CZTS is being introduced gradually in selected locations, beginning with areas in and around American military bases. Recently, General Electric announced development of an advanced behavior recognition system for use in crowded environments that uses computer software to analyze the images sent from surveillance cameras to interpret and predict the behavior of individuals and groups in social settings. The software, a form of intelligent video, can, for example, alert human operators to assaults from the moment they begin, and identify individuals whose behavior might indicate they are casing a retail establishment for criminal opportunities.[115] Future implementations of CZTS may involve nanocameras equipped with microminiaturized transmitters that can be spread over a city like grains of dust but that have the power to communicate relatively detailed information to local cellular-

Future implementations of CZTS may involve nanocameras equipped with microminiaturized transmitters that can be spread over a city like grains of dust.

like installations for entry into the CZTS network. The civil rights implications of local adaptations of DARPA's TIA and CZTS technology within the United States must be explored by any law enforcement agency considering the use of similar kinds of technologies.

Computer-Based Training

Computers provide an ideal training medium for criminal justice agencies. They allow users to work at their own pace, and they can be made available around the clock to provide off-site instruction to personnel whose job requirements make other kinds of training difficult to implement. Computer-based training (CBT) is already well established as a management training tool and is used extensively in law enforcement. CBT has the added advantage of familiarizing personnel with computers so that they will be better able to use them in other tasks.

Some of the more widely used computer-training programs include shoot/no-shoot decision-based software and police-pursuit driving simulators. The Atari Mobile Operations Simulator, firearms training simulation, and Robbec's JUST (Judgment under Stress Training) are just a few of the products available to police-training divisions. Recent innovations in the field of virtual reality (a kind of high-tech-based illusion) have led to the creation of realistic computer-based virtual environments in which law enforcement agents can test their skills.[116] Ever more advanced training tools are being developed for use in the criminal justice area. Recently, for example, the Law Enforcement Innovation Center at the University of Tennessee announced availability of a virtual reality simulator for training forensic investigators. Visit the simulator's home page at **http://leic.tennessee.edu/online/ivr.html.**

We have looked at just some of the most prominent uses of technology in criminal justice. Laser fingerprint-lifting devices, space-age photography, video camera–equipped patrol cars, satellite and computerized mapping,[117] field DNA-analysis kits, advanced chemical analysis techniques, chemical sniffers, and hair and fiber identification are all contemporary crime-fighting techniques based on new and emerging technologies. Field test kits for drug analysis, chemical sobriety checkers, and handheld ticket-issuing computers have also made the transition from costly high technology to widespread and relatively inexpensive use. As one expert has observed, "Police agencies throughout the world are entering an era in which high technology is not only desirable but necessary in order to combat crime effectively."[118]

On the Horizon

At the end of 2014, the Department of Homeland Security (DHS) submitted its semiannual report to Congress.[119] The report, which is available in its entirety at **http://justicestudies.com/pubs/DHS2014.pdf**, provides insight into some of the intrusion-detection technologies being used to help secure the nation's borders.

Various DHS semiannual reports have acknowledged concerns that weapons of mass destruction and other contraband of use to terrorists might enter the country through our nation's

Golden-i/Rex Features/AP Images

A model demonstrates use of the Golden-i headset computer. The wearable computer lets police see through walls using proprietary infrared technology and promises to give officers access to vital information without the need to use their hands or a keyboard. How can such technology enhance law enforcement capabilities?

seaports. Shipping containers are too numerous for each to be opened and visually inspected. Millions of such containers enter the country every year from ports around the world. The DHS notes that shipping containers are "highly vulnerable to exploitation by terrorists" and has begun to focus on the need to enhance container-inspection efforts.

Since the terrorist attacks of September 11, 2001, border security has expanded to include the use of high-technology equipment to search for radioactive materials, explosives, toxic chemicals, and dangerous biological materials. These pieces of equipment—which include various vehicle and rail X-ray systems, radiation-detection units, trace-detection devices, video systems, and the like—permit officers to inspect cargo and conveyances for contraband without having to perform the costly and time-consuming process of unloading cargo or drilling through or dismantling containers.

Trace-detection technology, which focuses on cargo, luggage, packages, containers, and vehicles, gathers and analyzes the minute amounts of vapors given off and the microscopic particles left behind when narcotics and explosives contraband are packaged and handled. Current technology provides security screeners with nonintrusive search capabilities.

Radiation-detection equipment is used at the nation's ports and border crossings to detect attempts to smuggle radioactive materials into the United States. Detection devices range from personal radiation detectors, which are somewhat limited in capability and not very costly, to more sophisticated, capable, and expensive portable radiation-detection systems.

Passengers, cargo handlers, seamen, and flight crews must also be screened to determine the level of risk they represent. The DHS notes that Customs and Border Protection routinely processes more than 1.1 million arriving passengers for entry into the United States at 324 air, land, and seaports every day. The Advance Passenger Information System (APIS) is a border enforcement tool used at our nation's airports to identify and detain high-risk travelers on flights bound for the United States. The system is intended to collect biographical information such as name, date of birth, and country of residence from international airline passengers and crew members entering the United States at airports around the country. Before arrival, travelers are

Raptorcaptor/Fotolia

A police surveillance drone in operation. What other new police technologies can you envision?

■ **augmented reality (AR)**   The real-time and accurate overlay of digital information on a user's real-world experience, through visual, aural, and/or tactile interfaces.[ii] The computer readouts superimposed on the visual fields of the fictional cyborgs in the *RoboCop* and *Terminator* movies provide an example.

matched against law enforcement databases to identify people who should be detained and examined for violation of U.S. law. All airlines serving the United States are required to provide APIS information to the Department of Homeland Security.

The Remote Video Inspection System (RVIS) used at border crossings is designed to expedite the clearance of low-risk travelers and to enhance security at remote border areas, including parts of the U.S.–Canadian border. The RVIS transmits images of a driver, vehicle, documents, and passengers to an inspector located miles away at a main port of entry that is monitored 24 hours a day.

Other security technologies now being employed sound like science fiction. For example, NASA is developing "non-invasive neuro-electric sensors," or brain-monitoring devices, that can receive and analyze brain-wave and heartbeat patterns from a distance.[120] The data are fed into a computer, which scrutinizes the information in order to "detect passengers who potentially might pose a threat."[121]

Especially intriguing technological advances can be found in the field of **augmented reality (AR)**.[122] Whereas virtual-reality systems generate audio and visual stimuli predicated on fictional scenarios and usually experienced by relatively passive viewers in situations not requiring interpersonal interaction, AR technology provides users with real-time fact-based information that can be accessed in the midst of real-world activity. Wearable AR systems, like those being developed by the U.S. military under the name Battlefield Augmented Reality System, provide visual, audio, and tactile overlays that can give the user critical information about the people he or she is facing and the situation in which he or she is involved. AR systems supply the user with data presented in a fashion similar to the science fiction visual readouts shown in *Terminator* films. There, the main character's computer-like brain automatically and continuously computes threat assessments by accessing stored databases and displays them in the character's visual field as easy-to-read schematics that are overlaid on the immediate surroundings. It is predicted that AR systems will soon be available that will provide "wired" officers with capabilities like these:

- Real-time intelligence about crime and criminals in the surrounding area
- Facial, voiceprint, and other biometric recognition data of known criminals, allowing for instantaneous identification
- Automated scans for chemical, biological, and explosive threats in the immediate area

- Real-time language translation to assist interaction with non-English-speaking people
- Three-dimensional maps, complete with building floor plans, sewer system schematics, and possible access and escape routes
- Advanced optics, including digital zoom and audio amplification for seeing and hearing at a distance
- Friend-or-foe identification technology to allow immediate recognition of "good guys"
- Coordinated deployment of robots and unmanned aerial vehicles (UAVs), including the ability to "see" and "hear" what the robots or UAVs encounter

Augmented-reality systems incorporating at least some of the features mentioned here are already a reality in police work. Xybernaut Corporation, for example, a leading provider of wearable computers, has teamed up with ZNQ3, a company that specializes in secure communications and dynamic identification, to provide wearable computers that enhance tactical awareness. According to Jeffrey Stutzman, founder and CEO of ZNQ3, "The secure communications and point-of-task computing power afforded by the joint Xybernaut/ZNQ3 solution allow first responders complete access to information providing critical situational awareness during a crisis."[123]

Thomas Cowper, whom we mentioned earlier in this chapter, poses some important questions about the practicality of augmented-reality applications in police work. How would "wired" officers be accepted by the public, given that their appearance would differ substantially from that of other officers? How cost-effective would AR technology be in police work? Who will pay for such systems, especially in smaller agencies? How can the accuracy of AR databases be ensured? What legal issues might arise?

Nanotechnology, or engineering and creating useful products on a molecular level, is another cutting-edge technology whose application to policing and the justice system is still largely in the realm of science fiction. Nonetheless, the National Science Foundation predicts that the field will be a $1 trillion industry in 2015. Nanotechnology may produce practical investigative applications in the near future. Microscopic cameras, motors, solar cells, recording devices, and high-frequency transmitters built with nanotechnology may have already resulted in the production of classified spy hardware such as a maneuverable mechanical mosquito able to fly into buildings and vehicles, providing its controllers with "fly-on-the-wall" observation capabilities.[124] Super sensors on such ultraminiaturized devices are said to be able to literally read over a person's shoulder and

■ theme   How might technological advances in investigative techniques threaten individual rights guaranteed under the Constitution? Which rights do you believe are most threatened, and why? Is the trade-off worthwhile?

■ **sentinel event**   A bad outcome that no one wants repeated and that signals the existence of underlying weaknesses in the system.

transmit visual, audio, global positioning system (GPS), infrared, and other data to remote recording and viewing devices, all the while remaining nearly invisible to those being targeted. The Institute of Nanotechnology says that miniaturized machines will soon be used to enhance tamper-prevention devices; bolster anticounterfeiting efforts; provide labs on a chip (sometimes called *dipstick technology*) for drug, food, explosives, and DNA testing; permit easy product tracking; and contribute to futuristic intruder-detection and intruder-identification systems.[125]

The Japanese news agency Kyodo reports that Hitachi Corporation is involved in talks with the European Central Bank to control counterfeiting and money laundering by embedding radio tags much smaller than a grain of sand in European bank notes (Euros).

A few years ago, the Japanese news agency Kyodo reported that Hitachi Corporation is involved in talks with the European Central Bank to control counterfeiting and money laundering by embedding radio tags much smaller than a grain of sand in European bank notes (Euros).[126] Radio-frequency identification (RFID) tags built with nanotechnology cannot be seen with the naked eye or felt by fingertips. The devices, called Mu-Chips, can authenticate bank notes that carry them and can even record details about the transactions in which they have been involved. RFID devices, which act much like digital watermarks, are queried by radio and use the energy of the incoming signal to generate a reply. Applicability of the technology was demonstrated at Japan's 2005 International Expo—an event that used RFID-tagged admission tickets. The Expo, which ran for five months, involved participants from 125 countries and drew nearly 15 million visitors.[127]

When agencies of the justice system use cutting-edge technology, it inevitably provokes fears of a future in which citizens' rights are abrogated in favor of advancing technology. Individual rights, equal treatment under the law, and due process issues all require constant reinterpretation as technology improves.

The Future of Criminal Justice

While no one knows exactly what the American justice system of the future will look like, we can be sure that it will continue to be characterized by the major subsystems of police, courts, and corrections. No doubt, the tensions between safety and

security that characterize the current system will continue to fuel efforts at reform and guide new developments.

In 2014–2015, the National Institute of Justice (NIJ) revealed a new framework for improving the system, and for keeping it true to the ideal of justice that underpins it. That framework was built around the concept of a **sentinel event,** or "a bad outcome that no one wants repeated and that signals the existence of underlying weaknesses in the system."[128] Anything that stakeholders agree should not happen again could be considered a sentinel event. Sentinel events are especially significant because they can lead to the public's loss of confidence in the system, and because of the perceived injustices that they create.

Some significant justice system sentinel events involve: (1) erroneous arrests; (2) wrongful convictions; (3) botched executions; (4) unnecessary police shootings of unarmed offenders or innocent bystanders; (5) inappropriate use of other forms of deadly force; (6) "wrongful releases" of dangerous or factually guilty criminals; (7) cold cases that stay unsolved too long; (8) DNA backlogs in forensic laboratories; (9) the unwarranted accumulation of unanalyzed rape kits over time; (10) failures to prevent domestic violence within at-risk families; (11) the mishandling of vulnerable mentally handicapped or physically ill arrestees; (12) careless police pursuits resulting in injuries or deaths; (13) unwarranted in-custody deaths and needless in-custody injuries; and (14) acquittals and dismissals of cases that at earlier points seemed solid.

Examples of recent newsworthy sentinel events include the shooting death of unarmed Ferguson, Missouri, teenager Michael Brown during an otherwise routine police stop; the death of New York City street vendor Eric Garner, who was placed into a chokehold by NYC officers; and the gruesome death of condemned Oklahoma prisoner Clayton Lockett. Lockett's execution took 43 minutes and involved numerous failed IV attempts.

The identification and analysis of sentinel events is common practice in the health care arena, where errors that are the end result of cumulative mistakes can produce life-threatening situations, and can result in enormous financial and physical costs. Our justice system, like the health-care system, is a complex social system; and bad outcomes in both are rarely the result of a single actor who makes a poor decision at a particular point in time. Rather, such outcomes are generally the consequence of multiple small errors that build up over time to combine and to produce negative events.

An examination of sentinel events shows that small errors can become big problems especially when exacerbated by exiting systemic weaknesses or agency inadequacies. Moreover, sentinel events are not the product of a single error, nor are they the fault of one operator or one investigative technique. Many things, for example, have to go wrong for a wrongful conviction to occur. Some of the things that may go wrong include mistaken eyewitness identification and testimony; crime scene evidence that is overlooked or improperly collected or which is inadequately tested in the laboratory; suspect interviews that are unrecorded or that result in tricked confessions; the selection of jurors who don't do their job; judicial mistakes; and distorted courtroom presentations of witness testimony and evidence.

Each error likely has some reason to occur. Tunnel vision—augmented by clearance rate and caseload pressures—may overwhelm investigators and prosecutors; poorly funded or untrained defense counsel may have failed to investigate alternative explanations or to execute effective cross-examination in the courtroom. Likewise, witnesses may have erred; the police may have erred; crime scene and laboratory technicians may have erred; the prosecutor may have been overzealous; the defense team was inadequate; the judge and the jury may have made mistakes; and even the appellate court may have erred—each for its own "reason."

Nonetheless, sentinel events in the justice system can serve a positive purpose. They can be used as "red flags" to alert us to the need for system change, including the need for better education or training, the implementation of enhanced operational procedures, and the development of a justice system culture that supports change in the pursuit of equity, justice, and fairness for everyone involved.

Unfortunately, sentinel events—especially in today's environment—are difficult to correct, causing them to reoccur in the future. This inability of the justice system to correct its own errors is largely due to *ascribing blame* to individual actors or to agencies within the system. A typical example of inappropriate blaming might be the immediate, instinctive, but unreasoned judgment that sometimes happens when an unarmed person is shot and killed by police officers who likely thought that they were in danger at the time the shooting took place. Media focus, social protests, the fear of lawsuits or enforced discipline, and blame-shifting, all conspire to virtually ensure that sentinel events are not objectively analyzed for the clues they can provide for future prevention. Instead of being used to reform the system and to eliminate future problems, they become fuel for public demonstrations fed by media pundits, and are often used for political positioning by unhelpful parties.

In its examination of sentinel events, NIJ says that by focusing exclusively on ascribing blame, "we drive many valuable reports of errors underground and leave latent system weaknesses unaddressed." Practitioners do not want to be blamed, and they do not want to become entangled in the unpredictable machinery of blaming colleagues. NIJ notes that "inevitably, in a blame-oriented system, less and less gets reported and less and less is learned."

Improving justice system response requires us to recognize that error is an inevitable accompaniment of the human condition, even among conscientious professionals with high standards. Errors must be accepted as evidence of system flaws, not character flaws. Through the adoption of a sentinel event model, NIJ says, we can begin to build "a culture of safety ... with a simple commitment to the routine, candid, nonblaming examination of as many errors—completed tragedies and "near misses"—as we can reach." NIJ notes, however, that unless the sentinel event process is honest and trustworthy, with adequate legal protections—including the use of immunity, privacy, confidentiality and nondisclosure agreements—system actors, "who have the very best information about how things really work and what really happened, will not be motivated to fully participate." Hence, the sentinel event review approach can only work if departments abandon the process of adversarial/punitive-based discipline, and instead adopt education-based" disciplinary procedures and policies.

As the NIJ sentinel event initiative recognizes, a culture of safety can only exist when an organization: (1) is informed about current knowledge in its field; (2) promotes the objective reporting of errors and near misses; (3) creates an atmosphere of trust in which people are encouraged to report safety-related information; (4) remains flexible in adapting to changing demands; and (5) is willing and able to learn about and adjust the way it performs. Read the entire report on sentinel event reviews at **http://justicestudies.com/pubs/sentinel.pdf.**

SUMMARY

- Old concepts of crime and criminality have undergone significant revision as a result of emerging technologies. Science fiction–like products that are now readily available either legally or on the black market have brought with them a plethora of possibilities for new high-stakes crimes. The well-equipped, technologically advanced offender in tomorrow's world will be capable of attempting crimes involving dollar amounts undreamed of only a few decades ago, and the potential for crime-caused human suffering will rise astronomically. Some of these crimes, like the theft of funds from electronic repositories or the ready availability of illegal goods and services, are much like traditional offenses, except that they use new communications technologies in their commission. The relentless advance of globalization is now combining with powerful emerging technologies to produce a new world of challenges for criminal justice agencies. Domestic and international terrorism, highly organized transnational criminal cartels, and changing social values are having a synergistic effect that is creating a complex tangle of legal, technological, and social issues.

- In response to new forms of crime and new technologies of crime commission, the crime-fighting abilities of police agencies will need to be substantially enhanced by cutting-edge surveillance and enforcement technologies and by international and interagency cooperation. A massive infusion of funds will be needed to support the adoption of new crime-fighting technologies such as laser and night-vision technologies, digital imaging, wearable computers, and thermography. Similarly, sophisticated personnel capable of operating in multicultural environments must be hired and trained to allow tomorrow's enforcement agencies to compete with the global reach of technologically adept criminals.

- Criminalistics refers to the use of technology in the service of criminal investigation and the application of scientific techniques to the detection and evaluation of criminal evidence. Law enforcement practitioners of the future will be aided in their work by a number of technologies, some of which are still in their infancy. These technologies include (1) DNA profiling and new serological/tissue identification techniques, many of which have already received widespread acceptability; (2) online databases for sharing digitized criminal justice information; (3) computer-aided investigations; and (4) computer-based training.

KEY TERMS

augmented reality (AR), 621	**forensic entomology,** 613
ballistics, 613	**hacker,** 604
biocrime, 603	**malware,** 606
biometrics, 612	**sentinel event,** 622
bioterrorism, 608	**social engineering,** 605
computer virus, 606	**software piracy,** 607
criminalist, 611	**spam,** 607
criminalistics, 611	**technocrime,** 603
DNA profiling, 615	**weapon of mass destruction**
expert system, 618	**(WMD),** 608
forensic anthropology, 613	

KEY CASES

MGM v. Grokster, 607   *Maryland v. King,* 617

QUESTIONS FOR REVIEW

1. Historically speaking, how have advances in technology affected society and criminal activity? What new kinds of crimes have technological advances made possible? Distinguish between new types of crimes produced by advancing technology and new ways of committing "old crimes" that have been facilitated by emerging technologies.

2. What role does technology play in the fight against crime? What new crime-fighting technologies hold the most promise for combating high-technology crimes?

3. What is criminalistics? Explain the interplay between advancing technology and methods used to gather evidence in the fight against crime.

QUESTIONS FOR REFLECTION

1. How has technology affected the practice of criminal justice in America during the past century? How has it affected the criminal law?

2. Why do criminal laws have to change to keep up with changes in technology? What modifications in current laws defining criminal activity might soon be necessary to meet the criminal possibilities inherent in new technologies?

3. What threats to individual rights might advanced technology create? Will our standards as to what constitutes admissible evidence, what is reasonable privacy, and so on undergo a significant reevaluation as a result of emerging technologies?

4. What is a "sentinel event"? How can sentinel events be used to improve the justice system?

NOTES

i. Centers for Disease Control and Prevention, "Bioterrorism: An Overview," http://www.bt.cdc.gov/documents/PPTResponse/laboverview.pdf (accessed July 5, 2011).

ii. Thomas J. Cowper and Michael E. Buerger, *Improving Our View of the World: Police and Augmented Reality Technology* (Washington, DC: Federal Bureau of Investigation, 2003), http://www.fbi.gov/publications/realitytech/realitytech.pdf (accessed October 7, 2009).

1. "Sony Hack: Obama Vows Response as FBI Blames North Korea," *BBC News*, December 19, 2014, http://www.bbc.com/news/world-us-canada-30555997 (accessed January 4, 2015).

2. Jake Miller, "FBI: North Korea Government Behind Sony Pictures Hack," *CBS News*, December 19, 2014, http://www.cbsnews.com/news/fbi-north-korean-government-behind-sony-pictures-hack (accessed January 5, 2015).

3. Levine, "Officials Warn Facebook and Twitter Increase Police Vulnerability."

4. Thomas J. Cowper, "Foresight Update 49," http://www.foresight.org/Updates/Update49/Update49.4.html (accessed August 5, 2011).

5. Ibid.

6. University of Minnesota Center for Infectious Disease Research and Policy, "All H2N2 Flu Virus Samples Destroyed, CDC Says," May 3, 2005, http://www.cidrap.umn.edu/cidrap/content/influenza/general/news/may0305h2n2.html (accessed July 10, 2008).

7. "Stem Cells Extracted from Human Clone," *MSNBC News*, February 12, 2004, http://www.msnbc.msn.com/id/4244988 (accessed July 8, 2006).

8. "President Bush Calls on Senate to Back Human Cloning Ban," White House press release, April 10, 2002.

9. "Bush Condemns Embryonic Cloning," Fox News, May 21, 2005, http://www.foxnews.com/story/0,2933,157163,00.html (accessed July 18, 2007).

10. H.R. 222, Human Cloning Research Prohibition Act.

11. Many other countries, such as England, permit therapeutic cloning, although they often criminalize or severely restrict human cloning efforts.

12. Dolly was euthanized in 2003 after falling ill with lung disease.

13. S. 658, Human Cloning Prohibition Act of 2005.

14. H.R. 1050, Human Cloning Prohibition Act of 2009.

15. House Committee on Energy and Commerce, Subcommittee on Health, "Prepared Witness Testimony," June 20, 2001, http://energycommerce.house.gov/107/hearins/06202001Hearing291/Allen449.htm (accessed August 15, 2006).

16. "Bush Backs Total Ban on Human Cloning: Declares Life Is a 'Creation, Not a Commodity,'" April 10, 2002, http://usgovinfo.about.com/library/weekly/aa041102a.htm (accessed August 10, 2006).

17. "Obama Says Government Will Not Open the Door for Human Cloning," Fox News, March 9, 2009, http://www.foxnews.com/politics/2009/03/09/obama-says-government-open-door-human-cloning/ (accessed April 3, 2013).

18. Robert Anderson, Jr., FBI Executive Asst. Director, Criminal, cyber, Response, and Services Branch, "Statement Before the Committee on Homeland Security and Governmental Affairs," Washington, DC, September 10, 2014.

19. Linda Rosencrance, "Cyberscam Strikes Massachusetts State Lottery," Computerworld, July 24, 2003.

20. "Are You Vulnerable to Cybercrime?" USA Today, February 20, 1995.

21. "Most Wanted Hacker Released from Prison," USA Today, January 21, 2000, http://www.usatoday.com/news/ndsfri02.htm (accessed January 28, 2006).

22. Elinor Abreu, "Kevin Mitnick Bares All," Industry Standard, September 28, 2000, http://www.nwfusion.com/news/2000/0928mitnick.html (accessed January 26, 2002).

23. Pia Turunen, "Hack Attack: How You Might Be a Target," CNN.com, April 12, 2002, http://www.cnn.com/2002/TECH/ptech/04/12/hack.dangers (accessed August 3, 2006).

24. Nikola Krastev, "East: Many Nations Lack Effective Computer Crime Laws," Radio Free Europe, December 19, 2000, http://www.rferl.org/nca/features/2000/12/15122000153858.asp (accessed April 28, 2006).

25. Ibid.

26. "'Love Bug' Prompts New Philippine Law," USA Today, June 14, 2000.

27. "Cybercrime Treaty Gets Green Light," BBC News Online, November 12, 2001.

28. Details for this section come from the Council of Europe, Convention on Cybercrime signatories website, http://conventions.coe.int (accessed April 8, 2011).

29. Susan Schaibly, "Files for Ransom," Network World, September 26, 2005, http://www.networkworld.com/buzz/2005/092605-ransom.html (accessed May 12, 2007).

30. Ibid.

31. Peter Grabosky, "Computer Crime: A Criminological Overview," paper presented at the Workshop on Crimes Related to the Computer Network, Tenth United Nations Congress on the Prevention of Crime and the Treatment of Offenders, Vienna, Austria, April 15, 2000, http://www.aic.gov.au/conferences/other/compcrime/computercrime.pdf (accessed January 12, 2007).

32. Kevin Johnson, "Hijackers' E-Mails Sifted for Clues," USA Today, October 11, 2001.

33. Robert Richardson, CSI Computer Crime & Security Survey 2010/2011 (New York: Computer Security Institute, 2011), http://gocsi.com/survey (accessed June 5, 2011).

34. Internet Crime Complaint Center, 2011 Internet Crime Report (Washington, DC: Bureau of Justice Assistance, 2012), http://www.ic3.gov/media/annualreport/2011_IC3Report.pdf (accessed July 20, 2013).

35. "Invasion of the Data Snatchers!" Time, September 26, 1988, pp. 62–67.

36. "Virus Infects NASA, Defense, University Computer Systems," Fayetteville (NC) Observer-Times, November 4, 1988, p. 19A.

37. Barbara E. McMullin and John F. McMullin, "Hacker Morris Sentenced," Newsbytes News Network, May 4, 1990, http://findarticles.com/p/articles/mi_m0NEW/is_1990_May_8/ai_9831055 (accessed June 23, 2007).

38. "First HTML Virus Detected," Andover News Network, http://www.andovernews.com/cgi-bin/news_story.pl?95529/topstories (accessed January 16, 2006).

39. Sophos Antivirus, "The First JAVA Virus," http://www.sophos.com/virusinfo/articles/java.html (accessed January 5, 2006).

40. Net IQ, "Virus Protection," http://marshal.netiq.com/0195/solutions_virusprotection.html (accessed August 1, 2010).

41. Gregg Keizer, "Microsoft Says Phishing Bad, Offers Little New for Defense," TechWeb News, March 15, 2005, http://www.techweb.com/wire/159900391 (accessed July 7, 2007).

42. AntiPhishing Working Group, Phishing Activity Trends Report: 2nd Quarter 2014, http://docs.apwg.org/reports/apwg_trends_report_q2_2014.pdf (accessed May 1, 2015).

43. Software Information Industry Association, "Report on Global Software Piracy, 2000," http://www.siia.net/piracy/pubs/piracy2000.pdf (accessed August 1, 2007).

44. MGM v. Grokster, 545 U.S. 913 (2005).

45. Sony Corporation of America v. Universal City Studios, Inc., 464 U.S. 417 (1984).

46. Public Law 108–187.

47. Peter Firstbrook, "META Trend Update: The Changing Threat Landscape," Meta Group, March 24, 2005, http://www.metagroup.com/us/displayArticle.do?oid551768 (accessed July 5, 2007).

48. Virginia Statutes, Section 18.2–152.3:1.

49. Jack McCarthy, "Spammer Sentenced to Nine Years in Prison," InfoWorld, April 11, 2005.

50. "Printable-Gun Instructions Spread Online after State Dept. Orders Their Removal," New York Times, May 10, 2013, http://thelede.blogs.nytimes.com/2013/05/10/printable-gun-instructions-spread-online-after-state-dept-orders-their-removal/?src=recg (accessed May 12, 2013).

51. Some of the technological devices described in this section are discussed in G. Gordon Liddy, "Rules of the Game," Omni, January 1989, pp. 43–47, 78–80.

52. Central Intelligence Agency Directorate of Intelligence, Terrorist CBRN: Materials and Effects (Washington, DC: CIA, 2003).

53. Radiological Weapons Working Group, Harvard Project on Managing the Atom.

54. The information in this paragraph comes from a June 30, 2003, General Accounting Office report. See "Continuing Radioactive Materials Seizures," Nuclear Threat Initiative website, http://www.nti.org/e_research/cnwm/overview/cnwm_home.asp (accessed August 1, 2003).

55. Matthew Bunn, Anthony Wier, and John P. Holden, Controlling Nuclear Warheads and Materials: A Report Card and Action Plan (Cambridge, MA: Nuclear Threat Initiative and Harvard University, 2003).

56. Fact Sheet: The Biological Weapons Convention (Washington, DC: Bureau of Arms Control, 2002), http://www.state.gov/t/ac/rls/fs/10401.htm (accessed August 8, 2010).

57. Ali S. Kahn et al., *Biological and Chemical Terrorism: Strategic Plan for Preparedness and Response* (Atlanta, GA: Centers for Disease Control and Prevention, April 21, 2000), http://www.cdc.gov/mmwr/preview/mmwrhtml/rr4904a1.htm (accessed August 2, 2007).

58. Council on Foreign Relations, "Terrorism: Questions and Answers—The Anthrax Letters," http://www.terrorismanswers.com/weapons/anthraxletters.html (accessed August 23, 2009).

59. See Rick Weiss, "DNA by Mail: A Terror Risk," *Washington Post*, July 18, 2002.

60. SMILE Conference, 2015, http://smileconference.com (accessed May 1, 2015).

61. "Inmates Provide Anonymous Tips with FaceCrook," *TechBeat*, Winter 2013.

62. Rosalio Ahumada, "California Police Use Twitter as Public Info Tool," *The Modesto Bee*, February 7, 2011.

63. Mike Levine, "Officials Warn Facebook and Twitter Increase Police Vulnerability," FoxNews.com, May 10, 2011, http://www.foxnews.com/scitech/2011/05/10/officials-warn-facebook-twitter-increase-police-vulnerability/#ixzz1Otq6y5F0 (accessed June 10, 2011).

64. Peter Eisler, "High-Tech 'Bait Cars' Catch Unsuspecting Auto Thieves," *USA Today*, November 29, 2004, p. 1A.

65. David Griffith, "LPR Under Fire," *Police Magazine*, April 17, 2014, http://www.policemag.com/channel/technology/articles/2014/04/lpr-under-fire.aspx (accessed March 1, 2015).

66. Toni Locy, "Thieves Target Auto Identification," *USA Today*, May 20, 2005, p. 1A.

67. For an excellent overview of technology in criminal justice, see Laura J. Moriarty and David L. Carter, eds., *Criminal Justice Technology in the Twenty-First Century* (Springfield, IL: Charles C. Thomas, 1998).

68. Alan Feuer, "Where Police Work Has a Tinge of Sci-Fi," *New York Times*, January 1, 2009, http://www.nytimes.com/2009/01/01/nyregion/01roomsmet.html (accessed June 4, 2009).

69. National Law Enforcement and Corrections Technology Center, electronic press release, April 7, 1995.

70. Lester D. Shubin, *Research, Testing, Upgrading Criminal Justice Technology*, National Institute of Justice Reports (Washington, DC: U.S. Government Printing Office, 1984), pp. 2–5.

71. U.S. Department of Justice press release, "Department of Justice and National Institute of Standards and Technology Announce Launch of National Commission on Forensic Science," February 15, 2013, http://www.justice.gov/opa/pr/2013/February/13-dag-203.html (accessed April 23, 2013).

72. Harry Soderman and John J. O'Connell, *Modern Criminal Investigation* (New York: Funk and Wagnalls, 1945), p. 41.

73. The system was invented by Lambert Adolphe Jacques Quetelet (1796–1874), a Belgian astronomer and statistician.

74. For more on Bertillon's system, see Alphonse Bertillon, *Signaletic Instructions* (New York: Werner, 1896).

75. Robert D. Foote, "Fingerprint Identification: A Survey of Present Technology, Automated Applications, and Potential for Future Development," *Criminal Justice Monograph Series*, Vol. 5, No. 2 (Huntsville, TX: Sam Houston State University Press, 1974), pp. 3–4.

76. Soderman and O'Connell, *Modern Criminal Investigation*, p. 57.

77. Ibid.

78. Francis Galton, *Finger Prints* (London: Macmillan, 1892).

79. Foote, "Fingerprint Identification," p. 1.

80. Office of Technology Assessment, *Criminal Justice: New Technologies and the Constitution: A Special Report* (Washington, DC: U.S. Government Printing Office, 1988), p. 18. Electro-optical systems for live fingerprint scanning were developed by Fingermatric, Inc., of White Plains, New York.

81. T. F. Wilson and P. L. Woodard, *Automated Fingerprint Identification Systems—Technology and Policy Issues* (Washington, DC: U.S. Dept. of Justice, 1987), p. 5.

82. Kristi Gulick, "Latent Prints from Human Skin," *Law and Order Magazine*, http://www.lawandordermag.com/magazine/current/latentprints.html.htm (accessed September 26, 2001); and "Murder Victims Finger Their Killer," *New Scientist*, May 10, 2008, p. 27.

83. Los Angeles Police Department, *Annual Report, 1985–1986*, p. 26.

84. Ibid., p. 27.

85. American National Standards Institute, *American National Standard for Information Systems—Fingerprint Identification—Data Format for Information Interchange* (New York: ANSI, 1986). Originally developed as the Proposed American National Standard Data Format for the Interchange of Fingerprint Information by the National Bureau of Standards (Washington, DC: NBS, 1986).

86. Dennis G. Kurre, "On-Line Exchange of Fingerprint Identification Data," *FBI Law Enforcement Bulletin*, December 1987, pp. 14–16.

87. Federal Bureau of Investigation, "30-Year-Old Murder Solved by the 'Hit of the Year,'" May 8, 2009, http://www.fbi.gov/page2/may09/iafis_050809.html (accessed May 9, 2009).

88. Jon Swartz, "Ins and Outs of Biometrics," *USA Today*, January 27, 2003, p. 3B.

89. In 1998, ruling for the first time on polygraph examinations, the U.S. Supreme Court upheld the military's ban on the use of polygraph tests in criminal trials. In refusing to hear a case, Justice Clarence Thomas wrote, "[T]he aura of infallibility attending polygraph evidence can lead jurors to abandon their duty to assess credibility and guilt."

90. Details for this story come from *USA Today*, Nationline, March 16, 2000.

91. "NYC Seeks to Indict Rapists by DNA Alone," *USA Today*, August 5, 2003.

92. Francis X. Clines, "DNA Clears Virginia Man of 1982 Assault," *New York Times*, December 10, 2001.

93. Public Law No. 109-162, Title X, Sec. 1002 (2005).

94. Public Law No. 109-162, Title X, Sec. 1004 (2005).

95. U.S. Department of Justice, *Understanding DNA Evidence: A Guide for Victim Service Providers* (Washington, DC: DOJ, 2001).

96. Seth Axelrad, "Survey of State DNA Database Statutes," http://www.aslme.org/dna_04/grid/guide.pdf (accessed July 4, 2007).

97. See Alec J. Jeffreys, Victoria Wilson, and Swee Lay Thein, "Hypervariable 'Minisatellite' Regions in Human Nature," *Nature*, No. 314 (1985), p. 67; and "Individual-Specific 'Fingerprints' of Human DNA," *Nature*, No. 316 (1985), p. 76.

98. Peter Gill, Alec J. Jeffreys, and David J. Werrett, "Forensic Application of DNA Fingerprints," *Nature*, No. 318 (1985), p. 577. See also Craig Seton, "Life for Sex Killer Who Sent Decoy to Take Genetic Test," *London Times*, January 23, 1988, p. 3. A popular account of this case, *The Blooding*, was written by crime novelist Joseph Wambaugh (New York: William Morrow, 1989).

99. Bureau of Justice Statistics, *Forensic DNA Analysis: Issues* (Washington, DC: BJS, 1991).

100. "Genetic Fingerprinting Convicts Rapist in U.K.," *Globe and Mail*, November 14, 1987.

101. Violent Crime Control and Law Enforcement Act of 1994, Section 210301.

102. "National DNA Index System Reaches 1,000,000 Profiles," FBI press release, June 14, 2002.

103. Public Law 108–405.

104. U.S. Code, Title 18, Chapter 213, Section 3297.

105. *Maryland v. King*, U.S. Supreme Court, No. 12-207 (decided June 3, 2013).

106. "Time Line '98," *Yahoo! Internet Life*, January 1999, p. 90. To access the database, visit http://www.publicdata.com.

107. William S. Sessions, "Criminal Justice Information Services: Gearing Up for the Future," *FBI Law Enforcement Bulletin*, February 1993, pp. 181–188.

108. OTA, *Criminal Justice*, p. 29.

109. Ibid.

110. For more on the system, see Craig Stedman, "Feds to Track Sex Offenders with Database," *Computerworld*, September 2, 1996, p. 24.

111. "Saving Face," *PC Computing*, December 1988, p. 60.

112. See Dawn E. McQuiston and Roy S. Malpass, "Use of Facial Composite Systems in U.S. Law Enforcement Agencies," http://eyewitness.utep.edu/Documents/McQuiston%20APLS%202000.pdf (accessed March 25, 2007).

113. "Security or Privacy? DARPA's Total Information Awareness Program Tests the Boundaries," InformationWeek.com, http://www.informationweek.com/story/showArticle.jhtml?articleID510000184 (accessed August 2, 2008).

114. Information in this paragraph comes from "U.S. Sensors Could Track Any Car, All Passengers in Foreign Cities," WorldTribune.com, July 30, 2003, http://www.worldtribune.com/worldtribune/breaking_8.html (accessed August 5, 2007).

115. Ming-Ching Chang, Weina Ge, Nils Krahnstoever, Ting Yu, Ser Nam Lim, and Xiaoming Liu, *Advanced Behavior Recognition in Crowded Environments* (Niskayuna, NY: GE Global Research, 2013).

116. See, for example, Jeffrey S. Hormann, "Virtual Reality: The Future of Law Enforcement Training," *FBI Law Enforcement Bulletin*, July 1995, pp. 7–12.

117. See, for example, Thomas F. Rich, *The Use of Computerized Mapping Crime Control and Prevention Programs* (Washington, DC: National Institute of Justice, 1995).

118. Matt L. Rodriguez, "The Acquisition of High Technology Systems by Law Enforcement," *FBI Law Enforcement Bulletin* (December 1988), p. 10.

119. Office of the Inspector General, Department of Homeland Security, *Semiannual Report to the Congress* (Washington, DC: DHS, 2014).

120. Frank J. Murray, "NASA Plans to Read Terrorists' Minds at Airports," *Washington Times*, August 17, 2002.

121. Ibid.

122. The information in this section comes from Thomas J. Cowper and Michael E. Buerger, *Improving Our View of the World: Police and Augmented Reality Technology* (Washington, DC: Federal Bureau of Investigation, 2003), http://www.fbi.gov/publications/realitytech/realitytech.pdf (accessed October 27, 2006).

123. "Xybernaut and ZNQ3, Inc. Team to Deliver Secure Mobile Wearable Computing Solutions to State and Local Governments," *Business Wire*, July 29, 2003.

124. See the fictional discussion of such an advanced device in Dan Brown, *Deception Point* (New York: Simon and Schuster, 2002).

125. See "Nanotechnology in Crime Prevention and Detection," Institute of Nanotechnology, http://www.nano.org.uk/crime2.htm (accessed August 5, 2007).

126. Winston Chai, "Radio ID Chips May Track Banknotes," CNET News.com, May 23, 2003, http://news.com.com/2100-1019-1009155.html (accessed August 12, 2005).

127. The 2005 World Exposition website, http://www1.expo2005.or.jp/en/whatexpo/index.html (accessed August 3, 2005).

128. *Mending Justice: Sentinel Event Reviews* (Washington, DC: National Institute of Justice, 2014), from which the information in this section is taken.

List of Acronyms

ABA	American Bar Association	CALEA	Commission on Accreditation for Law Enforcement Agencies	CZTS	Combat Zones That See
ACA	American Correctional Association			DARE	Drug Abuse Resistance Education
ACJS	Academy of Criminal Justice Sciences	CAN-SPAM	Controlling the Assault of Non-Solicited Pornography and Marketing	DARPA	Defense Advanced Research Projects Agency
ACLU	American Civil Liberties Union	CAPS	Chicago's Alternative Policing Strategy	DAWN	Drug Abuse Warning Network
ADA	Americans with Disabilities Act (1990)	CAT	computer-aided transcription	DEA	Drug Enforcement Administration
ADAM	Arrestee Drug Abuse Monitoring	CBT	computer-based training	DHS	Department of Homeland Security
		CCA	Corrections Corporation of America		
ADMAX	administrative maximum			DNA	deoxyribonucleic acid
AEDPA	Antiterrorism and Effective Death Penalty Act (1996)	CCE	Continuing Criminal Enterprise (statute) (1970)	DOJ	United States Department of Justice
AFDA	Association of Federal Defense Attorneys	CCIPS	Computer Crime and Intellectual Property Section	DPIC	Death Penalty Information Center
AFIS	automated fingerprint identification system	CDA	Communications Decency Act (1996)	DPRC	Drug Policy Research Center (RAND Corporation)
AI	artificial intelligence	CDC	Centers for Disease Control and Prevention	DUI	driving under the influence (of alcohol or drugs)
AIDS	acquired immunodeficiency syndrome	CFAA	Computer Fraud and Abuse Act (1986)	DWI	driving while intoxicated
AIMS	adult internal management system			EBP	evidence-based policing
		CFR	Council on Foreign Relations	ECPA	Electronic Communications Privacy Act (1986)
AJA	American Jail Association				
ALI	American Law Institute	CIA	Central Intelligence Agency	EPR	Emergency Preparedness and Response
AOUSC	Administrative Office of the United States Courts	CIAO	Critical Infrastructure Assurance Office		
				Europol	European Police Office
APIS	Advance Passenger Information System	CJA	Criminal Justice Act (England)	FBI	Federal Bureau of Investigation
APPA	American Probation and Parole Association	CJIS	Criminal Justice Information Services (FBI)	FCC	federal correctional complex
				FCI	federal correctional institution
AR	augmented reality	CLET	Certified Law Enforcement Trainer	FDA	Food and Drug Administration
ASC	American Society of Criminology	CMEA	Combat Methamphetamine Epidemic Act (2005)		
				FINCEN	Financial Crimes Enforcement Network
ASIS	ASIS International (formerly the American Society for Industrial Security)	CODIS	Combined DNA Index System (FBI)	FLETC	Federal Law Enforcement Training Center
		COPS	Community Oriented Policing Services	FLIR	forward-looking infrared
ASLET	American Society for Law Enforcement Training	CPO	Certified Protection Officer	FOP	Fraternal Order of Police
		CPP	Certified Protection Professional	FPC	federal prison camp
ATF	Bureau of Alcohol, Tobacco, Firearms and Explosives			FTCA	Federal Tort Claims Act
		CPTED	crime prevention through environmental design	FTO	foreign terrorist organization
AWDWWITK	assault with a deadly weapon with intent to kill			FWG	futures working group
		CRIPA	Civil Rights of Institutionalized Persons Act (1980)	GBL	gamma-butyrolactone
BJA	Bureau of Justice Assistance			GBMI	guilty but mentally ill
BJS	Bureau of Justice Statistics			GED	general equivalency diploma
BOP	Bureau of Prisons			GHB	gamma hydroxybutyric acid
BSEBP	British Society of Evidence-Based Policing	CRIPP	Courts Regimented Intensive Probation Program (Texas)	HEUNI	European Institute for Crime Prevention and Control
BTS	Border and Transportation Security	CSA	Controlled Substances Act (1970)	HIDTA	high-intensity drug-trafficking area
BWS	battered women's syndrome				
CAD	computer-assisted dispatch	CSC	Correctional Services Corporation	HIFCA	high-intensity financial crimes area
CAFA	Class Action Fairness Act				

628

HIV	human immunodeficiency virus	MDC	metropolitan detention center	NLADA	National Legal Aid and Defender Association
HRALEI	Human Rights and Law Enforcement Institute	MPC	Model Penal Code	NLECTC	National Law Enforcement and Corrections Technology Center
HSP	Heroin Signature Program	MROP	Mentally Retarded Offender Program (Texas)		
IACP	International Association of Chiefs of Police	MTF	Monitoring the Future (survey)	NLETS	International Justice and Public Safety Information Sharing Network
IAD	internal affairs division	NAACP	National Association for the Advancement of Colored People	NNICC	National Narcotics Intelligence Consumers Committee
IAFIS	Integrated Automated Fingerprint Identification System (FBI)	NACDL	National Association of Criminal Defense Lawyers	NOBLE	National Organization of Black Law Enforcement Executives
IAIP	Information Analysis and Infrastructure Protection	NADCP	National Association of Drug Court Professionals		
ICC	International Criminal Court	NADDIS	Narcotics and Dangerous Drugs Information System	NRA	National Rifle Association
ICE	Bureau of Immigration and Customs Enforcement			NSA	National Security Agency
		NCAVC	National Center for the Analysis of Violent Crime (FBI)	NSA	National Sheriffs' Association
IDRA	Insanity Defense Reform Act (1984)			NSDUH	National Survey on Drug Use and Health
ILC	International Law Commission	NCCD	National Council on Crime and Delinquency	NVAWS	National Violence against Women Survey
ILEA	International Law Enforcement Academy	NCCS	National Computer Crime Squad (FBI)	NW3C	National White Collar Crime Center
ILP	intelligence-led policing				
INCB	International Narcotics Control Board	NCEA	National Center on Elder Abuse	NYGC	National Youth Gang Center
Interpol	International Criminal Police Organization	NCIC	National Crime Information Center (FBI)	NYPD	New York City Police Department
IPES	International Police Executive Symposium	NCISP	National Criminal Intelligence Sharing Plan	ODCCP	Office for Drug Control and Crime Prevention (UN)
IPS	intensive probation supervision	NCJRS	National Criminal Justice Reference Service	OICJ	Office of International Criminal Justice
IRTPA	Intelligence Reform and Terrorism Prevention Act (2004)	NCSC	National Center for State Courts	OIG	Office of the Inspector General (DOJ)
		NCTC	National Counterterrorism Center	OJARS	Office of Justice Assistance, Research, and Statistics
ISC	International Society for Criminology	NCVC	National Center for Victims of Crime	OJJDP	Office of Juvenile Justice and Delinquency Prevention
IVS	International Victim Survey (UN)	NCVS	National Crime Victimization Survey	ONDCP	Office of National Drug Control Policy
JIC	Justice Information Center	NCWP	National Center for Women and Policing	PCIPB	President's Critical Infrastructure Protection Board
JJDP	Juvenile Justice and Delinquency Prevention [Act] (1974)	NDAA	National District Attorneys Association		
JTTF	Joint Terrorism Task Force	NDIC	National Drug Intelligence Center	PCP	phencyclidine
JUST	Judgment under Stress Training			PCR	police–community relations
				PDS	podular/direct supervision
JUSTNET	Justice Technology Information Network	NDIS	National DNA Index System (FBI)	PERF	Police Executive Research Forum
LAPD	Los Angeles Police Department	NETA	No Electronic Theft Act (1997)	PFI	Police Futurists International
LASD	Los Angeles County Sheriff's Department	NGCRC	National Gang Crime Research Center	PHDCN	Project on Human Development in Chicago Neighborhoods
LEAA	Law Enforcement Assistance Administration	NIBRS	National Incident-Based Reporting System (FBI)	PLRA	Prison Litigation Reform Act (1996)
LEAP	law enforcement availability pay	NIDA	National Institute on Drug Abuse	PORAC	Peace Officers Research Association of California
M-19	19th of April Movement				
MADD	Mothers Against Drunk Driving	NIJ	National Institute of Justice	POST	peace officer standards and training
		NIPC	National Infrastructure Protection Center		
MATRIX	Multistate Anti-Terrorism Information Exchange			PREA	Prison Rape Elimination Act (2003)
		NISMART	National Incidence Studies of Missing, Abducted, Runaway, and Thrownaway Children	PSI	presentence investigation
MCFP	medical center for federal prisoners			RFID	radio-frequency identification

RICO	Racketeer Influenced and Corrupt Organizations (statute) (1970)	SIIA	Software and Information Industry Association	UCR	Uniform Crime Reports
RID	Remove Intoxicated Drivers	SLATT	State and Local Anti-Terrorism Training Program	UN	United Nations
RISE	Reintegrative Shaming Experiments (Australian Institute of Criminology)	STG	security threat group	UNCJIN	United Nations Crime and Justice Information Network
RJC	real justice conferencing (Pennsylvania)	SVORI	Serious and Violent Offender Reentry Initiative	UNDOC	United Nations Office on Drugs and Crime
RLUIPA	Religious Land Use and Institutionalized Persons Act (2000)	SWAT	special weapons and tactics	UNICRI	United Nations Interregional Crime and Justice Research Institute
ROR	release on recognizance	TFJJR	Task Force on Juvenile Justice Reform	USCG	United States Coast Guard
RTTF	Regional Terrorism Task Force	TIA	Total Information Awareness	USCIS	United States Citizenship and Immigration Services
RVIS	Remote Video Inspection System	TIP	trafficking in persons	USNCB	United States National Central Bureau (Interpol)
SAMHSA	Substance Abuse and Mental Health Services Administration	TIVU	Terrorism and International Victims Unit (Office for Victims of Crime)	USP	United States penitentiary
SARA	scanning, analysis, response, and assessment	TVPA	Trafficking Victims Protection Act (2000)	USSC	United States Sentencing Commission
SARS	severe acute respiratory syndrome	TVPRA	Trafficking Victims Protection Reauthorization Act (2003)	VAWA	Violence against Women Act (1994)
SBI	State Bureau of Investigation	TWGECSI	Technical Working Group for Electronic Crime Scene Investigation	ViCAP	Violent Criminal Apprehension Program (FBI)
SCU	Street Crimes Unit	TWGEDE	Technical Working Group for the Examination of Digital Evidence	VOCA	Victims of Crime Act (1984)
SEARCH	National Consortium for Justice Information and Statistics	U.S.C.	United States Code	VWPA	Victim and Witness Protection Act (1982)
		UAV	unmanned aerial vehicle	WJIN	World Justice Information Network
		UCBE	unsolicited commercial bulk e mail	WMD	weapon of mass destruction

Glossary

The 18 chapters of *Criminal Justice Today* contain hundreds of terms commonly used in the field of criminal justice. This glossary contains many more. The terms in this glossary are explained whenever possible according to definitions provided by the Bureau of Justice Statistics under a mandate of the Justice System Improvement Act. That mandate was to create a consistent terminology set for use by criminal justice students, practitioners, and planners. It found its most complete expression in the *Dictionary of Criminal Justice Data Terminology*,[1] the second edition of which provides many of our definitions. Others (especially those in Chapter 2) are derived from the Uniform Crime Reporting (UCR) Program of the Federal Bureau of Investigation (FBI) and are taken from the most recent edition of the agency's *Uniform Crime Reporting Handbook*.[2] A second major source of standardized terminology used in the preparation of this glossary is the glossary provided by the website CrimeSolutions.gov, run by the National Institute of Justice (see http://www.crimesolutions.gov/Glossary.aspx).

Standardization of terminology is important because American criminal justice agencies, justice practitioners, and involved citizens now routinely communicate between and among themselves, often over considerable distances, about the criminal justice system and about justice-related issues. For communications to be meaningful and efficient, a shared terminology is necessary. Standardization, however desirable, is not easy to achieve—sometimes because of legal and technical distinctions between jurisdictions or because of variations in customary usage. In the words of the Bureau of Justice Statistics, "It is not possible to construct a single national standard criminal justice data terminology where every term always means the same thing in all of its appearances. However, it is possible and necessary to standardize the language that represents basic categorical distinctions."[3] Although this glossary should be especially valuable to the student who will one day work in the criminal justice system, it should also prove beneficial to anyone seeking a greater insight into that system.

1983 lawsuit A civil suit brought under Title 42, Section 1983, of the U.S. Code against anyone who denies others their constitutional right to life, liberty, or property without due process of law.

abused child A child who has been physically, sexually, or mentally abused. Most states also consider a child who is forced into delinquent activity by a parent or guardian to be abused.

acquittal The judgment of a court, based on a verdict of a jury or a judicial officer, that the defendant is not guilty of the offense or offenses for which he or she was tried.

actus reus An act in violation of the law. Also, a guilty act.

adjudication The process by which a court arrives at a decision regarding a case. Also, the resultant decision.

adjudicatory hearing The fact-finding process by which the juvenile court determines whether there is sufficient evidence to sustain the allegations in a petition.

ADMAX Administrative maximum. The term is used by the federal government to denote ultra-high-security prisons.

administration of justice The performance of any of the following activities: detection, apprehension, detention, pretrial release, post-trial release, prosecution, adjudication, correctional supervision, or rehabilitation of accused persons or criminal offenders.[4]

admission In corrections, the entry of an offender into the legal jurisdiction of a correctional agency or into the physical custody of a correctional facility.

adult A person who is within the original jurisdiction of a criminal court, rather than a juvenile court, because his or her age at the time of an alleged criminal act was above a statutorily specified limit.

adversarial system The two-sided structure under which American criminal trial courts operate. The adversarial system pits the prosecution against the defense. In theory, justice is done when the most effective adversary is able to convince the judge or jury that his or her perspective on the case is the correct one.

aftercare In juvenile justice usage, the status or program membership of a juvenile who has been committed to a treatment or confinement facility, conditionally released from the facility, and placed in a supervisory or treatment program.

aggravated assault The unlawful, intentional inflicting, or attempted or threatened inflicting, of serious injury upon the person of another. Although *aggravated assault* and *simple assault* are standard terms for reporting purposes, most state penal codes use labels like *first-degree* and *second-degree assault* to make such distinctions.

aggravating circumstances Circumstances relating to the commission of a crime that make it more grave than the average instance of that crime. See also **mitigating circumstances.**

alias Any name used for an official purpose that is different from a person's legal name.

alibi A statement or contention by an individual charged with a crime that he or she was so distant when the crime was committed, or so engaged in other provable activities, that his or her participation in the commission of that crime was impossible.

alter ego rule In some jurisdictions, a rule of law that holds that a person can defend a third party only under circumstances and only to the degree that the third party could legally act on his or her own behalf.

alternative sanctions See **intermediate sanctions.**

alternative sentencing The use of court-ordered community service, home detention, day reporting, drug treatment, psychological counseling, victim–offender programming, or intensive supervision in lieu of other, more traditional sanctions, such as imprisonment and fines.

anomie A socially pervasive condition of normlessness. Also, a disjunction between approved goals and means.

anticipatory warrant A search warrant issued on the basis of probable cause to believe that evidence of a crime, although not presently at the place described, will likely be there when the warrant is executed.

Antiterrorism Act See **USA PATRIOT Act.**

appeal Generally, the request that a court with appellate jurisdiction review the judgment, decision, or order of a lower court and set it aside (reverse it) or modify it.

appearance (court) The act of coming into a court and submitting to its authority.

appellant The person who contests the correctness of a court order, judgment, or other decision and who seeks review and relief in a court having appellate jurisdiction. Also, the person on whose behalf this is done.

appellate court A court whose primary function is to review the judgments of other courts and of administrative agencies.

appellate jurisdiction The lawful authority of a court to review a decision made by a lower court.

arraignment Strictly, the hearing before a court having jurisdiction in a criminal case in which the identity of the defendant is established, the defendant is informed of the charge and of his or her rights, and the defendant is required to enter a plea. Also, in some usages, any appearance in criminal court before trial.

arrest The act of taking an adult or juvenile into physical custody by authority of law for the purpose of charging the person with a criminal offense, a delinquent act, or a status offense, terminating with the recording of a specific offense. Technically, an arrest occurs whenever a law enforcement officer curtails a person's freedom to leave.

arrest (UCR/NIBRS) Each separate instance in which a person is taken into physical custody or is notified or cited by a law enforcement officer or agency, except those incidents relating to minor traffic violations.

arrest rate The number of arrests reported for each unit of population.

arrest warrant A document issued by a judicial officer that directs a law enforcement officer to arrest an identified person who has been accused of a specific offense.

arson (UCR/NIBRS) Any willful or malicious burning or attempting to burn, with or without intent to defraud, a dwelling house, public building, motor vehicle or aircraft, personal property of another, and so on. Some instances of arson result from malicious mischief, some involve attempts to claim insurance money, and some are committed in an effort to disguise other crimes, such as murder, burglary, or larceny.

Ashurst-Sumners Act Federal legislation of 1935 that effectively ended the industrial prison era by restricting interstate commerce in prison-made goods.

assault (UCR/NIBRS) An unlawful attack by one person upon another. Historically, *assault* meant only the attempt to inflict injury on another person; a completed act constituted the separate offense of battery. Under modern statistical usage, however, attempted and completed acts are grouped together under the generic term *assault*.

assault on a law enforcement officer A simple or aggravated assault in which the victim is a law enforcement officer engaged in the performance of his or her duties.

atavism A condition characterized by the existence of features thought to be common in earlier stages of human evolution.

attendant circumstances The facts surrounding an event.

attorney A person trained in the law, admitted to practice before the bar of a given jurisdiction, and authorized to advise, represent, and act for others in legal proceedings. Also called *lawyer; legal counsel.*

Auburn system A form of imprisonment developed in New York State around 1820 that depended on mass prisons, where prisoners were held in congregate fashion and required to remain silent. This style of imprisonment was a primary competitor with the Pennsylvania system.

augmented reality (AR) The real-time and accurate overlay of digital information on a user's real-world experience, through visual, aural, and/or tactile interfaces.[5] The computer readouts superimposed on the visual fields of the fictional cyborgs in the *RoboCop* and *Terminator* movies provide an example.

backlog (court) The number of cases awaiting disposition in a court that exceeds the court's capacity for disposing of them within the period of time considered appropriate.

bail The money or property pledged to the court or actually deposited with the court to effect the release of a person from legal custody.

bail bond A document guaranteeing the appearance of a defendant in court as required and recording the pledge of money or property to be paid to the court if he or she does not appear, which is signed by the person to be released and anyone else acting on his or her behalf.

bail bond agent A person, usually licensed, whose business it is to effect release on bail for people charged with offenses and held in custody, by pledging to pay a sum of money if the defendant fails to appear in court as required.

bail revocation A court decision withdrawing the status of release on bail that was previously conferred on a defendant.

bailiff The court officer whose duties are to keep order in the courtroom and to maintain physical custody of the jury.

balancing test A principle, developed by the courts and applied to the corrections arena by *Pell v. Procunier* (1974), that attempts to weigh the rights of an individual, as guaranteed by the Constitution, against the authority of states to make laws or to otherwise restrict a person's freedom in order to protect the state's interests and its citizens.

ballistics The analysis of firearms, ammunition, projectiles, bombs, and explosives.

battered women's syndrome (BWS) 1. A series of common characteristics that appear in women who are abused physically and psychologically over an extended period of time by the dominant male figure in their lives. 2. A pattern of psychological symptoms that develops after somebody has lived in a battering relationship. 3. A pattern of responses and perceptions presumed to be characteristic of women who have been subjected to continuous physical abuse by their mates.[6]

behavioral conditioning A psychological principle that holds that the frequency of any behavior can be increased or decreased through reward, punishment, and association with other stimuli.

bench warrant A document issued by a court directing that a law enforcement officer bring a specified person before the court. A bench warrant is usually issued for a person who has failed to obey a court order or a notice to appear.

bias crime See **hate crime.**

biased policing See **racial profiling.**

Bill of Rights The popular name given to the first ten amendments to the U.S. Constitution, which are considered especially important in the processing of criminal defendants.

bind over To require by judicial authority that a person promise to appear for trial, appear in court as a witness, or keep the peace. Also, the decision by a court of limited jurisdiction requiring that a person charged with a felony appear for trial on that charge in a court of general jurisdiction, as the result of a finding of probable cause at a preliminary hearing held in the court of limited jurisdiction.

biocrime A criminal offense perpetrated through the use of biologically active substances, including chemicals and toxins, disease-causing organisms, altered genetic material, and organic tissues and organs. Biocrimes unlawfully affect the metabolic, biochemical, genetic, physiological, or anatomical status of living organisms.

Biological School A perspective on criminological thought that holds that criminal behavior has a physiological basis.

biological weapon A biological agent used to threaten human life (for example, anthrax, smallpox, or any infectious disease).[7]

biometrics The science of recognizing people by physical characteristics and personal traits.

biosocial criminology A theoretical perspective that sees the interaction between biology and the physical and social environments as key to understanding human behavior, including criminality.

bioterrorism The intentional or threatened use of viruses, bacteria, fungi, or toxins from living organisms to produce death or disease in humans, animals, or plants.[8]

***Bivens* action** A civil suit, based on the case of *Bivens* v. *Six Unknown Federal Agents*, brought against federal government officials for denying the constitutional rights of others.

blended sentence A juvenile court disposition that imposes both a juvenile sanction and an adult criminal sentence upon an adjudicated delinquent. The adult sentence is suspended if the juvenile offender successfully completes the term of the juvenile disposition and refrains from committing any new offense.[9]

bobbies The popular British name given to members of Sir Robert (Bob) Peel's Metropolitan Police Force.

booking A law enforcement or correctional administrative process officially recording an entry into detention after arrest and identifying the person, the place, the time, the reason for the arrest, and the arresting authority.

Bow Street Runners An early English police unit formed under the leadership of Henry Fielding, magistrate of the Bow Street region of London.

broken windows theory A perspective on crime causation that holds that the physical deterioration of an area leads to higher crime rates and an increased concern for personal safety among residents.

Bureau of Justice Statistics (BJS) A U.S. Department of Justice agency responsible for the collection of criminal justice data, including the annual National Crime Victimization Survey.

burglary By the narrowest and oldest definition, the trespassory breaking and entering of the dwelling house of another in the nighttime with the intent to commit a felony.

burglary (UCR/NIBRS) The unlawful entry of a structure to commit a felony or a theft (excludes tents, trailers, and other mobile units used for recreational purposes). For the UCR/NIBRS Program, the crime of burglary can be reported if (1) an unlawful entry of an unlocked structure has occurred, (2) a breaking and entering (of a secured structure) has taken place, or (3) a burglary has been attempted.

capacity (legal) The legal ability of a person to commit a criminal act. Also, the mental and physical ability to act with purpose and to be aware of the certain, probable, or possible results of one's conduct.

capacity (prison) See **prison capacity.**

capital offense A criminal offense punishable by death.

capital punishment The death penalty. Capital punishment is the most extreme of all sentencing options.

career criminal In prosecutorial and law enforcement usage, a person who has a past record of multiple arrests or convictions for serious crimes or who has an unusually large number of arrests or convictions for crimes of varying degrees of seriousness. Also called *professional criminal.*

carnal knowledge Sexual intercourse, coitus, sexual copulation. Carnal knowledge is accomplished "if there is the slightest penetration of the sexual organ of the female by the sexual organ of the male."[10]

case law The body of judicial precedent, historically built on legal reasoning and past interpretations of statutory laws, that serves as a guide to decision making, especially in the courts.

caseload The number of probation or parole clients assigned to one probation or parole officer for supervision.

caseload (corrections) The total number of clients registered with a correctional agency or agent on a given date or during a specified time period, often divided into active supervisory cases and inactive cases, thus distinguishing between clients with whom contact is regular and those with whom it is not.

caseload (court) The number of cases requiring judicial action at a certain time. Also, the number of cases acted on in a given court during a given period.

certiorari See **writ of** *certiorari.*

chain of command The unbroken line of authority that extends through all levels of an organization, from the highest to the lowest.

change of venue The movement of a trial or lawsuit from one jurisdiction to another or from one location to another within the same jurisdiction. A change of venue may be made in a criminal case to ensure that the defendant receives a fair trial.

charge An allegation that a specified person has committed a specific offense, recorded in a functional document such as a record of an arrest, a complaint, an information or indictment, or a judgment of conviction. Also called *count.*

Chicago School A sociological approach that emphasizes demographics (the characteristics of population groups) and geographics (the mapped location of such groups relative to one another) and that sees the social disorganization that characterizes delinquency areas as a major cause of criminality and victimization.

child abuse The illegal physical, emotional, or sexual mistreatment of a child by his or her parent or guardian.

child neglect The illegal failure by a parent or guardian to provide proper nourishment or care to a child.

chromosomes Bundles of genes.

circumstantial evidence Evidence that requires interpretation or that requires a judge or jury to reach a conclusion based on what the evidence indicates. From the proximity of the defendant to a smoking gun, for example, the jury might conclude that he or she pulled the trigger.

citation (to appear) A written order issued by a law enforcement officer directing an alleged offender to appear in a specific court at a specified time to answer a criminal charge and not permitting forfeit of bail as an alternative to court appearance.

citizen's arrest The taking of a person into physical custody by a witness to a crime other than a law enforcement officer for the purpose of delivering him or her to the physical custody of a law enforcement officer or agency.

civil death The legal status of prisoners in some jurisdictions who are denied the opportunity to vote, hold public office, marry, or enter into contracts by virtue of their status as incarcerated felons. Although civil death is primarily of historical interest, some jurisdictions still limit the contractual opportunities available to inmates.

civil justice The civil law, the law of civil procedure, and the array of procedures and activities having to do with private rights and remedies sought by civil action. Civil justice cannot be separated from social justice because the justice enacted in our nation's civil courts reflects basic American understandings of right and wrong.

civil law   The branch of modern law that governs relationships between parties.

civil liability   Potential responsibility for payment of damages or other court-ordered enforcement as a result of a ruling in a lawsuit. Civil liability is not the same as criminal liability, which means "open to punishment for a crime."[11]

class-action lawsuit   A lawsuit filed by one or more people on behalf of themselves and a larger group of people "who are similarly situated."[12]

Classical School   An eighteenth-century approach to crime causation and criminal responsibility that grew out of the Enlightenment and that emphasized the role of free will and reasonable punishments. Classical thinkers believed that punishment, if it is to be an effective deterrent, has to outweigh the potential pleasure derived from criminal behavior.

classification system   A system used by prison administrators to assign inmates to custody levels based on offense history, assessed dangerousness, perceived risk of escape, and other factors.

clearance (UCR/NIBRS)   The event in which a known occurrence of a Part I offense is followed by an arrest or another decision that indicates that the crime has been solved.

clearance rate   A measure of investigative effectiveness that compares the number of crimes reported or discovered to the number of crimes solved through arrest or other means (such as the death of the suspect).

clemency   An executive or legislative action in which the severity of punishment of a single person or a group of people is reduced, the punishment is stopped, or the person or group is exempted from prosecution for certain actions.

closing argument   An oral summation of a case presented to a judge, or to a judge and jury, by the prosecution or by the defense in a criminal trial.

club drug   A synthetic psychoactive substance often found at nightclubs, bars, "raves," and dance parties. Club drugs include MDMA (Ecstasy), ketamine, methamphetamine (meth), GBL, PCP, GHB, and Rohypnol.

codification   The act or process of rendering laws in written form.

cohort   A group of individuals sharing similarities of age, place of birth, and residence.

Cohort analysis is a social science technique that tracks cohorts over time to identify the unique and observable behavioral traits that characterize them.

comes stabuli   A nonuniformed mounted law enforcement officer of medieval England. Early police forces were small and relatively unorganized but made effective use of local resources in the formation of posses, the pursuit of offenders, and the like.

commitment   The action of a judicial officer in ordering that a person subject to judicial proceedings be placed in a particular kind of confinement or residential facility for a specific reason authorized by law. Also, the result of the action—that is, the admission to the facility.

common law   Law originating from usage and custom rather than from written statutes. The term refers to an unwritten body of judicial opinion, originally developed by English courts, that is based on nonstatutory customs, traditions, and precedents that help guide judicial decision making.

community-based corrections   See **community corrections.**

community corrections   The use of a variety of officially ordered program-based sanctions that permit convicted offenders to remain in the community under conditional supervision as an alternative to an active prison sentence. Also called *community-based corrections.*

community court   A low-level court that focuses on quality-of-life crimes that erode a neighborhood's morale. Community courts emphasize problem solving rather than punishment and build on restorative principles like community service and restitution.

community policing   "A collaborative effort between the police and the community that identifies problems of crime and disorder and involves all elements of the community in the search for solutions to these problems."[13]

community service   A sentencing alternative that requires offenders to spend at least part of their time working for a community agency.

comparative criminologist   One who studies crime and criminal justice on a cross-national level.

compelling interest   A legal concept that provides a basis for suspicionless searches when public safety is at stake. (Urinalysis tests of train engineers are an example.) It is the concept on which the U.S. Supreme Court cases of *Skinner* v. *Railway Labor Executives' Association* (1989) and *National Treasury Employees Union* v. *Von Raab* (1989) turned. In those cases, the

Court held that public safety may sometimes provide a sufficiently compelling interest to justify limiting an individual's right to privacy.

compensatory damages   Damages recovered in payment for an actual injury or economic loss.

competent to stand trial   A finding by a court that the defendant has sufficient present ability to consult with his or her attorney with a reasonable degree of rational understanding and that the defendant has a rational as well as factual understanding of the proceedings against him or her.

complaint   Generally, any accusation that a person has committed an offense, received by or originating from a law enforcement or prosecutorial agency or received by a court. Also, in judicial process usage, a formal document submitted to the court by a prosecutor, law enforcement officer, or other person, alleging that a specified person has committed a specific offense and requesting prosecution.

CompStat   A crime-analysis and police-management process, built on crime mapping, that was developed by the New York City Police Department in the mid-1990s.

computer crime   See **cybercrime.**

computer virus   A computer program designed to secretly invade systems and either modify the way in which they operate or alter the information they store. Viruses are destructive software programs that may effectively vandalize computers of all types and sizes.

concurrence   The coexistence of (1) an act in violation of the law and (2) a culpable mental state.

concurrent sentence   One of two or more sentences imposed at the same time, after conviction for more than one offense, and served at the same time. Also, a new sentence for a new conviction, imposed upon a person already under sentence for a previous offense, served at the same time as the previous sentence.

concurring opinion   An opinion written by a judge who agrees with the conclusion reached by the majority of judges hearing a case but whose reasons for reaching that conclusion differ. Concurring opinions, which typically stem from an appellate review, are written to identify issues of precedent, logic, or emphasis that are important to the concurring judge but that were not identified by the court's majority opinion.

conditional release   The release by executive decision of a prisoner from a federal or state correctional facility who has not served his or her full sentence and whose freedom is contingent on obeying specified rules of behavior.

conditions of parole (probation) The general and special limits imposed on an offender who is released on parole (or probation). General conditions tend to be fixed by state statute, whereas special conditions are mandated by the sentencing authority (court or board) and take into consideration the background of the offender and the circumstances of the offense.

confinement In corrections, the physical restriction of a person to a clearly defined area from which he or she is lawfully forbidden to depart and from which departure is usually constrained by architectural barriers, guards or other custodians, or both.

conflict model A criminal justice perspective that assumes that the system's components function primarily to serve their own interests. According to this theoretical framework, justice is more a product of conflicts among agencies within the system than it is the result of cooperation among component agencies.

conflict perspective A theoretical approach that holds that crime is the natural consequence of economic and other social inequities. Conflict theorists highlight the stresses that arise among and within social groups as they compete with one another for resources and for survival. The social forces that result are viewed as major determinants of group and individual behavior, including crime.

consecutive sentence One of two or more sentences imposed at the same time, after conviction for more than one offense, and served in sequence with the other sentence. Also, a new sentence for a new conviction, imposed upon a person already under sentence for a previous offense, which is added to the previous sentence, thus increasing the maximum time the offender may be confined or under supervision.

consensus model A criminal justice perspective that assumes that the system's components work together harmoniously to achieve the social product we call *justice.*

constitutive criminology The study of the process by which human beings create an ideology of crime that sustains the notion of crime as a concrete reality.

containment The aspects of the social bond and of the personality that act to prevent individuals from committing crimes and engaging in deviance.

contempt of court Intentionally obstructing a court in the administration of justice, acting in a way calculated to lessen the court's authority or dignity, or failing to obey the court's lawful orders.

controlled substance A specifically defined bioactive or psychoactive chemical substance proscribed by law.

Controlled Substances Act (CSA) Title II of the Comprehensive Drug Abuse Prevention and Control Act of 1970, which established schedules classifying psychoactive drugs according to their degree of psychoactivity.

conviction The judgment of a court, based on the verdict of a jury or judicial officer or on the guilty plea or *nolo contendere* plea of the defendant, that the defendant is guilty of the offense with which he or she has been charged.

corporate crime A violation of a criminal statute by a corporate entity or by its executives, employees, or agents acting on behalf of and for the benefit of the corporation, partnership, or other form of business entity.[14]

corpus delicti The facts that show that a crime has occurred. The term literally means "the body of the crime."

correctional agency A federal, state, or local criminal or juvenile justice agency, under a single administrative authority, whose principal functions are the intake screening, supervision, custody, confinement, treatment, or presentencing or predisposition investigation of alleged or adjudicated adult offenders, youthful offenders, delinquents, or status offenders.

corrections A generic term that includes all government agencies, facilities, programs, procedures, personnel, and techniques concerned with the intake, custody, confinement, supervision, treatment, and presentencing and predisposition investigation of alleged or adjudicated adult offenders, youthful offenders, delinquents, and status offenders.

corruption See **police corruption.**

Cosa Nostra A secret criminal organization of Sicilian origin. Also called *Mafia.*

counsel (legal) See **attorney.**

count (offense) See **charge.**

court An agency or unit of the judicial branch of government, authorized or established by statute or constitution and consisting of one or more judicial officers, which has the authority to decide cases, controversies in law, and disputed matters of fact brought before it.

court calendar The court schedule; the list of events comprising the daily or weekly work of a court, including the assignment of the time and place for each hearing or other item of business or the list of matters that will be taken up in a given court term. Also called *docket.*

court clerk An elected or appointed court officer responsible for maintaining the written records of the court and for supervising or performing the clerical tasks necessary for conducting judicial business. Also, any employee of a court whose principal duties are to assist the court clerk in performing the clerical tasks necessary for conducting judicial business.

court disposition 1. For statistical reporting purposes, generally, the judicial decision terminating proceedings in a case before judgment is reached. 2. The judgment. 3. The outcome of judicial proceedings and the manner in which the outcome was arrived at.

court-martial A military court convened by senior commanders under the authority of the Uniform Code of Military Justice for the purpose of trying a member of the armed forces accused of a violation of the code.

court of last resort The court authorized by law to hear the final appeal on a matter.

court of record A court in which a complete and permanent record of all proceedings or specified types of proceedings is kept.

court order A mandate, command, or direction issued by a judicial officer in the exercise of his or her judicial authority.

court probation A criminal court requirement that an offender fulfill specified conditions of behavior in lieu of a sentence to confinement, but without assignment to a probation agency's supervisory caseload.

court reporter A person present during judicial proceedings who records all testimony and other oral statements made during the proceedings.

courtroom work group The professional courtroom actors, including judges, prosecuting attorneys, defense attorneys, public defenders, and others who earn a living serving the court.

courts of general jurisdiction courts of law with primary jurisdiction on all issues not delegated to lower courts. Most often called major trial courts, they most often hear serious criminal or civil cases. Cases are also designated to courts of general jurisdiction based on the severity of the punishment or allegation or on the dollar value of the case.

courts of limited jurisdiction courts of law that have jurisdiction on a restricted range of cases, primarily lesser criminal and civil matters, including misdemeanors, small claims, traffic, parking, and civil infractions. Such courts are also called inferior courts or lower courts. They can also handle the preliminary stages of felony cases in some states.

credit card fraud   The use or attempted use of a credit card to obtain goods or services with the intent to avoid payment.

crime   Conduct in violation of the criminal laws of a state, the federal government, or a local jurisdiction, for which there is no legally acceptable justification or excuse.

crime-control model   A criminal justice perspective that emphasizes the efficient arrest and conviction of criminal offenders.

Crime Index   A now defunct but once inclusive measure of the UCR Program's violent and property crime categories, or what are called *Part I offenses*. The Crime Index, long featured in the FBI's publication *Crime in the United States*, was discontinued in 2004. The index had been intended as a tool for geographic (state-to-state) and historical (year-to-year) comparisons via the use of crime rates (the number of crimes per unit of population). However, criticism that the index was misleading arose after researchers found that the largest of the index's crime categories, larceny-theft, carried undue weight and led to an underappreciation of changes in the rates of more violent and serious crimes.

crime prevention   The anticipation, recognition, and appraisal of a crime risk and the initiation of action to eliminate or reduce it.

crime rate   The number of offenses reported for each unit of population.

crime scene   The physical area in which a crime is thought to have occurred and in which evidence of the crime is thought to reside.

crime scene investigator   An expert trained in the use of forensics techniques, such as gathering DNA evidence, collecting fingerprints, photographing the scene, sketching, and interviewing witnesses.

crime typology   A classification of crimes along a particular dimension, such as legal categories, offender motivation, victim behavior, or the characteristics of individual offenders.

criminal homicide (UCR/NIBRS)   The act of causing the death of another person without legal justification or excuse.

criminal incident   In National Crime Victimization Survey terminology, a criminal event involving one or more victims and one or more offenders.

criminal intelligence   Information compiled, analyzed, or disseminated in an effort to anticipate, prevent, or monitor criminal activity.[15]

criminal investigation   "The process of discovering, collecting, preparing, identifying, and presenting evidence to determine *what happened and who is responsible*"[16] when a crime has occurred.

criminal justice   In the strictest sense, the criminal (penal) law, the law of criminal procedure, and the array of procedures and activities having to do with the enforcement of this body of law. Criminal justice cannot be separated from social justice because the justice enacted in our nation's criminal courts reflects basic American understandings of right and wrong.

criminal justice system   The aggregate of all operating and administrative or technical support agencies that perform criminal justice functions. The basic divisions of the operational aspects of criminal justice are law enforcement, courts, and corrections.

criminal law   The body of rules and regulations that define and specify the nature of and punishments for offenses of a public nature or for wrongs committed against the state or society. Also called *penal law*.

criminal negligence   Behavior in which a person fails to reasonably perceive substantial and unjustifiable risks of dangerous consequences.

criminal proceedings   The regular and orderly steps, as directed or authorized by statute or a court of law, taken to determine whether an adult accused of a crime is guilty or not guilty.

criminalist   A police crime scene analyst or laboratory worker versed in criminalistics.

criminalistics   The use of technology in the service of criminal investigation; the application of scientific techniques to the detection and evaluation of criminal evidence.

criminology   The scientific study of the causes and prevention of crime and the rehabilitation and punishment of offenders.

cruel and unusual punishment   Punishment involving torture or a lingering death or the infliction of unnecessary and wanton pain.

culpability   Blameworthiness; responsibility in some sense for an event or situation deserving of moral blame. Also, in Model Penal Code usage, a state of mind on the part of one who is committing an act that makes him or her potentially subject to prosecution for that act.

cultural defense   A defense to a criminal charge in which the defendant's culture is taken into account in judging his or her culpability.

cultural pluralism   See **multiculturalism.**

curtilage   In legal usage, the area surrounding a residence that can reasonably be said to be a part of the residence for Fourth Amendment purposes.

custody   The legal or physical control of a person or a thing. Also, the legal, supervisory, or physical responsibility for a person or a thing.

cybercrime   Any crime perpetrated through the use of computer technology. Also, any violation of a federal or state cybercrime statute. Also called *computer crime.*

cyberstalking   The use of the Internet, e-mail, and other electronic communication technologies to stalk another person.[17]

cyberterrorism   A form of terrorism that makes use of high technology, especially computers and the Internet, in the planning and carrying out of terrorist attacks.

danger law   A law intended to prevent the pretrial release of criminal defendants judged to represent a danger to others in the community.

dangerousness   The likelihood that a given individual will later harm society or others. Dangerousness is often measured in terms of recidivism, or the likelihood that an individual will commit another crime within five years following arrest or release from confinement.

dark figure of crime   Crime that is not reported to the police and that remains unknown to officials.

data encryption   The encoding of computerized information.

date rape   Unlawful forced sexual intercourse that occurs within the context of a dating relationship. Date rape, or acquaintance rape, is a subcategory of rape that is of special concern today.

Daubert standard   A test of scientific acceptability applicable to the gathering of evidence in criminal cases.

deadly force   Force likely to cause death or great bodily harm. Also, "the intentional use of a firearm or other instrument resulting in a high probability of death."[18]

deadly weapon   An instrument that is designed to inflict serious bodily injury or death or that is capable of being used for such a purpose.

deconstructionist theory   One of the emerging approaches that challenges existing criminological perspectives to debunk them and that works toward replacing them with concepts more applicable to the postmodern era.

decriminalization   The redefinition of certain previously criminal behaviors into regulated activities that become "ticketable" rather than "arrestable."

defendant A person formally accused of an offense by the filing in court of a charging document.

defense (to a criminal charge) Evidence and arguments offered by a defendant and his or her attorney to show why the defendant should not be held liable for a criminal charge.

defense attorney See **defense counsel.**

defense counsel A licensed trial lawyer hired or appointed to conduct the legal defense of a person accused of a crime and to represent him or her before a court of law. Also called *defense attorney.*

defensible space theory The belief that an area's physical features may be modified and structured so as to reduce crime rates in that area and to lower the fear of victimization that residents experience.

deliberate indifference A wanton disregard by correctional personnel for the well-being of inmates. Deliberate indifference requires both actual knowledge that a harm is occurring and disregard of the risk of harm. A prison official may be held liable under the Eighth Amendment for acting with deliberate indifference to inmate health or safety only if he or she knows that inmates face a substantial risk of serious harm and disregards that risk by failing to take reasonable measures to abate it.

delinquency In the broadest usage, juvenile actions or conduct in violation of criminal law, juvenile status offenses, and other juvenile misbehavior.

delinquent A juvenile who has been adjudged by a judicial officer of a juvenile court to have committed a delinquent act.

delinquent act An act committed by a juvenile for which an adult could be prosecuted in a criminal court but for which a juvenile can be adjudicated in a juvenile court or prosecuted in a court having criminal jurisdiction if the juvenile court transfers jurisdiction. Generally, a felony- or misdemeanor-level offense in states employing those terms.

delinquent child A child who has engaged in activity that would be considered a crime if the child were an adult. The term *delinquent* is used to avoid the stigma associated with the term *criminal.*

dependent child A child who has no parents or whose parents are unable to care for him or her.

desistance The cessation of criminal offending or other antisocial behavior.

design capacity The number of inmates a prison was intended to hold when it was built or modified. Also called *bed capacity.*

detainee Usually, a person held in local short-term confinement while awaiting consideration for pretrial release or a first appearance for arraignment.

detention The legally authorized confinement of a person subject to criminal or juvenile court proceedings, until the point of commitment to a correctional facility or until release.

detention hearing In juvenile justice usage, a hearing by a judicial officer of a juvenile court to determine whether a juvenile is to be detained, is to continue to be detained, or is to be released while juvenile proceedings are pending.

determinate sentencing A model of criminal punishment in which an offender is given a fixed term of imprisonment that may be reduced by good time or gain time. Under the model, for example, all offenders convicted of the same degree of burglary would be sentenced to the same length of time behind bars. Also called *fixed sentencing.*

deterrence A goal of criminal sentencing that seeks to inhibit criminal behavior through the fear of punishment.

deviance A violation of social norms defining appropriate or proper behavior under a particular set of circumstances. Deviance often includes criminal acts. Also called *deviant behavior.*

digital criminal forensics The lawful seizure, acquisition, analysis, reporting, and safeguarding of data from digital devices that may contain information of evidentiary value to the trier of fact in criminal events.[19]

diminished capacity A defense based on claims of a mental condition that may be insufficient to exonerate the defendant of guilt but that may be relevant to specific mental elements of certain crimes or degrees of crime. Also called *diminished responsibility.*

direct evidence Evidence that, if believed, directly proves a fact. Eyewitness testimony and videotaped documentation account for the majority of all direct evidence heard in the criminal courtroom.

directed patrol A police-management strategy designed to increase the productivity of patrol officers through the scientific analysis and evaluation of patrol techniques.

discharge To release from confinement or supervision or to release from a legal status imposing an obligation upon the subject person.

discretion See **police discretion.**

discretionary release The release of an inmate from prison to supervision that is decided by a parole board or other authority.

disposition The action by a criminal or juvenile justice agency that signifies that a portion of the justice process is complete and that jurisdiction is terminated or transferred to another agency or that signifies that a decision has been reached on one aspect of a case and a different aspect comes under consideration, requiring a different kind of decision.

dispositional hearing The final stage in the processing of adjudicated juveniles in which a decision is made on the form of treatment or penalty that should be imposed on the child.

dispute-resolution center An informal hearing place designed to mediate interpersonal disputes without resorting to the more formal arrangements of a criminal trial court.

district attorney (DA) See **prosecutor.**

diversion The official suspension of criminal or juvenile proceedings against an alleged offender at any point after a recorded justice system intake, but before the entering of a judgment, and referral of that person to a treatment or care program administered by a nonjustice or private agency. Also, release without referral.

DNA profiling The use of biological residue, found at the scene of a crime, for genetic comparisons in aiding in the identification of criminal suspects.

docket See **court calendar.**

domestic terrorism The unlawful use of force or violence by an individual or a group that is based and operates entirely within the United States and its territories, acts without foreign direction, and directs its activities against elements of the U.S. government or population.[20]

double jeopardy A common law and constitutional prohibition against a second trial for the same offense.

drug Any chemical substance defined by social convention as bioactive or psychoactive.

drug abuse Illicit drug use that results in social, economic, psychological, or legal problems for the user.[21]

drug court A special state, county, or municipal court that offers first-time substance-abuse offenders judicially mandated and court-supervised treatment alternatives to prison.

drug czar The popular name for the head of the Office of National Drug Control Policy

(ONDCP), a federal position that was created during the Reagan presidency to organize federal drug-fighting efforts.

drug-law violation The unlawful sale, purchase, distribution, manufacture, cultivation, transport, possession, or use of a controlled or prohibited drug. Also, the attempt to commit one of these acts.

drug trafficking Trading or dealing in controlled substances, including the transporting, storage, importing, exporting, or sale of a controlled substance.

due process A right guaranteed by the Fourth, Fifth, Sixth, and Fourteenth Amendments of the U.S. Constitution and generally understood, in legal contexts, to mean the due course of legal proceedings according to the rules and forms established for the protection of individual rights. In criminal proceedings, due process of law is generally understood to include the following basic elements: a law creating and defining the offense, an impartial tribunal having jurisdictional authority over the case, accusation in proper form, notice and opportunity to defend, trial according to established procedure, and discharge from all restraints or obligations unless convicted.

due process model A criminal justice perspective that emphasizes individual rights at all stages of justice system processing.

Electronic Communications Privacy Act (ECPA) A law passed by Congress in 1986 establishing the due process requirements that law enforcement officers must meet in order to legally intercept wire communications.

electronic evidence Information and data of investigative value that are stored in or transmitted by an electronic device.[22]

element (of a crime) In a specific crime, one of the essential features of that crime, as specified by law or statute.

embezzlement The misappropriation, or illegal disposal, of legally entrusted property by the person to whom it was entrusted, with the intent to defraud the legal owner or the intended beneficiary.

emergency search A search conducted by the police without a warrant, which is justified on the basis of some immediate and overriding need, such as public safety, the likely escape of a dangerous suspect, or the removal or destruction of evidence.

entrapment An improper or illegal inducement to crime by agents of law enforcement. Also, a defense that may be raised when such inducements have occurred.

equity A sentencing principle, based on concerns with social equality, that holds that similar crimes should be punished with the same degree of severity, regardless of the social or personal characteristics of the offenders.

espionage The "gathering, transmitting, or losing"[23] of information related to the national defense in such a manner that the information becomes available to enemies of the United States and may be used to their advantage.

ethnocentric Holding a belief in the superiority of one's own social or ethnic group and culture.

ethnocentrism The phenomenon of "culture-centeredness" by which one uses one's own culture as a benchmark against which to judge all other patterns of behavior.

European Police Office (Europol) The integrated police intelligence-gathering and intelligence-dissemination arm of the member nations of the European Union.

evidence Anything useful to a judge or jury in deciding the facts of a case. Evidence may take the form of witness testimony, written documents, videotapes, magnetic media, photographs, physical objects, and so on.

evidence-based policing (EBP) The use of the best available research on the outcomes of police work to implement guidelines and evaluate agencies, units, and officers.[24]

evidence-based practice Crime-fighting strategies that have been scientifically tested and are based on social science research.

ex post facto Latin for "after the fact." The Constitution prohibits the enactment of *ex post facto* laws, which make acts committed before the laws in question were passed punishable as crimes.

excessive force The application of an amount and/or frequency of force greater than that required to compel compliance from a willing or unwilling subject.[25]

exclusionary rule The understanding, based on U.S. Supreme Court precedent, that incriminating information must be seized according to constitutional specifications of due process or it will not be allowed as evidence in a criminal trial.

exculpatory evidence Any information having a tendency to clear a person of guilt or blame.

excuse A legal defense in which the defendant claims that some personal condition or circumstance at the time of the act was such that he or she should not be held accountable under the criminal law.

exemplary damages See **punitive damages.**

expert system Computer hardware and software that attempt to duplicate the decision-making processes used by skilled investigators in the analysis of evidence and in the recognition of patterns that such evidence might represent.

expert witness A person who has special knowledge and skills recognized by the court as relevant to the determination of guilt or innocence. Unlike lay witnesses, expert witnesses may express opinions or draw conclusions in their testimony.

extradition The surrender by one state or jurisdiction to another of an individual accused or convicted of an offense in the second state or jurisdiction.

federal court system The three-tiered structure of federal courts, comprising U.S. district courts, U.S. courts of appeal, and the U.S. Supreme Court.

federal law enforcement agency A U.S. government agency or office whose primary functional responsibility is to enforce federal criminal laws.

felony A criminal offense punishable by death or by incarceration in a prison facility for at least one year.

feminist criminology A developing intellectual approach that emphasizes gender issues in criminology.

filing The initiation of a criminal case by formal submission to the court of a charging document, alleging that a named person has committed a specified criminal offense.

fine The penalty imposed on a convicted person by a court, requiring that he or she pay a specified sum of money to the court.

first appearance An appearance before a magistrate during which the legality of the defendant's arrest is initially assessed and the defendant is informed of the charges on which he or she is being held. At this stage in the criminal justice process, bail may be set or pretrial release arranged. Also called *initial appearance.*

first plea See **initial plea.**

fixed sentencing See **determinate sentencing.**

fleeting-targets exception An exception to the exclusionary rule that permits law enforcement officers to search a motor vehicle based on probable cause and without a warrant. The fleeting-targets exception is predicated on the fact that vehicles can quickly leave the jurisdiction of a law enforcement agency.

force See **police use of force.**

foreign terrorist organization (FTO) A foreign organization that engages in terrorist activity that threatens the security of U.S. nationals or the national security of the United States and that is so designated by the U.S. secretary of state.

forensic anthropology The use of anthropological principles and techniques in criminal investigation.

forensic entomology The study of insects to determine such matters as a person's time of death.

forfeiture The authorized seizure of money, negotiable instruments, securities, or other things of value. Under federal antidrug laws, judicial representatives are authorized to seize all cash, negotiable instruments, securities, or other things of value furnished or intended to be furnished by any person in exchange for a controlled substance, as well as all proceeds traceable to such an exchange. Also called *asset forfeiture.*

forgery The creation or alteration of a written or printed document, which if validly executed would constitute a record of a legally binding transaction, with the intent to defraud by affirming it to be the act of an unknowing second person. Also, the creation of an art object with intent to misrepresent the identity of the creator.

fraud An offense involving deceit or intentional misrepresentation of fact, with the intent of unlawfully depriving a person of his or her property or legal rights.

frivolous suit A lawsuit with no foundation in fact. Frivolous suits are generally brought by lawyers and plaintiffs for reasons of publicity, politics, or other non-law-related issues and may result in fines against plaintiffs and their counsel.

fruit of the poisonous tree doctrine A legal principle that excludes from introduction at trial any evidence later developed as a result of an illegal search or seizure.

gain time The amount of time deducted from time to be served in prison on a given sentence as a consequence of participation in special projects or programs.

gender ratio problem The need for an explanation of the fact that the number of crimes committed by men routinely far exceeds the number of crimes committed by women in almost all categories.

gender responsiveness The process of understanding and taking into account the differences in characteristics and life experiences that women and men bring to the criminal justice system, and adjusting strategies and practices in ways that appropriately respond to those conditions.

general deterrence A goal of criminal sentencing that seeks to prevent others from committing crimes similar to the one for which a particular offender is being sentenced by making an example of the person sentenced.

genes Distinct portions of a cell's DNA that carry coded instructions for making everything the body needs.

globalization The internationalization of trade, services, investment, information, and other forms of human social activity. Also, a process of social homogenization by which the experiences of everyday life, marked by the diffusion of commodities and ideas, can foster a standardization of cultural expressions around the world.[26]

good-faith exception An exception to the exclusionary rule. Law enforcement officers who conduct a search or who seize evidence on the basis of good faith (that is, when they believe they are operating according to the dictates of the law) and who later discover that a mistake was made (perhaps in the format of the application for a search warrant) may still provide evidence that can be used in court.

good time The amount of time deducted from time to be served in prison on a given sentence as a consequence of good behavior.

grand jury A group of jurors who have been selected according to law and have been sworn to hear the evidence and to determine whether there is sufficient evidence to bring the accused person to trial, to investigate criminal activity generally, or to investigate the conduct of a public agency or official.

grievance procedure A formalized arrangement, usually involving a neutral hearing board, whereby institutionalized individuals have the opportunity to register complaints about the conditions of their confinement.

gross negligence The intentional failure to perform a manifest duty in reckless disregard of the consequences as affecting the life or property of another.[27]

guilty but mentally ill (GBMI) A verdict, equivalent to a finding of "guilty," that establishes that the defendant, although mentally ill, was in sufficient possession of his or her faculties to be morally blameworthy for his or her acts.

guilty plea A defendant's formal answer in court to the charge or charges contained in a complaint, information, or indictment, claiming that he or she did commit the offense or offenses listed.

guilty verdict See **verdict.**

habeas corpus See **writ of** *habeas corpus.*

habitual offender A person sentenced under the provisions of a statute declaring that people convicted of a given offense and shown to have previously been convicted of another specified offense shall receive a more severe penalty than that for the current offense alone.

hacker A computer hobbyist or professional, generally with advanced programming skills. Today, the term *hacker* has taken on a sinister connotation, referring to hobbyists who are bent on illegally accessing the computers of others or who attempt to demonstrate their technological prowess through computerized acts of vandalism.

hands-off doctrine A policy of nonintervention with regard to prison management that U.S. courts tended to follow until the late 1960s. For the past 50 years, the doctrine has languished as judicial intervention in prison administration dramatically increased, although there is now some evidence that a new hands-off era is approaching.

Harrison Narcotics Act The first major piece of federal antidrug legislation, passed in 1914.

hate crime (UCR/NIBRS) A criminal offense motivated, in whole or in part, by the offender's bias against a race, gender, gender identity, religion, disability, sexual orientation, or ethnicity, and committed against persons, property, or society. Also called *bias crime.*

hearing A proceeding in which arguments, witnesses, or evidence is heard by a judicial officer or an administrative body.

hearsay Something that is not based on the personal knowledge of a witness. Witnesses who testify about something they have heard, for example, are offering hearsay by repeating information about a matter of which they have no direct knowledge.

hearsay rule The long-standing precedent that hearsay cannot be used in American courtrooms. Rather than accepting testimony based on hearsay, the court will ask that the person who was the original source of the hearsay information be brought in to be questioned and cross-examined. Exceptions to the hearsay rule may occur when the person with direct knowledge is dead or is otherwise unable to testify.

heritability A statistical construct that estimates the amount of variation in the traits of a population that is attributable to genetic factors.

hierarchy rule A pre-NIBRS Uniform Crime Reporting Program scoring practice in which only the most serious offense was counted in a multiple-offense incident.

high-technology crime   Violations of the criminal law whose commission depends on, makes use of, and often targets sophisticated and advanced technology. See also **cybercrime.**

home confinement   House arrest. Individuals ordered confined to their homes are sometimes monitored electronically to ensure they do not leave during the hours of confinement. Absence from the home during working hours is often permitted.

homicide   See **criminal homicide.**

hot-spot policing   A contemporary policing strategy in which law enforcement agencies focus their resources on known areas of criminal activity.

Hudud **crime**   A serious violation of Islamic law that is regarded as an offense against God.

Hudud   crimes include such behavior as theft, adultery, sodomy, alcohol consumption, and robbery.

human smuggling   Illegal immigration in which an agent is paid to help a person cross a border clandestinely.

hung jury   A jury that, after long deliberation, is so irreconcilably divided in opinion that it is unable to reach any verdict.

hypothesis   An explanation that accounts for a set of facts and that can be tested by further investigation. Also, something that is taken to be true for the purpose of argument or investigation.[28]

identity management   The comprehensive management and administration of a user's individual profile information, permissions, and privileges across a variety of social settings.[29]

identity theft   A crime in which an impostor obtains key pieces of information, such as Social Security and driver's license numbers, to obtain credit, merchandise, and services in the name of the victim. The victim is often left with a ruined credit history and the time-consuming and complicated task of repairing the financial damage.[30]

illegally seized evidence   Evidence seized without regard to the principles of due process as described by the Bill of Rights. Most illegally seized evidence is the result of police searches conducted without a proper warrant or of improperly conducted interrogations.

illegal search and seizure   An act in violation of the Fourth Amendment of the U.S. Constitution, which reads, "The right of the people to be secure in their persons, houses, papers, and effects, against unreasonable searches and seizures, shall not be violated, and no Warrants shall issue, but upon probable cause, supported by Oath or affirmation, and particularly describing the place to be searched, and the persons or things to be seized."

incapacitation   The use of imprisonment or other means to reduce the likelihood that an offender will commit future offenses.

inchoate offense   An offense not yet completed. Also, an offense that consists of an action or conduct that is a step toward the intended commission of another offense.

incident-based reporting   Compared with summary reporting, a less restrictive and more expansive method of collecting crime data in which all of the analytical elements associated with an offense or arrest are compiled by a central collection agency on an incident-by-incident basis.

included offense   An offense that is made up of elements that are a subset of the elements of another offense having a greater statutory penalty, the occurrence of which is established by the same evidence or by some portion of the evidence that has been offered to establish the occurrence of the greater offense.

incompetent to stand trial   In criminal proceedings, a finding by a court that, as a result of mental illness, defect, or disability, a defendant is incapable of understanding the nature of the charges and proceedings against him or her, of consulting with an attorney, and of aiding in his or her own defense.

indeterminate sentence   A type of sentence imposed on a convicted criminal that is meant to encourage rehabilitation through the use of relatively unspecific punishments (such as a term of imprisonment of from one to ten years).

indeterminate sentencing   A model of criminal punishment that encourages rehabilitation through the use of general and relatively unspecific sentences (such as a term of imprisonment of from one to ten years).

index crime   See **Crime Index.**

indictment   A formal, written accusation submitted to the court by a grand jury, alleging that a specified person has committed a specified offense, usually a felony.

individual rights   The rights guaranteed to all members of American society by the U.S. Constitution (especially those found in the first ten amendments to the Constitution, known as the *Bill of Rights*). These rights are particularly important to criminal defendants facing formal processing by the criminal justice system.

individual-rights advocate   One who seeks to protect personal freedoms within the process of criminal justice.

industrial prison   A correctional model intended to capitalize on the labor of convicts sentenced to confinement.

information   A formal, written accusation submitted to the court by a prosecutor, alleging that a specified person has committed a specific offense.

infraction   A minor violation of state statute or local ordinance punishable by a fine or other penalty or by a specified, usually limited, term of incarceration.

infrastructure   The basic facilities, services, and installations that a country needs to function. Transportation and communications systems, water and power lines, and institutions that serve the public, including banks, schools, post offices, and prisons, are all part of a country's infrastructure.[31]

inherent coercion   The tactics used by police interviewers that fall short of physical abuse but that nonetheless pressure suspects to divulge information.

initial appearance   See **first appearance.**

initial plea   The first plea to a given charge entered in the court record by or for the defendant. The acceptance of an initial plea by the court unambiguously indicates that the arraignment process has been completed. Also called *first plea.*

insanity defense   A legal defense based on claims of mental illness or mental incapacity.

institutional capacity   The official number of inmates that a confinement or residential facility is housing or was intended to house.

intake   The first step in decision making regarding a juvenile whose behavior or alleged behavior is in violation of the law or could otherwise cause a juvenile court to assume jurisdiction.

intelligence-led policing (ILP)   The collection and analysis of information to produce an intelligence end product designed to inform police decision making at both the tactical and strategic levels.[32]

intensive probation supervision (IPS)   A form of probation supervision involving frequent face-to-face contact between the probationer and the probation officer.

intent   The state of mind or attitude with which an act is carried out. Also, the design, resolve, or determination with which a person acts to achieve a certain result.

interdiction The interception of drug traffic at the nation's borders. Interdiction is one of the many strategies used to stem the flow of illegal drugs into the United States.

interdisciplinary theory An approach that integrates a variety of theoretical viewpoints in an attempt to explain something, such as crime and violence.

intermediate appellate court An appellate court whose primary function is to review the judgments of trial courts and the decisions of administrative agencies and whose decisions are, in turn, usually reviewable by a higher appellate court in the same state.

intermediate sanctions The use of split sentencing, shock probation or parole, shock incarceration, community service, intensive supervision, or home confinement in lieu of other, more traditional, sanctions, such as imprisonment and fines. Also called *alternative sanctions*.

internal affairs The branch of a police organization tasked with investigating charges of wrongdoing involving members of the department.

International Criminal Police Organization (Interpol) An international law enforcement support organization that began operations in 1946 and today has 190 member nations.

international terrorism The unlawful use of force or violence by an individual or a group that has some connection to a foreign power, or whose activities transcend national boundaries, against people or property in order to intimidate or coerce a government, the civilian population, or any segment thereof, in furtherance of political or social objectives.[33]

interrogation The information-gathering activity of police officers that involves the direct questioning of suspects.

Islamic law A system of laws, operative in some Arab countries, based on the Muslim religion and especially the holy book of Islam, the Koran.

jail A confinement facility administered by an agency of local government, typically a law enforcement agency, intended for adults but sometimes also containing juveniles, which holds people detained pending adjudication or committed after adjudication, usually those sentenced to a year or less.

jail commitment A sentence of commitment to the jurisdiction of a confinement facility system for adults that is administered by an agency of local government and whose custodial authority is usually limited to people sentenced to a year or less of confinement.

judge An elected or appointed public official who presides over a court of law and who is authorized to hear and sometimes to decide cases and to conduct trials.

judgment The statement of the decision of a court that the defendant is acquitted or convicted of the offense or offenses charged.

judgment suspending sentence A court-ordered sentencing alternative that results in the convicted offender being placed on probation.

judicial officer Any person authorized by statute, constitutional provision, or court rule to exercise the powers reserved to the judicial branch of government.

judicial review The power of a court to review actions and decisions made by other agencies of government.

jural postulates Propositions developed by the famous jurist Roscoe Pound that hold that the law reflects shared needs without which members of society could not coexist. Pound's jural postulates are often linked to the idea that the law can be used to engineer the social structure to ensure certain kinds of outcomes. In capitalist societies, for example, the law of theft protects property rights.

jurisdiction The territory, subject matter, or people over which a court or other justice agency may exercise lawful authority, as determined by statute or constitution. See also **venue.**

jurisprudence The philosophy of law. Also, the science and study of the law.

juror A member of a trial or grand jury who has been selected for jury duty and is required to serve as an arbiter of the facts in a court of law. Jurors are expected to render verdicts of "guilty" or "not guilty" as to the charges brought against the accused, although they sometimes fail to do so (as in the case of a hung jury).

jury panel The group of people summoned to appear in court as potential jurors for a particular trial. Also, the people selected from the group of potential jurors to sit in the jury box, from which those acceptable to the prosecution and the defense are finally chosen as the jury.

jury selection The process whereby, according to law and precedent, members of a trial jury are chosen.

just deserts A model of criminal sentencing that holds that criminal offenders deserve the punishment they receive at the hands of the law and that punishments should be appropriate to the type and severity of the crime committed.

justice The principle of fairness; the ideal of moral equity.

justice model A contemporary model of imprisonment based on the principle of just deserts.

justice reinvestment A concept that prioritizes the use of alternatives to incarceration for persons convicted of eligible nonviolent offenses, standardizes the use of risk assessments instruments in pretrial detention, authorizes the use of early-release mechanisms for prisoners who meet eligibility requirements, and reinvests savings from such initiatives into effective crime-prevention programs.

justification A legal defense in which the defendant admits to committing the act in question but claims it was necessary in order to avoid some greater evil.

juvenile A person subject to juvenile court proceedings because a statutorily defined event or condition caused by or affecting that person was alleged to have occurred while his or her age was below the statutorily specified age limit of original jurisdiction of the juvenile court.

juvenile court A court that has, as all or part of its authority, original jurisdiction over matters concerning people statutorily defined as juveniles.

juvenile court judgment The juvenile court decision, terminating an adjudicatory hearing, that the juvenile is a delinquent, a status offender, or a dependent or that the allegations in the petition are not sustained.

juvenile disposition The decision of a juvenile court, concluding a dispositional hearing, that an adjudicated juvenile be committed to a juvenile correctional facility; be placed in a juvenile residence, shelter, or care or treatment program; be required to meet certain standards of conduct; or be released.

juvenile justice The policies and activities of law enforcement and the courts in handling law violations by youths under the age of criminal jurisdiction.[34]

juvenile justice agency A government agency, or subunit thereof, whose functions are the investigation, supervision, adjudication, care, or confinement of juvenile offenders and nonoffenders subject to the jurisdiction of a juvenile court. Also, in some usages, a private agency providing care and treatment.

juvenile justice system The aggregate of the government agencies that function to investigate, supervise, adjudicate, care for, or confine youthful offenders and other children subject to the jurisdiction of the juvenile court.

juvenile petition   A document filed in juvenile court alleging that a juvenile is a delinquent, a status offender, or a dependent and asking that the court assume jurisdiction over the juvenile or that an alleged delinquent be transferred to a criminal court for prosecution as an adult.

Kansas City experiment   The first large-scale scientific study of law enforcement practices. Sponsored by the Police Foundation, it focused on the practice of preventive patrol.

kidnapping   The transportation or confinement of a person without authority of law and without his or her consent or without the consent of his or her guardian, if a minor.

Knapp Commission   A committee that investigated police corruption in New York City in the early 1970s.

labeling theory   A social process perspective that sees continued crime as a consequence of the limited opportunities for acceptable behavior that follow from the negative responses of society to those defined as offenders.

landmark case   A precedent-setting court decision that produces substantial changes in both the understanding of the requirements of due process and in the practical day-to-day operations of the justice system.

larceny-theft (UCR/NIBRS)   The unlawful taking or attempted taking, carrying, leading, or riding away of property, from the possession or constructive possession of another. Motor vehicles are excluded. Larceny is the most common of the eight major offenses, although probably only a small percentage of all larcenies are actually reported to the police because of the small dollar amounts involved.

latent evidence   Evidence of relevance to a criminal investigation that is not readily seen by the unaided eye.

law   A rule of conduct, generally found enacted in the form of a statute, that proscribes or mandates certain forms of behavior. Statutory law is often the result of moral enterprise by interest groups that, through the exercise of political power, are successful in seeing their valued perspectives enacted into law.

law enforcement   The generic name for the activities of the agencies responsible for maintaining public order and enforcing the law, particularly the activities of preventing, detecting, and investigating crime and apprehending criminals.

law enforcement agency   A federal, state, or local criminal justice agency or identifiable subunit whose principal functions are the prevention, detection, and investigation of crime and the apprehension of alleged offenders.

Law Enforcement Assistance Administration (LEAA)   A now-defunct federal agency established under Title I of the Omnibus Crime Control and Safe Streets Act of 1968 to funnel federal funding to state and local law enforcement agencies.

law enforcement intelligence   See **criminal intelligence.**

law enforcement officer   An officer employed by a law enforcement agency who is sworn to carry out law enforcement duties.

lawyer   See **attorney.**

lay witness   An eyewitness, character witness, or other person called on to testify who is not considered an expert. Lay witnesses must testify to facts only and may not draw conclusions or express opinions.

learning organization   "An organization skilled at creating, acquiring, and transferring knowledge and at modifying its behavior to reflect new knowledge and insights."[35]

legal cause   A legally recognizable cause. A legal cause must be demonstrated in court in order to hold an individual criminally liable for causing harm.

legal counsel   See **attorney.**

legalistic style   A style of policing marked by a strict concern with enforcing the precise letter of the law. Legalistic departments may take a hands-off approach to disruptive or problematic behavior that does not violate the criminal law.

legalization   Elimination of the laws and associated criminal penalties associated with certain behaviors—usually the production, sale, distribution, and possession of a controlled substance.

less-lethal weapon   A weapon that is designed to disable, capture, or immobilize—but not kill—a suspect. Occasional deaths do result from the use of such weapons, however.

lex talionis   The law of retaliation, often expressed as "an eye for an eye" or "like for like."

life course perspective   An approach to explaining crime and deviance that investigates developments and turning points in the course of a person's life.

line operations   In police organizations, the field activities or supervisory activities directly related to day-to-day police work.

lone wolf terrorist   A domestic terrorist who perpetrates political violence by acting alone; who does not belong to an organized terrorist group or network; who acts without the direct influence of a leader; and whose tactics and methods are self-directed.

Mafia   See **Cosa Nostra.**

major crimes   See **Part I offenses.**

mala in se   Acts that are regarded, by tradition and convention, as wrong in themselves.

mala prohibita   Acts that are considered wrong only because there is a law against them.

malware   Malicious computer programs like viruses, worms, and Trojan horses.

mandatory release   The release of an inmate from prison that is determined by statute or sentencing guidelines and is not decided by a parole board or other authority.

mandatory sentence   A statutorily required penalty that must be set and carried out in all cases upon conviction for a specified offense or series of offenses.

mandatory sentencing   A structured sentencing scheme that allows no leeway in the nature of the sentence required and under which clearly enumerated punishments are mandated for specific offenses or for habitual offenders convicted of a series of crimes.

MATRIX   An acronym for the Multistate Anti-Terrorism Information Exchange, an Internet-based proof-of-concept pilot program funded by the Department of Justice and the Department of Homeland Security to increase and enhance the exchange of sensitive information about terrorism and other criminal activity between enforcement agencies at the local, state, and federal levels.

maximum sentence   In legal usage, the maximum penalty provided by law for a given criminal offense, usually stated as a maximum term of imprisonment or a maximum fine. Also, in corrections usage in relation to a given offender, any of several quantities (expressed in days, months, or years) that vary according to whether calculated at the point of sentencing or at a later point in the correctional process and according to whether the time period referred to is the term of confinement or the total period under correctional jurisdiction.

medical model   A therapeutic perspective on correctional treatment that applies the diagnostic perspective of medical science to the handling of criminal offenders.

medical parole   An early release option under which an inmate who is deemed "low risk" due to a serious physical or mental health condition is released from prison earlier than he or she might have been under normal circumstances.

mens rea The state of mind that accompanies a criminal act. Also, a guilty mind.

Miranda rights The set of rights that a person accused or suspected of having committed a specific offense has during interrogation and of which he or she must be informed prior to questioning, as stated by the U.S. Supreme Court in deciding *Miranda* v. *Arizona* (1966) and related cases.

Miranda triggers The dual principles of custody and interrogation, both of which are necessary before an advisement of rights is required.

Miranda warnings The advisement of rights due criminal suspects by the police before questioning begins. *Miranda* warnings were first set forth by the U.S. Supreme Court in the 1966 case of *Miranda* v. *Arizona*.

misdemeanor An offense punishable by incarceration, usually in a local confinement facility, for a period whose upper limit is prescribed by statute in a given jurisdiction, typically one year or less.

mistrial A trial that has been terminated and declared invalid by the court because of some circumstance that created a substantial and uncorrectable prejudice to the conduct of a fair trial or that made it impossible to continue the trial in accordance with prescribed procedures.

mitigating circumstances Circumstances relating to the commission of a crime that may be considered to reduce the blameworthiness of the defendant. See also **aggravating circumstances.**

mixed sentence A sentence that requires that a convicted offender serve weekends (or other specified periods of time) in a confinement facility (usually a jail) while undergoing probationary supervision in the community.

M'Naghten rule A rule for determining insanity, which asks whether the defendant knew what he or she was doing or whether the defendant knew that what he or she was doing was wrong.

Model Penal Code (MPC) A generalized modern codification considered basic to criminal law, published by the American Law Institute in 1962.

money laundering The process by which criminals or criminal organizations seek to disguise the illicit nature of their proceeds by introducing them into the stream of legitimate commerce and finance.[36]

moral enterprise The process undertaken by an advocacy group to have its values legitimated and embodied in law.

motion An oral or written request made to a court at any time before, during, or after court proceedings, asking the court to make a specified finding, decision, or order.

motive A person's reason for committing a crime.

motor vehicle theft (UCR/NIBRS) The theft or attempted theft of a motor vehicle. A *motor vehicle* is defined as a self-propelled road vehicle that runs on land surface and not on rails. The stealing of trains, planes, boats, construction equipment, and most farm machinery is classified as larceny under the UCR/NIBRS Program, not as motor vehicle theft.

multiculturalism The existence within one society of diverse groups that maintain unique cultural identities while frequently accepting and participating in the larger society's legal and political systems.[37] *Multiculturalism* is often used in conjunction with the term *diversity* to identify many distinctions of social significance. Also called *cultural pluralism*.

municipal police department A city- or town-based law enforcement agency. Also known as *local police*.

murder The unlawful killing of a human being. *Murder* is a generic term that in common usage may include first- and second-degree murder, manslaughter, involuntary manslaughter, and other similar offenses.

murder and nonnegligent manslaughter (UCR/NIBRS) Intentionally causing the death of another without legal justification or excuse. Also, causing the death of another while committing or attempting to commit another crime.

narcoterrorism A political alliance between terrorist organizations and drug-supplying cartels. The cartels provide financing for the terrorists, who in turn provide quasi-military protection to the drug dealers.

National Crime Victimization Survey (NCVS) An annual survey of selected American households conducted by the Bureau of Justice Statistics to determine the extent of criminal victimization—especially unreported victimization—in the United States.

National Incident-Based Reporting System (NIBRS) An incident-based reporting system that collects data on every single crime occurrence. NIBRS data will soon supersede the kinds of summary data that have traditionally been provided by the FBI's Uniform Crime Reporting Program.

natural law Rules of conduct inherent in human nature and in the natural order that are thought to be knowable through intuition, inspiration, and the exercise of reason, without the need for reference to created laws.

NCVS See **National Crime Victimization Survey.**

neglected child A child who is not receiving the proper level of physical or psychological care from his or her parents or guardians or who has been placed up for adoption in violation of the law.

negligence In legal usage, generally, a state of mind accompanying a person's conduct such that he or she is not aware, though a reasonable person should be aware, that there is a risk that the conduct might cause a particular harmful result.

negligent manslaughter (UCR/NIBRS) Causing the death of another by recklessness or gross negligence.

neoclassical criminology A **contemporary** version of classical criminology that emphasizes deterrence and retribution and that holds that human beings are essentially free to make choices in favor of crime and deviance or conformity to the law.

new-generation jail A temporary confinement facility that eliminates many of the traditional barriers between inmates and correctional personnel. Also called *podular jail*, *direct-supervision jail*, and *indirect-supervision jail*.

new police A police force formed in 1829 under the command of Sir Robert Peel. It became the model for modern-day police forces throughout the Western world. Also called *Metropolitan Police Force*.

night watch An early form of police patrol in English cities and towns.

NLETS The International Justice and Public Safety Information Sharing Network.

nolle prosequi A formal entry in the record of the court indicating that the prosecutor declares that he or she will proceed no further in the action. The prosecutor's decision not to pursue the case requires the approval of the court in some jurisdictions.

nolo contendere A plea of "no contest." A no-contest plea is used when the defendant does not wish to contest conviction. Because the plea does not admit guilt, however, it cannot provide the basis for later civil suits that might follow a criminal conviction.

not guilty by reason of insanity The plea of a defendant or the verdict of a jury or judge in a criminal proceeding that the defendant is not guilty of the offense charged because at the time the crime was committed, the defendant did not have the mental capacity to be held criminally responsible for his or her actions.

nothing-works doctrine   The belief, popularized by Robert Martinson in the 1970s, that correctional treatment programs have had little success in rehabilitating offenders.

no true bill   The decision by a grand jury that it will not return an indictment against the person accused of a crime on the basis of the allegations and evidence presented by the prosecutor.

occupational crime   Any act punishable by law that is committed through opportunity created in the course of a legitimate occupation.

offender   An adult who has been convicted of a criminal offense.

offense   A violation of the criminal law. Also, in some jurisdictions, a minor crime, such as jaywalking, that is sometimes described as *ticketable*.

offenses known to police (UCR/NIBRS)   Reported occurrences of offenses that have been verified at the police level.

opening statement   The initial statement of the prosecutor or the defense attorney, made in a court of law to a judge or jury, describing the facts that he or she intends to present during trial to prove the case.

operational capacity   The number of inmates a prison can effectively accommodate based on management considerations.

opinion   The official announcement of a decision of a court, together with the reasons for that decision.

opportunity theory   A perspective that sees delinquency as the result of limited legitimate opportunities for success available to most lower-class youth.

organized crime   The unlawful activities of the members of a highly organized, disciplined association engaged in supplying illegal goods or services, including gambling, prostitution, loan-sharking, narcotics, and labor racketeering, and in other unlawful activities.[38]

original jurisdiction   The lawful authority of a court to hear or to act on a case from its beginning and to pass judgment on the law and the facts. The authority may be over a specific geographic area or over particular types of cases.

parens patriae   A common law principle that allows the state to assume a parental role and to take custody of a child when he or she becomes

delinquent, is abandoned, or is in need of care that the natural parents are unable or unwilling to provide.

Parliament   The British legislature, the highest law-making body of the United Kingdom.

parole   The status of a convicted offender who has been conditionally released from prison by a paroling authority before the expiration of his or her sentence, is placed under the supervision of a parole agency, and is required to observe the conditions of parole.

parole board   A state paroling authority. Most states have parole boards that decide when an incarcerated offender is ready for conditional release. Some boards also function as revocation hearing panels. Also called *parole commission*.

parolee   A person who has been conditionally released by a paroling authority from a prison prior to the expiration of his or her sentence, is placed under the supervision of a parole agency, and is required to observe conditions of parole.

parole (probation) violation   An act or a failure to act by a parolee (or a probationer) that does not conform to the conditions of his or her parole (or probation).

parole revocation   The administrative action of a paroling authority removing a person from parole status in response to a violation of lawfully required conditions of parole, including the prohibition against committing a new offense. Parole revocation usually results in the offender's return to prison.

parole supervision   Guidance, treatment, or regulation of the behavior of a convicted adult who is obligated to fulfill conditions of parole or conditional release. Parole supervision is authorized and required by statute, is performed by a parole agency, and occurs after a period of prison confinement.

parole supervisory caseload   The total number of clients registered with a parole agency or officer on a given date or during a specified time period.

paroling authority   A board or commission that has the authority to release on parole adults committed to prison, to revoke parole or other conditional release, and to discharge from parole or other conditional release status.

Part I offenses   A UCR/NIBRS offense group used to report murder, rape, robbery, aggravated assault, burglary, larceny-theft, motor vehicle theft, and arson, as defined under the FBI's UCR/NIBRS Program. Also called *major crimes*.

Part II offenses   A UCR/NIBRS offense group used to report arrests for less serious offenses. Agencies are limited to reporting only arrest information for Part II offenses, with the exception of simple assault.

PATRIOT Act   See **USA PATRIOT Act.**

peace officer standards and training (POST) program   The official program of a state or legislative jurisdiction that sets standards for the training of law enforcement officers. All states set such standards, although not all use the term *POST*.

peacemaking criminology   A perspective that holds that crime-control agencies and the citizens they serve should work together to alleviate social problems and human suffering and thus reduce crime.

penal code   The written, organized, and compiled form of the criminal laws of a jurisdiction.

penal law   See **criminal law.**

penitentiary   A prison. See also **Pennsylvania system.**

Pennsylvania system   A form of imprisonment developed by the Pennsylvania Quakers around 1790 as an alternative to corporal punishments. This style of imprisonment made use of solitary confinement and encouraged rehabilitation.

peremptory challenge   The right to challenge a potential juror without disclosing the reason for the challenge. Prosecutors and defense attorneys routinely use peremptory challenges to eliminate from juries individuals who, although they express no obvious bias, are thought to be capable of swaying the jury in an undesirable direction.

perjury   The intentional making of a false statement as part of the testimony by a sworn witness in a judicial proceeding on a matter relevant to the case at hand.

perpetrator   The chief actor in the commission of a crime; that is, the person who directly commits the criminal act.

personality   The relatively stable characteristic patterns of thoughts, feelings and behaviors that make a person unique, and which influences that person's behavior.

petition   A written request made to a court asking for the exercise of its judicial powers or asking for permission to perform some act that requires the authorization of a court.

petit jury   See **trial jury.**

pharmaceutical diversion   The transfer of prescription medicines controlled by the

Controlled Substance Act by theft, deception, and or fraudulent means for other than their intended legitimate therapeutic purposes.

phrenology   The study of the shape of the head to determine anatomical correlates of human behavior.

physical dependence   A biologically based craving for a specific drug that results from frequent use of the substance. Physical dependence on drugs is marked by a growing tolerance of a drug's effects, so that increased amounts of the drug are needed to obtain the desired effect, and by the onset of withdrawal symptoms over periods of prolonged abstinence.[39] Also called *physical addiction*.

piracy   See **software piracy.**

plaintiff   A person who initiates a court action.

plain view   A legal term describing the ready visibility of objects that might be seized as evidence during a search by police in the absence of a search warrant specifying the seizure of those objects. To lawfully seize evidence in plain view, officers must have a legal right to be in the viewing area and must have cause to believe that the evidence is somehow associated with criminal activity.

plea   In criminal proceedings, the defendant's formal answer in court to the charge contained in a complaint, information, or indictment that he or she is guilty of the offense charged, is not guilty of the offense charged, or does not contest the charge.

plea bargaining   The process of negotiating an agreement among the defendant, the prosecutor, and the court as to an appropriate plea and associated sentence in a given case. Plea bargaining circumvents the trial process and dramatically reduces the time required for the resolution of a criminal case.

police–community relations (PCR)   An area of police activity that recognizes the need for the community and the police to work together effectively. PCR is based on the notion that the police derive their legitimacy from the community they serve. Many police agencies began to explore PCR in the 1960s and 1970s.

police corruption   The abuse of police authority for personal or organizational gain.[40]

police discretion   The opportunity for police officers to exercise choice in their enforcement activities.

police ethics   The special responsibility to adhere to moral duty and obligation that is inherent in police work.

police management   The administrative activities of controlling, directing, and coordinating police personnel, resources, and activities in the service of preventing crime, apprehending criminals, recovering stolen property, and performing regulatory and helping services.[41]

police professionalism   The increasing formalization of police work and the accompanying rise in public acceptance of the police.

police subculture   A particular set of values, beliefs, and acceptable forms of behavior characteristic of American police. Socialization into the police subculture begins with recruit training and continues thereafter. Also called *police culture*.

police use of force   The use of physical restraint by a police officer when dealing with a member of the public.[42]

police working personality   All aspects of the traditional values and patterns of behavior evidenced by police officers who have been effectively socialized into the police subculture. Characteristics of the police personality often extend to the personal lives of law enforcement personnel.

political defense   An innovative defense to a criminal charge that claims that the defendant's actions stemmed from adherence to a set of political beliefs and standards significantly different from those on which the American style of government is based. A political defense questions the legitimacy and purpose of all criminal proceedings against the defendant.

Positivist School   An approach theory that stresses the application of scientific techniques to the study of crime and criminals.

POST   See **peace officer standards and training (POST) program.**

postconviction remedy   The procedure or set of procedures by which a person who has been convicted of a crime can challenge in court the lawfulness of a judgment of conviction, a penalty, or a correctional agency action and thus obtain relief in situations where this cannot be done by a direct appeal.

postmodern criminology   A branch of criminology that developed after World War II and that builds on the tenets of postmodern social thought.

precedent   A legal principle that ensures that previous judicial decisions are authoritatively considered and incorporated into future cases.

predictive policing   A contemporary policing strategy that uses statistical techniques to analyze data in order to anticipate or predict the likelihood of crime occurrence in locations of interest.

preliminary hearing   A proceeding before a judicial officer in which three matters must be decided: (1) whether a crime was committed, (2) whether the crime occurred within the territorial jurisdiction of the court, and (3) whether there are reasonable grounds to believe that the defendant committed the crime.

preliminary investigation   All of the activities undertaken by a police officer who responds to the scene of a crime, including determining whether a crime has occurred, securing the crime scene, and preserving evidence.

presentence investigation (PSI)   The examination of a convicted offender's background prior to sentencing. Presentence examinations are generally conducted by probation or parole officers and are submitted to sentencing authorities.

presentment   Historically, unsolicited written notice of an offense provided to a court by a grand jury from their own knowledge or observation. In current usage, any of several presentations of alleged facts and charges to a court or a grand jury by a prosecutor.

presumptive sentencing   A model of criminal punishment that meets the following conditions: (1) The appropriate sentence for an offender convicted of a specific charge is presumed to fall within a range of sentences authorized by sentencing guidelines that are adopted by a legislatively created sentencing body, usually a sentencing commission. (2) Sentencing judges are expected to sentence within the range or to provide written justification for failing to do so. (3) There is a mechanism for review, usually appellate, of any departure from the guidelines.

pretrial detention   Confinement occurring between the time of arrest or of being held to answer a charge and the conclusion of prosecution.[43]

pretrial discovery   In criminal proceedings, disclosure by the prosecution or the defense prior to trial of evidence or other information that is intended to be used in the trial.

pretrial release   The release of an accused person from custody, for all or part of the time before or during prosecution, on his or her promise to appear in court when required.

prison   A state or federal confinement facility that has custodial authority over adults sentenced to confinement.

prison argot   The slang characteristic of prison subcultures and prison life.

prison capacity The size of the correctional population an institution can effectively hold.[44] There are three types of prison capacity: rated, operational, and design.

prison commitment A sentence of commitment to the jurisdiction of a state or federal confinement facility system for adults whose custodial authority extends to offenders sentenced to more than a year of confinement, to a term expressed in years or for life, or to await execution of a death sentence.

prison subculture The values and behavioral patterns characteristic of prison inmates. Prison subculture has been found to be surprisingly consistent across the country.

prisoner A person in physical custody in a state or federal confinement facility or in the personal physical custody of a criminal justice official while being transported to or between confinement facilities.

prisoner reentry See **reentry.**

prisonization The process whereby newly institutionalized offenders come to accept prison lifestyles and criminal values. Although many inmates begin their prison experience with only a few values that support criminal behavior, the socialization experience they undergo while incarcerated leads to a much greater acceptance of such values.

private prison A correctional institution operated by a private firm on behalf of local, state, or federal government.

private protective service An independent or proprietary commercial organization that provides protective services to employers on a contractual basis.

private security Self-employed individuals and privately funded business entities and organizations that provide security-related services to specific clientele for a fee, for the individual or entity that retains or employs them or for themselves, in order to protect people, private property, or interests from various hazards.[45]

private security agency See **private protective service.**

privatization The movement toward the wider use of private prisons.

probable cause A set of facts and circumstances that would induce a reasonably intelligent and prudent person to believe that a specified person has committed a specified crime. Also, reasonable grounds to make or believe an accusation. Probable cause refers to the necessary level of belief that would allow for police seizures (arrests) of individuals and full searches of dwellings, vehicles, and possessions.

probation A sentence of imprisonment that is suspended. Also, the conditional freedom granted by a judicial officer to a convicted offender, as long as the person meets certain conditions of behavior.

probation revocation A court order taking away a convicted offender's probationary status and usually withdrawing the conditional freedom associated with that status in response to a violation of the conditions of probation.

probation termination The ending of the probation status of a given person by routine expiration of the probationary period, by special early termination by the court, or by revocation of probation.

probation violation An act or a failure to act by a probationer that does not conform to the conditions of his or her probation.

probation workload The total set of activities required to carry out the probation agency functions of intake screening of juvenile cases, referral of cases to other service agencies, investigation of juveniles and adults for the purpose of preparing predisposition or presentence reports, supervision or treatment of juveniles and adults granted probation, assistance in the enforcement of court orders concerning family problems, such as abandonment and nonsupport cases, and other such functions assigned by statute or court order.

probative value The degree to which a particular item of evidence is useful in, and relevant to, proving something important in a trial.

problem police officer A law enforcement officer who exhibits problem behavior, as indicated by high rates of citizen complaints and use-of-force incidents and by other evidence.[46]

problem-solving policing A type of policing that assumes that crimes can be controlled by uncovering and effectively addressing the underlying social problems that cause crime. Problem-solving policing makes use of community resources, such as counseling centers, welfare programs, and job-training facilities. It also attempts to involve citizens in crime prevention through education, negotiation, and conflict management. Also called *problem-oriented policing.*

procedural defense A defense that claims that the defendant was in some significant way discriminated against in the justice process or that some important aspect of official procedure was not properly followed in the investigation or prosecution of the crime charged.

procedural fairness The process by which procedures that *feel* fair to those involved are made.

procedural law The part of the law that specifies the methods to be used in enforcing substantive law.

profession An organized undertaking characterized by a body of specialized knowledge acquired through extensive education and by a well-considered set of internal standards and ethical guidelines that hold members of the profession accountable to one another and to society.

professional criminal See **career criminal.**

property bond The setting of bail in the form of land, houses, stocks, or other tangible property. In the event that the defendant absconds prior to trial, the bond becomes the property of the court.

property crime A UCR/NIBRS summary offense category that traditionally includes burglary, larceny-theft, motor vehicle theft, and arson.

proportionality A sentencing principle that holds that the severity of sanctions should bear a direct relationship to the seriousness of the crime committed.

prosecution agency A federal, state, or local criminal justice agency or subunit whose principal function is the prosecution of alleged offenders.

prosecutor An attorney whose official duty is to conduct criminal proceedings on behalf of the state or the people against those accused of having committed criminal offenses. Also called *county attorney; district attorney (DA); state's attorney; U.S. attorney.*

prosecutorial discretion The decision-making power of prosecutors, based on the wide range of choices available to them, in the handling of criminal defendants, the scheduling of cases for trial, the acceptance of negotiated pleas, and so on. The most important form of prosecutorial discretion lies in the power to charge, or not to charge, a person with an offense.

prostitution The act of offering or agreeing to engage in, or engaging in, a sex act with another in return for a fee.

psychoactive substance A chemical substance that affects cognition, feeling, or awareness.

psychoanalysis A theory of human behavior, based on the writings of Sigmund Freud, that sees personality as a complex composite of interacting mental entities.

psychological dependence A craving for a specific drug that results from long-term substance abuse. Psychological dependence on drugs is marked by the belief that drugs are needed to achieve a feeling of well-being.[47] Also called *psychological addiction*.

psychological manipulation Manipulative actions by police interviewers that are designed to pressure suspects to divulge information and that are based on subtle forms of intimidation and control.

psychological profiling The attempt to categorize, understand, and predict the behavior of certain types of offenders based on behavioral clues they provide.

Psychological School A perspective on criminological thought that views offensive and deviant behavior as the product of dysfunctional personality. Psychological thinkers identify the conscious, and especially the subconscious, contents of the human psyche as major determinants of behavior.

psychopath A person with a personality disorder, especially one manifested in aggressively antisocial behavior, which is often said to be the result of a poorly developed superego. Also called *sociopath*.

psychopathology The study of pathological mental conditions—that is, mental illness.

psychosis A form of mental illness in which sufferers are said to be out of touch with reality.

public defender An attorney employed by a government agency or subagency, or by a private organization under contract to a government body, for the purpose of providing defense services to indigents, or an attorney who has volunteered such service.

public-defender agency A federal, state, or local criminal justice agency or subunit whose principal function is to represent in court people accused or convicted of a crime who are unable to hire private counsel.

public-order advocate One who believes that under certain circumstances involving a criminal threat to public safety, the interests of society should take precedence over individual rights.

public-safety department A state or local agency that incorporates various law enforcement and emergency service functions.

punitive damages Damages requested or awarded in a civil lawsuit when the defendant's willful acts were malicious, violent, oppressive, fraudulent, wanton, or grossly reckless.[48] Also called *exemplary damages*.

quality-of-life offense A minor violation of the law (sometimes called a *petty crime*) that demoralizes community residents and businesspeople. Quality-of-life offenses involve

acts that create physical disorder (for example, excessive noise or vandalism) or that reflect social decay (for example, panhandling and prostitution).

racial profiling Any police-initiated action that relies on the race, ethnicity, national origin, sexual orientation, gender or religion, rather than (1) the behavior of an individual, or (2) information that leads the police to a particular individual who has been identified as being, or having been, engaged in criminal activity. Also called **biased policing.**

Racketeer Influenced and Corrupt Organizations (RICO) A federal statute that allows for the federal seizure of assets derived from illegal enterprise.

radical criminology A conflict perspective that sees crime as engendered by the unequal distribution of wealth, power, and other resources, which adherents believe is especially characteristic of capitalist societies. Also called *critical criminology*; *Marxist criminology*.

rape Unlawful sexual intercourse achieved through force and without consent. More specifically, penetration, no matter how slight, of the vagina or anus with any body part or object, or oral penetration by a sex organ of another person, without the consent of the victim. *Statutory rape* differs from other forms of rape in that it generally involves nonforcible sexual intercourse with a minor. Broadly speaking, the term *rape* has been applied to a wide variety of sexual attacks and may include same-sex rape and the rape of a male by a female. Some jurisdictions refer to same-sex rape as **sexual battery**.

rated capacity The number of inmates a prison can handle according to the judgment of experts.

rational choice theory A perspective on crime causation that holds that criminality is the result of conscious choice. Rational choice theory predicts that individuals will choose to commit crime when the benefits of doing so outweigh the costs of disobeying the law.

reaction formation The process whereby a person openly rejects that which he or she wants or aspires to but cannot obtain or achieve.

real evidence Evidence that consists of physical material or traces of physical activity.

reasonable doubt In legal proceedings, an actual and substantial doubt arising from the evidence, from the facts or circumstances shown by the evidence, or from the lack of evidence.[49] Also, the state of a case such that, after the comparison and consideration of all the evidence, jurors cannot say they feel an abiding conviction of the truth of the charge.[50]

reasonable doubt standard The standard of proof necessary for conviction in criminal trials.

reasonable force A degree of force that is appropriate in a given situation and is not excessive. Also, the minimum degree of force necessary to protect oneself, one's property, a third party, or the property of another in the face of a substantial threat.

reasonable suspicion The level of suspicion that would justify an officer in making further inquiry or in conducting further investigation. Reasonable suspicion may permit stopping a person for questioning or for a simple pat-down search. Also, a belief, based on a consideration of the facts at hand and on reasonable inferences drawn from those facts, that would induce an ordinarily prudent and cautious person under the same circumstances to conclude that criminal activity is taking place or that criminal activity has recently occurred. Reasonable suspicion is a *general* and reasonable belief that a crime is in progress or has occurred, whereas probable cause is a reasonable belief that a *particular* person has committed a *specific* crime. See also **probable cause.**

recidivism The act of relapsing into a problem or criminal behavior during or after receiving sanctions, or while undergoing an intervention due to a previous behavior or crime. In criminal justice settings, recidivism is often measured by criminal acts that result in rearrest, reconviction, or return to prison.

recidivism rate A measure of the rate of reoffending (usually defined by arrest) for a given population of released prisoners, or for a group of criminally sanctioned offenders, over time. Rates of recidivism are generally calculated over a three or a five year time period.

recidivist A person who has been convicted of one or more crimes and who is alleged or found to have subsequently committed another crime or series of crimes.

reckless behavior Activity that increases the risk of harm.

recreational drug user A person who uses drugs relatively infrequently, primarily with friends, and in social contexts that define drug use as pleasurable. Most addicts begin as recreational users.

reentry The managed return to the community of an individual released from prison. Also, the successful transitioning of a released inmate back into the community. Also called *prisoner reentry*.

reentry courts "Specialized courts that help reduce recidivism and improve public safety through the use of judicial oversight to apply graduated sanctions and positive reinforcement, to marshal resources to support the prisoner's reintegration, and to promote positive behavior by the returning prisoners."[51]

reformatory style A late-nineteenth-century correctional model based on the use of the indeterminate sentence and a belief in the possibility of rehabilitation, especially for youthful offenders. The reformatory concept faded with the emergence of industrial prisons around the start of the twentieth century.

regional jail A jail that is built and run using the combined resources of a variety of local jurisdictions.

rehabilitation The attempt to reform a criminal offender. Also, the state in which a reformed offender is said to be.

release on recognizance (ROR) The pretrial release of a criminal defendant on his or her written promise to appear in court as required. No cash or property bond is required.

remote location monitoring A supervision strategy that uses electronic technology to track offenders who have been sentenced to house arrest or who have been ordered to limit their movements while completing a sentence involving probation or parole.

reprieve An executive act temporarily suspending the execution of a sentence, usually a death sentence. A reprieve differs from other suspensions of sentence not only in that it almost always applies to the temporary withdrawing of a death sentence, but also in that it is usually an act of clemency intended to provide the prisoner with time to secure amelioration of the sentence.

research The use of standardized, systematic procedures in the search for knowledge.

resident A person required, by official action or by his or her acceptance of placement, to reside in a public or private facility established for purposes of confinement, supervision, or care.

residential commitment A sentence of commitment to a correctional facility for adults in which the offender is required to reside at night but from which he or she is regularly permitted to depart during the day, unaccompanied by any official.

response time A measure of the time that it takes for police officers to respond to calls for service.

restitution A court requirement that an accused or convicted offender pay money or provide services to the victim of the crime or provide services to the community.

restoration A goal of criminal sentencing that attempts to make the victim "whole again."

restorative justice (RJ) A sentencing model that builds on restitution and community participation in an attempt to make the victim "whole again."

retribution The act of taking revenge on a criminal perpetrator.

revocation hearing A hearing held before a legally constituted hearing body (such as a parole board) to determine whether a parolee or probationer has violated the conditions and requirements of his or her parole or probation.

rights of defendant The powers and privileges that are constitutionally guaranteed to every defendant.

robbery (UCR/NIBRS) The unlawful taking or attempted taking of property that is in the immediate possession of another by force or violence and/or by putting the victim in fear. Armed robbery differs from unarmed, or strong-arm, robbery in that it involves a weapon. Contrary to popular conceptions, highway robbery does not necessarily occur on a street—and rarely in a vehicle. The term *highway robbery* applies to any form of robbery that occurs out doors in a public place.

routine activities theory (RAT) A neoclassical perspective that suggests that lifestyles contribute significantly to both the amount and the type of crime found in any society.

rule of law The maxim that an orderly society must be governed by established principles and known codes that are applied uniformly and fairly to all of its members.

rules of evidence Court rules that govern the admissibility of evidence at criminal hearings and trials.

runaway A juvenile who has been adjudicated by a judicial officer of juvenile court as having committed the status offense of leaving the custody and home of his or her parents, guardians, or custodians without permission and of failing to return within a reasonable length of time.

schizophrenic A mentally ill individual who suffers from disjointed thinking and possibly from delusions and hallucinations.

scientific jury selection The use of correlational techniques from the social sciences to gauge the likelihood that potential jurors will vote for conviction or for acquittal.

scientific police management The application of social science techniques to the study of police administration for the purpose of increasing effectiveness, reducing the frequency of citizen complaints, and enhancing the efficient use of available resources.

search incident to an arrest A warrantless search of an arrested individual conducted to ensure the safety of the arresting officer. Because individuals placed under arrest may be in possession of weapons, courts have recognized the need for arresting officers to protect themselves by conducting an immediate search of arrestees without obtaining a warrant.

search warrant A document issued by a judicial officer that directs a law enforcement officer to conduct a search at a specific location for specified property or a specific person relating to a crime, to seize the property or person if found, and to account for the results of the search to the issuing judicial officer.

security The restriction of inmate movement within a correctional facility, usually divided into maximum, medium, and minimum levels.

security threat group (STG) An inmate group, gang, or organization whose members act together to pose a threat to the safety of corrections staff or the public, who prey upon other inmates, or who threaten the secure and orderly operation of a correctional institution.

selective incapacitation A policy that seeks to protect society by incarcerating individuals deemed to be the most dangerous.

self-defense The protection of oneself or of one's property from unlawful injury or from the immediate risk of unlawful injury. Also, the justification that the person who committed an act that would otherwise constitute an offense reasonably believed that the act was necessary to protect self or property from immediate danger.

self-reports Crime measures based on surveys that ask respondents to reveal any illegal activity in which they have been involved.

sentence 1. The penalty imposed by a court on a person convicted of a crime. 2. The court judgment specifying the penalty imposed on a person convicted of a crime. 3. Any disposition of a defendant resulting from a conviction, including the court decision to suspend execution of a sentence.

sentencing The imposition of a criminal sanction by a judicial authority.

sentencing disposition 1. A court disposition of a defendant after a judgment of conviction, expressed as a penalty, such as imprisonment or payment of a fine. 2. Any of a number of alternatives to actually executed penalties, such as a suspended sentence, a grant of probation, or an order to perform restitution. 3. Various combinations of the foregoing.

sentencing hearing In criminal proceedings, a hearing during which the court or jury considers relevant information, such as evidence concerning aggravating or mitigating circumstances, for the purpose of determining a sentencing disposition for a person convicted of an offense.

sentinel event A bad outcome that no one wants repeated and that signals the existence of underlying weaknesses in the system.

sequestered jury A jury that is isolated from the public during the course of a trial and throughout the deliberation process.

service style A style of policing marked by a concern with helping rather than strict enforcement. Service-oriented police agencies are more likely to use community resources, such as drug-treatment programs, to supplement traditional law enforcement activities than are other types of agencies.

sex offense In current statistical usage, any of a broad category of varying offenses, usually consisting of all offenses having a sexual element except forcible rape and commercial sex offenses. The category includes all unlawful sexual intercourse, unlawful sexual contact, and other unlawful behavior intended to result in sexual gratification or profit from sexual activity.

sex offense (UCR/NIBRS) Any of various "offenses against chastity, common decency, morals, and the like," except forcible rape, prostitution, and commercialized vice.

sex trafficking The recruitment, harboring, transportation, provision, or obtaining of a person for the purpose of a commercial sex act.

sexual battery Intentional and wrongful physical contact with a person, without his or her consent, that entails a sexual component or purpose.

sheriff The elected chief officer of a county law enforcement agency. The sheriff is usually responsible for law enforcement in unincorporated areas and for the operation of the county jail.

sheriff's department A local law enforcement agency, directed by a sheriff, that exercises its law enforcement functions at the county level, usually within unincorporated areas, and that operates the county jail in most jurisdictions.

shock incarceration A sentencing option that makes use of "boot camp"—type prisons to impress on convicted offenders the realities of prison life.

shock probation The practice of sentencing offenders to prison, allowing them to apply for probationary release, and surprisingly permitting such release. Offenders who receive shock probation may not be aware that they will be released on probation and may expect to spend a much longer time behind bars.

simple assault (UCR/NIBRS) The unlawful threatening, attempted inflicting, or inflicting of less-than-serious bodily injury, without a deadly weapon.

smart policing A law enforcement initiative that makes use of techniques shown to work at both reducing and solving crimes.

smuggling The unlawful movement of goods across a national frontier or state boundary or into or out of a correctional facility.

sneak-and-peek search A search that occurs in the suspect's absence and without his or her prior knowledge. Also known as *delayed notification search*.

social control The use of sanctions and rewards within a group to influence and shape the behavior of individual members of that group. Social control is a primary concern of social groups and communities, and it is their interest in the exercise of social control that leads to the creation of both criminal and civil statutes.

social debt A sentencing principle that holds that an offender's criminal history should objectively be taken into account in sentencing decisions.

social development theory An integrated view of human development that points to the process of interaction among and between individuals and society as the root cause of criminal behavior.

social disorganization A condition said to exist when a group is faced with social change, uneven development of culture, maladaptiveness, disharmony, conflict, and lack of consensus.

social ecology A criminological approach that focuses on the misbehavior of lower-class youth and sees delinquency primarily as the result of social disorganization.

social engineering A nontechnical kind of cyberintrusion that relies heavily on human interaction and often involves tricking people into breaking normal security procedures.

social justice An ideal that embraces all aspects of civilized life and that is linked to fundamental notions of fairness and to cultural beliefs about right and wrong.

social learning theory A psychological perspective that says that people learn how to behave by modeling themselves after others whom they have the opportunity to observe.

social order The condition of a society characterized by social integration, consensus, smooth functioning, and lack of interpersonal and institutional conflict. Also, a lack of social disorganization.

social process theory A perspective on criminological thought that highlights the process of interaction between individuals and society. Most social process theories highlight the role of social learning.

social-psychological theory A perspective on criminological thought that highlights the role played in crime causation by weakened self-esteem and meaningless social roles. Social-psychological thinkers stress the relationship of the individual to the social group as the underlying cause of behavior.

sociopath See **psychopath.**

software piracy The unauthorized duplication of software or the illegal transfer of data from one storage medium to another. Software piracy is one of the most prevalent cybercrimes in the world.

solvability factor Information about a crime that forms the basis for determining the perpetrator's identity.

somatotyping The classification of human beings into types according to body build and other physical characteristics.

spam Unsolicited commercial bulk e-mail whose primary purpose is the advertisement or promotion of a commercial product or service.

span of control The number of police personnel or the number of units supervised by a particular commander.

specialized court A low-level court that focuses on relatively minor offenses and handles special populations or addresses special issues such as reentry. Specialized courts are often a form of community courts.

specific deterrence A goal of criminal sentencing that seeks to prevent a particular offender from engaging in repeat criminality.

speedy trial A trial that is held in a timely manner. The right of a defendant to have a prompt trial is guaranteed by the Sixth Amendment of the U.S. Constitution, which begins, "In all criminal prosecutions, the accused shall enjoy the right to a speedy and public trial."

Speedy Trial Act A 1974 federal law requiring that proceedings against a defendant in a federal criminal case begin within a specified period of time, such as 70 working days after indictment. Some states also have speedy trial requirements.

split sentence A sentence explicitly requiring the convicted offender to serve a period of confinement in a local, state, or federal facility, followed by a period of probation.

staff operations In police organizations, activities (such as administration and training) that provide support for line operations.

stalking Repeated harassing and threatening behavior by one individual against another, aspects of which may be planned or carried out in secret. Stalking might involve following a person, appearing at a person's home or place of business, making harassing phone calls, leaving written messages or objects, or vandalizing a person's property. Most stalking laws require that the perpetrator make a credible threat of violence against the victim or members of the victim's immediate family.

stare decisis A legal principle that requires that, in subsequent cases on similar issues of law and fact, courts be bound by their own earlier decisions and by those of higher courts having jurisdiction over them. The term literally means "standing by decided matters."

state-action doctrine The traditional legal principle that only government officials or their representatives in the criminal justice process can be held accountable for the violation of an individual's constitutional civil rights.

state court administrator A coordinator who assists with case-flow management, operating funds budgeting, and court docket administration.

state court system A state judicial structure. Most states have at least three court levels: trial courts, appellate courts, and a state supreme court.

state highway patrol A state law enforcement agency whose principal functions are preventing, detecting, and investigating motor vehicle offenses and apprehending traffic offenders.

state police A state law enforcement agency whose principal functions usually include maintaining statewide police communications, aiding local police in criminal investigations, training police, and guarding state property. The state police may include the highway patrol.

state-use system A form of inmate labor in which items produced by inmates may only be sold by or to state offices. Items that only the state can sell include such things as license plates and hunting licenses, whereas items sold only to state offices include furniture and cleaning supplies.

status offender A child who commits an act that is contrary to the law by virtue of the offender's status as a child. Purchasing cigarettes, buying alcohol, and being truant are examples of such behavior.

status offense An act or conduct that is declared by statute to be an offense, but only when committed by or engaged in by a juvenile, and that can be adjudicated only by a juvenile court.

Statute of Winchester A law, written in 1285, that created a watch and ward system in English cities and towns and that codified early police practices.

statutory law Written or codified law; the "law on the books," as enacted by a government body or agency having the power to make laws.

statutory rape Sexual intercourse with a person who is under the legal age of consent.

stay of execution The stopping by a court of the implementation of a judgment—that is, of a court order previously issued.

stolen property offense The unlawful receiving, buying, distributing, selling, transporting, concealing, or possessing of the property of another by a person who knows that the property has been unlawfully obtained from the owner or other lawful possessor.

stop and frisk The detaining of a person by a law enforcement officer for the purpose of investigation, accompanied by a superficial examination by the officer of the person's body surface or clothing to discover weapons, contraband, or other objects relating to criminal activity.

stranger violence Seemingly random violence perpetrated by assailants who were previously unknown to their victims. Stranger violence often results from rage, opportunity, or insanity.

strategic policing A type of policing that retains the traditional police goal of professional crime fighting but enlarges the enforcement target to include nontraditional kinds of criminals, such as serial offenders, gangs and criminal associations, drug-distribution networks, and sophisticated white-collar and computer criminals. Strategic policing generally makes use of innovative enforcement techniques, including intelligence operations, undercover stings, electronic surveillance, and sophisticated forensic methods.

street crime A class of offenses, sometimes defined with some degree of formality as those that occur in public locations and are visible and assaultive, that are a special risk to the public and a special target of law enforcement preventive efforts and prosecutorial attention.

strict liability Liability without fault or intention. Strict liability offenses do not require *mens rea*.

structured sentencing A model of criminal punishment that includes determinate and commission-created presumptive sentencing schemes, as well as voluntary/advisory sentencing guidelines.

subculture of violence A cultural setting in which violence is a traditional and often accepted method of dispute resolution.

subpoena A written order issued by a judicial officer or grand jury requiring an individual to appear in court and to give testimony or to bring material to be used as evidence. Some subpoenas mandate that books, papers, and other items be surrendered to the court.

substantive criminal law The part of the law that defines crimes and specifies punishments.

supermale A human male displaying the XYY chromosome structure.

superpredator A juvenile who is coming of age in actual and "moral poverty" without the benefits of parents, teachers, coaches, and clergy to teach right from wrong[52] and who turns to criminal activity. The term is often applied to inner-city youths, socialized in violent settings without the benefit of wholesome life experiences, who hold considerable potential for violence.

supervised probation Guidance, treatment, or regulation by a probation agency of the behavior of a person who is subject to adjudication or who has been convicted of an offense, resulting from a formal court order or a probation agency decision.

suspect An adult or a juvenile who has not been arrested or charged but whom a criminal justice agency believes may be the person responsible for a specific criminal offense.

suspended sentence The court decision to delay imposing or executing a penalty for a specified or unspecified period. Also, a court disposition of a convicted person pronouncing a penalty of a fine or a commitment to confinement but unconditionally discharging the defendant or holding execution of the penalty in abeyance upon good behavior. Also called *sentence withheld*.

suspicionless search A search conducted by law enforcement personnel without a warrant and without suspicion. Suspicionless searches are permissible only if based on an overriding concern for public safety.

sustainable justice Criminal laws and criminal justice institutions, policies, and practices that achieve justice in the present without compromising the ability of future generations to have the benefits of a just society.[53]

sworn officer A law enforcement officer who is trained and empowered to perform full police duties, such as making arrests, conducting investigations, and carrying firearms.[54]

Tazir **crime** A minor violation of Islamic law that is regarded as an offense against society, not God.

team policing The reorganization of conventional patrol strategies into "an integrated and versatile police team assigned to a fixed district."[55]

technocrime A criminal offense that employs advanced or emerging technology in its commission.

teen court An alternative approach to juvenile justice in which alleged offenders are judged and sentenced by a jury of their peers.

TEMPEST A standard developed by the federal government that requires that electromagnetic emanations from computers designated as "secure" be below levels that would allow radio receiving equipment to "read" the data being computed.

terrorism A violent act or an act dangerous to human life, in violation of the criminal laws of the United States or of any state, that is committed to intimidate or coerce a government, the civilian population, or any segment thereof, in furtherance of political or social objectives.[56]

testimony Oral evidence offered by a sworn witness on the witness stand during a criminal trial.

theft Generally, any taking of the property of another with intent to permanently deprive the rightful owner of possession.

theory A set of interrelated propositions that attempt to describe, explain, predict, and ultimately control some class of events. A theory is strengthened by its logical consistency and is "tested" by how well it describes and predicts reality.

three-strikes laws Statutes that require mandatory sentences (sometimes life in prison without the possibility of parole) for offenders convicted of a third felony. Such mandatory sentencing enhancements are aimed at deterring known and potentially violent offenders and are intended to incapacitate convicted criminals through long-term incarceration.

tort A wrongful act, damage, or injury not involving a breach of contract. Also, a private or civil wrong or injury.

total institution An enclosed facility separated from society both socially and physically, where the inhabitants share all aspects of their daily lives.

trafficking in persons (TIP) The exploitation of unwilling or unwitting people through force, coercion, threat, or deception.

traits stable personality patterns that tend to endure throughout the life course and across social and cultural contexts.

transfer to adult court The decision by a juvenile court, resulting from a transfer hearing, that jurisdiction over an alleged delinquent will be waived and that he or she should be prosecuted as an adult in a criminal court.

transnational organized crime Unlawful activity undertaken and supported by organized criminal groups operating across national boundaries. Also called *transnational crime.*

treason A U.S. citizen's actions to help a foreign government overthrow, make war against, or seriously injure the United States.[57] Also, the attempt to overthrow the government of the society of which one is a member.

trial In criminal proceedings, the examination in court of the issues of fact and relevant law in a case for the purpose of convicting or acquitting the defendant.

trial *de novo* Literally, "new trial." The term is applied to cases that are retried on appeal, as opposed to those that are simply reviewed on the record.

trial judge A judicial officer who is authorized to conduct jury and nonjury trials but who may not be authorized to hear appellate cases. Also, the judicial officer who conducts a particular trial.

trial jury A statutorily defined number of people selected according to law and sworn to determine, in accordance with the law as instructed by the court, certain matters of fact based on evidence presented in a trial and to render a verdict. Also called *petit jury.*

truth in sentencing A close correspondence between the sentence imposed on an offender and the time actually served in prison.[58]

UCR See **Uniform Crime Reporting Program (UCR).**

unconditional release The final release of an offender from the jurisdiction of a correctional agency. Also, a final release from the jurisdiction of a court.

undisciplined child A child who is beyond parental control, as evidenced by his or her refusal to obey legitimate authorities, such as school officials and teachers.

Uniform Crime Reporting (UCR) Program A statistical reporting program run by the FBI's Criminal Justice Information Services (CJIS) division. The UCR Program publishes *Crime in the United States,* which provides an annual summation of the incidence and rate of reported crimes throughout the United States.

USA PATRIOT Act A federal law (Public Law 107–56) enacted in response to terrorist attacks on the World Trade Center and the Pentagon on September 11, 2001. The law, officially titled the Uniting and Strengthening America by Providing Appropriate Tools Required to Intercept and Obstruct Terrorism Act, substantially broadened the investigative authority of law enforcement agencies throughout America and is applicable to many crimes other than terrorism. The law was slightly revised and reauthorized by Congress in 2006. Also called *Antiterrorism Act.*

use of force See **police use of force.**

vagrancy (UCR/NIBRS) An offense related to being a suspicious person, including vagrancy, begging, loitering, and vagabondage.

vandalism (UCR/NIBRS) The destroying or damaging of public property or the property of another without the owner's consent, or the attempt to destroy or damage such property. This definition of vandalism does not include burning.

venue The particular geographic area in which a court may hear or try a case. Also, the locality within which a particular crime was committed. See also **jurisdiction.**

verdict The decision of the jury in a jury trial or of a judicial officer in a nonjury trial.

victim A person who has suffered death, physical or mental anguish, or loss of property as the result of an actual or attempted criminal offense committed by another person.

victim-impact statement The in-court use of victim- or survivor-supplied information by sentencing authorities seeking to make an informed sentencing decision.

victimization In National Crime Victimization Survey terminology, the harming of any single victim in a criminal incident.

victimology The scientific study of crime victims and the victimization process. Victimology is a subfield of criminology.

victims' assistance program An organized program that offers services to victims of crime in the areas of crisis intervention and follow-up counseling and that helps victims secure their rights under the law.

vigilantism The act of taking the law into one's own hands.

violation 1. The performance of an act forbidden by a statute or the failure to perform an act commanded by a statute. 2. An act contrary to a local government ordinance. 3. An offense punishable by a fine or other penalty but not by incarceration. 4. An act prohibited by the terms and conditions of probation or parole.

violent crime A UCR/NIBRS summary offense category that traditionally includes murder, rape, robbery, and aggravated assault.

voluntary/advisory sentencing guidelines Recommended sentencing policies that are not required by law.

warden The official in charge of the operation of a prison, the chief administrator of a prison, or the prison superintendent.

warehousing An imprisonment strategy that is based on the desire to prevent recurrent crime and that has abandoned all hope of rehabilitation.

warrant In criminal proceedings, a writ issued by a judicial officer directing a law enforcement officer to perform a specified act and affording the officer protection from damages if he or she performs it.

watchman style A style of policing marked by a concern for order maintenance. Watchman policing is characteristic of lower-class communities where police intervene informally into the lives of residents to keep the peace.

weapon of mass destruction (WMD) A chemical, biological, or nuclear weapon that has the potential to cause mass casualties.

weapons offense The unlawful sale, distribution, manufacture, alteration, transportation, possession, or use, or the attempted unlawful sale, distribution, manufacture, alteration, transportation, possession, or use, of a deadly or dangerous weapon or accessory.

white-collar crime Violations of the criminal law committed by a person of respectability and high social status in the course of his or her occupation. Also, nonviolent crime for financial gain utilizing deception and committed by anyone who has special technical or professional knowledge of business or government, irrespective of the person's occupation.

Wickersham Commission The National Commission on Law Observance and Enforcement. In 1931, the commission issued a report stating that Prohibition was unenforceable and carried a great potential for police corruption.

witness Generally, a person who has knowledge of the circumstances of a case. Also, in court usage, one who testifies as to what he or she has seen, heard, or otherwise observed or who has expert knowledge.

work release A prison program through which inmates are temporarily released into the community to meet job responsibilities.

workhouse An early form of imprisonment whose purpose was to instill habits of industry in the idle. Also called *bridewell*.

writ A document issued by a judicial officer ordering or forbidding the performance of a specified act.

writ of *certiorari* A writ issued from an appellate court for the purpose of obtaining from a lower court the record of its proceedings in a particular case. In some states, this writ is the mechanism for discretionary review. A request for review is made by petitioning for a writ of *certiorari*, and the granting of review is indicated by the issuance of the writ.

writ of *habeas corpus* A writ that directs the person detaining a prisoner to bring him or her before a judicial officer to determine the lawfulness of the imprisonment.

youthful offender A person, adjudicated in criminal court, who may be above the statutory age limit for juveniles but is below a specified upper age limit, for whom special correctional commitments and special record-sealing procedures are made available by statute.

NOTES

1. Bureau of Justice Statistics, *Dictionary of Criminal Justice Data Terminology*, 2nd ed. (Washington, DC: U.S. Government Printing Office, 1982).
2. Federal Bureau of Investigation, *Uniform Crime Reporting Handbook, 2004* (Washington, DC: U.S. Dept. of Justice, 2005).
3. BJS, *Dictionary of Criminal Justice Data Terminology*, p. 5.
4. Adapted from U.S. Code, Title 28, Section 20.3 (2[d]). Title 28 of the U.S. Code defines the term *administration of criminal justice*.
5. Thomas J. Cowper and Michael E. Buerger, *Improving Our View of the World: Police and Augmented Reality Technology* (Washington, DC: Federal Bureau of Investigation, 2003), http://www.fbi.gov/publications/realitytech/realitytech.pdf (accessed October 7, 2007).
6. *People* v. *Romero*, 8 Cal. 4th 728, 735 (1994).
7. Technical Working Group on Crime Scene Investigation, *Crime Scene Investigation: A Guide for Law Enforcement* (Washington, DC: National Institute of Justice, 2000), p. 12.
8. Centers for Disease Control and Prevention, "Bioterrorism: An Overview," http://www.bt.cdc.gov/bioterrorism/overview.asp (accessed August 15, 2007).
9. Howard N. Snyder and Melissa Sickmund, *Juvenile Offenders and Victims: 2006 National Report* (Washington, DC: Office of Juvenile Justice and Delinquency Prevention, 2006).
10. *State* v. *Cross*, 200 S.E.2d 27, 29 (1973).
11. Adapted from Gerald Hill and Kathleen Hill, "The Real Life Dictionary of the Law," http://www.law.com (accessed June 11, 2007).
12. Hill and Hill, "The Real Life Dictionary of the Law" (accessed February 27, 2007).
13. Community Policing Consortium, *What Is Community Policing?* (Washington, DC: Community Policing Consortium, 1995).
14. Michael L. Benson, Francis T. Cullen, and William J. Maakestad, *Local Prosecutors and Corporate Crime* (Washington, DC: National Institute of Justice, 1992), p. 1.
15. Office of Justice Programs, *The National Criminal Intelligence Sharing Plan* (Washington, DC: U.S. Dept. of Justice, 2005), p. 27.
16. Wayne W. Bennett and Karen M. Hess, *Criminal Investigation*, 6th ed. (Belmont, CA: Wadsworth, 2001), p. 3 (italics in original).
17. Violence against Women Office, *Stalking and Domestic Violence: Report to Congress* (Washington, DC: U.S. Dept. of Justice, 2001), p. 5.
18. Sam W. Lathrop, "Reviewing Use of Force: A Systematic Approach," *FBI Law Enforcement Bulletin*, October 2000, p. 18.
19. Adapted from Larry R. Leibrock, "Overview and Impact on 21st Century Legal Practice: Digital Forensics and Electronic Discovery," http://www.courtroom21.net/FDIC.pps (accessed July 15, 2007).

20. Adapted from Federal Bureau of Investigation, "FBI Policy and Guidelines: Counterterrorism," http://jackson.fbi.gov/cntrterr.htm (accessed March 24, 2007).

21. Bureau of Justice Statistics, *Drugs, Crime, and the Justice System* (Washington, DC: BJS, 1992), p. 20.

22. Adapted from Technical Working Group for Electronic Crime Scene Investigation, *Electronic Crime Scene Investigation: A Guide for First Responders* (Washington, DC: National Institute of Justice, 2001), p. 2.

23. Henry Campbell Black, Joseph R. Nolan, and Jacqueline M. Nolan-Haley, *Black's Law Dictionary*, 6th ed. (St. Paul, MN: West, 1990), p. 24.

24. Lawrence W. Sherman, *Evidence-Based Policing* (Washington, DC: Police Foundation, 1998), p. 3.

25. International Association of Chiefs of Police, *Police Use of Force in America, 2001* (Alexandria, VA: IACP, 2001), p. 1.

26. Adapted from "Globalization," Encyclopedia Britannica, 2003, http://www.britannica.com/eb/article?eu5369857 (accessed July 23, 2003).

27. Black et al., *Black's Law Dictionary*, p. 1003.

28. *The American Heritage Dictionary and Electronic Thesaurus on CD-ROM* (Boston: Houghton Mifflin, 1987).

29. Adapted from Entrust, Inc., "Secure Identity Management: Challenges, Needs, and Solutions," p. 1, http://www.entrust.com (accessed August 5, 2007).

30. Identity Theft Resource Center website, http://www.idtheftcenter.org (accessed April 24, 2007).

31. Adapted from Dictionary.com, http://dictionary.reference.com/search?q5infrastructure (accessed January 10, 2007).

32. Angus Smith, ed., *Intelligence-Led Policing* (Richmond, VA: International Association of Law Enforcement Intelligence Analysts, 1997), p. 1.

33. Adapted from FBI, "FBI Policy and Guidelines: Counterterrorism."

34. Jeffrey A. Butts and Ojmarrh Mitchell, "Brick by Brick: Dismantling the Border between Juvenile and Adult Justice," in Phyllis McDonald and Janice Munsterman, eds., *Boundary Changes in Criminal Justice Organizations*, Vol. 2 of *Criminal Justice 2000* (Washington, DC: National Institute of Justice, 2000), p. 207.

35. David A. Garvin, "Building a Learning Organization," *Harvard Business Review* (1993), pp. 78–91.

36. U.S. Department of Treasury, *2000–2005 Strategic Plan* (Washington, DC: U.S. Government Printing Office, 2000), p. 1.

37. Adapted from Robert M. Shusta et al., *Multicultural Law Enforcement*, 2nd ed. (Upper Saddle River, NJ: Prentice Hall, 2002), p. 443.

38. The Organized Crime Control Act of 1970 (Public Law 91-451).

39. BJS, *Drugs, Crime, and the Justice System*, p. 20.

40. Carl B. Klockars et al., *The Measurement of Police Integrity*, National Institute of Justice Research in Brief (Washington, DC: NIJ, 2000), p. 1.

41. This definition draws on the classic work by O. W. Wilson, *Police Administration* (New York: McGraw-Hill, 1950), pp. 2–3.

42. National Institute of Justice, *Use of Force by Police: Overview of National and Local Data* (Washington, DC: NIJ, 1999).

43. National Council on Crime and Delinquency, *National Assessment of Structured Sentencing* (Washington, DC: Bureau of Justice Statistics, 1996), p. xii.

44. Bureau of Justice Statistics, *Prisoners in 1998* (Washington, DC: BJS, 1999), p. 7.

45. *Private Security: Report of the Task Force on Private Security* (Washington, DC: U.S. Government Printing Office, 1976), p. 4.

46. Samuel Walker, Geoffrey P. Albert, and Dennis J. Kenney, *Responding to the Problem Police Officer: A National Study of Early Warning Systems* (Washington, DC: National Institute of Justice, 2000).

47. BJS, *Drugs, Crime, and the Justice System*, p. 21.

48. Gerald Hill and Kathleen Hill, *The Real Life Dictionary of the Law* (Santa Monica, CA: General Publishing Group, 2000), http://dictionary.law.com/lookup2.asp (accessed February 28, 2007).

49. *Victor v. Nebraska*, 114 S.Ct. 1239, 127 L.Ed.2d 583 (1994).

50. As found in the California jury instructions.

51. Debbie Dawes, *The National Institute of Justice's Evaluation of Second Chance Act Adult Reentry Courts: Program Characteristics and Preliminary Themes from Year 1* (Washington, DC: Bureau of Justice Assistance, 2013).

52. The term *superpredator* is generally attributed to John J. DiIulio, Jr. See John J. DiIulio, Jr., "The Question of Black Crime," *Public Interest* (Fall 1994), pp. 3–12.

53. Melissa Hickman Barlow, "Sustainable Justice: 2012 Presidential Address to the Academy of Criminal Justice Sciences, *Justice Quarterly*, Vol. 30, No. 1 (2013), pp. 1–17.

54. Adapted from Darl H. Champion and Michael K. Hooper, *Introduction to American Policing* (New York: McGraw-Hill, 2003), p. 166.

55. Sam S. Souryal, *Police Administration and Management* (St. Paul, MN: West, 1977), p. 261.

56. Federal Bureau of Investigation, Counterterrorism Section, *Terrorism in the United States, 1987* (Washington, DC: FBI, 1987).

57. Daniel Oran, *Oran's Dictionary of the Law* (St. Paul, MN: West, 1983), p. 306.

58. Lawrence A. Greenfeld, *Prison Sentences and Time Served for Violence*, Bureau of Justice Statistics Selected Findings, No. 4 (Washington, DC: Bureau of Justice Statistics, April 1995).

Case Index

Name Index

Subject Index